APHRODISIAS XIV

THE PLACE OF PALMS:
AN URBAN PARK AT APHRODISIAS

Results of The Mica and Ahmet Ertegün South Agora Pool Project

Andrew Wilson and Ben Russell

Reconstructed view of the east end of the pool of the Place of Palms, with palm trees and North Stoa beyond, facing North-East (L. Aguilar).

NEW YORK UNIVERSITY
INSTITUTE OF FINE ARTS

UNIVERSITY OF OXFORD
FACULTY OF CLASSICS

APHRODISIAS XIV

RESULTS OF EXCAVATIONS AT APHRODISIAS IN CARIA
CONDUCTED BY NEW YORK UNIVERSITY

SERIES EDITOR: R. R. R. SMITH

REICHERT VERLAG WIESBADEN 2024

THE PLACE OF PALMS:
AN URBAN PARK AT APHRODISIAS

Results of The Mica and Ahmet Ertegün
South Agora Pool Project

Andrew Wilson and Ben Russell

With contributions by Allison Kidd, Angelos Chaniotis, Ahmet Tolga Tek, Hüseyin Köker, Joshua J. Thomas, Angela Trentacoste, Tim Penn, Hugh Jeffery, R.R.R. Smith, Erica Rowan, Muradiye Bursalı, Ulrike Outschar, Betül Teoman, Gültekin Teoman, and Mark Robinson

In memory of Mica Ertegün CBE, 1926–2023

REICHERT VERLAG WIESBADEN 2024

Cover:
photograph by I. Cartwright © New York University Aphrodisias Excavations.

Bibliographische Information der Deutschen Nationalbibliothek
Die Deutsche Nationalbibliothek verzeichnet diese Publikation in der Deutschen Nationalbibliographie;
detaillierte bibliographische Daten sind im Internet über http://dnb.dnb.de abrufbar.

Gedruckt auf säurefreiem Papier
(alterungsbeständig – pH 7, neutral)
© 2024 Dr. Ludwig Reichert Verlag Wiesbaden
ISBN: 978-3-7520-0692-6 (Print)
eISBN: 978-3-7520-0241-6 (eBook)
https://doi.org/10.29091/9783752002416
www.reichert-verlag.de
Das Werk einschließlich aller seiner Teile ist urheberrechtlich geschützt.
Jede Verwertung außerhalb der engen Grenzen des Urheberrechtsgesetzes ist ohne Zustimmung
des Verlages unzulässig und strafbar. Das gilt insbesondere für Vervielfältigungen, Übersetzungen,
Mikroverfilmungen und die Speicherung und Verarbeitung in elektronischen Systemen.

Contents

PREFACE XI
R. R. R. Smith

ABBREVIATIONS XV

NOTES TO THE READER XVII

1. **INTRODUCTION: FROM 'SOUTH AGORA' TO 'PLACE OF PALMS'** 1
   Andrew Wilson and Ben Russell

   A. EARLY INVESTIGATIONS, 18TH–20TH CENTURIES 1

   B. THE FIRST EXCAVATIONS, 1904–1905 AND 1937 4

   C. EXCAVATIONS BETWEEN 1969 AND 1991 5

   D. THE FUNCTION OF THE 'SOUTH AGORA' 8

   E. THE MICA AND AHMET ERTEGÜN SOUTH AGORA POOL PROJECT, 2012–2018 9

   F. FROM 'SOUTH AGORA' TO 'PLACE OF PALMS' 11

2. **POOL, STOA, PALM GROVE: DESIGN AND CONSTRUCTION, FIRST CENTURY AD** .. 15
   Andrew Wilson, Ben Russell, and Angelos Chaniotis

   A. ARCHITECTURE OF THE STOAS (BR, AW, & AC) 16

   B. THE POOL AND WATER SUPPLY (AW & BR) 23

   C. STRATIGRAPHIC EVIDENCE: GARDENS, POOL, AND NORTH STOA (AW & BR) ... 30

   D. HELLENISTIC AND METROPOLITAN MODELS: THE PLACE OF PALMS IN CONTEXT
      (AW & BR) 34

3. **USE, MAINTENANCE, AND MODIFICATION: FIRST TO FOURTH CENTURIES AD** .. 39
   Andrew Wilson, Ben Russell, Allison Kidd, Angelos Chaniotis, Ahmet Tolga Tek, and Hüseyin Köker

   A. THE PROPYLON (AW, BR, & AC) 39

   B. THE SOUTH SIDE: A SECOND STOA AND THE NEW BASILICA (AW, BR, & AK) . 41

   C. THE WEST STOA (AW & BR) 43

   D. THE NORTH STOA (BR, AW, AK, & AC) 48

   E. IMPERIAL-ERA COINS AND THE USE OF THE PLACE OF PALMS (ATT & HK) ... 55

   F. DISCUSSION: THE EVOLUTION OF A PUBLIC SPACE (BR & AW) 63

4. DESTRUCTION AND RENEWAL: THE PLACE OF PALMS REBORN, FIFTH TO SEVENTH CENTURIES AD 65
Andrew Wilson, Ben Russell, Allison Kidd, Angelos Chaniotis, Hugh Jeffery, Tim Penn, Hüseyin Köker, Ahmet Tolga Tek, Ulrike Outschar, Erica Rowan, and Mark Robinson

A. THE EPIGRAPHIC EVIDENCE: DOULKITIOS AND AMPELIOS (AC, AW, & BR) 65

B. REPAIRS TO THE POOL (AW, BR, AK, & ER) 67

C. ALTERATIONS TO THE PALM GROVE (AW & BR) 73

D. REPAIRS AND ALTERATIONS TO THE WEST STOA (AW, BR, & AC) 77

E. REPAIRS AND ALTERATIONS TO THE NORTH STOA (BR & AW) 77

F. THE NEW SOUTH STOAS (AK) 79

G. LATE ROMAN COINS FROM THE PLACE OF PALMS (ATT & HK) 91

H. LATE ROMAN CERAMICS (UO) 94

I. LATE ROMAN SMALL FINDS (TP & HJ) 104

J. ARCHAEOBOTANICAL EVIDENCE (ER) 105

K. A SHELL FRAGMENT OF *CHARONIA* SP. (TRITON'S TRUMPET) FROM A LATE ANTIQUE CONTEXT (MR) 113

L. A LATE FIFTH-CENTURY EARTHQUAKE (AW) 114

M. THE MAIOUMA FESTIVAL IN THE PLACE OF PALMS (BR & AW) 119

N. FURTHER ADJUSTMENTS IN THE SIXTH OR SEVENTH CENTURY (AW) 121

O. SEVENTH-CENTURY REPAIRS TO THE POOL AND MODIFICATION OF SUPPLY AND DRAINAGE (AW) 124

P. CONCLUSIONS (AW & BR) 125

5. INFORMAL WRITING, DRAWING, AND CARVING IN THE PLACE OF PALMS 127
Angelos Chaniotis, Andrew Wilson, and Ben Russell

A. INTRODUCTION (AC) 127

B. TEXTUAL GRAFFITI (AC) 128

C. PICTORIAL GRAFFITI (AC) 132

D. *TOPOS* INSCRIPTIONS (AC) 136

E. MASONS' MARKS (AC) 136

F. GAMEBOARDS (AW, BR, & AC) 140

G. INFORMAL WRITING AND THE SOCIAL LIFE OF THE PLACE OF PALMS (AC) 148

6.	**THE BASIN AT THE PROPYLON: STATUARY AND MYTHOLOGICAL RELIEFS,** *c.* AD 500–550	151
	R. R. R. Smith and Joshua J. Thomas	
A.	THE PROPYLON BASIN	151
B.	LOWER BASIN WALL: RELIEFS AND STATUE BASES	153
C.	UPPER BASIN WALL: MYTHOLOGICAL RELIEFS	154
D.	SEQUENCE OF THE RELIEFS	159
E.	THE STATUE	160
F.	CONCLUSION	162
7.	**THE SCULPTURAL LIFE OF THE PLACE OF PALMS, FIRST TO SEVENTH CENTURIES**	163
	Joshua J. Thomas	
A.	MYTHOLOGICAL STATUARY	163
B.	STATUES AND FOUNTAIN SCULPTURES ON THE POOL EDGE	166
C.	SCULPTURE FROM THE PROPYLON	167
D.	SCULPTURE FROM THE WEST STOA	172
E.	SCULPTURAL FINDS FROM THE POOL AND ITS SURROUNDINGS	175
F.	CONCLUSION	181
8.	**THE END OF THE PLACE OF PALMS, SEVENTH CENTURY AD**	183
	Andrew Wilson, Ben Russell, Allison Kidd, Ahmet Tolga Tek, Hüseyin Köker, Tim Penn, Hugh Jeffery, Erica Rowan, and Ulrike Outschar	
A.	STRATIGRAPHIC EVIDENCE (AK, BR, & AW)	183
B.	SEVENTH-CENTURY COINS (ATT & HK)	189
C.	CERAMICS FROM THE CLEARANCE DEPOSITS (UO, HJ, & TP)	192
D.	LATE ANTIQUE SMALL FINDS AND GLASS (TP & HJ)	195
E.	ARCHAEOBOTANICAL EVIDENCE (ER)	208
F.	A VIOLENT END: EARTHQUAKE, FIRE, AND THE SWORD (AW, AK, BR, ATT, & HK)	219
G.	CONCLUSIONS: THE END OF CLASSICAL APHRODISIAS (AW & BR)	228
9.	**AFTER ANTIQUITY: THE BYZANTINE TO OTTOMAN PERIODS**	229
	Allison Kidd, Ben Russell, Andrew Wilson, Tim Penn, Hugh Jeffery, Muradiye Bursalı, and Ulrike Outschar	
A.	HISTORICAL CONTEXT (AK, BR, & AW)	229
B.	STRATIGRAPHY OF THE MEDIEVAL AND EARLY MODERN SETTLEMENT (AK, BR, & AW)	230
C.	EARLY BYZANTINE CERAMICS (UO)	254
D.	MIDDLE BYZANTINE, SELJUK, BEYLIK, AND OTTOMAN CERAMICS (MB)	256

E. POST-ANTIQUE SMALL FINDS AND GLASS (TP & HJ) 258

F. CONCLUSIONS (AK & BR) 266

10. FAUNAL REMAINS FROM THE LATE ANTIQUE TO OTTOMAN PERIODS 269
Angela Trentacoste

A. MATERIALS AND METHODS 269

B. RESULTS 270

C. DISCUSSION 287

D. CONCLUSION 292

CONCLUSIONS 295
Ben Russell and Andrew Wilson

ÖZET 301

APPENDIX 1: INSCRIPTIONS FROM THE PLACE OF PALMS 307
Angelos Chaniotis

A. INSCRIPTIONS CONCERNING THE CONSTRUCTION AND RESTORATION
OF BUILDINGS AND THEIR DECORATION 307

B. HONORIFIC INSCRIPTIONS FOR EMPERORS AND IMPERIAL OFFICERS 315

C. HONORIFIC DECREES AND HONORIFIC INSCRIPTIONS FOR CITIZENS 319

D. SCULPTORS' SIGNATURES ON HONORIFIC STATUES 324

E. DEDICATORY INSCRIPTIONS 325

F. EPITAPHS 327

G. FRAGMENTS 331

**APPENDIX 2: CATALOGUE OF INFORMAL WRITING, GRAFFITI, MASONS' MARKS,
AND GAMEBOARDS FROM THE PLACE OF PALMS** 333
Angelos Chaniotis

A. POOL 333

B. NORTH STOA 341

C. WEST STOA 350

D. SOUTH STOA 352

E. THEATRE WALL 354

F. PROPYLON 354

G. LOOSE FRAGMENTS 355

APPENDIX 3: CATALOGUE OF GREEK, ROMAN, AND BYZANTINE COIN FINDS FROM THE PLACE OF PALMS 357
    Ahmet Tolga Tek and Hüseyin Köker

- A. A GENERAL CONSPECTUS OF COIN FINDS FROM THE PLACE OF PALMS 357
- B. GREEK COINS 358
- C. ROMAN PROVINCIAL COINS 359
- D. UNIDENTIFIED ROMAN PROVINCIAL COINS 360
- E. ROMAN IMPERIAL COINS 360
- F. UNIDENTIFIED LATE ROMAN COINS 366
- G. BYZANTINE COINS 367
- H. MEDIEVAL EUROPEAN COINS 372

APPENDIX 4: CATALOGUE OF ISLAMIC COIN FINDS 373
    Betül Teoman and Gültekin Teoman

- A. SULTANATE OF RÛM 373
- B. AYDINIDS 373
- C. GERMIYANIDS 374
- D. KARAMANIDS 374
- E. MENTESHE 374
- F. SARUHANIDS 374
- G. OTTOMAN EMPIRE 375
- H. ORNAMENTAL MANGIRS 376
- I. UNIDENTIFIED ISLAMIC COINS 378
- J. MODERN COINS 379

APPENDIX 5: LATE ROMAN AND EARLY BYZANTINE CERAMICS – TABLES 381
    Ulrike Outschar

APPENDIX 6: CONTEXT DESCRIPTIONS 389
    Allison Kidd and Ben Russell

BIBLIOGRAPHY 397

IMAGE CREDITS 427

INDEX 429

FOLDOUT: STATE PLAN OF THE PLACE OF PALMS SHOWING LOCATIONS OF INSCRIPTIONS

PLATES

Preface
The Mica and Ahmet Ertegün South Agora Pool Project

During a visit to Aphrodisias in July 2011, Mrs Mica Ertegün was fascinated by a grand Versailles-like pool, 170 m in length, that runs down the middle of what was then known as the city's 'South Agora'.[1] Excavations in the 1980s had unearthed both ends of the pool, but most of it remained unexcavated, unresearched, and little understood. Mrs. Ertegün was intrigued by an honorific poem inscribed on the Propylon of the complex, a columned facade facing the east end of the pool, that describes a 'place of palms' that had been restored in *c*. A.D. 500 by a great local benefactor called Ampelios:

'... we Nymphs are grateful, because he (Ampelios) gave wonder and splendid beauty to the place of palms, so that anyone who, among our waters, turns his glance around, may always sing the praise both of him and that of the place, and of the Nymphs as well.' (*ALA* 38; Appendix 1, ln 10)

A first hypothesis was that the Nymphs in the poem could be connected to the long pool and that 'the place of palms' probably referred to the whole complex—presumably named after an extensive grove of palm trees. These exciting possibilities were then explored with a generous gift from Mrs. Ertegün in the 2012 campaign. The excavation in that year discovered strong evidence for the palm grove: palm material preserved in wet earth at the bottom of the pool, and planting trenches outside the pool on its north side, between the colonnade and the pool edge.

Thus was born *The Mica and Ahmet Ertegün South Agora Pool Project*. The 2012 season was a 'year zero' of the full project that began in 2013 with a magnificent gift by Mrs. Ertegün of five years of further funding to excavate the pool and to research its complex character, long life, and function. This extraordinary generosity made the excavation of this unusual complex possible, and this volume presents the publication of its results.

The project has shown that the complex was not an agora, but a grand tree-lined urban park with its long pool surrounded by Ionic colonnades. Its earliest part, the North Stoa, was dedicated by a local aristocrat Diogenes to the emperor Tiberius (AD 14–37), and the conception of the whole complex goes back to this period. The leading notables of Aphrodisias were well-connected in Rome and often visited the imperial centre as ambassadors to maintain their city's standing with the emperors. There they seem to have been impressed by a new kind of urban facility, the *porticus* complexes, such as the *Porticus Liviae* in the Subura district and the *Porticus Pompeiana* adjoining the theatre of Pompey in the Campus Martius, which combined colonnades, tree-plantings, water features, and high-quality statues. It seems these *porticus* in Rome were a direct inspiration for the Urban Park at Aphrodisias, a new and exciting form of public facility that no regional competitors in western Asia Minor matched. They are known to us primarily from literary sources and the Severan *Forma Urbis*, a marble map of the city. The Aphrodisias example, though it contains many local adjustments, gives us an entirely new sense of what these complexes were like.

The Park was laid back to back with the Agora to its north, and it became an urban hub, giving access to the Hadrianic Baths and Basilica at its west end and to the Tetrapylon Street and Theatre at its east end. The east end was closed by a massive columned facade, the Propylon (formerly known as the Agora Gate), re-dated here to the late first century AD, which led to the street behind through tunnels under its lateral towers (*pyrgoi*). The short north end of the huge Civil Basilica, built in the years around AD 100, opened directly onto the Park at its southwest corner. The Baths then rose above and behind the square's new West Stoa in the Hadrianic period. Entrance to the Theatre was through a stairway (now blocked), up and through a tall retaining wall at the southeast corner of the square.

The relationship to the Theatre is of some interest in the planning and conception of the new complex. The Theatre hill originally extended to the north, across the space later occupied by the Park. A first massive engineering task was to cut this hill back to the current line of the Park's south side, and to support it with a huge 20m-tall ashlar retaining wall which supports the auditorium of the Theatre, which lies above and to the south. A staircase was constructed through the retaining wall that rose to the level of the Theatre's *diazoma* or walkway between its two tiers of seating. The result was a carefully conceived and constructed citizen route across the public-political centre of town, from the Bouleuterion where the Council met to the Theatre where the *demos* met. Notables and citizens could walk across the Agora, into the Park by its central north door, round the pool either in the cool north colonnade or under the palm trees, and ascend the monumental staircase up and into the heart of the Theatre—always staying within the charmed elegant colonnaded architecture of the Agora and the Park without setting foot in vernacular street space outside. (Colonnaded streets were a long way in the future at this point in Aphrodisias.) The new complex linked the two poles of the city's political life, Council House and Theatre.[2]

This design gives some insight into a question posed from a modern perspective: what was this complex for? It is often not a good question for ancient building projects. The Urban Park was not for any particular function or designed to meet any

---

1 As described by this writer in Smith *et al.* 2016, 76.

2 This aspect was discussed in Smith 1996, 45–9.

pressing need. It was a public amenity, a beautiful calm shaded space in the centre of town, with colonnades, statues, trees, and a pool across which any light breeze would produce a cooling effect. It was an attractive place for the pleasure and enjoyment of the citizen—it was citizen space. In antiquity, the ideal of citizenship was not to work, to have leisure, and to live off rents and one's property. In such a garden-park, one could relax, sit, talk, walk, enjoy one's status, and transit between different parts of the city.

This aspect of citizen pleasure, without practical function, is superbly attested in the complex by another of its remarkable features, its 'graffiti' or semi-public writing, published here in detail by Angelos Chaniotis. The edges of the pool and the porticoes are covered in more than 500 items of chiselled drawings, gameboards, and personal text messages. Other buildings in Aphrodisias and elsewhere, such as stadia and theatres, have seat inscriptions, but none has the density and variety of this Place of Palms. In most of the city's inscriptions, the elite speak down to their compatriots in large dedications and public documents. In the assembled graffiti of the pool complex, we see and hear citizens of all levels speaking to each other and upwards to their betters. It is an extraordinary body of material from all through the complex's long life; it both animates the space and testifies to its intense and prolonged use as a place of idling citizen relaxation.

The complex had carefully designed origins in the early first century AD, and like most ancient structures it had a long later life. It is one of the key aspects of this publication that it is able to demonstrate phases of repair and re-modelling much longer than might be expected. Like the Hadrianic Baths, their pool complex was deeply loved by the Aphrodisians and was maintained with great effort and expense up to the widespread urban collapse of the early-mid seventh century. The late antique period saw an intense proliferation of gameboards carved on the pool perimeter. After it went out of use, the pool began to be used for successive waves of debris and dumped material thrown in from the pool edges. It is these dump layers that produced such an extraordinary panoply of finds of marble, metal, ceramic, glass, and wood. Heavy marble items, such as portrait heads and the tail of Troilos' Horse, could not be thrown far and were found close to the edges. Lighter items were found thrown further in, in diminishing quantities, towards the middle of the pool.

The carefully recorded excavation also allows a detailed narrative of what happened in this space after the pool went out of use, from its filling up to transformation into agricultural space, from the seventh century to the Ottoman period. This is a long, painstakingly-won archaeological story.

Research in the area started with the very first excavations at Aphrodisias in 1904–5, when Paul Gaudin, a railway engineer, and the talented archaeologist Gustave Mendel, excavated much of the West Stoa, which they treated as part of the Hadrianic Baths, their main focus. Giulio Jacopi's single season of pre-war excavation in 1937, with the noted scholar of Roman architectural history Luigi Crema, excavated much of the North Stoa (the Portico of Tiberius) with its mask-and-garland frieze. Kenan Erim's excavations (1961–1990) continued work in the southern part of the West Stoa in 1969. Part of the pool's south perimeter was discovered in 1984, and in 1988 further excavation discovered both of its curved ends. In 1979, Nathalie de Chaisemartin began work on the garland friezes of Aphrodisias, and has produced many interesting studies of the friezes of the Urban Park, sometimes with diverging views of its function.[3]

The naming of the complex has had several changes, from Portico of Tiberius, to South Agora, now to the Place of Palms, a name attested for it in the verse inscription of late antiquity mentioned above. 'Place of Palms' is a poetic and evocative name. The purpose of the complex is better captured by the term Urban Park. This is intended as a modern English equivalent of the specialized Roman use of the term *porticus* which seems so visibly to have inspired its design. Luigi Crema had seen the complex was not an agora, and his term 'Portico of Tiberius', so long employed to refer to the whole complex by Kenan Erim, as well as to the North Stoa, also comes close to its ancient character.

The excavation of the pool in five long campaigns, 2013–2017, and the documentation of the whole complex was a great opportunity to study an active city centre over a very long period, both its life as an ancient park from the first to the seventh century and its long later life after the pool no longer functioned and was filled and forgotten from the seventh century onwards. The project was highly collaborative in nature. A large international team of experts from six countries made specialist studies, represented in the chapters here, of numismatics, ceramics, architecture, epigraphy, statuary, and faunal and archaeobotanical remains. The aim is an integrated archaeological study framed by historical questions. All the recovered remains and their study are tied to the rigorous, in-phase stratigraphic excavation of the whole previously unexcavated area of the pool. That is, the excavation went down in each layer across the whole area at the same time. The excavation was designed and overseen by Andrew Wilson and Ben Russell, ably assisted in the field with organization and documentation by Andrew Ward in 2012–2013, John Sigmier in 2013, and Allison Kidd in 2013–2017.

The main research and writing of the chapters of this publication were carried out at Aphrodisias in 2018 and 2019, in part of the excavation house called the Quiet Room, in which contributing scholars work in peace without further duties in the field. The gathering of the main authors in these seasons allowed fruitful interaction and swift collective decisions on narrative and interpretation, as well as the creating and collecting of the illustrations needed. Further seasons were devoted to refining, editing, and completing the chapters, drawings, and documentation.

The Aphrodisias Excavations are a collaborative project of New York University and its Institute of Fine Arts and of Oxford University and its Classics Faculty. It has further invaluable support from foundations, individuals, and the following groups of friends: the Geyre Vakfı in Istanbul (President, Ömer Koç), the Friends of Aphrodisias Trust in London (President, John Scott), and the Aphrodisias Sevenler Derneği in Izmir (President, Mizyal Toktay). Key supporters include: the Malcolm H. Wiener Foundation; the Leon Levy Foundation; the

---

3   de Chaisemartin 1987; 1989a; b; de Chaisemartin and Lemaire 1996; de Chaisemartin 1998; 1999; forthcoming.

Headley Trust; the British Institute at Ankara; Lucien Arkas; Murat Ülker and pladis; the Merops Foundation; the Faculty of Arts and Science of New York University; the Shuffrey Fund of Lincoln College, Oxford; and the Craven Fund of the University of Oxford. Valuable funding for the publication of this volume has been given by the following: the Loeb Classical Library Foundation, Harvard University; All Souls College, Oxford; the Craven Fund of the University of Oxford; the Leverhulme Trust; and the School of History, Classics and Archaeology of the University of Edinburgh. Much of the work on this volume by Ben Russell was made possible by a Philip Leverhulme Prize. It is a pleasure to record profound gratitude to all these institutions and supporters.

I would like finally to thank Linda Wachner who has been a guiding angel of the project; Baron Lorne Thyssen-Bornemisza and the Augustus Foundation who have contributed generously to the research; Ömer Koç, who is the generous sponsor of a multi-year post-excavation programme of conservation of the delicate marble perimeter of the pool (2018–2024); and most importantly, the late Mica Ertegün, who sadly passed away while this volume was in press. Without Mrs Ertegün, none of the detailed story of this truly remarkable ancient complex would have seen the light of day. I offer warmest thanks to these dear and generous friends.

R. R. R. Smith
Oxford, January 2024

Abbreviations

ALA	Roueché, C., *Aphrodisias in Late Antiquity* (Society for the Promotion of Roman Studies, London 1989).
ala2004	Roueché, C, *Aphrodisias in Late Antiquity*, electronic second edition (2004), http://insaph.kcl.ac.uk/ala2004/
AR	Reynolds, J., *Aphrodisias and Rome* (London 1982).
BMC I	Mattingly, H., *Coins of the Roman Empire in the British Museum*, vol. 1: *Augustus to Vitellius* (London 1923).
BMC Caria	Head, B. V., *Catalogue of the Greek Coins of Caria, Cos, Rhodes, &c.* (British Museum Catalogues of Greek Coins, 18. London 1897).
BMC Ionia	Head, B. V., *Catalogue of the Greek Coins of Ionia* (A Catalogue of Greek Coins in the British Museum. London 1892).
BMC Lydia	Head, B. V., *Catalogue of the Greek Coins of Lydia* (British Museum Catalogues of Greek Coins, 22. London 1901).
BMC Mysia	Wroth, W., *Catalogue of the Greek Coins of Mysia* (British Museum Catalogues of Greek Coins, 15. London 1890).
BMC Vandals	Wroth, W., *Catalogue of the Coins of the Vandals, Ostrogoths and Lombards, and of the Empires of Thessalonica, Nicaea and Trebizond, in the British Museum* (London 1911).
CIG	*Corpus Inscriptionum Graecarum*, 4 vols. (Berlin 1828–1877).
DOC I	Bellinger, A. R., *Catalogue of the Byzantine coins in the Dumbarton Oaks Collection and in the Whittemore Collection*, vol. 1: *Anastasius to Maurice, 491–602* (Dumbarton Oaks Catalogues. Washington, D.C. 1966).
DOC II.1	Grierson, P., *Catalogue of the Byzantine Coins in the Dumbarton Oaks Collection and in the Whittemore Collection*, vol. 2.1: *Phocas I and Heraclius (602–641)* (Dumbarton Oaks Catalogues. Washington, D.C. 1968).
DOC II.2	Grierson, P., *Catalogue of the Byzantine Coins in the Dumbarton Oaks Collection and in the Whittemore Collection*, vol. 2.2: *Heraclius Constantine to Theodosius III (641–717)* (Dumbarton Oaks Catalogues. Washington, D.C. 1968).
DOC III.2	Grierson, P., *Catalogue of the Byzantine Coins in the Dumbarton Oaks Collection and in the Whittemore Collection*, vol. 3.2: *Leo III to Nicephorus III, 867–1081* (Dumbarton Oaks Catalogues. Washington, D.C. 1973).
DOC IV.1	Hendy, M., *Catalogue of the Byzantine Coins in the Dumbarton Oaks Collection and in the Whittemore Collection*, vol. 4.1: *Alexius I to Alexius V (1081–1204)* (Dumbarton Oaks Research Library and Collection. Washington, D.C. 1999).
GRPC Lydia II	Kurth, D., *Greek and Roman Provincial Coins. Lydia*, vol. 2: *The Bronze Coinage of Lydia: Acrasus-Klanudda* (Istanbul and Loxahatchee 2020).
IAph2007	Reynolds, J., Roueché, C., and Bodard, G., *Inscriptions from Aphrodisias*, http://insaph.kcl.ac.uk/iaph2007/
LIMC	*Lexicon iconographicum mythologicae classicae* vols. I–VIII (Zurich 1981–)
Lindgren I	Lindgren, H. C. and Kovacs, F. L., *Ancient Bronze Coins of Asia Minor and the Levant from the Lindgren Collection* (San Mateo, CA 1985).
LSA	*Last Statues of Antiquity* database, http://laststatues.classics.ox.ac.uk/
MAMA 8	Calder, W. M. and Cormack, J. M. R. (eds.), *Monumenta Asiae Minoris antiqua* VIII: *Monuments from Lycaonia, the Pisido-Phrygian Borderland, Aphrodisias* (Manchester 1962).
LRBC I & II	Carson, R. A. G., Hill, P. V., and Kent, J. P. C. *Late Roman Bronze Coinage* (New York 1978, reprinted 1989).
MBR	Buzdugan, G. Luchian, O., and Oprescu, C. C. *Monede și banknote românești* (București, 1977).
MIBE I	Hahn, W. and Metlich, M., *Money of the Incipient Byzantine Empire, Anastasius I – Justinian I, 491–565*. 2nd edn. (Vienna 2013).

MIBEC II	Hahn, W. and Metlich, M., *Money of the Incipient Byzantine Empire Continued, Justin II – Revolt of the Heraclii (565–610)* (Vienna 2009).
MIB III	Hahn, W., *Moneta Imperii Byzantini*, vol. 3, *von Heraclius bis Leo III / Alleinregierung (610–720)* (Vienna 1981).
Paris I	Morrisson, C., *Catalogue des monnaies byzantines de la Bibliothèque nationale*, vol. 1: *D'Anastasie Ier à Justinien II (491–711)* (Paris 1970).
Paris II	Morrisson, C., *Catalogue des monnaies byzantines de la Bibliothèque nationale*, vol. 2: *De Philippicus à Alexis III (711–1204)* (Paris 1970).
RIC I	Sutherland, C. H. V., *The Roman Imperial Coinage*, vol. 1: *From 31 BC to AD 69*. 2nd edn. (London 1984, reprinted 1999).
RIC V.1	Webb, P. H., *The Roman Imperial Coinage*, vol. 5.1: *Valerian to Florian* (London 1927).
RIC V.2	Webb, P. H., *The Roman Imperial Coinage*, vol. 5.2: *Probus to Amandus* (London 1933).
RIC VI	Sutherland, C. H. V., *The Roman Imperial Coinage*, vol. 6: *From Diocletian's Reform (AD 294) to the Death of Maximinus (AD 313)* (London 1967).
RIC VII	Bruun, P. M., *The Roman Imperial Coinage*, vol. 7: *Constantine to Licinius* (London 1967).
RIC VIII	Sutherland, C. H. V., *The Roman Imperial Coinage*, vol. 8: *The Family of Constantine I* (London 1981).
RIC IX	Pearce, J. W. E., *The Roman Imperial Coinage*, vol. 9: *Valentinian I to Theodosius I* (London 1951).
RIC X	Kent, J. P. C., *The Roman Imperial Coinage*, vol. 10: *The Divided Empire and the Fall of the Western Parts 395–491* (London 1994).
RPC I	Burnett, A., Amandry, M., and Ripollès, P. P., *Roman Provincial Coinage*, vol. 1: *From the Death of Caesar to the Death of Vitellius (44 BC–AD 69)*, 2 vols. (London and Paris 1992).
RPC II	Burnett, A., Amandry, M., and Carradice, I., *Roman Provincial Coinage*, vol. 2: *From Vespasian to Domitian (AD 69–96)*, 2 vols. (London and Paris 1999).
RPC III	Amandry, M. and Burnett, A., *Roman Provincial Coinage*, vol. 3: *Nerva, Trajan and Hadrian (AD 96–138)*, 2 vols. (London and Paris 2015).
RPC IV	*Roman Provincial Coinage*, vol. 4: *From Antoninus Pius to Commodus (AD 138–192)*. Online at https://rpc.ashmus.ox.ac.uk/
RPC VI	*Roman Provincial Coinage*, vol. 6: *From Elagabalus to Maximinus Thrax (AD 218–238)*. Online at https://rpc.ashmus.ox.ac.uk/
RPC VII.1	Spoerri Butcher, M., *Roman Provincial Coinage*, vol. 7.1: *De Gordien Ier à Gordien III (238–244). Province d'Asie*, 2 vols. (London and Paris 2006).
RPC VIII	Mairat, J. and Spoerri Butcher, M., *Roman Provincial Coinage*, vol. 8: *Philip I (AD 244–249)* (2020). Online at https://rpc.ashmus.ox.ac.uk/
SNG Ashmolean IX	Ashton, R. H. J., and Ireland, S., *Sylloge Nummorum Graecorum: Great Britain*, vol. 5: *Ashmolean Museum (Oxford)*, part 9: *Bosporus-Aeolis* (London 2007).
SNG Ashmolean XI	Ashton, R. H. J., and Ireland, S., *Sylloge Nummorum Graecorum: Great Britain*, vol. 5: *Ashmolean Museum (Oxford)*, part 11: *Caria to Commagene (except Cyprus)* (London 2013).
SNG Aul. Karien	Kraft, K., and Kienast, D., *Sylloge Nummorum Graecorum: Deutschland. Sammlung von Aulock*, Heft 7: *Karien* (Berlin 1962).
SNG Cop. Caria I	Breitenstein, N., *Sylloge Nummorum Graecorum: Denmark. The Royal Collection of Coins and Medals, Danish National Museum*, part 25: *Caria 1: Alabanda-Orthosia* (Copenhagen 1947).
SNG Cop. Caria II	Breitenstein, N., *Sylloge Nummorum Graecorum: Denmark. The Royal Collection of Coins and Medals, Danish National Museum*, part 26: Caria 2: *Sebastopolis-Trapezopolis* (Copenhagen 1947).
SNG Cop. Mysia	Breitenstein, N., *Sylloge Nummorum Graecorum: Denmark. The Royal Collection of Coins and Medals, Danish National Museum*, part 19: *Mysia* (Copenhagen 1945).
SNG München 22	Baldus, H. R., *Sylloge Nummorum Graecorum: Deutschland. Staatliche Münzsammlung München*, Heft 22: *Karien* (Berlin 2006).
SNG München 23	Leschhorn, W., *Sylloge Nummorum Graecorum: Deutschland. Staatliche Münzsammlung München*, Heft 23: *Lydien* (Berlin 1997).
SNG France 5	Levante, E., *Sylloge Nummorum Graecorum: France*, vol. 5: *Bibliothèque nationale de France: Mysie* (Paris and Zurich 2001).
SNG Tübingen 5	Mannsperger, D., *Sylloge Nummorum Graecorum: Deutschland. Münzsammlung der Universität Tübingen*, Heft 5: *Karien und Lydien* (Berlin 1994).
Von Aulock Phrygiens I	Hans von Aulock, *Münzen und Stadte Phrygiens*, Teil I (Tübingen 1980).

Notes to the reader

A range of numbering conventions is used throughout this study that warrant some explanation:

- *Notebooks*:
  Excavation notebooks held in the Aphrodisias archive are referenced according to their Nbk number, title, author and date (for example Nbk 209: *NW Sebasteion I* (K. Erim, 1981)).

- *Site code*:
  The site code for the excavations in the Place of Palms was SAg (for South Agora).

- *Trench numbers*:
  The trenches opened in the various excavation seasons are labelled by the site, year, and then number, for example, SAg. 14.1.

- *Context numbers*:
  Contexts (or stratigraphic units) are labelled in bold using a four-digit number (for example **1015**, **4480**); where duplicate numbers were used in different trenches, the trench number is added to the front of the context number (**17.2.5024**). The same sequence of numbers was used for deposits, cuts and structures. A list of the most important contexts, with a description of each, is provided in Appendix 6. Since excavations in the Place of Palms were carried out over multiple seasons and a large area, many contexts were found to equal other ones. Where this is the case, it is noted in Appendix 6. Where a single context has multiple context numbers, the number that refers to the greatest excavated part of it is used in both the text and Appendix 6 (for example **4482** equals **4484**, **5029**, **5031**, and **5032**, but in the text this context is referred to as just **4482**). Since find numbers provide a connection to materials in the on-site depots, the context numbers in these are not updated; as a result context **4482** can contain finds with context numbers **4484**, **5029**, **5031**, and **5032** in their labels.

- *Feature numbers*:
  In the stratigraphic discussion of the post-antique phases of the Place of Palms, in Ch. 8 and 9, built structures (such as field walls, platforms, trackways), are provided with feature numbers to facilitate discussion of them. These are labelled by phase and placed within square brackets, with their equivalent context numbers provided in a footnote, for example wall [5.1]: **4300/4440** or wall [6.1]: **4152/4297**.

- *Find numbers*:
  Finds were labelled during excavation with a code comprising site code, trench number, context number, and then find number, with the last of these preceded by an 'F' for small finds, a 'C' for coins, or an 'M' for marble finds (for example SAg.16.1.4342.F583). Since nearly all of the finds referred to in Ch. 8 come from trench SAg.17.1, that trench number is omitted from the finds numbers in Ch. 8, which are given as context number and then find number, for example 4482.F868 instead of SAg.17.1.4482.F868.

- *Inventory numbers*:
  Conserved small finds and finds of particular importance were provided with an inventory (Inv.) number, comprising the year of their discovery and a unique number, for example Inv. 16-065. In the text, inventoried finds are provided with both their find number and inventory number (for example SAg.16.1.4342.F583 (Inv. 16-065)).

- *Coin numbers*:
  In addition to their find numbers, coins were given a unique coin number following analysis by our numismatists; this comprises a 'C', followed by the date of discovery and a unique number (for example, C2016.005, which had the find number SAg.16.1.4203.C101). The coins found in the Place of Palms are included in this study in two catalogues, of non-Islamic coins (Appendix 3) and Islamic coins (Appendix 4), organized by date. The numbering system used in these catalogues runs across these two appendices and it is the catalogue number of individual coins that is referred to in the text (for example, Cat. 21).

- *Ceramic catalogue numbers*:
  Various fragments of ceramics were catalogued during the excavations and are discussed in Appendix 5. These are labelled using the trench number, context number, and then a unique identifying number (for example, 12.2.2015.1).

- *Epigraphic numbering conventions*:
  Inscriptions from the Place of Palms catalogued in Appendix 1 are labelled 'In' followed by a number (for example, In6). Informal texts, graffiti, masons' marks and gameboards catalogued in Appendix 2 are labelled according to their location: P (Pool), NS (North Stoa), WS (West Stoa), SS (South Stoa), and TW (Theatre Hill retaining wall); loose fragments are listed separately (L). Following each location code a separate numbering sequence is employed (for example, P1–513, NS1–360, WS1–115, SS1–32, TW1–10, L1–6).

- *Sculpture numbering conventions*:
In Ch. 6 the different elements of the sculpture associated with the sixth-century basin are labelled using the following conventions, each with a separate numbering sequence: **B** for the reliefs and statue bases used in the lower basin wall; **R** for the mythological reliefs; **P** for pillars; and **St** for the statue. In Ch. 7, **Bs** is used for statue base settings (for example, **Bs**-1), with all other sculpture and bases catalogued by a number in bold (for example, **119**). The inventory numbers of all these sculpted objects are listed in the catalogues in Ch. 6 and 7.

- *Architecture numbering conventions*:
The columns in the North, West and South Stoas are provided with separate numbers to facilitate the locating of architectural features and inscriptions relating to or in proximity to them. The columns of the North Stoa are labelled N1–70 (with N71 being the first column of the West Stoa, W1), running from east to west. The columns of the West Stoa are W1–20, running from north to south. The columns of the South Stoas, which have not been fully excavated, are labelled with a unique catalogue number according to the geographic location within which they were found and the type of block according to its position within an architectural order. The labels that correspond to geographic locations within each excavated area are: SE = southeast, SC = south-central, SCWTh = south-central, west of the Theatre Hill (pertaining only to column drums in the area that have been excavated but not reerected), SW = southwest, SWP = 'South West Portico' (column drums in the area that have been excavated but not re-erected), SG = 'South Gate/Propylon Gate', and NS = 'North Stoa' (blocks belonging to the South Stoas but moved at some point during excavation to the north). Within each geographic indicator, blocks are identified by a number sequence according to the location in which they were found, following east to west, and by element type, with aa = stylobate, a = base, b = column, c = capital, d = entablature, e = second-storey base, f = second-storey colonnette, and g = second-storey capital. Thus, SE1aa refers to the first stylobate block located in the southeastern section of the excavated area.

Contributors

The names of authors of each chapter are given in full beneath the chapter title. Authors of subsections of chapters are identified by their initials in parentheses following the relevant subheadings. If no initials are listed it can be assumed that the all authors of the chapter co-authored the subsection in question.

Initials	Name
AC	Angelos Chaniotis
AK	Allison Kidd
AT	Angela Trentacoste
ATT	Ahmet Tolga Tek
AW	Andrew Wilson
BR	Ben Russell
BT	Betül Teoman
ER	Erica Rowan
GT	Gültekin Teoman
HJ	Hugh Jeffery
HK	Hüseyin Köker
JJT	Joshua J. Thomas
MB	Müradiye Bursalı
MR	Mark Robinson
RRRS	Bert Smith
TP	Tim Penn
UO	Ulrike Outschar

In addition to those listed above, a wide range of colleagues and students contributed to the Place of Palms project. Andrew Ward, Valeria Riedemann, Hazal Avci, Onur Özdemir, Gabrielle Thiboutot, John Sigmier, Paige Chandler, Amanda Sharp, Allison Macintosh, Marlee Miller, Ayçe Gökdağ, Miłosz Klosowski, Christian Niederhüber, Martin Hallmannsecker, Ilknur Busra, Kelley Stone, Lisa Machi, Molly Daunt, Katherine Halcrow, Doğuş Coşar, Alis Altinel, Doğa Aras, Nefeli Piree-Iliou, Anja Schwarz, Hannah Simon, and Mariam Farooqi worked on the excavations, with occasional assistance from Blake Coleman, Jella Karademir, Hüseyin Burak Soy and Aydin Algül. Support for various aspects of the excavation was also provided by Alexander Sokolicek and in particular Ine Jacobs, who helped enormously in 2016 and 2017 especially. Architectural documentation was undertaken by Seth Dugger, Emily Davidson, Jacob Anderson, Yasmeen El-Jayyousi, Lindsay Wong, Amrita Ghosh, Kirk Webb, Pennie Liu, Lauren Aguilar, Lillian Candela, Jacob Anderson, Emma Brown, Robert Foy, Lior Melnick, Mary Tsai, Kate Jones, Sarah Beth McKay, Peter John Martinez, Alyssa Olson, and Dillon Horwitz, under the supervision of Harry Mark, who also provided support and advice throughout the project. Photography was carried out by Ian Cartwright and Defne Gier. The conservation team, who handled finds from the excavations, consisted of Federica Di Vita, Lucy-Anne Skinner, Buşra Ari, Kent Severson, Brian Castriota, Bermet Nishanova, Christine Haynes, Ariel O'Connor, and Soon Kai Poh. Deniz Burç assisted Ulrike Outschar and Muradiye Bursalı with the ceramics analysis. Takashi Fujii (2014–2015), Benjamin Wieland (2015), Masataka Masunaga (2015), Georgios Tsolakis (2018), and Özge Acar (2019) worked with Angelos Chaniotis on the identification and registration of the informal writing and drawings in the Place of Palms. Miranda Gronow helped with locating nineteenth- and early twentieth-century images of the site. Mark Robinson provided expert archaeobotanical skills and advice on planting pits and trenches, and sampled and identified material from organic deposits in the pool. Logistical assistance was given by Thomas Kaefer, Gerhard Paul, and Trevor Proudfoot. Useful discussion of architectural issues took place with Jim Coulton, Arzu Öztürk, Philip Stinson, and Brian Rose.

CHAPTER 1

Introduction: From 'South Agora' to 'Place of Palms'

Andrew Wilson and Ben Russell

The Aphrodisian complex that has been known since the 1930s as the 'South Agora' occupies a low, flat area in the centre of the city, between the southern flank of the Agora and the northern edge of the Theatre Hill (Fig. 1). In its most extensive form it was a large public piazza, surrounded on four sides by a combination of stoas and public buildings, with a monumental pool running down its centre (Pl. 1.A–B; Pl. 2.A). Rather than a single structure, it is a mosaic of different buildings which gave it the appearance of increasing unity over time. These constituent elements are the open area of the piazza itself and its pool, the stoas along the north, west, and south sides, and the monumental façade known as the 'Agora Gate' at its east end (Fig. 2). This was a nodal point in the urban plan of Aphrodisias: the Basilica opens on to the southern side of the space at its western end, the Hadrianic 'Olympian' Baths lie just to the west of the complex (Pl. 2.B), the Agora (sometimes called the 'North Agora') to its north, and the Theatre was accessible via a staircase off the eastern end of its south side (Pl. 3.A–B).

Since the labels assigned to the various elements of the complex have evolved over time, here we propose standardizing them: the stoas we refer to throughout as the North Stoa (previously the 'Portico of Tiberius'), West Stoa, and South Stoa, and the 'Agora Gate' as the Propylon; the choice of *stoa* and *propylon* is driven by the fact that the inscriptions on the monuments themselves use these terms. Our decision to dispense with the term 'South Agora' requires further explanation, given in sections D and F below.

A. EARLY INVESTIGATIONS, 18TH–20TH CENTURIES

The first reference in scholarship to the area occupied by the so-called 'South Agora' can be found in Richard Pococke's description of central Aphrodisias, which he visited in 1740. In this passage, which is quoted in full in the later publication of the Society of Dilettanti's expedition, Pococke notes that the space between the Theatre and the Temple (which he identified as that of Bacchus) was filled with colonnaded spaces: 'I saw remains of such pillars extending [from the Temple] to the Theatre and the other temple [probably the Hadrianic Baths], all which were probably covered, and made spacious shady walks for the great number of people that resorted to this place…'.[1]

Pococke's account includes no images of the site but the British expedition to Aphrodisias in 1813, sponsored by the Society of Dilettanti in London, spent considerable time documenting the monuments of the city centre. These were published in the third volume of their *Antiquities of Ionia* in 1840.[2] This expedition identified the series of columns noted by Pococke as the remains of the Agora, which they reconstructed as a rectangular piazza ringed by porticoes with interior colonnades on four sides.[3] Beyond these porticoes they proposed the existence of a further, outward-facing portico. While they were correct to assign most of these colonnades to the Agora, the columns that they interpreted as an external portico are actually those of the North Stoa of the 'South Agora'. This is confirmed by the fact that the 'Order of the Columns of the Exterior Portico of the Agora' depicted in Plate VI in the Society of Dilettanti volume includes a mask-and-garland frieze of the sort found in the 'South Agora' (Pl. 4.A), while the 'Elevation of the Portico of the Agora' in Plate V has a frieze of putti-and-garlands of the sort used in the Agora.[4] That there was some difficulty distinguishing between the columns of the two stoas is further shown by a comment in the caption to Plate V, which notes that some of the columns assigned to the Agora were inscribed with the name of ΚΛ. ΑΝΤΩΝΙΑ, which is true of two shafts from the North Stoa of the 'South Agora' but none in the Agora proper (see Ch. 3 §D).[5] Plate VI in the Society of Dilettanti publication, therefore, is the earliest representation we have of the architecture of this complex.

Of the various other nineteenth-century visitors to the ruins of Aphrodisias, Charles Texier and Charles Fellows add little to the picture sketched out by Pococke and the Society of Dilettanti expedition with regard to this space; they again identify just one agora, with an Ionic colonnade.[6] Alexandre Laborde, however, shows two views of the area of the Agora, one facing North that shows two columns of the North Stoa of the 'South Agora' with the Agora itself beyond.[7] A second image shows the standing columns at the South-East corner of the Agora facing South, with the retaining wall of the Theatre Hill in the background (Pl. 4.B).[8]

---

1 Pococke 1745, 69–70.
2 Society of Dilettanti 1840, 45–74.
3 Society of Dilettanti 1840, ch. II, Pl. IV.
4 Society of Dilettanti 1840, ch. II, Pl. V & VI.
5 Society of Dilettanti 1840, 64.
6 Texier 1849, 164–165; Fellows 1852, 251–257.
7 Laborde 1838, 98, Pl. LVII, 112.
8 Laborde 1838, 98, Pl. LVII, 111.

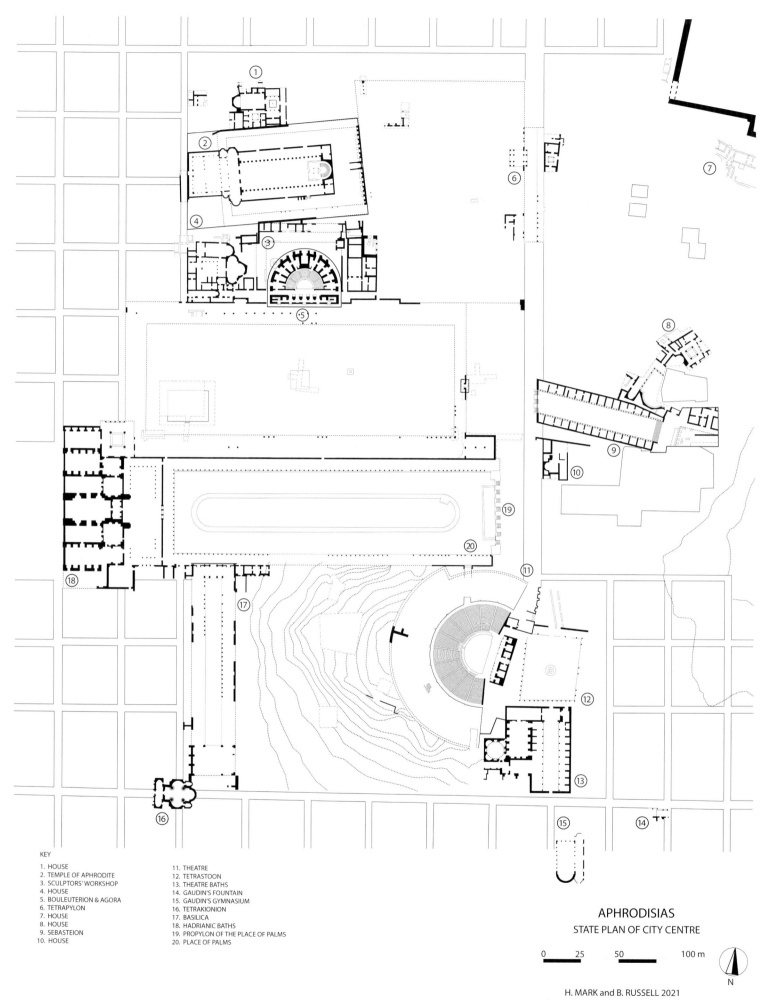

Fig. 1. State plan of the city centre of Aphrodisias.

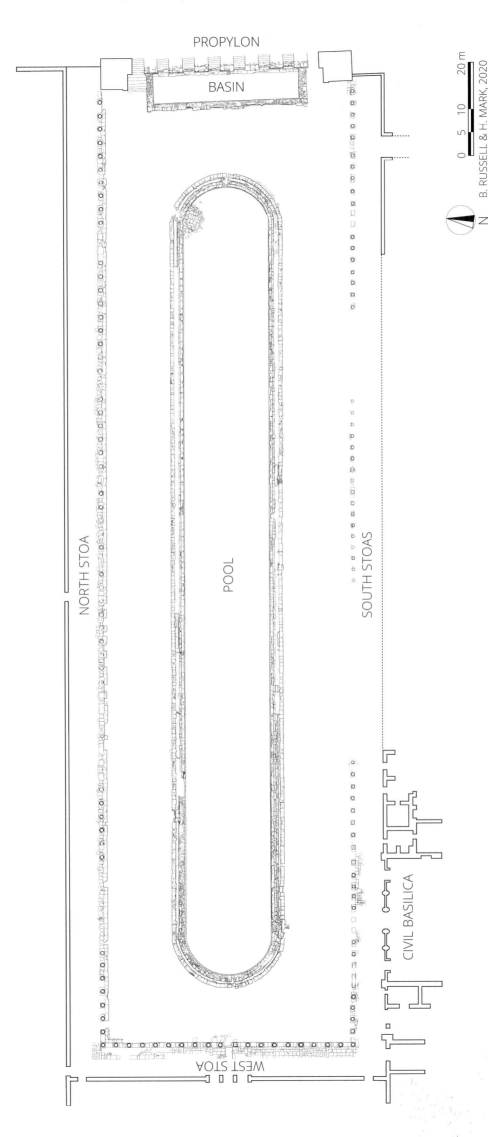

Fig. 2. State plan of the Place of Palms.

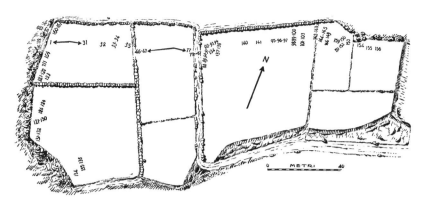

Fig. 3. Plan of mask-and-garland findspots,
as documented by Jacopi in 1937.

B. THE FIRST EXCAVATIONS, 1904–1905 AND 1937

The first excavations in the vicinity of the 'South Agora' were undertaken in 1904 and 1905, under the direction of Paul Gaudin and Gustave Mendel.[9] These concentrated on the Hadrianic Baths but extended as far east as the front of the West Stoa, which was at that point designated the 'Galerie de l'Est' of the Baths.[10] André Boulanger continued this work in the Hadrianic Baths in 1913 but did not venture any further to the east than Gaudin and Mendel.[11]

Excavations to the east of the Hadrianic Baths were eventually picked up by the Missione Archeologica Italiana in Anatolia in 1937, led by Giulio Jacopi.[12] Recognising the importance of the structures earlier identified, the Italian mission continued the excavations of the West Stoa and found its connection to the North Stoa; they then exposed c. 25 m of the latter and found most of the architectural elements in the position in which they had fallen (Fig. 3).[13]

The Italian team also found the architrave blocks with the dedicatory inscription on, as well as a substantial quantity of mask-and-garland frieze blocks.[14] This inscription showed that the building was dedicated to Aphrodite, the divine Augustus, Tiberius, Livia, and the *demos* at some point between AD 14 and 29, by a certain Diogenes son of Menandros (see Ch. 2 §A; Pl. 10.B). The structure has since become known as the 'Portico of Tiberius', despite the fact that the inscription specifically calls the building a 'stoa' and Tiberius was just one of the dedicatees.

Luigi Crema, who was responsible for the architectural analysis on this project, provided a detailed description of the architecture of the North Stoa and oversaw the taking of a series of casts of two columns and their entablature for the Museo della Civiltà Romana in EUR, Rome.[15] Crema also documented the architecture of the main colonnade of the West Stoa and observed the presence of a further colonnade along the south side of the piazza, the South Stoa (which we identify as multiple stoas), for the first time.[16] He proposed that the colonnades along the north, west and south sides of the space would have incorporated 175 columns, rising to 189 if there was also a stoa along the east side.[17] Considering that he was estimating the lengths of the structures he was fairly close: the total was probably c. 170–172 by the time the late antique South Stoa was added to the space (see Ch. 4 §F): 70 in the North Stoa, 20 in the West Stoa, and c. 80–82 in the South Stoa, depending on whether the two late antique parts of the latter had a gap between them or not.

Jacopi was the first to identify this complex as a commercial agora, and labelled it the 'South Agora' to distinguish it from the main Agora to the north; this name has been used in much of the subsequent literature.[18] Crema, however, noted in the same publication that the designation of this space as an agora was specious.[19] He raised the possibility that it could have functioned as part of a bath-gymnasium complex along with the Hadrianic Baths, but pointed out that it could only have been planned as such if a pre-Hadrianic bathhouse was located on the same site, for which there is currently no evidence. Here Crema referenced Silvio Ferri's brief note, published a year earlier, which proposed a possible connection between the epigraphically-attested Gymnasium of Diogenes (*Diogenianon*) and the recently-excavated North Stoa, which was dedicated by a Diogenes.[20] In the end, Crema argued against this proposal; the 'South Agora', he concluded, would have been simply too large a gymnasium for a city of this size, could not have been built directly with the Hadrianic Baths, and was connected to too many other structures to be a suitable venue for athletics. He left open the possibility, however, that excavations at the east end of the complex might shed new light on the function of the complex; a temple in this zone, he reasoned, would make this space appear much more like a Roman forum—a 'Foro di Tiberio'—than a traditional agora.

---

9   On these excavations Collignon 1904; 1906; Mendel 1906; Erim 1987, 8.
10 Mendel 1906, 159 (pl. 1), 164.
11 Boulanger 1914.
12 Jacopi 1939.
13 Crema 1939, 284.
14 Jacopi 1939, 85–96.
15 Crema 1939, 284–288, fig. 51–53.
16 Crema 1939, 288–292 (South Stoa), 292–295 (West Stoa).
17 Crema 1939, 295.
18 Jacopi 1939, 95–96; a view followed by Erim 1970, 92; Waelkens 1987; de Chaisemartin 1987.
19 Crema 1939, 296–304.
20 Ferri 1938, 59–60; the inscription is *CIG* II, 2782.

C. EXCAVATIONS BETWEEN 1969 AND 1991

Systematic excavations in the 'South Agora' were resumed by the New York University project, under the direction of Kenan Erim, in 1969. By this date the entire space, as opposed to just the North Stoa, had become generally referred to as the 'Portico of Tiberius'; this is the term used on the excavation notebooks for this sector of the city.

In 1969, work concentrated on the West Stoa and on its connection with the South Stoa, the existence of which Crema had first noted (Pl. 4.C).[21] It was in this year that much of the fallen colonnade and especially the inscriptions mentioning Albinos' restoration works were documented (see Ch. 4 §D).[22] In 1970 and 1971 the excavators worked from west to east along the line of the South Stoa and here encountered the façade of the Basilica and numerous panels of Diocletian's Edict on Maximum Prices that had been inscribed on it.[23] These discoveries convinced Erim that the 'Portico [of Tiberius] was indeed part of the marketplace of the city', as Jacopi had originally proposed. In 1972, during further work on the Basilica and its relationship with the 'South Agora', Erim was able to conclude that what remains of the South Stoa was late antique and that originally the Basilica did not have a colonnade along its front.[24]

Much of the northern half of the West Stoa, an area partially excavated already in the early twentieth century, was then cleaned in 1974 and 1975.[25] In 1984 the southern half of the structure was cleaned and a trench opened at its northern end, where it joins the North Stoa.[26] Finally, in 1988 a sondage was excavated by Ali Önce in the north-west corner of the open area of the complex, which showed that the West Stoa's sub-structures abutted those of the North Stoa, confirming that it was later.[27] The latter building was fully excavated between 1984 and 1985.[28] The excavations in 1984 confirmed that much of the architecture of the North Stoa lay where it had fallen: 'it is clear that some of the column drums have been scattered a little, yet many of them are more or less in the vicinity of their original location, along with capitals, architrave and occasionally frieze fragments' (Pl. 4.D–E).[29] Three carved marble seats were also found in the North Stoa 'neatly aligned at one point in front of the backwall of the portico.'[30] The re-erection of the fragments of the North Stoa's colonnade was also begun in 1985.[31]

In 1975, while work was going on in the West Stoa, investigations at the other end of the complex discovered the Propylon.[32] Excavation of this structure continued in 1977 and 1980, when a number of the late antique interventions, including the inscriptions mentioning Ampelios and Doulkitios, were first found (Pl. 5.A).[33] These discoveries, and the excavation of a large basin in front of the structure (see Pl. 58.A–B), led Erim to propose that the Propylon was turned into a *nymphaeum* in late antiquity, an interpretation that was accepted until recently. The structure continued to be excavated between 1983 and 1987.[34] At the same time, work resumed on the south side of the 'South Agora', and in 1984 the stairway up to the Theatre was identified.[35]

Much of the eastern end of the South Stoa, and a substantial section of its centre, was excavated in 1986 and many of its columns re-erected (Pl. 5.B).[36] Erim astutely dated this stoa to late antiquity, proposing the fifth century specifically, and concluded that 'the south flank of the Portico of Tiberius [that is, the 'South Agora'] was either not completed in early Imperial times, or thoroughly overhauled or rebuilt after serious damage caused by the late fourth century earthquake.'[37]

While most of the excavations conducted in the 1970s and early 1980s in the 'South Agora' concentrated on the structures around the edge of this space, several trenches did touch on its interior area. Those carried out in 1984 at its western end discovered that the original ground level was much lower than the stylobates of the surrounding stoas. Erim concluded that the ground level had been raised in late antiquity and the excavators identified a series of terracotta pipes laid in this fill.[38] These interventions were connected by Erim to a supposed fourth-century earthquake and restoration work in its wake. Excavations

---

21 Erim 1970, 92–93; Nbk 76: *NE Nymphaeum / SW Portico of Tiberius* (S. Kulaklı, 1969).

22 See also Erim 1975, 78.

23 Erim 1972, 58–59; 1973, 65–66; see Nbk 82–84: *Baths of Hadrian/Portico of Tiberius, Books 1–3* (S. Crawford and J. Gary, 1970); Nbk 85: *Portico of Tiberius: Catalogue of Architectural Finds* (S. Crawford and J. Gary, 1970); Nbk 100–102: *Portico of Tiberius, Books 1–3* (P.F.M. Zahl, 1971).

24 Erim 1974, 41; Nbk 134–137: *Portico of Tiberius/'Basilica', 1–4* (P. McDermott, 1972).

25 See Nbk 153: *W Portico of Tiberius* (1974); Nbk 164: *SE Corner Tetrastoon (Piazza); E Tetrastoon; E Theatre Baths (Aula Thermale); Clearing Portico of Tiberius* (A.A.W.J., K.T. Erim, 1975).

26 Erim 1985, 180; see Nbk 256: *N Portico of Tiberius, Book 1* (N. de Chaisemartin and T. Çıkış, 1984); Nbk 257: *N Portico of Tiberius, Book 2* (T. Çıkış, 1984).

27 Nbk 300: *Portico of Tiberius NCE I* (A. Önce, 1988), 5; noted in de Chaisemartin and Lemaire 1996, 153.

28 Erim 1985, 180; see Nbk 256: *N Portico of Tiberius, Book 1* (N. de Chaisemartin and T. Çıkış, 1984); Nbk 257: *N Portico of Tiberius, Book 2* (T. Çıkış, 1984).

29 Nbk 259: *Portico of Tiberius: North-Central East* (K. Erim, 1984), 3; for photographs showing the collapsed colonnade, see Nbk 269: *Portico of Tiberius NE II, Book 2* (A. Önce, 1985), 2; Nbk 272: *Portico of Tiberius: North-Central East 1985* (K. Erim and J. Gorence, 1985), 60.

30 Erim 1986a, 179; see Nbk 268: *Portico of Tiberius NCE I; NE I; NE II, Book 1* (A. Önce, 1985), 13; Nbk 272: *Portico of Tiberius: North-Central East 1985* (K. Erim and J. Gorence, 1985), 54.

31 On work in the North Stoa in 1985, see also Nbk 269: *Portico of Tiberius NE II, Book 2* (A. Önce, 1985); Nbk 270: *Portico of Tiberius NE III; NE IV* (A. Önce, 1985); Nbk 272: *Portico of Tiberius: North-Central East 1985* (K. Erim and J. Gorence, 1985).

32 Erim 1976, 28–29; restoration Erim 1984, 206; 1985, 179.

33 Erim 1981, 180–181.

34 Erim 1984; Nbk 253: *S Agora Gate I-84, Book 1* (B. Rose, 1984); Nbk 254: *S Agora Gate I-84, Book 2, also containing I-85* (B. Rose and A. Önce, 1984); Nbk 280: *E Agora Gate* (S. Doruk, 1986); Nbk 287: *Agora Gate Basin I* (B. Odabaşı and E. Üçbaylar, 1987).

35 Erim 1985, 180; see Nbk 253: *S Agora Gate I-84, Book 1* (B. Rose, 1984); Nbk 254: *S Agora Gate I-84, Book 2, also containing I-85* (B. Rose and A. Önce, 1984); Nbk 271: *Portico of Tiberius S I; S II* (A. Önce, 1985).

36 Nbk 278: *Portico of Tiberius SE I; SW I* (J. Gorence and K. Erim, 1986); Nbk 279: *Portico of Tiberius SE I, Book 2* (K. Erim and J. Gorence, 1986).

37 Erim 1986a, 180.

38 Erim 1985, 180.

in front of the North Stoa in 1985 confirmed the observations made to the west two years earlier: the stylobate was raised on top of a course of seat blocks above the original ground level of the space, and this area was filled in late antiquity, with new pipes laid across it.[39]

The focus on the peripheries of the 'South Agora' meant that the final feature of the complex to be identified archaeologically was the monumental pool that ran down its centre. A stretch of the southern walls of this structure was discovered in 1984, eighty years after the first excavations in the area, but at this point their significance was not appreciated. In her notebook on the excavations of her Trench B in the middle of the 'South Agora' in 1984, Juliette de La Genière describes simply the discovery of 'two rows of re-used blocks in an east–west direction', which were interpreted as the remains of a 'road' or pathway across this marshy area.[40] The large number of inscriptions and gameboards on the blocks was noted, as was the similarity of at least one of the reused blocks with the seat blocks from the Theatre.

In 1985, a section of the northern pool walls, near the centre of the pool, was uncovered by Ali Önce during his work on the clearance of the North Stoa (Pl. 5.C).[41] Only in 1988, when work in front of the Propylon, overseen by Francis Thode, discovered the eastern end of the pool, was its full scale appreciated.[42] At this point a substantial section of the northern portion of the east end of the pool walls was explored and the channel between them excavated; the hydraulic arrangements at this end of the structure were also carefully documented. A trench at the western end confirmed the extent and precise configuration of the pool, and Önce's earlier trench was also re-opened and expanded.[43] The discovery of the pool in 1988 was a surprise: as Erim put it, 'at the present state of investigation, this unexpected feature of the Tiberian portico cannot be fully explained.'[44] The fact that the exterior edges of the pool walls were treated as seats, like the blocks beneath the stylobates of the stoas, encouraged Erim to question the validity of Jacopi's identification of the area as an agora.

This renewed interest in the function of the 'South Agora' prompted a series of interventions between 1988 and 1990 in the pool itself, which exposed the eastern and western ends of the structure for distances of c. 18 m and c. 50 m respectively (see Fig. 4).[45] At the east end a late ramp of stone blocks was located in 1989 (a probable 'cattle ramp'; see Ch. 8 §A; Pl. 80.D).[46] Also from the east end of the pool came a well-preserved carved wooden panel decorated with a meander pattern, probably part of the architecture of the North Stoa (see Pl. 12.B).[47] In 1990, three trenches were opened by Nathalie de Chaisemartin and Dinu Theodorescu within the North Stoa, with the specific aim of testing the theory that this structure could have been part of a gymnasium.[48] In the first of these (1990-S1), the excavators identified what they argued was a sunken floor running along the centre of the stoa, which had a surface of marble chips set in a light mortar; on either side of this they recognized raised walkways, into which terracotta pipes were cut in late antiquity, with the southernmost of these walkways partially supported by a row of rough blocks below the level of the stylobate. A second sondage (1990-S2) further east identified some of the same features, though again it was noted that the interior of the North Stoa was heavily modified in late antiquity.[49] A third trench cleared the central doorway between the 'South Agora' and the Agora proper, where the row of marble seats had previously been found re-used as part of the back wall of the North Stoa.[50]

In 1991, the same excavators, with Anca Lemaire, opened a further five trenches to investigate the relationship between the components of the complex and the date of them.[51] The first of these trenches (1991-S1) targeted the north-east corner and showed that the North Stoa originally turned here, probably for two intercolumniations or c. 4.5 m, before the Propylon was built.[52] This was confirmed by a trench inside the basin in front of the Propylon (1991-S4), which found no trace of an earlier stoa.[53] A third trench (1991-S2) explored the join between the South Stoa and the Propylon. This confirmed the late date of most of what remains of the South Stoa but also identified the sub-structures of an earlier stoa, which does not seem to have turned to the north beneath the later Propylon.[54] At the north-west corner of the complex, a further trench (1991-S5) was opened inside the West Stoa, just to the west of the 1988 sondage excavated by Önce, which confirmed that the seat blocks and *euthynteria* of the North Stoa originally continued further to the west.[55] Finally, a trench (1991-S3) was opened against the exterior of the northern wall of the pool itself, which first iden-

39 See Nbk 257: *N Portico of Tiberius, Book 2* (T. Çıkış, 1984), 10 for a plan of these pipes; Nbk 259: *Portico of Tiberius: North-Central East* (K. Erim, 1984), 4–5.
40 Nbk 252: *S Agora/Temple of Aphrodite/Acropolis (Höyük)* (J. de La Genière, 1984), 6–10.
41 Nbk 269: *Portico of Tiberius NE II, Book 2* (A. Önce, 1985), 17–18, 23.
42 Nbk 298: *Agora Gate: Basin Front II* (F. Thode, 1988), 14–16.
43 Nbk 293: *Portico of Tiberius W I* (A. Tulga et al., 1988); Nbk 300: *Portico of Tiberius NCE I* (A. Önce, 1988).
44 Erim (1990, 20) correctly noted the exceptional size of the structure and drew comparisons with the pools in the Library of Hadrian at Athens, the Villa of the Papyri at Herculaneum, and the Canopus of Hadrian's Villa at Tivoli (see Ch. 2 §D).
45 , 13. For 1988: Nbk 299: *Agora Gate: Basin II* (E. Üçbaylar et al., 1988). For 1989: Nbk 304: *Portico of Tiberius W I* (A. Page and F. Thode, 1989); Nbk 305: *Portico of Tiberius W II* (A. Page and F. Thode, 1989); Nbk 306: *W Portico of Tiberius; SW Pool* (K. Görkay, 1989); Nbk 307: *SW Portico of Tiberius* (F. Thode, 1989); Nbk 308: *Portico of Tiberius SI & II* (A. Page, 1989); Nbk 309: *Portico of Tiberius SIII* (A. Page, 1989); Nbk 310: *E Portico of Tiberius: Basin 89-I* (A. Önce, 1989). For 1990: Nbk 316: *Portico of Tiberius: W Pool, Book I; E Pool* (A.T. Tek, 1990); Nbk 317: *Portico of Tiberius: W Pool, Book II* (A.T. Tek, 1990); Nbk 318: *Portico of Tiberius: E Pool* (A. Önce, 1990).
46 Nbk 310: *E Portico of Tiberius: Basin 89-I* (A. Önce, 1989), 24.
47 Smith 1996, 1920, fig. 11.
48 For all trenches, see Nbk 319: *Portico of Tiberius: Sondage 1; Sondage 2; NCE Porte Centrale* (N. de Chaisemartin and D. Theodorescu, 1990); see also, de Chaisemartin and Lemaire 1996, 150 fig. 1, 167–171.
49 de Chaisemartin and Lemaire 1996, 167, fig. 18.
50 de Chaisemartin and Lemaire 1996, 171, fig. 20; de Chaisemartin 1989a, 73.
51 For all trenches, see Nbk 323: *Portico of Tiberius Sondages* (D. Theodorescu et al., 1991).
52 de Chaisemartin and Lemaire 1996, 152–3 fig. 3.
53 de Chaisemartin and Lemaire 1996, 158, fig. 9.
54 de Chaisemartin and Lemaire 1996, 157–8 fig. 8.
55 de Chaisemartin and Lemaire 1996, 153–4 fig. 6.

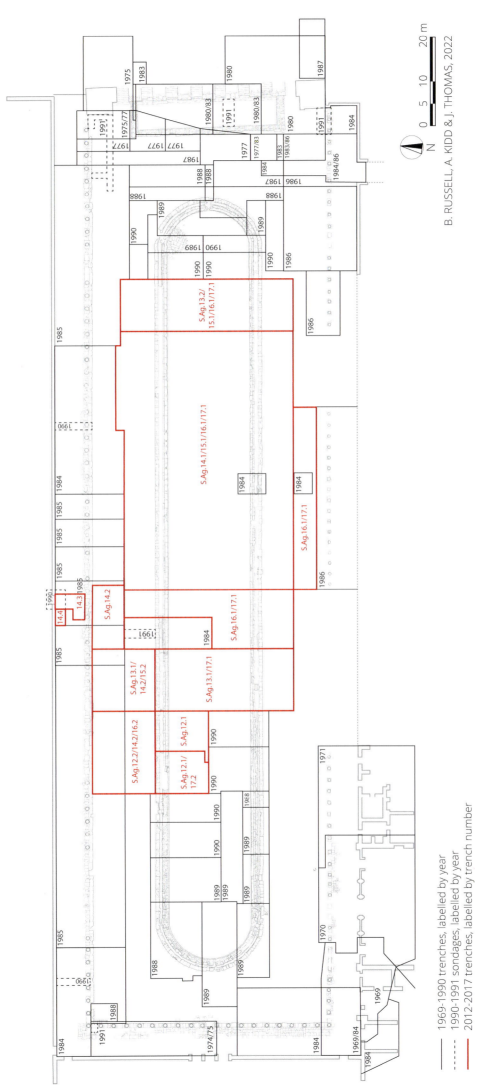

Fig. 4. Outlines of trenches in the Place of Palms.

tified the fact that the pool walls were raised in late antiquity in a second phase of building.[56] This information has proved vital for reconstructing the development of the area over time.

D. THE FUNCTION OF THE 'SOUTH AGORA'

In the wake of the discovery of the pool and the excavations between 1988 and 1991, the possibility that the 'South Agora' could in fact have been built as a gymnasium, an idea proposed by Ferri and explored but dismissed by Crema in 1939, began to gain traction again. In 1989, de Chaisemartin, who had worked on the mask-and-garland frieze of the 'South Agora' since 1979, published a key article arguing once more for the identification of the entire complex as a gymnasium, based primarily on its plan and the iconography of its architectural ornamentation.[57] This was followed up in 1996 by a fuller discussion of this proposal.[58] The key additional pieces of evidence that de Chaisemartin and Lemaire marshalled in support of their argument were: first, the dimensions of the space (which they compared to hellenistic gymnasia elsewhere)[59] and its connection with the Hadrianic Baths and their putative predecessor; second, the archaeological evidence that they identified within the North Stoa in 1990 and interpreted as a sunken exercise track; and third, the inscription mentioning a Gymnasium of Diogenes that Ferri had first connected to this space.[60]

The first of these bodies of evidence had already been partially dismissed by Crema, while Christopher Ratté has shown that the overall dimensions of the complex were largely determined by those of the earlier Agora; so while it is true that the space was large enough to have been used for certain athletic events, it remains unlikely that the complex was built with these in mind.[61] There is also as yet no evidence that another set of baths existed on the site of the later Hadrianic Baths.[62]

The archaeological evidence from within the North Stoa is more complicated. Using the data from the 1990 excavations, de Chaisemartin and Lemaire argued that this structure was built as a covered exercise area or *xystos*, a portico type that Vitruvius tells us was commonly associated with gymnasia and enabled athletics, especially wrestling, to be carried out undercover during winter months.[63] Vitruvius says such a portico should have walkways of at least 10 feet along either side, with a sunken area between them not less than 12 feet wide. If he means that each walkway should be 10 feet wide then this implies a total minimum internal width of 32 Roman feet or *c.* 9.44 m. The features identified by de Chaisemartin and Lemaire are much narrower than this, but they argue that Vitruvius means that the walkways together should have a width of 10 feet, in which case the deposits they document in the North Stoa are of broadly the correct dimensions.[64] This seems however to force an unlikely meaning from the Latin, and since Vitruvius specifies later in his text that the *xystos* is a portico of large dimensions, it is overwhelmingly more likely that he means that each walkway should be 10 feet wide, *c.* 3 m, rather than just 1.5 m.[65] The North Stoa, as Bert Smith noted at the time, with its internal width of 6.59 m, is simply not large enough to accommodate such activities.[66] The other features identified during the excavations can also be explained differently: the layer of marble chips interpreted by de Chaisemartin and Lemaire as an exercise track is more likely a layer of construction debris related to the erection of the building; the rough blocks beneath the back of the stylobate are also simply part of the foundations of the colonnade.[67] Other features of the interior of the North Stoa that are mostly late antique are examined further in Ch. 4 §E.

The third piece of evidence referenced by de Chaisemartin and Lemaire is the inscription, found in the area of the Theatre, mentioning a Gymnasium of Diogenes.[68] Ferri first connected this text to the 'South Agora' because of the mention of a Diogenes. However, this inscription, honouring Marcus Ulpius Carminius Claudianus, dates to the second century AD, as shown by Anne-Valérie Pont,[69] and Angelos Chaniotis has argued that the gymnasium in question was named after a sponsor, Lucius Antonius Claudius Diogenes Dometeinos, who provided funds for the *gymnasiarchos* in eternity in *c.* AD 175.[70] The exact reference in the text is also to the construction of an anointing room (ἀλειπτήριον) in the gymnasium and so probably to part of a bath complex; Chaniotis suggests that the obvious structure to connect this text to is the second-century Theatre Baths.

Two other observations count against the gymnasium proposal. While Erim considered the possibility that the pool could have had 'a practical as well as an aesthetic purpose', further exploration of it suggested it was probably too shallow, at maximum *c.* 0.94 m (see Ch. 2 §B), to be a swimming pool, the *natatio* that de Chaisemartin and Lemaire also refer to;[71] in comparison most *natationes* in Roman bathhouses are between 1 m and 2 m deep, while the swimming pool in the Hasmonean

---

56 de Chaisemartin and Lemaire 1996, 158–9, fig. 9.
57 de Chaisemartin 1989b. For a full publication of the mask and garland frieze, and similar friezes elsewhere in the city, see de Chaisemartin forthcoming; in that volume de Chaisemartin has not revised her interpretation in the light of new evidence, and continues to identify the 'South Agora' as a gymnasium.
58 de Chaisemartin and Lemaire 1996.
59 de Chaisemartin 1989a; b; de Chaisemartin and Lemaire 1996, 170.
60 For an extended, and more recent, discussion of the gymnasium proposal, see Maiuro 2007, 203–209; Ismaelli 2011, 167; de Chaisemartin forthcoming.
61 Ratté 2002, 16.
62 A later suggestion by Joyce Reynolds (1995) that an inscription found in the Hadrianic Baths relates to a pre-Hadrianic bath building is to be rejected; see Wilson 2016a, 182.
63 de Chaisemartin and Lemaire 1996, 167–170. On this building type, Vitruvius, *De Arch* V.11.3–4,.
64 de Chaisemartin and Lemaire 1996, 170.
65 Vitruvius, *De Arch* VI.7.5; *De Arch* V.11.3 reads: *ita facta, uti in partibus, quae fuerint circa parietes et quae erit ad columnas, margines habeant uti semitas non minus pedum denum mediumque excavatum, uti gradus sint in descensu marginibus sesquipedem ad planitiem, quae planities sit non minus pedes xii*, and the translation F. Granger gives in the Loeb series is 'On the sides which adjoin the walls and those which adjoin the columns, they are to have borders ten feet wide to serve as paths.'
66 Smith 1996, 45.
67 Smith 1996, 45.
68 de Chaisemartin 1989a, 73.
69 Pont 2008.
70 Chaniotis 2008b, 72–3.
71 Erim 1990, 20; de Chaisemartin and Lemaire 1996, 164.

winter palace complex at Jericho was 4 m deep.[72] Instead, as Smith has put it, the pool's 'primary purpose was surely ornamental—it was a grand civic "amenity" providing nothing more practical than an impressive display and cooler air in the summer heat within the complex.'[73]

The key final point about the 'South Agora' that is never truly dealt with by de Chaisemartin and Lemaire is its position within the city plan. This was a public space of high traffic and a vital lynchpin in the urban plan, quite unlike a gymnasium (see Fig. 1; Pl. 2.B, 3.A–B). The Basilica opens on to it; the Propylon is oriented towards its interior; it is directly connected to the Theatre, Hadrianic Baths, the Agora proper, and the Tetrapylon Street. By the second century it had three entrances from the north, two from the east, at least four from the south, and three from the west; in its first phase it appears to have been completely open at its eastern end and across much of its southern side. The construction of the enormous set of stairs up through the Theatre Hill retaining wall, at the point at which the whole area was first laid out, is testament to the envisaged role of this area as one of high connectivity.[74] As Smith has noted, 'a gymnasium was a private space in which youths exercised naked and which could, at least in principle, be closed.'[75] For Ratté the 'South Agora' was, in contrast, essentially a thoroughfare: its location 'in the centre of the city with useful buildings all around it meant that it was actually on the way from one place to another, and so probably more often passed through, than visited in its own right'; he compares it to key street intersections in places like Miletos or Ephesos, which gradually developed into focal points in their respective urban armatures.[76]

If the area was not a gymnasium, was Jacopi correct that it was a second commercial agora? This interpretation is also problematic. *Topos* inscriptions, seemingly identifying the locations of stallholders in the stoas, certainly do attest to commercial activity here in late antiquity,[77] but the complex is unlikely to have been built as a marketplace: the Agora was presumably the city's main commercial space. Instead of an agora the more obvious parallels for the complex are in fact the grand *porticus* of late republican and imperial Rome. Crema first noted this 'Roman' connection in the 1930s and the proposal has been further developed by Smith: this was 'a second public square, a grand piazza, progressively equipped with lavish marble architecture, fine marble decoration, a sumptuous aedicular "gate", and a magnificent pool – none of it for any particular function (rather the reverse, all conspicuously useless), but, like the great *porticus* of Rome, designed for the pleasure and well-ordered leisure of all good citizens with the means and free time to enjoy it.'[78] Ratté draws a parallel with Central Park in New York and highlights the significance of the complex in the urban development of the city. Following the major phase of construction at Aphrodisias in the Augustan period under C. Julius Zoilos, the famous freedman of Octavian, this central urban complex was one of the key structures of a Tiberian building programme that was sponsored by a new range of local elites, who Joyce Reynolds proposed were consciously asserting themselves in the post-Zoilos era.[79] Ratté notes the scale of the undertaking, which required the cutting back the Theatre Hill, and its significance for urban foot traffic, providing a key connection between Theatre and Temple via the Agora for the first time.[80]

E. THE MICA AND AHMET ERTEGÜN SOUTH AGORA POOL PROJECT, 2012–2018

One set of data from the 'South Agora' that was never integrated into these various discussions of its function is the late antique inscriptions on the façade of the Propylon. These texts honour those responsible for the reconstruction of the complex in the late fifth/early sixth century AD. They are discussed in detail below (in Ch. 4 §A and Appendix 1), but a key point from the northernmost of the three inscriptions (In10) is relevant here.[81] This text gives thanks on behalf of the nymphs to a certain Ampelios 'because he gave wonder and splendid beauty to this place of palms, so that anyone who, among our waters, turns his glance around, may always sing the praise both of him, and of the place, and of the Nymphs as well.' Only in 2011 was the implication of this inscription first appreciated: the composer of this text was assuming that whoever who was reading it was standing in the 'Place of Palms', which must therefore be the open area of the so-called 'South Agora'. The 'waters' mentioned are presumably those of the pool, since the basin in front of the Propylon, as will be shown below (see Ch. 4 §A, §N), was added after the inscription.

By late antiquity, then, the so-called 'South Agora' was apparently called the 'Place of Palms'. Whether it had this name from the beginning is impossible to know. However, there certainly was a palm grove in the city earlier, as a first- or second-century inscription attests, and it seems unlikely that the city had two complexes known in this way.[82] This raised the possibility that, exactly like the *porticus* of Rome referenced by Smith, this complex was not just a grand piazza, striking for the scale of its surrounding architecture and its pool in particular, but also a green space, planted with trees and bushes to provide shade—an urban park, not like New York's Central Park in appearance though similar in function.

In 2012, a pair of test trenches was opened to see whether the theory that this was a planted area could be proven (Fig. 4). Two contiguous trenches were opened at the western end of the unexcavated area of the pool (to the west of the middle of the pool), one within it and one covering the area between it and the North Stoa. Inside the pool, these excavations enabled the various phases of filling and silting-up of the structure in the post-Roman period, which had first been documented in the

---

72 Nielsen 1990, 155; for example, the *natationes* in the Baths of Caracalla, 1.20–1.40 m deep (Yegül 1992, 158), and the Hadrianic Baths at Lepcis Magna, 1.73 m deep (Bartoccini 1929, 31). Jericho: Netzer 1975, 92.
73 Erim 1990, 20; Smith 1996, 13.
74 On this point, Smith 1996, 45; Ratté 2002, 15; Raja 2012, 38.
75 Smith 1996, 49.
76 Ratté 2002, 24.
77 Roueché 1989, 237–9 (nos 199–206); see also Ch. 5 §D.
78 Smith 1996, 49.
79 Ratté 2002, 16; Reynolds 1987.
80 Ratté 2002, 16; also Raja 2012, 38, 51.
81 *IAph2007* 4.202.i.
82 *MAMA* VIII.448 = *IAph2007* 12.204.

late 1980s and early 1990s, to be carefully recorded. Outside the pool, the late antique raising of the ground level that Erim had first identified and the imperial period ground level beneath it were uncovered. The discovery of two parallel rows of planting trenches in this area confirmed the hypothesis that this was a garden or planted space.[83] The 2012 excavations also confirmed the preservation of some organic matter, including a piece of Cretan date palm (*Phoenix theophrasti*) in the very lowest layers of the fill of the pool.[84] In response to these promising results, an ambitious 5-year project was launched in 2013 to study this complex fully. This new project was generously sponsored in the name of Mica and Ahmet Ertegün and its overall aims were to complete the excavation and documentation of the complex, conserve the newly-exposed structures, and organize the area into visitor-friendly space with appropriate signage and walkways—to make it more intelligible to visitors, in other words (for the appearance of the complex in 2011, see Pl. 6.A–B).

The more specific aims of the excavators with regard to each of the areas of the complex were as follows:

1. The pool: to excavate the remaining fill, recover and sample more organic material, and document all the finds, in order to examine what they reveal about the abandonment of the complex; to document and analyse its walls, floor and hydraulic fittings, as well as evidence for alterations made over time; to record graffiti, gameboards, preparation settings for statue bases, fountain fixtures, and other fittings around the edges of the pool in order to investigate the sculptural programme and the social use of space.
2. The piazza: to investigate the planting trenches discovered in 2012 and associated early ground surfaces (see Pl. 6.C); to date and assess the late antique changes to the ground surface around the pool and the stimulus for them.
3. North, West, and South Stoas: to analyse the architecture of each of these structures, their phasing, and the evidence for their evolution over time; to study the marble revetment from the North Stoa; to record graffiti and gameboards.
4. Propylon: to provide a new assessment of the epigraphy of this structure and its possible date; to re-assess the evidence for late antique interventions, especially the date of the basin. Although further architectural study of this monument is a key desideratum, it was beyond the scope of the present project.
5. Post-antique levels: to date the destruction of the complex and its causes; to record and date all of the medieval and later field walls and structures in the area to understand the post-antique inhabitation and agricultural use of the area.

In 2013, trenches were opened immediately to the east of the 2012 trenches and adjacent to them, as well as at the eastern end of the unexcavated area of the pool (Pl. 7.A). Work continued in these trenches in 2014, with the latter being expanded to the west, leaving just a thin strip of unexcavated area between the two trenches (Pl. 7.B). A sondage in the central section of the North Stoa was also undertaken in this year. In 2015, work focused on the centre of the complex, the area above the pool and its walls, where significant remains of later settlement were uncovered (Pl. 7.C), as well as on the upper level of the late antique raised ground level to the north, where further traces of a late phase of planting, comprising pits rather than trenches, were exposed. In 2016 the last remaining strip of unexcavated land across the middle of the pool was excavated so that the fill of the pool could be removed stratigraphically across its full remaining extent in phase (Pl. 8). This work was completed in 2017, when the lowest deposits in the pool were excavated (Pl. 9.A) and conservation began in 2018 (Pl. 9.B–C).

Alongside the excavations, a full architectural study of the complex was undertaken. New state plans and elevations were produced of the stoas along the north, west and south sides of the space, the remains of the western side of the Propylon and its basin, the Theatre Hill retaining wall, and the walls of the pool itself, as they were uncovered. The architecture of the stoas and the pool, including its hydraulic infrastructure, was re-analysed. The sculptural finds from the entire complex, most of them made in the 1970 and 1980s, were plotted and catalogued, and the reliefs from the Propylon basin re-examined. Numismatic, archaeobotanical, and zooarchaeological analysis was carried out alongside work on the ceramic and small finds assemblages. At the same time, a full epigraphic survey of all the marble surfaces of the complex revealed a colossal number of formal and informal texts testifying to the intensive use of the space.

Excavation methodology and recording, and stratigraphic considerations

The excavation, cleaning, and recording of trenches as large as those opened in the 'Place of Palms' (which eventually became one trench in 2016 and 2017) present considerable challenges, exacerbated in this case by the number of post-antique drystone-wall structures built across the filled-in pool, and the expanse of rubble dumps from earlier excavations to the south of the limit of the pool, below the Theatre Hill.

On the one hand, the stratigraphic integrity of most of the soil layers excavated across the open area of the 'Place of Palms' above the levels of the pool walls, corresponding to the post-antique levels in the main, was poor. There was a particular problem, the result of taphonomic processes, in relating soil layers to structural phases. The soil layers excavated were all silty deposits that had accumulated by alluviation or colluviation from the Theatre Hill, and although brown when moist (after rain), quickly turned grey on drying and with exposure to the sun. New contexts could be distinguished by greater amounts of inclusions (especially brick/tile and rubble), but for the most part soil layers might be 10–20 cm thick, composed of grey silt with relatively few cultural inclusions. Such layers represent the accumulation of alluvial deposits over a considerable period of time, and changes between them are often unclear; distinctions between such contexts during excavation are necessarily arbitrary, and based in part on the levels of bases of walls belonging to post-antique—medieval or post-medieval—structures or field

---

[83] For a summary of the 2012 excavations, see Wilson, Russell, and Ward 2016.
[84] See Robinson 2016.

systems built over the filled-in pool. Yet the walls that the soil layers abut or cover represent almost discrete events within these longer processes of soil formation; changes in sedimentation regime sufficient to be recognised as a new soil context do not necessarily coincide with the events relating to the construction or destruction of walls or buildings. Associated surfaces were remarkably hard to identify; although we expected to find, and looked for, beaten earth floors within buildings, for the most part they were not recognised, perhaps because the buildings used wooden floors on the dwarf wall foundations, or rugs or carpets.

A number of groups of post supports was recognised by one or more (usually three or four) stones set in the ground on edge at an angle. The same technique is still used locally for wooden structures, such as the temporary shelters (çardaklar) built on site to provide shade for the excavators. Normally one would expect to identify the postholes in which these were set, but the soil within them was visually identical to that around them, and it was only the characteristic setting of the stones on edge that was diagnostic. The result was that the post-settings had to be excavated in reverse stratigraphical order, pedestalled during the excavation of a soil layer, with the resultant risk of contamination of the soil context by intrusive material that might have been within the post-hole but outside the post supports. Moreover, if wooden chocks were sometimes used (as is also the case today), such arrangements would be entirely missed.

Pottery from most of the post-antique layers was mixed, each unit spanning several centuries within the period between the twelfth and seventeenth or eighteenth centuries. While this in part may reflect the extended life of several of the occupation phases, it seems also to reflect the use of much of the area as gardens, orchards or fields at some phases; cultivation and tilling of the soil means that these layers cannot be regarded as sealed contexts, and there is clearly intrusive material. This is likely to be exacerbated by further unrecognised postholes, and also by the activity of moles and perhaps other burrowing animals in the area. During excavation in 2013, 2014, and 2015, there were particularly active moles who would throw up new molehills during the course of excavation and overnight. On one occasion the activity of a single mole overnight produced enough soil to fill a wheelbarrow; careful examination of the soil recovered seven pottery sherds, showing the potential for upward movement of material. Downward, intrusive, movement of material within the stratigraphy could easily occur through the collapse of animal burrows.

On the other hand, some methodological advances were made during the process of excavation. For the relatively rapid cleaning of large areas of rubble deposit, drystone walls, or even the very rubble-rich late-antique dumped fill to the north of the pool, we used a petrol-driven leaf blower to blow earth away and clean the features. This worked well when aimed downwind and away from active work in the rest of the trench. For the rapid and accurate planning of rubble deposits and drystone walls, we experimented in 2015 with automated planning techniques using a drone-mounted camera. The drone used was a DJI Phantom 3 Professional quadcopter, with which we obtained a series of vertical and oblique digital photographs covering the trench or the area to be mapped. These were then processed with Agisoft Photoscan software and geo-referenced from the site grid to create a 3-D photogrammetric model, from which an ortho-rectified photo (or orthophoto) could be produced. These formed the basis for stone-by-stone drawings and other base plans, which could then be used for the rapid and accurate manual plotting of finds within the trench, and were especially useful when excavating the rubble deposits at the bottom of the pool in 2017 which produced very large quantities of finds whose exact findspot needed to be recorded.

F. FROM 'SOUTH AGORA' TO 'PLACE OF PALMS'

Our multi-method approach to this enigmatic urban space has shed new light on its function in the heart of the city over at least six centuries (Fig. 5).

The North Stoa and the retaining wall of the Theatre Hill were part of a single phase of development and were designed to create a large open space centred on the monumental pool, which can also be connected to this phase; in fact, building work in this area would probably have been impossible without this water feature and, crucially, its associated drains, which dealt with the high water table that otherwise turns the area into a swamp for much of the year. A first-phase South Stoa is also likely, though probably only in the eastern half of the complex, along the side of the Theatre Hill. Work on these structures began some time between AD 14 and 29, though they could well have been worked on for decades. The open space around the pool was planted and was potentially planted with palms from the beginning.[85] This was never a commercial agora—the city already had a large agora immediately to the north—nor was it designed as a gymnasium. From the beginning, this complex combined monumental architecture with water and greenery, providing, like the *porticus* of Rome, a tranquil oasis in the heart of the city.

In a first-century AD provincial context the similarity of this project to metropolitan examples is striking, but perhaps even more so are the extent of the modifications, additions, and renovations made to the complex over time. New architectural, stratigraphic, and epigraphic analysis shows that in the first century alone the South Stoa was probably re-built, along with much of the Theatre Hill retaining wall, the Propylon added (not in the second century as previously thought), and the Basilica constructed. In the second century the Hadrianic Baths were built, with the new West Stoa providing a link between the two complexes. Modifications were made to the North Stoa at the end of the second century and then both this structure and the West Stoa were extensively re-modelled in the fourth century, with the latter given a mosaic floor and its colonnade filled in with doors.

Perhaps the most surprising and intensive intervention in the area, however, is also the latest. At the end of the fifth or early in the sixth century, following a massive earthquake, al-

---

85 Chaniotis 2008b, 73–4 includes the palm grove as one of his 'Twelve buildings in search of locations', discussing the earlier inscription *MAMA* VIII.448 but not the later *IAph2007* 4.202.i. See Wilson 2016b, 129.

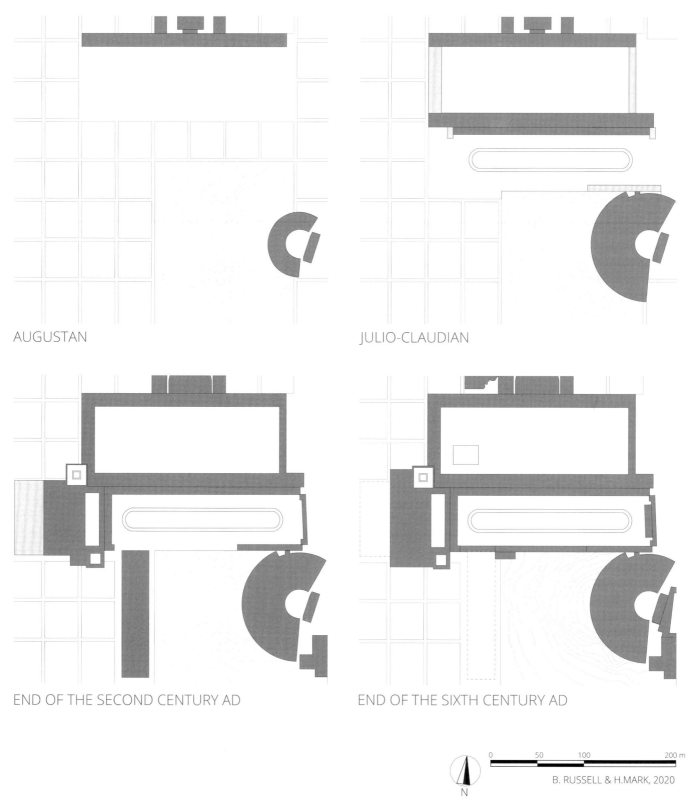

Fig. 5. Restored phase plans of Place of Palms between the first and sixth centuries AD.

most every part of the complex was renovated or re-built: at either end the Propylon and the West Stoa were re-erected, both inscribed with texts honouring their new donors; a new South Stoa—or series of stoas—was extended along the whole of the southern side of the complex—reaching its longest length in this period; the pool walls were patched up and their heights adjusted, and the pool floor repaired; and the ground level of the whole of the open space was raised. The fact that new planting pits were dug into this raised ground level shows that the area was still a garden at this late date; this was a vital civic space, lovingly cared for, for more than half a millennium. This was not, however, just a transitional space—it was certainly a thoroughfare, connecting many of the most important public spaces in the city centre, but the graffiti and the gameboards that cover the surfaces of the seats around the pool and along the stoa show that this was also a space for relaxation and leisure; in fact, the largest concentration of gameboards known from the Roman empire comes from this complex.

What should this complex be called, then? It was not an agora, so the term 'South Agora', though inoffensively generic, is not accurate. This was a *porticus* of the sort found at Rome and in some respects, therefore, Erim's use of the term 'Portico of Tiberius' for the entire space is appealing, though the term is not found in the site epigraphy, and as noted above the North Stoa in fact had four other dedicatees besides Tiberius. The only epigraphically-attested label for this complex that we have, therefore, is the 'Place of Palms', χώρος φυνικόεις. Since the area appears to have been planned from the beginning as a planted space, with its trees, monumental pool, and stoas providing cool air and shade, it clearly functioned as a garden *porticus* or urban park. While the 'Place of Palms' name is late, and possibly poetic, it captures the function of this space well and we therefore use it here, alongside the more generic descriptor 'Urban Park', with the caveat that we cannot be sure what the complex was called prior to the late fifth century.

While the new analysis of the 'Place of Palms' complex focused on its development between the imperial and late antique period, the excavations between 2012 and 2017 also provided vital insights into both the destruction of the area, in the seventh century, and the extensive settlement that developed over this area in the medieval period and later. Although the excavation notebooks from the 1970s and 1980s make frequent references to post-Roman structures and Byzantine, Beylik, and Ottoman finds, these had never been studied, and indeed when exposed in small-scale trenches were difficult to interpret. A series of interesting medieval structures—including a probably Ottoman house and field walls—was carefully documented at the eastern end of the 'South Agora' in 1988 during the excavations undertaken by Francis Thode, for instance.[86] Ali Önce also documented a late wall made of re-used column drums on the north side of the pool in 1990.[87] The extent to which these buildings were part of a wider settlement was unclear in the late 1980s and early 1990s, however. Larger-scale open area excavation, especially between 2013 and 2016, showed in fact that the area of the former 'Place of Palms' was eventually occupied by an agricultural village that was in use for at least three centuries. Its layout and the finds from it provide a clearer picture of the late history of Aphrodisias than any other area of the site excavated so far.

---

86 Nbk 297: *Agora Gate: Basin Front I* (F. Thode, 1988), 12–18; Nbk 298: *Agora Gate: Basin Front II* (F. Thode, 1988), 14–16 showing a field wall lying over the pool walls.

87 Nbk 318: *Portico of Tiberius: E Pool* (A. Önce, 1990), 35, 37, 39.

CHAPTER 2

Pool, Stoa, Palm Grove: Design and Construction, First Century AD

Andrew Wilson, Ben Russell, and Angelos Chaniotis

Prior to the early imperial period the area occupied by the Place of Palms seems to have been an empty space. Deep sondages dug by J. de La Genière in the centre of the complex found no trace of earlier occupation.[1] The northward projection of the Theatre Hill at this date still covered much of the eastern end of the space.[2] It has also been proposed that a tributary of the Morsynos river originally ran across this area, skirting the north side of the Theatre Hill; indeed the plan produced by the Society of Dilettanti expedition in 1812 shows a stream running south of the Agora.[3] Even after the construction of the city, this was probably a boggy area for much of the year and regularly covered by flood water; a spring in the north-eastern corner of the complex continues to well up periodically between autumn and early summer.

The decision to develop this zone was presumably driven by a desire to provide a connection between the area of the Agora, Bouleuterion, and Temple, to the north, and the Theatre, to the south, the two main foci of monumentalization in the Augustan city. In order to open up and regularise this awkward gap in the urban plan, a substantial portion of the northern slope of the Theatre Hill was cut back—as much as was possible without affecting the existing Theatre, roughly equivalent to two city blocks—and a massive retaining wall built (see Fig. 5).[4] The Theatre Hill retaining wall is one of the most striking stretches of masonry still visible at Aphrodisias and was planned or built in the late Augustan or early Tiberian period (see Pl. 13.A).[5] The terracing work necessary for the creation of this new space would have intercepted the water-table in what would already have been a damp area, necessitating substantial drainage works; if there were a pre-existing watercourse it would also have had to have been canalised.

While the Theatre Hill retaining wall defined the southern limits of the new complex, its northern edge was delineated by the North Stoa (the so-called 'Portico of Tiberius'). This was built at the same time as the southern stoa of the Agora, providing a clear division between it and the new complex to the south; the dedicatory inscription on this monument provides the best evidence for the date of this first phase of the Place of Palms. Despite previous assumptions that it must have been a later, probably second-century, addition to the complex,[6] we can be confident too that the pool running down the centre of the space also dated to this first phase, for reasons that will be outlined below; the ring drain around the pool would have been vital for keeping this area dry and making it useable.[7]

Whether a southern stoa ran in front of the Theatre Hill retaining wall at this date, mirroring the North Stoa, is less certain. The extant remains of the South Stoas largely belong to late antiquity, though the cuttings on the retaining wall of the Theatre Hill indicate that two earlier stoas also existed on this side of the complex.

Understanding the arrangement of the eastern and western ends of the Place of Palms in its first phase is complicated by the presence of later structures. The Propylon (known in earlier scholarship as the Agora Gate), now known to have been finished by the reign of Nerva, obscures any evidence of the original layout at the east end.[8] Some traces of the possible stylobate of an earlier stoa were noted in earlier excavations in the northeast corner of the complex, however, and will be discussed below. At the other end, the West Stoa was erected in its present position in the Hadrianic period, to accommodate the Hadrianic Baths behind it; it is possible that this stoa was a first-century structure that was simply moved eastwards in the Hadrianic period but analysis of the architectural decoration instead suggests that it was built new in the second century, with an elaborate central portal and raised columns to emphasise the entrance to the Hadrianic Baths from the east. These later structures will be discussed further in Ch. 3; this chapter focuses on those features that can be dated to the first phase of construction.

The excavations between 2012 and 2017 focused primarily on the area of the pool (see Fig. 4), with the aim of connecting the two end sections that had already been excavated between 1988 and 1990. A trench was also opened midway along the north side of the space, running between the north edge of the pool and the stylobate of the North Stoa. A small sondage inside the North Stoa was excavated in 2014. The new excavations have clarified certain details of the architecture of the stoas and the pool in their first phase; they have also provided essential new information about the use of the open area between the pool and its flanking stoas.

---

1 de Chaisemartin and Lemaire 1996, 158–159; Ratté 2002, 15–16.
2 See Ratté 2008, fig. 10a.
3 On an earlier river, see de Chaisemartin and Lemaire 1996, 158–161; for the later stream, Society of Dilettanti 1840, Ch.II Pl. I.
4 Ratté 2008, 17, fig. 10a–b.
5 Smith 2013, 7.
6 On the pool as a later addition, perhaps contemporary with the Hadrianic Baths, see Ratté 2002, 23; Raja 2012, 40.
7 On the vital importance of drainage, see de Chaisemartin and Lemaire 1996, 159–160; Wilson 2016b, 120, 135.
8 On the date of the Propylon, see Wilson 2016b, 107, and further discussion below, Ch. 3 §A.

A. ARCHITECTURE OF THE STOAS (BR, AW, & AC)

North Stoa

Of the three stoas, the North Stoa (Pl. 10.A) is the best understood and best preserved; Crema described its architectural elements also as 'artisticamente i migliori.'[9] Its architecture has been discussed fully and in passing by Crema, Bingöl, Waelkens, and de Chaisemartin.[10] Gaudin's excavations first revealed the northwest corner of this stoa but it was not until 1937 that it received particular attention. Beginning in this northwest corner, Jacopi's excavations followed the colonnade eastwards, exposing a series of fallen architectural elements. Their arrangement indicated that they had originally fallen towards the southwest, apparently following the destruction of the complex by an earthquake. The Italian project also found the key entablature blocks of the central section of the North Stoa on which the dedication of the structure to Aphrodite, the divine Augustus, Tiberius, Livia, and the *demos* is recorded in a single line (the *hastae* or vertical divisions in the text given below mark block divisions) (Pl. 10.B). The main surviving part of this text reads as follows (for full details, see Appendix 1, In1):

Ἀφροδίτηι καὶ | Αὐτοκράτορι Καίσαρι Θεῶι | [Σεβαστῶι Διὶ Πατρώωι καὶ | Αὐτοκ]ράτορι Τιβερίωι Καίσα[ρι | [Θεο]ῦ Σε|βαστοῦ υἱῶι Σεβαστῶι · καὶ · Ἰουλίαι Σεβασ|τῆι · καὶ τῶι Δήμωι τὴν στό[αν] | Διογένης Μενάνδρου τοῦ | [Δ]ιογένους τοῦ Ἀρτεμιδώρ|[ου καὶ ·· c. 13 ·· ἱέρ]ηα Ἀφροδίτης · καὶ · Μένανδ[ρος ·· ? ··]¹¹

To Aphrodite and to the Imperator Caesar Divus Augustus Zeus Patroios, and to the Imperator Tiberius Caesar son of Divus Augustus, and to Iulia Augusta, and to the People, Diogenes, son of Menandros, grandson of Diogenes, great-grandson of Artemidoros, and [- - -], priestess of Aphrodite, and Menandros [- - - ?... dedicated] the stoa ...

Since Livia is named as Iulia Augusta the dedication must date between Augustus' death in AD 14 and Livia's in AD 29. The structure, identified as a *stoa* in the inscription, was dedicated by Diogenes son of Menandros. Diogenes also dedicated the southern stoa of the Agora and indeed the two stoas share the same back wall and are effectively two sides of the same enormous structure.[12] Two doorways in this spine wall connected the two stoas and, via them, the Agora and the Place of Palms; one of these is located at the northern end of what is now the West Stoa and the other is aligned with the intercolumniation between columns N37 and N38 of the North Stoa.[13] A third doorway was probably located at the eastern end, in the intercolumniation between columns N5 and N6, but the rear wall in this area is poorly preserved.

The construction of one of these stoas is mentioned in an unpublished honorific decree for Diogenes.[14] The relevant passage reads (ll. 6–9): καὶ τὴν | πρὸ τοῦ Διὸς στοὰν ἀτελῆ τυνχάνουσαν καὶ τὸ σῶμα τῆς πόλεως ὑβρίζουσαν | ἐκ τῶν ἰδίων μετὰ πολλῶν ἀναλωμάτων κατασκευάσας ἐνεδείξατο διότι διὰ τὸ τῆ[ς] | π[ατ]ρίδος αὐτὸ ποιεῖ κάλλος, οὐ διὰ τὰς ἰδίας τῆς τειμῆς ἐπιγραφάς ('and the stoa in front of (the temple/statue of) Zeus, which happened to be incomplete and was an insult for the body of the city, he constructed using his own fortune with many expenses and showed that he does this for the beauty of the city, and not for the inscriptions that honour him'). The location of the stoa is indicated with the phrase πρὸ τοῦ Διός, that is, in front of a statue or, more likely, a shrine, of Zeus (probably Zeus Nineudios). If this construction stood in the Agora (as the mention of its unfinished nature being 'an insult to the city' strongly suggests), then the stoa 'in front' (πρό) of it must be the southern stoa of the Agora.[15]

In its current form, the North Stoa is 204 m long and comprises 70 columns (N1–70, or 71 if one includes the northernmost column of the West Stoa, which we label W1); it is, on average, 7.65 m deep, measured from the front of the stylobate to its rear wall, 6.59 m from the back of the stylobate. At its eastern end, the excavations in 1991 confirmed that the *euthynteria* of the North Stoa turned to the south, probably for two intercolumniations, at the point at which the Propylon was later constructed (Fig. 6).[16] The construction of the Propylon, therefore, must have led to the removal of this projecting section of the North Stoa and one column to the east of the current column N1. At its western end, in contrast, excavations in the same year found the stylobate and *euthynteria* course of the North Stoa continuing under the paving of the West Stoa (Pl. 10.C; Fig. 7).[17] How far the North Stoa originally extended to the west is uncertain. The middle of its three existing doorways is located between columns N37 and N38, which means it currently has 37 columns to the east of it, while the line of the West Stoa is 34 columns to the west. This would seem to suggest that the North Stoa originally extended for a further three columns to the west.[18] If we include the column at the east end removed by the construction of the Propylon, however, then we would need to add four columns to the west end. This would take the North Stoa beyond the back wall of the later West Stoa, where the ground rises 1.2 m to the level at which the East Court of

---

9 Crema 1939, 284.
10 Crema 1939; Bingöl 1980; Waelkens 1987; de Chaisemartin 1989a; b.
11 *IAph2007* 4.4i = *SEG* 1980, 1244 = *AE* 1980, 870. Further fragments read:
   ii [·· ? ··]ΑΙΙΑΛ[·· ? ··]
   iii [·· ? ··]ΤΑ[·· ? ··]
   iv [·· ? ··]ΤΙ[·· ? ··].
12 Ratté and Smith 2008, 720.
13 The seventy columns in the North Stoa are numbered from east to west.
14 This inscription, found in 1994, was not included in *IAph2007*. The text was read by Angelos Chaniotis (last revision in August 2017); see Chaniotis 2021, 188 n. 22 (and also 187 n. 17).
15 It is tempting to wonder if a square structure in the centre of the Agora (Ratté and Smith 2004, 153–7) is the shrine or temple of Zeus referred to in this inscription.
16 Nbk 323: *Portico of Tiberius Sondages* (D. Theodorescu et al., 1991), description of Sondage IA Extension C (unnumbered pages); de Chaisemartin and Lemaire 1996, 153–154, fig. 6; de Chaisemartin 1989b, 30–2.
17 Nbk 323: *Portico of Tiberius Sondages* (D. Theodorescu et al., 1991), description of Sondage V (unnumbered pages); de Chaisemartin and Lemaire 1996, 153, and 154, fig. 6.
18 On this point, de Chaisemartin and Lemaire 1996, 151–153.

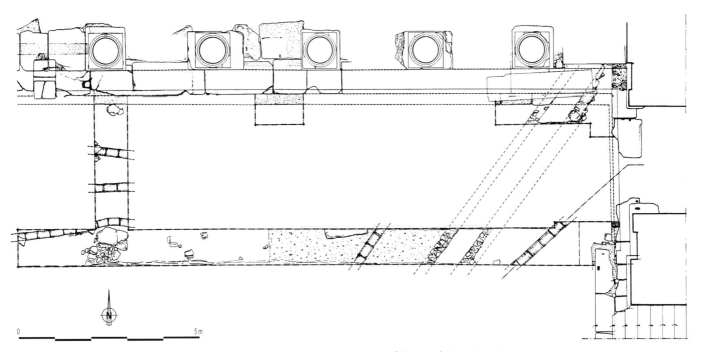

Fig. 6. Plan of sondage S1 at the east end of the North Stoa (1991).

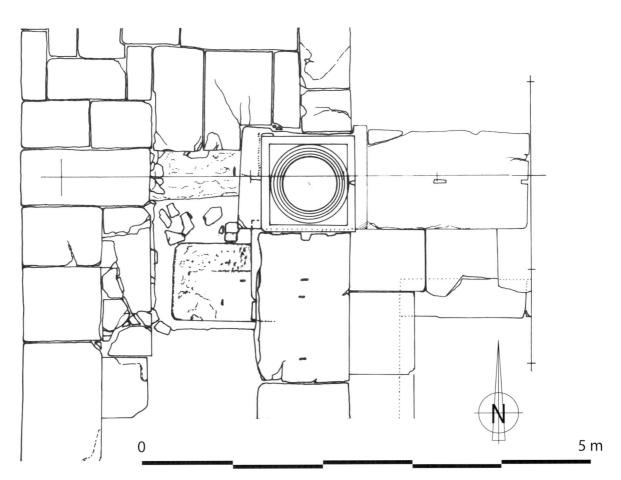

Fig. 7: Sondage S5 at the west end of the North Stoa (1991).

the Hadrianic Baths was built. Either this ground level was only raised later or the North Stoa was originally cut into the side of the slope of the rise on which the baths were built.

This reconstruction assumes that the middle doorway in the North Stoa belongs to this first phase and so is a reliable guide to reconstructing the original length of the building. As is shown below (see Ch. 4 §E), however, this central section of the rear wall of the North Stoa seems to have been dismantled and re-built in late antiquity. At least 3 m of the wall to the west of the doorway, where a series of marble seats was used to chock it up, and as much as 10 m to the east of it have been substantially altered. This helps explain why the doorway is very narrow for the main access point to the Place of Palms from the north and is not aligned with the central axis of the intercolumniation between columns N37 and N38. The exact location or arrangement of the original doorway between the Agora and Place of Palms, therefore, can only be guessed at. However, a clue to what it may have looked like is provided by the doorway between the later West Stoa and Hadrianic Baths. This was a three-aisled structure, sufficient to allow significant pedestrian traffic between the complexes. If a similarly grand entranceway existed in the North Stoa then its central axis would align with the intercolumniation between columns N36 and N37. If this was the case, the original North Stoa may only have extended two columns beyond the line of the later West Stoa, making it 74 columns long in total (if the one lost column from the east end is added in). In such a reconstruction the North Stoa would not have extended beyond the back wall of the later West Stoa. If this line did mark the edge of a slope, it is likely that the stoa did not turn to the south as at its eastern end. Although the North Stoa of the Place of Palms was built at the same time as the southern stoa of the Agora and by the same person, there is no necessary reason for their western ends to align, especially since they do not align at their eastern ends.[19]

As both Crema and Waelkens note, the architectural decoration of the North Stoa is reasonably homogenous (Fig. 8). The 70 Ionic columns that survive from the original phase are arranged with an interaxial spacing of 2.89 m on average, equivalent to 10 Aphrodisian feet.[20] The overall order measures 7.54 m in height (26 Aphrodisian feet). The columns of the North Stoa are raised above the ground level of the interior of the Place of Palms on three courses of ashlar masonry: the *euthynteria* course, the top 0.14–0.16 m of which would have been visible above the imperial-period ground level; a course of seat blocks, 0.37–0.38 m high, with a projecting upper lip and a depth of 0.66–0.68 m; and the course of the stylobate itself, 0.36–0.38 m high. The seat blocks of the North Stoa mirrored the seat blocks of the exterior of the pool walls and provided a continuous bench of 205 m, punctuated in four places by stairs (in the intercolumniations between Columns N5–6, N21–22, N37–38 and N54–55); these connected the stylobate to the *euthynteria* level of the exterior via three steps, each 0.16–0.18 m high (Pl. 10.D). Two of these sets of steps align with doorways to the Agora. The seat blocks either side of these steps are ornamented with lions' claws, similar to seat blocks from the Theatre and Bouleuterion.[21]

De Chaisemartin argued that the presence of game boards on the seat blocks and stylobate of the North Stoa indicated that this was a popular spot for sitting and relaxing in the shade provided by the roof of the stoa.[22] The stoa roof would certainly have shaded these seats at certain times of the day, but the planting scheme in front of the stoa would have been more important in providing relief from the sun: for much of the day the steps would have been in full sunlight were it not for the screen of palm trees in front (see below, and Ch. 5 §F). The interior of the North Stoa might well originally have been unpaved, as is discussed below; its ground level was significantly lowered at a later date, at which point most of the stylobate blocks not directly supporting the columns of the stoa were also removed.

A total of 55 largely complete bases belonging to the North Stoa survives, while four base fragments are preserved in the area behind the North Stoa and a further ten were found during excavation (Pl. 11.A). All are Attic in form and vary slightly in height, between 0.35–0.38 m, with a lower width of 0.93–0.95 m.

The column shafts of the North Stoa are not monolithic but, as is typical at Aphrodisias, are divided into two or three long drums. Each shaft is 5.58 m in height, with a lower diameter of 69.75 cm and upper diameter of 58.5 cm (62.5 including astragal).[23] The ratio of lower diameter to height of exactly 1:8 is typical of the Ionic order. The bottom third of each shaft is smooth, while the upper two-thirds are ornamented with a series of twenty-four flutes; as Stinson has noted, this is a standard arrangement on colonnades in the city.[24] Each shaft terminates with an astragal decorated with bead-and-reel. Over 200 lengths of column drum longer than 0.50 m are preserved, including those re-erected, as well as a further 50 smaller fragments. Sixty of the pieces are at least partially unfluted and so belong to the lower end of shafts. The remainder are fluted for their entire length and so belong to the upper two-thirds of shafts. The actual length of each drum varies considerably. The lower drums always include all of the unfluted sections of the shafts but often also incorporate a portion of the lower part of the fluting. The shortest preserved lower drum measures just 1.72 m, with its upper surface marking the transition between the unfluted and fluted sections. The longest lower column drum, in contrast, measures 3.38 m, and is therefore fluted for most of its upper half. The fluted drums comprising the upper portions of the shafts also vary in length, with the shortest being just 97 cm and the longest extant example measuring 3.29 m. No attempt was made to standardize the lengths of these column drums, although a joint in the unfluted section of the shaft was always avoided.

The Ionic capitals of the North Stoa are mostly fragmentary but enough survive to reconstruct their form. A total of 35 are preserved from previous excavations in the Place of Palms, while 25 fragments were found during the current excavations, many of them re-used in post-antique field walls. Crema first noted

---

19 For an alternative reconstruction of the North Stoa further to the west, but also with a southward projection, see Ratté 2008, fig. 10b.
20 de Chaisemartin and Lemaire 1996, 151; de Chaisemartin 1999, 264.

21 de Chaisemartin 1989a, 64.
22 de Chaisemartin 1989a, 64.
23 Crema 1939, 284.
24 Stinson 2016, 34.

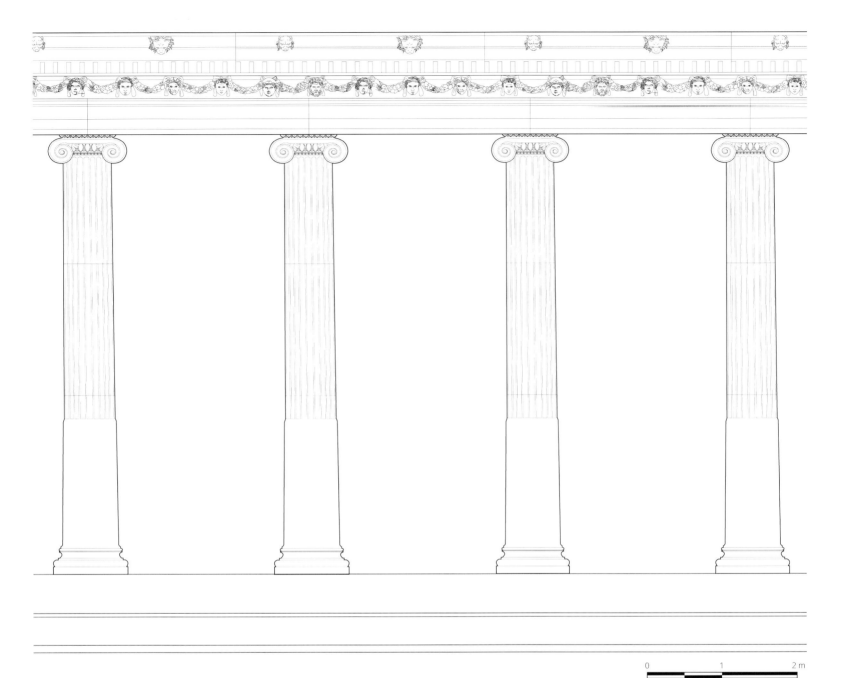

Fig. 8. Reconstruction of the south elevation of the North Stoa.

the overall characteristics of these capitals and provided a reconstruction of their decorative schemes.[25] The majority of the capitals follow a standard model (Pl. 11.B): the echinus is decorated with an egg-and-tongue moulding, five eggs wide, with the eggs pointed towards their base; a Lesbian cyma adorns the abacus; on the sides, the pulvinus is carved with alternating horizontal acanthus and reed leaves, while the balteus is ornamented with vertical laurel leaves framed by single bands of bead-and-reel. Subtle differences in the carving of individual capitals are evident; indeed Waelkens identified four variations on the Lesbian cyma.[26] There is also variation in the balteus decoration, with twisted ropes rather than bead-and-reel used as a frame on nearly half of the examples on which this feature is preserved. While the laurel leaves on the balteus usually point upwards, in one instance they face the other way and a single capital has a unique balteus form consisting of interlocking fillets (Pl. 11.C). Differences in the handling of the acanthus leaves on the pulvinus can also be noted, with some carvers working in deep relief and detailing the eyelets with single drill holes and others preferring a flatter form.

25 Crema 1939, 284, fig. 54.

26 Waelkens 1987, 130.

These details of the capitals reveal the hands of different craftsmen or working groups rather than chronological differences. Similar differences in technique as well as quality can be noted in the mask and garland carvings on the frieze, which evidently occupied the attentions of a large number of individual carvers.[27] The style of the capitals is consistent with a date in the first half of the first century AD and there is no reason to think that these are not the capitals of the original Tiberian phase of the North Stoa erected by Diogenes. This is supported by the fact that the Ionic capitals of the North Stoa are broadly similar to those of the southern stoa of the Agora, which was also funded by Diogenes—in fact, it is effectively the same structure. The major difference between these stoas is that the Agora stoa was a double stoa, with its central row of columns in the Corinthian order, a feature found in none of the stoas of the Place of Palms. The relatively early date of the North Stoa's columns and capitals is also indicated by the fact that the Ionic columns of the Flavian-era Civil Basilica seem to draw inspiration from those of the North Stoa: the column shafts are fluted in a similar way; the three components of the entablature are split across three blocks and the specifications of the architrave and frieze blocks are basically identical; the mask-and-garland decoration follows exactly the same spacing arrangement; the cornice is extremely similar. The capitals from the interior of the Basilica largely follow the format of those of the North Stoa, though with certain discernible differences: the acanthus leaves on the pulvini are arranged upright rather than on their sides, the volutes are carved more deeply (4–5 cm rather than 3–4 cm), and darts rather than tongues are used between the eggs of the echinus.[28]

The entablature of the North Stoa follows the standard Ionic format, consisting of architrave, frieze, and cornice, each carved on separate blocks. Their heights are 48 cm, 38 cm, and 50 cm respectively. The exterior face of the architrave blocks consists of three fasciae below bands of astragal, ovolo, and cavetto mouldings, all undecorated. The upper fascia carries the dedicatory inscription that adorned the central portion of the colonnade. The interior face consists of a single flat plane surmounted by a plain sloping crown moulding. The soffit of each architrave block is decorated with a recessed panel. These blocks are each approximately 2.88–2.90 m long, equivalent to the interaxial distance between the columns, 0.57–0.58 m deep at their base and 0.75–0.77 m deep at their top. Each architrave block was fixed to its neighbours with a pair of substantial clamps.

The frieze blocks are the most famous and most studied feature of the architecture of the North Stoa. Excavated and studied by Jacopi in the 1930s, they are decorated with a continuous relief of alternating masks and garlands (Pl. 11.D).[29] A considerable literature already exists on this mask and garland frieze and this does not need repeating.[30] Several features of the frieze decoration are worth highlighting here, however. First, the mask and garland format was a favoured scheme at Aphrodisias and was also used for the stoas of the Agora, around the Temple, in the Theatre, and on the interior order in the Civil Basilica.[31] Second, the masks and garlands vary in technique and possibly also in their date, indicating that some frieze blocks were replaced over the lifespan of the North Stoa. The actual arrangement of the frieze shows some further variety with the distance between masks ranging considerably.[32] Despite this, the blocks are positioned so that one mask is located directly above the central axis of each column shaft, with three in between.[33] Since the weight of the frieze blocks is supported by the architraves, there was no need to produce them in standard lengths and they vary between 0.90 and 2.10 m.[34] De Chaisemartin has noted that the numerals (in the form of single Greek letters) carved into the top of each frieze block indicate that work progressed eastwards and westwards from the central point of the North Stoa and was divided between at least two workshops; these letters are listed in Appendix 2 (NS350–360).[35]

The entablature was topped by cornice blocks dentillated in the typical Ionic style and surmounted with a thin band of cyma reversa before a cyma recta crown moulding (Pl. 11.E–F). The water spouts take the form of feline heads, alternating between lions and either lionesses or panthers, and are spaced at 1.41–1.46 m. The blocks themselves measure between 1.13 and 1.75 m long, always terminating at their right-hand end with a dentil. Their depth also varies considerably, between 0.75–0.87 at the base and 0.97–1.08 m at the top. On the upper surfaces the cornice blocks have inset guttering carved along their front halves, immediately behind their projecting lips.

The roofing of the North Stoa can be reconstructed based on the location of the rafter or beam holes in the rear sides of the frieze and cornice blocks.[36] On the frieze blocks these slots, 0.57–0.75 m wide and 0.15–0.22 m deep, are carved down the whole height of the block and arranged 2.11–2.40 m apart. They allow for the end of either a horizontal beam or a sloping rafter to be inserted into the back of the frieze blocks and supported on the top of the architrave blocks. The placement of these slots was marked out during the carving process with a chiselled outline but rarely did the final carved slot fill the delineated box, suggesting that the carvers responsible reacted to the size of the available roof timbers. A second set of pitched rafters, supporting the roof tiles themselves, slotted into cuttings in the rear of the top surface of the cornice blocks. The first phase of these consisted of wide slots (27–40 × 30–40 cm long and 10–15 cm deep) spaced 32–42 cm apart. Smaller slots were added later, perhaps in a second phase of roofing (see Ch. 3 §D) (Pl. 12.A). In 1989 a carved wooden panel, decorated with a meander pattern, was recovered from the east end of the pool and could be part of the original ceiling of the North Stoa, though its exact display context is impossible to deduce (Pl. 12.B).[37]

The other end of the roof rafters would have connected to cuttings in the North Stoa's rear wall. The rear wall of the North

---

27 On this point, de Chaisemartin 1999, 264–265.
28 Stinson 2016, 34, pl. 33a–d; for Flavian parallels at Hierapolis, see De Bernardi Ferrero 2002, 20–1, fig. 34.
29 Jacopi 1939.
30 See especially de Chaisemartin 1987; 1989a; b; 1999; forthcoming.
31 Stinson 2016, 66, fig. 35 for distribution of these elements; for a full study, de Chaisemartin forthcoming.
32 Crema 1939, 284.
33 de Chaisemartin 1999, 264.
34 Crema 1939, 285.
35 de Chaisemartin 1999, 265.
36 Crema 1939, 285–6, fig. 52.
37 Inv. 89-1; it measures c. 1 m in length and is c. 30 cm wide. See Smith 1996, 19–20, fig. 11.

Stoa is preserved nowhere higher than 1.40 m. It was constructed of a *euthynteria* course of roughly tooled grey marble ashlar blocks, 30–42 cm high. This base course, the top of which is the same height as the top of the stylobate of the stoa, supported a second course of larger grey marble orthostats, 75–80 cm in height. Above the *euthynteria* this wall was constructed as a line of casemates, probably packed with earth, with these orthostats forming the exterior face and smaller blocks traversing the wall roughly every two orthostats. A second course of horizontally laid ashlar blocks (28–30 cm high) topped this first course of orthostats, running the full thickness of the wall; these are now only visible at the western end. Above this point the wall was probably constructed entirely in small blockwork, now largely robbed or fallen away. The orthostats and the horizontal blocks above them have neatly worked faces and were probably intended to be visible in their first phase. At a later date, however, marble revetment was added to the wall, as numerous pin holes show (see Ch. 3 §D). While the rear wall of the North Stoa was constructed mostly in grey marble ashlar and small blockwork, the doorways through had marble doorframes, which echoed the arrangement of the architraves of the stoa (Pl. 12.C).

West and East Stoas?

Twenty columns constitute the West Stoa (W1–20), which runs for 55.2 m north-south alongside the East Court of the Hadrianic Baths. Nineteen of these columns were fully or partially re-erected in the 1970s and 1980s (Pl. 12.D), although before that it seems that they had been re-set at least once during the repairs carried out by Albinos in late antiquity (see Ch. 4 §D). The exact date of the original construction of this stoa is debated. As noted above, it certainly encroaches on the west end of the Place of Palms, presumably to accommodate the Hadrianic Baths and their East Court, with the result that the West Stoa is closer to the west end of the pool than the Propylon is to its east end. There is no evidence that there was a full West Stoa contemporary with the first phase of the North Stoa, though only full excavations beneath the current West Stoa could confirm this. The West Stoa that currently stands is not simply a Tiberian structure moved eastwards to accommodate the Hadrianic Baths. Instead, the architecture of the West Stoa indicates that it was a new creation of the Hadrianic period (see Ch. 3 §C). If a pre-existing stoa did frame the west end of the Place of Palms it was removed entirely to accommodate this new one.

As noted already, there is also no evidence for an East Stoa prior to the construction of the Propylon in the late first century AD. De Chaisemartin noted that the *euthynteria* and seat blocks of the North Stoa turn southwards at the east end for two intercolumniations but there is no evidence for a structure between this point and the line of the South Stoa (on which more below) prior to the construction of the Propylon.[38] In its first phase, therefore, the Place of Palms appears to have been open at both its east and west ends, communicating directly with the north-south streets running through these areas (see Fig. 5).

The Theatre Wall and a South Stoa

Along the eastern portion of its southern flank the Place of Palms is dominated by the imposing Theatre Hill retaining wall, one of the finest examples of extant masonry at Aphrodisias (Pl. 13.A). In its first phase this wall was constructed entirely in large ashlar blocks of varying sizes with bevelled edges. The stone used was a cream-yellow limestone rather than the white marble preferred for architectural decoration.[39] This wall was at least 9.3 m high in its first phase and its original masonry is preserved for at least 36 m from its eastern end. At 12.7 m from this same eastern end, a monumental stairway, 4.6 m wide, provided a direct connection between the Place of Palms and the Theatre. The stairway had an arch above it, supported by a pair of projecting corbels 5.2 m above ground level. At the western end of the surviving ashlars there is clear evidence for the collapse and repair of the original retaining wall above its bottom five courses. Two sections of walling are evident but these may well both belong to the same phase of construction. The lower courses of the wall were rebuilt in cut-down ashlar blocks (doubtless reused from the damaged masonry that had collapsed). A row of recesses was built into this new wall but the holes are too large to have taken timbers for roof structures and may originally have held ornamental fittings of some sort, perhaps marble consoles. Above this point, the wall was continued in coarser rubble walling, which was carried up above the original ashlar courses that are still in place at the eastern end of the wall. Probably dating to the same period as these repairs are the series of barrel vaults laid out further west, perpendicular to the line of the Theatre Hill retaining wall but with their entrances aligned with it (see Pl. 13.A; Fig. 9).

The uncovered section of the Theatre Hill retaining wall preserves on its surface a series of cuttings and sockets, most of them for roof structures, which constitute our best evidence for the existence of a series of stoas along this side of the Place of Palms (Fig. 9). Four rows of cuttings can be observed:

1. A row of downward-sloping rafter holes, each with a capping stone, running along the top of the highest ashlar course of the Theatre wall, neatly cut into the blocks of the eastern end of the wall and built into the coarser rubble walling to the west (Pl. 13.B); this row of holes runs parallel to the courses of ashlar blocks.
2. Cut into the bottom of the same course of ashlar blocks is a row of more widely-spaced downward-sloping rafter holes (Pl. 13.C). These continue into the rubble walling to the west but seem to be cut into this wall rather than built into it. The bulk of these holes align with the columns of the late antique Stoa South, though several additional holes were added at the end of the first stretch of ashlar wall, before the staircase into the Theatre, and in the first stretch of rubble walling. This row of holes slopes slightly down from east to west.
3. Running along the bottom of the third ashlar course down from the top of the wall is a row of triangular slots for upward-angled struts (Pl. 13.D). These slots continue into the

---

38 de Chaisemartin and Lemaire 1996, 153, fig. 3–4.

39 On the possible source of this limestone, see Stearns 2012, 158–159.

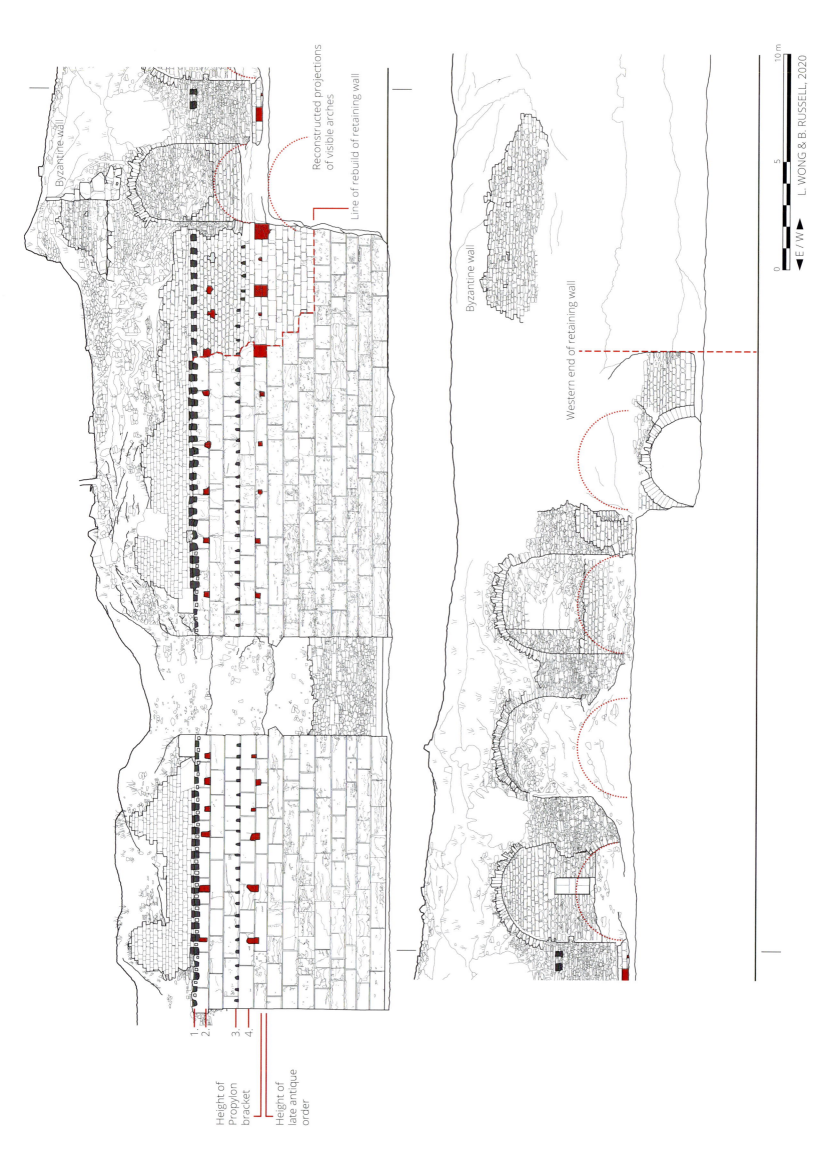

Fig. 9. North elevation of the Theatre Hill, showing arrangement of cuttings in the retaining wall and the vaults to the west.

rubble walling. These slots are aligned vertically with the highest row of rafter holes (1, above) and like them they are aligned with the courses of ashlar blocks, except in the rubble walling to the west, where they step down one course of blocks half way along the preserved section.

4. A final row of holes, aligned vertically with the second row of cuttings (2, above) and with the columns of the late antique South Stoas, straddles the join between the fourth and fifth ashlar courses down from the top of the wall (Pl. 13.E). These are large square or rectangular cuttings for horizontal beams. Like the second row of cuttings, they again slope downwards from east to west. These holes are aligned with the square recesses built into the second phase wall but are certainly later than them. While the recesses seem to have been re-used at this stage, two shallower cuttings were added between these earlier recesses to continue the row of beam slots.

The first and second of these rows of cuttings supported downward-sloping rafters, the third row upward-facing struts, and the fourth row horizontal beams. While theoretically all of these cuttings could have been made at the same time, their alignment suggests we are looking here at two or possibly three phases of roof system, relating to multiple iterations of a South Stoa. The first and third row of cuttings align with each other vertically, while the same is true of the second and fourth rows. These latter rows of cuttings must belong with the late antique South Stoas, the architecture of which is still preserved. The discovery of burn marks and charred timbers in these cuttings during excavation in 1984 demonstrates that they were in use when the final South Stoas were destroyed (Pl. 14.A–B).[40] These cuttings, and this phase of the South Stoas, therefore, are discussed in Ch. 4 §F.

The first and third rows of cuttings, which do not seem to have been in use in late antiquity, must therefore relate to an earlier stoa or, perhaps more likely, to two earlier stoas. The suggestion that there were two phases of stoa is provided by the horizontal alignment of the cuttings. The first and third rows of cuttings on the ashlar section of the Theatre Hill retaining wall are perfectly aligned with the courses of its blocks, suggesting that the base of the stoa that these relate to was completely level; it was at the same height at its eastern and western ends, in other words. When the western portion of the Theatre wall was rebuilt, however, and these cuttings were extended across the new sections of walling, their arrangement and even their sizes were slightly altered. The top of the upper row of cuttings was brought down, and the third row of cuttings was dropped down a course of stones after four slots. The stoa that post-dated this rebuild stepped gradually downwards from east to west, therefore. If a stoa had been built for the first time in this place only after the rebuild of the Theatre wall, one might expect all of the cuttings in the first and third rows respectively to be placed on a single line sloping to the west, as the late antique cuttings were, but this is not the case. Although this evidence is slight, it would seem to indicate that there was a South Stoa already in place before the Theatre Hill retaining wall collapsed and that when this wall was rebuilt a second stoa, probably identical in dimensions,

was put back up. Both stoas were single-storey and the height of the rafter cuttings would suggest they were of roughly the same dimensions as the North Stoa.

The arrangement of these cuttings in the Theatre wall is significant because the collapse and repair of this structure is most likely datable to the late Julio-Claudian or early Flavian period, as will be discussed in Ch. 3 §B. This means that any stoa pre-dating this event was broadly contemporary with the North Stoa and so belongs in the first phase of construction of the Place of Palms. No marble architecture survives of this first-phase stoa, but the overall plan of the Place of Palms and its constituent elements further suggest that a southern stoa was envisaged from the earliest stages of the planning process. The distance between the stylobates of the North and South Stoas is on average 53.5 m and the pool is equidistant between them, its walls c. 14.6 m from the former and c. 14.7 m from the latter. While the pool is not equidistant between the back wall of the North Stoa (22.2 m) and the Theatre Hill retaining wall (21.4 m), the placement of the stoas seems to have masked this fact (the South Stoa being correspondingly narrower).

This original first-century South Stoa, however short-lived it was, is unlikely to have continued all the way along the southern side of the Place of Palms.[41] When this stoa was rebuilt later in the first century AD, the new building probably only ran along the northern side of the Theatre Hill, stopping at the northwest corner of the hill. The Civil Basilica, with its elaborate façade, seems to have been inserted into a gap along the south side of the Place of Palms; a stoa here would have had to have been demolished or, if left in place, would have entirely blocked the Basilica from view. The South Stoa was only extended along the whole southern side of the Place of Palms in late antiquity when the Basilica was in ruins.

B. THE POOL AND WATER SUPPLY (AW & BR)

The discussion of the architecture above has demonstrated that the Place of Palms was delineated in its first phase by stoas running the full length of its north side and probably part of the way along its south side. The west and east ends of the space were monumentalized later, as discussed below (Ch. 3 §A–C), while its southern side underwent a number of developments between the first and sixth centuries AD. The various structures flanking the Place of Palms enclose an area of c. 11,000 m². The central and dominant feature of this space is its vast ornamental pool, surrounded by inward- and outward-facing marble seating, and fed by fountains at the east end and at several points around the edge. It measures 168 m long × 18.4–18.8 m wide internally, and 173.8 m × 23.9–24.3 m externally,[42] and is from 0.95–1.15 m deep (with a water depth of up to 0.94 m).[43] With a surface area of just over 3,000 m² it is one of the largest ex-

---

40 Nbk 253: *S Agora Gate I-84, Book 1* (B. Rose, 1984), 53.

41 Wilson 2016b, 107.

42 de Chaisemartin and Lemaire 1996, 158, give rounded dimensions of 169 m and 19 m wide; the dimensions given by Erim 1988, 748 of 145 m long by c. 40 m wide are wrong.

43 All measurements taken to the top of the flat foot-rest ledge for the inner seats: 0.95 m at the east end; 1.10 m the around the middle of the north and south sides; somewhat less than 1.15 m at the west end

cavated ornamental pools in the Roman world and forms an elaborate monumental display of water that is impressive even by the standards of cities in the Roman East (see Pl. 2.A).

The Pool Walls

The inner face of the pool is lined with vertical marble slabs capped with flat marble slabs surmounted by a row of marble blocks that form a continuous inward-facing bench (Pl 14.C). Outside this, separated by a gap orginally covered with marble slabs since robbed, another row of marble blocks, shaped as a seat, creates an outward-facing continuous bench running around the pool (Pl. 14.D). Beneath the seat blocks a pair of drystone masonry walls runs in parallel all around the pool, enclosing a drainage channel, 0.65 m wide. As currently visible, the pool is essentially late antique, as all of the seat blocks have been re-set, and many of the seat blocks and the wall revetment slabs are in fact material that has been reused in the late repairs (see Ch. 4 §B). The essential design of the pool and the walls beneath this marble surface, however, appears to be early imperial in date; and some of the seating blocks preserve an original rebate at the rear, over the drain, that was not cut in the blocks of the rebuilt phase.

The inner pool wall, 1.21 m wide in total, was built on the side facing the drain as a drystone masonry wall of schist stones, while the side facing the pool was revetted with marble slabs 0.68–0.77 m high, varying between 0.465 and 2.203 m in length; their thickness also varied considerably, from 0.195 to 0.32 m, as many were reused. The space between the drystone face and the revetment slabs was filled with earth (mainly) and some rubble (stones and tile fragments). Each slab was clamped to its neighbour by an iron clamp 15 cm long and 1.5 cm wide, set in lead (Pl. 15.A). They rested on a marble socle 0.11–0.38 m high, offset by 0.16–0.205 m on the inside of the pool. The revetment slabs were capped by a ledge of flat marble slabs 7.5–8.3 cm thick surmounting the inner wall of the ring drain, that served as a footrest for the inward-facing seats, whose seat blocks, 0.35 m high, originally rested on the ring drain wall directly behind the slabs, thus giving the seat itself a height of c. 0.27 m. The inner seat blocks varied in length between 0.42 and 2.21 m, and were 0.33–0.335 wide; while their visible surfaces were polished smooth, the rear face, facing the ring drain, was left rough below a rebate 3–8 cm deep to take marble cover slabs whose other ends rested in an answering rebate on the rear face of the outward-facing seat blocks. These slabs were systematically robbed in antiquity and none remains.

The outer seat blocks measured 0.36 m high × 0.79–1.04 m wide (including the rough back edge) and varied in length from 0.43 to 3.36 m (this latter block being a re-used architrave block, in the rebuilt phase). Their outer face was undercut in a concave curve echoing the seat blocks located beneath the stylobate course of the surrounding stoas, to allow people to sit comfortably with their heels slightly under the seat, further back than their knees. The upper surface was slightly dished, again to provide a more comfortable seat. They rested originally directly on top of the outer wall of the ring drain, which was 0.65 m wide and again built in unmortared masonry of schist stones, allowing groundwater to enter the ring drain.

The Ring Drain

The drain between these two parallel walls of the pool was originally covered, by a lower level of schist slabs resting on top of the drystone walls and by a second level of marble slabs, now robbed, placed in rebates in the upper rear surface of the marble seat blocks (Pl. 15.B). The schist cover slabs of the drain are visible in places on the south-eastern curved end of the pool, but elsewhere they were removed in late antiquity. The height of both the inner and outer walls of the pool was raised when the exterior ground level was adjusted in late antiquity (see Ch. 4 §C). The width of the drain channel varies from 0.56–0.57 m in the south-east part of the pool, to 0.52–0.53 m along the south side, and 0.71 m by the centre of the north side. The depth of the ring drain increases from 0.55–0.68 m at the east end to 1–1.20 m in the west part, and 1.70 m at the very west end, reflecting the fact that the outflow drainage from the ring drain was at the west end.[44]

The channel itself had a solid floor, made of schist slabs with mortar between them (Pl. 15.C), but the drystone masonry construction of the walls of this drain shows that they were intended to let water infiltrate and that the main purpose of this channel was to drain the naturally high groundwater table in the area. The terracing of the area by cutting back the Theatre Hill to create a level space for the Place of Palms at its east end would have intercepted the water-table and seasonal flooding would have occurred (as it does today, now that the ancient city drains have long been blocked), periodically turning the Place of Palms into a swamp. The ring drain around the pool was therefore an essential part of the solution to the problem of managing local groundwater to enable the creation of a public space here.

In a sondage within the drain on the north side of the pool the lowest deposit found, immediately on top of the drain's floor, was a 20 cm thick layer of alternating silt and sand, which contained numerous fresh water snail shells, indicating that it formed in flowing water. The drain was clearly functioning when this deposit accumulated. While it was originally identified as context **1033**, closer inspection showed it comprised four layers (**1040–1043**). The few ceramics found date it to the first and second century AD but a pair of unidentifiable late Roman coins also came from these deposits, testifying to the continued use of the drain over several centuries.[45] The ring drain was deliberately filled in the late fifth or early sixth century AD and the environmental evidence extracted from this drain—both from the usage deposits and the fill—is discussed in Ch. 4 §J.

There is no evidence in the sections excavated that the ring drain received feeder drains from the stoas or area around the

(1.15 to the base of the offset basal course, but the floor itself is missing at this point). Erim 1988, 748 gives 1.24 m, which is incorrect.

44 For depth measurements, see Nbk 307: *SW Portico of Tiberius* (F. Thode, 1989), 35.
45 Cat. 159 and 160.

pool in the first phase, although the modifications to the area in late antiquity did include the creation of a drain from the eastern end of the Place of Palms feeding into the ring drain on the southeast side (see Ch. 4 §B).

The Pool Floor

The pool floor, as fully excavated at the end of the 2017 season,[46] showed signs of extensive repairs in late antiquity, attributable to the reconstruction works of Ampelios, *c.* AD 500 (see Ch. 4 §B; Fig. 23). The original floor, however, seems to have consisted of three elements:

1. A substrate (**1034**) of irregular flat stones, marble, schist, and limestone,[47] laid in at least two layers, apparently set directly in the earth into which the pool had been excavated, without mortar (Pl. 16.A).
2. A layer of small stones and tile fragments laid over the substrate of flat stones (**1035**), measuring from 3 × 2 to 9 × 11.5 cm. Against the very edges of the pool, pebbles and tile fragments (*c.* 9–14 cm long × 2–5 cm wide × 6–7 cm high) had been carefully laid on edge and parallel to each other for a distance of 44–46 cm from the pool walls (Pl. 16.B); elsewhere the stones of this layer were laid flat and more haphazardly. This layer of stones seems to have been set in a pinkish red mortar, now much degraded and largely disappeared.
3. A layer of *cocciopesto* mortar (**1036**), whose aggregate consisted of small angular pebbles and fragments of tile, 1.5–5 cm across, in a pinkish grey mortar. The upper surface had been smoothed with a charcoal-rich dark grey mortar skim, and polished (Pl. 16.C).

The upper, *cocciopesto*, surface was preserved only across areas of the central stretch of the pool, but had been entirely lost at the western end, and much damaged at the eastern end. The middle layer, of pebbles, had disappeared entirely in the western third of the pool, where only the substrate of flat stones survived. The substrate was missing in patches only at the very western end of the pool where a late drain outlet appeared to have been dug through it, and in a linear stretch along the north side of the pool towards the east end, where it had been filled (in the seventh century?) with rubble.

In the western third of the pool, where the substrate was largely revealed, two parallel rows of stones are set in lines east-west and 30–34 cm apart (Pl. 16.D). If this feature is projected through the curved western end of the pool, it coincides precisely with a remnant of terracotta pipeline exposed at the base of the ring drain at the southwest curved end of the pool. Evidently the linear settings of the substrate stones abut and line this pipeline on either side; and the pipeline, which presumably fed a structure in some part of the city to the west or south-west of the pool, was laid under the pool floor at the time the pool was dug. Laying the pipeline beneath the pool, the space for which had already been dug out, rather than around one of the sides, would have minimised effort, saving the need to dig a separate 200 m-long trench 1.5 m deep to bury the pipeline at the same depth below streets and ground surfaces.

Water Supply and Fountains

The main water supply to the pool was at the centre of the east end, where the bottom of the outward-facing seat block on the long axis of the pool is cut, apparently to accommodate either the upper part of a channel block (now gone) or several terracotta pipelines that would have run underneath it in the original phase (Pl. 16.E; Fig. 11: B). It was earlier suggested that a large stone channel block carved in the shape of the prow of a ship flanked by dolphins, found by the Triconch Church near the south end of the basilica in 1962,[48] may have been the original inflow channel.[49] This suggestion was based partly on a block lying in the still-flooded eastern end of the pool excavated in 1988, whose shape suggested that it could have supported the ship's-prow channel block. On completion of the pool excavations in 2017, however, and drainage of the eastern end of the pool, it became apparent that this block did not fit the channel block, weakening the argument for association between the pool and the original location of the channel block (for which the Hadrianic 'Olympian' Baths remains another and perhaps better possibility). If there had been a channel block at the eastern end of the pool then it had been moved in late antiquity, as its original position on the east axis of the pool is now occupied by a distributor block of a later (sixth-century) phase of supply. Alternatively, and perhaps more likely, all the supply to the pool may have been delivered by terracotta pipelines to fountains.

A void space, *c.* 0.25–0.28 m high and 0.58–0.91 m wide between the schist slabs that roofed the ring drain and the marble slabs forming the surface of the edging around the pool and seats, served as a duct in which were laid terracotta water pipes that supplied fountains at several other points on the rim of the pool seating (Pl. 17.A). Although the terracotta pipes had all been recuperated when the marble slabs linking the seat blocks were robbed, their existence can be securely inferred from pipelines entering the duct at the east centre of the pool, and from inner seat blocks whose rear face was carved with a socket to take a pipe entering from the duct, and pierced through to the upper surface to feed the water through an ornamental fountain spout; in at least one case the clamp fittings for the fountain sculpture are visible on the upper surface of the block. Such fountain blocks were found at two points on the curved eastern end of the pool, one in the middle of the north side, and one at the western end (Pl. 17).

---

46   The eastern and western ends had been exposed in 1988–1990, and two sondages in the middle of the pool, against the south and north sides in 1985 and 1988 respectively, had also reached the floor (see Ch. 1 §C). The 2012 excavations had exposed an area of the floor (8.2 × 9 m).
47   Sample dimensions (cm): 8 × 10; 9 × 9.5; 11 × 23.5; 14 × 28.5.
48   M. Bell, unpublished typescript: Summary of the 1962 SWC Excavations, p. 5. Cf. Commito and Rojas 2012, 292 fig 41.
49   Wilson 2016b, 111–112.

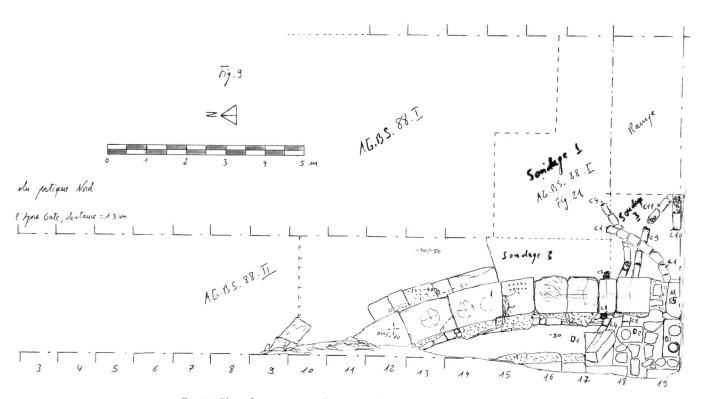

Fig. 10. Plan of terracotta supply pipes at the east end of the pool (1988).

Flanking the position of the presumed channel block on the middle of the east end of the pool, excavations in 1988 revealed three phases of terracotta pipelines that supplied fountains (Fig. 10). The first phase consisted of three pipelines, two running east–west (C8 and C10 in the numbering of the 1988 excavations), and one running southeast to northwest (C11), discovered heading towards the pool just north of the centre of the east curved end.[50] Later phases of supply had truncated them, and removed the evidence for how the fountain supply was organised in the first phase: C8 was found only where it ran across the outer wall of the ring drain (Pl. 17.B), under the seat blocks which had been re-laid here in the late fifth/early sixth century, and C10 and C11, found a metre to the east of the pool's outer wall, were truncated by the cutting for the third-phase pipeline C1. Presumably one of the three pipelines fed a fountain immediately to the north of the central inflow channel spout, and the other two ran within the duct described above to supply the two fountains that existed on the curved northeast end, and halfway down the north side. Outside the pool, to the south of the centreline of the curved end, excavation in 1988–9 was not carried down to a level to determine whether other pipelines entered here, although it seems likely, by symmetry, that a pipeline would have fed another fountain flanking the south side of the inlet channel, and another pipeline must have fed the fountain on the southeast curve of the pool.

The evidence for the situation of the fountains fed by the piping in the duct above the ring drain is (with each labelled using a capital F followed by a number):

– F-1. Around the midpoint of the southeast curve of the pool, one of the inward-facing seat blocks has a circular hole 0.18 m in diameter cut in its rear face to take a terracotta pipe from the duct (Fig. 12: F-1). This hole passes through the block as an elbow-joint to emerge in the upper surface as a nearly square aperture, 0.115 × 0.12 m, whose inner profile slants at 45 degrees upwards towards the pool (Pl. 17.C; Fig. 11, A). Two clamp holes, 5.5 cm wide and 8.5 and 11 cm long respectively, show that a small fountain sculpture was set here, that would have delivered a jet of water into the pool from the pipeline carrying water under pressure.

– F-2. There appears to have been a similar block on the northeast side of the curved end of the pool (Fig. 12: F-2); the block at the exactly corresponding position has been removed when a post-antique ramp was constructed down into the pool, but it seems to have been replaced a few metres to the west, where a slightly curved block obviously originally from the curved east end of the pool has been re-set in late antiquity on top of the beginning of the straight section of the north wall of the pool. A cutting near its east end is now broken but was clearly again designed to take a terracotta pipe from the void space in a circular socket (c. 0.20 m in diameter) in its north face. The hole changes to a rectangular cross-section about 10 cm wide, and is again angled upwards at c. 45 degrees to deliver a stream of water arcing upward and into the pool, presumably through a bronze spout fitting (Pl. 17.D; Fig. 11, C).

– F-3. In the middle of the north side of the pool, in front of the central doorway connecting the Place of Palms to the Agora, is a double elbow-joint block with two cuttings through the rear face and upper surface (Pl. 17.E; Fig. 11,

---

50 Nbk 298: *Agora Gate: Basin Front II* (F. Thode, 1988), 34, fig. 9.

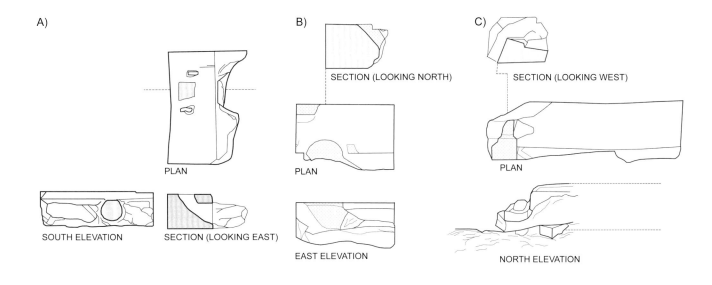
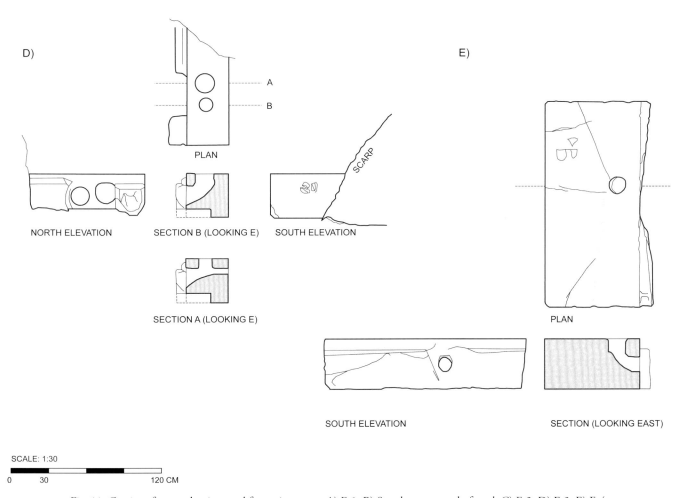

Fig. 11. Cuttings for supply pipes and fountain spouts: A) F-1; B) Supply at east end of pool; C) F-2; D) F-3; E) F-4.

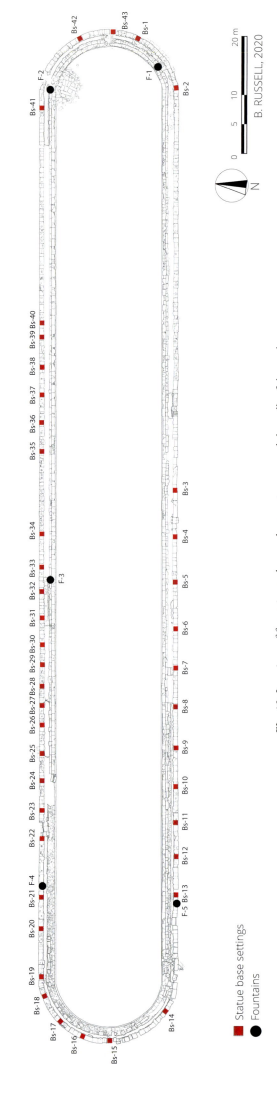

Fig. 12. Locations of fountains and statue base settings around the walls of the pool.

D; Fig. 11: F-3). Of the two cuttings, that to the east is roughly circular, measuring 0.15 m diameter in the south (rear) side of the block, and 0.16 m diameter in the top surface. A second cutting only 4 cm to the west measures 0.17 × 0.16 m in the rear face of the block and 0.105 × 0.11 in the top; there is also a small hole 3 cm wide and 5.5 cm high going through the block to emerge on the front side facing the pool, with two sockets immediately west of it to secure a metal fountain spout. It is possible either that both cuttings are contemporary, or that the west one is later than the east one, replacing it at a period when water could no longer be delivered under sufficient pressure to create a jet of water above the level of the pool surround, and so had to be delivered through the side of the block instead. There was no corresponding arrangement opposite, on the south side of the pool,[51] at least as the south side now survives, although since the southern side was almost entirely replaced in late antiquity (see Ch. 4 §B), this does not entirely exclude the possibility that there had been a matching fountain sculpture there in the original phase.

– F-4. On the straight north side of the pool towards the west end there is another elbow joint cut into the rear of a seat block, but this time on the north or *outside* of the ring drain (Fig. 12: F-4). The hole on the south side of the block to take the terracotta supply pipe is roughly circular and measures 0.125 × 0.11 m, and 0.15 × 0.14 m on the upper surface of the block (Pl. 18.A; Fig. 11, E). Again, this must have supplied a fountain; possibly a fountain facing away from the pool, but more likely a fountain that took the form of a sculptural group sufficiently large that it sat across the drain, with the pipe running up through the back of the sculpture to emerge on the side facing the pool.

– F-5. On the south side of the pool, also towards the west end and nearly but not exactly opposite the block just described on the north side, a seat block has a cutting on its external (south) side fed by a pipe from outside the pool (not from within the piping duct over the drain) (Fig. 12: F-5). This indicates another fountain feature, fed this time by a pipe coming from the south (Pl. 18.B).

The evidence of the cuttings for fountain emplacements thus shows that there was probably a pair of fountains closely flanking the main inlet at the mid-point of the east end of the pool, and another pair part-way around the arc of the east end, as well as further fountains on the north side—in the centre, and towards the west end—and also towards the west end of the south side (Fig. 12).

No fountain sculptures were found *in situ* in association with the cuttings for the pipes that fed them, but it is possible to recover something of the decorative programme from the findspots of several fountain sculptures found either within the pool or in its general vicinity. During excavations of the eastern end of the pool in 1990 there was found a statuette in fine-grained white marble of a boy riding a dolphin, with the dolphin's mouth acting as a fountain spout for a channel carved within its body (see Pl. 76.F).[52] The piece is second- or third-century in date. The boy's penis has been deliberately chiselled off, no doubt in late antiquity by Christians who found it offensive, which would suggest that this sculpture was still visible into the Christian period. This could have been one of the fountains flanking the main inlet at the east end. It has been suggested that the pristine surface of this statue, which shows little sign of weathering, indicates that it was displayed inside or under cover (see Ch. 7 §E). While this might be true, this figure certainly does not belong to the first phase of the complex and could have been added to the pool edge at a later date.

Two frogs carved in veined blue and white local marble are also candidates for fountain sculptures from the east end of the pool, as one of them, a frog squatting on a shell, hollowed out inside for a fountain, was found in the southeast part of the Place of Palms in 1986 (see Pl. 76.D), outside the pool. Only the left-hand half of this sculpture survives, 17 cm wide, broken across a line of weakness introduced by the fountain tube that ran inside it.[53] A rectangular clamp hole (1.5 × 2.5 cm) on the left side, shows how it would have been fixed to its support, presumably the fountain surround. A second frog sculpture, also in the same blue-veined marble and with the mouth serving as a spout, and of similar dimensions, was found in the excavations of the central *skene* area of the Theatre,[54] where it seems to have been reused in late antique or early medieval constructions (Pl. 18.C). Since the now fragmentary frog was found in the Place of Palms to the southeast of the pool, it is tempting to think that it went on the southeast side of the pool curve. The clamp holes of the fountain emplacement here are only 25 cm apart, but if the missing part of the frog was not too wide it might have fitted here.[55] The complete frog, 32 cm wide, cannot have gone on the southeast curve of the pool but might have fitted on the northeast arc. However, the association with the pool is not certain: the notebook recording the find of the fragmentary frog sculpture does not make clear whether it was found near the late antique ground level of the Place of Palms or among collapse from the Theatre Hill,[56] and it remains a possibility that both frogs may have decorated the Theatre rather than the pool (see Ch. 7 §E).[57]

Drainage Arrangements

All drainage from the pool, whether overflow or floor-level evacuation drainage, went into the ring-drain surrounding the pool, towards the west end. In its first phase the pool was equipped with an overflow in the middle of the west end (Pl. 18.D), an

---

51 Contrary to expectations in Wilson 2016b, 114.
52 Aphrodisias Inv. No. 90–5; Smith 1996, 20 and 22, fig. 14. Fragmentary: max. surviving dimensions: H 41 cm, W 21 cm, D 23 cm.
53 Aphrodisias Inv. No. 86–75 A. (Pieces B–F, registered under the same inventory number, do not belong to this sculpture). H 26.5 cm, W 20 cm (broken), D 43.5 cm.
54 Inv. 71–331. Nbk 126: *Theatre: Central Skene 4* (T. Egilmez, 1971), find CS.71.657. Dimensions: H 12 cm, W 32 cm, D 28 cm.
55 *Contra* the suggestion in Wilson 2016b, 117, which seemed to rule it out.
56 Nbk 278: *Portico of Tiberius: SE I, SW I* (J. Gorence, 1986), 64.
57 Wilson 2016b, 117.

oblong opening 13.5 cm wide by 7 cm deep, set 7 cm below the top of the lower seat block curved hemicycle. This overflow opened into a small channel, 22 cm wide and 22 cm deep, left as a void in the mortared rubble core of the wall, which was lined with a thin layer of pinkish *opus signinum*, of which traces remain; and this channel ran through the thickness of the wall into the ring drain. Since the pool was being constantly fed, constant overflow would have been necessary; and this would also have created a current across the surface of the water in the pool that would have militated against stagnation. The height of the overflow indicates a water level *c.* 94 cm above the base of the pool in this first phase. In practice such a depth of water would have been just enough to swim in; although the pool does not appear to have been designed principally as a swimming pool, it is easy to imagine people swimming in it from time to time (and for discussion of the Maiouma festival, see Ch. 4 §M).

The pool must have had an exit drain at the base in the first phase. At the base of the pool wall at the centre of the west end is a now broken block with a circular hole surrounded by a square rebate, probably for a metal filter. Through this water would have emptied into a built drain 0.46 m wide that ran through the thickness of the pool wall into the ring drain. Sited originally over this drain (and now lying in it) one of the coping blocks of the pool surround, with a slot 0.23 × 0.13 m in section cut through it, presumably held a stopcock or some kind of mechanism for opening and closing the drain outflow (Pl. 18.E). The arrangements here have been damaged and partly obscured by crude undercutting in late antiquity for the reinstatement of a drain in the third phase of drainage arrangements (see Ch. 4 §B).

The outflow drain that leaves the ring drain at the centre of the west end of the pool is probably a later addition (see Ch. 4 §B); the original exit drain, with walls in *petit appareil* and roofed by schist slabs, departs at an angle from the ring drain some 4 m south of the west end of the pool (Pl. 18.F). It heads to the south-west, and appears to be joined by another drain running north–south from the Hadrianic Baths or the West Stoa. This must have fed into the collector drain under the street along the west side of the basilica.

Paving around the Pool

The pool was surrounded by a marble paved path 2.81 m wide (as a remnant surviving at the west end shows), edged by a rounded kerb 8 cm wide (Pl. 19.A). Excavation in 2012 showed that the path was a few centimetres higher than the surrounding ground surface, to keep it drier in wet weather.[58] At the east end only a single row of paving slabs survives, and along the long (straight) sides the paving has been almost entirely removed.

C. STRATIGRAPHIC EVIDENCE: GARDENS, POOL, AND NORTH STOA (AW & BR)

Although much of the structure of the pool appears to have been re-set in late antiquity, some stratigraphic evidence for the construction of the pool and the early layout of the Place of Palms was discovered in excavations in 2012, while a sondage in the interior of the North Stoa in 2014 was carried out to understand the function of this structure.

The Paved Path around the Pool

In trench SAg. 12.2, a little to the west of the middle of the North Stoa, an area of 16.5 × 14 m was opened up between the pool and the stoa (Fig. 13). The earliest level encountered here was a layer of clean sticky mid yellowish brown clay (**2025**) that probably represents the natural layer into which the Place of Palms was terraced, somewhat disturbed during construction with fragments of tile trodden into it. Into this had been cut the ring drain whose walls formed the surround of the pool, and against the northern wall of the pool the natural was covered with a preparation layer (**2013**) of two courses of large rubble stones set in loose to firm mid greyish brown silty clay with frequent lumps of greyish white mortar (Pl. 19.B). Its upper elevation lay between 515.65 and 515.79 m. a.s.l. This was 26–30 cm thick and extended for a width of 2.80 m north of the pool wall, equal to the width of the marble-paved path and its kerbed edge where this still survives at the curved western end of the pool. The preparation is clearly the packing for the marble slabs of the path that surrounded the pool, as further shown by remains of an uneven layer of light grey mortar (**2011**) surviving in places on top of it, and two square marble paving slabs left *in situ* against the northern wall of the pool—the rest had been robbed, no doubt when the ground level was raised here in late antiquity.[59]

In 1991 a sondage was dug against the centre of the north side of the pool and encountered the same preparation layer, at the time interpreted as the bedding for what was assumed to be the paving of the 'agora'. Cleaning in 2012 of the eastern section of this sondage confirmed that this packing extended only 2.80 m from the edge of the pool, and not all the way across the space to the north, and that it was in fact the bedding for the paved path.[60]

Dating of the Pool

The date of the pool can be suggested indirectly from architectural considerations, and directly by some (limited) stratigraphic evidence. In architectural terms, the pool cannot pre-date the

---

58 Wilson, Russell, and Ward 2016, 78.
59 Three coins (Cat. 103, 108 and 125) dating to the fifth century were found on this mortar surface and provide a *terminus post quem* for the stripping of its paving; they were presumably deposited when **4028** was built up over this area.
60 Wilson, Russell, and Ward 2016, 78.

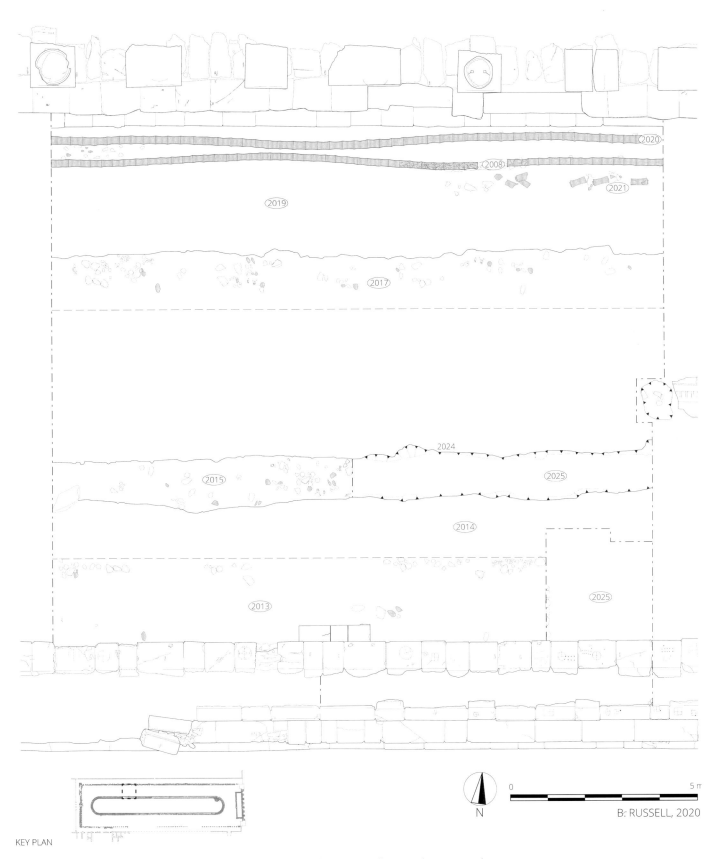

Fig. 13. Plan of trench SAg. 12.2 showing planting trenches.

North Stoa (started AD 14–29) and the creation of the area to the south of it, which was made by cutting back part of the Theatre Hill. On grounds of position, the pool should pre-date the Hadrianic 'Olympian' Baths. It is centrally situated between the colonnades of the North and South Stoas, but is not symmetrical between the West Stoa and the most westerly point of the Propylon: it is nearly 6 m closer to the former. This implies that the pool was laid out before the construction of the Hadrianic Baths, whose construction forced changes to the Place of Palms that disrupted this original symmetry. If the North Stoa was extended two columns to the west of where it currently ends, which is proposed above, the pool would be equidistant between the two ends of its straight section and a triple-aisled doorway aligned with its central axis. Although the original dimensions of the North Stoa, or the arrangement of its central doorway, cannot be proven, a date for the pool in the first century AD, prior to the construction of the baths, remains likely on architectural grounds.

Such a dating is supported by evidence from excavation: in 1991 a sondage against the centre of the north side of the pool found within what we now understand to be the stony bedding for the paving of the path around the pool pottery described in the excavation notebook as 'à engobe brune' and dated to the first century AD, probably meaning Eastern Sigillata B wares.[61] This should provide a *terminus post quem* for the pool too. No coins were recovered from layers datable to the construction phase of the pool.

A first-century dating raises the possibility that the pool formed a part of the original scheme for the area in the reign of Tiberius; and indeed the practicalities associated with the creation of the porticoed space virtually require that the pool was part of the design from the outset. Because the level space for Place of Palms was created partly by cutting back the northern flank of the Theatre Hill, the works disrupted the natural drainage of the area and risked intercepting the local groundwater—nowadays, with the city's drains blocked and out of service, water wells up periodically between autumn and early summer in the northeast corner by the Propylon, and sometimes floods the entire area of the Place of Palms. Significant drainage arrangements are therefore a *sine qua non* for the creation of a public space at this point, and the only drainage arrangement known here is the ring drain around the pool. And since the ring drain presupposes the pool which it surrounds, and is of one build with it, it follows that the pool must have been part of the original design for the area as a monumental space in the reign of Tiberius.

A Tiberian date for the pool also implies that Aphrodisias must already have had an aqueduct by this point in the Julio-Claudian period, since the pool was fed by pipelines under pressure that must have derived ultimately from aqueduct supply. The existence of the Eusebian Baths, built by a benefactor of the Julio-Claudian period, supports this deduction. The Aphrodisias Regional Survey identified three known aqueduct systems of the Roman period that fed the city.[62] The longest and latest one is the Hadrianic Timeles aqueduct coming from the Tavas valley. The other two came from Işıklar to the north, and Seki to the east. The Julio-Claudian aqueduct should be the Işıklar system, as it is the shortest (7 km) and therefore most probably the earliest, while the Seki aqueduct would then be identified with the water supply scheme attested by an inscription of the Domitianic period.[63]

Ground Level and Planting Beds

To the north of the preparation layer **2013** the presumed natural clay (**2025**) was covered by a layer of firm sticky redeposited light greyish brown clay, 14–27 cm thick, with inclusions of brick, tile, and pottery (**2014**), interpreted as the original ground surface of the Place of Palms. About 1.5 m north of the edge of the preparation layer for the path, this layer and the clay beneath it were cut by a straight-sided linear trench (**2024**) running east–west parallel to the pool wall for the full length of the excavation trench, 1.10–1.30 m wide and 0.45 m deep. The lower 6–10 cm of this was filled with a firm dark greyish brown silty clay with frequent large (fist- to double-fist-sized) stones and fragments of tile, and abundant potsherds, to form a free-draining substrate (**2028**). The upper part of the trench above this was filled with a mixture of dark reddish brown soil and light greyish/brownish pink sandy soil mixed with crushed brick dust (**2015**), 0.39 m thick, and containing frequent stones and fragments of tile, and some animal bone. The fill was very compact in the upper part, becoming looser and easier to work lower down. The eastern half of trench **2024** and its fills was excavated for length of 8.36 m (Pl. 19.C).

A parallel feature (**2017**) was identified about 4.5 m to the north of **2024**, also running east–west across the full exposed length of the excavation trench. Its edges were much harder to define, as its upper surface appeared to have had a mounded profile and its edges therefore dived down under the soil surface that had accumulated against it. This feature was not excavated but its upper surface was exposed and it consisted of the same pinkish earth with brick dust and abundant stone and tile inclusions as **2015**; it was up to 1.65 m wide in places.

Both features **2024** and **2017** are interpreted as planting beds filled with looser soil with a deliberate admixture of brick dust over a free-draining stony substrate, to enable trees and plants to root more easily than would have been possible in the poorly draining sticky natural clay into which they were cut. The fills themselves contained late antique material and indeed, as will be shown in Ch. 4 §C, there is good evidence that they stayed in use up until at least the late fifth or early sixth century and were even re-cut. However, the southernmost of these trenches (**2024**) is originally cut from the imperial ground level, not a higher level, and so we can be reasonably certain that the first phase of these planting beds belongs to the imperial phase of the Place of Palms; gardening and re-digging of the planting beds could easily have introduced later material. It was presumably in these planting beds that the palm trees mentioned in the early imperial inscription found reused in the city wall (*IAph2007* 12.204) and the late antique inscription of Ampeli-

---

61 Nbk 323: *Portico of Tiberius Sondages* (D. Theodorescu et al., 1991), final (unnumbered) written page; cf. Wilson 2016b, 127.
62 Commito and Rojas 2012.
63 Wilson 2016b, 101–102.

os (*IAph2007* 4.202.i) were planted, forming two lines of trees parallel to the long sides of the pool (Pl. 20.A).

Between the two planting beds the Roman ground surface (**2016**) was exposed but not excavated; it was seen in the west section (Pl. 20.B). Here it was heavily compacted, and traces of a white stony lime layer *c.* 0.36 cm thick were visible in the section edge but had been largely truncated by Jacopi's excavations in 1937 and the excavation of the North Stoa in 1985, and by subsequent wear and tear. This feature is interpreted as an unpaved path, *c.* 3.08–3.90 m wide, that would have run between the avenue of palm trees. To the north of planting bed **2017** was exposed an ancient ground surface of firm sticky dark greyish brown silty clay (**2019**), similar to **2014** to the south, with occasional pottery and tile inclusions but far fewer than within the fills of the planting trenches. This ran up to and abutted the euthynteria course of the north portico, whose top surface lay at 515.88 m a.s.l. The rough surface of the preparation layer **2013** after the robbing of most of the paving slabs, the ground surfaces **2014** and **2019**, the path **2016**, and the planting beds **2015** and **2017** were all covered by a stony dumped fill which represents the raising of the ground level of the entire area in late antiquity (see Ch. 4 §C).

The mounded surface of the planting trenches in the Place of Palms and the compacted path between them find parallels in the planting beds of the Great Peristyle of the Villa Arianna at Stabiae,[64] whose burial by *lapilli* of the Vesuvian eruption of AD 79 has allowed for clearer definition and the casts of the roots of the various species planted there.[65] The Villa Arianna garden contained both wide planting beds for shrubs, with mounded surfaces, and separate lines of plants, including trees. The wide beds here were arranged along the northern and southern sides of the garden and framed three east-west lines of plants, which in turn separated a series of four paths, or *ambulationes*.[66] On the northern side, the two sets of wide beds (PB1 and PB2 to the east and PB7 to the west) were separated by a semicircular pool, which aligned with a north-south path cutting across the garden.[67] These beds were 5 m wide and contained an array of small plants arranged both in lines and clusters; these were mostly herbaceous plants and small shrubs but also some small trees. Post holes in PB1 indicate fences with panels of reed or wicker. These were designed to create what Gleason calls a 'tableaux arrangement' comparable to those visible on contemporary wall-paintings from the Vesuvian sites.[68] Elsewhere, post holes aligned with plant cavities reveal the line of trained shrubs or vines or perhaps hedges. Compacted earth paths ran around these beds but the four best defined of these ran east-west down the centre of the garden and are divided by the narrow lines of plants. It is these beds, 83–84 m long, that provide the closest parallels for the beds in the Place of Palms. The paths between them measured 3.5–4 m wide, similar in width to the path discussed above. The beds themselves were 0.5–1 m wide, slightly narrower than the beds at Aphrodisias. The plants in them, to judge from the root cavities, were arranged 4–4.5 m apart and comprised (1) large and apparently old shade trees (plane or pine), (2) smaller cavities with associated post holes for new trees or vines, (3) compact cavities, possibly for palm trees, and (4) clusters of cavities, possibly for coppiced woody plants.

At the Villa Arianna, the presence of palm trees is proposed on the basis of the size and formation of certain root cavities but also on the basis of phytolith sampling. This identified phytoliths which could belong to palms, though they were not defined enough to be certain about this.[69] Our interpretation of the planting trenches as being for palm trees around the pool receives some support from the identification by Mark Robinson in 2012 of a fragment of Cretan date palm (*Phoenix theophrasti*) in the lowest levels of the silting of the pool.[70] This fragment comes from a much later context, datable to the first half of the seventh century AD. Since the pool was regularly cleaned out, no waterlogged contexts dating to the early imperial period, in which such evidence might have been preserved, were found and so this find does not in itself provide evidence that palms were planted in this area prior to late antiquity. However, the mention of a palm grove in the inscription of Artemidoros Pedisas, discussed below, shows that such a space existed in the city in the first century AD.

Date and Function of the North Stoa

In 1990 a sondage excavated by de Chaisemartin across the width of the North Stoa close to its western end also exposed early imperial levels.[71] The aim of this trench was to explore whether the North Stoa might constitute a covered exercise area or *xystos*, a portico type that Vitruvius tells us was commonly associated with gymnasia and enabled athletics, especially wrestling, to be carried out undercover during winter months.[72] De Chaisemartin identified what she believed to be a sunken 'track', 3.7 m wide (or twelve and a half Attic feet), the upper surface of which was marked by a white stratum on a thicker layer of preparation. Raised 'walkways' or earth banks ran along either side of this 'track'. The lowest level exposed in 1990 was a deposit of marble chips, which the excavators connected to the construction of the North Stoa. At least two late antique pipelines cut into the top of the earlier deposits were also identified. A second sondage further east identified some of the same features, though again noted that the interior of the North Stoa was heavily modified in late antiquity.[73] Three elegant marble thrones found re-used as part of the back wall of the North Stoa just west of its central doorway in 1989 were identified by de Chaisemartin as judges' seats and used to support her suggestion that the area was used for athletics, despite the fact that they were actually set below the ground level of the stoa.[74]

---

64 Gleason 2010.
65 Gleason 2016.
66 For plans of the layout, see Gleason and Sutherland 2016, 26, fig. 3.1.1; 2016, 67 fig. 6.1.1.
67 Gleason 2016, 67–68.
68 Gleason 2016, 71.
69 Ryan 2016, 105.
70 Robinson 2016, 94–95.
71 de Chaisemartin and Lemaire 1996, 167–171.
72 The *xystos* proposal is made in de Chaisemartin 1989a; b. On the function, Vitruvius, *De Arch* VI.7.5, V.11.4.
73 de Chaisemartin and Lemaire 1996, 167–171.
74 de Chaisemartin and Lemaire 1996, 171, fig. 20; de Chaisemartin 1989a, 73.

Sondage 14.3 was opened in 2014 across the North Stoa in line with the central doorway to the Agora in order to test whether the deposits identified in 1990 could be traced further east. The earliest level exposed here was a grey silty fill (**14.3.5003**) abutting the back of the seat blocks beneath the stylobate, which seems to date to the period of the initial construction of the stoa. No traces of the white stratum identified by de Chaisemartin were apparent. The seat blocks, however, were found to project substantially northwards beyond the line of the stylobate. The relatively flat rear sides of the stylobate blocks, which lack the rebates found on the corresponding blocks of the West Stoa might support de Chaisemartin's argument that the North Stoa was never paved. However, the *euthynteria* blocks of the back wall do have a shallow rebate cut into their southern faces and a series of large grey marble paving slabs, ranging in size between 80 × 60 cm and 110 × 90 cm, were found out of context in the North Stoa; these slabs are 20–23 cm thick and are cut along one side to fit a rebate 10 cm deep. These slabs are considerably larger than those used in the later West Stoa and do not belong to any of the other architectural components of the complex.

The sondage 14.3 revealed that the interior of the North Stoa was extensively remodelled in late antiquity, probably in the late fifth or early sixth century AD, and it was at this time that the marble thrones were reused in the foundations of the rear wall (see Ch. 4 §E). Substantial repairs were made to the back wall of the building and two new pipelines were cut down into the fill running between the seat blocks and the back wall. No traces of a running track were discovered and indeed the evidence from the *euthynteria* of the back wall might indicate that the stoa was paved in at least one of its iterations prior to late antiquity, at which point its interior ground level was lowered. It is possible that some of the features identified in the sondages in 1990 could belong to structures pre-dating the North Stoa. The late antique alterations and the reasons for them will be discussed in Ch. 4 §E.

D. HELLENISTIC AND METROPOLITAN MODELS: THE PLACE OF PALMS IN CONTEXT (AW & BR)

Rather than an open space for commerce or exercise, as has been previously argued (see Ch. 1 §D), the identification of the pool in 1988 and the excavation of the planting trenches in 2012 show that this was a green space, planted to act as a large-scale urban park with its enormous ornamental pool adorning nearly half of its total surface area. We can in fact go a step further and identify this area with the palm grove known from two inscriptions. The earlier of these, dated on the grounds of letter forms to the first or second century AD, was found re-used in the mid-fourth-century city wall, and is therefore not in its original location. It records the dedication by Artemidoros Pedisas of several statues, in marble and gilded bronze (apparently), which he had promised during the building of the palm grove:[75]

Ἀφροδείτῃ καὶ θεοῖς
Σεβαστοῖς καὶ τῷ Δήμῳ
Ἀρτεμίδωρος Διονυσί-
ου φύσει δὲ Ἀρτεμιδώ-
ρου τοῦ Διογένους
vv. Πηδίσας *vv.*
ἐκ τῶν ἰδίων ἀνέθηκε
τὸν Ἑρμῆ καὶ τὴν ἐπίχρυ-
σον Ἀφροδείτην καὶ τοὺς
παρ' ἑκάτερα Ἔρωτας λαμ-
παδηφόρους καὶ τὸν πρὸ
αὐτοῦ Ἔρωτα μαρμάρινον
καθὼς ὑπέσχετο καὶ αὐτὸς
κατασκευαζομένου τοῦ
φοινεικοῦντος ἐν τῷ τῆς
στρατηγίας αὐτοῦ χρόν[ῳ]

'For Aphrodite and for the Divi Augusti and for the People, Artemidoros Pedisas son of Dionysios, biological son of Artemidoros son of Diogenes, at his own expense set up the Hermes, and the gilded Aphrodite, and the Erotes carrying torches on either side, and the marble Eros in front of the statue of Hermes, as he also promised when the palm grove was being constructed at the time in which he served as a strategos.'
(tr. Roueché and Reynolds, modified A. Chaniotis)

This inscription does not tell us the original location of the palm grove, which is here called a φοινεικοῦς,[76] but a later inscription allows us to pinpoint its location with some precision, working on the assumption that the city did not have two palm groves. This text is the northernmost of three inscriptions carved into the façade of the Propylon honouring those responsible for its reconstruction in the late fifth/early sixth century AD.[77] The exact nature of the text and its context are discussed in detail in Ch. 4 §A and Appendix 1 (In10) but the key detail here is that it gives thanks on behalf of the nymphs to a certain Ampelios 'because he gave wonder and splendid beauty to the place of palms (χῶρος φυνικόεις), so that anyone who, among our waters, turns his glance around, may always sing the praise both of him, and of the place, and of the Nymphs as well.'

The implication of this inscription is that the reader of it was standing in the Place of Palms. The planting beds provide confirmation that the area was indeed cultivated and aside from the marble pavement running around the pool the whole area was left unpaved. Whether palm trees extended the length of the complex is unknown but only a small number of trees could have been accommodated at the eastern end alone; indeed the size of the planting trenches discussed above suggests that trees were distributed through the complex. Crucially, trees would also have provided shade to the seating arranged around the exterior walls of the pool and along the lengths of the stoas—without shade, the space is not somewhere to linger in the summer months. Maintaining a large-scale garden of this sort would have required gardeners. These might have been public slaves

---

75 *MAMA* VIII.448 = *IAph2007* 12.204. What this group might have depicted is discussed in Ch. 7 §A.

76 On this term, Chaniotis 2008b, 74.
77 *IAph2007* 4.202.i.

but an association of professional gardeners (*kepouroi*) is also attested on the seat inscriptions in the Stadium at Aphrodisias.[78]

Palm groves are attested in literary sources and papyri in the Levant and Egypt, where they mostly seem to be agricultural units.[79] An inscription from Smyrna dated to *c.* AD 125, however, provides a parallel for a monumental palm grove like the Aphrodisian example.[80] This text gives a list of benefactors who have promised donations to the city, including individuals tasked with the construction (or reconstruction) of a palm grove, φοιν(ε)ικών, among other projects. The donations are listed in order of importance and allow some reconstruction of the capital investment poured into monumentalizing the complex. The first entry specifically relating to the palm grove notes that Chersiphron the Asiarch promises to pay for its gardens. Since Chersiphron's contribution is listed below a promise of 70,000 *denarii* and above an entry promising 50,000 *denarii* from Lucius Pompeius for the palm grove generally, the work on the gardens probably amounted to an investment between these sums. Among other contributions are a temple, various sums of money, and 52 marble columns along with their capitals and bases for the palm grove. The Smyrna palm grove, therefore, combined lavish architecture and gardens. A minimum sum equivalent to 127,500 *denarii* was spent on this complex but it could also have been much more; 230,000 *denarii* listed in the inscription are not assigned to any specific project and might have been funnelled into the palm grove project. These are large sums: even the minimum total is only slightly lower than the highest recorded sum spent on a building in North Africa (150,000 *denarii*), where the listing of costs was a more established practice.[81] The theatres at Calama and Madauros cost considerably less.[82] No archaeological remains of the palm grove at Smyrna survive so we have no sense of its size compared to the Aphrodisian one. However, since the Smyrna inscription mentions just 52 columns and the North and West Stoas of the Place of Palms comprise 90 columns, we can assume that the Aphrodisias complex was at least as large as, and potentially much larger than, the one at Smyrna.

The fact that Chersiphron spent quite so much on just the gardens of the palm grove at Smyrna might be explained by the palm trees that it contained. These will have been *Phoenix theophrasti* or Cretan date palm, the only species of the tree native to Europe: it is found on Crete, Amorgos, Anaphe, and on the Datça, Bodrum, and Kumluca peninsulas in southern Türkiye (Pl. 20.C).[83] The Aphrodisian palms would have been the same variety. *Phoenix theophrasti* can grow up to *c.* 10 m tall, with trunks *c.* 0.5 m thick; the leaves, 2–2.5 m long, provide considerable shade and over time the trees will tend to form clumps, with old trunks being replaced by new ones.[84] These slow-growing trees would have had to be imported to the palm groves at both Smyrna and Aphrodisias, transplanted as mature trees, and set in tree pits or trenches. Since *Phoenix theophrasti* do not have tap roots but rather cable-like roots from the base of the tree, which are continually replaced, this kind of transplantation would have been feasible.[85] The remainder of the space around these trees could then have been planted in whatever way was felt most appropriate, with other trees, shrubs or flowers.

The scale of the Place of Palms is striking; nothing like it is known from Asia Minor at this date. However there are clear parallels for urban green spaces of this sort from Rome. The late republican and Augustan *porticus*-monuments of Rome were probably all planted.[86] Vitruvius, in fact, assumes that such open complexes were planted with greenery ('*viridibus*').[87] Although the monumental buildings of these complexes have attracted most attention in scholarship, their planting was a vital aspect of their function and appeal. Indeed, as Taylor, Rinne, and Kostoff have put it, 'ancient Rome's greatest urban investment was not in its streets and buildings, but in its staggering patrimony of cultivated greenspace', in which these *porticus*-monuments played a prominent role.[88] Among the Roman porticoes, several in particular offer parallels for the formal planting of trees flanking shaded walks. The Porticus of Pompey was planted with plane trees and the Porticus Vipsania with laurels.[89] It has been suggested that the Porticus of Philippus was also planted with trees, based on analysis of its representation on the Severan marble plan, though this remains debated.[90] Post-dating the Place of Palms but showing the continuation of the tradition are the longitudinal structures in front of the Templum Pacis at Rome, which have been variously identified as either pools of flowing water (*euripi*) or, more reasonably, raised flowerbeds.[91] Others have argued that the whole space was extensively planted, with Pollard describing the compound as replete with 'colonial botanical gardens', though in practice the scope of planting is unclear.[92] This kind of planting was not limited to public spaces in the capital. Planting pits for plane trees were identified in front of the porticoes of the Palestra Grande at Pompeii, which dates to the Augustan period.[93]

The planting schemes in these *porticus*-monuments would have provided shade, a backdrop for the display of statuary and paintings, and framed the associated architecture, but they may also have had religious connotations. Stands of trees were often associated with Roman shrines and sanctuaries.[94] In Rome, planters, probably for laurels, were built around the Temple of *Divus Iulius* in the Roman Forum.[95] At Pompeii planting com-

---

78 *IAph*2007 10.29.
79 For a list of references, see Hallmannsecker 2017, 120 n. 71.
80 *IGR* IV 1431; *I.Smyrna* 697; Chandler 1763, 78 no. 48; cf. Chaniotis 2008b, 74; Bowie 2012; Hallmannsecker 2017, 120–122.
81 Duncan-Jones 1982, 67–69.
82 400,000 and 375,000 *sesterces* respectively: Duncan-Jones 1982, 77.
83 Boydak 1985; 1987; Yaltirik and Boydak 1991; Boydak and Barrow 1995; 2000.
84 Riffle and Craft 2003, 400–406; Chao and Kruger 2007, 1078.

85 Robinson 2016, 94–95; on moving trees, see Pliny *HN* 12.16.
86 On the verdantness of these complexes, Taylor, Rinne, and Kostoff 2016, 103–108; Hallett 2021.
87 Vitr. *De arch.* V.9.5; on which, see Fox 2023, 112–114.
88 Taylor, Rinne, and Kostoff 2016, 103.
89 Porticus of Pompey: Gleason 1994; Martial 11.47; Propertius 2.32.20. Porticus Vipsania: Martial 1.108.1; on trees in these and other *porticus*-monuments, see Fox 2023, 115–124.
90 Richardson 1977, 359; for the identification of these features as statue bases, see Coarelli 1977, 474–476.
91 Anderson 1982, 105; Coarelli 1999; Meneghini and Santangeli Valenzani 2006, fig. 54; Tucci 2017, 58–61. For other examples, see Hallett 2021.
92 Pollard 2009, 312; on the idea of 'botanical imperialism', see also Marzano 2022, 50–87; and on Rome as an 'arboreal cosmopolis', see Fox 2023, 26–31.
93 Jashemski 1979, 160–1, fig. 246.
94 Taylor, Rinne, and Kostoff 2016, 105–106; Carroll 2018, 154–155,
95 Gros 1976, 90–91.

prising part of a possible sacred grove (*nemus*) has been identified in the precinct of the Temple of Venus, contemporary with the structure's construction in the first century BC.[96] Comparable planting holes for trees, cut into the bedrock, have been identified at the Sanctuary of Juno at Gabii.[97] Planting pots have also been recovered from the open area of the Augustan *tropaeum* at Nikopolis in north-western Greece, where Strabo also tells us there was a nearby sacred grove.[98]

The inspiration for these grand planting schemes, in both *porticus* and sanctuary, can be traced back to the hellenistic period. The monuments at Pompeii and Gabii, as well as Nikopolis, were consciously modelled on the grand cultic centres of the hellenistic East, raised on terraces with panoramic views. While no gardens have been excavated at the well-known sanctuaries at Lindos or Kos, third-century BC plantings have been identified in the grounds of the Hephasteion next to the Athenian Agora; the planting pits containing *ollae perforatae* here indicate that this garden was replanted at least three times and continued to be tended to well into the Roman period.[99] Planting also featured heavily in the *paradeisoi* of hellenistic palaces. Herod's Winter Palace at Jericho provides a glimpse of the continuation of this tradition. Planting pits from various areas of the lower terrace of the site show that this was a landscaped garden.[100] The Herodian tradition also seems to have influenced nearby Nabataea, where the Garden and Pool Complex at Petra, containing planting pits, *ollae perforatae*, and a small ornamental swimming pool was laid out prior to the Roman annexation.[101]

Water features played a role in many of these complexes and the late antique inscription on the Propylon of the Place of Palms indeed refers not just to trees but also to water (a feature not mentioned on the text from Smyrna). These waters must be the central pool and it is this enormous water feature that makes sense of the reference to the nymphs in the same text. The only other water feature in this area is the basin in front of the Propylon but this was only added some time after the inscription was carved and actually obscured it from view.[102] The pool, in fact, is the most striking architectural feature of the complex and is quite exceptional for its date size, shape, and concept (Fig. 14). It has been compared to the Canopus at Hadrian's Villa and it is in villa and palatial contexts that some of the clearest parallels for pools of this scale are found.[103] The Canopus (Pl. 20.D), though, while of similar width, is rather shorter than the Aphrodisian pool; the pool of the Poecile at Hadrian's Villa is also smaller.[104] Nero's *stagnum* in the grounds of the Domus Aurea, another villa pool, was probably larger (*c.* 200 × 200 m), but it is again later in date.[105] The peristyle pool of the Villa of the Papyri near Herculaneum, while earlier (first century BC), is much smaller (*c.* 66 m long) and belongs to a private context.[106]

These pools, in villas and palaces, drew on a hellenistic tradition of lavish water displays, often set within gardens, which in turn looked back to the *paradeisoi* of near eastern palatial complexes.[107] Documented examples include the artificial lake at the second-century BC Tobiad palace at Araq el-Emir in Jordan;[108] the series of pools in the Hasmonean winter palaces at Jericho;[109] and the more formally arranged rectangular pool at Herod's Third Winter Palace at Jericho, measuring 90 × 42 m.[110] Further large swimming pools were incorporated into the Herodian complexes at Herodeion (69 × 45 m) and Caesarea (35 × 18 m).[111] Even if the structures do not survive, Josephus' description of Herod's palace in the Upper City of Jerusalem refers to groves of trees, walkways, canals, and pools, into which fountains poured.[112] The influence of these projects can be seen elsewhere in the Levant: in the Garden Pool Complex at Petra, which has again been identified as a royal palace, and in the pair of monumentalised reservoirs at Birketein, just outside Jerash in Jordan, 88.5 × 43.5 m (Pl. 21.A);[113] these latter pools will be returned to in Ch. 4 §M.

Large-scale pools in public urban contexts are much scarcer. Agrippa's *stagnum* on the Campus Martius was probably the largest of these urban pools, though it no longer survives. It is estimated at 180 × 220–300 m.[114] This was not simply a monumental pool, however, but rather an annexe to Agrippa's baths and later became the *natatio* of Nero's baths. Different in function from the pool in the Place of Palms was also Augustus' *naumachia*, which was probably the largest pool anywhere in the Roman world.[115] One urban pool, set within an architectural complex, that has been compared to the pool of the Place of Palms is the cruciform pool of the 'Gymnasium' at Herculaneum, but it is appreciably smaller.[116] The portico of the Library of Hadrian at Athens also contains an ornamental pool, with curved ends much like the Aphrodisian example and the Canopus at Hadrian's Villa, but again this is considerably shorter, as well as later.[117]

106 The pool in the Villa of the Papyri is *c.* 66 m long (Deiss 1985, 62: 217 ft long by 23 ft wide).
107 Nielsen 1999; 2001; on the Achaemenid water features at Pasargadae and comparanda, Stronach 1990; on Egyptian gardens with pools, Wilkinson 1998; Kappel and Loeben 2011, 7–12; on the possible Babylonian influences on Herodian garden design, Taylor 2014, 156–157. On the connection between palatial architecture and luxury villa architecture, especially with regard to water, see Zarmakoupi 2014, 146–150.
108 Nielsen 1999, 138–46, 284–6.
109 Netzer 1986; 1996a.
110 Netzer 2001, 48–64; Macaulay-Lewis 2017, 119.
111 Netzer 1981; 1996b; Taylor 2014, 171–172; for an overview of all of these sites, Netzer 1999.
112 Josephus *BJ* 5, 180–181; on this text, Taylor 2014, 153.
113 On Petra, Bedal 2004; Kropp 2009; on the Birketein, Seigne 2004, 175–8; Lichtenberger and Raja 2016, 105, 107.
114 Coarelli 1977, 807–846; Roddaz 1984, 254–255; Coleman 1993, 50–51.
115 Taylor 2014, 176.
116 The longer arm of this cruciform pool measures *c.* 49 m (160 ft) in length (Deiss 1985, 152).
117 Sisson 1929, 58.

96 Carroll 2010, 74–81.
97 Coarelli 1993, 48–51.
98 Zachos 2003, 81, fig. 24; Strabo 7.7.6.
99 Thompson 1937, 404–411; Macaulay-Lewis 2006, 215.
100 Gleason 1993, 159–161.
101 Bedal 2004.
102 Wilson 2016b, 133; for more on this basin, see Ch. 4 §N.
103 Erim 1990, 27; de Chaisemartin 1989b, 41, 44.
104 119 m long × 18 m wide (Jashemski and Salza Prina Ricotti 1992, 580).
105 Panella 1995.

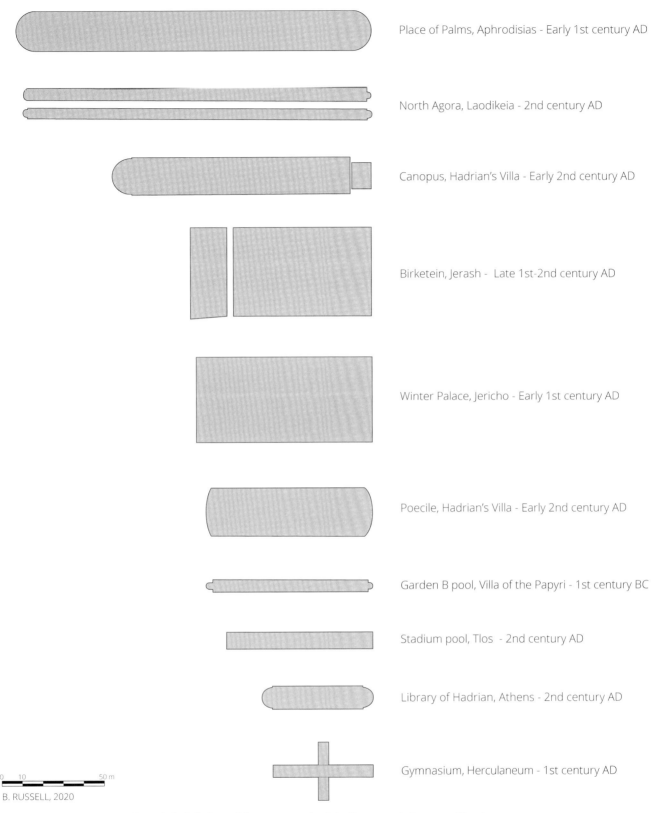

Fig. 14. Scaled plans of decorative pools of the Roman period, arranged by size.

In Asia Minor, monumental linear water cascades running down the middle of colonnaded streets are known from Perge and Antioch in Pisidia;[118] but these too are substantially later than the pool at Aphrodisias. The only comparable pools in public spaces but not part of a bath complex that come close to matching the size of the pool in the Place of Palms are the pool adjacent to the stadium at Tlos and the pair of pools in the North (Sacred) Agora at nearby Laodikeia.[119] The Tlos pool was added to the stadium area in the second half of the second century AD and measured 72 × 8.30 m (Pl. 21.B); it was refurbished in the second half of the third century but then went out of use in the fourth century. At Laodikeia the two pools are roughly the same length of the pool in the Place of Palms but are considerably narrower, *c.* 5 m (Pl. 21.C). They are arranged running along the east and west sides of this square rather than along its centre, which seems to have been occupied by a temple or other large rectangular structure. The whole complex is dated to the second century AD. The length of the pools at Laodikeia and the site's proximity to Aphrodisias suggest a degree of neighbourly emulation.

The Place of Palms at Aphrodisias would have been a shady open space in a city centre which was otherwise densely built-up (see Frontispiece). The combination of marble architecture, gardens, and water on a massive scale, and publicly accessible, is unique outside Rome in this period. In the capital, the grand new porticoes of the Late Republic and Augustan period translated what had previously been private palatial designs into public landscapes. Unlike the temple groves, these enclosed piazzas were intended, as Carroll puts it, to 'create a rather more introverted complex of gardens, art displays and opportunities for relaxation and public interaction.'[120] The Place of Palms, as Smith first noted, was an Aphrodisian take on these metropolitan porticoes; it was yet another way for the prominent citizens of the city to assert their connections with the capital.[121] In this sense the financing and construction of this complex, in the wake of Zoilos' restructuring of the city centre, was a local response to what Hallett has called the 'greening' of Augustan Rome.[122] However, this was not solely about emulation. While in scale and layout the Place of Palms rivalled the most famous complexes in Rome, providing a green haven at the heart of the city, this was also a more open and interconnected space. Its large-scale use of water, with its connections to palatial and villa architecture, was also unparalleled, its ornamental pool perhaps the largest of its sort anywhere at the time of its construction.

---

118 Perge: Abbasoglu 2001, 179–80; Antioch (probably Hadrianic): Owens 2002, 341–2.
119 Tlos: Korkut 2015, 21–28; Laodikeia: Şimşek 2013, 286–296.
120 Carroll 2010, 82.
121 Smith 1996, 49.
122 Hallett 2021; also on this phenomenon, Favro 1996, 176–180; and on the Augustan 'horticultural revolution', Marzano 2022, 88–129.

CHAPTER 3

Use, Maintenance, and Modification: First to Fourth Centuries AD

Andrew Wilson, Ben Russell, Allison Kidd, Angelos Chaniotis, Ahmet Tolga Tek, and Hüseyin Köker

Although the Place of Palms assumed its monumental aspect in the Julio-Claudian period, its form continued to evolve throughout the following centuries. Between the Flavian and Trajanic periods, the Civil Basilica was added to the western end of the south side, its façade and main entrance opening directly on to the Place of Palms.[1] The colossal columnar monument, described in its inscription as a *propylon*, was added at the east end not later than the reign of Nerva. At roughly the same point, a new South Stoa appears to have been added along the north side of the Theatre Hill. In the Hadrianic period, the west end of the piazza was extensively remodelled when the Hadrianic 'Olympian' Baths were built, with the West Stoa apparently moved eastwards to accommodate the new palaestra court of the baths.[2] Alongside these new additions, one or possibly two earthquakes in the second century provoked sufficient damage to necessitate repairs, to statuary and to colonnades; some of this work can be identified epigraphically and some archaeologically.[3] There is also evidence for fourth-century repairs and alterations to the North and West Stoas. Architecturally, this was a complex in continual flux but also one that was routinely invested in and updated. Coin evidence provides some additional insight into the use of the Place of Palms through these centuries.

A. THE PROPYLON (AW, BR, & AC)

The most dramatic new building to be added to the Place of Palms after its initial construction was built at the eastern end of the complex towards the end of the first century AD. This elaborate columnar façade monument is known in modern scholarship as the 'Agora Gate' or the 'East Agora Gate'.[4] Since the 'South Agora' is no longer an appropriate name for the Place of Palms, and the dedicatory inscription calls the building a *propylon*, we prefer to designate this monument the Propylon of the Place of Palms (not to be confused with the Propylon of the Sebasteion, a short distance further north along the Tetrapylon Street).

The Propylon consisted of a two-storey columnar façade raised on a stepped base perforated at either end by a pair of barrel-vaulted tunnels (Fig. 15; Pl. 22.A). The columnar façade is divided into eight bays framing seven sets of *aediculae*. At each end, north and south, it terminates in two projecting towers or *pyrgoi*, which extend over the tunnels. Although the structure is no longer standing above its stepped base, enough survives of its architectural elements to tentatively reconstruct its elevation. The first-storey columns were in the Ionic order and the upper in the Corinthian. The first bays from each end seem to have been roofed with broken pediments, the second and third by bridging Syrian gables, while the central bay was probably topped with a flat roof. The structure merits further study but it is beyond the scope of this project. A preliminary reconstruction published in the 1980s is illustrated here (Fig. 16).[5] An unusual detail of the structure is that it does not run perfectly perpendicular to the lines of the North and South Stoas: the face of its southern tower is built *c*. 1.8 m to the east of the corresponding face of its northern tower. Nothing to the west of the Propylon explains this arrangement but it is possible that it responded to structures on other alignments to its east, which have not been excavated.

Much of the dedicatory inscription (In2) can be reconstructed from among the fragments that collapsed into the east end of the Place of Palms when the structure was destroyed in an earthquake after antiquity. It records the construction of the Propylon (τὸ πρόπυλον) and its towers (τοῖς πύργοις) and the 'honours' (ταῖς τειμαῖς), presumably statues, of the emperors by Diogenes son of Menandros son of Diogenes, nicknamed 'the Younger'.[6]

Τῇ προμήτορι Ἀφροδίτῃ καὶ Θεοῖς Σεβας[τοῖς] καὶ τῷ δήμῳ Διογένης Μενάνδρ[ου] τοῦ Διογένους νεώτερος ἀνέθηκεν καὶ ἔκτισε[ν ἐκ τῶν] ἰδίων τὸ πρόπυλον ἐκ θεμε[λίων] σὺν τοῖς πύργοις καὶ ταῖς τειμαῖς τῶν Σεβαστῶν καὶ τῷ λοιπῷ κόσμῳ παντ[ὶ - -]

To the ancestral mother Aphrodite and the Divi Augusti and to the People, Diogenes 'the Younger', son of Menandros son of Diogenes, dedicated and constructed from his own finances the propylon from its foundations with the towers and the honours (statues) of the Augusti and all the rest of the decoration [- -].

The name of the reigning emperor is missing from the fragments of the inscription that have so far been found. A statue base of the emperor Nerva, set up during his reign (AD 96–98),

---

1 Stinson 2016, 16–19.
2 On the date and construction of the baths, see Wilson 2016a.
3 Wilson 2018a, 473–474.
4 Erim 1986b, 123–130; Ratté 2002, 23–24; Wilson 2016b, 130–133.
5 Erim 1986b, 182–3.
6 Unpublished: AphCat 70–9 pp. 69 and 72: items 77.47 + 77.48, 80.15, 27, 30, 31, 32, 83.?; 84.?; 77.134. A transcription of much of the inscription is given in Nbk 253: *S Agora Gate I-84, Book 1* (B. Rose, 1984), 13, which is supplemented here with the first block (77.134).

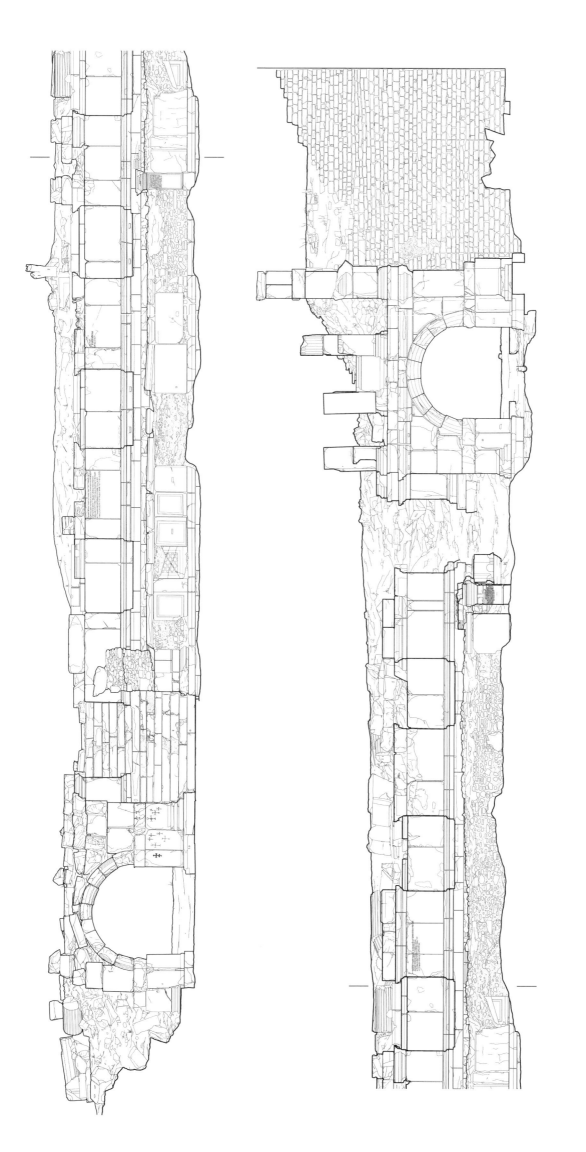

Fig. 15. West elevation of the Propylon of the Place of Palms.

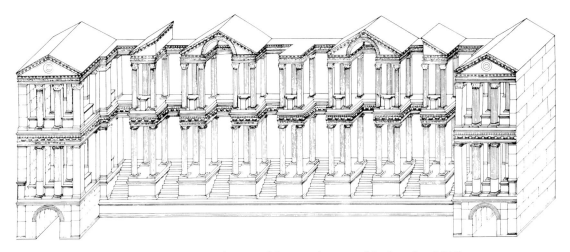

Fig. 16. Reconstruction drawing of the west elevation of the Propylon (1986).

records that the statue was paid for from a bequest of Diogenes the Younger; two more, to Hadrian and Antoninus Pius, were put up later still by the *demos*, the latter with funds promised by Adrastos son of Adrastos, the son of Apollonios the son of Andron Attalos (*IAph2007* 4.201). The monument has generally been dated to the Hadrianic or Antonine period on grounds of architectural style,[7] and the statue bases from the façade have been used to support a date in the reign of Antoninus Pius (AD 138–161) (see Ch. 7 §C). But the epigraphic evidence shows this dating is impossible. The Propylon and the statues of the Augusti on it were erected during the lifetime of Diogenes the Younger. The statues of the Augusti should have been statues of emperors before Nerva, since Diogenes was dead before the statue of Nerva was erected, evidently during Nerva's reign; the statue was erected from Diogenes' bequest. The dedication and the monument thus date before AD 96. The statues of Nerva, Hadrian, and Antoninus Pius were erected later. The inscription provides a *terminus ante quem* of c. AD 96; on grounds of architectural style it would be difficult to date the Propylon as early as the middle of the first century AD. A Flavian date for the period of its construction thus seems likely.

Given the persistence of names within the leading families of Aphrodisias, we can be reasonably certain that the builder of the Propylon, Diogenes 'the Younger' son of Menandros son of Diogenes, was related to the Diogenes son of Menandros who had built the North Stoa in the reign of Tiberius; he is perhaps more likely to have been his grandson rather than a homonymous younger brother (see In2). It was thus fitting that he should further adorn the space which his ancestor had funded by giving it a monumental columnar entrance screen in the most up-to-date fashion.

The Propylon of the Place of Palms develops the columnar screen format which had already been used a short distance to the north in the mid-first-century AD Propylon of the Sebasteion, and takes it to a new scale. It also foreshadows a wider set of elaborate columnar screen monuments common throughout Asia Minor in the second century AD, notable examples of which include the Market Gate from Miletos and the Library of Celsus at Ephesos, and is contemporary with or earlier than columnar nymphaea at Miletos, Ephesos, Side, Perge, and Aspendos, to list just a short selection.[8] The Propylon of the Place of Palms at Aphrodisias anticipates many of these better-known monuments by a decade or more and is a striking example of the precociousness of Aphrodisian architecture. Like these other monuments, the primary function of the Propylon was to provide a monumental backdrop to civic life and a venue for epigraphic and statue displays, the evidence for which is discussed in Ch. 7.

B. THE SOUTH SIDE: A SECOND STOA AND THE NEW BASILICA (AW, BR, & AK)

The limited evidence for a lost first-phase South Stoa was outlined in Ch. 2. The key features that point to the existence of such a structure are the cuttings on the Theatre Hill retaining wall and the overall layout of the Place of Palms. The cuttings on the Theatre wall, however, also indicate that after this first-phase stoa, and probably quite soon after it, a second stoa was constructed along the south side of the complex. This stoa had the same dimensions as the first-phase stoa and indeed may even have re-used some of its architectural elements. Its construction can be dated to the same period as the rebuilding of the Theatre Hill retaining wall, since the upper row of cuttings supporting the rafters for its roof were built into its structure; in other words, the stoa was planned from the beginning. The square recesses built into the new wall would have been within this stoa but their function is not clear; they are too large for roof beams and cannot have supported a second storey, since they are immediately beneath the row of cuttings for roof struts. At this stage, our best guess is that they were sockets for decorative elements of some sort.

Also contemporary with these repairs are the series of barrel vaults that extend west from the original ashlar Theatre wall (see Pl. 13.A). These vaults served both as supports for the extended

---

7 Erim 1986b, 123–30.

8 On columnar screen architecture of this sort, see Ward-Perkins 1981, 288–302; Quatember 2011, 90–94.

upper cavea of the Theatre, and as buttresses for the Theatre Hill, perhaps to prevent further collapses. Beneath them the rubble walling continues with at least one decorative niche built into it. This new Theatre Hill retaining wall, comprising ashlar, rubble walling and vaulting, continued for a total distance of 70.5 m from the preserved eastern end of the original ashlar wall, at which point it turned to the south for a short distance. It is unclear what originally lay on the line of the Theatre Hill retaining wall to the west. The late antique (third) iteration of the South Stoa, which was probably several stoas, certainly continued beyond the end of this wall and its rear must have been supported by a structure of some sort. It is possible that it fronted a row of shops or other buildings, like those uncovered just east of the Basilica.

Since the vaults built into the rebuild of the Theatre wall provided the support for the upper section of the auditorium they must belong to the extension of the Theatre by Hermas, the adoptive son of Aristokles Molossos, who completed this work according to his foster-father's will in either the third or the fourth quarter of the first century AD.[9] The extension of the Theatre and the construction of this second South Stoa, therefore, occurred at roughly the same date as the construction of the Propylon.

While none of the marble elements of the first phase South Stoa survives, a line of *euthynteria* and seat blocks, exposed in a sondage in 1991, probably belongs to this second-phase stoa. These were found at the eastern end of the stoa where it meets the Propylon (Pl. 22.B).[10] These blocks are at the same height as the corresponding blocks of the North Stoa and certainly predate the late antique phase of the structure, since the rubble fill that was used to raise the late stylobate is placed on top of these blocks.[11] It is possible that they come from the first-phase stoa, but the seat blocks are not handled in the same way as those of the North Stoa; instead of curved fronts to their projecting sections they have flat ones, while the fronts of the *euthynteria* blocks are irregularly worked. The structure is similar, in both respects, to the later West Stoa. On this basis, de Chaisemartin and Lemaire proposed that this phase of the South Stoa (which they considered the first) was later than the North Stoa, perhaps even contemporary with the West Stoa.[12]

There is no reason, however, to push the date of the stoa this late and there are two pieces of evidence to suggest that the construction of the second-phase South Stoa took place at broadly the same time as work on the Propylon, which was certainly finished by c. AD 96. First, a bracket projecting from the western side of the southern tower of the Propylon, built into the structure of the monument, supported the architrave of the South Stoa (Pl. 22.C); the Propylon, therefore, was designed and built to connect to a stoa running along the northern side of the Theatre Hill. It could be argued that this bracket was added to accommodate a planned but not yet started stoa, of course. However, the arrangement of the juncture between the seat blocks of the South Stoa and the foundations of the Propylon indicate that work had in fact already started on the former when the latter was begun. If the two monuments were begun at the same time, one would expect a neat join between the first of the seat blocks and the foundations of the Propylon. Instead, the most easterly seat block appears to have been lifted, shaped to fit a corresponding block on the Propylon and then re-inserted. This could simply indicate that the builders of the Propylon had got their measurements wrong—and, as discussed above, the Propylon is not set at exactly 90 degrees to the line of the North or South Stoas—but even in this case it seems to suggest that the *euthynteria* and seat blocks of the South Stoa were in place before the Propylon was built. This does not mean that the South Stoa was finished before the Propylon was begun; if it had been then its eastern end would have to have been dismantled anyway to allow for the adjustment to its seat blocks and, presumably, stylobate, as well as the setting of the architrave on the bracket of the Propylon.

The most plausible chronology would seem to be that the rebuilding of the Theatre Hill retaining wall, and the work overseen by Hermas, were begun in roughly the middle of the first century AD (perhaps after the same earthquake that damaged the Sebasteion during its construction in the Julio-Claudian period, in the AD 40s or 50s),[13] with the second-phase South Stoa being laid out as soon as was possible, and then the Propylon being added while this stoa was still being worked on. Most of the work on both the South Stoa and Propylon, above stylobate level, was therefore probably completed at the same time, and probably in the Flavian period.

How long this second-phase South Stoa remained standing is unclear. It was certainly rebuilt in the late fifth or early sixth century AD (see Ch. 4 §F). Whether this Flavian stoa stayed in place until that date is uncertain. It could have been damaged just before these late antique interventions, in the late fifth-century earthquake that prompted the rebuild, or it could have fallen down and its remains could have been cleared away before this. A major earthquake did hit the city in the fourth century, probably necessitating repairs to the West Stoa and Hadrianic Baths as well as to the Basilica (by Flavius Constantius), as is outlined below (see Ch. 3 §C).[14] However, this fourth-century earthquake provoked repairs, not a full-scale rebuild, of the West Stoa, Hadrianic Baths and Civil Basilica, so it is unlikely to have completely destroyed the South Stoa. It is entirely possible, therefore, that like the Propylon, the second-phase South Stoa remained in place until the late fifth century AD.

This second-phase South Stoa was supported along its rear side by the Theatre Hill retaining wall and so is unlikely to have extended westwards beyond the northwest corner of this hill. Indeed, if this stoa did extend further to the west it would have obscured the façade of the Civil Basilica. Only during the late fifth- or early sixth-century refurbishments of the whole of the Place of Palms was the South Stoa, in a third iteration, extended along the whole length of the complex and in front of the Basilica, which at this point was in ruins. In Philip Stinson's formulation, this late stoa might even have been used to 'mask' the collapsed Basilica from the still bustling Place of Palms.[15] At this

---

9 de Chaisemartin *et al.* 2017, 43–44. *IAph2007* 8.108, 8.112, 8.113.
10 de Chaisemartin and Lemaire 1996, 157, fig. 8.
11 de Chaisemartin 1998, 221 and fig. 17; Wilson 2016b, 107.
12 de Chaisemartin and Lemaire 1996, 157–158; also, de Chaisemartin 1989a, 65.

13 Wilson 2018a, 470, 472–473.
14 Wilson 2018a, 474–476.
15 Stinson 2016, 82–84.

late date it seems to have been two storeys high for at least some of its length, perhaps in the central section of the southern side of the Place of Palms, to the west of the vaults supporting the Theatre substructures. This late antique rebuilding of the South Stoa probably occurred at the same time as Albinos' interventions in the West Stoa, and other major works throughout the Place of Palms in the late fifth or early sixth century (Ch. 4 §D–F).[16]

While the first-century rebuild of the northern side of the Theatre Hill and the construction of the second South Stoa and Propylon were massive building projects, the largest new structure to be added to the Place of Palms was the Civil Basilica. This building has been well studied and published by Stinson and so only needs to be revisited here in brief.[17] Ceramics from excavations within the building, the style of the architectural decoration, and the epigraphic evidence from the structure indicate that it was constructed in the last quarter of the first century AD; it was probably started during the reign of Titus and completely finished by the early years of Trajan's reign.[18] Work on the Basilica, therefore, probably began after work had started on the Propylon, even if the two projects must have run in parallel for some time. This overlap might have put a strain on the labour force but if correctly arranged would have been manageable: teams responsible for groundwork and basic masonry could have been moved from these earlier projects to the Basilica initially, with marble-carvers following later; the numbers of marble-carvers in the city may even have been so large that elements for both the Propylon and the Basilica could have been worked on at the same time.

The Civil Basilica itself occupied three city blocks immediately west of the Theatre Hill, with its North Façade opening directly on to the Place of Palms (see Fig. 1). This façade contained three doorways and remained the main entrance to the building throughout its history; it was this façade, in the early fourth century AD, that was inscribed with the texts of Diocletian's Edict on Maximum Prices and his Currency Edict or Currency Revaluation.[19] The Basilica was, therefore, oriented towards the Place of Palms from its inception. This connection was further emphasised in the primary Ionic order of its interior, which was modelled on that of the earlier North Stoa of the Place of Palms, while the mask-and-garland frieze, to quote Stinson, 'seems to enter the building' from the complex beyond.[20] Like all of the other structures around the Place of Palms, the construction of the Basilica was financed by members of the local elite: fragmentary names of two, C. Laikanios and a Paulleina, siblings or husband and wife, were included on the dedicatory inscription.[21] The fact that these individuals chose to build the Basilica opening on to the Place of Palms and not in a space adjacent to the North Agora shows how the urban park had cemented itself as a vital civic space within little more than half a century.

What the Basilica added to the developing Place of Palms complex beyond its imposing façade was an enormous 4,200 m^2 of indoor space, which could have been put to varied uses: business, legal affairs, assemblies during inclement weather, or simply leisurely strolling.[22] The structure also provided direct covered access to the Place of Palms from the major east-west road running south of the Theatre Hill to which the Basilica connected at its southern end. In this way the building acted, as Stinson notes, 'as an extended entrance sequence into the heart of the city from the south'; the statues that were later erected inside the northern vestibule of the building even faced to the south, as if oriented towards passers-by heading towards the Place of Palms rather than those entering the building itself from the north.[23]

C. THE WEST STOA (AW & BR)

As noted in Ch. 2, there are good reasons to think that the West Stoa (see Pl. 12.D) was a new creation of the Hadrianic period rather than simply a first-century stoa moved to accommodate the baths. The West Stoa appears to have remained standing until at least the late fifth century AD, when it either collapsed or was damaged and was then re-erected by Albinos—a phase of activity discussed in Ch. 4 §D. Cuttings on the stylobate blocks, bases, column drums and capitals of the West Stoa, however, show that the structure underwent a substantial transformation at some point between the second and fifth centuries AD. In this phase of activity the colonnade of the stoa was enclosed with doorways and a new mosaic floor was added in the interior, turning it into a long hall. A series of fourth-century bases and statues from the West Stoa provide the best dating evidence for this transformation.

The Hadrianic stoa

The West Stoa has a colonnade twenty columns long. Sixteen of these columns—W1–8, 13–20—are the same dimensions, 5.17 m with a lower diameter of 69.5 cm, slightly shorter and squatter than those of the North Stoa. Their different proportions can be explained by the fact that unlike the North Stoa columns, they are raised on pedestals, 83 cm tall. The middle four columns of the West Stoa (W9–12), however, are taller, 5.34 m with a lower diameter of 79.5 cm, and are raised on pedestals 1.33 m in height. Together these four central columns form a portal (a more modest form of 'propylon' than that at the eastern end of the Place of Palms).[24] On at least two of the four central columns (W9 and W10) the Attic column bases are carved out of the same block of stone as the rest of the pedestal, the tops of which are adorned with deep rectangular recesses, which make base and pedestal appear separate components (Pl. 22.D); on column W12 of the central group, however, base and pedestal are separately carved,

16 Wilson 2016b, 108.
17 Stinson 2016.
18 Stinson 2016, 16–19.
19 On the North Façade, Stinson 2016, 2–6 (with fig. 4), 21–26; on the edicts, Stinson 2008, 91–6; 2016, 73–75; Reynolds 1989; Crawford 2002; Chaniotis and Fujii 2015; Crawford and Stinson 2023.
20 On the influence of the North Stoa, Stinson 2016, 88.
21 Stinson 2016, 123–125 (Doc 1).

22 Stinson 2016, 8–11.
23 Stinson 2016, 89.
24 de Chaisemartin and Lemaire 1996, 155: a 'pseudo-propylon'.

Fig. 17. Reconstruction of the east elevation of the West Stoa and its central gateway.

while the top of the other pedestal (W11) is missing.[25] On all the other columns the base and pedestal are separately worked. The interaxial spacing of the columns of the West Stoa is 3.02 m, slightly wider than in the North Stoa, though the central bay is wider, resulting in an interaxial spacing of 3.46 m.

The four larger columns of the central portal supported a pediment with Syrian gable that roofed and drew attention to the three-aisled gateway behind it, which connected the West Stoa to the East Court of the new Hadrianic Baths. Projecting brackets on the first and fourth columns of the central group supported the architraves of the north and south ends of the colonnade, managing the difference in heights of the columns (Pl. 22.E). A similar arrangement occurred on the façade of the Flavian Civil Basilica, on which the entablatures of the east and west wings were lower than the entablature of the central portal that they flanked. To accommodate this difference in heights, the side columns of the Basilica propylon were carved to receive the ends of the architrave blocks, and preserve large mortise holes in their flanks; their capitals have indents on one side of their lower bell to receive the frieze blocks of these lower entablatures.[26] Stinson points to parallels from Delos and from Ptolemais in Cyrenaica.[27] He also notes that Vitruvius' description of a 'Rhodian' peristyle includes colonnades of different heights being incorporated into the same structure, in this case with one stoa being higher than the other three.[28] The bracket that joined the Propylon at the eastern end of the Place of Palms and South Stoa performed a similar function, facilitating the juncture between adjacent structures of different heights.

From the West Stoa, little survives of the Syrian gable and its pediment itself, aside from three blocks of the arch and three blocks of raking cornice.[29] The arch blocks comprise three fascias topped with a crown moulding decorated with egg-and-dart. These fragments and the spacing of the four central columns of the West Stoa allow a reconstruction to be proposed (Fig. 17).[30] The facts that the arch blocks that survive relate to an architrave, and no frieze or cornice arch blocks have been found, suggest that the arch sprung from above the horizontal cornice blocks and comprised just an architrave, similar to the scheme later employed on the pediment of the Tetrapylon.[31] Arzu Öztürk proposed an identical formulation of this portal in her work on the reconstruction of the Hadrianic Baths.[32] She also reconstructed the architecture of the three-aisled gateway behind this propylon, which provided access to the East Court of the Hadrianic Baths beyond. The four pedestals of this gateway remain *in situ* and enough of the entablature blocks survive for its appearance to be reconstructed; even though no capitals survive, the piers

25   Crema 1939, 293.
26   Stinson 2016, 26.
27   For these parallels, see Winter 2006, 172–174, fig. 365; Pesce 1950, pls. 7b, 10.
28   Vitruvius, *De Arch* 6.7.3.
29   The blocks of the arch are currently stored in the West Stoa and the sections of raking cornice in the south-west corner of the Place of Palms; these blocks were first identified by Gaudin (see Mendel 1906, 164).
30   A similar reconstruction can be found in Stinson 2016, 74 fig. 37.
31   On the Tetrapylon, Paul 1996; Outschar 1996b.
32   Öztürk 2016, 202–204, fig. 12.14.

probably had Corinthian capitals to tie in with the order of the East Court beyond.[33] Since the East Court is 1.2 m higher than the West Stoa, this gateway was accessed by a set of five steps. De Chaisemartin and Lemaire propose that the central propylon of the West Stoa is a later intervention, perhaps Hadrianic, while the rest of the colonnade could be earlier, but as noted already, there is no convincing evidence for a pre-Hadrianic stoa at this end of the complex.[34] All of this architecture—stoa with its central portal—probably dates to the Hadrianic period and can be connected with the construction of the Hadrianic Baths.

Despite the addition of pedestals and the central portal, much of the rest of the architecture of the West Stoa follows the scheme of the earlier North Stoa, to which it connected at its northern end. While the architrave and frieze blocks of the West Stoa are largely identical to those of the North Stoa, the cornices show slight differences, with the moulding beneath the cyma recta crown moulding being treated as a plain band rather than the cyma favoured on the North Stoa; the water spouts are simplified and squatter on the West Stoa cornice but the differences would hardly have been discernible from the ground.

At least two types of capital were also integrated into the West Stoa, half following the format of the North Stoa capitals and half with egg-and-dart echinuses (Pl. 22.F). The former could date to any time between the Julio-Claudian and the Hadrianic period, while the latter seem more obviously Flavian to Hadrianic.[35] In practice, they probably all date to the Hadrianic construction of the stoa and the variation in the echinus mouldings simply reflects different workshop habits, of the sort noted on the *balteus* mouldings of the North Stoa capitals. Differences are also observable on the seat blocks beneath the stylobate, the upper lip of which is flat rather than curved as on the North Stoa, and on the *euthynteria* blocks, which are left rough on their face; these details are comparable to the treatment of the corresponding blocks belonging to either the first (Julio-Claudian) or second (Flavian) phase of the South Stoa.[36]

One interesting detail on the West Stoa colonnade is the addition, on column W13, of a club of Herakles, 42 cm high, carved into the base of the middle flute of its eastern side (Pl. 22.G); this might be a mason's signature, since Herakles is often associated with architecture, or even a reference to an association with, or a nickname (for example Ἡρακλᾶς, Ἡρακλείδης, Ἡράκλειος) of, the possible commissioner of the stoa, who was a military officer, as discussed below.

As in the case of the North Stoa in its first phase, it is not clear whether the West Stoa was paved inside in the Hadrianic period. The evidence for probable paving in the North Stoa, however, suggests that it was; indeed it was certainly paved in its later phases, first with mosaic and then with grey marble slabs.

The rear wall of the West Stoa is constructed of similar grey marble blocks to the rear wall of the North Stoa and is punctuated by the central three-aisled doorway, as well as two doorways at its northern and southern ends. As in the North Stoa, these doorways are framed in white marble but unlike in the North Stoa they are approached by flights of stairs, a result of the elevated position of the East Court of the Hadrianic Baths to the west.[37] The lintel blocks of these doorways were inscribed on the sides facing the East Court with dedicatory inscriptions datable to the reign of Hadrian.[38] Aside from these doorways, the rear wall of the West Stoa, like the rear wall of the North Stoa, was revetted in marble, the evidence for which is discussed further below in connection with the North Stoa. Consoles also projected through the rear wall of the West Stoa, probably at ceiling height, their decorated faces extending out into the East Court of the Baths.[39]

A fragmentary building dedication on an architrave block of the first or second century AD (Pl. 23.A) was found in the southwest corner of the Place of Palms, in front of the Civil Basilica.[40] This architrave block is smaller than those used in the main architrave of the West Stoa, but could be part of the interior architecture that connected the propylon and its Syrian gable with the gateway to the baths beyond. Alternatively, it might come from another area of the Hadrianic Baths. Its mitred left end shows that it belongs to the first (left-hand) block of a series. This text and its dating are discussed in full in the catalogue of inscriptions (Appendix 1, In5). The inscription reads, 'To Imperator Caesar Divus Augustus [father of the fatherland? …], Antipatros the *primipilarius* [together with - - -].' Although the emperor's name is lost, the inscription is probably Hadrianic if (as is overwhelmingly likely) the donor, Antipatros, a *primipilarius*, is the same individual as M. Cocceius Antipatros Ulpianus, *primipilarius*, the father of a woman who dedicated a caryatid in the adjacent East Court of the baths;[41] the same man is probably also the sponsor of another building.[42] This architrave block tells us that this individual was active in this sector of the city in the Hadrianic period, even if it cannot be certainly connected to the West Stoa.

Fourth-century interventions

The West Stoa seems to have remained standing in its Hadrianic form for perhaps two hundred years. The next clear evidence for alterations to it is a series of cuttings on the stylobate blocks, pedestals, bases, and columns. These features pre-date the late fifth-century re-erection by Albinos, since the columns were slightly moved at this later point and their pedestals placed over some of these cuttings, rendering them useless. At the same date, the interior of the West Stoa seems to have been paved with a mosaic floor, on which a series of statue bases was set.

Five main types of cuttings can be identified along the length of the West Stoa, some of which have parallels on the North Stoa (Fig. 18). Four of these can be associated with the insertion of doors and doorframes into the colonnade of the stoa.

First, in the top surface of the stylobate blocks of each of the nineteen intercolumniations of the West Stoa are a series of sockets relating to door mechanisms. These consist of regular sets of cuttings at both ends of each intercolumniation, com-

---

33 Öztürk 2016, 203–204, fig. 12.16.
34 de Chaisemartin and Lemaire 1996, 155–156.
35 de Chaisemartin 1989a, 64.
36 de Chaisemartin and Lemaire 1996, 155.
37 On these doorways, Öztürk 2016, 18, fig. 12.14.
38 *IAph2007* 5.207–208; see Wilson 2016a, 185.
39 On these figured consoles, Thomas 2022.
40 *IAph2007* 4.3.
41 Smith 2007, B21; cf. Wilson 2016a, 187 no. 14.
42 Chaniotis 2004, 397 no. 19; *SEG* LIV 1027.

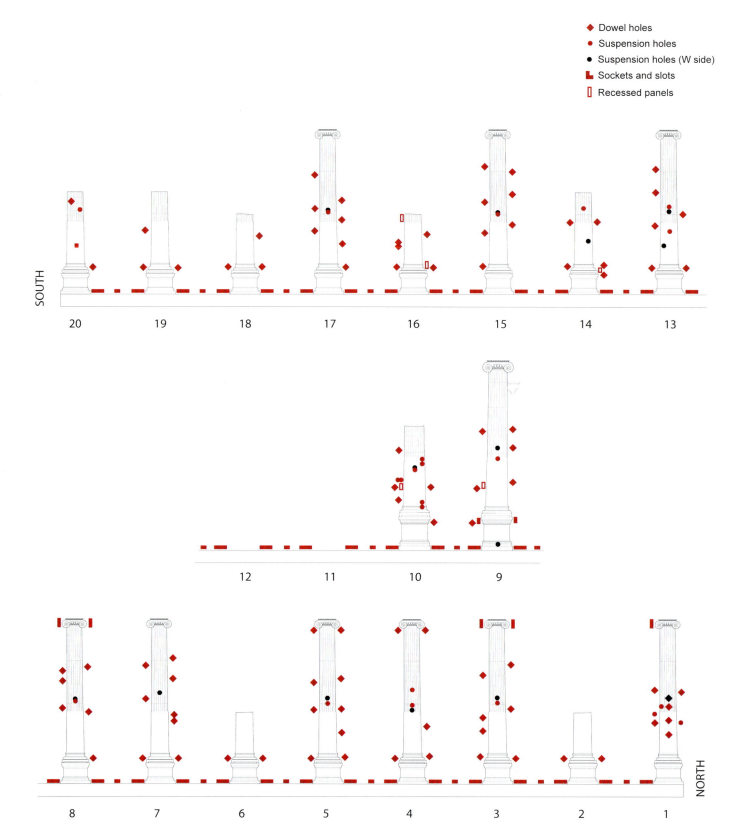

Fig. 18. Distribution of cuttings of various types on the colonnade of the West Stoa.

prising a central square socket (10–11 × 9–11 cm), located 3–6 cm out from the edge of the pedestal, framed by either two or four rectangular dowel holes (7–10 × 3–5 cm) closer to the edge of the pedestal (Pl. 23.B). The square sockets are designed to receive the metal fixtures (*cardines*) in which the leaves of a door would have pivoted, while the dowels would have held upright wooden doorframes in place. At least one central groove (6–9 × 2–3 cm) can be seen in the upper surface of each stylobate block attesting to the presence of a vertical bolt on one or both of the door leaves for locking them from the inside. Since some of the pedestals re-erected by Albinos were placed over the cuttings for doorframes and *cardines*, these features can certainly be dated to before the late fifth century AD, as can those cuttings discussed below that go with them.

Second, vertical lines of between three and five dowel holes are observable on the north and south sides of all of the preserved column shafts of the West Stoa (see Pl. 23.C). These are aligned with the square sockets in the stylobate and seem to indicate the points at which wooden doorframes or the metal vertical support for some other form of closing system were fixed to the shafts. The lowest holes in each series are usually cut into the column base or the bottom of the lowest drum of the shaft at a height of between 1.13 and 1.28 m above the stylobate; these lowest holes are all circular (1–2 cm in diameter). The holes above are always square (*c.* 3 × 3 cm) and on those columns where a full run of holes is preserved (W13 and W15) they are located between 1 and 1.9 m apart, with the highest being cut into the very top of the fluting or into the astragal of the shaft. The remains of iron pins are preserved in multiple holes.

The third set of cuttings can be found on seven columns (W4, W9, W10, W13–16), where narrow strips (8–12 cm wide) of the surface of the base or column shaft have been cut back to form a flat panel (see Pl. 23.C). These features are always aligned with the square sockets in the stylobate and the vertical lines of dowel holes on the shafts. When placed on the base they tend to cut through the upper torus moulding back to the line of the face of the column shaft and were clearly designed to receive a flat element, presumably the edge of the doorframe.

Finally, two of the capitals of the West Stoa (on W3 and W8) have their *balteus* cut away on both sides to form a deep groove for the insertion of an upright element (for an example from the North Stoa, see Pl. 27.A). On the capital on W1, only the south side of the capital has received this treatment and the same is true of a capital now preserved on the stylobate block between W8 and W9. Similar cuttings are found on a number of the capitals of the North Stoa, as will be discussed below; in these cases, however, dowel holes are associated with these cuttings, a feature not found on the West Stoa. Herrmann observed similar cuttings on a fourth-century Ionic capital now in the courtyard of Santa Maria dell'Anima in Rome. He remarks on the neatness of this cutting and suggests that it was for the insertion of the 'frame of a window.'[43] Similar cuttings are visible on some of the Ionic capitals of the colonnade in front of the Byzantine shops at Sardis.[44] In the case of the West Stoa, these cuttings should be connected to the continuation of the upright wooden doorframes held in place lower down by the fixings attested on both the column shafts and the stylobate blocks. A wooden beam would presumably have been fixed across the top of the intercolumniation at the height of the capitals. The fact that not every *balteus* was removed from every capital along the length of the West Stoa shows that not every frame was taken to the same height. The actual lintels of the doors installed in these intercolumniations could have been at any height within the overall frame and the space above filled with a grille or shutters, but since all of these features would have been fixed to the wooden frame no traces of them are now visible.

As well as these various cuttings associated with the installation of doors, two sets of cuttings relate to the provision of either lighting or other adornment. First, a series of dowel holes for the insertion of metal elements is also visible on multiple shafts. On columns W13 and W14 these holes are at the same height, 2.38 m, and both face west (that is, inwards into the stoa). On W10, four sets of holes face east (outwards), at 1.97, 2.15, 3.97, and 4.05 m. These holes are different from the vertical series found on the north and south of columns and could conceivably be for projecting hooks from which oil lamps or other adornment could have been suspended. Secondly, suspension holes cut through the fillets of the fluted sections of the column shafts are found on 12 of the 14 columns preserved to the height of their fluting (see Pl. 23.C). These holes (*c.* 2 cm in diameter) are always found on the east and west sides of the columns and no more than one is found per column face. They range in height between 2.82 and 4.54 m, with a mean height of 3.81 m. These holes could not have supported lamps since these would have hung awkwardly against the fluting; it is more likely that they were for the attachment of garlands or some other form of temporary decoration, or conceivably even for wooden tablets with some form of advertisement or *topos* inscription.

The first collection of cuttings outlined above shows that at some point after its construction in the Hadrianic period the colonnade of the West Stoa was fitted with doorways. The second set of cuttings could date to the same period or to Albinos' later interventions, and attests to lighting and decorative installations. The addition of doors effectively transformed the interior of the stoa into an enclosed hall, which would have required artificial lighting. In 1969, excavations in the south-western corner of the West Stoa, in the vicinity of the fallen statue base honouring a certain Menander, uncovered a patch of mosaic flooring, which was covered by the later grey marble flooring that certainly dates to Albinos' restoration (Pl. 23.D).[45] The Menander statue base, which can be dated to the late fourth century AD, stood on this mosaic floor.[46] The geometric design of this mosaic is comparable to the mosaics from the Basilica, funded by Flavius Constantius in the middle of the fourth century AD.[47]

It is tempting to connect the cuttings on the colonnade of the stoa and the installation of this mosaic and date them both to the mid fourth century AD. As will be discussed in Ch. 7 §D, this hall became one of the main venues for the display

---

43 Herrmann 1988, 94, fig. 170–1.
44 Whether these cuttings were made when these capitals were re-used here or prior to this, when they were part of another structure, is not clear; they are not discussed in Crawford 1990.
45 Nbk 76: *NE Nymphaeum / SW Portico of Tiberius* (S. Kulaklı, 1969), 36, 41.
46 Lenaghan forthcoming.
47 Stinson 2016, 75–78, pl. 47a–b.

of statuary, new and old, in late antique Aphrodisias; the most significant sculptural finds from this structure are the group of Theodosian emperors, suggesting that the space had already taken on this new function by the late fourth century AD. An inscription, carved on the upper fascia of a small-scale cornice block, recorded by Boulanger in the northern part of the West Stoa, might relate to this phase of rebuilding or repair.[48] The text is discussed fully in Appendix 1 (In8); it states that 'Helladios set me here also, the renovator of the splendid metropolis', and probably refers to a statue. This inscription is dated to the 'early or middle of the fourth century' by Roueché and Reynolds.[49] Helladios was a governor (ἡγεμών) of Karia known from two other inscriptions at Aphrodisias.[50] He was involved in repair work in the Hadrianic Baths (*IAph2007* 5.118) and so may also have intervened in the adjoining West Stoa.

It is possible that the repairs to the Hadrianic Baths and the changes apparent in the West Stoa may have been prompted by an earthquake around the middle of the fourth century. This possibility is suggested not only by extensive repairs to the Basilica's floor at that same time, financed by another governor, Flavius Constantius, but also by material from public buildings reused in the city walls constructed in the years between AD 355 and 362, including an *ethnos* base from the Sebasteion and the original base of the Blue Horse statue from the Basilica.[51] While we cannot certainly connect Helladios to the West Stoa or definitively date these changes to the structure to the fourth century, it is certainly tempting to connect developments in the West Stoa to those in the neighbouring Hadrianic Baths and Basilica, which are more concretely dated to this period. Although the enclosing of the West Stoa seems to have turned it into a hall, one of whose functions became the display of statuary, it is worth noting that in the tenth century the emperor Romanos is said to have added doors and wooden screens or boarding to stoas at Constantinople to provide better shelter against the cold and snow for the homeless who slept there.[52]

Unsurprisingly, considering its long lifespan, a number of the architectural elements of the West Stoa show signs of repair. Two sections of fluting on W16 were removed and replaced with new inserts. The column base of W14 is a later replacement, carved in much more schematic style and in a greyer marble than the original elements. The bases of W13 and W14 also preserve clamp holes, which held them to the lower end of the shaft above; one is visible on the west side of W13 (though this should be rotated 180 degrees to put it back in its original location) and three on the east side of the base of W14. Dating these repairs is difficult; they could belong with the fourth-century interventions described or above or perhaps the phase of reconstruction funded by Albinos later. The best candidates for late fifth-century repairs are the patches on W16 and the new base for W14, which shares some similarities with the bases of the late phase of the South Stoas (on which, see Ch. 4 §F). What these repairs attest to, however, is the continual upkeep of the structure over at least three centuries and perhaps longer.

D. THE NORTH STOA (BR, AW, AK, & AC)

The North Stoa, along with the pool running down the centre of the complex, was the most long-lived architectural feature of the Place of Palms. Evidence from its surviving architectural elements and material recovered from the excavations, however, show that, like the West Stoa, it continued to be updated and repaired over the course of its life. In the early second century AD, when the West Stoa was constructed, the North Stoa's western end was truncated; this probably necessitated removing at least part of its roof and then joining the replacement roof with that of the new West Stoa. Probably contemporary with this phase of activity, the rear wall of the North Stoa was covered in new marble revetment. In the same century and perhaps later, several of the columns of the stoa were repaired and the structure perhaps partly or wholly re-roofed. Later still, but prior to the late fifth century, the North Stoa underwent a similar, though less systematic, transformation to that experienced by the West Stoa, with new fittings or screens added into the intercolumniations of its colonnade.

Marble revetment

As already noted, the rear wall of the North Stoa was originally constructed in a combination of grey marble orthostats and small blockwork. The carefully smoothed faces of the grey marble blocks suggest that these were meant to be seen and in its first phase the rear wall was probably not further adorned. Evidence for the later addition of marble revetment, however, is provided by holes (*c.* 2 × 2 cm) for revetment pins, which are visible across the exterior faces of all the orthostats still in place (Pl. 23.E). Some examples of the T-shaped pins originally secured in these holes were recovered from the excavations, in stratigraphic units which also produced substantial quantities of revetment (see Ch. 8 §D). The placement of these pin holes provides some insight into the revetment scheme employed. A horizontal row extends the entire length of the preserved sections of the rear wall, 20–23 cm above the top of the *euthynteria* course, which seems to have corresponded to the interior floor level of the stoa. At roughly regular intervals, 1.60 m apart, vertical lines of pin holes extended upwards from this horizontal row, suggesting that the rear wall was broken into panels of decoration. In addition to these pin holes, the external faces of the ashlar blocks of the second course were point-chiselled with small divots to prepare them for the application of mortar. The relatively limited number of pin holes and their wide spacing show that most of the revetment was held in place by mortar, with these pins providing additional support for the largest panels or other decorative elements. Since none of the wall is preserved above 1.40 m the arrangement of revetment on its upper

---

48 *IAph2007* 4.120.
49 *IAph2007* 4.120; *ala2004* II.35.
50 *IAph2007* 1.131; 5.118.
51 On the Basilica, Stinson 2016, 75–78; on the Blue Horse, Smith and Hallett 2015; on the wider evidence for earthquake damage, Wilson 2018a, 474–476.
52 Georgios Monachos Continuatus, *Chronicon breve* (*Patrologia Graeca* 100, p. 1173 lines 15–26).

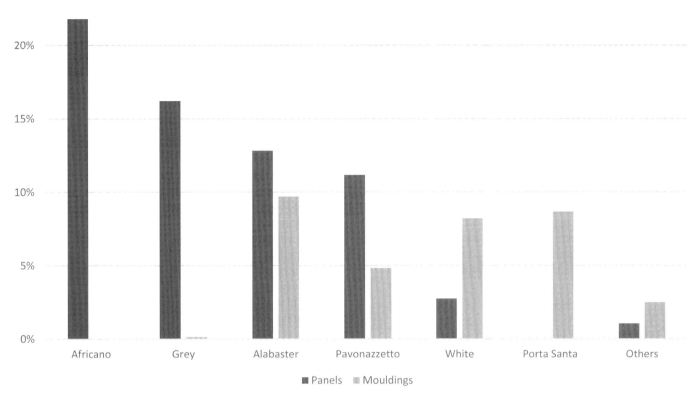

Fig. 19. Graph of marble types present in the wall revetment assemblage from the lowest deposits in the pool.

portions is unclear. Some indications of the decorative scheme, however, are provided by finds from the excavations.

The various deposits of dumped material found inside the pool along its northern edge yielded large quantities of marble revetment, as well as fragments of flat pilaster shafts and pilaster capitals—over two tonnes in total. These deposits date to the seventh century and are discussed in detail in Ch. 8. They represent the result of clearance activities following substantial damage to, and then the eventual destruction of, the North Stoa. Nearly five tonnes of roof tiles were also recovered from these dumps. The analysis of the marble from the main stratigraphic units associated with these dumps and the silt at the bottom of the pool (**4328**, **4442**, **4448**, and **4482**) shows that the decorators of the North Stoa (and probably also the West Stoa) used substantial quantities of decorative stones, the range of which is revealing of the city's economic connections and local aesthetic concerns.

The revetment can be divided into two categories: flat panels and mouldings. A total of 1,524 kg of flat panel fragments and 792 kg of moulding fragments was documented from the five stratigraphic units noted above. The breakdown of the lithotypes represented is plotted in Fig. 19. In the case of the flat revetment, 94% was in only four materials: *africano* (*marmor luculleum*) from Teos and its vicinity (33%), *alabastro fiorito* (19%) from the region around Hierapolis and Tripolis in Phrygia, a mottled grey marble (25%), and a variety of bluish marble similiar to *pavonazzetto* (*marmor phrygium*) (17%). These latter two are both from Aphrodisian territory, the grey probably from the Yazır quarries (11 km west of the city) and the *pavonazzetto*-like marble from Çamova Tepe, not far from Karahisar (22 km east).[53] While the *africano* and *alabastro fiorito* fragments were not ornamented in any way, both the mottled grey and *pavonazzetto* fragments belonged to large rectangular panels with scotia mouldings running down either both or one of their long sides. A further 4% of the revetment from these contexts was in local white marble. Other imported stones are attested in much lower quantities (<1% of the total each), in some cases in a few fragments only: among the Greek materials are *cipollino* (*marmor carystium*) from Euboea, *verde antico* (*marmor thessalicum*) from Thessaly, *serpentino* (*marmor lacadaemonium*) from Lakonia; from Asia Minor, a single piece of *cipollino rosso* from Iasos; from North Africa, *giallo antico* (*marmor numidicum*); and from a range of possible sources, *nero antico* and *rosso antico*. Materials from imperially-controlled sources are extremely scarce: *porfido rosso* is limited and there are single pieces each of *grantio bianco e nero* and *granito della Sedia* from the Eastern Desert.

Among the fragments of moulding recovered some slight differences in the range of lithotypes can be noted. Four main materials are used for mouldings: *alabastro fiorito* (28%), *portasanta* from Chios (25%), local white marble (24%), and Çamova Tepe *pavonazzetto* (14%). A clear relationship between lithotype and moulding type is also apparent. *Portasanta* was used for both fluted flat pilaster shafts, of which 201 kg were recovered (Pl. 24.A

---

53 On these regional quarries, see Stearns 2012; Long 2012. On Aphrodisian *pavonazzetto*, Attanasio *et al.* 2015, 754 (sample no. 4–5).

& Colour Pl. 1.A), and for a shallow moulding that might well have been used as a base for the pilaster shafts; *pavonazzetto* was used for a shallow cavetto and quarter-round crown moulding (see Pl. 24.B & Colour Pl. 1.B); *alabastro fiorito* was employed for both a crown moulding and an architrave moulding comprising three fascias; and the local white marble for a cyma recta crown moulding, a fillet with rounded profile, and two forms of moulding into which coloured marble panels were set—the first with a longitudinal recess and the second a fillet with diagonal recesses across it, 2 cm wide. Shallow panels of *serpentino* with bevelled rear edges were found among the assemblage that fit the first of these inset moulding types, while small lengths of porphyry were similarly cut to the diagonal recesses on the fillet, to create the impression of red and white twisted cabling.

Among this assemblage a small quantity of moulding fragments in the mottled grey Yazır marble was found that seem to be replacements for elements originally carved in other stones. These include some sections of a fluted pilaster shaft, similar in form to those carved in *portasanta*, a section of architrave moulding identical to the alabaster versions, and four lengths of crown moulding of the same form as the sections carved in white marble. These pieces suggest that the revetment scheme in the North Stoa was patched up over time and that the local Yazır grey was the favoured marble for this work.

Figured capitals

The final element of this revetment scheme uncovered during excavation is a series of figured Corinthian pilaster capitals. Twenty fragments of these pilaster capitals were found in the dumped deposits at the base of the pool, especially along its northern side, while a substantial number of fragments that can be tied to this group (more than 50 in total) were recovered from other contexts, many of them built into the system of Beylik to Ottoman field walls described fully in Ch. 9. These capitals are all carved in local white marble and follow a standard Corinthian format with acanthus leaves and egg-and-dart moulding along their bottom edge. They have lower widths and heights of *c.* 32 cm. While the bulk of the fragments preserve part of the acanthus leaves, abacus, or base moulding, the four most complete examples show that these capitals were populated by winged erotes engaged in a range of activities: holding a thyrsos (Pl. 24.C),[54] hunting (Pl. 24.D–E),[55] and harvesting grapes (Pl. 24.F).[56] A finely carved head of an eros with neatly curled hair probably also comes from one of these capitals (Pl. 24.G).[57]

This group of capitals can be connected to a series of six figured pilaster capitals found in the Place of Palms during the 1980s and published by Sheila Dillon.[58] One of these (Dillon's C5) was found in excavations in the North Stoa and the other three (C4, C7, C8) in the open area of the Place of Palms and in the pool. Two other capitals published by Dillon that have no recorded findspot (C1 and C9) also belong to this group.[59] Dillon dates these pieces to the second century AD and notes their stylistic similarity to the 'peopled scrolls' from both the Hadrianic Baths and the Theatre Baths.[60]

One other figured pilaster capital published by Dillon (C6), depicting Artemis, was found in the South Stoas of the Place of Palms but it is technically quite different from the erotes series and later in date. This could come from a late antique phase of the South Stoa, the evidence for which is discussed in Ch. 4 §F. A capital of similarly schematic quality showing an eros either hunting or harvesting, found in the pool in 2017, might also belong to a later group of pilaster capitals (Pl. 24.H).[61] The Artemis capital has close affinities with the series published by Dillon from the North Temenos House, which she dates to the third to fourth centuries AD at the earliest.[62]

Decorative scheme of the rear wall

The exact arrangement of these various revetment elements on the back wall of the North Stoa can only be speculated at. The fact that we have flat pilasters, pilaster capitals, and mouldings with fascias indicates an architectural scheme. Since the rear wall is preserved nowhere above 1.40 m, the spacing of the pin holes reveals only that there was a base course of small panels beneath a row of larger panels, which together make up a dado. Four complete panels in white marble of the right size to belong to the base panel have been recovered, while the largest flat panels preserved (up to 47 × 94 cm) are all in Yazır grey and would fit above this base course. Beyond this any reconstruction must be tentative but we can locate a certain number of the mouldings and flat panels with some degree of certainty (Pl. 25.A & Colour Pl. 1.C). The white marble crown moulding is the only one deep enough to support the bases of the pilaster shafts and so must belong to the top of the dado. The flat panels of *pavonazzetto* belong to two lines running horizontally, one with scotia moulding top and bottom, the other with them just along the top; no corner sections of the scotia moulding were found, indicating that they do not turn. These must belong to the bottom half of the composition since the top comprises mostly alabaster mouldings. An appealing possibility is that one line of these panels was located at the top of the dado, between the panels of Yazır grey and the white crown moulding, and the other above the dado, topped by the *pavonazzetto* crown moulding, and broken into sections by the pilaster shafts.

To judge from the width of the pilaster shafts and the height of their capitals (32.5 cm and 32 cm), their original height was

---

54 SAg.17.1.4329.M1622 (Inv. 17-29).
55 SAg.17.1.4328.M2710 (Inv. 17-149)/SAg. 17.1.4328.M2696 (Inv. 17-150)/SAg.17.1.4328.M2657 (Inv. 17-152) and SAg.12.1.1032 (Inv. 12-24).
56 SAg.17.1.4328.M2759 (Inv. 17-155)/SAg.17.1.4328.M2739 (Inv. 17-157)/SAg.17.1.4281.M1048 (Inv. 17-153). Another fragment of a harvesting eros (SAg.17.1.4328.M2699) shows that this theme was repeated.
57 SAg.17.1.4448.MM2578 (Inv. 17-62).
58 Dillon 1997, 762–767, no. C4 (eros holding thyrsos), C5 (winged eros), C7 (winged eros), C8 (winged eros harvesting grapes).
59 Dillon 1997, C1 (standing eros) and C9 (dancing eros).
60 Dillon 1997, 762.
61 Inv. 17-54.
62 Dillon 1997, 743.

probably around 2.8 m (an estimate determined by using a ratio of height to lower width of 8:1); they were capped by an astragal moulding also in *portasanta*. If these pilasters corresponded to the free-standing columns of the colonnade in front of them they would have had an interaxial spacing of 2.89 m. Two small fragments of the top of bases in white marble survive; these might have been raised on the white marble blocks with longitudinal insets mentioned above. The field between the *portasanta* shafts must have been primarily occupied by the *africano* panels, given their quantity. Indeed a number of these are cut to fit around the edge of the pilaster capitals, showing that there was no border between the pilasters and these panels and that this field extended to the top of the capitals.

The final elements that can be located with reasonable confidence are the alabaster mouldings: the architrave panels must go above the capitals and were probably topped by the crown moulding in the same stone; the white marble fillet with diagonal recesses, apparently imitating a twisted cord moulding, should belong to this mock entablature too, perhaps beneath the architrave. Finally, the large quantity of flat alabaster panels must belong to fields between the pilasters; they are too shallow to belong with the architrave and since none of them is cut to fit around vertical elements, it seems likely that they belong to panels set within the *africano* surround.

Rather than employing a full-height pilaster order, then, the designers of the revetment scheme on the rear wall of the North Stoa preferred to use shallow mouldings in a range of stones to give the impression of an architectural scheme, with the only real architectural elements being the pilaster shafts and capitals. Interestingly, the arrangement seems to have been designed to showcase imported materials to maximum effect. Local Aphrodisian stones were used primarily in the dado (white, Yazır grey, and Çamova Tepe *pavonazzetto*). The bulk of the central field of the wall was adorned with *africano* and *portasanta*, while *alabastro fiorito* was divided between the central field and the entablature. The inset porphyry and *serpentino* elements would have added a flash of colour at the top of the dado and the bottom of the entablature; these were the only materials in the ensemble that were sourced from beyond Asia Minor or its immediate vicinity. The other lithotypes recovered are attested in much smaller quantities and possibly belong to later repairs or to other structures around the Place of Palms.

Dating

This marble revetment does not belong to the Tiberian phase of the North Stoa and indeed displays of polychrome marble are rare at Aphrodisias in the Julio-Claudian period. The structures containing the largest concentrations of these materials are all later: the Flavian-Trajanic Civil Basilica, the Hadrianic Baths, and the mid second-century Theatre Baths. Some of the materials used for the revetment of the North Stoa are not attested at all, in fact, in pre-Flavian structures. Leah Long notes that the *pavonazzetto*-like Çamova Tepe marble is first attested in the Civil Basilica, while the mottled grey from Yazır is not found before the early to mid second century AD.[63] Even at Rome, porphyry and *serpentino* are only found from the Augustan period onwards, with the former not becoming popular until the late Julio-Claudian period; *verde antico* too is not common before the second century AD.[64]

This elaborate marble cladding, therefore, was probably only added to the rear wall of the North Stoa roughly a century after its initial construction, at some point in the early second century AD. The Hadrianic Baths contain large quantities of *africano*, *portasanta*, and *alabastro fiorito* revetment and flooring, while the Theatre Baths used Yazır marble for monolithic columns and substantial quantities of *alabastro fiorito* paving. The figured pilaster capitals are also dated to the second century and find their closest parallels in the 'peopled scrolls' of the Hadrianic Baths and Theatre Baths.

The construction of the Hadrianic Baths certainly prompted substantial intervention in the Place of Palms. As noted above, the North Stoa was shortened and then connected to the new West Stoa, creating a unified structure around the northern and western edges of the complex. The new rear wall of the West Stoa was also clad in marble revetment, to judge from pin holes in the sections that survive, and so it would make sense if this revetment was carried along the North Stoa at this point. The exact decorative scheme of the West Stoa revetment can only be guessed at, since no record survives of the marble finds from the west end of the pool, but it is plausible that it matched the new scheme in the North Stoa. The rear wall of the North Stoa by the Hadrianic period measured *c.* 210–215 m (accepting that the exact position of its eastern end is unclear); the rear wall of the West Stoa would have added a further 55 m of marble decoration to this.

Some of this marble revetment, and indeed probably the bulk of it, seems to have remained in place on the rear wall of the North Stoa until the seventh century AD. Only at this point was it cleared away and dumped into the pool (Ch. 8 §A). The replacement elements in Yazır grey indicate, however, that the rear wall revetment was patched up over time. This is further suggested by the fact that some marble revetment panels were found re-used in late antique repairs to the pool floor (see Ch. 4 §B). These repairs date to the late fifth or early sixth century AD. Second-hand marble revetment panels were also cut down to be used as game counters (see Ch. 8 §D). What collapsed in the seventh century, then, was whatever remained of the originally second-century decorative scheme and any replacement pieces added in the fifth or sixth century.

Epigraphic evidence for repairs to the North Stoa

While the revetment on the rear wall of the North Stoa provides the clearest evidence for post-Tiberian alterations, inscriptions on the structure and other details of its architecture indicate that this building received continual attention over its lifespan.

On drums of columns and on the stylobate blocks of the eastern part of the North Stoa one reads the names of mem-

---

63 Long 2012, 194–5.
64 Gnoli 1988; Pensabene and Bruno 1998.

bers of prominent Aphrodisian families (Appendix 2: NS43, NS47, NS48, NS51, NS55, NS59, NS60, L2). The relevant texts are concentrated in a relatively small area between columns N15 and N20 and should be discussed as a group. The texts on drums of columns were engraved with large deep letters (NS51, NS59, NS60, L2); by contrast, those on the south face of the stylobate are lightly incised. Most of these texts can be dated to the first four centuries AD but at least one of the texts (NS55) is distributed over two non-contiguous stylobate blocks suggesting that it was engraved after the removal of the intercolumnar stylobate blocks in late antiquity; as will be shown below, however, this is unlikely to have been the case.

One name is well preserved: Κλ(αυδία) | Ἀντω|νία (NS51, NS59, NS60) (Pl. 25.B–C). Since the name is in the nominative, it designates the agent of an act—more likely a sponsor than a contractor. The nominative (not genitive) excludes the possibility of ownership of the column or of a *topos* inscription, and the deep carving and elegant lettering clearly distinguishes these inscriptions from graffiti or masons' marks and brings them close to inscriptions on the columns of the temple of Aphrodite naming the donors or columns.[65] Names in the nominative on column inscriptions (not graffiti) always designate dedicants, but unlike the inscriptions of Antonia and Capitolinus (discussed below) they are also accompanied by a short text reporting the construction or dedication.[66] The identity of this Claudia Antonia can be inferred from the context: the name on another column drum from the same stoa (L2: ΤΩΛ) can be restored as [Καπε]|τωλ[ῖ]|νος (Pl. 25.D). The only name in Aphrodisias in which one finds the sequence ΤΩΛ is Καπιτωλῖνος/Capitolinus, written also as Καπετωλεῖνος and Καπιτωλεῖνος, but not Καπειτωλεῖνος.[67] A Claudia Antonia and a Capitolinus are mentioned in the same context in two statue dedications (one from the Bouleuterion and one reused in the City Walls): Claudia Antonia Tatiane was the person honoured and Τιβέριος Κλαύδιος Καπιτωλεῖνος, son of Tib. Claudius Smaragdos, supervised the dedication.[68] Tib. Claudius Capitolinus and Claudia Antonia Tatiane were, therefore, certainly somehow connected. That people who were related were engaged in the same building project is well attested in Aphrodisias.[69]

The donation of columns by Claudia Antonia and Claudius Capitolinus must be connected with repairs in the east section of the North Stoa. The date can be approximately determined on prosopographical grounds. Tatiane was a niece of the senators Tib. Claudius Attalos and Tib. Claudius Diogenes,[70] whose *floruit* falls in the early Severan period. Capitolinus' son, the orator Tib. Claudius Aurelius Ktesias (*IAph2007* 12.324), was honoured during the Severan period (possibly after AD 212), as the addition of the *nomen* Aurelius to his name indicates). The repairs should, therefore, be dated around AD 200. The replacement of several columns must have necessitated dismantling and re-erection of the associated architraves and the corresponding section of the roof.

The other inscriptions that can be associated with sponsors of repairs to the North Stoa are written on stylobate blocks under columns N15–N17. Although the style of writing, with lightly incised letters, is very different from the inscriptions on the columns, another consideration suggests placing these texts into the same historical context: both *nomina gentilia* inscribed on the stylobates of columns N15, N16, and N17, namely Antonia (NS43: Ἀν[τω]νίας; NS48: Ἀν[τωνίας?]) and Claudius (NS47: Κλαυδίου), are exactly the same as those appearing on the column drums N18, N19 and probably N20, immediately to the west. In view of the location it is tempting to identify Antonia and Claudius with Claudia Antonia Tatiane and Tib. Claudius Capitolinus respectively.

Finally, a third name also lightly incised on the stylobate blocks is known to have been used by elite families from the first century BC to the late second century AD but not in late antiquity: Μύων (NS55) (Pl. 26.A–B). In the early first century AD Myon Eusebes Philopatris was one of the most important sponsors of public buildings.[71] Under Trajan, Myon Adrastos served as priest of Divus Nerva (*IAph2007* 11.508). In the second half of the second century AD, several members of the boy choruses sent to Klaros had this name.[72] The name is not attested after the end of the second century AD. The problem with this text is that it is inscribed across two stylobate blocks which have had the block between them removed. This block was removed in late antiquity, which might indicate that the inscription is also late antique. However, considering the likely date of the name Myon, it is also possible that these blocks were moved around after the second century AD as part of repairs to the stoa or that the inscription originally continued across the now lost middle block and so read differently. Since it is very unlikely that this inscription belongs to the late antique phase of the stoa, it may well name a third sponsor of the restoration work in the late second century AD.

These inscriptions are not *topos* inscriptions, but texts somehow associated with repairs to the North Stoa. The shallow carving of the inscriptions on the stylobates shows that their function was very different from that of the carefully carved and clearly visible texts on the column drums. They probably were of a temporary and not a commemorative nature, possibly designating sections of the stoa that were funded by different sponsors.

One final group of inscriptions that probably reveal repairs to the North Stoa are the series of 'assembly marks', or better 're-assembly marks', found on some of the column drums and the architrave blocks of the structure (these are discussed more fully in Ch. 5 §E). These comprise single letters that were added to architectural elements to ensure that they were erected in the proper order and joined to the correct neighbouring elements. The fact that these marks were not added during the original phase of construction (as true 'assembly marks') is suggested by the fact that they are not found on every architectural element in the North Stoa; instead, they seem to have been added to just

---

65 *IAph2007* 1.4–1.9.
66 A few examples from the imperial period: *SEG* XXVI 1470; XXVIII 1427; LIII 726; LXIII 951. Names in the nominative appear also in Christian prayers on columns (for example *IAph2007* 1.21–1.26).
67 *IAph2007* 2.13a, 4.306, 8.711, 11.57, 12.323, 14.13.
68 *IAph2007* 2.13 and 12.323. Tib. Claudius Capitolinus is also mentioned in *IAph2007* 14.13.
69 Chaniotis 2021.
70 PIR² C 796 and 851; *IAph2007* 2.16.
71 Chaniotis 2018b.
72 Ferrary 2014, 336 no. 86 l. 3 and 488–9 no. 205 l. 2 (three individuals).

those elements that had come down and could be re-erected, to ensure they were put back correctly.

Architectural evidence for maintenance

Physical evidence for the re-erection of columns in the North Stoa is provided by recut dowel holes and pouring channels and by the presence of lewis holes. On seven columns (N3, N10, N13, N15–18), all at the eastern end, at least one, and in some cases both, of the dowel holes on the tops of their column bases have had their pour channels re-carved (Pl. 26.C). In each case, this new pour channel cuts through an area of breakage, presumably caused by either the collapse of the column shaft or its twisting on its base. In order to re-set these shafts, the old dowel and its lead casing either had to be removed entirely and replaced or new lead had to be added; in either scenario a new pour channel was required. Lewis holes on the upper surfaces of column drums also attest to the re-erection of shafts. During the original construction of the North Stoa lewis holes were not used to lift column drums and twenty-six of the drums now stored in the North Stoa, whose upper surfaces are preserved, have no lewis hole and a pair of dowel holes (or no dowel holes at all, in the case of the top drums). A total of twenty-seven drums preserved in the North Stoa, however, have lewis holes cut into the middle of their upper surfaces, between the dowel holes, showing that they were re-erected at some point in their history. In every other way the drums with lewis holes are identical to those without; there is no sign that these drums were particularly damaged and they do not appear to have been newly carved inserts. All of this suggests that the North Stoa did not collapse completely until it finally came down in the eleventh century (as discussed in Ch. 9 §A). Instead, sections of the colonnade (and no doubt also the roof) seem to have sustained damage during one or more events and were dismantled and re-erected, while other sections appear to have survived largely intact.

While most, if not all, of the column shafts of the North Stoa seem to have been used continually from the Tiberian period onwards, some of the capitals are later additions. Most of the capitals from the North Stoa follow a standard Ionic scheme belonging to the first phase of the structure. Three examples, though, are quite different. These have an egg-and-dart rather than egg-and-tongue moulding on their echinus (Pl. 26.D). Two of them have the same scheme, but this time with upward facing darts, on their abacus, while the third has a Lesbian cyma. Bingöl was the first to draw attention to these, arguing that they represent later repairs.[73] He identified seven capitals with egg-and-darts (only three are now visible in the North Stoa) and argued that the egg-and-dart motif only becomes common in Asia Minor in the mid second century. Waelkens suggested this date could be pushed earlier, even into the Julio-Claudian period, though he acknowledges that the motif does not become common until after the Flavian period.[74] The particular formulation of the egg-and-dart on the echinus makes these capitals look even later than the Hadrianic capitals of the West Stoa and it is tempting to connect them to the same phase of activity as Claudia Antonia's columns, that is around the turn of the second to third centuries AD. The single capital with a unique balteus form (see Pl. 11.C) could also be a later replacement; its echinus follows the standard form of the first-phase capitals but the leaves of its pulvinus are much more deeply carved and its balteus is unparalleled in the structure.

Other capitals of the original Julio-Claudian type show evidence for repairs. On one a small metal pin was used to re-attach a portion of the echinus moulding in the area of the central egg. Two drill holes can be noted on the volute of one of the later capital types; these seem to have been used to pin two parts of the volute back together or to affix a replacement piece (Pl. 26.E–F). On eleven capitals, the echinus was carved away. This was not a universal policy and so appears not to have been done proactively for aesthetic reasons. It could be a response to damage suffered to the decoration, perhaps during a collapse of part of the stoa. The delicate and projecting elements of the echinus would have been especially vulnerable to damage on impact with the ground. It might have been felt preferable to remove this moulding altogether rather than re-erect capitals with broken and patchy echinuses. Comparable evidence for secondary interventions is apparent in the south stoa of the Agora. Waelkens observes that the Ionic capitals on the standing columns in the southeast corner of the Agora date to two phases. These columns belong to the outer colonnade of the south and east stoas of the complex. Five of these capitals are similar in form to the capitals of the North Stoa of the Place of Palms (on the only standing column of the east stoa, on the corner column, and on the second, third and seventh columns of the south stoa). They have the same echinus arrangement, similar pulvinus ornamentation and comparable handling of the abacus. The volutes are also similar, with the channels being semi-circular in profile. The remaining capitals have only three rather than five eggs on their echinus moulding, much more schematic ornamentation on the pulvinus, and a different handling of the channels on their volutes. A late first- or second-century date for these capitals seems plausible.

One final piece of evidence to indicate that the North Stoa was at least partially re-erected at some point following its initial construction is provided by the cuttings for roof beams in both the rear side of the frieze blocks and the tops of the cornice blocks. On the frieze blocks, more than one example of a secondary slot, located out of sequence with the first phase of beam slots can be identified. On the cornice blocks a secondary series of smaller slots (20–24 × 20–24 cm and 10–15 cm deep) spaced 20 cm apart and sometimes re-using or partially cutting the larger slots of the first phase can also be linked to a replacement roof (see Pl. 12.A). There is no way of dating these features; they could date to the same phase of activity as the construction of the West Stoa, when the North Stoa and this new building were joined, or they could be much later.

This new roof, the repairs to the column shaft of N27, and the re-erection of other shafts could all date to the same period as Claudia Antonia's inscriptions, dated above to *c.* AD 200. However, there is no reason to assume that all of these repairs and adjustments represent responses to a single event; and there

---

73 Bingöl 1980, 170–2 no. 46–53.
74 Waelkens 1987.

is evidence also for substantial repairs to the North Stoa in the late fifth/early sixth century (see Ch. 4 §E), during which it is very likely that columns were also reset, and certain that the roof must have been dismantled and repaired as the rear wall underwent substantial re-erection. This venerable structure will have required periodic upkeep, and occasionally quite substantial maintenance.

Cuttings for doorframes

As well as evidence for repairs and the replacement of certain elements, cuttings on the various blocks of the North Stoa show that, like the West Stoa, its colonnade was embellished with a number of attachments and inserts (Fig. 20a–b). Unlike the West Stoa, where anastylosis has been carried out on all but one of the 20 column shafts, only 43 of the 70 columns of the North Stoa have been either partially or fully (9) re-erected above their base. This makes understanding how this stoa was adapted and enclosed more difficult, though certain general similarities and the occasional difference with the situation in the West Stoa can be noted. It should also be noted that some of the column shafts that have been re-erected were rotated during this process; on Fig. 20a-b the original orientation of the shaft, as indicated by the surviving cuttings and their alignment, is shown.

As on the West Stoa, most of the columns of the North Stoa seem to have had wooden doorframes attached to their east and west sides, held in place by iron pins. The holes left by these pins are visible on 21 of the re-erected shafts and all but two of those preserved above 1 m in height. The fact that at least some shafts do not have these holes, however, shows that the installation of these doorframes was undertaken in a less systematic manner in the North Stoa compared to the West Stoa. This is further supported by the number of holes on even those shafts that have been completely re-erected, which ranges from one to four per side. Cut-back strips (5–13 cm wide) for receiving the sides of doorframes are found on 10 shafts, usually alongside holes for iron pins (Pl. 26.G). In two cases, however, these strips are found on shafts lacking holes for the addition of iron pins, indicating that an alternative form of fixing these features in place was occasionally employed.

Other adjustments connected to these wooden frames are apparent on the bases and capitals. On four capitals the *balteus* is removed on both sides and on a further four on only one side (Pl. 27.A); on two other examples with the *balteus* removed only one side is preserved. The cuttings left behind measure 10–12 cm wide and 5–8 cm deep. Rectangular holes (2–3 × 3–4 cm), a feature not found on the West Stoa, are cut into the side of the *balteus* in one case or the flat side of the capital above the *pulvinus* in two cases (Pl. 27.B). Rust on the inside of these holes shows that they were used for metal fixings. In both of the cases where these cuttings are found above the *pulvinus* the *balteus* beneath has been cut back. Slots of the same width as those found cut into the sides of some of the capitals are also apparent on ten bases, a feature not seen on the West Stoa colonnade (Pl. 27.C–D). These slots measure 3.5–5 cm wide and 3–4 cm deep. Six of the nine bases with these cuttings on are in a line at the west end of the North Stoa (N65–70) and the northernmost column of the West Stoa (W1) has a similar cutting in the east side of its plinth.

While all of these cuttings show that at least some of the intercolumniations of the North Stoa were filled with doorframes, cuttings in the stylobate blocks relating to door mechanisms are less frequently attested than on the West Stoa. Sockets for *cardines*, in fact, are not visible on any sections of the stylobate. Instead, shallow grooves with roughly point-chiselled surfaces, 15–20 cm wide and running the full width of the intercolumniation, are found on the top of the stylobate blocks between columns N5 and N6, N12 and N13, N37 and N38, and N51 and N52 (Pl. 27.E). These grooves could have supported wooden thresholds on top of the stylobate, into which either *cardines* were then inserted or perhaps along which some form of shuttering was slid. Two of these grooves, between columns N5–6 and N37–38, were located in intercolumniations accessed by steps from the ground level of the Place of Palms. Deeper and shorter rectangular slots are found on the stylobate blocks in the westernmost six intercolumniations of the North Stoa (running from N65 to W1). These slots are flush with the column bases at either side of the intercolumniation and correspond to cuttings through the edge of the bases. They measure 5–14 cm long, 2–4 cm wide and 1–3 cm deep. In the intercolumniation between columns N68 and N69 a third slot is found in the middle (Pl. 27.F). These slots could not have held *cardines* but could have been used to secure wooden thresholds in place.

Considering the abundant evidence for the addition of doorways between the columns of the North Stoa, it is surprising that there is little evidence for north–south barriers within the stoa. Only on the north side of the stylobate behind column N52 are two cuttings visible that might relate to the installation of a division of some sort here (Pl. 27.G). If there were further north–south dividing walls within the North Stoa they must have been supported by posts embedded into the floor of the stoa, which has since been removed and lowered—a point that will be returned to in Ch. 4 §E.

Dating these features of the North Stoa precisely is difficult. It would be tempting to see them as part of the same phase of work as the comparable cuttings in the West Stoa, which is probably fourth-century in date and was certainly carried out prior to Albinos' restoration in the late fifth or early sixth century (on which, see Ch. 4 §A). They certainly date to before this later period since the equivalent late antique activities in the North Stoa lowered the ground level and removed many of the stylobate blocks; the doorways between the columns would have been rendered useless by this work. The presence of gameboards carved over some of the grooves on the stylobate blocks further indicates that whatever fixtures these features were designed to support were later removed and were not part of the final phase of the North Stoa. A date after the restoration work at the end of the second century but before the late fifth century, therefore, seems most likely; and it is most economical to see them as contemporary with the probably mid fourth-century alterations to the West Stoa.

Although the efforts to enclose the North Stoa were less systematic than on the West Stoa, these adjustments would still have led to a drastic alteration of the structure's appearance and, possibly, function. While the North Stoa was an open, clearly public, structure in the earlier imperial period, these alterations indicate that it became more and more closed off to through-traffic later. The fact that this blocking of the colonnade was less systematic and apparently less heavy-duty than that observed in the West Stoa might indicate that these alterations were made by a range of individuals over time rather than as part of a single intervention.

One possible purpose of this closing of the colonnade, at least in places, could have been the subdivision of the structure into separate units intended for commercial or other uses. Sixteen (possibly seventeen) *topos* inscriptions have been documented in the North Stoa, all on column shafts, except one which is carved into the top of a seat block (see Ch. 5 §D).[75] Not all of these can be dated but those that can are all late: NS15 is dated to the third century AD, NS52 to the fifth or sixth century, and NS58 and NS78 (see Pl. 43.A) were carved alongside Christian crosses. These inscriptions are also concentrated in areas where the cuttings described above are visible: NS6, NS10, NS67, NS165, NS190, NS243, NS330, NS341, NS344, and NS349 are found on columns with cuttings for doorframes (respectively N6, N7, N26, N39, N41, N52, N67, N69, and N71); NS38 comes from the stylobate next to N14, one intercolumniation along from one of the preserved threshold cuttings; while NS52 on column N18 and NS67 on N26 were found directly above holes added to the south face of the shafts for suspension of something or installation of a light fitting.

If this association between the *topos* inscriptions and the architectural cuttings for wooden fittings is accepted, then it further constrains the dates of the *topos* inscriptions, to *before* the end of the fifth century, since the wooden elements were removed and no longer accommodated in the rebuilding of the stoa at this time. The correspondence between *topos* inscriptions and architectural details would seem to suggest that the North Stoa acquired a more distinctively commercial function over the course of the third to fifth centuries. It was subdivided or altered to suit this new purpose, with fittings for doorways or shop counters or stalls; but these alterations were quite different from the arrangements observed in the West Stoa, which remained a unified space.

E. IMPERIAL-ERA COINS AND THE USE OF THE PLACE OF PALMS (ATT & HK)

Something of the lengthy use and frequentation of the Place of Palms may perhaps be inferred from the coin finds, many of which will represent losses by users of the area in antiquity. The coins discussed in this section were all found in late antique contexts, but are discussed here for the light they shed on coin circulation in the region in the early imperial period. They are either residual in the contexts in which they were found, or they attest the re-use of hellenistic and early Roman coins as small change in late antiquity.

75 NS6, NS11, NS15, NS19, NS38?, NS52, NS58, NS63?, NS67, NS78, NS165, NS190, NS243, NS330?, NS341, NS344, NS349.

Coin finds from the hellenistic to the Julio-Claudian periods

Only ten hellenistic coins, all from the late hellenistic period, were excavated from the Place of Palms. The mints and types represented are mostly consistent with those coins excavated at Aphrodisias between 1961 and 1973 and published by MacDonald in 1976.[76] Among the new finds, six are from the civic mint itself.

MacDonald's catalogue of coins from Aphrodisias lists 151 late classical and hellenistic coins (plus two hoards), but we could not use all of these examples as a comparative data group here, because of the inclusion in MacDonald's publication of 'stray' coins brought in by workers.[77] As was the custom in those years when there were few local museums (and no site museum at Aphrodisias), archaeological teams paid extra money to their workers who brought in artefacts found in the local vicinity. Although MacDonald seems to presume that the stray coins he catalogued were found within the site or its immediate vicinity, this was probably not the case for all the coins. Seasonal workers came to Aphrodisias from many villages in the surrounding area, and they also sometimes worked on farms and fields away from their villages in months when there were no excavations, which would have allowed them to find artefacts from other sites as well. The prospect of bonus pay for bringing in artefacts also incentivised others (family members, friends) to collect them from various sources and to give them to excavation workers to be sold to the excavation team. Coins purchased by Louis Robert between the 1930s and 1960s from Geyre, Karacasu, and various villages around Aphrodisias like Bingeç show that ancient coins were commodities worth collecting by villagers, for sale to visitors or middlemen in the antiquities trade.[78] One would expect such an antiquities trade network already in place since the nineteenth century or even earlier; MacDonald's comments about the area and its inhabitants being 'relatively isolated and innocent' in regard to the trading of antiquities should be considered naïve. We do appreciate the value of such 'purchased' coins with local provenances in understanding the coinage used in Karia in general, and even in a regional manner if the absolute find spots at the village level are known; but we believe that using such evidence alongside scientifically excavated archaeological material would be misleading to some extent. Wherever these coins were brought from, they disrupt the picture that can be gained from 'excavated' examples only; especially as some may have come from other sites either nearby or further away where earlier material is better represented than in the Aphrodisias city centre.

Thus, when the 'stray' finds are removed, the pre-Roman 'excavated' examples are 52 coins and two hoards. Fig. 21 below shows a major difference between old and new finds: old-

76 Alabanda (cat. 2), Tabai? (cat. 9) and Magnesia ad Sipylum (cat. 10) are represented for the first time with hellenistic coins at Aphrodisias, with these new finds.
77 MacDonald 1976, 2.
78 Geyre: Delrieux 2011, 297; Karacasu: Delrieux 2011, 307; Bingeç: Delrieux 2011, 294. One might also wonder that if workers were receiving bonus payments for items they brought in, what would have stopped them from also taking items secretly from the trenches they were excavating to get the bonuses?

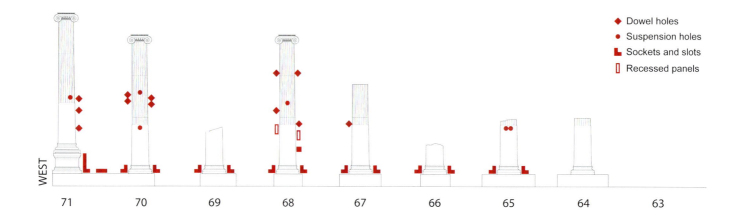
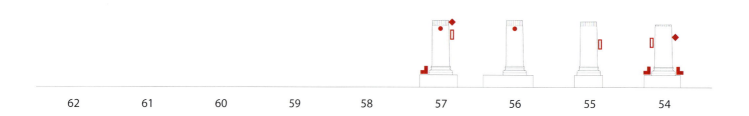
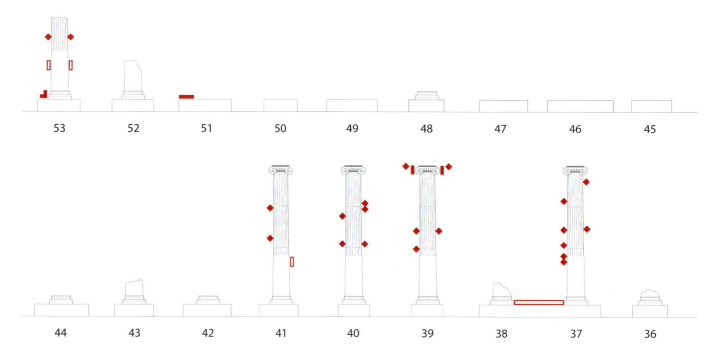

Fig. 20a. Distribution of cuttings of various types on the western half of the colonnade of the North Stoa.

Fig. 20b. Distribution of cuttings of various types on the eastern half of the colonnade of the North Stoa.

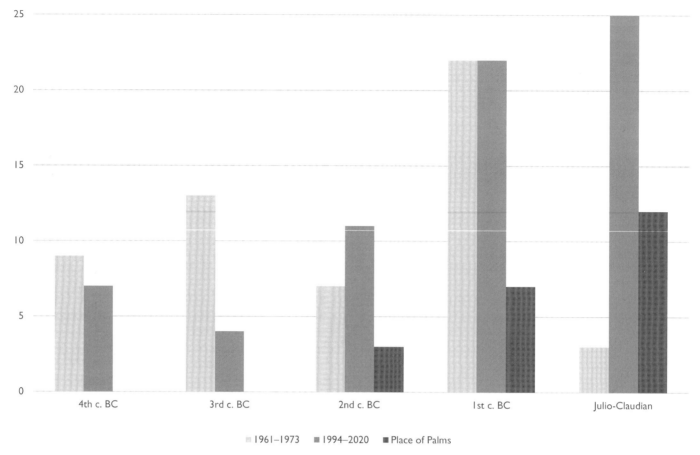

Fig. 21. Pre-Roman to Julio-Claudian coin finds at Aphrodisias (145 coins = 52 coins + 2 hoards counted as single (latest) coins in the graph, 'excavated' from 1961–1973 + 69 coins found between 1994–2020 from other sectors + 22 coins from the Place of Palms).

er coins from the fourth and the third centuries BC are better represented among the excavated group from the 1961–1973 seasons that MacDonald studied than in the new group examined by us found between 2002–2018 and the reverse is true for Julio-Claudian examples.[79]

Fig. 21 illustrates the chronological distribution of all recorded pre-Roman to Julio-Claudian coins from Aphrodisias. There is a similar number of coins by century from the fourth to second centuries BC when Aphrodisias used either hellenistic royal coinages, or foreign coins mostly from neighbouring mints. But in the first century BC, there is a very distinct increase in finds, connected to the monumentalisation of the city, with the local mint providing most of the examples catalogued.

Coins of Plarasa and Aphrodisias constitute 82.6% of the total finds in the first century BC when the local mint started operating.[80]

None of the early coins found in the Place of Palms comes from the construction phases of the area. All of the hellenistic coins were found in fills from later periods. These early coins may simply be residual in later contexts, the result of earth containing them being dug from earlier levels during reconstruction of the area, or brought in from places like the Theatre Hill where earlier layers existed, to raise the ground level surrounding the pool. But there is also the possibility that some early coins, especially small ones, were used as fifth-century AD *nummi*, as hoard evidence from Aphrodisias[81] and elsewhere in Asia Minor suggests.[82] This may be the case for cat. 6 and 7,

---

79 This difference may be caused by where in the city the coins had been excavated from. MacDonald mainly worked on coins from excavations of the mound (Theatre Hill / 'acropolis') and the Temple of Aphrodite area. Both areas provided older archaeological and numismatic material (including two hellenistic hoards) than the rest of the city. The Temple of Aphrodite itself may have had an entirely different coin usage from the rest of the city, with its own and probably independent treasury, and foreign coins may also have been dedicated to and kept in the temple area, while they were being taken out of circulation (or prevented from circulating) in trade by the local government via its *trapeza* in the rest of the city. Julio-Claudian coins are better represented in newer finds, as most of these come from the city centre where many of the excavated buildings in their earliest phases date to this period.

80 Tek 2019, 166.

81 A late Roman hoard from *c.* AD 400, discovered in 1966 about 1 km outside the city walls of Aphrodisias, contained *c.* 8,000 coins of only the smallest format, among which a second-century BC Rhodian coin was also observed: Lauritsen 1984.

82 An early fifth-century AD hoard found inside an earthenware vessel, excavated at Arykanda in Lykia by one of the authors (A. T. Tek), contained a fourth-century BC bronze coin (of the dynast Perikles of Zemuri/Limyra), the same size as the 28 coins, all fifth-century *minimi*, with which it was found. Another hoard of 259 coins from Arykanda, buried in the AD 450s, contained four Lycian Federation units from the 1st century BC, of similar format, size and weight to late Roman coins (Sancaktar 2011, 224). At Sardis, five coins dating from the first

which were excavated from contexts that contain predominantly fifth-century AD coins; both coins are very worn and hardly recognizable, and have diameters of 9/10 mm and 11/12 mm which would make them the same size as fifth-century AD *minimi* and passable as them.

We can safely presume that the coins minted by Plarasa and Aphrodisias in the late hellenistic period would still have been in the circulation pool of the city in the first century AD, as the city continued to mint similar-sized bronze units in three denominations (roughly 23, 19 and 13–15 mm diameters) during the Julio-Claudian period,[83] and in four denominations (roughly 25, 23, 21, 14 mm) during the Flavian period.[84] Another piece of evidence showing that older coins remained in circulation in the first century AD is the existence of a countermark that was used on hellenistic issues possibly during the Augustan period (or slightly later) rendering the old worn coins easily recognizable as local.[85] Cat. 19 and 20 are examples of these coins.[86]

For the classification of coins of Plarasa and Aphrodisias we have followed *RPC* I: the earliest Augustan issue is under Plarasa-Aphrodisias (*RPC* I, 2837),[87] but subsequently Plarasa was absorbed and only the ethnic of Aphrodisias was used on the coinage and also on public documents. Therefore, most of the coins without imperial heads that carry the Plarasa-Aphrodisias ethnic should be from the late hellenistic period. Although not included in *RPC*, three types in MacDonald have only the ethnic of Aphrodisias on them,[88] while earlier versions of two of the types carry the double ethnic.[89] This usage of the single ethnic suggests that these types should also be listed as Augustan, among the earliest types issued in this reign, after *RPC* I, 2837 and before *RPC* I, 2838. The Plarasa–Aphrodisias ethnic seen on the other and older reverses of these three types may well be contemporary with *RPC* I, 2837; that is, early Augustan.

We have preferred to list all issues with the single ethnic use of Aphrodisias as Roman provincial coins (cat. 15–29). Such a dating would also provide a date for various types of sigmas employed on late hellenistic and early imperial coins of Aphrodisias. On hellenistic series, 4-bar sigmas (Σ) were used (MacDonald types 1–36[90]). These are replaced with 3-bar sigmas (C or Ϲ) on later coins of Augustus and Tiberius (*RPC* I, 2838–2843), reverting to a 4-bar sigma under Caligula (*RPC* I, 2844–2845[91]).

Among coins belonging to other mints, cat. 1 is a coin of Pergamon from the 'temple coinage' series, of the temple of Athena Nikephoros for which we have adopted the dates newly proposed by Jérémie Chameroy, in light of the recent finds at Pergamon.[92] Cat. 10 is a very worn and broken coin of Magnesia ad Sipylum, with a countermark. The condition of the coin makes it lighter than the references cited. None of the examples cited has a countermark, but a coin seen in trade has the same countermark as our coin, which was identified as a thunderbolt, but looks also like a scorpion, a common symbol used on later types of the city and as countermarks.[93]

---

century BC to the third century AD were found in the Sardis 1982 hoard which contained 685 coins in total and dated to the fifth century AD (Burrell 2008, 160); one of the early coins was a Lycian Federation unit from Phellus, minted in the first century BC, but again the same size and same weight as Later Roman *minimi* among which it could be passed (Burrell 2008: 169, note 68). The same situation, where earlier small-format coins of similar format and weight exist among late Roman coin assemblages, was also observed in Israel (Bijovsky 1998, 77; 2002, 197–202). Jane DeRose Evans has discussed this phenomenon, referring to further examples from Greece and elsewhere, with an emphasis on Sardis: Evans 2013, 140–141.

83 Johnston 1995, 63, table 2; *RPC* I, 2837–2845.
84 *RPC* II, 1221–1225.
85 Howgego 1985, 147, cmk. 227; MacDonald 1992, 47–50, pl. XXXII, cmk. 13.
86 Although MacDonald dates this countermark to the later part of the first century AD, we believe it should be earlier, maybe dating to the mid/late Augustan or the early Tiberian period. MacDonald (1992, 48) wrote that the coins with this countermark he observed are from 'the time of Augustus, judging from the module and traces of portrait'. The two coins we observed with this countermark, however, seem to belong to late hellenistic issues of Plarasa-Aphrodisias (MacDonald, type 28), with the eagle's wings partly visible, and Aphrodisias continued to issue *RPC* coins using the same hellenistic units and standards; therefore in a similar 'module'. Traces of portraits not safely identified can be misleading; but as no emperors other than Augustus (if MacDonald's identifications of the traces of imperial portraits are correct) have yet been identified on these particular coins, then the date for the usage of this countermark should be sought in the mid/late Augustan period or maybe the early years of Tiberius, but not later; certainly not in the later first century AD. The countermark was probably used to validate earlier and worn, almost unrecognizable, hellenistic and early Augustan issues. In our view, how long a particular coin remained in active circulation cannot be calculated from its state of wear.
87 *RPC* I, 2837 has on its reverse a head of Aphrodite, facing right. She wears a *stephane* and her hair is open (without veil and not turreted). This representation is also seen on earlier coins of Plarasa and Aphrodisias, and may illustrate a more hellenized, older or different cult image of the goddess. Some hellenistic bronzes where a standing figure of the goddess are seen (MacDonald, type 35) seem to have this head and not a turreted one. This head type appears finally on coins of Caligula (*RPC* I, 2845). Another and older head type of the goddess appears on hellenistic silver and bronze issues of Plarasa and Aphrodisias (MacDonald, type 1–27), this time veiled and wearing a *stephane*. From *RPC* I, 2839 onwards (apart from *RPC* I, 2845 mentioned above), Aphrodite is shown veiled and turreted, like the better-known type of 'Aphrodite of Aphrodisias'.
88 MacDonald 1992, type 35-R108, type 36-R116/117 and type 37-R118.
89 MacDonald 1992, type 35-R108-110, type 36-R112-115.
90 Including types MacDonald 1992, 35b and 36b-c where Aphrodisias was named alone without Plarasa.
91 *RPC* I, 2845 is dated to 2 BC – AD 4 and identified as Gaius Caesar (MacDonald 1992, type 39), but this identification was corrected by A. Johnston (1995: 45) who preferred the identification as Caligula following *RPC*. This coin also has a 4-bar sigma similar to and contemporary with *RPC* I, 2844.
92 Chameroy 2012, 173, tab. I, type 37. Another coin of Pergamon, again from a temple series, the temple of Asklepios, was also excavated at Aphrodisias (MacDonald 1976, 8, no. 276). Chameroy recorded 12 more coins of Pergamon at the Aphrodisias Museum (Chameroy 2012, 166); their provenance is unknown, but they may have arrived at the museum also from villages in the vicinity and possibly even from beyond. A small hoard of *cistophoroi* excavated in 1973 from the surroundings of the Bouleuterion at Aphrodisias, containing one issue of Pergamon and two of Tralles, attests to the second-century BC usage of Pergamene royal coinage in Aphrodisias (MacDonald 1976, 2, nos. 1–3).
93 Gorny & Mosch Giessener Münzhandlung 2010, Auc. 191, lot 1590 (11 October 2010).

Table 1. List of first- to third-century AD coin finds from the Place of Palms.

Authority	Date	Number of coins found (total: 41)	Aphrodisias (total: 15)	Other *RPC* (total: 12 + 5 unidentified)	*RIC* (total: 5 + 4 barbarous)
Augustus	27 BC – AD 14	5	Nos. 15–18	No. 36 (mint?)	
Mid/late Augustus or early Tiberius	Early first century AD	2	Nos. 19–20		
Tiberius	14–37	1			No. 43
Caligula	37–41	2	Nos. 21–22		
Nero? or early Flavian	Later first century AD	2	Nos. 23-24		
Vespasian	69–79	1		No. 33 (Sardis)	
Domitian	81–96	1		No. 31 (Tabai)	
Trajan	98–117	1		No. 12 (Antioch ad Maeandrum)	
Hadrian	117–138	2		No. 11 (Ephesos), No. 35 (Hydrela)	
Antoninus Pius	138–161	1		No. 30 (Apollonia Salbake?)	
Marcus Aurelius	161–180	1		No 34 (Tripolis)	
Septimius Severus	193–211	3	No. 25	No. 32 (Hypaepa), No. 37 (mint?)	
Macrinus	217–218	1	No. 26		
Gordian III	238–244	2	No. 27	No. 13 (Antioch ad Maeandrum)	
Philip I	244-249	1		No. 14 (Antioch ad Maeandrum)	
Salonina	253–268	2	Nos. 28–29		
Claudius II	268–270	2			Nos. 45–46
Aurelian	270–275	1			No. 47
Barbarous Radiates	*c.* 270s–280s	4			No. 48–51

Coin finds from the first to third centuries AD

Thirty-six coins found in the Place of Palms represent the first to third centuries AD (Julio-Claudian examples until the Tetrarchic period). Among them are thirty-two Roman provincial, five Roman imperial coins, and four 'barbarous radiates'. Fifteen of the coins are issues of Aphrodisias, twelve are from other cities, and five could not be attributed to any mint because of their conditions. Table 1 summarises these finds according to their dates.

Of these 36 early Roman coins, only six (cat. 12, 18, 19, 27, 50, and 51) came from meaningful contexts; all the rest were found in medieval to modern levels. As with the hellenistic examples, the six coins discussed here were found in the phase 2 levels of the Place of Palms, that is in levels identified as the late Roman restoration phase (see Ch. 4 §C). Once again, most of these coins have very small diameters and could have easily passed as late Roman *nummi*; they may have had a second usage period just as those small-format hellenistic issues discussed above.

For those coins found in later medieval contexts, one suspects that the same kind of secondary usage may have happened again. During the Beylik period in particular, the production of bronze coin was very haphazard and it is quite possible that ancient coins worn beyond recognition or those that fitted the same sizes as current coins could have easily passed as units of '*manghir*' among regular Beylik coinage. Eighteen of the Roman coins were in fact found in contexts that also contained Islamic coins. But more evidence is needed before such a theory could be proven, as all of these coins might have been easily removed from deeper levels by late medieval farming activities, or could have arrived by erosion and landslides from the Theatre Hill.

In Fig. 22, we have combined all published and recently recorded first- to third-century coins excavated at Aphrodisias. Noticeable peaks seen during the reigns of Augustus, Septimius Severus, and Valerian/Gallienus correspond to large outputs of coinage by the local Aphrodisias mint. Although not shown on the graph, out of the 161 Roman coins with provincial mints fully identified, 59.6% of the coin finds from the first to third centuries at Aphrodisias are from the local civic mint and 38.5% come from neighbouring mints around the Maeander Valley and in a 150-km radius around the city. Only 1.8% of the finds are from more distant places. The representation of other mints is probably the effect of people travelling through the neighbourhood; most of the longer-distance, higher-value trade would have been conducted in silver coinage, rarely represented in site finds.[94]

---

94 See Tek 2019 for a more detailed discussion on the circulation and related maps. The percentages given here are developed further with more recent research on the finds.

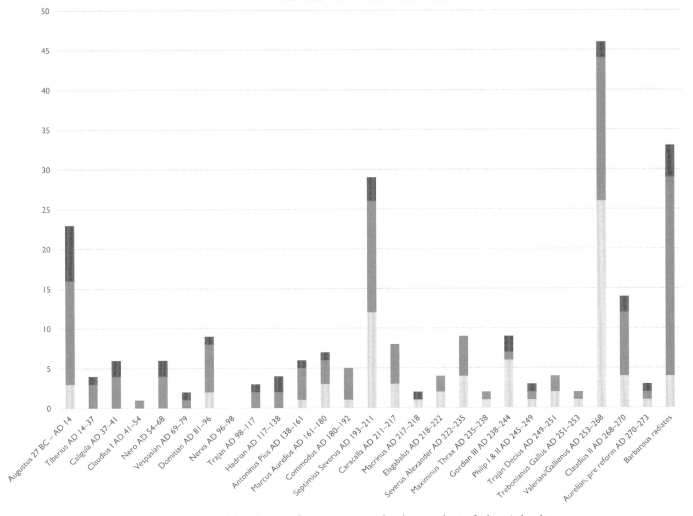

Fig. 22. Chronological distribution of Roman provincial and imperial coin finds at Aphrodisias.

Of the coins of Aphrodisias found in the Place of Palms, cat. 15–17 correspond to MacDonald 1992, type 35. As explained above, these coins must be among the first types to be minted under Augustus after 27 BC as their earlier version carries the double ethnic name showing that this type was in circulation when this change happened. The type represented by cat. 23–24 seems to be a massive issue with 40 examples and several different dies recorded by MacDonald (MacDonald 1992, type 48; *RPC* II, 1221). This type has a 4-bar sigma, but also omegas shaped as 'Ω'. The same omegas are seen on *RPC* II, 1222–1225, all dated to the Flavian period with some doubt, especially in the case of *RPC* II, 1225, which could be of Nero and Agrippina, instead of Domitian and Domitia. In our view, this issue could fill a gap of several years if it started under Nero, replacing as the base small unit all the now certainly worn small-unit coins that had been circulating in the city since the late hellenistic period. The usage of many different obverse and reverse dies could mean either that the coin type was issued continuously for some years or that there was a massive simultaneous issue using different dies at the same time to meet the demand. For cat. 25 and 27, and the dating of anonymous issues of Aphrodisias with *Demos*, *Synkletos*, *Boule* and other various types, we have used Ann Johnston's article on the subject.[95]

Regarding other mints represented at Aphrodisias, our attribution of cat. 30 to Apollonia Salbake is not certain. There is little doubt that the emperor on the obverse is Antoninus Pius.[96] The reverse type is very similar to *RPC* III, 2278 Apollonia Salbake, with Apollo and Artemis standing face-to-face, and Apollonia did indeed issue denominations of such small size. That is why we have favoured this town for the attribution, being unable to find any other similar coins from elsewhere in this denomination. For the coin of Tripolis in cat. 34, the dating is problematic.[97] As Johnston proved, there is a correlation between denominations and coin types and their average diameters and weights.[98] Twelve examples of this coin type have an average diameter of 20 mm and weight of 4.62 g, which

95 Johnston 1995: 90–99, appendix I.
96 We thank Prof. Michel Amandry for examining this coin from its photos and verifying the obverse identification.
97 In general catalogues this coin type is very loosely dated: *BMC Lydia*, 22, is listed among coins dated as 'Septimius Severus to Gallienus'; *SNG* Cop. 723 is merely listed as 'imperial times'; *SNG* München, 794 is put into the '2nd/3rd centuries AD'.
98 Johnston 2007.

only fits the denominations of Marcus Aurelius at Tripolis, and the style of the obverse and reverse types also fit better with a second-century AD date than a third-century date. The Athena type on the obverse is closer in style to *RPC* III, 2559, dated to the reign of Trajan, than to *RPC* VI, 5558–5561 (temp.), anonymously dated to AD 218–238. This coin type was added to the *RPC* III website after the publication of the book as *RPC* III, 2559A, therefore favouring a Trajanic or Hadrianic dating now, but we still think it should be dated to Marcus Aurelius' reign. A detailed study of the issues of the mint of Tripolis of Lydia is however needed to confirm such a dating.

Among the coins found at Aphrodisias between 1961 and 1973 and published by D. J. MacDonald, Roman republican and Roman imperial coinages and their copies are represented by 34 excavated examples, mostly in silver units (*denarii* and *antoniniani*),[99] with one *sestertius*. The present catalogue adds nine more examples to this sum (cat. 43–51). Among them, the *denarius* of Tiberius (cat. 43) would have been interesting had it marked early construction activities in the Place of Palms, but unfortunately the coin does not come from a meaningful context. Cat. 45–47 are imperial *antoniniani* of Claudius II and pre-reform coinage of Aurelian. Cat. 48–51 are all barbarous radiates.

The monetary reform of Aurelian in AD 274 seems to have provoked a distinct division of coin usage in Aphrodisias and the rest of the Maeander Valley and surrounding regions.[100] Although some regions of Asia Minor like Pamphylia and Pisidia continued minting provincial issues well into the reign of Aurelian, provincial mints in Western Asia Minor stopped operating in c. AD 265–270, with most mints including Aphrodisias minting with a large final output in the reign of Gallienus and a very small number of mints continuing into the reign of Claudius II. This large output may have been an attempt to cope with rising inflation and the collapse in the value of the imperial silver coinage.

But another factor usually overlooked for the ending of the provincial coinage in Western Asia Minor would have been the effect of the barbarian attacks and invasion. Goths and other tribes were very active in the Aegean, attacking unfortified cities and looting temples, with the most famous example being the looting and destruction of the Temple of Artemis at Ephesos in *c.* AD 268. Apart from the destruction of some famous cities and sanctuaries, we do not know the exact extent of the Gothic raids into Asia Minor that continued between AD 255–276. But one may imagine that the attacks would have caused large-scale destruction in the territories of the cities, and loss of human life, which would have multiplied with the Plague of Cyprian, which was more virulent in the cities.[101] These conditions would certainly have affected the economy in general, and coin production and supply as well. Aphrodisias also seems to have suffered from these conditions as there is an almost 25-year gap in the production of sculpture, sarcophagi, and inscriptions corresponding to these years,[102] suggesting economic contraction or some sort of unrecorded calamity affecting the city population. Rich cities around the fertile Maeander Valley would have been obvious targets for the migrating tribes, and even an area to think of occupying and settling in.

Whatever the actual cause, the result of the ending of the minting of local coinage and the demonetization of these earlier issues,[103] and possibly, interruption in the arrival of newly issued imperial money from centralized mints,[104] perhaps due to barbarian activities in the region, seems to have caused a shortage of coinage in Western Asia Minor, notably at Aphrodisias, but also at other places. This gap seems to have been filled by the import of Gallic Empire imitations via North Africa,[105] and quite a number of Gallic issues and their contemporary copies have been excavated in Aphrodisias.[106] These are also known

---

99 MacDonald 1976 contains the following 'excavated' coins: nr. 428 (fourré *denarius*, Roman republican), nr. 435 (*denarius*, Trajan), nr. 439 (*denarius*, Antoninus Pius), nr. 440 (*denarius*, Lucius Verus), nr. 445 (*sestertius*, Severus Alexander), nr. 446 (*denarius*, Severus Alexander?), nr. 449–450 (2 *antoniniani*, Philip I), nr. 454 (*antoninianus*, Trebonianus Gallus), nr. 456–518 (of which 15 *antoniniani* have been excavated, Gallienus and Salonina), in nr. 520–547 (of which 6 *antoniniani* have been excavated, Claudius II), in nr. 603–555 (4 barbarous radiates).

100 Aurelian's coinage reform, which included demonetization, was described by Zosimus among the events of AD 274: Zosimus, *New History* (Ἱστορία Νέα) (1.61.3): ἤδη δὲ καὶ ἀργύριον νέον δημοσίᾳ διέδωκεν, τὸ κίβδηλον ἀποδόσθαι τοὺς ἀπὸ τοῦ δήμου παρασχεύασας, τούτῳ τε τὰ συμβόλαια συγχύσεως ἀπαλλάξας. (Greek text from 1887 Mendelssohn edition.) 'Now he officially issued new money (*argyrion neon*) after arranging for the state to buy in the debased coinage (<*argyrion*> *kibdelon*) to avoid confusion in financial dealings.' (English translation from the 1982 Ridley edition, brackets inserted our own).

101 On the Plague of Cyprian, see Harper 2015.

102 The decline in sarcophagus production at Aphrodisias is discussed at length by Öğüş (2014, 148–152).

103 A coin hoard containing 3,995 *antoniniani* was brought to Aphrodisias Museum from the local vicinity (from outside the city walls of Aphrodisias, but within its territory) in 2016. Although we have examined only some of the coins at random and not the whole hoard, the coins we saw in the hoard belong to Gallienus, Salonina, Claudius II, and Aurelian (pre-reform). It is interesting that these issues with a very low silver content were hoarded as though in a savings hoard, but the actual reason may have been their demonetization with the reform of AD 274. Another hoard of 542 *antoniniani* containing similar coins ending with pre-reform issues of Aurelian has been found at Arykanda in Lycia (Tek 2002, 394), again connected with similar reasons. Another hoard of 10 *antoniniani* with the latest issue belonging to Valerian I, found at Karacasu in the territory of Aphrodisias, in 1980 (Lauritsen 1993), is probably unconnected with the later demonetization of AD 274, but is within the time period of the Gothic attacks.

104 The closing of the central mint at Smyrna (Chameroy 2018, 399) may well be connected to a Gothic attack on the city and destruction of the mint facilities, or difficulties in transportation while the Goths were active in the Aegean and coastal areas.

105 Chameroy 2018.

106 Probably not as many as previously supposed. In the table in MacDonald 1974, 279 and catalogue in 285; 63 Gallic imitation coins and two other coins of Tetricus I and II found at Aphrodisias are listed. In 1976, he seems to have changed some identifications: MacDonald 1976, 15, nr. 601 Tetricus I; no coin at nr. 602; nrs. 603–665 barbarous radiates, that is 63 coins listed instead of the earlier sum of 65, with only four coins labelled as 'excavated'. We do not know where the other 59 coins were found, and whether they should be labelled as 'from Aphrodisias'. Thirty-three of these coins are illustrated in Chameroy 2018, 402, fig. 10. Besides four more found in the Place of Palms (cat. 48–51), 26 others have been excavated at Aphrodisias between 1994–2020, bringing the total from the scientific excavation of the site to 34.

from other sites in Western Asia Minor.[107] When the contexts are examined, only one coin (cat. 50) comes from a meaningful context that could be dated to or shortly after the third century AD; all the rest (cat. 48–49, 51) were found in late Roman and early Byzantine contexts. The small format of Gallic Empire imitations means that they fit easily into the format of fifth-century AD *nummi*; in fact one example from Parion was recorded in a fifth-century hoard. As the Gallic Empire imitations from Sardis were also found in fifth-century contexts,[108] one wonders whether their arrival in Western Asia Minor happened in the late third century AD or much later in the fifth century AD.

F. DISCUSSION: THE EVOLUTION OF A PUBLIC SPACE (BR & AW)

The Place of Palms, as constructed in the early Julio-Claudian period, did not remain unchanged for long. This was a continually evolving space comprising a series of self-contained but connected architectural ensembles, which was added to, updated and repaired on a regular basis. A minimum of four phases of work can be reconstructed between the late first century AD and the end of the fifth century (see Fig. 5).

Flavian to Trajanic: At some point in the third quarter of the first century AD, the first-phase, single-storey South Stoa was replaced, following the probable partial collapse of the Theatre wall and the expansion of the Theatre itself, with a new structure. This new South Stoa was probably erected at roughly the same time as the Propylon, which was completed before AD 96 but must have been started much earlier. This monumental screen enclosed the east end of the Place of Palms for the first time. In the southwest corner of the complex the Civil Basilica was added, also in the Flavian era, though it may not have been finished until the early Trajanic period. Most of this side of the Place of Palms, therefore, must have been a construction site for much of the second half of the first century AD.

Hadrianic: The next changes occurred at the western end of the complex, where the construction of the Hadrianic 'Olympian' Baths necessitated the adjustment of the west end of the North Stoa and the creation of the new West Stoa, with a grand archway at its centre. At the same time, the North Stoa, by then a century old, was updated according to the latest marble fashions.

Severan: The epigraphic evidence from the North Stoa indicates substantial repairs to this building at the end of the second century AD, apparently as a result of earthquake damage to some of the columns, though other evidence of architectural repairs might point to more than one phase of interventions.

Fourth-century: Alterations to the West Stoa, including its flooring in mosaic, as well as Flavius Constantius' work in the Basilica, belong to a phase of fourth-century activity that was possibly undertaken in response to an earthquake. It is possible that the various cuttings in the columns and stylobate of the West and North Stoas date to the fourth century, though they are impossible to date closely and could have been started earlier; the West Stoa does seem to have been enclosed by the Theodosian period, however. In the case of the North Stoa the cuttings to take wooden elements appear to be in relation to *topos* inscriptions, indicating shop counters or stalls, and thus an increasing commercial use of the stoa.

The evidence outlined above shows that the Place of Palms was a key venue for investment on the part of local benefactors. By the second century AD two of the city's largest civic buildings, the Civil Basilica and the Hadrianic Baths, opened onto it, while at its eastern end the new Propylon was the largest columnar façade monument erected in the city, dwarfing the earlier Propylon of the Sebasteion and the *skene* in the Theatre. Continual maintenance and adjustment of the complex's constituent structures occurred throughout the first to fourth centuries AD.

Much of the architecture erected in and around the Place of Palms was exceptionally precocious, to a degree not previously recognized. The pool, as noted in Ch. 2, was one of the largest, if not the largest, decorative pools in the Roman world, larger than anything in Rome and longer than the more famous pools of Hadrian's Villa, which date almost a century later. The palm grove itself, although clearly inspired by the layouts of planted porticoes in Rome, predates by about a century the monumental palm grove at Smyrna known from a Hadrianic inscription;[109] was Smyrna imitating Aphrodisias in this respect? The Propylon, now redated to the Flavian period, is broadly contemporary with the nymphaeum at Miletos and earlier than other, more famous columnar screen monuments of the coastal cities of Asia Minor, like the Library of Celsus at Ephesos, by at least a decade. Indeed, the monumental Propylon of the Place of Palms extends and elaborates on a model already built at Aphrodisias in the Julio-Claudian Propylon of the Sebasteion in the mid first century AD. The Hadrianic 'Olympian' Baths built at the western end of the complex in the 120s–130s were closely contemporary with such large *thermae* of the 'Asia Minor type' as the Theatre Baths and the East Baths of Ephesos, and perhaps slightly earlier than the Baths of Alexandria Troas attributed to Herodes Atticus.[110] These port cities on the coast—Alexandria Troas, Smyrna, Ephesos, Miletos—were all much larger than Aphrodisias, with populations several times its size and thus more wealthy patrons and strong inter-provincial connections

---

107 Chameroy 2018: 400, table 1. More Gallic Empire and imitation coins can be added to the table: new examples from Sardis (Evans 2018: 152–152, nos. 296–310); from Smyrna agora (Ersoy, Önder, and Turan 2014: 30–32, no. 21–29); from Stratonikeia (Tek, Köker, and Sariiz 2015: 138, 140, fig. 8); from Anaia (Ünal and Bülbül 2005: 117, no. 3); from an early fifth-century AD late Roman hoard found in Parion (Keleş and Oyarçin 2019: 193, 196, nr. 1); and one found in Sinop now in Sinop Museum [Casey 2010: 50, no. 517]. A brockage coin of Postumus and another coin of Tetricus I were published from Ankara Anatolian Civilizations Museum, but their find places are unknown (Arslan 1992, 94–96, nos. 176 and 179). We also recorded several Gallic imitations at Tripolis in Lydia. Apart from the Sinop example, all of these coins with known findspots are restricted to Western Asia Minor. We have not seen them at the Lycian, Pamphylian, Pisidian, and Cilician sites that we have worked at (e.g. Arykanda, Phaselis, Side, Perge, Tarsus, Kelenderis).
108 Evans 2018, 34.
109 *IGR* IV 1431; *I.Smyrna* 697; see Ch. 2 §D.
110 Wilson 2016a, 172–173.

via maritime trade. What explains the precocity of public architecture at Aphrodisias?

Several factors may be suggested, all of which probably operated to various degrees. First, Aphrodisias's privileged connections with Rome, dating back to the time of Zoilos and renewed at least on the accession of every new emperor when the city sent embassies to Rome to confirm its status as exempt from imperial taxation. This would help explain the early architectural influence of Rome on Aphrodisias—in for example the Theatre built by Zoilos, or the palm grove and pool reminiscent of the shady porticos of late republican and Augustan Rome—but it would not directly explain the innovation. The sense of a special connection with Rome might however have fuelled a sense of architectural ambition; and the realisation of such ambition must surely have been assisted by the availability of high-grade marble next to the site, and its role in the local economy. It seems virtually certain that the owners of the various marble quarries were among the local elite who formed the town council; many of the city's leading families were involved in the donation, construction, and repair of major building projects over several generations.[111] The local architectural economy clearly gave rise to a sizeable workforce of skilled sculptors, masons, and, crucially, architects. Many of the powerful voices on the town council had a direct interest either in the marble quarries or in other aspects of the building industry. Euergetism at Aphrodisias could go further, as it were, for the same cash value, if building material came straight from the donor's quarries. Moreover, for projects funded or part-funded from civic funds (like the 'Olympian' Baths), the city's exemption from imperial tax collection must have helped the city's finances considerably.

The building work carried out around the Place of Palms in the first to fourth centuries AD, though architecturally impressive, was largely piecemeal and *ad hoc*. This was a complex that continually evolved. As we shall see in the next chapter, however, a massive earthquake in the fifth century led to a substantial overhaul of the whole of the Place of Palms, the results of which unified the complex in a way not seen before this date.

---

111 On this point, see Russell 2013, 53–55; and on the case of Carminius, see Pont 2008.

CHAPTER 4

Destruction and Renewal:
The Place of Palms Reborn, Fifth to Seventh Centuries AD

Andrew Wilson, Ben Russell, Allison Kidd, Angelos Chaniotis, Hugh Jeffery, Tim Penn,
Hüseyin Köker, Ahmet Tolga Tek, Ulrike Outschar, Erica Rowan, and Mark Robinson

Epigraphic, structural, and stratigraphic evidence combine to indicate a programme of major repairs to and restoration of the entire Place of Palms in the late fifth or early sixth century AD; this involved extensive repairs to the pool itself, restoration and modification of the North Stoa, re-erection of the West Stoa, the complete rebuilding of the South Stoa in front of the Theatre Hill, the construction of another stoa along the western half of the southern side of the Place of Palms, and repairs to the Propylon. We shall argue below (§K) that the evidence of material recycled from other buildings in these repairs suggests that the restoration followed a devastating earthquake in the late fifth century that impacted all, or nearly all, of the major public buildings of the city.

Further structural evidence indicates one or more separate sets of repairs to the pool in the course of the sixth century and also in the seventh century, and modifications to its water supply, including the construction of a large reservoir header tank against the Propylon (§M, discussed further in Ch. 6). We propose that among the reasons for the continued vitality and maintenance of the Place of Palms in late antiquity was not merely that it was a pleasant and enjoyable public park in the heart of the city, but also that it was the location for the celebration of the Maiouma festival, involving nocturnal revelries and aquatic shows, for which the pool was well suited.

A. THE EPIGRAPHIC EVIDENCE: DOULKITIOS AND AMPELIOS (AC, AW, & BR)

Three inscriptions were carved in late antiquity on the second, third, and fifth of the projecting piers of the Propylon (see Fig. 15). All three are in verse, and while the lettering of the Ampelios inscription is more carefully cut, they clearly go together. They honour two individuals, Ampelios, *pater civitatis*, and Doulkitios, governor of Karia, who played a key role in the late antique refurbishment of the complex.

The northernmost of the three inscriptions (In10), in hexameters, honours Ampelios, with a cross pattée above it (Pl. 28.A):[1]

+
ἴδμονι θεσμοσύνης γλυκερῷ γενετῆρι τιθήνης
Ἀμπελίῳ Νύμφαι χάριν ἴσχομεν οὕνεκα θάμβος
χώρῳ φυνικόεντι καὶ ἀγλαὸν ὤπασε κάλλος

ὄφρα καὶ ἡμετέροις τις ἐν ὕδασιν ὄμμα τιταίνων
αὐτὸν ἀεὶ καὶ χῶρον ὁμοῦ Νύμφας τε λιγαίνοι.
Τραλλιανὸς ῥητὴρ τάδ' ἐγράψατο Πυθιόδωρος.

'To Ampelios, learned in law, sweet father of his nurse, we Nymphs are grateful, because he gave wonder and splendid beauty to the place of palms, so that anyone who, among our waters, turns his glance around, may always sing the praise both of him and of the place, and of the Nymphs as well.
Pythiodoros, the orator from Tralles, wrote this.'

It is this inscription, as noted in Ch. 2, that draws the direct connection between the location where the reader was standing – the east end of the complex – the pool or waters of the Nymphs, and the palm grove, and refers poetically to the large porticoed space as a χῶρος φυνικόεις, a 'palmy place' or 'place of palms'.

Ampelios is known from other inscriptions as πατὴρ τῆς πόλεως (*pater civitatis*, 'father of the city'), a post which involved the supervision of civic finances and building projects. The poem plays on this role with the oxymoron 'father of his nurse', where Aphrodisias is the 'nurse' or native city that raised him. Ampelios' involvement in construction or reconstruction work is recorded at the Bouleuterion, Theatre Baths, and City Walls (see Appendix 1, discussion of In10). These projects were all probably undertaken in this official capacity as none of these inscriptions states that he paid for the works out of his own money.

The other two inscriptions on the Propylon are both in elegaic couplets, and refer to a governor of Karia, Doulkitios, who was apparently instrumental in rebuilding the Propylon itself and also perhaps much of the rest of the Place of Palms. The first, lacunose, appears to refer to the reconstruction of something apparently called a *temenos* (In11) (Pl. 28.B):

καὶ τόδε [?Νυμφάων τ]έμενος Κ[άρεσσι?]ν ἔγειρε
Δουλκί[τιος ?κτίστη]ς τῆς Ἀφ[ρ]οδισιάδος
οὐδὲν [φεισάμενος] πλούτου δόξης χάριν ἐσθλῆς·
ἥδε γὰρ [ἀίδ]ιον μ[ν]ῆμα βροτοῖσιν πέλει.

And Doulkitios, [?builder] of Aphrodisias, raised up this *temenos* [?of the Nymphs] [?for the Karians]; he [was unsparing] of wealth for the sake of good reputation, which is [?a permanent] memorial for mortals.[2]

---

1 Roueché 1989 (*ALA* 38) = *IAph2007* 4.202.i. See also Appendix 1, In10, with further bibliography and brief discussion.

2 Roueché 1989 (*ALA* 39) = *IAph2007* 4.202.ii. See also Appendix 1, In11, with further bibliography and brief discussion.

The second inscription commemorating Doulkitios, which has surviving traces of rubrication, must refer to the reconstruction of the Propylon (In12) (Pl. 28.C):

τὸν καὶ ἀγωνοθέτην καὶ κτίστην καὶ φιλότιμον καὶ Μαϊουμάρχην
  Δουλκίτιον, ξεῖνε, μέλπε τὸν ἡγεμόνα
ὅστις κἀμὲ καμοῦσαν ἀμετρήτοις ἐνιαυτοῖς
  ἤγειρεν κρατερὴν χεῖρ' ἐπορεξάμενος.

Stranger, sing of Doulkitios, the governor, giver of games and founder and lover of honour and Maioumarch, who, stretching out his strong hand, raised me too, who had suffered for unnumbered years.[3]

The inscription itself is speaking, and therefore the 'me' must refer to the Propylon on which it is carved. It would suggest that Doulkitios took down and re-erected much of the columnar structure of the Propylon, presumably because it had become unstable. A new display of statuary, as discussed in Ch. 7, was added to the building at this date too.

The three inscriptions form a coherent group; although the metre of the Ampelios inscription, in hexameters, differs from the elegiac couplets of the two Doulkitios inscriptions, the two latter are both connected with the previous texts by the particles καὶ (In11) and κἀμὲ (In12), and the left-to-right arrangement of the texts leaves no doubt that the καὶ of In11 means that the previous text is In10, the poem to Ampelios. It is possible therefore that the orator Pythiodoros may have composed all three texts.[4] In any case, they clearly refer to building works and renovations that are connected.

It has generally been assumed that the *temenos* of the second Doulkitios inscription refers to some kind of enclosure (as in the use of the word for a temple precinct), and that what is being poetically referred to here should be the stoas around the Place of Palms; and we too have followed this interpretation in earlier publications.[5] Yet this is not entirely straightforward, and other interpretations are also possible. Doulkitios demonstrably did *not* reconstruct the West Stoa, since that was done by Albinos (see §D); and the only directly attested epigraphic evidence for the construction of the two new South Stoas mentions one Philip, who roofed either two of the sections, or perhaps rather both stoas. Moreover, the obvious place to commemorate the reconstruction of the stoas would be on the architraves of the stoas themselves. *LSJ* defines a *temenos* (sense II) as 'a piece of land marked off from common uses and dedicated to a god, precinct', noting uses where the Pythian race course at Delphi is called a *temenos* (Pindar, *P*.5.33), the lake formed by the river Cephisus is the τέμενος Καφισίδος (Pindar, *P*.12.27), or where sacred groves are referred to as a *temenos* (Tim. *Pers.* 211; *h.Ven.*267). It might therefore be legitimate to wonder whether in the highly poetic language of the inscription, if τόδε [?Νυμφάων τ]έμενος has been correctly restored, the *temenos* of the Nymphs might be not the surrounding colonnades, but either the pool itself, or the palm grove more generally (see also Appendix 1, In11).

The interpretation of what Doulkitios restored is partly dependent on how one reads the Ampelios inscription: are the nymphs grateful to Ampelios because he restored their pool, and it was the restoration of the pool that gave 'wonder and beauty to this place of Palms'; or are they grateful because he restored the palm grove around the pool, which one sees by looking around from within the pool? One could perhaps defend either an interpretation in which Ampelios restored the palm grove and Doulkitios the pool, or *vice versa*. Or possibly the studied ambiguity of the verse inscriptions hints at both men having a hand in both projects.

These inscriptions indicate a date in the late fifth century or even the early sixth century for the rebuilding of the Propylon; Ampelios is a *pater civitatis*, an office attested in inscriptions and laws from the 460s onwards (but which appears to have existed even before then) and throughout the sixth century.[6] Doulkitios is referred to as *hēgemōn* (= Latin *praeses*), suggesting a date before the end of the reign of Anastasius (AD 491–518), as at some point before the end of his reign the office was upgraded and Karia was thereafter governed by a consul (*hypatikos*).[7]

A monogram on a column of the South Stoa that is identical with that of the emperor Anastasius (see Appendix 2, SS24; Pl. 54.C) supports this date; as we shall see (section §F) the South Stoas were rebuilt at the same time. The mention of the emperor and the possible mention of an ὕπαρχος (*praefectus praetorio per Orientem*) on columns used for the construction of the eastern South Stoa (SS15, SS17, SS20, SS22; see Pl. 54.D–E) raises the question of the funding used for the repairs in the Place of Palms. While Albinos is explicitly praised for using private funds for the West Stoa (WS9, WS13, WS15, WS20, WS21, WS23, WS24) and the governor Doulkitios is praised for his generosity in spending his own riches (In11), things are different in the case of Ampelios (see Appendix 1, In10). As πατὴρ τῆς πόλεως (*pater civitatis*) he supervised the civic finances and construction works. The 'palaestra' of the Bouleuterion was constructed and the city walls were repaired 'under' Ampelios (ἐπί Φλαβίου Ἀμπελίου), that is under his supervision, not with his funds; Ampelios was involved in these building projects as the governor's agent. In the case of the Place of Palms, the governor not only authorized the use of civic funds but also used private means (οὐδὲν [φεισάμενος] πλούτου), and there are other parallels for a combination of civic and private funds in construction work in this period.[8] We should explain Anastasius' and the praefect's monograms in this context: after a devastating earthquake, Anastasius may have provided some financial assistance for rebuilding or supplied building materials.

---

3   Roueché 1989 (*ALA* 40) = *IAph2007* 4.202.iii.
4   For a much earlier instance of a hexameter text followed by a text in elegiac couplets by the same poet, see *CIL* 8.211 from the early second-century mausoleum at Kasserine in Tunisia; lines 1–90 are in hexameters, and lines 91–110, which the poet claims are added as an afterthought, are in elegiac couplets, with each pentameter indented. See Groupe de Recherches sur l'Afrique antique 1993 for this monument and the inscription.
5   Roueché 1989, 89; Wilson 2016b, 133–134; 2016; 2018a, 478.
6   Roueché 1979, 176–185.
7   Roueché 1989, 66–7, although she erroneously considers that this must mean Doulkitios held office before the *start* of the reign of Anastasius (AD 491).
8   See Roueché 1979, 178 no. 3 and 183.

The nature of Ampelios and Doulkitios' works somewhat obliquely referred to in these verse inscriptions has been clarified by the excavations between 2012 and 2017, which not only allow us to identify the archaeological correlates of these inscriptions, but also to see why this extensive programme of restoration had become necessary. We shall return to the significance of Doulkitios' title of 'Maioumarch' in §M towards the end of this chapter.

B. REPAIRS TO THE POOL (AW, BR, AK, & ER)

The pool was extensively repaired in late antiquity, as became apparent already during excavation in 2013, when some evidently re-used material in the pool walls was exposed, but the full extent of these repairs only became clear during the post-excavation conservation programme in 2018–2019.

Structural repairs to the pool: re-setting of the seats and pool walls

The conservation work of 2018–2019 aimed to stabilise the marble surround of the pool, especially where it had been damaged by post-antique earthquakes (Ch. 9), and in many places along the southern side and around the eastern end this involved lifting the inner seat blocks in order to take up, repair, and consolidate the flat slabs below them. At some points too the slabs forming the pool walls needed to be re-set, which required digging out the fill of the pool wall between the facing slabs and the ring drain edge. All this work revealed that along the south side of the pool in particular, and also to a considerable extent at the eastern end, as well as in places elsewhere, the pool walls and seats include a substantial quantity of material that does not belong to the original phase of the pool (Fig. 23: a), and much of it consists of recycled architectural elements from other buildings—including from the Basilica, the previous phase of the South Stoa, and either the Theatre or the Bouleuterion.

The material re-used from other public buildings in the outward-facing bench seating includes an architrave block, cracked and recarved with its upper surface slightly dished to serve as an outer seating block on the south side (Pl. 29.A), and a column drum, split and reused as an outer seating block with the flat side uppermost, reused over the new exit drain (Pl. 29.B). In the inward-facing pool seats, several bench seating blocks were reused from the stylobate of a stoa (probably the South Stoa before its late antique rebuilding), identifiable by the tell-tale concave curved profile of the front underside, with the front lip trimmed off (Pl. 29.C–D); and several seat blocks with lions'-claw feet (Pl. 29.E), which could derive either from the upper cavea of the Theatre (which may have collapsed with parts of the vaulted substructures on the Theatre Hill), or from the Bouleuterion, where the front rows of seats were removed in late antiquity for the enlargement of the orchestra. Reused material in the wall of the pool includes, most obviously, part of a cut-down base with a dedicatory inscription on the visible face, possibly from a sanctuary of Asklepios (Pl. 30.A; Appendix 1, In31). The word ἀφετηρία, 'starting point', on another block built into the pool walls was seemingly inscribed when this block was used in a different context (Appendix 2, P167; Pl. 47.A).

Where the flat slabs of the inner seating are missing or were removed during conservation, it could be seen that many of the blocks now forming the edge of the pool wall all along the southern side, and on the northern curve of the western end of the pool, and the western part of the north side, are late repairs, cut down from stylobate bench-seating blocks (identifiable from remnants of the concave curved profile of their original underside), or Theatre or Bouleuterion seat blocks, with traces of lions'-claw feet. During conservation works on the pool edge in 2018, in order to stabilise a section of the pool edge towards the eastern end of the southern side, where the blocks were leaning inward towards the pool as a result of post-antique earthquake damage (Ch. 9), the earth fill between the slabs of the pool wall and the masonry of the ring drain was dug out, exposing the backs of the slabs. The rear faces of two of these slabs were seen to have been regularly sawn, with traces indicative of the use of a mechanical (water-powered) saw, and on one of these was visible a remnant of the curved underside of a stylobate bench block that had been trimmed back (Pl. 30.B). Evidently these too had been reused from material from other buildings.

The seat blocks of the repairs can be distinguished from those of the original pool wall even when the new blocks are not obviously identifiable as particular architectural elements of other buildings. The original blocks have a very irregular rough-hewn rear edge, and often a wide rebate for the marble cover slabs that originally covered the duct for the fountain pipelines. The blocks of the repair phase have a much narrower rebate, or lack it entirely (in which case the cover slabs, if still present, must have been supported on smaller stones or earth fill set within the duct); this is conditioned by the narrower width of the blocks that were reused. Their rear face is usually more neatly cut, resulting from trimming down of architectural elements.

Also apparently later additions are a large number of slabs laid flat as the foot-rests for the inward-facing bench seats. These are identifiable by their different material as well as the late antique masons' marks on many of them. The original foot-rests of the first phase of the structure were all carved in white Aphrodisian marble, like all of the other elements of the pool. On the heavily repaired southern side, however, the foot-rests are a mixture of white and blue-grey marble slabs. By virtue of their different material, these blue-grey slabs can be identified as later additions (Pl. 30.C). This is further confirmed by the fact that many bear masons' marks of the same sort as are found on the paving of the West Stoa, the late antique paving of the Tetrapylon Street, and on the paving of the Tetrastoon; the function of these marks is discussed further in Ch. 5 §E. Whether these are re-used slabs, taken from paving elsewhere, such as inside the North Stoa or from a neighbouring structure, or newly cut slabs specifically produced for repairing the pool is uncertain but the latter option is a distinct possibility.

This blue-grey marble comes from the quarries at the very southern tip of the Taşkesiği ridge of the City Quarries, especially Quarry H, immediately north of the city, where new marble extraction continued until at least the fifth century and possibly

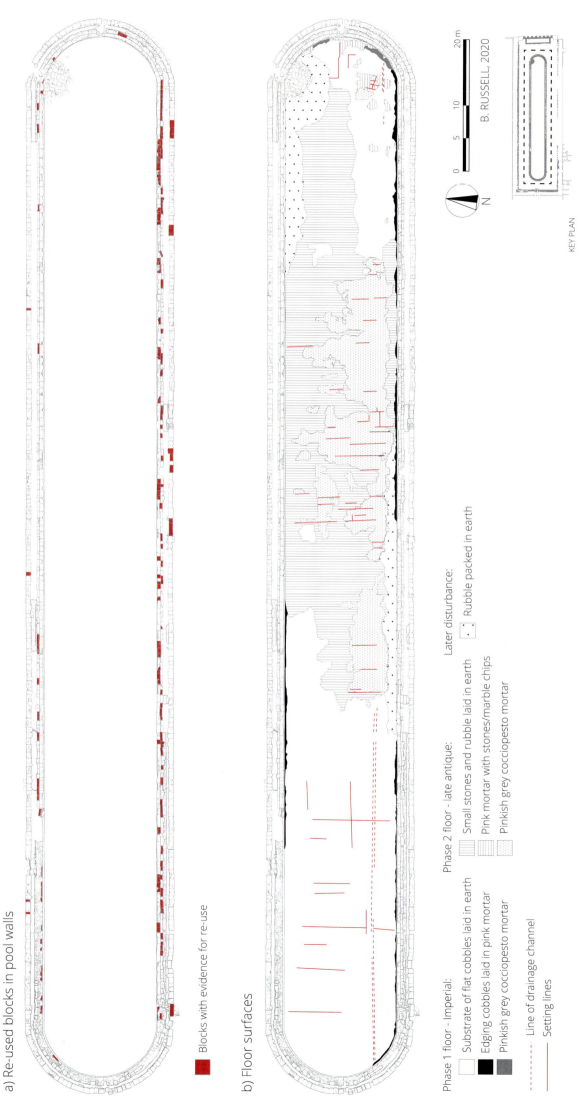

Fig. 23. Distribution of re-used blocks and repairs to pool floor.

later.[9] The other instances in which this blue-grey marble is used for large-scale paving in the city all date to the fourth century and later. If the pool slabs were re-used then they must have come from a project that had only recently been completed, therefore, and it seems more likely that, like the paving stones of the West Stoa, they were newly produced. Those responsible for the reconstruction of the pool, therefore, seem to have drawn on a combination of re-used elements from surrounding structures for the more substantial components of the pool walls and new paving slabs for these foot-rests.

Overall, the repairs were evidently far more extensive along the southern side of the pool, where most of the seat blocks and the edge of the pool appear to have been replaced, than they were on the northern side, where original blocks are much more common (see Fig. 23: a). The greater damage that evidently occurred to the southern edge may have been caused by the collapse onto it of the two-storey second-phase South Stoa (see §F).

Where repairs to the pool wall were less extensive, for example on the northern side of the pool as seen in trenches SAg.12.1 and SAg.12.2, a layer of roughly mortared rubble (**1037**) was added on top of the dry stone masonry (**1038**) of both walls of the ring drain and then the original marble seating blocks were replaced (Pl. 30.D). Originally, when the pool was constructed the top of the seat blocks had been 37–38 cm above the surrounding path. After the ground level of the Place of Palms was raised during the late antique renovation works (see §C), the outer seats were raised perhaps 5–10 cm by setting them on the stones and rubble **1037**; but even so they were only some 23–26 cm above the new higher ground level (as shown in the 2012 and 2013 trenches near the middle of the north side).

Pool floor

Much of what survives of the walls of the pool, therefore, is actually the result of late antique reconstruction work. This is also true of the pool floor, which was extensively re-surfaced in this period. This work, like much of the work on the pool walls, could only have been done with the pool empty.

As noted in Ch. 2, the floor of the pool in its first phase consisted of a substrate of large flat stones laid in mud, covered with a layer of smaller stones set in a friable mortar, and then surfaced by a layer of waterproof *cocciopesto* mortar. This final layer of original, presumably first-century, *cocciopesto* survives only in patches and is almost completely lost towards the ends of the pool (see Fig. 23: b). In its place, across most of the central section of the pool a new late antique surface can be identified, which was presumably intended to replace the degraded earlier floor and prevent leakage. This surface consisted of a thick layer of *cocciopesto* into which were set a range of materials, including small stones, broken roof tile, marble, and even bone (Pl. 31.A–C). Among the marble components are fragments of a range of revetment panels that came from the second-century scheme of the rear wall of the North Stoa, including pieces of the distinctive *portasanta* pilaster shafts and alabaster architrave

9 Russell, B. 2016, 266.

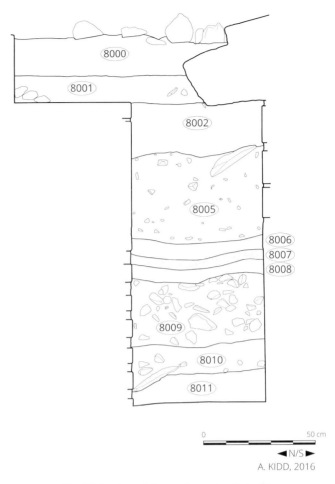

Fig. 24. Section of the southern ring drain fill.

mouldings (see Ch. 3 §D). The presence of this material in this repair surface shows that the rear wall of the North Stoa was substantially damaged prior to the late fifth-/early sixth-century reconstruction of the Place of Palms; it would make sense if this damage occurred during the same earthquake that caused such widespread destruction in the city centre and necessitated this campaign of renewal. Most of the marble revetment in the North Stoa seems to have survived this event and, as noted in Ch. 3, the decorative scheme was patched up with newly cut panels in grey marble from Yazır. Those panels that were dislodged and broken, however, and could not be re-used directly made ideal aggregate for the new pool floor.

Filling of the ring drain

At the same time as the late antique repair work on the walls and floor of the pool, the structural evidence for which is discussed above, the ring drain running around the pool was deliberately filled. This had already been noted in the excavations of 1989,[10] and in 2012 and 2013 two sondages were excavated to explore the nature of this fill, one on the north side of the pool (as part of trench SAg. 12.1; see Fig. 27) and one on the south side (as an extension to trench SAg. 13.1) (Fig. 24).

10 Nbk 307: *SW Portico of Tiberius* (F. Thode, 1989), 32–37.

In the northern ring drain, a series of usage deposits, consisting of alternating sandy and silty layers, directly overlay the floor slabs (see Fig. 27). These were identified in 2012 and initially removed as a single stratigraphic unit (**1033**) but on closer inspection of the section they were divided into four separate sedimentation layers (**1040–1043**). Four of these layers were sampled for archaeobotanical analysis, the results of which are presented below (§J). These layers are all individually quite thin and together are nowhere thicker than 10 cm. While they might have built up gradually over a long period during the life of the Place of Palms, dating them is difficult and the environmental material from them is consequently best considered as late antique.

The usage deposits were sealed by a compact deposit of clay, 60 cm thick, with stones and brick tile fragments, and occasional pottery (**1030**). All of the pottery from these deposits dates this event to the last quarter of the fifth or the first quarter of the sixth century; the single coin (cat. 158), an unidentified late Roman bronze, is consistent with this.[11] The depth of this deposit and its compact nature with abundant fragments of pottery and building rubble shows that it was not a gradual accumulation of silting, but a deliberate infilling of the drain, inserted after the schist slabs that originally topped the ring drain had been removed. Above it, the fill consisted of two thin layers of grey clay, both full of tile and pottery (**1029** and **1022**), which together filled the space corresponding to the original pipe duct.

In the southern ring drain, a somewhat different sequence was identified (Fig. 24). There were no alternating sandy and silty layers, nor large quantities of carbonized remains found on the bottom. Instead it was intentionally filled to roughly the halfway point, then used temporarily as a drain before an additional layer of fill was added. At the base, resting on the schist slabs (**8012**) was a 14.5 cm deep deposit of light grey, thick, dense silt (**8011**). There were very few fragments of pottery, marble and bone, and less than 1 kg of tile. The lack of finds within this context along with the dense consistency of the soil, indicates that it is the natural fill that accumulated directly on the bottom of the drain. Over it the drain had been deliberately filled with rubble, although several stages could be distinguished based on the different characteristics of the layers in the deposit. The lowest layer of the deliberate fill (**8010**) was only 7 cm deep, and contained fewer large stones and significantly less pottery and tile (11.1 kg compared to 1.1 kg) than the layer above (**8009**). Based on a bowl fragment, the context can be dated to the fifth century AD. Over it, a fill deposit (**8009**) contained, in addition to stones, a range of marble fragments, roof tiles, glass and ceramic slag, pottery and a very small quantity of bone. Two fragments of worked marble, one from a column and one piece of revetment were recovered. A bone object was the only notable small find. Overlying **8009** a rubbly layer (**8008**) contained fifth-century ceramics. The decreasing quantity of rubble in this layer indicates that it is the top of the intentional fill levels.

This sequence of dumped fills was covered by a thin sandy deposit (**8007**), apparently representing water-borne deposition while water flowed through the partly filled drain before the second episode of filling. Above this were two further intentional fills. A layer of fill (**8006**), up to 12.5 cm thick, contained more and larger fragments of pottery, and finer ceramic types but fewer fragments of tile (only 1.1 kg) than the layer above. Two late Roman coins were found in **8006**. The first can be dated to AD 355–361, in the reign of Constantius II (cat. 64), while the second is unidentifiable but certainly late Roman (cat. 203). The pottery however is fifth-century. The bottom of the context contained a rich layer of organic material that was sampled in full. Covering **8006** a thick fill deposit (**8005**) contained numerous rocks of varying shapes and 6.2 kg of small tile fragments and abundant mortar. A late Roman A1 amphora fragment gives a *terminus post quem* of the end of the fourth century but in fact the date is pushed into the fifth century by the date of the deposit below it.

Two layers of silty fill (**8002**, and over it, **8001**) containing substantial quantities of tile and mortar sealed **8005** and filled the space corresponding to the original pipe duct. These contained ceramics ranging in date from the first to fifth centuries. The final level of fill in the drain (**8000**) was a layer of rubble and topsoil that had been disturbed by previous investigations in this area and so was not sampled. Archaeobotanical samples were taken from all of the other contexts (**8001–8011**) and the results of their analysis are discussed below (§J).

The decision to fill the ring drain involved the deliberate removal of the lower schist cover slabs for the drain, which would also have entailed removal of the marble seat blocks and the upper slabs covering the drain, and the terracotta pipelines in the duct. Except on the south-east curve of the eastern end of the pool, where it seems that part of the drain was rehabilitated, these schist cover slabs were never replaced. Nor is there any evidence that the terracotta pipes were replaced either. It seems likely, then, that this drain was filled at the same time as the water supply arrangements were re-done (below), the seating was repaired and replaced and the height of the pool walls was adjusted and the external ground level raised (below). If the upper cover slabs, in marble, across the drain were replaced after this operation, as seems likely, then they were evidently later robbed as none has been found *in situ*. Where the replacement seat blocks either side lacked rebates, the cover slabs could have rested on the earth fill of the drain and former duct.

The deliberate blocking of the ring drain with a dumped fill—for a total length of a little over 200 m—clearly involved considerable effort, and cannot be explained simply by the drain having become redundant.[12] Rather, it seems like an effort to staunch leakage through the sides of the pool into the ring drain. The sedimentary and archaeobotanical evidence (**8007**) also suggests that for a short period of time (perhaps during the reconstruction works) the southern side of the ring drain was temporarily used as a drain or sewer channel, probably coming from the drain on the north-south Tetrapylon Street, directing food and garden waste from houses, shops and temples situated east of the pool area. This explanation is fully consistent with the need to extensively repair the pool walls and seats following an

---

11 Context **1031**: Late cooking pot – fifth century AD. Context **1030**: late Roman unguentarium, late fifth century AD; local imitation of ARS form 99, *c.* AD 500 (± a decade or two). See Wilson, Russell, and Ward 2016. Cf. PT.SW.I.89-F95, F96, F97 and F99, and PT.W.I.89-F145: Nbk 307: *SW Portico of Tiberius* (F. Thode, 1989), 31–33).

12 The drain is 152 m long along the north and south sides of the pool and each curved end is 33 m long, so the total length of the drain is 370 m.

earthquake, and with the modifications to the overflow arrangements discussed below.

Modifications to the water supply and drainage of the pool

Excavations in 1988 of the northern half of the eastern curve of the pool surround showed that the three terracotta pipelines C8, C10, and C11 of the first phase of supply were replaced by at least two pipelines: C4, from the northeast, and C9 from the east, which reached the pool to the north of the east end.[13] Both pipelines were laid across the top of the drain wall (rather than running through it as the first-phase supply pipes had), and to install them the marble seating must have been taken up and relaid, apparently associating the replacement of the supply pipelines with the extensive repair works to the marble seating surround of the pool and the raising of the level of that seating.

Both of the new pipelines entered a stone elbow joint pipe block on its rear face (C4 into D1, the northernmost block, and C9 into D2), and then continued from the upper surface of the distributor block (Pl. 31.D–E).[14] From the northern of the two elbow joint blocks, D1, a terracotta pipe must have been set in a cutting angled upwards in the rear face of a block of the inner coping of the pool, feeding a fountain feature (Pl. 31.F), perhaps incorporated into a sculptural group at the east end of the pool. The arrangements immediately south of the centre-line of the east end of the pool are not clear, as detailed records of the excavation here in 1988 do not exist,[15] but it is likely, by symmetry, that a similar arrangement may have existed here too. To the east of the pool, the pipelines C4 and C9 of the second phase were sealed by the dumped fill layer which raised the ground level of the Place of Palms.

Since the filling of the ring drain would have necessitated the removal not only of the marble cover slabs over the pipeline duct running around the pool, but also the schist cover slabs of the ring drain, the pipelines running in this duct supplying fountains around the pool must have been taken up at this point too. It is unclear whether the pipelines to the fountains around the pool were re-laid on top of the earth fill of the ring drain, and then subsequently removed in the third phase of supply arrangements (below), or whether they were removed and not replaced already in this second phase.

The southern part of the ring drain seems however to have continued in use as a drain, or to have been rehabilitated as such. A drain which was probably added when the ground level around the pool was raised is seen entering the ring drain at an angle to the south of the centre of the eastern curved end of the pool (Pl. 31.G), and from here, around the southeast curve of the pool and along the eastern part of the southern side for at least 25 m, the schist cover slabs are still in place (or, more correctly as regards the southeast curve of the pool, have been replaced after excavation of a part of the drain here in 1989). The upper fill of the ring drain has not been completely excavated along the southern side between the limits of the portions dug out in 1989–1990, but it is clear that the schist slabs are missing again by the time one reaches the sondage of 1985 which exposed the gameboards of Eusebios (Appendix 2, P110–P111) and the acclamation for the litter-carriers (Appendix 2, P106). It would appear that a portion of the ring drain from the southeast curve of the pool along the eastern part of the southern side was either maintained in use, or rehabilitated, to carry a drain from the eastern part of the Place of Palms—or probably in fact a drain connected to the street drain of the north-south Tetrapylon Street in the vicinity of the Propylon of the Sebasteion—for some distance along the southern side of the pool before diverting it through the southern wall of the ring drain and presumably into some other pre-existing drain along the southern side of the area. One imagines that the motivation for this would be that the digging and construction of several dozen metres of drain channel could be saved by reusing this portion of the ring drain. Whether this part of the ring drain was never filled in, or whether it was dug out and rehabilitated once the flooding problems became apparent and the ground level raised, is not entirely certain; but evidently it is connected with the modifications to the arrangements for drainage of the Place of Palms in the late fifth or early sixth century.

At the western end of the pool, the overflow arrangements were modified. The original overflow in the centre of the west end was blocked by filling it with compact clayey silt, stones and fragments of tile and pottery, and a new overflow was made at a level 25 cm lower down, two blocks to the north. Here a cutting 10 cm wide and 6 cm deep in the facing slabs of the pool edge, 0.33 m below their top, gives onto a drain 40 cm deep and 27–28 cm wide cut through the ring drain wall at an angle running from northeast–southwest (Pl. 32.A; Fig. 25). This drain was both floored and roofed with tiles, four of the cover tiles being preserved at the northeast end, nearer the pool. The overflow drain continued within the now-blocked ring drain to an exit drain in the middle of the west end as a tile-covered channel built within the fill of the ring drain (Pl. 32.B–C), showing that the second-phase outflow cannot be earlier than the blocking of the ring drain. It makes sense to see the modification of the outflow arrangements as contemporary with the other repairs to the pool structure and with the blocking of the ring drain. The lower elevation of the new overflow, at 0.69 m above the floor of the pool, suggests that it was no longer possible to maintain the water level in the pool at its original depth of 0.94 m, perhaps because of leakage through the walls which we have suggested was a motivating factor in the blocking of the ring drain.

The new overflow drain leaves the ring drain through an exit drain 0.37 m wide in the centre of the west end, which appears be a late antique addition. It may be the case that this drain continues as the east-west drain seen some distance to the west that runs out towards and under the West Stoa, debouching into the end of the service corridor of the Hadrianic baths, although the intervening space remains unexcavated. Certainly this latter drain is a late antique addition, laid within the raised late antique ground level that covers the original seat/stylobate

---

13 Nbk 298: *Agora Gate: Basin Front II* (F. Thode, 1988), 34.
14 D1: 0.61 m north–south × 0.385 m east–west × 0.51+ m high; diameter of hole for pipe, 0.17 m. D2: 0.695 m north–south × 0.32–0.33 m east–west; height not usefully measurable (considerably over 0.15 m); the pipe hole in the upper surface is 0.105 m from the north end, and is 0.195 m in diameter.
15 Nbk 299: *Agora Gate: Basin II* (E. Üçbaylar et al., 1988) gives very little information.

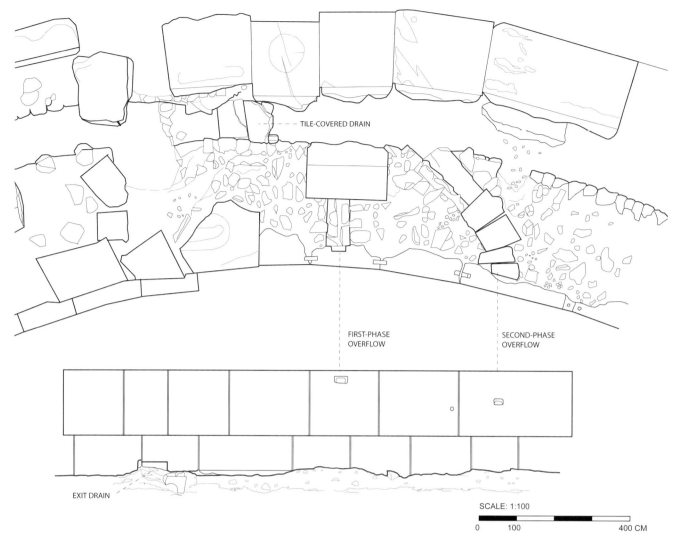

Fig. 25. Plan and elevation of first- and second-phase overflows at west end of pool.

of the West Stoa (visible immediately south of the drain). Presumably it fed into the drain below the service corridor of the baths rather than into the service corridor itself.

Alterations were also made to the arrangements to allow the pool to be completely drained for cleaning. A new exit drain was cut through the south wall of the pool to the east of the curve by the western end. Concave vertical grooves 4.5 cm wide and 2.5 cm deep cut into the edge of the two slabs of the pool wall that flank this drain show that they were fitted with a sluice gate 0.50 m wide that could be raised to allow the pool to be drained (Fig. 26; Pl. 33.A). This exit drain passed through the ring drain, whose floor slab was cut through at this point and incorporated into the west wall of the exit drain, and passed through the outer wall of the ring drain into an exit drain 1.80 m deep, heading southwest towards the street that ran along the west side of the Basilica.[16] Where it passes under the outer wall of the ring drain, the exit drain is covered by a split column shaft reused from the Basilica or the second-phase South Stoa, which serves as one of the outward-facing seat blocks of the pool, its curved side downwards (see Pl. 29.B). The reuse of this column shaft, and the reuse of a seat block originally from the pool edge in the east wall of the exit drain as it crossed the ring drain,[17] associate these alterations to the drainage arrangments with the wider programme of repairs to the pool that we argue were prompted by a severe earthquake that damaged not only the Place of Palms but also many buildings in the city (§L).

The new exit drain arrangements were probably necessitated by the blocking of the ring drain, which also blocked the original exit drain at the west end and the communication to it from the block with the rebate for a filter grille, in the drain through the west wall of the pool which we suggested in Ch. 2 could be controlled by a stopcock mechanism (see Ch. 2 §B). The insertion of the sluice gate, a more visible arrangement than the discrete stopcock, would arguably have required siting the new exit drain on the southwest side of the pool to avoid spoiling the appearance of the western curve of the pool, so important to the effect of the view along the pool from the eastern end.

16 Nbk 307: *SW Portico of Tiberius* (F. Thode, 1989), 34–5.

17 Not noted in Nbk 307: *SW Portico of Tiberius* (F. Thode, 1989).

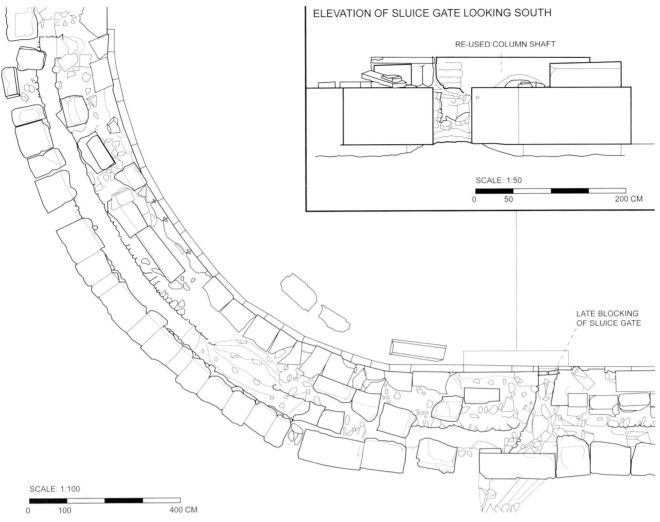

Fig. 26. Plan of second-phase exit drain and sluice gate.

C. ALTERATIONS TO THE PALM GROVE (AW & BR)

Contemporary with and soon after the filling of the ring drain and the alterations to the pool's water system, more substantial late antique works were undertaken in the open area around the pool. The first phase of these concentrated on the earlier planting trenches, exposed in trenches SAg. 12.2, 13.1, 15.2 and 16.2. Although the upper surface of the northern planting trench **2017** was disrupted by earlier excavation and restoration work in the area in front of the North Stoa, evidence from the southern planting trench suggests it was partly re-cut. This cut, **16.2.5010**, contained a rubbly fill (**16.2.5001**) that included fragments of architectural elements from the North Stoa.[18] This confirmed the observation made in 2012 that this southern planting trench's upper fill, **2015**, contained late Roman material: ceramics from the fifth century (see Appendix 5) and a coin of Marcian (cat. 104, AD 450–457). The fact that fragments of material from the North Stoa were found in **16.2.5001** indicate that this re-cutting of the planting trench was part of the wider refurbishment of the Place of Palms in the late fifth century AD. That such changes were made at this date indicates that the restoration of the planting scheme was considered crucial to the overall project. Soon after these adjustments, however, a more drastic intervention was required, which put these linear planting trenches out of use entirely.

Raising of the ground level

Since the purpose of the ring drain had been to deal with the high water table of the Place of Palms, filling it in would have caused the area of the park to become wet and boggy. Apparently in response to this self-inflicted problem, those responsible for the restoration decided to raise the ground level across the whole of the open area of the Place of Palms by between 30 and 40 cm (Pl. 33.B; Fig. 27). This covered over the linear planting trenches discussed above, forcing a new solution to be found for the planting schemes (as discussed below). This dumped de-

---

18 A fragment of the *balteus* of an Ionic capital or a garland from the mask and garland frieze (SAg.16.2.5001.M1) and a fragment of a flute from a column shaft (unnumbered). Also from this deposit came a copper alloy arrowhead: SAg.16.2.5001.F001 (Inv. 16-040).

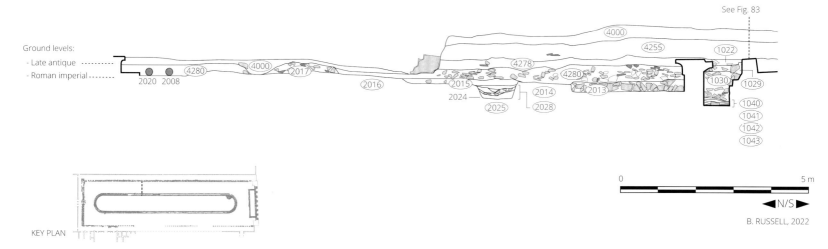

Fig. 27. North-South section drawing across trench SAg. 12.2 between the North Stoa and the northern pool wall, facing East.

posit (**4280**) was identified in trenches SAg. 12.2, 13.1, 15.2 and 16.1 and fully excavated in 12.2 and 13.1. It contained substantial quantities of brick and tile fragments, stones, chunks of mortar, and relatively limited amounts of pottery and bone—evidently deriving from the cleaning-up of earthquake demolition material.

The ceramics found in this deposit confirm a late fifth- or early sixth-century date (see Appendix 5). Sixty-four coins were recovered from this deposit.[19] To these we can add the three found on the stripped marble preparation surface of the path running around the pool (**2011**), over which the dumped deposit accumulated.[20] The vast majority of these coins date before the end of the fifth century, though there are seven which go later, including two datable to the reign of Phocas. These later coins are all from the upper part of the deposit (above 516.00 m; none is from the lowest 25 cm of the deposit below this), and doubtless come from the usage of the park in the sixth and early seventh centuries—this is not a fully sealed context and one can see how coins might have been trodden into the ground surface, or even dug further in during gardening work. The lowest levels of the overlying deposit, **4278**, that built up immediately on top of the raised late antique ground level **4280**, contained sixth- and seventh-century ceramics, as well as coins that also run up to the reign of Phocas.[21]

In SAg. 12.2 and 13.1, where the late antique dumped deposit was fully excavated, it was laid directly on top of the preparation surface (**2013**) of the path adjacent to the pool, from

19 Cat. 12, 18, 27, 51, 58, 77, 80, 88, 94, 95, 101, 102, 112, 115, 118–122, 126, 131, 133, 163–193, 205–208, 238, 248, 262, 263, 269, 271, and 286.
20 Cat. 103, 108 and 125.
21 This thick alluvial deposit, up to 25 cm deep, covered much of the area north of the pool walls. It was severely disrupted by earlier excavations in this sector (by both Jacopi and Erim), as well as the movement of vehicles along the north side of the Place of Palms complex during previous restoration work. The ceramics and coins (cat. 15, 132, 209–221, 237, 254 and 267), however, suggest that the lowest levels of this deposit built up from the sixth century onwards and that it continued to accumulate after the collapse of the North Stoa and even into the Beylik period.

which the paving slabs had been stripped, and on the earlier ground surface. This dumped deposit raised the ground level flush with the top of the continuous line of seat blocks running along the North and West Stoas, beneath the level of the stylobate, and the original level of those running around the edge of the pool—which, as shown above, were raised in response.

Three terracotta pipelines (**2008**, **2020**, **2021**) were laid at the same time as this dump was deposited, running east-west across the northern part of the trench parallel to the *euthynteria* of the North Stoa (Pl. 33.C). The two pipelines closest to the stoa (**2008** and **2020**) are intact, both sealed internally with white mortar and externally with pink *opus signinum*.[22] Fragments of broken tile stuck to this *opus signinum* show that the make-up deposit was packed around and over them before the mortar had set. The southernmost pipeline (**2021**) was broken in antiquity and only survived in fragmentary form in the eastern part of the trench.[23] No cuts were visible in the dumped deposit for these pipelines, which were evidently laid on the existing ground surface and the deposit to raise the ground level immediately dumped around them.

The deposit dumped to raise the ground level covered the entire Place of Palms around the pool. It was encountered and recorded also by Francis Thode by the eastern end of the pool,[24] and is visible also in the sondage conducted by Nathalie de Chaisemartin by the south-eastern corner of the Place of Palms, where it is seen to fill the gaps between the late column foundations. Several drains were laid within this raised ground surface. One, near the northeast corner of the Place of Palms, was found in the sondage excavated in this area in 1991 (see Fig. 6), its walls built of mortared masonry, with an internal width of *c.* 0.5

22 Dimensions: **2008**, pipe sections 27–30 cm long, external diameter 18 cm at ends, 16 cm at waist, ribbed externally. **2020**, pipe sections 31–32.5 cm long, external diameter 23 cm at ends, 21 cm at waist, ribbed externally.
23 **2021**: external diameter 17.8 cm.
24 Nbk 297: *Agora Gate: Basin Front I* (F. Thode, 1988), 68–70 ('couche de déstruction', *c.* 50 cm thick); Nbk 298: *Agora Gate: Basin Front II* (F. Thode, 1988), 19–20 ('couche très compacte', *c.* 40–50 cm thick).

m.[25] It must originally have been covered by slabs, now missing. This drain ran under the stylobate of the North Stoa and must have taken street drainage from the north-south street running in front of the Sebasteion Propylon southwards into the Place of Palms. It cannot have run eastward along the northern side of the pool, as excavation in 2012 between the north wall of the pool and the North Stoa, near the centre of the Place of Palms, found no trace of late drains. It is very probable that it connected with the drain mentioned above that entered the ring drain of the pool by the eastern end, and seems to have been carried by the ring drain around the southeast curve of the pool and for some distance along the southern side. Another late drain, also laid within the raised ground surface, was encountered in a sondage in 1988 in the northwest corner of the Place of Palms,[26] running under the North Stoa (ultimately coming from the Agora?); if it continued southwards (as it must have done, since it can hardly have gone anywhere else), we would expect it to have connected with the late exit drain running westward from the west end of the pool towards the service corridor.

This raising of the ground level was not limited to the Place of Palms. A similar deposit, containing late fifth-century coins, was laid across the Agora and a collecting basin added to its southwest corner to assist with the groundwater problems.[27] Similar steps were taken along the line of the Tetrapylon Street to prevent flooding.[28] This raising of the ground levels across the city centre involved a massive investment of labour and materials. In the area of the Place of Palms alone at least 2,010–2,680 m³ of rubble and soil were used.[29] However, since much of this rubble consisted of roof tiles and mortar, as well as probably mudbrick, presumably from structures damaged in the preceding earthquake, the need to raise the ground level of these various public spaces also provided an opportunity for the clearing-up and redepositing of substantial quantities of earthquake demolition material, which would otherwise have had to have been transported out of the city.

A new late antique planting scheme

The raising of the ground level put the linear planting trenches out of use. However, evidence from the upper surface of the late antique deposit that raised the ground level indicates that a new solution to planting was found. Although poorly preserved in trench SAg. 12.2, where it had been partially removed and disturbed by the earlier excavations of Jacopi in 1937 and Erim in 1985, and by subsequent activity in the area relating to the maintenance of the site, this surface was well preserved in SAg. 15.2. Here careful trowelling revealed a large circular pit (**3061**), overlapping in plan with the line with the southernmost planting trench (Pl. 34.A; Fig. 28). This could well be for the planting of a tree; it measured 1–1.10 m in diameter and was *c.* 35–45 cm deep. The fill (**3062**) of this pit contained ceramics of the same range as the dumped deposit. A second planting pit (**16.2.5003**) was found to the north-west of **3061** in SAg. 16.2; it had a similar diameter of 1.04 m to **3061** but was shallower, at only 28.5 cm. It did not overlie either of the earlier planting trenches. In addition to these two large pits, a line of smaller holes (**3063, 3065, 3067, 3069, 3071, 3075, 3077**), running north of the line of the southernmost of the two earlier planting trenches, was also cut into the upper surface of this new late antique ground level (Fig. 28). These holes run on an east-west line roughly equidistant between the two larger pits, **3061** and **16.2.5003**. Their fills (**3064, 3066, 3068, 3070, 3072, 3076, 3078**) again contained ceramics of the same date as the dumped deposit. These pits were all cut from the level of the raised ground surface, with **4078**—the lowest levels of which represent the use of the space after the late fifth century—building up over the upper surfaces of their fills.

The two large pits excavated, both *c.* 1 m in diameter, were presumably for trees. In the Great Peristyle garden of the Villa Arianna at Stabiae, which has been discussed already in Ch. 2, the tree cavities were smaller than this.[30] However, at Stabiae these cavities reveal the size of the plant or tree growing in this space when the eruption of Vesuvius struck in AD 79. In the Place of Palms we are dealing with planting pits and so we would expect them to be wider than whatever was planted in them. Their fills were in both cases of a fine silty clay. In contrast to these larger pits, the seven smaller holes that run between them may represent planting places for shrubs or smaller herbaceous plants; alternatively they might be post holes for a trellis of some sort along which trailing plants could have been grown. Parallels for both lines of shrubs and other plants and for low fences over which foliage could be trained come again from the Villa Arianna.[31] Two of these holes, **3071** and **3075**, are larger than the other five and it is possible that these two represent actual planting pits, with the rest being post holes for a trellis; a line of broken tile and stone extending westwards from these smaller holes and on axis with them could represent a continuation of this feature, the top layer of which has been disturbed by later activity.

These late antique planting pits and associated stake holes reveal a crucial aspect of the interventions by Doulkitios and Ampelios in the Place of Palms, which is that the Place of Palms remained a green space. Even after the raising of the ground level, which buried the earlier planting trenches, new pits were dug for both trees and smaller shrubs or other plants. The two larger pits that were excavated must have been for new trees or for existing trees transplanted, since they had compacted bases; in other cases, however, the late antique fill could have been packed around the trunks of still-standing mature trees. The series of smaller holes confirm that this was not simply a space for trees but was also planted with smaller species of plants, perhaps trained along fences or trellises. This may well

---

25 Nbk 323: *Portico of Tiberius Sondages* (D. Theodorescu et al., 1991); de Chaisemartin and Lemaire 1996, 152–153.
26 Nbk 300: *Portico of Tiberius NCE I* (A. Önce, 1988), 5.
27 Ratté and Smith 2008, 720; Wilson 2019, 201.
28 Wilson 2019, 201.
29 The calculation here takes the area enclosed by the stoas (10,811 m²) minus the area of the pool (4,110 m²), which comes to 6,700 m², and assumes an even depth of fill 0.30–0.40 m.
30 Gleason 2016; the exact dimensions of the various cavities excavated are not provided in this publication but the photographs and discussion suggest than the tree cavities are below 1 m in diameter, sometimes quite considerably below this.
31 Gleason 2016, 67–69.

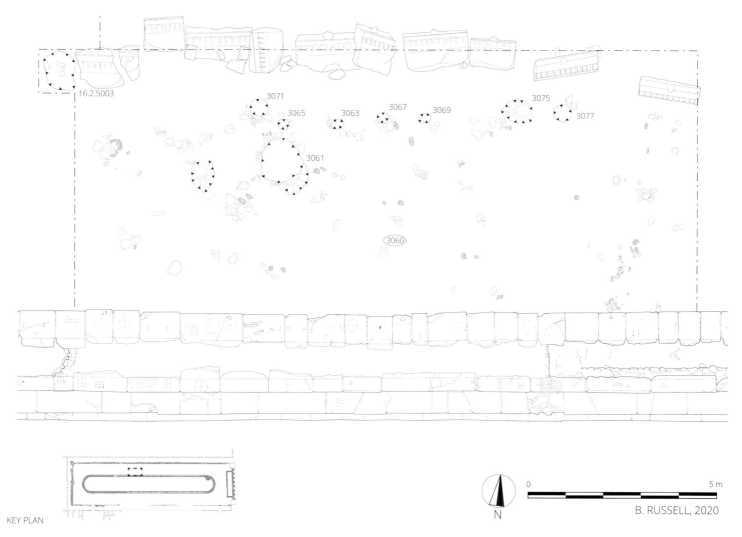

Fig. 28. Plan of trenches SAg. 15.2 and 16.2 to the north of the northern pool walls showing late antique planting pits, with line of fallen cornice blocks from the North Stoa to the north.

have been the case in the imperial period too—we cannot be certain about how the planting was actually arranged within the planting trenches at this earlier date, but the continuous planting trenches with a mounded surface suggest flowerbeds between trees. Following the raising of the ground level, those responsible for the maintenance of the open areas of the Place of Palms preferred to dig individual planting pits rather than long trenches, presumably because the rubble fill was awkward to dig out. Despite this, they appear to have aimed for a similar aesthetic, a mix of tall shade-giving trees and lower ornamental shrubs or bushes. So essential was this garden to the functioning of the Place of Palms that for Ampelios and Doulkitios to return this space to its 'wonder and splendid beauty' they also had to oversee its re-greening.

Waterlogged and carbonized material recovered from the bottom of the pool provides some support for this picture. The most notable find was a 1 mm fragment of palm leaf recovered from a sondage at the northern edge of the pool in 2012.[32] Although only one piece of palm leaf was found, these deposits formed in the seventh century, at which date any trees planted in the area, even as part of Ampelios and Doulkitios' renovations, would have been hundreds of years old. Furthermore, this leaf only survived because it was waterlogged. The fact that any palm leaf was recovered at all, therefore, is noteworthy. Finds from other contexts, however, indicate that the palms were not the only vegetation in the Place of Palms. The two most abundant tree species found in the drain were pine and cypress; but as argued in §J below, these probably are waste from ritual burning, and do not reflect the planting around the pool. A single date stone was also found along with numerous buds and leaves of the Kermes oak. Pine, cypress and Kermes oak all currently grow around and within the site. While Kermes oak can grow into a shade-giving tree, it is more commonly found in the area growing as a bush. Thus the planting trenches may have been filled with palms, with Kermes bushes growing between them. The hardy nature of pine cones, cypress branches and seed pods, and the leaves of the Kermes oak, mean that they are better able to survive the carbonization process than a date tree, especially the leaves. Similarly, unless their seeds are present, more delicate flowering plants do not readily become carbonized, and so while they may also have been planted between the

32 Robinson 2016, 94.

trees, there is not enough evidence within the archaeobotanical record to confirm their presence.

D. REPAIRS AND ALTERATIONS TO THE WEST STOA (AW, BR, & AC)

While the inscriptions suggest that Ampelios and Doulkitios were responsible for the archaeologically-attested work on the pool and the wider Place of Palms, other individuals took credit for refurbishing the other structures in the complex. The inscriptions that were carved on the twenty columns (nineteen of which survive) of the West Stoa are a series of acclamations to the *clarissimus* Albinos (Appendix 2 WS1, WS4–6, WS8–10, WS13–18, WS20–25; *ALA* 83; see also Ch. 5 §B), that praise him as the κτίστης, 'builder' or 'founder', of the stoa—in reality, of course, the rebuilder (Pl. 34.B). The acclamations progress from God through the emperors, prefects, senate, Aphrodisias, and then focus on Albinos himself; they read, from north to south:

'In the entire world, there is one God!'
'Many years for the emperors!'
'Many years for the prefects!'
'Many years for the senate!'
'Many years for the metropolis!'
'Look around, Albinos! May the builder of the stoa prosper!'
'Lord, lover of the fatherland, may you remain for us!'
'Your buildings, Albinos, lover of building works, are an eternal reminder'
[… *clarissimus* Albinos]
'Look around, Albinos, see what you have donated']
'The entire city says this: "Your enemies to the river!" May the great god grant us this!'
'May Albinos prosper! The *clarissimus* to the senate!'
'Envy shall not prevail over fortune!'
'May Albinos prosper, the builder also of this work!'
'You disregarded (your) property and obtained glory, Albinos, *clarissimus*!'
'Lover of the fatherland, following your ancestors, Albinos, *clarissimus*, may you receive plenty!'
'[- -] providing to the city, he is being praised in acclamations [in this]'.
'With your buildings you have brightened the city, Albinos, lover of the fatherland!'
'The entire city, having praised you in acclamations in one voice, says: "He who forgets you, Albinos, *clarissimus*, does not know God".'

Albinos was also honoured with a statue, whose base was found in the southern part of the West Stoa, in return for his (building) works and the 'untold gold' which he gave to the city (*ALA* 82; Appendix 1, In28).

As we have seen in see Ch. 3 §C, the pedestals on which the columns of the stoa sit now cover some of the cuttings in the floor which belong to the presumably fourth-century modifications when doors and screen fittings were inserted between the columns, and this suggests that the columns were at some point taken down and re-erected. It is reasonable to see this as the work for which Albinos was commemorated. Taking down the columns would of course mean removing the roof, or what remained of it. Such a large operation of dismantling and re-erecting must imply that the building had been severely damaged and become structurally unsound. Consonant with that deduction is evidence that substantial repair work was also done to the back wall of the West Stoa, which formed the common wall between it and the palaestra court of the Hadrianic 'Olympian' Baths. A number of marble architectural elements from the baths (architrave members and door frame surrounds) which show traces of mechanical sawing on their side or rear faces result from a late antique programme of trimming them back to fit properly after the building they formed part of had shifted out of alignment.[33] These include a door surround from the northern doorway between the West Stoa and the palaestra court of the baths, and this would imply that the west wall of the West Stoa had shifted out of true. Since other blocks with the same sawing traces are found in the walls of the pool of the Place of Palms, this should put Albinos' repair works to the West Stoa, and the repairs to the pool and the Hadrianic Baths all at the same period, in response to the widespread earthquake damage for which we argue in this chapter.[34]

The floor of the West Stoa was also repaved, and many of the marble paving slabs laid new at that time bear masons' marks, with sixteen different abbreviated names (Ch. 5 §E). Among these are eight slabs with the abbreviations Ἀλβ(ῖνος) and Ἀλβῖν(ος), concentrated particularly in the northern part of the stoa (Appendix 2 WS33, WS37, WS39, WS41, WS44, WS47, WS49, WS54). This suggests that Albinos' repair works involved not only his paying for the work, but also supplying material from his own quarry or workshop.

E. REPAIRS AND ALTERATIONS TO THE NORTH STOA (BR & AW)

Two sets of evidence combine to indicate a substantial rebuild of the North Stoa in late antiquity. Stratigraphic evidence from two sondages near the middle of the North Stoa (SAg. 14.3 and SAg. 14.4) showed that the floor level of the stoa was lowered in antiquity, with the imperial level floor removed at the time that many of the stylobate blocks were also removed. The north wall was, if not completely rebuilt, at least partly dug out and underpinned by the insertion of four seat blocks taken from another building, potentially the Bouleuterion, and the threshold of the central doorway was re-set, which must also have necessitated the re-setting of the door frame and dismantling and re-erection of the immediately surrounding parts of the wall. The marble revetment of this rear wall was re-set in this period and patched up with the fragments of Yazır grey noted in Ch. 3 §D; panels that were too damaged to be useable ended up in the new pool floor, as discussed above. Less closely datable, but probably to be

---

33 Wilson, Russell, and Proudfoot in preparation.
34 See also Wilson 2018a.

associated with this rebuilding, are architectural signs of damage to and resetting of the columns of the stoa.

Late antique works identified in Trenches SAg. 14.3 and 14.4

In late antiquity the ground level inside the North Stoa was lowered. In trench SAg.14.3 the upper fill of what is presumed to be the initial construction of the stoa, **14.3.5003**, a compact grey silty fill abutting the stylobate, was cut in two places by trenches running east-west (from south to north: **14.3.5016** and **14.3.5011**) into which two pipes were laid (**14.3.5022** and **14.3.5008**) (Pl. 34.C).

The cut for the southern pipe, **14.3.5016**, measured from 1.8 to 2.1 m wide and 19 cm deep. In it lay a ceramic pipeline, **14.3.5022**, of which eight pipe sections were uncovered within the trench, each 42–45 cm long and 13.5–15 cm in diameter at the ends and 10.5–13.5 cm diameter at the waist. The directions of the male and female joints indicated that the pipeline flowed from east to west, with the last pipe section exposed bending appreciably towards the south. The pipe trench was filled with a compact orange-brown layer full of bricks and roof tile fragments, **14.3.5019**, including an unidentified late Roman coin (cat. 200), and sealed by a light grey mortar layer generally 3–4 cm thick (but in places up to 7 cm) containing numerous pieces of rubble (**14.3.5018**). This seems to be the first of a series of construction dumps covering the pipe trench: over it were a compact grey silty surface, **14.3.5013**, up to 7 cm thick, a thin grey mortar layer, **14.3.5012**, up to 1 cm thick, concreted to a friable pinkish mortar surface, **14.3.5002**, 2–3 cm thick, with inclusions of small brick/tile fragments and pieces of wall plaster and revetment, that lay immediately above it, and a thin (2–3 cm) layer of grey silt, **14.3.5001**, which included glass, and some small fragments of marble revetment, as well as four coins.[35] While the only identifiable one of these coins (cat. 56) was dated to AD 337–340, the ceramics from these fills are dated to the fifth and sixth centuries AD, and fourth-century coinage continued to circulate in Aphrodisias until the late fifth century. Since these construction layers surmount a water pipe trench that cuts the original construction make-up, they must date from the late antique reconstruction of the stoa.

Running east–west to the north of the centre of the trench was a second cut, **14.3.5011**, *c*. 0.70 m wide (but in places up to 1.10 m) and *c*. 0.30 m deep, for another terracotta pipeline, **14.3.5008**. Part of four pipe sections were exposed, measuring between 36 and 46 cm in length and 19.5–20 cm in diameter at the ends, and 17–17.5 cm at the waist. The pipeline had been packed around with a dark brown silt, **14.3.5004**, up to 25 cm thick, which included stones and large fragments of an earlier ceramic pipeline which it had probably replaced. The upper 3–8 cm of the cut had then been filled with a compact grey silty fill, **14.3.5005**, containing abundant fragments of tile.

North of these two later cuts for the insertion of pipes was a third, sharply sloping cut, 60 cm wide and 40 cm deep, running along the south side of the rear wall of the North Stoa, **14.3.5014**. This cut severed a pre-existing pipeline, probably

35 Cat. 56, 225–227.

to be equated with the northernmost of the pipelines identified in the 1990 sondage. Since the two fills of this northern cut—**14.3.5015** and **14.3.5007**—run under the threshold of the central door through the back wall, this cut would seem to relate to the rebuilding of the back wall of the North Stoa (Pl. 34.D). Among the ceramics in this fill were four fragments of a fifth-century large closed vessel. The row of three marble thrones noted by De Chaisemartin and reinvestigated in trench SAg.14.4 (below) was actually placed in this cut, at a slight angle so that their broken tops were propping up the superstructure of the wall and reinforcing its foundations. Exposed at the bottom of the cut **14.3.5014** is the upper surface of a still unexcavated deposit, **14.3.5020**, at 515.7 m, a dark greyish brown layer of clay with inclusions of charcoal, mortar and tile.

All ancient layers within the North Stoa have been truncated by the cut **14.3.5009** for Kenan Erim's excavation of the portico in 1985, since when a thin layer of topsoil had accumulated over the whole area. During the cleaning of the topsoil a small oil lamp of Asia Minor type (F1), dated to the fifth or sixth century was discovered in a crack between two of the blocks beneath the stylobate level on the south side.

To the west of trench SAg.14.3, trench SAg.14.4 was opened to investigate the three winged marble griffin or sphinx thrones and one plain marble seat, situated below the imperial floor level and placed against the rear wall of the North Stoa, which had been exposed in excavation in 1990 and 1991 (Pl. 34.E). SAg.14.4 was opened in an effort to understand when and why they had been placed there. The earliest context uncovered in this sondage was a medium to dark grayish-brown compact clay surface, **6004**, exposed in a small area (0.5 × 1.5 m). This deposit goes beneath the marble thrones and seat and is probably the same as the layer **14.3.5020** at the bottom of the cut running along the south side of the rear wall. The (re)construction cut for the late antique works on the rear wall seems to have cut down to this layer and the fact that the marble thrones and seat were placed on this deposit indicates that they were wedged deliberately into the base of the cut. The actual fill of the cut consisted of a deposit of compact, medium grayish-brown clay with inclusions of brick, mortar, and charcoal, **6002**, with an upper elevation of 515.64–515.70 m. This layer contained a range of ceramic fragments, including late Roman cooking wares. Trampled into the upper surface of this deposit were spills of hard, medium brownish-gray mortar, **6003**, ranging in size from 60 × 20 cm to 15 × 7 cm, which testify to building activity in this area. A final deposit above this, consisted of greyish-yellow clay, **6001**, had been highly disturbed by the excavations here in the 1990s.

What the excavations in SAg. 14.4 showed was that the marble thrones were re-used in the North Stoa not as thrones but as building blocks. The backs of their seats are broken and set under the basal course of the back wall of the North Stoa, while their bottoms are wedged into the base of the (re)construction trench. These were convenient pieces of marble used to prop up the back wall and only their tops would have been visible above ground level. They could have been brought from somewhere else in the city and indeed the Bouleuterion is a possible candidate, since it was refurbished in the late fifth or early sixth centuries, at the same time and by the same person as the Place of Palms. This suggestion is supported by the fact that the undecorated seat at the east end of the row is from either the Bouleuterion or Theatre.

Despite the limited extant stratigraphy in the North Stoa, it is clear that substantial alterations were made to the lower portions of this structure in late antiquity. The floor level was lowered, with the imperial-level floor removed entirely. At the same time, and presumably in response to a need for building stone, most of the stylobate blocks that could be removed from beneath the colonnade without disrupting it—that is those that did not run directly beneath a column—were taken away; only those in the intercolumniations between columns N5–6, N12–13, N37–38, and N70–71 were left in place. Some stylobate blocks—like that inscribed with the name of Myon (NS55), discussed in Ch. 3 §D—were perhaps also moved around at this point. It is likely that the decision to remove these stylobate blocks led to the decision to lower the ground level inside the North Stoa, since the stylobate acted as one side of the original imperial-era floor and the latter could not have survived in place without the former. It is worth noting that in the West Stoa, where none of the stylobate blocks could have been removed without disrupting the colonnade, Albinos was responsible for a new paved floor, laid over the mosaic that seems to have been installed in the fourth century (see Ch. 3 §C). At the same time, in the North Stoa a series of new pipes was added beneath the new late antique floor level and a (re)construction trench dug along the south side of the rear wall, to add new supports to it and consolidate it. The ceramics indicate that all of this work occurred in the late fifth or early sixth century, at the same time as the raising of the ground level of the open area of the Place of Palms and the wider campaign of renovations led by Doulkitios and Ampelios, though no epigraphic evidence like that from the West Stoa reveals who was directly responsible for the North Stoa alterations.

Re-erection of the columns of the North Stoa

In several of the column bases of the North Stoa (N3, N10, N13, N16, N17, N18), the pouring channels for solder for the dowels have been re-cut, indicating that the columns originally set on them had been re-set at some point in antiquity. The stylobate of column N15 was cracked in antiquity and clamped on its western side. On column shaft N27, the lowest drum has sheared off diagonally along its upper surface (Pl. 35.A). Cuttings for four large clamps, three on the south side and one on the west side, show that this drum had begun to crack and was repaired before it finally split and collapsed. The holes left by these clamps measure 4–5 cm wide and are 1 cm deep; this was a serious intervention. The fact that these clamps are only found around half of the shaft, however, suggests that this crack did not pass all the way through the shaft and in fact this repair was probably carried out while the column was standing. Other columns (N2, N4, N7) bear stress marks which suggest that they had been subjected to severe lateral stress, probably without collapsing.

This damage and repair work is not itself closely datable, and it is possible that the re-setting of some of the columns may belong to the late second-/early third-century repairs of Claudia Antonia and Tiberius Capitolinus, which seem to have involved columns N15–N20 (see Ch. 3 §D). But the repairs with highly visible iron clamps to the cracked column N27 would seem to be much more in keeping with late antique repairs, rather than the wholesale replacement of damaged columns by Claudia Antonia and Tiberius Capitolinus. Some of the evidence for column repairs many therefore be reasonably associated with the stratigraphic evidence for late antique repairs from trenches SAg.14.3 and 14.4. Indeed, excavations in the Agora found the original inscribed architrave and some cornice blocks lying where they had fallen, and buried in a late antique layer of dumped fill, which shows that the colonnaded South Stoa of the Agora had collapsed; and this is of course the same building as the North Stoa of the Place of Palms. It is no surprise, then, that the common wall of these stoas needed consolidation, underpinning, and repair.

In combination, the evidence suggests that the North Stoa of the Place of Palms had been shaken in an earthquake with a south-to-north thrust that threw down the columns north of the spine wall, but the columns on the side of the Place of Palms had not (or not entirely) collapsed, being braced by the roof timbers that connected them to the rear wall. The damaged and unsound structure had to be partially dismantled, involving taking down and re-setting the columns, re-setting the threshold (and presumably therefore the entire door surround) of the central entrance through to the Agora, and underpinning at least a part of the rear wall of the stoa to the west of this entrance. Clearly these repairs to the columns and back wall would have necessitated the dismantling and rebuilding of the roof as well, if it had not actually collapsed in the earthquake.[36] It is possible that the assembly/re-assembly marks found on some of the column drums and the architrave blocks of the North Stoa (mentioned in Ch. 3 §D and discussed in Ch. 5 §E) might belong to this phase of activity.

F. THE NEW SOUTH STOAS (AK)

While the North Stoa seems to have been partially dismantled, repaired, and re-erected, the South Stoa was entirely destroyed and built anew from its foundations in the late fifth or early sixth century AD. In terms of scale, materials employed, and manner of execution, the building work along the southern side of the Place of Palms is a testament to the achievements of monumental construction in western Asia Minor during this period. Unlike in the preceding phases, in late antiquity the colonnades here mirrored the North Stoa by running along the southern edge of the Place of Palms for 205 m from the Propylon to the West Stoa. Although previous discussions have referred to a single 'South Stoa', the following analysis of the architectural elements suggests that we are probably dealing with two, or perhaps more, sections of stoa here, which were constructed in different ways. Given the late date of this stoa and its complicated

---

36 Wilson 2018a, 478; 2019, 200.

architecture, a more extended treatment of the remains is given here than have been provided for the North and West Stoas.

Together, these new stoas contributed an important aesthetic to the urban milieu of the late Roman and early Byzantine city; while their construction at this late date expressed Aphrodisias's enduring civic identity, the use of newer and older elements is symptomatic of the changes that occurred in the urban life of Aphrodisias during this period. This section provides an architectural analysis of the buildings to demonstrate how various financial determinants, aspects of patronage, and aesthetic preferences dictated the parameters for their construction. By tracing the choices made throughout the building process, this section explores the way in which patrons and craftsmen at Aphrodisias consciously maintained classical paradigms to the end of the antique period while 'modernising' the south side of the Place of Palms according to contemporary urban needs and expressive concerns.

Overview of the architecture

Only portions of the South Stoas have been excavated: one area extending eastward from the West Stoa during 1960–1971 and 2018–2019, and another area in two trenches extending westward from the Propylon in 1984–1986.[37] The majority of the blocks identifiable as from these stoas was uncovered during these excavations, with a few additional elements revealed within the area of the pool in 2013–2017.[38] Surviving architectural elements from the South Stoas include sculpted marble blocks, some other types of roughly shaped stone, roof tiles, and even wood, recovered from a waterlogged context in the pool in 2017.[39] A far greater quantity of brick, tiles, and worked limestone and schist blocks from its structure must have been encountered in previous excavations, but these were neither documented nor preserved, though some are visible in the exposed profiles that remain from these investigations. All marble elements were carved from local Aphrodisian marble; over half of them were newly carved for this project, as proven by their dimensions, technical execution, and uniformity of select motifs.

Although many blocks were moved in the process of reconstruction efforts supervised by Kenan Erim and during later site maintenance, most are near their original find spots, where they fell. The sequence in which they are presented here follows the order in which they are currently positioned along the south side of the Place of Palms, proceeding westward from the Propylon.[40] First-hand analysis of each block was conducted and full measurements were taken whenever possible (measurements were unavailable for those blocks that have been re-erected, and thus too high to reach, and those that remain partially unexcavated or obscured by subsequent erosion and siltation). A summary of these measurements is provided in Tables 2 and 3 below.

The architectural elements uncovered in the two trenches extending westward from the Propylon are all broadly of the same format and reveal that the South Stoa here (the 'eastern South Stoa') was an Ionic colonnade constructed using newly sculpted architectural elements (Fig. 29). The series of cuttings in the face of the Theatre Hill retaining wall, discussed in Ch. 2 §A and Ch. 3 §B, show that this late antique eastern South Stoa was single-storeyed at least as far as the western end of the Theatre Hill retaining wall (see Fig. 9). It was roofed differently from the earlier South Stoas, however. New holes for downward-sloping rafters were punched into both the ashlar and petit appareil sections of the Theatre wall and corresponding holes for horizontal beams added below these (rows 2 and 4, as discussed in Ch. 2 §A); the earlier recesses built into the western stretch of the Theatre wall were also repurposed as beam holes at this date. Burnt wooden remains were found in these holes when the wall was revealed during excavation in 1984, matching the evidence for the seventh-century destruction of the stoa found within the pool.[41] The rafters probably connected to the beams at their northern end, rather than slotting into the rear of the entablature (and indeed most of the surviving architrave blocks, apparently the sole element of the entablature, have no cuttings in them). The lower order of the eastern South Stoa certainly continued beyond the western end of the Theatre Hill retaining wall, for at least a further 15 columns, but the arrangement of its rear side and its elevation to the west of the Theatre wall—an area that has not been excavated—is uncertain.

To the west, the excavations in front of the Basilica identified a separate stretch of stoa built of reused elements (the 'west-

---

37 See excavation journals: Nbk 76: *NE Nymphaeum / SW Portico of Tiberius* (S. Kulaklı, 1969); Nbk 82–84: *Baths of Hadrian/Portico of Tiberius, Books 1–3* (S. Crawford and J. Gary, 1970); Nbk 85: *Portico of Tiberius: Catalogue of Architectural Finds* (S. Crawford and J. Gary, 1970); Nbk 100–102: *Portico of Tiberius, Books 1–3* (P.F.M. Zahl, 1971); Nbk 134–137: *Portico of Tiberius/'Basilica', 1–4* (P. McDermott, 1972); Nbk 254: *S Agora Gate I-84, Book 2, also containing I-85* (B. Rose and A. Önce, 1984), 177; Nbk 271: *Portico of Tiberius S I; S II* (A. Önce, 1985), 28–29, 30, 32–33, 35 (Finds M41, M49, M55, M65); Nbk 278: *Portico of Tiberius SE I; SW I* (J. Gorence and K. Erim, 1986), 55 (Find M118); Nbk 279: *Portico of Tiberius SE I, Book 2* (K. Erim and J. Gorence, 1986), 12–13, 18; Nbk 577: *BSAg 18.1* (D. Çosar and M. Gronow, 2018): BSAg.18.1.M12-M14, BSAg.18.1.M29, BSAg.18.1.M35-M36, BSAg.18.1.M78, BSAg.18.1.059.M128-M129.

38 Nbk 561: *SAg 15.1 (Field Notebook I)* (A. Kidd et al., 2015), 169, 174 (SAg.15.1.4000.M647, currently remains *in situ* within **4358**). Nbk 567: *SAg 16.1, BkD* (A. Kidd et al., 2016), 53 (SAg.16.1.4293.M768); Nbk 567c: *SAg 16.1 (Field Notebook II)* (A. Kidd et al., 2016), 60, 70; Nbk 574a: *SAg 17.1 (Field Notebook & Binder Data I)* (A. Kidd et al., 2017); Nbk 575a: *SAg 17.1 (Finds Notebook I)* (A. Kidd et al., 2017), SAg.17.1.4440.M1589, SAg.17.1.4440.M1590. For those belonging to the second storey, see nn. 61–66 below.

39 Brick and roof tiles (377 kg), worked stone, and wooden material were recovered from the excavations of the pool in 2017 from **4471** (see Ch. 8 §A). The wooden remains include SAg.17.1.4471.F738 and SAg.17.1.4471.F739. Some burnt wooden timber beam ends were also discovered in 1984 inside the cuttings made into the face of the Theatre Hill retaining wall, where the stoa's second storey and roof would have been attached: Nbk 253: *S Agora Gate I-84, Book 1* (B. Rose), pp. 53, 69–73; Wilson 2019, 215–216.

40 Each architectural member has been given a unique catalogue number according to the geographic location within which it was found and the type of block according to its position within an architectural order, as explained in the Notes to the Reader (pp. XVII–XVIII above).

41 Nbk 253: *S Agora Gate I-84, Book 1* (B. Rose, 1984), 53, 69–73; Wilson 2019, 215–216.

Fig. 29. Reconstructed northern elevation of the late antique South Stoa's Ionic colonnade, east end.

ern South Stoa'). This stoa ran along the front of the Basilica and the row of late antique shops to its east. This western South Stoa was probably single-storeyed in front of the Basilica, but again its precise configuration to the east of this point is uncertain. Although the area between the documented sections of the eastern and western South Stoas remains uncertain, we can make some hypotheses about the arrangement of the structure in this zone. First, since the eastern and western stretches of stoa were aligned with each other in plan, it seems likely that the line of the stoa was continued between them. Between the west corner of the Theatre wall and the north-east corner of the Basilica, however, the stoa must have been built differently, since it had no pre-existing structure behind it for its roof beams to slot in to. One possibility is that the shops east of the Basilica might have continued as far as the Theatre wall and would have provided a suitable support structure for the stoa. An alternative is that the stoa could have fronted a blank wall in its eastern stretch (behind the 15 most westerly preserved columns of the eastern South Stoa) and shops only at its western end. Where the junction occurred between the eastern and western South Stoas is also uncertain; however, given their architectural differences they were probably separated from each other, perhaps by a street entering the Place of Palms from the south. What is likely is that at least part of this central section of stoa had a second storey. As we shall see below, architectural elements of dimensions considerably smaller than the main order of the stoas have been documented across the south-central area of the Place of Palms and provide good evidence for a second storey in at least part of the structure.

Table 2. Dimensions of the South Stoa's Lower Colonnade.

	Bases				Columns			Capitals			Architrave			
	#	W/D	H	Diam	#	Total Shaft H	Up&Lo Diam	#	W/D	H	#	L	Depth	H
East Sector (newly sculpted)	SE1a-10a, SE13a-19a, SC1a-16a, SW1a	0.67–0.74	0.29–0.57	0.60–0.63	SE1-19b, SC1-11b	4.44*	Lo 0.58–0.62 Up 0.46–0.51	SE1a-19a	0.59–0.69	0.18–0.52	SE1d-37d	2.44–2.46	Up 0.56 Lo 0.49	0.33–0.37
West Sector (reused)	SW2a-9a, SW16a-21a	0.71–0.86	0.26–0.39	0.55–0.60	SC12-17b, SW1-4b, SW16-17b, SW20-23b	4.65–5.06*	Lo 0.57–0.62 Up 0.44–0.60	-	-	-	SW38d-41d, SW43d-59d	1.72–2.71	Up 0.48–0.85 Lo 0.46–0.60	0.35–0.57
West Sector (newly sculpted)	SW10a-13a	0.75–0.80	0.39–0.47	0.60	SW5b-7b, SW9b-12b	4.73–5.53*	Lo 0.58–0.67 Up 0.56–0.61	-	-	-	SW42d, SW60d	1.93–2.28	Up 0.60 Lo ----	0.34–0.37

Measurements given in metres. *Explanation of Abbreviations*: H (height); W (width); D (depth); Diam (diameter); L (length); Up (upper); Lo (lower). For those numbers for which only one measurement is given, this is an average. Estimates are indicated by an asterisk *

Table 3. Dimensions of the South Stoa's Upper Colonnade.

	Bases				Columns			Capitals			
	#	W/D	H	Diam	#	Shaft H	Diam	#	W/D	H	LoDiam
Colonnettes	SC1e-2e	0.23–0.30	0.15–0.25	0.23	SC1f-9f	[0.19–0.51] 1.44*–2.48*	0.18–0.31	SC1g-4g	0.16–0.34	0.15–0.26	0.15–0.21
Double Engaged Columns	SC3e-6e	D 0.41–0.68 W 0.29–0.40	0.19–0.25	UpD 0.36–0.57 UpW 0.25–0.30	SC10f	2.40*	L 0.45 W 0.30	SC5g-8g	D 0.47–0.74 W 0.22–0.35*	0.20–0.30	LoD [0.30]–0.44 LoW 0.19–0.23

Partially preserved measurements are indicated by brackets [ ]. The estimated full extent is indicated by an asterisk *

Stylobate

Because of the raising of the ground level in the Place of Palms during the late fifth/early sixth century, the new stylobate of the eastern South Stoa was laid 49–64 cm above the pre-existing ground level and 7 cm above the stylobate of the preceding phase. This is evident at the southeast corner of the Place of Palms, where a sondage conducted in 1991 revealed an earlier phase of the South Stoa, comprising *euthynteria* slabs at its base, followed by a course of four seat blocks and capped by a single remaining stylobate block (Pl. 35.B).[42] These are in turn covered by the late antique make-up layer, within which the foundation of the new stoa is embedded. Portions of this foundation are visible at the east and west ends of the stoa, where it consists of a low rubble wall, bound by a coarse *opus caementicium*. In most cases, this foundation wall supports the stylobate blocks, though at the westernmost end of the western South Stoa the stylobate blocks rest directly on blocks belonging to either the Civil Basilica's paving or a *euthynteria* step leading from the Place of Palms to the Basilica (Pl. 35.C).

As with the late antique version of the North Stoa, these stylobate blocks do not run continuously for the length of the stoas but rather are set in isolation from each other. The gaps between the blocks are filled by the late antique make-up layer, which rises gently from the pool's edge to the top of the stylobate blocks, thereby providing a gradual ramp rather than a step into the stoa's interior.[43] The newly laid stylobate blocks are generally rectangular but have different lengths, widths, and heights, in blue-grey, grey, or cream-coloured marble, indicating that most of these blocks have been recycled from other buildings. For example, although SE1aa–10aa are in blue-grey marble of similar dimensions, their prior use is indicated by their shape, two of which feature the contours of tympanum blocks that are comparable to the missing tympanum blocks from the interior of the Civil Basilica.[44] Other blocks demonstrate an even clearer example of reuse. SC9aa is a cream-coloured mar-

---

42 de Chaisemartin and Lemaire 1996, 157.

43 The height difference of the late antique make-up layer between the pool's edge and the late antique stylobate ranges between 0.21–0.61 m. The difference between the two is inconsistent because, as with the North Stoa, the South Stoa slopes downward as it extends west although the levels of the pool structures remain constant.

44 Stinson 2016, 32.

ble stylobate block that has been taken either from a preceding phase of the South Stoa or from within the North Stoa,[45] while at the western end columns SW15aa–16aa and SW21aa–22aa are founded on blocks that originate from the Basilica, including a relief panel from the Basilica's tympanum screen, and two cornice blocks.[46]

Bases

All 55 bases excavated within the South Stoas are variants of the Attic-Ionic type. The 34 bases belonging to the eastern South Stoa were newly sculpted, as indicated by their style, finishing treatment, and lithotypes in either blue-grey or cream-coloured marble. While the majority follow the standard Attic-Ionic typology found in the North and West Stoas, many feature mouldings that are merely evocative of the norm established in preceding centuries (Pl. 36.A). As with the North and West Stoas, these bases were sculpted with the plinth from the same block. However, here in the eastern South Stoa, all mouldings are set within the parameters of the plinth, with the torus and intermediate astragals reduced to flat bands. The only classicizing element among the group is the scotia, though it exists as hardly more than a one-third round. With regard to size, these bases have similar upper diameters and square proportions for the plinths but vary significantly in their heights.

All visible dowel holes on these bases are circular, measuring 5–8 cm in diameter and 5.5–8 cm deep. Apart from the width, depth, and general height of the plinth, no consistent proportions are maintained among the group, with all elements either elongated or shortened to accommodate the height of the shaft above. While some mouldings are more pillowy than geometric, there is an extreme range in the level of execution. Two anomalies within the group omit all mouldings above the initial torus; it is possible that these two may be unfinished, as their shapes have been roughed out only at the initial stages of the sculpting process. For all others within the group, the uppermost mouldings have been smoothed of most tool marks, though some feature light vertical and horizontal chisel marks. The plinths, however, display much texture resulting from the use of a tooth chisel.

The 21 bases belonging to the western South Stoa comprise a mixture of reused (SW2a–9a, SW16a–21a) and newly carved bases matching those of the east (SW1a, SW10a–13a). Two others are recycled pedestal bases (SW22a–23a). Those that are reused are carved in cream-coloured marble and are stylistically consistent with high-imperial models. The torus and scotia are moulded in one-half rounds, separated from each other by rounded astragals. Except for the pedestal bases, the overall proportions of the group are quite squat. Two stylistic anomalies are noticeable on SW7a and SW9a: SW7a features a hidden recess at the bottom of its plinth whereas SW9a has horizontal striations on its upper torus. Variations in the shape of their dowel holes suggest different construction teams.[47] There is also a level of incompletion and reworking: SW22a–23a are only half-finished, a boss remains on the plinth of SW9a, and many have vertical recesses cut into either both or one of their sides for the insertion of partitions (SW6a, SW7a, SW18a, SW19a).

Columns

The column shafts of the South Stoas all match the same general typology of their counterparts in the West and North Stoas (Pl. 36.B), but are thinner and less smoothly executed. Flutes are confined to the upper portion of the column; some begin and terminate with a simple U-shaped moulding whereas others feature a Π-shaped moulding. The only ornamentation that appears consistently throughout the group is a simple, flat collar at the bottom of the lower shaft.

All shafts belonging to the eastern South Stoa are composed of drums of varying heights in blue-grey or cream-coloured marble, with typically three to four drums fitted together to achieve an approximate height of 4.44 m. The height of the unfluted drums ranges between 1.12 and 1.74 m, the height of the drums in the middle of the shaft is between 1.15 and 1.55 m, and that of the uppermost drums is between 0.78 and 0.99 m. Such height variations demonstrate that shorter blocks were consistently positioned higher up the shaft. An exception within the group is SE16b, whose lower drum measures 3.08 m tall, thereby constituting over two-thirds the overall column height. Although entasis is not applied to these columns, the shafts do taper, with their upper diameter measuring approximately 5/6 their lower diameter, a standard typical of earlier classical Ionic design. Most of the shafts have 20 flutes, though one has 16.[48] The fillets and flutes, which typically begin 1.74 m up the shaft, are broad and flat. Each fillet measures 2 cm wide and each flute is shallow, at 0.5–1.5 cm deep and 5.5–7 cm wide. On eight examples a hole cuts through the fillet, 3.02 and 3.08 m up the shaft, each 2.5 cm in diameter. These are similar to those on the shafts of the North Stoa, made for the insertion of suspension rods, either for hanging garlands, commercial goods sold in stalls and shops within the stoa, or other fittings such as lamps.

The surface finish on these columns matches that of the newly carved bases and architrave blocks, with the texture of the tooth chisel applied over the whole of the shaft. On the unfluted portions, it was applied in vertical strokes to the ends of the drum, at which point the strokes run horizontally across the drum's diameter in a manner that is at times clumsily achieved. Such tool marks suggest that the drums were shaped to this state prior to their erection. As with the bases within the eastern South Stoa, these column drums have circular dowel holes, averaging 4.5 cm in diameter and 5.5 cm deep.

---

45 The depth of this block is 0.99 m, measuring only 0.11 m shorter than several of those documented within the North Stoa.
46 Stinson 2016, 85; Wilson 2018a, 477 fig. 36.8, and 478. Stinson (2016, 84–87) states that the South Stoa was constructed 'almost entirely of spolia.' However, his review of the stoa was limited to the portion immediately adjacent to the Civil Basilica. Most other stylobate blocks of the stoa's west end also appear to be reused elements given their shape and the evidence of prior cuttings and tool marks.
47 SW6a has a square dowel hole (5.5 × 5.5 cm with a depth of 4 cm) whereas SW3a, SW8a–9a, and SW19a–20a have circular dowel holes (averaging 5 × 5 cm with a depth of 4.5 cm).
48 SAg.15.1.4085.M768.

The column shafts from the western South Stoa consist of shafts that have been recycled from multiple other buildings and a few shafts that may have been freshly carved for the late antique stoa. Unlike drums belonging to the eastern part, which were carved predominantly from blue-grey marble, the drums here were carved from cream, white-grey, or grey marble, all of them Aphrodisian. These drums were rarely documented in their findspots during previous excavations, with several found reused in later Byzantine fortifications and Ottoman dwellings.[49] On average, the lower diameter of the unfluted drums is larger than the diameter of the drums to the east, suggesting that the total height of one shaft in the west probably reached 4.65–5.53 m.[50] These shafts were thus higher than those to the east, a factor that may have been compensated by the elimination of column capitals in this area. The flutes here also begin at a lower height than in the east, 1.44–1.64 m up the shaft. The taper of the shafts matches those to the east, with the uppermost diameter measuring 5/6 that of the base, although there are some signs of entasis and the height of each drum is more evenly distributed throughout the shaft.

Beyond these proportional details, the greatest difference between these columns and those to the east is the fluting, which consists of 24 fillets (measuring 1.5 cm wide) and more rounded, deeply carved flutes (2 cm deep, 4.8–7.5 cm wide). Such stylistic and technical characteristics indicate an earlier period of production. Anathyrosis is evident on the bottom and top of five drums, three drums are unfinished, two feature rounded rather than flat apophyges, and another has a flare at its top. With regard to the fluting, only one terminates with a U-shaped moulding whereas another features lunette mouldings within the uppermost flutes. Within the group both square and circular dowels were employed, with one exceptional example featuring three square dowel holes, another featuring one circular and one square dowel hole on either end, and three with no dowel holes. The dowel holes are, for the most part, larger than those of the eastern part of the South Stoa, measuring 5–9.5 cm wide and 6–8 cm deep.

Capitals

Only 13 complete and 6 fragmentary late antique capitals that with certainty belong to this late antique building have been found in the Place of Palms; all come from the eastern South Stoa. They are Ionic and are the most expressive element of the building, described by de Chaisemartin as 'chapiteaux rustiques et décorés de manière fantaisiste' (Pl. 37.A–J and 38.A–I).[51] Capitals of identical craftsmanship have been documented in the post-antique alterations of the *frigidarium* and *tepidarium* of the Hadrianic 'Olympian' Baths, indicating that many of these elements were dispersed throughout the area for later construction works after the stoa had fallen into disuse.[52] It is possible that capitals from the western part may also have been relocated since antiquity. However, it is also possible that the western South Stoa never made use of capitals; the taller columns here would have precluded the use of capitals if the entablatures were to remain at the same height in both the eastern and western sections of the stoa.

The set of capitals belonging to the eastern South Stoa was carved in blue-grey, cream, and white, grey-streaked marble. While the widths and depths of each capital are quite similar, there is a wide range in their heights. At least three of those in cream-coloured marble were carved from recycled blocks (SE1c, SE6c, SE15c), as evidenced by sets of cuttings on either their top or bottom surfaces that predate the carving of the capitals. A deep, circular channel with a central boss appears on the top of SE1c; two offset, perpendicular lewis holes and a setting line on the top of SE6c; a rectangular clamp cutting and two square dowel holes on the bottom and part of the front of SE15 (Pl. 39.A). The overall size of SE15c and the additional square dowel holes match that of the bases for the columns of the North Stoa.[53] It is therefore probable that at least this capital was carved from a column base, perhaps belonging to a former phase of the South Stoa.

Stylistically, the capitals may be dated to the late fifth century.[54] Unlike the Ionic capitals of the North Stoa, the depth of their moulding is significantly reduced, retaining much of the shape and density of the rectangular blocks from which they were sculpted. As with other late antique examples at Aphrodisias and elsewhere in Asia Minor, such as those of the Tetrapylon Street and those documented at Ephesos in the city's agora and the Church of St. John, much of the volume of the echinus, bolster, and neck of each capital is bound to the overall mass of the block, resulting in a thick and bulky form.[55] The capitals thus align well with John Herrmann's observations on late antique Ionic capitals in Asia Minor as being bold, powerfully articulated, and simple.[56] Although stylistically coherent, the ensemble nevertheless forms a highly individualized group whose variations in detail recall the effect of spoliated elements. Their uniformity is achieved through the application of a limited set of stylistically similar motifs on the constituent parts of each capital. However, no two capitals are alike; motifs are distributed among the group with no perceivable regularity. In several instances, the decorative scheme of a single capital varies between each face. Even when these motifs are replicated, the evidence suggests that individuals tasked with the carving of this group had varying levels of skill. Six capitals were left unfinished, most with the bolster incomplete. This diversification among the group demonstrates that a number of sculptors

---

49 Nbk 278: *Portico of Tiberius SE I; SW I* (J. Gorence and K. Erim, 1986), p. 75. Many of these currently remain *in situ* in the south-central sector of the urban park.
50 An estimate determined by using the Vitruvian ratio of 8 1/6: 1 for the height to the unfluted drums' lower diameter.
51 de Chaisemartin 1989a, 65. For a full review of the capitals, see Kidd 2018.
52 McDavid 2016, 216.
53 The average dimensions for a column base from the North Stoa and its dowel hole cuttings are as follows: H: 34.6, Diam.: 81.4; distance from outer edges of square dowel holes: 47.1; dowel holes: 6.7 × 6.2, D: 6.1. The comparative dimensions for SE15c are as follows: H: 31.5, D: 61.4, Diam.: 50.6; distance from outer edges of square dowel holes: 45.2; dowel holes: 7.5 × 6.2, D: 4.1; 5.5 × 6, D: 4.1.
54 See Kidd 2018 for a comprehensive analysis and catalogue of these capitals.
55 Herrmann 1988, 18, Figs. 163, 333.
56 Herrmann 1988, 148–152.

were involved and that they were permitted a range of flexibility in their interpretation and execution of the overall decorative scheme.

The most consistent features of the group are the abacus and volutes. The abacus is undecorated and square in shape, averaging 60 cm wide and deep and 5 cm tall. In most examples it extends slightly beyond the full length of the bolster and reaches the same width as the volutes along each face. In all examples, the volutes were carved in flat, shallow relief, turning three or four times before reaching the eye and varying only in that they may be either regularly or irregularly spaced as they turn.

Four distinct motifs were carved on the echinus. The egg and dart pattern is predominant, with two or three eggs set below a fillet, upward-pointing darts, and a basic bead and reel pattern below. Vaguely resembling the egg and dart is the motif of *godrons taillés* and dart, in which three *godrons* span the width of the echinus and two small, upward-pointing darts fill the two void spaces below, both of which are positioned above a bead pattern. Two capitals feature a six-petalled rosette set within a circle. On one the motif is flanked by laurels and bordered to the bottom by a broad band, while that on another is flanked by upward-pointing unfinished darts. The single anomaly of the group is SE14c (Pl. 38.C), which features a meticulously crafted egg and dart with deeply carved and fully rounded eggs alternating with downward-pointing darts. The capital's other side features two four-leafed plants that spring from a single stem toward each volute. This example exhibits refined balance and precision, and its style is compatible with other sixth-century examples, particularly in the rigidity of the vegetal pattern and in the shallow ovolo moulding of the echinus.[57]

The bolster, cylindrical in shape and bowing slightly at its centre, is largely engaged with the core of the capital. Its decorative details maintain the least diversity and greatest precision among the group. Perhaps as a consequence of such exactitude, the bolster is often left unfinished. A majority display an overlapping scale-like leaf pattern, accompanied by a simple, undecorated double- or triple-banded astragal for its balteus. Three examples have a concave leaf pattern, in which single leaves are positioned within four vertical registers that wrap around the bolsters, each separated by a simple band moulding and a double-banded astragal as the balteus. The one exception again is SE14c. Its bolsters, which have greater bowing and levity than the others, feature a leaf motif arranged in overlapping bands that grow larger as they extend toward the volutes.

Entablature

The only surviving elements belonging to the stoa's entablature are architrave blocks; no cornice or frieze blocks have been found among the excavated materials and it is not clear that the late antique South Stoas ever incorporated these elements.

The architrave blocks belonging to the eastern South Stoa are simple and straightforward in design (Pl. 39.B). Carved from blue-grey and cream marble, they feature three plain fasciae on one face and an undecorated soffit. For those that are unbroken, the length of the architrave block matches precisely the colonnade's interaxial intercolumniation. Most examples have no clamp, dowel, or lewis holes. However, one example has cuttings for four clamps and a lewis hole while another has a large cutting on its back, possibly for the insertion of a beam. Because such cuttings are found on only two blocks, it is probable that they were not made for the construction of the late antique South Stoa but rather evidence the blocks' prior use. The tooth chisel was applied over the whole of the architrave's surface except for the top, which remained rough and unfinished.

The architrave blocks of the western South Stoa consist of both newly carved and reused architrave blocks in blue-grey, cream, and white-grey marble. The six that were newly carved match the same style as those to the east, although their dimensions are less consistent and they feature a simple soffit pattern. The remaining blocks are of varying quality, style, and type. Some of the larger blocks are carved on both sides, featuring an elaborate design on one face consisting of bead and reel, egg and dart, and anthemion mouldings surmounted by a rinceaux frieze and displaying an overlapping leaf pattern on the soffit. Others that are carved on both sides feature a plain, crisp design and have no upper frieze; one of these bears an inscription dated to the second century AD,[58] while another is inscribed with a text, 'Νείκη Σεβαστῶν', with letter-forms datable to the late first century AD (see Appendix 1, In3). Of those that are carved on only one face, three have no fascia mouldings, and one of these features a schematic, overlapping leaf pattern on its soffit. In stark contrast to those to the east, five blocks have beam holes carved at the back measuring 13–19 cm wide and 18–31 cm deep.

Considering these stylistic and technical details, those blocks featuring the rinceaux motif and the inscriptions probably derived from the Civil Basilica, whereas those others that are more straightforward in design were probably taken from a building close by that had been renovated after the Severan period but which collapsed in the late fifth century, perhaps part of the Hadrianic 'Olympian' Baths to the west, or the earlier phase of the South Stoa that stood against the Theatre Hill.[59] As dis-

---

57 The closest parallels may be found on the echinus of Ionic capitals from the Church of St John in Ephesos (Justinianic) and from Hagia Eirene in Istanbul (*c.* AD 548) as well as on the bolster and impost of Ionic impost capitals from the palaestra within the Bath-Gymnasium Complex at Sardis (late fifth / early sixth century) and from Basilica A at Nea-Anchialos (second quarter of the sixth century). Among these, that at Aphrodisias is probably the earliest known example.

58 *IAph2007* 4.3.
59 The epigraphic and archaeological record attests that a series of renovations were made to the baths in late antiquity, some of this precipitated by earthquake damage to the building (Wilson 2016a, 192–193; 2018a, 481–483; 2019, 201–202; McDavid 2016: 215–217, 220–224). The reduction of the building's overall size following the collapse of its western part, probably due to the same earthquake that prompted the reconstruction of the Place of Palms (Wilson 2018a, 476–479; 2019, 201–202), no doubt rendered available many architectural blocks for the construction of the South Stoa.

cussed in Ch. 3, there may have been renovations to the South Stoa following a mid-fourth-century AD earthquake.[60] If these simpler architrave blocks derived from that work, they would be the only known architectural evidence from that phase.

Postulated second-storey scheme

Although the cuttings in the Theatre Hill retaining wall suggest that the eastern South Stoa, like its predecessors, was single-storeyed in this area, additional, smaller architectural finds suggest that at least one part of the late antique stoas in this area had two storeys—apparently the section in front of the vaults on the side of the Theatre Hill. These elements were found in the central sector of the south side of the Place of Palms or nearby within the pool (Fig. 30).

In general, these blocks are more heavily damaged than the blocks belonging to the first storey, further suggesting that they fell from a much higher level. They include colonnettes in white and blue-grey marble as well as in granite and double-engaged columns in cream and grey-speckled marble. Fragments belonging to the colonnettes consist of nine shaft fragments,[61] four Corinthian or fluted capitals,[62] and two bases.[63] Those belonging to the double-engaged columns are four bases,[64] one column,[65] and four fluted capitals, one of which features a cross embedded within the flutes.[66] Two consoles matching the proportions of the colonnettes have also been found along the south side of the Place of Palms, one of which has an egg and dart motif on its abacus that precisely matches the style of the same feature on the capitals of the lower storey.

Apart from the consoles, the variety of types, sizes, styles, and technical execution within the group suggests that these elements had been reused from other buildings. Even so, their sculpting technique and design indicate a late antique date; their mouldings are shallow and broad with much of the modelling of the rigid forms achieved by a freehand approach with no sign of drilling, characteristics that are broadly indicative of local styles in western Asia Minor from the mid-fourth to fifth centuries.[67] Together, the group would have resulted in a row of at least 13 columns, with one double-engaged column alternat-

60 See Ch. 3 §B.
61 Six were found during previous excavations, two in 2016 (SAg.16.1.4293.M1281, SAg.16.1.4360.M1332), and one remains *in situ* (in **4358**).
62 Three were revealed during previous excavations, the other in 2016 (SAg.16.1.4277.M973).
63 One was found during previous excavations, the other in 2015 (SAg.15.1.4182.M860).
64 Two were found during previous excavations, the other two in 2013 and 2015/2016 (SAg 13.1.3013.M50, SAg.15.1.4182.M856/SAg.16.1.4134.M895).
65 This is embedded *in situ* near the Civil Basilica.
66 All four were recovered during previous excavations.
67 For comparison, see Peschlow 1998 (especially evidence from the 'Bishop's Church' at Limyra, Taf. 18.3,4) and Niewöhner 2007 for a comprehensive analysis of local styles in the architectural ornamentation of Lycia and Phrygia. Pensabene 1973 dates similar pieces found in Ostia (especially Cat. 657 and Cat. 661) to the early fourth century, but these are without provenance.

ing for every three colonnettes. Given that there are no known entablature elements belonging to this upper storey, it is probable these columns supported an arcade, presumably in brick.

Discussion

The construction of the late antique South Stoas was contemporary with the refurbishment of the Place of Palms by Ampelios and the rebuilding works by Doulkitios. As discussed more fully below (§L), these interventions were probably a response to a major seismic event.[68] While the North Stoa seems to have largely survived this disaster, albeit not unscathed, the south side of the Place of Palms was badly hit. The pool was particularly damaged along its southern side judging from the extent of repairs to it (see §B). The fact that some of the blocks used to repair it include an architrave and a column in cream-coloured marble, which probably come from the second-phase South Stoa, also suggests that this structure was brought down by the earthquake.

While the second-phase South Stoa had probably terminated at the end of the Theatre Hill retaining wall, in this late antique phase the full southern extent of the urban park was furnished with colonnades; this effectively obscured from view the ruins of the Basilica, which was never rebuilt after its destruction in the late fifth century.[69] Even if a number of blocks had survived from the earlier stoa and could be redeployed for use in the new one, the creation of a new colonnade along the western part of the south side of the Place of Palms necessitated additional materials. As discussed above, the architectural elements of the preserved eastern and western stoas had similar proportions, but the eastern one comprised newly sculpted materials, and the western largely reused elements. The two stretches of stoa, therefore, were broadly unified, at least in the appearance of their columns, in the treatment of their stylobate and adherence to a general module. Had it run uninterrupted for the full length of the south side of the Place of Palms, the lower storey would have comprised an estimated 82 fluted columns, judging from the exposed bases and stylobate blocks.[70] The true figure should be somewhat lower, perhaps 80, if the two stoas were separated by a street.

That the South Stoas have several more columns than their counterpart to the north is due in part to the size of their columns, whose diameter is approximately four-fifths of those of the North Stoa. This proportional reduction also permits a tighter interaxial columnar distance within the South Stoas, which averages 2.45 m in the eastern South Stoa and 2.58 m in the

68 See below, Ch. 4 §L, and Wilson 2016b, 108, 124, 134; 2018a.
69 Using ceramic evidence from the Basilica excavations, Stinson (2016, 85–86, 90) dates the first signs of dilapidation of the basilica to the fifth century AD. Wilson 2018a, 478 connects the abandonment of the basilica with the late fifth-century earthquake that prompted large-scale rebuilding across the city.
70 Crema 1939, 291 reconstructed 86 columns along the length of the south side, assuming that the central portion was not adorned with a stoa.

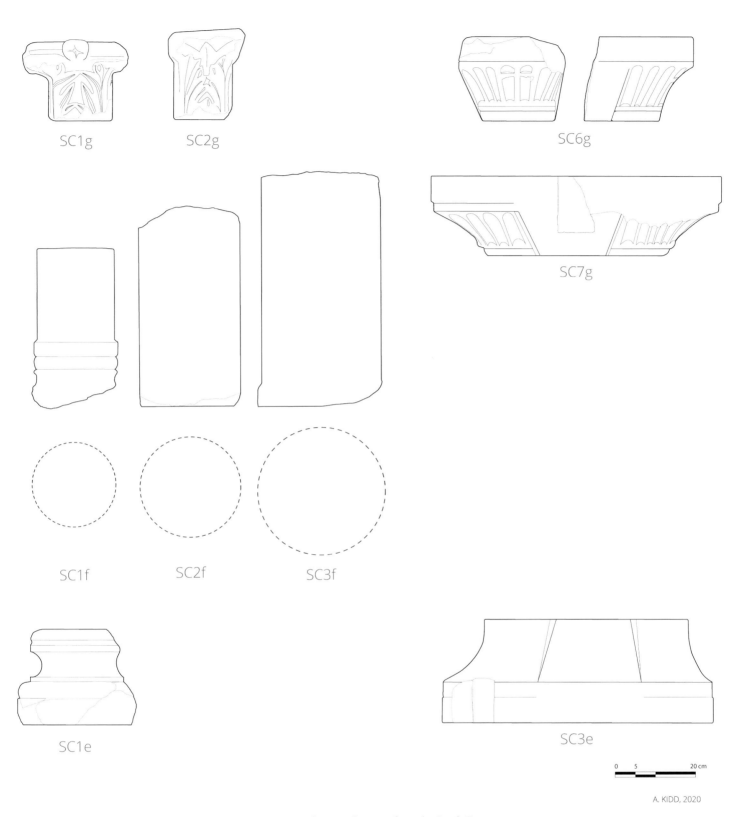

Fig. 30. Second-storey elements from the South Stoas.

western South Stoa.[71] The sole exception is between SE5b and SE6b, where a wider space of 3.86 m was maintained for continued access to the staircase leading up to the Theatre, which was still in use at this time and may also have hosted events in conjunction with the Maiouma festival (§M below).[72] The total order of this lower storey reached approximately 5.87 m in height, 0.28 m lower than the North Stoa. To match this height in both stoa sections, the heights of each architectural element (bases, drums, capitals) were varied as needed. In the western South Stoa, capitals seem to have been eliminated altogether.

Overall, the proportions of the Ionic order in the eastern South Stoa are slender when compared to established designs in Roman Asia Minor, a feature that is exaggerated by the absence of entasis on the column shafts. A module based on the lower diameter of the columns guided some aspects of the order even though there is a degree of internal flexibility among its constituent elements. In the eastern South Stoa, the ratio of the lower diameter to the combined height of each base, shaft, and capital is approximately 9:1, and to the average interaxial intercolumniation of the colonnade 4:1. While the lower diameter is slightly less than twice the height of the architrave, this measurement usually corresponds to the width and depth of the abacus of the capitals. Nine of the capitals maintain some internal coherence with common proportional standards. In such instances, the ratio of the abacus height to echinus height is approximately 1:3. The shape of the abacus also appears to guide the height of the capital from the bottom of the volute to the top of the abacus to a certain degree. Unlike the Vitruvian standard, which sees the height of the capital equal 1/2 the depth of the abacus, these capitals feature a set of proportions where this height ranges from approximately 1/3 the depth of the abacus to 2/5 the depth of the abacus. No further proportional logic can be identified among the group. This suggests that while a paradigm may have guided sculptors in their execution of each block, craftsmen were not strictly held to this model nor were they bound to follow the formulae that once governed the proportions of the Ionic order. In the western South Stoa, recycled blocks of similar styles and dimensions were hand-picked from different buildings, dating to different periods, to compose a colonnade that maintained a metrological standard that roughly matched that of the east. A few rudimentary bases, column shafts, and architrave blocks were freshly carved to supplement the arrangement.

A similar procedure of selection was applied in the second-storey, which comprised reused elements that were arranged to create a coordinated whole, not unlike the way in which various elements were redeployed in the construction of the fifth-century Northeast Street Stoa at Aizanoi.[73] Although no full column shaft is preserved, the height of the total order for both the colonnettes and double-engaged columns would have been at most approximately 2.80 m.[74] Unlike earlier second-storey schemes in the hellenistic East as well as near-contemporary examples such as the narthex and transept of the Church of St John at Ephesos, whose heights were typically between 2/3 and 4/5 that of the lower order,[75] the height of the upper order from the South Stoa was much smaller, measuring a little over 1/2 the height of the lower order. Despite the small scale of the colonnettes, the second storey would have been strengthened by the addition of the thick double-engaged columns.

For the newly sculpted eastern South Stoa, similarities in the modular system, style, and technical execution of various elements confirm that this was a single commission, executed either by one workshop or a group of workshops under a single contractor, which worked within a pre-determined set of parameters and were thus responsible for the execution of either a single order within the colonnade, from base to capital, or specific tasks within the order, such as the fluting, the bolsters, or the echinus. The application and execution of motifs among the capitals of the group represent a range of styles and models implemented by many different carvers, some of whom may not have been comfortable with, or competent in, the sculpting of architectural ornamentation. Even so, the consistent application of the tooth chisel across the whole surface of all elements as well as the presence of circular dowel holes, all of similar dimensions, verify that a uniform system of techniques was applied by the craftsmen.

The indiscriminate use of cream, white-grey, and blue-grey marble throughout the colonnade indicates that these elements were sourced from a selection of different marble blocks that were readily available at the time. The wholesale elimination of the frieze and cornice may further attest to a limitation in the availability of resources. Given that many, if not all, elements in cream-coloured marble seem to have been carved from recycled blocks, it is plausible that damaged blocks from the former South Stoa may have supplied marble for the project. SE15c, as discussed above, seems to have been carved from a pre-existing base. Other cream-coloured capitals, even the tallest at 51.8 cm (SE5c), fit well within the depth of an architrave block, such as the broken example found reused as a seat in the pool walls,[76] and could have thus been carved from similarly broken fragments. Likewise, the cream-coloured column drums

---

71 de Chaisemartin and Lemaire 1996, 157 note that the intercolumniation in the western sector of the stoa varies widely, ranging between 2.35–2.79 m. The present study has found an even greater degree of variation, with extremes as low as 2.12 m and as high as 3.14 m in this area. Excavation records from the east and west ends of the South Stoa demonstrate that the column bases here were displaced in a major destruction event and during subsequent reuse, at times quite drastically. Considering that these areas were subject to reconstruction and anastylosis work by K. T. Erim's team the original spacing of the columns here is not easily calculated. The south-central section of the eastern South Stoa, however, remained relatively untouched and so provides the best evidence for the position of the columns *in situ*; here the intercolumniation is most consistent, ranging between 2.40–2.45 m. Since most of the columns of the western South Stoa were moved around and have been re-erected, the calculation of 2.58 m given above for this stretch of the stoa is based on the intercolumniations of just the four easternmost columns, which seem not to have been moved.

72 For more on the Maiouma and its setting in the urban park, see section §M below and Wilson 2016b, 132–135. For a broader discussion of the festival and its connection with both water features and theatre during the late antique period, see Weiss 2014, 139–140, 233.

73 Rheidt 1995, 700–705.

74 An estimate derived by taking the average diameter of the colonnette bases and the width of the double column bases.

75 Coulton 1976, 130–131; measurements for the Church of St John taken from Hörmann 1951, 129–164.

76 See above, §B.

of the late antique stoa could have been carved from columns of the former stoa; considering their average lower diameter of approximately 60 cm, these could easily have been cut down from columns of similar dimensions to those of the North Stoa (which had a lower diameter of 66 cm), particularly ones that sustained damage only to their fluting. In addition to the ruined stoa, the adjacent Basilica by this time lay partly in ruins and could have served as an on-site quarry for both the western and eastern South Stoas.[77]

The use of recycled blocks in the restoration of the monumental pool and seat blocks that might come from the Bouleuterion in the patching up of the North Stoa[78] confirms that reuse was deemed an acceptable, cost-efficient solution within the larger restoration project. This prevalence of reuse and recycling should not be deemed as a negative characteristic of the Place of Palms restoration project—such practices were typical even of contemporary projects that received imperial funding, such as the Church of St John at Ephesos, where several Ionic impost capitals were carved from an earlier Ionic frieze block and large column drums. Beyond the redeployment of architectural blocks, the South Stoas' evidence also suggests that the blocks in blue-grey marble had been freshly quarried. Especially with regard to the architrave blocks and the column drums, the blocks in blue-grey marble are much more uniform in their dimensions and sculptural execution. This parallels the use of blue-grey marble in other repair work undertaken in the Place of Palms, where blue marble slabs were extensively used to replace the white marble slabs that originally lined the inner ledge of the pool walls along its south side, as well as the widespread use of blue-grey marble paving slabs within the South and West Stoas.[79]

While direct reuse was deemed appropriate in the construction of the western South Stoa and within the second storey, a much more elaborate effort was desired for the eastern South Stoa adjacent to the theatre. Such variations in design between the two stoas suggest that two or more patrons were responsible for the completion of the different stoas, each working under the umbrella of the area's larger restoration project. A dedicatory inscription on an architrave block from the western South Stoa provides epigraphic evidence for the cooperative funding of the stoa (Appendix 1, In9). The text reads: † Φίλιππος Ἡροδιαν(οῦ) ὁ θαυμ(ασιώτατος) εὐχαριστῶν τῇ οἰκίᾳ πατρίδι τὰ βʹ διάχορα ἐσκέπασεν, '† Philippos, son of Herodian, *admirandissimus*, returning thanks to his own fatherland, covered the two sections.'[80] The implication is clearly that some other body or bodies paid for the elements of the stoa below the roof.

Although this text has previously been taken to mean that Philippos roofed only two intercolumniations, this seems a small intervention, and in fact 'διάχορα' need not indicate intercolumniation, since the term is rarely attested and has broad meaning; it could signify that he roofed both sections of the stoas, east and west, or possibly that he roofed the two-storey section of the stoa. On the basis of prosopography and letter-forms, Rouché used this inscription to date the stoa's construction to the late fifth century AD. The simple face moulding of the architrave block, with two fasciae and a simple canted upper moulding, indicates that this was a new element created in late antiquity, and indeed this form is found all along the remaining length of the South Stoas' entablature. Notably, this is the only architrave block from the South Stoa bearing an inscription contemporary with its late antique construction. Considering the block's findspot, a highly visible location near where the eastern and western stoas would have met, perhaps where a street would have entered the Place of Palms, it is possible that the 'two sections' mentioned in the text refer more broadly to the eastern and western South Stoas. It is tempting to wonder whether, just as Albinos contributed paving slabs for the West Stoa from his own quarries or workshop, Philippos might have owned a tile factory or timber yards from which he contributed roofing materials.[81]

However the Philippos inscription is interpreted, it is clear that the project was a joint initiative. A series of 28 inscriptions on both newly carved and directly re-used elements, placed on the upper and/or lower surfaces of 21 column drums and the upper surface of six bases (see Ch. 5 §E),[82] indicates that many of the stoas' materials had been sourced from, or produced by, many of the same individuals. These inscriptions consist of either a single letter (see Pl. 54.L), a combination of two to three letters, or more elaborate block monograms with names given in the genitive, ranging between 5 and 12.5 cm in height. A *beta* occurs with the most frequency, nine times on five columns and three bases. The block monograms, which occur on four column drums and one base from the eastern South Stoa, can be dated stylistically to the late fifth/early sixth century, further corroborating Rouché's dating of the stoa. They feature the name of an individual, Ἀναστάσιος (occurring once, SS24, see Ch. 5 §E; Pl. 54.C) and probably a title, ὕπαρχος (four times, SS15, SS17, SS20, SS22, see Ch. 5 §E; Pl. 54.D–E).[83]

Accepting that a few of these marks may be masons' marks that remained on reused elements within the South Stoas, the selection of letters overall is too homogenous to have provided the builders with an accurate indication of a block's placement within the colonnade. Their placement on areas of the blocks that had already been dressed further suggests that these cannot be *notae lapicidinarum*. Rather, they are similar to marks recorded on paving slabs within the West Stoa and the Tetrastoon, where abbreviated names and individual letters mark ownership or donation of the block, or the workshop of manufacture.[84] As

---

77 Stinson's analysis of the basilica's interior colonnade demonstrates that the basilica had been heavily robbed of its building materials; while the building would have once featured 74 Ionic columns, only seven have been recovered (Stinson 2016, 34). Some smaller blocks from the building, such as fragments of the Price Edict and a figural relief panel, were incorporated into the conversion of the Cathedral of St Michael around the same time as the construction of the South Stoa (Stinson 2016, 86).
78 See above, Ch. 4 §E.
79 See above, Ch. 4 §B.
80 *ALA* 108–9, doc. 66, pl. 17. Appendix 1, In9, with corresponding numbers SS20, SS17, and SS15 respectively.
81 Appendix 1, In9. See also *ALA* 108 f.
82 There are probably more of these marks, but the re-erection of a majority of the blocks in the stoa's eastern portion prohibit a view of their tops and bottoms.
83 See also Chaniotis 2015a, 11.
84 See Chaniotis 2015a, 8–11.

such, the letters and monograms appear to denote the names of patrons or contractors who had purchased the blocks on behalf of patrons or the workshops that repurposed them for this new construction. They are revealing of a highly organized system of municipal management akin to that which is attested in contemporary Rome, Hierapolis, and even in other building projects at Aphrodisias,[85] as they indicate that blocks from dilapidated buildings were available for purchase, rather than for free use, and were then marked to denote their transferral of ownership before being recycled.

The monograms in particular are important. Although the name Anastasius is also attested twice at Aphrodisias on architraves in the late fifth-/early sixth-century conversion of the Temple of Aphrodite into the cathedral Church of St Michael as that of a wealthy donor,[86] the Anastasius monogram is a precise visual match with the monogram of the emperor Anastasius (r. AD 491–518) as found on his pre-reform coinage,[87] and as such appears to indicate some level of imperial involvement in the project (see Appendix 2, SS24). (Conceivably the Anastasius mentioned in the inscription from the Church of St Michael might be the emperor rather than a local donor, as hitherto assumed.) Another monogram that appears on three columns and one base of the South Stoa (SCWTh14, SCWTh17, SCWTh18, SC10a) may be resolved as ὑπάρχου and is similar to monograms of *praefecti praetorio per Orientem* of this period.[88] One can see that any imperial funds for post-earthquake reconstruction would have been channelled through the governor, Doulkitios, and perhaps even obtained at his request. This is thus a hint that the eastern South Stoa might have been included in the works falling under Doulkitios' reconstruction of the *temenos* of the nymphs (above, §A), whether or not one takes *temenos* in the strictly narrow sense of enclosure, or as referring to the place as a whole.

To what extent the availability of funds or materials, or a combination thereof, guided patrons' decisions and thus resulted in different treatments of the eastern and western South Stoas, remains to be determined. Considering the limited evidence for the use of freshly quarried or carved marble in the city's urban building projects after AD 300 compared to earlier imperial periods,[89] it is probable that the project would have incurred a great cost. It is thus noteworthy that time and funds were allocated for the carving and re-carving of blocks for large portions of the building. The recycling of blocks from neighbouring dilapidated buildings for use within the two stoas would have been a cost-effective solution, and we find that even

in the realization of the newly sculpted architecture measures were taken to keep costs low. There is little volumetric rendering of the sculpted blocks, which retain much of their original dense, rectangular shape, and the moulded depth of the ornamentation is shallow. Such technical alterations helped reduce the project's costs in terms of the amount of materials used and time spent carving, not to mention the skill required for the task.[90] They may also explain why the selection and execution of ornamental motifs varied to such a degree among the Ionic capitals, why certain details from the classical canon were omitted, and why the heights of blocks varied to such a degree within the order. Costs were mitigated by the flexible homogeneity of the project, facilitated by the work of different carvers with varying levels of proficiency, with some demonstrating a high degree of artistic production and others quite rudimentary in skill.[91] While it has already been established that Aphrodisias maintained its sculptural workshops well into the late antique period,[92] this considerable range in artistic production suggests that the city struggled to provide sufficient training for the number of craftsmen needed for a project of this magnitude, perhaps a consequence of fewer opportunities for construction work in the preceding century, or simply of the scale of city-wide reconstruction for which we argue in §L below. Even with the diverse skills of artisans, many of the capitals and bases were put in place at varying levels of incompletion, suggesting that the project proceeded with a certain rapidity or indifference, or a combination thereof.

While quarrying activity was reduced in late antiquity,[93] its continued operation nevertheless made new monumental architecture possible and offered patrons and artisans the freedom of aesthetic choice in new construction projects. Typically the Corinthian order, impost capitals, and brick arcades were predominant among other fifth- and sixth-century building projects of the Mediterranean East.[94] And, apart from Near Eastern sites like Apamea and Skythopolis, newly constructed buildings of late antiquity increasingly utilised unfluted monolithic columns no taller than 3.5 m.[95] Therefore, the design at Aphrodisias *ex novo* of an Ionic colonnade comprising 4.44 m fluted columns and a marble architrave demonstrates a prevailing local loyalty to classical traditions.[96] It specifically alludes to Aphrodisias' past legacy by recalling elements of the Ionic order as it appeared on

---

85 Chaniotis 2008b, 68; Pensabene 2017, 185–186, 194; Marsili 2019, 114–116. See also legal regulations outlined in the *Codex Theodosianus* (15, 1, 10 and 15, 1, 36).

86 *ALA*, doc. 94 and 95.

87 This monogram appears on the reverses of copper *nummi* minted at Constantinople between AD 491 and 498 (Bellinger 1966, 15.1 and 28).

88 See Appendix 2, SS15, SS17, SS20, and SS22.

89 See Smith 1999a, 157–159, Ratté 2001, and Dalgıç and Sokolicek 2017, table 23.1. While Aphrodisias saw an intensive period of city-wide building activity around the turn of the fifth to sixth centuries AD (§L below), most of these projects involved the post-earthquake maintenance, restoration, and embellishment of existing structures, thereby minimising the quantities needed of newly carved marble.

90 Herrmann 1988, 160.

91 Jacobs 2013, 447–449 connects the deterioration of skilled sculpting with the unemployment, and subsequent shortage, of stone carvers and other skilled artisans from the third century onwards, as suggested by *Cod. Theod.* 13, 4, 2, *Cod. Theod.* 13, 4, 4, and *Cod Theod.* 13, 4, 3. Even so, sculptors were probably more plentiful in the fifth and sixth centuries than they were in the later third and fourth centuries.

92 Smith 1999a.

93 For continued use of the local quarries of Aphrodisias during the fifth century, see Long 2012, 188, 192–193 and Russell 2013, 266.

94 Jacobs 2013, 170–171, 182–184.

95 Jacobs 2013, 168.

96 Most colonnaded public spaces in the late antique East featured the Corinthian order, which had been established as the predominant order as early as the early–middle imperial period. It was during the fifth century onward that the impost capital gained popularity in colonnaded streets and plazas. For more, see Jacobs 2013, 170–172.

other civic monuments.[97] The most prominent references are the three-banded fascia on the architrave, the half-fluted columns, and the egg-and-dart motif and the scale-like leaf pattern on the capitals. Whereas most of these elements are ubiquitous among the earlier architecture within the Place of Palms, the scale-like leaf pattern on the Ionic capitals is thought to have appeared for the first time in Asia Minor on several capitals belonging to the Temple of Aphrodite at Aphrodisias.[98] Its use in the South Stoa may reference this building, which was around the same time being converted into the Church of St Michael. The motif also duplicates the garland that decorates the friezes belonging to the North and West Stoas, and the Propylon.

These ties to established styles, however, should not be mistaken for staunch conservatism. They were not simply copied from earlier monuments but were integrated with newly-introduced designs. The columns of the eastern South Stoa were more slender and the diversity of the capitals' motifs, which introduce upward-pointing darts, rosettes, *godrons*, and splayed acanthus leaves to the traditional egg-and-dart canon, lend the stoa a robust heterogeneity.[99] The stoa's variety and innovation were further amplified in the second-storey section, where alternating orders and coloured marbles were probably coordinated within a brick arcade. These variegated elements are visually striking in their contrast with each other, especially when compared with the relatively homogeneous assemblage of the Ionic column shafts, bases, and architraves of the first storey. Though to a much lesser degree, the same visual juxtaposition is illustrated in the pre-existing architecture of the Place of Palms. During the Tiberian period, the entire length of the North Stoa was decorated with a frieze of masks and garlands that was so varied that no two reliefs were alike.[100] An additional mask and garland frieze was extended to the east during the second century AD with the erection of the Propylon. The many alterations made to these buildings over time added further diversity. The North Stoa underwent at least one stage of repairs before AD 500 and thus contained two different iterations of the Ionic capital.[101] Such evidence seems to disprove the traditional view that heterogeneity, or *varietas*, was a 'central [aesthetic] concept of late antiquity and the Middle Ages.'[102] Rather, the heterogeneity of the South Stoas' late antique design augments and redefines the same *varietas* that had already existed in this space, thereby modernising the southern vista of the Place of Palms with a vibrant visual display.

The manner in which traditional and novel approaches were seamlessly interwoven in the eastern South Stoa's architectural design befitted the edifice's new late antique setting.[103] This quotation of established decorative motifs in new designs can be identified elsewhere, such as in the Bath-Gymnasium Complex at Sardis, which displayed the newly carved Ionic impost capitals featuring a distinctly local and traditional 'open and closed palmette' motif, or along the southern extension of the Cardo at Jerusalem, where the new addition was fitted with Corinthian capitals to match the structure's pre-existing design but the format was updated with more geometric mouldings and Latin crosses added to the abacus' central boss.[104] What is more, the application of one of the oldest architectural orders of the Greco-Roman world among the stoa's newly sculpted elements on such a monumental scale was an expression comparable to few other contemporary works; the closest parallel may be Skythopolis' Palladius Street.[105] That the South Stoas may be compared to these examples, many from much larger cities that enjoyed imperial benefaction, is revealing of the resources that Aphrodisias could mobilise even in late antiquity. Urban display was clearly considered a worthwhile investment in a city that had by this date become the capital of the new province of Karia. Within the larger restoration project of the Place of Palms, Doulkitios, as governor of Karia, and Ampelios, as *pater tēs poleōs*, were no doubt influential if not directly involved in the construction of the eastern South Stoa, and perhaps also the western one, in order to ensure that the city of Aphrodisias was visually worthy of its regional pre-eminence.

G. LATE ROMAN COINS FROM THE PLACE OF PALMS (ATT & HK)

Among the coin finds from the Place of Palms, 183 coins are from the late Roman period, from Tetrarchic issues to the early fifth century AD (cat. nos. 52–234). Ninety-five of these can be attributed to the late Roman period only by their formats (thin and small flans, diameter and weight). Some are corroded beyond recognition by the waterlogged conditions in the area, but many were worn, clipped (for example cat. no. 82), badly struck or have blank unstruck flans/disks.[106] One lead disk of 10/12 mm (cat. no. 139) was also recorded, which probably also passed as a coin.[107]

As the recent excavations in the Place of Palms uncovered surfaces and layers belonging especially to the late fifth century AD, most of our finds are from these decades, providing a good insight into the coins in circulation at the time. Eighty-six per cent of the dated late Roman coin finds are those minted after

---

97 Smith 1999a notes this penchant for conservatism also in the production of statuary in late antique Aphrodisias.
98 Bingöl 1980, 90, Cat. 28, 34–36.
99 For more, see Kidd 2018.
100 Jacopi 1939; de Chaisemartin 1989b, 36–41; de Chaisemartin and Lemaire 1996, 161–164.
101 See Ch. 3 §E; Crema 1939, 216–220; Waelkens 1987.
102 Brenk 1987, 105; Onians 1988, 60–69; Saradi-Mendelovici 1990, 52–53; Lindros Wohl 2001, 92–98; Hansen 2001, 76–80; Coates-Stephens 2003, 343.
103 For variety in reused elements in late antique colonnaded streets, see Jacobs and Waelkens 2013, 249; also Jacobs 2013, 136–145 for a comprehensive overview of colonnaded streets in late antique and early Byzantine Asia Minor.
104 Yegül 1974, 271–272; Gärtner 2012, 104.
105 Tsafrir and Foerster 1997, 121–122.
106 Burrell (2008: 168) noticed that among the 1982 Sardis Hoard, consisting of 695 coins she studied, almost half of the coins were illegible/blank, although the coins were in good shape, indicating that they were flans which were never minted. Blank flans cast or cut from sheets of bronze were also observed in Israel; see Bijovsky 2002: 197–202.
107 At least one lead example recently excavated at Side seems to have a diademed imperial head on the obverse, which suggests that some of these lead pieces were issued to pass as coins; blank lead flans were also observed among late Roman finds in Israel; see Bijovsky 2002: 197–202

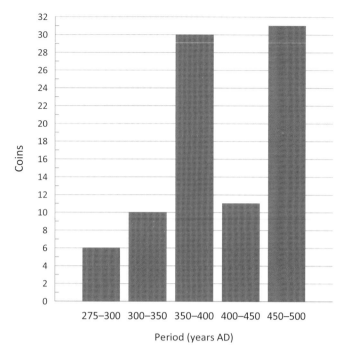

Fig. 31. Dated late Roman coins from the Place of Palms, by period (n = 88).

the AD 350s, and around 50% of the identified total belong to the fifth century AD (Fig. 31). From AD 425 until the coinage reform of Anastasius I in AD 498 the most common denomination found in excavations in the Eastern Mediterranean is the smallest, the *minimus*, usually 10 mm in diameter and weighing less than 1 g. But apart from contemporary *minimi*, the same levels excavated at Place of Palms yielded several older coins that would pass as *minimi* in size and weight, or examples purposefully clipped to fit in, and several unstruck flans or disks as described above. A similar pattern of circulation and coin usage (especially the presence of many older coins in late fifth-century contexts) was observed in the re-examination of two contemporary purse hoards previously published from Aphrodisias.[108]

108 Hoover 2000: Hoards 1 and 3. We re-examined all the coins in Hoover 2000: 295, Hoard 1 = (The Stadium) Arena Hoard, identifying some more coins from it and correcting some of those previously identified, which changes its proposed burial date drastically. The corrected list is as follows (using numbers in Hoover 2000): A1: Constantius II, VIRTVS – AVGG NN, TRPS *RIC* VIII, Trier 87; *LRBC* I, 121 (AD 337–340); A2: Constantine deified, chariot CONSA, *RIC* VIII, Constantinopolis 37; *LRBC* I, 1041 (AD 337–340); A12–19?: *Gloria Exercitus*, 1 standard, obverse worn (335–341); A3: Valentinianus II, GLORIA REI – PVBLICAE, camp gate, Thessalonica, *RIC* IX, Thessalonica 59a; *LRBC* II, 1856 (AD 383–388); A5: Theodosius I, *Salus Rei Publicae* type 1, SMNA, Nicomedia, *LRBC* II, 2428 (AD 383–392); A7: Theodosius I, *Salus Rei Publicae* type 1, ANTA, Antioch, *LRBC* II, 2764 (AD 383–392); A8: Arcadius, VOT V, SMKΓ, Cyzicus, *LRBC* II, 2562 (AD 383); A6: Arcadius, *Salus Rei Publicae* type 1 (AD 383–392); A9, A10, A11: Various emperors, not identifiable, *Salus Rei Publicae* or *Victoria Auggg* types (AD 383–392); A4: Theodosius II, cross within wreath, *RIC* X, 440–455 (AD 425–435); A12–19?: Leo I, emperor and captive, *RIC* X, 698–712 (457–474

Coin finds from the Place of Palms generally fit with the pattern of yearly loss from the other areas excavated at Aphrodisias between 1995 and 2020 (Fig. 32). This is perhaps to be expected as the coins we have studied from these periods were generally found in sectors close to the Place of Palms (for example, the Tetrapylon Street). One major peak that does not fit the rest of Aphrodisias is visible in the graph, in the fourth century during the period AD 383–395. At first sight this seems to indicate periods of higher usage (and hence coin loss) of the Place of Palms during these years. But such a statement would disregard the fact that these coins very probably remained in circulation much longer. In fact, most of these coins are small-format issues like the *Vota* and *Salus Rei Publicae*[109] issues of AD 383, and were probably still in circulation among *minimi* issued in those years. A slight peak during the period AD 355–361 is caused by the presence of reduced *Fel Temp Reparatio* falling horseman types, struck during this period but which probably remained in circulation for a long time because of their smaller formats.[110]

MacDonald published 51 pre-reform and post-reform coins dating to the Tetrarchy from Aphrodisias;[111] we can add only

AD); A12–19?: Leo I, Verina standing, *RIC* X, 713–718 (AD 457–474); A12–19? (two coins): Libius Severus, VICTO – AVG, Rome, *RIC* X, 2714 (AD 461–465); A12–19 three coins: illegible. This purse hoard thus closed with these 19 examples of the later fifth century. We identified one more coin from A20–A22 that come from 'outside the door' as Islamic; and another Islamic coin and a Byzantine coin of Constans II mentioned in Hoover 2000 also come from this area, which indicates a mixed context, independent of the hoard, whereas the 19 coins listed above were found together. The newly identified coins belonging to Theodosius II, Leo I, and Libius Severus show that the hoard does not belong to 'sometime after AD 393–395' as Hoover supposed, but much later, to the AD 460s–470s at the earliest, and contains a number of earlier coins, almost 130/40 years after their minting period, precisely fitting the pattern observed in the Place of Palms and at other sites like Sardis, mentioned below.

109 F. M. Lauritsen reported that among the 6,000 coins he examined from the 1966 late Roman hoard of 8,000 bronze coins from Eymir (1 km from the city walls of Aphrodisias), half of the specimens were from this type (Lauritsen 1984).

110 The survival of fourth-century AD coins in fifth-century AD contexts has been recorded at several sites, indicating their long persistence in circulation (Bijovsky 2002; Burrell 2008: 159, note 4). Barbara Burrell observed from the Sardis 1982 hoard of 695 coins that almost a tenth of the hoard consisted of fourth-century AD coins (Burrell 2008: 169). Jane DeRose Evans also published another hoard from Sardis (the Sardis MMS-II 1986 Hoard) in which a reduced and not clipped FEL TEMP REPARATIO coin was present together with later issues; the hoard is dated to AD 475 (Evans 2013: 144–145); in her new Sardis publication, she lists several more fifth-/sixth-century AD hoards with earlier coins in them from various sites in the East Mediterranean (Evans 2018: 94–96, table 3.15). A purse hoard consisting of 170 coins from Parion, dated AD 420–430s, contains some coins from the AD 270s onwards (Keleş and Oyarçin 2019); in a similar hoard of 259 coins from Arykanda with its latest coin issued by Marcian (AD 450–457), most of the coins belong to the fourth century (Sancaktar 2011); another hoard from Ephesos that is dated to c. AD 520–530 consisting of 160 coins contained issues from AD 350s onwards (Schindel and Ladstätter 2016).

111 MacDonald 1974; 1976, 16, nos. 668–719 and 46–47, fig. 4. This number contains not only excavated coins, but also those bought from workers, although neither publication states how many of which. In MacDonald 1976, only eight coins were labelled as excavated. As with the Greek and Roman provincial finds, coins could have

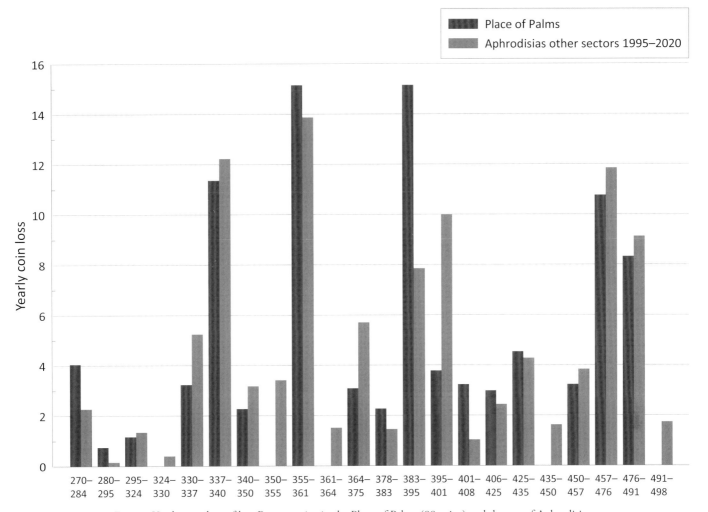

Fig. 32. Yearly coin loss of late Roman coins in the Place of Palms (88 coins) and the rest of Aphrodisias (817 coins; data compiled from finds between 1995–2020) calculated as: finds per period / length of period × 1000 / total.

two more (cat. 52–53) to these from the Place of Palms. In fact, these two coins represent the only coins from the Place of Palms dating to the 37 years between AD 284 to 321, although they are paralleled from other excavated areas of the city that we have so far studied. Such a decline in coin finds throughout the entire site may suggest several things at once, but none of them easy to prefer to the others, or to prove: a local or province-wide economic collapse? One or several unrecorded calamities that reduced the population and thereby reduced coin loss? One could easily appeal to local effects of later third-century plagues and the Gothic incursions to Western Asia Minor here as obvious reasons for disruption in the AD 260s–280s, and it may have taken some time to recover afterwards.

One must also add the fact that we do not know how long older Roman provincial issues remained in circulation until they were completely de-monetized; the generally accepted terminal year for this is Aurelian's coinage reform of AD 273, and minting ceased at Pamphylian and Pisidian cities in his reign. Aphrodisias stopped minting earlier, with a final grand output during the reign of Gallienus. But how long these coins remained in circulation is not clear; the end of minting does not mean the absolute ending of use. Still, when one thinks of the extant copies of the Diocletianic edicts on coinage reform and on maximum prices inscribed on the walls of the Basilica at Aphrodisias, we would have expected the Tetrarchic issues to be better represented at the site. Instead, it is possible that the use of Gallic Empire imitative coins at Aphrodisias (cat. 48–51) may have continued until the coinage reform of AD 294, an idea first suggested by MacDonald and later developed by J. Chameroy with more evidence collected from Western Asia Minor.[112] These coins are followed by various issues from the House of Constantine, including cat. 55, from the Londinium

---

been brought from other sites with different histories of monetary usage and representation, and these cannot therefore be used to make correct deductions about coin use at the excavated site of Aphrodisias.

112 MacDonald 1974; 1976, 46; Chameroy 2018; the small format of these barbarous radiates made it possible for them to pass as late Roman units together with earlier smaller-format coinage.

mint.[113] The small quantity of coinage dated before AD 330 from the Place of Palms is not a factor peculiar to here, but is common also in the rest of the city centre, as seen in Fig. 32—these coins were probably already and successfully de-monetised, but being larger in format, were also unsuitable for re-use in the fifth century AD as well.

Some of the coins described above from the House of Constantine onwards show signs that they were clipped and made into smaller coins: cat. 82, a *Virtus Exercitus* type of Arcadius, is a good example. The coin was clipped in such a way that it has lost most of the inscribed areas with only a small part of the inscription remaining, but the type and imperial head are visible.[114]

A major peak visible in Fig. 32 for both the Place of Palms and the rest of the city centre dates to AD 457–474, during the reign of Leo I.[115] This peak seems to correspond to the last phase of the area before the late antique restoration, with ten examples of Zeno from AD 476–491 also present (cat. 123–132). Although no pre-reform coins of Anastasius I are represented, coins of Leo I and Zeno would still have been in circulation until AD 498. Interestingly, several examples of the pre-reform coinage of Anastasius were recorded from the Agora next door;[116] their non-representation among the finds from the Place of Palms may be simply the result of chance.

The mint representation in the Place of Palms, even though the sample is very small, is what might be expected (Table 4; Fig. 33): Western mints are seldom represented[117] with the relatively high percentage for them (among the identifiable mints) in Fig. 33 in being caused by Gallic imitative coins. Balkan

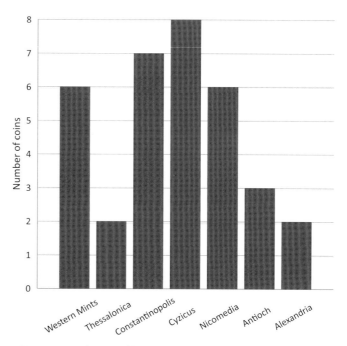

Fig. 33. Distribution of late Roman coins from the Place of Palms coins by identifiable mints (n = 34).

mints are also seldom represented, but of course Constantinople was one of the main suppliers of late Roman coinage to Aphrodisias together with Cyzicus and Nicomedia. As Aphrodisias lay in the Diocese of Asiana, Cyzicus would have been the official mint to supply the city, but coins of these three mints are always found in closely similar percentages in sites in Western Asia Minor. Antioch and Alexandria are, as would be expected, each represented by very few examples.

Ninety-six coins and one lead tessera produced to pass as a coin remained unidentified due to their condition or because they were badly struck (or the flans were not struck at all), but are attributed to the late Roman period by their general features like weight, thickness, and size (cat. 139–234). Eighty-five of these coins have diameters between 6–15 mm and these fit into the general sizes observed for the *minimi*; they may therefore more probably belong to the fifth century AD and not the fourth century AD, which fits again with the identified and dated issues.

H. LATE ROMAN CERAMICS (UO)

A small selection of diagnostic pottery fragments is presented here, based on analysis of material from the four sets of late Roman stratified contexts excavated in the Place of Palms:

1. The secondary fills of the first phase of the planting trenches in the open area of the Place of Palms (contexts **2015, 2017** and **3079**);
2. The deposit of rubble dumped across this area in late antiquity after the late fifth-century earthquake to raise the ground level (**4280**);

---

113 Issues of western mints, especially of Londinium, are generally rare among the late Roman coin finds from Asia Minor, but are quite possibly connected to Constantine's military operations; some from the AD 320s had arrived in Asia Minor together with issues of Arelate, Trier, Ticinum, Augusta Treverorum, Aquileia, and Rome. It is worth listing those of Londinium known to us from Türkiye: one from Arykanda (Tek 2002: cat. no. 1297); two from Sardis (Buttrey *et al.* 1981 cat. no. 160; Evans 2018: cat. no. 364); one from Side (unpublished, recorded by the authors in 2018); and one from Tarsus (Cox 1950: no. 304). There are also single finds of the Londinium mint from Mambre and Capernaum in Israel (Evans 2006: 43). Altogether, Western issues of the AD 320s, especially those of Londinium, did not play an important part in the general circulation pattern of bronze coinage at the time in Asia Minor or anywhere else in the Eastern Mediterranean, but their presence here is a good example of documenting numismatically a historically known military deployment.

114 Older and clipped coins were also observed in fifth-century AD hoards from Sardis (Evans 2013: 138, 140, note 16)

115 Admittedly that the 'lion' or 'emperor and captive' types of Leo I are relatively easier to identify in comparison to monogrammed examples issued in these decades, but comparing these issues with monogrammed ones whether identified or unidentified, the peak under Leo I is clearly not an artificial one, but real.

116 For example, C2002.013, C2003.071, C2003.093, C2003.114, all from Agora trenches.

117 Although among the fifth-century AD coins the mints identified are predominantly Eastern, a few examples from the West are also represented at Aphrodisias. There are coins of Johannes (two coins), Valentinian III (eight coins), Libius Severus (two coins) and Odovacar (three coins) from the mints of Rome and Ravenna recorded from other sectors at Aphrodisias; and another coin of Odovacar comes from the Place of Palms (cat. 138).

Table 4. The mint and date distribution of the 71 late Roman coins from the Place of Palms where mints and/or dates could be determined.

Year	Western Mints	Balkan Mints	Heraclea	Constantinople	Nicomedia	Cyzicus	Antioch	Alexandria	?	Total
c. 275–280s (barbarous radiates)	4									4
284–293										0
293–305					1	1				2
305–321										0
321–324	1								1	2
324–330										0
330–337					1				1	2
337–340				1	1		1			3
340–347										0
347–350					1	1				2
350–355										0
355–361				1		1	1		4	7
361–364										0
364–375				1	1					2
375–383									1	1
383–395		2				2			11	15
395–401									2	2
401–408					1	1			1	3
408–423									1	1
423–435									3	3
435–450										0
450–457					1	1				2
457–474				6				2	13	21
474–491	2					1				3
Total	3	2	0	9	7	8	2	2	38	71

3. The fills of the planting pits cut into this new raised ground level (contexts **3062**, **3067**, **3076**, **3078**, and **3081** contained some pottery);
4. The lowest levels of **4078**, which built up immediately on top of the late antique ground level;
5. The fills of the ring drains (contexts **8009**, **8010**, and **8011** produced diagnostic ceramics).

None of these contexts is an occupation layer; most of them comprise large dumps of mixed materials. Joining fragments are rare and only a few are large enough to enable the reconstruction of the complete form of the vessel. The surface and texture of the sherds also show the long-term effects of groundwater. Several of the deposits were disturbed by later agricultural activity which led to the intrusion of some post-antique ceramics.[118]

A full breakdown of the ceramics from these deposits is provided in Appendix 5, Table 27. Some general points can be noted here. The ceramics from these deposits provide only very general dating evidence: in most cases the material is extremely homogenous in both fabric and form. Indeed the bulk of late Roman ceramics at Aphrodisias were produced locally and are similar to those produced across much of western Asia Minor; the same is true, in fact, for all periods from the hellenistic through to the Byzantine.[119]

118 On these post-antique ceramics, see Ch. 9 §C–D.
119 Hudson 2008, 333; De Staebler 2012, 59.

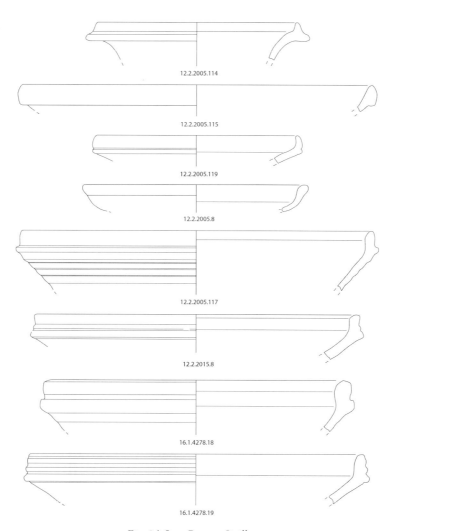

Fig. 34. Late Roman Sigillata.

Imported pottery

Distinctive imports are very rare at Aphrodisias generally and in many contexts entirely absent, no doubt reflecting the costs of transport to an inland site far from the coast.[120] This general picture is clearly reflected in the late Roman material from the Place of Palms: among hundreds of diagnostic fragments only a handful are identifiable as imports.[121] The few fragments of imported pottery belong to three groups: Late Roman Sigillata and table wares—two sherds of African Red Slip (ARS) and Cypriot Sigillata; and three sherds of Late Roman C ware (LRC, also known as Phocaean Red Slip ware)—,[122] unguentaria, and amphorae. All except one of the imported sherds come from contexts equivalent to **4280**, the late Roman dumped fill which raised the ground level of the Place of Palms, and **4278**, the occupation layer on top of this ground level; the exception is a LRC form 3 (12.2.2015.8) from one of the planting beds, context **2015**.

Late Roman Sigillata: the two pieces of African Red Slip are a sherd of ARS C ware form 99, and a fragment which is either a variant of ARS/C Form 74 (?) or possibly a fragment of a lid (cf. Atlante 1981, pl. 31, n. 10), of the late fifth–sixth century AD (12.2.2005.114 &115, Fig. 34). Two of the three sherds of LRC ware are variants of LRC Form 3, of the later fifth or sixth century AD, while the third is without known parallel (12.2.2005.8 &117, 12.2.2015.8, and 12.2.2005.8 & 119, Fig. 34). They seem however, to come from a production centre other than Phocaea;[123] the colour of the fabric is more pale and rather pinkish-red than brownish-red; general texture and characteristics, as for example the smokey grayish rim, are instead very similar. Other production centres of LRC ware are known, including one next to Priene,[124] and given the location of Aphrodisias it makes sense that its LRC imports might have come from a production site somewhere in the lower Maeander valley rather than from Phocaea to the north of Izmir. Both sherds of Cypriot Sigillata are variants of Hayes Form 9 (16.1.4278.18–19,

---

120 This seems to be unusual for sites in Asia Minor in general—for distribution patterns of imported Fine Ware in Asia Minor see Lund 1996, 109–110.
121 All of the imports are listed in the catalogue (marked in bold), while pottery fragments of local or regional production are considered only as a representative selection.
122 Hayes 1972 and Atlante 1981, *s.v.* African Sigillata and LRC.

123 For production of LRC at Phocaea/Foça, see Hayes 1980, lix.
124 Vaag 2003; Ladstätter and Sauer 2005a; Yılmaz 2008 (for production next to Priene).

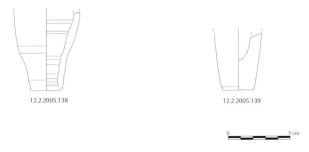

Fig. 35. Late Roman unguentaria from fifth- and sixth-century contexts.

Fig. 34), with a grooved rim.[125] This is a form dated to the late sixth or seventh century, which fits well with the stratigraphic observation that **4278**, the context in which they were found, built up on top of the raised late antique ground level.

Unguentaria: The non-local unguentaria are of a type first classified by Hayes in 1971,[126] represented by two sherds of similar fabric and form (12.2.2005.138–139, Fig. 35).

Amphorae are represented here by two fragments of Late Roman 1 (LRA 1) (12.2.2005.120–121, Fig. 36), a type thought to have been produced at a number of centres in Cyprus, the south coast of Asia Minor (bay of Iskenderun), and northern Syria.[127] These imports can be broadly dated to between the late fifth and early seventh centuries AD, although again their context date suggests the late fifth/early sixth century.

Local wares

As far as plain wares and coarse wares are concerned the vast majority of the material can be attributed to local production and is characterized by the same basic clay composition and the same technological repertoire that distinguishes the productions of the western Maeander valley in general.[128] The extent and output of local production at Aphrodisias itself are still unclear,

---

125 Hayes 1972, 379–382, grooved variants of Form 9; see also: Kenkel 2007.
126 Hayes 1971; further research and distribution in the Eastern Mediterranean see Hayes 1992, 8, Metaxas 2005, and Degeest 2000, 88; for local production of a similar type near Ephesos see Lochner, Sauer, and Linke 2005 and Ladstätter and Sauer 2005b; for distribution and trade connections regarding western provinces see Fernández 2014, 384, 529. According to Metaxas 2005, differences in the form of the base (flat or pointed) are not of chronological importance as initially suggested by John Hayes.
127 LRA 1: Peacock and Williams 1986, Form 44; further research see Williams 2005; van Alfen 1996 and Arthur 1998, 164–165; Bezeczky 2013, 158, Type 52; Reynolds 2018.
128 The late antique and early Byzantine repertoire of types and forms corresponds to the general picture in Asia Minor and the Western Mediterranean; since general aspects and characteristics are already described in depth by Hudson 2008 and De Staebler 2012 the repertoire is discussed here only briefly in comparison with well documented and dated contexts in Aphrodisias itself and from selected places like Samos or Ephesos. For useful overviews of the material from Ephesos see for instance Turnovsky 2005a; b; Ladstätter 2008; 2010, 265; Waldner and Ladstätter 2014; 2016, *s. v.* late antique contexts *passim*.

---

as no pottery kilns or waste deposits of the Roman and late antique period have yet been found, although mis-fired pieces and pieces of poor quality are proof of potters' activities near the site for the supply of the local market. Large clay deposits next to Aphrodisias and in the Dandalas valley are known and are still in use today. The production and export of clay vessels in Aphrodisias as well as their import was obviously never an important economic factor in antiquity,[129] although from middle Byzantine to classical Ottoman times the situation might have changed.[130]

The following description of common wares or fabrics found at Aphrodisias is based only on macroscopic observations and was established by the author together with Peter De Staebler at the beginning of pottery studies at the site in 1999–2000.[131] The material discussed (apart from the handful of imports already mentioned) constitutes only pottery of presumably local and regional production, and occurs in two fabrics.

Tan Micaceous Ware (TMW) is a rather fine fabric with large amounts of mica visible in the core as well as on the surface. The amount of levigation depends on the size and thickness of the wall. The clay contains small white (lime?) inclusions, which occasionally spall the smooth surface with small reaction voids. In large vessels the fabric tends to be porous but generally the clay is hard-fired and dense. When hard-fired, the breaks have a jagged surface; when soft-fired, a laminated structure is often visible. Normally the colour of the core and the surface is the same; thick-walled fragments may have a grey core due to the firing process. The colour ranges from pale orange-brown to cinnamon (Munsell 6/6–2.5YR to 5/6–2.5YR to 5/6–5YR). The repertoire of vessels produced in this fabric in different qualities shows a wide range of forms including storage vessels and amphorae, kitchen and plain table wares, as well as pots, dishes, bowls, jugs, jars and pitchers. This fabric was used for pottery production at the site over many centuries.

Gritty Cook Ware (GCW) is a rather coarse and hard-fired fabric, commonly used for all varieties of cooking vessels as there are pots, pans, and casseroles. The fabric is slightly micaceous with small to medium sized grey and tan inclusions of sand and particles of quartz. The walls of the vessels are generally quite thin, tending to become thicker towards the rim. The texture along the breaks is dense and has a jagged structure. Exterior surfaces are smooth with occasionally fine scratches from tempering and often show traces of a second finish with a sponge before drying and firing; inner surfaces are slightly ridged with a less smooth finish. Mica is visible on the surfaces, which are often smoked grey from the firing procedure in the reducing atmosphere of the kiln. With frequent use they become dark gray, nearly black, especially on the bottom and the outside edge of the rim. The surface colour ranges from dark brownish-red (Munsell 10R 4/6) to grey, the colour of the core from brick-red to brownish-red. The fabric is most common in late antiquity and the early Byzantine period.

---

129 A more detailed study of the imported amphorae found in Aphrodisias should at least provide more information about goods imported from abroad, although—based on personal observation—fragments of imported amphorae are only present in modest quantities.
130 See Öztaşkın 2017 and this volume, Ch. 9 §C–D.
131 See more detailed discussion in De Staebler 2012, 61–73.

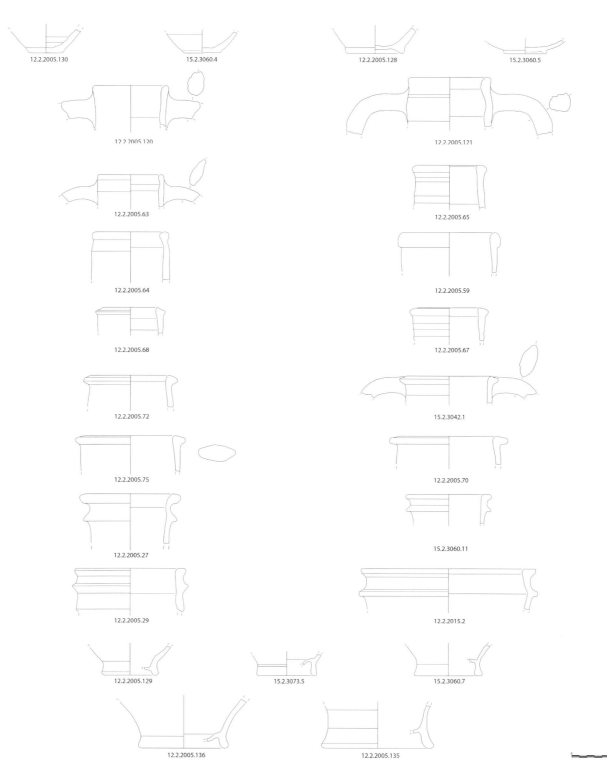

Fig. 36. Late Roman amphorae.

The repertoire of vessels in both wares found in the late Roman contexts corresponds to what one would expect in the inventory of simple household kitchens or public cook shops,[132] and is limited to the following categories.

Bowls: these have been found in large quantities. Except for one fragment of a simple rim bowl (12.2.2005.19, Fig. 37),[133] all of the examples are either bowls with a steep, slightly carinated rim imitating LRC Form 3, with horizontal lips imitating Cyp-

---

132 The lack of frying pans and dining plates might be coincidental but might reflect also eating habits in late antiquity—soups and stews could have been preferred dishes; the relatively large quantity of bowls found in our contexts seems to support this idea.

133 De Staebler 2012, fig. 10 and Hudson 2008, 326 fig. 10, 328–329 (contexts 1, 2 and 3, late fourth to early sixth century AD)—our fragment is not made of Local Brittle Ware as usual but of TMW. See also Outschar 2016, 118, no. 86, fig. 61.

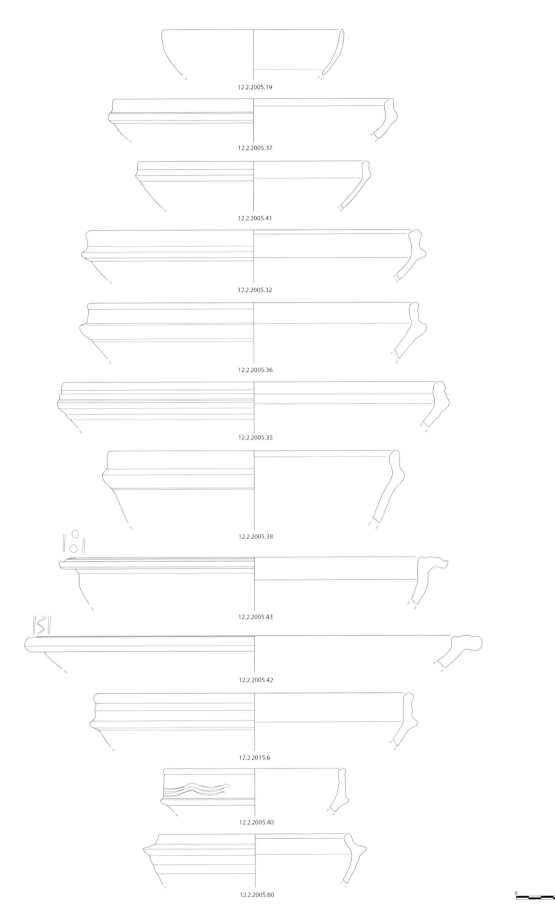

Fig. 37. Late Roman bowls (1).

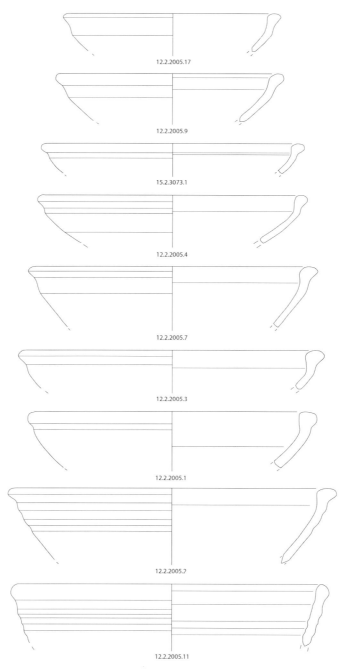

Fig. 38. Late Roman bowls (2).

riot Sigillata Form 9 (Fig. 37),[134] or bowls with a thickened rim (Fig. 38), which are well known from sixth- and seventh-century contexts in Aphrodisias.[135] Horizontal rims decorated with waves or dots are typical for late antique examples.[136] Another form is represented by 12.2.2005.60 (Fig. 37), which could easily also be the upper part of a funnel instead of a bowl.[137]

Basins: basins are represented in many fragments belonging to vessels of various dimensions, with diameters ranging from 24 cm to approximately 40 cm (Fig. 39). They all have horizontal rims, either plain and simple or slightly accentuated with shallow grooves or stepped.[138] All variations are common in late antique contexts and are well known already from later imperial times—in Aphrodisias they are all in TMW.

---

134 Hayes 1972, 379 and fig. 82.
135 Hudson 2008, 324, 329, 341 context 4, 1–11 (late sixth to mid seventh century AD) and De Staebler 2012, fig. 8.
136 See for the repertoire at Aphrodisias De Staebler 2012, fig. 5; further parallels, for example Jantzen 2004, no. 1593–94 (first quarter of the seventh century AD); Ladstätter 2008, K 435–436, 456–457, 559 on pp. 160–161, 170 and Taff. 312–313 and 322; Ladstätter 2010; Waldner and Ladstätter 2014; Waldner 2016, *passim*.
137 For a close parallel from an earthquake deposit (AD 551) in Beirut see Hayes 2005, fig. 17.
138 See Hudson 2008, 338 context 3, 17–18 (early sixth century AD) and 342 context 4, 16; De Staebler 2012, fig. 5, 1–6.

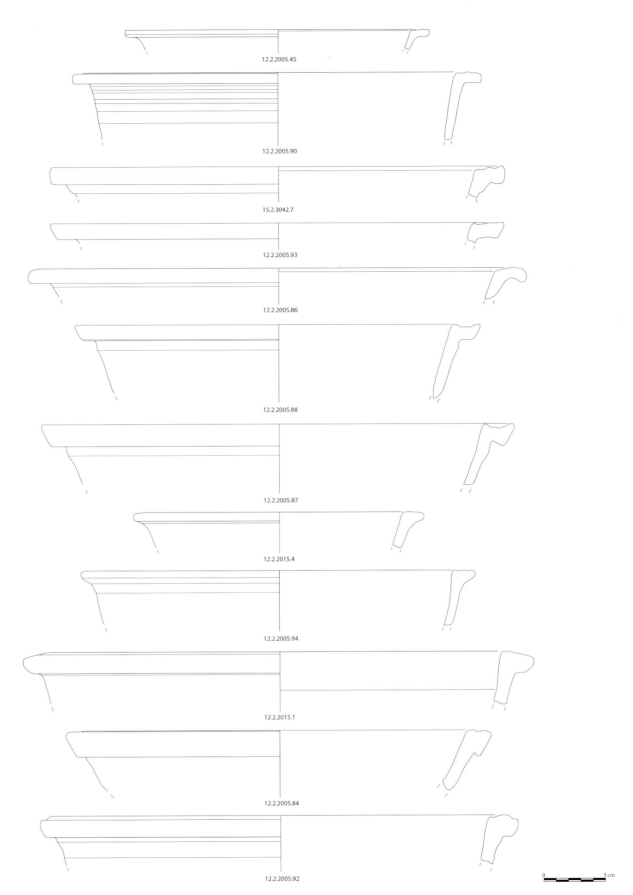

Fig. 39. Late Roman basins.

101

Fig. 40. Late Roman cooking pots and lids.

Cooking pots and lids: although few fragments were large enough to reconstruct the whole form, the majority of cooking vessels discussed in this context are globular or sack-shaped pots with out-turned rims, normally with a seating for a lid, and pairs of smaller or wider strap handles. They are local imitations in the tradition of late antique Aegean cooking pots. Most of them are in GCW fabric, with a few (12.2.2005.108, 51, 55, 33, 53 & 105; 15.2.3073.3, Fig. 40) in coarse TMW; since the latter do not show any traces of secondary firing they might have been used for storage and serving purposes rather than cooking over an open fire. A single fragment of coarse GCW (12.2.2005.99) has a cylindrical neck without a separately defined rim and belongs to cooking ware known from the fifth

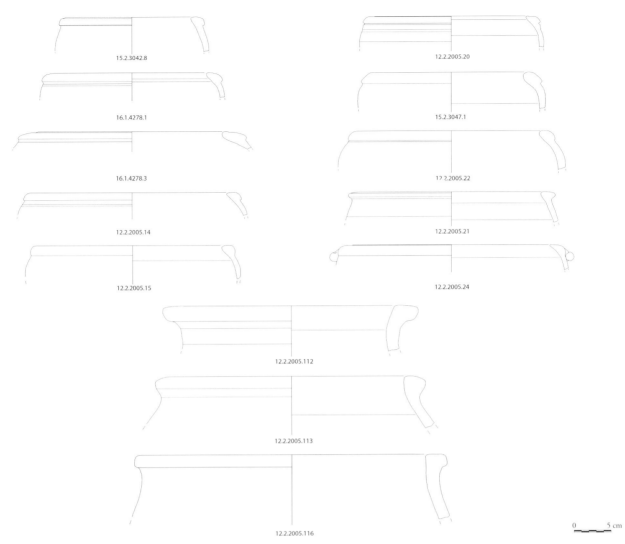

Fig. 41. Late Roman storage vessels.

and sixth centuries AD.[139] Lids are represented by only two fragments (15.2.3047.2 and 12.2.2005.124, Fig. 40) in TMW, and belong to types common in late antique Aphrodisias.[140]

Storage vessels: a homogeneous group of small storage (?) vessels in TMW, present only in the late Roman contexts outside the ring drain (Fig. 41),[141] has an inverted rim marked by a more or less accentuated groove on the outside separating the rim from the presumably ovoid or globular body—this groove could have been helpful to fix a string or wire when covering the spout with a flexible material like smooth leather or cloth. One, perhaps earlier (?), example (12.2.2005.24, Fig. 41) has small horizontal handles attached next to the rim. Three rim fragments (12.2.2005.112, 113 & 116, Fig. 41) belong to dolia or pithoi.[142]

Local amphorae, jugs and jars: the huge amount of spout fragments found particularly in the late Roman contexts outside the ring drain could be attributed to locally produced amphorae or to large jugs, since most of them are only rims and upper parts of the neck without handles. Form and volume remained more or less the same for centuries and slight variations of the rim profile[143] do not provide a chronological distinction. Handles are attached either directly to or under the rim and on the shoulder (see for example 15.2.3042.1, Fig. 36). They

---

139 For the repertoire in general De Staebler 2012, fig. 13 and Hudson 2008, 341, fig. 21 (sixth century AD) and 343, fig. 22 (seventh century AD); for further parallels see for instance Gassner 1997, 174–175, no. 720–721; fig. 35 Type PW-XII (late fifth–sixth century AD); Jantzen 2004, no. 1926 from a seventh-century AD context.

140 De Staebler 2012, fig. 9 and Hudson 2008, 338, context 3.19–22; Outschar 2016, 116, no. 87–93, fig. 61; Jantzen 2004, no. 1651 and 1653 (first quarter of the seventh century AD).

141 De Staebler 2012, fig. 3 (here as cooking pots)—since some of the fragments are in coarse TMW a function as cooking pots as well as storage vessels is possible. The form is common from imperial times to late antiquity and is reflected also in cooking ware of later periods in the eastern provinces—see Gogräfe 2016, Abb. 90.

142 They are of no chronological importance since they are usually of long-term use; their characteristic features are more or less the same during the centuries.

143 Either the rim has a small triangular or round thickened profile or the neck ends slightly everted—see for example 17.1.4448.2, 12.2.2005.72, 73 or 12.2.2005.63. For parallels see Jantzen 2004, no. 1344 and 1348 (first quarter of the seventh century AD).

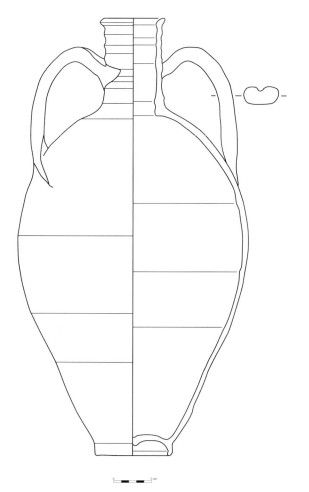

Fig. 42. Late Roman local amphora (example from elsewhere at Aphrodisias).

are common in Aphrodisias; Fig. 42 shows a complete example from elsewhere on the site with a base corresponding to base fragments from our contexts presented here on Fig. 36.[144] A third group with double carinated rims (12.2.2005.27 & 29, 15.2.3060.11 and 12.2.2015.2, Fig. 36) is also represented only in the late Roman contexts outside the ring drain and is also of local production.[145]

The late Roman (late fifth-/early sixth-century) contexts show that although the vast majorty of the pottery at this inland site was local, occasional imports of Mediterranean finewares—ARS, Late Roman C, and Cypriot Sigillata—did reach Aphrodisias. Most of the pottery consisted of local plain and coarse wares for storage, food preparation and cooking, and eating. Since the majority came from large dumped fills redeposited as post-earthquake clearance and clean-up, they may not imply anything about usage of the Place of Palms itself.

I. LATE ROMAN SMALL FINDS (TP & HJ)

This section discusses those few finds from the late antique contexts dated to the beginning of the sixth century or earlier (artefacts of late antique manufacture recovered from the seventh-century dumps within the pool are discussed in the small finds commentary for those contexts in Ch. 8 §D).

A stratigraphically early find within this late antique period is an iron object recovered from the fill of the southern planting bed, **2015**, for which a coin of Marcian (cat. 104) gives a *terminus post quem* of AD 450–457; the context is sealed by the late fifth-/early sixth-century dump above it but, as noted above, probably dates to immediately before it (Pl. 39.C). The function of this item is unclear; it has a hammerlike head and a thin, rounded stem, possibly broken towards the bottom.[146] A rounded perforation in one of the terminal ends of the head may suggest this was some kind of tool, though it does not conform to any established typologies.[147] It could perhaps be a distant ancestor of a late Byzantine or early Ottoman leather-cutting tool excavated at Pergamon.[148] However, the perforation may be the result of post-depositional damage and the item may instead simply be a T-clamp for securing wall revetments or for holding in place a ceramic stud.[149] From **16.2.5001**—again a late antique fill of the southern planting trench—also came a copper alloy arrowhead with a curved broadhead blade terminating in two barbs, a diamond-shaped section and a circular socket (Pl. 39.D).[150]

Two notable finds come from late fifth-/early sixth-century fills of the ring drain. A fragment of a lathe-turned bone object came from **8009**.[151] This item is broken at one end and has a central circular perforation (∅: 0.3 cm); it could be a small spindle whorl but also a handle or similar fixture. Another part of the fill of the ring drain, excavated during the 1990 season and dating to the same period, yielded a single, well-preserved glass vessel (∅: 13.2 cm).[152] This is a thin-walled hemispherical bowl with a fire-rounded, slightly inward-turned rim, probably in a colourless fabric (see Fig. 65). The bowl is broadly comparable to two slightly smaller examples (∅: 10.0 cm and 7.0 cm respectively) from Sardis, the larger of which has been dated to the fifth to early seventh centuries.[153] A similar example from Thessaloniki is dated to the fourth to fifth centuries.[154]

A few finds were also uncovered in the lower part of the fills which represent the raising of the ground level of the urban park in late antiquity, equivalent to **4028**, dated to within a decade or so of AD 500. A copper alloy belt buckle was cast as one frame, D-shaped with a thin bar and slight point at the tongue rest (Pl.

---

144 Garage House Depot 3 ex 1997. See also De Staebler 2012, 63 fig. 4; Hudson 2008, 337 context 3.4, fig.14 and context 6.13, 14 fig. 25 (early sixth and seventh century AD).
145 For parallels see Hayes 1992, deposit 30, 140, fig. 48, no. 182, seventh/eighth century AD.
146 SAg.12.2.2015.F2017: H: 18.0 cm, W (head): 5.5 cm, ∅ (head exterior): 1.3 cm, ∅ (head interior): 0.6 cm, W (stem): 0.5–0.7 cm.
147 Owen Humphreys (pers. co, November 2019).
148 Gaitzsch 2005, 183. LE 9.
149 For example Manning 1985, 132, plate 62, R65.
150 SAg.16.2.5001.F001 (Inv. 16-040): H: 4.0 cm, W: 1.8 cm, D: 0.8 cm.
151 Inv.16–038: L: 2.0 cm, ∅: 1.1 cm.
152 PTSW.90.F63: H: 6.3 cm, ∅: 13.2 cm. N.B. the state of preservation means that the less probable possibility, an opaque white fabric, cannot be excluded.
153 Von Saldern 1980, 62–63, cat. 395–6; pl. 24.
154 Antonaras 2010, 385, fig. 2.

39.E).[155] The tongue is attached through a loose loop. The type is very simple and therefore not particularly diagnostic, though fair parallels may be found at Sardis.[156] Also found was a small length of fine copper alloy chain composed of figure-of-eight links (Pl. 39.F).[157] Several chains for late antique scale weights at Sardis were manufactured in the same technique.[158] A thin sheet of copper alloy plate was folded so as to accommodate a round profile leading to a sharp point, either as the terminal of a sheath for a tool or as cladding for a wooden implement.[159] The finds in these contexts represent the detritus of a bustling city centre in the period prior to the late fifth-century earthquake.

J. ARCHAEOBOTANICAL EVIDENCE (ER)

The long life and later renovations of the Place of Palms mean that the only archaeobotanical evidence that can be securely dated to the fifth and sixth centuries comes from the ring drain surrounding the pool. The assemblage from the ring drain, however, is relatively well preserved and its mixture of foodstuffs and ritual/pruning waste makes it an exemplary source of evidence for the use and maintenance of plants in the city. Moreover, this assemblage provides a first glimpse into diet in Aphrodisias and, more broadly, contributes to our very fragmentary knowledge of food consumption practices in late antique Asia Minor. This section provides an overview of the finds, followed by an in-depth analysis of the foodstuffs and decorative plants, and a discussion of the formation of the assemblage and Aphrodisias' relationship to its hinderland and other Anatolian cities.

The ring drain assemblages

The assemblages from the ring drains come from the two sondages whose detailed stratigraphy is described above (§B), one in the north ring drain and one in the southern one. Both assemblages are formed almost exclusively of carbonized material. There was a very small number of mineralized remains recovered from both sondages, which does suggest that the drain was at one time used as a sewer for waste removal. The formation of the assemblages will be discussed later.

The material from the north side was located immediately above the floor of the drain. A roughly 2 m stretch of the drain fill was sampled over the course of two seasons. This section of the drain had already been partially excavated and sampling took place after a small area of organic material was discovered during cleaning in 2013. The material collected in 2013 has been labelled QA (Quadrant A) while material collected in 2014 has been labelled QB. Four deposits from the lower portions of the northern ring drain were sampled: **1040–1043**. As these four contexts were the same in both quadrants, identical context numbers have been used. Although there are clear distinctions between the different contexts (sandy or silty), the presence of food remains and charcoal in each of the layers suggests that they were filled with the same type of fuel and cooking waste. Soil, in as large quantities as possible, was collected from each context.

Unlike the material on the north side, the organic material on the south side was sandwiched roughly halfway up the drain channel between layers of intentional fill. However, there is a difference of roughly 0.7 m in depth between the south and north sides of the drain, the southern side being lower. The filling of the south side with natural clay followed by an intentional rubble fill layer brings the carbonized material in the south side to within roughly 20 cm of the level of the carbonized material on the north side. The consistency in the dating of the ceramics from both sides of the drain suggests that the carbonized material from the two sides should be considered contemporaneous.

Excavation and sampling of the south side sondage began in 2015 but had to be stopped due to the high water level that season. The remaining contexts were excavated in 2016. Large samples were collected from each context within the ring drain while the two obvious organic layers (**8006** and **8007**) were sampled in full (see Fig. 24). Unlike these two organic-rich contexts, the flotation samples from the lower contexts (**8008–8011**) contained very little carbonized material, demonstrating that there was only one period in which this drain was used as a sewer.

In the case of **8006**, the bottom of the context contained a rich layer of organic material. At the time of excavation, the bottom of the context was situated just above the water level and it was clear that as a result of waterlogging, the botanical material was in a good state of preservation. Consequently, the lowest portion of the context was sampled in full. In total eight samples, one from the top, one from the middle and six from the bottom of this context were collected and processed. The processing of the flotation samples helped clarify the nature of the context. The samples from the bottom were extremely rich in charcoal and archaeobotanical finds. There was some archaeobotanical material recovered from the middle context sample (8006.2), but not in the same quantity as the material from the bottom. These findings suggest that the bottom of the context represents the final period in which the drain was used as a sewer channel to move waste out of the Place of Palms. The finds from the middle of the context represent the upward movement of the carbonized material, probably due to shifting water levels causing this already buoyant material to seep into the intentional fill above whenever the water level rose. Ceramic evidence dates the fill levels both above and below **8006** and **8007** to the late fifth century or perhaps the very early sixth century. We can therefore assume that the archaeobotanical assemblage was deposited when the pool and the surrounding areas were undergoing reconstruction following the earthquake.

Archaeobotanical sampling procedures

Standard archaeobotanical sample processing procedures were used to extract the carbonized material from the ring drain, the

---

155 SAg.12.2.2005.F.2014: L: 2.8 cm, W: 2.7 cm, D: 1.1 cm.
156 Waldbaum 1983, 121, no. 709.
157 SAg.12.2.2010.F.2013: L: 7.5 cm, L (link): 1.2 cm, W: 0.7 cm.
158 Waldbaum 1983, 81–81, nos. 435, 436, 437, 444.
159 SAg.12.2.2010.F.2015: L: 4.3 cm, W: 2.1 cm, D: 1.1 cm.

pool fill and the planting trenches. The sampling and processing of the waterlogged material from the bottom of the pool are discussed in Ch. 8 §E. Alterations and improvements in methodology took place over the course of the various seasons and are noted in the text.

Wherever possible, at least 10 litres of soil were taken from each context sampled, and all large samples were collected in blue garbage bags. Samples were labelled in the order they were collected, for example 8006.1, 8006.2, so that it would later be possible to differentiate between the top and bottoms of the contexts. All samples were processed using the on-site machine-assisted flotation device. During the 2013 season strong fine mesh or thin fabric was not available to line the tank, and thus three layers of window screen mesh were used instead. The following year 255 μm nylon flotation mesh was purchased and used to line the tank in all subsequent seasons. Material that floated was caught on 0.5 mm and 0.3 mm Endecotts sieves. The flots from each sieve were combined, placed into bags and allowed to dry in the sun. The remaining heavier residue material was then washed over a 2 mm sieve. The residues were placed on trays and left to dry before being sorted in the conservation lab. Bone, glass, shell, eggshell, and small finds were sorted into separate containers for future analysis. Diagnostic ceramic sherds were also kept. The material from the ring drain was at first also washed over a 1 mm sieve. Subsamples from the 1 mm trays were examined, but as little was found and no mineralized material was visible the practice was discontinued after the first few samples.

North drain results

The eight samples examined from the north side of the drain produced 13 taxa and 122 identifiable items. As can be seen in Table 5, cereals were represented by wheat and barley, and legumes by lentil and bitter vetch. There were a total of five fruit and nut species and four weed and tree taxa. Four buds, probably from the Kermes oak (*Quercus coccifera*), were found in context **1043**. Fragments of olive endocarp (stone) were the most common find followed by walnut shell fragments and cereal grains. Density levels were low throughout, varying only from 1.1 to 0.05 seeds per litre. Context **1043** in Quadrant B contained the greatest quantity and variety of finds, followed by context **1041** in Quadrant A. The total number of samples collected is too small to suggest any significant differences between the two quadrants or even between contexts. The uppermost context, **1040**, had the fewest finds, which is not surprising as material may have been washed away by later water flow in the drain.

South drain results

The twenty samples examined, representing material from all nine contexts within the drain, produced a total of 40 taxa and 895 identifiable individual items. As on the north side, both wheat and barley were found (Table 6). Legumes were similarly represented by lentil and vetch. However, on this side of the drain a wider range of fruits and nuts was recovered, six and four taxa respectively. One seasoning, black mustard, was found in context **8007**. The south side of the drain also contained a wider range of weed and tree taxa. The 21 weed seeds represent a mixture of species that grow on agricultural land and/or waste ground. In addition to larger quantities of pine and cypress, the south side also had the burnt leaves and buds of Kermes oak. Wild grass seeds and the buds from the Kermes oak were the most common finds, followed by seeds of field madder, the twigs and seeds of cypress, walnut shells, and cereal grains.

As expected, the density levels varied dramatically, from zero to 41.6 seeds per litre (Fig. 43). Samples from contexts **8006** and **8007** contained by far the greatest variety and quantity of finds, confirming the hypothesis that the drain was only used as a sewer for a short time between periods of intentional infilling. Samples collected from the middle of **8006** and the middle of **8007** had the greatest number of finds. Material from the upper and lower portions of these contexts, represented by samples 8006.2 and 8007.5 had significantly fewer finds. The carbonized remains in these samples probably represent material that became mixed into the fill layers above and below when water levels rose and fell. The small number of finds in sample 8006.7 is probably due to the high water levels during excavation as context **8006** was above the water table during the 2015 season.

Archaeobotanical finds

Although the taxonomic range and density levels of the finds from the two sides varied, their similar dates and depositional histories mean that the two assemblages can be amalgamated to provide a more detailed picture of diet and plant management practices in Aphrodisias. In the following sections the finds from the north and south sides of the ring drain have been combined.

Cereals and legumes. The cereal assemblages from both sides of the drain are dominated by free-threshing wheat and barley. The identification of a single hexaploid free-threshing rachis fragment confirms the presence of *Triticum aestivum*. Since wheat and barley were recovered in almost equal numbers, we can tentatively state that similar quantities of free-threshing wheat and barley were consumed at Aphrodisias. The moderate quantity of emmer wheat, along with two additional grains of hulled wheat from the south side of the drain also suggests the consumption of hulled wheats and not accidental inclusions in the free-threshing wheat crop. A much smaller number of legumes was recovered. However, legumes do not preserve as well as cereals and the overall level of preservation within the drain was not excellent. The five lentils represent food waste while the vetch and bitter vetch, found in very low numbers, were probably cereal contaminants or fodder.

Fruit and nuts. The fruit assemblage is made up of a combination of the standard Mediterranean staples: figs, olives, and grapes, and a range of stone fruit. The small number of fruit finds is not unexpected as they do not require cooking prior to consumption and the two assemblages do not represent any sort of catastrophic burning event. The presence of both carbonized

Table 5. North drain taxa list.

		Context	1040		1041		1042		1043		Total
		Quadrant	QA	QB	QA	QB	QA	QB	QA	QB	
		Volume (L)	11.4	5	11	8	12.3	16	11.2	20	94.9
Cereals	**Common name**	**Component**									
Hordeum vulgare sl.	Barley	Caryopsis		1	1	1	3			3	9
Triticum aestivum/durum	Free-threshing wheat	Caryopsis	2	1				1		1	5
Triticum sp.	Wheat	Caryopsis			2		1			1	4
Triticum sp.	Wheat	Glume frag.			1						1
Cerealia	Cereal	Caryopsis	4			1	3		2	2	12
Pulses											
Lens culinaris	Lentil	Seed					1				1
Vicia sp.	Vetch	Seed					1				1
Fruits and nuts											
Juglans regia	Walnut	Shell (frag.)			1		1	1	3	7	13
Olea europaea	Olive	Endocarp (whole)			1			1			2
Olea europaea	Olive	Endocarp (frag.)	2		14	7	6	7	8	10	54
Pinus sp.	Pine	Seed			1						1
Vitis vinifera	Grape	Pip (whole)								2	2
Vitis vinifera	Grape	Pip (frag.)								1	1
Prunus dulcis	Almond	Shell fragment								1	1
Weeds and other taxa											
Cupressus sp.	Cypress	Twig			1						1
Cupressus sp.	Cypress	Seed								1	1
Poaceae	True grasses	Caryopsis					1	1		1	3
Fabaceae	Legume family		2							4	6
Bud	N/A	Bud								4	4
		Total	10	2	22	9	17	11	13	38	122

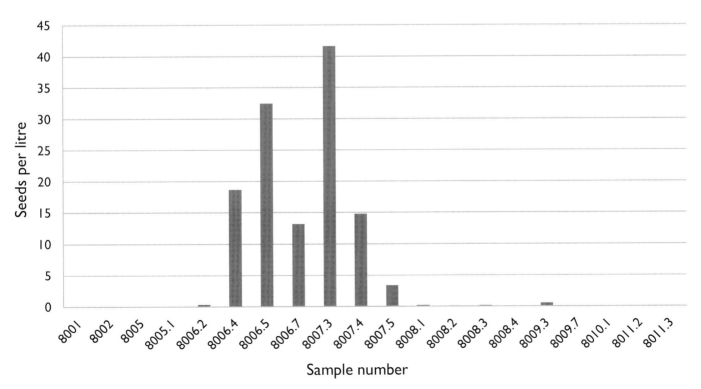

Fig. 43. Density of finds from the south drain samples.

Table 6. South drain taxa list.

Samples from the organic-rich layers **8006** and **8007** are shown individually in order to highlight differences in the upper and lower portions of the contexts. For each of the remaining contexts the samples have been consolidated.

		Context	8001	8002	8005	8006.2	8006.4	8006.5	8006.7	8007.3	8007.4	8007.5	8008	8009	8010	8011	TOTAL
		Volume (L)	18	11	31	20	10	8.1	5	4.3	10	7.7	44.4	19	14	33	235.5
Cereals	**Common name**	**Component**															
Hordeum vulgare sl.	Barley	Caryopsis		1			8	4		1	5	3		2	1		25
Hordeum sp.	Barley	Rachis					1	1		1							3
Triticum aestivum sl.	Bread wheat	Rachis								1							1
Triticum dicoccum	Emmer wheat	Caryopsis					5				2						7
Triticum aestivum/durum	Free-threshing wheat	Caryopsis				1	9	5		4	1			1			21
Triticum aestivum/durum	Free-threshing wheat	Rachis									10						10
Triticum sp. *spelta/dicoccum*	Spelt or durum wheat	Caryopsis						1									1
Triticum sp.	Wheat	Caryopsis					1	4	3	1	3						12
Triticum sp.	Wheat	Rachis					1	20	2			1					24
Cerealia	Cereal	Caryopsis			1	1	10	9	1	8		1					31
Pulses																	
cf. *Lens culinaris*	Lentil	Seed						3									3
Lens culinaris	Lentil	Seed									1						1
Vicia ervilia	Bitter vetch	Seed							1								1
Fruit																	
Ficus carica	Fig	Pip									1						1
Ficus carica	Fig	Flesh									1						1
Olea europaea	Olive	Endocarp	1			1		1	1	4	1		1				10
Phoenix sp. *theophrasti/dactylifera*	Date	Endocarp									1						1
Prunus avium	Sweet cherry	Stone						1									1
Prunus persica	Peach	Stone									6						6
Vitis vinifera	Grape	Pip					1			1							2
Vitis vinifera	Grape	Flesh									1						1
Nuts																	
Corylus avellana	Hazelnut	Shell frag.							3								3
Juglans regia	Walnut	Shell frag.					6	2	1	9		1					19
Pinus pinea	Stone pine	Nut						2									2
Pinus sp.	Pine	Nut									8	1					9
Pinus sp.	Pine	Bract					1	2									3
Prunus dulcis	Almond	Shell frag.					1	8				1					10
Nutshell	N/A	Shell frag.					2			3	2	1					8
Seasonings																	
Brassica cf. *nigra*	Black mustard	Seed								1							1

		Context	8001	8002	8005	8006.2	8006.4	8006.5	8006.7	8007.3	8007.4	8007.5	8008	8009	8010	8011	TOTAL
Trees																	
Coniferae	Conifer	Cones								1			2				3
Cupressus sp.	Cypress	Seed					1	8	5	2	6	2					24
Cupressus sp.	Cypress	Twig						6	1	10	7						24
Cupressus sp. or *Juniperus* sp.	Cypress/ Juniper	Twig					1										1
Quercus coccifera	Kermes oak	Bud					1	31	32		29						93
Quercus coccifera	Kermes oak	Leaf frag.								2	37						39
Weed seeds																	
Apiaceae	Parsley family												1				1
Avena sp.	Wild oat	Caryopsis						1		1							2
cf. *Avena*	Wild oat	Caryopsis					1										1
Chenopodiac-eae	Goosefoot family								1								1
Chenopodium sp.	Goosefoot								1								1
Cyperaceae	Sedges									1							1
Fabaceae	Legume family						1	4	2	3	4	4	2				20
Fallopia convolvulus	Black-bindweed								1								1
Galium aparine	Cleaver							5			1						6
Medicago sp.	Medick	Pod							1								1
Medicago/ Melilotus sp.	Medick/ Melilot							9	2	12	1		1				25
Papaveraceae	Poppy	Capsule								1							1
Plantago sp.	Fleaworts							3		1							4
Poaceae	True grasses							67	77	27	54	30	4		1		2	262
Polygonaceae	Knotweed family							1		1							2
Polygonum cf. *aviculare*	Knotgrass										1						1
Raphanus sp.	Wild radish									2							2
Rubiaceae	Madder family							7		2							9
Rumex sp.	Dock									1							1
cf. *Rumex acetosella*	Sheep's sorrel							1									1
Sherardia arvensis	Field madder							19	18	4	9	4	2					56
Veronica sp.	Speedwell								2	1							3
Weed seed	N/A					1	2	8	45		15	17			3			91
Other taxa and unidentified material																	
Stalk	N/A							1		1							
		TOTAL	1	1	2	7	187	263	66	179	148	26	5	7	1	2	895

grape and fig flesh in the south side of the drain does suggest ritual burning, which will be discussed in detail later. Although olive stone fragments dominate the assemblage, the numbers are too small to suggest fuel use and instead reflect either ritual burning or the burning of table waste. The date stone fragment could not be identified to species level and therefore may represent either an imported and consumed item from a date palm (*Phoenix dactylifera*), or may have come from one of the Cretan date palms (*Phoenix theophrasti*) that grew in the Place of Palms (Pl. 40.A) (see §C for planting patterns).

The nut assemblages, from both sides of the drain, are made up primarily of walnut shell fragments, followed by the nuts and bracts of stone pine (Pl. 40.B). The walnut, almond, and hazelnut shells undoubtedly represent consumption of these nuts. The shells may have been burnt as fuel, especially the oily walnut shells, or simply as a way to dispose of waste. While the pine nuts may have been consumed, pine nuts and cones were frequently used in rituals in the Roman world and it is more probable they reflect ritual burning practices.

Seasonings. The only seasoning found was a single seed of *Brassica nigra* or black mustard. This species is native to the region and was probably collected locally. Herbs and seasonings do not usually carbonize well and the general absence of seasonings in the samples has more to do with preservation than a lack of desire or opportunity for the inhabitants of Aphrodisias to flavour their food.

Trees. Compared to the foodstuffs, an almost equally large quantity of arboreal remains was found, particularly from the south side of the drain. The north side had only one twig and one seed of cypress but the sample sizes, compared to the south side, were considerably smaller. The south side contained numerous fragments of cypress and large quantities of carbonized leaves and buds of Kermes oak. Like pine, cypress was thought to have special ritual significance in the Roman world.[160] Consequently, the combination of pine and cypress, along with the oak, suggests either ritual burning or the burning of pruning waste and will be discussed in detail in the following section.

Weeds. The weed seed category is the most varied and consists of a range of taxa that can be found growing in a broad array of soil types and habitats. Wild grass seeds (Poaceae) made up 53.1% of the entire weed assemblage followed by *Sherardia arvensis* (n=56), *Medicago* or *Melilotus* sp. (n= 25) and Fabaceae (n=20). The remaining taxa were found in counts of nine or less. The Fabaceae, *Medicago* sp. and *Melilotus* sp. may have been grown as fodder crops while *Sherardia arvensis* can be found growing in pastures. Since these taxa are the most numerous it is possible that part of the weed seed assemblage reflects dung fuel. The use of dung as fuel has been identified archaeobotanically at both Gordion and Sagalassos.[161] However, the ratio of weed seeds to charcoal, necessary to determine the presence of dung fuel, was not calculated at Aphrodisias and therefore we cannot be certain. Some of the taxa, such as the wild oat, goosefoot, medick, wild grasses, and field madder probably grew amongst the cereals and would have been burnt during food preparation or cereal cleaning. Because the assemblage is mixed it is impossible to tell which grew amongst the wheat and which amongst the barley. However, all of these species except the oats could equally have been growing on abandoned or disturbed ground. The sorrels are ruderals and grew on uncultivated soil, perhaps around the pool. There are three taxa, the sedges, the cleavers, and the plantains, that prefer wet or poorly drained soil. At Gordion seeds from the Cyperaceae (sedge) family dominated the weed assemblage, which Marston and Miller interpreted as signs of crop irrigation.[162] However, the quantities from Aphrodisias are too small to suggest that similar practices were taking place. Some of the seeds may have been carbonized if the plants, particularly those with colourful flowers, were also burnt for ritual purposes. In sum, the weed seed assemblage, at least for the southern side of the drain, may reflect a combined use of fuel, perhaps derived from dung, with plants burnt as part of food preparation practices, garden maintenance, or ritual.

Diet and food production in Aphrodisias and its hinterland

The archaeobotanical finds from the ring drain around the pool in the Place of Palms are our first evidence for diet in late antique Aphrodisias. Although 150 km from the Aegean coast, the region has a Mediterranean climate with hot dry summers and cool wet winters.[163] The fertile Dandalas (Morsynos) river valley and the gently sloping hillsides ensured that a diverse range of cereals, pulses, fruits, and nuts could be produced in the city's hinterland. The valley floor, in which Aphrodisias is situated, is between 450–650 m asl, low enough to allow the cultivation of a broad range of items. Little, except for desired rather than required luxuries such as wine, seems to have been imported.[164] Consequently, the Aphrodisian diet, for the most part, reflects the local production of the relatively standard set of items grown in the Mediterranean during the Roman period.

As with many cities in the Eastern part of the empire, both wheat and barley were the staple crops. Free-threshing wheat is more susceptible to drought than emmer or barley and as a naked wheat more susceptible to loss by wind and bird predation. Therefore the presence of three different cereal types suggests careful agricultural risk management, at least initially, although by late antiquity cultural preference may have also played a role with different cereals performing different functions.[165] Pulses formed a part of the diet although it is difficult to estimate their importance. Extensive survey in the Dandalas river valley suggests that cereals were produced in the low-lying areas close to the river while the northern and steeper parts of the valley were probably used for pastoralism.[166] At least twelve farmsteads, occupied during the imperial and late Roman periods, were found in low-lying parts of the valley.

Grapes were grown for consumption and for wine while olives were grown both as table olives and for oil. The regional survey identified 90 points of interest with evidence for olive oil or wine production, with 33 of those sites located within one kilometre of the city walls. Because of the need for crushing mills and basins in addition to presses, there is more secure evidence for olive oil than wine production. At least 22 crushing mill basins, five runner stones from olive mills, and 67 press counterweight blocks were found around the city, attesting to the widespread production of olive oil and probably also wine. The iron-rich soil in certain areas of the valley means that the area is particularly good for growing olives, and olive groves can still be found throughout the valley today.[167]

---

160 Rovira and Chabal 2008.
161 Putzeys *et al.* 2004, 49–52; Marston and Miller 2014, 765–769.
162 Marston and Miller 2014, 767.
163 Stearns 2012, 135.
164 Adkins 2012, 93–94.
165 For example, the use of free-threshing wheat for bread but the less glutinous emmer to make porridge.
166 Adkins 2012, 102–106
167 Lockey 2012, 203–204. It is interesting to note that despite widespread olive oil production it does not appear that the urban inhabitants of Aphrodisias were using the pressing waste as a fuel. The use of olive pressing waste (pomace) as a fuel was a common practice throughout the Mediterranean, North Africa, and the Near East both before and after the Roman period (Rowan 2015). Only 54 olive fragments were recovered from the north drain and 10 from the south; not enough to suggest anything other than table or ritual waste. Except for a few major centres such as the nearby Yolüstü settlement with its minimum of 11 presses, most pressing seems to have taken

Nuts and stone fruit were produced either by trees grown in the city or in nearby orchards. The recovery of peach stones suggests nearby cultivation as they bruise easily in transport over long distances. Although some stone fruit, and especially peaches, are known to have been expensive luxury items elsewhere in the Empire, the proximity of production probably ensured that fruit was inexpensive at Aphrodisias.[168] While few seasonings were found that is more likely the result of preservation than a true absence.

The archaeobotanical evidence from Aphrodisias in its Anatolian context

Few archaeobotanical assemblages from late Roman cities and sites in Anatolia have been studied, and therefore we are able to make an important contribution to understanding and comparing dietary and agricultural practices in this part of the Roman Empire.[169] Urban Anatolian sites which have so far yielded archaeobotanical evidence for Roman and late antique diet are limited to Sagalassos, Gordion, and Ephesos. Climatically, Aphrodisias is most similar to Ephesos, followed by Sagalassos. Gordion is situated in central Anatolia, a significantly drier region, meaning that comparison only with the most standard staple foods is possible.

Ephesos, on the western coast of Anatolia, also has a Mediterranean climate. Archaeobotanical samples from the Roman and late Roman periods have come primarily from the terrace houses and in particular Terrace House 2, unit 7. The samples from this unit date from the first century BC to the third century AD. A large mid first-century AD pit, containing a mixture of public feasting and votive offerings, has also recently been excavated in Terrace House 2, unit 3/5, room 12a.[170] As at Aphrodisias, the Ephesian diet seems to have been based predominantly on free-threshing wheat, followed by hulled barley and a limited amount of hulled wheat and legumes such as lentils. No chaff was found, which indicates cereals were processed outside the city.[171] Fruit finds are dominated by figs, olives, and grapes, followed by smaller quantities of pomegranate, pear, and mulberry.[172] The stone fruits are missing from Ephesos. It may be that horticulture was not practised near the city but it may also be due to the nature of the samples as all the samples, except those from the pit, were collected as part of a rescue excavation. An almost identical range of nuts was recovered, including pine nuts, hazelnuts, and walnuts. Palynological data from the near-by lake Bafa (Bafa Gölü) indicate that walnut and olive trees were growing in the region.[173]

The city of Sagalassos lies at 1,450–1,600 m asl in the western Taurus Mountains, in the Oromediterranean climatic zone.[174] Despite colder temperatures, and therefore somewhat different agricultural conditions, pollen data suggest that a similar range of crops and trees was grown in the fertile soil that surrounded the city.[175] Sections of the city have been thoroughly sampled for archaeobotanical remains, although the assemblages remain only partially published. There is material from a large late antique/early Byzantine house, a public latrine in the imperial-period baths, and other unspecified sections of the site.[176] The material from the latrine came from two phases, one dating from AD 130–350 and another from AD 420–600.

At Sagalassos, as at Aphrodisias and Ephesos, free-threshing wheat followed by barley and emmer formed the staple crops.[177] Millet became increasingly popular from the fifth century AD onwards, a practice that does not seem to have developed at Aphrodisias, at least at the time that the ring drain deposits formed.[178] Lentils and peas were found in the late antique elite town house, although the lentils may have been imported as it is too cold to grow them nearby. Common fruits at Sagalassos during the Roman period included figs, plums, grapes, and hackberry.[179] Only a small number of olive stones have been recovered, which led Baeten et al. to suggest that olives were not an important part of the diet,[180] although pollen data from Sagalassos has revealed that olive trees were grown extensively in the surrounding territory, probably for olive oil.[181] While a limited number of olive stones was also recovered from Aphrodisias, at both sites it is more probable that olives simply were not being burned on site.

Compared to Sagalassos, Aphrodisias seems to display a wider range of stone fruits, although plums were found at Sagalassos but not Aphrodisias. Nut taxa, including chestnut, hazelnut, almond, pistachio, and walnut, were recovered from Sagalassos, and pollen evidence indicates that walnut trees, along with plum, were grown within the city.[182] It is possible that a similar practice was taking place at Aphrodisias. Unlike at Aphrodisias, however, hazelnut and pine would have to be imported into Sagalassos.[183] Mineralized seeds of coriander and dill have tentatively been identified from the public latrine at Sagalassos, attesting the use of seasonings.[184]

---

place on a small scale (Lockey 2012, 216–219). Consequently, it is probable that the small farms used the pressing waste themselves, outside the city. The larger production sites are somewhat farther from the town and their pomace may have been used at these sites and the nearby farms and settlements.

168 Pliny *HN* 15.40. Peaches, figs, and grapes grow in abundance around the site today and are very inexpensive at local markets when in season.
169 Çakırlar and Marston 2019, 92.
170 Heiss and Thanheiser 2020.
171 Heiss and Thanheiser 2016, 630.
172 Heiss and Thanheiser 2020.
173 Knipping, Müllenhoff, and Brückner 2008; Heiss and Thanheiser 2016, 635.
174 De Cupere *et al.* 2017, 5.
175 Donners *et al.* 2000, 723–26; Baeten *et al.* 2012, 2.
176 Waelkens, Donners, and van Thuyne 2003; Putzeys *et al.* 2004; Baeten *et al.* 2012; Fuller *et al.* 2012.
177 De Cupere *et al.* 2017, 11.
178 Baeten *et al.* 2012, 14.
179 Putzeys *et al.* 2004.
180 Baeten *et al.* 2012, 12.
181 Waelkens, Donners, and van Thuyne 2003, 54.
182 Waelkens, Donners, and van Thuyne 2003, 57; Vermoere 2004, 189; Baeten *et al.* 2012, 13.
183 Waelkens, Donners, and van Thuyne 2003, 57; De Cupere *et al.* 2017, 11.
184 Baeten *et al.* 2012, 13.

Gordion, on the edge of the Sakarya river, is located in the semi-arid environment of the central Anatolian steppe. Although once a thriving Phrygian city, during the Roman period it was used primarily as a military base with a small civilian settlement next to the camp.[185] Archaeobotanical samples were collected from the entirety of the Roman period, which lasted from AD 50 to the early fifth century when the site was abandoned. The samples come primarily from mixed domestic contexts and represent the remnants of dung fuel, accidental cooking fires, and the intentional burning of crop processing waste. As at the other Anatolian sites, free-threshing wheat was the most popular crop, followed by hulled barley and lentil. A small number of Foxtail millet seeds (*Setaria italica*) were found and may have been a secondary crop during the Roman period. However, unlike the other sites, emmer was not grown or consumed.[186] The range of fruit and nut species produced and eaten is significantly narrower than at Aphrodisias, primarily due to the limited amount of rainfall.[187] Both olive oil and wine were not produced in the region and had to be imported.[188] Grape was the only fruit found in the Roman-period samples,[189] although small quantities of fig, cherry, pistachio, almond, and hazelnuts were found in earlier deposits. Marston has suggested that these fruit and nut trees did not grow in any large quantity around Gordion and instead the remains represent either the product of scattered garden trees, the collection of wild fruit, or in the case of hazelnut, imports.[190]

The samples from Ephesos, Sagalassos, and Gordion cover several centuries and the number of samples is limited compared to some other well studied sites in the Roman Empire such as Pompeii. Nevertheless, in combination these datasets present us with a rough idea of late antique diet in Anatolia, and we can now tentatively situate Aphrodisias within its wider dietary context. For the most part, consumption patterns at Roman and late Roman urban Anatolian sites seem relatively similar, despite vast geographical and sometimes climatic differences. The staple crops at all sites were free-threshing wheat and barley. Barley was recovered from the feasting context at Ephesos, and in large enough quantities from the remaining three sites to suggest consumption rather than fodder. While planting a more weather-resistant cereal in addition to the more sensitive free-threshing wheat makes good agricultural sense, the consumption of both may reflect both the Greek and Roman culture of ancient Anatolia. The consumption of emmer at Aphrodisias is in line with the evidence from both Ephesos and Sagalassos. The lack of millet is interesting but the fertility of the Morsynos valley may have negated the need to grow an additional cereal. Lentils were the dominant legume. A wide range of fruit and nuts, except at Gordion, seems to have been plentiful and readily available at all the sites. Walnuts, based on both the macrobotanical and palynological data appear to have been particularly prevalent, followed by pine nut and hazelnut.

Unsurprisingly, grapes, olives, and figs were the most popular fruits as they are both culturally significant and well suited to the varying climates. For the remaining fruits, consumption patterns vary based on climatic constraints. Peach was found only at Aphrodisias. Frost will harm the flowers of the peach tree and so its absence from Sagalassos, where there are periods of frost in the winter, is not unexpected.[191] Instead, plums, better suited to Sagalassos' higher elevation, were more popular, while pomegranate was common at Ephesos. Berries rather than stone fruit were eaten at Ephesos and it is interesting that no stone fruit was recovered from the well-preserved feasting pit as the region is climatically suitable for stone fruit. Luxury imported items, such as rice or black pepper were not found at any of the sites, and while this may be due to sampling bias, especially at the coastal site of Ephesos, it is equally possible that such items were not available or desired. The fertile hinterland surrounding all the sites appears to have been able to provide the inhabitants with an abundant and varied diet, especially in the range of cereals, fruits, and nuts. Aphrodisias and its hinterland, however, did have its own specialities or preferences, such as peaches, based on climate and perhaps local popularity.

Ritual and garden waste

As alluded to above, the drain assemblages probably represent a combination of food consumption and ritual and/or garden waste. Roman votive deposits typically contain a mixture of common foodstuffs, food items burned whole, and inedible material such as leaves and twigs.[192] Within the assemblage from the southern side of the ring drain at least five kinds of items suggest ritual waste (Pl. 40.C). Firstly, there are the edible items; the fragment of carbonized grape and fig flesh, which originally would have been burnt whole. Then there are the remains of inedible plants including cypress twigs and seed pods, and the numerous fragments of pine bracts. There is artistic and archaeobotanical evidence from around the empire for the ritual significance of pine cones in Roman society.[193] Similarly, the olive stones could represent food waste, but they are also frequently found in burnt offering pits from Pompeii.[194]

Lastly, there are the burnt leaves and buds of the Kermes oak. It is possible that the oak leaves and buds, along with the cypress and pine, simply represent the burning of pruning waste from trees that were growing around the pool or elsewhere on the site. However, the recovery of almost 600 fragments of forest/woody macchia plants including hundreds of Kermes leaves from the first-century AD pit in Ephesos does seem to suggest a ritual function. Heiss and Thanheiser have argued that the pit represents the remains of a public feast and votive offering that took place during a single event. In addition to a wide range of fruit, the pit also contained 86 carbonized lumps of

---

185 Marston and Miller 2014, 763; Çakırlar and Marston 2019.
186 Marston and Miller 2014, 765–766.
187 The site receives on average less than 350 mm of rain per year: Miller 2011, 312.
188 Marston and Miller 2014; Marston 2017, 115–118.
189 There was no evidence, however, for wine pressing in the area.
190 Marston 2017, 115.

191 Donners *et al.* 2000, 723.
192 Robinson 2002; Rottoli and Castiglioni 2011; Reed and Leleković 2019.
193 Ciaraldi and Richardson 2000; Robinson 2002, 97; Zach 2002; Lodwick 2015.
194 Ciaraldi and Richardson 2000; Robinson 2002, 995; Rowan 2014.

processed cereals, probably bread, numerous fragments of pine bracts, cypress twigs, and the buds of a member of the genus *Erica*.[195] There were also a large number of fish bones, fragments of imported wine amphorae, and over 600 dishes and plates.[196] Because the assemblage has undoubtedly become mixed as it moved down the drain, it is impossible to say for certain that the ring drain assemblage from Aphrodisias reflects a similar event or events. However, the presence of Kermes leaves in the ritual deposit from nearby Ephesos, combined with the other ritual components found in the drain, does suggest that at least some of the assemblage is votive in nature. This would suggest that pagan rituals were still taking place in the city, a fact also indicated by the evidence for religious tensions that is discussed further below (§M).

Formation of the ring drain assemblage

Now that the nature of the archaeobotanical assemblages have been determined, it is possible to hypothesize about the formation processes that led to their creation. In other words, how did kitchen waste and ritual offerings end up in a drain originally designed to collect ground water in a public part of the city? The length of the drain and the quantity of the carbonized material do not suggest a single burning event but rather the accumulation of material. Since the fill levels both above and below the organic layer on the south side have an identical date range, it is clear that the ring drain was not used as a sewer for very long. It is probable that the earthquake that took place just before AD 500 damaged the city's drainage system and for a short time the ring drain was used as a sewer, carrying water introduced into it by the angled drain added at this period south of the eastern end, which itself may have been connected to the drains of the Tetrapylon Street to the north-east. The date of the earthquake and the date of the fill levels on the south side (AD 475–525) are in alignment. On the north side, the lower fills which produced the archaeobotanical material accumulated soon before that side was intentionally filled in. On the south side, the drain was opened up, partially filled, as stated above, to stop pool water leaking out, used for a while as a sewer, and then the remainder of the drain was filled in. Water and waste from the more elevated areas of the site, such as the Tetrapylon Street and Sebasteion, would have flowed into the ring drain at the eastern end and drained out at the western end. The water in the original pipelines that supplied the pool's fountains flowed in a similar direction (see Ch. 2 §B).

Finally, large fragments of charcoal suggest that material flowed into the ring drain from elsewhere on the site. The pieces are too big to fit between any cracks in the marble cover slabs and so were not deposited from above by people sitting and eating around the pool. It was originally hypothesized that material was thrown into the drain during the repairs to the Place of Palms that took place following the earthquake. However, the clear upper and lower limits of the organic layer, combined with its horizontal extent, presumably along the length of both

[195] Heiss and Thanheiser 2020.
[196] Galik *et al.* 2020.

the north and south sides, negated this idea. The ring drain may have been partially open during repairs, but if used as a sewer to clear away food, garden, and, following the typical pattern of Roman sewers, human waste, it was probably at the very least covered with wooden boards while repairs were in progress. Instead, the material flowed through the sewer, pushed along by waste and probably rain water, and eventually settled into the narrow, concentrated band clearly visible in the south side. While the area around the pool was certainly planted with trees and possibly flowers and shrubs, because of the formation of the ring drain deposit, we cannot definitely state that the ritual or pruning waste comes directly from the Place of Palms.

Conclusions on the archaeobotanical material

In sum, the material from the north and south sides of the ring drain presents us with our first glimpse of diet and also ritual burning in Aphrodisias. Following patterns found elsewhere in the Empire, pine, cypress, fig and grape were used in burnt offerings. The more unusual contribution, although perhaps not in Roman Anatolia, are the leaves of Kermes oak. The Aphrodisian diet was based on the local production of a range of cereals, legumes, fruit, and nuts. Regional survey evidence suggests that cereals were produced in the Morsynos valley while presses and counterweights attest to the nearby production of wine and vast quantities of olive oil. Fruits and nuts may have been grown in the city or in orchards nearby. When compared to other urban sites in Anatolia with secure datable archaeobotanical evidence, the diet appears in line with consumption patterns found in the rest of late antique Türkiye, namely local but varied and based on free-threshing wheat and barley. Aphrodisias' Mediterranean climate and fertile hinterland enabled the inhabitants to exercise choice and cultivate a wide range of foods similar but not identical to those seen in other urban centres. Peaches were found only at Aphrodisias while other seemingly common items, such as pomegranate, were absent. The sample sizes, however, remain small and undoubtedly further sampling and research will continue to enhance and expand our understanding of life in this corner of the Roman world.

K. A SHELL FRAGMENT OF *CHARONIA* SP. (TRITON'S TRUMPET) FROM A LATE ANTIQUE CONTEXT (MR)

Aphrodisias was sufficiently distant from the coast that marine shellfish played little if any part in the diet. Only a limited number of shells of marine molluscs were found during the excavation of the deposits in the pool, as discussed in Ch. 10 §B. In the late antique contexts outside the pool, however, part of the columella (internal spiral) of a very large gastropod (sea snail) was found on top of context **2011**; this is the stripped mortar surface of the walkway around the pool and so, in practice, this shell fragment was part of **4280**, the late antique dump that raised the ground level of the Place of Palms. The columella (Pl. 40.D) was identified by comparison with modern shells in the Oxford University Museum. Since the columella is largely obscured unless the shell is broken, this required the use of a small mirror. Fortunately, there are few very large Old World gastropods and the fragment could be attributed to a member of the genus *Charonia* (Triton's trumpet) (Pl. 40.E).

Two species of *Charonia* can be found in the Mediterranean, *C. seguenzae* (Aradas & Benoit), which was formerly known as *C. variegata* or *C. tritonis variegata*; and *C. lampas* (L.), which now includes *C. nodifera*.[197] A third species, *C. tritonis* (L.) occurs in the Red Sea.[198] They are large shells, growing to a length of 40 cm or more. The primary habitat of the genus is at the edge of shallow water reefs where they occur on sandy and hard seabeds, feeding on echinoderms, particularly Asteroidea (starfish).[199] *Charonia* spp. are occasionally by-catches of netting but are most readily captured by diving. The most common use to which these shells are now put is for ornament but in the recent past in the Mediterranean region, they have been made into signal trumpets by cutting off the apex and, in some instances, attaching a metal mouthpiece.[200] The animals are rarely eaten.

The use of *Charonia* spp. shells as trumpets was widespread in antiquity. Of the 61 largely intact shells of *C. seguenzae* and *C. lampas* excavated from AD 79 levels at Pompeii and Herculaneum, over half showed working of the apex which would have enabled them to be blown.[201] *Charonia seguenzae/lampas* features in Graeco-Roman mythology as the 'conch' blown by the sea god Triton to calm the seas and is considered to be his symbol, hence the English name of Triton's trumpet.[202] A Roman mosaic now in the Bardo Museum, Tunis, shows Triton heralding the birth of Aphrodite by blowing on a shell which, assuming it represents a Mediterranean species, best matches *C. seguenzae*. There is a carved arcaded sarcophagus from Aphrodisias itself with a Triton blowing a *C. seguenzae*-like conch above a column at each front corner.[203]

Given the lack of evidence for other shellfish consumption at Aphrodisias, it is most unlikely that the *Charonia* sp. fragment was from a specimen imported as food. It could have been from a signal or ceremonial trumpet used elsewhere in the city that was discarded once broken and so ended up in the rubble dumped across the Place of Palms. The presence of another fragment of *Charonia* sp. in the first clearance deposit at the base of the pool (see Ch. 10 §B), however, might indicate that such shells were used in ornamental and ceremonial ways in relation to the pool.

L. A LATE FIFTH-CENTURY EARTHQUAKE (AW)

The discussion above has made passing references to the likelihood that the far-reaching repair programme attested both epigraphically and archaeologically was a response to severe damage caused to the city in a late antique earthquake. This section brings together the evidence in support of this hypothesis.

Evidence

We have seen that in the late fifth or very early sixth century there were extensive repairs to and rebuilding of the pool surround, with alterations to the water-supply and drainage arrangements, the filling of the ring drain, and the raising of the ground level across the entire Place of Palms, involving also the construction of new drains in the area. There is structural and stratigraphic evidence too for repairs to the North Stoa and its back wall (and the collapse of its colonnade on the Agora side), and also for the construction of two new South Stoas, one of which was continued across the front of the now-ruined Basilica. The West Stoa too was dismantled and rebuilt, and this operation also entailed repairs to the palaestra court of the Hadrianic 'Olympian' Baths, which involved taking down and re-setting parts of its architrave, and some marble door surrounds. Epigraphic evidence also attests a rebuilding of the Propylon of the Place of Palms, by the governor Doulkitios.

These operations were all contemporary. We have presented above (§B) the stratigraphic and structural evidence that links the repairs to the pool walls and the re-setting of the pool seats with the changes to the water supply and drainage arrangements, and the filling of the ring drain. We have also argued that the raising of the ground level was a response—perhaps undertaken within months, and certainly during the course of the overall rebuilding operations—to the flooding of the area that was a perhaps unforeseen consequence of the filling of the ring drain around the pool (§C). Material for this dumped layer doubtless derived from earthquake debris across the city. The epigraphic evidence of the late antique inscriptions on the Propylon assures the contemporaneity of repairs to the pool and/or the Place of Palms by Ampelios and of the repairs to the *temenos* and the rebuilding of the Propylon itself by Doulkitios (§A). The construction of both new South Stoas happened simultaneously with these works, as shown by the fact that the columns of the new South Stoas are set on foundation blocks which are themselves raised up on a level of rubble above the level of the earlier stoa's stylobate because the ground level in the area had been raised; and the dumped fill for this raised ground level abuts them. Similarly the repairs and alterations to the North Stoa involved the removal of stylobate blocks that were not directly supporting columns, so that the walking surface of the North Stoa was now the same as that of the raised ground level of the Place of Palms. If further proof of contemporaneity were needed, the repairs to the North Stoa's rear wall included the reuse of marble thrones that must come from an auditorium of some sort, with the Bouleuterion, which was also extensively remodelled by the same Ampelios (*ALA* 43) who restored the Place of Palms, a possible candidate—we shall return to this below.

We are therefore seeing nothing less than a wholesale rebuilding of the civic centre of Aphrodisias (Fig. 44). Not only were these building operations all contemporary with each other, but they were also causally linked. The repairs to the pool

---

197 Doxa *et al.* 2019, 49; Parenzan 1970, 156.
198 Hall *et al.* 2017, 14.
199 Hall *et al.* 2017, 15, 27–28.
200 Hall *et al.* 2017, 29–30; Reese 2002, 295; Borg-Cardona 2013.
201 Reese 2002, 293–294.
202 Borg-Cardona 2013, 187–188.
203 Smith and Ratté 1998, 245–246.

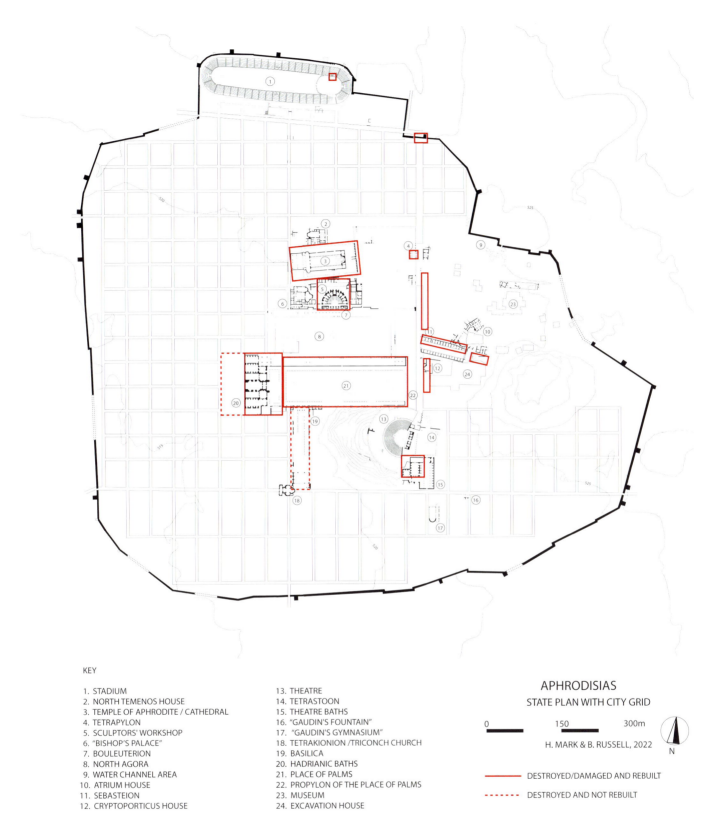

Fig. 44. Areas of Aphrodisias with evidence for damage by earthquake at the end of the fifth century AD.

walls use a striking number of architectural elements recycled from other public buildings—an architrave block, cut-down stylobate bench-blocks, and a split column drum, all presumably from a stoa, and most probably the second-phase South Stoa (§B). Seats with lions'-claw feet were also reused in the inner seat surround and cut down for use in the side slabs of the pool; these must derive either from the Theatre or the Bouleuterion. The columns of the South Stoa at its western end were founded on two cornice blocks and a carved screen block from the Basilica, which was evidently therefore ruined, and was never rebuilt (§F). It is very clear not only that the pool itself required repair, especially along the southern side where the two-storey second-phase South Stoa appears to have collapsed forward onto it, but also that the buildings which provided the material recycled in the repairs and in the foundations of the new South Stoas had been destroyed or severely damaged. Serious structural damage is also implied by the need to take down and re-set the West Stoa, the North Stoa, and the Propylon—all colonnaded structures susceptible to seismic shocks. It is hard to escape the conclusion that Aphrodisias was hit by a major earthquake in the late fifth century.

Dating

The dating of the earthquake and the repairs which followed it is given by two sets of evidence, epigraphic and stratigraphic, which can be combined to narrow the chronological window further. The inscriptions commemorating the repair works of Ampelios and Doulkitios carved on the Propylon suggest a window of *c.* AD 450–518: Ampelios' office of *patēr tēs poleōs* is not attested before the middle of the fifth century, while Doulkitios, as governor, is described as *hēgemōn*, indicating a date before the governorship of Karia was upgraded to consular rank before the end of the reign of Anastasius, after which governors were called *hypatikos*.[204] The monogram of Anastasius on one of the column drums of the eastern South Stoa shows that work on this structure was carried out during his reign (491–518).

The stratigraphic evidence consists of ceramics and coins from the fill of the ring drain around the pool, and from the extensive fill dumped across the Place of Palms to raise the ground level. The pottery both from the ring drain and from the dumped fill dates to *c.* AD 475–525. The numismatic evidence from the Place of Palms terminates with coins of Zeno (AD 474–491) (cat. 123–132), apparently giving a *terminus post quem* close to the start of the bracket indicated by the ceramic material. The absence of coins post-dating the coinage reform of Anastasius (AD 498) also suggests that we are dealing with the earlier rather than the later part of the ceramic dating bracket.

Combining the epigraphic and the stratigraphic evidence therefore gives a chronological range of 475–518. Within this range, two possibilities for refining the date further are suggested by the indiction-dated inscription from the Bouleuterion which records Ampelios' conversion of it into a *palaistra*; and as we have seen this work must be broadly contemporary with the repair of the rear wall of the North Stoa, and presumably also with Ampelios' repairs to the pool. The Bouleuterion conversion is dated to the tenth year of an indiction cycle, for which the options within the bracket of 475–518 are either 486/7 or 501/2. (A third option, 516/17, can be excluded because after Doulkitios but before the death of Anastasius in June 518 one has to fit in at least two governors with the rank of *hypatikos*, Flavius Ioannes,[205] and Procopius who held the office in 518.[206]) The date of 501/2 for the Bouleuterion works would fit very well if the earthquake that devastated the city centre of Aphrodisias was the same one as the earthquake of AD 494 which Marcellinus Comes says destroyed Hierapolis, Laodikeia, and Tripolis.[207] On the other hand the numismatic evidence would also allow the earlier date of 486/7, as the identifiable coins from the Place of Palms stop with Zeno (AD 474–491), though it should be noted that there are many coins of the second half of the fifth century that cannot be more closely identified than to the period 450–498. None comes from after the Anastasian reform of 498. But a coin of Anastasius, dating before his coinage reform (so AD 491–498), from what we believe is a contemporary deposit in the Agora, may take the date of at least some of the repair works into the 490s, although the earthquake could have been a few years earlier.[208] The monogram of Anastasius from a column of the eastern South Stoa confirms that repair work was (still) going on in his reign. In any case the earthquake and the extensive works of restoration and repair that followed it should fall between AD 475 and the very early 500s; and such a large-scale programme of restoration would in any case have taken many years.[209]

Extent

If the city suffered a major earthquake, we should expect its effects to have been felt beyond the Place of Palms and adjacent stoas, and indeed that is exactly what we do find (see Fig. 44). There is evidence to implicate in the earthquake damage and subsequent rebuilding also the Agora proper (the 'North Agora'), the Bouleuterion, the stoas and Sculptor's Workshop to the north of the Bouleuterion, the Hadrianic 'Olympian' Baths, probably also the Theatre Baths, Tetrapylon, and certainly the City Walls.[210] Less certain, but highly probable, is that the Temple of Aphrodite was also damaged and that its conversion into a Christian church formed part of the post-earthquake reconstruction.

---

204 Roueché 1989, 66–67 (although the *terminus ante quem* for the upgrade in rank is in fact AD 518, the *end* of the reign of Anastasius, and not its beginning in 491), and 320.
205 Roueché 1989, 320, *v. magn., comes et consularis* on milestones at Halicarnassus and Beypınar: *SEG* 16.665 and 16.694.
206 *SEG* 52.991 and 55.1509.
207 Marcellinus Comes, Annales, anno 494 (ii Asterii et Praesidii): *Laudicia, Hierapolis et Tripolis atque Agathicum uno tempore unoque terrae motu conlapsae sunt.* ('Laodikeia, Hierapolis and Tripolis, as well as Agathicum, collapsed at the same time and in a single earthquake.')
208 C2002.013, NAg 02.3, B3 (pers. comm. A. T. Tek).
209 Wilson 2016b, 134; Wilson, Russell, and Ward 2016, 89–90; Wilson 2018a, 479; 2019, 203.
210 The evidence is discussed more fully in Wilson 2018a, 476–484.

In the Agora, the South Stoa (which is of course the same building as the North Stoa of the Place of Palms, sharing a common spine wall) collapsed, falling to the north, and was rebuilt. We have seen already that the spine wall of this building was rebuilt in late antiquity and propped up with throne seats, probably from the Bouleuterion (see §E). Four cornice blocks, and an architrave block with part of the original dedicatory inscription mentioning Diogenes, the builder of the stoa in the reign of Tiberius, were found during excavations in 2002 (trench N.Ag.02.3), lying where they had fallen, and then buried in a dumped fill containing large quantities of building rubble and eighty-four late Roman coins, the latest of which is a pre-reform issue of Anastasius (AD 491–498).[211] Clearly the South Stoa of the Agora had collapsed—and this would be consistent with an earthquake shock in a north-south direction: the South Stoas of the Place of Palms and of the Agora, unsupported by bracing structures to their north, collapsed, while the North Stoa of the Place of Palms was badly shaken, with some columns cracked, but ultimately held up by its roof beams and rafters braced against its north wall. Pieced repairs to the cornice and architrave blocks of the stoa at the south-east corner of the Agora show that the colonnade here was damaged and repaired at some point after its construction, and some of the mask-and-garland frieze blocks are clearly late replacements. While these repairs are not in themselves closely datable, inscriptions show that some of the columns here were re-erected in late antiquity, one of them by the governor Flavius Pelagius Ioannes, whose title of *hēgemōn* (rather than *hypatikos*) places him before 518 at the latest.[212] As with the Place of Palms, a thick dumped fill was laid across the whole of the Agora, and the problem of drainage was solved by the creation of a collecting pool in the south-western corner.[213]

The Bouleuterion was extensively repaired and remodelled by the same Flavius Ampelios who restored the Place of Palms, and these works saw the removal of the front rows of seats and the conversion of the orchestra into a small arena for wrestling matches—the *palaistra* of Ampelios' inscription here (*IAph2007* 2.19 = *ALA* 43, dated in the tenth year of an indiction cycle, as discussed above).[214] It was potentially these works that made available the thrones and seats used to prop up the rear wall of the North Stoa of the Place of Palms / South Stoa of the Agora. The building seems to have lost its roof at this point, and holes cut into the surviving seating indicate that it was now covered by an awning supported on poles. An architrave block from the stage building, with a mechanically sawn upper surface, might belong to the same operations of trimming marble decorative and structural elements during repair works so that they would fit back into place in buildings whose walls had shifted somewhat during the earthquake.[215] All of Ampelios' modifications to the Bouleuterion, converting it into a *palaestra* for wrestling, would therefore be consistent with a response to massive damage to the building in an earthquake.

The destruction of the Sculptor's Workshop and other shops or workshops in the rear of the stoa north of the Bouleuterion should also be dated to this period.[216] It is clear that the workshop did not simply cease operations,[217] but was suddenly destroyed: a life-size male portrait statue had fallen face-down off an overturned column base in the middle of one of the rooms, that may have served as a working base; the c. 75 sculptural fragments found scattered around the room in the 1969 season are also consistent with damage to the workshop. Iron tools (three point chisels, 20–28 cm long) were found still lying on the floor in the doorway between the two rooms of the workshop;[218] if the workshop were simply abandoned one would expect these to have been recuperated and reused or recycled. The ground level over the workshop and the former stoa to its south, and the space between this and the Bouleuterion, was raised by c. 75 cm with a dumped fill, closely reminiscent of the situation in the Agora and the Place of Palms. This served as the new ground level for structures that incorporated numerous other fragments of sculpture from the workshop and appear thus to have immediately succeeded it. The stratigraphy thus indicates a sudden and violent destruction of the workshop and a wholesale subsequent transformation of the area. It is likely that this transformation of the area included the dismantling and removal of the columns of the stoas to the north and west of the Bouleuterion.[219] A date for the destruction and the ensuing reconstruction works is given by coins from the ground level of the stoa immediately adjacent to the workshop; the recent re-examination of a hoard and other coins from the context by Ahmet Tolga Tek and Hüseyin Köker shows that the latest coin in this context dates to the late fifth century.[220] The destruction and redevelopment of the Sculptor's Workshop, and the area between and the Bouleuterion is thus exactly contemporary with the other major renovations following apparent earthquake destruction discussed here. (An interesting corollary is that the Sculptor's Workshop was in full activity towards the end of the fifth century; and that contrary to previous interpretations, it did not close because of lack of demand at this period.)

Flavius Ampelios is also attested on a fragmentary inscription from the Theatre Baths (*IAph2007* 8.609 = *ALA* 44), which

---

211 Ratté and Smith 2008, 720 and fig. 7 p. 721. Latest issue: C2002.013, NAg 02.3, B3 (pers. comm. A. T. Tek).
212 Wilson 2018a, 479–481; for Flavius Pelagius Ioannes, see *IAph2007* 3.6 = *ALA* 29, with comments on the dating in Wilson 2018a, 480 n. 37.
213 Wilson 2018a, 479, for the arguments for interpreting this as a pool rather than a 'sunken court', and for dating it to the late Roman period rather than to the early imperial period.
214 Ampelios's name is restored in this fragmentary inscription, but it is almost certainly confirmed by his title of 'most eloquent *scholasticus* and father [of the city]'. On the conversion of the building, see Hallett and Quatember 2018, 355–356, cf. Wilson 2018a, 479.
215 This material will be discussed in more detail in a future study.
216 The publication of the Sculptor's Workshop (Van Voorhis 2018) is unclear on both the date and reasons for its destruction.
217 *Contra* Van Voorhis 2018, 10, 20.
218 Van Voorhis 2018, 14.
219 Van Voorhis 2018, 7 and 17, following Berenfeld 2009, assumes that the colonnades of the north and west stoas were removed at the time of the construction of the Bouleuterion in the Severan period, but no evidence is presented in support, other than apparently the supposition that they might have been too close to the Bouleuterion. Cf. also Berenfeld 2019, 23 for the same dating.
220 This hoard was first published by Hoover (2000, 296–297), who gave the closing date as AD 425–450; Tek and Köker have now revised this date to 408–423. A coin of Zeno that is not from this hoard but was found in this same context in a neighbouring trench allows us to push the date of this context later, however.

may suggest repairs to those baths too; and an inscription from the North East Gate of the City Walls records his restoration of the gate in the eighth year of an indiction (*IAph2007* 12.101. ii = *ALA* 42), two years before his inscription in the Bouleuterion, assuming the same indiction cycle (thus either 484/5 or 499/500 on the chronology argued above). Reused material originating from the Place of Palms and thus implying damage to buildings there, including the block recording Artemidoros Pedisas' donation of a gilded statue of Aphrodite and statues of Hermes and Erotes, and mask-and-garland frieze blocks from one of the stoas there, could derive either from the original mid-fourth century construction of the City Wall, or the late fifth-century repairs.

Ampelios may also have been involved in the construction of a fountain against the front of the podium of the former Temple of the Sebasteion, as suggested by the abbreviated forms of his name inscribed on column drums there (see Ch. 5 §E).

The late fifth-century earthquake must also be the context in which to situate the extensive late antique changes to the Hadrianic 'Olympian' Baths. These baths, originally built following the 'Asia Minor imperial thermae type' with an ambulatory surrounding a *frigidarium* or *natatio* in their western half, and the now visible row of vaulted *tepidaria* and *caldarium* in their eastern half, were remodelled in the late Roman period after the western half collapsed. The ambulatory was blocked off and a cold pool inserted into room 6 of the baths (originally the end of the ambulatory, immediately north of the northern tepidarium). This pool is paved with reused marble including parts of an architrave block which carried the dedicatory inscription of the baths, which has been sawn into slabs. If this architrave block was available for reuse, it must imply that serious structural damage to the building had occurred.[221] The palaestra court of the baths was extensively restored: Pytheas rebuilt the south stoa of the palaestra court (*ALA* 58 = *IAph2007* 5.303), and Dionysios the doctor (*ALA* 67 = *IAph2007* 5.219), who paid for repairs 'up to the tiled roof' of the palaestra colonnade, is commemorated on an inscribed architrave of the court. These repairs should be associated with the rebuilding that we can infer not only from the reconstruction of the common wall between the palaestra court and the West Stoa of the Place of Palms, but also from the marble architraves and doorway surrounds that show traces of mechanical sawing, trimmed to fit them back into a structure that had shifted out of true.[222]

To the south of the Propylon of the Sebasteion, the Tetrapylon Street, which runs north-south towards the eastern side of the Propylon of the Place of Palms has a colonnade which collapsed in an earthquake in the early seventh century AD. The column bases of this colonnade are founded on reused cornice blocks from more than one monument, and ceramics and coins from the fill point towards a late fifth-century date for the colonnade's construction, contemporary with the other post-earthquake building works. The surface of the street was raised considerably at the same period, by up to 1.1 m in front of the Sebasteion Propylon.[223]

More tentatively, evidence from the Stadium, the Tetrapylon, the Triconch House, and the Temple-Church may also be associated with destruction and, in the latter two cases, rebuilding, after the late fifth-century earthquake. The small purse hoard of 19 coins which was found in the northern refuge of the late Roman arena within the Stadium beneath elements of collapse, and which has recently been redated by Tek and Köker to the AD 460s/470s, provides a *terminus post quem* for the disuse and partial collapse of the arena and may be related to the destruction of the late fifth century.[224]

Tek and Köker's redating of the Stadium arena hoard, and their demonstration that late fourth-century coinage continued circulating at Aphrodisias until the late fifth century (§G above), also prompts a reconsideration of the date of the late antique reconstruction of the Tetrapylon. During the modern anastylosis of the Tetrapylon monument two bronze coins were discovered between the stylobate and one of the pedestals of the columns, showing that the monument must have been taken down and put back up again already in the late Roman period.[225] This observation was confirmed by the discovery of two keystones for the west side of the Tetrapylon's arch, of different sizes; when the monument was re-erected in late antiquity, it was not perfectly done and the original keystone would not fit, so a new one had to be carved.[226] Of the two bronze coins found set under the pedestal of one of the columns, the one that has been identified is a bronze of Arcadius (AD 395–401), of VIRTVS EXERCITVS type, *RIC* X, nos. 56–76.[227] Until now this has always been seen as evidence for the re-erection of the Tetrapylon around AD 400. But since coins of Arcadius were actually circulating until the late fifth century, as indicated by their presence along with other late fourth-century coins in the Stadium Arena hoard whose *terminus post quem* is now understood to be the 460s/470s (above), then it becomes entirely possible that the dismantling and re-erection of the Tetrapylon dates not to *c.* AD 400, but to the late fifth century—that is, exactly the time that other columnar buildings, such as the North and West stoas of the Place of Palms, and the Propylon, were being taken down and re-set because of structural damage. Indeed, this scenario would remove the problem of having to find an explanation both for why the Tetrapylon alone should have had to have been rebuilt around AD 400, and for why it was not apparently rebuilt in the late fifth century when most other public buildings suffered damage.

By the same token, the Triconch House, whose construction is conventionally dated *c.* AD 400, is merely given a *terminus*

---

221 Wilson 2018a, 483. For the original configuration of the baths, see Wilson 2016a.
222 Wilson 2019, 202.
223 Smith 2018b, 1–3.
224 Find circumstances of the hoard: Nbk 373, 136–137; Smith and Ratté 2000, 226. Hoard: Hoover 2000. For the redating to the AD 460s/470s, see n. 108 above.
225 Paul 1996, 208.
226 Paul 1996, 212–213.
227 Paul 1996, 208, gives the details as: coin no. 84/189: diam. 0.017 m. Obv. ARCADIVS PF AVG, diademed draped bust of emperor r.; Rev. Arcadius standing facing, head r., crowned by Victory (GLORIA ROMANORVM). But Arcadius issued no such GLORIA ROMANORVM types and in fact the reverse inscription on this coin was not read. The description fits the VIRTVS EXERCITVS type, *RIC* X, nos. 56–76 (information: A. T. Tek).

post quem by a coin of Theodosius I (AD 379–395);[228] but this coin too could have circulated until Anastasius's coinage reform of 498, and the construction of the Triconch House might therefore be dated as late as the end of the fifth century.

The conversion of the Temple of Aphrodite into a church has generally been assumed, largely on stylistic grounds, to have occurred in the fifth century and it has even been suggested that it might have been prompted by the visit of Theodosius II to the city in AD 443, and that imperial assistance might have been provided.[229] But if as we have seen the city was capable of major rebuilding works in the late fifth century, there is no need to invoke imperial funding and a mid-fifth-century context for the conversion. In fact, the outer narthex of the church of St Michael is given a *terminus post quem* of the late fifth century by coins of Leo I (457–474) found in the construction trench of its north wall, and it and the adjoining atrium to the west may therefore belong to the post-earthquake renovation works.[230]

The two large marble basins or *louteria*, one of which is now in the atrium, and the other now lies immediately north of the church but presumably had also been placed in the atrium,[231] probably derive originally from the Hadrianic 'Olympian' Baths and were moved to the church when parts of the baths were ruined in the late fifth century and the outer narthex and atrium were built.[232] The outer narthex is structurally later than the inner narthex and the church itself,[233] but this may simply result from the sequence of construction rather than imply any significant lapse of time between the events. Indeed, Robin Cormack pointed out that the colonnaded atrium (and thus the outer narthex) would be 'a feature essential in a church of the early Byzantine period, when the holy liturgy generally began with the assembly of the congregation here.'[234] Further research on the question is required, but the possibility is seriously to be considered that the late fifth-century earthquake and subsequent major rebuilding works across the city provided the opportunity for the ambitious conversion of the temple structure into the church involving the re-setting of its colonnades.

A further important discovery in relation to the question of a late-antique earthquake was the recognition that a number of the architectural blocks around the site have been sawn with a mechanical, and therefore water-powered, saw.[235] Twenty-seven such blocks have been catalogued, including two used in the repair of the pool; the remainder all come from buildings also known to have been reconstructed in the late fifth or early sixth century (Hadrianic Baths, Bouleuterion, Propylon of the Place of Palms), and it appears that in most cases these blocks have either been cut for reuse, or have been trimmed to size during re-erection works where they would not quite fit their original context because walls or other elements had shifted somewhat. For this to have been worthwhile, the water-powered saw must have been located somewhere in the city centre (aqueduct water supply would have been no problem), and was possibly even set up during the major rebuilding works following the late fifth-century earthquake for which we now have increasing evidence. The significance of this discovery is that it shows something of the extent of use of water-power for stone sawing around AD 500; and indeed the traces of mechanical sawing recognised on a third-century sarcophagus and large quantities of veneer panels, some dating from the second century AD, push the evidence for widespread water-powered marble sawing at Aphrodisias back into the high imperial period. This is of great importance in establishing the normality of the use of relatively complex water-powered machinery in the imperial period, making Aphrodisias something of a type-site in the history of mechanical technology.[236]

M. THE MAIOUMA FESTIVAL IN THE PLACE OF PALMS (BR & AW)

The fact that Doulkitios is given the title of 'Maioumarch' in the second of his inscriptions on the base of the Propylon could well explain a key function of the Place of Palms, at least in late antiquity. This title is added outside the metre of the verse, at the end of the first line of the text, which led Roueché and Reynolds to argue that it was therefore added after the epigram was composed but before it was inscribed.[237] They suggest that this particular element of Doulkitios' titulature was probably added by the town council and so was significant to them. As Maioumarch, Doulkitios was the official who presided over the celebration of the Maiouma, but this is the only attestation of this title anywhere.[238]

The Maiouma festival itself, which seems to have originated in Syria, became popular across a wide area, especially in late antiquity. Antioch, Ostia, and possibly Constantinople all hosted versions of the festival, according to the literary sources, and there is epigraphic evidence for it at Nicaea, Tyre, and Jerash.[239] The Nicaean text is third-century in date, while the text from Jerash refers to a festival in the year 535. John Malalas (writing a little after the mid sixth century) talks about the Maiouma at Antioch in relation to new regulations introduced under the reign of Commodus, showing that it was not exclusively late antique.[240] He records that the festival was triennial, consisted of night-time processions, theatrical performances recalling the mysteries of Dionysos and Aphrodite, and banquets; he also says that it was named after the month of May in which it occurred, an etymology that is dubious.

The emperor Julian was critical of the Maiouma at Antioch for bringing together male, female, and adolescent performers

---

228 Berenfeld 2009, 212; 2019, 31: a coin of Theodosius, C00.230, and another unidentified fourth-century coin, C00.231, found in the packing below the floor of the triconch hall.
229 Cormack 1990b, 83–84.
230 Smith and Ratté 1995, 44, 46; Hebert 2000, vol. 1, 27–28; vol. 3, 362.
231 Hebert 2000, vol. 1, 61.
232 Wilson 2019, 202–203.
233 Smith 2018a, 272.
234 Cormack 1990b, 80.
235 A full study of this material is in preparation.
236 On ancient use of water-power in general, see Wilson 2020.
237 *ala*2004 IV.25.
238 Roueché 1989, 71–73; 1993, 188–189 (no. 65).
239 Preisendanz and Jacoby 1930, 610–613; Belayche 2004a, 14–19. Nicaea: Roueché 1989, 9–14, no. 11; Tyre: Rey-Coquais 1977, no. 151; Robert and Robert 1978, no. 522 p. 499; Jerash: Welles 1938, 470–471, no. 279.
240 John Malalas, *Chronographia* 284–5.

and he railed against its licentiousness; he also says that huge sums of money were wasted on the banquets that also took place at the festival.[241] Libanius probably also had the Maiouma in mind when he complained about a festival involving shameful processions, which he connected to the Antiochene suburb of Daphne.[242] The festival certainly seems to have been carried out over multiple days—the inscription from Tyre notes that 'those who celebrate the Maiouma in this place have pleasant days'[243]—as well as nights; it was the nocturnal antics, in fact, that particularly troubled John Malalas and Severus of Antioch (writing between AD 512 and 518), who seem to describe the same festival.[244]

Although these sources do not mention water-based performances, other evidence suggests that the Maiouma was at least in part a water festival. Its name probably in fact derives not from May, but from the Semitic words *mai*, 'waters', and *yamma*, 'sea'.[245] John the Lydian notes that the Ostian version of the festival involved cavorting in the sea and it was probably the Maiouma that John Chrysostom had in mind when he complained about his congregation being distracted by the performances of naked actors in the flooded theatre.[246] Greatrex and Watt argue that the Brytae festival at Constantinople, despite its different name, was probably related to the Maiouma.[247] It took place in the theatre, which was flooded for the occasion, and certainly involved dancing.

What the religious content of the Maiouma was is unclear. Belayche in fact argues that it had no specific religious connotation, and was principally a festival of revelries involving water.[248] It was certainly banned for a while because in 396, under Arcadius and Honorius, an edict was promulgated re-permitting its celebration, providing that it was carried out in a decent fashion.[249] Three years later it was banned once more; apparently it failed to meet the required standard and had become synonymous with wantonness.[250] Since the later Justinianic Code leaves out the second of these Theodosian edicts, the one banning it again, this would suggest the prohibition did not last.[251] These bans relate to the immodesty of the festival, however, and not to its religious character. Indeed the two edicts in the *Codex Theodosianus* are not listed in the section on paganism (XVI, 10) and Roueché notes that the fact that Julian condemns the festival suggests that the problem was not that it was pagan.[252] John Chrysostom was concerned about his congregation attending, and Severus of Antioch complained that good Christians should not engage in such pursuits.[253] These Christian sources were primarily concerned with the indecency of the Maiouma—its naked, or at least scantily-clad, performers and the revelry they inspired—not its paganism. Even the Brytae festival at Constantinople, banned by Anastasius in 501, was curtailed not because of its religious character but because of two outbursts of factional violence, in 499 or 500 and 501, which led to the deaths of large numbers of people, many of them drowning in the waters of the theatre.[254]

The majority of the sources above associate the festival with theatres. In the fourth century a number of cities did convert their theatres or odea to accommodate some kind of aquatic shows by deepening and waterproofing their orchestra pits,[255] and it has been plausibly suggested that this phenomenon is directly connected with the increasing popularity of the Maiouma.[256] The inscription from Jerash, in fact, was found near the small 'festival theatre' north of the city centre, at the Birketein.[257] The defining feature of this locale, however, is not this theatre itself but the pools after which it is named (*birketein* meaning 'two pools' in Arabic), which have already been mentioned in Ch. 2 §D; these are actually a single large reservoir, 88.5 × 43.5 m and 3 m deep, divided in two by a wall (see Pl. 21.A).[258] This reservoir seems to have been built in the late first or at some time during the second century and either served public monuments in the city or was used for irrigation, but it would also have made a perfect setting for aquatic performances. The reservoir was certainly monumentalised, with a portico around it built in the Severan period.[259] An inscription from the Birketein, dating from November 535, was initially thought to refer to the lifting of a ban on the festival, but has been re-interpreted as a reference to the refurbishment of the pools.[260] The inscription itself was found on the west pier of a gateway at the south end of this pool and so provides clear support for this structure as the venue for the Maiouma.[261] McCown draws a parallel between the role of the Birketein, a 'semi-sacred pleasure ground' outside the city of Jerash, and the relationship of the suburb of Daphne to the city of Antioch.[262] These were both bucolic settings, rich in water, beyond the city centre and it is striking that both Libanius and Severus of Antioch describe festivals at Daphne similar to the Maiouma, although without naming them explicitly.[263]

At Aphrodisias a similarly suitable venue for the Maiouma, of course, already existed, and it lay directly in front of the inscription naming Doulkitios as Maioumarch. The large

---

241 Julian, *Misopogon* 346c, 362d.
242 Libanius, *Orationes* 41.16.
243 Rey-Coquais 1977, no. 151; Robert and Robert 1978, no. 522 p. 499; Greatrex and Watt 1999, 10.
244 John Malalas, *Chronographia* 284–5; Severus of Antioch, *Homily* 95.
245 *ala2004* IV.26; Greatrex and Watt 1999, 13; this etymology is also noted by John the Lydian, *De Mensibus* IV.80.
246 John the Lydian, *De Mensibus* IV.80; John Chrysostom, *Homiliae in Matthaeum* VII.6.
247 Greatrex and Watt 1999.
248 Belayche 2004b.
249 *Codex Theodosianus* XV, 6, 1.
250 *Codex Theodosianus* XV, 6, 2. Roueché 1989, 72.
251 *Codex Justinianus* XI, 45.
252 Roueché 1989, 72.
253 John Chrysostom, *Homiliae in Matthaeum* VII.6; Severus of Antioch, *Homily* 95.
254 Greatrex and Watt 1999, 1–4.
255 Traversari 1960.
256 Godefroy 1665 [*non vidimus*], cited by Roueché 1989, 72–3; Roueché *ala2004*.
257 Greatrex and Watt 1999, 13; on this theatre, McCown 1938a.
258 Seigne 2004, 175–8; Lichtenberger and Raja 2016, 105, 107.
259 Kraeling 1938, 58–59; Welles 1938, no. 153: the portico was dedicated during the emperorship of Septimius Severus, Caracalla and Geta, AD 209–211.
260 McCown 1938b, 686; reinterpretation: Mentzu-Meimare 1996, 69–73.
261 McCown 1938a, 159.
262 McCown 1938a, 159.
263 Libanius, *Orationes* 41.16; Severus of Antioch, *Homily* 95.

and shallow pool in the Place of Palms, equipped with a marble bench around its edge and with space for more spectators beyond, shaded by trees, was a ready-made aquatic auditorium. The Theatre and Bouleuterion at Aphrodisias were never converted to host aquatic spectacles but then the presence of this pool rendered such conversions unnecessary; they could be put to other uses instead, and the former was adapted for gladiatorial shows in the second century and the latter for wrestling in late antiquity. The proximity of the Theatre at Aphrodisias to the pool in the Place of Palms echoes the arrangement of pool and theatre at the Birketein outside Jerash; revelry in one venue could easily have spilled over into the other.

Whether the title of Maioumarch meant that Doulkitios actively organised or even financed the Maiouma is not certain. It might simply have been the title of a prestigious office that the city decided to bestow on the governor. Since nobody else is known to have held this title, however, it is tempting to think that this was a title that reflected Doulkitios' personal patronage of the festival, in a venue that he helped to restore—this would be especially appropriate if his restoration of the *temenos* in fact referred to the pool, as suggested above. The Maiouma certainly received high-level official support elsewhere. Malalas notes that at Antioch the praetorian prefect Antiochus Chuzon gave money to the city for horse races, the celebration of the Olympian festival, and the Maiouma in 430–431.[264] The Brytae festival at Constantinople was hosted by the praetorian prefect Helias in 499 or 500 and his successor, Constantine Tzouroukkas, in 501.[265] Even the earlier text from Nicaea seems to be part of an inscription honouring someone connected to the festival.[266]

Whether the Maiouma was as controversial among the Christian population at Aphrodisias as in other areas of Asia Minor and the Levant is not clear from the present state of the evidence. Religious tensions in the city are well-documented.[267] Some benefactors in this period were defiantly pagan. The Pytheas, mentioned above, who was involved in the rebuilding of the Hadrianic Baths (*ALA* 58 = *IAph2007* 5.303) is a case in point. An honorary epigram on the base of a statue set up for this same Pytheas, probably in the Bouleuterion, begins with the words 'City of the Paphian goddess and of Pytheas' (*ALA* 56), referring to his building activity as a 'first-fruit offering', a pagan religious term. This could be interpreted as a specific response to the conversion of the Temple of Aphrodite into a church in this period.[268] At the same time, the rebuilder of the West Stoa of the Place of Palms, Albinos, was defiantly Christian, as the acclamations honouring him make clear (§D). His building project was just over the wall from Pytheas' in the Hadrianic Baths, a point that perhaps explains the vehemence of some of the inscribed acclamations.

Doulkitios, as Maioumarch, was presumably not himself Christian. The case of Ampelios is less clear. The verse inscription commemorating his repairs makes use of pagan imagery such as the nymphs, though this need have no great significance beyond the poetic,[269] and there is a cross inscribed above the inscription, centred with it and of the same size of the letters (see Pl. 28.A). If the cross is contemporary with the inscription, as it appears to be, he was presumably a Christian, but if so his faith did not prevent him appealing perhaps to the pagan community through the reference to nymphs, whose poetic context may have defused potential offence to the Christian community. The fact that Christians like Albinos and perhaps also Ampelios were happy to invest in the rebuilding of the West Stoa of a complex seemingly associated at that date with the Maiouma would suggest that the festival was simply part of Aphrodisian civic life and not explicitly religious. The numerous informal texts inscribed on the pool's edges and the stylobates of the North and West Stoas, which are discussed in detail in Ch. 5, show that the Place of Palms was frequented by individuals from the full spectrum of the city's religious communities. Christian prayers are common, as are inscribed crosses, as well as Jewish menoroth, in all of these places, often associated with longer texts. There is some indication of religious conflict, however. In one instance a phallus is inscribed next to a menorah (Appendix 2, P407, P409; see Ch. 5 §C). Another text, on a gameboard, explicitly denigrates the governor and Maioumarch—'Eusebios buggers/buggered Doulkitios'—and might have been inscribed by a Christian (Appendix 2, P110; Pl. 43.G).

These various texts and symbols—as well as the work by Albinos—show that the Place of Palms was certainly not a no-go area for Christians. That being said, the large number of inscribed crosses on the walls of the north tunnel leading through the Propylon into the space, a location that otherwise has fewer of the kinds of informal texts and symbols on the pool and in the stoas, is striking (Fig. 45). While crosses are common throughout Aphrodisias, the concentration of them in the monumentalized entrance to the Place of Palms makes it appear as if some in the Christian community felt that this was space that needed to be marked, perhaps even cleansed—as though they were taking almost literally Doulkitios' appellation of it as a *temenos*.

N. FURTHER ADJUSTMENTS IN THE SIXTH OR SEVENTH CENTURY (AW)

Several sets of modifications to the Place of Palms and its pool can be attributed to the period after the restorations of the late fifth/early sixth century, but before the pool went out of use and began to be filled in, in the mid seventh century. These include: the construction of a large basin against the west face of the Propylon; repairs to the walls of the pool; and further alterations to the supply and drainage of the pool. These must, broadly, date to the sixth century, or in some cases perhaps to the early seventh.

---

264 John Malalas, *Chronographia* 362.
265 John of Antioch, frg. 214c; Greatrex and Watt 1999, 1–2.
266 Robert 1936, 9–14, no. 11.
267 Chaniotis 2008a; Wilson 2019, 207–208.
268 We are grateful to A. Chaniotis for this suggestion.

269 For the use of pagan mythology by Christians, see Uytterhoeven 2009; Graf 2011; Leppin 2015.

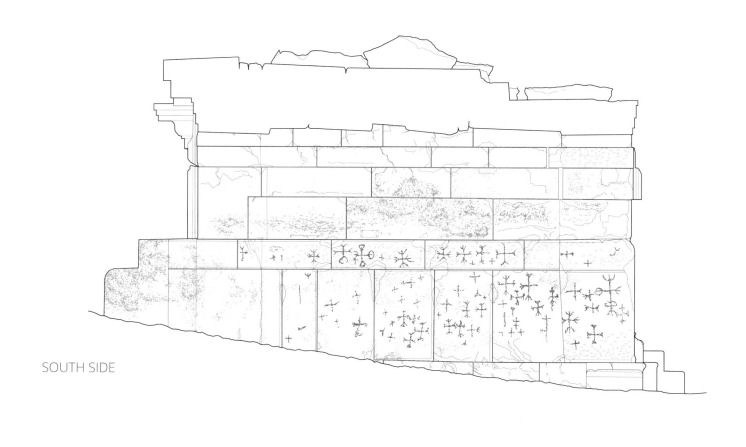

SOUTH SIDE

NORTH SIDE

Fig. 45. Crosses inscribed on the north and south walls of the north tunnel of the Propylon.

The basin against the Propylon

The large basin constructed against the Propylon, with thick masonry walls incorporating much re-used material and surmounted by a series of mythological reliefs recycled from an earlier Roman building, is fully described in Ch. 6. Here it suffices merely to emphasise four main points, and to discuss the water supply to the basin.

First, the basin is not contemporary with the inscriptions commemorating the repair work by Ampelios and Doulkitios which are carved on the Propylon above it. The height of the basin wall and the mythological reliefs surrounding the basin parapet would have completely obscured the inscriptions from the viewpoint of anyone standing in the Place of Palms in front of the Propylon, and two of the pipelines that supplied the basin delivered water directly over the inscriptions. The basin must belong to a period in the sixth century sufficiently after the restoration project of Ampelios and Doulkitios that it was acceptable to obscure their inscriptions in this way.[270]

Second, the basin is not, as was claimed in works published between its discovery in 1986 and 2016, a late antique fountain nymphaeum.[271] Its walls are far too high (*c.* 3 m) and too thick (1.48–1.57 m on the north side, 1.82 m on the south side, 1.66 m on the west side) to allow people standing on the ground beside it to draw water from it.[272]

Third, the basin instead seems to have served as a large reservoir tank to collect water from several different pipelines, and it can hardly have served any function other than as a header tank to supply water under pressure to fountains at the east end of the pool in the third and final phase of supply, described below.

Finally, the functional aspects of the basin go hand-in-hand with a sculptural programme, that included not only mythological reliefs (Gigantomachy, Amazonomachy, and Centauromachy scenes) set between Eros pillars, but also re-purposed statuary, including a seated statue of a himation-clad figure set on a reused base for a governor of *c.* AD 300; the honorand was presumably the benefactor who had not only built the basin (Ch. 6), but reorganised and restored the supply to the pool (below).

The basin measured 31.5 × 6.6 m internally, by up to 3 m deep, for a total volume of *c.* 890 m³. It was fed by at least ten different pipelines. Seven discharged into it from the east, three pairs laid in cuts hacked through the upper ashlars of the piers supporting the columns of the Propylon, and the seventh laid in a cut across the never-completed blocked stairs between the second and third piers from the south, emerging at an angle into the basin at the top of the second pier. Three more pipelines supplied the basin under pressure from the south. One came diagonally across the southeast corner of the Place of Palms from the South Stoa, laid well above the original ground surface, and thus within the late antique raised ground level, and runs up the south wall of the basin at the southeast corner, running through the wall just before the top to discharge into the basin. Two more pipelines, one of which at least seems to have come through the southern tunnel of the Propylon, met in a pressurised stone junction box made from a hollowed-out octagonal base, with two sockets for the pipelines at the bottom of it (Pl. 40.F). The upper surface of this octagonal block was worked as a male pipe joint and it was originally surmounted by a second octagonal block worked to take a lid, probably in metal (Pl. 41.A). From it a pipe fed into the basin, just east of the middle of its south side. Together, these pipelines show a considerable effort to fill the pool with water from a number of different sources (and perhaps originating from more than one of the city's aqueducts) in order to maintain a sufficient volume and head of water in the tank to supply the pool.

Modifications of the water supply and drainage of the pool

There is evidence of further work on the supply and drainage arrangements of the pool in the centre of the Place of Palms during the course of the sixth century or the early seventh. Certainly post-dating the second phase of water supply and drainage arrangements, attributed to Ampelios' restoration work of the late fifth century, is a third phase of modifications to the pool's supply and drainage which should date to some time during the sixth century. It is this phase that is likely to be contemporary with the construction of the basin against the Propylon.

In this third phase, pipelines C4 and C9 of the second phase were replaced by a larger, single pipeline, C1, laid or cut within the dumped levelling layer that raised the ground level to the east of the pool and sealed the second-phase pipelines. Pipeline C1 approached the pool from the north-east and reached the pool at the centre of the east end, where the seats are interrupted, one having been taken up and relaid upside-down. Here it fed into the east face of a large marble distributor block, D3,[273] which had two sockets 0.21 m in diameter in its north face (perhaps for pipelines directly replacing C4 and C9 to their fountain outlets?), and two circular openings in its upper face, also 0.21 m in diameter. These openings on the upper face were not for pipelines, but presumably allowed for cleaning or removal of any blockages within the distributor block; they were originally closed with circular lids made from cut-down tiles or hypocaust *pilae*, of which the westernmost was found *in situ* in 1988, and the other was found during cleaning in 2017 (Pl. 31.D–E and 41.B–C).[274] In the west face of the distributor block a larger hole, 0.28 m in diameter, was for the main feeder pipe into the pool. Since there were no sockets for pipelines in the south face of the block, it appears that in this third phase there were no pipes circulating in the void duct space over the drain to supply fountains along the south side of the pool. Since both of the outlets from the distributor block D3 on its north side seem to be accounted for by the recuts for the two fountains earlier fed by C4 and C9, and there is no room for extra pipes to enter the void space, it appears that there were no pipelines running around the north side of the pool either. If the pipelines running around the pool had been relaid in Phase 2 (Ampelios'

---

270 Wilson 2016b, 132–133.
271 For example Erim 1986b, 10; 1987; Roueché 1989, 67–73; Linant de Bellefonds 1996, 174 and 186; Ratté 2001, 136; Jacobs and Richard 2012, 15–16.
272 Wilson 2016b, 132.

273 D3: length 0.85 m × width 0.525 m × height 0.55 m.
274 Nbk 297: *Agora Gate: Basin Front I* (F. Thode, 1988), 68, figs 20–21.

repairs) on top of the earthen fill of the ring drain, then they must have been removed in Phase 3. All this suggests that the header tank built against the Propylon supplied no more than two or three fountains at the east end of the pool.

The reasons that prompted these various alterations, evidently substantially later than the wholesale refurbishment of the area under Doulkitios and Ampelios, are unclear. The need to create a large header tank, fed by multiple pipelines, to maintain pressure to the fountains at the east end of the pool, may imply a reduction in the flow of some or all of the city's aqueducts that had hitherto supplied the fountains.

O. SEVENTH-CENTURY REPAIRS TO THE POOL AND MODIFICATION OF SUPPLY AND DRAINAGE (AW)

Several other repairs and changes to the supply and drainage arrangements—brick patching to damage in the marble slab lining of the north side of the pool; a late and low-level large diameter pipeline entering the pool on the south-eastern arc, and changes to the drainage arrangements, seem to be even later than the basin against the Propylon. We cannot with certainty date them more closely than between some time in the sixth century, after the repairs of Ampelios and Doulkitios, and after the construction of the Propylon basin, and before the filling of the pool in the mid seventh century, after AD 643/644; but we think it most likely that these very late repairs postdate the earthquake of *c.* AD 620, for reasons discussed below.

Some unsightly brickwork repairs filling patches of damage to the marble slabs of the pool walls (Pl. 42.A) must surely postdate the repairs of Ampelios, when the pool walls had been fully replaced in marble.

In the side wall of the southeast curve of the pool, a large circular hole was cut through the marble slab to allow a large terracotta pipe, which traversed the still-used or reinstated portion of the ring drain here, to discharge into the pool just 29 cm above the floor (Pl. 42.B). This seems to be a last attempt to keep a sufficient amount of water in the pool, by using pipelines from whatever source even if they lacked the pressure to feed fountains on the surround; water delivered through this pipeline must have entered the pool at or just below the water level that was now being maintained. This should be later than the third-phase supply arrangements, and suggests that the basin against the Propylon had ceased to function effectively as a header tank. But this late supply pipe must predate the pool's ceasing to function as an ornamental feature in the mid seventh century (after AD 643/644, the *terminus post quem* given by the latest coin in the lowest deposits filling the pool; see Ch. 8).

It was presumably also at this same time as the major alterations to the water supply that the drainage arrangements of the second phase were further modified, with the blocking of the sluice gate for the exit drain at the southwest of the pool, in masonry using small stones and tiles (in 1989 the excavators left *in situ* the lowest course in flat stones and two brick courses above it), and the side facing the pool was then plastered over with pink waterproof tile mortar. The same pink mortar was applied to seal the joints between the marble revetment slabs forming the side walls of the pool in this southwest part of the basin. The second-phase overflow at the west end was blocked with a fill of earth, stones, and fragments of tile. These measures suggest continued or even worsening problems with retaining a sufficient level of water in the pool.

As the sluice-gate exit had now been blocked up, the original floor-level drain at the west end of the pool was reinstated, but this time by a crudely hacked opening which partly cut through the original drainage exit block with its rebated circular socket (for a filter?), and the hole underneath enlarged by undermining the basal socket of the pool wall (Pl. 42.C); at this point too the concrete floor of the pool was missing, and sand and stones were found here instead.

The repairs to the pool walls indicate damage to some of the marble lining slabs, particularly at joins between slabs. The significant changes to the water supply indicate that the water supply from the header tank against the Propylon no longer functioned properly, and that water now had to be brought in from a lower-lying pipeline, presumably run through the southern tunnel arch of the Propylon. Changes to the drainage arrangements also suggest problems with maintaining the water level in the pool, which would be consistent with damage to the pool walls or floor that was causing water to leak.

A hypothesis that would explain these various points might be that a further earthquake had damaged the pool walls, and that it had put out of action either the supply lines to the Propylon basin, or the basin itself. In theory this could have happened at any point in the sixth century, or the first half of the seventh century, before the filling of the pool in the mid seventh century, after AD 643/644.

Although an otherwise unknown sixth-century or early seventh-century earthquake cannot be entirely excluded, we do have independent evidence for an earthquake around AD 620, the characteristics of which are consistent with the late damage and repairs discussed here. The evidence for the earthquake of *c.* 620 is discussed more fully in Ch. 8; it destroyed the colonnades of the north-south Tetrapylon Street, many columns of which fell to the west, while some of the upper brick arcading fell to the east. The Propylon collapsed to the west in this earthquake, as did a wall of the shops against the west side of the ruined civil basilica. Unlike the earthquake of the late fifth century, then, whose main thrust was south-to-north, the earthquake of *c.* 620 had a mainly east-to-west and west-to-east shaking movement. This would explain the damage to marble panels of the north side of the pool, which were compressed together by such a force and cracked at one point, necessitating the brickwork repairs seen in Pl. 42.A. Since the Propylon collapsed westward into the basin that had been built against its west side, which was found full of architectural elements from the Propylon when it was excavated, this basin would no longer have functioned as a header tank after this earthquake, and a new supply pipe would have been needed at this point. Moreover, as the archaeobotanical evidence discussed in Ch. 8 demonstrates, the pool was kept clear with water flowing through it until the moment when rubble deposits were dumped into it during a clean-up of the Place of Palms after a fire in the mid seventh century, not earlier than AD 643/644. This implies that there must have been sufficient maintenance of the pool after the earthquake of *c.* AD 620 for water to have continued to flow through the pool; and these repairs are precisely the kind of work that would have been needed.

Rather than postulate another earthquake in the sixth century, then, we prefer to explain these late repairs as motivated by the earthquake of *c.* 620. The significance of this tentative dating is that the city—or rather its population—was still willing and able to undertake such repair work, aesthetically crude as it was, in the 620s. This is later than many people might have been expected—but as has been pointed out, because of a relative lack of epigraphic evidence from cities in Asia Minor which can be securely dated to the seventh century, a common tendency is to date generically 'late' works to the sixth century and not the seventh because of a presumption that total decline had set in by the seventh century.[275] The lack of known seventh-century activity thus reinforces the picture in a circular argument. Such assumptions need to be tested, not simply taken on trust; and it is precisely through stratigraphic archaeology, where the recovery of coins can refine dating sequences more precisely, that such testing is possible.

One might add that it is possible (though not certain) that the seventh-century repairs to the marble flooring of the Hadrianic Baths, which are given a *terminus post quem* by a coin of Phocas (602–610) found in the mortar beneath the floor, might also post-date the *c.* 620 earthquake.

P. CONCLUSIONS (AW & BR)

At some time in the last two decades of the fifth century Aphrodisias was hit by a devastating earthquake. Buildings across the city were damaged, and the public buildings of the city centre either collapsed or required major structural repairs; much of the columnar architecture that had not collapsed needed to be dismantled and re-erected. Besides the Place of Palms with its pool and surrounding stoas, buildings damaged included at least the Basilica, the Hadrianic 'Olympian' Baths, the Agora, probably the Bouleuterion and stoas/shops to its north including the Sculptor's Workshop, parts of the City Walls, the stoas along the north-south street to the south of the Tetrapylon, and possibly also the Tetrapylon, the Temple of Aphrodite, and the area of the Triconch House. Stratigraphic, epigraphic, and numismatic evidence combines to place the earthquake and ensuing reconstruction work somewhere between 475 and the very early 500s; reconstruction work on this scale across the city will have taken a decade or more, hence no doubt the phrase in the epigram commemorating Doulkitios' reconstruction of the Propylon that it had stood 'neglected for unnumbered years'.

Work on this scale is exceptional, in the present state of research on late antique cities in Asia Minor; but may perhaps prove to be less so than currently appears. At Sagalassos, major reconstruction was undertaken in the early sixth century following an earthquake *c.* AD 500.[276] Laodikeia, Hierapolis, and Tripolis were devastated by an earthquake in AD 494, but public buildings there were rebuilt too. It is possible that Aphrodisias and Sagalassos were hit by the same earthquake which struck Laodikeia, Hierapolis, and Tripolis; but it is also possible that the decades around 500 were seismically very active—there is a known tendency for earthquakes in a region to cluster chronologically.[277] The capacity of these cities, at least, to recover from massive earthquake damage is a testament to continued urban vitality at these sites.

The reconstruction of the Place of Palms was undertaken by the governor Doulkitios in the reign of Anastasius, under the supervision of the *pater tēs poleōs* Flavius Ampelios, who is also attested in several of the other building reconstructions at the same time. In addition to the use of civic funds, there may have been some imperial assistance for post-earthquake reconstruction, attested by Anastasius's monogram on the eastern South Stoa; Doulkitios appears to be celebrated for having contributed some of his own wealth too, and other individual benefactors certainly contributed, such as Albinos in the West Stoa, and Philip for the roofing of the South Stoa(s). The works in and immediately around the Place of Palms included wholesale rebuilding of the South Stoa against the Theatre Hill retaining wall, the construction of a new stoa along the western stretch of the south edge of the Place of Palms, running across the front of the Basilica which was not rebuilt; the dismantling and re-erection of the Propylon; the taking down and re-erection of at least some of the columns of the North Stoa and parts of its back wall, and of columns to the north that formed the South Stoa of the Agora proper; the re-erection and repaving of the West Stoa, by Albinos, and repairs to the Hadrianic 'Olympian' Baths further west by several other individuals. The marble walls and seating around the pool were extensively replaced, especially on the south side where the second-phase South Stoa had collapsed onto the edge of the pool, and the water supply and drainage arrangements were altered, with the ring drain filled in to prevent leakage. The ground level of the whole area was raised by some 40–60 cm with a dumped fill of earth and rubble from the earthquake damage; similar thick dumped fills of the same kind of composition are found across the Agora and the area to the north of the Bouleuterion. This raising of the ground level was both a means of disposing of the vast amount of rubble from the destruction caused by the earthquake, and dealing with problems of groundwater drainage caused by the filling of the ring drain around the pool and perhaps also damage to parts of the city's under-street drainage network. The rebuilding of the West Stoa and North Stoa involved the removal of screen fittings and other fixtures, opening up intercolumniations again to return the visual aspect of the colonnades to something closer to their early imperial form.

The extensive reconstruction programme in the Place of Palms, and indeed across the city more generally, shows the continued vitality of urban life at Aphrodisias at the opening of the sixth century. The governor and *pater tēs poleōs* were able to organise the repair and rebuilding of most of the city's public buildings, and the tradition of élite euergetism was still alive and well, and capable of being directed towards this massive rebuilding programme. The extraordinary level of activity, in-

---

275 Roueché 2007a, 186.
276 Jacobs and Waelkens 2013.
277 On earthquake clustering, see Wilson 2018a, 471 fig. 36.1; Fentress and Wilson 2021.

cluding the construction with new architectural elements of the eastern South Stoa, indicates the importance of the Place of Palms in the urban life of Aphrodisias—it was reconstructed, whereas the Civil Basilica was left in ruins, merely screened by the new western South Stoa. One of the reasons for the importance of the Place of Palms, besides its central nodal location within the city plan, may have been that its enormous pool was used for the aquatic revelries of the Maiouma festival, presided over by Doulkitios the governor.

The excavated levels from the late antique reconstruction works yielded stratified finds that both help date this activity and shed light on the nature of urban life and material culture at the time of the earthquake and the ensuing building works. Coin finds not only help to show that the rebuilding work occurred around the end of the fifth century, but also that fourth-century coins continued to circulate at Aphrodisias almost to the end of the fifth century—a realisation with important implications for the use of fourth-century coins to date other construction activity at the site: they merely provide a *terminus post quem*, and the actual date of loss, and thus of deposition in the contexts in which they were found, could be a century later. The pottery is overwhelmingly local, with very few imports from outside the immediate region—a picture highly unusual for Roman cities, even in landlocked regions (Sagalassos has a far greater quantity of non-local material). This appears to point to Aphrodisias's self-sufficiency in basic foodstuffs and also in commodities like olive oil and wine, a picture reinforced by the botanical remains.

The archaeobotanical evidence also suggests the ritual burning of figs and grapes as food offerings, and also of cypress, pine, and perhaps Kermes oak. Some of this material probably entered the ring drain via a sewer or drain that was connected to it in the late antique repairs, and thus this material probably derives from elsewhere in the city. But if this is indeed ritual waste, it would indicate the active continuation of pagan ritual at Aphrodisias at this late date.

Later sixth-century (or even later) repairs to the pool and alterations to its water supply, including the addition of a large water tank against the Propylon, were perhaps caused by a further earthquake or tremor, but much less severe. They demonstrate continued maintenance of the Place of Palms, and show that the city was still capable of organising and funding considerable construction projects well into the sixth century and even into the early seventh century. This is consistent with evidence that shows the Hadrianic 'Olympian' Baths had their marble flooring renewed or repaired as late as the reign of Phocas (602–610) or later.[278] Despite earthquakes and the Justinianic Plague of the mid sixth century, Aphrodisias was still a thriving urban centre into the early seventh century. Ch. 8 will examine when and how that changed; the next three chapters, however, pull together the evidence for informal writing, graffiti, and gameboards, and what they suggest about the use of the Place of Palms; the sculptural programme of the Propylon basin in late antiquity; and the sculptural finds from the area between the first and seventh centuries AD.

---

278 Smith 2018a, 280; Wilson 2019, 211–212.

CHAPTER 5

Informal Writing, Drawing, and Carving in the Place of Palms

Angelos Chaniotis, Andrew Wilson, and Ben Russell

A. INTRODUCTION (AC)

Images, texts, and individual letters scratched or chiselled on the surface of pavements, steps, and walls are a very common sight in ancient city-scapes; sometimes they are also found carved on rocks in the countryside. Gameboards of different types are also very common, especially in the imperial-era and late antique contexts. Researchers have recognized their importance. However, these different types of informal writing and drawing tend to be studied separately and are rarely included in epigraphic corpora; masons' or assembly marks are treated by students of architecture, textual (and sometimes pictorial) graffiti by epigraphers, gameboards by researchers of ludic practices, and so on. The Place of Palms, the largest known assemblage of such items in a single architectural complex in the Roman East and one of the largest in the Roman empire, presents a unique opportunity to study them together and exploit the information that they offer for the history of the site and the people who visited it. A total of 1,059 of these informal inscriptions of various sorts was documented in the Place of Palms, roughly half of them gameboards; all of these are described in Appendix 2.

Definitions

The texts and images engraved or carved—in one case, painted (TW1)—on the surface of the seats and blocks of the pool, the pavement of the stoas that surround it, the stylobates of the columns, and the columns themselves, should not indiscriminately be labelled 'graffiti'. The texts and images in the Place of Palms comprise many different types of informal writing,[1] drawing, and carving: textual and pictorial graffiti, *topos* or place inscriptions, names of sponsors of buildings, masons' marks, and gameboards.

Graffiti proper are texts and images incised, engraved, painted, or written with charcoal on a surface whose primary function was not to be the bearer of a text or an image.[2] An account concerning the expenses of a celebration written on the wall of a public building or a stele is not a graffito, and the same applies to an account written on a piece of papyrus, an ostracon, or a wax tablet; walls, stelae, papyri, ostraka, and wax tablets were meant to be used for the purpose of inscribing such texts. By contrast, when an account of expenses for a feast is scratched on the plaster of the wall of a private house (for example *SEG* LV 117), then it is a graffito, because the primary function of the wall of a house is not to be the bearer of texts. Similarly, an acclamation written on a dedication or recorded on a stele is not a graffito; but when exactly the same acclamation is written on the pavement of the road or on a column, then it is. A religious symbol (a cross or a menorah) is not a graffito when it appears on a dedication, an epitaph, a lamp, or an amulet, but it is a graffito when it is scratched on a wall.

According to this definition of graffiti, inscriptions that serve a function directly connected with the surface on which they have been written are not graffiti. This applies to inscriptions that designate a space as belonging to or used by a merchant or another professional. Such '*topos*' or 'place inscriptions' are informal, sometimes also unauthorized texts, but they are not graffiti. The same applies to masons' marks and names of contractors and sponsors of buildings that served a purpose precisely in connection with the surface on which they were written. Not all gameboards were graffiti. From Aphrodisias we know elaborate gameboards on blocks that were carved for this purpose and name the man who donated them.[3] These are not graffiti; but all the gameboards on the seats of the pool and on the pavement and the stylobates of the stoas are.

With these distinctions in mind, we shall now examine the various types of informal writing, drawing, and carving along with the information that they provide for activities that took place in the Place of Palms. The informal texts and gameboards are all catalogued in Appendix 2 and plotted on the Foldout; their catalogue numbers are prefixed by P for Pool, NS for North Stoa, WS for West Stoa, SS for South Stoas, TW for Theatre Wall, and Pr for Propylon.

Graffiti clusters and interplay of text and image

In the Place of Palms graffiti rarely appear in complete isolation, with the exception of some graffiti and *topos* inscriptions on columns that tend to be clearly separated from another. Graffiti and gameboards on seats and blocks of the pool are usually engraved in close proximity to each other.[4] When they overlap,[5]

---

1 On informal writing, in general, see Bagnall 2011.
2 On the definition of graffiti see Langner 2001, 12; Chaniotis 2011b, 193–196; Keegan 2014, 4–8; Lohmann 2018, 3–11.
3 Rouché 1989, pl. XV.59, XVI.69.
4 Graffiti clusters are a common phenomenon; see Huttner 2019, with special discussion of examples from gymnasia.
5 For example: P197; P200 and P201; P209; P433 and P434; NS49 and NS50; NS 91–94 and NS95; NS100; NS114 and NS115; NS153 and NS154; NS171–NS173; NS194 and NS195; NS207; NS267 and NS268; NS274 and NS275; NS319 and NS320; NS322 and NS323; NS332.

we can assume that they were engraved in succession. But in most cases, it is not possible to determine their chronological or other relation—for example, whether one graffito responds to another or if a text accompanies a drawing. Sometimes (P88 and P89) gameboards were engraved exactly parallel to each other. In a few exceptional cases, we can recognize combinations of text and image, text and gameboard, or clusters of related specimens of informal writing. Here, I will present both the clear and probable cases of graffiti clusters.

A well-attested phenomenon, not only in Aphrodisias, is the combination of textual and pictorial graffiti.[6] The best-documented example in the Place of Palms is a combination of two busts, probably of athletes, and the prayer of a goldsmith (P33; Pl. 46.A; see Ch. 5 §C). In this case, we can be quite confident that texts and images belong together because there is a similar conjunction of text and image on a seat of the theatre. The text, certainly written by the same hand, names the same goldsmith, and the image is, again, a bust (Pl. 46.B). Another close association of a textual and pictorial graffito can be observed in NS78 (Pl. 43.A). It consists of an abbreviated personal name (Ἀνα†τόλ(ιος) or Ἀνα†τολ(ίου)) combined with a drawing that resembles a table or the lintel of a building.

We may assume a connection between text and image also in the case of the word πελαργός, 'stork' (P79; Pl. 43.B) which is inscribed near the representation of birds (P81, P90, and P91; Pl. 43.C–E). In the same context, one sees two lines of unclear text (P95; Pl. 43.F). It consists of syllables starting with *kappa* (to be read as κο κρ | κου κ.. or κο κε | κου κ...). One is tempted to recognize here the effort of the author to imitate the sound of birds, as in a rupestral graffito in Koresia that shows the image of a bird and next to it the sounds τιότ τιό τι.[7] A mosaic from Tarsus (first-/second-century AD) shows a bearded man throwing a stone at a crow seated on a sundial; the crow's cry is recorded above the bird's head: κρα κρα.[8] Aristophanes' comedy *Birds* provides a lot of evidence for the way the cries of birds were represented in writing: for example ποποποποποποποῖ, ἰὼ ἰὼ ἰτὼ ἰτὼ ἰτώ (ll. 227–228), τοροτοροτοροτοροτίξ, κικκαβαῦ κικκαβαῦ, τοροτοροτοροτορολιλιλίξ (ll. 260–262), and τιὸ τιὸ τιὸ τιὸ τιὸ τιὸ τιοτίγξ (l. 738). The closest parallel for the Aphrodisian graffito is provided by an Archaic Rhodian cup from Kamiros that depicts goslings and next to them the graffito φοφο (κωκω).[9]

More common is the combination of texts and gameboards (P110, P111, P227; Pl. 43.G–J). It is reasonable to see such combinations in the context of ludic mood. In the case of P111 (Pl. 43.I) and P227 (Pl. 43.J) the graffiti are acclamations of the '*nika*' type ('the fortune of NN prevails/shall prevail') accompanied by personal names. But it is also possible that gameboards, regarded as symbols of competition and, therefore, victory and defeat, were chosen for inscribing a text that alludes to victory more generally and not in the narrow context of playing a game on the seats of the pool. This is how I am tempted to interpret the graffito P110 that refers to the victory of Eusebios over Doulkitios using an obscene expression ('Eusebios buggered/buggers Doulkitios'; Pl. 43.G–H). If this Doulkitios is indeed to be identified with the provincial governor of the late fifth century (see Ch. 4 §A), the text may refer to a political or religious conflict and not to a game (see Ch. 4 §M).

We find a cluster that unambiguously demonstrates the connections between graffiti and gameboards on a seat on the north side of the pool (Pl. 44.A). One sees, in sequence (from east to west), two gameboards (P405, P406), a menorah (P407), and another gameboard (P408). The drawing of an erect phallus completes this cluster (P409). The phallus most likely was intended as an aggressive comment against the Jews, an act of humiliation. As observed in connection with obscene texts (see §B), obscenity was a common weapon in conflicts, attributing to an opponent the passive part in anal sex.

On several occasions, one may observe how a gameboard was transformed into a pictorial graffito. The most sophisticated instance is a mancala gameboard (P398; Pl. 44.B); two apses with small crosses were added to either end of the two rows of holes, transforming the gameboard into the outline of a church, with the rows of holes resembling columns. The addition of lines and shapes turned two cross-in-square gameboards (NS152 and NS195) into unclear pictorial graffiti. The transformation of Christian crosses into gameboards is also attested (cross-in-square: NS72; cross-in-circle: N265; Pl. 44.C and 46.F). In the case of P408 (Pl. 44.A), the base of a menorah was turned into a cross-in-square board. It is possible that the caricature of a man (NS163; Pl. 44.D) originally was a calligraphic *alpha* (as in NS235 and P396; Pl. 44.E–F) turned into a caricature with additional lines.

A sophisticated interplay of text and image is presented by a graffito on the top of the seat blocks of the North Stoa (NS231; Pl. 44.G). At first sight, the text is a partial abecedary consisting of the first eight letters of the alphabet; however, two letters (Z and H) are taken out of their normal position and placed laterally, flanking a cursive B (which resembles a cursive omega with a line above). In this way, the text is transformed into an image, the image of a cross. But it is also a 'talking' image, since the horizontal bar of the cross can be read as the word ζωή, which is a well attested Christian acclamation, usually combined with φῶς (Φῶς, Ζωή; see In18 ii). In this case, text and image merge into one. Such 'Buchstabenbilder', letters creating images, are quite common among graffiti.[10] Was this graffito made by a crypto-Christian who wanted to leave a memorial of his faith without revealing it? Since the Christian nature of the invocation Ζωή was known, it is more likely that we have an open display of faith.

B. TEXTUAL GRAFFITI (AC)

Acclamations

The recording of acclamations in inscriptions is quite common, especially in late antiquity, both in graffiti and in official in-

---

6   For example, Roueché 1993, pl. XIII.46 F.18, pl. XIV 46 H.9.i, pl. XVI 46 J.8.
7   *IG* XII.6.1213. For the bird sound cf. Aristophanes, *Birds* 237 and 738.
8   *SEG* LXIV 1497.
9   Jacopi 1932, 56 no. 2; Segre and Pugliese Carratelli 1952, 276, no. 192u. For this bird sound see Oellacher 1948, with examples from literary sources.

10 Langner 2001, nos. 1–31.

scriptions.[11] As we can judge from the best documented cases, acclamations were engraved on stone to commemorate events in which these acclamations really took place, that is, gatherings of groups that praised a benefactor, showed their support for a circus faction, or wished good fortune for a professional association.

The acclamations typically consist of the verbs αὔξω (αὔξι, 'may prosper');[12] or νικάω (νικᾷ, 'prevails') followed by the word τύχη ('fortune') and the name of the person or group (circus faction, professional groups etc.), whose fortune shall prevail.[13] Another common acclamatory phrase represented among the material from the Place of Palms is the phrase πολλὰ τὰ ἔτη ('many years') followed by the name of an individual or an institution (WS4, WS5). Acclamations invoking fortune and victory may also consist of the words νίκη and τύχη followed by a designation of a group or a personal name (NS20: Νίκη! Τύχη το[ῖς - - ?]).

The largest group of acclamations from Aphrodisias, and one of the largest groups from the Roman Empire, consists of the acclamations for the benefactor Albinos on the columns of the West Stoa of the Place of Palms (see Ch. 4 §D). Their careful, deep carving and the large size of the letters clearly distinguishes them from ordinary graffiti. The inscribing of these acclamations must have been authorized by the city. The acclamations proceed in a hierarchical order from the Christian God (WS1) and the emperor (WS4), to the prefects (WS5), the senate (WS6), and the city (WS8). Some acclamations use standard phrases (αὔξι: WS9, WS17, WS20; πολλὰ τὰ ἔτη: WS4–WS6, WS8) and a variant of the common religious acclamation εἷς θεός (WS1: εἰς τὸν † κόσμον | ὅλον εἷς ὁ θεός).[14] However, most of the texts are very individual, highlighting the benefactor's building activities (WS9, WS13, WS20, WS24), asking him to look around and see his work (WS9, WS15), praising his patriotism (WS10, WS22), generosity, and love of glory (WS21), condemning his enemies (WS16, WS25) and those who were envious of him (WS18), wishing him advancement to the rank of a senator (WS17) and prosperity (WS22), and expressing the people's expectation of further services (WS10). Despite the repeated references to unanimity (WS16: ὅλη ἡ πόλις τοῦτο λέγι; WS25: ἡ πό[λις ὅλ]η ὁμοφώνως εὐφη[μ]ή{σα}σα λέγι), the acclamations for Albinos also allude to enmity, violent conflicts, envy, and ingratitude (WS16: 'your enemies to the river!'; WS18: 'envy shall not prevail over fortune!'; WS25: 'he who forgets/does not acknowledge you, Albinos, *clarissimus*, does not know God'). This atmosphere of division may be connected with the religious conflicts of the late fifth century.[15]

A small loose fragment found in the pool may be part of an acclamation (L3; Pl. 45.A). One recognizes a reference to a sponsor of buildings (L. 2: κτί]στης τῶν), and in the next line a vocative: πολῖτα. It probably is part of the honorific attribute φιλοπολίτης, well attested in Aphrodisias.[16] It is followed by a word that starts with κυ-. This constellation of κτίστης, a praising attribute composed with φιλο-, and κύρι(ο)ς appears in the Place of Palms in the acclamations for Albinos and is otherwise unparalleled: W9: αὔξι ὁ κτίστης τῆς στοᾶς; WS10: φιλόπατρει κύρι; WS13: φιλοκτίστα; WS20: αὔξι Ἀλβῖνος ὁ κτίστης καὶ τούτου τοῦ ἔργου; WS22: φιλόπατρι. Since the lettering of L3 is very different from that of the acclamations on the columns of the West Stoa, this may be an acclamation for another sponsor of a building or for another building sponsored by Albinos. A possible restoration of ll. 2–3 is [αὔξι ὁ κτί]στης τῶν | [- - - φιλ]οπολῖτα κύ[ρι |- - -]. Given the honorific nature of this text, one cannot exclude the possibility of an honorific epigram.

The largest group of acclamations, apart from those for Albinos, consists of acclamations for circus factions. They are known from various locations in Aphrodisias: the Stadium, the Bouleuterion, the Theatre, the Tetrapylon, and the Place of Palms.[17] In the Place of Palms they are found on seats and blocks of the pool (P377; Pl. 45.B), on the pavement of the West Stoa (WS12; Pl. 45.C) and on the bases of columns (NS227, NS244, NS260). Two acclamations celebrate the Reds (P377: Ν[ι]κ[ᾷ] | ἡ Τύ|χη | τῶν | Ῥου|σέων; WS12: Νικᾷ [ἡ τύχη] | τῶ Ῥουσέων),[18] another one the Greens (NS227: Νικᾷ ἡ τύχη τῶν | (Πρασίνων)), and another one the Blues (NS244: Νικᾷ ἡ τύχη τῶν | (Βενέτων)); the circus faction mentioned in another acclamation (NS260; Pl. 45.D) cannot be determined.

There are also acclamations for the fortune of the city (NS233: Αὔξι ἡ τύχη τῆς πό(λεως); WS28: νικᾷ ἡ | τύχη | τῆς πό|λεως; SS30: Νικ[ᾷ ἡ Τύ]|χ[η τῆς] | πόλ[εως]; Pl. 45.E; TW8: Νικᾷ ἡ τύχη τῆς πόλε[ω]ς) and of a professional group, the chair-bearers (P106: νικᾷ | ἡ τύ|χη | τῶν | σελ|λοφό|ρων; Pl. 45.F). An acclamation remained unfinished (NS235; Pl. 44.E); in two cases the identity of the group to which the benediction is directed cannot be determined (P112: Αὔξι | ἡ τύχη | τῶν | ΔC[- - -]; NS20: Νίκη | Τύχη ΤΟ; Pl. 45.G–H).

In some cases, the acclamation for an individual is written near a gameboard and seems to refer to the game (P111: Νικᾷ ἡ Τύχη το[ῦ?] and Νικᾷ [ἡ Τύχη τοῦ] Εὐσεβίου; Pl. 43.I; P227: Νικᾷ ἡ | τύχη τ[οῦ Ἀγ[αθοκλῆ; Pl. 43.J). If the letters ΑΧΗΛΙ (P384; Pl. 45.I) are to be read as Ἀχηλῖ (Ἀχιλλεῖ), this may be an acclamation. The name Ἀχιλλεύς is well attested in Aphrodisias.[19] It was sometimes used by gladiators and athletes, including a famous pankratiast from Aphrodisias.[20] Given other evidence for the commemoration of athletes in this area (see §C), this

---

11 On acclamations in late antique Aphrodisias see Roueché 1984; 1989, 116–122. Generally on acclamations see Wiemer 2004; Kruse 2006; Kuhn 2012. On religious acclamations see Chaniotis 2009a.

12 P112, NS233, NS235, WS9, WS17, WS20. For an acclamation of this type in the Bouleuterion see Roueché 1993, 42 no. 12.

13 P106, P377, NS227, NS260, WS28, SS29, TW8. For such acclamations in other locations see *ALA* 1.1.iii; 3; 8.e; 9.a; 10; 11.iii; 46.B.1, E.2b, E.9.i, E.11, E.20, G4, G.12.i, J.8, J.13, X.4, X.7, X.15 (Theatre); 11.iii (Bouleuterion); 45.3.V.ii; 45.36.Y.ii (Stadium).

14 On this acclamation and its diverse meanings in various contexts see Peterson *et al.* 2012.

15 Chaniotis 2008a.

16 *IAph2007* 8.23, 9.25, and 12.308 (restored in 13.7).

17 Roueché 1989, 219–228.

18 The otherwise unattested form Ῥουσέων corresponds to Ῥουσίων (cf. *SEG* LII 998 ll. 25f., fourth/fifth century?: φακτ(ί)ωνα ῥουσί|α(ν)). Cf. Ῥόσεον, Ῥοσέου, and Ῥοσέους in defixiones against charioteers: Audollent 1904, nos. 235, 237, and 246.

19 *IAph2007* 12.524, 12.908, 13.303; *SEG* LIV 1061.

20 *IAph2007* 5.214. This Aurelius Achilleus is probably to be identified with Achilleus, nicknamed 'the camel', chief-secretary of the international association of athletes, whose sarcophagus was found in 2015 (Chaniotis, Field Reports 2015, I 15.10. Ἀχιλλεύς is a common name

text may be an acclamation in the dative for an athlete.[21] Finally, depending on whether the vocative κύριε in the graffito Κύριε ΑΠΟΛΙΩ (P448) refers to a member of the elite or Jesus, the text may be an acclamation for a man or a Christian invocation.

The presence of acclamations is directly associated with the function of the Place of Palms as a place of public gatherings for celebrations and announcements. It may have been the place where members of associations held regular meetings.[22] One of the place inscriptions marked the place of Eugraphios, the *phylarch* (NS341), possibly the chairman of a professional association (see §D); Roueché has plausibly argued that the inscribed acclamations for the city and the factions in the Place of Palms record the voiced acclamations of an actual ceremony,[23] perhaps a gathering of the factions and the professional associations.

Prayers and invocations

Prayers are a distinctive group of epigraphic texts in late antique Aphrodisias, originating from both Christians and Jews.[24] Although there is Jewish evidence among the graffiti in the Place of Palms (representations of menoroth), all the prayers whose religious origin can be determined are Christian. The longest text is the prayer of the head goldsmith Kolotron (P33: † Κολοτρον προταυράριος | οὗ Θεὸς μνήσετε, 'Kolotron, the first *aurarius*, whom God shall remember'; Pl. 46.A). This goldsmith is also commemorated in a graffito from the Theatre (Pl. 46.B).[25] The prayer is of the μνήσεται-type as in an epitaph from Sicily: μνησετή σοι ὦ θε(ὸς) εἰς [αἰῶνα].[26] This formula goes back to commemorative graffiti of the μνησθῆ-type, which are very common in pilgrimage sites, houses, anchorages, burial caves, and quarries.[27] In both pagan and Christian contexts the formula requests divine attention and protection. As already discussed, a partial abecedary (NS231; Pl. 44.G can be read as the Christian invocation Ζωή.

A Christian prayer invokes Jesus to protect a certain Primus (P452: Κύριε βοήθι Πρίμω; Pl. 46.C). The vocative κύριε in the graffito Κύριε ΑΠΟΛΙΩ (P448) may be an invocation of Jesus. An abbreviated invocation of the Mother of God can be recognized on the base of a column (NS54: Μή(τηρ) † Θε(οῦ); Pl. 46.D).[28] The reading of P45 (Pl. 46.E) and NS36 as one word, that is the Christian invocation Θεέ, often attested as part of the prayer Θεὲ βοήθει, is not certain. The Christian symbol ΑΩ, an appellation of Christ in the Book of Revelation (1:8, 21:6, 22:13) can be read in NS264, close to a cross that was turned into a gameboard (NS265; Pl. 46.F). The same symbol appears in connection with a christogram in NS1; the reading ΑΩ in P73 is not certain.

The only prayer that may not be Christian, because of the lack of a cross, was inscribed on the Theatre Hill retaining wall (TW10). It consists of the word εὐχή followed by the name of a man in the genitive. This formula was common among the Christians—usually accompanied by a cross or another distinctively Christian symbol or text—,[29] but it is also attested in Jewish contexts.[30] The fact that this text lacks a cross does not automatically make the dedicant a Jew or a sympathizer,[31] since another prayer of this type without a cross at Aphrodisias is clearly Christian.[32]

'Labels'

Here, we define 'labels' as texts that explain an image or the function of a space. For example, the text πε|λα|ργός ('stork', P79; Pl. 43.B) written near the drawings of birds may be a text explaining or commenting on the images. A sequence of syllables starting with the letter kappa (P95; Pl. 43.F) may be related to these images, if these syllables were intended to imitate the voice of birds.

An entirely different kind of a 'label' is the word ἀφετηρία (P167; Pl. 47.A), the designation of the starting point of a race. Its presence on a block near the middle of the south side of the pool is puzzling. The best explanation is that this word had been inscribed on the block during the block's first use in a different context, that is, before the block was used for the pool. Given the text's location, and the extensive repairs to the south side of the pool, it is less probable that the text stands at the starting point of a race of (necessarily very small) boats that took place in the pool. A boat race is famously described by Vergil in the fifth book of the *Aeneid* in connection with the funeral games for Anchises (5.140–280), and aquatic displays are attested in the Roman Empire.[33] It would be surprising if the possibilities offered by the pool in the Place of Palms had not been exploited for water spectacles. It should be mentioned in this context that there may be a representation of a boat on a block of the opposite (north) side of the pool (P319; see §C).

The text ἐδίκτου ('of the edict'), crudely engraved on the moulding of the base of one of the piers dividing the central staircase that leads from the West Stoa to the Hadrianic Baths (WS30; Pl. 47.B), can be best interpreted as a 'label' defining the use of this particular space. In this interpretation, this in-

---

or nick name of athletes; see Ameling 1987, 6–7. For gladiators see *SEG* LXVI 509.

21 Examples of acclamations in the dative: for example Εὐμήλῳ με[γάλῳ κη]-δεμόνι Πυλειτῶν (*SEG* XXXVIII 1172); Ἀσίας πρώ|τοις Βε|νεβεντά|νοις] (*SEG* LVII 915); Ἀσίας πρώτοις (*SEG* LXI 965); καλαῖς Μυτιλιναίαις (*SEG* XLVIII 400).
22 Chaniotis and De Staebler 2018, 39.
23 Roueché 1989, 228.
24 Roueché 1989, 172–190 (Christian prayers); Chaniotis 2002a (Jewish prayers).
25 *ALA* 46 J.8; *IAph2007* 8.61.8.i.3.
26 *IG* XIV 537. For μνήσεται in a non-Christian context see *I.Milet* I.364.
27 Rehm 1941; for example *SEG* XXXVIII 1663–1668; XXXIV 1014; XXXV 1536; XLV 1985; XLVI 1730; LVII 561.
28 This is a very common invocation, abbreviated in different ways: ΜΡ ΘΥ (Homolle 1892, 423 no. 90); ΜΘ (for example *SEG* LIV 991); Μ†Θ (*SEG* XXX 803 m); ΜΗΡ ΘΥ (*I.Muz.Iznik* 491); ΜΗ ΘΥ (*IGLS* V 2478); ΜΗ ΘΕ (Jarry 1967, 177 no. 88).

29 For example, *IAph2007* 1.20 and 11.225.
30 See, for example, Horbury and Noy 1992, 30–32 no. 19; Noy 1993, 244–245 no. 181.
31 This is tentatively assumed for the dedicant of another prayer of this type, Flavius Damocharis (*IAph2007* 11.64) by Reynolds and Tannenbaum 1987, 138; but see Chaniotis 2002a, 224.
32 *ALA* 137 iii a (the prayer of Stephanas).
33 Vergil: Feldherr 1995. Aquatic displays: Coleman 1993; Rogers 2018, 46–55, 70–75.

scription informed the users of this space that the pillar would be used for the temporary display of an edict (or edicts), probably inscribed on wooden tablets. The lettering suggests a date in the imperial period (not in late antiquity).

Finally, if the reading λάκος is correct (NS261), the graffito written on a column designated the place where either clothes (τὸ λάκος) or wine (ὁ λάκ(κ)ος) were stored or sold.

Obscene texts

Obscene texts and images (see §C) belong to the most common and best studied types of graffiti.[34] In Aphrodisias they are found in several locations: in the Theatre, the Bouleuterion, and on a block of the City Walls.[35] In the Place of Palms, there are two texts of the πυγίζω-type ('I bugger', 'so-and-so buggers'). The longest is P110, written on a block toward the east end of the pool (Pl. 43.G–H). The text is written inside an eight-spoke wheel gameboard, with the text distributed between two segments of the circle. The text probably reads: [π]υγί[[ζει] or [ἐπ]ύγι[σεν] ὁ Εὐ|[σέ]βις | Δουλ|κίτιν ('Eusebi(o)s buggers/buggered Doulkiti(o)s)'). The omission of the omikron in names ending in -ιος is very common in late antiquity. An Eusebios is mentioned in an acclamation written, again, in association with a gameboard immediately to the east of this graffito (P111). Although Eusebios is a common late antique name, especially among Christians, the proximity of the two graffiti and the shared combination of text and gameboard strongly suggests that we are dealing with the same individual. The identity of the second man is easier to determine. Doulkitios must be the provincial governor of Karia, known from three inscriptions (see Ch. 4 §A). He was involved in restoration work in the Place of Palms, and as a Μαϊουμάρχης (IAph2007 4.202 iii), he was responsible for the water festival of the Maiouma that must have taken place in and around the pool (see Ch. 4 §M).

In graffiti, the use of obscene verbs is not to be taken literally, indicating an actual homosexual relationship between two men, but metaphorically, indicating the victory of the man represented as playing the active part in anal sex and the humiliation of his opponent.[36] One can, therefore, take the text to mean that Eusebios defeated the governor in a game. But one may also consider the possibility that Doulkitios' defeat did not occur in a game played on the seats of the pool but in conflict or dispute that took place on Aphrodisias' public stage. One might think of a dispute concerning religious or political issues. If we follow this interpretation, a gameboard was selected for the graffito because of its association with competition, victory, and defeat. The second graffito using the verb πυγίζω is on a column of the North Stoa; it remained unfinished (NS53: πυγιζ; Pl. 47.C).

Commemorative graffiti

One particular type of commemorative graffiti are texts that publicly declare one's affection towards another individual. It is one of the few types of graffiti that are referred to in literary sources. Plutarch explicitly mentions the commemorative character of such graffiti, advising his readers not to bother about them: 'Nothing useful or pleasant is written on the walls; simply that so-and-so commemorates so-and-so wishing him well (ἐμνήσθη ἐπ' ἀγαθῷ) or that another one is the best of friends (φίλων ἄριστος)'.[37] In Aphrodisias we find such graffiti that use the verb φιλῶ in the Theatre,[38] the Sebasteion,[39] and the Place of Palms (NS283; Pl. 47.D). In all these cases, the exact meaning of φιλῶ ('I am a friend of NN' or 'I love NN') cannot be determined, but we certainly are not dealing with obscenity but with the display—genuine or theatrical—of affection. At least in some cases φιλῶ expresses the affectionate loyalty of an individual to a person of authority (as in the honorific titles φιλοσέβαστος and φιλοκαῖσαρ or the attributes of slaves φιλοκύριος and φιλοδέσποτος).[40]

Names, abbreviations, and monograms

Although simple name-graffiti are very common, their meaning and motivation—commemoration, acclamation, writing exercise, label, topos inscriptions—can never be determined with certainty.[41] When they are in the genitive, they probably are place inscriptions of shop-keepers (see §D), but this may also be the case with names in the nominative (NS7: Εὐτυχία; NS18: Εὐδοξία). The name Εὐτύχης (L1; Pl. 47.E) is probably a commemorative graffito. The letters ΑΧΗΛΙ (P384; Pl. 45.I), possibly the misspelled personal name Ἀχιλλεύς in the dative (Ἀχηλῖ for Ἀχιλλεῖ), may be an acclamation.

Many graffiti are abbreviated words or names. The letters ΛΑΓΑ (P101; Pl. 47.F) might be the beginning of the word λάγανον, a cake, but also a variant of λάχανον, vegetable,[42] rather than a name. In that case, this inscription would designate the stand of a seller of cakes or vegetables. In another late antique inscription from Aphrodisias the occupation of a greengrocer is abbreviated as ΛΑΧΑ.[43]

In some cases, the abbreviation can be interpreted as a name. If P396 is an abbreviated name starting with Ἀλ-, written under the drawing of a pediment, there are many possibilities (for example Ἀλβῖνος, Ἀλέξανδρος, Ἀλύπιος etc.). If the reading ΕΙ (P366) is correct, it may be the abbreviation for Εἰρηναῖος or

---

34 For a selection of textual graffiti see Chaniotis 2019, 18–21; cf. Keegan 2014, 255–259; pictorial graffiti: Langner 2001, nos. 252, 292, 293, 297–310, 331, 733, 1260–1291.
35 Theatre: ALA 46.A.6, 46.K.9; Bouleuterion: ALA 11.A.i. City Walls: Chaniotis 2011b, 204. See also Bain 1997.
36 Chaniotis 2011b, 204–205.
37 Plut., Mor. 520 d–e. For φιλῶ-graffiti in Smyrna see Bagnall et al. 2016, nos. T5.1. On graffiti and sexuality see Keegan 2014, 252–259.
38 ALA 7b = IAph2007 8.10b and Chaniotis 2011b, 205: φιλεῖ Θεοδᾶτος Ὑψικλέα.
39 Four unpublished graffiti on columns of the North Building (mentioned in Chaniotis 2011b, 205): 1) Φιλῶ. 2) Φιλῶ | Ἐπικράτη (sic). 3) Φιλῶ | Ἀπολ|λώνιον κύρι|ον. 4) Φιλῶ | Ἀπολλώ|νιον ΑΝ|ΤΙΛΟΜΑ.
40 Chaniotis 2011b, 205 and 2020.
41 For example, Bagnall et al. 2016, no. T1.2.
42 For this form in late antique Antioch see IGLS III.1.865.
43 Reynolds and Tannenbaum 1987, 118.

Εἰρηνίων.[44] The abbreviation NI (NS9) can be the beginning of numerous names composed with νίκη. The letters ΟΠ contained within a circle appear twice in close proximity to each other (P66 and P67; Pl. 47.G); this graffito perhaps represents an abbreviation (the name Ὅπλων is attested in Aphrodisias). For AN (P302, NS48), ΠΕ (NS12, NS191), and ΠΟ (NS270; cf. TW3) there are numerous possibilities. The letters ΚΕ with a line above them (P194; Pl. 47.H) certainly represent an abbreviation; a straight line above letters is often used as an abbreviation symbol. ΚΕ is a common abbreviation for κ(ύρι)ε, but there are other possibilities (for example Κ(ωνσταντῖν)ε). The letters ΘΕ (NS36) may be the beginning of an abbreviated theophoric name. A graffito of two lines (NS230; Pl. 47.I) consisting of five groups of two letters each (ΑΗ | ΑΝ ΠΗ ΚΕ ΒΟ) followed by a single letter (B) more likely is a cluster of abbreviated names. Some abbreviations probably are place inscriptions (see §D). Other abbreviations (NS280: IN; WS7: HNK or HNIC) are hard to interpret.

Monograms were used for the names of the circus factions of the Greens and the Blues (NS227, NS244; cf. NS141; Pl. 47.J–K) in acclamations[45] as well as for the names of contractors or supervisors of building projects, written on column drums (SS15, SS17, SS20, SS22, SS24). There are several Christian monograms, with letters attached at the ends of the bars of the cross (P17?, P309?, P465, NS45?, NS277?; Pl. 47.L–M and 48.A), a monogram with letters attached to a *psi*-like shape (P324), and ligatures of letters that may be monograms (P16, P64; cf. P410; Pl. 48.B–C). The names cannot be identified, except perhaps for Κυ(ριακός) (P16). The letter M (P439) combined with a cross may also be a monogram. The significance of these monograms—commemoration of individuals or place inscriptions—cannot be determined.

Individual letters and undetermined texts

In the case of individual letters (apart from the masons' marks discussed below, §E), we can not be certain whether they represent abbreviations or numerals. The following single letters are attested: Α (P182, P216, P307, NS340, NS346); Β (NS207?, NS246?) or the magical symbol known as 'Brillenbuchstabe'; Γ (P231?, NS14, NS21, NS247?, NS343); Δ (NS3, NS269); Ε (P78, P170?, P239?, P392, NS254?, NS39?); Η (P114?, P148?); Θ (P170?, P423, P427); Θ or Φ (P135, P147); Κ (NS26); Μ (P439?, NS262); Ν (P114?, P148?, NS232); Ο (P463?, NS116?, NS343); Π (P231?); Σ (C: P149?, P210?, P231?, P425, P439?); Τ (NS2, NS46, NS343); Υ (P15, NS343); Φ (WS29); Ω (P239?, NS39). In the case of three drawings that resemble the letters Β, Γ, and Ε and are written in this sequence in close proximity, one may consider the possibility of an abecedary (NS254; cf. NS231).

In many cases, textual graffiti cannot be read with certainty (P22, P65, P103?, P115, P127, P450, NS203, NS211, NS268) or do not make any sense (P51, P74, P114; Pl. 48.D), even when they consist of several lines (P96; Pl. 48.E; P169: two lines; P284: three lines).

---

44 Εἰρηνίων is attested for a gladiator: *IAph2007* 8.701.
45 For box-monograms of circus factions see also *ALA* 46.E.9 and 46.E.11.

C. PICTORIAL GRAFFITI (AC)

Religious symbols

Religious symbols have been recorded in many locations in Aphrodisias, especially in the area of the Temple/Church and the Tetrapylon, the Sebasteion, the Bouleuterion, the Hadrianic Baths, the Theatre, and the Tetrastoon. Unsurprisingly, Christians are omnipresent in a city that was later renamed the 'City of the Cross', Stavropolis, but there are also Jewish symbols,[46] and representations of double axes that can be associated with the Karian Zeus—if they are not symbols of masons.[47] Christian crosses and Jewish menoroth also appear in large numbers in the Place of Palms, on seats of the pool, on columns and on the pavement of the stoas, and in the tunnel through the Propylon.

The Christian cross is the most common religious symbol (54 cases, possibly another 6). It appears mostly alone,[48] but also close to other crosses (P1 and P2, P253 and P254, P267 and P268, P479 and P480, NS126 and NS127, NS281 and NS282, WS3; Pl. 48.F) and a menorah (P212; Pl. 48.J), and as part of Christograms (see below), monograms (P17?, P309?, P465, NS45?), textual graffiti (P33, P96, P132, NS18, NS54, NS58, NS78, SS4, SS9, TW2), and pictorial graffiti (NS143, NS271). The Christian cross appears in different shapes. The more elaborate versions have small circles (NS32 and NS126) or triangles (NS143) at the end of the arms. The cross P256 is within a circle. P422 may be a cross with a triangular base, but this is far from certain (Pl. 55.F). One of the crosses is painted with red paint (TW1). The size of crosses varies from 5.5 cm (NS86) to 41 cm (NS32).

The highest concentration of Christian crosses in the area of the Place of Palms in fact occurs on the Propylon. While the various inscribed symbols on this building have not been systematically collected and studied as part of this publication, at least 104 crosses were inscribed on the walls of the northern tunnel through this building, 73 on the south side and 31 on the north side (see Fig. 45). At least 12 further examples were inscribed on the west façade of the Propylon just to the south of this tunnel (see Fig. 15). The concentration of crosses here may indicate that this boundary of the Place of Palms acquired some signficiance for the local Christian community, as discussed in Ch. 4 §M. Some of these crosses might also be quite late—perhaps Byzantine—in date since the base of the Propylon remained standing and visible into the medieval period.

There are other Christian symbols, sometimes in combination with texts, as already mentioned. In one case (P398), crosses and arches were added on either side of a mancala gameboard, making it resemble a church (Pl. 44.B). In another case (NS231; Pl. 44.G) the first eight letters of the alphabet are arranged in the shape of a cross whose horizontal arm reads ΖΩΗ ('life'). An elaborate 'eight-spoke-wheel' gameboard is decorat-

---

46 Chaniotis 2002a.
47 Chaniotis 2008a, 259.
48 P23, P37, P48, P104, P119, P126, P134, P142, P154, P160, P180, P193, P238, P244, P251?, P256, P275, P277, P278, P422?, P437, P438, P507, NS16, NS22, NS32, NS86, NS89, NS97, NS126, NS143, NS253, TW1, TW5, TW6.

ed with eight crosses (NS317; Pl. 57.C). There are also a few instances of Christograms (NS1, NS8?, NS345, WS2). The best preserved (NS1; Pl 48.G) consists of a cross, the letters ΑΩ—symbols of beginning and end—attached at the left and right end of the horizontal bar, and the letter P, from the name Χριστός, on the top.

In two cases the cross was not engraved on the conspicuous surface of a seat or a block of the pool, but on the underside of the inner seat slab (P154) and the rim of a seat (P180). There are a few obvious concentrations of crosses in particular areas, especially on the south wall of the north corridor of the Propylon (see above). Other clusters of crosses can be observed on columns of the North Stoa (NS1, NS8?, NS16, NS22, NS32, NS281 and NS282) and on seats/blocks of the pool (P251, P253, P254, P256).

Menoroth are widely distributed in many locations around the pool (P189, P208, P213, P264, P266, P407, P446?; Pl. 44.A and 48.H–M), on the top of the seat blocks of the North Stoa (NS137; Pl. 48.N), on two columns of the West Stoa (WS11, WS29; Pl. 49.A), and on pillars of the Sebasteion.[49] This distribution reflects the importance and visibility of the Jewish community in late antique Aphrodisias.[50] Sometimes they are found in proximity to crosses. The cross P212 is directly under the menorah P213 (Pl. 48.J). P189 (Pl. 48.H) is close to the cross P193; the menorah P266 is near the crosses P267 and P268 (Pl. 48.L). The drawings of menoroth are usually very large. One representation is particularly detailed, including the representation of shofar (horn) and probably ethrog (citrus; P208; Pl. 48.I).[51] In one case a menorah has ten branches (P189; Pl. 48.H).

A possible case of religious insult or conflict can be observed in the case of a cluster of graffiti and gameboards (P405–409; Pl. 44.A), in which an erect phallus was engraved near the representation of a menorah (see above §B).

Human figures and faces

Graffiti with human figures appear both isolated and in compositions that represent actions in many locations, especially in the Theatre and the Bouleuterion.[52] Faces in profile view and busts are also very common types of pictorial graffiti.[53]

The best executed and preserved graffito of this kind in the Place of Palms is the representation of two large male busts (P33; Pl. 46.A), recognized by Bert Smith as images of athletes (probably boxers).[54] The bearded man on the left possibly wears a wreath on his bald or shaved head; but the short lines radiating from his head may also represent an elaborate hairstyle. His muscular body, indicated through raised shoulders, and his nakedness make his identification with an athlete more likely than his identification with the goldsmith Kolotron, who wrote the prayer next to these images. The man on the right has shaved face and head, with just one strand of hair extending from his head. Another relatively large pictorial image (36 cm) shows a standing figure with a raised, extended arm (P245; Pl. 49.B), possibly holding a branch. It may be the representation of a victorious athlete (or of the statue of an athlete) or gladiator with *palma* in his hand.[55] A human figure with an extended arm holding an object (P139) may also be a similar representation (Pl. 49.C). A pictorial graffito of a human figure on the stylobate of the south colonnade of the Tetrapylon Street (opposite the Tetrapylon) resembles these two graffiti and may also be a victorious athlete with raised arms (Pl. 49.D). The presence of these images in the Place of Palms may be associated with the place where the fans of athletes and circus factions gathered to celebrate their idols.

Apart from the two busts of athletes mentioned above (P33), one recognizes the outline of a bust (P107; Pl. 49.E) and three rather poorly executed human faces (NS4, NS204, NS288; Pl. 49.F–G). One is a caricature of a man, which is difficult to interpret (NS163; see Pl. 44.D). The upper part of a dressed body supports a bald head with indication of mouth, nose and eyes. The head is flanked by a circle and a triangle (left) and a semicircle and an oblong strip (right), perhaps indicating big ears and clothing items; an oval object is on top of the bald head. Some other graffiti that may represent human figures or busts (P29, P270, P321, P343) are too unclear to allow an interpretation. Two other figural graffiti appear to represent statues and are discussed separately below, under 'Sculpture'.

Animals

Representations of animals are very common among pictorial graffiti,[56] and such representations have been recorded in various locations in Aphrodisias.[57] Most graffiti representing animals have been found in the Place of Palms. That most of these representations are images of birds (P29, P81, P90, P91, P94, P422?, NS142, NS272, NS273?, NS289, NS333; Pl. 43.B–E, 49.H–L) is certainly connected with the fauna that the visitors saw in the park here.[58] One recognizes with certainty at least

---

49 For the Sebasteion, see Chaniotis 2002a, 221–222.
50 See Reynolds and Tannenbaum 1987; Chaniotis 2002a.
51 For similar representations in the Sebasteion, see Chaniotis 2002a, 237 nos. 14 and 16.
52 *ALA* 46.D.15; 46.E.10; 46.H.3, 4, 6, 9, and 26; 46.J.3, 4, and 8; 46.K.1; 46.L.9; Chaniotis 2011b, 204; Keegan 2014, 73–76; Chaniotis and De Staebler 2018, 41 no. 17.
53 For example, Langner 2001, nos. 187–632; Bagnall *et al.* 2016, nos. D1.3, D8.4, D11.4, D12.2, D19.2, D20.1, D21.1, D22.1, D25.4, D29.3, D29.4, D29.5, D32.3, DP54.1, DP.109.1.
54 For a possible representation of a wrestler in the Theatre see *ALA* 46.J.3. On athletic imagery, especially of boxers, in late antiquity, see Dunbabin 2017.

55 Langner 2001, nos. 919–926. On this imagery see Dunbabin 2017, 154–156, 163.
56 Langner 2001, nos. 1379–1843.
57 Chaniotis and De Staebler 2018, 36–37. For the representation of a scorpion in the theatre, see *ALA* 46.B.23.
58 For birds in graffiti see Langner 2001, nos. 1634–1747; Bagnall *et al.* 2016, nos. D29.9., D29.10, DP73.1, DP84.1, D29.8, DP94.1 (doves, ducks, herons, parrots, swans). For bones of birds found in the Place of Palms see Ch. 10. For domesticated birds in antiquity, see Mynott 2018, 131–149. I would like to thank C. Lunczer for his assistance in identifying the birds.

one peacock (NS333; cf. NS142, NS272, NS289),[59] two storks or herons (P81, P90; cf. the textual graffito P79);[60] the identity of other birds, in more generic images (P91, P422?, NS273), remains obscure. If P29 (Pl. 49.H) is the representation of an ostrich, it is connected with *venationes*.[61]

This is certainly the case with a second group of representations of wild animals.[62] There are two such sets of representations, both on columns of the North Stoa. On one column one recognizes the roughly depicted outlines of three running lions (NS331; Pl. 50.A) with shaggy manes and waving tufted tails. Since lions were imported to cities for the purpose of staging *venationes* and since *venationes* are known to have taken place in Aphrodisias, it is reasonable to assume that this representation was inspired by a scene that had actually taken place or by images of *venationes* on works of art (on mosaics, paintings, lamps, etc.).[63]

A cluster of images on the same column is too unclear to allow a secure interpretation (NS332; Pl. 50.B–C); an association with *venationes* is only a possibility. According to a very tentative interpretation, the cluster consists of the representation of a gladiator (left) engaged in a fight with an ostrich (right), represented from the back. In this interpretation, the head of the figure on the left is only outlined, since it is encased within his helmet. The horizontal lines on his torso indicate either a shield or a *manica* protecting his arm. The figure on the right may be an ostrich, represented from the back: the long legs support a round body, with a long neck projecting on top of it and turning to the right.[64] P29 may be another representation of a man and an ostrich and NS273 a representation of a man and a bird (Pl. 50.D), but both images are too crude to allow certainty.

The second relevant graffito (NS295; Pl. 50.E) shows two animals running toward the left, one above the other. The animal below can be recognized as an antelope, a gazelle, or a wild goat in view of the characteristic long horns. A similar representation has been recorded in the Stadium (Pl. 50.F). Of the animal above only the front part is preserved. It may be a dog or a horse. Although the two creatures are not in proportion, the proximity of the two animals that run in the same direction suggests interpreting this as one scene, often represented in graffiti: a dog chases the antelope or wild goat.[65] P470 seems to be the outline of an animal, with a tail, back legs, body, and head (Pl. 50.G).

Fish representations are not common among pictorial graffiti.[66] The somewhat crude but detailed drawing of a fish (P449; Pl. 50.H) may be a representation of a fish seen in the pool (or a sculpted fountain decoration; see below). The fish has a large trapezoidal tail, oblong body, and a large head with oval eye and open mouth; the pelvic and anal fins are clearly represented; three small cavities above the mouth might indicate bubbles. There are similar fish representations in graffiti.[67] Two sketchy fish representations on a pillar of the Theatre stage should be noted.[68] The fish are represented in outline, with lines indicating the separation of head from body and body from tale. They may be Christian symbols: ΙΧΘΥΣ (fish) is the acronym for Ἰησοῦς Χριστὸς Θεοῦ Υἱὸς Σωτήρ ('Jesus Christ, son of God, saviour').

Phalluses

The phallus is a common symbol that defies a single interpretation. It may have an apotropaic meaning; it may suggest manly potency; or it may be used to humiliate the defeated party in a conflict (see §B). In the context of the Place of Palms, exactly as in other locations in Aphrodisias and, more generally, in ancient pictorial graffiti,[69] the last of these is the most likely meaning. Surprisingly, there are only two phallus representations. In one case an erect phallus is found in isolation (P159; Pl. 51.A), in another it is part of a cluster of gameboards and a menorah (P409; Pl. 44.A). In the latter case, the juxtaposition suggests that the phallus may have been intended as an insult against the Jews.

Sculpture

The makers of pictorial graffiti often represented something that they had experienced (for example, a gladiatorial combat)[70] or something that they were looking at, for example a building, a work of art or a musical instrument.[71] Among the graffiti on the wall of the corridor behind the Bouleuterion of Aphrodisias one finds representations of organs (*hydrauleis*) and possibly works of art.[72] The drawing of a fountain in the shape of a vase was en-

---

[59] Cf. Langner 2001, nos. 1693–1708; for representations of peacocks in Aphrodisias see Chaniotis and De Staebler 2018, 40–41 nos. 5, 13, 18, 24. For peacocks as domesticated birds, see Mynott 2018, 131–137.

[60] Cf. Langner 2001, no. 1634 (Alexandria) and 1713 (Aphrodisias, theatre). On storks and herons in ancient culture, see Mynott 2018, 170–177, 287–288.

[61] Cf. Langner 2001, no. 1652, 1657; for another graffito representing an ostrich in Aphrodisias, see Chaniotis and De Staebler 2018, 41 no. 22.

[62] *Venationes* in graffiti: Langner 2001, nos. 1063–1103, 1105, 1114–1119, 1122–1127; Bagnall *et al.* 2016, nos. D29.2, D29.6, D29.13.

[63] *Venationes* in Aphrodisias: Roueché 1993, 61–64, 72–80; cf. Hrychuk Kontokosta 2008, 223–227 nos. 34–38; 228 no. 40. Lions in graffiti in the context of *venationes*: Langner 2001, nos. 1063, 1068, and 1069; Bagnall *et al.* 2016, nos. D8.7, D29.2, D29.8, D29.13, D30.1; cf. Adam-Veleni 2012.

[64] Chaniotis and De Staebler 2018, 34–35, who also consider the possibility of a gladiatorial combat.

[65] For a similar theme (dog attacks deer) cf. Langner 2001, nos. 1100, 1102, 1108–1110.

[66] Langner 2001, nos. 1786–1814; Bagnall *et al.* 2016, nos. DP12.1, DP15.1, DP76.1.

[67] Cf. Langner 2001, nos. 1804 (head), 1806 (head, tail, fins).

[68] Langner 2001, nos. 1808–1809.

[69] Aphrodisias: Theatre: *ALA* 46.D.16; 46.F.18; 46.G5; 46.J.4. City wall: Chaniotis 2011b, 204. Phalluses in graffiti: for example Bagnall *et al.* 2016, nos. D5.2, D8.1, D8.2, D11.5, D16.1, D24.1, D24.2, D24.3, D25.1, D25.2, D25.3, D25.9, D26.2, D29.7, D29.12, DP100.1.

[70] For example, Langner 2001, nos. 1003–1056, 1228; Chaniotis and De Staebler 2018, 33–34.

[71] Works of art and musical instruments: Langner 2001, nos. 2341–2369.

[72] Organs: Langner 2001, nos. 2364–2369. The images of emperors, interpreted by Roueché 1993, 41–42, as representations of pantomimes (cf. Langner 2001, nos. 2348–2350), may have been inspired by representations of seated emperors in sculpture, on medallions, or perhaps on textiles.

graved on the wall of a square pool or basin in the atrium north of the Hadrianic Baths.[73]

Two pictorial graffiti on columns of the West Stoa may be representations of statues that decorated the Place of Palms or the Hadrianic Baths. The first graffito (WS19) shows a naked female figure with raised arms, resembling depictions of Aphrodite Anadyomene (Pl. 51.B).[74] A statue of Aphrodite is known to have decorated the Place of Palms.[75] The second image is more difficult to interpret (WS26; Pl. 51.C). It is a seated male figure with outstretched legs and a disproportionally large, monstrous head. The figure holds an object in the outstretched left hand and brings his right arm behind the shoulder. The posture gives the impression of an archer, holding a bow with the left hand and reaching to the quiver with the right hand to pull out an arrow. However, the position of the outstretched, open legs closely corresponds to that of images of seated or reclining satyrs.[76] The big head, with large eyes and two projecting ears, also resembles the representation of a satyr's head, for example the head of a satyr playing the flute from Aphrodisias.[77] In this interpretation, the object in the left hand may be a flute.

Finally, one might speculate that the drawing of a fish (P449; Pl. 50.H) was inspired by sculpture that decorated the pool, perhaps a water-spout in the shape of a fish.[78] A marble statuette of a boy and a dolphin was used as a fountain spout in this area, and two sculptures of frogs may have been part of fountain decoration in the Place of Palms (see Ch. 2 §B); for further discussion of the sculptural finds from the space, see Ch. 7.[79]

Buildings and other constructions

Buildings, other constructions, architectural elements, and plans of buildings are not as common as other pictorial graffiti,[80] but they are attested in Aphrodisias.[81] A drawing consisting of two concentric elliptical lines, ending in a curve at one end and a straight line at the other (P300) resembles the plan of the pool (Pl. 51.D).[82] A problem with this interpretation is the fact that the second curve is missing. Should one assume that at some point one of the two ends of the pool was covered, perhaps only temporarily (for example, with wooden planks during the restoration of the West Stoa)? Other pictorial graffiti consisting of simple outlines that resemble structures may be vague representations of buildings (P313; Pl. 51.E; cf. the drawing of a pediment: P396; Pl. 44.F). An arch, added on a pre-existing gameboard (P331; Pl. 51.F) may represent a building;[83] crosses and apses were added on either side of a mancala gameboard, making it resemble a church (P398; Pl. 44.B). Also, the gameboard NS152 was turned into a pictorial graffito resembling a structure (Pl. 51.G). Another graffito resembles a ladder (NS23; Pl. 51.H).[84]

Measures

Measures, that is lines corresponding to one foot or two feet, have been recorded on the back wall of the South Stoa (TW9; Pl. 51.I) of the Place of Palms, as well as on the outer face of the south wall of the Temple/Church (east end).[85] They were probably used for the measurement of textiles.

Various objects and geometrical designs

An oblong object (P319) may be the representation of a boat with rudder and a small cabin at the stern (Pl. 51.J).[86] Representations of boats, with and without sails, are very common among pictorial graffiti.[87] A *tabula ansata* (P230; Pl. 52.A; cf. P231?) probably depicts an object that was seen by the ancient visitors to this area: wooden or bronze tablets attached on the walls of the stoas and inscribed with announcements. This *tabula ansata* does not contain an inscription (unless the inscription was written with paint). *Tabulae ansatae* were occasionally used as decorative frames around the text in stone inscriptions[88] and in the graffiti of Smyrna.[89] Also the rough drawing of a pediment (P396; Pl. 44.F), under which an abbreviated name (?) is inscribed, may represent the top of a pedimental stele or the pediment of a building.

Many drawings are partly preserved, unclear or vague,[90] and others, consisting of simple geometrical shapes or lines, circles,

---

73 Chaniotis 2018a, 83.
74 Chaniotis 2018a, 86. Cf. Rouché 1989, 128: 'a small naked female figure—perhaps Tyche?'.
75 *IAph2007* 12.204 (1ˢᵗ/2ⁿᵈ century): ἀνέθηκε τὸν Ἑρμῆ καὶ τὴν ἐπίχ[ρυ]σον Ἀφροδείτην.
76 For example, Stewart 1990, II, 676; cf. the Barberini Faun and the Sleeping Faun from Herculaneum: e.g. Pollitt 1986, 134 and 162; images of satyrs on the coins of Naxos: for example *SNG* Lloyd no. 1151.
77 Smith 1998, 257.
78 Chaniotis 2018a, 85.
79 Wilson 2016b, 116–117.
80 Langner 2001, nos. 2268–2340.
81 The most elaborate is a Christian shrine: see Rouché 1989, 187 no. 142; a similar graffito connected with a prayer is found on a block unearthed in the Tetrapylon Street (Chaniotis, Field Reports 2015, I 15.14). For other graffiti with buildings see Chaniotis 2018a, 81–84.
82 Chaniotis 2018b, 83–84.
83 Arches in graffiti: Langner 2001, nos. 2280–2281.
84 Cf. Langner 2001, no. 2773.
85 Rouché 1989, 172, where one of these drawings is interpreted as a design of an altar or table. But see Chaniotis 2011b, 202. For drawings of measures (different lengths of foot) see *MAMA* XI 254 (Laodikeia Katakekaumene, fourth-/fifth-century AD).
86 Suggested to me by B. Russell and A. Kidd.
87 Langner 2001, nos. 1844–2196. For the Aphrodisian image cf. esp. his no. 2184 (helm and cabin); see also his nos. 2152, 2178, 2181, and 2183. For ships among the graffiti of Smyrna see Bagnall *et al.* 2016, nos. DG4.1, D2.1, D4.1, D5.1, D6.1, D8.3; see also Keegan 2014, 79–80.
88 For example, Rouché 1989, pl. XXXVII no. 157. For an earlier example see Chaniotis 2015b, 121–122.
89 See Bagnall *et al.* 2016, nos. TG6.1, TG6.4.
90 P47 (animal?, P49, P87, P120, P133, P143, P149, P177, P261, P389, NS40, NS115, NS122, Pr13; unfinished?: P103, P310, P446, P463, NS314.

semicircles, and squares[91] may be unfinished gameboards; but one cannot exclude the possibility that vague designs are abstract representations of objects; for example, the circles may represent wreaths.

D. *TOPOS* INSCRIPTIONS (AC)

A *topos* inscription can be expected in any location where a space could be used for a specific purpose, for example, as a seat in a theatre or a stadium, as a permanent or temporary shop, or as the place where a professional could exercise his trade.[92] It is possible that other types of informal inscriptions, such as prayers and acclamations, also fulfilled the function of place inscriptions,[93] reserving a space for a tradesman or for the members of an association, but they should be considered separately.

The *topos* inscriptions in the Place of Palms are usually written on columns of the stoas (NS7, NS10, NS15, NS18, NS38?, NS52, NS58, NS63?, NS67, NS165, NS190, NS243, NS330?, NS341, NS342, NS344, NS349, WS27, SS4), but are also found on the stylobate of the North Stoa (NS78), on the base of a column (SS7), on the Theatre wall (TW2, TW4?, TW7), and on a seat of the pool (P132). These *topos* inscriptions suggest that the shaded and sheltered space offered by the stoas was used by traders as shops for their merchandize, both temporary and more permanent, but also by other professionals (for example, teachers, see below), and possibly also by homeless people.[94]

Usually, they consist of the word τόπος and a personal name in the genitive (P132: Παύλου τόπος; NS6: τόπος Παπ[ία?]; NS341: [τό]πος | Εὐγρα|φίου | φυλάρ|χου; NS342: τόπος | Ζωτικοῦ | [[...]] | [[...]]; NS349: Ζωτικοῦ τόπος; Pl. 52.B–E), but they may also have the form of a name in the genitive (NS10: Ἀντιόχου; NS15: Διονυσί|ου καὶ Πα|πίου; NS58: Θεοκτίστου; NS344: Ἑκαταίου; WS27: Πάπα?; SS7: Καλλινίκου †; cf. TW4; Pl. 52.F–I, 53.D–E), an abbreviated name (NS63: Κησ., possibly Κησ(ωνίου); NS67: Θεοκ(τίστου); NS78: Ἀνα†τολ(ίου)?; NS165: Πισιθέ(ου)?; NS190: Εκ., for example Ἐκ(άτωνος) or Ἐκ(αταίου); NS330: Ἐπι.; SS4: † Μ(- -)|ου; Pl. 43.A, 52.J–O)), and a name and an occupation (NS52: Ἰωάνν(ου) | ἐλλ(ογιμωτάτου); TW2: τόπος | Ζοτικοῦ | καπήλου † | εὐτυχῶς †; TW7: [Τ]όπ|ος Ἀρτέ[μω]νο|[ς κα]|πήλου; Pl. 52.P and 53.A–B), or simply an occupation without a name (NS19: σοφιστοῦ; Pl.

53.C), always in the genitive.[95] It is possible that some of the abbreviated names and monograms served as *topos* inscriptions (see §D). Also names of women in the nominative may be place inscriptions of owners of shops (N7: Εὐτυχία; NS18: Εὐδοξία; Pl. 53.D–E). In some cases, a space was not occupied by an individual but by a group. The letters ΤΩΝ in NS11 probably belong to the designation of a group in the genitive plural: Τόπ[ος—23– -]|τῶν. In two cases, the same individual is recorded in more than one *topos* inscription (NS58 and NS67: Θεόκτιστος; NS342, NS349, and TW2: Ζωτικός).

The *topos* inscriptions provide only limited information on the use of specific spaces. In the case of NS19 (σοφιστοῦ), the *topos* inscription designates a place as belonging to/being used by a 'sophist', that is a teacher of rhetoric. Ioannes, designated as ἐλλογιμώτατος (NS52), must also have been a teacher of rhetoric or a lawyer. If Zotikos, recorded on two adjacent columns of the North Stoa (NS342 and NS349), is the same person as the κάπηλος of the same name, who had a stand near the retaining wall of the theatre (TW2), he must have been a retail trader or, perhaps more probably, a tavern keeper.[96] Another κάπηλος, Artemon, also had his stand nearby in the South Stoa (TW7). The occupation of the φύλαρχος Eugraphios (NS341) cannot be determined; φύλαρχος usually means the chairman of a civic tribe, but in this case it may designate the chairman of a professional guild.[97] If the letters ΛΑΓΑ (P101; Pl. 47.F) belong to the word λάγανον (cake or vegetable), the graffito may designate the place reserved for a seller of food-stuffs (possibly to be read as λαγα(νοπώλου)).

NS78 is an elaborate *topos* inscription (Pl. 43.A). One recognizes the abbreviated personal name Ἀνα†τόλ(ιος) or Ἀνα†τολ(ίου) written under a drawing that may represent a table. It consists of an oblong band supported by two poles. We may have the representation of the stand (counter?) of a trader by the name of Anatolios.

E. MASONS' MARKS (AC)

The general label 'masons' marks' comprises several different categories of texts, numerals, and signs connected with the production and placement of building material. In Aphrodisias, masons' marks have been recorded in many buildings, on blocks of walls, columns, and pavement plaques. In the Place of Palms, they appear on the pavement of the West Stoa, on blocks of the pool, on columns of the South Stoa, and (in smaller numbers) on the North Stoa. For their interpretation, we also adduce the masons' marks that were recorded in the Tetrastoon, because this (still unpublished) material provides useful insights into the use of masons' marks.

---

91 Parallel lines: P211, P402, P410, NS64; line: NS17; a wavy line: P104, NS254?; circles: P108, P192, P196, P259?, P354, P412, P469, P473, P509, NS100, NS210, NS220?, NS223, NS238, NS245, Pr7, Pr12, Pr14; semicircles: P149, P196, P223, P386, P463, Pr9; squares: P184, P188, P231?, P303, P365?, P376, NS168, NS180, Pr4, Pr23; a circle, a square, and an irregular shape: NS205; an oval: NS248.

92 *Topos* inscriptions in Aphrodisias: Roueché 1989, 229–241. On *topos* inscriptions and the evidence they provide, see Van Nijf 1997, 209–240; Lavan 2012, 338–340 (on trade); Dey 2015, 99 (place reservations for processions); Saliou 2017 (typology and evidence for the use of public space).

93 Robert 1971, 82–84; cf. Saliou 2017, 125 with note 5.

94 On shops in late antique cities, especially in porticos and squares see Lavan 2012. For homeless people finding shelter in porticos in Constantinople see Symeon Logothetes, *Chronicon* 136.57 ed. Wahlgren 2006.

95 Cf. the typology of Saliou 2017: τόπος + name of a person in the genitive (type Ia) or τόπος + an ethnic or a profession in the genitive plural (type Ib); name in the genitive (type II); name in the nominative (type III); verb that indicates place reservation (type IV).

96 Saliou 2017, 145 note 175, tentatively suggests that Zotikos may have successively set up his shop in different locations. However, the lettering of the two inscriptions is very different.

97 Roueché 1989, 196–197.

In the pool, the masons' marks mainly appear on the upper surface of blocks,[98] rarely on the surface that faces the interior of the pool (rim of the seat) and was not visible by the visitors to the park.[99] In the North Stoa they are on architrave blocks (NS350–NS360), in the flutes of columns (NS290, NS296, NS297, NS339; Pl. 54.J), on the foundation, below the robbed stylobate (NS35), on the surface of the columns (NS3), and on the euthynteria (NS240). In the West Stoa masons' marks were carved on the plaques of the pavement (WS31–WS115), in the South Stoa on the top or bottom of column drums (SS1–SS3, SS5, SS6, SS10–SS12, SS14–SS18, SS20, SS22, SS23–SS28, SS31, SS32)—sometimes on both top and bottom (SS13, SS19, SS21) —, or in the flutes (SS6).

The masons' marks consist of one, two, or three letters—in one case, five letters (WS39)—or of monograms (SS15, SS17, SS20, SS24), or complete names (L4). The size of letters varies (usually 5–6 cm), but there are also very large marks (10–16 cm); usually, the monograms are large (9–13 cm). We can often recognize different hands, with individual features in the lettering. For example, the masons' mark M on blocks of the pool is always cursive; in the mark ΕΥ, the upsilon is always written higher than the epsilon, the sigma in the mark ΕΥC is cursive, the mark ΗΛΙ is sometimes written from right to left (Pl. 53.L–M, P). In the case of ΕΡΩ, the letter *rho* is written upside down in relation to the other two letters (Pl. 53.J). This confirms the hypothesis that such abbreviations were used as signatures.

Abbreviated names and monograms

The interpretation of marks with two or more letters as abbreviated names is certain. First, most such sequences cannot represent one number (for example, ΘΕ). Second, most of the sequences of two or more letters correspond to the beginning of personal names, usually names attested in Aphrodisias:

ΑΛ: P43.

ΑΛΒ and ΑΛΒΙΝ (Pl. 53.G): WS33, WS37, WS39, WS41, WS44, WS47, WS49, WS54. These two abbreviations certainly stand for Ἀλβῖνος, who can be identified as the man responsible for the reconstruction of the West Stoa (see In28 and Ch. 4 §D). The marks were written by two or three different hands, and this clearly distinguishes them from the other marks.

ΓΕ: WS91, WS104. Possibly the name Γεώργιος (cf. *IAph2007* 1.33 ii, 1.36, 8.57.26 i, 11.67) or Γέμελλος (cf. *IAph2007* 11.55 b 21).

ΕΙΩ (Pl. 53.H): WS103, WS108, WS109, WS114. This is probably the abbreviated name Εἰω(άννης) (for Ἰωάννης). It always appears in combination with Κοι.

[98] P3, P4, P9, P18–P20, P25, P28, P30–P32, P34, P38, P39, P41–P43, P46, P50, P52, P53, P59–P61, P63, P66?, P67?, P70, P76, P77, P83–P86, P93, P98, P99, P121–P123, P125, P128, P129, P136, P138, P156–P158, P162, P165, P168, P174, P179, P191, P203, P220, P228, P229, P232, P233, P237, P242, P243, P248, P252, P271–P274, P286, P287, P289, P290, P292–P294, P338, P360, P441, P488.

[99] P173, P441, P458, P483, P486, P491.

ΕΝΙ (Pl. 53.I): P338, P360, P488. Names starting with Ἐνι- are rare. This may be an abbreviated word.

ΕΡΩ (Pl. 53.J): P9, P38, P53. The names Ἔρως and Ἐρωτικός are attested in Aphrodisias,[100] but there are other personal names that could have been abbreviated in this way.

ΕΥ (Pl. 53.K–L): P3, P18, P19, P20, P25, P30, P31, P32, P77, P83, P84, P128, P129, P138, P156, P158, P229, P232, P237, P243, P272, P274, P293, P294. Many names are composed with εὐ. The use of the abbreviation ΕΥΣ for Εὐσ(έβης) or Εὐσ(έβιος) and ΕΥΤ for Εὔτυχος or Εὐτύχης (see below) suggests that we are dealing with a different name, for example Εὔ(δαμος), Εὐ(έλπιστος), Εὔ(μαχος). One notices a concentration of this mason's mark in the southeast section of the pool.

ΕΥΣ (Pl. 53.M): WS31, WS71. This is certainly the abbreviation of Εὐσ(έβιος) or Εὐσ(έβης), both very common names. One wonders whether this provider of material is identical with the homonymous individual mentioned in two graffiti (P110 and P111c).

ΕΥΤ (Pl. 53.N–O): WS32, WS34, WS35, WS38, WS40, WS43, WS45, WS46, WS48, WS50, WS51, WS66, WS69, WS74, WS83, WS93, WS94, WS95, WS98, WS101, WS102, WS105, WS107, WS111. This is the abbreviation for Εὔτυχος or Εὐτύχης. It sometimes appears in combination with ΚΦ (WS98, WS107, WS111).

ΗΛΙ (Pl. 53.P): WS65, WS68, WS70, WS75, WS79, WS80, WS81, WS86, WS87, WS90. This is sometimes written sinistrorsum (WS79, WS86). In one case, it is combined with ΚΟΙ (WS68). It most likely is the abbreviated name Ἡλιόδωρος, attested for a builder in late antiquity (*IAph2007* 13.508), rather than Ἡλίας, unattested in Aphrodisias.

ΘΕ (Pl. 47.A and 53.Q): P63, P93, P99, P157, P168, WS42, WS76. This is the beginning of a personal name composed with θεός.

ΚΑ: WS112. This is the abbreviation of one of many names starting with κα- or καλλ-.

ΚΟΙ (Pl. 53.H): WS64, WS68, WS103, WS108, WS109, WS114. This abbreviation appears together with Εἰω(άννης) (WS64, WS103, WS108, WS109, WS114) and ΗΛΙ (WS68); it probably is the abbreviated praenomen Κόϊντος (Quintus) used as a personal name. In Aphrodisias, it is also attested in the form Κόϊνθος (*IAph2007* 11.11).

ΚΟΥ (Pl. 53.R): WS99. It appears in combination with Π. The nickname Κουρέων (for Κουρίων?) is attested in a late antique inscription (*IAph2007* 8.603).

ΚΦ: WS92, WS98, WS107, WS111, WS115. This abbreviation (or the number 520?) appears alone (WS115) or in combination with Εὐτ. (WS98, WS107, WS111) and Π (W92).

ΛΕ: WS58. This is the abbreviation of either Λέων or Λεόντιος, both of which are attested in Aphrodisias in late antiquity (Λέων: *IAph2007* 1.19 ii, 1.25 ii, 1.29 i, 1.32, 12.718 i; Λεόντιος: 11.55 b 21, 15.345).

ΜΑΡ (Pl. 53.S): WS62, WS97, WS106. There are numerous names in Aphrodisias that start with these letters (Μαργαρέτης, Μάργαρος, Μαρδαητος, Μαρίων, Μάρκελλος, Μαρκιανός, Μαρσύας, Μάρτιος, Μάρων), the most common

[100] Bourtzinakou 2012, nos. 1017, 1018 (Eros), 1019 (Erotikos).

of which is Μᾶρκος. Both Μαρκιανός (*IAph2007* 2.516) and Μαρδαητος (*IAph2007* 8.272) are attested in late antiquity.

ΝΟΝ (Pl. 53.T): WS36, WS77, WS85. The name Νόννος is attested in late antiquity in Aphrodisias (*IAph2007* 13.107 ii).

ΣΕ: WS84. Of the numerous names starting with Σε-, Σεβῆρος and Σεραπίων are attested in a late antique context (*IAph2007* 11.55 b 2 and 13).

ΥΤ: WS63. If this is to be read from right to left, it may be the name Τυχικός, attested in Aphrodisias in late antiquity (*IAph2007* 11.55 b 44).

ΦΙ: WS96?, WS100. There are numerous common names starting with φιλ- (Φιλέρως, Φιλήμων, Φίλιππος, Φιλόθεος, Φιλόκαπος, etc.).

With the exception of the abbreviation ΘΕ, the masons' marks on the pool are not the same as those on the pavement of the West Stoa. This may be explained by the fact that the repairs of the pool and of the West Stoa were assigned to different constructors or used different providers of material.

Usually, an abbreviated name appears alone, but in the West Stoa and in the Tetrastoon we also find cases of marks consisting of two separate groups of letters. In the West Stoa, we find the combinations ΕΙΩ ΚΟΙ (WS64, WS108, WS109, WS114), ΗΛΙ ΚΟΙ (WS68), ΕΥΤ ΚΦ (WS98, WS107, WS111), and Π ΚΦ (WS92). Combinations of two (in some cases, three) abbreviations are more common in the masons' marks on the pavement plaques of the Tetrastoon: ΦΩ ΠΟ, ΝΙ ΑΛ, ΦΙ ΑΡΙ, ΑΛΕ ΕΥΣ, ΝΙ ΑΛ Ζ, ΛΕ ΑΛΕ ΖΗ, and ΛΕ ΠΟ ΑΛΕ. The abbreviated names and individual letters that are found on pavement plaques both in the West Stoa and the Tetrastoon do not follow any clear pattern as regards their location, although there are some concentrations of the same abbreviations (for example, ΑΛΒ in the northernmost and ΕΙΩ in the southernmost parts of the West Stoa, ΗΛΙ in the middle). It is certain that the marks were carved before the plaques were placed in the pavement. In the Tetrastoon, in one case the mark is partly under the stylobate of a colonnade; therefore, it could not have been added after the completion of work. We may, therefore, conclude that these marks were made in the process of the cutting of the plaques, either in a quarry or in a workshop. They were not instructions concerning the placement of the plaques but, instead, they marked the work completed by a worker, a group in a quarry, or a workshop, or the plaques delivered by a provider of material or contractor.[101]

In cases in which two abbreviated names are combined (for example Ειω. Κοι.), the one name perhaps indicates the owner of the workshop or the contractor, the other the mason. We may infer this from the fact that in the masons' marks from the Tetrastoon we find a large number of plaques in which the first abbreviation remains the same and the second changes. I provide two examples: ΑΛΕ (2 plaques), ΑΛΕ ΔΑ (1), ΑΛΕ ΕΥ (3), ΑΛΕ ΕΥΣ (2), ΑΛΕ Ζ (1), ΑΛΕ ΖΗ (1), ΑΛΕ ΟΝΗ (2), and ΑΛΕ ΠΟ (1). Presumably, Ἀλέ(ξανδρος) was the owner of the workshop or the leaseholder of the quarry or the contractor and for example Δα(μᾶς), Εὐ(τύχης), Εὐσ(έβιος), Ζ(ωτικός), Ζή(νων), Ὀνή(σιμος), and Πο(λυχρόνιος) were masons or team leaders. The same applies to plaques that combine the abbreviation ΛΕ with a second and sometimess a third abbreviation: ΛΕ Α ΖΗ (1 plaque), ΛΕ ΑΛ (1), ΛΕ ΑΛΕ (3), ΛΕ ΑΛΕ ΖΗ (3), ΛΕ ΑΡ (1), ΛΕ Ζ (10), ΛΕ | ΖΗ (6), ΛΕ ΠΟ ΑΛΕ (2). In this case, we can speculate that for example Λε(όντιος) was the owner or contractor, employing various masons: Ἀλ(ύπιος), Ἀλέ(ξανδρος), Ζή(νων), Ἀρ(τεμᾶς), Ζ(ωτικός), and Πο(λυχρόνιος). But we cannot exclude other explanations, and only the complete comparative study of all masons' marks on pavements (including those of the Tetrapylon Street that have not been recorded yet) may provide more certainty.

In one case, we observe a connection between the abbreviated name and the project for which the plaques were destined. On eight plaques of the pavement of the West Stoa we find the abbreviated name of the man who supervised this construction, Ἀλβ(ῖνος) and Ἀλβῖν(ος), written by two, possibly three, different hands. This man surely is Albinos, the sponsor of the rebuilding of the West Stoa *c*. AD 500, known from acclamations written on its columns and from an honorific epigram (In28). The names of sponsors of building projects appear as mason's marks also in two other cases at Aphrodisias. On the surface of three bases from the temple of the Sebasteion we find the abbreviated name of Ἀνπέ(λιος), that is Flavius Ampelios (Pl. 54.B). Ampelios is known as the man who supervised various building activities and repairs of buildings in the late fifth century/early sixth century AD: the 'palaestra' in the Bouleuterion, work in the Place of Palms, the Theatre Baths, and the Walls (see In10). The column bases were marked with Ampelios' name by three different masons. This indicated that the bases were to be used in a project sponsored by him. Finally, the abbreviation Κω. is found on six blocks used for the construction of the late antique City Walls (Northeast wall, west-east stretch, 'water channel'). It is reasonable to associate this abbreviation with the governor Fl. Constantius, who built the Walls (*IAph2007* 6.41). In all these cases, we are not dealing with owners of workshops or leaseholders of quarries, but with the men responsible for building projects. Their abbreviated names on the plaques, columns, and blocks are to be understood as 'for (the project of) Albinos, Ampelios, or Constantius' or, more likely, 'acquired by (or, on behalf of) Albinos, Ampelios, or Constantius'. In the case of the column bases and the blocks for the walls we are dealing with recycled building material,[102] that was acquired by the sponsors of the buildings, either purchased by them or given to them by the civic authorities.[103]

A similar interpretation can be suggested for names, written in full, abbreviated, or represented through monograms and carved on the surface of column drums of the South Stoa: a monogram that certainly represents the name Ἀναστάσιος (SS24; Pl. 54.C); an unclear monogram (SS15, SS17, SS20, SS22; Pl. 54.D–E) that probably represents the title ὕπαρχος (see Pl. 54.F for comparanda); the name of Κρισπῖνος in the genitive (L4; Pl. 54.G); the abbreviated name of a certain Ξάνθ(ος?) (L5);

---

101 For similar observations in Pergamon, see Bachmann and Lorentzen 2017.

102 For epigraphic evidence on the use spolia from older buildings see Chaniotis 2008b, 66–70; for the use of spolia in the late antique city wall see De Staebler 2008, 312–314.

103 Columns of a stoa were given to the sponsors of the archive on the basis of a civic decree: *IAph2007* 12.1006 LL. 15–17: μετενηχότα δὲ [εἰς | ταύτη]ν καὶ τῆς παλαιᾶς στοᾶς κατὰ τὸ γενόμ[ενον] | ψήφισμα διάσ] τυλα ὀκτώ.

and the mark Κρίσπου on a column drum found in the Tetrapylon Street (Pl. 54.H). The identification of this Ἀναστάσιος as the emperor of this name is discussed in Ch. 4 §A and F. Unlike Ampelios and Albinos, none of the other men is known as a sponsor of a building or a benefactor. They may have been contractors of building projects who acquired building material, possibly from demolished buildings, to use it (or re-use it) for the building of the South Stoa—and in the case of Krispos, the colonnade of the Tetrapylon Street. This is a phenomenon known from Rome, where blocks from dismantled buildings carry inscriptions indicating ownership.[104] But it is also possible that these men were supervisors of public works appointed by the city. During the reign of either Constantine or Constantius II, civic property that generated revenues (*redita fundorum iuris rei publicae*), especially land, was confiscated by the fiscus.[105] As a result, many cities were not in a position to fund building projects and carry out the necessary repairs of buildings. To confront this problem, the proconsul of Achaia Publius Ampelios issued an edict that returned part of these revenues to the cities in the form of building material placed under the responsibility of supervisors of building works (ἐπιμεληταί, *curatores operum publicorum*).[106] An inscription from Chalkis recording his edict gives a list of the men who were appointed as ἐπιμεληταί, the projects for which they were responsible, and the material that each one of them received.[107] If similar measures were taken in Aphrodisias, the men whose names appear on column drums may well be *curatores operum publicorum*.

Single letters

Marks consisting of only one letter are found on blocks of the pool, plaques of the stylobate and the *euthynteria* of the North Stoa, columns of the North and South Stoa, column drums, and architrave blocks of the North Stoa.[108] A particular group are the marks that were engraved within the fluting of columns of the North Stoa (NS290, NS296, NS297, NS339; Pl. 53.F and 54.J). One of these marks consists of the letter X inscribed three times within a frame (NS296). The following single letters are attested:

A: P76, P121 (two marks on adjacent plaques; Pl. 54.I), P125, NS240, NS350, NS360, WS56.
B: NS351, NS360, WS53, WS61, SS6, SS13, SS14, SS16, SS21 (Pl. 54.L), SS27, SS28.
Γ: NS14, NS21, NS352, WS52, SS3, SS19, SS23.
Δ: NS3, NS35, NS353, WS60, SS5, SS10, SS11, SS12, SS26.
E: P4?, P123, P173, NS354, SS5, SS31.
Ϛ (*stigma*, for the numeral six): NS355.
Z: NS356, SS11.
H: NS357.
Θ: NS297, NS359, WS57, SS2.
I: NS358.
K: P441, P458.
M (Pl. 54.M): P28, P34, P39, P41, P42, P46, P50, P52, P59, P60, P61, P70, P85, P86, P98, P122, P136, P162, P165, P174, P179, P191, P203, P220, P228, P233, P242, P248, P252, P271, P273, P286, P287, P289, P290, P292.
O: SS6, SS25.
Π: P441, P483, P486, P491, NS290, NS339, WS55. This letter appears also in combination with ΚΦ (WS92) and ΚΟΥ (WS99).
P: SS32.
Φ: WS72, WS73, WS78, WS82, WS88, WS89, WS110, WS113.
X (Pl. 54.J): NS296, SS18.
Ϡ (Pl. 54.K): WS59.

These marks may have served different purposes. Some of the single letters are numerals connected with the construction of a building, indicating the position of a column, a column drum, or a block. Such 'assembly marks' have been recorded in many places, including Aphrodisias, and are sometimes associated with repairs of buildings or the re-use of building material.[109] The letters B, Γ, Δ, E, and Z on the surface of column drums of the South Stoa (SS3, SS5, SS6, SS10–SS14, SS16, SS19, SS21, SS23, SS26–SS28, SS31) are certainly numerals. Sometimes the same numeral (B and Γ) is written on both surfaces of a drum (SS13, SS19, SS21), certainly indicating the sequence of drums ('second', 'third', etc.).[110] In three cases, two numerals are carved on a drum: Γ E (SS3), Δ E (SS5), and Δ Z (SS11). These numerals may indicate the position of a drum from bottom to top, as in the house of Leukatios in Ptolemais:[111] 'third drum out of five', fourth drum out of five', 'fourth drum out of seven'. But since the columns of the South Stoa usually consist of three (maximum four) drums, these marks may originate in an earlier use.

Masons' marks (numerals) on plaques sometimes indicate the position of adjacent plaques. In the pool, the letter Π is written on a seat block and repeated on the plaque in front of it (P441); the same mason's mark (A) is written on adjacent plaques of the pool (P121). The same applies to the numerals on architrave blocks of the North Stoa (NS350–NS359) that indicate the position of the blocks (from one to ten). Another architrave block from the North Stoa (NS360, now stored behind the stoa, around the middle of the stoa) has two numerals, A

---

104 Meneghini and Santangeli Valenzani 1996, 78–80; 2004, 71. I owe these references to Bert Smith.
105 Jones 1964, 732 and 1301 note 44.
106 The edict: *IG* XII.9.907. Discussions of its impact: Heil 1995, 163–165.
107 *IG* XII.9.907 LL. 18–21: ὅσων ἔργων ἐπιμεληταὶ κατέστησαν καὶ ὅσον | ἕκαστος διετυπώθη λαμβάνειν ἀπὸ τῶν πο|λιτικῶν προσόδων καθ' ἕκαστον ἐνιαυτὸν ὑποτέ|τακται ('the building works for which they appointed supervisors and what each one of them has been determined to receive annually from the public revenues is written below').
108 For an assembly mark on a relief panel re-used in the late antique basin in front of the Propylon, see In7.
109 There are numerous such examples in the foundation of the cavea of the Theatre and the pillars of the North Building of the Sebasteion. See now the comprehensive study by Weber 2013. Other examples: Vallois 1923, 34–37 (Portico of Philip in Delos); Klimek 2013 (house of Leukatios, Ptolemais); Weber 2014 (sanctuary of Klaros); Varkıvanç 2017 (theatre of Kaunos).
110 See for example Weber 2014, 77 (temple of Apollo at Klaros).
111 Klimek 2013.

and B, indicating that it is the first block and the second should be placed to its right. The letter B is inscribed upside-down, therefore, certainly before the block was placed in its position.

By contrast, the letters O, Π, P and X would be very high numbers. The same applies to single letters written by the same hand on different plaques and blocks found in different locations (for example, M). These letters are unlikely to indicate the number of a block or a plaque and its position; in that case, one would have expected the same mason to have written different numerals, not repeat the same numeral. For these letters or marks we need a different interpretation. The association of one letter with one 'hand' or one mason strongly suggests that these letters were either abbreviated names (for example, mason M(enandros)) or, less probably, *signa* of masons (M = mason no. 40). The letter Π carved in the fluting of two columns of the North Stoa is a case in point. It is unlikely that it was a numeral, since we cannot explain why two columns are marked with the same number (80) in a stoa that only had 71–74 columns. These Πs must, therefore, be some sort of signs connected with the production of the columns. The same applies to the three X inscribed within a frame (NS296), possibly also to the letters O and X (SS18 and SS25, see above). The sign S (WS59) certainly is a *signum*. Of course, individual letters might also be numerals connected with the production or cutting of plaques or blocks, for example indicating the numbers of items produced in a workshop or the project for which the items were made.

In summary, the different groups of masons' marks identified in the Place of Palms had different functions and belonged to different periods. The small letters on the architecture of the North Stoa possibly relate to its construction or more likely phases of repairs, and so were inscribed in the first three centuries AD. The letters on the architecture on the South Stoa probably also relate to its construction, which occurred in the late fifth or early sixth century AD. In contrast, the masons' marks on the blocks of the pool walls and the paving of the West Stoa are not contemporary with the construction of these structures and relate to restoration work. The paving slabs in the West Stoa, as shown by those inscribed with the name of Albinos, were inserted during the *c*. AD 500 refurbishment of this structure. On the pool walls, the masons' marks seem also to be found only on blocks added in late antiquity. Some of these are certainly re-used blocks, as noted in Ch. 4, and many were not even white marble, but a blue-grey marble that was more widely used in late antique construction. In fact, half of the masons' marks on the pool are found on blue-grey marble blocks that are certainly later additions.[112]

F. GAMEBOARDS (AW, BR, & AC)

The seats of the pool, and the seat blocks and stylobate of the North Stoa, are covered with a profusion of incised gameboards as well as the textual and pictorial graffiti discussed above. In total, 532 certain or probable gameboards have been documented in the Place of Palms, 291 on the walls of the pool, 226 in the North Stoa, and 15 on the steps of the Propylon (Fig. 46). These comprise five different gameboard types: cross-in-circle (172 cases), mancala (162 cases), and cross-in-square gameboards (134 cases) are best represented, while eight-spoke-wheel (42 cases) and *duodecim scripta* (22) gameboards are far less common.[113] This count does not include a gameboard for 'Nine Men's Morris', cut on an architrave block of the North Stoa (see In1); its date cannot be determined, since it could have been carved before or during the reconstruction of the North Stoa after the earthquake of *c*. AD 500 or after the final collapse of the stoa in the eleventh century. This same game is possibly attested on an inscribed roof tile, found in a seventeenth-century context in the Place of Palms, though it is probably residual (see Ch. 9 §E); this piece is a reminder that the population of Aphrodisias also made use of portable gameboards.

The games of *duodecim scripta*, mancala, and a three-in-a-row game similar to tic-tac-toe, which was played on the cross-in-square gameboard, are all well-understood, while the nature of play of the cross-in-circle and the so-called 'round merels', with a board like an eight-spoked wheel, is less certain. These designs are all found in other public places in Aphrodisias too, notably the Theatre, the Stadium, and the paving to the west of the Tetrapylon, but also in Room 7 of the Hadrianic Baths, and sometimes on street paving, as on Tetrapylon Street to the south of the Tetrapylon, and the late street paving and steps in front of the Temple of the Sebasteion. They are common in Roman or late Roman cites across Asia Minor, and further afield.[114] We describe first the different kinds of boards in the Place of Palms, and then their chronology and distribution. Charlotte Roueché has published a typology of gameboards and pavement designs;[115] this does not correspond to any functional grouping of the games themselves, but we give cross-references to her types where relevant. We start with the types of boards whose games are confidently identifiable, and then the boards where the nature of play is more speculative or disputed.

Duodecim scripta / tabula / alea

A rectangle with three parallel rows of holes; each row has a total of 12 holes, six on either side of a larger circle in the middle.[116] This middle circle is occasionally highlighted in different ways, sometimes with a larger size, sometimes taking a different shape. For example, in NS90 (Pl. 55.A), the central row has a

---

112 This is the case with P25, P28, P30–32, P34, P38, P39, P41–43, P52, P53, P60, P61, P63, P83–85, P121–123, P128, P129, P136, P138, P156, P162, P168, P174, P191, P203, P233, P271–274, P289, and P290.

113 These numbers include uncertain but probable gameboards; excluded are examples that are really very unclear (for example P108, P231, P365, NS100, NS102, NS210, NS314).
114 For a recent discussion of the Byzantine evidence, see Crist 2021.
115 Roueché 1993, 249–52; updated and expanded 2014; see also Bell and Roueché 2007; Roueché 2007b. We do not give any credence to Roueché's suggestion that some of these boards may have been *topos* markers or represent places where people might stand on occasions of festivals or processions.
116 P75, P111, P116, P124, P304, P415, P417, P455, P456?, NS33, NS37, NS83?, NS90, NS147, NS149, NS214, NS216, NS279, NS285, NS291, NS311?, NS323. Cf. Roueché type 3Rows.1–12.

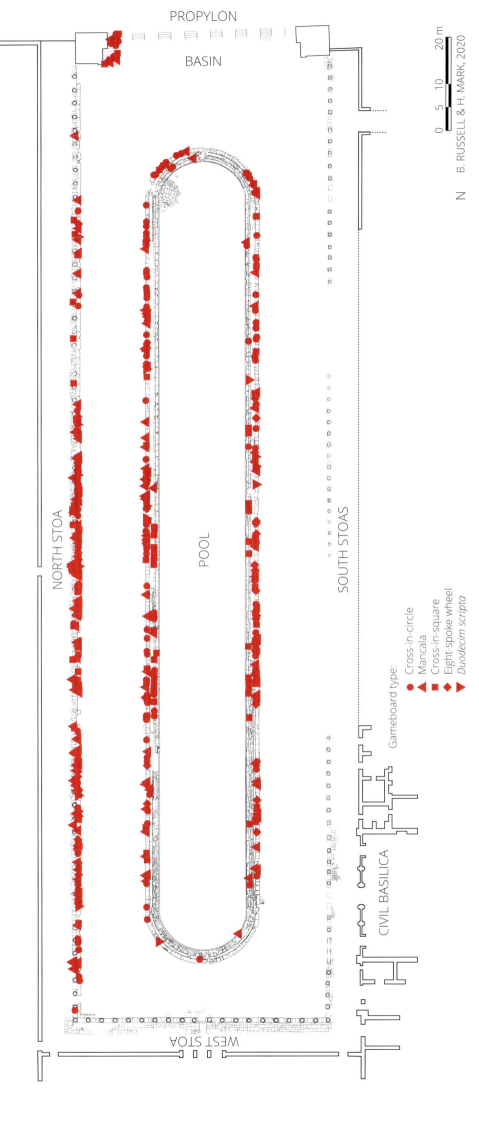

Fig. 46. Distribution of gameboards in the Place of Palms.

circle in the middle, the lateral rows have semicircles (cf. P111; Pl. 43.I). In NS147 (Pl. 55.B), the middle circle of the middle row is replaced by a rhombus, while the lateral rows have larger circles; P417 has circles instead of holes. In a more elaborate variant, a cross divides the quadrangle into four sections. The vertical, long bar of the cross consists of 12 holes with a circle in the middle. The lateral rows of holes are attached to the long sides of the quadrangle. Each row has six holes on either side of a semicircle in the middle of the row; these two semicircles are at either end of the horizontal bar of the cross. NS279, NS285, and NS291 are variants of this scheme (Pl. 55.B–C): a square is divided with a cross into four segments. There are three rows, of twelve (NS285, NS291) or six 'holes' each (NS279); the holes of the lateral rows are represented by small circles. In NS279, the middle row, which is one of the arms of the cross, has six pairs of small circles, arranged on either side of the arm of the cross; in NS285 and NS291, at the point where the arms of the cross intersect there is a bigger circle, while at the points where the arms reach the sides of the rectangle there are large semicircles. P116 lacks the circles/semicircles in the middle of the rows; instead, a horizontal line divides the three vertical rows into two parts. P417 is within a frame.

This type of gameboard is common across the Roman empire and in the western provinces the holes are often replaced by three rows of twelve letters, making a sentence.[117] It has been identified as the game of *duodecim scripta* mentioned by Ovid, and Austin argues that it was an early game of the backgammon type, played with six-sided dice (three according to Austin; two according to Schädler), and fifteen pieces for each player.[118] Austin reconstructs the rules by analogy with backgammon and on the basis of a board found at Ostia (*CIL* 14.5317) where the letters on each 'table' indicate the sequence of play:

```
C C C C C C    B B B B B B
A A A A A A    A A A A A A
D D D D D D    E E E E E E
```

Austin's reconstruction is worth quoting in full:[119]

> This, evidently a board of primitive type for the use of beginners, strongly suggests that the direction of play followed the letters of the alphabet: the pieces would be entered on the middle row (marked A . . . A), by alternate throws of the dice, of which three were used. The game must certainly have conformed to the rules common to its type: thus, if either player had a single man ('blot') on any point, and his opponent's throw enabled him to move a man to that point, the latter could take the 'blot', removing it from the board and substituting his own man; but two or more pieces on one point were immune from capture, and prevented the enemy from using a throw to that point; a piece taken in the manner described had to be re-entered by the dice before its owner could move again. These rules would apply not only to the game proper in progress, but also to the preliminary procedure of entering the men, which would thus often occupy a considerable time. Neither player could begin to advance his pieces until all were so entered on the middle row; movement then took place, through B to C, then down to D; when one player had brought all his pieces to the last six points of the board (that is E . . . E) he could then, and then only, begin to play them off the board according to the throw of the dice—but if meanwhile any 'blot' was captured, it had to be re-entered as before and brought back to the E table before this playing-off process could be resumed. The winner was he who succeeded in thus playing all his men off the board while his opponent still had pieces remaining on it.

Elaborate gameboards carefully carved on reused statue bases were set up at Aphrodisias in the palaestra court of the Hadrianic Baths, three given by the *pater tēs poleōs* Flavius Photius, one by an *exceptor* (clerk), and one by a *magnificentissimus*, in the late fifth/early sixth century AD.[120] Professionally cut gameboards are also known from Ephesos, Miletos, Kibyra, Laodikeia, Sagalassos, Side, Perge, and Çarşamba in Phrygia.[121] In Asia Minor, while this sort of game attracted the most elaborate gameboards, we do not (usually) see the use of epigrams using letters for the game spaces, as is quite common in the Latin-speaking West. In the East, examples with letters are known only from Kos and various sites in Asia Minor.[122] Peter Talloen argues that the boards without letters in Asia Minor are a later development and should be considered a different game from *duodecim scripta*;[123] but while it is to a large extent true that the lettered boards from the western provinces are often earlier than the boards from Asia Minor, this need not indicate that the game was necessarily different. Roueché observes that in the western provinces, it is usually the examples with letters that have been published, 'with a passing reference to those without letters'[124]—in other words, boards without letters in the West have been largely overlooked, though they certainly existed.[125]

In the early Byzantine period, *duodecim scripta* was supplanted by, or developed into, the game of *tabula* or τάβλη, also known simply as *alea* ('dice'). *Tabula* is described by Isidore of Seville and in Agathias's epigrammatic account of the closing stages of a famous game of it played by the fifth-century Emperor Leo (*Anth. Pal.* IX.483); it was similar to *duodecim scripta* but had only two rows of dots, players moving through the board in directions opposite to each other.[126] It developed eventually into the games of the backgammon family known today, which in Greece are still called τάβλι (*tavli*).

One possible example of a *tabula* board exists in the Place of Palms, on an outer seat slab of the pool's north wall (P455); it has two rows of 12 points, divided 6 and 6 in each row by a D-shaped symbol (but missing the centre of its upright: Pl. 55.E).[127] Since the seat block in question is much smaller than

---

117 Ihm 1890; 1891; Lamer 1927, 2004–2012; *ILS* 8626 and 9453; Purcell 1995.
118 Austin 1935a, 32–34. Cf. Schädler 1998, 17.
119 Austin 1935a, 33–34.
120 *IAph2007* 5.10, 5.13, 5.14, 5.15, 15.351; Roueché 2007b, 101.
121 Talloen 2018, 117; Miletos, Side and Perge: Roueché 1989, 111–112.
122 Talloen 2018, 103–106; *IG* XII.4.3409; *MAMA* X 330; *SEG* 59.1384.
123 Talloen 2018.
124 Roueché 1989, 111.
125 For example Ihm 1890, 225.
126 Austin 1934; 1935b, 76–79.
127 Roueché type 2Rows.1.

its two neighbours, and appears to have been inserted between them, it is very possible that the board was actually a *duodecim scripta* board that has lost its third row when the seat block was cut down. If so, that would date the *duodecim scripta* board to before the late fifth-century reconstructions of the pool.

The apparent absence, or near-absence, of *tabula* boards at Aphrodisias, when the game was known to be popular in the late fifth century (for example with Leo I), is at first sight surprising. But it would be possible to play *tabula* on a *duodecim scripta* board, by ignoring the central line of places and just using the outer two rows. Indeed, Austin suggested that *tabula* was 'originally played on a xii scripta board in which the middle row was not used for movement'.[128] A board at Sagalassos may also have been cut down from a 3-row *alea* or *duodecim scripta* board for a *tabula* board; and two-row boards are known also from Sardis and Didyma.[129]

Mancala

Numerous instances of boards for games of mancala are also found in the Place of Palms, consisting of two parallel rows of (usually five) holes (Pl. 55.F–I).[130] In a variant, the rows of holes are placed within a rectangle that resembles a grid (P298, P326, P419, P420, P421, NS107; Pl. 55.F; cf. P461 that has, however, only four holes in each row; Pl. 55.G),[131] or in a simple rectangle (P234, P317, NS113; cf. P320, P373); in P330 a line divides a rectangle into two parts, each of which is subdivided into five sections; holes are visible only in two of these sections. In a variant, two rows of five holes each are connected with lines (NS316). In one case (P14; Pl. 55.H), there is an additional hole, in the middle, between the third hole of the left and right row. P218 (Pl. 55.I) is placed within a circle, which seems to have been made separately. P364 (Pl. 55.J) is a gameboard in the shape of a grid, consisting of four rows of five sections each. A few boards have two somewhat larger holes offset diagonally to the side, one at the end of each row (see below). Often only a few holes remain of such a gameboard, and for this reason gameboards of this type may be hard to recognize. In the case of partly preserved gameboards that were incised next to each other, it is often difficult to assign holes or rows of holes to individual gameboards.

Mancala is a class of games including many variants with differing rules, but all involve numerous small pieces—pebbles, seeds, shells, or glass counters, for instance. At the start of the game a set number of pieces is placed in each cup, and players take turns in 'sowing' the pieces from a cup one by one into consecutive cups, counter-clockwise around the board. In a two-row game, each player owns one row, and when the last piece of his turn falls in an empty cup on his own side, he captures those pieces from the opposite cup in his opponent's row. Captured pieces are put to one side, nowadays, often in a larger cup that serves as the player's store at the right-hand end of his row, but these larger receptacles are absent from many of the Aphrodisias boards. When one player has no more pieces on his side, the winner is the player who has the most pieces.[132]

Until the late 1990s, when boards for two-row mancala were recognised at a number of ancient sites in Asia Minor including Aphrodisias, mancala was not considered as a game that had been played in classical antiquity.[133] Since then, ancient mancala boards have also been recognised at Palmyra, those with rows of five holes being considered Roman, and some with rows of seven holes, found only within the Temple of Baal which was transformed into a fort in or after the seventh century, considered an Arab introduction.[134]

Mancala boards at Aphrodisias were often placed lengthwise between the players, as at Palmyra, although this is uncommon today.[135] Most lack the larger receptacles at the ends of the rows that served as each player's store, but some boards have a pair of larger receptacles, one at each end and offset to different sides of the board (see, for example, Pl. 44.C).[136] This suggests that while dedicated receptacles for the players' stores were not a feature of the early form of Roman mancala, they developed during the period when the Place of Palms was still a usable space, that is before the mid seventh century AD. The sizes of the cups or holes in the boards at Aphrodisias are so small that very small counters must have been used—grape pips?

Cross-in-square – simplified 'small merels'

A cross divides a square into four segments (Pl. 43.J, 44.A and 56.A).[137] In one case two squares with a cross share one of their

---

128 Austin 1934, 203.
129 Talloen 2018, 112–113, 121 and n. 113.
130 P11, P12, P14, P26, P44, P55, P89, P113, P118, P127?, P153, P166, P197, P214, P218 (two rows of 4 holes), P219, P224, P234, P235, P250?, P262, P263, P265, P280, P281, P291, P295, P296, P298, P299, P312, P314, P315, P317, P320, P326, P329, P330, P332?, P336, P348, P349, P353, P364?, P373, P380, P382, P395, P398, P400, P419, P420, P421, P424, P426, P430, P434, P436, P442, P444?, P445?, P447, P460, P461?, P467, P471?, P472, P474, P489?, P512, P513, NS5, NS24, NS28, NS31, NS42, NS44, NS50, NS61, NS65, NS73, NS75, NS76, NS77, NS91, NS92, NS93, NS94, NS96, NS105, NS106, NS107?, NS111, NS112, NS113, NS118, NS119, NS124, NS125, NS128, NS129, NS131, NS139, NS146, NS148, NS150, NS155, NS156, NS157, NS158, NS161, NS162, NS164, NS177, NS182, NS183, NS186, NS187, NS188, NS189, NS194, NS196, NS197, NS198, NS200, NS208, NS215, NS217, NS219, NS221, NS222, NS224, NS228, NS229, NS234, NS236, NS237, NS251, NS252, NS258, NS266, NS267, NS275, NS278, NS286, NS287, NS292, NS294, NS298, NS306, NS309, NS316, NS325, NS334, NS335, NS336, NS348, Pr5, Pr19, Pr21; cf. NS311. Mancala boards at Aphrodisias most commonly take the form of Roueché's types H4, H11, H12, R1, R5, R6 (all with rows of 5 holes); but there are also variants with other numbers of holes: H2, H3, H4, H5, and R2 (6 holes), R3 (8 holes), (and possibly also H1, with 3 holes).
131 Cf. Roueché 1993, 251, type R6.
132 de Voogt 2010, 1056–1057.
133 Schädler 1998, who also notes that these boards could have been used to play the attested game *pente grammai*, 'five lines'.
134 de Voogt 2010.
135 Cf. de Voogt 2010, 1060 for Palmyra.
136 P218, P235, P353, P419, P467, NS73, NS96, NS146?, NS148, NS150?, NS177, NS197, NS215, NS234.
137 P5, P7, P21, P40, P68, P80, P88, P100, P102, P117, P130, P131, P137, P145, P146, P150, P152?, P155, P175, P181, P190, P198,

sides, creating a rectangle with eight segments (P249; Pl. 56.B); three gameboards are joined into one long series of three squares with crosses (NS133–NS135). In a variant, small holes were added within each square (P145; Pl. 56.C); P257 combines the features of P145 and P249 (eight segments and holes; Pl. 56.D). P202 (Pl. 56.F) has a small cross in one of the squares. In a variant (NS103) a cross with two horizontal arms divides the square into six sections.

This is a game similar to tic-tac-toe or 'noughts and crosses', and is probably the game mentioned twice by Ovid as having as its goal to get three counters in a row.[138] Players have three counters and take turns in placing them on the board, at points where lines intersect; once all counters are on the board, players use their turn to move a piece to an adjacent vacant position. The aim is to get three in row, and to block your opponent from doing the same. Versions of this game are found around the Roman world, often with additional diagonal lines (giving two further possibilities of three-in-a-row lines), which are lacking in the examples from Aphrodisias.[139]

Cross-in-circle boards

The cross-in-circle game is represented by Roueché's types C2, C7, CC5, CC8 (a dual-purpose board that could be used to play either this game or the eight-spoke wheel game). In the case of P256 (Pl. 56.G) the cross does not touch the periphery; it is not certain that this is a gameboard and not an encircled Christian cross. In the case of P260 (Pl. 56.H) and NS324, the gameboard in enclosed within a large circle. In P369 and NS313 a small circle is attached to the gameboard; NS312 has a line attached to its periphery. In the case of NS166 and NS167 (Pl. 56.I), two gameboards, a small and a big one, are attached to each other. In P97, a circle was incised on one of the spokes, resembling the letter theta (Pl. 56.N).

A cross divides a circle into four segments (Pl. 46.F).[140] P171 (Pl. 56.K), P257, P308, P325, P337, and P418 have semicircles at the point where the four spokes touch the periphery (cf. P432); P205 (Pl. 56.J) has two small cross-in-circle drawings in two of the segments. A variant (NS66; Pl. 56.L) has two concentric circles instead of one. In one case (NS260) the gameboard is enclosed within a circle. In another (P339) an additional line (parallel to one of the arms of the central cross) separates a small segment. The shape of P494 resembles that of a fruit (neither square nor circle), while P468 (Pl. 56.M) is heart-shaped. P495 has a line attached to it (like a 'tail').

The design of a cross in a circle is also commonly found alongside gameboards of all the other types discussed in this chapter, both in the Place of Palms and in other buildings of Aphrodisias where gameboards are common, including the Theatre and Stadium. It is not a game of a type still played or still known, and doubt has been cast on whether it is in fact a gameboard, since if played as a three-in-a-row game with players simply taking turns to place counters, it will always result in stalemate. As there are only five spaces on the board, Player 1 will be able to place all three counters, but Player 2 can only place two. Player 2 can never make a line of three counters, but could perhaps win by preventing Player 1 from forming a line. Player 1 would invariably take the centre, Player 2 places a counter on any one of the places around the edge; Player 1 puts a counter on a space on the edge at 90⁰ to Player 2's piece, and Player 2 then prevents Player 1's line being completed by putting a counter in the space diametrically opposite the counter just placed by Player 1. The only remaining space can be filled by Player 1, but again it will not produce a line of three as the other end of the line is occupied by Player 2's first piece. The only way in which a different outcome could be achieved is for Player 2, through stupidity or kindness, to let Player 1 win by not blocking Player 1's line in the second move. This will never produce a satisfactory game, and it cannot therefore be a straightforward three-in-a-row game with counters simply placed on the board in alternating turns.

This has led to doubt over whether the cross-in-circle design is in fact a gameboard at all: in 1991 Andrew Fear interpreted examples from the amphitheatres at Italica and Mérida in Spain as religious graffiti, perhaps associated with the goddess Nemesis,[141] and we ourselves had wondered whether at Aphrodisias it might be a Christian symbol calqued on the merels boards that are so common, or a game of unknown type.[142] Yet if it were a Christian symbol, it is strange that it is found only on horizontal surfaces, and never on vertical ones—and this is true both of

P202, P204, P217, P221, P226, P227, P246, P249, P257, P276, P283?, P285, P316, P318, P322, P340, P346, P355, P358, P359, P361, P362, P363, P368, P370, P374, P378?, P385, P387, P388, P393, P401, P405, P406, P408, P414, P443?, P478, P492, P501, P503, NS29, NS30, NS34, NS41, NS56, NS62, NS69, NS70, NS71, NS72, NS79, NS80, NS81, NS82, NS85, NS95, NS101, NS103, NS104, NS108, NS109, NS117, NS120, NS121, NS123, NS132, NS133, NS134, NS135, NS140, NS151, NS152, NS154, NS159, NS172, NS173, NS174, NS175, NS176 (unfinished), NS184, NS185, NS193, NS195?, NS201, NS202, NS206, NS209, NS212, NS213, NS218, NS225, NS242, NS249, NS250, NS255 (unfinished), NS256, NS257, NS276, NS293, NS300, NS302, NS303, NS304, NS318, NS319, NS321, Pr3, Pr6, Pr16, Pr18, Pr22. Cf. Roueché 1993, 251, type S3.

138 Ovid, *Ars Amatoria* III.365–6; *Tristia* II.481–2.
139 Austin 1935b, 79–80.
140 P6, P8, P13, P24, P35, P36, P54, P56, P57, P58, P62, P69, P71?, P72, P87?, P97, P109, P151, P164, P171, P172, P178, P185?, P195, P197?, P201, P205, P206, P207, P209, P215, P222, P223?, P225, P236, P240, P255, P258, P259?, P260, P279, P282?, P297, P301, P305?, P306?, P308, P323, P325, P328?, P331?, P334, P335, P337, P339, P341, P342, P344, P345, P347, P350, P351, P352, P356, P357, P367, P369, P371, P372, P375, P379, P381, P383, P390,
P391?, P394, P399, P403, P404, P411, P413, P418, P428, P429?, P431, P432, P433, P435, P440, P451, P453?, P454?, P457, P459, P464, P466, P468, P476, P477, P481, P482, P484, P485, P487, P490, P493, P494, P495, P496, P497, P498, P499, P500, P502, P504, P505, P506 (unfinished), P508, P510, P511, NS25, NS49, NS57, NS66, NS74, NS87, NS88, NS98, NS99, NS100, NS110, NS114, NS145, NS153, NS160, NS166, NS167, NS169, NS170, NS171, NS179, NS181, NS192, NS199, NS207, NS220?, NS226, NS239, NS265, NS284, NS305, NS307, NS308, NS312, NS313, NS315, NS320, NS322, NS324, NS326, NS327, NS329, NS337, NS338, NS347 (unfinished), Pr2, Pr8, Pr10, Pr11, Pr15, Pr17, Pr20. Cf. Roueché 1993, 249, type C2.
141 Fear 1991.
142 Wilson, Russell, and Ward 2016, 84; cf. Jacobs 2013, 618–619.

Aphrodisias and other sites.[143] Responding to Fear's paper, Richard Rothaus pointed out that the motif was always found on flat, horizontal surfaces—on steps, in doorways, porches and other places where people might sit—and in association with gameboards of other types, and so argued that it must be a gameboard, citing examples at Aphrodisias, Sardis, and Didyma.[144] To this list we can add Stratonikeia and Laodikeia,[145] and doubtless a systematic search would produce examples from other sites too.

The variations on the design of the board also provide support for the view that it is not primarily a religious motif or symbol. While the most common form is a simple cross in a circle, variants include ones with additional straight lines joining the ends of the arms of the cross, making a cross in an angled square within a circle, ones which mark the junctions of the diameter lines with the circumference with segments of circles, as on some eight-spoke wheel boards (P186), and ones which dispense with the cross altogether, marking the points with a small central circle and segments of circles on the circumference where the arms of the cross would touch the circle had they been drawn. None of these variants would affect the playability of the game, as they do not alter the basic design of a central point surrounded by four points at 90° angles, but the latter variant shows that the design is *not* primarily a Christian symbol, as it can exist without the cross. Nonetheless, although the design is a gameboard rather than a religious symbol, it is entirely possible that its popularity at Aphrodisias in late antiquity (and elsewhere in Asia Minor, where these boards may also all be late antique) may have been connected with the fact that most variants of the board included an obvious cross.

Since the board could not be played with a simple three-in-a-row game in which players alternate putting pieces on the board, if it is a three-in-a-row game, as might be suggested from its similarity to the other merels and cross-in-square boards, an additional element would have to be involved. This could be achieved by introducing the factor of chance: if one had to throw a particular throw of a die in order to place each piece on the board (evens? odds? six? etc.), this randomises the choice of whoever takes the centre spot, and it is not a foregone conclusion that the second player to get a piece on the board could block the first. One might even consider a rule that a player could not take the centre spot until they had already placed two pieces on the circumference. The game would then become one much more of chance than strategy, though there is still a strategic component involved. It must be stressed that this is an entirely speculative reconstruction, but one could at least play a game satisfactorily on this board in this particular way.

An alternative and perhaps preferable solution is suggested by a threshold panel mosaic from Piazza Armerina, showing children playing games of throwing stones or game pieces into particular patterns (Pl. 56.O). On the right, a boy has thrown a stone to make a line of five; on the left, a boy has been throwing stones onto a board identical to our cross-in-circle boards. One stone is in the centre, and the other four occupy the blank spaces in each quarter. Schädler identifies the scene in the mosaic as a game similar to 'franc du carreau', attested in France from the sixteenth century AD onwards, in which one throws coins or counters on to a square board divided into four by either vertical and horizontal, or diagonal, lines, with the aim being to throw a piece either onto the centre, or to get as close to the centre as possible without touching a line.[146] Schädler's argument is in fact made in the context of an attempt to reinterpret the eight-spoke wheel boards (below), but his observation would actually apply very well, indeed better, to the cross-in-circle boards at Aphrodisias. It is easy to imagine how these could be played using coins, with the winner scooping the board. But a 'franc du carreau' game would not work for the boards which lack the cross and instead have a small central circle and segments of circles on the circumference.

Eight-spoke wheel boards
(Round merels, Rundmühle, Radmühle)

A very common design is a circle divided into eight equal segments by four diameter lines, like a wheel with eight spokes (Pl. 57.A–C).[147] Variants on this type might embellish or emphasise the centre with a small circle (NS68, NS259; cf. P311),[148] the segments are marked by semicircles attached to the periphery of the circle (P140, P186, NS27, NS68; cf. P311); in P333 a wavy line stretches along the periphery of the circle; P462 resembles a hexagon enclosed within the circle. The most elaborate variant is NS317 (Pl. 57.C). Instead of one circle, it consists of four concentric circles, the smallest one representing the center of the outer periphery. Four diameters divide the periphery into eight segments, as in the main type. However, at the point where the radii touch the outer periphery there is a semicircle; crosses decorate the spaces between these semicircles. In the case of P141, a spoke divides one of the segments into two, resulting in a total of nine (not eight) segments (Pl. 57.A); the same phenomenon appears in NS136, whereby there are two segments divided into smaller ones, creating a circle with ten segments.

This type of board is commonly found on Roman sites, at for example Rome (Basilica Julia, porch of the Oratory of the Forty Martyrs, pavement of the Horrea Agrippiana, Trajan's Markets), Ostia, Lepcis Magna, Ephesos, Stratonikeia, and Didyma.[149]

In 1918 Carl Blümlein proposed rules for this game, assuming that it is the game referred to twice by Ovid who talks about a small board with three counters for each player, and winning consists of getting them in a straight line.[150] According to Blümlein's reconstruction, players alternately place counters

---

143 The 'mill' game mentioned by Jacobs (2013, 619) as carved on an architrave of the North Stoa is actually a Nine Men's Morris board, not a cross-in-circle: Roueché 2007b, 103 no. 13.
144 Rothaus 1992.
145 A. Wilson, personal observation, 2013 (Stratonikeia) and 2015 (Laodikeia).
146 Schädler 2018, 89–90.
147 P10?, P27?, P82, P92, P110, P140, P141, P144, P161, P163, P176, P183, P186, P187, P199, P200, P241, P269, P288, P311, P327, P333, P397, P416, P462, P464, P475, NS27, NS68, NS84, NS130, NS136, NS138, NS178, NS241, NS259, NS263, NS274, NS299, NS301, NS310, NS317. This game is represented at Aphrodisias by Roueché's types C4, C5, C6, CC2, CC6, CC7, CC8, CCC1, CCC2, and apparently also H10.
148 Roueché type CC2.
149 A. Wilson, personal observation.
150 Blümlein 1918; Ovid, *Ars Amatoria* III.365–6; *Tristia* II.481–2.

on the board, and once all counters are on the board, each player's turn consists of moving one of their counters to an adjacent free space. If a player cannot move, they have lost.

Blümlein's suggested rules produce an initially playable game and his reconstruction has until recently been generally accepted. It has been called into question, however, by two independent studies.

Florian Heimann identified a starting situation which can lead to an infinite loop in the game;[151] and consequently Schädler doubted that the game was played according to Blümlein's rules. Separately, in 2014 Claudia-Maria Behling argued that players will quickly see through the tactics needed to win, and that Ovid's three-in-a-row game was played not on a circular board but on the cross-in-square board described above.[152] Instead, she proposed that the eight-spoke wheel board was used for a throwing game similar to 'franc du carreau' with a circular board (cf. above). It is possible that one could play such a game on many of these boards. But it encounters the problem that some of the boards have the intersections with the circumference marked out as semicircles, and the central point with a circle; and elsewhere, for example in the Old Forum at Lepcis Magna, these points are neatly hollowed out as cups, evidently for placing a counter in. This looks like a game where one places counters at specified points, not where one throws to avoid lines. That observation is confirmed by a gameboard from the Tetrapylon Street, just south of the Tetrapylon, at Aphrodisias where the board consists entirely of cup-like depressions, without the lines connecting them (Pl. 57.D). This could only be played as a game where counters were placed in the cups, to make lines of three; it could not be a throwing game where one had to avoid the lines, for the simple reason that there were no lines.

Despite the doubts expressed by Behling and Schädler, the demonstration[153] that some circumstances can lead to infinitely repeated loops does not in our view prove that Blümlein reconstructed the game incorrectly: first, by no means all starting situations lead to these loops; second, many casual players (rather than game theorists) do not necessarily spot the flawless play that would result in these loops,[154] and make a mistake allowing their opponent to win, so a game may conclude satisfactorily; third, other successful games may result in a stalemate from time to time. Part of the appeal of these boards in the early Christian period may have lain in the fact that, as Jacobs points out, the letters of I X Θ Y Σ can be traced on a board with six or eight spokes.[155]

Boards and pieces

The elaborate gameboards inscribed into the surfaces around the Place of Palms possibly imitate boards made of wood with inlays from other materials—a gameboard with ivory inlay is mentioned by Martial.[156] Besides the aforementioned elaborate decoration, one occasionally finds elements added to gameboards. In P97, a circle was incised on one of the spokes, resembling the letter theta (Pl. 56.N). In P100, letters were added (Pl. 56.E); P495 has a line attached to it (like a 'tail'). A cross-in-circle gameboard was turned into an eight-spoke wheel gameboard with the addition of irregular spokes (P464). A cross (NS89) touches a cross-in-circle gameboard (NS88; Pl. 57.F). A cross-in-square gameboard was transformed into a *duodecim scripta* board (NS279; Pl. 55.C): one of the bars of the cross was turned into the central row of a *duodecim scripta* board through the addition of 6 (instead of 12) holes and a circle in the middle; also, two later rows (with 6 holes each) were added. In the case of P330 a cross-in-square gameboard was combined with a mancala gameboard.

An interesting phenomenon that can be occasionally observed is the transformation of a gameboard into a pictorial graffito through the engraving of additional elements. So, crosses and arches were added on either side of a mancala board (P398; Pl. 44.B), making it resemble a church, and an arch was added to a cross-in-circle board (P331; Pl. 51.F); in another instance, the base of a menorah was turned into a cross-in-square board (P408; Pl. 44.A).

Many of the gameboards listed above required counters to be played and indeed the deposits within the bottom of the pool have produced a large quantity of these, as discussed in Ch. 8 §D. In the Place of Palms, these counters are circular and are mostly made of cut-down marble revetment panels, though some in ceramic were also recovered. The range of polychrome marbles used would have allowed different players to employ different colour palettes of counters, allowing them to be distinguished on the board. But these counters are also indicative of a level of investment on the part of these gamers in their equipment. Among the counters found are examples in the full suite of polychrome marbles, including exotic imports like Egyptian porphyry and *serpentino* from the Peloponnese. These counters might have been cut from second-hand material but trimming a set of (approximately) round counters from a panel of stone requires considerably more effort than cutting back a fragment of pottery or collecting a pebble. Like the gameboards themselves, some of which must have taken considerable effort to carve, these counters show that the Place of Palms gamers took their leisure pursuit seriously.

Chronology

The date of many of these gameboards is not precisely fixable but can be approximately deduced in many cases from the architectural context of the blocks on which they are carved. Many of the games on the surround of the pool are demonstrably later than the rebuilding of the pool, as they are carved on blocks reused in the repair of the pool's seats, and only make sense in their current position.[157] For the North Stoa the situation is often less clear, but there are certain cases where a gameboard (for

---

151 Heimann and Schädler 2014.
152 Behling 2014.
153 Schädler 2012; Heimann and Schädler 2014; Schädler 2018.
154 Heimann's proof used formal analysis looking up to eight moves ahead to prove the loop: Heimann and Schädler 2014.
155 Jacobs 2013, 619, fig. 217.
156 Martial 13.1.8. On elaborate gameboards, see Austin 1935b, 80.

157 This is true of P24, P26, P27, P55, P56, P130, P131, P144, P145, P146, P231, P285, P351, P352, P361, P362, P363, P378, P379, and P455.

example NS5, NS30, NS31, NS148, NS149) is carved over one of the grooves in the intercolumniations for doorframes which we have argued (Ch. 3 §D) were inserted perhaps in the fourth century; and since the board can only have been carved after the doorframe was removed again, it must date to after the repairs and rebuilding of the late fifth century. Several gameboards (for example NS61, NS183, NS192, NS193, NS221, NS266, NS294) were also carved after the stylobate blocks between the columns were removed, which probably happened in the same period.

Two other pieces of evidence support this late date. The inscribed gameboards P110, P111, and P201 are probably all late antique. P110 can be dated closely to the late fifth or early sixth century AD, since it mentions Doulkitios. The marble counters also suggest a post-fifth century date for much of this gaming activity. The most likely sources for the marble of these counters are the rear walls of the North and West Stoas (and perhaps also the South Stoa) of the Place of Palms. The rear walls of the North and West Stoas were revetted in polychrome marble in the early second century, as explained in Ch. 3 §D. The range of lithotypes used on these decorative schemes is broadly reflected in the game counters. To judge from the discovery of revetment panels used in late antique repairs to the pool floor, the rear walls of these stoas were damaged in the late fifth-century earthquake, patched up, and any material from them too fragmentary to be put back up was re-used for other purposes. Just at the moment that the Place of Palms was refurbished in the late fifth or early sixth century, and indeed as a result of this work, there was an injection of polychrome revetment, neatly suited to the production of game counters, onto the second-hand market. It is unlikely that many of the marble counters found in the pool deposits date to before the late fifth century.

This does not mean that all of the gameboards in the Place of Palms date to the period after the late fifth century. Along the line of the North Stoa, in fact, most of the recovered gameboards that are not on the stylobate blocks are on the top of the seat blocks in front of them; only a minority were carved on the surface from which the stylobate blocks between columns were removed. This would suggest that many of these gameboards were carved prior to the late fifth century. However, they may not be much earlier in date than this. The fact that no gameboards were found on the stylobate of the West Stoa (or those few sections of its seat blocks that have been uncovered), a structure that was closed off in the fourth century AD, might suggest that gameboard carving was not common prior to this date. The fact that so many gameboards are found on the North Stoa is probably a reflection of its quite different character from the fourth century onwards compared to the West Stoa (as discussed in Ch. 3 §C).

Based on the above evidence, we can say that the datable gameboards and the bulk of the recovered game counters can be placed between the end of the fifth century and the early seventh century, while many of the others, especially on the North Stoa, are probably datable to after the fourth century. This does not mean that gaming did not occur in the Place of Palms prior to this point, simply that the majority of this activity that remains visible was late antique.

Distribution

The distribution of the gameboards, as with much of the rest of the graffiti, is not even across the Place of Palms (see Fig. 46). There are just 15 on the northern steps of the Propylon but since the southern steps of the structure are lost this represents a relatively high concentration. In the North Stoa there are 226 gameboards, while, as noted above, there are none in the West Stoa. Around the pool, there are 291, of which 144 are on the north side, 120 are on the south side, 22 on the east end, and just 5 on the west end.

While there is no obvious preference for the north side or the south side, around the length of the pool walls there are some clear concentrations of gameboards and notable gaps in the distribution. The south-east, north-west and north-east curves of the pool ends have very few gameboards. On the south side, there are gaps in the spread of gameboards for the first 15 m from the east end, the 20 m just east of the halfway point, and then again for 15 m three-quarters of the way along. Even in the area of the densest clustering of gameboards, the 30 m west of the halfway point, one finds concentrations of 5–10 gameboards across 3–7 seat blocks then a gap of two or three seats blocks before the next cluster. On the north side, large gaps can be noted one-third of the way along from the east end, just west of the halfway point, and at the western end, with smaller breaks in the distribution as noted on the south side all the way along. On the North Stoa, the pattern is even more marked. The first third of the stylobate from the east bears very few gameboards; in fact there is just one on the stretch between columns N1 and N10, and just three between columns N18 and N25. In contrast, the central and western half of the stylobate, with the exception of the far western end, contains the highest concentration of gameboards in the whole complex. The densest clustering is between columns N30 and N45, in front of and either side of the doorway through to the Agora.

Where the gameboards are actually located on the different parts of the structures they adorn offers some further insight into why they were carved where they were and how they were played. Although the paving of the North Stoa and the cover slabs running between the pool walls are now lost, the distribution of gameboards on what survives indicates that they were concentrated in areas of seating. On the North Stoa, the majority are on the top of the outward-facing seat blocks, even where sections of the stylobate are still in place. The few grey marble paving slabs that survive, out of context, in the North Stoa, do not have gameboards on them. Over 80% of the gameboards around the pool are located on the outward-facing seats of the exterior pool wall; those located on the inner pool wall are all found on the seat block and not the foot rest, with just four exceptions.

How do we explain this distribution? The fact that the gameboards recorded were not evenly spread across the different parts of the various structures of the Place of Palms and along their full length suggests that the gamers responsible for these boards were not congregating here simply because it afforded them suitable flat surfaces for incising; there were, in fact, other areas in the city that provided much more extensive flat surfaces (for example the Tetrastoon and the Hadrianic Baths). Instead, what the concentration of gameboards reveals are those areas where people liked to gather and to spend time, and from this a number of conclusions can be drawn.

First, gamers favoured those areas already provided with comfortable seats. Gameboards were not carved on the paving of the path around the pool or, as far as we can tell, inside the stoas, presumably because these were thoroughfares, where groups of gamers occupying floor space would have been in the way. The Place of Palms provided a vast length of purpose-built seating designed specifically for relaxation. That these gamers sought out comfortable places to play might seem obvious, but it was not true everywhere. Thédanat's, and more recently Trifilò's, work on the distribution of gameboards in the Forum Romanum at Rome shows a different picture.[158] Here most of the gameboards located to date come from the floor of the interior colonnades of the Basilica Julia; fewer than 20% of those from the Basilica Julia are located on the steps that link the complex to the Via Sacra and the open *area* of the forum beyond. Eleven gameboards were found on the travertine paving of the *area*, concentrated towards its south-western corner, and a further seven in the side walkways of the Arch of Septimius Severus. The vast majority of these examples, therefore, were situated on flat floor surfaces rather than steps, which would have provided more natural seating; the gamers playing them would have squatted on the floor or possibly leaned against nearby columns or walls. At Aphrodisias, more comfortable spots were preferred.

The second point that can be made about the gameboards in the Place of Palms relates to visibility. For Trifilò this was the key driving factor in the distribution of the gameboards at Rome: they are concentrated in areas of high traffic, as close to major thoroughfares, especially the Via Sacra, as possible; in his view, the gamers who used these boards wanted to be seen.[159] Trifilò finds support for this argument in the five examples of gameboards from the forum of Timgad, three of which are located immediately in front of the main entrances to the complex, with the other two inside the basilica.[160] In the Place of Palms, the concentration of gameboards in the central section of the North Stoa probably also reflects the fact that this was an area of high traffic; the doorway from the Agora was likely to have been one of the main entrances to the complex and indeed there is a particularly dense cluster of gameboards either side of the steps between columns N37 and N38. At the same, however, there were entrances in to the Place of Palms through the Propylon, from the Theatre, the Basilica, the Hadrianic Baths, and both the south-west and south-east corners of the Agora and yet in the areas in front of all of these entrances, on either the North Stoa or the pool walls, there are no obvious concentrations of gameboards. If traffic in and out of the complex was the prime driver for the distribution of gameboards we might expect concentrations at either end of the pool, as well as in the central section of the north side; the ends of the pool, in fact, as already noted, contain relatively few gameboards. It is also possible that temporary constructions, for example wooden constructions that have left no signs of their existence, prevented people from using certain spaces for gameboards.

Instead of traffic through the complex, a more plausible explanation for the distribution of gameboards can be found in the defining feature of the Place of Palms itself—that is, its palms. This was an urban park. Its pool and its vegetation made it a cool and pleasant place to relax. This is why it was provided with such extensive seating in the first place; it was designed to encourage people to linger. The gameboards (and inscribed texts) reveal what people, especially in late antiquity, did with their time while they lingered. The central section of the North Stoa was certainly favoured as a venue for gaming because it was an area of high traffic but also because it was probably shady.[161] Double rows of trees along the north and south sides of the pool would have provided shade to much of the North Stoa and the south side of the pool for all of the day and the north side of the pool in the early morning and evening; depending on how high the trees were, they might even have shaded the north pool wall during the middle of the day too. Gaps between trees, and in the resulting shade cover, could then explain the gaps in the gameboard distribution along the pool walls.

The fact that few gameboards were found at the eastern end of the pool would seem to indicate that this area was not planted with trees, though the façade of the Propylon would have provided some shade in the morning. The western end of the pool would only ever have been in shade in the late afternoon and evening. Since the gameboards mostly date to late antiquity, what we see here is potentially a reflection of the tree cover after the fourth century and especialy following the late fifth- or early sixth-century refurbishments; whether this provided more or less shade than the earlier iteration of the space can only be guessed at, but the arrangement of the planting pits might seem to indicate that the general amount of vegetation in the complex was reduced in this later phase.

G. INFORMAL WRITING AND THE SOCIAL LIFE OF THE PLACE OF PALMS (AC)

With the exception of a painted cross (TW1), all the texts, images, and gameboards were chiselled on stone. We have to assume that texts and images made with paint or charcoal—a very common practice[162]—have been lost.

There are only very few clues concerning the date of graffiti and mason's marks. The inscriptions on column drums from the North Stoa that name Claudia Antonia Tatiane, Claudius Capitolinus, and Myon (Ch. 3 §D) can be dated to around AD 200. These inscriptions are the only items that predate late antiquity with certainty; also the inscription P167 seems to have been engraved on the stone in the second or third century, that is during the first use of the stone in a different structure. There

---

158 Thédenat 1923; Trifilò 2011.
159 Trifilò 2011, 328–331.
160 Trifilò 2011, 313–315; this analysis is based on the original documentation by Boeswillwald, Cagnat, and Ballu 1905.
161 On gameboards often being located in the shade, see Crist 2021, 348.
162 For example Bagnall *et al.* 2016, DG4.1, D1.4, DP12.1, D12.3, D19.2 etc. In Aphrodisias, painted inscriptions are preserved in the theatre (*ala2004* 76), the Hadrianic Baths (*ala2004* 61), on columns of the Tetrastoon (*ala2004* 75), on columns of unknown provenane (*ala2004* 77 and 78), and on fallen columns in the Tetrapylon Street (discovered in 2018). See also Roueché 2007a.

are many indications that the bulk of the graffiti and masons' marks belong the fourth to sixth centuries. Both Albinos, mentioned in the acclamations on the columns of the West Stoa and on plaques of its pavement, and Doulkitios (P110), are known from other inscriptions and belong to the late fifth century. The masons' marks on the West Stoa and on the slabs of the pool all belong to late repairs, of the late fifth or early sixth century. Christian graffiti (crosses, texts accompanied by crosses, prayers) postdate the Christian prosecutions and are more likely to be dated in the fifth and sixth centuries, when Christianity was firmly established in Aphrodisias. References to circus factions can be expected in a late antique context. The lettering of the graffiti can be broadly dated to late antiquity (c. 300–600), but the dating of informal writing, with its preference for cursive forms, often differs from that of official inscriptions.

The onomastic material as well—leaving aside abbreviated names—can be best reconciled with late antique onomastic practices. Ἀλύπιος ('free of sorrow'; P111) was hitherto unattested in Aphrodisias but it is found in other places in late antique Asia Minor.[163] Together with Ἀδόλιος ('free of cunning') and Ἀχόλιος ('free of bile, anger') it belongs to a group of names composed with the alpha privative that express positive hopes or positive qualities.[164] Εὐσέβιος is a common name in late antiquity, attested for both Christians and Jews.[165] Other Christian names include Εὐδοξία (NS18), Θεόκτιστος (NS58, NS67), Ἰωάννης (NS52), Κυριακός (P16), and Παῦλος (P132). Ἀνατόλιος (NS78) and Εὐγράφιος (NS341), with the typical late antique ending -ιος, also point to a date in the fourth, fifth, or sixth century.

The abundance of texts and drawings carved or simply incised on stone with sharp instruments is striking. The best explanation for it is the fact that a significant part of the population of Aphrodisias was in one or other form associated with stoneworking, as masons, sculptors, and builders. A late antique list of donors, Jews and sympathisers, includes a stone-cutter (λατύπος), a marble-worker (λευκουργός), and a carpenter (τέκτων) as well as men employed in metal- and woodworking (bronze- and goldsmiths).[166] We may assume that the people who frequented the Place of Palms came here with their tools, and this enabled them to carve on stone. With the exception of very few names of women—possibly *topos* inscriptions—all the texts, and perhaps the images too, seem to have been made by men.

Most texts and images are made in a very crude manner and were temporary in nature. Many times, gameboards are superimposed. Texts and pictorial graffiti that make no sense to us had some meaning for the men who scratched them on the stone, and for the onlookers. Only the *topos* inscriptions and the acclamations are more carefully carved, because they were meant to be seen for a longer period of time. We also encounter a few cases of graffiti that show the effort of masons to imitate calligraphic letters (NS235, P396; possibly P105; Pl. 44.E and Pl. 57.E). Very few of the pictorial graffiti are skilfully made: two busts of athletes (P33; Pl. 46.A), most likely made by a goldsmith, a stork or heron (P90; Pl. 43.D), and three galloping lions (NS331; Pl. 50.A). A few gameboards are also elaborately decorated. The circles of the gameboards N226 and NS347 were made with the use of a compass (Pl. 57.G). Most of the texts and images studied here were ephemeral, and in this way they give us snapshots of life in this area.

The graffiti provide information about occupations and groups that were present in this area and their activities. Two teachers had their 'booths' in the North Stoa: near column N18, a certain Ioannes, characterized as ἐλλογιμώτατος,[167] probably a teacher of rhetoric and lawyer (NS52: Ἰωάνν(ου) | ἐλλ(ογιμωτάτου)), and near column N9 a teacher of grammar and rhetoric (NS19: cοφιcτοῦ). There is also evidence for retail salesmen and tavern keepers (NS342, NS349, TW2, TW7),[168] and the measures engraved on the South Wall (one foot and two feet) were probably used by textile merchants. A prayer (P33) names a goldsmith, who is also known from a prayer in the theatre. The drawings of busts next to both graffiti, executed in the way a smith would have engraved an image on a metal sheet, suggest that the drawings were made by the goldsmith. Perhaps he was making a demonstration of his skills, but one cannot exclude the possibility that he had a shop in the Place of Palms. The acclamation for the professional association of the chair-bearers or litter-carriers (P106) attests yet another group, and it is possible that professional associations had their headquarters or club houses in this area.

The urban park was a clearly 'gendered' space, a space dominated by men in everyday life, by women perhaps only on the occasion of the Maiouma festival. One recognizes only very few women in the area, apart from Claudia Antonia Tatiane, who sponsored repairs in the North Stoa (see Ch. 3 §D). The names of women are written in the nominative on columns of the North Stoa: Εὐτυχία (NS7), Εὐδοξία (NS18). They may be the names of shop-keepers.

Apart from everyday commercial activities the graffiti give some information on leisurely interactions among the visitors to the Place of Palms, who played games seated around the pool, made aggressive or friendly jokes, commemorated themselves and their friends in texts and caricatures, watched peacocks and other birds, admired the statuary decoration, and commented on *venationes* that they had seen in the stadium.

The Place of Palms was also an area where important documents were posted (WS30) and probably public announcements were made. We may infer this from a pictorial graffito representing a *tabula ansata*, an object that was obviously seen in this area (P230) and from the graffito ἐδίκτου (WS30). The acclamations for circus factions (P377, NS227, NS244, WS12) reflect gatherings of their fans, when invitations to chariot races and other contests were announced and afterwards, in order

---

163 Seven attestations in *LGPN* Va-c (fourth-century and later); cf. the short form Ἀλύπις (3 attestations, fourth to sixth centuries). The female form Ἀλυπία is attested since the late hellenistic period. For related names (Ἀλύπητος, Ἀλυπιανός, Ἄλυπος) see Kanavou 2013, 181.
164 For Adolios and Acholios see Chaniotis 2002a, 233.
165 Chaniotis 2002a, 234.
166 Reynolds and Tannenbaum 1987, 116–123.

167 Another ἐλλογιμώτατος in Aphrodisias is Flavius Ampelios (*ALA* 42 and 43), a σχολαστικός. The epithet ἐλλογιμώτατος typically characterizes a σχολαστικός, an orator, usually expert in legal matters; see also *CIG* 4438; Germer-Durand 1899, 23 no. 29 (Gerasa).
168 On taverns in late antique cities see Putzeys and Lavan 2008, 97–100 with bibliography.

to cheer the victorious charioteers and athletes (cf. P33, P245, P247?). It is possible that voluntary associations had their headquarters in this area.

The graffito ἀφετηρία, 'starting point of a race' (P167; Pl. 47.A), would seem to suggest some sort of a race in the pool, perhaps of boats—real or miniature. But the position of the plaque makes this hypothesis unlikely. Rather, the mason's mark on the plaque suggests that it was taken from another location to be reused in the pool. Also, the letter-forms suggest a date in the second or third century AD and not in late antiquity. It is, therefore, far more likely that the inscription indicated the starting point of a race, for example in a gymnasium, a hippodrome, or another location that hosted races (probably not the stadium).

In late antiquity, a period of strong, sometimes violent, religious competition, the Place of Palms, as other important public spaces, was also used by pious people as a stage for the display of their beliefs. The Jews, a very strong community in Aphrodisias in the fourth to sixth centuries, engraved their religious symbols, especially menoroth, and the Christians engraved crosses, christograms, and prayers. The acclamations for Albinos allude to enmities, political or religious in nature (WS16; cf. WS25), and the drawing of a phallus near the drawing of a menorah (P407 and P409) possibly reflects religious conflicts. If the joke at the expense of the governor Doulkitios (P110: 'Eusebi(o)s buggers/buggered Doulkiti(o)s') is not connected with the governor's defeat in a game, it may be evidence for political controversies, for which there is both literary and epigraphic evidence in the late fifth century.[169]

Graffiti were ephemeral texts and images, addressed to contemporary audiences, not to the future historian. Only those who knew names and contexts could understand references to these people and their situations or appreciate their jokes. As unofficial texts and images, graffiti are expressions of thoughts and feelings of ordinary people. If they serve as a unique source of information for the social, religious, and economic history of this city, it is because in areas such as the Place of Palms they can be studied in a closed archaeological context.

---

[169] Chaniotis 2002b.

CHAPTER 6

The Basin at the Propylon: Statuary and Mythological Reliefs, *c.* AD 500–550

R. R. R. Smith and Joshua J. Thomas

In the sixth century the continuing maintenance and renovation of the complex water system of the Place of Palms required the building of a huge new holding basin at its east end (see Ch. 4 §N). This chapter presents recent research on the long lives of disparate earlier statuary, statue bases, and mythological reliefs re-used in its construction and embellishment. It is part of the ambitious late history of the Place of Palms and a perhaps striking new case study in the growing scholarly discourse around 'spolia' and recycled antiquity.[1] The basin offers an unusually well-preserved and well-documented example of thoughtful, strategic deployment of high-quality earlier monuments in effective new combinations. Any appearance of re-use, we will find, was probably the least of the sixth-century builders' priorities. We see a confident plan to provide a huge new reservoir for the park's long pool and to decorate it with the best reliefs and statuary its builders could acquire.

Three objects or sets of objects of different dates from the wall of the holding basin have been published in three different monographs: (1) an extensive set of mythological parapet reliefs of the later second century,[2] (2) an inscribed base honouring a provincial governor of *c.* AD 300,[3] and (3) a seated statue of a bare-chested intellectual-looking figure of the first or second century AD.[4] These monuments are of course interesting in themselves, and have already been well studied in their own right. Other perspectives however are available. We will see that as excavated, in the last phase of their respective lives, they functioned in close proximity as part of a single monument of the first half of the sixth century AD. The mythological reliefs and the tall re-used base provided the frame for the seated statue.[5]

A. THE PROPYLON BASIN

The Propylon was a colossal façade-building of the late first century built across the east end of the Place of Palms, turning the complex into a fully enclosed 'interior' space (see Ch. 3 §A). It consisted of a two-storeyed aedicular façade, framed by massive projections called 'towers' (*pyrgoi*) in its inscribed dedication (In2). The two storeys were raised on a substantial basement, and under the north and south 'towers' this basement was pierced by vaulted entrance tunnels. In the main façade, the stairs between the aediculae were from the beginning closed by marble panels set between the podia of the aediculae. These stairs were never used in the imperial period and were perhaps a redundant part of a borrowed design.

The building was restored in the later fifth century, as recorded in one of the three verse texts inscribed on the podia of the second, third, and fifth aediculae (see Ch. 4. §A). The work was carried out by the provincial governor Doulkitios, in conjunction with a far-reaching restoration of the whole park complex by the local grandee Ampelios.[6] The restored façade displayed heterogenous statues that may have been brought here from other contexts.[7]

In a second intervention of the sixth century, a large, thick-walled basin was added in front of the building (Pl. 58.A–B and 59.A–B).[8] The basin was 31.5 m long north to south, and 6.6 m wide with returns that did not extend all the way to the framing towers (*pyrgoi*) but rather abutted against the first and seventh podia of the aediculae. In the space between the basin's short return walls and the *pyrgoi*, the northernmost and southernmost stairs were now opened and completed down to the park's ground-level.

The intact lower part of the basin wall was 1.80 m high, on average 1.72 m thick,[9] and built of rough mortared rubble that was faced on the exterior with various recycled marble blocks. We will see that the wall was originally even higher (*c.* 3.00 m), and was much too tall and massive to have been a usable fountain basin. It surely functioned instead as a header tank for the fountains supplying the long pool at the centre of the Place of Palms.[10] The marble facing and the impressive display of re-deployed monuments investigated here were designed to give a prestigious classical-looking appearance to this functional structure.

The date of the basin's construction is not given by any sure external means. An economical hypothesis would see the basin as part of the same restoration of the Propylon and Place of Palms carried out by Ampelios and Doulkitios in the late fifth century.[11] Against this chronology, however, it can be observed (a) that the three verse texts of these benefactors on the podium of the Propylon would be obscured by the new 3 m-high basin wall for anyone looking from ground level in the Place of Palms, and (b) that supply pipes feeding the new header basin were inserted crudely from behind over the top of the second and third po-

---

1 See for example: Kinney 2006; Brilliant and Kinney 2011; Kristensen and Stirling 2016; Ng and Swetnam-Burland 2018.
2 Linant de Bellefonds 2009.
3 *ALA* 7; *LSA* 195.
4 Smith *et al.* 2006, no. 52.
5 Preliminary discussion in Smith 2018c, 333.

6 *ALA* 38 (Ampelios), 39–40 (Doulkitios).
7 Smith *et al.* 2006, nos. 3, 17, 53–58, 85, 86, and 202. See Ch. 7 §C.
8 For further discussion of this structure, see Ch. 4 §N.
9 The basin wall varied in thickness as follows: 1.57 (north), 1.76 (west), 1.82 m (south).
10 Demonstrated by Wilson 2016b, 130–135; see also Ch. 4 §N.
11 As argued by Roueché in *ala2004* commentary IV.34.

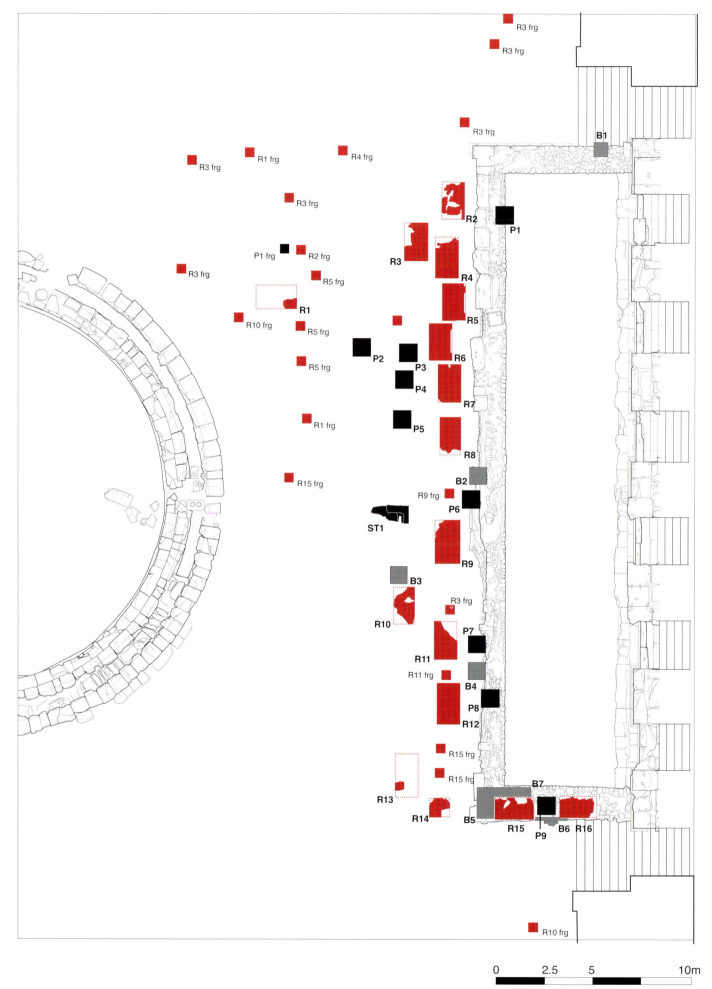

Fig. 47. Diagram reconstructing find positions of mythological relief panels (red), Eros pillars and statue (black), and bases and other items built into basin lower wall (grey).

dia of the Propylon and discharged into the basin directly over the verse inscriptions beneath. Since both of these factors impinge directly on the legibility and standing of the verse texts, it seems likely that the installation of the pipes and so of the basin took place in a separate second phase, after that of Ampelios and Doulkitios.[12] There is no way of telling how much later this second intervention might have taken place, but continued building activity, especially connected with water facilities and baths, can be documented elsewhere on the site into at least the mid-sixth century. We may say that the first half of the sixth century or the years around the middle of the sixth century is the most likely period for the construction of the basin, although we cannot entirely exclude a date later in that century.

B. LOWER BASIN WALL: RELIEFS AND STATUE BASES

The thick basin wall has a well-built stone-block footing at ground level and a varied lower course of recycled blocks (Pl. 59.B): some moulded, some plain, some seat-blocks (on the short north side, these are probably seat-shaped blocks recycled from the intercolumnar stylobates of the North Stoa of the Place of Palms – Pl. 59.C). Above this, the wall was faced with assorted recycled marbles and panels, about seven to eight on the short north side, perhaps thirty to thirty-five on the long west wall (well-preserved only in its northern half), and about five to seven on the short south side. Some are moulded panels recycled as they were; one has an open-work fence-screen motif carved in shallow relief; others were plain blocks that had panel mouldings carved into them probably for this new context; and a few on the short north side have large crosses scratched on them (probably later) to protect the faithful as they passed through the much-used access passage on this side. These panels were finished by a crowning course at a single, carefully-controlled level. The crowning course has a simple bevel moulding of probably contemporary, late antique manufacture.

Among these recycled blocks, there is a series of 'higher-grade' re-used elements: a small Eros pillar of a kind we will meet more of later, *in situ* in the north wall (**B 1**, visible in Pl. 59.B), four inscribed statue bases in the centre and southern stretch of the long west wall (**B 2–5**), and a relief from the Sebasteion in the south wall (**B 6**). They may be listed briefly as follows, **B 1–6**, and are plotted on the find-plan (Fig. 47) with these numbers (**B** = bases and other spolia in the lower part of the basin wall):

North side:
B 1. Eros pillar, *in situ*, partly concealed by stairs (Pl. 60.A). W: 45, figure H: 58.5 cm. Frontal winged Eros strides to viewer's left, right hand raised, bow in left hand.

West side:
B 2. Statue base for governor T. Oppius Aelianus Asklepiodotos, *c.* AD 250—280 (Fig. 48, Pl. 60.B). Tall, heavily-moulded three-part base, with raised circular contact

---

12 See Wilson 2016b, 133; and for the wider sixth-century context, Wilson 2019, 208–9.

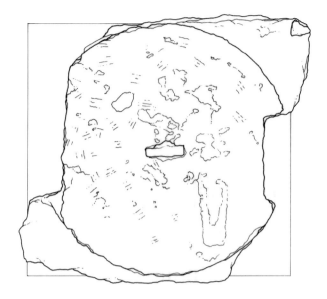

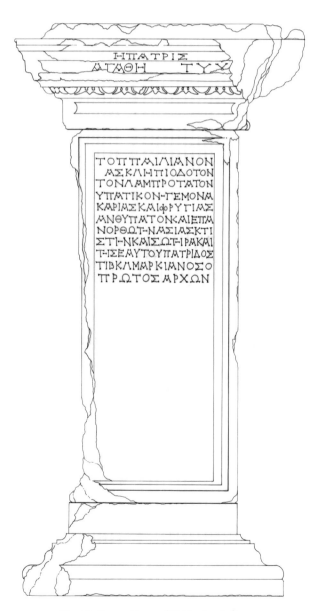

fig. 48. Re-used base of T. Oppius Aelianus Asklepiodotos, governor, *c.* AD 250—280.

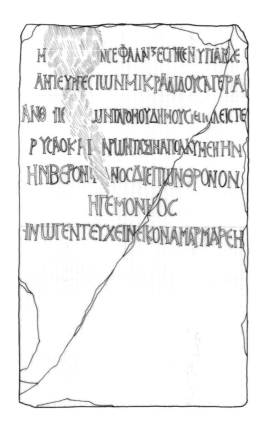

Fig. 49. Re-used base of Praetorian Prefect Anthemios, AD 405–414.

disc on top, as if for a round bronze plinth. H: 153, W: 83.5, D: 82, Letter H: 2 cm. *In situ* in exact centre of basin wall. The upper surface rises 27 cm above the level of the crown moulding. *ALA* 7; Appendix 1, In16.

B 3. Statue base for Praetorian Prefect Anthemios, AD 405–414 (Fig. 49, Pl. 60.C). Plain shaft from a recycled high-imperial base, with Christian invocation roughly carved on viewer's right side. Found in front of southern stretch of basin's west wall. Probably displayed with right side facing out. H: 102, W: 61, D: 57, Letter H: 3.5 cm. *ALA* 36; Appendix 1, In18.

B 4. Statue base for Marcus Lepidus from the Propylon? of the Sebasteion, AD 37–41 (Pl. 60.D). Tall, one-piece base with unpanelled shaft and simple upper and lower mouldings. Found in front of southern stretch of west wall of basin. H: 115.5, W: 63, D: 42, Letter H: 4 cm. Smith 2013, P-base 16.

B 5. Statue base for the restored 'statues of the Cyclops', AD 102–116 (Pl. 61.A). H: 69.5, W: 62, L: 221, Letter H: 2 cm. Long plain block with simple lower moulded fillet, missing its upper and lower moulded elements. *In situ* at southwest corner of basin wall, inscribed on short end facing west and on long side facing north. *IAph2007* 4.308; Appendix 1, In4.

South side:

B 6. Relief of *ethnos* from Sebasteion North Building (Pl. 61.B). The full relief was originally too tall for the basin wall, so *c.* 22 cm was cut off from the lower part of the panel and the figure's lower legs. H: 150, W: 147, D: 41 cm. Smith 2013, B5.

The Eros pillar (**B 1**) probably came from the same unknown source as the seven Eros pillars that we will meet shortly re-used on top of the wall. While its upper moulding is narrower, its Eros figure is of the same scale and style as the others.

It is interesting that statue bases for a governor of the later third century and especially a Praetorian Prefect of the early fifth century were already available for re-deployment in the sixth century (**B 2–3**). The statue of the Prefect had been standing for little over 100 years. The base for 'the statues of the Cyclops' restored in the early second century is a long and imposing block that forms the south-west corner of the lower basin wall (**B 5**). Given its size it might most easily have come from somewhere in the adjoining park complex.[13] The *ethnos* relief (**B 6**) was from the North Building of the Sebasteion, much of which had already collapsed by the mid-fourth century. It came from wherever the collapsed marbles from the building had been stored between the mid-fourth century and the early sixth century. It had to be cut down for its position in the basin wall.

C. UPPER BASIN WALL: MYTHOLOGICAL RELIEFS

A grand series of mythological parapet reliefs was uncovered in 1977 in front of the basin's long west wall, and two further reliefs were excavated at the short south wall in 1983.[14] The reliefs were well published by P. Linant de Bellefonds in 2009. In an Epilogue, Linant de Bellefonds briefly considered their

13 So Thomas 2018, 160–162.
14 Linant de Bellefonds 2009.

154

late antique context: 'It is probable therefore that these panels comprised the exterior decoration of the basin.'[15] She saw too that they should be combined with the Eros pillars also found in front of the basin but which she did not study or publish. Later research on their late antique position has been able to demonstrate with certainty that the mythological reliefs and Eros pillars were disposed precisely *on top of* the basin wall in a continuous parapet screen. This raises the restored height of the basin surround to at least *c.* 2.98 m.

The decisive proof for the reconstruction of the reliefs and pillars on top of the wall is in the excavation notebook 240 of 1983 by Gerhard Paul that records the unearthing of the short south wall of the basin.[16] The notebook has a plan (Fig. 50) and photos (Pl. 58.C) demonstrating that half an Amazonomachy relief (**R 15**) and a full Centauromachy relief (**R 16**) divided by one of the Eros pillars (**P 9**) were found *in situ* on top of the short south wall of the basin. The other, left part of the Amazonomachy relief survives (with Herakles at left), and it is easy to see from its documented position that the full relief fitted at the west end of the south wall, with a second, missing pillar at the angle.

It is clear then from this documented find-context that the redeployed mythological parapet reliefs were used to decorate the top of the basin wall, separated by small Eros piers. The basin wall was sufficiently wide to have supported a strong masonry wall behind the reliefs so that the holding tank could have been filled up to the full 3 m height, to the level of the top of the reliefs, without the water pressure bursting the reliefs outwards. The stubs of masonry walls on top of the east side of both the north and south short sides of the basin where they abut the Propylon provide clear evidence for this 'inner' masonry support behind the reliefs (Pl. 59.B).

On top of the masonry wall abutting against the Propylon on the north side, a recycled cornice block is preserved *in situ* (visible at left in Pl. 59.B). There are a dozen or so high-imperial cornice blocks of the same type, found in front of the basin during the original excavation, and still in the block field immediately west of the basin. They have boldly carved acanthus decoration and 'sloping' dentils and include a sima carved with palmettes. These recycled cornice blocks probably once crowned the reliefs and the backing masonry wall all around the three sides of the basin.

It remains to see how the reliefs and pillars were sequenced around the basin. A full reconstruction (Fig. 51) can be achieved with remarkable precision from the find-plan (Fig. 47) and by careful measurement. The main parts of each relief were found fallen in front of the basin, marked in large red rectangles on the plan. Smaller fragments known to belong to the reliefs are marked as small red squares, and their scatter further from the basin wall shows they are of less help in reconstructing the sequence of the main pieces. The Eros pillars and two further members that may also have been used as dividing piers between reliefs are marked as black squares. The sequence of reliefs and piers should follow their find positions.

---

15 Linant de Bellefonds 2009, 121.
16 Nbk 240: *South East Agora Gate (SEAG) I* (B. Rose and G. Paul, 1983), 74–79.

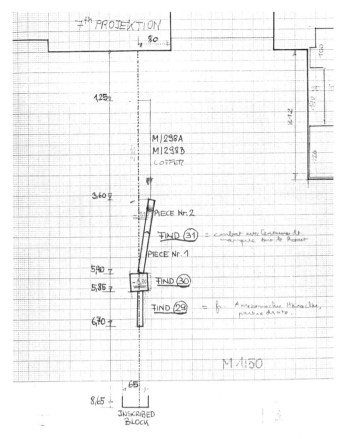

Fig. 50. Short south wall of basin (North is to left), with relief **R 15**, Eros pillar **P 9**, and relief **R 16** (marked as Finds 29–30) *in situ* on top of basin. Measured sketch from excavation notebook (Nbk 240: *South East Agora Gate (SEAG) I* (B. Rose and G. Paul, 1983), 77).

Starting at the north, we can see that the place for a relief on the short end wall can only be filled by a panel surviving in fragments found further out from the northwest corner of the basin (**R 1**, Artemis and Giants, known in four fragments, only two of which have find-places). This was a full major panel for which there is no space on the west front, whose relief sequence we will see follows with much greater ease.

In positioning the reliefs on the basin's long west wall, we need first to be aware of its central feature. The re-used base from a time-expired statue of the governor T. Oppius Aelianus Asklepiodotos (**B 2**) sat at the front of the basin's west wall at its very centre and rose above the wall's crown moulding by some 27 cm. This was clearly an important and prominent central feature of the whole basin display. The only surviving monument this central base could carry that was found anywhere near it is the large redeployed seated himation statue (**St 1**). It was excavated immediately in front of the base, and should be restored on it.

With an alternating sequence of Eros pillars and relief panels, there is enough space for at least six reliefs to either side of the central statue. Of well-preserved reliefs with good find-places, seven were excavated in front of the northern part of the basin's west wall (**R 2** – **R 8**) and five in front of the southern part (**R 9** – **R 12** and **R 14**), together with a small part of a further relief (**R 13**). Only one adjustment has then to be made

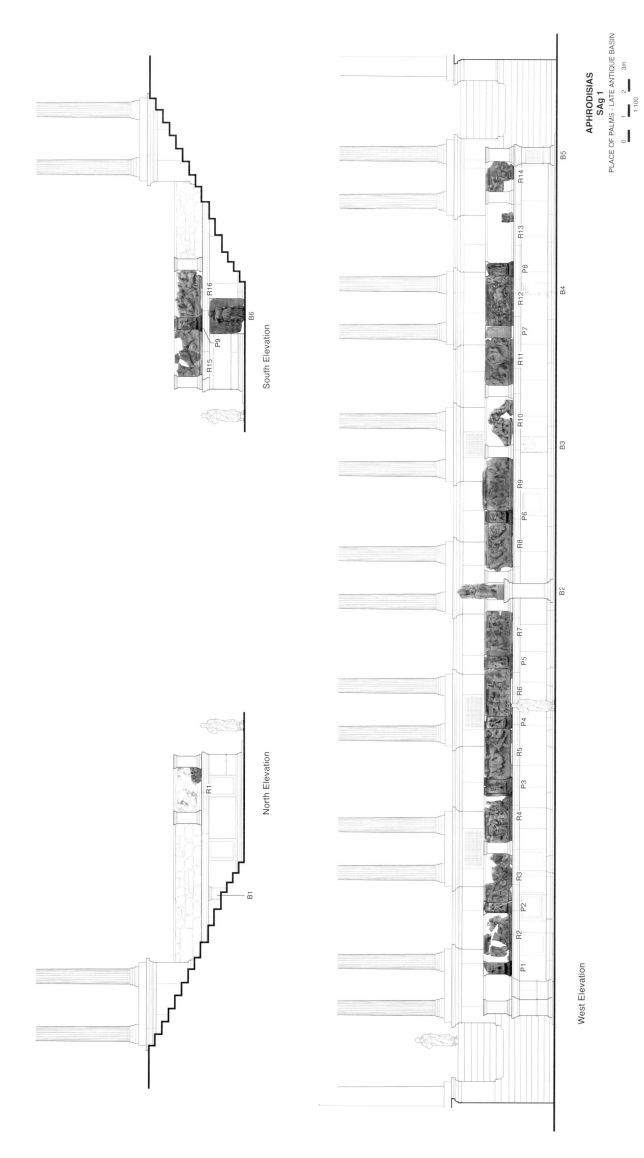

Fig. 51. Reconstruction of basin walls.

in the sequence suggested by the find-positions—that is, one relief (**R 8**) needs to move to the other side of the statue. That there were in fact six and *a half* reliefs in each of the north and south wings is demonstrated in a striking manner. The last relief from the south end of the west wall (**R 14**)—it has a 'strong' find-place—does not survive as a fragment, as it might appear, but as a section from the right-hand half of an Amazonomachy relief that was cut down to fit precisely the available space before the angle (Pl. 63.G). It was cut down by a little less than a half of the full panel width (surviving W: 109 cm). A half relief does not survive for the corresponding position at the north end, but the same narrower final space has to be reconstructed in order for the whole surviving reliefs that were found here to fit on the basin wall.

Within these parameters, the reliefs and pillars can be disposed around the basin on top of its lower wall according to the find-plan, as shown in the reconstruction, in the following sequence (**R** = reliefs, **P** = pillars, **St** = statues, and those without a bibliographic reference are unpublished).

Mythological reliefs

The relief panels were carved from single marble blocks, and are on average H: 118, W: 200, and D: 30 cm, with moulded frames above and below. They are carved with scenes from much-loved mythology—principally from the Gigantomachy, Amazonomachy, and Centauromachy—in a dynamic hellenistic style and in the technical manner of the later second century AD.

Each panel carries between three and eight figures disposed in vigorous action groups. The heads of many of the divinities seem to have been deliberately removed, and the exposed male genitals of *all* naked male figures are missing—no doubt deliberately removed, as for example on the Sebasteion reliefs.[17] Intentional defacing can be verified in some places. The recording of the exact circumstances of deposition of each relief and its constituent fragments is not consistent. Some were excavated in water and have less clear find positions; others were found face-up, others face-down, but not often with clear orientations. The find-map (Fig. 47) combines differential information into a single, simplified, and partly diagrammatic plan.

Short north side:
R 1. Gigantomachy with Artemis (Fig. 52). Relief, preserved in four small fragments. Three have precise find-locations, at north end of basin. Dimensions based on typological reconstruction of scene, H: 118, W: 195, D: 27 cm. Artemis in deer-drawn chariot, two giants, one attacked by dog. Linant de Bellefonds 2009, 39, G6.

Long side (north)
R 2. Gigantomachy with Hades (Pl. 62.A). Most of relief survives but made up of 26 fragments, found mostly close to north end of basin wall. H: *c.* 117.5, W: 191, D: 20 cm. Hades fights two giants with Cerberus-dog, two

17 Defacing in Sebasteion: Smith 2012.

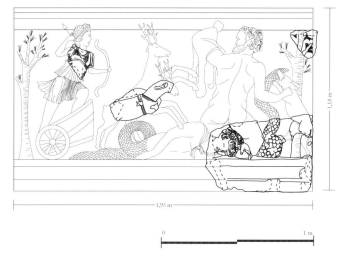

Fig. 52. Reconstruction of Gigantomachy relief **R 1**.

trees, one pine, in background. Linant de Bellefonds 2009, 26, G3.

R 3. Gigantomachy with Hephaistos (Pl. 62.B). Most of relief survives, made up of 14 fragments, of which main pieces found at north end of basin. Hephaistos holds hammer and launches two fiery projectiles at two giants, pine tree in background. H: 115.5, W: 195, D: 21 cm. Linant de Bellefonds 2009, 31, G4.

R 4. Amazonomachy (Pl. 62.C). Well-preserved panel; main part and fragments found at north end of basin wall. H: 119, W: 195, D: 28 cm. Two young armoured Greek heroes fight three Amazons. Linant de Bellefonds 2009, 87, A1.

R 5. Centauromachy with Apollo (Pl. 62.D). Full panel, main part and fragments found at north end of basin wall. H: 118, W: 194, D: 25 cm. Naked Apollo and bearded Lapith fight two centaurs. Linant de Bellefonds 2009, 68, C2.

R 6. Centaurs carousing (Pl. 62.E). Fully preserved panel, found in two main parts at middle of north wing of west basin wall. Two young and two older centaurs lie in rocky landscape; from left to right, one blows trumpet, one drinks from huge bowl, one holds small kithara, and one drinks from a horn(?). H: 117, W: 198, D: 31 cm. Linant de Bellefonds 2009, C3.

R 7. Centauromachy with Herakles (Pl. 62.F). Fully preserved panel, found in three fragments at middle of north wing of west basin wall. H: 119, W: 190, D: 26 cm. Herakles and two young heroes (Theseus and Perithoos?) fight two older centaurs. Linant de Bellefonds 2009, 64, C1.

Long side (south)
R 8. Amazonomachy with Dionysos and Pan (Pl. 63.A). Almost complete panel found in one piece near centre of west basin wall. H: 117, W: 203, D: 32 cm. Dionysos and Pan fight against a mounted Amazon each. Linant de Bellefonds 2009, 96, A3.

R 9. 'Pastoral scene' (Pl. 63.B). Full panel in 5 joining fragments found near centre of west basin wall. H: 126, W:

218, D: 41 cm. Uncertain subject: Aphrodite or nymph on rock with goats watches startled hero-shepherd with sheep and huge dog (Aphrodite and Anchises?). Upper fillet inscribed: [....]*einos huios Kapitol*[*einou* …], letter H: 3 cm. Linant de Bellefonds 2009, 105, P1; Appendix 1, In6.

R 10. Gigantomachy with Apollo (Pl. 63.C). Large part of panel in 2 main joining pieces, found near middle of south wing of basin's west wall. H: 105, W: 190, D: 30 cm. Apollo's griffin-drawn chariot rides down two giants. Linant de Bellefonds 2009, 35, G5.

R 11. Gigantomachy with the Dioskouroi (Pl. 63.D). Full panel in 4 main fragments, found at middle of southern wing of basin's west wall. H: 121.5, W: 191, D: 37 cm. Mounted Dioskouroi ride down a giant each, trees in background, one a pine. Linant de Bellefonds 2009, 21, G2.

R 12. Gigantomachy with Selene and Nyx (Pl. 63.E). Full panel in single piece, found towards south end of basin in front of west wall. H: 119, W: 206, D: 26 cm. Selene in bull-drawn biga driven by Eros, drives at two giants, supported behind by Nyx. Linant de Bellefonds 2009, 15, G1.

R 13. Amazonomachy (Pl. 63.F). Single piece of relief and lower moulded frame, found at south end of basin's west wall. H: 52, W: 42, D: 24 cm. Not a fragment but part of panel cut down into large block-like form, probably later(?). Two fallen Amazons in front of a mounted Amazon riding to right in background. Linant de Bellefonds 2009, 104, A5.

R 14. Amazonomachy (Pl. 63.G). Right half of panel, cut down at left, found in front of basin's west wall, at its south end. H: 117, W: 109, D: 24 cm. The left side is worked, and the original central lewis hole is preserved on top near the current left side. Additional cutting of uncertain purpose and date at lower right corner. A youthful armoured Greek warrior hero fights two Amazons falling from their horses. Linant de Bellefonds 2009, 100, A4.

Short south side:

R 15. Amazonomachy with Herakles (Pl. 64.A). Badly broken panel made up of 5 main pieces; the right-hand third of the panel with hero and mounted Amazon was found *in situ* on top of the south wall of the basin abutting Eros pillar **P 9** on its west side. Other main fragments were found in front of basin near south corner. H: 114, W: 194, D: 19 cm. A naked Herakles and a naked hero frame two mounted and one dead Amazons. Linant de Bellefonds 2009, 91, A2.

R16. Centauromachy (Pl. 64.B). Full panel, missing upper moulding, broken in several places but found *in situ* on top of the south wall of the basin abutting Eros pillar **P 9** on the other, east side. H: 112, W: 186, D: 26 cm. Four Lapiths in violent combat with four centaurs. Linant de Bellefonds 2009, 76, C4.

Statue

St 1. Seated himation statue (Pl. 66.A–B). Preserved in one piece, found fallen immediately in front of basin's west wall at its centre. H: 177, W: 68, D: 71 cm. Plinth H: 16, W: 53, D: 59 cm. Figure wears himation without chiton, elaborate sandals, and ring on third finger of left hand and sits hunched forward on animal-legged stool with thick cushion. Smith *et al.* 2006, no. 52.

Pillars

On the Eros pillars, the figures are carved in relief on the front face, standing on rough projecting ground lines (Pl. 65). The Erotes are naked, long-haired, frontal figures, moving to left or right in dynamic action postures. Some have their chlamys wrapped around their lower left arm, in the manner of heroic hunters, and they are probably all conceived as hunting Erotes. Their genitals are all missing, probably deliberately removed. At one point in the southern stretch of the upper basin wall, the inscribed shaft of a statue base of comparable dimensions (**P 7**) seems to have been used in the place of an Eros pillar.

West side:

P 1. Eros pillar (Pl. 65.A). Two joining pieces, one found at north end of west basin wall, the other about 10 m in front of west wall. Top left corner broken off. H: 106, W: 56.5, D: 43 cm. Long-haired wingless putto wearing chlamys, moves to viewer's left, right hand raised. Inv. 77-52, with Nbk 297: *Agora Gate: Basin Front I* (F. Thode, 1988), Find 6.

P 2. Eros pillar (Pl. 65.B). One piece, top broken, found in front of northern wing of west basin wall. H: 116, W: 44.5, D: 39 cm. Winged Eros wearing chlamys moves to viewer's left, right hand raised. Nbk 287: *Agora Gate Basin I* (B. Odabaşı and E. Üçbaylar, 1987), Find 9.

P 3. Eros pillar (Pl. 65.C). One piece, with lateral panels, found in front of basin's west wall at centre of northern wing. H: 117.5, W: 84, D: 34 cm. Winged Eros wearing chlamys moving to viewer's left with raised right hand. Chlamys is wrapped around lower left arm and held in left hand. Legs have soft fat infant forms. Widely spaced inscribed letters on plinth: Θ Κ Γ Β (Letter H: 4.5 cm). Inv. 77-51.

P 4. Eros pillar (Pl. 65.D). One piece, upper moulding broken, found in front of basin towards middle of west wall. H: 116, W: 54, D: 46 cm. Winged Eros wearing chlamys moving to viewer's left with raised right hand holding short spear, stands on thick projecting ground line. Chlamys is wrapped around lower left arm and hand—like a hunter. Inv. 77-49.

P 5. Eros pillar (Pl. 65.E). One piece, upper moulding broken, found in front of basin towards middle of west wall, south of **P 4**. H: 117, W: 55.5, D: 48 cm. Winged Eros moves to viewer's left, has quiver on back and strap for

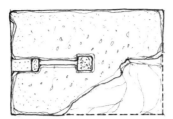

Fig. 53. Top of statue base, **P 7**, with cuttings for lateral clamps. Front faces down. W: 50 cm.

it across chest, holds bow in left hand, right hand raised (right arm broken off below elbow). Inv. 77–50.

P 6. Eros pillar (Pl. 65.F). One piece, with narrow side panel on viewer's left side. Found immediately south of central statue base **B 2**, in front of west wall. H: 119, W: 56, D: 45 cm. Winged Eros wearing chlamys moving to viewer's right, with raised right hand. Chlamys is wrapped around lower left arm and held in clenched left hand. Faint traces of inscribed letters on upper plinth (letter H: 2 cm). Inv. 77-65.

P 7. Statue base (Pl. 65.G). Inscribed shaft of second-century base for statue overseen by Ulpius Zenon. Found in front of basin's west wall, towards south end. H: 109, W: 50, D: 43. Letter H: 2 cm. To function in the same series as the Eros pillars it would require an added lower plinth of *c*. 8–10 cm. Lateral clamp cuttings in the upper surface and rough cuttings on both sides are secondary and probably for fixing reliefs (Fig. 53). Smith *et al.* 2006, 90, no. 181; Appendix 1, In27.

P 8. Muse pillar (Pl. 65.H). One piece, upper moulding broken. Found in front of basin's west wall near south end. H: 117, W: 62, D: 48 cm. Frontal Muse figure, heavily draped, with raised right hand (holding missing staff?) and tragic mask in left hand, so Melpomene. Inv. 77-114.

South side:

P 9. Eros pillar (Pl. 65.I). One piece, found *in situ* on top of short south wall of basin. Upper moulding broken, face and left hand missing. H: 113, W: 56, D: 46 cm. Winged Eros wearing chlamys moving to viewer's left, right hand raised. Chlamys is wrapped around lower left arm. Inv. 83-74.

The sequence of mythological reliefs and the statue at the centre is clear from the find-plan. The pillars are less well-preserved and are placed again according to their find sequence. Whether there were pillars either side of the statue, as restored in the elevation, is not known. We may be sure only that an element of similar dimensions was required to make a transition between statue and reliefs.

Two of the pillars require further comment. **P 7** presents a difficult case: it is the inscribed shaft of a second-century statue base found as marked on the plan, in front of the west basin wall towards its south end. It is of course entirely different in form from the other pillars, and it could have belonged below as facing in the lower basin wall with the Anthemios and M. Lepidus bases (**B 3** and **B 4**). With the addition of a plinth below of 8–10 cm, it is however of the correct height and width to function as one of the pillars. It also has rough cuttings on both sides and deep lateral clamp cuttings in its upper surface that make no sense for its life as the shaft of a statue base (Fig. 53). They are secondary and most likely for fixing relief panels to either side.[18] The *lectio difficilior* is preferred here, and the inscribed base is placed in the parapet as a divider between two reliefs.

P 8 is a pillar of nearly identical form to the Eros pillars, decorated with a relief figure of the tragic Muse Melpomene. It was found towards the south and can be incorporated in the reconstruction there without difficulty. The implication of these two items seems to be that the basin builders had difficulty in sourcing sufficient numbers of the Eros pillars. From their use in other buildings[19] and find-places elsewhere in the city,[20] we know there was, by contrast, no shortage of the mythological parapet reliefs. It is both possible and likely that the mythological reliefs and the Eros pillars belonged together in their original, later second-century display context. The apparent shortage of Eros pillars available for re-use in the sixth century would be due simply to their greater suitability for various later building contexts.

D. SEQUENCE OF THE RELIEFS

It might seem that there is no rhyme or reason to the sequence in which the reliefs were re-deployed on the basin wall. Indeed, Linant de Bellefonds comments: '… the builders made little attempt to group the panels thematically. … (The) reliefs were laid out without any consideration of the themes represented: Centauromachies, Gigantomachies, and Amazonomachies alternated in complete disorder.'[21] At one level this is clearly correct, but does it mean that the late antique basin designer and sponsor acted randomly, without considerations of any kind? It is of course possible that the reliefs were simply installed on the basin wall as they arrived from storage or direct from the source monument, as was most convenient in terms of the work flow, and that their only agreed purpose was to give the vernacular basin an exciting, dynamic figured crown, in a classic style that represented prestige and authority.

We might ask however if there might not be, in addition, some further rationale for their sequence, other than the simple themes found on the source monument. Looking at their subjects another way, one might see a different set of choices. All but two or three of the complete relief panels have the dominating presence of a major classical divinity, and it seems as though the choice of reliefs has been designed to foreground their roles. In this perspective, the series highlights the following:

---

18 Certainly secondary: one of the clamp cuttings (on viewer's left) interrupts the pour channel for the central dowel hole.
19 Three reliefs from the same series were re-used in 'Gaudin's Fountain', a monumental late antique fountain building at a crossroads in the southeast part of the city: Öğüş 2015.
20 Four isolated pieces were found (1) in the area southeast of the Theatre, (2) in the western and (3) southern stretches of the City Wall, and (4) in a well northeast of the Sebasteion: see Linant de Bellefonds 2009, 3–5.
21 Linant de Bellefonds 2009, 121.

Short north side: *Artemis* (**R 1**)
Long side (north): *Hades* (**R 2**), *Hephaistos* (**R 3**), *Apollo* (**R 5**), *Herakles* (**R 7**)
Long side (south): *Dionysos* (**R 8**), *Aphrodite*(?) (**R 9**), *Apollo* (**R 10**), *Dioskouroi* (**R 11**), *Selene* (**R 12**)
Short south side: *Herakles* (**R 15**).

For most of late antiquity, the old gods remained harmless in mythological narratives—provided scenes avoided representation of the hated act of sacrifice and incorporated no solitary, frontal divine images that could be taken as invitation to direct activation through prayer.[22] The Sebasteion had survived with only a couple of its *c.* 50 mythological reliefs defaced in conformity with such radical Christian thinking.[23] Some—perhaps many—conservative, classically-educated members of the city elite argued to save the Sebasteion mythological display, and some now, we may imagine, took an interest and some pleasure in re-arranging the mythological reliefs to foreground prominent images of favourite classical gods safely engaged in a variety of traditional and uplifting old stories. It might be too much to say that such an idea and its execution were covert, but it was at least deniable.

In this sequence, the Apollo in **R 5** and the Apollo in **R 10** are in corresponding central positions respectively in the northern and southern stretches of the west wall. Herakles (**R 7**) and Dionysos (**R 8**) are in the very centre, on either side of the statue (**St 1**), and the good-time theme of the Centaurs carousing (**R 6**) is matched by the scene of Aphrodite and her hero-shepherd lover(?) (**R 9**). Various scenes of gods and giants more or less correspond in the 'outer' parts of the west wall. Such a set of 'divine' choices would be deniable: it could legitimately have been said, as above, that the reliefs were simply built in without regard for old pagan mythological coherence, that their function was merely that of classical-looking decoration devoid of story-telling or further religious content. That the gods in the relief panels were perceived, however, by some at least, at some point, as real functioning deities is perhaps suggested by the later violent removal or defacing of several of their heads.[24] This brief discussion of other possibilities is perhaps enough to suggest that the careful and expensive fitting of these old 'classic' reliefs to the upper basin wall was not random or unconsidered in its sequencing of the redeployed components.

E. THE STATUE

As we have seen, the archaeology of the basin wall shows that its centrepiece was a tall inscribed recycled base for the statue of a governor of *c.* AD 300 (Fig. 48, Pl. 60.B) whose honour was no longer current and functioning at the time the basin was constructed. It is a complete base in three parts, with tall shaft between strongly projecting moulded upper and lower elements. That the base was moved and redeployed whole shows it was also to have a pronounced honorific function in its new context.

The base rises above the basin wall and its crown moulding by some 27 cm, projecting into the zone occupied on the basin wall by the relief panels. It was clearly then a strong focus of the whole basin display. The find-plan shows that only one statue was excavated in a potential relationship to the base—that is, the old recycled seated statue (**St 1**).[25] It was found fallen in front of the base at the centre of the basin's west wall (Fig. 47), and should be restored on this base, rising high above the surrounding parapet composed of Eros pillars and mythological relief panels (Fig. 51).

The statue is a remarkable and animated figure of a bare-chested intellectual or cultural figure wearing only a himation, perched forward on a thick cushion on a tall narrow stool which is supported on each side by two crossed animal legs with cloven hooves (Pl. 66.A–B). The figure had one foot forward (now lost), the other back with the heel raised and leaning against the block supporting the stool. It wears a most elaborate kind of civilian Greek sandals. The thick himation is draped over the left shoulder and chest and from under the right arm is wrapped around the lower left arm. The left hand wears a ring on the third finger and rests in the lap. The right forearm is broken off and was carved in the round extending over the left hand. The right hand probably made a speaking gesture. The contingent action and implied narrative of the figure is clearest in the strong turn to the proper right of the figure's head seen now in the prominent asymmetrical neck tendons. The exposed right chest and upper abdomen have the sagging elderly forms that had been common for older thinkers, orators, and citizen honorands since the statue of Demosthenes of 280 BC.[26] This was a high-quality statue of the early imperial period whose honorific function had expired—a statue of at least 400 years before the basin parapet was composed.

We can deduce some things about its significance in its new setting. First, it was not an old monument that was moved and redeployed with its old subject and meaning intact—as the Troilos and Achilles group in the Civil Basilica or the Achilles and Penthesilea group in the Hadrianic Baths.[27] Either the original head was removed and replaced with a new head, or the original head was broken and repaired. The head was attached or re-attached on a line immediately under the chin, perhaps with a beard worked in the round hanging in front to conceal the connection. It was attached with a large dowel set in the deep irregular rectangular dowel cutting still visible in

---

22 These two rules can be deduced from the negotiated choices made in what was kept and what was defaced in the great relief display of the Sebasteion: Smith 2012.
23 Smith 2012.
24 The heads of the following have been removed or deliberately defaced: Apollo (**R 5**), Aphrodite(?) (**R 9**), both Selene and Nyx (**R 12**), and Herakles (**R 15**), possibly also Pan (**R 8**) and the Dioskouroi (**R 11**). The heads of Hades (**R 2**) and Hephaistos (**R 3**) were left untouched, perhaps because of their more 'human' appearance: so Linant de Bellefonds 2009, 5 n.17. The heads of Herakles (**R 7**) and Dionysos (**R 8**) were also untouched, perhaps unrecognised in their similarity to other young heroes and warriors in the reliefs. The reliefs re-used in 'Gaudin's Fountain' were defaced in the same manner: Öğüş 2015, 322–324.

25 See also find plan in Smith 2009, 59, fig. 15.
26 Smith 1991, 37–38, fig. 39; Zanker 1995, 83–89, figs. 48–49.
27 Troilos and Achilles: Smith and Hallett 2015. Achilles-Penthesilea: Smith 2007, 215–18; Gensheimer and Welch 2013.

the broken neck stump. The cutting measures 4.5 × 5 cm and was at least 5 cm deep. Its large size and irregular, asymmetrical position were probably determined by the head's animated turn to its right.

Possible head

In the final phase of excavation of the long pool in the Place of Palms in 2017, a badly worn and damaged male portrait head was found in two pieces near the bottom of the pool close to its north side towards the east end, about 70 m from the Propylon basin (inv. 17-53 and 17-112, H: 28 cm; see Ch. 7 §E, no. 74) (Pl. 66.C–D). It has short lank hair lying flat on the brow in a curving fringe and a beard with a heavy moustache. The form of the emphatically drilled eyes suggest a date in the late second or early third century. The underside of the head has been heavily re-worked for later attachment to a statue. The underside was hollowed out leaving a flat horizontal 'soffit' surface at the level of the ears into which was cut a long vertical dowel hole, rectangular in section, half of which has broken away with most of the back of the head.

The large dowel and elaborate recycling of the head for a new body make it an attractive candidate for the missing head added to the seated statue from the basin. The head and the statue are of the same scale, share a fixing technique, and are similarly weathered. Although the shattered neck and chin of the head are missing and cannot now connect to the statue, a trial fitting of the head on the statue was carried out in 2018. The trial mounting showed that the head *could* have belonged to the statue (Pl. 67).

Given the uncertain nature of the connection, further questions may be redundant, but it remains unclear if the head would have been the *original* head of the seated figure that was repaired or whether it was a recycled head from another statue used on the seated figure for the early sixth-century monument. The deep square dowel hole into the statue and the invasive working of the underside of the head look more like the addition of an 'alien' recycled head. Either the statue had lost its original head by this date, or a different kind of head was needed for the benefactor honoured on the basin wall. In essence, the effect of this portrait head as reconstructed in Pl. 67 is to reduce the overtly 'intellectual' claim of the statue and to place the honorand in a more 'normal' civic environment.

Honorand

We can be sure that the portrait did not represent the governor of *c.* AD 300 on whose base the statue sat. That is, the statue cannot originally have represented him and been moved with the base—for a simple reason: the statue's dress costume and cultural posture are emphatically inappropriate for a Roman governor of any period, whether high imperial or late antique. The statue monument at the centre of the basin wall represents, then, a new combination of two separate recycled components. As attested for example at Ephesos, the original inscribed text of the base was surely covered with stucco, so that it could carry a painted text to commemorate a new honorand.[28]

Who then might be honoured in such a statue in the early to middle sixth century? One might perhaps think first of a figure closely involved in this precise context, at the Propylon and in the Place of Palms. There are two such grand, well-documented figures who worked on this project, both of whom left a strong mark at Aphrodisias. One is the governor Doulkitios known from an inscribed statue honour from the Theatre (*ALA* 41) and from two of the three verse texts inscribed on the Propylon, both of which refer to the restoration of the building on which the texts are written, namely the great Propylon facade itself (*ALA* 39–40) (see Ch. 4 §A). The other is the local grandee Ampelios who is recorded carrying out building and restoration work in the Theatre Baths (*ALA* 44), at the North East Gate of the city (*ALA* 42), in the Bouleuterion (*ALA* 43), as well as in the Place of Palms (*ALA* 39). This last text is the first of the three verse inscriptions on the Propylon, and its claim to have made a far-reaching restoration of the Place of Palms has been fully confirmed by recent research and excavation (for example, the entire marble surround of the pool was raised and re-set: see Ch. 4 §B).

If we were deciding between Doulkitios and Ampelios for the subject of the seated statue, the decision would not be difficult. The costume is wrong for Doulkitios as governor. His statues would need to wear the late antique chlamys or the dress toga. A himation is attested once for a governor's statue,[29] but the aged, bare-chested himation posture of our seated figure would be jarring for such a subject. This kind of statue stands for the power of education and *polis* culture as something distinct and different from the power of imperial office and Constantinople. It would well suit Ampelios or someone of the same kind of city profile as him. It would still be an unexpected choice for such a statue, but we could understand it from what we know of the political-cultural demeanour of such men.

For the statue to represent Ampelios himself, we would need to suppose either that the basin was still part of his renovation of the whole complex (which we saw there were good arguments against) or that the statue commemorated his work as the towering benefactor of the complex in a later generation. It is however less important to give the statue a precise name than to specify what we can of the *kind* of honorand represented and to bring together the recorded offices, virtues, and titles of such men on the one hand with the signifying components of the statue on the other. The inscribed careers of Ampelios and several other similar figures of the period 500–550 bring out the interesting interaction of this old 'thinking' statue and contemporary sixth-century ideals.

Ampelios is an excellent example of a kind of locally-based non-imperial-office-holding grandee of which Aphrodisias has several from the fifth into the sixth century, acting alongside the governor. He was *patēr tēs poleōs*, so in charge of city building projects, and he carried the resonant title of *scholastikos*, the equivalent of an advanced educational award—Roueché compares it to the title of PhD (*ala2004* IV.22). He is also praised as

---

28 Ephesos: Quatember, Scheibelreiter, and Sokolicek 2009, 119, n. 62.
29 Himation statue of Alexandros in North Agora: Smith 1999a, 165–167, figs. 5 and 7; Smith *et al.* 2006, no. 49.

'most eloquent' (*ellogimōtatos*: *ALA* 42). Although they are not connected by any evidence to the basin, inscriptions record several other local grandees of this period with similar city profiles. Some are 'fathers of the city' (*ALA* 62, 69, 85, 89, and 238), several are known to have been important builders (Philippos *ALA* 66, Albinos *ALA* 82, Rhodopaios *ALA* 85–87; see Ch. 4 §A and §F). Others like Pytheas (*ALA* 55–59) had central imperial rank but also the well-developed character of a local city benefactor. Pytheas was a man of culture and learning who also had the added aura of a strong religious traditionalist of the kind that we suspected may have motivated the selection and sequencing of the mythological reliefs. More than six of these local figures in this period (c. 500–550) received statues for their benefactions (*ALA* p. 114). The career and honours of Rhodopaios illustrate this kind of figure in strong and clear terms: he has an accumulation of city-based titles, such as *patēr*, *euergetēs*, *philopatris*, and *ktistēs*, and he received no less than *three* statue honours (*ALA* 85–87).[30]

The himation of the seated statue would suit a civic benefactor; the seated and bare-chested 'intellectual' aspect would suit a figure of high education and cultural attainments; and the dynamic posture of the sharply-turned head and the 'speaking' gesture of the right arm would create a narrative of eloquence and intense engagement. The position of the statue, on top of the basin wall at its exact centre, could suit Ampelios or another benefactor of the same kind of the next generation. The statue faced the Place of Palms whose restoration Ampelios had carried out—excavation has documented that this was a major undertaking, and the statue might still have commemorated him in the next generation. Alternatively, it might represent another benefactor of this well-attested category who was responsible precisely for the basin construction. The reliefs which frame the statue would be an appropriately high-toned and 'educated' commentary and set of comparisons for what the great benefactor had achieved—like the classical heroes of old.

What is perhaps important to recognise is that while we can make sense of the statue in relation to the recorded careers, virtues, and titles of these early sixth-century city grandees, the choice of this old, hunched, hellenistic-style 'intellectual' figure without chiton represented a daring and radical choice. Its semantic force and essential meanings lie at one end of the range of desirable personal attributes for such men. It accentuates and sharpens one cluster of ideas in their portfolio of public roles and personal virtues. We should not doubt that the meanings and effects of such statues were alive and precisely understood still in this period.

F. CONCLUSION

In the sixth century (probably early or middle), a large, thick-walled holding basin was added in front of the Propylon. It was much too tall and massive to have been a usable fountain basin and functioned instead as a header tank for the long pool. It also incorporated and displayed in a striking new collocation the disparate components discussed here. It is clear from the documented find-contexts and recent work on the basin that the mythological parapet reliefs were re-used to decorate the top of the basin wall, separated by small Eros piers, while the handsome old base honouring an earlier governor was positioned in the centre of the basin wall, probably with its inscription plastered over and re-written. The base carried the seated 'intellectual' statue found fallen close by in front of it. The statue's head was repaired or more probably replaced using a deep neck dowel. We see here a striking example of how carved marbles made in the first to third centuries could have long unpredictable lives in complicated, evolving configurations from the fourth to the sixth centuries.

A wide and deep new holding-tank in front of its Propylon was an essential and functional late addition to the Place of Palms, but it was also given the appearance of a 'classic' city monument of the high empire by facing its thick functional masonry walls with re-used marble blocks and a series of brilliant hellenistic-style mythological reliefs. At its centre stood a great hellenistic-style thinker statue reconfigured as the late antique builder-founder (*ktistēs*) of the whole magnificent construction. As modern historians we are intensely interested in such vigorous re-purposing of the past, but it is seriously doubtful how far its contemporary sixth-century viewers would have been aware of or interested in the earlier history of its constituent components. Its primary interest and effect were those of a monument as useful and as beautiful as the great city amenities of the city's glorious past.

---

30 Recently on Rhodopaios: Lenaghan 2019.

CHAPTER 7

The Sculptural Life of the Place of Palms, First to Seventh Centuries

Joshua J. Thomas

Since the early twentieth century, excavations in the Place of Palms have unearthed nearly a thousand separate sculptural finds, ranging from small de-contextualised fragments to fully preserved statue monuments. As part of the Mica and Ahmet Ertegün South Agora Pool Project, all of the available information concerning the find locations of these pieces was collated and consolidated, resulting in the production of a find distribution map (Fig. 54). As the map itself clearly demonstrates, particularly dense concentrations of statue, statue base and relief finds were excavated in the area of the Propylon, in the West Stoa, and in the rubble deposits from within the pool, especially at its east and west ends.

While a comprehensive study of all these sculptural finds lies beyond the scope of this volume, the present chapter has two main aims. The first is to group together sculptural finds that can be associated with particular display contexts in the Place of Palms, and to consider how they might have functioned within these spatial settings. The second is to make a preliminary presentation of new pieces from the recent campaigns in the context of their excavation in the complex. We shall see that the Place of Palms served as one of the most important sculptural display centres in Aphrodisias over the course of some six centuries, and that some telling threads can be woven through the large corpus of surviving material.

A. MYTHOLOGICAL STATUARY

Our only secure evidence concerning the statuary displayed in the Place of Palms during its earliest years is supplied by a first-century AD inscription that was later re-used in the city wall (discussed also in Ch. 2 §D).[1] The text records the dedication of a series of mythological statues by a local benefactor named Artemidoros Pedisas:[2]

> 'For Aphrodite and for the Divi Augusti and for the People, Artemidoros Pedisas son of Dionysios, biological son of Artemidoros son of Diogenes, at his own expense set up the Hermes, and the gilded Aphrodite, and the Erotes carrying torches on either side, and the marble Eros in front of the statue of Hermes, as he also promised when the palm grove was being constructed at the time in which he served as a *strategos*.'

Although no fragments of the statues mentioned in the inscription have yet been identified,[3] the text implies that they were originally set up somewhere in the Place of Palms. This has two important implications for our understanding of the statuary set up in the complex at this early stage.

Firstly, both the explicit reference to a 'gilded Aphrodite' and the implicit contrast between the 'marble Eros' and other—presumably bronze—Erotes indicate that a portion of the statues set up in the Place of Palms would have been made from bronze.[4] These bronze statues would have been particularly appropriate to the decoration of the open areas surrounding the pool, where they would have been less susceptible to weathering and erosion than marble statues decorated with paint. No fragments of large-scale bronze statuary have been excavated in the Place of Palms, although a bronze leg belonging to a statuette of an athletic male figure was found at the west end of the pool in 1990 (**98**).

Secondly, the fact that Artemidoros Pedisas dedicated a group of statues depicting Hermes, Aphrodite and three Erotes suggests that mythological subjects were considered well-suited to the decoration of the complex during this early period. This inference accords well with our evidence for the decoration of comparable complexes in Italy, which, as we saw in see Ch. 2 §D, would have been well known to the foremost citizens of Aphrodisias:

(1) The Portico of Pompey at Rome housed mythological statues including a group depicting Apollo and the Muses, a group of personified cities, and a fountain sculpture depicting the satyr Maron, who supplied Odysseus with the wine that he would later use to sedate the Cyclops Polyphemos.[5]

(2) Also in Rome, the Temple of Peace housed mythological statues including a Ganymede made by the famous fourth-cen-

---

1   Inscription and dating: *MAMA* 8.448; *IAph2007* 12.204; Wilson 2016b, 132–133. Fourth-century city wall and spolia: De Staebler 2008.
2   Text tr. Roueché and Reynolds, modified A. Chaniotis. Artemidoros Pedisas prosopography: Bourtzinakou 2012, 202 no. 498.
3   It is possible that the group depicted Hermes' seduction of Aphrodite. For this episode see: Pseudo-Hyginus, *Astronomica* 2.16; *Fabulae* 271; Diod. Sic. 4.6.5; Cic., *Nat. D.* 3.21–23; Ov., *Met.* 4. 288ff.
4   Epigraphically attested bronze sculpture at Aphrodisias: Reynolds 1997, 423–428. Surviving bronze portrait head from Aphrodisias: Snijder 1935.
5   Sculpture in *Porticus Pompeiana*: Prop. 2, 32, 11–15; Plin. *HN* VII 34, XXXVI 41; Suet. *Vit. Ner.* 46; Tatian, *ad. Gr.* 33–34. For commentary on these texts and for finds tentatively associated with the Porticus: Coarelli 1972, 99–122; Fuchs 1982; Sauron 1987; Kuttner 1999; Russell, A. 2016, 176–178; Davies 2017, 229–232. Relationship of Maron and Odysseus: Homer, *Od.* 9.97f. Correspondences between Porticus Pompeiana personifications and Sebasteion *ethnos* reliefs: Smith 2013, 114–115.

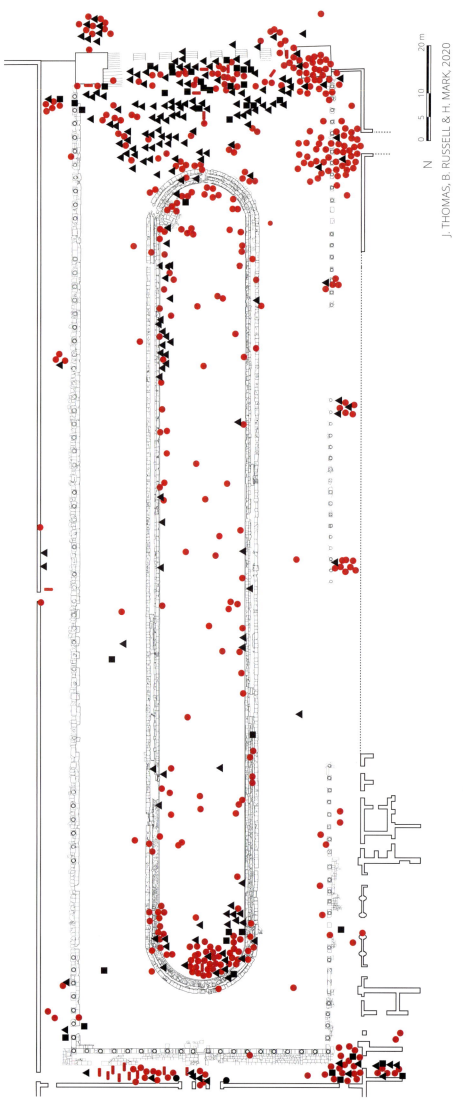

Fig. 54. Scatter plan of sculptural finds from Place of Palms. Red dots represent statuary finds, black squares represent statue bases, and black triangles represent architectural and relief sculpture.

tury BC sculptor Leochares, and a celebrated statue of the goddess Venus by an artist whose name has not survived.[6]

(3) Many mythological statues were excavated in the 'Canopus' of Hadrian's Villa at Tivoli, a complex centring on a long ornamental pool surrounded by a colonnade.[7] On the western side of the pool, six support statues took the place of columns in the colonnade: four Caryatids copying those from the Erechtheion at Athens, and two Silenoi. Along the northern edge of the pool, meanwhile, copies of famous classical statues were set up within the intercolumniations, including an Ares, a Hermes, an Athena, and two Amazons. Within the pool itself, a group depicting Skylla devouring the companions of Odysseus was set up on a large base.

While we are unable to connect any other mythological groups to the Place of Palms with certainty, our evidence is sufficient to advance one or two possibilities. It has recently been suggested, for instance, that a remarkable statue group depicting Achilles ambushing the Trojan prince Troilos—which was re-erected in the Civil Basilica in the mid fourth century—might originally have been set up somewhere in the Place of Palms, since the palm tree had long been associated with the plains of Troy.[8] The best-preserved component of this group is a galloping horse carved from a single block of blue-grey marble, which originally supported a separately carved statue of Troilos in white marble. Our understanding of this group was enriched in 2017 by the discovery in the pool of a large portion of the horse's tail, which joins break-to-break with the creature's hindquarters (**88**). The tail has a lively, aerated appearance, achieved through a series of long, deep drill channels divided by perforated 'bridges' that separate the individual strands of hair. This aeration lends the statue a momentary quality: the horse is in the process of bolting, having been startled by Achilles' aggression towards the Trojan prince. Suffice to say, none of the other animal statues excavated in the Place of Palms approaches the same level of technical virtuosity (compare, for example, **85**, **86**, **87**, **96**).

Also significant, in this context, is a large statue base shaft re-used in the sixth-century holding basin constructed in front of the Propylon (Ch. 6, cat. **B 5**).[9] One of the texts inscribed on the base informs us that it was crowned originally by 'the statues of the Cyclops' (τοὺς ἀνδριάντας τοῦ Κύκλωπος; Appendix 1, In4), presumably a multi-figured statue group incorporating a representation of the Cyclops Polyphemos. Nothing of this statue group has yet been excavated, but two marble statuettes surviving from elsewhere in Aphrodisias may constitute small-scale versions of the original composition:[10] a figured table leg depicting the seated Polyphemos eviscerating a companion of Odysseus; and a statuette fragment depicting the nude, muscular torso of a seated male figure, which may be another version of the same iconographic scheme.[11]

Several considerations suggest that the Cyclops monument might originally have numbered among the mythological statue groups displayed in the Place of Palms.[12] Most compelling is the observation that several other Polyphemos statue groups surviving from antiquity are known to have been displayed next to—or to have formed part of—extravagant water installations. In nearby Ephesos, for example, a Polyphemos group was re-purposed for the decoration of an apsidal fountain building constructed by Calvisius Ruso, the proconsul of Asia, during the reign of Domitian.[13] Other Polyphemos groups associated with water displays have been excavated in imperial residences in Italy: at the Villa of Tiberius at Sperlonga, the Ninfeo della Punta dell'Epitaffio at Baiae, the Villa of Domitian at Castelgandolfo, and Hadrian's Villa at Tivoli.[14] The Tivoli group offers a particularly interesting point of comparison, since it may have been set up in the vicinity of the long 'Canopus' pool or the adjacent dome-shaped *cenatio*.[15] In light of these parallels, it seems likely that the Aphrodisias Cyclops monument was originally set up close to an extravagant water installation, making the Place of Palms and its pool an attractive possibility.

Together with the Achilles and Troilos group, then, the Cyclops base suggests that the Place of Palms might originally have been decorated with high-toned mythological statue groups depicting episodes borrowed from Homeric epic.[16] It would therefore be interesting to know how many of the mythological statue fragments excavated in the Place of Palms proper also belonged to statues set up in the complex during antiquity. This question is difficult to answer, not only because of the lack of specific information concerning the original display contexts of the majority of fragments, but also because the neighbouring Hadrianic 'Olympian' Baths emerged as an important locus for the display of mythological statuary during late antiquity.[17] These considerations are well illustrated by the head of a flute-playing satyr excavated in the West Stoa of the Place of Palms, which is a virtuoso version of a well-known hellenistic type,[18] combining a careful study of the satyr's sub-human physiognomy with an evocative representation of the physical effort required to play the double-flute (*aulos*) pressed to his lips (**54**). A strong case can be made that the head originally belonged to a statue set up on one of bases dedicated by Fl. Zenon in the East

---

6 Sculpture in Templum Pacis: Darwall-Smith 1996, 58–65; Coarelli 1999, 67–70; Tucci 2017, 216–258.

7 Sculptural decoration of the 'Canopus' at Tivoli: Raeder 1983, 299–315; Duthoy 2012, esp. 52–77; Neudecker 2014, 133–134.

8 Achilles and Troilos group: Smith and Hallett 2015. Possible display context in Place of Palms: Smith and Hallett 2015, 167.

9 Cyclops statue base: Reynolds 1980, 74–76 no. 3; AR no. 55; *IAph2007* 4.308; Thomas 2018.

10 'Miniaturisation' of large scale statuary at Aphrodisias: Smith 1996, 58–63; 1998; 2011, 72–74; Klar Phillips 2008, 258; Gensheimer and Welch 2013; Van Voorhis 2018, 31–34, 42–43.

11 Polyphemos *monopodium* leg: Klar Phillips 2008, 280–281 cat. 20; Feuser 2013, 255–256 cat. 130; Thomas 2018, 151. Polyphemos(?) statuette: Thomas 2018, 153.

12 Fuller discussion of the Cyclops base: Thomas 2018.

13 Fountain of Domitian at Ephesos: Fleischer 1971; Andreae 1977; 1982, 69–90; Andreae 1985; 1999; Aurenhammer 1990, 168–77; Alvino 1996, 205–207; Lenz 1998; Longfellow 2011, 62–76.

14 Polyphemos groups in imperial residences: Andreae 1982; Lavagne 1988, 515–616; Viscogliosi 1996; Carey 2002.

15 So, for example, Lavagne 1988, 612.

16 Mythological statuary in Aphrodisias more broadly: Chaniotis 2009b.

17 Mythological statuary in Hadrianic Baths: Smith 2007, 210–218; Gensheimer and Welch 2013.

18 Version in New York: Richter 1954, 108 no. 211. Version in Copenhagen: Poulsen 1951, cat. 483; Möbius 1970, 51–53; Moltesen 2000, 290–291 cat. 95.

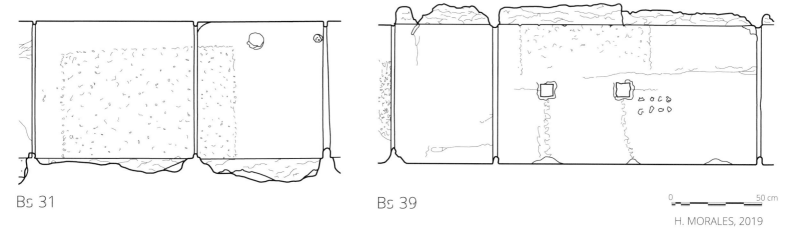

Fig. 55. Statue base setting **Bs-31** on north pool wall, identified by the anathyrosis treatment of the marble surface, and **Bs-39**, identified both by the anathyrosis and by the pendant pair of clamp holes used for affixing a base above.

Court of the Baths,[19] since the piece exhibits stylistic and technical affinities with several statues associated with the workshop owned by Zenon and his compatriot Fl. Andronikos in the early to mid fourth century (**94**, for example).[20]

B. STATUES AND FOUNTAIN SCULPTURES ON THE POOL EDGE

While our understanding of the mythological statue fragments excavated in the Place of Palms is affected by a lack of knowledge concerning their original contexts of display, we encounter the opposite problem when assessing the statue base settings on the marble pool walls. These settings provide us with the precise display contexts of monuments set up in the complex,[21] but we lack the bases and statues originally displayed on top.

In total, some forty-three certain and possible statue base settings remain visible on the outer pool wall (plotted on Fig. 12), all but two of which were for quadrangular bases (the exceptions are **Bs-22** and **Bs-34**, for circular bases).[22] These settings can be identified by the anathyrosis treatment of the marble surface of the pool wall (Fig. 55, **Bs-31**) and/or by the presence of one (or more) pairs of clamp holes for attaching a statue base on top (Fig. 55, **Bs-39**). In three cases (**Bs-2**, **Bs-20** and **Bs-40**) only a single clamp hole is preserved, but this can be explained by the replacement of the adjacent seat block—and so pendant clamp hole—when the pool was repaired during late antiquity. The typological variety of the settings suggests that the statuary display around the pool continued to evolve over an extended period of time. Still, there is no way of knowing whether the statue monuments originally faced inwards towards the pool itself or outwards towards the rest of the complex—or whether there was any consistency in this respect. It seems likely that any honorific portrait monuments would have faced outwards, so that their inscribed dedications remained easily legible. Mythological statues, by contrast, might easily have faced inwards, where they could have been admired by those relaxing on the opposite pool edge. Alternatively, there may have been a preference for subjects that could be appreciated from multiple viewpoints.

The distribution of these settings is significant: of forty-two, some twenty-seven are positioned along the northern pool wall, set for the most part at approximately regular intervals (see Fig. 12). This suggests that the northern side of the pool was the more important for the display of large-scale statuary, and there are in fact two further observations that support this conclusion. Firstly, the settings on the north pool wall are on average larger and more deeply cut than those on the south, suggesting that larger statue monuments tended to be displayed on this side. Secondly, there are six settings on the north pool wall that have two sets of clamp holes and/or other signs of re-use (**Bs-17**, **Bs-29**, **Bs-38**, **Bs-39**, **Bs-40**, **Bs-41**), presumably because their associated statue monuments were re-erected or replaced when the pool was repaired during late antiquity.

Five further sets of cuttings on the pool edge can be associated with fountain sculptures that supplied water to the pool during antiquity. These fountain settings were discussed in Ch. 2 §B in the context of the role that they played in distributing water to the pool. Here it will be useful to consider them in conjunction with two fountain sculptures found during the excavation of the complex.

The first is a high-quality, highly polished statuette depicting a nude, pudgy boy riding on the back of a dolphin, found at the east end of the pool in 1990 (**108**). Given its find location, it is tempting to infer that this statuette was set up on

---

19 Fl. Zenon bases: Erim and Roueché 1982; *ALA* nos. 11–12; Smith 2007, 214–215, 227 cats. B26, B27.
20 Workshop of Fl. Zenon and Fl. Andronikos: Smith 1996, 58–63; 1998; 2007, 213–215; 2011, 72–74; Bergmann 1999, 14–17; Moltesen 2000; Russell 2013, 339–344; Van Voorhis 2018.
21 Other types of decorative sculpture might also have been set up on the pool walls: see for instance a marble sundial of the second or third century AD (**107**).
22 Note that there are also two sets of clamp cuttings on the inner pool wall on its southern side. The four possible but uncertain statue base setting are **Bs-5**, **Bs-16**, **Bs-19**, and **Bs-43**; remains of point chiselling or possible clamp holes in these locations might indicate base settings, or they could relate to other features.

the outer pool wall at its eastern arc,[23] but its small scale and its excellent state of preservation speak against this possibility. It is more likely that the piece belonged to a covered fountain located somewhere in the vicinity: for argument's sake, in one of the surrounding stoas or somewhere in the Hadrianic Baths. Wherever it was set up, the deliberate chiselling away of the boy's genitals indicates that the statuette remained on display into late antiquity.[24]

A second fountain sculpture excavated in the eastern part of the South Stoa of the Place of Palms was discussed briefly in Ch. 2 §B. It depicts a frog perching on a rocky base, carved from local blue-grey marble (**109**). Only the proper left half of the sculpture is preserved, but enough survives to indicate that its inside was originally hollowed out to accommodate a water fitting, and that the mouth of the frog served as a fountain spout. A second frog fountain sculpture, also carved from blue-grey Aphrodisian marble, was found during the excavation of the stage building of the Theatre (but apparently reused in late antique or early medieval constructions).[25] While this second frog seems more schematic and two-dimensional than its counterpart from the Place of Palms, the two pieces are sufficiently close in scale, subject and material to suggest that they might originally have been displayed in the same context. Whether or not this context was the pool edge is more difficult to determine. On the one hand, the dimensions of both frog sculptures accord reasonably well with the dimensions of the fountain settings positioned around the pool. On the other, the frog excavated in the South Stoa might easily have fallen from the adjacent Theatre Hill, in which case we might envisage a display context for both pieces somewhere in the Theatre itself.[26]

C. SCULPTURE FROM THE PROPYLON

Imperial period

As we saw in Ch. 3 §A, the Propylon was a monumental columnar façade building constructed in the late first century AD, which connected the Place of Palms to the arterial north-south Tetrapylon Street bordering it to the east.[27] A large number of sculptural pieces was discovered during excavations in front (to the west) of the building (Fig. 56, which does not include those belonging to the basin, shown on Fig. 47).

Although the architecture of the Propylon awaits a full and detailed study, excavations revealed a series of ornamental architectural sculptures that clearly belonged to the building during antiquity. Particularly striking are a pair of large figural consoles, which were both found fallen in front of the fourth podium of the building, and so presumably decorated the central *aedicula* positioned directly above (**36, 37**). These consoles have richly carved projecting portions, each depicting an Eros riding on the back of a dolphin in a scheme familiar from elsewhere in Aphrodisias and from other sites in the Roman East.[28] Similarly grandiose are three large marble acroteria that originally crowned the building's Corinthian upper storey, which are modelled on large, krater-like vessels of the kind used to store large volumes of liquid during antiquity (**38, 39, 40**). Together with the consoles, these acroteria indicate that the architectural sculpture of the Propylon had a pronounced aquatic dimension, and this choice seems appropriate to the pool lying at the heart of the Place of Palms.

The *aediculae* of the Propylon would have been decorated by a series of freestanding statues, much like those of the Sebasteion Propylon located a short distance to the north-east.[29] Important information concerning these statues is supplied by the building's dedicatory inscription, discussed already in Ch. 3 §A. The relevant section of this text records that Diogenes Neoteros ('the Younger') paid for the construction of the Propylon itself, and that he was also responsible for 'the honorific statues of the Augusti' (ταῖς τειμαις τῶν Σεβαστῶν; Appendix 1, In2) and the building's other decoration. Bases belonging to three of these honorific statues were excavated in front of the Propylon, honouring Nerva (**1**), Hadrian (**2**) and Antoninus Pius (**3**) respectively. We saw in Ch. 3 §A that the statue of Nerva was set up during his reign using a bequest from Diogenes Neoteros. Statues of Hadrian and Antoninus Pius—and presumably also one of Trajan—were then added during their reigns.[30] A possible candidate for the missing Trajan base is the re-used base honouring Anthemios, the praetorian prefect of AD 405–414, which was built into the holding basin in front of the Propylon in the mid sixth century (see Ch. 6 §B, **B 3**). The dimensions of this base correspond with those of the other bases in the imperial series.

While the (separately carved) upper plinth of the Antoninus Pius base has not yet been found, the cuttings and clamp holes on the Nerva and Hadrian bases indicate that they originally supported colossal portraits made from bronze rather than marble.[31] These bronze portraits have not survived, but a series of marble statue pieces excavated in the same area that originally belonged to large-scale imperial portraits may offer some sense of the grandeur and quality of the missing statues. Two of these pieces are already well known: a colossal, headless statue of a cuirassed emperor, which was excavated in precisely the same area as the Antoninus Pius statue base, and which has traditionally been identified as the portrait of this emperor that stood on top (**10**); and a near-colossal head of Nerva, which stands out on account of its energetic, hellenistic-style re-working of this emperor's metropolitan portrait type (**24**). A third, less well-known example is supplied by a large fragment of an over-life-size statue of a seated, partially nude male figure wearing a hip mantle, which was excavated in the open area to the east of the pool (**31**). The scale and costume of this statue indicate that it represented either a seated divinity in the Zeus or Asklepios

---

23 So Wilson 2016b, 116.
24 Responses to classical statuary in late antiquity: Jacobs 2010.
25 Frog fountain sculpture from the Theatre (Inv. 71-331): Wilson 2016b, 116–117, fig. 7.23.
26 So already Wilson 2016b, 117.
27 Propylon: Erim 1986b, 123–130; Ratté 2002, 23–24; Öğüş 2015, 306–307; Wilson 2016b, 35.

28 Comparanda from Ephesos: Aurenhammer 1990, 89–91 cats. 69–71.
29 Sebasteion Propylon and its statues: Reynolds 1996; Smith *et al.* 2006, 44–47; Lenaghan 2008; Smith 2013; 55–70.
30 Imperial statue groups featuring Trajan and his predecessors and/or successors: Deppmeyer 2008, 46–48.
31 Noted already by Smith *et al.* 2006, 58, 127, 161.

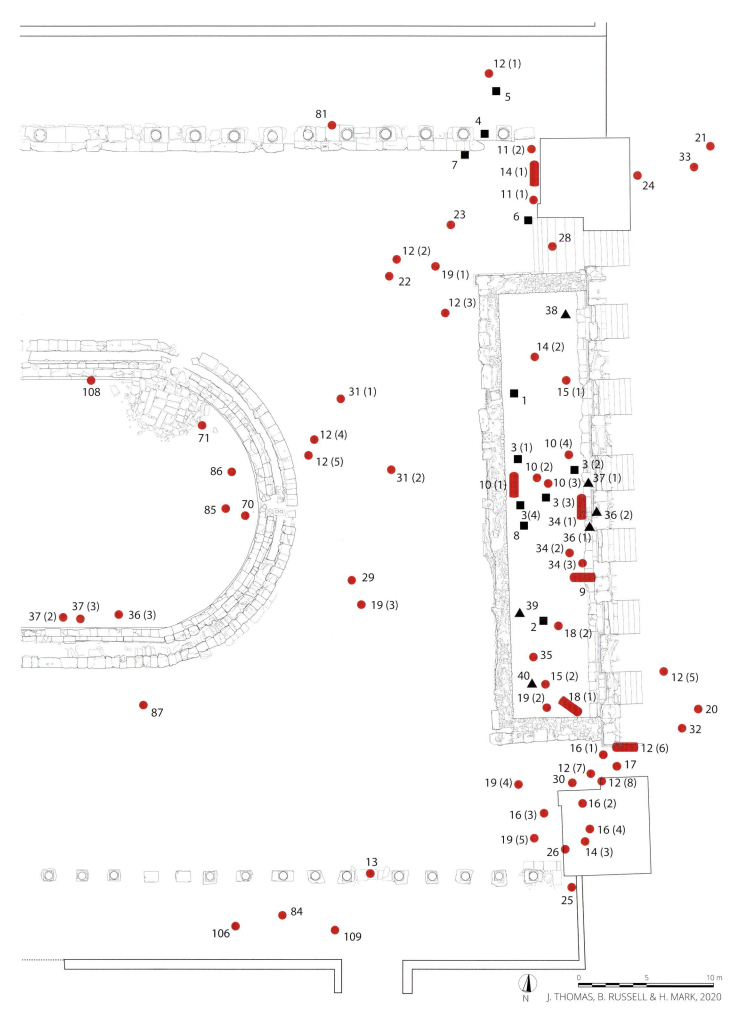

Fig. 56. Scatter plan of catalogued sculptural finds from east end of Place of Palms, not including those from the basin, shown on Fig. 47. Red dots represent statuary finds, black squares represent statue bases, and black triangles represent architectural and relief sculpture.

mould, or else an enthroned emperor dressed in the so-called 'Jupiter costume', comparable to the seated statue of Augustus from the Basilica at Ephesos and a fragmentary statue of an unidentified seated emperor from Ankara.[32]

As well as the bases for Nerva, Hadrian, and Antoninus Pius, excavations in front of the Propylon also uncovered four bases of the high imperial period commemorating private (that is, non-imperial) benefactors, some of which were surely displayed on the building during antiquity (4, 5, 6, 7). All four bases list the Aphrodisian Council of Elders (*gerousia*) as an awarding body, either alone or in conjunction with the *boulē* and the *dēmos*. This concentration is strikingly high, and requires an explanation. One possibility is that the meeting place of the Council of Elders was located somewhere close to the Propylon, and that this spatial proximity contributed towards the large number of bases. Support for this hypothesis is supplied by a semi-circular statue base built into the Niche Building located a short distance to the north of the Propylon, facing onto the arterial Tetrapylon Street. The text on this base records statue honours for Myon Eusebes, one of the builders of the Sebasteion,[33] on account of his construction of 'the first bathhouse for the Council of Elders'.[34] Recent excavations of the façade of this building—a short distance to the north of the Propylon—have uncovered the remains of a bathing facility, presumably the Gerousian bathhouse mentioned in the inscription.

In any case, it is likely that these non-imperial bases originally supported some of the portrait statues that were likewise excavated in front of the Propylon (9–32), although the discrepancy between the number of surviving bases (four) and the number of surviving statues (at least ten) renders it difficult to propose more specific associations.

Late antiquity

The decoration of the Propylon continued to be updated in late antiquity. Excavations in front of the building unearthed a fragmentary marble plaque carrying an inscription honouring a late antique emperor with the *nomen* Flavius, who should probably be identified as Julian (r. AD 361–363) (8).[35] This plaque was surely affixed to the front face of a statue base belonging to an honorific monument commemorating this emperor. Other statue-base plaques honouring Julian have been excavated in Samos, Salamis, Rome, and Aceruntia.[36] In Aphrodisias, meanwhile, a second honorific statue monument for Julian was set up in the Tetrastoon in front of the Theatre, although it was later re-used for Theodosius I or II.[37]

It may be significant that the width of this plaque is virtually identical to that of the Antoninus Pius statue base shaft already discussed (plaque: 74; base: 75.5 cm). This observation, together with the fact that the plaque and the base were excavated in such close proximity, suggests a new hypothesis: that the plaque was affixed to the front face of the Antoninus Pius base during the reign of Julian. In this case, the two large clamp holes cut into the right and left sides of the base could have supported a pair of large, bracket-like clamps used to affix the plaque to its front face. This suggestion also bears on our appreciation of the colossal marble portrait of a cuirassed emperor also excavated in close proximity to the Antoninus Pius base, traditionally identified as Antoninus Pius himself (10). It opens the possibility that this statue was re-purposed to represent Julian in the fourth century. We might compare, in this respect, other cuirassed portraits re-used to commemorate emperors in Asia Minor during the late third and fourth centuries: the tetrarchs at Side and Perge, and the portraits of Constans and Constantius II set up by Caelius Montius in Ephesos.[38]

We saw in Ch. 4 §A that the Propylon was renovated by Doulkitios during the late fifth or early sixth century.[39] This late antique renovation has important implications for our understanding of the statue and statue-base finds excavated in front of the building. Indeed, we are led to consider whether these finds necessarily decorated the Propylon during its original phase, or whether some of them were first displayed on the building only *after* Doulkitios' intervention, having been recycled from elsewhere in the city.[40]

The problem is exemplified by the best-known portrait excavated in front of the Propylon: an over-lifesize statue of a young *togatus* (9), which was found fallen immediately in front of the fifth projecting podium and so presumably displayed in the *aedicula* above following Doulkitios' reconstruction of the building. While this figure has sometimes been interpreted as 'a late-antique pastiche' representing a personification or a mythological figure,[41] the statue is rather a portrait of the early to mid second century depicting a young local benefactor. His toga, his plain leather boots and the ring on his left hand all indicate that he belonged to the equestrian order at Rome.

None of the statue bases excavated in front of the Propylon can be associated with this portrait: and indeed, there can be no

---

32 Seated portraits of Roman emperors in 'Jupiter costume': Hallett 2005, 166–172, 318–320. Seated Augustus from Ephesos: Rose 1997, 175 no. 115, pl. 214; Boschung 2002, 9 no I.II, pl. 8.2.4. Ankara seated emperor: Maderna 1988, 174 cat. JT 15, with further bibliography.
33 Myon Eusebes and the Sebasteion: Smith 2013, 13–18.
34 Pylon building and statue base for Myon Eusebes: Sokolicek 2016, 59–65; Chaniotis 2018b. Himation statue that originally stood on Myon Eusebes base: Smith 2016c, 293–294.
35 The imperial honorand was previously identified as Justinian: see *ALA* no. 81; *IAph2007* 4.311.
36 Samos: *LSA*-818 (U. Gehn); Salamis: *LSA*-868 (U. Gehn); Rome: *LSA*-1498 (C. Machado); Aceruntia: *LSA*-1697 (C. Machado).
37 Tetrastoon monument for Julian/Theodosius: *ALA* no. 20; Smith 1999a, 161–162; 2001.
38 Side armoured tetrarch: İnan and Alföldi-Rosenbaum 1966, 86 no. 63; LSA-244 (J. Lenaghan). Perge armoured tetrarchs: Özgür 2008, 142–145 nos. 61–62; Akçay-Güven 2018; LSA-2543 and LSA-2544 (both J. Lenaghan). Ephesos Constantinian statues: Heberdey 1912, cols. 174–177; LSA-1122 and LSA-1123 (both J. Auinger).
39 Reconstruction of Propylon in late antiquity: *ALA* no. 40; *IAph2007* 4.202iii; Wilson 2016b, 133.
40 Possibility of late antique re-use: Smith *et al.* 2006, 58–60; Lenaghan 2007, 166–168; Smith 2016a, 154. Comparable late antique 'recycling' of earlier statuary in the Bouleuterion: Smith *et al.* 2006, 62; Bier 2008, 153–154; Hallett and Quatember 2018, 356–358.
41 Late antique personification theory: Hannestad 1994, 160; 2001, 138–139; 2012, 83–86. Refutation of theory: Smith *et al.* 2006, 32; Borg 2007, 586–587.

guarantee that it actually stood on one when it was set up on Doulkitios' reconstructed building.[42] This makes it difficult to assess both the identity of the represented figure and the nature of the statue's relationship with the structure. It is conceivable that the portrait was first set up in the generation or so following the construction of the building, much like the statue monuments for Hadrian and Antoninus Pius already discussed. In this case, we might imagine that it represented a wealthy local citizen who contributed towards the beautification of the Propylon or the Place of Palms in the early to mid second century. Even if so, it would not necessarily follow that the statue still 'represented' this second-century benefactor following Doulkitios' reconstruction project. Rather, it may have been re-used at this juncture to commemorate a new, contemporary honorand. Another possibility is that the statue was displayed on the Gate for the first time only during late antiquity, having been recycled from elsewhere in the city. In this case, too, the statue surely would have commemorated a new, late antique honorand.

It is interesting, in this context, that the portrait was set up directly on top of the podium inscribed with the verse text commemorating Doulkitios' intervention.[43] This setting raises the tantalising possibility that ancient viewers were supposed to connect the inscription and the re-used statue standing above, in which case the latter might have been understood as representing Doulkitios. Some support for this hypothesis is provided by the inscription itself, which tells us that Doulkitios re-erected the Propylon by 'stretching out his mighty hand' (κρατερὴν χεῖρ' ἐπορεξάμενος; In12). This evocative language resonates with the iconography of the portrait itself, since the elongated, lowered right arm 'extends away from the body, with the hand and forearm worked fully in the round'.[44] It is possible, then, that the iconography of the repurposed statue had some impact on the wording of the honorific inscription, or that the wording of the inscription had some bearing on the choice of statue being repurposed. The choice of a togate figure would also be appropriate for the representation of a Roman governor, even if the portrait has none of the Constantinopolitan fashion elements that we associate with newly made portrait statues of the late fifth and early sixth centuries AD.

Not all of the statues that decorated the Propylon during its final phase were portraits. Indeed, an under-lifesize statue of a youthful river god was found fallen directly in front of the fourth podium of the building, and may have been displayed in the *aedicula* immediately above (34). The god is shown reclining on a rocky plinth, supporting his weight on his left arm and holding a long reed with lanceolate leaves in his left hand. He wears only a himation wrapped around his waist, and a wreath made of reeds around his head. His face is youthful and idealising, framed by long hair that falls in a series of wavy, water-drenched strands separated by deep drill channels. Its style and technique place the statue in the second century, making it later than the Propylon itself. This fact, together with the statue's horizontal orientation and the high level of finish on its rear, suggests that it was not originally designed for the decoration of an *aedicula*. Perhaps then it was also repurposed for this late antique display context. Given its aquatic iconography, it is possible that the statue was originally set up somewhere in the Place of Palms or in the Hadrianic Baths. That river god statues were sometimes erected in recreational complexes like the Place of Palms is suggested by the statue of the Nile set up in the Temple of Peace in Rome,[45] and the statues of the Nile and Tiber excavated in the area of the 'Canopus' at Hadrian's Villa in Tivoli.[46]

Clearly the statue represents a personification of a river from the region surrounding Aphrodisias. Numismatic comparanda from the late second and third centuries suggest two possibilities: the River Morsynos and the River Timeles.[47] Both rivers are depicted on Aphrodisian coinage as youthful, beardless personifications reclining with the lower parts of their bodies draped. Of the two, the Timeles is perhaps the more likely candidate, since an important new aqueduct constructed during the Hadrianic period carried water from this river into the city.[48] In either case, the statue adds an important new example to our corpus of high imperial river god statues surviving from the Greek *poleis* of Asia Minor. We might compare, for instance, the statue of the River Maeander from the *frigidarium* of the Baths of Faustina at Miletos, the statue of the River Kestros that decorated the northern nymphaeum at Perge, and the statues of the river Kaystros (?) from the *frigidarium* of the Vedius Gymnasium at Ephesos.[49]

Propylon: bases, statuary, ornament

Inscribed bases

1. Base for colossal bronze statue of Nerva, awarded by the *dēmos*, funded by Diogenes Neoteros, son of Menandros, son of Diogenes. H: 130, W: 86, D: 77, Letter H: 5.5–6 cm. AD 96–98. Found 1977 in Propylon holding basin. Inv. 77-034. Smith *et al.* 2006, 58, 78 H24, 127, 261; Appendix 1, In13 (Pl. 95.C).

2. Base for colossal bronze statue of Hadrian, awarded by the *dēmos*. H: 129, W: 61, D: 66, Letter H: 5.5–6 cm. *c.* AD 117–123. Found 1983 in Propylon holding basin. Inv.

---

42 Compare the statues without bases excavated in front of the stage building of the Bouleuterion: Smith *et al.* 2006, 61–65; Bier 2008, 153–154.
43 Noted already by Smith *et al.* 2006, 111 n. 1.
44 Smith *et al.* 2006, 109.
45 Nile statue in *Templum Pacis*: Plin., *HN* XXXVI 58.
46 Tivoli river gods: Raeder 1983, 89 cats. I 86, I 87.
47 River Morsynos coins: Imhoof-Blumer 1923, 290 no. 290; MacDonald 1992, 115 Type 140; *LIMC s.v.* Demos no.19 (O. Alexandri-Tzahou). River Timeles coins: Imhoof-Blumer 1923, 290–291 nos. 291–292; MacDonald 1992, 89 Type 77, 100 Type 107, 115 Type 141, 149 Type 231; *LIMC s.v.* Demos no.19 (O. Alexandri-Tzahou); *LIMC* VIII *s.v.* 'Timeles' (P. Linant de Bellefonds). Timeles was also depicted on coins and a votive relief from Herakleia Salbake in the neighbouring Tavas plain: Imhoof-Blumer 1923, no 295; Sheppard 1981.
48 Timeles aqueduct: *IAph2007* 11.412; *IAph2007* 12.1111; Reynolds 2000; Coleman 2008; Pont 2008; Commito and Rojas 2012, esp. 253–275, 286–291; Wilson 2016b, 101–102.
49 Miletos river god: Bol 2011, 109–110 cat. VI.22. Perge north nymphaeum and associated statuary: Dorl-Klingenschmid 2001, 228–229 cat. 85; Longfellow 2011, 156–161. Ephesos river gods: Aurenhammer 1990, 105–109 cats. 86, 87. River god statues in the Roman world: Klementa 1993.

83-075. Smith *et al.* 2006, 58, 78 H25, 127; Appendix 1, In14 (Pl. 95.D).

3. *Base for colossal statue of Antoninus Pius*, awarded by the *dēmos*, funded by Adrastos, son of Adrastos, son of Apollonios, son of Andron Attalos. Missing: separately-carved upper plinth. H: 115, W: 75.5, D: 62, Letter H: 4.5–6 cm. AD 138–161. Found 1980 in Propylon holding basin, broken into four fragments. Inv. 80-024. Smith *et al.* 2006, 78 H25, 126–127 cat. 17; *IAph2007* 4.301; Appendix 1, In15. (Pl. 68.A).
4. *Base for Adrastos, son of Hierokles*, awarded by the *gerousia*. H: 28, W: 94, D: 60, Letter H: 2.5 cm. First century. Found 1987 in front of north *pyrgos* tunnel of Propylon. Inv. 87-371 = I-76. Smith *et al.* 2006, 80 H50.
5. *Base for Hierokles, son of Hierokles*, awarded by the *gerousia*, *boulē* and *dēmos*. H: 28, W: 73, D: 58, Letter H: 1.5–2 cm. Second century. Found 1987. Inv. 87-372 = I-77. Smith *et al.* 2006, 84 H103.
6. *Three non-joining fragments of base for [Teimok]les, son of Apollonios*, awarded by the *gerousia*, *boulē* and *dēmos*. H: 29.5, Letter H: 2 cm. First–second century. Largest fragment found 1975 in front of north *pyrgos* tunnel of Propylon. Inv. 64-117, 75-198. Smith *et al.* 2006, 87 H142; Appendix 1, In21 (Pl. 96.A–B).
7. *Base for Ammia, daughter of Zenon*, awarded by the *boulē*, *dēmos* and *gerousia*. H: 28.5, W: 79, D: 60, Letter H: 2.5 cm. Second century. Found 1989 at east extremity of North Stoa. Inv. I-160 = 89a. Smith *et al.* 2006, 93 H226.
8. *Fragmentary statue base plaque honouring late antique emperor, probably Julian.* H: 76; W: 74: D: 2.5, Letter H: 9.5 cm. AD 361–363. Found 1983 in Propylon holding basin, broken into 8 fragments. Inv. 83-127. *ALA* 81; *IAph2007* 4.311; Appendix 1, In17 (Pl. 68.B).

Portrait statuary
9. *Statue of youth wearing toga.* Early second century. Inv. 83-064. Smith *et al.* 2006, 108–112 cat. 3, pls. 8–10 (Pl. 68.C).
10. *Cuirassed statue of Roman emperor ('Antoninus Pius'), possibly re-purposed to represent Julian in fourth century.* Mid second century(?). Inv. 80-024, 80-025. Smith *et al.* 2006, 126–128 cat. 17, pl. 17 (Pl. 68.D).
11. *Two non-joining fragments of himation statue (Eretria type).* First to early second century. Inv. 75-196, NAgPY 89-I.1. Smith *et al.* 2006, 182 cat. 53, pl. 49.
12. *Himation statue signed by Apellas Koblanos.* First to early second century. Inv. 77-030, 83-063, 87-338, 87-445, T-448. Smith *et al.* 2006, 182–183 cat. 54, pls. 50–51; Appendix 1, In29.
13. *Head of young priest.* First century. Inv. 86-029. Smith *et al.* 2006, 183–184 cat. 55, pl. 51.
14. *Headless himation statue.* First to early second century. Inv. 75-219, 80-020, 83-204, T-57. Smith *et al.* 2006, 184 cat. 56, pls. 52–53.
15. *Torso and plinth of himation statue.* First to early second century. Inv. 80-033, 83-062. Smith *et al.* 2006, 185 cat. 57, pls. 52–53.
16. *Himation statue in arm-sling pose.* Second century. Inv. 83-060A, 83-061, 83-203. Smith *et al.* 2006, 185–186 cat. 58, pl. 54.
17. *Head of young priest.* Late first or early second century. Inv. 83-191. Smith *et al.* 2006, 186–187 cat. 59, pl. 55.
18. *Statue of veiled woman, signed by sculptor Menodotos.* Late first or early second century. Inv. 83-122. Smith *et al.* 2006, 204–205 cat. 85, pls. 65–67; Appendix 1, In30.
19. *Two non-joining parts of draped female statue.* First century. Inv. 77-032, 83-060B, 83-192A-B, 87-420. Smith *et al.* 2006, 205–207 cat. 86, fig. 26, pl. 68.
20. *Female torso in Ephesos Kore-Persephone type.* First to early second century. Inv. 83-065. Smith *et al.* 2006, 207 cat. 87, pl. 68.
21. *Thighs of over-lifesize draped female statue.* Imperial period. Inv. 75-027. Smith *et al.* 2006, 207–209 cat. 88, pls. 69–70.
22. *Chest of under-lifesize chlamys bust.* Third–fourth century. Inv. 87-389. Smith *et al.* 2006, 227 cat. 122, pl. 94.
23. *Fragmentary himation bust.* Second century. Inv. 77-025. Smith *et al.* 2006, 240 cat. 128, pl. 96.
24. *Near-colossal head of Nerva.* Late first century. Inv. 75-193. Smith *et al.* 2006, 260–261 cat. 164, pl. 113.
25. *Head of youth.* First century. Inv. 85-157. Smith *et al.* 2006, 275–276 cat. 178, pl. 125.
26. *Male hair fragment.* Second–third century. Inv. 83-199. Smith *et al.* 2006, 283 cat. 196, pl. 133.
27. *Two non-joining fragments of veiled female head.* Not plotted on find-spot plans because fragments found during basket sorting. First–second century. Inv. 83-171. Smith *et al.* 2006, 287 cat. 203, pl. 138.
28. *Fragmentary female head with crown braid.* Late third to early fourth century. Inv. 75-228. Smith *et al.* 2006, 296–297 cat. 220, pl. 151.
29. *Fragmentary head of male youth: Westmacott Ephebe type.* H: 20, W: 18, D: 12 cm. Late first or early second century. Found 1987 in front of Propylon holding basin. Inv. 87-369. Lenaghan 2007, 163–169.
30. *Fragment of lower right torso of over-lifesize nude male figure.* H: 30.5, W: 23, D: 24 cm. First–second century. Found 1983 in rubble adjacent to south *pyrgos* tunnel of Propylon. Inv. 83-196. Unpublished (Pl. 69.A).
31. *Fragment of over-lifesize seated male statue in heroic nude costume with hip mantle.* H: 72, W: 79, D: 60 cm. First–second century. Found 1987 in front of Propylon holding basin. Inv. 87-417. Erim 1986b, 20 (Pl. 69.B).
32. *Fragmentary neck and head of over-lifesize male portrait with stubbled beard and shallow neck socket (with central dowel hole) for insertion into statue body.* H: 20, W: 16, D: 19 cm. Late fifth or early sixth century. Surface find in 1983 immediately to the east of the Propylon. Inv. 83-126. Nbk. 240: *South East Agora Gate (SEAG) I* (B. Rose), p. 20. Unpublished.

Mythological and votive statuary
33. *Fragmentary lifesize head of goddess or personification.* H: 22, W: 19, D: 20 cm. First century. Found 1975 to the

east of the north *pyrgos* tunnel of the Propylon, built into later wall. Inv. 75-070. Unpublished (Pl. 69.C).

34. *Under-lifesize statue of youthful, reclining river god, probably the Timeles or Morsynos.* H: 84, W: 150, D: 50.5 cm. Second century. Body found 1980 fallen in front of fourth projecting bastion of Propylon; head and R hand found 1983 in approximately the same area. Inv. 80-021, 83-086, 83-086A. Unpublished (Pl. 69.E).

35. *Battered under-lifesize head of satyr wearing wreath.* H: 25, W: 16, D: 18 cm. High imperial? Found 1983 in later fill of stones inside Propylon holding basin. Inv. 83-128. Unpublished (Pl. 69.D).

Architectural sculpture

36. *Console with Eros riding dolphin*, with projecting part decorated with acanthus scroll relief on L side and left in quarry state on R side. H: 74, W: 58, L: 187 cm. Late first century. Console found 1980 fallen in front of north corner of fourth projecting bastion of Propylon. Eros head found 1990 at east end of pool. Inv. 80-016 (console), 90-009 (Eros head). Smith 1996, 20, 23 fig. 15 (Pl. 70.A–B).

37. *Console with Eros riding dolphin*, with projecting part decorated with acanthus scroll relief on R side and left in quarry state on L side. H: 73, W: 44, L: 182 cm. Late first century. Console found 1980 fallen in front of south corner of fourth projecting bastion of Propylon. Eros head found 1990 at east end of pool. Inv. 80-023 (console), 90-008 (Eros head). Smith 1996, 20, 23 fig. 15 (Pl. 70.C–D).

38. *Krater-like acroterion with egg-and-dart surface decoration, moulded foot and conical lid.* H: 116, W: 78, D: 78 cm. Late first century. Found 1983 fallen in front of Propylon. Inv. 83-047 (Pl. 71.A).

39. *Krater-like acroterion with fluted surface decoration and no lid.* H: 70, W: 66, D: 62.5 cm. Late first century. Found 1983 fallen in front of Propylon. Inv. 83-048 (Pl. 71.B).

40. *Krater-like acroterion with fluted surface decoration, volute-like handles and conical lid.* H: 88, W: 60 cm. Late first century. Found 1983 fallen in front of Propylon. Inv. 83-049 (Pl. 71.C).

D. SCULPTURE FROM THE WEST STOA

Another nodal point for the display of honorific portraiture was the West Stoa of the Place of Palms (Fig. 57), which was constructed in tandem with the adjoining Hadrianic 'Olympian' Baths during the reign of Hadrian (AD 117–138).[50] As demonstrated in Ch. 3 §C, at some point later, probably in the fourth century AD, the colonnade of the West Stoa was blocked with doorways and a new mosaic floor was added to the interior. These changes effectively turned the previously open building into an enclosed hall. The stoa only returned to its original 'open' form following the renovations undertaken by Albinos in the late fifth or early sixth century (see Ch. 4 §D).

Four large female portrait statues of the imperial period were excavated in the northern half of the stoa. Three of these seem earlier than the building itself on stylistic and iconographic grounds: a headless *pudicitia* figure of the late hellenistic or early imperial period (**47**) and two well-preserved over-lifesize statues of female honorands with carefully arranged Trajanic fashion hairstyles (**45**, **46**).[51] This chronological discrepancy suggests that the West Stoa may not have been the original display context of these statues. Rather, they were probably repurposed during late antiquity, either when the stoa was enclosed in the fourth century or following Albinos' work.[52] It would be interesting to know whether any of the first- and second-century portrait fragments excavated in the west end of the pool likewise belonged to re-used statues that were displayed in the stoa during late antiquity (**75**, **76**, **77**, **78**).

Less difficult to interpret are the late antique portrait monuments excavated in the West Stoa. Together these pieces indicate that the West Stoa was 'the single most important setting for late antique statue honours' at Aphrodisias, together with the adjoining East Court of the Hadrianic Baths.[53] The stoa seems to have acquired this importance as early as the Theodosian period, probably soon after its transformation described above.

Since the late antique portrait finds from the stoa will be presented fully in a forthcoming volume on late antique portrait statuary from Aphrodisias, it will suffice here to introduce the key pieces in outline only. The earliest dated monument is a Theodosian imperial group, erected in front of the central stairway leading into the East Court of the Hadrianic Baths by Fl. Eutolmius Tatianus, the Praetorian Prefect of the East, in AD 388–392.[54] Four re-used columnar bases belonging to this group have been found: three carrying inscriptions honouring Valentinian II (**41**), Arcadius (**42**), and Honorius respectively;[55] and a fourth with an erased inscription that surely once honoured Theodosius I.[56] Excavations in the stoa also uncovered two newly carved, highly polished statues of outstanding quality that belonged to this Theodosian group. Although neither statue can be associated with a particular base with certainty, the figures have sometimes been labelled 'Valentinian II' (**57**) and 'Arcadius' (**58**), designations retained here for the sake of consistency. The two emperors are dressed in the same manner, wearing closed senatorial boots (*calcei patricii*), a sleeved under-tunic, an over-tunic, and a distinctive kind of short, late antique toga that recurs in two other statues from the site (including **119**, as we shall see below).[57] While the head of the

---

50 Construction of West Stoa: de Chaisemartin 1989, 30–32; Wilson 2016b, 107. Dating of the Hadrianic Baths: Wilson 2016a, 181–192; McDavid 2016, 209–210.

51 A Trajanic bust found in the vicinity (**49**) might also have pre-dated the West Stoa.

52 So, more fully, Smith 2007, 209–210.

53 Quotation: Smith 2016a, 156.

54 Theodosian group: Smith 2007, 218; 2016a, 150; 2018c, 338–339.

55 Honorius base: *ALA* no. 25; Smith 2007, 229 cat. B31; *IAph2007* 5.217; LSA-167 (J. Lenaghan).

56 Deduced from the fact that Fl. Eutolmius Tatianus also set up groups honouring these four emperors at Side and Antinoopolis. Side: *CIG* III 4350; Nollé 1993, no. 52; LSA-267 (U. Gehn). Antinoopolis: Bernand 1984, 102–104 no. 19, pl. 8; LSA-876 (U. Gehn).

57 Toga costume in late antique Aphrodisias: Smith 1999a, 178–181; 2016a, 17–20. Unfinished *togatus* excavated in the Sculptor's Work-

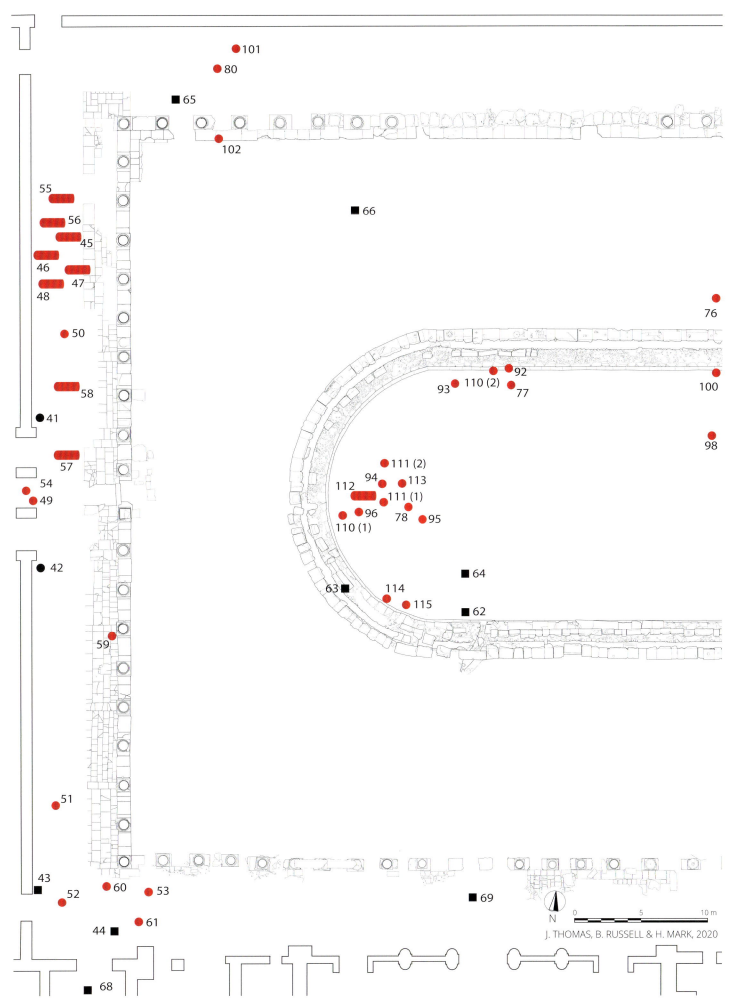

Fig. 57. Scatter plan of catalogued sculptural finds from west end of Place of Palms.
Red dots represent statuary finds, black squares represent statue bases, and black triangles represent architectural and relief sculpture.

'Arcadius' was broken from the statue, the head of the 'Valentinian II' survives intact. This emperor has a youthful, clean-shaven face, with a jewelled imperial diadem sitting atop his plain fringe of hair.

Two further fragments excavated elsewhere in the Place of Palms probably also belonged to this Theodosian group. The first is a 'slice' of a diademed portrait head excavated at the west end of the pool, which has precisely the same kind of straight, brushed forward hairstyle as both the 'Valentinian II' and Theodosian imperial portrait heads excavated elsewhere (**110**).[58] Its scale suggests that it might have belonged originally to the 'Arcadius' portrait. The second fragment is the right ankle of a high-quality, late antique *togatus*, who wears *calcei patricii* with 'hanging' straps very similar to those worn by 'Valentinian II' and 'Arcadius' (**118**).

A further statue base of the Theodosian period was found in the southern part of the West Stoa, immediately adjacent to the southern doorway leading into the East Court of the Hadrianic Baths (**43**).[59] This base was set up by the *boulē* for one Menandros, possibly the vicar of Asia in AD 385–388, to thank him for reducing the city's tax burden. Although the statue that stood on top of this base has not yet been identified, three portrait heads of the late fourth and fifth centuries found in the southern half of the West Stoa offer a vivid taste of the kind of vigorously individualised portrait with which Menandros is likely have been honoured (**59, 60, 61**). The most sumptuous is the head of a mature, full-faced, clean-shaven man, with short hair combed onto his brow (**61**), which can be dated to the later fourth century on account of its stylistic and technical affinities with the Theodosian imperial portraits already discussed.[60]

Whereas for Menandros we have a statue base lacking an associated statue, excavations in the northern half of the West Stoa uncovered a pair of high-quality, well-preserved *chlamydatus* portrait statues that lack their bases, sometimes referred to as the 'Elder Magistrate' (**56**) and the 'Younger Magistrate' (**55**). It is possible that these statues originally stood to either side of the northern doorway leading into the East Court of the Hadrianic Baths, in much the same way that the Theodosian family group framed the central doorway and the Menandros statue flanked the southern doorway.

The latest statue monument excavated in the West Stoa is a columnar base of the late fifth or early sixth century honouring Albinos himself (**44**). This base was found close to the Menandros base: that is, at the southern end of the stoa, in the vicinity of the doorway leading into the East Court of the Baths. The inscription on the base records that the city honoured Albinos for his 'works' (ἔργοις), a formulation referring to his restoration of the West Stoa.[61] It is likely that comparable portrait monuments would have been erected for the other individuals who paid for large-scale repairs in the Place of Palms at approximately the same time: Ampelios, who sponsored wholesale renovations in the complex; Doulkitios, who paid for the re-construction of the Propylon; and Philippos, who was responsible for repairing or building at least part of the structures of the South Stoas (see Ch. 4 §F).[62]

Given that the West Stoa of the Place of Palms became an important location for the display of honorific portraiture in late antiquity, it would be interesting to know whether the same was also true of the North and South Stoas of the complex. The evidence from the partially excavated South Stoas is limited in this respect: we have only a handful of statue and bust fragments (**83, 84**) and a fragment of a second-century statue base honouring one Julia Faustina (**69**). The majority of finds from the North Stoa are likewise fragmentary (**80, 81, 82**) but excavations here also uncovered one larger piece that should be considered in more detail: the body of a late antique *togatus* with a neck socket for the insertion of a separately carved head (**119**). This body was excavated immediately in front of the central passageway between the North Stoa of the Place of Palms and the South Stoa of the Agora, suggesting that it might once have belonged to a statue monument that flanked this passageway to one side. It is doubtful, however, that this was the original display context of the *togatus*, since the figure wears precisely the same distinctive kind of short toga as the 'Valentinian II' and 'Arcadius' statues already discussed, and was surely originally part of the same Theodosian group.[63] The more limited statuary finds from the North and South Stoas might reflect the fact that neither of these structures was enclosed in the same way as the West Stoa.

West Stoa: bases and statuary

Statue bases

41. *Base for Fl. Valentinianus (II)*, aged 17–21, set up by Fl. Eutolmius Tatianus, praetorian prefect of the East, AD 388–392. H: 103, Diam.: 54, Letter H: 3.5–7 cm. Found 1905 in West Stoa, on north side of central stairway leading to East Court of Hadrianic Baths. *ALA* no. 27; Smith 2007, 229–230 cat. B32; *IAph2007* 4.11; LSA-166 (J. Lenaghan).

42. *Base for Fl. Arcadius*, aged 11–15, set up by Fl. Eutolmius Tatianus, praetorian prefect of the East, AD 388–392. H: 66, Diam.: 56.5, Letter H: 3–4 cm. Found 1905 in West Stoa, on south side of central stairway leading to East Court of Hadrianic Baths. *ALA* no. 26; Smith 2007, 230 cat. B33; *IAph2007* 4.10; LSA-164 (J. Lenaghan).

---

shop dressed in the same short late antique toga: İnan and Alföldi-Rosenbaum 1979, 224–226 no. 195; Smith 1999a, 162, pl. I 2; Van Voorhis 2018, 69–70 cat. 1.
58 Theodosian imperial portraiture: İnan and Alföldi-Rosenbaum 1966, 89–90; İnan and Alföldi-Rosenbaum 1979, 138–140; Stichel 1982, esp. 27–58.
59 Julia Lenaghan is preparing an article on this base, building on a paper she delivered at the following conference: *Iscrizioni metriche nel tardo impero romano: società, politica e cultura fra Oriente e Occidente. Settant'anni dopo Louis Robert, Hellenica IV (1948)*, Sapienza Università di Roma, 18–19 November 2019.
60 Compare also figures with similar hairstyles depicted on the Theodosian obelisk base of AD 388–392: Bruns 1935; Kiilerich 1998.

61 Repair of West Stoa by Albinos: *ALA* no. 83; *IAph2007* 4.21.
62 Philippos' renovations: *ALA* no. 66; *IAph2007* 4.19.
63 For the re-use of existing statue monuments in late antiquity, see, for example Smith 2016b, 4, 20; Hallett 2017, 883–884.

43. *Base for Menandros, vicar of Asia in AD 385–388(?),* awarded by the *boulē*. H: 145, Diam.: 55, Letter H: 5–6.5 cm. Late fourth century. Found 1913 in the Baths, possibly in current location in south wing of West Stoa. *ALA* no. 24; Smith 2007, 230–231 cat. B44; LSA-191 (J. Lenaghan).
44. *Fragmentary base for Albinos,* awarded by the *polis*. H: 40, Diam.: 50, Letter H: 4–4.5 cm. Sixth century. Found in south wing of West Stoa. Inv. 84-078 = I-161. *ALA* no. 82; Smith 2007, 231 cat. B45; *IAph2007* 4.20; LSA-191 (J. Lenaghan); Appendix 1, In28.

Portrait statuary: imperial period
45. *Statue of woman in Ceres type with tall Trajanic fashion hairstyle.* Early second century. Found 1905 in north wing of West Stoa. Istanbul, Arch. Mus. inv. 2269. Smith *et al.* 2006, 207–209 cat. 89, pls. 69–70; Smith 2007, 222 cat. A9.
46. *Statue of woman wearing peplos with tall Trajanic fashion hairstyle.* Early second century. Found 1905 in north wing of West Stoa. Istanbul, Arch. Mus. inv. 2268. Smith *et al.* 2006, 209–211 cat. 90, pls. 69 and 71; Smith 2007, 222 cat. A10.
47. *Headless statue of woman in pudicitia type.* First century. Found 1905 in north wing of West Stoa. Istanbul, Arch. Mus. inv. 2267. Smith *et al.* 2006, 211–212 cat. 91, pl. 72; Smith 2007, 222 cat. A11.
48. *Lower body of female statue in Large Herculaneum type.* Late second to third century. Found 1905 in north wing of West Stoa. Ödemiş, Arch. Mus. inv. 719. Smith *et al.* 2006, 212–213 cat. 92, pl. 72; Smith 2007, 222 cat. A12.
49. *Trajanic bust of clean-shaven man with sword strap and chlamys.* Late first to early second century. Found 1965 in service tunnel beneath central staircase leading from West Stoa into East Court of Hadrianic Baths. Inv. 65-224, 65-513. Smith *et al.* 2006, 232–233 cat. 111, pls. 89–91; Smith 2007, 221 cat. A5.

Mythological and votive statuary
50. *Over-lifesize ideal female head with bow-knot hairstyle: caryatid from East Court of Hadrianic Baths?* H: 49, W: 29, D: 27.5 cm. Second century. Found 1974 during clearing of north wing of West Stoa. Inv. 74-291. Smith 2007, 224 cat. A20 (Pl. 71.D).
51. *Over-lifesize ideal female head with bow-knot hairstyle: caryatid from East Court of Hadrianic Baths?* H: 45 cm. Second century. Found 1905 in south wing of West Stoa. Istanbul, Arch. Mus. inv. 1614. Smith 2007, 224 cat. A22.
52. *Over-lifesize head of stephane-wearing ideal female figure, with open 'singing' mouth and back of head hollowed out.* H: 37, W: 32, D: 21 cm. Second or early third century. Found 1969 in south wing of West Stoa. Inv. 69-430. Unpublished (Pl. 71.E).
53. *Fragmentary under-lifesize head of ideal female figure with bow-knot hairstyle.* H: 19, W: 16, D: 17 cm. First–second century. Found 1969 in southwest corner of South Stoa, seemingly resting on the marble of the stylobate. Inv. 69-218. Unpublished (Pl. 71.F).
54. *Satyr head blowing double flute.* H: 31, W: 18, D: 22.5 cm. Later second century or fourth century. Found 1965 in service tunnel beneath central staircase leading from West Stoa into East Court of Hadrianic Baths. Inv. 65-236. Smith 1998, 257, figs. 12–13; Smith 2007, 224 cat. A26 (Pl. 71.G).

Portrait statuary: late antiquity
55. *Chlamydatus statue ('Younger Magistrate').* H: 176, W: 58 cm. Fifth century. Found 1904–1905 in north wing of West Stoa. Istanbul, Arch. Mus. inv. 2266. Smith 2007, 228 cat. A35; LSA-170 (R. R. R. Smith).
56. *Chlamydatus statue ('Elder Magistrate').* H: 181, W: 54, D: 30 cm. Fifth century. Found 1904–1905 in north wing of West Stoa. Istanbul, Arch. Mus. inv. 2255. Smith 2007, 228 cat. A36; LSA-169 (R. R. R. Smith).
57. *Theodosian imperial togatus statue ('Valentinian II').* H: 188, W: 66, D: 34.5 cm. AD 388–392. Found 1904–1905 near the centre of the West Stoa, at the steps leading into the East Court of the Hadrianic Baths. Istanbul, Arch. Mus. inv. 2264. Erim 1967, 243, pl. 72 fig. 26; Smith 2007, 228 cat. A37; LSA-163 (R. R. R. Smith) (Pl. 72.A).
58. *Headless Theodosian imperial togatus statue ('Arcadius').* H: 147, W: 54.5, D: 31 cm. AD 388–392. Found 1975 in West Stoa ('at about the central point of the portico': so *ALA* p. 48). Inv. 75-248. Smith 2007, 228 cat. A38; LSA-165 (R. R. R. Smith).
59. *Portrait head with squinting left eye and light beard.* H: 23.5, W: 21.5, D: 20 cm. Fifth century. Recomposed of two fragments, one found 1905 in the Hadrianic Baths, the other found 1985 in West Stoa. Inv. 85-040. Smith 2007, 229 cat. A39; LSA-174 (J. Lenaghan).
60. *Portrait head of gaunt man with thick hair and neck pillar.* H: 26, W: 23, D: 24 cm. Fifth century. Found 1969 at south end of West Stoa. Inv. 69-431. Smith 2007, 229 cat. A40; LSA-181 (J. Lenaghan).
61. *Portrait head of fleshy-faced, clean-shaven man.* H: 26, W: 14, D: 14.5 cm. Mid to late fourth century. Found 1969 at south end of West Stoa. Inv. 69-210. Smith 2007, 229 cat. A41; LSA-180 (J. Lenaghan) (Pl. 72.B).

E. SCULPTURAL FINDS FROM THE POOL AND ITS SURROUNDINGS

Finds from the pool

Excavations inside the pool in the Place of Palms have revealed a very large number of sculptural finds, the majority of which formed part of the rubble dump that was deposited when the structure was filled in during the seventh century AD (see Fig. 56–58; Pl. 78.A–B; Ch. 8 §A). These finds can be usefully divided into two categories: those whose original display contexts can be established with a high level of probability; and those whose original display contexts are unknown.

We have already encountered several finds belonging to the first category: the tail of the 'Blue Horse' from the Achilles and Troilos group (**88**), the imperial head fragment from the Theodosian group in the West Stoa (**110**), and the Eros pilaster capitals from the North Stoa discussed in Ch. 3 §D, for example. But there are also other finds in this category that should be enumerated here. We might mention, for instance, two joining fragments of a high-quality portrait head of a young male honorand excavated at the east end of the pool, whose fringe and physiognomy indicate a date in the early imperial period (**72**). Both the over-lifesize scale of this head and its icy, classicising physiognomy suggest that it might originally have belonged to one of the Julio-Claudian imperial portrait statues set up in the *aediculae* of the Sebasteion Propylon. In this case, the head probably represented an imperial prince of the Tiberian period.[64]

At the opposite, western end of the pool, excavations unearthed a series of finds that can be associated with the Hadrianic Baths. Best known, perhaps, is the head of the *Old Fisherman* statue (**94**), the body of which was excavated in the East Court of the Baths. But we should also mention three inscribed bases recording the dedication of (unspecified) statues by one Ammia(?) (**63**), by Klaudia Melitine, the wife of Tiberius Attalos Agatheinos (**62**), and by an anonymous high priestess who was also a 'daughter of the city' (**64**). All three bases—and four others excavated elsewhere in the Place of Palms (**65, 66, 67, 68**)—belong to a series of more than twenty bases dedicated by women from the leading families of Aphrodisias, which were originally set up in the East Court of the Baths.[65] The subject of the statues that stood on top is given by an exceptional base in the series recording the dedication of 'the caryatid' (τὴν καρυατιν) by Titus Flavius Athenagoras Agathos on behalf of his deceased wife Flavia Attalis Ailiane.[66] The most plausible 'caryatid' candidates are a series of over-lifesize ideal female heads excavated in the Baths and elsewhere, many of which have cuttings in the backs and/or tops of their heads that suggest an architectural function. Five such heads have been excavated in the Place of Palms itself: two ideal over-lifesize female heads with elaborate bow-knot hairstyles found in the West Stoa (**50, 51**); a battered female head excavated in the western portion of the North Stoa (**101**); and two heads with classicising physiognomy and carefully hollowed-out crowns found at the western end of the pool (**92, 93**).

Viewed together, then, the finds in this category offer a useful conspectus of some of the sources of the rubble deposited in the pool when the structure began to be filled in the mid seventh century. Much of the sculptural debris seems to have been collected from structures located in the immediate vicinity of the Place of Palms: the Propylon, the North and West Stoas, the Hadrianic Baths, the Civil Basilica, and the Sebasteion Propylon.

We have no way of determining the original display contexts of many of the other finds excavated in the pool: the most we can say is that they *may* have been set up in the Place of Palms or its surrounding buildings during antiquity. This conclusion applies to the majority of portrait statue finds excavated in the rubble deposit(s) at the bottom of the pool, many of which have already been well-studied. Particularly striking are two late antique finds from the pool's west end, originally thought to belong to a single statue but since dissociated:[67] a male portrait head with a stubbled beard pecked into his cheeks and an undercut 'mop' hairstyle of the kind fashionable in court circles in Constantinople in the early sixth century (**111**); and a lifesize statue of a seated, himation-wearing figure, which was made in the fourth century but then repaired and re-used at a later stage (**112**). The former is precisely the kind of head that we would expect to find on a portrait of one of the aristocrats who funded the regeneration of the Place of Palms in the late fifth or early sixth century. The latter is one of two seated portrait statues excavated in the park, the other being the recycled seated himation statue displayed at the centre of the basin at the Propylon (Ch. 6 §E, cat. **St. 1**). It would be interesting to know whether these two seated statues were configured in some kind of direct visual relationship at opposite ends of the long pool.

In addition to such well processed finds (see also **113, 114, 115**), recent excavation campaigns in the Place of Palms uncovered four further portrait heads whose original identities and display contexts are again lost to us, but which attest the astonishing quality and variety of Aphrodisian portrait production throughout antiquity:

(1) A fragmentary, over-lifesize female portrait head with a deep socket drilled into the neck for its attachment into the shoulders of a statue (**73**).

(2) A badly worn, over-lifesize male portrait head of the late second or early third century found in two joining parts, which depicts a mature figure with a fleshy face, flat hair and a thick moustache (**74**). This head was discussed in detail in Ch. 6 §E.

(3) An excellently preserved male portrait head of the Theodosian period found lying face-up in the rubble fill adjacent to the northern pool wall (**116**). The head has a neck tenon with a central dowel hole for insertion into the shoulders of a draped statue, and depicts a broad-faced figure with narrow eyes, a thick beard, and hair brushed forwards into a dense fringe. It also has a tiny covert inscription carved behind the beard at the top of the neck: 'ΧΜΓ', short for Χριστὸν Μαρία γεννᾷ ('Maria gives birth to Christ'). This Christian acronym is found on other portraits of the same period,[68] but is usually inscribed on the crown of the head. It may have constituted a covert expression of faith on the part of the Christian sculptor.

---

64 Portrait statues of Julio-Claudian princes: Massner 1982, 95–97; Fittschen and Zanker 1985, 19–33 cats. 19–26. Alternatively, the head might have belonged to a portrait of a young man from a local aristocratic family that had secured Roman citizenship: for a comparandum from the Theatre, see Smith *et al.* 2006, 104–107 cat. 2.

65 Caryatids in East Court of Hadrianic Baths: Erim and Reynolds 1989, 521–522; Reynolds 2002; Smith 2007, 210–213 with cats. A16–A24, B11–B25; Öztürk 2016, 200–202; Wilson 2016a, 189–192.

66 For this base, see Reynolds 2002.

67 Dissociation of head and statue: Smith 1999b, 718–719.

68 Comparanda: *ALA* no. 145; Smith 2002, 150–153; Cahill 2010, 575 cat. 219.

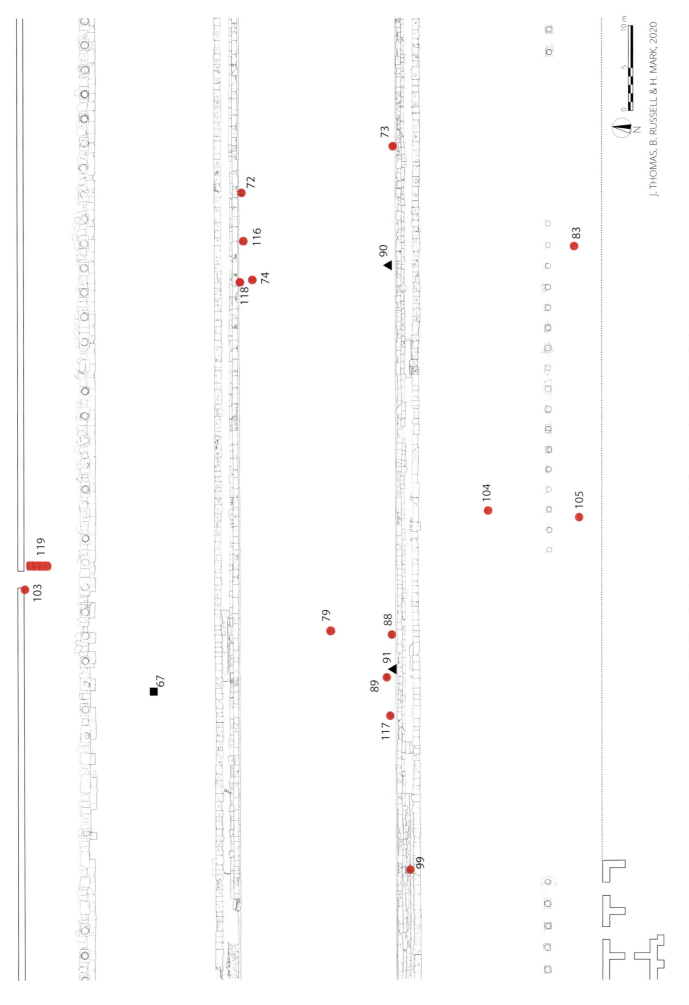

Fig. 58. Plan of catalogued sculptural finds from central part of Place of Palms.
Red dots represent statuary finds, black squares represent statue bases, and black triangles represent architectural and relief sculpture.

(4) A lifesize male portrait head of the early sixth century depicting a local notable with stubbled beard, creased forehead, and a remarkable combination of a bald pate with the fashionable Constantinopolitan 'mop' hairstyle (**117**). The figure's eyes have the same 'raised-disc' pupils as several other high-quality portraits belonging to the latest phase of statue production at Aphrodisias, including the famous portrait of the governor Fl. Palmatus set up in the Tetrastoon in front of the Theatre.[69]

Similarly difficult to contextualise are the many fragments of mythological and votive sculpture excavated in the pool. Among the most technically accomplished is an attractive, under-lifesize head of a lean-faced, *stephane*-wearing goddess excavated in the ring drain, which can be dated on stylistic and technical grounds to the first century (**99**). The goddess has finely pierced earlobes for the addition of metal earrings, and her hair is tied into an elaborate chignon at the nape of her neck. More recently discovered examples include a highly polished relief carved from imported white marble, which depicts the expressive face of a 'barbarian' with tufty hair and overtly 'non-Greek' physiognomy (**90**); and a battered, under-lifesize head of a goddess or personification, whose upper part was clearly worked and added separately (**89**).

While many of these finds clearly belonged to large-scale, public monuments, excavations in the pool also brought to light a handful of finds that are smaller in scale and more personal in conception. A good example is a small votive plaque depicting the eyes and brows of a face, which was surely dedicated to a healing divinity by an individual whose eyes had been cured (**91**).[70] Higher in quality is a statuette depicting a pagan priestess, which can be dated to the fourth or fifth century on account of its highly polished finish (**97**). The priestess is shown wearing a long, thick chiton and a himation pulled over the back of her head to form a veil, which is held in place by a flat fillet with a round central bust-crown. This statuette might have been produced for a wealthy pagan patron at a time when the political influence of Christians was growing in Aphrodisias.[71] The same might also be true of a small marble headdress (*polos*) belonging to a statuette of Aphrodite of Aphrodisias, which, judging by its sculptural finish, was likewise carved during late antiquity (**95**).

Finds from the surrounding stoas

Whereas the Aphrodite of Aphrodisias statuette would have depicted the goddess in her local guise as a stiff, archaising Anatolian fertility deity, another statuette excavated in the eastern half of the South Stoa showed Aphrodite in a rather different format, wearing a clinging, translucent chiton (**106**). This second Aphrodite is one of a series of miscellaneous finds excavated in the stoas surrounding the pool that are difficult to associate with particular display contexts, much like many of the finds from the pool itself. Other examples include a fragmentary torso of an under-lifesize naked male figure wearing the chlamys (**103**); an over-lifesize head of a *stephane*-wearing goddess with an expressive, open mouth and architectural cuttings in the back of her head (**52**);[72] and a battered double-herm depicting a pair of bearded male figures (**105**).

Pool and surrounding areas: bases, statuary, reliefs

Statue bases

62. *Caryatid base dedicated to the* dēmos *by Klaudia Melitine, wife of Tiberius Attalos Agatheinos, and signed by the sculptor Andronikos son of Mousaios.* H: 66.5, W: 61.5, D: 60.5, Letter H: 3.8–4.0 cm. Late Hadrianic. Found 1989 at west end of pool. Inv. I-162. Smith 2007, 226 cat. B24; Wilson 2016a, 187 cat. 13.

63. *Caryatid base dedicated to the* dēmos *by Ammia(?), daughter of […].* H: 70, W: 52, D: 53, Letter H: 4.5–5 cm. Late Hadrianic. Found 1989 at west end of pool. Inv. I-165. Smith 2007, 226 cat. B23; Wilson 2016a, 187 cat. 15.

64. *Fragmentary Caryatid base dedicated to the* patris *by […], high priestess, daughter of the city.* H: 65, W: 58, D: 57, Letter H: 4.5 cm. Late Hadrianic. Found 1989 at west end of pool. Inv. I-163. Smith 2007, 226 cat. B25b; Wilson 2016a, 187 cat. 18.

65. *Caryatid base dedicated to the* patris *by Ulpia Apollonia.* H: 60, W: 62, D: 53, Letter H: 4 cm. Late Hadrianic. Found 1984 in westernmost part of North Stoa. Inv. 84-055 = I-75. Smith 2007, 226 cat. B25a; Wilson 2016a, 186 cat. 2.

66. *Fragmentary Caryatid base, dedicated to the* patris *by […], priestess for life of the goddess Aphrodite and flower bearer, daughter of the city.* H: 64, W: 56, D: 55, Letter H: 5–6 cm. Late Hadrianic. Found 1984 in front (to the south) of Column N65 of North Stoa. Inv. I-79. Smith 2007, 226 cat. B22; Wilson 2016a, 187 cat. 17.

67. *Fragmentary Caryatid base, possibly dedicated by Flavia Attalis Ailiane.* H: 24, W: 27, D: 20 cm. Late Hadrianic. Surface find north of pool in 2015, in trench 15.2. Inv. 15-027. Unpublished.

68. *Caryatid base, dedicated by Aelia Stateilia Stratonike.* H: 64, W: 59, D: 54, Letter H: 5.5 cm. Late Hadrianic.

---

69 Other 'raised disc' pupils: Smith 1999b, 714–716; 1999a, 168–169; 2016c, 300–302 no. 4; LSA-173 (J. Lenaghan); LSA-177 (R. R. R. Smith); LSA-198 (R. R. R. Smith); LSA-219 (R. R. R. Smith). Comparanda from Ephesos: LSA-697 and LSA-707 (both J. Auinger).
70 Three comparable votive plaques were excavated in the Hadrianic Baths in the 1960s (Inv. 63-568, 65-215), two of which were inscribed with dedications to Asklepios. Further comparanda from the Asklepeion at Pergamon: Petsalis-Diomidis 2010, 257–260.
71 So Smith 1996, 20–21, comparing the statuette to late antique statuettes of Kybele and Asklepios excavated in the House of Kybele. Compare also a small head of Helios from the Theatre Baths, for which see Smith and Lenaghan 2008, 310 cat. 41.
72 This head resembles an over-lifesize female head with a similarly expressive open mouth excavated in the *cavea* of the Theatre: Erim and Smith 1991, 86 no. 22, 87 fig. 24.

Found 1984 in the area immediately south of the south corner of the West Stoa, adjacent to the Civil Basilica. Inv. 84-071 = I-80. Smith 2007, 226 cat. B25; Wilson 2016a, 187 cat.16.

69. *Base for Julia Faustina, set up by her husband.* H: 45, W: 55, D: 26, Letter H: 5.5–7 cm. Second century. Found 1970 in South Stoa, in front of Civil Basilica. *IAph2007* 4.118; Appendix 1, In23.

Portrait statuary: imperial period

70. *Bearded portrait head.* Mid second century. Found 1988 at east end of pool. Inv. 88-002. Smith *et al.* 2006, 268–269 cat. 170, pls. 116–117.
71. *Veiled female head.* First century. Inv. 89-008. Found 1989 at east end of pool. Smith *et al.* 2006, 287 cat. 202, fig. 26, pl. 137.
72. *Over-lifesize Julio-Claudian portrait head, possibly depicting an imperial prince.* H: 34, W: 22, D: 23.5 cm. First century. Recomposed of two fragments, found 2016 and 2017 close to north pool wall towards its east end (in **4328**). Inv. 16-052, 17-033. Unpublished. (Pl. 72.C)
73. *Fragment of over-lifesize female portrait head with deep socket in neck for attachment to a statue.* H: 29, W: 16, D: 20 cm. First–second century. Found 2016 adjacent to south pool wall (in **4341**). Inv. 16-061. Unpublished (Pl. 72.F).
74. *Male portrait head with lank hair, heavy moustache and bearded cheeks.* H: 28, W: 20, D: 20.5 cm. Late second or early third century. Two joining fragments found 2017 in rubble deposit adjacent to north pool wall (in **4328**). Inv. 17-053, 17-112. Unpublished (Pl. 66.C–D and 67).
75. *Head of young priest wearing diadem.* First century. Found 1988 at west end of pool. Inv. 88-005. Smith *et al.* 2006, 187–188 cat. 60, pl. 56.
76. *Battered head of youth.* First century. Found 1990 in 'north side of the rubble wall' adjacent to excavation trench. Inv. 90-011. Smith *et al.* 2006, 276–277 cat. 181, pl. 127.
77. *Head of girl.* First century. Found 1988 at west end of pool. Inv. 88-026. Smith *et al.* 2006, 286 cat. 200, pls. 134–135.
78. *Draped upper torso of female statue with head broken away.* H: 40, W: 54, D: 29 cm. First–second century. Found 1989 in rubble deposit at west end of the pool. Inv. 89-014. Smith 1996, 19 fig. 9, 20.
79. *Lower torso fragment of lifesize naked male figure.* H: 32, W: 37, D: 38 cm. First–second century. Found 2017 built into later field wall above the area of pool (**4399**). Inv. 17-009. Unpublished (Pl. 72.D).
80. *Right hip of draped female statue.* First century. Found 1984 towards west end of North Stoa. Inv. 84-060. Smith *et al.* 2006, 213 cat. 93, pl. 72.
81. *Fragment of chlamys bust.* Second–third century. Found 1972 in east part of North Stoa. Inv. 72-168. Smith *et al.* 2006, 235 cat. 116, pl. 93.
82. *Chest fragment of female bust with rosette tabula.* Second–third century. Surface find in 1971 in North Stoa. Find no.: PT 71.57. Smith *et al.* 2006, 248 cat. 146, pl. 104.
83. *Unfinished male head broken from bust.* First century. Found 1986 in the central part of the South Stoa, in front of the Theatre Hill. Inv. 86-030. Smith *et al.* 2006, 249 cat. 153, pl. 105.
84. *Fragment of upper right torso of cuirassed male figure.* H: 31, W: 16, D: 21 cm. Imperial period. Stray find during excavation of east part of South Stoa in 1986. Inv. 86-068. Unpublished (Pl. 72.E).

Mythological and votive sculpture

85. *Under-lifesize head of horse.* H: 24, W: 16, D: 27 cm. Pendant piece to **86**. First–second century. Found 1988 in rubble deposit at east end of pool. Inv. 88-003. Unpublished (Pl. 73.A).
86. *Under-lifesize head of horse.* H: 34.5, W: 22, D: 27.5 cm. Pendant piece to **85**. First–second century. Found 1989 in rubble deposit at east end of pool. Inv. 89-007. Unpublished (Pl. 73.B).
87. *Headless eagle standing on triangular plinth.* H: 57, W: 28, D: 39 cm. First–second century. Found 1990 close to the southeast curve of the pool. Inv. 90-017. Unpublished (Pl. 73.C).
88. *Tail of 'Blue Horse' from Achilles and Troilos statue group.* H: 37, W: 15, D: 14 cm. First century. Found 2017 in rubble deposit adjacent to south pool wall (**4471**). Inv. 17-036. Achilles and Troilos group: Smith and Hallett 2015. Tail: Smith 2021 (Pl. 73.D–E).
89. *Battered lower part of under-lifesize head of female divinity or personification*: upper part of head originally carved and added separately. H: 18, W: 22, D: 22 cm. Second–third century. Found 2017 in rubble deposit adjacent to south pool wall (**4471**). Inv. 17-060. Unpublished (Pl. 74.A).
90. *Fragment of relief carved from imported marble depicting head of barbarian with tufty hair.* H: 25, W: 15.5, D: 9 cm. Second century? Found 2017 in rubble deposit at bottom of pool (**4461**). Inv. 17-049. Unpublished (Pl. 74.C).
91. *Votive plaque with representation of eyes and brow.* H: 11, W: 6.8, D: 3.2 cm. High imperial period? Found 2017 in rubble deposit at bottom of pool (**4448**). Inv. 17-063. Unpublished (Pl. 74.B).
92. *Over-lifesize ideal female head with classicising physiognomy, centrally parted hair fastened by chignon, and hollowed out top of crown.* H: 32, W: 27, D: 33 cm. Second century. Found 1988 in rubble deposit at west end of pool. Inv. 88-004. Erim 1988, 751 fig. 12; Erim 1990, 20 fig. 24; Smith 2007, 211–213, 224 cat. A23 (Pl. 74.D).
93. *Over-lifesize ideal female head with classicising physiognomy, hair 'folds' over ears, and hollowed out top of crown.* H: 30.5, W: 27.5, D: 25.5 cm. Second century. Found 1988 in rubble deposit at west end of pool. Inv. 88-025. Erim 1988, 752 fig. 13; Erim 1990, 20 fig. 23; Smith 2007, 211–213, 224 cat. A24.

94. *Head of Old Fisherman statue.* H: 24, W: 17.5, D: 21.5 cm. Joins with body of same statue found 1965 in Hadrianic Baths. Late second century or fourth century. Found 1989 in rubble deposit at west end of pool. Inv. 89-003. Wiegand 1916; Smith 1996, 58–63; Smith 1998, 253–260; Smith 2007, 213–214, 225 cat. A27; Van Voorhis 2018, 34–35.
95. *Miniature marble headdress* (polos) *belonging to Aphrodite of Aphrodisias statuette.* H: 4.7, W: 3.3, D: 2.9 cm. Third–fourth century. Found 1989 in rubble deposit at west end of pool. Inv. 89-010. Smith 1996, 19 fig. 10, 20; Brody 2007, 18–19 cat. 7.
96. *Body fragment of harnessed, under-lifesize quadruped, probably a horse.* H: 23.5, W: 15, D: 48 cm. Imperial period. Found 1989 in rubble deposit at west end of pool. Inv. 89-015. Unpublished. (Pl. 74.E)
97. *Highly polished statuette of veiled priestess.* H: 16, W: 6.5, D: 4.5 cm. Fourth–fifth century. Found 1990 in rubble deposit at west end of pool. Inv. 90-001. Smith 1996, 20–23, 24 figs. 17–18. (Pl. 74.F)
98. *Bronze leg of under-lifesize male statue.* H: 16, W: 6.5, D: 4.5 cm. Imperial period. Found 1990 in rubble deposit at west end of pool. Inv. 90-006. Smith 1996, 19 fig. 13, 20. (Pl. 75.A)
99. *Under-lifesize head of goddess or personification wearing rosette stephane.* H: 25, W: 19, D: 20 cm. First century. Found 1990 in ring drain between the inner and outer pool walls at west end of pool. Inv. 90-010. Smith 1996, 20, 21 fig. 12. (Pl. 75.B)
100. *Battered head of long-haired, under-lifesize male figure.* H: 21, W: 12.5, D: 13.5 cm. First–second century? Found 1990 in rubble deposit at west end of pool. Inv. 90-012. Unpublished. (Pl. 75.C)
101. *Battered head of over-lifesize ideal female figure with back of head hollowed out: caryatid from East Court of Hadrianic Baths?* H: 29, W: 24, D: 24 cm. Second century. Found 1984 in westernmost part of North Stoa. Inv. 84-049. Unpublished. (Pl. 75.D)
102. *Battered under-lifesize head of ideal male figure wearing wreath.* H: 18.5, W: 17, D: 16.5 cm. High imperial? Found 1984 near to westernmost part of North Stoa. Inv. 84-048. Unpublished. (Pl. 75.E)
103. *Torso of under-lifesize male figure dressed in heroic nude costume with chlamys.* H: 34, W: 28, D: 16 cm. First–second century. Found 1985 built into modern field wall constructed directly on top of rear wall of North Stoa. Inv. 85-101. Unpublished. (Pl. 76.A)
104. *Under-lifesize head of a wreath-wearing ideal male youth.* H: 23, W: 20, D: 20 cm. First century. Found 2018 in rubble deposit immediately south of the pool. Inv. 18-074. Unpublished (Pl. 76.B).
105. *Battered double-herm with back-to-back heads of two bearded male figures.* H: 23.5, W: 17, D: 19 cm. First–second century. Found 1985 in central part of South Stoa. Inv. 85-158. Unpublished (Pl. 76.C).
106. *Statuette of Aphrodite (Venus Genetrix type).* H: 30, W: 18.5, D: 4 cm. First century. Found 1986 in eastern part of South Stoa. Inv. 86-141. Unpublished (Pl. 76.E).
107. *Marble sundial dedicated by Kl. D[…], broken across the dial.* H: 35, W: 32, D: 21 cm. Second–third century. Found 1992 in spoil heap immediately to the east of the Place of Palms. Inv. 92-053. Smith 1996, 65, fig. 67; *IAph2007* 4.114; Appendix 1, In35a.

Fountain sculpture
108. *Fountain statuette depicting naked boy riding on a dolphin.* H: 38.5, W: 19, D: 22.5 cm. Second–third century. Found 1990 in rubble deposit at east end of pool. Inv. 90-005. Smith 1996, 20, 22 fig. 14; Wilson 2016b, 116 (Pl. 76.F).
109. *Fountain sculpture depicting frog standing on plinth,* made from local blue-grey marble. H: 26.5, W: 20, D: 43.5 cm. First–second century. Found 1986 in easternmost part of South Stoa. Inv. 86-075. Wilson 2016b, 116–117 (Pl. 76.D).

Portrait statuary: late antiquity
110. *Two joining fragments from upper part of diademed Theodosian imperial head.* H: 24.5, W: 21, D: 13 cm. AD 388–392. Belongs to same statue as **58**. Found 1988 at west end of pool. Inv. 88-027. Smith 2007, 229 cat. A42; LSA-168 (J. Lenaghan).
111. *Separately carved portrait head with light stubble beard and undercut Constantinopolitan 'mop' fashion hairstyle.* H: 31, W: 24, D: 25 cm. Late fifth to early sixth century. Found 1989 at west end of pool. Inv. 89-002A. Smith 1999b; Smith 2007, 229 cat. A43; LSA-173 (J. Lenaghan).
112. *Headless seated himation statue.* H: 135, W: 71.5, D: 58 cm. Fourth century. Found 1989 at west end of pool. Inv. 89-002B. Smith 1999b; Smith 2007, 229 cat. A44; LSA-172 (J. Lenaghan) (Pl. 76.G).
113. *Portrait head with short beard and balding brow.* H: 26, W: 17, D: 19 cm. Fifth century. Found 1989 at west end of pool. Inv. 89-004. Smith 2007, 229 cat. A45; LSA-182 (J. Lenaghan).
114. *Fragmentary upper part of portrait head with brushed forward hair.* H: 26, W: 20.5, D: 21.5 cm. Fifth century. Found 1989 at west end of pool. Inv. 89-005. Smith 2007, 229 cat. A46; LSA-184 (J. Lenaghan).
115. *Fragmentary portrait with bald pate, stubble beard, and neck worked for insertion into a socket.* H: 31, W: 21, D: 17.5 cm. Fifth century. Found 1989 at west end of pool. Inv. 89-006. Smith 2007, 229 cat. A47; LSA-530 (J. Lenaghan).
116. *Over-lifesize male portrait head with Theodosian hairstyle and beard, neck tenon for insertion, and covert 'ΧΜΓ' inscription at top of neck.* H: 33.5, W: 23.5, D: 25 cm. Late fourth or early fifth century. Found 2017 lying face-up in rubble deposit adjacent to north pool wall (**4328**). Inv. 17-059. Unpublished (Pl. 77.A).
117. *Male portrait head with stubble beard, bald pate and Constantinopolitan 'mop' hairstyle.* H: 27.5, W: 28, D: 23.5 cm. Sixth century. Found 2017 in rubble deposit adjacent to south pool wall (**4471**). Inv. 17-070. Unpublished (Pl. 77.C).

118. *Ankle and scroll support fragment belonging to late antique togatus.* H: 35, W: 28, D: 15 cm. Late fourth to fifth century. Found 2015 built into field wall constructed in area above pool (**4028**). Inv. 15-017. Unpublished (Pl. 77.B).

119. *Torso of over-lifesize late antique togatus statue.* H: 101, W: 62, D: 35 cm. Late fourth to early fifth century. Found 1985 in North Stoa, in front of entrance to southern stoa of the Agora. Inv. 85-100. Nbk 272: *Portico of Tiberius 'North-Central-East'* (K. Erim and J. Gorence), 33–35. Unpublished.

F. CONCLUSION

Viewed together, the sculptural finds from the Place of Palms remind us that the complex—as excavated—dates to the early seventh century AD. Indeed, the majority of finds that can be associated with specific display contexts belong to statue assemblages that were curated during late antiquity, notably Doulkitios' reconstructed Propylon and the honorific portrait gallery in the West Stoa. Doubtless there were other important statue assemblages in earlier times, as can be seen from the large number of statue base recesses on the pool edge that date from before late antiquity. In the present state of our evidence, however, these earlier assemblages cannot be reconstructed with the same level of certainty.

Although a large portion of the sculptural finds from the complex can no longer be contextualised, the sheer quantity and variety of the surviving material is instructive. This wide-ranging selection of finds offers a fascinating snapshot of the extraordinary scale and scope of the consumption of marble statuary and sculpture in Aphrodisias throughout antiquity.

CHAPTER 8

The End of the Place of Palms, Seventh Century AD

Andrew Wilson, Ben Russell, Allison Kidd, Ahmet Tolga Tek, Hüseyin Köker,
Tim Penn, Hugh Jeffery, Erica Rowan, and Ulrike Outschar

The Place of Palms, as restored in the late fifth and early sixth century AD, served as a revitalised urban park, with some service and perhaps commercial activities, and a grand display of urban aesthetics in late antique Aphrodisias. A century and a half later, however, it met a violent and dramatic end. This chapter presents the stratigraphic evidence for the first phases of filling in the pool, and what the material recovered from them allows one to deduce about the timing and the nature of the processes that brought the monumental life of this area to a close. The conclusions have a bearing on the seismic history of Karia in the seventh century, and also on the much-discussed question of the end of the classical city in Asia Minor, the degree to which it may have been connected with Persian invasions in the early seventh century, and with Arab raids in the middle and later seventh century. It was during this period also that the city's name was changed from Aphrodisias to Stavropolis, 'City of the Cross'.

A. STRATIGRAPHIC EVIDENCE (AK, BR, & AW)

The catastrophic end of the Place of Palms as a monumental public space is evidenced most clearly by two successive phases of deposits within the monumental pool, representing artificial dumps of debris resulting from large-scale clearance activities after extensive damage to much of the architecture in the wider complex.[1]

The first clearance deposit

The first deposit found within the pool comprises an extensive scatter of finds lying directly on its floor across its central and southern sectors (**4482**; Fig. 59; Pl. 78.A). This yielded substantial quantities of materials from the surrounding architecture of the Place of Palms, mostly the North and South Stoas: 910 kg of roof tiles, 230 kg of marble revetment (already discussed in Ch. 4 §D), fragments of Ionic capitals from the North Stoa, as well as numerous waterlogged and charred wooden planks and rafters, many of which preserved evidence of nail holes, cut marks, and flat-sawn ends; the longest of these was 1.46 m long, 10 cm wide, and 4 cm thick.[2] Nails (26 in total) and revetment pins (7) originating from the stoas were also recovered.[3] Among the other finds were glass lamp fragments[4] and a gold glass plaque,[5] metal tools and blades (4),[6] metal architectural fittings (5),[7] metal objects related to commercial activities such as parts of balance scales (3),[8] a coin weight,[9] copper alloy bells (2),[10] a copper alloy buckle,[11] an iron cross,[12] a stirrup,[13] and weapons, including what were probably javelins (8).[14] Sculptural finds, including a section of drapery and a foot, probably come from statuary displayed on the pool edge or in the stoas.[15] This range of finds matches the kinds of assemblages excavated on the pool bottom at its eastern and western ends in the late 1980s and in 1990. All of these materials were distributed fairly evenly across the pool floor. Coins from this deposit dated from AD 541/2 in the reign of Justinian I to an issue of Constans II, 643/4 (Table 7).

Along the north side of the pool and deposited at the same time as the material discussed above was a very substantial accumulation of material, again lying directly on the pool floor (**4328**; Pl. 78.2). This deposit was found across the whole of the north side of the pool, with a maximum thickness of 49

---

1 Since nearly all of the finds referred to in this chapter are from trench SAg.17.1, that trench number is omitted from the finds numbers here, which are given as context number and then find number, for example 4482.F868 instead of SAg.17.1.4482.F868. Finds from other trenches are given their full trench and find number.

2 4482.F868. For the other wooden planks and rafters, 4482.F887, 4482.F888, 4482.F891. A series of other wooden elements were assigned in the field to the context above **4482**—the silt layer labelled **4448**—but they were found close to the pool floor and excavated out of sequence because of their extreme fragility, and so are listed here: 4448.F719, 4448.F770 to 4448.F772, 4448.F777.

3 Nails: 4482.F860, 4482.F883, 4482.F885 (4 nails as bulk find), 4482.F893, 4482.F897 (6 nails as bulk find), 4482.F918, 4482.F922, 4482.F929, 4482.F938, 4482.F942, 4482.F945, 4482.F955, 4482.F958, 4482.F959 4482.F1053, 4484.F944, 4484.F948, 4484.F949. Revetment pins: 4482.F898, 4482.F899, 4482.F901–902, 4482.F904, 4482.F915, 4482.F920.

4 For example 4482.F953.
5 4482.M2648.
6 4482.F914, 4482.F939, Inv. 17-122 (4482.F951), 4482.F957.
7 4482.F900; 4482.F903; 4482.F905–906; 4482.F917; 4482.F919.
8 Inv. 17-119 (4482.F913); Inv. 17-120 (4484.F946); Inv. 17-121 (4402.F962).
9 4482.C240/241/242.
10 Inv. 17-169 (4482.F875); Inv. 17-175 (4484.F963).
11 4482.F954.
12 Inv. 17-090 (4482.F886).
13 Nbk 316: *Portico of Tiberius: W Pool, Book I; E Pool* (A.T. Tek, 1990), F24, Photo 22; Penn, Russell, and Wilson 2021.
14 Nbk 307: *SW Portico of Tiberius* (F. Thode, 1989), F82–85; F87, 28–9; Nbk 304: *Portico of Tiberius W I* (A. Page and F. Thode, 1989), 66, F150; Inv. 17-083 (4482.F876). See below for further discussion.
15 Inv. 17-072 (4482.M2662), Inv. 17-073 (4482.M2666), Inv. 17-103 (4482.M2640), Inv. 17-104 (4482.M2648).

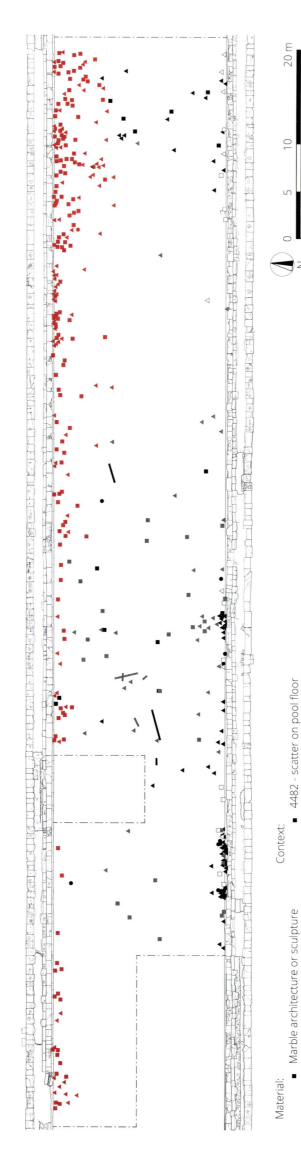

Fig. 59. Plan of finds in clearance deposits at bottom of pool.

Table 7. Coins from the floor of the pool and first clean-up deposit.

Catalogue number	Context	Year excavated	Description	Date
233	4482	2017	Late Roman, unidentified	
240	4482	2017	Justinian I, Constantinople mint	541/2
255	PT.W.88.I floor of pool	1988	Tiberius II, Constantinople mint	578/9
257	PT.W.88.I floor of pool	1988	Tiberius II, Nicomedia mint	580/1
270	4482	2017	Phocas, Nicomedia mint	605/6
274	4482	2017	Heraclius, Constantinople mint	613
275	4482	2017	Heraclius, Constantinople mint	613 or 613/4
278	4328	2017	Heraclius, Constantinople mint	631/2
279	4482	2017	Heraclius, Constantinople mint	632/3 or 633/4
280	4328	2017	Heraclius, Constantinople mint	634/5
289	4482	2017	Constans II, Constantinople mint	643/4

cm against the pool wall, tapering away towards the south for a maximum distance of 7.39 m from the interior pool wall; the highest concentration of debris was found at the eastern end of the excavated area. This evidently represents a dump of debris, which had been cleared from the surrounding area and thrown into the pool from the north side. It must have resulted from extensive damage to, or destruction of, the North Stoa and the Propylon, and perhaps other surrounding architecture as well.

The finds in this deposit were consistent with those from the scatter across the pool floor but were much more concentrated. They include 5,446 kg of roof tiles, a similar quantity of building stone, 1,202 kg of marble revetment, and a substantial but somewhat smaller quantity of structural and decorative marble architectural fragments, as well as a significant amount of disintegrated mortar and charcoal. Those architectural elements that could be identified came from the North Stoa and the Propylon. Among these were fragments of Corinthian pilaster capitals, decorated with erotes, from the North Stoa; these have been discussed already in Ch. 3 §D and other examples of them were also found as residual in later contexts.[16] The roof tiles show signs of weathering commensurate with long use. Worked pieces of wood in the form of planks and rafters (4), again with evidence of nail holes and saw marks, were also recovered, the largest of which was 50 cm in length and 6 cm thick;[17] importantly, many of these showed burning or extensive charring. None of these fragments was decorated, unlike the carved panel found in the pool in 1989,[18] though it is likely they all came from the ceiling and roof of the North Stoa.

While architectural remains dominated this deposit, several utensils,[19] glass fragments,[20] and a substantial number of metal objects were found: nails (8 in total),[21] iron architectural fittings (4),[22] an iron stylus,[23] iron buckle,[24] blades (7),[25] a glass pendant,[26] copper alloy tools (2),[27] two copper alloy weights,[28] copper alloy cross pendant,[29] copper alloy vessel,[30] copper alloy bell,[31] copper alloy buckle,[32] copper alloy hinge,[33] rolled lead scrolls (4),[34] and weaponry including arrowheads (3)[35] and a spearhead;[36] the most important of these finds are discussed further below (§D). These objects give us an insight into the activities taking place around the pool in the final phase of the Place of Palms and some of them point toward commercial activity.

---

16   Corinthian pilaster capital fragments: Inv. 17-054 (4328.M2291), Inv. 17-062 (4448.M2578), Inv. 17-106 (4329.M2387), and Inv. 17-148 to Inv. 17-152 (4328.M2737, 4328.M2710, 4328.M2696, 4328.M2727, 4328.M2657), Inv. 17-154 to Inv. 17-157 (4328.M2671, 4328.M2759, 4328.M2672, 4328.M2739), Inv. 17-160 to Inv. 17-164 (4328.M2699, 4466.M2761, 4466.M2770, 4328.M2736, 4466.M2760), Inv. 17-166 (4328.M2705), Inv. 17-168 (4466.M2795), 4328.M2674, as well as Inv. 85-124, Inv. 85-125, Inv. 12-24, and Inv. 17-030 (4329.M1623).
17   4466.F996. For the other planks: 4466.F998; 4466.F1008 (with nail holes); 4328.F862.
18   Smith 1996, 19–20, fig. 11; see Pl. 12.B.
19   Such as a marble pestle (4466.M2777).
20   For example 4466.F966; 4466.F1001; 4466.F1042.
21   4328.F730, 4328.F979, 4328.F991, 4466.F1025, 4466.F1036, 4466.F1041, SAg.17.2.5033.F23, SAg.17.2.5033.F24.
22   4466.F1005; 4466.F1006; 4466.F1032; 4328.F971.
23   Inv. 17-127 (4466.F1018).
24   4328.F984.
25   Three blades with tang attached: 4466.F1013, 4466.F1014, 4466.F1019; and four other blades: 4328.F985, 4328.F986, 4466.F1020, 4466.F1048.
26   Inv. 17-124 (4328.F976).
27   Inv. 17-134 (4466.F1024); Inv. 17-170 (4328.F981).
28   Inv. 17-085 (4328.F747); Inv. 17-128 (4466.F1027).
29   Inv. 12-023 (SAg.12.1.1032.F1027).
30   Inv. 17-173 (4466.F1037).
31   Inv. 17-176 (4466.F1017).
32   Inv. 17-174 (4466.F1010).
33   4328.F749.
34   Inv. 17-77 (4328.F731), Inv. 17-78 (4328.F729), Inv. 17-80 (SAg.17.2.5027.F20), Inv. 17-81 (SAg.17.2.5027.F21).
35   4328.F972, 4328.F974, 4466.F1033.
36   4466.F1031.

Alongside these more humble items were found glass paste mosaic fragments and tesserae with preserved gold leaf (8),[37] as well as a number of impressive marble sculptural fragments. These included three portrait heads, one foot, and a male statuette, representing the full chronological range of sculptural production at Aphrodisias from the first to fifth centuries AD (discussed in Ch. 7 §E).[38] Despite the extent of this deposit, there was comparatively little pottery (11.1 kg) and relatively few bones (14.8 kg), though the recovery of numerous horse bones, including a partial equid cranium, as well as several oyster, Atlantic triton, and murex shells, is noteworthy (see Ch. 10 §B).[39] The debris that constitutes the bulk of this deposit was evidently thrown into the pool in a single event; we are not looking here at the slow accumulation of refuse over time.

Archaeobotanical analysis indicates that there was no sedimentation or overgrowth within the pool when the materials outlined above were deposited; the pool had been kept clean up until this moment. This evidence will be discussed further below (§E). Here it should be noted simply that several peach stones (2),[40] pine cones (15),[41] and traces of fig, grape, blackberry and burrs were among the archaeobotanical remains found in 2017 within the artificial dump to the north and within the spread of materials lying directly on top of the pool floor; this recalls the discovery in 1990 of several peach stones and fig seeds directly on the pool floor, or wedged between the stones of the floor, towards the eastern end.[42] All samples taken from only the north side of the pool within the artificial dump yielded *Chara* sp. oospores (a type of algae), with some *Schoenoplectus lacustris* (bulrush). These aquatic plants indicate that the pool still contained running water and was not yet overgrown when the deposits along the north side were dumped in; the additional presence of terrestrial plants and foodstuffs within these layers, however, indicates that a certain amount of vegetation and perhaps also rubbish from around the pool was deposited concurrently with the debris or shortly thereafter. This material probably came from **4278**, the occupation deposit on top of the late antique ground level north of the pool (see Ch. 4 §C), which continued to build up through this period and into the early medieval period.

Towards the eastern end of the pool, on the north side, an area of subsidence of the pool floor and a long and deep crack between the pool floor and the north wall, was filled with material from the first clean-up deposit. The crack and subsidence are most likely to have been caused by earthquake damage. Although the earthquake of *c.* AD 620 for which we argue below (§F) might be a possible cause, two points argue against it. First, this would imply a gap of several decades between the earthquake and the dumping of the deposit over it (after 643/4); yet the archaeobotanical evidence shows that water was still flowing through the pool, which sits ill with the idea of a major crack in the pool floor. Second, the main thrust of the *c.* 620 earthquake was east-to-west, and the crack is more consistent with a south-to-north thrust. It is perhaps therefore more likely that the crack was caused by a later earthquake, probably that in the 11th century (see Ch. 9 §A), and the material from the first clearance deposit already lying on the pool floor simply settled into the crack that opened up.

Sedimentation and a second clearance deposit

Following the depositing of the contexts described above, a layer of natural sedimentation accumulated across the whole of the pool, sealing the objects scattered over the area and covering the lowest 10–15 cm of the dump along the north side. This layer (**4448**) comprised thick, dark grey silt and yellowish-tan clay and represents the first major build-up of silt in the pool (Pl. 79.A–B). This layer yielded scant ceramics (6.41 kg), as well as small finds embedded within the matrix, such as moulded coloured marble revetment and architectural fragments belonging to the North Stoa, worked wooden remains,[43] fragments of statuary,[44] metal vessels and tools (11),[45] architectural fittings (4),[46] copper alloy vessels (2),[47] loomweights (9),[48] a glass lamp fragment,[49] glass with gold leaf appliqué,[50] and projectile weapons (2).[51] The distribution and variety of these small finds and ceramics seem to suggest that they had been deposited sporadically into the pool as refuse, rather than with the main clearance dump thrown in from the north side.[52]

Archaeobotanical materials from this layer consisted mainly of many freshwater snail shells and aquatic plants, such as bul-

---

37 Inv. 17-109 (4466.F1016), Inv. 17-135 to 17-137 (4466.F1039, 4466.F1045, 4466.F1046), Inv. 17-140 to 17-143 (4329.F973, 4466.F1026, 4466.F1043, 4466.F1044).

38 The back of a first-century male portrait head (Inv. 17-033), which joins with a portrait face (Inv. 16-052) found at the east end of the same deposit; a third-century male portrait head, found in two parts (Inv. 17-053 and Inv. 17-112); an early fifth-century bearded male portrait, probably of a Theodosian governor, with ΧΜΓ inscribed on the underside of its chin (17-059); two marble feet, one sandalled and one bare (Inv. 17-061); and a male statuette (Inv. 17-111). See Ch. 7 §E for further details.

39 See Ch. 10 for further details. For the cranium: 4328.F968; for the shells: 4466.F993, 4466.F1002, 4466.F1003, 4466.F1011.

40 4328.F734, 4482.F932.

41 4328.F735, 4328.F737, 4482.F866, 4482.F867, 4482.F872, 4482.F923, 4482.F927, 4482.F940, 4482.F941, 4482.F947, 4482.F965, 4328.F969, 4328.F983, 4328.F987, 4466.F1000.

42 Nbk 316: *Portico of Tiberius: W Pool, Book I; E Pool* (A.T. Tek, 1990), 13, 57.

43 4448.F685, 4448.F799, 4448.F801, 4448.F802, 4448.F815.

44 Inv. 17-048 (4448.M1934), Inv. 17-056 (4448.M2413), Inv. 17-063 (4448.M2606), Inv. 17-100 (4448.M2527), Inv. 17-102 (4448.M2633).

45 4448.F686, 4448.F795, 4448.F837, 4448.F850, 4448.F853, 4448.F854, 4448.F863, 4448.F881, 4448.F916; 4448.F1062; 4448.F1063.

46 4448.F848; 4448.F873, 4448.F874, Inv. 17-117 (4448.F879).

47 Inv. 17-171 (4448.F808), Inv. 17-172 (4448.F821).

48 4448.F774, 4448.F779, 4448.F797, 4448.F842, 4448.F849, 4448.F851, 4448.F852, 4448.F855, 4448.F937.

49 For example 4448.F840. See Ch. 8 §D for further discussion.

50 Inv. 17-088 (4448.F836).

51 Inv. 17-074 (4448.F826); Inv. 17-082 (4448.F844).

52 This siltation layer (**4448**) was difficult to distinguish from the layer above, **4480**, especially in the northern and central sections of the pool; only along the southern side of the pool, where the second clearance deposit (**4471**, see below) fell on to **4448** and was overlain by **4480**, could a clear interface be identified. It is possible, therefore, that some finds from **4448** were deposited after the second clearance deposit and settled down into the silt.

rushes (the aforementioned *Schoenoplectus* (Scirpus) *lacustris*), demonstrating that the layer had formed while fresh water still flowed through the pool.[53] Plants and foodstuffs were found, primarily at the east end of the pool, including pine cones,[54] large quantities of grape fragments, as well as carbonized cereal grains. Since these terrestrial plants and foodstuffs could not have grown within the pool, these remains are indicative of human activity in the area outside the pool. Since it was noted over the course of the excavations (between 2012 and 2017) that between 2 and 5 cm of silt would accumulate in the area between each excavation season, it is possible that this layer built up during a short period of time, perhaps within the span of a few years after the pool had fallen out of use.

Although this silt accumulated naturally, it was directly overlain by another artificial clearance deposit, this time along the south side of the pool's interior (**4471**) (Pl. 79.B). Similar to the first clean-up dump to the north, yet on a much smaller scale and at a higher level and thus later, this deposit sloped down from a thickness of 50 cm at the southern pool edge and extended northwards for a maximum of 1.66 m. Several marble sculptural finds were recovered from within this dump: a female head (probably of a divinity), an early sixth-century male portrait head, and a section of the tail of the blue horse from the Troilos and Achilles sculptural group from the Civil Basilica (all discussed in Ch. 7).[55] This deposit also included a coin of Heraclius overstruck between AD 660 and 685 with an Arab countermark (cat. 281); this gives a *terminus post quem* for this second clean-up of AD 660 at the earliest.[56]

This second clearance deposit produced burnt timber remains and ceramic building materials (377 kg), as well as some building stone.[57] The brick and tiles from this southern clearance deposit were so well-preserved that they can be divided into three typological groups: 1) worn tiles matching those recovered from the artificial deposit to the north that demonstrate evidence of significant burning; 2) long and rectangular cut bricks that are unworn in appearance;[58] and 3) square, unworn cut bricks.[59] The latter two typological groups are commensurate in size and age with the type of ceramic building materials that should be associated with the sixth-century phase of the South Stoa, which was constructed only a little over a century before the deposition of this material. The only sculpted architectural elements from the layer seem to belong to the Propylon.[60] Given that bricks and tiles were documented across the entire length of the south side of the pool, with only the marble architectural elements from the Propylon and burnt wood found at the eastern end, it is probable that this deposit resulted mainly from a partial clean-up of damage to the South Stoa.

Structural evidence for late activity after the abandonment of the pool

The clearance dumps within the pool provide proxy evidence for activities in the area outside the pool. This can be supplemented with additional evidence, hinting at the nature of the activity in the area of the former Place of Palms after the pool had ceased to be maintained as a monumental feature, provided by cuttings in the pool walls and structures added to it.

Along the north side of the pool, a series of 13 circular holes (6–8 cm in diameter) was cut into the north ledge of the outer pool seat; these holes are spaced at intervals which vary between 1.85 and 7.13 m (see Pl. 79.C).[61] Immediately to the east of where the cuttings in the pool seat blocks end, are a series of post-supports built against the edge of the north side of the pool, spaced at intervals of 4.49 to 9.82 m towards its eastern end (**4286, 4287, 4288, 4289, 4290**).[62] The fact that these post-supports appear to continue the line of holes in the pool seats suggests that these features were part of the same phase of activity. The post-supports are cut directly into the late antique make-up layer (**4280**) that abuts the north side of the outer pool wall; one re-uses a broken pilaster capital fragment from the back wall of the North Stoa as a chock stone.

A similar series of 12 cuttings was noted along the south side of the pool, which are spaced at intervals of 1.83 to 10.91 m (see Pl. 79.C and 80.A).[63] There are none around the east end and only one at the west end of the pool. The possibility that these were fixtures installed when the pool was in use, perhaps to hold poles for awnings shading the pool's edges, can be ruled out, since in two instances these cuttings are found in areas previously occupied by statue bases, and the fragment of pilaster capital in one of the post supports shows that this post-dates damage to the North Stoa. The dimensions of these cuttings and post-supports closely match some of the longer and thinner wooden poles recovered from the silt within the pool (**4448**) (Pl. 80.B).[64] These wooden poles, unlike the rafters and planks found at lower levels, were not burnt. These poles, and their corresponding cuttings, were probably used to support awnings and perhaps temporary stalls along the north and south sides of the pool.

Further evidence for stalls is supported by the recovery of several platform-like features (**4282, 4291, 4292**) interspersed between the post-supports and built directly against the north side of the outer pool wall, possibly serving as built surface-extensions of the pool wall (see Pl. 79.C). The fact that the deposit within which the poles were found in the pool post-dates the

---

53 Wilson, Russell, and Ward 2016, 86.
54 4448.F828, 4448.F890.
55 Inv. 17-036 (4471.M2476), Inv. 17-060 (4471.M2464), Inv. 17-070 (4471.M2609). On the Troilos and Achilles sculpture: Smith and Hallett 2015.
56 See below, §B.
57 SAg.17.1.4471.F738, 4471.F739.
58 Measuring L: 0.29 m, W: 0.15 m, Thickness: 0.04 m.
59 Measuring L: 0.36 m, W: 0.36 m, Thickness: 0.04 m.
60 4471.M2610, 4471.M2639.
61 Distances between holes on north side of pool: 7.13 m = 24.1 RF; 4.99 m = 16.74 RF; 5.28 m = 17.72 RF; 4.51 m = 15.13 RF; 3.45 m = 11.58 RF; 4.84 m = 16.24 RF; 5.7 m = 19.13 RF; 4.82 m = 16.17 RF; 1.85 m = 6.21 RF; 2.13 m = 7.14 RF; 5.26 m = 17.65 RF; 4.29 m = 14.4 RF.
62 Distances between post supports: 9.82 m = 33.2 RF; 4.49 m = 15.2 RF; 7.65 m = 25.8 RF.
63 Distances between holes on south side: 10.91 m = 36.9 RF; 9.24 m = 31.2 RF; 4.7 m = 15.87 RF; 3.65 m = 12.33 RF; 3.9 m = 13.18 RF; 3.39 m = 11.45; 3.04 m = 10.27 RF; 4.12 m = 13.92 RF; 2.65 m = 8.95 RF; 1.83 m = 6.18 RF; 4.13 m = 13.95 RF; 4.16 m = 14.05 RF.
64 4448.F802, 4448.F830. One pole was also found in a siltation deposit (4479) over the collapse that sealed this phase: 4479.F804.

first clearance dump suggest that these temporary structures appeared only once the Place of Palms had ceased to play a role as an urban park. The function of these temporary structures is unclear but the finds from the deposit within the pool suggest that commercial activity took place in the space and it is possible that the area between the pool and both the North and South Stoas was turned into an open-air marketplace at this date.

As well as these cuttings and post-supports, two structures were also added to the pool shortly after it went out of use, which might again hint at a utilitarian change in function. On the south side, a stone basin (**4464**) was constructed within the pool, just to the east of where the cuttings in the pool seats terminate (see Pl. 79.C and 80.C). This basin was built after the deposition of the first clearance dump (**4328**) but before or during the subsequent phase of siltation (**4448**), and measured 1.59 m long, 1.1 m wide, and 82 cm tall. It abutted the south pool wall, with west, north, and east walls made of three marble slabs removed from the adjacent inner ledge of the pool; an additional sculpted marble revetment slab lined its base. The basin was probably intended to facilitate access to water, that could filter in through the joints between the slabs, after the pool had begun to silt up.

The basin belongs to the same broad phase of activity as a substantial ramp, which was added to the north-east corner of the pool (see Pl. 79.C and 80.D). This ramp, constructed of gently sloping marble blocks, their surface scored or corrugated, leads to the pool floor from the socle blocks of the inner pool wall. The ramp is best explained as a means of permitting hoofed animals easy access to drinking water; the outer and inner seat blocks of the pool were pushed aside from their original positions at the top of the ramp in order to ensure it was flush with the ground level beyond. The scorings on the marble blocks were presumably intended to stop the animals slipping on the wet stones. The ramp was excavated in 1989 without the detailed recording of stratigraphy,[65] but it rests on the pool floor rather than on a layer of silt, and it would have been half-covered by the time of the construction in the interior of the pool of the trackway of Phase 5 discussed in Ch. 9 §B, dated to the thirteenth century. It should therefore fit between the disuse of the pool as a monumental feature, and the second clearance dump, by which time the siltation within the pool would have covered the lower end of the ramp. That would put it between the early seventh century at the earliest and perhaps the end of the seventh century, given that the Arabic-countermarked coin from the second clean-up dump is unlikely to have circulated much after 685 (see discussion on chronology below).

Dating and interpretation of the stratigraphic sequence

The stratigraphic sequence outlined above shows three phases of activity: a first phase of clearance and dumping of debris into the pool along its north side, with some material scattering into the central and southern parts of the pool; a phase of siltation within the pool, the development of temporary installations outside it, and the construction of the cattle ramp and small basin; and then a second clearance deposit along the south side. The dates of these deposits provide key information about the timing and nature of the events which saw the end of the Place of Palms as a monumental space, and indeed of the transformation not only of the space of the city centre, but of the nature of life at the site.

The majority of the pottery from the two lowermost deposits, belonging to the first phase listed above, dates to the sixth to seventh centuries AD (§C below). The seven coins found in **4482**, directly on the pool floor, which range in date from the 540s to 643/4, give a *terminus post quem* for the dumping of this material on the pool floor.[66] Further corroboration of this chronology comes from the many metal objects found within the first dump along the north side of the pool, the details of which are discussed below (§D). Broadly datable to the sixth century by style and iconography is a circular silver pendant depicting a rider-saint spearing a nude female demon.[67] Further finds include a lead seal with a monogram giving the owner's name and official title: Θεοδώρου μητροπολίτου ('[Seal] of Theodore the Metropolitan [bishop]'). The seal is dated by letter forms and artistic style to the late sixth to early seventh century.[68] A lead weight and the fragmentary parts of small, hand-held scales are all comparable to weights and scales found in the 'Early Byzantine' shops at Sardis.[69]

These finds together point to a seventh-century date for the abandonment of the pool. The silt (**4448**) that formed over the first clearance deposit also yielded ceramics of the sixth to seventh centuries AD. The single coin from this context, of Justinian (AD 539/540), provides no further refinement of the deposit's seventh-century stratigraphic date.[70] From the later clearance deposit on the south side, the recovery of a coin of Heraclius, datable between 632 and 635 but with an Umayyad countermark (AD 660s–685?), confirms that this phase of activity probably occurred within a few decades of the clearance along the north side.[71]

The datable evidence from the excavated deposits, therefore, suggests that the pool was effectively put out of use by the first clearance dump along its north side in or soon after the AD 640s. The space of the Place of Palms was then turned over to temporary activities, probably mercantile in character, for at least several decades until the later part of the seventh centu-

---

65 Nbk 310: *E Portico of Tiberius: Basin 89-I* (A. Önce, 1989), 22–24.

66 These coins are: cat. 233 (unidentified late Roman); cat. 240 (AD 541/2); cat. 270 (AD 605/6); cat. 274 (AD 613); cat. 275 (AD 613 or 613/4); cat. 279 (632/3 AD); cat. 289 (AD 643/4).

67 Inv. 17-108 (4466.F1012).

68 Inv. 17-094 (4328.F990). The form of the μητροπολίτου monogram is identical to that of Laurent (1963) Corpus V/1a 947, for which the date given is seventh century. For more on this and other Byzantine seals from Aphrodisias, see Jeffery 2020. On grounds of style, this seal appears too early to be that of the Bishop Theodore of Stavropolis who attended the Sixth Ecumenical Council in AD 680 (cf. Roueché 1989, 381; Yıldırım 2016, 47), and may refer to a different Theodore (not an uncommon name for churchmen of this period).

69 The Byzantine Shops at Sardis yielded nine complete steelyards, with four additional steelyard parts (Waldbaum 1983: 81–2). Further evidence for contemporary steelyards has been found at Pliska, Amorium, and Skythopolis (Morrisson 2012: 381).

70 Cat. 246.

71 Cat. 281.

ry when a second campaign of clearance took place along its southern side.

What events prompted these clearance activities and effectively terminated the life of the Place of Palms? The unstratigraphic nature of the recording of the excavations of the North and South Stoas in the 1980s means that our evidence for the chronology and nature of their destruction comes not from the excavated areas within the stoas themselves, but has to be inferred largely from their architectural elements found in deposits within the pool. The nature of the debris within the first and second dumped deposits within the pool shows that considerable damage was caused to the architecture of the Place of Palms at some point in the seventh century AD. The roof tiles, revetment, wood and architectural elements in the first deposit belong almost exclusively to the North Stoa. Burning was found on many of the roof tiles, wooden rafters and planks, as well as some of the architectural elements. The North Stoa did not completely collapse in this period—most of its columns and entablature remained standing until a much later earthquake in perhaps the eleventh century (see Ch. 9 §A)—but it clearly suffered substantial damage. It lost its roof, its back wall seems to have lost most of its marble revetment, and at least some of its columns came down—among the architectural finds of the first clearance deposit were small pieces of cornice and architrave blocks (7), garland fragments from the mask and garland frieze (2), a column section, the various fragments of pilaster capital discussed above, and large quantities of tiles. The presence of architectural elements from the Propylon in the same clearance deposit show that this structure had also been similarly damaged around the same time, though none of the fragments from this building showed signs of burning. The South Stoa suffered ruin comparable to the North Stoa, as it too did not completely collapse at this time but sustained considerable damage. The same range of debris is found in the second clearance deposit as in the first and traces of burning are again evident.

Additional evidence for a conflagration along the south side of the Place of Palms is provided by the traces of burning in the beam and rafter holes on the Theatre Wall, discussed in Ch. 2 §A and Ch. 4 §F .[72] The crucial point about this debris is that it shows that both the North and South Stoas suffered from burning, lost their roofs and some of their surface decoration, but at the same time their colonnades mostly remained standing, and only collapsed along their full length several centuries later. The coin evidence from the pool shows that the debris of the North Stoa was collected and dumped into the pool sometime after AD 643/4. The partial ruins of the South Stoa were cleared out in the late seventh century. Both phases of clearance were probably undertaken to make further space available for foot-traffic and whatever commercial activities were hosted in the area. The date of the destructive activities that prompted these clearances, however, is less certain. We return to this question in §F below, after a review of the finds from these deposits.

B. SEVENTH-CENTURY COINS (ATT & HK)

Seventy-four Byzantine and two related coins were recorded from the Place of Palms: 56 of these are from the early Byzantine period up until the mid seventh century AD, and 18 are later (Fig. 60). Seventy-two of the coins are in AE, 1 billon (cat. 308) and 1 AR (cat. 309) units. As with the pre-reform coinage of Anastasius, his post-reform coinage is not represented in this area;[73] our finds start with Justin I (cat. 235–237) and continue with Justinian I (cat. 238–247).

Cat. 245–246 are issues of Justinian from the Carthage mint, and cat. 247 is a Vandal coin from Carthage possibly minted just prior to Belisarius' operations there.[74] In a recent study, Andrei Gândila listed 44 coins of Justinian I minted at Carthage recorded at various sites and museums in Türkiye.[75] The Aphrodisias finds are thus not surprising and all of these coins from Türkiye show connections with North Africa; indeed some could well document deployments of Belisarius' army after the conquest of Carthage and their return to Asia Minor. A later coin of Constans II of AD 650/1, cat. 291, from Syracuse,[76] is another example of western issues travelling to the East. Apart from these, all other early Byzantine coins come predominantly from the Constantinople mint, with a few examples from Thessalonica, Nicomedia, Cyzicus, and Antioch (Table 8).[77] Alexandria is not represented among the coins catalogued

---

73 During the 1995–2021 seasons 10 pre-reform and 3 post-reform coins of Anastasius were recorded from Aphrodisias. Interestingly, 5 pre-reform coins and 1 post-reform coin come from trenches in the Agora, just next door to the Place of Palms.

74 The small *nummi* with palm tree (*BMC Vandals*, 26, nos. 68–72) have been attributed to Vandal-period Carthage, as the palm was a symbol of the city's Punic coinage, and numerous examples have been excavated there (Asolati 1995, 191 and note 17). The dating of these coins has been much debated; see Bijovsky 2012: 317–320 for attribution problems and references. Palm tree coins have also been excavated from the East; Bijovsky 2012, 320–321, lists 229 examples found at various sites in Israel. From Türkiye, they have been published only from Antioch (Waage 1952, 147, no. 2057), Sardis (Evans 2018, 234, no. 1108), and we recorded two examples in Side in Pamphylia; their lesser representation here in comparison to Israel may lie in the fact that the type is not very well known to numismatists in Türkiye.

75 The list published in Gândila 2016, 170–172 covers 19 find spots and museum collections from Türkiye; Gökalp 2018, 96, table 7 lists 10 more coins from the Carthage mint found at various sites in Western Asia Minor; for more examples from Ephesos, Schindel 2009, 228, no. 187–193, 231, no. 230–231; more examples from Sardis, Evans 2018, 230, no. 1055 (4 coins), 234, no. 1106–1122 (27 coins); two examples found in the Milas area in Karia, from the Carthage mint, exist in Bodrum Archaeological Museum (Uygur 2017, 63, nos. 32–33). For a general evaluation of the Carthage mint and its circulation, see Morrisson 1990.

76 The mint of Syracuse is represented with merely a few examples in Türkiye: two examples have so far been published, one from Pergamon (Voegtli 1993, 58, no. 811) and the other from Miletos (Sancaktar *apud* Niewöhner 2016, 270, no. 145). We recorded one more example at Side. These coins could be evidence for an unknown military deployment against Arab raids into Asia Minor.

77 The mint distribution of the coins we studied is similar to that published by Morrisson 2017, 74, note 22, from a sample of 67 Byzantine coins found at Aphrodisias in earlier years; calculating this sample from percentages given in the publication, 39 from Constantinople, 18 from Nicomedia, 9 from Cyzicus, 6 from Antioch and 9 from Thessalonica

---

72 Nbk 253: *S Agora Gate I-84, Book 1* (B. Rose, 1984), 53, 69–73.

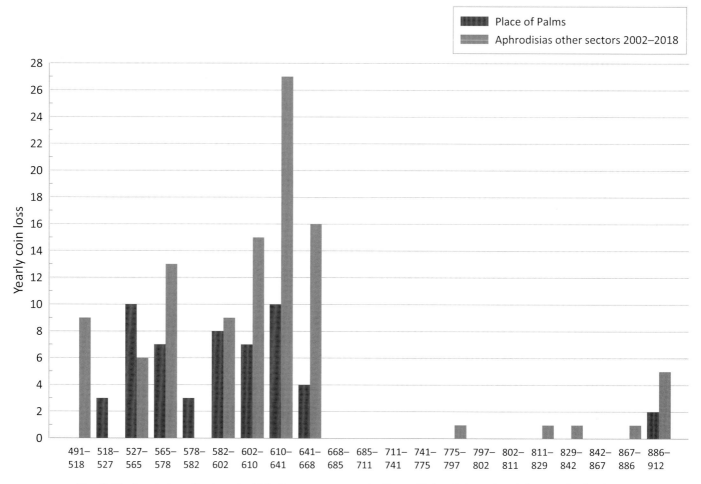

Fig. 60. Yearly coin loss of early and middle Byzantine coins in the Place of Palms (54 coins) and the rest of Aphrodisias (104 coins); data compiled from finds between 2002–2018) calculated as: finds per period / length of period × 1000 / total.

Table 8. Mint distribution of 56 (+1) early Byzantine and related coins from the Place of Palms.

Numbers in brackets are nos. 247 (Vandals of North Africa) and 281 (Heraclius coin with Umayyad countermark).

Year	Carthage	Syracuse	Thessalonica	Constantinopolis	Nicomedia	Cyzicus	Antioch	?	Total
491–518									0
518–527				3					3
527–565	2 (+1)			4	1		2		9 (+1)
565–578			1	4	1		1		7
578–582				2	1				3
582–602				4	1	1	1	1	8
602–610				4	2	1			7
610–641				8 (+1)		1			9 (+1)
641–668		1		3					4
?					1			4	5
Total	2 (+1)	1	1	32 (+1)	7	3	4	5	55 (+2)

from the recent excavations at Aphrodisias, although a peculiar hoard of Alexandrian *dodekanummia* is known from the earlier excavation of the Theatre.[78]

These coins are followed by issues of Justin II (cat. 248–254) which are rather regular, of types that may be expected from any site in Asia Minor. Three examples of Tiberius II (cat. 255–257) from the pool are statistically interesting within such a small sample given the rareness of his coinage,[79] but these may represent contents of a small contemporary purse hoard; the coins seem to have been found separately in close proximity, not together. Maurice (cat. 258–265) and Phocas (cat. 266–272) are also each represented with several examples and many of these may have been still in circulation in the early seventh century AD. The most numerous representation at Aphrodisias is of coins of Heraclius, represented at the Place of Palms by ten examples (cat. 273–282). These issues are followed by coins of Constans II (cat. 288–291), during whose reign (AD 641–668) coin finds at Aphrodisias stop entirely for more than a century (Fig. 60). This break in coin losses may reflect drastically decreased economic activity related either to an Arab destruction of the site or to Arab raids affecting coin distribution from Constantinople, unless cat. 292 (which remains unidentified) is a later coin and not one of Constans II, though the latter is more likely. On five early Byzantine coins (cat. 283–287), the emperors could not be identified due to the conditions of the coins, but the sizes, flans, and letter shapes of the units suggest that these are of emperors between Anastasius and Heraclius.

The most interesting context concerning Byzantine coins is that directly over the floor of the pool (Table 7 above). Context **4482** yielded seven coins (cat. 233, 240, 270, 274, 275, 279, 289), dated to the late Roman period, AD 541/2, AD 605/6, AD 613, AD 613 or 613/4, AD 632/3 or 633/4, and AD 643/4 respectively. To these we can add two coins dated AD 578/9 and 580/1 (cat. 255 and 257), found in excavations of the western part of the pool in 1988 (trench PT.W. 88.I), which the excavators noted were found directly on the floor. Two more coins (cat. 278 and 280) come from dumped deposits along the north side of the pool, **4328**, which are dated to AD 631/2 and 634/5.[80]

The presence of no coins here earlier than the mid/late sixth or early seventh century probably shows that the pool was maintained and cleaned regularly up to when these coins accumulated in it. If the accumulation was gradual during and after this period, then we are seeing a pattern of coins dropped in the pool starting from the reign of Justinian, which may also mean the pool floor itself was thoroughly cleaned at the time.[81] But one must remember that sixth-century AD coins could still have been in circulation in the early seventh century AD, and dropped then.

On the other hand, as most of the coins are from the seventh century AD, maybe we should think of them (including the older ones still in circulation) as accumulating there only in the seventh century. As the seventh-century material starts with a coin of Phocas (cat. 270), this brings to mind another coin of Phocas dated AD 605/6 (C2016.099) found in 2016 'mortared in place under marble flooring of the caldarium',[82] indicating repairs or alterations in the Hadrianic 'Olympian' Baths at the time. We may speculate that the pool was also cleaned at this time with some minor repairs done to it,[83] and a fresh accumulation of dumped material and silt containing coins occurred afterwards.

The latest coin from the pool floor is cat. 289, dated to AD 643/4, which provides a *terminus post quem* for the clean-up after a major destruction event; the question of whether this represents a generation's time-lag before cleaning up after a Persian sack, or a later disaster such as an Arab raid in the mid/late seventh century, is discussed below (§F). A coin recovered from the second clearance deposit in the pool (cat. 281), context **4471**,[84] is a regular Imperial coin (not a pseudo-Byzantine issue)[85] countermarked with an Arabic legend in the Levant area. This is the first such coin to be recorded from Asia Minor, to our knowledge; its historical significance is discussed below (§F).[86]

---

field notes; but some of the dates are corrected here after subsequent research.

81 These alterations may have been repairs after earthquake damage, which brings to mind, for example, the earthquake that destroyed the city of Cos somewhere between AD 554–558 (Ruggieri 2005, 251; 2009, 214) which must have affected other parts of Karia as well. A mid-sixth-century earthquake affecting Aphrodisias had already been suspected (Wilson 2018a, 484–495).

82 Smith 2018a: 270; Wilson 2019: 212.

83 Wilson 2019: 209.

84 We would like to thank Drs Wolfgang and Ingrid Schulze, Dr Anthony Goodwin, Dr Donald Ariel and Dr Gabriela Bijovsky for examining the coin from photos and sharing their thoughts on it. It was with their combined effort that this difficult coin could be identified correctly.

85 The so-called pseudo-Byzantine or Arab-Byzantine coinage is a local coinage struck in Syria during the Persian control of the area in the AD 610s–620s that copies Byzantine types, possibly to supply money to the local markets which could not receive coinage from official Byzantine mints during the invasion. It continued under the Arabs from the 640s onwards either by countermarking existing coins, or minting new ones that closely resemble contemporary Byzantine coins, until the coinage reform of AD 685. The classification and relative dating of this coinage has been debated by several scholars since 1950s; the classification now most commonly used is that of Pottier, Schulze, and Schulze 2008.

86 One may expect to encounter pseudo-Byzantine/Arab coinage at places like Antioch, Karrhae/Harran, Urfa/Edessa and even in Cilicia, the

---

mint. Thirty of these coins date to the reign of Heraclius (Morrisson 2017, 75, note 30). Prof. C. Morrisson derived these data from unpublished notes of Prof. M. Hendy on Byzantine coin finds at Aphrodisias. Morrisson 2017, 75, note 30, 77, fig. 5.1; 80, fig. 5.3 also gives data on Aphrodisias finds. As we have not had access to these notes, or seen the coins themselves, we cannot at the moment compare these two find groups.

78 The hoard excavated in the 'South Post Scaenam' trench of the Theatre in 1972 was described thus by Kenan Erim: 'The coins, 100 in number, all copper dodecanummia of the mint of Alexandria, range in date from Justinian I to Maurice Tiberius and even perhaps Phocas. They are rarely found outside of Egypt and must represent the contents of a purse, namely the value in copper of a simple fraction of the gold solidus', Erim 1974, 39. The same hoard (hoard 328) is also listed together with seven more Byzantine hoards from Aphrodisias in Morrisson, Popović, and Ivanišević 2006, 393–396, hoards 326–333.

79 Only one other coin (C1995.018) of Tiberius II was recorded at Aphrodisias among Byzantine coins found between 1995–2021.

80 Destruction deposits described in Wilson 2019, 215–217; these coins are specifically mentioned in Wilson 2019, 216, note 12, using our

The context above the second clearance deposit, **4442**, which is fully discussed in the next chapter, also produced several seventh-century coins. Cat. 291 dates to AD 650/1, while cat. 292 is probably another issue of Constans II, but because we can only see a small size M on it, we have dated it between 641–720 when these M's are present in the same format on the coinage. Seven further coins found in excavations in other parts of Aphrodisias between 2002–2018 belong to Class V and VI types of Constans II and continue up to AD 655/6 or 656/7. The latest coin of Constans II recorded at Aphrodisias dates to AD 658, after which there is a gap in the finds sequence (Fig. 60) up to the next coin, dated to AD 792–797, found in the Tetrapylon Street; and we may therefore suspect a successful Arab raid on Aphrodisias shortly after AD 658, a suggestion discussed further below (§F). Whether the coin gap means the abandonment of Stavropolis (as Aphrodisias was called in the later seventh century) during this period of continuous warfare with the Arabs is not clear; numismatic evidence might seem to point in that direction, but on the other hand the attestation of bishops of Stavropolis in the 660s, 680, and 692, together with the evidence of the cattle ramp, water tank, and postholes for awnings or stalls, indicates continued activity and that some kind of settlement survived. But if so, one would have to imagine that it was greatly reduced in the eighth century AD, leaving no numismatic traces at least among the material we have studied.

C. CERAMICS FROM THE CLEARANCE DEPOSITS
(UO, HJ, & TP)

Substantial quantities of ceramics were recovered from the first clearance deposit within the pool, both from the deposits scattered across the whole pool (**4482**) and the larger accumulation of material along its northern side (**4328**), as well as the siltation deposit (**4448**) that built up after these dumps. A full breakdown of the ceramics from these contexts is provided in Appendix 5, Table 28. Also included in the discussion in this chapter are the late Roman ceramics found, as residual material, in the later siltation deposits that accumulated in the pool (**4480**, **4461**, **4329** and **4442**); these are listed in Appendix 5, Table 29, while the main discussion of these deposits is in Ch. 9 §B. The general picture they provide is similar to that derived from the materials excavated in the late Roman deposits outside the pool and in the ring drain.

The bulk of the ceramics from these contexts are locally-produced kitchen wares, which can be broadly dated to the late fifth to seventh centuries AD, and in particular the first half of the seventh century. Among these wares are basins in TMW with a thickened, almost rectangular rim (see 17.1.4466, 2–4, Fig. 61) that are not found in the late Roman contexts outside the pool.[87] Cooking pots with an everted and grooved rim are also only found in these contexts within the pool, though they remain rare (17.1.4328.2).[88] Locally-produced handled amphorae or jugs similar in form to those discussed in Ch. 4 §H were also found in these contexts (see, for example, 17.1.4448.2, Fig. 61). Definite jugs are represented only by two neck fragments (17.1.4448.1 & 4, Fig. 61), with a quite narrow 'squashed' spout and broad strap handles.[89]

The few imports that can be identified from the deposits in the pool, however, are slightly later in date than those discussed in Ch. 4 §H, mostly coming from the sixth and seventh centuries. These include a fragment of Phocaean Red Slip/LRC (17.1.4482.8, Fig. 61) datable to the sixth century, a base fragment of a Yassi Ada 159 C19 amphora (17.1.4442.F790, Fig. 62) datable to the first half of the seventh century but residual in a later context,[90] and several fragments of Peacock and Williams Class 45/Late Roman 3 amphorae, including one of the latest versions (17.1.4448.5, Fig. 61), which is dated to the late sixth to seventh centuries AD.[91]

A large number of fragments of unguentaria was also found in these contexts (12.1.1032.1, 17.1.4482.1–7, 17.1.4448.8; Fig. 63). These are primarily datable to between the early sixth and early seventh century on form alone. Nine of these fragments of late Roman unguentaria have monogram stamps and a further fragment found in the late Roman make-up layer (**2005**, equivalent to **4280**) outside the pool is included in this discussion (Fig. 64).[92] These are spindle-shaped vessels with a narrow neck, generally between 18 and 21 cm in height. They were manufactured in huge quantities between *c.* AD 520 and 650,

---

regions of Asia Minor that were the first to be conquered by Arabs in the seventh century. Among the published finds from Karrhae/Harran, four examples could be pseudo-Byzantine instead of regular imperial issues (the two illustrated give that impression) though none is countermarked (Heidemann 2002, 279–280, no. 1–4, 290, Taf. 1); there are some published examples from Antioch (Waage 1952, 165–166) but none is countermarked with Arabic countermarks. Another example with a Heraclian Greek monogram countermark is published from Tell Kurdu near Antioch (Vorderstrasse 2006). Two coins from Niğde Museum have been identified as Arabo-Byzantine (Métivier and Prigent 2010, 591, note 76, 614, table 2), and one coin from Tyana is again identified as such (Asolati and Crisafulli 2015, 242, tab. 5, 246, no. 13). All the known examples listed above therefore come from sites in Asia Minor controlled by Arabs or those directly close to or on the border. Outside the borderland between Arabs and Byzantine Empire, such coins have only been reported from Sardis. Two coins from Sardis were published as "fals?", meaning pseudo-Byzantine/Arab issues (Evans 2018, 46, 242, no. 1235–1236). If these are correctly identified, then these would be another piece of evidence to add to the results from Aphrodisias for the presence of these coins in western Asia Minor and possible connections with Arab raids.

---

87 See Jantzen 2004, no. 1593–94 (first quarter of the seventh century AD).
88 For parallels, see Jantzen 2004, no. 1483; Hayes 1992, 108 deposit 34 and 35 (no. 52 and no. 12), and Japp 2007, 64, Kat. No. 29—late fifth century AD and later.
89 For close parallels see Jantzen 2004, no. 1428 and no. 1430—first quarter of the seventh century AD.
90 On the Yassi Ada amphorae, see van Alfen 1996; Arthur 1998, 169–70.
91 Peacock and Williams 1986, 188–190, Class 45; Outschar 1991, 317; Outschar 1993; 1996a, 60, n. 198 and 199; Bezeczky 2013, 164–166, Type 55. Several centres of production in western Asia Minor have been supposed, for example the region of Ephesos and the Maeander valley.
92 Some of these finds were assigned find numbers during excavation: 4448.F435; Inv. 17-110 (4466.F1038); Inv. 17-084 (4442.F751; residual in a later deposit); Inv. 17-093 (4482.F956); Inv. 17-087 (4448.F825). Others were recovered as bulk finds in the following contexts: P.T.SW.89 / 2.8.1989; SAg.12.1.1032; SAg.12.2.2005; 4482; 4482.

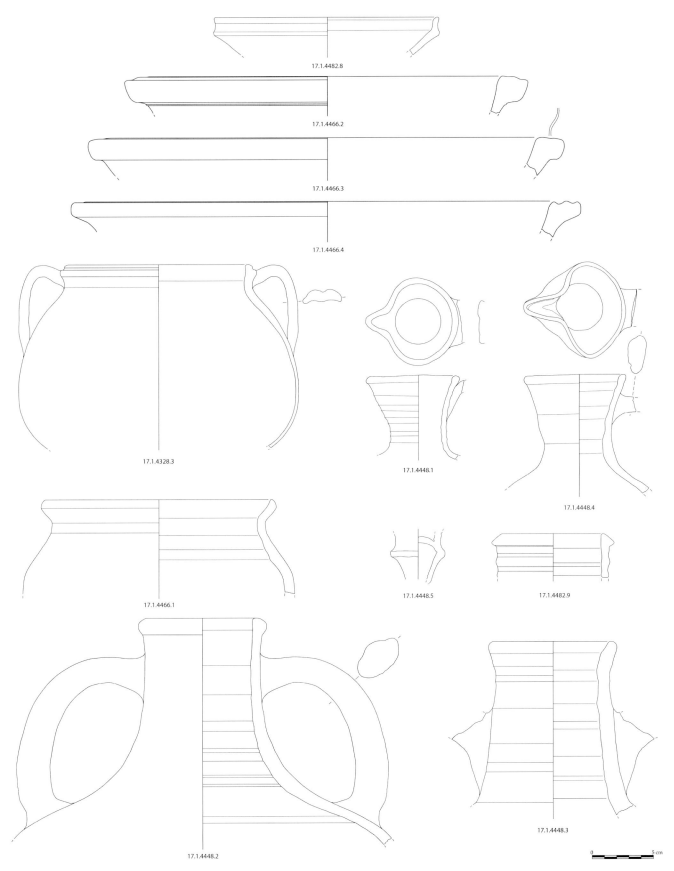

Fig. 61. Ceramics from the earliest deposits in the bottom of the pool.

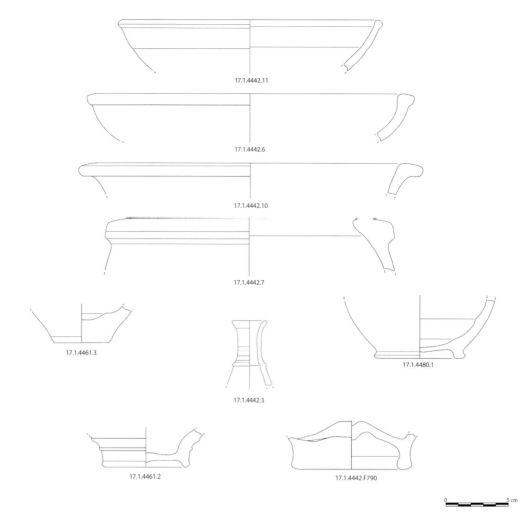

Fig. 62. Residual late Roman ceramics in Phase 4–6 deposits.

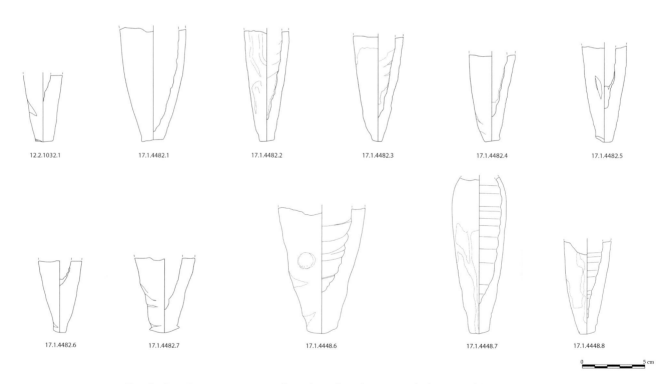

Fig. 63. Late Roman unguentaria from the earliest deposits in the bottom of the pool.

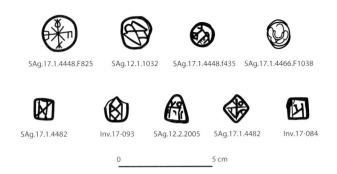

Fig. 64. Unguentaria stamps.

and are found across the eastern Mediterranean.[93] Studies have demonstrated the existence of several urban workshops making unguentaria in southwestern Asia Minor.[94] They are sometimes assumed to have served a paraliturgical function in a manner similar to the flask-like ampullae in contemporary circulation.[95] Stamped impressions are frequently found near the bases of the unguentaria. Though figural images and Christian and magical symbols are occasionally employed, the most common form of stamp is a monogram, sometimes resolving as a name or title in the genitive.

The most unusual of the examples from the Place of Palms consists of a crescent within a hexafoil frame.[96] Three more employ oblique and orthogonal lines focusing on one or more 'X' motifs.[97] Hayes noted that the type was particularly common in a deposit from the Agora at Athens dating to the middle of the sixth century.[98] It is unclear whether this type of monogram was intended to be read phonetically.[99] Four unguentaria display box monograms of sixth-century types. One, the example from outside the pool, positions several letters around a central *pi*; the stamp was triangular with rounded corners.[100] The monogram is similar to examples from Ephesos, though the impression is so worn that it is difficult to read any more letters than Ο-Π-Υ.[101] An unusual monogram based on a central *chi* set on a square stamp was impressed so that the four arms were vertical and horizontal.[102] In addition to the X, one reads Α(?)-Δ-Ε-Λ-Ο-Υ. Another box monogram on a square stamp—this time found on a residual fragment in a later context—may be a simple graphic sign similar to those discussed above.[103] The best preserved of the box monograms centres on an *epsilon* and was impressed using a circular stamp.[104] Possible letters include Ε-Η-Θ-Ι-Μ-Ο-Π-Ρ-Τ-Υ. Similar examples are known from Constantinople, Iasos, and Ephesos.[105] Metaxas suggests either the proper name Θεοπέμπτου or the office Μητροπολίτου for a comparable monogram at Ephesos.[106]

The two remaining unguentaria were impressed with cross monograms on circular stamps.[107] Both resolve as Ἐπάρχου—[stamp/unguentarium?] of the Eparch. The eparch, or urban prefect, was responsible for criminal prosecution and the regulation of the marketplace. His seal on the unguentaria may point towards a commercial role in addition to any ritual function. Parallels may be found at Constantinople, Iasos, Knidos, Limyra, Ephesos, Sagalassos, and Kibyra.[108] The last of these sites is of particular interest, since the monogram published by Dündar is so similar to that from Aphrodisias that they may derive from the same stamp.[109] The observation is intriguing since Kibyra fell within the administrative province of Karia, of which Aphrodisias was capital.

D. LATE ANTIQUE SMALL FINDS AND GLASS
(TP & HJ)

Small finds from the fills within the monumental pool illustrate over a millennium of life at Aphrodisias. In this section we discuss a curated selection of minor artefacts rather than providing a comprehensive catalogue, aiming to cast light on the various activities occurring in and around the Place of Palms. Presentation broadly follows the stratigraphic sequence outlined above, but rigid adherence to such a neat stratigraphic periodisation would belie the residual nature of many of the finds. This is especially true of the seventh-century deposits, which contain both material generally relevant to civic life at the end of antiquity and military equipment perhaps reflecting two apparently violent sacks of the city.[110] We therefore discuss these two categories of evidence separately. A number of significant finds that date from the seventh century, but which were recovered in contexts substantially later than their date of manufacture, are discussed here as residual material; their contexts—mostly **4442** and **4480**—are discussed in Ch. 9 §A.

Many of the artefacts sealed within the dumped deposits on the pool floor illuminate the lives of the citizens of Aphrodisias in the decades before the traumatic events of the early to mid seventh century. Dropped gaming tokens and the instruments of commerce reflect activities that may be localised within the Place of Palms. Accoutrements of dress, adornment and of personal piety provide the backdrop—a broader characterisation

---

93 Hayes 1968, 214; 1971, 243. See distribution map at Metaxas 2005, 77 fig. 7.
94 Cottica 1998; Lochner, Sauer, and Linke 2005; Dündar 2007.
95 Hayes 1968, 214 cf. Vroom 2017, 190.
96 Inv. 17-110 (4466.F1038).
97 The fragment from SAg.12.1.1032 with comparable examples at Constantinople, Ephesos, Limyra, and Kibyra: Hayes 1992, pl. 16 no. 11; Metaxas 2005, 79 no. 6; Eisenmenger and Zäh 1999, fig. 5. no. 8; Dündar 2007, 174 nos. U4, U5. The fragment from **4482** with comparable examples at Ephesos and Iasos: Metaxas 2005, 78 nos. 3–4; Baldoni and Franco 1995, fig. 3 nos. 18–27. Inv. 17-093 (4482.F956).
98 Hayes 1992, 9.
99 Dündar 2007, 154.
100 This is the example fom SAg.12.2.2005.
101 Metaxas 2005, 80 nos. 13–16.
102 This is the example fom **4482**.
103 Inv. 17-084 (4442.F.751).

104 4448.F435.
105 Hayes 1992, Pl. 17 nos. 31–32; Baldoni and Franco 1995, fig. 1 no. 3; Metaxas 2005, 82 no. 26b.
106 Metaxas 2005, 82 no. 26a.
107 Bulk find from P.T.SW.89 / 2.8.1989; Inv. 17-087 (4448.F825).
108 Hayes 1992, Pl. 17 nos. 45–46; Baldoni and Franco 1995, 115–116 nos. 2–5, 12–13, 18; Degeest *et al.* 1999, 260; Metaxas 2005, 83–84, nos. 28–29; Dündar 2007, 158 U6.
109 Dündar 2007, 158 U6, cf. Inv. 17-087 (4448.F825). Note in particular the warped omicron of the ου ligature.
110 Contexts **4328**, **4448**, **4471**, **4482**.

of vernacular material culture. We address this material thematically, associating objects through social practices such as commerce, leisure, ritual and dress.

Before considering this material we must make some preliminary remarks about the composition of these assemblages. Though the objects recovered from within the pool are by no means numerically insignificant, the quantities involved do not amount to what we might expect to find in a vibrant late antique public space. At least two hypotheses might be advanced in order to explain this quantitative limitation. First, we might suppose that the Place of Palms had, by the end of late antiquity, ceased to have been used as intensively as before. However, this view is unsupported by the rich variety exhibited in the recovered material. It seems more probable that the materials dumped into the pool are those items that were either missed or deemed of little value by the workforce undertaking the clean-up. Furthermore, we cannot exclude the possibility that additional material was not also dumped elsewhere or retrieved for recycling. Such an interpretation has the merit of explaining the relatively limited number of metal and glass finds related to the large quantities of roof tiles and other building materials recovered from the same contexts. The materials analysed below nevertheless hint at some of the activities undertaken in this area of Aphrodisias in the late sixth and early seventh centuries.

Glass

The vessel glass recovered from the clean-up dumps (**4328**, **4471**, and **4482**) and the overlying siltation layer(s) (**4448**, **4442**, **4480**) in the pool should be treated together due to its coherent stylistic and typological nature; the pieces are residual in the overlying layers. Comprising a minimum of 52 vessels, the modest size of this assemblage probably reflects the selective recovery and recycling of material during the clean-up process. Most of these vessels are extremely fragmentary and not all are readily identifiable. Still, this assemblage is comparable with glass finds from across the Mediterranean, with vessels including beakers, goblets, lamps, long-necked bottles, and flasks.[111] No comprehensive study of glass from Aphrodisias is available at present. Although analysis of a larger glass assemblage from the Agora is currently in preparation,[112] a site-wide systematic study is very much needed. We may nevertheless make some preliminary remarks about the nature of this late antique glass assemblage from the Place of Palms, and its value for our understanding of this area of the city late antiquity.

A substantial proportion of these glass vessels relate to lighting. Most easily identifiable are hollow stemmed lamps, of which six examples were recovered. These come in a range of colours, including shades of pale yellowish-green (Fig. 65, 4448.F840, 4442 (bulk find 1)),[113] mid blueish-green (Fig. 65, 4442 (bulk find 2)),[114] and pale greenish-blue (Fig. 65, 4480.

111 François and Spieser 2002, 595–6.
112 Katherine Larsson *pers. comm.* (October 2018).
113 4448.F840: ⌀ base: *c.* 2.2 cm H: 2.7 cm, ⌀ (stem): 1.9 cm; 4442 (bulk find): ⌀ base: 0.9 cm, H: 4.5 cm, ⌀ (stem): 2.2 cm.
114 4442 (bulk find): ⌀: 1.75 cm, H: 3.0 cm, ⌀: 1.7 cm.

F782, 4482.F953).[115] Comparable vessels, generally dated to the fifth to seventh centuries, are known at numerous sites around the Mediterranean, with notable examples including Constantinople,[116] Elaiussa Sebaste,[117] Amorium,[118] Nicaea,[119] Tarsus,[120] Anemurium,[121] and Sardis.[122] Although these lamps are very frequently found in church contexts, their use in a domestic context at Anemurium and in the (former) theatre in Nicaea suggests that the same forms could be employed in a variety of settings. Their presence in a public space like the Place of Palms is therefore unsurprising.

The presence of five glass handles may also relate to lighting. These comprise vertically ribbed handles with a sub-triangular section in a pale yellowish-green glass (Fig. 65, 4482 (bulk find 1)),[123] which may have attached to the body and/or rim of a lamp. Comparable examples are known at numerous late antique sites, including Constantinople,[124] Elaiussa Sebaste,[125] Amorium,[126] Tarsus,[127] and Iasos.[128] Other handles in the form of applied coils affixed to the bodies of lamps were found in later layers, such as in the case of a very pale blue example with a round section recovered in an Ottoman context (**4048**) (Fig. 65, SAg.15.1.4048 (bulk find 9)).[129] However, coiled handles are typically of late antique date, as shown by examples from Istanbul,[130] Elaiussa Sebaste,[131] and Amorium.[132] This handle from Aphrodisias, and others like it, may therefore be in secondary deposition and might originally have been used to illuminate the Place of Palms or other public or private spaces in late antiquity. Both types allow for chain-suspended lighting systems, which were probably employed throughout the Place of Palms—it has been noted above (Ch. 3 §C–D) that holes for metal fittings in columns of the North and West stoas might have served for the attachment of hanging lamps. Indeed, Leslie Dossey relates the invention of the glass hanging lamp to the spread of public street lighting in late antiquity.[133]

Glass goblets are among the other highly recognisable forms recovered from the fills of the pool,[134] with at least ten examples identified. A range of styles is illustrated here in order to

115 4482.F953: ⌀: *c.* 2.0 cm H: 3.2 cm, ⌀ (stem): 1.9 cm; 4480.F782: ⌀ (base): *c.* 2.0 cm, H: 3.75 cm, ⌀ (stem): *c.* 2.2–2.9 cm.
116 Canav Özgümüş 2009, 22, fig. 9.
117 Gençler-Güray 2010, 237–9, especially 238, fig. 214.
118 Gill 2002, 37, cat. 21–24 with 63, fig. 1/2.
119 Özgümüş 2008, 730 with 729, tab. I.3.
120 Olcay 2001, 83, fig. 2.
121 Russell 1982, 137.
122 Von Saldern 1980, 49–52, type 3, especially cat nos. 274 and 280; pl. 23.
123 For example 4482 (bulk find): H: 3.1 cm, D: 0.5–1.3 cm.
124 Canav Özgümüş 2009, 22, fig. 5.
125 Gençler-Güray 2010, 237, fig. 213.
126 For example Gill 2002, 35–36, cat. 2–4, with 63, fig. 1/2, nos. 2–4.
127 Olcay 2001, 83, fig. 4a–h.
128 Contardi 2009, 130, fig. 4.
129 SAg.15.1.4048 (bulk find): H: 2.4 cm, W: 1.9 cm, D: 0.32 cm.
130 Canav Özgümüş 2009, 22, fig. 5.
131 Gençler-Güray 2010, 237, fig. 213.
132 Gill 2002, 36, cat. 10 with 63, fig. 1/2, no. 10; 123–133, cat. 13–17 with 169, fig. 2/1, nos. 13–17.
133 Dossey 2018; cf. Wilson 2018b, 71–72 for the suggestion of public lighting in the Place of Palms.
134 Isings 1957, 139–140, form 111.

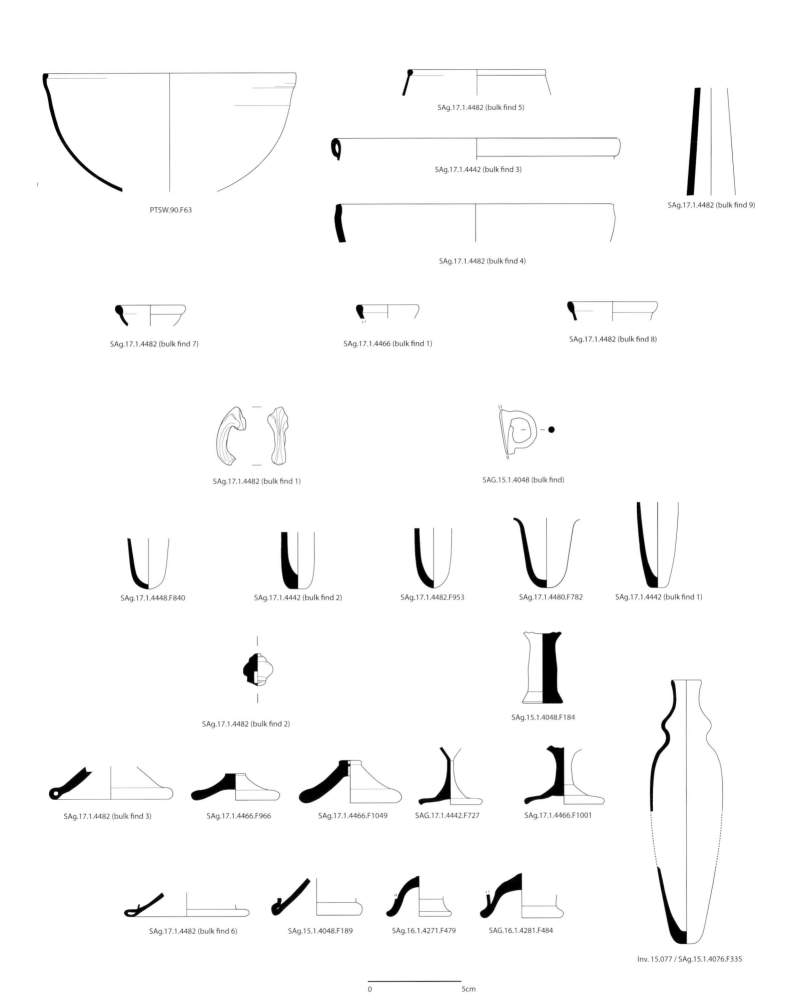

Fig. 65. Vessel glass and associated finds.

give an idea of the wide variety of goblets in circulation in late antiquity. Beaded stems are represented by a hollow example in pale yellowish-green glass (Fig. 65, 4482 (bulk find 2)).[135] Undecorated, filled stems are represented by two examples in a pale greenish-blue fabric as illustrated here; one of these is residual in a later context (Fig. 65, 4442.F727, 4466.F1001).[136] Another highly residual pale greenish-blue stem, likely belonging to the same period, was recovered in the same Ottoman context mentioned above (4048); it is included here to give a broader view of the typological variety of glass goblets of probable late antique date represented at Aphrodisias (Fig. 65, SAg.15.1.4048.F184).[137] Other goblet feet, sometimes still attached to their stems, and made from light blueish-green (Fig. 65, 4482 (bulk find 3)),[138] and mid-blueish green glass (Fig. 65, 4466.F966, 4466.F1049),[139] were also recovered from parts of the earliest fills of the pool (equivalent to 4482 and 4328). While most of the illustrated examples feature sloping feet with plain edges, at least one had a folded edge (Fig. 65, 4482 (bulk find 3)).[140] Goblets with both straight and beaded stems are attested at Istanbul,[141] Elaiussa Sebaste,[142] Amorium,[143] Nicaea,[144] Myra,[145] Sardis,[146] Iasos,[147] and across the wider late Roman world.

Yelda Olcay suggests that while the straight, filled-stem variants of this form appear to have been in use from at least the fifth century down to the present day, the knobbed variety are typically of a fifth- to eighth-century date.[148] The same scholar argues forcefully that such vessels served primarily as lamps,[149] and were sometimes fitted with handles similar to those discussed above. But the diversity of the forms observed in even the small number of vessels recovered in the Place of Palms suggests that stemmed goblets of differing sizes and finenesses may have had disparate uses, with some serving as vessels and others to provide lighting.

The glass evidence for lighting is also supplemented by a single metal find. This lead wick holder comprises a central roundel with a perforation for supporting the wick, from which radiate two arms terminating in gentle hooks for anchoring the device over a vessel rim (Fig. 66, Inv. 17-122).[150] This type of wick holder is also attested at Elaiussa Sebaste in a seventh-century collapse layer.[151] With a span of c. 16 cm, the object from the Place of Palms would be suitable for use in conjunction with hemispherical bowl lamps (see below). The significance of such substantial evidence for lighting is twofold. Firstly, it suggests that considerable activity was taking place in this public space in the hours of darkness, or that the stoas were poorly supplied with natural light. Secondly, the range of different coloured fabrics in which these lamps appear should encourage us to think about the subtle polychrome effects of the light may have been emitted by these lamps against the marbles of the stoas, even if, at present, it is not possible to establish whether these differently coloured lamps were originally commingled or zoned by colour.

Other open-form glass vessels could have served as lamps, perhaps in conjunction with wick holders of the type described above, or might simply relate to the use of the Place of Palms as a market place or hint at the consumption of food and drink. Several hemispherical bowls were recovered.[152] These include a deep bowl with an outward folded rim in pale greenish-blue glass which is broadly paralleled at Amorium (Fig. 65, 4442 (bulk find 3)).[153] A bowl with a broken-off and ground rim in a light green-blue fabric may be similar to another item from Amorium (Fig. 65, 4482 (bulk find 4)).[154] These vessels could have been used either for the display of perishable goods or for serving either on a daily basis or during public events.

Beakers are represented by, for example, a specimen in a dark blue fabric with an inward-folded rim and slightly outward-flaring body (Fig. 65, 4482 (bulk find 5)).[155] A comparable beaker form (although in a different fabric), is known at Amorium.[156] Another form connected to drinking may include at least one tubular folded base in a pale greenish-blue fabric (Fig. 65, 4482 (bulk find 6)).[157] Similar bases recovered from fifth- to eighth-century layers in Istanbul have been described as tumblers by Canav Özgümüş.[158] Several pushed-in bases from later layers (equal to 4255 and 4281, which are discussed in Ch. 9 §C) may also belong to a similar beaker type dating to late antiquity, though the question of their dating may be resolved by future compositional analysis (Fig. 65, SAg.16.1.4271.F479, SAg.16.1.4281.F484).[159] This small quantity of beakers and tumblers together suggest that some drinking activities may have taken place in the Place of Palms, though the small number of individuals recovered does not allow us to comment on the scale of this undertaking. It would be consistent, however, with the evidence for κάπηλοι trading from the eastern South Stoa near the stairs up to the Theatre (see Ch. 5 §D: TW2, TW6), if these are tavern-keepers rather than retail sellers (the word can mean both).

---

135 4482 (bulk find),: ⌀: 1.6 cm, H: 1.7 cm.
136 4442.F727: ⌀: 3.6 cm, H: 3.05 cm (residual); 4466.F1001: ⌀: 4.4 cm, H: 3.1 cm.
137 SAg.15.1.4048.F184: ⌀. 1.57 cm H: 3.67 cm.
138 4482 (bulk find): ⌀: 6.0 cm, H: 1.7 cm.
139 4466.F966: ⌀: 4.4 cm, H: 1.4 cm; 4466.F1049: ⌀: 4.8 cm, H: 2.6 cm.
140 4482 (bulk find): ⌀: 6.0 cm, 1.7 cm.
141 Canav Özgümüş 2009, 22, fig. 11.
142 Gençler-Güray 2010, 240; 241, fig. 218.
143 For example Gill 2002, 38–43, cat 34–87 with 64–66, figs. 1/4 to 1/7.
144 Özgümüş 2008, 732, table II.7–9; taf. XXVII, fig. 3; Olcay 2001, 83, fig. 2a–h.
145 Olcay 2001, 87, fig. 7.
146 Von Saldern 1980, 53–60, cat 300–373; pl. 24.
147 Contardi 2009, 130, figs. 5–9.
148 Olcay 2001, 87.
149 Olcay 2001, 86–87.
150 Inv. 17-122, L: 16.0 cm, W (roundel): 1.3 cm, W (arm): 0.5 cm, D: 0.13 cm.
151 Gençler-Güray 2010, 237; 236, fig. 212.
152 Isings 1957, 113–114, form 96.
153 4442 (bulk find): ⌀: 15 cm, H: 1.2 cm, ⌀: 15.0 cm. Cf Gill 2002, 149, cat. 173 with 175, fig. 2/11, no. 173.
154 4482 (bulk find): ⌀: 14.4 cm, H: 2.0 cm. Cf Gill 2002, 46, cat. 125 with 69, fig. 1/11, no. 125.
155 4482 (bulk find): ⌀: 7.2 cm H: 1.4 cm. This rim could also relate to a lamp; the flaring body makes this unlikely, though not all lamps are straight-sided.
156 Gill 2002, 146, cat. 156 with fig. 2/10, no. 156.
157 4482 (bulk find): ⌀: 6.0 cm, H: 1.3 cm.
158 Isings 1957, 137–8, form 109b-c. For Istanbul see Canav Özgümüş 2009, 22, fig. 14.
159 SAg.16.1.4271.F479: ⌀: 3.2 cm h: 2.1 cm; SAg.16.1.4281.F484: H: 2.4 cm, ⌀: 4.2 cm.

Closed-form vessels from these contexts may provide further evidence for commercial activity in the Place of Palms during the late sixth and early seventh centuries. Small flasks or bottles, generally in pale yellowish-green fabrics, include at least three examples with tightly folded rims, turned both inward (Fig. 65, 4466 (bulk find 1)),[160] and outward (Fig. 65, 4482 (bulk find 7), 4482 (bulk find 8)).[161] Although the fragmentary nature of these objects means we cannot discuss their overall form in detail, bottles with broadly comparable rims are present, for example, at Amorium,[162] Sardis,[163] and Ephesos.[164] One larger closed-form vessel is attested by the cylindrical neck of a bottle in a pale greenish-blue fabric (Fig. 65, 4482 (bulk find 9)),[165] though its fragmentary state and the absence of a rim make it difficult to find close comparanda. These vessels, whether they contained oils, perfumes, or medical products, suggest that a variety of goods may have been on sale within the North Stoa before its collapse, or indeed elsewhere in the Place of Palms.

Finally, limited quantities of glass production debris, including small chunks of raw glass, several possible moils, and probable glass slag, were recovered in context **4482**, overlying the pool floor, and (probably as residual material) in the higher siltation deposit **4442**, which is discussed in Ch. 9 §B.[166] This production waste was predominantly pale yellowish-green, comparable in colour to some of the vessels discussed above. Several fragments of turquoise glass cakes, probably architectural inlays similar to the glass *sectilia* excavated at Kenchreai,[167] but which could also be (re-)used in small quantities as glass colouring agents, were also recovered. This evidence is insufficient to suggest that glass manufacturing was taking place in the Place of Palms in late antiquity, but it may be added to a growing body of evidence for glass manufacture within the city limits. Production waste has also been found scattered in late antique contexts in the North Agora,[168] and a small furnace in the easternmost room (S1) of the Sebasteion's south portico has been dated to the fifth to seventh centuries.[169] It therefore seems probable that at least some of the glass vessels in the Place of Palms assemblage may have been manufactured nearby. The presence of this waste may also show that small quantities of industrial waste were introduced into the pool at the same time as the main clean-up, or that a further glass workshop remains unexcavated or was missed by earlier excavations in the Place of Palms or its immediate vicinity.

Metal architectural fittings

A range of metal fittings helps to extend our understanding of the architecture of the urban park in late antiquity. Finds include: wedge-shaped iron dowels with rectangular sections (Pl. 81.A);[170] several U-shaped iron clamps for the holding together of marble blocks,[171] one of which is still encased in its lead packing (Pl. 81.B);[172] and other lead overspills.[173] Comparable clamps are known, for example, at Sardis,[174] and at Pergamon.[175] Twelve revetment pins with T-shaped heads probably held marble panels to the rear wall of the North Stoa.[176] Several hundred iron nails in a variety of sizes and shapes including round, square, and rectangular flathead nails were also recovered.[177] Some of these nails probably formed part of the timber roofing system of the same stoa, while others may have been utilised in door construction.

The presence of doors is also suggested by two iron loops with sub-circular section, now heavily corroded (for example, see Fig. 66),[178] as well as two objects comprising a square-sectioned iron rod bent into an omega-shape with a narrow or closed loop (Pl. 81.C).[179] At Pergamon, similar objects have been thought to belong to a Roman-period door handle in an elite house,[180] with comparable examples attested in both ancient and Byzantine contexts.[181] Further evidence for doors or shutters may be provided by at least five hairpin-like iron objects with square sections (Pl. 81.D);[182] similar objects have been interpreted at Nysa as door hinges,[183] though at Pergamon further comparanda are identified simply as attachments for iron loops.[184] Although the doorframes added in the intercolumniations of the North and West Stoas in the fourth century were removed during the late fifth-/early sixth-century rebuilding works, there were doors from the North Stoa into the Agora, and from the West Stoa into the Hadrianic 'Olympian' Baths, and if these fittings are door handles then it is possible that they come from these doors, which were still in place into the early seventh century. A copper alloy hexagonal ring with a rectangular section

---

160 4466 (bulk find): ⌀: 3.0 cm, H: 0.7 cm.
161 4482 (bulk find): ⌀: 3.4 cm, H: 1.1 cm; 4482 (bulk find), ⌀: 4.6 cm, H: 1.0 cm.
162 For example, Gill 2002, 56, cat. 251–252 with 74, fig. 1/18, nos.251–252.
163 For example, Von Saldern 1980, 70–72, cat. nos. 476–499; pl. 26.
164 Fünfschilling 2014, 142, fig. 15.4.
165 4482 (bulk find): ⌀: 2.6 cm, H: 5.7 cm.
166 Glass slag: 4442.F721.
167 Ibrahim, Scranton, and Brill 1976.
168 Katherine Larsson *pers comms* (October 2018).
169 Smith and Ratté 1998, 238; Çakmaklı 2014, 133.

170 4482.F917: L (maximum): 12.0 cm, W: 2.3 cm, D: 1.1 cm; 4328.F971: L: 17.5 cm, W (maximum): 2.0 cm, D: 0.7 cm.
171 4448.F848: L: 8.5 cm, H: 2.5 cm, D: 2.5 cm.
172 4466.F1032: L: 0.9 cm, W: 0.3 cm, D: 3.5 cm.
173 For example, 4328.F748; 4466.F1009.
174 Waldbaum 1983, 67, Cat.287.
175 For example, Gaitzsch 2005, 167, BK 1.
176 Found in **4482**. As a representative example of dimensions, the well-preserved pin SAg.17.4442.F865, residual in a later context measures L: 3.5 cm, W: 3.4 cm, D: 0.1 cm.
177 Waldbaum 1983, 68, types 2–4.
178 4466.F1006: ⌀ (exterior): 4.9 cm, ⌀ (interior): 3.4 cm, D: 0.3 cm; Cf. 4466.F1005.
179 4448.F873: L: 9.0 cm, W: 10.0 cm, D: 1.2 cm; 4448.F874: L: 8.0 cm, W: 5.3 cm, D: 1.0 cm.
180 Gaitzsch 2005, 55–60, especially 57, Abb. 13.
181 Gaitzsch 2005, 194, Ö 1–2, Ö 9.
182 4482.F900: L: 8.0 cm, W: 1.9 cm, D: 1.0 cm. Other examples include 4482.F898; 4482.F903; 4482.F905–906.
183 Tamsü Polat 2014, 151, cat. 278–280 and Taf. 72, 9–11.
184 Gaitzsch 2005, 194, Ö 5–6, though it is worth noting that these have been assigned a late Byzantine and therefore significantly later chronology.

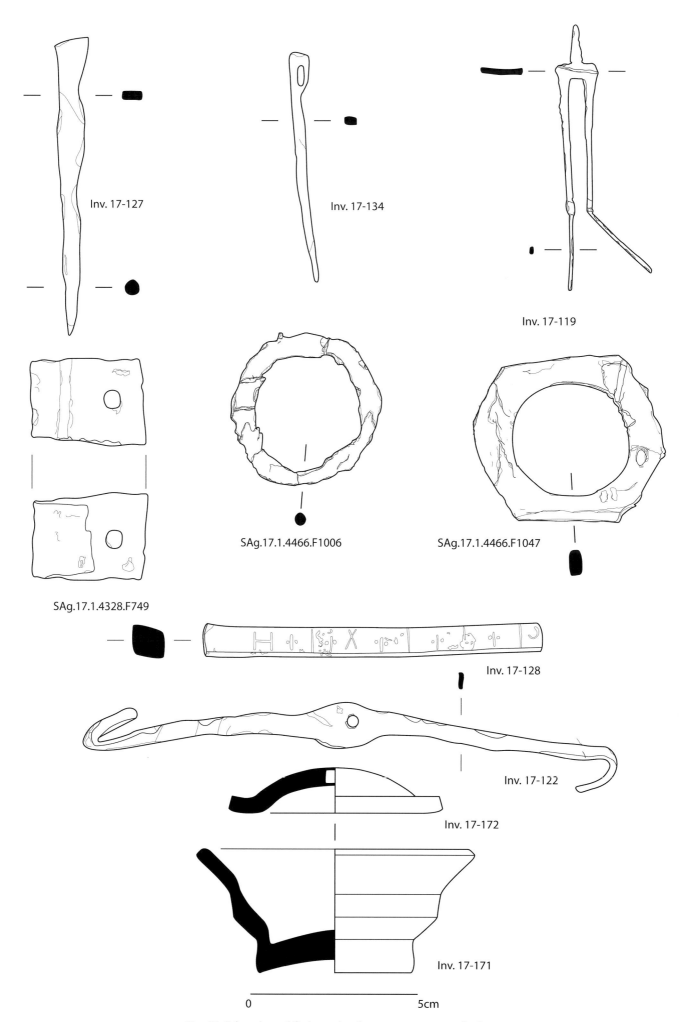

Fig. 66. Selected metal finds: marketplace accoutrements and others.

might also be a door handle, but alternatively it may have been a furniture fitting (Fig. 66, 4466.F1047).[185]

Two heavily corroded iron objects, both forged, cannot be confidently identified but may have been either furniture fittings or utility devices, perhaps connected to the fixed architecture of the stoa.[186] The first object has an open shape formed by bending a single sheet of metal through two approximately 90-degree angles to produce a square bracket (Pl. 81.E–F).[187] The exposed edges are serrated with irregular teeth, though these do not appear sharp and were not necessarily intended for cutting. The interior of this object also has two possible bolts running across the interior. These bolt-like objects may have served as anchoring points. A small hook found with the object may have originally been attached to the exterior side of the middle face. The second object is shaped similarly to the first, though it differs by apparently lacking the serrated edges and bolts described above.[188] Other finds may relate to the lighting provision for the West or North stoas, where cuttings in the columns are at a height to suggest the suspension of lamps. An iron hook with a square section may have served for the suspension of some of the glass lamps discussed above.[189]

Glass architectural fittings

Small quantities (31 fragments, total weight 256.8 g) of glass window panes in various fabrics were recovered, ranging in colour from colourless to pale blue to varied hues of blueish-green, greenish-blue, greenish-yellow, and yellowish-green.[190] While it is possible that some of these variations in colour may result from differing glass thicknesses, the range of colours represented, which cannot have all belonged to the same pane, suggests that there were windows in at least one of the stoas. The only obvious candidate is the upper storey of part of the South Stoa, unless glass panes were set in the doors inserted into the West and North Stoas, which by the seventh century had probably gone. The small amounts of window glass identified imply that much material pertaining to the stoas was recovered and recycled, or simply missed, during the clean-up and therefore not deposited into the various fills of the pool.

Fine tesserae in turquoise, green-yellowish, and dark blue glass hint at revetments covering parts of the walls and/or ceiling of the north stoa. As these tesserae were not recovered *in situ*, reconstruction of the precise decorative scheme is not possible. The decoration nevertheless must have been relatively lavish. There is a significant quantity of gold sandwich glass decorations comprising sheets of gold leaf applied to a thicker glass cake and then fixed in place by the addition of a further, thinner, layer of glass. Extant examples of decorations made using this technique include tesserae (ranging in size from *c.* 0.8–1.2 cm by 0.7–1.0 cm and 0.6–0.7 cm deep),[191] but five larger, highly fragmentary gold glass plaques in the same fabric and made using the same technique were also recovered (Pl. 81.G; Colour Pl. 2.A).[192] Particularly noteworthy among these is an oval-shaped gold glass plaque in a mid orangeish-brown fabric, of which around half survives (Pl. 81.H; Colour Pl. 2.B).[193] This plaque is far larger than the cube-shaped tesserae with a width of 5 cm and a preserved length of 6.5 cm.

While small, square glass tesserae are relatively common finds in monumental late antique building contexts, the presence of these larger plaques is rarer.[194] It is noteworthy that these gold glass plaques are hitherto attested primarily in ecclesiastical contexts, such as the church of St Polyeuktos in Constantinople,[195] and the basilica of St Demetrios in Thessaloniki;[196] or else they have been found at elite residences, with examples recovered in the Topkapı Palace Courtyard excavations in Istanbul.[197] As such, their presence in the Place of Palms, a secular public space, is unusual and underlines the richness of the decorative schemes which must have marked the late antique restoration of this part of the city.

Marketplace accoutrements

The recovery of several weights (*exagia*) reinforce the evidence from informal writing (Ch. 5 §D) that the Place of Palms served as a venue for economic activity during the sixth and early seventh centuries. Two smaller weights hint at high-value exchange, whether purchases involving gold coinage or money changing. The first is a small circular copper alloy weight, originally thought to be three fused coins, but which is probably a coin weight (Pl. 81.I). At 8.98 g it corresponds approximately to two *nomismata/solidi*.[198] Although the weight's obverse is now heavily corroded, rendering any lettering illegible, examples of comparable denomination are known from Athens[199] and from the Yassi Ada shipwreck.[200] The second is an approximately disk-shaped weight in a dark blue fabric with a rolled rim enclosing a bust of a figure holding an object, probably a *mappa*, in his

---

185 4466.F1047: L: 5.5 cm, W: 4.7 cm, ⌀ (interior): 3.4 cm.
186 An alternative interpretation of this object as a curry-comb used for horse grooming was advanced by workmen involved in the excavation, but it has not been possible to adduce close comparanda in time or space—the nearest parallels come from medieval London: Clark 1995, 163, fig. 120.
187 Inv. 17-117 (4448.F879): L: 17.0 cm, W: 6.0 cm, D: 4.0 cm.
188 4466.F1042: L: 17.0 cm, W: 4.1 cm, plate thickness: *c.* 0.3 cm.
189 4482.F919: L: 11.7 cm, W: 1.0 cm, D: 0.5 cm.
190 These glass panes were from contexts **4328**, **4482**, and **4442** (where they are residual).
191 For example, Inv. 17-139 (4442.F759); Inv. 17-140 (4329.F973); Inv. 17-141 (4466.F1026); Inv. 17-142 (4466.F1043); Inv. 17-143 (4466.F1044).
192 Inv. 17-088 (4448.F836): H: 6.5 cm, W: 5.0 cm, D: 1.0 cm; Inv. 17-104 (4482.M2648): H: 2.7 cm, W: 2.5 cm, D: 0.4 cm; Inv. 17-135 (4466.F1046): H: 1.5 cm, W: 1.2 cm, D: 0.3 cm; Inv. 17-136: H: 2.2 cm, W: 1.7 cm, D: 0.8 cm; Inv. 17-137 (4466.F1039) is too fragmentary to measure accurately.
193 Inv. 17-88 (4448.F836).
194 Gorin-Rosen 2015 with further bibliography.
195 Harrison and Gill 1986, 174.
196 Antonaras 2012, 303, type 1, figs. 1–5.
197 Atik 2012.
198 4482.C240/241/242, ⌀: 1.8–2.0 cm. We thank Ahmet Tolga Tek and Hüseyin Köker for this identification. On weights, Waldbaum (1983, 85) gives the weight of two *nomismata* as 9.10 g.
199 Bendall 1996, 52, cat. 147–148.
200 Sams 1982, 204, w7.

right hand (Pl. 81.J; Colour Pl. 2.C).[201] Faint traces of lettering are detectable around the figure but the pressing was poorly executed and these are largely illegible.[202] The item, which weighs 4.49 g, equal to one *nomisma,* belongs to the 'bust of an eparch and inscription' type.[203] Weights of this type are dated broadly to between the reigns of Justin I (AD 521–527) and Heraclius I (AD 610–641), though the poor state of the lettering means we cannot identify which eparch issued this weight.

These objects seem to have been used for checking the approximate weights of gold coins. They have been found in commercial contexts in the Byzantine shops at Sardis (where three glass weights were found in association with other weights, scale pans, a steelyard, and balance beams),[204] and at Tel Naharon in Palestina Secunda.[205] Recent compositional analysis of comparable weights held in the British Museum suggests that glass weights of this type were probably produced in Constantinople before being distributed across the empire for use in local markets, as might be expected in the case of an item issued by the eparch.[206] The weight therefore probably reflects ongoing imperial regulation of commerce in Karia into late antiquity.

Two larger weights were also recovered. One is a square-sectioned copper alloy bar, one surface of which appears to preserve traces of lightly etched Greek lettering: an *eta* to the left of the piece and a possible *chi* in the centre (Fig. 66, Inv. 17-128).[207] The letters are interspersed with etched vertical dividing lines running the whole height of the object, sometimes flanked on either side by a single dot.[208] Side A features three long and two short vertical lines, side C has three short vertical lines which divide two dots. Its weight (*c.* 81 g) corresponds approximately to three ounces or 18 *nomismata* and we therefore cannot exclude that it was used as a commercial or coin weight. However, the markings seem to correspond to measurement divisions on complete steelyard arms known, for example, at Sardis.[209] On comparison with extant examples, this represents around a fifth of the original object, which is estimated to have been 18 inches (45.72 cm) in length.[210] Such an interpretation cannot therefore be excluded, though the clean breaks at either end make it more likely this was a weight or scale than a steelyard arm.

The final weight is a copper alloy discoid weight, convex on one side, flattened on the other, and weighing 51 g (Pl. 81.K).[211] This corresponds very broadly to either a two-ounce commercial weight[212] or a 12-*nomisma* coin weight (that is 54.6 g).[213] This slight disparity in weight may result from corrosion on this heavily weathered object. In its present state of conservation and in the absence of any visible lettering it is impossible to discern whether this weight was destined for money-changing or more generalised use in exchange, though it cannot be excluded that little distinction was made in practice.

Other elements of weighing equipment were recovered alongside this weight. These include the suspension device of a balance scale, with a moulded upper part terminating in a flattened loop (Fig. 67, Inv. 17-120). Below the moulding, one leg is preserved, ending in a perforation at the lower end, which would have originally received the attachment pin holding the scale pointer in place.[214] This instrument is similar to a balance-scale suspension device attested at Sardis, dated to a late Roman–early Byzantine phase.[215] Also recovered from the pool was a copper alloy balance pivot with two thin prongs with two square sections, becoming flattened towards the ends. The prongs attach to a flattened rectangular plate with curved shoulders (Fig. 66, Inv. 17-119).[216] From the top of this plate protrudes a small, tapering projection, while from the bottom extend two square-sectioned prongs, transitioning to a rectangular section halfway down their length. This is similar to a late Roman object excavated at Corinth and originally published as a hairpin, but now reinterpreted as a balance pivot, and to a balance found in the Saraçhane excavations in Istanbul.[217]

Tools and containers

A few tools and implements also attest to the economic and social activities taking place in the Place of Palms in late antiquity. Finds from the fills of the pool included a copper alloy flat chisel with a circular socket, possibly for light engraving work on metal, leather or wood (Pl. 82.A),[218] and a copper alloy needle with an elliptical eyelet (Fig. 66, Inv. 17-134).[219] These items suggest either that manufacturing, perhaps small-scale, may have been taking place, or that these items were being sold in or near the stoas. Also recovered was a possible iron stylus with circular section tapering to a point at one end, and at the other end a flattened wedge, perhaps for erasing text on wax tablets (Fig. 66, Inv. 17-127).[220] Accordingly, we might envisage that scribal activities were undertaken in this space. An iron sickle or pruning hook may indicate maintenance of foliage in the urban park, or

---

201 Inv. 18-55 (4448.F911), ⌀: 2.2–2.4, H: 0.6 cm.
202 Entwistle and Meek 2015, 2.
203 Entwistle and Meek 2015, 3–4, 12–13, cat. 11–29; Bendall 1996, 60–62, cat. 184–188.
204 Petzl 2019; 86, figs. 464–468 and 477–482.
205 Vitto 1980, 214.
206 Entwistle and Meek 2015, 11.
207 Inv. 17-128 (4466.F1027): L: 10.0 cm, W: 1.0 cm, D: 1.0 cm.
208 This object is discussed in Angelos Chaniotis's internal report, *Epigraphic Research in Aphrodisias 2018.*
209 Waldbaum 1983, 81, no. 437.
210 Vikan and Nesbitt 1980, 32.
211 Inv. 17-85 (4328.F747): H: 0.67 cm, ⌀: 4.0 cm.
212 For example, Bendall 1996, 46, cat. 119–122.
213 For example, Bendall 1996, 50, cat 134–135.

214 Inv. 17-120 (4484.F946): H: 9.5 cm, ⌀ (upper part, maximum): 0.7 cm, W (leg): 0.35 cm, D (leg): 0.2 cm. N.B. there is little trace of the other leg, so an outside chance remains that this object may have instead served another purpose, for example as a hair pin, but this seems unlikely given the overall design. Another possible part of a balance scale is represented by Inv. 17-121 (4402.F962) (see also Figure 8.8, 17-121).
215 Waldbaum 1983, 84, cat. 460.
216 Inv. 17-119 (4482.F913): H: 7.8 cm, W (plate): 1.3 cm, W (prong): 0.1 cm, D: 0.13–0.2 cm.
217 Original publication at Corinth: Davidson 1952, 282, cat. 2288. Reinterpretation as a pivot: http://ascsa.net/id/corinth/object/mf%20658?q=balance&t=object&v=list&sort=&s=12 (Last accessed 24/9/2018); Saraçhane: Harrison 1986, 257, cat. 466.
218 Inv. 17-170 (4328.F981): H: 8.7 cm, W: 1.0 cm, D: 0.7 cm.
219 Inv. 17-134 (4466.F1024): L: 6.8 cm, W (head): 0.55 cm, W (body): 0.35 cm, D: 0.28 cm.
220 Inv. 17-127 (4466.F1018): H: 8.8 cm, W: 3.7–5.6 cm, D: 2.7–3.4 cm.

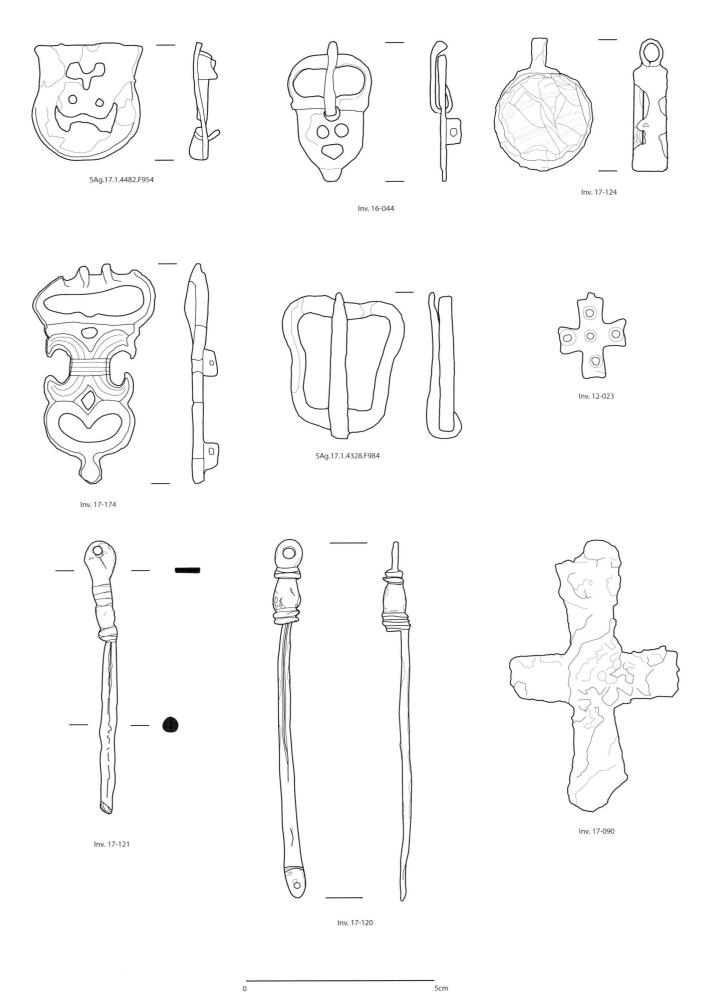

Fig. 67. Selected metal finds: marketplace accoutrements and items of personal adornment.

could simply have been on sale for use in agricultural activities, whether in gardens or outside the city limits (Pl. 82.B).[221]

Other items indicate food preparation. An iron pan with a poorly-preserved U-shaped pan and a rectangular-sectioned handle was recovered during the 1990 season (Pl. 82.C). It seems to have been found in one of the lower fills of the pool, though its precise elevation cannot be reconstructed with certainty.[222] At least five blades were found in the deposit dumped along the north side of the pool, 4328 and its equivalent contexts.[223] To these we may add two recovered from the scatter of material lying directly on the pool floor (4482),[224] and three in the siltation layers which seal the material deposited during the clean-up (4448),[225] some of which probably reflect material disturbed from below. Three such knives are illustrated here to give an idea of the range of items recovered (Pl. 82.D–F).[226] It is probable that these blades relate to food preparation activities or other productive activities (for example, working of textiles or leather, or for butchery in a market context), as they are common finds on Roman and late antique sites. They are known from Sardis in numerous public and domestic contexts without a clear link to a military presence.[227] At the same time, however, it cannot be excluded either that these knives represent weapons of last resort seized by the inhabitants of Aphrodisias in response to the violent events possibly implied by the assemblage of weaponry discussed below (see §F).

Storage, presumably for prestige goods or other valuables, may have been provided by boxes or chests. This is suggested by a lightweight copper alloy hinge formed by the folding of a single sheet and featuring a circular perforation (ø: c. 0.5 cm) on one side, which was found in the first clean-up dump (4328) (Fig. 66, 4328.F749).[228] More small-scale storage functions may also have been fulfilled by a copper alloy vessel recovered in the siltation layer overlying the clean-up dump (4448), but which could be residual from an earlier phase of activity (Fig. 66, Inv. 17-171).[229] This object is characterised by a pronounced foot and carinated body terminating in a slightly everted rim; this fits a domed copper alloy lid with a slightly everted rim and a circular central perforation (ø: 0.6 cm) (Fig. 66, Inv. 17-172).[230] That a second nearly identical lid was also recovered from the bottom 5 cm of the first clean-up dump in the pool again suggests that these items were of late antique date.[231] A similar small bowl, albeit with a straight-sided body, has been dated to the early Byzantine period at Sardis.[232] A thinner domed copper alloy lid of early Byzantine date has been recovered at the same site, fitted with a small hook and button inserted into the perforation to allow it to be suspended from a small chain,[233] though such a chain is missing from the examples from the Place of Palms.

Gaming counters

Frequent finds in the clean-up fills of the pool and in later layers (4482) as well as the overlying siltation layers (4448) were sub-circular, roughly recut fragments of marble wall revetment panels (for examples, see Pl. 82.G; Colour Pl. 2.D). Some still preserve traces of mortar on the unfinished side. The objects vary in diameter from c. 2.9 cm to 11.5 cm or larger. Stones represented include the local white Aphrodisian marble, *greco scritto*, a dark grey *bigio*, *portasanta*, and at least one example of porphyry. The revetment panels from which the circular pieces were cut probably originally decorated the rear wall of the North Stoa, and were removed prior to the refurbishments of Doulkitios and Ampelios; similar fragments of marble are employed in repairs to the pool floor. Recut brick or ceramic vessel fragments also appear in the same contexts, some of which are quite small and irregular (c. 4.0 cm in the illustrated example), while others are more carefully recut and circular in shape (with diameters of c. 9.4 cm and 11.3 cm). Similar finds have been interpreted as vessel stoppers elsewhere, but they are usually much thicker, acting almost as corks;[234] the disks from the Place of Palms are more likely to be game tokens or counters.

These objects are part of a long tradition of makeshift gaming pieces, dating back at least as far as the archaic period; Kurke has identified examples of geometric pottery reused in this way from the Athenian Areopagos.[235] The numerous gaming boards carved into marble seats and surfaces around this public space suggest that a large number of such counters would have been in circulation in this public space, even if not all of these boards were in use at precisely the same time (Ch. 5 §F). Moreover, the varied tones offered by the coloured marble counters may have facilitated games, such as *duodecim scripta* and merels, in which it is essential for smooth gameplay for a player to be able to distinguish between their pieces and those of their opponent(s). In either case, these items suggest a pragmatic attitude to the material culture of earlier periods and the willingness of late antique populations to repurpose available resources to meet needs in the present.

Religious items

Small finds often open windows onto the more personal devotional practices of past actors. However, the first artefact to be considered under this heading, a lead seal recovered in the clean-up dump in the pool (4328) and therefore predating the

---

221 4448.F795: H: 31.0 cm, W: 2.5 cm, D: 0.5 cm.
222 Nbk 316: *Portico of Tiberius: W Pool, Book I; E Pool* (A.T. Tek, 1990), 9, f9: H (total surviving): 30.5 cm, H (handle): 9.3 cm, W (handle): 0.9 cm, D (blade): 0.3 cm, W (shaft/blade): 1.6 cm, D (handle): 0.4 cm.
223 4466.F1013; 4466.F1019; 4466.F1020; 4328.F985; 4328.F986.
224 4482.F914; 4482.F957.
225 4448.F837; 4448.F850; 4448.F863.
226 4328.F985: L: 14.0 cm, W: 2.0 cm, D: 0.5 cm; 4448.F863: L: 19.5 cm, W: 1.6 cm, D: 0.2 cm; 4448.F850: L: 21.0 cm, W: 3.1 cm, D: 0.2 cm.
227 Waldbaum 1983, 56–58, nos. 183–204.
228 4328.F749: L: 3.5 cm, W: 2.5 cm, D: 0.4 cm.
229 Inv. 17-171 (4448.F808): H: 3.9 cm, ø: 8.0 cm.
230 Inv. 17-172 (4448.F821): H: 1.3 cm, ø: 6.8 cm.
231 Inv. 17-173 (4466.F1037): H: 1.3 cm, ø: 7.2 cm.
232 Waldbaum 1983, 88, cat. 490; pl. 31.

233 Waldbaum 1983, 95, cat. 551, pl. 36.
234 Zemer 1977, 89–93; Witte 2012, 243–245.
235 Kurke 1999, 264, fig. 1.

640s, speaks to a more authoritative and institutional form of religion.[236] Seals could be used both to validate documents and to secure their contents. A thread attached to the object that was to be sealed was passed between two circular lead blanks, which were then struck by tongs cut with imagery or inscriptions unique to their owner. The obverse and reverse of our example display cruciform monograms in wreath borders, resolving as Θεοδώρου μητροπολίτου: '[Seal] of Theodore the Metropolitan [bishop]' (Pl. 82.H). The palaeography and form of the monograms corroborate a date in the second half of the sixth or in the seventh century.[237] The style and context are probably too early for the bishop Theodore of Stavropolis known to have attended the Sixth Ecumenical Council in AD 680, and the seal may belong to an earlier bishop of the same name; there is certainly room enough for one in the *fasti* compiled by Roueché.[238] It should be noted however that Theodore's metropolitan see is not specified.

These deposits also yielded two cross pendants. The first is a very small cast copper alloy plate from the northern clean-up deposit (Pl. 82.I; Fig. 67, Inv. 12-23).[239] The vertical arm is slightly longer than the transverse, and all arms flare slightly. One side is decorated with small circles in each arm and at centre. It is a fairly crude example of a well-documented type. Khairedinova classifies these as type 3 variant 3 within her typology of crosses from the Crimea, and demonstrates that they are associated with burials of the late sixth and early seventh centuries in the Eski-Kermen necropolis.[240] Ferrazzoli likewise dates two examples from Elaiussa Sebaste to the sixth or seventh centuries.[241] A minor category of belt buckle dating to the sixth to seventh centuries incorporates crosses of just this type as plates.[242] A close parallel in an eleventh-century grave at Hierapolis demonstrates that the type may have been quite long-lived, or that individual crosses might remain in circulation for centuries.[243] The second cross found on the pool floor (4482) is a rudimentary iron piece fashioned from two flat rods (Fig. 67, Inv. 17-090).[244] Similar iron crosses have been recorded in medieval graves at Sagalassos and at Zeytinlibahçe Höyük.[245] Yet our example was evidently produced in late antiquity, and such a crude device could conceivably belong to any Christian era.

A circular silver pendant was uncovered within the lowermost 5 cm of the clean-up dump.[246] A small hoop for suspension is set perpendicular to the two faces, both of which display scenes that identify the pendant as an amulet (Pl. 83.A). The iconography is cast in low relief. Details are difficult to discern on account of repeated polishing. On one side, a mounted figure rides from left to right. He is positioned above a supine form with recognisable torso and head, again facing right. The horseman aims his lance aggressively towards the lower figure. On the reverse we encounter another supine individual. Above and at centre is an irregular shape, out of which emerges a vertical shaft surmounted by a Greek cross in a circular frame. The cross is flanked by human figures to left and right. Only their torsos, heads, and arms are depicted. They incline and gesture towards the cross. The worn condition of our example may indicate that it was already quite old at the time of deposition in the seventh century. Its form is very similar to that of three late antique copper alloy amulets from Sagalassos depicting the Holy Rider.[247] The horseman may have been identified as Solomon, who was associated with exorcism in Judeo-Christian magical traditions.[248] Alternatively he could represent a variety of military saints, such as Sissinos or George, depending on the narrative framework most familiar to the user of the amulet.[249] The prostrate figure is probably the daemon Gylou, who might otherwise be known as Abyzou or as the Lilith of the Hebrew tradition.[250] This female daemon was supposedly enraged by her own infertility, and exacted a spiteful revenge on mothers and newborn infants. On later Byzantine amulets Holy Rider iconography is often coupled with depictions of the womb.[251] It is possible that this silver pendant was as an exorcising medical aid intended for a woman. The iconography on the reverse of the amulet is more unusual. The key to its elucidation may lie in its partial reflection of the obverse, since the balanced compositions imply a single identity for the two supine figures. A provisional interpretation might see the daemon Gylou bound by the power of the cross.

Two small copper alloy bells from similar contexts on the pool floor (equivalent to 4328 and 4482) may also belong to this sphere of magical protection (Pl. 83.B–C). The first has a flared body with an oval profile, surmounted by a heavy loop for suspension.[252] The second is more typically 'bell-shaped', with a rounded upper body and slight lower flare, again with a large suspension loop.[253] Bells of this size are often identified as *tintinnabula*, and appear frequently in both domestic and funerary contexts.[254] John Chrysostom provides a disapproving reference to 'bells which are hung upon the hand[s] of children as a protective measure, and the archaeological contexts of *tintinnabula* are often indicative of domestic ritual rather than animal herding.[255] At Salamis small bells clustered in and around the Campanopetra basilica.[256] Nevertheless it cannot be ruled out that very similar bells might be placed on the collars of small sheep or goats, or even strung on horses' bridles, as Waldbaum suggests.[257] A much larger copper alloy bell also recovered from

---

236 Inv. 17-94 (4328.F990); Jeffery 2020, no. 25.
237 Cf. Laurent 1963, no. 947; Dumbarton Oaks BZS.1958.106.5559.
238 http://insaph.kcl.ac.uk/ala2004/narrative/fasbis.html (last accessed 07/12/18); see n. 67
239 Inv. 12-23 (SAg.12.1.1032.F1027): H: 2.2 cm, W: 1.7 cm.
240 Khairedinova 2012, 426.
241 Ferrazzoli 2012, 294.
242 Schulze-Dörrlamm 2009, 193, cf. Kazanski and Blanc 2003, 46.
243 Arthur 2006, 92 fig. 35.2.
244 Inv. 17-090 (4482.F886): H: 7.5 cm, W: 4.5 cm, D: 0.4 cm.
245 Cleymans and Talloen 2018, 287; Dell'Era 2012, 404.
246 Inv. 17-108 (4466.F1012): ⌀: 2.7 cm.

247 Waelkens and Poblome 1997, 337–338.
248 Spier 1993, 33–44; Vikan 1984, 79–81.
249 Bonner 1950, 208–11; Greenfield 1989.
250 Russell 1995, 40–41.
251 For example, Spier 1993, no. 33.
252 Inv. 17-176 (4466.F1017): H: 5.2 cm, W: 4.5 cm, D: 2.2 cm.
253 Inv. 17-175 (4484.F963): H: 6.0 cm, W: 4.5 cm, D: 4.0 cm.
254 Waldbaum 1983, 43, nos. 93, 100, 102 (found in the House of the Bronzes); Davidson 1952, 338, no. 2898; Chavane 1975, nos. 422–424; Gill 1986, 258, no. 474; for comprehensive bibliography see Goldman 1950, 393.
255 *Hom 1 Cor. 12:13* (PG 61.105–106); Russell 1995, 42.
256 Chavane 1975, 147–148.
257 Waldbaum 1983, 42.

the clean-up deposits on the pool floor (**4482**) is surely a bell for cattle, sheep, or goats; it should serve as a reminder of the regular presence of domesticated animals in late antique cities (Pl. 83.D).[258]

Seven tightly rolled sheets of lead may well be inscribed with demands for the intervention of divine powers in personal affairs (Pl. 83.E). They were found in the lowermost deposits of the pool (equal to **4328**) and in other subsequent clean up deposits within the pool (equal to **4442**, **4480** and **4329**).[259] This was a common ritual strategy attested across the entire Roman world. Invocations, magical formulae and potent graphic signs would be engraved upon a thin metal sheet, which was subsequently rolled up and either deposited at a special location or worn upon the person.[260] For now we must await the delicate unravelling of these sheets.

A rectangular marble plaque representing two wide eyes flanking the bridge of a nose belongs to the Roman period, but was found in the earliest siltation layers above the early seventh-century deposits (**4448**), and would have been offered as a votive in anticipation of healing (see Ch. 7 §E no. 91, and Pl. 74.B).[261] Three other marble votive plaques, one with eyes and two with a pair of breasts, and a votive base, all dedicated to Asklepios, have been found in or near the Hadrianic Baths where there may have been a shrine or cult area of Asklepios, and this plaque too should be regarded as having come originally from the same shrine.[262]

Items of dress

Belted trousers would have been worn by men of all social classes in late antique Aphrodisias.[263] Indeed, an inscription on a doorjamb in the eastern colonnade of the Temple-Church precinct proclaims the work or retail place of a certain Kyriakos, trouser-maker.[264] Four buckles, three of copper alloy and one iron, illustrate costume around the turn of the seventh century. The most elaborate of the copper alloy buckles was found within the seventh-century dump (contexts equivalent to **4328**). It consists of two frames divided by an elaborate openwork plate, all cast as a single piece (Fig. 67, Inv. 17-174).[265] The frame to the left is tall and oval with a pointed tongue-rest, while that to the right is heart-shaped and may be a decorative element. The plate takes the form of two sharp crescents reflected across a central axis. A short bar across the join imitates a textile or rope tie. There are two attachment lugs on the reverse. The form is highly unusual and finds no clear parallel in Schulze-Dörrlamm's exhaustive typology. The symmetrical crescents are found on her types E14 and E5, dating to the seventh and eighth centuries.[266]

The two further copper alloy buckles may be attributed to Csallany's *Maskenschnallen* type, produced in the second half of the sixth and the early seventh century.[267] The first of these is a slightly bulbous shield-shaped plate the cast frame of which has broken away (Fig. 67, 4482.F954).[268] It was likewise recovered from the seventh-century deposit (**4482**). There are three reverse attachment lugs: one at the point, two at the top corners. Openwork cuttings create a mask with short hair, small round eyes and a trefoil arrangement for mouth and nose. The composition finds a very close parallel on a contemporary rectangular buckle from Sardis.[269]

The second buckle is very small but complete (Fig. 67, Inv. 16-044).[270] Its plate and frame are cast as a single piece with an attached tongue. There are two reverse attachment lugs. The frame is a slim and elongated oval with a slightly raised tongue-rest. The plate is shield-shaped, terminating in a small pointed projection. Three perforations form the eyes and mouth of the mask. The form corresponds to Type 6 of Russell's typology of buckles from Anemurium produced in the early seventh century.[271] An almost exact parallel is currently in the possession of the Afyon Museum, and a similar piece has been found at Sardis.[272] The buckle was discovered within the occupation layer between the north wall of the pool and the North Stoa (**4278**), a deposit that began to accumulate in the sixth century and continued through the Byzantine period. The iron buckle, found in the seventh-century deposit (**4328**), is a single trapezoidal frame with curved outer corners (Fig. 67, 4328.F984).[273] A tongue with a sharp tip is attached through a simple loop.

An interesting pendant was found in the same context as the iron buckle (**4328**) (Fig. 67, Inv. 17-124).[274] A flat, circular piece of cut blue/green glass is set within a fairly deep copper alloy frame. A small loop for suspension is welded above. Though its surfaces are now dulled by cracks and patina, this inexpensive

---

258 Inv. 17-169 (4482.F875): H: 11.0 cm, W: 7.7 cm, D: 5.3 cm. For livestock at late antique Sagalassos, see Degryse *et al.* 2004.
259 **4442**: Inv. 17-075 (4442.F712), Inv. 17-076 (4442.F716); **4328**: Inv. 17-077 (4328.F731), Inv. 17-078 (4328.F729); **4479**: Inv. 17-079 (4479.F786); **5027**: Inv. 17-080 (SAg.17.2.5027.F20), Inv. 17-081 (5027.F21); **4329**: Inv. 17-066 (4329.F692), Inv. 17-138 (4329.F682).
260 Cf. Gager 1992; Kotansky 1994. The folded lead sheets bear some similarity to a type of fishing weight known as 'net sinkers', which were affixed to a net in order to prevent it from floating. Examples of net sinkers from elsewhere are usually more rounded in form, rather being folded like the examples from the Place of Palms (see Galili, Zemer, and Rosen 2013, 153, figs. 10 and 12). This distinction in form could be post-depositional, since lead is soft and liable to be deformed after burial, or it could be because the function is different. However, at present and in the absence of evidence for large quantities of fish from the pool, the presence of a weighted fishing net defies explanation, and it remains possible that all these lead objects were curse tablets.
261 4448.M2606 (Inv. 17-063): L: 10.0 cm, W: 6.0 cm, D: 3.0 cm. See also Ch. 7 §E.
262 *IAph2007* 15.240 (eyes); 5.112 (breasts); 5.117 (breasts); 4.113 (base, found in 1990 during excavation of the pool)
263 Russell 1982, 145–146.
264 *ala2004* 189.
265 Inv. 17-174 (4466.F1010): H: 5.8 cm, W: 3.2 cm, D: 0.28 cm.
266 Schulze-Dörrlamm 2009, 18, 43.
267 Csallány 1954, 347.
268 4482.F954: H: 3.0 cm, W: 2.8 cm, D: 0.35 cm.
269 Waldbaum 1983, 119, no. 696.
270 Inv. 16-044 (SAg.16.1.4278.F454): L: 3.7 cm, W: 2.3 cm, D (plate): 0.4 cm.
271 Russell 1982, 133–165, nos. 11–13.
272 Lightfoot 2003, no. 7; Afyon Museum Inv. 12658; Waldbaum 1983, 119, no. 693.
273 4328.F984: L: 3.5 cm, W: 3.5 cm, D: 0.4 cm.
274 Inv. 17-124 (4328.F976): ⌀ (pendant): 2.6–2.8 cm, D: 1.1 cm, H (suspension loop): 0.8 cm.

pendant must once have been extremely reflective. Moreover, the copper alloy backplate would have lent a deeper, more yellowish tint to the glass.

Weaponry

A small but significant collection of weapons was recovered from the lowest fills of the pool and the overlying siltation layers. The assemblage comprises, in total, three arrowheads, several instances of a type of javelin, and a spearhead; all are made of iron. Discussion of these items is complicated by their poor state of preservation and the limited comparanda available for most Roman and Byzantine weapons post-dating the mid-fifth century, alongside the paucity of extant general typologies.[275]

The assemblage of weapons might reflect a particular violent event, either a raid during the Persian invasions of Asia Minor between AD 615 and the early 620s or another conflict later in the century. Duman has argued that a spearhead and two arrowheads discovered in destruction contexts of the early seventh century at Tripolis on the Maeander represent a Persian raid.[276] These finds from Aphrodisias are typologically distinct from those found in burnt layers at Tripolis, though our limited understanding of weaponry typologies in the late antique eastern Mediterranean militates against the attribution of specific types to Sasanian or East Roman soldiers, or indeed to other groups.[277]

Two arrowheads found in the first artificial clean-up layer in the pool (**4328** and its equivalent contexts) are reasonably well preserved. The first has a leaf-shaped blade with a flat section and terminates in a flaring socket, from which protrudes the remains of an iron tang (Pl. 83.F).[278] This corresponds to a broad type of leaf-bladed, socketed arrowheads widely attested across the ancient world. Such arrowheads are found both inside and outside Roman-controlled territory, and date to the fourth through seventh centuries.[279] In Asia Minor broadly similar examples are known from Sardis, where an arrowhead of this type has been tentatively dated to the Byzantine period (that is after AD 395), and also from Amorium.[280] The second of the Aphrodisias arrowheads at present lacks close comparanda. It has an elongated lanceolate blade with a midrib on both sides and a circular-section tang (Pl. 83.G).[281] A third very fine arrowhead was recovered immediately above the pool floor (Pl. 83.H). This item may have originally featured a triangular or square-sectioned blade and a circular tang,[282] corresponding to a type known at Bahçe Birecik (Urfa) and associated with some seventh-century or later material.[283]

Other projectile weapons may have been recovered in the fills of the pool. The 2012–2017 excavations recovered three long iron rods with circular sections. The longest was slightly bent at both ends, though it is unclear whether this was a deliberate feature of its manufacture or post-depositional damage.[284] Of the two others, both of which are considerably shorter, one is also bent at both ends while the other is straight.[285] To these may be added several objects recovered during the 1989 excavation season from the western end of the pool in the Place of Palms. In that year, the excavator Francis Thode referred to six finds recovered resting on the pool floor as iron javelins, while only partly differentiating between those with a clear blade and those which simply have a point.[286] Two of these iron objects have been located in the site depots. Though the objects are broadly similar, comprising long, circular-section shanks, only one appears to terminate in a blade (Pl. 83.I). This blade is broadly leaf-shaped in form, with a rhomboid profile.[287] The item may represent the evolution of the earlier imperial *pilum*. Vegetius in the fifth century informs us about several types of javelin, namely the *spiculum* and *verutum,* both with metal heads of nine Roman inches (20 cm) in length, and connecting to wooden shafts.[288] However, Coulston and Bishop have demonstrated that javelins with considerably longer shanks are known from parts of the Western Empire: Carvoran, Lauriacum, and Vindonissa have yielded iron-shanked weapons of comparable length (ranging between 54.9 cm and 59 cm) to our item from Aphrodisias, albeit with double-barbed heads which differ from our leaf-bladed example.[289] Unfortunately, these items have not been closely dated, but they serve to underline the possibility of identifying this item with a sort of late antique javelin.

While the other iron rods cannot be conclusively identified as weapons they may represent javelins that have lost their bladed heads upon impact. The possible spearhead in this assemblage is less well preserved. A highly corroded iron object found immediately above the floor of the pool in the clean-up dump begins with a conical tip, which is square in section about the body, before terminating in a circular socket (Pl. 83.J).[290] This item may have been a spearhead comparable to a type known from Avar contexts featuring thin, pointed blades terminating in a conical socket, appearing from AD 630 onwards.[291] Similar examples are also known in late antique contexts at Ivillino in Northern Italy, although the excavator viewed them as catapult projectiles.[292] Csiky, however, rejects this interpretation, arguing

---

275 Theotokos 2018, 441, though on the Balkans see now Glad 2015.
276 Duman 2018, 359.
277 Duman 2018, 359, fig. 18.
278 4328.F972: L: 5.6 cm. W: 1.1 cm, D: 0.4 cm.
279 Glad 2015, 234, type A2; 238, fig. 44.
280 Waldbaum 1983, 39, cat. 79; Harrison *et al.* 1993, 159, fig. 2.
281 4328.F974: L: 7.5cm, W: 1.1cm, ⌀ (exterior base): 0.17cm, ⌀ (interior base): 0.8 cm.
282 4466.F1033: L: 4.0 cm, W: 1.2 cm, D: 0.5 cm.
283 Dell'Era 2012, 399 and 400, fig. 6e.
284 Inv. 17-074 (4448.F826): L: 175 cm, W: 1.5 cm, D: 1.0 cm.
285 Inv. 17-083 (4482.F876): L: 41.5 cm, W: 1.5 cm, D: 1.0 cm; Inv. 17-082 (4448.F844): L: 58 cm, W: 1.5 cm, D: 0.8 cm.
286 Nbk 307: *SW Portico of Tiberius* (F. Thode, 1989), 28–29, F82-5; F87; Nbk 304: *Portico of Tiberius W I* (A. Page and F. Thode, 1989), 66, F150. To date two of these objects (F83, F85) have been located.
287 *Pilum*, PTW.SW.89.1.13.F83: L (total): 67.5 cm, ⌀: 0.5 cm, L (blade): 8.5 cm, W (blade): 1.8 cm, D: 0.5 cm.
288 For the *spiculum* and *verutum* see Vegetius, II.15. The evidence is now also summarised by Theotokos 2018.
289 Bishop and Coulston 2006, 200.
290 4466.F1031: L: 10.5 cm, W: 2.3 cm, D: 0.5 cm. An alternative interpretation of this item as a tool remains possible.
291 For example, Csiky 2015, 109, fig. 35, nos. 1 and 4.
292 Bierbrauer and Bosio 1987, 170–171; II. Taf. 58: 1–10, Taf. 59: 1–5.

forcefully for their status as thrusting weapons.[293] Without other evidence for projectile artillery in use at late antique Aphrodisias, this object is perhaps best viewed as some kind of offensive thrusting weapon, though again the parallels to other published material remain relatively loose.

These weapons do not necessarily indicate the presence at Aphrodisias of troops of a particular ethnic group, whether Avars, Sasanians, or others. Rather, they demonstrate that weapons across the late antique and early medieval world took similar forms; there was probably a high degree of knowledge exchange between opponents in war. The transfer of military technology from the Avars to the Eastern Roman Empire is explicitly acknowledged by the late sixth-century *Strategikon*,[294] and Haldon has argued that the late Roman military may have adopted some originally Avar equipment, including some types of small shields, slings, javelins, and bows.[295] However, we should not necessarily assume that all weapon types were Avar innovations, and it remains possible that their origins belong within the bounds of the Empire. Further work on this subject at Aphrodisias and elsewhere within the territory claimed by the Roman state is a pressing desideratum.

Earlier excavations of the pool also yielded a stirrup (Pl. 84.A).[296] According to a notebook from the 1990 excavations, this item was 'from the floor of the pool', a statement corroborated by a black-and-white photograph of the item *in situ* (Pl. 84.B) and by A.T. Tek, one of the contributors to this volume, who excavated it.[297] The stirrup's arms and foot plate were probably cast, but the suspension loop was created through the attachment of an additional iron coil; this part of the item suffered the heaviest corrosion, obscuring some details of its original form. The rounded arms of the object terminate in a flat, horizontal foot plate. The D-shaped suspension loop terminates in trailing ends which coiled around the arms, perhaps for decorative purposes or additional durability.

Two objects of a comparable type have been identified in late sixth- or early seventh-century contexts at Caričin Grad in Serbia.[298] Another possible example was discovered at the late antique fortress at Rupkite/Ripkit, near Karasura in Bulgaria, though unfortunately it was not illustrated.[299] Two mentions of stirrups in the *Strategikon* demonstrate that this technology was indeed known in the Eastern Empire in late antiquity.[300] The first of these prescribes the appropriate gear for cavalrymen, including stirrups; the second uses the same word to describe an arrangement of saddle tack that corpsmen could use to help wounded soldiers mount horses and thereby carry them to safety. Florin Curta has argued that this textual evidence, combined with 'apple-shaped' stirrups found in Avar funerary contexts from AD 600 onwards, suggests that stirrups were introduced by the Avars during their conflicts with the Roman state in the sixth century.[301] He further argues that stirrups with D-shaped forms, like this example from Aphrodisias, were not true stirrups but mere mounting platforms, citing the above-mentioned passage of the *Strategikon*.[302] Alternatively, Werner has suggested that these objects are too lightweight to function as true stirrups, aiding in mounting or standing in the saddle, but instead served as footrests during riding.[303]

While the merits of these arguments are treated at greater in length in a separate study, two principal grounds for identifying these items as stirrups can be briefly summarised here.[304] First, the same word (σκάλας) is used to refer to both passages of the *Strategikon,* and the text therefore suggests no clear typological differentiation between the stirrups and mounting platforms. Secondly, the footplates of apple-shaped stirrups can sometimes be just as thin as those of D-shaped stirrups, and as a consequence there is no evidence to suggest that either type has a better claim to work as 'functioning' stirrups.[305] In view of this evidence, we interpret this D-shaped item along with other examples from the Balkans as stirrups. It is also worth noting that the three Balkan examples have been found in contexts with strong military connotations. The identification of this stirrup at Aphrodisias may, therefore, provide further evidence for action of a military nature in the Place of Palms at some point around the middle of the seventh century.

E. ARCHAEOBOTANICAL EVIDENCE (ER)

The archaeobotanical evidence from the lowest deposits within the Place of Palms' pool provides a range of insights into the nature of water flow and vegetation in this structure prior to and immediately following the first clearance deposit in the seventh century AD. It also tells us about the plants growing on the debris dumped into the pool at this date and offers information about other undergrowth and food consumption around this space in the decades following. Although the pool was a single structure in antiquity, from an archaeobotanical perspective it is an enormous and multi-zonal space. While samples taken from across its excavated area show that the first clearance deposit prompted the silting up of the pool, they also show that this happened unevenly. The north side of the pool began to silt up and become overgrown first, with the centre and southern side developing vegetation later; indeed some parts of the pool may even have been kept deliberately clear of plants to allow access to the water.

This section begins with a summary of targeted archaeobotanical work carried out in the pool in 2012. This is followed by an explanation of the sampling strategy used in 2017 in order to ensure thorough coverage of the deposits from across the full exposed extent of the pool floor. Following a presentation of the

---

293 Csiky 2015, 110.
294 *Strategikon* 1.2.
295 Haldon 2008, 475.
296 PTE.1.1990.F24: Overall, H: 11.9 cm, W: 12.5 cm. Arms: W: 0.9 cm. Foot plate: L: 10.5 cm, W: 1.9 cm, D: 0.4 cm. Suspension loop: H: 1.7 cm; W (at base): 2.0 cm.
297 Nbk 316: *Portico of Tiberius: W Pool, Book I; E Pool* (A.T. Tek, 1990), F24, Photo 22; Penn, Russell, and Wilson 2021.
298 Ivanišević and Bugarski 2012, 135–136 and 272, fig. 1.
299 Herrmann 1992, 175.
300 *Strategikon* 1.2; 2.9.

301 Curta 2008, 302–303.
302 Curta 2008, 307–308; repeated more recently at Curta 2013, 818, and n. 30.
303 Werner 1984.
304 Penn, Russell, and Wilson 2021.
305 Ivanišević and Bugarski 2012.

carbonized and waterlogged material is a detailed discussion of the silting of the pool.

Archaeobotanical sampling in 2012

During the 2012 season Mark Robinson excavated three sampling pits in Trench 12.1 in order to establish the full sediment sequence.[306] The first of these (12.A) was opened close to the centre of the pool, at the far southern edge of Trench 12.1. The second (12.B) was located immediately adjacent to the northern side of the pool. The third (12.C) was positioned between 12.A and 12.B.[307] Examining both the archaeobotanical and mollusc remains, Robinson concluded that prior to the deliberate deposition of the first clearance deposit in the seventh century AD, the pool was still functioning.[308] The water was clean and probably slow-moving. There was some vegetation in the form of *Chara* sp. (stonewort algae), *Potamogeton* sp. (pondweed), and *Schoenoplectus lacustris* (bulrushes), but the pool would not have appeared overgrown; *Lemna* sp. (duckweed) was absent. Following the first clearance deposit, however, the silting regime in the pool changed markedly. This area of the pool became increasingly overgrown and silty. Even when it was largely filled with silt, the molluscs indicate that this remained a damp area, in which water regularly accumulated.[309]

Limited quantities of waterlogged seeds recovered from these sampling pits also offered some insights into what was growing around the pool in the seventh century AD. These were concentrated in Sampling Pit 12.B, adjacent to the pool walls, indicating that most of them were local. Since the pool appears to have been kept clean prior to the seventh century AD, these finds reveal what was growing, or had recently been growing, in the Place of Palms at this date. Most of the seeds were from herbaceous plants and suggest that the area around the pool was grassy or partly vegetated. *Verbena officinalis* (vervain) was the best represented, but *Papaver* sp. (poppy), *Malva* sp. (mallow) and *Asteraceae* (daisy) were also present. The most pertinent find was the discovery from Sampling Pit 12.A, of a fragment of palm leaf. The stomated cell pattern and the round crenate phytoliths of this fragment are characteristic of palm and closely match modern samples from *Phoenix theophrasti* or Cretan date palm.[310] The significance of this find has been discussed in Ch. 2 and 4.

Taken from a much larger area of the pool, the 2017 pit samples have created the opportunity to expand upon these original findings and provide a more nuanced and detailed history of the use-life of the pool immediately prior to and after the seventh-century demise of the Place of Palms.[311]

306 Robinson 2016.
307 Robinson 2016, 91 fig. 6.1. These sampling pits have been re-labelled 12.A-C to distinguish them from the sampling pits opened in 2017 (17.A-Q).
308 Robinson 2016, 96.
309 Robinson 2016, 96–97.
310 Robinson 2016, 94–95 fig. 6.7.
311 In both the 2012 and 2017 samples, the degree of waterlogged preservation was found to be of an adequate but not of an excellent quality (Robinson 2016).

Sampling strategy in 2017

The size of the pool required the implementation of a sampling strategy that ensured maximum coverage of all areas of the pool floor. Three deposits cover the pool floor: **4482**, a scatter of debris across the whole area of the pool; **4328**, a thick sloping layer of detritus that was pushed into the pool from its northern edge; and **4448**, a thin siltation layer, covering **4482** and **4328**. This final deposit formed prior to the dumping of the second clearance deposit (**4471**) along the south side of the pool. These deposits were sampled via 17 individual sampling pits, each 1 m². These were marked off during excavation and labelled 17.A-Q (Fig. 68). Since **4482** represents a scatter of material, without any associated sediments, all of the archaeobotanical samples were taken from **4328** and **4448**. The sampling pits were aligned in five rows of three so that the middle and sides of the pool would be sampled at various points. It was hoped that the samples would be compositionally different, allowing us to better understand the nature of each fill and the degree of human involvement in the filling of the pool. Two additional sampling pits, 17.P and 17.Q, were opened on the north side of the pool, where the thick clearance deposit was deepest and where Robinson's earlier Sampling Pit 12.B had produced evidence of palm. Sampling Pits 17.M–Q, along the north side of the pool, were all from **4328**. The remaining pits sampled **4448**.

Sample processing. All of the soil from the sampling pits was collected, which produced samples ranging in size from 13 to 36.25 L. Since it would not have been possible to keep the samples wet beyond the end of the excavation season, they were processed in full in order to best preserve the archaeobotanical material; despite their large size with respect to traditional waterlogged samples. Since the material from the pool floor was waterlogged it needed to be treated differently from the archaeobotanical samples taken elsewhere on the site. Soil from the sampling pits was washed over a 0.8 mm sieve to remove any large rocks and to collect larger snail shells and pieces of charcoal. Any charcoal or seeds caught on the sieve were placed on the residue tray. Shells, carbonized material, bone, glass, and metal were also kept. Ceramic building material, marble fragments, and pottery were discarded, regardless of size. Water was then added to the tank and the material gently stirred to break up any clumps of soil. Material that floated was caught on 1 mm and 0.3 mm sieves. In order to make microscope scanning faster and easier the 1 mm and 0.3 mm flots were always kept separate. After flotation the flots were washed into small plastic containers and then transferred to glass jars in the lab. Water was added to the samples to ensure that they remained constantly submerged. Depending upon the sample size, for every 12–14 L of processed material, the flots were kept in separate bags. In other words, a 30 L sample would have two bags for the 1 mm flot and two for the 0.3 mm flot. In order to keep the samples wet but free from mould a 70% ethanol solution was added to the contents of each jar once sorting was finished.

The material that did not float, the residue, was washed through a 2 mm sieve. Half of the residue material (i.e. the first 12–14 L) was also washed through a 1 mm sieve. The 2 mm and 1 mm residues were left to dry on trays. The 2 mm residues were

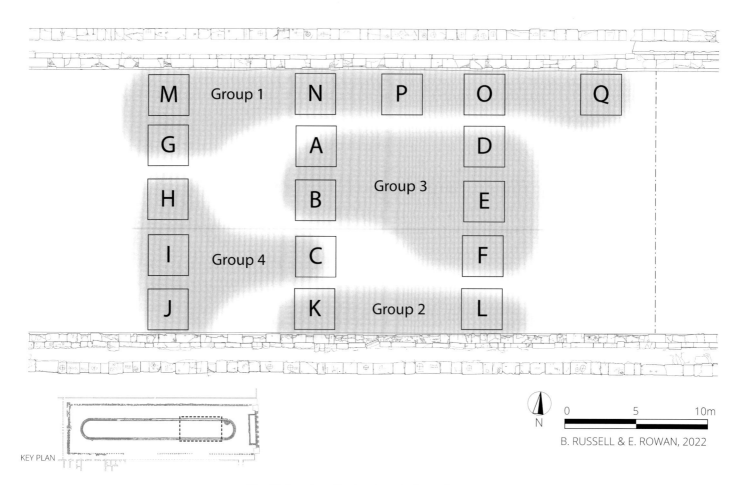

Fig. 68. Location of archaeobotanical sampling pits.

sorted in full. Two of the 1 mm residues were scanned and it was determined that a sufficient quantity of material was present in the 1 mm flot that a full sorting of the 1 mm residue material was not necessary.

Sorting and quantification procedures. For all 17 sampling pits the 1 mm flot was scanned in full while 2–3 petri dishes of the 0.3 mm flot were examined. Due to time constraints and the enormous quantities of waterlogged material present, scales of abundance rather than raw counts were recorded. The 0.3 mm samples rarely contained anything but the most common taxa such as *Chara* sp. oospores and there was no need to pick out items such as the *Schoenoplectus lacustris* seeds when they often ran into the hundreds or thousands. Three scales of abundance were used, taxa with 1–10 finds, 11–100 and 101–1000. The general characteristics of each test pit were also recorded in a notebook. As no physical reference collection was available, identifications were made using the Digital Plant Atlas project, images from the 2016 publication of the original pool sondages, and other online images.[312]

Results

In total 73 taxa were identified, including 11 aquatic species, 53 terrestrial taxa, and an additional 9 carbonized waterlogged taxa (see Tables 9 and 10). As Robinson had earlier noted, most of the aquatic material came from only three species and comprised the seeds of *Schoenoplectus lacustris* (bulrushes) and *Potamogeton* sp. (pondweed) and the oospores of *Chara* sp. (stonewort algae) (Pl. 84.C).[313] The stonewort oospores were found in every sampling pit while the bulrushes were identified in 15 sampling pits, and the pondweed in nine. For all three taxa the quantities varied depending upon the sampling pit and its location within the pool.

Ubiquity levels also varied significantly for the terrestrial species. The four most ubiquitous taxa were *Ficus carica* (fig), *Vitis vinifera* (grape), *Rubus fruticosus* (blackberry) and the burrs of *Medicago polymorpha* (burr medick), while 26 of the taxa were found in only one test pit. The varying ubiquity levels and the ratio of aquatic to terrestrial plants shed light on the different formation processes that took place to create the deposits within each sampling pit. Sampling pits displaying similar ratios and characteristics have been organized into groups, since these particular areas, rather than the individual sampling pits, highlight areas of human or environmental activity (see Fig. 68).

312 Jacomet 2006; Robinson 2016; Cappers, Neef, and Bekker 2019.

313 Robinson 2016, 95.

Table 9. Waterlogged material from the 17 test pits. Abundance: x = 1–10 finds; xx = 11–100 finds; xxx = 101–1000 finds.

	Test pit	A	B	C	D	E	F	G	H	I	J	K	L	M	N	O	P	Q
	Context	4448	4448	4448	4448	4448	4448	4448	4448	4448	4448	4482	4448	4466	4466	4466	4466	4466
	Volume (L)	31	30.5	24.5	20.25	36.25	36	22.1	23.5	15.25	13	20.25	20	14	23.25	20	18	30.5
Aquatic taxa	**Common name**																	
Alismataceae	Water-plantain		x															
Apium cf. *nodiflorum*	Fool's watercress				xxx	xx	x											
Chara sp.	Stonewort (oospore)	xxx	xxx	xxx	xxx	xxx	xx	x	xxx	xx	xxx	xxx	x	xxx	xxx	xxx	xx	x
Cyperaceae	Sedge		x		x	x	x		xx									
Lemna sp.	Duckweed	x			x		x		x				x	x			x	
Lycopus sp.	Water horehound				x													
Nasturtium sp.	Watercress				x													
Phragmites australis	Common reed	x																
Potamogeton sp.	Pondweed	x	xx	x	xx		xxx			xx	xx	xx						x
cf. *Schoenoplectus lacustris*	True bulrush	xxx	xxx	xx	xxx	xx	xxx	x	x	xx		x	xx	xx	xx	x		x
Zannichellia sp.	Horned pondweed				x		x	x		x		x						
Terrestrial taxa																		
Agrimonia sp.	Agrimony						x											
Apiaceae indet.	Carrot family				x			x					x	x				
Asteraceae indet.	Daisy family		x		x		x					x						x
Ballota nigra	Black horehound						x											
Ballota nigra cf. subsp. *meridionalis*	Black horehound																	x
Ballota sp./*marrubium* sp.	Horehound				x	x												
Boraginaceae	Borage family				x													
Brassica sp.	Cabbage family (pod)																	x
Calendula sp.	Marigold												x					
Carduus/Cirsium sp.	Thistle		x		x		x					x	x					x
Chenopodium album	Goosefoot				x	x												xx

211

	Test pit	A	B	C	D	E	F	G	H	I	J	K	L	M	N	O	P	Q
Chenopodium sp.	Goosefoot		x		x	x							x	x			x	
Cyperaceae/Polygonaceae	Sedge/Knotweed		x		xx			x		x		x						x
Euphorbia helioscopia	Sun spurge					x				x	x		x				x	
Ficus carica	Fig	x	xx	x	xxx	xx	x					x	x	xx		x		
Fumaria sp.	Fumitory		x															
Galium aparine	Cleaver									x								
cf. Gymnospermae	Conifer													x				
Hyoscyamus sp.	Henbane				x													
Juglans regia	Walnut																	x
Lamiaceae	Mint family		x		x									x				
Lepidium sp.	Peppercress											x						
Lithospermum sp.	Gromwell											x						
Malva sp.	Mallow	x					x											
Medicago polymorpha	Burr medick	xx	x		xx	x								x	x	x	x	
Medicago sp.	Medick					x												
Nutshell	Nutshell	x				x												x
Olea europaea	Olive				x													
Persicaria sp.	Knotweed				x													
Pinus pinea	Stone pine (bract)				xx	x							x		x			x
Poaceae	Wild grass					x	x						x					
Portulaca sp.	Purslane				x	x											x	
Prunus persica	Peach					x												
Quercus coccifera	Kermes oak (leaf frag.)											x						
Quercus ilex	Evergreen oak (leaf frag.)										x							
Quercus sp.	Oak (leaf frag.)												x					x
cf. *Raphanus raphanistrum*	Wild radish			x														
Ranunculus cf. *parviflorus*	Small flower buttercup				x									x				
Ranunculus parviflorus	Small flower buttercup		x		xx	x	x											x

212

	Test pit	A	B	C	D	E	F	G	H	I	J	K	L	M	N	O	P	Q
Raphanus raphanistrum	Wild radish	x						x										
Reseda sp.	Weld				x													
Rubus fruticosus agg.	Blackberry	x	xx		xx	x	x	x		x	x	x	x	x				x
Rubus sp.	Blackberry (thorn)		x		x		x											
Rumex acetosella	Sheep's sorrel	x			xx		x											x
Salix sp.	Willow				x													
Sambucus sp.	Elder	x			x	x												
Scrophulariaceae	Figworts	x												x				
Solanum cf. *nigrum*	European black nightshade		x		x		x	x										
Solanum sp.	Nightshade			x							x		x	x				x
Stellaria sp.	Chickweed																x	
Urtica sp.	Nettle				x							x						
Valerianella sp.	Corn salad											x						
cf. *Verbascum* sp.	Mullein	x			x									x	x			
Verbascum sp.	Mullein																	x
Verbena officinalis	Vervain		x		xx	x						x		x				
Vitis vinifera	Grape	x	x	x	xx	x	xx					x	xx	x				xx

**all finds were in the form of seeds, pips, achenes and so forth. No plant testa was identifiable.

Group 1: Sampling Pits 17.G, 17.M–Q. This group of sampling pits was located along the northern edge of the pool. Sampling Pits 17.N–P were located in the most concentrated areas of the first clean-up deposit **4328**, while 17.M and 17.Q were positioned at its eastern and western edges. Although 17.G is more centrally located, and sampled the overlying silt layer **4448**, it displayed the characteristics found in the others. All of these test pits contained few waterlogged plants and a moderate variety of terrestrial species and foodstuffs (Pl. 84.D). The absence of both a variety and quantity of waterlogged plants supports Robinson's earlier suggestion that the pool's water was largely still clean prior to the dumping of the first clearance deposit in the seventh century AD.[314] The presence of *Lemna* sp. (duckweed) in Sampling Pits 17.M and 17.P, however, suggests that the water was starting to become stagnant when this debris was deposited or soon thereafter. Moving water would have helped skim this small plant from the surface.[315]

Some of the terrestrial plants noted in these samples, such as the *Ballota nigra* subsp. *Meridionalis* (Black horehound) and the *Verbascum* sp. (Mullein), are typical of species that grow on waste ground and it is likely that they were growing in and around the debris prior to its deposition into the pool. This lends some support to the idea that the North Stoa had been substantially damaged some time prior to the deliberate clearance operation that lead to the accumulation of the first clearance deposit (**4482** and **4328**). The numerous finds of waterlogged fig and grape, along with the carbonized remains of several food items, especially in Sampling Pits 17.Q and 17.M, make it clear that human activity was still taking place in the area when this clearance operation was carried out. There was also a considerable variety of weeds of cultivated crops such as *Euphorbia helioscopia* (Sun spurge), *Stellaria* sp. (Chickweed) and *Chenopodium* sp. (Goosefoot) in the sampling pits, which suggests the presence of agricultural activity nearby (see below for a more detailed discussion).

314 Wilson 2019, 217.
315 Robinson 2016, 96.

Table 10. Charred material from the 17 waterlogged test pits. Abundance: x = 1–10 finds; xx = 11–100 finds.

Taxonomic Name	Common name	Component	Test pit	A	B	C	D	E	F	G	H	I	J	K	L	M	N	O	P	Q
			Context	4448	4448	4448	4448	4448	4448	4448	4448	4448	4448	4482	4448	4466	4466	4466	4466	4466
Cereals and legumes																				
Hordeum vulgare sl.	Hulled barley	Caryopsis							x					x	x					
cf. *Lens culinaris*	Lentil	Seed															x			
Triticum dicoccum	Emmer wheat	Caryopsis													x					
Triticum aestivum/durum	Free-threshing wheat	Caryopsis						x		x					x					
Triticum aestivum/durum	Free-threshing wheat	Rachis								x										
Vicia/Lathyrus sp.	Vetch or pea	Seed									x									
Cerealia	Cereal	Caryopsis		x											x					x
Fruit and nuts																				
Fabaceae	Wild legume				x															
Juglans regia	Walnut	Shell			x		x	x												x
Olea europeae	Olive	Stone					x	x									x			x
Pinus pinea	Stone pine	Bract													x					x
Pinus pinea	Stone pine	Nut			x		x	xx		x										xx
cf. *Punica granatum*	Pomegranate	Seed																		x
Nut shell	N/A						x	x	x											x
Weed seeds and trees																				
Avena sp.	Oat	Caryopsis											x							
Cupressus sp.	Cypress	Twig										x								
Galium aparine	Cleaver									x					x					
Medicago sp.	Medick											x								
Poaceae	Wild grass						x			x					x					x
Quercus sp.	Oak	Bud							x											
Total number of taxa (waterlogged (Table 9) and carbonized)				17	22	7	42	22	26	13	7	9	7	22	17	18	7	4	7	27

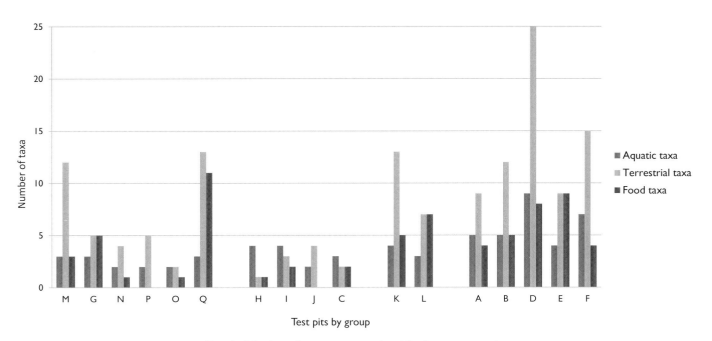

Fig. 69. Number of aquatic, terrestrial and food taxa per test pit.

Group 2: Sampling Pits 17.K, 17.L. Group 2 consists of two pits that sampled the silt layer **4448** beneath the debris of the second clearance deposit (**4471**) on the south side of the pool. These two sampling pits contained a larger and more varied range of aquatic plants compared to Group 1, but an equally broad mixture of terrestrial plants and food remains. Since **4448** accumulated in the pool after the deposits on the northern side (**4328**), it is not surprising to find a greater number of aquatic plants (Fig. 69). Over time the pool continued to fill with sediment and became increasingly vegetated. Nevertheless, the amount of pondweed and bulrushes in these test pits is relatively low, showing that the pool still contained somewhat clean, slow-moving water. The wide range of terrestrial taxa on this side of the pool probably relates to the fact that wild plants would have grown on the side of the Theatre Hill to the south. The fragment of Kermes oak leaf, a species with sharp spiky leaves, as well as the blackberries, might have arrived here with the debris deposited as part of **4471**, which was pushed down on top of and into **4448**. The edible plants represent discarded food waste, presumably thrown into the pool from its southern edge.

Group 3: Sampling Pits 17.A, 17.B, 17.D–F. The samples from the pits in this group are characterized by the greatest variety of aquatic, terrestrial and food plants (see Fig. 69). It is clear from the excavations that this area was never covered by rubble deposits of the sort found along the northern (**4328**) and southern (**4471**) sides of the pool. Consequently, the area remained more open and was allowed to slowly fill with sediment (**4448**) and aquatic plants. These include pondweed, algae, fool's watercress (*Apium nodiflorum*) and bulrushes (see Pl. 84.C). Small quantities of duckweed were found in three of the sampling pits, again suggesting that the water was turning stagnant as **4448** accumulated. Figs and grapes were present in all the samples while carbonized walnuts, pine nuts, and cereals were found in multiple test pits.

The foodstuffs suggest continued occupation either in or near the Place of Palms. As in the samples from Group 1, the terrestrial plants represent a mixture of ruderal plants growing on waste or disturbed ground and the weeds of cultivated crops. The ubiquity of *Rubus fruticosus* (blackberries),[316] *Rumex acetosella* (Sheep's sorrel) and *Verbena officinalis* (Vervain), all ruderal plants, suggests that the area around the pool was not kept clear of weeds and was becoming increasingly overgrown (Fig. 70–71). Sampling Pit 17.D had a larger quantity and variety of plants than the rest, probably because some of the terrestrial plants dumped into the pool with the debris in **4328** may have shifted down into the centre of the pool in this area. The remains of dung beetle were found in Sampling Pits 17.D and 17.F. These were also found by Robinson and suggest the nearby presence of domestic animals.[317]

Group 4: Sampling Pits 17.C, 17.H–J. These four sampling pits are at the westernmost end of the 2017 excavations. They had the lowest species diversity, especially in terms of terrestrial plants and foodstuffs. There were fewer bulrush and pondweed seeds in these pits than in those in Group 3, suggesting that the area contained slow-moving yet still relatively clean water. The absence of most terrestrial plants and the almost complete absence of foodstuffs might indicate abandonment of the area outside the pool here earlier than elsewhere. It is also possible that this area, which had a basin inserted into it later, was kept clear of sediment and vegetation to allow access to the water (see §A).

In sum, the pool began to fill in slowly over time, but this process did not start until the middle of the seventh century AD. Prior to this the pool contained primarily clean, slow-moving water, even if some vegetation was present. The limited quantities of aquatic material found in the debris deposits of

---

316 Blackberry plants can be used for food yet also quickly take over an area of open ground.
317 Dung beetle was also found in Sampling Pit I: Robinson 2016, 97.

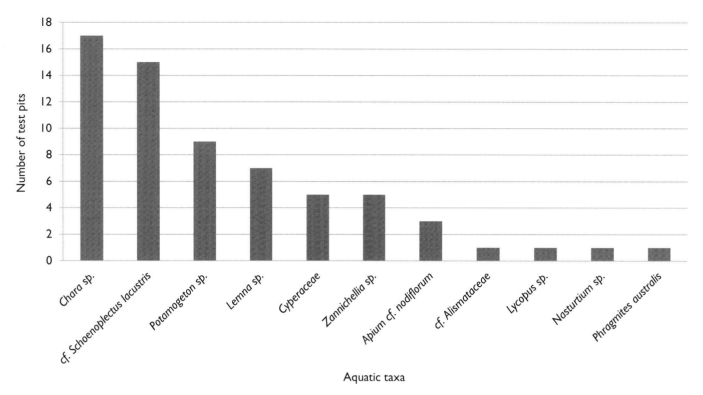

Fig. 70. Ubiquity of the aquatic taxa.

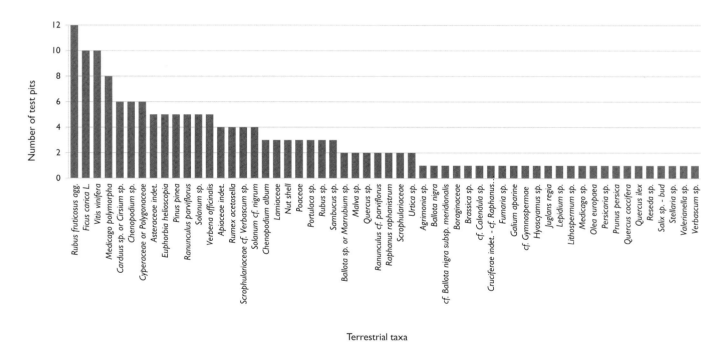

Fig. 71. Ubiquity of the terrestrial taxa (excluding the carbonized remains).

4328 suggest that the pool was actively cleaned on a regular basis. No deposits built up on the pool floor that might offer some insight into what was growing in the Place of Palms prior to the seventh century AD. The first clearance deposit hindered proper cleaning and undoubtedly increased the speed of sedimentation. The eastern section of the pool, although still relatively open, started to clog with bulrushes soon after the formation of this deposit. The combination of terrestrial plants and food remains at the eastern end of the pool suggests that this area of the Place of Palms was still in use, although no longer as a monumental urban park. By the time the second clearance deposit, along the south side of the pool, further filled it up, there are signs that the water was becoming increasingly stagnant. The centre of the pool remained clean and open longest. Although

Table 11. Identification of the waterlogged wood.

Context	Finds Number	Function	Latin Name	English Name	Türkçe Adı
4448	F719	Timber	*Cupressus sempervirens*	Mediterranean cypress	Akdeniz servisi
4448	F770	Timber	*Pinus brutia*	Turkish red pine	Kızılçam
4448	F771	Timber	*Pinus brutia*	Turkish red pine	Kızılçam
4448	F772	Timber	*Cupressus sempervirens*	Mediterranean cypress	Akdeniz servisi
4448	F777	Timber	*Juniperus* sp.	Juniper	Ardıç
4448	F815	Timber	*Pinus brutia*	Turkish red pine	Kızılçam
4328	F996	Timber	*Cupressus sempervirens*	Mediterranean cypress	Akdeniz servisi
4471	F739	Timber	*Castanea sativa*	Chestnut	Kestane
4480	F804	Pole	*Pinus brutia*	Turkish red pine	Kızılçam
4482	F868	Timber	*Ulmus* cf. *minor*	Field elm	Karaağaç

it is impossible to determine the exact time lag between these various silting events, all the artefactual evidence from the pool suggests that the deposits sampled here had formed by the end of the seventh century.

Waterlogged wood and hand-picked finds. As the above discussion has shown, organic material from the bottom of the pool was found in a state of waterlogged preservation. Larger, hand-picked waterlogged finds included wooden branches and beams, whole pine cones, and peach stones. There were 21 pieces of waterlogged wood recovered from the pool (see Pl. 80.B). The majority of these came from the deposits on the pool floor (**4482**, **4328**, and **4448**) and comprised building timbers; most of them had evidence of cut marks, while some had sawn ends and nail holes. Many of these timbers were carbonized. Several similar timbers were found in **4471** (the second clearance deposit, on the south side). Alongside these larger timbers, a series of thinner poles were also found in **4448** and **4479** (the silt covering the second clearance deposit); as noted above, these were perhaps for awnings associated with occupation of the space around the pool in the period between and after the clearance deposits (see §A). Nine of the largest fragments of waterlogged wood were sampled and sent to Prof. Ünal Akkemik of the Istanbul University Faculty of Forestry for identification (Table 11). Due to their size, the bulk of the samples were taken from timbers rather than poles. Four of the nine wood samples were identified as Turkish red pine, the remaining samples as Mediterranean cypress, juniper, chestnut, and field elm. While we cannot be sure where the timbers in the deposits from the pool floor came from, most of the other debris recovered from these levels, and especially the contexts **4328** and **4448**, is associated with the North Stoa. The timber from **4471**, in contrast, presumably came from the South Stoa. The evidence for burning on the timbers matches the evidence for burning found on some of the marble architectural elements in these deposits. This suggests that the timbers found on the pool floor came from the stoas and were presumably part of their roofs, which came down in the early to mid seventh century AD.

The other plant remains found in the bottom of the pool, due to their extremely well preserved nature, were easy to iden-

Table 12. Quantities of waterlogged pine cones (*Pinus pinea*, Eng. Stone pine, Turk. Fıstıkçamı) and peach stones (*Prunus persica*, Eng. Peach, Turk. Şeftali).

Context	Number of pine cones	Number of peach stones
4448	3	0
4328	7	3
4482	8	2

tify on site (Table 12). The pine cones all come from the species *Pinus pinea* (stone pine) (Pl. 84.E). The peach stones probably represent food waste as carbonized finds of peach were recovered from the ring drain, an assemblage made up of kitchen and ritual waste (see Ch. 4 §J) (Pl. 84.F). There is, however, an interesting discrepancy between the numerous finds of *Pinus pinea* cones, the complete absence of *Pinus brutia* cones, but the recovery of *Pinus brutia* wood. An explanation is required since *Pinus brutia* produces a large number of pine cones on an annual basis and both species grow native in the region.[318] A combination of ecological requirements, wood characteristics, and Roman cultural practices probably explain the lack of *Pinus brutia* pine cones. Turkish red pine grows on south-facing slopes up to 1200 m asl and on north-facing slopes up to 900 m asl.[319] It also does well with large amounts of rainfall, roughly 900–1000 mm annually. Crucially, for architectural purposes, it is somewhat fire-resistant.[320] Its frequent presence in the pool suggests that it was a preferred building material, at least more so than stone pine. Less well suited to the flat plain of the Morsynos river valley, Turkish red pine was probably imported from the nearby slopes of the Baba Dağı and Karıcalı ridges, which would have provided the ideal habitat.[321] The mean an-

[318] Atalay, Efe, and Soykan 2008, 16; Atik, Ortaçeşme, and Erdoğan 2011, 110.
[319] Donners *et al.* 2000, 738.
[320] Kirmaci, Agcagil, and Aslan 2013, 31.
[321] Stearns 2012, 135.

nual rainfall in the modern province of Aydın, in which Aphrodisias is located, is 672.7 mm, though it is undoubtedly greater than this mean in the mountains.[322] Therefore, the absence of *Pinus brutia* pine cones can be explained by the fact that none of these trees would have been growing in the city. Stone pine trees, however, probably were growing in and around the site. The presence of carbonized pine nuts in the ring drain and waterlogged pine nuts at the bottom of the pool attests to their use as a foodstuff. As discussed in Ch. 4 §J, stone pine is also a species associated with Roman ritual and burial practices. Similarly, cypress trees, which also have ritual significance,[323] and whose seed pods were found in the ring drain, were also growing in or around Aphrodisias.

The pool and its surroundings in the seventh century AD

The data collected from the test pits located at the bottom of the pool not only reveal how the pool eventually filled but provide crucial information regarding its immediate surroundings in the seventh century AD. The carbonized foodstuffs and the terrestrial taxa are particularly revealing.[324] The large number of terrestrial taxa, and the many plants that grew on disturbed ground or in open grasslands, indicate that this area of the city was overgrown and perhaps partially abandoned prior to the large-scale clearance operation represented by deposits **4482** and **4328**.[325] Some of these wild plants, such as the *Medicago polymorpha, Ranunculus parviflorus, Verbena officinalis, Rumex acetosella,* and *Malva* sp, may have come from the ruins of the Basilica or even the Agora, which seems to have been abandoned as a monumental space and perhaps used for agriculture by this date. The waterlogged weeds of cultivated cereals, including *Raphanus raphanistrum, Euphorbia helioscopia, Chenopodium* sp., present in the pool does suggest agricultural activities taking place nearby. These findings, of partial urban abandonment and/or repurposing for agriculture are in line both with other archaeological evidence from the site and with evidence from other cities in Anatolia.[326] This is a period associated with the slow reduction in settlement size at many sites.[327]

The presence of charred foodstuffs, concentrated in particular areas of the pool, as stated above, does suggest continued human occupation in this part of the city. Unlike some of the waterlogged fruit remains, which may have simply come from fig trees or grape vines growing nearby,[328] the carbonization of the material requires human action. Although more narrow in range than the food remains from the ring drain, which date to the late fifth and early sixth centuries AD (see Ch. 4 §J), these finds suggests that staple items, including cereals, legumes, fruits and nuts, seemed to have remained the same in the seventh century. The combination of barley, free-threshing wheat, and emmer wheat is identical to that found in the ring drain, suggesting no major changes in crop selection. Similarly, the presence of carbonized and waterlogged walnut and pine nut, figs, grapes, olives, and peaches suggests that horticulture was still practised either in or near the city. Interestingly, survey work done outside the site found that while some farmsteads were still operating in the seventh century AD, none continued after this date; after this, farmers returned to the pre-Imperial trend of living up on the plateaux south of the Morsynos valley where it was safer.[329] Consequently, agricultural and horticultural production may have started to take place within the city walls from the seventh century AD onwards.

This pattern of rural abandonment and increased urban agriculture can also be seen at Sagalassos.[330] Pollen samples from the Byzantine phases (mid fifth to seventh centuries AD) of a latrine contained chestnut, hazel, walnut, and plum, suggesting that these trees were probably growing in the city. From the fifth century AD onwards there is also archaeobotanical evidence of cereal threshing taking place close to the city and both millet and barley being grown in the city itself.[331] Archaeobotanical evidence from a large urban house in the city, occupied into the seventh century, also demonstrates the slow abandonment of both the house and the city. In addition to the recovery of carbonized food and kitchen waste in the utilitarian area of the house, the excavators found an increase in the number of wild plant taxa, indicating that this part of the site and sections of the house itself had become overgrown. Many of these wild plant taxa, including *Chenopodium album, Solanum nigrum,* and *Rumex* sp. were also found in the pool samples.

Conclusions

The combination of aquatic, ruderal, agricultural, and edible plant taxa recovered from the pool floor show that both the pool and the surrounding area underwent dramatic changes in the mid seventh century. Up to this point the Place of Palms was still used as an urban park and the pool was actively maintained and kept clean. Following the traumas of the seventh century (the nature of which is discussed below), activity in the Place of Palms did not entirely cease, but its nature changed radically, with a more utilitarian focus. The dumping of the debris from the clearance of the ruins of the North Stoa into the pool marked the beginning of the end of this structure as a monumental water feature. The pool started to silt up at this point, eventually turning into a swamp filled with pondweed and bulrushes. The entire southern side of the pool was abandoned or used only for water collection. Food remains indicate that the northeastern corner remained in use with human and probably animal activity taking place nearby. This area was later provided

322 Kirmaci, Agcagil, and Aslan 2013, 31.
323 Rovira and Chabal 2008.
324 The enormous size of the pool meant that it was probably a catchment area for more than just the Place of Palms, and material from the Agora and even possibly the area around the South Avenue may well have blown in. Deposition of material by animals and especially birds also undoubtedly played a role.
325 For a more detailed discussion of the abandonment of other areas and buildings within the city, see Wilson 2019a.
326 Ratté 2001, Wilson 2019.
327 Cassis *et al.* 2018, 384.
328 Both currently grow in abundance on the site.

329 Ratté and De Staebler 2011, 136.
330 Baeten *et al.* 2012; Vanhaverbeke *et al.* 2011.
331 Baeten *et al.* 2012, 1156.

with a cattle ramp, which gave access to the still-flowing water that remained in the pool (discussed in §A). The large number of non-edible terrestrial plants, and highly aggressive taxa such as blackberry, suggests that the area around the pool was becoming overgrown. Increasing agricultural activity nearby can also be traced, perhaps in the Agora.

This shift in the urban character of this part of the city is not uncharacteristic of cities in Anatolia at this time, and archaeobotanical and zooarchaeological evidence from Sagalassos reveal an almost identical pattern. Evidence from the Bouleuterion and the Tetrapylon Street show, however, that life at Aphrodisias nevertheless continued, albeit in a different form. The continued consumption of a range of cereals, legumes, fruits, and nuts at Aphrodisias, points to an increase in agriculture and horticulture within the city walls. Once the sediment in the pool was sufficient to remain dry for most of the year, this space was able to be used in an entirely new capacity during the Beylik period.

F. A VIOLENT END: EARTHQUAKE, FIRE, AND THE SWORD (AW, AK, BR, ATT, & HK)

The debate over the end of the ancient city in Asia Minor

In most of the cities of Asia Minor it is evident that the maintenance of major public buildings was carried through into the seventh century but not beyond.[332] In 1975 Clive Foss first proposed the theory that the decline of the ancient city in Byzantine Asia was precipitated by several Sasanian Persian invasions in the wake of the defeat of Heraclius near the Cilician Gates in 613. In 615 a Persian army marched across Asia Minor and captured Chalcedon, camping on the shores of the Bosphorus opposite Constantinople. Even though they withdrew in the same year, as Foss remarks, 'the extent and duration of the campaign suggests that the defences of Asia Minor had collapsed'.[333] The Persians took Ancyra and Rhodes in 623.[334] Historical accounts attest the destructive nature of these raids and the massacre and/or enslavement of local populations. Foss also argued, on the evidence of burning from cities such as Ephesos and Sardis, the prevalence of coin hoards of this period (including two near Tralles/Aydın), and the sharp drop in numbers of coins reaching cities including Aphrodisias after AD 615/616, that a Sassanid Persian army had passed along the Maeander Valley in AD 615/616.[335] A key site in this argument is Sardis, where the baths-gymnasium complex was partially burned and an associated two-storey colonnade of shops destroyed by fire; in and under the destruction layers were 888 coins dating from AD 498–616; and a hoard of over 200 copper coins buried in the Temple of Artemis closed with issues of 615. Foss argued that the Persians had sacked Sardis in the spring campaigning season of 616.[336]

Foss's theory encountered opposition. Frank Trombley argued that destruction on the Greek islands, the Aegean coast of Asia Minor, and the Maeander Valley was caused not by Persians, but by Avars or Slavs (although the date of their known incursions into the Cyclades had previously been thought to be prior to AD 615).[337] James Russell argued that rather than a sudden collapse in the early seventh century, urban life at cities in Asia Minor declined gradually but steadily over a long period, and rejected the interpretation of the evidence from Sardis as reflecting an attack by the Persians.[338] He and others stressed structural changes in economy and society,[339] and the effects of the Justinianic plague of the mid sixth century; and more recently the difficulty of attributing destruction events to particular ethnic invaders (Persians, as opposed to Avars or Arabs) has been emphasised.[340]

Other scholars preferred to place the blame for the end of the monumental glory of the classical city on destructive earthquakes, for which there is seventh-century evidence at a number of sites including Ephesos and Aphrodisias. At Ephesos, Hermann Vetters attributed the destruction of the two Hanghäuser, or terrace house complexes, excavated by the Austrian team, to an earthquake in the early seventh century.[341] In the 1980s, Kenan Erim attributed the many destruction levels of the seventh century found in excavations across Aphrodisias to a large earthquake which he believed had destroyed the city in the reign of Heraclius, putting an end to monumental urban life there.[342] In his view, among the buildings destroyed by this earthquake were the Sebasteion, the Theatre stage building, the Bouleuterion, and the Propylon of the Place of Palms (then referred to as the Agora Gate in the Portico of Tiberius).[343] In 2001, however, Chris Ratté cast doubt on Kenan Erim's theories of widespread destruction by an early seventh-century earthquake, arguing that the evidence both for an earthquake and for the chronology of the destruction of many of these buildings was limited; he preferred, like Foss, to ascribe the decline of the city to the Persian invasions, concluding: 'At Aphrodisias, there is no good reason to believe that an earthquake played a significant rôle'.[344]

The debate over the 'Foss thesis' continues. Although initially destruction layers with coins dating up to AD 616 at Sardis were thought to indicate a Persian sack of those cities, doubt has been cast on that idea by James Russell, who argued that the fire that destroyed the Byzantine shops might have been

---

332 The problem of the end of classical urbanism in seventh-century Asia Minor is treated at greater length in Wilson 2022.
333 Foss 1975b.
334 For the chronology, which has been clarified since Foss wrote, see Howard-Johnston 2021, 211.
335 Foss 1975b; 1976. For two coin hoards supposedly closing *c.* 615 found near Aydın (Tralles), see Grierson 1965: 209–218, Foss 1975b, 731, 743; 1976, 53–55. Schindel 2009, 207–211, in fact argued that these hoards contain coins issued in or after 616 and cannot therefore be associated with a Persian invasion in 615 or 616. In fact, the recognition that the invasion probably occurred in 617 (Wilson 2022) now restores the possibility that they might be associated with it.

336 Foss 1975a, 14–15, 20–21. For the destruction of the Byzantine shops at Sardis, see Crawford 1990, 2, and 22–101 for the detailed evidence; also Bates 1971, 1–2.
337 Trombley 1985; *contra* Oeconomides and Drossoyianni 1989, 165–166.
338 Russell 2001.
339 Whittow 2001; cf. Whittow 2018, 43–48.
340 Greatrex 2018.
341 Vetters 1977a, 17, 26, 28; 1977b, 17; 1981, 257–258; 1982, 147.
342 Erim 1986b, 35, 87, 111, 120 and 170; 1990, 18 and 20.
343 Erim 1986b, 111.
344 Ratté 2001, 144 (quote) and 145–147.

an accidental conflagration, since no weapons were found.[345] Marcus Rautman accepts that the drop in coin finds at the site reflects the disruption of trade by Persian invasions after 615, although he stays silent on the question of whether Sardis itself was sacked.[346] Destruction of late Roman houses in 'Field 55' in the area of the Roman imperial cult sanctuary is attributed by the present excavators primarily to early seventh-century earthquakes, with a *terminus post quem* given by coins of 611/612: 'The scenario is complex and has yet to be worked out in detail, but probably includes at least two earthquakes and a conflagration in some rooms.'[347] In fact, it seems that a fire *preceded* the earthquake(s), and burned human remains and weapons (swords and a spearhead) from the late Roman houses in Field 55 appear suggestive of a violent sack.[348]

At Ephesos, opinion among the excavation team has, until recently, appeared divided. Destruction layers on the colonnaded street called the Arkadiane, and the Curetes Street, the Theatre, and the Church of Mary the Mother of God, have been dated by coins to 615 or 616. There is no evidence that this seventh-century destruction at Ephesos was caused by earthquake—the earthquake which destroyed the terrace houses (Hanghäuser) and which Hermann Vetters had seen as putting an end to urban life in the early seventh century is now dated to the third century. The destruction layers from the Curetes Street, and some of the coins within them, were certainly burned. In 2009 Nikolaus Schindel argued powerfully that the extensive destruction at Ephesos was the result of a Persian sack in 616.[349] Sabine Ladstätter, however, argued that this may need rethinking. A building south of the Church of St Mary was destroyed in or after the mid seventh century, on the evidence of coins; but it also produced numerous coins of earlier years of Heraclius (610–641), which may therefore have been in circulation until the mid seventh century. She suggested therefore that other destruction deposits which yielded relatively few coins of the early years of Heraclius' reign may need to be redated to after the Persian wars.[350] However, the discovery in 2022 of several shops and workshops destroyed by fire, with, among the destruction later, arrows and spearheads, and several hundred coins of which the latest issues are of 614/615, dramatically confirmed the idea of a violent destruction in the early seventh century.[351] It seems likely in fact that Ephesos suffered two destructive events, one in or shortly after 616 at the hands of the Persians, and another in the reign of Constans II, perhaps by an Arab raid.[352]

Yet just as the original type-sites for the Foss thesis were being called into question, new archaeological evidence from other sites was coming to light that seems to support basic elements of his original view.[353] At Stratonikeia an attack is suggested not only by the coin profile of the site, but also by destruction layers in two buildings outside the walls. In the Erikli Kilise, a church outside the walls, a thick burned layer was found on the floor, containing coins up to AD 616,[354] and a building outside the city walls by the north gate was burned, with a lot of metal artifacts *in situ* (steelyard weights and balance); the latest coin was of AD 613.[355] At Tripolis, close to the confluence of the Meander and Lykos, just north-west of Hierapolis and Laodikeia, a burned layer over the ground level of the western stoa of the Colonnaded Street and the late Roman agora, including the stoa's carbonised roof timbers, included a spearhead and arrowheads and is attributed by the excavators to a Persian sack in the early seventh century; and they report a gap in the coin record between Phocas (603–610) and 630.[356]

More generally there are two peaks of coin finds from various sites in Karia: one corresponds to AD 613/4, marking the start of the Persians' Asia Minor campaign; the second peak at AD 629/630 marks the end of the war.[357] The total lack of coin finds at some sites and the few examples represented at others in the intervening years is probably more a result of the Persian campaigns affecting coin supply to the region; yet some sites seem to have been continuously able to receive coins, for example Myndos, which probably was not affected by a Persian raid (or an Avar or Slav one affecting the Aegean coasts). The same situation is visible at Side, where the supply of fresh coins continued up to AD 622/3, although diminished in comparison to the decade before, but was cut when Pamphylia itself suffered a Persian raid from the sea.[358] The sites which show an abrupt break in coin finds in these decades should be examined with more care and some might indeed have been destroyed by Persian raids; Stratonikeia seems to have been, from the evidence excavated there.

Painstaking research by James Howard-Johnston on the written sources for 'the last great war of antiquity' between the Byzantine and Sasanian empires has added a new piece of evidence to the debate. The *Armenian History* of Pseudo-Sebeos mentions a double invasion of Asia Minor by two different Persian forces, one under the general Shahin, who was sent west from the Persian court, reaching Theodosioupolis (Karin) in summer, and then capturing Melitene before pushing further west into Pisidia, where he joined up with an army under the general Shahrvaraz. The *Armenian History* appears to place this episode after Shahin broke out of Caesarea in Cappadocia, where he had been besieged in 611–612, after which he wintered in Armenia before being recalled to the Persian court; but Howard-Johnston points out that a double invasion deep into south-west Asia Minor is inconceivable before the collapse of the defences of Asia Minor with the Byzantine defeat at the

---

345 Russell 2001.
346 Rautman 2017, 234.
347 Cahill 2019, 132–135; quotation from p. 132.
348 Wilson 2022, 580–581, drawing on information in Greenewalt 2007, 745 and 753 fig. 8; Cahill 2018, 336; Cahill 2019, 130, 132.
349 Schindel 2009, 193–212, followed by Külzer 2010, 524; 2011, 31; 2013, 7–8. For burnt coins from the destruction layers on the Curetes street, see Schachinger 2014, 535.
350 Ladstätter 2017, 245.
351 Sabine Ladstätter, *pers. comm.* October 2022; press release at https://www.oeaw.ac.at/en/news/ephesos-more-than-1400-year-old-area-of-the-city-discovered-under-a-burnt-layer-2.
352 Wilson 2022, 582–583.

353 Wilson 2022.
354 Tek, Köker, and Sariiz 2019, 176 n. 3. Above the destruction layer were two later coins, dated AD 619/620 and 629/630. Cf. Wilson 2022, 583.
355 Tek, Köker, and Sariiz 2019, 176 n. 5.
356 Duman 2018, 359; the dating evidence for the layer with the weapons has not yet been published, but the implication is that the coins of Phocas provide a *terminus post quem*.
357 Tek, Köker, and Sariiz 2019, 185–186, especially fig. 5.
358 Tek 2015, esp. 131 fig. 3; Tek 2016, 247–248.

Cilician Gates in 613. Shahin's westward adventures after being recalled to the Persian court must be misplaced in the *Armenian History*, and should have occurred after 613. The known locations and campaigning activities of both Shahin and Shahrvaraz exclude the years immediately following; the earliest they could both have been present in Pisidia is 617, a more likely candidate than the next year, 618, when the Persians were preparing for the full-scale invasion of Egypt in 619.[359] Thus, instead of Foss's otherwise unrecorded invasion of 616, we have a record of a double invasion in 617, which puts both generals and their forces in Pisidia, a region close to the cities of Karia for which there is evidence of destruction around this time. A Persian invasion in 617 would be entirely consistent with the numismatic *termini post quos* of AD 616 from Sardis, Ephesos, and Stratonikeia.

The recent excavations at Aphrodisias both in the Place of Palms and on the nearby Tetrapylon Street have produced further evidence bearing on the debate, which, coupled with a reassessment of site-wide evidence for seventh-century destruction in the site notebooks, allows us to begin to disentangle the events which devastated Aphrodisias in the early seventh century. The picture is more complicated than it appeared before; we shall argue that there is evidence suggesting at least one sack of the city, and certain traces of an earthquake in the early seventh century; there appear also to have been *two* further destructions by assault around or shortly after the middle of the seventh century.

Evidence for fire at Aphrodisias

Evidence of extensive destruction by fire in the seventh century has been found in at least five areas within the city walls: the Tetrapylon Street between the Tetrapylon and the Sebasteion Propylon, the Bouleuterion, the House of Kybele (formerly called the 'Water Channel' House) near the north-east sector of the city wall, the north building of the Sebasteion, and now the Place of Palms (Fig. 72).

Along the east portico of the Tetrapylon Street to the north of the Sebasteion, excavated in 2008–2016, a heavily burned layer from some of the shops of the porticoes along the eastern side of the street (roof-tiles, bricks, revetment, marble floor-tiles, columns, and burned timbers) sealed coins of Phocas and the early part of the reign of Heraclius, the latest being an issue of 613/616.[360] This fire was discontinuous suggesting that not all the shops burned, and parts of the burned deposit had subsequently been cleared away to make a path through the debris, but before this work could be completed the rubble that remained was covered by a level of unburned destruction debris from the collapse of the two-storey façade of the stoa on the other side of the street. The extent and pattern of the brickfall show that this façade collapsed all in one go, and more likely as a result of earthquake than structural weakness of a dilapidated ruin. In the upper part of the earthquake collapse was found a hoard of 340 coins (Justinian to Heraclius), closing in AD 618, that had been kept in a textile bag, fragments of which survived, unburned;[361] it seems most probable that the money had been kept in the upper storey of the portico. The hoard provides a *terminus post quem* of 618 for the destruction by earthquake, and a *terminus ante quem* of, let us say, c. 620 for both the fire destruction and the subsequent earthquake collapse (any later than that and we should expect coins later than 618 in the hoard).

To the south of the Sebasteion, excavations in 2018 on the Tetrapylon Street confirmed beyond doubt the destruction of the colonnade of the eastern stoa here by earthquake (and not fire), as the columns and brick arcading had all fallen to the west in a single collapse.[362] The excavations on the Tetrapylon Street therefore establish a sequence of destruction by fire followed not long afterwards by an earthquake, both events falling within the window AD 613/616–c. 620.

Very close by, the late antique shops built over the north building of the Sebasteion were destroyed by fire; the deposit of roof tiles and burned timbers sealed coins of AD 565–578, 582–602, and 603–610 on the stylobate and pavement slabs in front of the north building.[363] Further north-east, just inside the city wall, the House of Kybele also burned down, its destruction deposit sealing seven coins of Heraclius found on the floor; the four legible ones provide a *terminus post quem* of AD 614. The building had burned while it stood, and then collapsed; bricks had vitrified and fused to material onto which they had fallen, and one of the intercolumnar bronze screens from an upper-storey colonnade had partly melted and fused to the marble pavement onto which it had fallen. The collapsed columns and capitals were reddened and cracked by fire.[364] Excavations in the Bouleuterion show that the North Stoa of the Agora adjoining the Bouleuterion, and the backstage corridor of the Bouleuterion itself, were also destroyed by fire; the pottery indicates a date in the early seventh century, but the date cannot be narrowed further by coin finds.[365] Parts of the surviving masonry of the Hadrianic Baths also show extensive damage by fire, though this is undatable,[366] and the baths ceased operation in the seventh century.

---

359 Ps-Sebeos 113, trans. Thomson p. 66 (ch. 34); Thomson, Howard-Johnston, and Greenwood 1999, 203–204. See now Wilson 2022, 570.

360 For full details, see Yıldırım 2016: 46–47, Sokolicek 2016: 65–69, and Dalgıç and Sokolicek 2017: 274–265. Coin C2008.936, mentioned by Yıldırım (2016, 46 n. 21) as coming from the burned destruction deposit, is a class II nummus (M) of Heraclius datable to AD 613/616.

361 Trench NAve 11.4, C2011.536-873; Öğüş 2016: 55. Identification of further coins in the hoard by Hüseyin Köker and Ahmet Tolga Tek in 2018 pushed its terminal date to AD 618.

362 Excavations under the supervision of Ine Jacobs; preliminary report in Smith 2018b, 1–2, and figs. 2, 4–6.

363 Nbk 210: *Sebasteion: North Portico I* 1981 (B. Rose, 1981), 54, 56, 61; Nbk 228: *Sebasteion: N Central Portico I* (B. Rose, 1982), 54–55, and 76–80. A coin of AD 629/630, found on the other side of a later wall built after the destruction by fire, does not seem to be from the same context: Nbk 210: *Sebasteion: North Portico I* (B. Rose, 1981), 63–5 (coin of Heraclius I, Anno XX), 78 (wall B is later than wall A).

364 Nbk 262: *Water Channel, Book 3* 1984 (J. Gorence, 1984), 1–6; Nbk 263: *Water Channel* (J. Gorence, 1984), 28–31.

365 Nbk 15: *Odeion (Bouleuterion), I* (J. Coleman, 1963), pp. 19–22, 24–6, 28, 30, 60–1, 65, 67, 86, 95, 98, 100–1, 105–7; Nbk 16: *Odeion (Bouleuterion), II* (J. Coleman, 1963), 3–4, 9, 11, 35, 52, 54, 60.

366 Especially on the north face of the south wall of Room 7, rebuilt in the late fifth century; the fire damage must post-date the rebuild. Cf. Erim 1986b, 99.

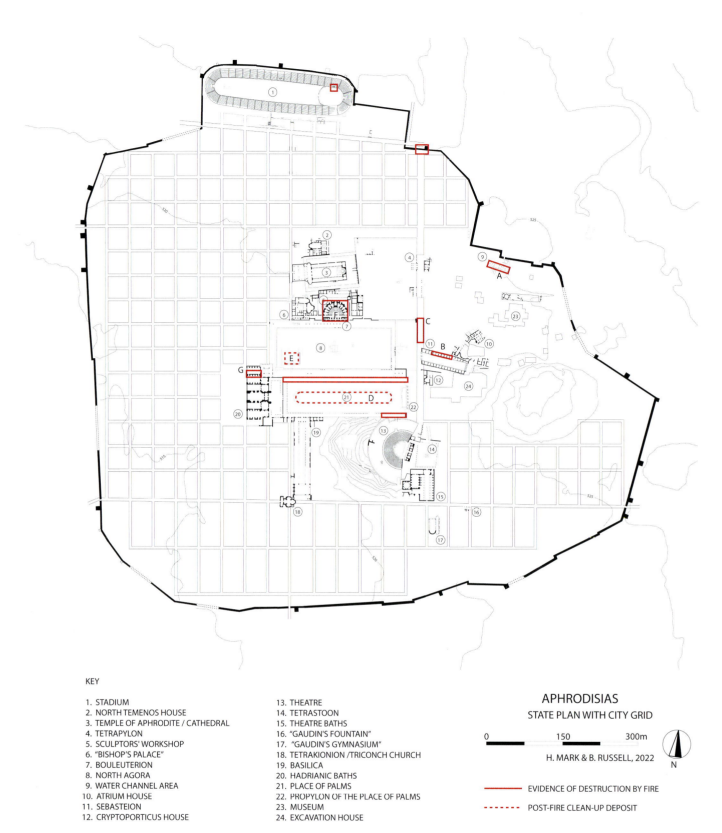

Fig. 72. Areas of seventh-century fire destruction at Aphrodisias. Key (with dates of destruction in parenthenses) A: House of Kybele (*terminus post quem* AD 614). B: Sebasteion, north building (*terminus post quem* AD 603–10). C: Tetrapylon Street (AD 613–618/620). D: Place of Palms (clean-up *terminus post quem* AD 643/4). E: Agora, late antique collecting pool. F: Bouleuterion (7th-c., not closely dated). G: Hadrianic 'Olympian' Baths (probably 7th-c.).

In the Place of Palms, as noted above, the evidence for destruction by fire includes the charred ends of roof timbers found in the beam holes cut into the Theatre Hill retaining wall for the roof of the final phase of the South Stoa, and the less direct evidence from two large-scale clean-ups of the area, which saw charred timbers and architectural fragments, many of them reddened or cracked by fire, dumped into the pool in two clearance deposits in the seventh century. The lower of these deposits also included some weaponry. This is discussed further below (§ Interpretation of the Place of Palms evidence).

Evidence for earthquake

Several areas of Aphrodisias have yielded evidence for earthquake damage in the seventh century (Fig. 73). We have seen above that recent excavations have now provided certain evidence for an earthquake along the Tetrapylon Street, both north and south of the Sebasteion Propylon, and that this should be dated to around AD 618–620 on the evidence of the coin hoard. The thrust of this earthquake caused a fall of columns to the west, and it may be expected therefore that the Propylon, a columnar structure oriented north–south and therefore unsupported to east and west, should have collapsed at this time; and indeed its collapse is also dated to the early seventh century, though not precisely.[367] Many of its elements were found fallen on its western side, in and over the late antique basin built against it (see Ch. 6 §A). The fall pattern of the mythological reliefs from the top of the basin wall is also consistent with this destruction (see Fig. 47). A substantial amount of architectural material from the Propylon is found in the first clean-up deposit at the eastern end of the pool, showing that the building was in ruins by the mid seventh century. Potentially also datable to this period is the substantial crack and area of subsidence identified in the pool floor, at its eastern end, where it joins the north pool wall, filled by material from the first clearance deposit; we think it more likely, however, that this results from a later earthquake and the material from the clearance deposit simply settled into the crack (above, Ch. 4 §O).

Excavation in 1994 of the row of shops running north-south along the west side of the Civil Basilica found coins beneath thick debris of the collapse of the tiled roofs, the latest being a *follis* of Heraclius and Heraclius Constantine of AD 619/620 (Inv. C94-12).[368] This could associate the destruction of these shops with the earthquake, supporting a date of *c.* 620, as suggested by evidence in the Tetrapylon Street.

Evidence for an earthquake in the early seventh century AD has also been claimed in the Theatre and the Tetrastoon.[369] The columns of the east stoa of the Tetrastoon alongside the Theatre, and of the eastern side of the basilical hall of the Theatre Baths immediately south of the Tetrastoon, were found fallen to the west.[370] The Theatre stage building collapsed, sealing material including coins dating into the reign of Heraclius.[371] The rear wall of the stage building was blocked when the Theatre was incorporated into seventh-century fortifications built on the Theatre Hill, which also re-used material from the collapsed Tetrastoon.[372] The collapse of the Theatre and Tetrastoon, though not in themselves precisely dated, would fit very well with the earthquake now attested *c.* AD 620, both in terms of chronology and direction of fall.

Evidence for a strong earthquake of the early seventh century AD that caused destruction on a massive scale has been recognised at Laodikeia, Hierapolis, and Tripolis in the Lykos valley (at Hierapolis there is also evidence for an earthquake in the second half of the seventh century).[373] At Laodikeia, the excavators date this earthquake to the reign of Phocas (602–610) on the basis of the latest coins reported as having been sealed by the collapse in House A, on 'House A Street', and apparently also in the collapse of the South Tower of the Byzantine East Gate.[374] If this is correct, the earthquake that devastated the cities of the Lykos Valley in the early seventh century should not be the same one as that which struck Aphrodisias around AD 620. But the full contexts for the coins from Laodikeia have not yet been published, and this picture may change; and in any case the coins merely provide a *terminus post quem*, which could indeed be consistent with an earthquake of *c.* 620.

Interpretation of the Place of Palms evidence

Two questions must be posed: (1) were the fires in the Tetrapylon Street, Sebasteion, the House of Kybele, and Bouleuterion related to each other, and to the destructive fire attested in the Place of Palms? and (2) were these fires accidental, or started deliberately, for example by hostile action?

The fires in the Tetrapylon Street, the north building of the Sebasteion, and the House of Kybele could, on coin evidence, all be exactly contemporary with each other, in a window between their latest *terminus post quem* of 614 (or even 616, if the issues of 613/616 are late in their possible dating window), and the *terminus ante quem* suggested by the hoard from the Tetrapylon Street of *c.* 620. The destruction of the Bouleuterion could also be part of the same event, but is less closely dated. As for the evidence from the Place of Palms, of burned timbers, architectural debris, and weapons all cleared into the pool, we need to distinguish between the date of the fire, and the date of the clean-up event, which may not be the same thing. The clean-up of the area and the dumping of fire-affected rubble and debris from the North Stoa into the north side of the pool is dated around the mid-seventh century by coins, the latest being of 643/4. The fire might have happened shortly before the clean-up, or some considerable time before. In other words, if the fire in the Place of Palms was contemporary with the fires

---

367 Erim 1990, 20.
368 Smith and Ratté 1995, 16; Ratté 2001, 139 n. 71.
369 For the Theatre, see Erim 1986b: 35, 87, 111.
370 Cf. Erim 1986b, 88 and photograph on p. 89.
371 Cormack 1991, 120.
372 Erim 1986b, 87–88.
373 Wilson 2022, 584–585, 588. Laodikeia and Hierapolis: Kumsar *et al.* 2016.
374 Şimşek 2008, 412–413, 417 (latest coin in House A), 418 (latest coins on 'House A Street'); Şimşek 2009, 106 (Byzantine East Gate); Şimşek 2014, 33, 42. Cf. Kristensen 2018, 73–74.

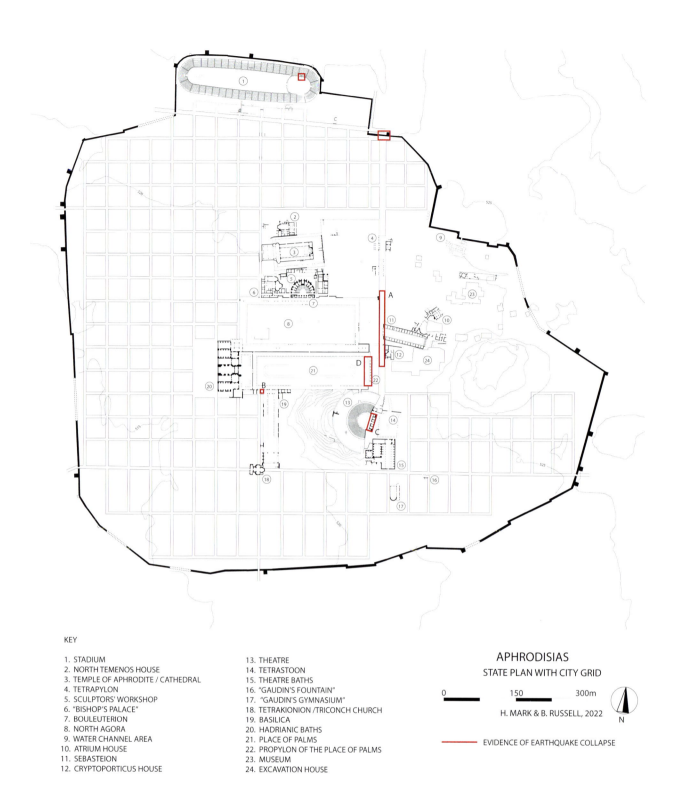

Fig. 73. Areas of Aphrodisias showing evidence of destruction by earthquake in the early seventh century. A: Tetrapylon Street. B: shops against west side of Basilica. C: Theatre stage building. D. Propylon of the Place of Palms.

that destroyed the Tetrapylon Street and, apparently the House of Kybele and Sebasteion north building, then the clean-up did not happen for a generation or so—which might speak to the extent of devastation and possible depopulation associated with it. If on the other hand we think this first scenario gives too long an interval between destruction and clean-up, we would need to postulate a second scenario with at least *two* major destructive fires in the city—one affecting areas of the north and east of the city and dated by the Tetrapylon Street evidence before *c.* 620, and a second one, which affected the Place of Palms, in the years before or not too long after AD 643/4.

As to the cause, while no weapons were found in the Tetrapylon Street, Sebasteion, House of Kybele, and Bouleuterion excavations, it might be thought to stretch credulity that four serious fires in different parts of the city all occurring within a few years of each other, at the most, were completely unrelated accidents. If we also include the Place of Palms in this list, the weapons and military equipment found at the bottom of the pool are suggestive (above, §D). In 1988 seven iron objects described as 'javelins de fer', three fragments with their points, and four fragments of shafts without points, were found lying on the floor of the pool towards the west end, the three points and three of the shaft fragments within the same 2 m² area.[375] Three fragments were re-located in 2018 and one is very clearly a weapon, with a bladed point. Found on the floor of the pool towards the eastern end in 1990 was an iron stirrup, possibly the earliest archaeological find of a stirrup in Asia Minor, and certainly a piece of military, rather than civilian, equipment at this mid-seventh-century date.[376]

From the new excavations, we can add another iron spearhead and three iron arrowheads (see §D above). Two long thin metal objects, somewhat bowed or bent, are probably best interpreted as shafts of javelins or pilum-type weapons of the sort found in 1988.[377] The other metal finds from the pool mostly relate to mercantile or utilitarian activities and the presence of weaponry of this sort is difficult to explain unless soldiers were present in the area or armed conflict took place here. Finds of weaponry are not limited to the Place of Palms. A stratigraphic sequence similar to that within the pool of the Place of Palms was documented in 2003–2004 during the excavations of the late antique collecting pool at the south-west corner of the Agora. Found within this was a layer of debris that had been deposited from the south over its wall and onto a clean, paved marble surface.[378] The debris includes a concentrated amount of marble architectural fragments, rubble, and ceramic building materials, apparently deriving from the surrounding stoas, that had been cleared into the pool. The stoas from which they must originate include the South Stoa of the Agora, which is of course the same building as the North Stoa of the Place of Palms. Lying directly on the pavement of the pool in the Agora were seven well-preserved iron knives, comparable in size, shape, and design to those found on the floor of the pool in the Place of Palms.[379] These layers were then sealed by a thick layer of silt that, as Ratté suggests, had gradually accumulated during the late antique through early Byzantine periods.[380] If we accept the first scenario outlined above, and assume that the Place of Palms fire occurred at the same time as those identified elsewhere in the city, these weapons suggest deliberate destruction; and the pattern of probably discontinuous but apparently simultaneous fires in different parts of the city would fit the pattern of a sack of the city, with soldiers torching buildings after they looted them.

This first scenario is the most economical solution to explain the evidence from the Place of Palms and elsewhere in the city. According to this reconstruction a sack occurred between AD 614 and 620, and thus, on chronological grounds, most probably by the Persians in 617,[381] followed swiftly and also by *c.* 620 by an earthquake, the combined effect of which was so devastating that the (returning? reviving?) population did not begin to rehabilitate the city centre for a generation. The earthquake caused substantial damage along the Tetrapylon Street, and was responsible also for the collapse of the Propylon and probably the shops on the western side of the Basilica. It did not entirely bring down the columns of the North or South Stoas of the Place of Palms (most of which remained standing until the eleventh century), but probably caused damage to the structures; it may also have caused the large crack in the floor of the pool along the north side towards the eastern end described above. Large-scale clearance of the debris caused by this destruction was only carried out in the Place of Palms some time after AD 643/4, presumably to open up the area again. The installation of a cattle ramp on the north side of the pool, before any siltation built up within the pool (and thus before the second clean-up event relating to the destruction of the South Stoa later in the seventh century), and temporary awnings or stalls around the pool's edge, indicate an attempt to use the Place of Palms as a utilitarian and commercial zone.

While this first scenario is economical, it is perhaps too much so, and there are potential problems with it. That there was something of a gap between the destruction event that brought down the roof of the North Stoa and its clearance is indicated by the presence of ruderal plant remains among the rubble of the first clearance deposit. However, such plants will grow up over piles of rubble within a year or two; they need not necessarily indicate decades of abandonment and the emergence

---

375 Nbk 307: *SW Portico of Tiberius* (F. Thode, 1989), 30. F80, F83–5; F87–8; PT.W.89-I, F150.
376 Nbk 316: *Portico of Tiberius: W Pool, Book I; E Pool* (A.T. Tek, 1990), 27, and photo 22, F24; Penn, Russell, and Wilson 2021.
377 Inv. 17-074, Inv. 17-082.
378 Ratté and Smith 2004, 157.
379 Knives: Inv. 2000-055, Inv. 2000-056, Inv. 2004-23, Inv. 2004.32–5; see Nbk 435: *N.Ag.04.1* (H. Awan, 2004), 46, 63, 66, 68, 80. Despite the statement in the preliminary report that an oak board dated to the ninth century AD was found in this deposit directly on the floor of the pool (Ratté and Smith 2008: 721), it is clear from the excavation notebooks that the ninth-century wood was found at a considerably higher level in the silted fill: Nbk 425: *N.Ag.03.2* (M. Berenfeld, 2003), 155, 161, and Nbk 435: *N.Ag.04.1* (H. Awan, 2004), 44, give elevations of between 514.71 and 515.79 m asl for the various pieces of wood, while the pool floor lay at 514.2 m asl. They do not therefore provide a ninth-century *terminus post quem* for the rubble deposit and the knives deposited on the floor of the pool; and the deposit appears similar in nature to the clean-up dump in the pool of the Place of Palms.
380 Ratté and Smith 2008, 721, 723.
381 Too early for an Arab raid; and a raid by Slavs is highly unlikely this far inland in Asia Minor.

of a wasteland. Furthermore, the botanical evidence from the bottom of the pool indicates that the water was still moving and the structure largely clean at the moment the first clearance deposit was dumped into it. It is hard to think that the pool would have been maintained if the city had been abandoned for a generation.

Moreover, we have presented in Ch. 4 §O the evidence for very late repairs to the pool and modifications to its water supply before it was filled in, and our reasoning for thinking that these repairs probably post-date the earthquake of c. 620 rather than proposing to associate them with an otherwise unknown earthquake in the sixth century. In particular, the east-to-west or west-to-east shaking movement could explain the cracking of marble slabs in the north wall, compressed against each other by such an earthquake; and the creation of the new large pipeline entering the pool at a low level on the south-eastern arc of the pool is explicable by the basin against the Propylon that had acted as a header tank for the fountains now being out of service as the Propylon had collapsed into it. These late repairs are precisely the kind of work that would have been needed to keep water flowing in the pool, as the archaeobotanical evidence indicates it was, after the earthquake of c. 620.

The botanical evidence instead implies that at least the initial clean-up of the Place of Palms, as represented by the first clearance deposit along the north side of the pool, occurred fairly soon after the destructive event that necessitated it, and not a generation later. The second scenario outlined above, therefore, needs to be given serious consideration: the destruction of parts of the city (but not the Place of Palms) by fire, probably at the hands of the Persians in AD 617, and then by earthquake c. 620, was then followed by some late repair work to the pool and modifications of its water supply; and then, some time after 643/4, by another fire that did affect the Place of Palms, and burned the North Stoa. The clean-up following this event, with material dumped into the pool, effectively put an end to the pool as a monumental feature; a cattle ramp was installed near the eastern end, and the pool began to silt up. There was then *another* destructive event, this time involving the burning of the roof of the South Stoa, later in the seventh century. If we separate out these events then the weapons from the Place of Palms and Agora cannot be used to argue that the c. 614–620 fire was a result of military action, even if the distribution of burned deposits across the city still indicates this and would fit the idea of a Persian sack in AD 617. However, the weapons from the Place of Palms and the Agora do strongly indicate that the first of the proposed later destructions resulted from hostile action—perhaps an Arab raid in the second half of the seventh century (see below). The second destruction event may also reflect an Arab raid.

Two further lines of evidence point in favour of this second scenario—that the two clean-up events represented by the first clearance deposit on the pool floor, and the second one somewhat later, over the initial silting layer, may have resulted from attacks on the in the second half of the seventh century. These are a city-wide gap in coin finds dating between AD 658 and 792/7, and an Arab-countermarked coin from the second clean-up deposit, on the south side of the pool.

Arab raids into Asia Minor began in the 640s, as summer raids; they reached Amorium in 645/6 and al-Mara near Melitene in 653/4. There was a pause in raiding when the early caliphate was then involved in a bitter civil war (the 'First Fitna') from 656–61; but raids resumed in 662/3, now on a more or less annual basis until at least 680/1, this time with Arab forces striking deeper and wintering in Asia Minor.[382]

Although the latest coin from the first clearance deposit on the pool floor (cat. 289) is dated to AD 643/4, it could have circulated well into the 660s or 670s and merely provides a *terminus post quem* for the clean-up of the area to the north of the pool. It might therefore be easiest to associate the destruction debris thrown into the pool with Arab raids in the late 640s/early 650s (although there is no other evidence that they penetrated as far inland as Aphrodisias this early), or after AD 662, instead of the aftermath of a Persian attack some 30 or 40 years earlier. Serious disruption to the economic life of the city in or shortly after the late 650s is indicated by a city-wide break in coin finds starting then. At the time of writing, only the coin finds from the excavations at Aphrodisias between 2002–2018 have been fully studied; these show a total gap in coin finds from the site starting after the Class VI coins of Constans II, around AD 655/6 or 656/7, after which the next coin recorded is of Constantine VI from AD 792–797 (C2009.107). Cécile Morrisson gives the coin gap at Aphrodisias as AD 658 to AD 829, dates derived from unpublished notes of the late M. Hendy.[383] Combining both sets of evidence we have a complete gap in coin finds across the city from AD 658 to 792/7. It is very possible that we are seeing here the effects of one or more destructive Arab raids on Aphrodisias shortly after AD 658, and probably after the end of the 'First Fitna', thus in the early 660s. This created a gap in coin finds until the end of the eighth century AD. Indeed, the destruction debris observed on the pool floor in the Place of Palms, and in the collecting pool in the

---

382 Kaegi 2006; Wilson 2022, 569–570. For a general outline of the Arab raids into Asia Minor see Lilie 1976, 60–96 and Brandes 1989, 51–62. With the end of peace in AD 653 or 654, the Arab fleet took Rhodes, Kos, and Crete, and attacked the coasts of Asia Minor (Halikarnassos, Smyrna and Ephesos were specifically mentioned as cities taken); Arabs are even mentioned in Chalcedon, across the Bosphorus from Constantinople in the same year. With the destruction of the Byzantine fleet in 655 at Phoenix in Lycia, there was no power left to prevent them going further (Brandes 1989, 55–60). In AD 663, Pergamon, Smyrna, and maybe Chios were attacked, among other places. In AD 670/671, the Arab fleet was once more in the Aegean for an expedition reaching Constantinople and laying siege to the city which lasted seven years until 677/678. In AD 670/1 Arabs were wintering at Cyzicus, while in 672/3, a second fleet landed and wintered at Smyrna and a third fleet wintered in Lycia and took Rhodes again. In AD 674/5, Arabs could winter in Crete, even though one navy and a land army had suffered a defeat by the Byzantines in Lycia the previous year (Brandes 1989, 55–60). Arabs settled in Rhodes and held the island, attacking the Byzantines from here until they were removed by Caliph Yazid, son of Mu'awiya, after Mu'awiya's death in AD 680 (Ruggieri 2005, 249; 2009, 211, n. 27). But Arabic graffiti discovered at Knidos (Ruggieri 1992; 2005, 249; 2009, 211, 217–218) dated to year H98 = AD 716/17 and mentioning troops from Palestine (Imbert 2013, 734–745), indicate a continuing Arab military presence on the coasts of Karia. Other Arabic graffiti from Kos mention an 'expedition against infidels', and 'troops', and are dated to H98 = AD 716 and H99 = AD 718/9 (Imbert 2013, 746–750). Further Arabic graffiti recorded at Iasos, Didyma, and Halikarnassos could be related to these; the graffito from Iasos mentions a mosque (Ruggieri 2005, 249; 2009, 211, 218).
383 Morrisson 2017, 76.

Agora, could easily belong to the clean-up undertaken immediately or soon after such an event.

The Arabic-countermarked coin of Heraclius (cat. 281) from the second clean-up deposit on the south side of the pool in the Place of Palms, whose deposition must date to the 660s or later, provides some evidence for the presence of Arabs in the area. A countermarked coin would have not been legal tender in Byzantine Asia Minor and so could hardly have arrived by trade. Since it was found in the second clean-up deposit, well above the first clean-up deposit, it raises the question of whether the burning of the South Stoa implied by the second clean-up deposit was caused by another of the Arab raids on Asia Minor. Such countermarked coins would probably have been taken out of circulation when true Arab coinage started with the coinage reform in AD 685. The presence of this coin here among the second clean-up deposit may be evidence either for another Arab raid on the capital of Karia, or for pseudo-Byzantine issues entering Karian circulation from Arabs wintering in the southwest of the region. Although it is very tempting to imagine that the coin was dropped by an Arab raider, that might be pushing fantasy too far; yet this is one coin whose circulation would probably not have been permitted in Byzantine Asia Minor, with its obvious Arabic countermark, and none has been previously recorded from any sites here, and therefore it must be linked directly to an Arab presence in the region.

Coin gaps like that at Aphrodisias exist at many other published sites in Asia Minor, and debate continues as to whether these sites were destroyed and totally abandoned as a result of Arab raids, indicating a mass depopulation of many of the classical cities, or whether occupation continued at those sites and it was coin production and supply that suffered during the Arab raids, and older issues continued to be used.[384] The coin gap does not mean that the city was abandoned for a century or more as numismatic finds might at first sight suggest. Bishops of Stavropolis are attested in the early 660s, 680, and 692,[385] though of course this does not mean they were actually present in the city. More compelling is the archaeological evidence from the Place of Palms, notably the clearance deposits in the pool, the cattle ramp, basin, and cuttings in the pool wall for awning poles, which show that this area was still used, perhaps as a marketplace. What the coin gap does show is that after one or more catastrophic events which we might connect with Arab raids, economic life must have suffered so badly that no numismatic evidence has been left at the buildings excavated in the last two decades. The missing years may be present among other unstudied older finds, but even if so, they would most probably represent a very small percentage of the finds, reflecting a very small community surviving at Aphrodisias in the aftermath of successful Arab raids affecting all of Asia Minor.

At Sagalassos, where the city centre was abandoned at some point in the seventh century AD, after which the settlement was reduced to a village and maybe a fortified garrison, several villages in the countryside continued in existence, indicating that there was not a complete depopulation of the territory.[386] This may be a cultural change where old metropoleis were abandoned or reduced to villages (after their destruction?) in favour of smaller and pastoral settlements organized around a church.[387] However, around Aphrodisias the effects of the Persian invasion and then the seventh-century Arab raids may have been more serious and long-lasting; the rural survey showed that while some of the farmsteads around the city were still occupied into the seventh century, none survived its end. What settlement did persist was on the higher and less accessible plateau south of the Morsynos river.[388] The implication appears to be that not only were the city's physical buildings burned and ruined by earthquake, but that its agricultural base was also decimated by Persian and Arab forces.

To sum up, there is now evidence to indicate that the city suffered a series of destructive events in the seventh century. Fire damage is documented in the Tetrapylon Street, Sebasteion, House of Kybele, and probably also the Bouleuterion, between c. 614 and 620. The spread of this devastation could well indicate that it resulted from enemy action, most probably a Persian sack during the double invasion of Asia Minor by the armies of Shahrvaraz and Shahin in AD 617. In the immediate aftermath of this event, and before the damage could be fully cleaned up, a major earthquake hit the city, around 620. While it is tempting to connect the clearance deposits in the pool of the Place of Palms to these events (the first scenario described above), the botanical remains in particular suggest this is unlikely. The first clearance deposit must have been dumped into the pool soon after the event that prompted it—there was no intervening period of abandonment—and the coin evidence shows that this event can only have occurred after 643/4. The weapons from the pool floor, therefore, are not connected to the fire damage documented elsewhere in the city between c. 614 and 620 and must be related to another attack on the city after 643/4, either in the late 640s/early 650s, or in the 660s. The chronology would suggest that this was an Arab raid. While no evidence for a later assault on the city was found in the excavations in the Tetrapylon Street, Sebasteion, or House of Kybele, these areas of the city had already been destroyed by this date, and were evidently not rebuilt after the events of 617 and c. 620. The burning attested in the Hadrianic Baths could belong to either an early or a mid or late seventh-century destruction event.

The Place of Palms seems to have survived the putative Persian sack of 617, even if the Propylon was probably brought down by the c. 620 earthquake (we do not have independent evidence for the date of destruction of the West Stoa). The still-standing North and South Stoas would have represented obvious targets for any attackers after this date. Following the destruction of the North Stoa (mid 640s–660s), the large-scale clearance of the detritus from it—and its dumping into the pool—was prompted by a desire to clear the north side of the former Place of Palms. The cattle ramp was inserted after this clear-up, as were the series of temporary structures, perhaps

---

384 Lightfoot 2002, 231–235; Morrisson 2017, 75–79.
385 *Notitia* 1, Jankowiak 2013, 438–444; Theodore of Stavropolis is attested at the Sixth Ecumenical Council in Constantinople in AD 680 (*PBE* I, Theodoros 30), and Sisinnios attended the Council 'In Trullo' at Constantinople in 692 (*PBE* I, Sisinnios 9).
386 Vanhaverbeke *et al.* 2009.
387 Brandes 1989 remains the standard work discussing this period in Asia Minor, including a discussion of the numismatic finds and coinage (Brandes 1989, 143–149).
388 Ratté and De Staebler 2011, 136.

stalls with awnings. The second clearance deposit, on the south side of the pool and relating to the destruction of the South Stoa, is dated by the Arabic-countermarked coin to the 660s or later in the seventh century, and strongly suggests that the city suffered a *second* Arab raid in the later seventh century. The new evidence from the Place of Palms shows that this major urban space suffered extensive damage, probably three times, at the hands of hostile forces, in the early, middle, and late seventh century. After the double blow of the Persian sack in 617 and an earthquake shortly afterwards, it never regained its monumental character and developed into an open-air marketplace and convenient location for watering cattle; but the North and South Stoas were still standing apparently with their roofs on, until they were burned, separately, in two Arab raids in the second half of the seventh century.

G. CONCLUSIONS: THE END OF CLASSICAL APHRODISIAS (AW & BR)

The end of ancient Aphrodisias was a series of mutiple blows: a sack by an invading force, probably Sasanid Persians, followed swiftly by earthquake, and later still by one or more Arab raids. The ruined monuments, colonnades, and shops were never rebuilt, and the character of the city changed forever—not only in physical appearance, but also in function and administrative power. The contrast with the preceding century is stark: the city had been devastated by a severe earthquake in the late fifth century, but had responded to this disaster with a vigorous city-wide programme of rebuilding. Further strenuous efforts were made to keep the pool and its water supply functional during the sixth century, including the construction of the basin against the Propylon; and the Hadrianic 'Olympian' Baths were renovated, with a newly laid marble floor in at least one of the rooms, in or after the reign of Phocas. In the first decade of the seventh century, Aphrodisias was still a city able to maintain its public buildings; after c. 620, it was not. And yet, extraordinarily, even though the buildings of the north-south Tetrapylon Street and public monuments like the Propylon of the Place of Palms were not repaired, repairs *were* made to the pool and its water supply arrangements were restored, to keep water flowing to it and through it even after the Propylon basin that served as a header tank for the fountains had been ruined by the collapse into it of the Propylon itself.

If much of the city centre remained in ruins from c. 620 onwards, the place can scarcely have continued to serve in any effective sense as the seat for the governor of the province of Karia; and indeed we have no surviving evidence for a governor of Karia after the sixth century.[389] Indeed, the system of Byzantine themes which emerged from the 640s onwards, first as field armies stationed within a territory, and eventually becoming territorial administrations in their own right, appears to have replaced the provincial system in the wake of the Persian wars. One wonders therefore if the cleaning up of the Place of Palms in the mid to late seventh century, and apparently of the Agora too, was undertaken at the impulse of the theme army, as part of the effort to fortify the Theatre Hill with the construction of a defensive wall across the rear of the stage building of the Theatre; material that could be reused in the fortifications was salvaged, and the remainder thrown into the pool. If the clean-up was not undertaken by the theme army, then it was presumably done at the behest of the bishop, who must have stepped into the administrative void left by the effective disappearance of the governor from the city. In either case, it is tempting to see the utilitarian use of the Place of Palms after this clean-up event as an attempt to revitalize the ruined city centre, at least to a certain degree. The Place of Palms, and apparently part of the Agora as well, offered the convenience of a pool into which a considerable amount of rubble and debris could be deposited to clear a field of fire below the new fortifications on the Theatre Hill and to make space for essential commercial activities required by the remaining populace and the new military units present on the Theatre Hill. Other spaces within the city that had been more densely built up during previous periods would have offered no such easy clearance strategy.

It was at some time in this period that the city's name was changed from Aphrodisias, City of Aphrodite, to Stavropolis, City of the Cross.[390] The new name appears over the North East Gate of the City Wall, carved into an erasure where the original name once was. This renaming should post-date the composition of Sophronius of Jerusalem's account of the miracles of John and Cyrus, written between 610 and 619, which still refers to the city as Aphrodisias, but predates 660 by which time the city is called Stavropolis in *Notitia* 1.[391] The suggestion is attractive that the renaming of the city was connected with the return of the True Cross from Persia as part of the peace settlement of AD 629.[392] One can see how with the end of the Persian wars in 629 and the return of the True Cross, the recent memory of the double disaster of violent sack and earthquake might have convinced the population that they needed both the physical protection of a *kastron*, and the protection of a more Christian name. Even that did not save the city from further raids and destruction at the hands of the Arabs in the second half of the seventh century.

---

389 Roueché 1989, 321–322.
390 Roueché 1989, 149–151; 2007a, 186–189.
391 Jankowiak 2013, 438–444 argues that *Notitia* 1 is to be dated around AD 660.
392 Gelzer 1901, 548.

CHAPTER 9

After Antiquity: The Byzantine to Ottoman Periods

Allison Kidd, Ben Russell, Andrew Wilson, Tim Penn, Hugh Jeffery, Muradiye Bursalı, and Ulrike Outschar

Following the destructive events that occurred in the Place of Palms in the late antique period the gradual siltation of the pool and its surrounding areas was punctuated by several massive earthquakes in the centuries following. These two natural processes had a profound effect on the topography of the former Place of Palms, shaping occupation within the area for the next millennium. The new excavations provide remarkable insights into the development of this space and the emergence of a new post-antique settlement at Stavropolis or Karia, as Aphrodisias was now increasingly called. What they reveal is that the Place of Palms ceased to serve as an urban park, and indeed as any kind of monumental space, in the seventh century. It remained a largely empty sector of the city through the Byzantine period, only being reoccupied in the thirteenth to fourteenth centries, at which point the pool and its walls had entirely disappeared from view. The open area of the former Place of Palms was then divided into fields in the Seljuk and early Beylik periods. Out of the fieldwalls and tracks of this period emerged a fully-fledged village in the late Beylik and early Ottoman periods, which provides us with our most detailed evidence to date of life at the city in the post-antique period.

A. HISTORICAL CONTEXT (AK, BR, & AW)

After the city of Aphrodisias was renamed Stavropolis at some point during the second or third quarter of the seventh century, the city features little in the historical sources between the eighth and the eleventh centuries. Bishops of Stavropolis are attested, but by the eighth century an alternative name for the city, Karia, was already emerging, from the name of the province or *eparcheia* of which it had been the capital. At the Council of Nicaea of 787 the deacon Theophylact signed himself 'deacon and exarch, and representative of the throne of Stavropolis, that is Karia'.[1] Thereafter, from the ninth century until 1278, we find bishops subscribing to conciliar acts as bishops of 'Karia', although the name Stavropolis was not entirely eliminated: it occurs in episcopal lists, and the see is called Stavropolis on a dedicatory cross of 1172.[2]

Six years after the Byzantine defeat at Manzikert in 1071, the Sultanate of Rûm seceded from the Great Seljuk Empire, forming an independent state in central Anatolia, centred on Konya. By the 1180s the western borders of this state had been expanded into Karia, and Stavropolis found itself in the borderlands of the Byzantine Empire, and indeed suffered a raid at the hands of Theodoros Mankaphas and Turkish plunderers between AD 1188 and 1194, in which the cathedral of St Michael was burned down.[3] In AD 1197, the Seljuks under Sultan Kay Khusraw of Iconium attacked the city, took its inhabitants as prisoners and resettled them at Philomelion in Phrygia.[4] The extent to which the city had already declined is indicated both by the fact that the Byzantine commentator Niketas Choniates refers to Karia as a κωμοπόλις, a compound word literally meaning 'village-city', and by the fact that the population shipped off into captivity numbered fewer than 5,000. Of the Byzantine seals from the site published by Nesbitt and Jeffery, four belong to the eighth century, one to the eighth or ninth, four to the ninth, thirteen to the tenth century, and nine to the eleventh century; as Nesbitt notes, 'the sigillographical record of Karia ends well before Theodoros Mankaphas' attack on the city in 1188'.[5] Choniates says that the people did not resist resettlement, although the accuracy of his account has been questioned.[6] The city of Karia has generally been considered to have been abandoned for a while after this, although our excavations now suggest some continued occupation. We shall see, however, that the city had also suffered a major earthquake in the tenth or eleventh century.

The extent to which Karia/Stavropolis was formally under Seljuk rule in the mid to late thirteenth century is unclear. In the wake of the Seljuk defeat by the Mongols at the battle of Köse Dağ in 1243, Seljuk power waned, and during the second half of the thirteenth century the Sultanate of Rûm disintegrated into a series of beyliks, principalities or petty kingdoms governed by Beys. Karia lay in the territory of the Menteshe beylik, which emerged between 1260 and 1290, and whose capital was at Milasa. Control of many sites in this region oscillated between the Byzantines and Seljuks;[7] although George Pachymeres says that Karia had already been lost to the Turks by AD 1278,[8] the city was still formally recognized as part of the Byzantine Empire until AD 1282,[9] and evidence for Byzantine ceramic production into the thirteenth century indicates some

---

1 Nesbitt 1983.
2 Nesbitt 1983, 159 n. 7; Roueché 1989, 151, 167.
3 Niketas Choniates, *Historia*, p. 400 (van Dieten 1971).
4 Niketas Choniates, *Historia*, p. 495 (van Dieten 1971). The number given for the population at Aphrodisias (Karia) also includes the inhabitants of Tantalos, which Roueché (1989, 167) suggests is the nearby site of modern-day Dandalas.
5 Nesbitt 1983 (quote from 159); Jeffery 2020.
6 Jeffery 2019, 16–17.
7 Beihammer 2017, 21.
8 Pachymeres, *De Michaele et Andronico Palaeologis* VI.20, p. 468 Bonn edition (Niebuhr 1835).
9 *Ducas* 2.2; Roueché 1989, 167.

continuity of a Byzantine population within the city throughout this period.

There was still an episcopal see of Karia in the reign of Andronikos II (r. AD 1282–1328), though its status appears reduced as its position in the episcopal *Notitiae* drops from twenty-first to twenty-sixth place.[10] Bishops are attested into the late fourteenth century, although by this time they seem to be absentee bishops of a titular see, whose name reverted to Stavropolis. Around 1394 the metropolitan bishop of Stavropolis was also given the bishopric of Rhodes, Kos, and the Cyclades since he could not exercise his function in his own see.[11] However, the titular see of Stavropolis appears to have continued beyond this date: Isaias of Stavropolis attended the Council of Florence in 1439, from which he fled to avoid signing the decree of union which would recognise papal supremacy over the Eastern churches.[12]

In the early fourteenth century the Aydinid beylik took over the northern part of the Menteshe beylik, including Güzelhisar (formerly Tralles), which was renamed Aydın, and Karia; a Turkish satrap of Karia is first mentioned in AD 1329.[13] The Beylik of Aydın was first absorbed into the growing Ottoman state, as it expanded into western Anatolia, in 1390, but Tamerlane's victory over the Ottomans in 1402 and the ensuing civil war that lasted until 1413 meant a period of turmoil. Ottoman control over western Anatolia and the area within which Karia (Stavropolis) lay was not firmly established until 1425.

A settlement of some kind persisted at the site, called Gerye (from Karia), and then more recently Geyre. By the mid twentieth century it was a village of part-stone, part-timber houses, concentrated around what is now the open space in front of the museum, the original *meydan* (opposite which several of the traditional houses have been renovated), over the cavea and stage building of the Theatre, and the higher ground above the Propylon of the Place of Palms and the area further east, and stretching northward along Tetrapylon Street. In the early 1960s, as large-scale excavation work began under Kenan Erim, the surviving village was relocated to a new location half a kilometre to the west, which has kept the name of Geyre.

B. STRATIGRAPHY OF THE MEDIEVAL AND EARLY MODERN SETTLEMENT (AK, BR, & AW)

Challenges during excavation

Problems of stratigraphy and dating are especially difficult when interpreting the archaeology of the post-antique period in the Place of Palms. Not only are ceramic sequences less well understood than for the Roman and early Byzantine periods, and coins more scarce, but local taphonomic processes mean that we have less clearly defined stratigraphic horizons. Because earlier excavation had truncated most post-antique layers outside the pool without any clear stratigraphic record, we must largely rely on areas within the boundaries of the pool walls for these phases, except for an area to the south. Until the fourteenth or fifteenth century this area was still swampy and wet. Therefore, the sedimentary deposits within the area of the grand ornamental pool cannot be regarded as sealed contexts. It was visually very difficult to discriminate with precision sub-units within this silting sequence (see Ch. 1 §E), and the division between stratigraphic units is often necessarily either arbitrary or somewhat imprecise. Moreover, objects sink into wet silt, and may thus be intrusive into deposits that are stratigraphically earlier. The problem was further compounded by disturbance from animal burrows and tunnelling moles; this could easily lead to older material being thrown up into later deposits, while the opposite could occur as burrows or mole-runs collapsed, resulting in downward movement of soil and artefacts contained within it, leading to the possibility of later material intruding into earlier deposits, which is even more problematic for dating (see Ch. 1 §E). Furthermore, since the area of the former pool was swampy, we are not seeing direct occupation for the phases during which the pool was filling up, but rather a reflection of such occupation by way of what was cleared or thrown into the wet ground of the former pool.

The field walls that define later settlement in this area were built in drystone walling, a construction technique which does not lend itself to any sort of longevity in such a consistently wet area. The repeated collapses of such drystone walls are not necessarily signs of disregard or decay, but perhaps simply a result of poor or less stable construction and the consequent need for frequent renewal. The more substantial houses and structures also had foundation courses or dwarf walls of drystone construction, but evidently were partly constructed in wood, as shown by the existence of numerous postholes. These were recognizable as settings of one, two, three, or four stones which had been placed on end to wedge the upright timber in its posthole. The resolution of such postholes into coherent patterns that would reliably suggest a house plan has frequently eluded us. Replacement of timbers over time could lead to several features in close proximity to each other but all relating to essentially the same architectural layout. Post-settings such as these could easily be missed in excavation, and it is likely that some have been; moreover, if wooden elements were used to chock timbers in their postholes, they would leave no trace (see Ch. 1 §E).

The following stratigraphic discussion should be read with the phase plans in Figs 74, 76–79, and 81–82, and the section drawings in Fig. 83. To simplify the explanation of the complex layers of walls and structures that define the post-antique settlement, the various stratigraphic units (labelled in bold) have been grouped together into features, numbered according to their phase and enclosed in square brackets ([4.1], [4.2], etc.), and it is these that are labelled on the accompanying phase plans. Further information about each context can be found in Appendix 6. The main phases are summarised in Table 13; we number the construction and use of the pool as Phase 1, the late antique repairs as Phase 2, and the sequence of destruction and abandonment in the seventh century as Phase 3. This chapter therefore starts with Phase 4.

---

10 Gelzer 1901, 598, 613; Roueché 1989, 167–8, 324.
11 Roueché 1989, 168, 325–6.
12 Ostroumov 1861, 31, 154; Gill 1958, 30.
13 Cantacuzenus I, p. 388 lines 16–17 Bonn edition (Schopenus 1828).

Table 13. Chronological phases identified during the excavations in the Place of Palms.

Phase	Key features	Period	Date Range
1	Construction and use of Place of Palms	Roman imperial	1st to 5th/6th cent. AD
2	Restoration and continued use	Late antique	5th/6th to 7th cent. AD
3	Destruction, clearance, and change of use of area around pool	Late antique – early Byzantine	7th to 8th cent. AD
4	Pool as a swamp, limited occupation around it; collapse of stoas	Middle Byzantine	8th cent. to 1197
5	Drying out of pool, paths laid across it	Seljuk	Late 12th to late 13th cent.
6	Division of area into agricultural plots for the first time	Beylik	Late 13th to late 14th cent.
7	Further development of land units and trackways across area	Late Beylik – early Ottoman	Late 14th to early 15th cent.
8	First phase of village	Early – classical Ottoman	Early 15th to mid 16th cent.
9	Later phase of village	Classical to late Ottoman	Mid 16th to 17th cent.
10	Limited occupation of village area	Late Ottoman	17th to 18th cent.
11	Field walls	Late Ottoman	19th to early 20th cent.
12	Field walls and modern excavation	Turkish Republic	1923 to present

Phase 4, 8th–12th centuries AD: limited Byzantine activity and collapse of the stoas (Fig. 74)

Most of the evidence for the period between the eighth and the twelfth centuries comes from within the area of the former pool, which limits what can be said about Byzantine activity here. Earlier excavations by Jacopi and Erim to the north of the pool had truncated post-antique layers in the North Stoa and to the south of it. Similarly, to the south of the pool earlier excavations by Erim truncated post-antique layers in many parts of the South Stoa; in the remaining areas where these layers are preserved our excavation could not be taken below the eleventh-century layers of rubble collapse because of the need to preserve vehicular access for a crane and for spoil removal. Outside the pool, therefore, evidence for activity in this area came from a narrow strip over and immediately north of the pool's north wall. Within the pool, following the accumulation of the second clearance deposit on the south side, discussed in the previous chapter, this phase is characterised by the gradual infilling of the pool by siltation, and the final collapse of what remained of the surrounding architecture, some time prior to the late eleventh century.

Across the area of the pool, a 15–20 cm thick compact layer of fine-grained greyish-brown silt (**4480**) accumulated in the centuries following the seventh-century clearance operations, building up around around the basin and cattle ramp discussed in Ch. 8 §A. This layer was mostly indistinguishable from **4448** beneath, except along the south side of the pool where it overlay the second clearance deposit (**4471**).[14] Sampling of this deposit along the northern side of the pool by Mark Robinson in 2012 revealed a high concentration of freshwater snails, though not as many as in **4448**, indicating that the pool was still wet at this date.[15] The latest coin, dated to the reign of Constans II (cat. 288) does not help date the accumulation any further.

This period of slow siltation in the pool is punctuated by two events: the collapse of the North and South Stoas and damage to the pool walls in a major earthquake, and the clearance of the resulting debris into the pool. This earthquake caused the colonnade of the North Stoa to fall southwards, and excavations in the 1980s found long stretches of the entire order of the stoa lying as it had collapsed in the earthquake (see Pl. 4.D–E).[16] Kenan Erim had many of the columns re-erected, but left a stretch of architrave and cornice blocks where they were, where we planned them at the start of our excavation (Fig. 75). Within the area of our excavations, the collapsed entablature blocks (**3001**) were found lying on the top of the late antique make-up layer **4280**. This suggests that despite siltation within the pool, the area north of it had been kept mostly clear of debris.[17]

The east segment of the South Stoas, in contrast, fell in on itself, presumably because the thrust of the earthquake came from the north and the stoa was supported along its rear side by the Theatre Wall. This earthquake also caused substantial damage to the pool walls, especially along the south side of the pool, where the seat blocks and uprights were buckled and broken, and many of them displaced by the tremors. It may have been this earthquake which caused the large crack along the north side of the pool towards the eastern end (Ch. 4 §O); if so, then

---

14 Among the limited finds in this deposit were two metal implements (SAg.17.1.4480.F796 and SAg.17.1.4480.F833), a loomweight (SAg.17.1.4480.F824), and a fragment of glass lamp (SAg.17.1.4480.F782). These finds are similar to those found in 4448 and the fragment of glass lamp is discussed with another fragment of a similar design from 4448 in Ch. 8 §D.

15 Wilson, Russell, and Ward 2016, 86; Robinson 2016, 92–93.

16 Jacopi's excavations in 1937 had trenched along the fallen colonnade and removed only the mask-and-garland frieze blocks, leaving the columns, architrave, and cornice blocks behind.

17 Previous excavations in the South Stoa confirm this situation, with little to no accumulated soils or debris beneath where the blocks had fallen. Nbk 82: *BHadPortTib1* (S. Crawford and J. Gary, 1970), 6, 8, 64; Nbk 254: *SAgGate I-84*, Bk 2 (B. Rose, 1984), 175–183; Nbk 271: *Portico of Tiberius S. I-85* (A. Önce, 1985), 23–35, 45–46; Nbk 278: *Portico of Tiberius SE I-86, SW I-86* (J. Gorence, 1986), 21–23, 39, 78–79–83, 87–88; Nbk 279: *Portico of Tiberius SE I-86*, Bk 2 (J. Gorence and K.T. Erim, 1986), 1–19.

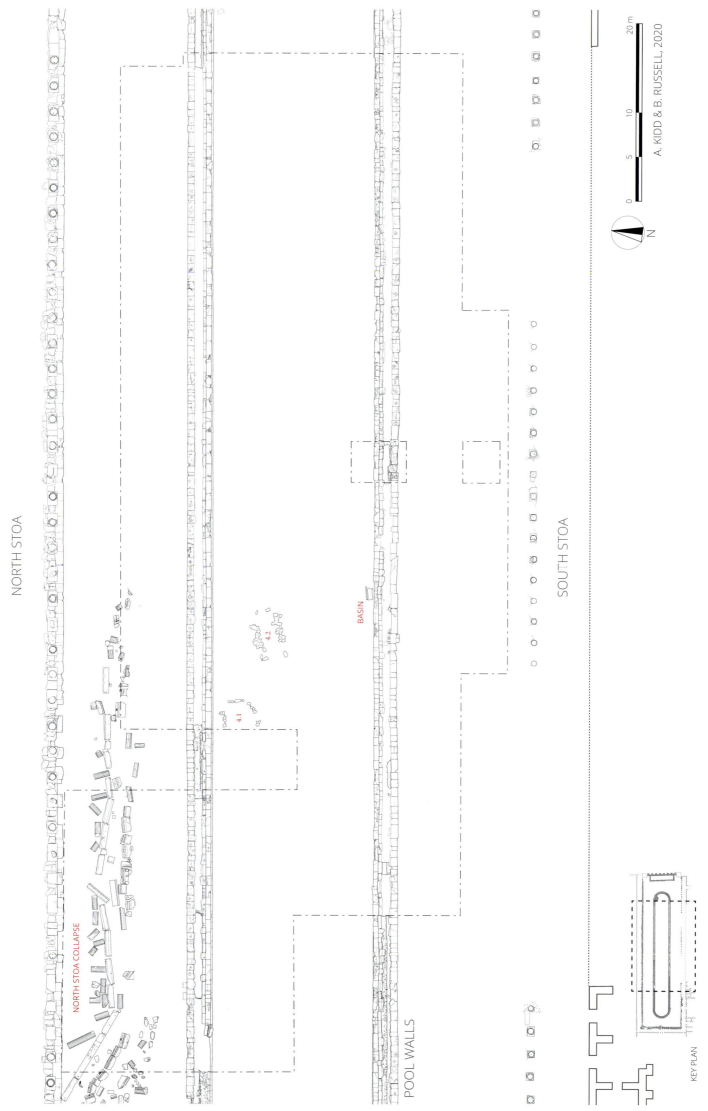

Fig. 74. Plan of post-antique occupation, Phase 4.

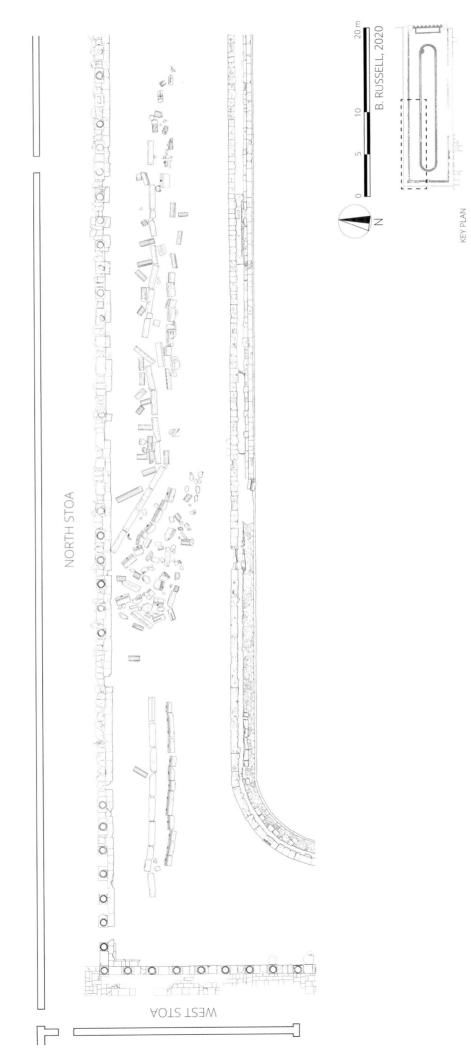

Fig. 75. Plan of fallen North Stoa architrave and cornice blocks.

the debris of the first clearance deposit which was found filling it would have collapsed into it at this point. Elsewhere on the site, the effects of the same earthquake may be recognised by the collapse of the statues of L. Antonius Claudius Diogenes Dometeinos and his niece Claudia Tatiana Antonia, which were found toppled forward (that is southward) from their bases in the North Stoa of the Agora (against the Bouleuterion). They had fallen onto a thick accumulation of earth that had built up over the late antique surface of the Agora.

Whatever remained standing of the Propylon must have also finally collapsed at this time, since debris from the North and South Stoas as well as from the Propylon were dumped into the pool, on top of the silt 4480. These new clearance deposits ran the entire length of the pool, along both its north (4329) and south sides (4461), partially overlapping the inner pool walls and sloping down into the partly filled pool to a maximum distance of 6.52 m and 10.46 m from the north and south pool walls respectively (Pl. 85.A–B). The deposit along the north side (4329) was up to 42 cm thick and comprised numerous fragments of architectural elements: column and capital fragments, marble revetment panels, and figured capitals from the North Stoa, while towards the eastern end of the pool came numerous fragments of screen and frieze blocks originating from the Propylon.[18] The limited quantity of brick and tile (just 231 kg) can be explained by the fact that the North Stoa had probably already lost its roof in the seventh century and had been standing without it, as a skeleton of a colonnade, since then.

Along the south side the corresponding clearance deposit (4461) was thinner, just 20 cm thick, and contained fewer architectural elements. Finds from these layers provide limited dating information but were mostly concentrated in the area around the stone basin that had been built against the south side of the pool soon after the abandonment of the pool (see Ch. 8 §A); this might indicate that this continued to be a point of access to the partially silted-up pool, like the cattle ramp built in the north-east of the structure.[19] The ceramics and coins are largely late Roman residual finds. Some ceramics found in 2012, in the corresponding context 1019, were dated as late as the tenth or eleventh century, although it was noted that coarse wares at the site change very little between the seventh and eleventh centuries.[20] This middle Byzantine earthquake can thus be broadly dated to the tenth or eleventh centuries.

Following the depositing of these clearance dumps, the general regime of siltation within the pool continued, with a 20–25 cm layer of sticky grey silt accumulating uninterrupted over them across the pool (4442). Apart from a considerable amount of tile and brick (7,431 kg), probably scatter from the post-earthquake clean-up, this deposit was largely sterile, with the few finds recovered mostly coming from the areas nearest the pool walls.[21] As with the layer below, most of the ceramics in these layers can only be dated generally to the late Roman period, with the exception of an eighth-century pilgrim flask, discussed in more detail below (§C). The latest coin from this layer dates between AD 641 and 720.[22]

The lower number of freshwater snails (*planorbidae* and *sphaerium*) in this layer indicate that it formed in either stagnant or swampy rather than running water, demonstrating that the pool, by this date, was beginning to dry out.[23] As this layer accumulated to the point where the interior of the pool had become more or less dry land, we find the first structures built within the pool (see Fig. 74). The first feature, [4.1], though truncated by previous excavation in 1988,[24] consisted of a circle of re-used architectural fragments and schist blocks, roughly 4 m in diameter.[25] The second, [4.2], located southeast of the first, was a pair of parallel lines of marble and schist blocks, as well as ten marble paving slabs, running northeast-southwest.[26] These are not walls but might mark out a pathway through the boggy ground that the pool had become. The repositioning of a seat block within the pool walls near these structures and an accompanying deposit sloping down into the pool (17.2.5025) may have served to provide access down into the area from the higher ground beyond the pool walls to the south.

As a whole, the paucity of finds within these layers appears consistent with the evidence for the middle Byzantine period elsewhere in the city. Following the tumultuous seventh centu-

---

18 Among the pilaster capitals were SAg.17.1.4329.M1622 (Inv. 17-029), SAg.17.1.4329.M1623 (Inv. 17-030), SAg.17.1.4329.M2387 (Inv. 17-106), SAg.17.1.4329.M2477 (Inv. 17-167).

19 Notable finds from 4329 include several sculptural fragments (SAg.17.1.4329.M1743 (Inv. 17-045), SAg.17.1.4329.M2337, SAg.17.1.4329.M2338 (Inv. 17-099)), metal tools and accessories, such as a hook (SAg.17.1.4329.F691), a ring (SAg.17.1.4329.F704), and two blades (SAg.17.1.4329.F705, SAg.17.1.4329.F763), a loomweight (SAg.17.1.4329.F778), and two further rolled lead scrolls (SAg.17.1.4329.F682 (Inv. 17-066), SAg.17.1.4329.F692 (Inv. 17-138)). While only a limited quantity of animal bones was recovered, a partial cattle cranium did come from this deposit (SAg.17.1.4329.F/06). In 4461, four joining fragments of Diocletian's Edict on Maximum Prices were found (SAg.17.1.4461.M2444–2447) but the deposit was otherwise much less rich in finds than 4329, except in the area surrounding the water tank (4464), where a particularly high concentration of refuse was discovered, including animal bones, charcoal, numerous pieces of water pipe, loomweights (SAg.17.1.4461.F810–812), a glass vessel (SAg.17.1.4461.F813), and 218 kg of brick/tile; also recovered were sculptural fragments (SAg.17.1.4461.M2010 (Inv. 17-049), SAg.17.1.4461.M2431 (Inv. 17-058)) and a series of large screen panels featuring figural designs, one (SAg.17.1.4461.M2543 (Inv. 17-115)) carved in blue marble and featuring an animal's paws and tails, another (SAg.17.1.4461.M2064 (Inv. 17-050)) in white marble and decorated with a male head, possibly a barbarian.

20 Wilson, Russell, and Ward 2016, 86–87.

21 These included several loomweights (SAg.17.1.4442.F694–697, SAg.17.1.4442.F722, SAg.17.1.4442.F725, SAg.17.1.4442.F758, SAg.17.1.4442.M2620), stamped unguentaria (SAg.17.1.4442.F707, SAg.17.1.4442.F745, SAg.17.1.4442.F751 (Inv. 17-084)), sculptural fragments (SAg.17.1.4442.M1607 (Inv. 17-043), SAg.17.1.4442.M1641 (Inv. 17-044), SAg.17.1.4442.M2142 (Inv. 17-051), SAg.17.1.4442.M2466 (Inv. 17-067)), rock crystal (SAg.17.1.4442.F701), possible stone projectiles (SAg.17.1.4442.F715, SAg.17.1.4442.F743), as well as metal tools (SAg.17.1.4442.F709, SAg.17.1.4442.F755), glass vessels (SAg.17.1.4442.F727, SAg.17.1.4442.F754), two lead scrolls (SAg.17.1.4442.F712 (Inv. 17-075), SAg.17.1.4442.F716 (Inv. 17-076)), a mother of pearl game piece (SAg.17.1.4442.F710), a glass paste tessera with gold leaf decoration (SAg.17.1.4442.F759 (Inv. 17-139)), an antler (SAg.17.1.4442.F760), and a spearhead (SAg.17.1.4442.F757 (Inv. 17-086)).

22 Cat. 292.

23 Wilson, Russell, and Ward 2016, 87.

24 Nbk 300: *PorTibNCE I* (A. Önce, 1988), 1–4, 6–9.

25 [4.1]: 4476.

26 [4.2]: 4477, 4478.

ry, excavations to date have identified few areas of middle Byzantine occupation at the site.[27] In the tenth to twelfth centuries, activity was concentrated in the area around the Cathedral of St Michael and the so-called Bishop's Palace.[28] Architectural blocks were also recycled for the construction of a fortification on the summit of the Theatre Hill, mostly dating to the twelfth century, and there was limited occupation within the ruins of the Civil Basilica.[29] It is generally assumed that much of the rest of the city was abandoned and indeed a pattern of ruralisation is attested at other urban centres in Asia Minor.[30] A similar sequence of events has been recorded at Hierapolis, where a major earthquake (possibly the same one?) also seems to have struck at some point during the tenth or eleventh century. This led to the ruralisation of much of the urban area there, with Byzantine activity concentrated around the newly-built *kastron*.[31]

Parallels can also be found at Pergamon, Miletos, Laodikeia, and sites along the Maeander where a major earthquake, or series of earthquakes, at the end of the middle Byzantine period caused significant destruction of urban architecture and where fortified *kastra* were built during the Komnenian period (1071–1185) in response to Seljuk and Turkomen incursions.[32] Limited middle Byzantine finds in the pool in the former Place of Palms might support this picture at Stavropolis, but not necessarily. The seventh-century clearance deposits show that attempts were made to open up and use this space in some way. As noted in Ch. 8 §A, cuttings in the pool walls imply the erection of temporary structures, possibly with awnings. The cattle ramp and basin also belong to this phase of activity. Further clearance dumps in *Phase 4* are indicative of later attempts to keep the space open and useable; and even after the eleventh-century earthquake clear efforts were made to remove debris from beyond the pool. The absence of domestic debris in the pool shows that the former Place of Palms was not turned into a residential zone in this period, but at this date the pool was still effectively a swamp. The only structures that were built were ephemeral. Even in a bustling middle Byzantine city, we would probably not expect this to have been an area of intense occupation.

Phases 5–6, late 12th – late 14th centuries: Seljuk and early Beylik use of the space

Although historical sources imply that the city was abandoned at the end of the twelfth century, after Sultan Kay Khusraw of Iconium had taken its population into captivity in AD 1197, structures began to be built in the area of the former Place of Palms in the mid to late thirteenth century, during the Seljuk period. Identified as *Phase 5* in the stratigraphic sequence, this marks the beginnings of the repurposing of the space for agricultural ends, which led eventually to the emergence of an Ottoman village landscape in the area. Moreover, the nature of middle Byzantine ceramics found at the site implies some continuity of population, rather than a complete break (below, §C).

Phase 5 (Fig. 76). The first of these new post-Byzantine structures, [5.1], is a long wall running roughly east-west across the eastern sector of the pool before curving northward towards the area of the cattle ramp, which though partially buried by this date still represented the easiest access point to the interior of the pool (Pl. 85.C).[33] Preserved to a height of three courses in several areas, this wall contained numerous re-used architectural blocks, including 291 paving slabs, and two Ionic capitals from the South Stoa.[34] Contemporary with this wall was a major clearance deposit to the west (**4434**), which comprised broken architectural fragments, paving slabs, moulded screen panels, and two fragments of Diocletian's Edict on Maximum Prices, all elements identifiable as having belonged originally to the Civil Basilica.[35]

This is all indicative of efforts to regulate the south-west corner of the former Place of Palms, tidy it up, and provide access through it. This work can be dated by the ceramics within the silt (**4420**) that built up around and over these deposits, and around the collapse (**4429**) of wall [5.1]; this siltation layer reached the level of the pool's interior ledge. Although this layer contained few small finds, the ceramics indicate that it formed during the Seljuk and early Beylik periods, which at Aphrodisias are conventionally dated to the mid to late thirteenth century.[36] The low numbers of freshwater snail species (*planorbidae*) in this deposit show that it was still a boggy environment, at least during periods of heavy rain, even if it was much drier than in earlier periods.[37] This is the last deposit that formed in this aquatic marshy environment, however. From this level upwards, the few *planorbidae* recovered in the deposits were found alongside land

---

27 Dalgıç and Sokolicek 2017. For a full overview of the evidence from this period, see Jeffery 2022.
28 Berenfeld 2019; Jeffery 2019, 35, 50–54.
29 For the fortification atop the Theatre Hill, see Jeffery 2019, 96–97; Erim 1969; 1971. For occupation levels within the area of the former Civil Basilica, see Jeffery 2019, 82–83; Nbk 10: *Martyrion* 1 (M. Bell, 1962), 7–8.
30 For recent research, see Commito 2019; Niewöhner 2017a, 260–263; Niewöhner 2017b; See also Koder 2012.
31 Arthur 2012, 285–287.
32 For more, see Jeffery 2019, 168–171; Koder 2012; Arthur 2012, 285–295; Niewöhner 2017b, 41.

33 [5.1]: **4300/4440**. Part of this wall was also excavated in 1990, though its precise position is unclear. For more see Nbk 316: *Portico of Tiberius: W Pool, Book I; E Pool* (A. T. Tek, 1990), 17–18.
34 SAg.17.1.4440.M1589 – M1590. Other finds include a red stone vessel (SAg.17.1.4300.F690) and a stamped unguentarium (SAg.17.1.4300.F713).
35 **4434** = **3025**. The Price Edict blocks are SAg.17.1.4434.M1689, SAg.17.1.4434.M1693, SAg.17.1.4434.M1696, SAg.17.1.4434.M1699, SAg.17.1.4434.M1707, SAg.17.1.4441.M1712 (Inv. 17-032), for comparison to other similar blocks of Diocletian's Edict found in the area of the Civil Basilica, see Stinson 2016, Ph. 21B, 22A, 22B, and 23B.
36 Among the significant finds were nine loomweights (SAg.17.1.4420.F669–671, SAg.17.1.4420.F673, SAg.17.1.4420.F674, SAg.17.2.5015.F4–5), an iron spearhead (SAg.17.1.4420.F665 (Inv. 17-025), an iron pickaxe SAg.17.1.4420.F675 (Inv. 17-065)), one tool (SAg.17.1.4420.M1514), rock crystals (SAg.17.1.4420.F663, SAg.17.1.4420.F667, SAg.17.2.5015.F6), raw glass, a die (SAg.17.1.4420.F672 (Inv. 17-064)), as well as a ring and earring (SAg.17.1.4420.F677 and SAg.13.1.3033.F027 (Inv. 13-138)).
37 Wilson, Russell, and Ward 2016, 87.

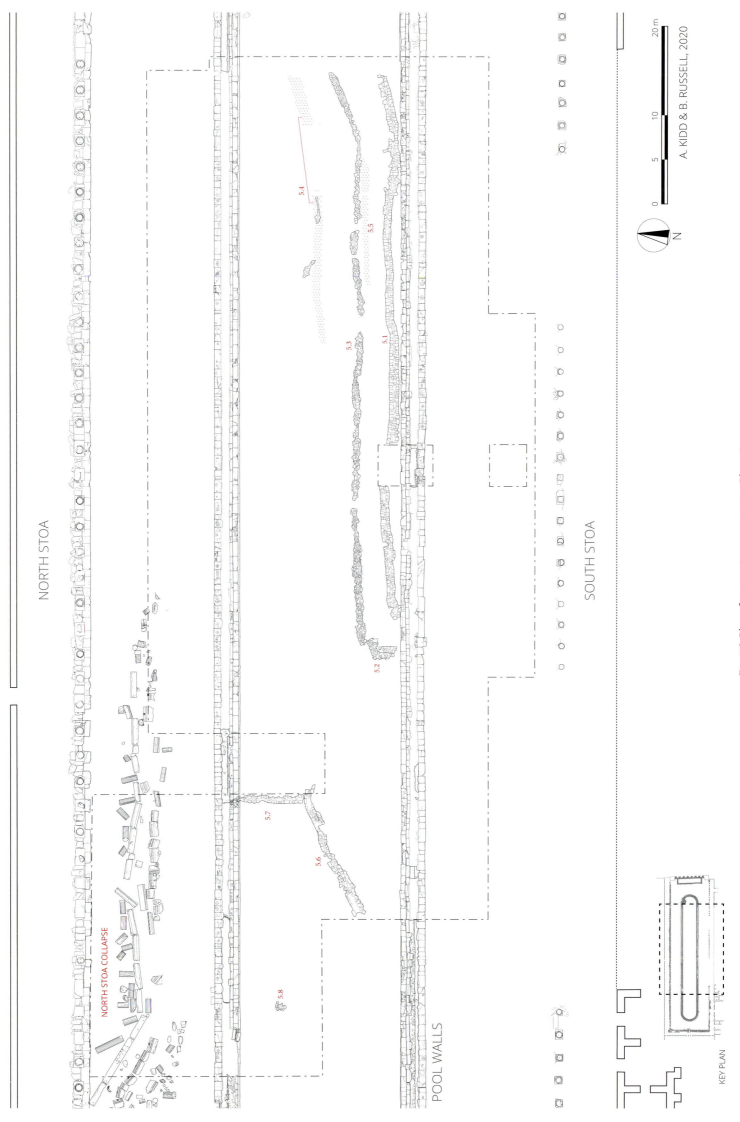

Fig. 76. Plan of post-antique occupation, Phase 5.

snails from the family *helicelidae*.[38] This marks a change from a damp, boggy landscape to a terrestrial regime, a transformation that made the area of the former pool of the Place of Palms habitable for the first time.

Later in this phase, as the silt (**4420**) continued to accumulate but while portions of the upper courses of wall [5.1] were still visible, a series of walls was constructed around it. At its western end this included [5.2].[39] Following a trajectory parallel to [5.1], [5.3] was then constructed.[40] Unlike other documented field walls, this wall was composed of stone rubble that, rather than being laid flat in courses, was inserted into the ground at 45-degree angles. This wall was built on **4420** and so is later than [5.1] but together the two walls framed a trackway that ran broadly east-west (Pl. 85.D). Coinciding with the construction of [5.3] two long sandy deposits, [5.4] and [5.5], were made to follow alongside [5.1] and [5.3]. These deposits contained crushed ceramics, mortar, and nutshells, and seem to have been designed as drainage channels, perhaps to keep the area, and the route through it, dry.[41] Piles of stone scattered across the area close to these walls (**4435**, **4443**, **4444**) might represent further attempts to fill particularly boggy hollows. This phase of Seljuk and early Beylik activity came to an end shortly following the construction of the walls listed above when part of the Theatre Hill and the structures on top of it collapsed (**4358**).[42] Some of the debris from this collapse was cleared and dumped (**4341**) over the southern pool walls.[43] To the northwest of these features, a pair of walls, [5.6] and [5.7], provides evidence for either an additional trackway or perhaps incipient settlement in this area.[44] A sturdy, stone-lined pit, [5.8], was constructed near the rubble remains of what may have once served as a wall (Pl. 86.A).[45] These features again made use of predominantly smaller, broken architectural components from the nearby North Stoa and Civil Basilica. These are the only features hinting at activity in the western portion of the pool at this date.

Phase 6 (Fig. 77). The next phase of activity in this area, *Phase 6*, can be dated to the Beylik period proper. Like *Phase 5*, it began with the construction of a long wall, [6.1], this time running north-south across the whole width of the pool and over both the northern and southern pool walls (Pl. 86.B).[46] This wall was preserved in places up to three courses and consisted of regular faces with rubble infill of medium- to large-sized limestone, schist, and marble blocks recycled from the debris of the surrounding stoas and the Propylon. It dips down notably from where it runs over the pool walls into the lower-lying space within the limits of the former pool. This wall divided the space in two and might well have been a field wall or property boundary. The only other evidence for human activity across the pool area during this phase are scattered rubbish heaps, apparently dumped into the area when it was still a marshland, possibly again to fill up damp hollows (**4314**, **4344**).[47] A cluster of structures, [6.2], comprising one long wall running southeast-northwest and three stubs of walls, was excavated overlying the south pool walls, which might indicate that some more permanent structures were built outside the pool along its southern side in this period;[48] the area to the south was not excavated but could reveal more of possible settlement in this area. Another wall excavated in 1989 to the west, following the same north-south trajectory as [6.1], may also have served to subdivide the area.[49]

As in earlier periods, silty deposits (**4316**) continued to accumulate inside the pool during *Phase 6*, eventually covering the lowermost courses of the aforementioned walls and their collapses (**4298**, **4453**), as well as the earlier clearance deposit (**4341**).[50] The upper level of this silty deposit finally covered the pool walls, concealing the structure for the first time. Along the south side of the pool a mixed deposit of colluvial material formed by erosion from the Theatre Hill and the clearance of debris (**4438**) mixed with the southern extent of the silty deposit (**4316**).[51] To the north, the alluvial deposit **4278**, the earliest levels of which accumulated on the late antique ground

---

38 Wilson, Russell, and Ward 2016, 87.
39 [5.2]: **4449**.
40 [5.3]: **4352/4459**.
41 [5.4]: **4353/4354/4374/4430**; [5.5]: **4427**.
42 The upper surface of this collapse unit was exposed and cleaned but not excavated. A sculpted marble head visible within this unit was removed and documented, however (Inv. 18-074).
43 This deposit comprised mostly rubble, river stones and ceramic building materials (757 kg); among the small finds were loomweights (SAg.16.1.4342.F563, SAg.16.1.4342.F566, SAg.16.1.4342.F572, SAg.16.1.4342.F577–578), a game piece (SAg.16.1.4342.M1339), faceted crystal pieces (SAg.16.1.4342.F565, SAg.16.1.4342.F562, SAg.16.1.4342.F583 (Inv. 16-065)), a possible stone projectile (SAg.16.1.4342.F549), an over-life-size sculptural head (SAg.16.1.4342.M1338 (Inv. 16-061)), a fragment of the Price Edict (SAg.17.1.4441.M1712 (Inv. 17-032)), and tools, including a knife blade and a grinding stone (SAg.16.1.4342.F561 and SAg.16.1.4342.F571).
44 [5.6]: **3030/3032**; [5.7]: **3031**.
45 [5.8]: **17.2.5013, 17.2.5016/17.2.5017/17.2.5018/17.2.5019**
46 [6.1]: **4152/4297**.
47 Though these consisted primarily of rubble and ceramic building materials, one yielded a heavily corroded iron arrowhead (SAg.16.1.4314.F513).
48 [6.2] = **4190** (long wall), **4437**, **4451**, **4452**.
49 **4190** = **4299**; Nbk 309: *Portico of Tiberius S* III 1989 (A. Page, 1989), 31–32.
50 The lowermost level of an alluvial deposit excavated in 2012 (**1007/1023**) also matches this layer, but since this layer was particularly wet, contained few structures, and had been partially exposed for several decades, it was difficult to differentiate any stratigraphic change between this deposit and the layer above or isolate the layer from external contamination. **4316** was 15 cm thick and contained 898 kg of ceramic building materials, numerous small architectural pieces and some sculptural fragments, including an under life-sized hand (SAg.16.1.4298.M1293 (Inv. 16-060)), and a foot (SAg.16.1.4316.M1180 (Inv. 16-042); other finds include ten loomweights (SAg.16.1.4298.F574, SAg.16.1.4316.F545, SAg.16.1.4339.F546–548, SAg.16.1.4339.F553, SAg.17.1.4409.F636–637, SAg.17.1.4409.F656, SAg.17.1.4409.F714), a spindle whorl (SAg.16.1.4339.F554), and a few agricultural tools, such as an iron billhook (SAg.16.1.4339.F550 (Inv. 16-055)).
51 Notable finds in this deposit include 325 kg of ceramic building materials, fragments of the Price Edict (SAg.17.1.4438.M1580–M1581 (Inv. 17-040–17-041)), a horseshoe (SAg.17.1.4438.F683), game pieces (SAg.16.1.4319.F584, SAg.16.1.4320.M1322), a copper-alloy thimble (SAg.16.1.4319.F579), and a sculptural fragment (SAg.16.1.4320.M1327 (Inv. 16-062)). The upper 5 cm of a contaminated deposit excavated from above the ring drain of the north and south sides of the pool (**4485** and **4486**) also belongs to this layer. However, its lower

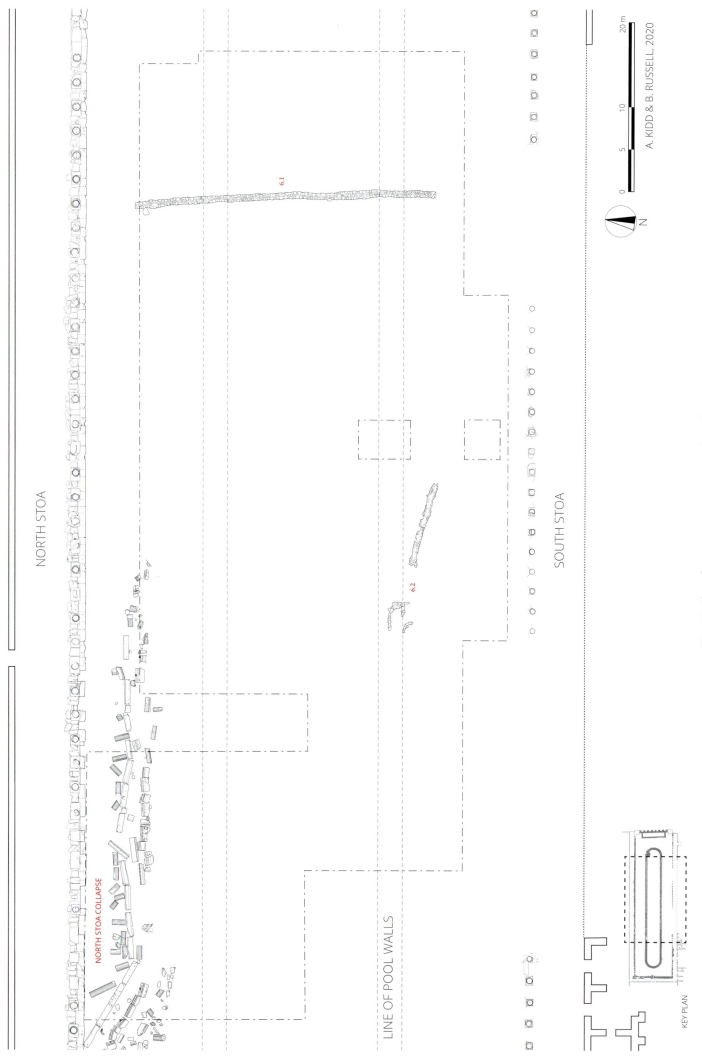

Fig. 77. Plan of post-antique occupation, Phase 6.

level (see Ch. 4 §C), continued to build up over the debris of the collapsed North Stoa; no clear distinction in the stratigraphy could be noted here due to the intensely disrupted nature of this deposit.[52] While sixth- and seventh-century coins were recovered from the bottom of this deposit, ceramics of Beylik date, ranging up to the fourteenth century were found in its upper portion.[53] It is evident that this later layer comprised several centuries of post-antique siltation that had accumulated at a much lower rate than inside the pool.

Further activity in this area at this date was disrupted by another major collapse of material from the Theatre Hill, probably prompted by a substantial earthquake which brought down the Byzantine fortification walls that had been constructed on the north-west corner of the hill at some point in the twelfth century. This resulted in a considerable build-up of debris (**4089**) sloping down to the north along the south side of the pool, which was partly cleared immediately after its formation. The debris comprised massive quantities of smooth river stones and worked *petit appareil* blocks, broken architectural fragments, 2,678 kg of ceramic building materials, as well as ceramics, three rings, a pectoral reliquary cross, and a bread stamp all dated to the middle Byzantine period.[54] The large river cobbles, *petit appareil* blocks and bricks are all characteristic of the building material of the standing remains of the Byzantine fortification on the Theatre Hill immediately to the south (Pl. 86.C), and although this deposit evidently formed in the Beylik period, the material within it clearly derives from the walls and interior of the Byzantine fortification on the Theatre Hill.

While evidence for human activity during *Phases 5* and *6* was limited, the clearance deposits and construction of walls within the area nevertheless signify the beginning of the re-settlement of this area. The clearance of debris represents a concerted effort during the thirteenth and fourteenth centuries to reclaim areas that had fallen out of use after the seventh century. During this time, portions of the former Civil Basilica were re-occupied and building activity resumed along the former Tetrapylon Street, where a Seljuk or Beylik-period bathhouse was constructed above the ancient street level.[55] The pathways built across the pool in the thirteenth century effectively connected these other areas of Seljuk-Beylik settlement. This construction, alongside the presence of glazed table wares, storage wares, kitchen wares, and imported glazed table wares, suggests that for the first time since the seventh century the former Place of Palms was again a bustling area. A close parallel can be noted at Hierapolis, where in the Seljuk phase 'winding tracks linking patches of human settlement' have been noted.[56] And indeed at various other urban centres renewed activity can be identified in the Seljuk period, as the Seljuks solidified their control over inland Asia Minor.[57]

Phase 7, late 14th – early 15th centuries: late Beylik and early Ottoman occupation (Fig. 78)

In the century following the collapse of the north side of the Theatre Hill that brought down the Byzantine fortifications, siltation continued across the area of the former Place of Palms, but so too did the gradual re-organisation of the space, and particularly its sub-division into distinct parcels of land, presumably for cultivation.

The thick silt (**4281**) that accumulated over the Theatre Hill debris (**4089**) varied in depth between 15 and 35 cm and contained within it finds dating to the Beylik and early Ottoman periods.[58] Among the numerous glazed ceramics, one fragment

---

levels, which yielded several late Roman coins, belong to the upper late antique fill of the ring drain.

[52] Among the finds of potentially late date were glass vessels (SAg.16.1.4278.F448 (Inv. 16-031), SAg.16.1.4278.F449), a loomweight (SAg.16.1.4278.F466), a belt buckle (SAg.16.1.4278.F454 (Inv. 16-044), which has been discussed in Ch. 8 §D), and an iron blade (SAg.16.1.4278.F455 (Inv. 16-039)).

[53] For the coins, cat. 237, 254, and 267.

[54] The rings are SAg.16.1.4309.F531–532, SAg.17.1.4309.F631, the cross SAg.17.1.4416.F649 (Inv. 17-034), and the bread stamp, SAg.16.1.4293.F560 (Inv. 16-056). Other finds include 39 loomweights (SAg.16.1.4089.F515, SAg.16.1.4089.F516, SAg.16.1.4293.F522, SAg.16.1.4293.F529, SAg.16.1.4309.F517–520, SAg.16.1.4309.F523–524, SAg.16.1.4309.F526–528, SAg.16.1.4309.F534–535, SAg.16.1.4309.F555–557, SAg.16.1.4317.F536–538, SAg.16.1.4317.F573, SAg.17.1.4393.F630, SAg.17.1.4408.F652–653, SAg.17.1.4416.F638–642, SAg.17.1.4416.F644, SAg.17.1.4416.F646–648, SAg.17.1.4416.F650, SAg.17.1.4419.F655, SAg.17.1.4419.F657–658, SAg.17.1.4424.F660), three possible stone projectiles (SAg.16.1.4309.F559, SAg.17.1.4393.F632, SAg.17.1.4416.F645, SAg.17.1.4426.F661), three marble game pieces (SAg.16.1.4089.M1096, SAg.17.1.4416.M1424, SAg.17.1.4419.M1428), two horseshoes (SAg.16.1.4393.F530, SAg.17.1.4419.F654), several sculptural fragments, for example SAg.15.1.4089.M845 (Inv. 15-078); as well as SAg.16.1.4293.M1141 (Inv. 16-035), SAg.16.1.4317.M1140 (Inv. 16-051), SAg.17.1.4393.M1405 (Inv. 17-037)), a fragment of the Price Edict (SAg.15.1.4089.M844 (Inv. 15-063)), tools including a copper alloy vessel handle (SAg.17.1.4393.F633), an iron handle (SAg.17.1.4416.F643), a blade (SAg.16.1.4309.F559), and a stone threshing tool (SAg.17.1.4416.M1423).

[55] The results of these excavations, under the direction of Ine Jacobs, are being prepared for publication. See also Nbk 566: *South Avenue* (I. Jacobs, 2016), Nbk 573: *South Avenue* (I. Jacobs, 2017), Nbk 579: *South Avenue* (I. Jacobs, 2018), Nbk 584: *South Avenue* (I. Jacobs, 2019).

[56] Arthur 2012, 295.

[57] Beihammer 2017, 223.

[58] Large quantities of ceramic building materials (1,436 kg) and numerous small finds came from this layer, including 21 loomweights (SAg.16.1.4281.F457–458, SAg.16.1.4281.F467, SAg.16.1.4281.F485–490, SAg.16.1.4281.F493–494, SAg.16.1.4281.F500–502, SAg.17.1.4403.F612, SAg.17.1.4404.F607, SAg.17.1.4404.F625, SAg.17.1.4405.F615, SAg.17.1.4405.F617, SAg.17.1.4405.F620, SAg.17.1.4405.F623, SAg.17.1.4415.F629), three spindle whorls (SAg.17.1.4404.F600/SAg.17.1.4404.F605 (Inv. 17-010), SAg.17.1.4404.F624, SAg.17.1.4405.F616 (Inv. 17-016)), metal and glass slag (SAg.16.1.4281.F473 (Inv. 16-027)), ten iron blades (SAg.13.1.3020.F18 (Inv. 13-092), SAg.16.1.4281.F463, SAg.16.1.4281.F469, SAg.16.1.4281.F472 (Inv. 16-049), SAg.16.1.4281.F480–481 (Inv. 16-048), SAg.16.1.4281.F506, SAg.17.1.4404.F601, SAg.17.1.4404.F604), two beads (SAg.12.1.1007.F1010, SAg.12.1.1007.F1013), a range of horseshoes (SAg.16.1.4281.F491, SAg.16.1.4281.F503, SAg.16.1.4281.F507, SAg.17.1.4404.F603 (Inv. 17-012), SAg.17.1.4411.F627, SAg.12.1.1007.F1008), iron arrowheads (SAg.16.1.4281.F461, SAg.16.1.4281.F476, SAg.17.1.4403.F608 (Inv. 17-014), SAg.17.1.4404.F619 (Inv. 17-019)), bronze rings and an iron hook

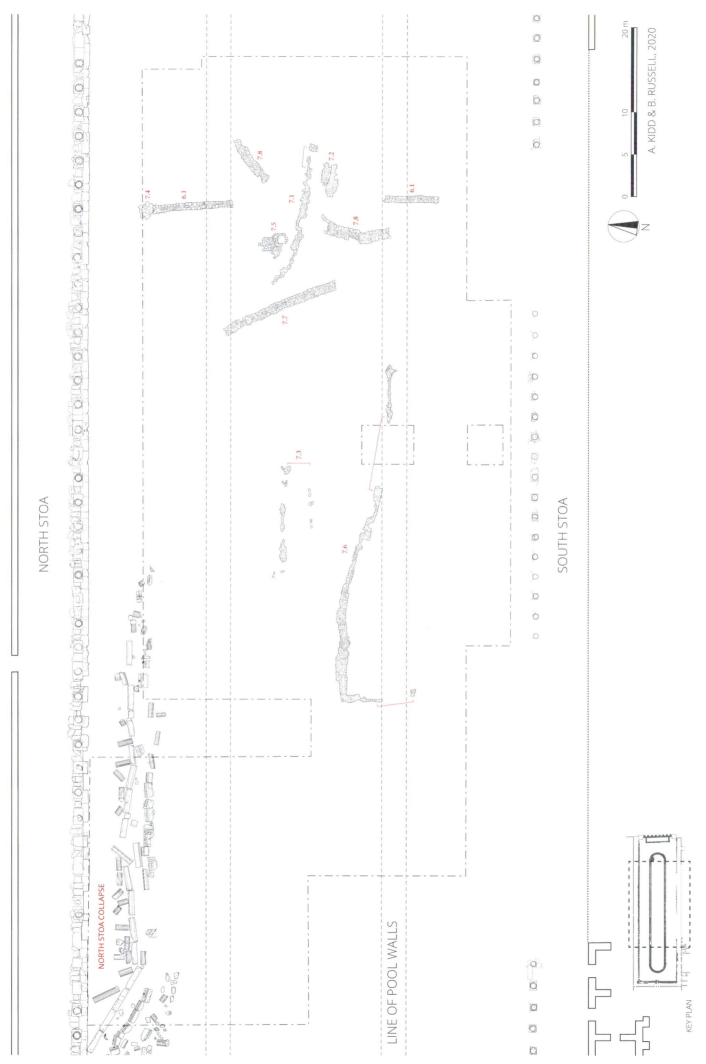

Fig. 78. Plan of post-antique occupation, Phase 7.

was moulded and features an image of a striding horse.[59] Several coins dating up to AD 1461 indicate a late Beylik to early Ottoman date.[60] One particularly notable numismatic find was a medieval eastern European coin from Wallachia (modern-day Romania) dating to AD 1386–1418.[61] This may have found its way to the site following Ottoman campaigns in Wallachia in the 1440s, possibly therefore some time well after the coin's issue date. A cast musket ball from this deposit, a significant find from a context of this date, is discussed further below.[62]

Few structures were built early in this period. Across the middle of the pool, the northern and southern ends of the wall [6.1] remained visible from the earlier *Phase 6*, where they were built on the higher ground outside the former pool. The first new structures built in *Phase 7* were a series of walls running east-west down the centre of the pool, preserved to just one course: [7.1] and [7.2] in the east, the latter abutted by a platform, and [7.3] in the west.[63] A further platform-like structure, [7.4] was added to the northern end of [6.1].[64] Various other features within this space, [7.5], include two circular stone arrangements, each measuring 1.5 and 0.85 m in diameter, and a platform featuring a recess that may have served to anchor a device of some sort.[65] Given the comparative diversity of small finds in the siltation layer 4281 surrounding this area, which included metal and glass slag and several metal tools, it is probable that these features denote an area of production of some sort.

At the east end of the pool, in the area most drastically affected by the collapse of the Theatre Hill, collapse debris (4089) was levelled and partially cleared for the construction of several field walls and associated features at a slightly later date during this phase. One of these, [7.6], was a long east-west wall, which turned south at its western end; it seems to have been a boundary wall that divided the central section of the area into northern and southern tracts of land.[66] Two other substantial walls, oriented northwest-southeast ([7.7]) and northeast-southwest ([7.8]) were built at the same time in the east and would be further developed in *Phase 8*.[67] These walls were built of rubble and large architectural elements from the collapsed Theatre Hill and the North Stoa.[68] They seem to have delineated routes across the area of the former pool, between the Theatre Hill debris and the still damp areas of ground.

Together, the rich assemblage of artefacts and the emergence of several field walls and features during *Phase 7* denote heavy and continued use of the area, the first human activity of this nature since the late antique period. It was located between key nodes in the emerging Beylik settlement. The boundary walls and trackways of *Phase 7* suggest that, by this date, the area of the former Place of Palms had been turned over to agriculture or arboriculture and production whereas the distribution of finds indicates that there was no one particular area of concentrated occupation. Moreover, the range in type and function of the finds denotes increased social engagement, connectivity, and perhaps even prosperity during the period; the presence of the Wallachian coin even hints at inter-regional connections, providing some insight about this settlement at a time when other historical sources remain silent.

Phase 8–9, early 15th–17th centuries: an Ottoman village

Phase 8 (Fig. 79)
The open, largely flat area that the former Place of Palms had become by the fifteenth century continued to silt up through the Beylik and into the classical Ottoman period. Over this period, however, the area became more built-up, with the earlier field walls developed into a series of structures that can be more easily recognised as village houses and enclosures, separated by lanes, in *Phase 8*.

Around the collapsed remains of the Beylik field walls from the previous phase another thick layer of silt accumulated (4255).[69] The ceramics and coins indicate an early Ottoman date for this accumulation, with the coins dating up to 1461.[70]

(SAg.13.1.3020 (Inv. 13-102) and SAg.16.1.4281.F459), a copper alloy bell (SAg.12.1.1007.F1007 (Inv. 12-021)), a ring (SAg.12.1.1007.F1016 (Inv. 12-018)), a metal utensil or handle (SAg.17.1.4405.F614), a metal fitting (SAg.16.1.4275.F442), a star-shaped bronze pendant (SAg.13.1.3020.F021 (Inv. 13-093)), a worked gemstone (SAg.17.1.4403.F610), faceted crystal (SAg.17.1.4403.F606, SAg.17.1.4404.F618, SAg.17.1.4415.F628), glass bangle and bead fragments (SAg.13.1.3020.F022–23, SAg.13.1.3020.F016 (Inv. 13-098–100), SAg.16.1.4281.F464), glass vessels (SAg.16.1.4281.F484, SAg.16.1.4281.F495, SAg.16.1.4281.F504), and a ceramic tripod (SAg.16.1.4281.F505.). Also recovered were residual items, including gaming paraphernalia, such as a limestone die (SAg.16.1.4281.F499), a brick incised with a merels board (SAg.16.1.4281.F492), and three game pieces (SAg.16.1.4281.M1065, SAg.16.1.4281.M1068, SAg.17.1.4405.F611), as well as a ceramic object shaped and incised in imitation of an Ionic column (SAg.17.1.4405.F622 (Inv. 17-017)), a stamped unguentaria fragment (SAg.17.1.4404.F621), and a marble sculptural fragment (SAg.17.1.4403.M1369 (Inv. 17-013)). A single seventeenth-century coin (cat. 365) must be intrusive.
59 SAg.16.1.4281.F460.
60 Late Beylik coins from this layer include cat. 316 and 324, while Ottoman ones include cat. 334, dated to the reign of Murad II, and cat. 344 and 345 to the reign of Mehmed II.
61 Cat. 309.
62 SAg.17.1.4403.F602 (Inv. 17-011).
63 [7.1]: **4296**, **4303**; [7.2]: **4313**, **4312**; [7.3]: **4294**, **4295**.
64 [7.4]: **4273**.
65 [7.5]: **4307** and **4308** (the two circular stone features, respectively), **4305** (the platform with recess).
66 [7.6]: **4299**, **4221/4219/4276/4400/4425**; this latter wall was abutted by a platform-like structure, **4414**.
67 [7.7]: **4073**; [7.8]: **4159**, **4270/4272**.
68 A blade (SAg.16.1.4221.F446), an arrowhead (SAg.16.1.4270.F444), a game piece (SAg.16.1.4221.F447), a theatre seat block (SAg.16.1.4219.M896) and a marble table support featuring a linx head (SAg.16.1.4270.M963) were also built into the walls.
69 Collapse deposits from field walls of the previous phase include **3014**, **4252/4261**, **4269**, **4274**, **4304**, **4310**, **4311**, **4394**, **4275**, **4407**, **4412**, **4413**; a further deposit of debris to the north comprised **4395** = **4406**.
70 The latest coin, dated to the reign of Mehmed II is cat. 349. Other finds include 1,435 kg of ceramic building materials, 16 loomweights (SAg.16.1.4245.F399, SAg.16.1.4251.F390, SAg.16.1.4251.F397, SAg.16.1.4251.F407, SAg.16.1.4255.F439, SAg.16.1.4266.F413, SAg.16.1.4266.F416, SAg.16.1.4269.F443, SAg.16.1.4271.F425–426, SAg.16.1.4271.F428, SAg.16.1.4271.F432, SAg.16.1.4271.F435, SAg.16.1.4271.F477, SAg.17.1.4388.F592–593), items pertaining to jewellery or jewellery manufacture, such as two pen-

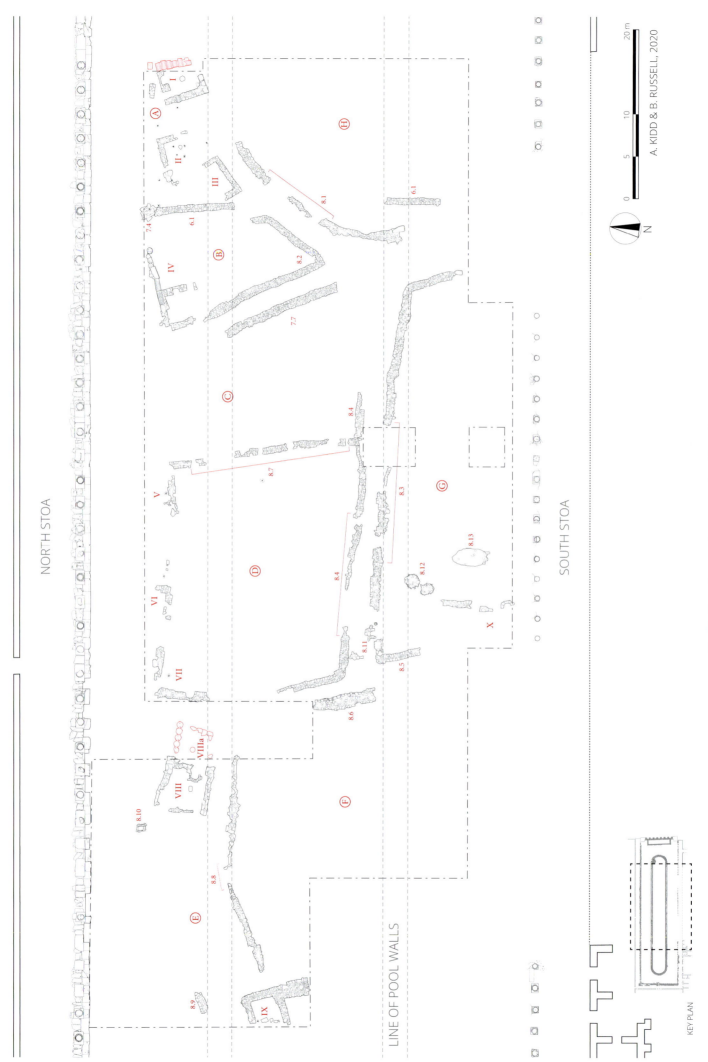

Fig. 79. Plan of post-antique occupation, Phase 8.

Eroded debris from the Theatre Hill also accumulated during this phase along the southern side of the excavated area. This loose and sandy colluvial deposit (**4095**), approximately 15 cm deep, mixed with the silt deposit to the north (**4255**).[71] The coins recovered from this deposit appeared to be residual, with one Saruhanid coin of İshak Bey dating to the second half of the fourteenth century,[72] since the ceramics included material ranging up to the early Ottoman period.

The first walls built in *Phase 8*, as **4255** was accumulating and on top of it, were a series of new drystone walls, which filled in, were built on top of, or responded to the remains of still-visible walls built during *Phases 6* and *7*. These walls served to divide the usable land of the former Place of Palms into distinct plots separated by lanes. They were made primarily of rubble and reused marble architectural elements from the collapsed

North Stoa and Theatre Hill.[73] Towards the east of the excavated area, wall [7.8] was rebuilt and expanded at its southern end, to create a new, nearly continuous wall, [8.1], curving from the southern edge of the pool towards the north-west.[74] North of this, and parallel to it another new wall was built, [8.2], which turned northwards at its western end to run parallel to [7.7].[75]

Together these new and old walls defined a pair of lanes that converged at the southernmost point of [8.2] (Pl. 86.D). A further lane ran west from this point, flanked on its southern side by [8.3], *c.* 57 m long, and on its northern side by [8.4].[76] The former effectively acted as a retaining wall, roughly following the line of the pool wall below it. These long east-west walls turned north and south respectively at their western ends to form the eastern boundary of a further lane, orientated nearly north-south and bounded to the east by [8.5] and the west by [8.6].[77] Although most of these new walls were poorly preserved, surviving only in one course of stones, wall [8.6] was preserved for up to three courses and incorporated the marble torso of an over life-sized male statue (Pl. 87.A; see Ch. 7 §E no. 79).[78] A wall running north-south in this central section of the trench, [8.7], divided the area north of [8.4] into two distinct enclosures, which will be discussed further below.[79] In the western area of the excavations the arrangement of these new boundary walls is less clear but various sections of walling, [8.8] and [8.9], indicate that a similar arrangement of lanes and enclosures was expanded into this zone.[80]

These various drystone walls divided the flat area of the former Place of Palms into parcels of land between which ran narrow lanes. Eight enclosures can be identified, which have been labelled A–H (see Fig. 79). Within four, or potentially five, of these enclosures at least one small rectilinear building was uncovered; these buildings are numbered I–X. The cleaning of debris left from previous excavations revealed the upper courses of at least two further buildings probably belonging to this phase, which were either located within Enclosure F or in a further enclosure south of F and west of G. However, this area has not been excavated and thus awaits further stratigraphic documentation.

Within the easternmost enclosure (A), two, possibly three, rectilinear structures were uncovered. The first of these, Building I, in the northeast corner of the trench excavated between 2013 and 2017, comprised one sturdily built L-shaped wall and a second wall featuring a niche; another wall was found just to the north (Pl. 87.B; see Fig. 80).[81] Excavation in 1990 immediately to the east had uncovered an adjacent wall composed entirely of reused column drums and an Ionic capital from the North Stoa, which must represent the eastern side of Building

---

dants (SAg.16.1.4266.F414 (Inv. 16-028), SAg.16.1.4255.F398), two beads (SAg.16.1.4255.F384, SAg.16.1.4255.F389), worked gemstone (SAg.16.1.4233.F386), faceted crystal (SAg.16.1.4255.F388, SAg.16.1.4255.F453, SAg.16.1.4271.F430, SAg.16.1.4271.F440), and two glass bangles (SAg.16.1.4271.F471 (Inv. 16-045), SAg.17.1.4388.F594), several stone and metal tools, including a pestle and a soapstone blade sharpener (SAg.16.1.4266.F412 and SAg.16.1.4266.F418 respectively), a blade (SAg.16.1.4255.F438 (Inv. 16-046)), a blade sheath (SAg.16.1.4255.F401 (Inv. 16-024)), and metal chains (SAg.16.1.4251.F403, SAg.16.1.4255.F400, SAg.16.1.4255.F402, SAg.16.1.4255.F431, SAg.16.1.4275.F441 (Inv. 16-025)), as well as hand-crafted terracotta accoutrements, including a bird-shaped whistle (SAg.16.1.4255.F424 (Inv. 16-011)), a mould decorated with the image of a fish (SAg.16.1.4255.F482 (Inv. 16-029)), a perforated jug stopper (SAg.16.1.4271.F427 (Inv. 16-026)), a vessel foot (SAg.17.1.4388.F662 (Inv. 17-006)), a stone lid (SAg.17.1.4407.F613), and a lid with incised décor (SAg.16.1.4236.F380). Also recovered were three murex shells (SAg.16.1.4251.F395, SAg.16.1.4255.F434, SAg.16.1.4266.F415, SAg.17.1.4388.F591 (Inv. 17-007)), four game pieces (SAg.16.1.4255.F436, SAg.16.1.4266.F417, SAg.16.1.4271.M1038), two possible stone projectiles (SAg.16.1.4255.F437, SAg.16.1.4266.F419), an arrowhead (SAg.16.1.4255.F420), a worked bone spool (SAg.16.1.4233.F383 (Inv. 16-005)), and two marble sculptural fragments (SAg.16.1.4271.M1047 (Inv. 16-030), SAg.17.1.4388.M1354 (Inv. 17-008)). The more disturbed contexts produced a wide variety of finds, including some that are clearly intrusive: a bullet (SAg.12.1.1004.F1005) a bullet casing (SAg.13.1.3005.F5), a metal chain (SAg.13.1.3004.F13), a key (SAg.12.2.2001.F2006), metal fittings (SAg.12.1.1004.F1006, SAg.12.2.2001.F2004, SAg.13.1.3004.F10), a wooden pallet (SAg.13.1.3004.F11 (Inv. 13-090)), a ceramic vessel (SAg.13.1.3005.F8–9), glass bangles ((SAg.13.1.3004.F12 (Inv. 13-101), SAg.13.1.3004.F13, SAg13.1.3005.F7), the metal sole of a shoe (SAg.12.1.1004.F1003), and various sculptural fragments (SAg.12.1.1004.M3 (Inv. 12-30), SAg.12.1.1004.M4 (Inv. 12-25), SAg.12.1.1004.M5).

71 Finds include several glass vessel fragments (SAg.15.1.4095.F341, SAg.15.1.4095.F342, SAg.15.1.4095.F343), seven glass bangle fragments (SAg.15.1.4095.F323, SAg.15.1.4095.F324, SAg.15.1.4095.F330, SAg.15.1.4095.F344, SAg.15.1.4095.F345, SAg.15.1.4095.F346, SAg.15.1.4095.F347), seven loomweights (SAg.15.1.4095.F319, SAg.15.1.4095.F338, SAg.15.1.4095.F339, SAg.15.1.4095.F340, SAg.16.1.4384.F590, SAg.17.1.4398.F595, SAg.17.1.4398.F597), a metal bowl (SAg.15.1.4095.F336), a metal hinge (SAg.15.1.4095.F334), a game piece (SAg.16.1.4369.F586), and faceted rock crystal (SAg.15.1.4095.F329).

72 Cat. 328.

73 Other artefacts built into the walls included a blade (SAg.16.1.4113.F429, a game piece (SAg.17.1.4391.M1368), and a fragment of a male portrait sculpture (SAg.12.1.1011.M37 (Inv. 12-19)).

74 [8.1]: **4159/4270/4272, 4078**.

75 [8.2]: **4036, 4055**.

76 [8.3]: **4087/4113/4134/4391**; [8.4]: **4151, 4176/4372/4401**.

77 [8.5]: **4355/4362**; [8.6]: **4399**.

78 SAg.17.1.4399.M1364 (Inv. 17-009).

79 [8.7]: **4068/4175/4186/4188/4189**.

80 [8.8]: **3003, 1011**; [8.9]: **2002**.

81 Building I: **4020, 4104, 4105**.

Fig. 80. Ottoman houses in the area of the former Place of Palms.

I (Pl. 87.C).[82] These enclosed a space that measured c. 4.29 by 3.97 m, with an overturned Ionic capital, presumably serving as a post-support, neatly centred between the two walls (Pl. 87.D). The other two buildings (II and III) in this enclosure each survived as three sides of a rectangle, measuring between 3.72 and 5.21 m in length (Pl. 87.E; Fig. 80).[83]

To the west, a second enclosure (B) contained another small rectilinear structure in its northwest corner (IV) (Fig. 80). The northern wall of Building IV was, like Building I, composed of reused column drums from the North Stoa (Pl. 88.A). This was abutted by an L-shaped north-south wall featuring a niche and an entryway frame of some sort. Together with wall [8.2] to the west, these features enclosed a space measuring approximately 3.90 by 4.38 m, and it is probable that a second room was situated on the east side of the niched wall.[84]

No structures were found in Enclosure C, to the west, but Enclosure D contained several more small structures on its northern side. Although these were largely truncated by previous excavations targeting the North Stoa, still preserved were three sets of adjoining walls and a semi-circular structure, each measuring between 1.30 and 2.45 m. Together these form one certain building (VI) and perhaps the remains of another two (V and VII) (Fig. 80).[85]

Within the westernmost excavated enclosure (E), another small structure was discovered (VIII). This was the best preserved of the series, comprising four walls, which enclosed a space, measuring 6.25 by 4.86 m; it also included a semi-circular feature, measuring 1.07 m and an overturned capital situated in the middle of the structure (Fig. 80).[86] An extension of this structure, labelled here as VIIIa, was excavated immediately west of this in 1985; it was also rectilinear in plan and its walls were composed almost entirely of fragmentary column drums and a frieze block, with a further column drum positioned in the centre of the structure.[87] Other segments of walls and portions of dwellings, evidently belonging to this phase on the basis of construction technique and stratigraphic sequence, were identified in previous excavations.[88] The precise location of these, however, was not documented.

Finally, at the western edge of Enclosure E, a 3.1 m wide well-built quadrangular structure was constructed, Building IX (Pl. 88.B; Fig. 80). The base of this building's walls was constructed at a lower depth that the walls of other structures of this phase. This could indicate that the building was built early in this period or that it sank into the deposit **4255** to a greater extent than the other buildings of this phase. As discussed below, this is the only building constructed in *Phase 8* inside the area of the former pool, where the ground would have been wetter and softer. It is even possible that this building was initially constructed in *Phase 7*, on the previous siltation layer (**4281**), though given the absence of other buildings in that phase we have opted to include it in *Phase 8*.[89] What survives of Building IX comprised three walls that enclosed a floor of large flagstones,[90] its western wall have been truncated by excavations in 1990.[91] The structure's walls were constructed using drystone masonry comprising medium to large limestone, schist, and recycled marble blocks from the North Stoa for external linear faces and rubble infill. Given that earlier had truncated the structure, it is difficult to determine its function.

Buildings I–VIII were all constructed on the strip of land between the now-concealed northern pool walls and the collapsed remains of the North Stoa (see Fig. 79). This corridor of land was presumably both drier than the area of the former pool to the south and freer from debris than the zone to the north. Certain blocks from the North Stoa collapse were repurposed for the walls of these buildings, especially those small enough to be moved by hand or which could be rolled into place, like column drums. In several instances these re-used blocks were purposefully situated to be visible from the exterior of the building or were used as significant structural features within the building itself, such as for doorframes, working surfaces, or as central post-supports or tables in the case of the two overturned capitals mentioned above. Where the walls survive they are straight, arranged at right angles to each other, and range in thickness between 0.64 and 0.76 cm.

Only in Building IX, which was built to the south of the northern pool walls, were the walls much thicker, up to 1.1 m wide, perhaps to support the structure on a less stable, wetter surface. As noted above, this building was either the first to be constructed in this phase or its walls seem to have sunk into the ground on which it was built, perhaps a direct result of their heavier load; either way, the builders of Buildings I–VIII chose to locate their structures further to the north.

None of the surviving walls of these buildings is preserved for more than three courses, but it is likely that they were designed from the beginning as dwarf walls for superstructures in mudbrick or another form of earth construction. Buildings I, IV, VIII and possibly also VII and X (discussed below) had niches, a distinctive feature of these *Phase 8* structures (see Fig. 80). Only one surface, the flagstone floor within Building IX, was revealed among these dwellings. No other surfaces, such as beaten earth floors, or occupation deposits were found. An uneven compact deposit (**4018**) containing two nails, identified just above the lower portions of Building II, may be interpreted as disintegrated mudbrick or a preparation layer for a later floor. Even the accumulated soils within and immediately outside the walls of these buildings (**4019**, **4237**, **4238**, and **3012**) produced only scant evidence of occupation.[92]

---

82 Nbk 318: *Portico of Tiberius: E Pool* (A. Önce, 1990), 35–37.
83 Building II: **4025**, with **4263** and **4264**; Building III: **4022**,
84 Building IV: **4061** (column drum wall), **4080** (niche wall), **4130** (entranceway), **4130**.
85 Building V: **4109**, **4110**, **4111**, **4112**; Building VI: **4070**, **4071**, **4072**, **4361**; Building VII: **4324**, **4431**.
86 Building VIII: **3006**, **3009**, **3010**, **3011** (walls), **3008** (niche).
87 Nbk 269: *Portico of Tiberius NE II Book 2* (A. Önce, 1985), 13–21.
88 Nbk 318: *Portico of Tiberius: E Pool* 1990 (A. Önce, 1990), 9–10.
89 It should again be noted that this area of the pool was much wetter when it was excavated in 2012, which made disentangling the stratigraphy of the pool fills harder than in other areas of the pool in later years.
90 Building IX: **1008**, **1025**, **1026** (walls), **1006/1027** (floor).
91 Nbk 317: *PorTibWPool* I 1990 (A.T. Tek, 1990); Nbk 309: *Portico of Tiberius S III 1989* (A. Page, 1989), 31–32.
92 Finds include two blades (SAg.16.1.4238.F406, SAg.16.1.4238.F411), a loomweight (SAg.16.1.4238.F408), horse tackle (SAg.16.1.4238.F382 (Inv. 16-010)), a bronze ring (SAg.16.1.4237.F387 (Inv. 16-032)), and a cylindrical metal object (SAg.16.1.4238.F409). Several

The documented stone walls, however, constitute only part of these one- or two-room buildings. Postholes containing rings of chocking stones were documented both within and around most of these structures. These include a pair between Buildings I and II, a series within Building II and to the northwest of it, and other examples in the vicinity of Buildings V, VI, VII, and IX (all marked on Fig. 79 and 80).[93] These postholes could represent lines of fence posts, perhaps marking out pens for animals. However, the fact that they are generally positioned close to the walls of buildings seems to indicate that they supported timber uprights for porches, verandas, or lean-to structures or annexes that were extensions to the buildings themselves.

The enclosures in which Buildings I–IX were located presumably encircled also market gardens and/or space for animals. Their built structure and spatial design share many of the characteristics of Ottoman vernacular dwellings at other settlements in western Anatolia, such as Eskihisar (ancient Stratonikeia), Alaşehir (ancient Philadelphia), Menemen, Manisa, and Hierapolis.[94] Such early dwellings usually had earth floors and walls comprising repurposed ancient architectural fragments or other stone elements, which supported timber frames stabilized with mudbrick. These one- to two-room units were often situated at the edge of large, enclosed gardens that could be accessed via narrow streets or lanes. The earliest varieties of these houses integrated elements of nomadic tent-like spaces by featuring semi-open, multipurpose spaces on their ground floors, which could be extended into the garden through the use of timber verandas.[95] These ground floors and verandas were typically used for cooking, keeping livestock, weaving, and various other domestic tasks. Living space was located on a second storey, which was supported by timber uprights. That the early Ottoman buildings at Aphrodisias relied on a particularly local vernacular design is evidenced by later eighteenth- and nineteenth-century dwellings recorded in Kuyucak, Bozdoğan, Kavaklı, and even the nearby town of Karacasu, where many of the earliest known stone and timber multipurpose courtyard units also featured a niche in one wall for storage, of the sort seen in Buildings I, IV, and VII.[96]

Also belonging to this classical Ottoman phase are a series of other notable features. Northwest of Building VIII, a well [8.10] was uncovered, which cuts into a fallen cornice block from the North Stoa as well as through the late antique raised ground level (Pl. 89.A).[97] The well was rectangular in plan, its opening measuring 0.52 by 0.45 m, and was lined with stones and reused architectural elements, including an Ionic capital. Its fills (**3085**, **3084**, **3083**) contained Roman, Beylik, and Ottoman pottery dating up to the second half of the fifteenth century, including much of a glazed plate and a green-glazed jug recovered from its uppermost fill.[98]

To the south, another two enclosures (F and G) were distinguished. In the southernmost of these, Enclosure G, several features were identified that together constitute some sort of a working area, possibly with an associated dwelling (Building X). The working areas can be divided into three. Feature [8.11] comprised a compact working surface, 1.67 by 1 m in plan, which was surrounded by a stone and tile wall, through which a sloping exit channel cut, suggesting it was used for cleaning, washing, or processing liquids of some sort (Pl. 89.B); nearby were a group of stones arranged in a semi-circle 1.88 m across, a single course of stones arranged in a rough U-shape, measuring 1.98 by 1.42 m with its opening facing south, and a circle of stones 0.41 m in diameter.[99] Although no burnt remains were discovered, the U-shaped feature may have served as a hearth and the circular feature as a base for an upright device of some sort. To the southeast, a pair of working surfaces, [8.12], were identified, each elliptical in plan, measuring 1.61 m and 1.65 m in length, and composed of small- to medium-sized blocks of schist, limestone, and marble, and rubble infill, with the larger stones arranged as a border.[100] A third surface, [8.13], was more irregular in shape and comprised only small stones as well as crushed brick, tile and ceramics.[101]

To the east were two further walls, which followed the contours of the Theatre Hill collapse, and another semi-circular feature, which perhaps belongs to a structure, tentatively identified as Building X (see Fig. 80).[102] Apart from the semi-circular structures, none of these features resembles the buildings along the north side of the space in *Phase 8* and it is possible that Enclosure G contained an industrial area, perhaps associated with agricultural production.

Phase 9 (Fig. 81)
Most of the structures along the south side of the excavated area, as well as many of the field walls, were short-lived. Several fell down soon after construction, and their collapses were gradually covered by a thick layer of firm, dark brownish-grey silt (**4012**), similar to the various deposits that filled the area of the former pool.[103] The build-up of this silt implies a hiatus in the growth of the village, after which we can identify a renewal of building activity and occupation, in what we refer to as *Phase 9*. **4012** contained a wide range of Ottoman domestic and agricultural objects, as well as a reasonable quantity of residual, fragmentary items, suggesting intensive use of the land and perhaps

---

coins were found here but require further analysis to see if they are legible.
93 These postholes include **4228**, **4229**, **4230**, **4231**, **4239**, **4241**, **4254**, **4256**, **4259**, **4262**, and **4267** (in Enclosure A); **4234** and **4347** (in Enclosure D) and **5003** (in Enclosure E).
94 Avşar and Genç 2016; 2018; Erdem and Yergün 2016, 61–72; Karaman and Zeren 2015, 79–83; Arthur *et al.* 2012, 12–15; Gülmez 2007, 330.
95 Erdem and Yergün 2016, 57; Kuban 1965, 92; Taşdöğen 2006, 55; Erdim 1985.
96 Taşdöğen 2006, 56, 228.
97 [8.10]: **3082**.

98 SAg.15.2.3083.F11 (Inv. 15-084).
99 [8.11]: **4364** (working surface), **4350/4361** (stone and tile wall), **4383** (channel), **4368** (semi-circular feature), **4379** (U-shaped feature), **4380** (circular feature).
100 [8.12]: **4096**, **4097**.
101 [8.13]: **4093**.
102 Building X: **4047**, **4049** (walls), **4050** (niche).
103 The collapses of the *Phase 8* walls are **1017**, **2004**, **3007**, **4021**, **4023**, **4242**, **4243**, **4257**, **4258**, **4363**, **4377**, **4397**, **17.2.5006**, **17.2.5008**, and **17.2.5009**.

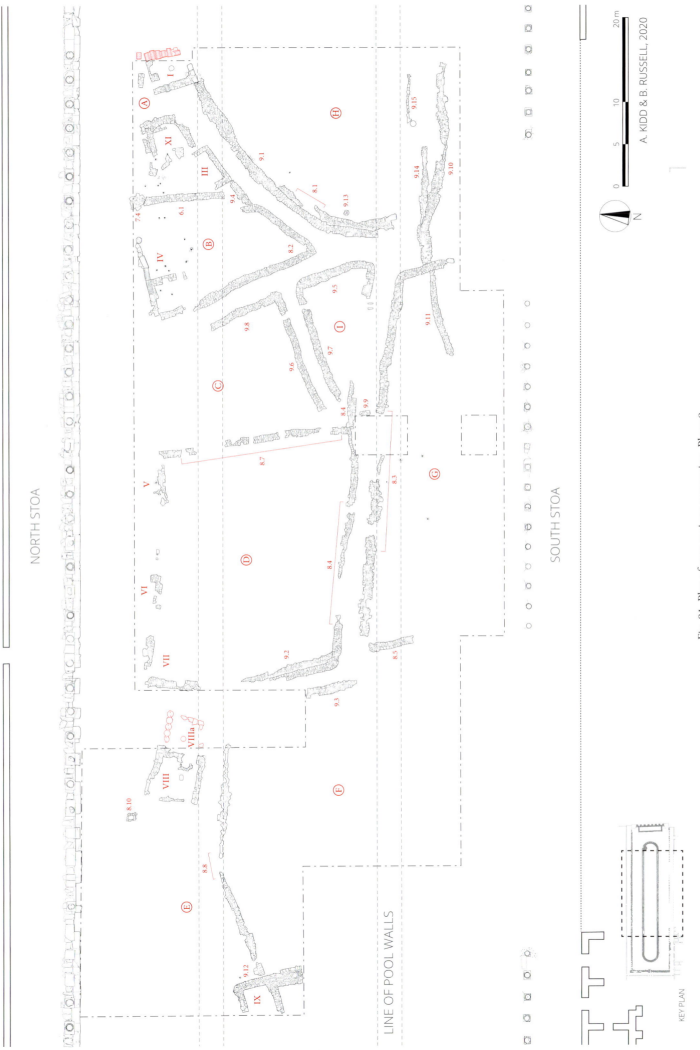

Fig. 81. Plan of post-antique occupation, Phase 9.

ploughing.[104] The earliest coin found was hellenistic, the latest an ornamental mangir of Tire, c. AD 1444–1512.[105]

During *Phase 9* many of the plot boundary walls of the Ottoman village were repaired, strengthened, and adjusted to respond to the rising ground surface. In the east, wall [8.1] was overbuilt by a wider wall, [9.1].[106] In the west, the northern extension of [8.4] was widened and lengthened, [9.2].[107] Parallel to this wall, [8.6] was overbuilt by wall [9.3].[108] New walls were also added to fill in spaces between earlier structures and to create new lanes through the village (Pl. 89.C). A short wall, [9.4], was built to close the gap between the field wall [8.2] and Building III, thereby further enclosing the lane running northeast-southwest between [8.2] and [9.1].[109] In the centre of the excavated area, wall [7.7] was overbuilt by new structures [9.5] and [9.8], both of which curved to the west.[110]

A pair of new walls, [9.6] and [9.7], was built perpendicular to and extending from [9.5]/[9.8], with space for a trackway left between them.[111] This trackway separated Enclosure C from a new enclosure, I, to the south, which was probably entered both through a gap at the eastern end of [9.7] and via a pair of upright stones to the south. The western edge of this enclosure is probably represented by a short length of wall, [9.9], which abutted [8.4] and [8.3].[112] This long retaining wall was further supplemented by [9.10] and [9.11], which followed the contours of the collapsed Theatre Hill and thus formed a boundary between the useable land of the central and northern parts of the former Place of Palms and the debris to the south.[113] Two piles of stones (**4133** and **4178**), probably rubbish heaps, were situated in this area on either side of [8.3] and [9.9]. New walls were also built to fill gaps in the existing network of lanes in the west of the excavated area, where [9.12] was constructed to fill the space between [8.8] and Building IX.[114]

Although changes were made to the drystone walls and the lanes that they enclosed between *Phases 8* and *9*, most of the buildings constructed during *Phase 8* continued to be used during *Phase 9*. The exception was Building II, in Enclosure A, which was built over by a new structure, Building XI (Pl. 89.D; Fig. 80).[115] This new building was much like the others in that its walls were built of largely unshaped rubble to provide footings for a superstructure in mudbrick and/or timber.[116] Unlike Buildings I–IX, which were all rectilinear, Building XI had a curved eastern wall. It was also larger than the earlier buildings, measuring 5.58 by 4.4 m internally.

While Building XI represents the only new stone-footed building that can be dated to *Phase 9*, numerous new post-supports were documented in this phase. These were mostly clustered to the west of Building XI in Enclosure A and to either side of Building IV in Enclosure B (see Fig. 81).[117] New post-supports were also documented in Enclosure G, the area of the possible workshop, even though no stone-built structures can be assigned to this enclosure in this phase.[118] Further post-supports were found distributed throughout the area with no connection to a specific built structure, though in some cases the post-holes were built into the stone walls of the two phases.[119] Within Enclosure H and to the west of [9.1] a circular feature [9.13], 0.71 m in diameter, built of upright stones, may have served as either a large post-support or a pit for anchoring a timber device of some sort.[120] Within Enclosure B, just to the south of Building IV, a large storage vessel was discovered (F137), firmly secured in an upright position in the soil (Pl. 90.A and Colour Pl. 7).

The structures that can be dated to *Phases 8* and *9* show that early Ottoman settlement at Aphrodisias was more ex-

---

104 Just 567 kg of ceramic building materials were documented in this layer, but the small finds included items of jewelry or its manufacture, such as three glass bangles (SAg.15.1.4015.F308, SAg.15.1.4091.F301, SAg.15.1.4177.F369.), faceted crystal (SAg.15.1.4091.F304, SAg.16.1.4203.F379), four bronze rings (SAg.12.2.2004.F2008 (Inv. 12-22), SAg.13.2.4015.F020 (Inv. 13-142), SAg.15.1.4076.F309, SAg.16.1.4203.F378 (Inv. 16-032)), and two glass beads (SAg.13.2.4012.F17, SAg.15.1.4076.F143); domestic items such as four loomweights (SAg.15.1.4016.F321, SAg.15.1.4091.F300, SAg.15.1.4091.F303, SAg.16.1.4222.F478), a copper alloy needle (SAg.15.1.4076.F316 (Inv. 15-048)), a bone pin (SAg.13.2.4015.F014 (Inv. 13-134)), and two spindle whorls (SAg.13.2.4012.F13, SAg.15.1.4076.F318), metal tools and fittings, including a fluted rotary blade (SAg.13.2.4016.F021 (Inv. 13-140)), a set of hinges (SAg.15.1.4076.F328), four blades (SAg.15.1.4076.F310, SAg.16.1.4244.F404, SAg.16.1.F405, SAg.16.1.4346.F576), a utensil (SAg.15.1.4076.F332), two horseshoes (SAg.15.1.4076.F331, SAg.15.1.4076.F333), an iron ring (SAg.15.1.4091.F307), chains (SAg.13.2.4015.F018 (Inv. 13-139), SAg.15.1.4091.F311), as well as nine other unidentified metal tools (SAg.13.2.4012.F15, SAg.15.1.4016.F322, SAg.15.1.4076.F313, SAg.15.1.4076.F314, SAg.15.1.4076.F325, SAg.15.1.4076.F326, SAg.15.1.4076.F327, SAg.15.1.4076.F337, SAg.15.1.4091.F302, SAg.15.1.4091.F305, SAg.15.1.4091.F312); and several items intended for local manufacture and production, such as three millstones (SAg.15.1.4076.M830, SAg.15.1.4076.M838, SAg.15.1.4076.M841), flint (SAg.16.1.4220.F375), and a large ceramic vessel (SAg.15.1.4076.F137). Other items include, probably residual: three glass vessels (SAg.15.1.4091.F297, SAg.15.1.4076.F335 (Inv. 15-077), SAg.15.1.4177.F335), a probable stone ballista ball (SAg.15.1.4016.F299, an arrowhead (SAg.13.2.4012.F016 (Inv. 13-136)), a game piece (SAg.15.1.4076.M842), glass slag (SAg.15.1.4076.FF298), and two murex shells (SAg.13.2.4015.F19, SAg.15.1.4091.F306).
105 The earliest is cat. 9, the latest cat. 360.
106 [9.1]: **4014/4041/4056/4121**. A surprising discovery, an alabaster phallus (SAg.15.1.4121.M869 (Inv. 15-072)), was found directly beneath this wall where it was possibly placed as a type of foundation deposit. See Ch. 9 §E for further discussion.
107 [9.2]: **4373, 4378**.
108 [9.3]: **4335**. Artefacts built into this wall included a blade (SAg.17.1.4335.F599), a loomweight (SAg.17.1.4335.F598), and an anonymous coin (SAg.17.1.4335.C208 (C2017.004)), which provides a broad *terminus post quem* of AD 1307–1426 for its construction.
109 [9.4]: **4158**.
110 [9.5]: **4084, 4059**; [9.8]: **4083**.
111 [9.6]: **4082**; [9.7]: **4088**.
112 [9.9]: **4150**.
113 [9.10]: **4108**; [9.11]: **4182**.
114 [9.12]: **1014/17.2.5005**.
115 Building XI: **4013/4017**.
116 A bone spool (SAg.16.1.4013.F381 (Inv. 16-006)) and an iron arrowhead (SAg.15.1.4017.F273 (Inv. 15-047)) were also recovered from within the wall.
117 The relevant post-supports are 4160, 4179, 4180, 4181, and 4235 (in Enclosure A); 4161, 4162, 4163, 4164, 4165, 4166, 4167, 4168, 4169 (in Enclosure B).
118 4171, 4172, 4173 and 4174/4315.
119 The relevant post-supports are 4170, 4226, 17.2.5007.
120 [9.13]: **4129**.

tensive than previously thought (see Fig. 79 and 81). At this date the settlement was a substantial village, which seems to have occupied the space between the city's eastern gate and the Theatre Hill, clearly also extending, along its western edge, into the area of the former Place of Palms.[121] Indeed cadastral records note the emergence of a new village in this location at this time. Whereas no settlement is mentioned in this area in the first Ottoman survey in the 1460s, a village called 'Gerye' (the name probably deriving from 'Karia', the middle Byzantine alternative name to Stavropolis, from the city's former Byzantine *eparcheia*), with a bazaar, is cited in the survey of 1530.[122] The flat area of the former Place of Palms, which was largely dry by this date, was well suited to horticulture or the planting of clusters of trees and small-scale market gardening; indeed, the high groundwater table noted in this area in Ch. 2 §B continued to ensure the land here was kept well-watered. However, evidence for manufacturing at this date shows that a range of activities took place in this area.

Some of these activities might also have included recycling and/or refuse dumps. Deposits of refuse and debris (**4048**) were made in the southeast of the area during this phase.[123] A considerable amount of glass, including 86 glass bangle fragments[124] and 16 pieces of glass vessels, was also found in this deposit.[125] Considering that none of these fragments matched precisely in shape, colour, or size, and that they were recovered along with abundant inclusions of charcoal, mortar, and metal slag,[126] it is likely that this area served as a location where the recycling of glass took place, or at least an area where glass that could not be repurposed was thrown out. The continued accumulation of colluvial deposits (**4092**) in this southernmost area made this an ideal location for such dumping of glass and other refuse, since it could be used for little else.[127] Various attempts to contain the colluvial debris are indicated by the construction of least two retaining walls ([9.14] and [9.15]).[128] However, these walls were covered by this same colluvial deposit not long after their construction.

Despite the rapid growth of this Ottoman village, development was ultimately interrupted by yet another catastrophic seismic event. Previous investigations conducted by Kenan Erim within the area of the South Stoa had revealed that an entire portion of the Theatre Hill retaining wall, and with it much of the Theatre's *summa cavea*, collapsed northwards.[129] Our excavation of this collapse layer (**4085**) revealed several larger marble architectural elements, such as seat blocks and a fluted column drum from the South Stoa that had probably been repurposed in the Byzantine fortifications on top of the Theatre Hill (Pl. 90.B).[130] Further finds included a fragment of an inscription,[131] a glass vessel fragment,[132] a metal tong,[133] and two spindle whorls.[134] The only coin from within the layer was residual, dating to the early fifteenth century, while the ceramics provide only a broad date through the classical Ottoman period. Few other notable finds were documented in the layer, as it seems to have been heavily disturbed by later activity.[135] The exact date of this earthquake is hard to pinpoint but finds from deposits above (**4007**) and below (**4012**) would seem to indicate that it occurred in the late sixteenth or early seventeenth

---

121 For material dating to this period, see Nbk 114: *Theatre: Surface Area II* (J. Conger, 1971): 9; Nbk 88: *Theatre: Ramp 1-Ramp 2, Surface, Vol. 1* (K. J. Linser, 1970): 37, 38, 54, 332–333; Nbk 46: *Theatre* (E. Rosenbaum, 1966): 9; Nbk 67: *Theatre Trench VII* (E. Schraml et al., 1968): 3; Nbk 73: *Theatre, Vol. 1* (Hambrusch et al., 1969): 19. See also Jeffery 2019, 94.

122 Howard 2017, 2. For the records of 1530, see *166 Numaralı Muhâsebe-i Vilâyet-i Anadolu Defteri (937/1530)*. Ankara, 1995. 459, 464. For the 1460s records, see Erdoğru and Bıyık, eds. *T.T. 001/1 M. Numaralı*.

123 A very large quantity of ceramic building material was recovered in these deposits (too high to count in **4107** and 713 kg in the other contexts), as were high inclusions of charcoal, mortar, metal slag (SAg.15.1.4048.F70). Other finds, mostly domestic in character, were probably residual and include 11 loomweights (SAg.15.1.4048.F112, SAg.15.1.4048.F290–F293, SAg.15.1.4048.F196, SAg.15.1.4048.F290–F293, SAg.15.1.4051.F215), a pestle (SAg.15.1.4048.F69), two spoon handles (SAg.15.1.4048.F178 (Inv. 15-045), SAg.15.1.4107.F273), a copper alloy ear spoon (SAg.15.1.4048.F210 (Inv. 15-042)), a metal tong (SAg.15.1.4048.F186 (Inv. 15-039)), as well as intact ceramic (SAg.15.1.4048.F38, SAg.15.1.4048.F187) and metal (SAg.15.1.4048.F115) vessels; objects for agricultural and manufacturing purposes, include two millstones (SAg.15.1.4048.F214, SAg.15.1.4048.M754), a sickle (SAg.15.1.4107.F266), a chain (SAg.15.1.4107.F281), and various other metal (SAg.14.1.4048.F36 (Inv. 14-072), SAg.15.1.4048.F294, SAg.15.1.4048.F294, SAg.15.1.4107.F279), ceramic (SAg.15.1.4048.F194), and stone tools (SAg.15.1.4048.F37, SAg.15.1.4048.F50, SAg.15.1.4048.F88); and items for personal adornment, include four faceted crystal fragments (SAg.15.1.4048.F71–F72, SAg.15.1.4048.F229, SAg.15.1.4052.F68), a conical teal-coloured jewelry piece (SAg.15.1.4048.F226), and a bead (SAg.15.1.4107.F258). Other small finds included a game piece (SAg.15.1.4048.M804), and an inscription dated to the fourth century AD (SAg.15.1.4053.M653 (Inv. 15-8)). Like these small finds, the coins recovered were also residual finds and provide no accurate date for the layer.

124 SAg.15.1.4048.F46, F73–77, F80–85, F87, F98, F100–103, F105–109, F117–122, F126–129, F175, F177, F179, F181–183, F190–193, F195, F197–F204, F207, F209, F216–223, F227–228, F233–236, SAg.15.1.4051.F205–206, F208, F211, SAg.15.1.4107. F259, F261, F265, F268–272, F274–278, F282.

125 SAg.15.1.4048.F79, F86, F113–114, F176, F184–185, F188–189, F169, F232, SAg.15.1.4051.F212–213, SAg.15.1.4107.F267, F280, F287.

126 For a particularly large fragment of metal slag, see SAg.15.1.4048. F70.

127 Finds from this colluvial layer include a Byzantine stamp (SAg.15.1.4092.F251 (Inv. 15-037), rock crystal (SAg.15.1.4092. F224), two glass bangle fragments (SAg.15.1.4092.F249, SAg.15.1.4092.F253), a glass vessel fragment (SAg.15.1.4092.F252), loomweights (SAg.15.1.4092.F250, SAg.15.1.4092.F254), and a metal fitting (SAg.15.1.4092.F225).

128 [9.14]: **4094**; [9.15]: **4103**.

129 Nbk 278: *Portico of Tiberius: SE I, SW I* (J. Gorence, 1986): 25–49, 66. In addition to sizeable chunks of the Theatre Hill's retaining wall, these investigations catalogued 32 theatre seat blocks within the collapse layer (M53–54, M57, M59, M61, M63, M67–M70, M72–M73, M75–M76, M78, M81–M84, M86–M87, M90–M99, M101), as well as numerous orthostat and *petit appareil* blocks belonging to the retaining wall.

130 SAg.15.1.4005.M797, SAg.15.1.4005.M798, SAg.15.1.4005.M768.

131 SAg.15.1.4005.M808 (Inv. 15-076).

132 SAg.15.1.4005.F315.

133 SAg.15.1.4085.F247 (Inv. 15-038).

134 SAg.13.2.4005.F6, SAg.13.2.4005.F10.

135 See discussion of **4086** below.

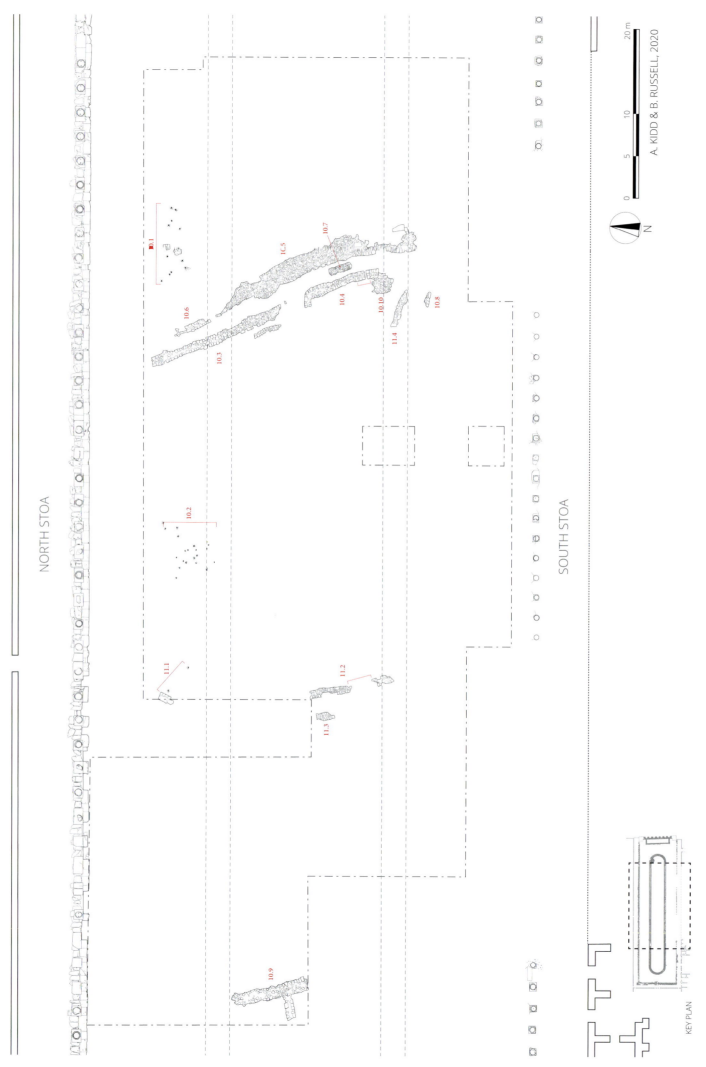

Fig. 82. Plan of post-antique occupation, Phases 10 and 11.

century;[136] it certainly led to the collapse of other walls in the area.[137]

Phase 10–11, 17th–20th centuries: from village to the gardens of Geyre

Phase 10 (Fig. 82)

The major Ottoman earthquake largely brought an end to village life in the area of the former Place of Palms. A new alluvial deposit (**4007**) again built up over the area, measuring 30–40 cm in depth. This deposit contained significant quantities of animal bones, especially in the northeast sector of the area (totalling 120 kg), as well as of small finds, most of which can be associated with Ottoman village life.[138] A surprising find was a terracotta phallic pendant, probably an apotropaic amulet.[139] This is probably a residual find of Roman date. Ceramics recovered from this layer consist primarily of classical Ottoman table wares with some residual Byzantine and Beylik materials (though it is also possible that Beylik forms continued to be used into the Ottoman period). Although numerous coins were found in this deposit, they range in date between the hellenistic period and the end of the sixteenth century.[140] It is probable therefore that this layer accumulated in the early seventeenth century. Importantly, the large number of artefacts from **4007** was concentrated in the northeast and south-central sectors of the area, the point at which major paths through the area intersected. This is distinct from the documented pattern of *Phases 8* and *9*, when finds were recovered from all across the excavated area, and suggests that during *Phase 10* the area of the former Place of Palms was once again a thoroughfare, rather than an area of settlement.

Although the stone-footed buildings of *Phases 8* and *9* were all abandoned by *Phase 10*, and no new stone-footed buildings were constructed during this phase, the large number of post-supports documented in the northeast ([10.1]) and in the north-central ([10.2]) zones suggest that a series of timber structures were constructed in roughly the same area as the earlier stone-footed buildings.[141] These timber structures could be animal pens or small storage buildings; they were less substantial than the earlier buildings, but it is also possible that the greater emphasis on timber construction was a response to the earthquake that appears to have destroyed the previous phase—a comparable response is known at Smyrna after the earthquake of 10th July 1688.[142]

A new series of field walls was also constructed in *Phase 10*, some on top of pre-existing walls and others altering the course of the pathways running through the area (Pl. 90.C). These include remnants of walls situated between [10.1], which were truncated by earlier excavations within the North Stoa.[143] The most significant changes were made in the centre of the area, however, where [9.5] was partially dismantled and built over by a series of new walls, [10.4], and [9.8] was extended to form [10.3].[144] These new walls delimited the western edge of a trackway, running for at least 34 m on a northwest-southeast orientation, which was limited to the east by [10.5], built out of the collapse of many of the *Phase 9* walls in this area; [10.6] continued this structure to the north.[145] At some point a short wall ([10.7]) composed entirely of long, flat stones laid on their

---

136 Among the list of historically known earthquakes in Türkiye in the late sixteenth and seventeenth centuries (Ambraseys 2009, 462–528), there are various possible candidates. Perhaps the best is an earthquake at Smyrna on 23 February 1653, which affected the Maeander valley at least as far as Aydın as well (Ambraseys 2009, 491–492). But of course the sixteenth- or seventeenth-century earthquake that hit Aphrodisias may have been another earthquake not otherwise recorded.

137 **1009**, **1013**, **4008**, **4024**, **4114**, **4325**. Two non-architectural artefacts from within these layers include an iron tool (SAg.16.1.4325. F587) and a blade with a tang (SAg.16.1.4325.F588).

138 These range from objects of personal adornment, including several glass bangles (SAg.15.1.4065.F130, SAg.15.1.4075.F156–F157, SAg.15.1.4075.F161, SAg.15.1.4075.F171–F172, SAg.15.1.4075. F284, SAg.15.1.4075.F286), beads (SAg.15.1.4075.F135, SAg.15.1.4075.F140, SAg.15.1.4075.F170), finger rings, two of which are stylistically closely related (SAg.15.1.4075.F133 (Inv. 15-018), SAg.15.1.4075.F149 (Inv. 15-036), SAg.15.1.4101. F245), and rock crystal (SAg.15.1.4065.F141, SAg.15.1.4065. F260, SAg.15.1.4075.F138, SAg.15.1.4075.F146, SAg.15.1.4075. F151, SAg.15.1.4075.F164, SAg.15.1.4075.F239); metal tools and utilitarian objects, such as three horseshoes (SAg.15.1.4065. F248, SAg.15.1.4075.F162, SAg.16.1.4356.F580), bronze and iron rings (SAg.15.1.4065.F93, SAg.15.1.4065.F91, SAg.15.1.4075. F131, SAg.15.1.4075.F158), chains (SAg.15.1.4065.F96–F97, SAg.15.1.4075.F132, SAg.15.1.4075.F256, SAg.15.1.4077.F256), a blade (SAg.15.1.4075.F159), a metal hook (SAg.15.1.4065. F93), as well as other assorted equipment, fittings (SAg.15.1.4065. F90, SAg.15.1.4065.F95, SAg.15.1.4065.F104 (Inv. 15-041), SAg.15.1.4065.F263, SAg.15.1.4075.F124, SAg.15.1.4077.F160), and utensils (SAg.15.1.4065.F92 (Inv. 15-022), SAg.15.1.4075. F240); stone tools, including grinding stones (SAg.15.1.4060. F116, SAg.15.1.4075.F169), two millstones (SAg.15.1.4075. M737, SAg.15.1.4075.M748), a pestle (SAg.15.1.4077.F153), a stone cylinder (SAg.15.1.4065.F78), worked stone piece with handle (SAg.16.1.4202.F377), and flint (SAg.15.1.4075.F238); and domestic tools, such as ivory spools (SAg.15.1.4007.F12 (Inv. 13-135), SAg.15.1.4075.F150), spindle whorls (SAg.15.1.4065. F99, SAg.15.1.4075.F154), a loomweight (SAg.16.1.4356.F582), and a stamped terracotta handle (SAg.16.1.4202.F376). Other finds include several glass vessel fragments (SAg.15.1.4065.F139, SAg.15.1.4065.F264, SAg.15.1.4075.F283) and several residual artefacts, including a mould-made Roman-period terracotta mask of a female visage (SAg.15.1.4075.F262 (Inv. 15-016)), three murex shells (SAg.15.1.4075.F136, SAg.15.1.4075.F148, SAg.15.1.4075. F155), five gamepieces (SAg.15.1.4060.F180, SAg.15.1.4065. M699, SAg.15.1.4075.M739, SAg.15.1.4075.F237, SAg.15.1.4077. FM820).

139 SAg.15.1.4077.F320 (Inv. 15-055). See Ch. 9 §E for further discussion.

140 The earliest is a coin of Pergamon dated to the second century BC (cat. 1) and the latest a mangir of Sultan Mehmed III, minted in Sidrekapsi in AD 1594/5 (cat. 364).

141 [10.1]: **4124**, **4125**, **4126**, **4127**, **4128**, **4135**, **4136**, **4137**, **4138**, **4187**; [10.2]: **4115**, **4116**, **4117**, **4118**, **4119**, **4120**, **4139**, **4140**, **4141**, **4142**, **4143**, **4144**, **4145**, **4153**, **4154**, **4155**, **4156**, **4183**, **4184**, **4185**.

142 Stiros 1995, 735, 727; Ambraseys 2009, 522–524.

143 **4131** and **4132**.

144 [10.3]: **4029/4224**; [10.4]: **4031**, **4032**. The small wall to the west of [10.3] is **4062**.

145 [10.5]: **4033**; [10.6]: **4036**.

side in two parallel rows partially blocked this new trackway and was perhaps used as a working surface of some sort.[146]

To the south of this new trackway, the remains of one east-west wall ([10.8]), now truncated due to later interference in the area, was constructed to serve as a terrace retaining wall to prevent the further downward movement of colluvial accumulation from the Theatre Hill.[147] Near the western limit of our excavation, a large field wall running north-north-west to south-south-east and a smaller wall perpendicular to it, [10.9], were built over the remains of Building IX.[148] This north-north-west to south-south-east wall must have been a major dividing wall, as it prolongs a series of field walls uncovered recently in the excavation of the area in front of the Civil Basilica and was still visible by the time of Jacopi's excavations in 1937.[149]

Although no dwellings survive from *Phase 10*, apart perhaps from the clusters of post supports, there is evidence for activity, possibly agricultural production, in the southeastern area of the space. A levelling cut (**4090**) and layer of debris (**4086**), probably the result of ploughing, was made above the aforementioned earthquake collapse layers. Immediately to the north of this was a distinct feature associated with wall [10.4] (Pl. 90.D). A gap in the wall, measuring 25 cm wide, was flanked by large stone blocks built into the walls. Too small for the passage of a human being or animal, it probably represents the negative space left by a timber element, possibly a beam or anchoring device. Adjacent to this gap was a platform, [10.10], measuring 1.13 by 0.35 m, composed of small stones, tiles, and marble pieces.[150] This installation was possibly for the processing, perhaps pressing, of agricultural produce. Contemporary with this installation are a series of other features. These include a makeshift fire pit or hearth built into the northeastern face of wall [10.6], which contained a deposit (**4058**) rich in charcoal. Several burnt marble fragments were also uncovered in this layer, including a revetment slab[151] and seven flutes that had been shaved off the column drums previously used in nearby Building IV. These flutes were probably used to support objects above a fire, with the east face of [10.6] serving as the hearth's back wall.

The construction of new field walls, the evidence for processing activities, and the fact that most of the ceramics recovered from *Phase 10* deposits outside the major trackways were very fragmentary and included a mixture of classical Ottoman table wares with Byzantine and Beylik materials all seem to indicate that the space was devoted primarily to cultivation following the late sixteenth- or early seventeenth-century earthquake; the concentration of artefacts along the main routes implies heavy foot traffic through the area. The remains of the earlier buildings were systematically cleared in this period, except for their stone footings, which became silted over. No trace was found of timber or mudbrick, though any useable materials were probably removed elsewhere. The various enclosures that characterized *Phases 8* and *9* were consolidated in this period and the land split into large parcels. This would seem to indicate a gradual contraction of the village of 'Gerye' between the fifteenth and seventeenth centuries, accompanied by an increase in the size of individual landholdings; at some point during this period the settlement (whose focus was now located outside the excavated area, further east) probably also acquired its modern name Geyre.

Phase 11 (see Fig. 82)
The general character of the area at the end of *Phase 10* would remain largely unchanged through to the twentieth century. Further build-up of alluvial deposits (**4006**) occurred across the area into the eighteenth century. The substantial alluvial layer, **4006**, that defines the beginning of *Phase 11* seems to have been heavily ploughed, with objects churned up from the layers beneath and mixed with debris from field walls which had fallen into disrepair.[152] While many of the finds from the layer were residual or difficult to date precisely, a copper alloy belt buckle could be dated to the seventeenth or eighteenth century,[153] and the latest coin dates to the reign of Sultan Ahmed III, specifically to AD 1703–4.[154]

Some of the *Phase 10* field walls were maintained to a certain degree into *Phase 11* (such as [10.10]) but a new north-south pathway was constructed across the central sector of the area, extending from the area of the former Agora towards the Theatre Hill. Although no beaten earth or cobblestone paving was discovered, two post-supports and a short length of wall, [11.1], and segments of two parallel drystone walls were revealed, [11.2] and [11.3], constructed using reused architectural blocks.[155] A short section of wall to the east, [11.4], shows that retaining walls to hold back the northern edge of the Theatre Hill also continued to be built at this late date.[156]

Despite the broad dating of the ceramic and coin finds from *Phase 11*, early accounts by antiquarians who visited Aphrodis-

---

146 [10.7]: **4042**.
147 [10.9]: **4030**.
148 [10.10]: **1002**, **1010**.
149 Nbk 582: *BSAg* (M. Gronow, 2019); Wilson, Russell, and Ward 2016, 89; Jacopi 1939, 85, fig. 6.
150 [10.11]: **4043**. The platform also included among its rubble conglomerate a decorative iron hinge (SAg.15.1.4043.F66 (Inv. 15-021)).
151 SAg.15.1.4058.M668.
152 The collapse deposits are **1012**, **4028**, **4040**, and **4360**. Finds from **4006** and associated collapse deposits include 988 kg and 33 kg of ceramic building materials and animal bones respectively, weapons, tools, and evidence of production, among them an iron arrowhead (SAg.15.1.4064.F60 (Inv. 15-017)), a leather-cutting knife with curved blade (SAg.15.1.4064.F59 (Inv. 15-040)), blades (SAg.15.1.4067.F55, SAg.16.1.4323.F570, SAg.16.1.4331.F564), a leather sheath for a small knife or dagger (SAg.15.1.4064.F61 (Inv. 15-020)), a key (SAg.14.1.4027.F16), a spatula (SAg.16.1.4323.F568), as well as fittings (SAg.13.2.4006.F22, SAg.15.1.4028.F165–166, SAg.15.1.4067.F56, SAg.16.1.4331.F575) and metal slag (SAg.14.1.4027.F7); stone weapons and tools, such as a spherical projectile (SAg.15.1.4064.F58) and a pestle (SAg.14.1.4027.F39); domestic items, including a loomweight (SAg.16.1.4323.F569), a spindle whorl (SAg.16.1.4331.F554), glass (SAg.15.1.4064.F54) and ceramic vessels (SAg.16.1.4323.F576). Other miscellaneous finds include a glass bangle (SAg.15.1.4067.F57), a bone bead (SAg.15.1.4028.F173), rock crystal (SAg.15.1.4028.F53, SAg.15.1.4064.F62, SAg.15.1.4064.F64, SAg.15.1.4064.F67, SAg.15.1.4064.F110), several game pieces (SAg.14.1.4027.M655-M656, SAg.15.1.4064.M680, SAg.15.1.4067.M676, SAg.16.1.4323.M1290) and a sculptural fragment (SAg.15.1.4028.M718 (Inv. 15-007)).
153 SAg.14.1.4006.F47 (Inv. 15-044).
154 Cat. 366.
155 [11.1]: **4321**, **4322**, **4333** (wall); [11.2]: **4326**, **4340**; [11.3]: **4336**.
156 [11.4]: **4040**.

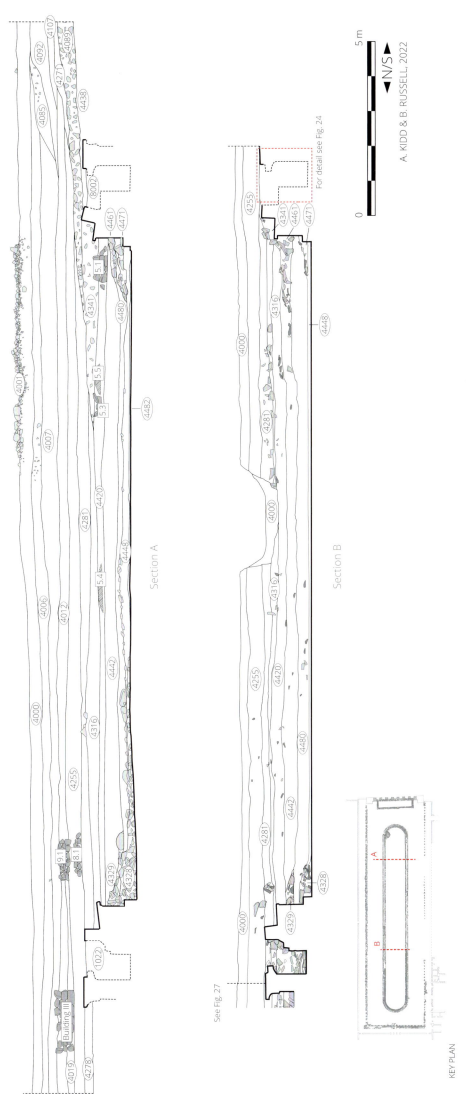

Fig. 83. North-South sections across the post-antique deposits in the Place of Palms, facing East.

ias during the nineteenth century help to flesh out the picture of settlement in this area. They describe the zone to the north of the Theatre Hill as separated into gardens, fed by a water channel, which they called the 'Timeles', routed along the back wall of the North Stoa (and indeed the walls of this channel remain to this day).[157] In their publications, several accompanying plates illustrate the total absence of Ottoman buildings in this area by this date.[158]

Phase 12, twentieth century: the impact of earlier excavations

The final phase within the former Place of Palms revealed by the recent excavations relates to modern cultivation activity and archaeological interventions. The drystone walls documented in *Phase 11* certainly remained in use into the twentieth century. The walls [11.2] and [11.3] apparently correspond to those flanking a track documented by Jacopi in 1937, from which he extracted several blocks of the North Stoa's mask and garland frieze.[159] This track, and a series of other walls, are visible on his plan of the area (see Fig. 3). It connected to an east-west road that rose above the south side of the former Place of Palms and skirted the north of the collapsed Theatre Hill. Some of these features are also still visible in a balloon photograph of the area taken in the early 1960s (Pl. 90.E) and other photographs from the early years of the excavations directed by Kenan Erim (Pl. 90.F). By the time our excavations commenced in 2012, several field walls and a few trees survived over the fill of the pool, including a walnut tree.

In terms of the stratigraphic sequence, the first layer encountered during the new excavations was a thick topsoil (**4000**), which extended across the entire surface of the area and ran to a depth ranging between 0.30 and 0.60 m. It was characterized by crumbly soil with a high amount of vegetal material and ceramics of mixed date with a great deal of evidence for modern intrusions. Collapse debris from abandoned walls and a large amount of residual artefacts were recovered, including a considerable quantity of marble architectural fragments, as well as modern objects, including a screw and the metal sole of a shoe.[160] The layer also yielded 37 coins, which range in date from the Augustan period to the modern Republic of Türkiye.[161]

The various trenches opened by Jacopi and Erim over the course of the twentieth century, not all of which are documented, were also located (Fig. 4). These include cuts made for excavations within the North Stoa (then called the 'Portico of Tiberius') (**3015, 3044, 3046, 4010, 4044**), the South Stoa (**4046, 4090**), the Propylon (**4099**), as well as sondages within the pool (**4038/4348/4349, 4039**). To these we may add five wheelbarrow cuts, one leading to the North Stoa (**4002**), one to the South Stoa (**4034**), and two leading toward the Propylon (**4003, 4004**). Spoil heaps from earlier excavations (**2006, 3036, 3037, 4001, 4011, 4277**), mainly comprising marble architectural fragments that had not been catalogued and stone rubble, were also documented.[162]

C. EARLY BYZANTINE CERAMICS (UO)

Presented in this section and the following one are the pottery finds ranging from the Byzantine to Ottoman periods uncovered during the excavations in the area of the Place of Palms in Aphrodisias. This material consists primarily of glazed and unglazed domestic wares, and provides some insight into the nature of the settlement that occupied this space in different periods after antiquity. The aim here is to present a brief overview of the ceramics from the new excavation; it is not an exhaustive study of post-antique ceramics from Aphrodisias more generally. That being said, the finds from the area of the Place of Palms constitute the largest assemblage of post-antique ceramics excavated stratigraphically from the site. In fact, the bulk of ceramics from the Place of Palms date to the post-antique period: the ratio of Roman to post-antique material is approximately 1:6.

There are almost no ceramic finds from the area of the Place of Palms that can be dated to between the mid-seventh century and the mid-eleventh centuries, roughly equivalent to *Phase 4* above. As noted above, and in the previous chapter, there is little archaeological evidence for any settlement in the area during these centuries. This is not true elsewhere in the city, where limited amounts of unglazed local coarse ware fragments, of storage and kitchen wares, dating to the ninth and tenth centuries remind us that there was early middle Byzantine activity at Aphrodisias, especially north of the former Place of Palms—along the Terrapylon Street, in the Bouleuterion and the neighbouring Bishop's Palace, as well as around the Cathedral.[163] However, the general scarcity of local coarse wares in the earliest Byzantine layers in the Place of Palms supports the hypothesis that the area of the pool was essentially a swamp in this period.

The ceramics from the *Phase 4* contexts, listed in Appendix 5, Table 29, therefore, are mostly residual material and have been discussed in Ch. 8 §C (see Fig. 62). The one striking find from *Phase 4* is a completely unique pilgrim flask (Fig. 84), which was found in **4442**, the major alluvial deposit that built up after the collapse of the stoas.[164] No parallels for a large pilgrim flask of this sort are known from Asia Minor.[165] The form, and the position of the handles in particular, are unusual: while the handles of other known pieces from Asia Minor are attached

---

157 Society of Dilettanti 1840, 46; Laborde 1838, 98.
158 Society of Dilettanti 1840, Ch. II, Pl. I, XXIV; Laborde 1838, 98, Pl. LIV, 105.
159 Jacopi 1939, 86 fig. 6.
160 SAg.14.1.4000.F18 and SAg.17.1.4200.F746 respectively.
161 The latest coin is cat. 407, a 50 kuruş dated to 2005, though other twentieth-century coins were recovered (cat. 404, 405, 406).
162 The few artefacts recovered from the spoil heaps, apart from architectural finds, included an oyster shell (SAg.14.2.3036.F1), a terracotta toy (SAg.14.2.3036.F3), a sculpted lock of hair possibly belonging to a console from the Hadrianic Baths (SAg.14.2.3037.M23 (Inv. 14-069)), and a game piece (SAg.13.1.4001.M663).
163 For a general description and typology of medieval and Ottoman glazed pottery in Aphrodisias, see Öztaşkın 2017; for classification of Ottoman pottery, François 2001.
164 SAg.17.1.4442.2
165 Most of them are unpublished. A good overview is given by www.antike-tischkultur.de *s.v.* Pilgerflaschen—see especially examples from the museums in Muğla and Aphrodisias; an example in the museum of Ödemiş shows a similar form but has strap handles attached directly to the neck and painted circles marking the centre of the body.

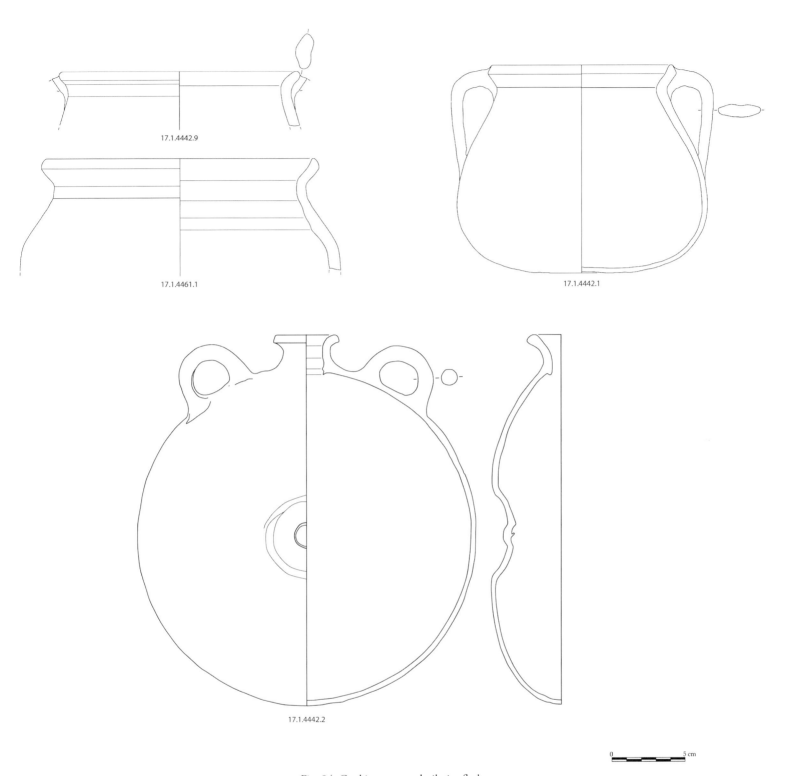

Fig. 84. Cooking pots and pilgrim flask.

directly to the spout and the neck, the handles of our example are attached directly on the upper part of the shoulder as 'eyelets' for a string or shoulder strap. The clay is medium-hard, dense and gritty with small quartz and lime inclusions and of deep reddish-brown colour; no mica is visible and the surface without any slip has been carefully smoothed before drying. The body is lentil-shaped in section and composed of two separately turned parts symmetrically attached to one another. Regarding shape, fabric, and characteristic details a striking parallel comes from Ḫirbat al-Minya in Palestine and belongs to an Umayyad context of the eighth century AD.[166] A smaller, but very similar example, has been found in Antioch, unfortunately without precise dating.[167] Also of Near Eastern origin is an example

166 Bloch 2006, 1–69. The fabric of our example corresponds to her description of 'Biscuit Ware', the most common fabric for plain coarse ware at the site and belongs to Type 2. Further examples of this type of pilgrim flask are said to be known from other sites in Palestine—all from Early Islamic, Umayyad contexts.
167 http://users.stlcc.edu/mfuller/antiochpottery.html: 'pilgrim flask form pottery vessel discovered when removing a tree over the Ro-

found in an Umayyad context from Hippos-Sussita.[168] These similarities in form and characteristic features suggest the provenience of our piece from one of the Roman provinces in the Near East as well. Near the large fragments of the pilgrim flask was found a cooking pot of the seventh century AD (Fig. 84)—these were two of only a small number of completely reconstructable vessels found in the Place of Palms.[169]

D. MIDDLE BYZANTINE, SELJUK, BEYLIK, AND OTTOMAN CERAMICS (MB)

Middle Byzantine and Seljuk ceramics

In contrast to the scarcity of early Byzantine ceramics, middle Byzantine material datable to the second half of the eleventh century and the twelfth century was recovered during the excavations. All of these ceramics, however, come from deposits that accumulated in the Beylik and Ottoman periods, *Phases 6–9* in the stratigraphic discussion above, and must be residual.[170] This middle Byzantine material is not associated with structures in the Place of Palms itself but instead appears to have been redeposited here from the Byzantine fortified settlement on the Theatre Hill. The earliest deposit in which middle Byzantine material is found (4089) is in fact the major layer of collapse from the Theatre Hill running along the south side of the Place of Palms. The Ottoman contexts in which middle Byzantine ceramics were found are thick alluvial layers, which again contained material eroded off the Theatre Hill. The Byzantine settlement on the hill developed after the seventh century and by the twelfth century most of the summit of the hill appears to have been covered in housing.[171] The various collapses of the fortifications on the Theatre Hill led to substantial quantities of Byzantine material being washed into the area of the Place of Palms. Although these finds are divorced from the original contexts in which they were deposited, the ceramics are primarily of a domestic character and what they reveal are increasing connections between Byzantine Aphrodisias and elsewhere in Asia Minor and the Mediterranean.

The earliest fragment of middle Byzantine pottery from the Place of Palms is a base fragment of a glazed plate, so-called White Ware, which comes from an alluvial siltation context which accumulated during the early classical Ottoman period (4266) (Colour Pl. 3, 1). The hard white fabric contains small red inclusions and the whole surface is covered with light green glaze. This particular fabric is classified, according to finds from Saraçhane, as White Ware III.[172] This type of pottery was in circulation between the second half of the eleventh century and the middle of the twelfth, and our base fragment probably comes from a workshop in the vicinity of Constantinople. The bulk of the middle Byzantine ceramics from the area of the Place of Palms can be dated more firmly to the twelfth century. Among these are a range of glazed local and imported table wares and unglazed local storage wares. The imported glazed wares are represented mainly by middle Byzantine wares: Green and Brown Painted Ware (Colour Pl. 3, 2–3), Painted Fine Sgrafitto Ware (Colour Pl. 3, 4–5), Fine Sgrafitto Ware (Colour Pl. 3, 6), Manganese Stained Sgrafitto Ware (Colour Pl. 3, 7), Brown Stained Ware (Colour Pl. 3, 8), Aegean Ware (Colour Pl. 3, 9), and Slip-Painted Ware (Colour Pl. 3, 10).

Although these groups of wares were produced in different techniques, shipwreck assemblages from the Mediterranean, as well as archaeometric analysis, show that they were probably produced in the same workshops, the locations of which remain unknown.[173] The fact that these wares are still found at Aphrodisias in the second half of the twelfth and the beginning of the thirteenth century, indicates that a Byzantine population remained in the city, even after the city was raided by the Seljuks. All these wares have coarse bodies contrasted with sophisticated inner decorations. The clay is pinkish-brown with large lime and quartz inclusions. The white slip is thick and creates a smooth background. In terms of painting techniques, the ornament is added with a green or manganese glaze and brown paint under transparent glaze. The forms attested are variations of shallow bowls and dishes. Among all the middle Byzantine fragments, there is only one piece of Aegean Ware (Colour Pl. 3, 9). Aegean Ware has wide sgrafitto lines including stylized animal figures, floral and abstract motifs. The light green glazed fragment found during the excavations is decorated with a stylized wheat motif. A small number of Zeuxippus Ware fragments dating to the beginning of the thirteenth century was also found (Colour Pl. 4, 1–2). Typically, this ware has creamy or pinkish slip and orange-brown coloured glaze. The features of the clay of our fragments are typical for imports from workshops in northern Asia Minor.

The vast bulk of middle Byzantine pottery from the area of the Place of Palms, more than 95% of the total, is locally produced. The mass production of local glazed pottery starts in the second half of the twelfth century. The local glazed wares include Fine Sgrafitto Ware (Colour Pl. 4, 3–4), Sgrafitto with Relief Ware (Colour Pl. 4, 5–6), Green and Brown Painted Ware (Colour Pl. 4, 7), and Slip-Painted Ware (Colour Pl. 4, 8). The local glazed wares share the same ornamental style and techniques with imported Middle Byzantine pottery, but they can easily be distinguished from the imports by the fact that their clay contains lots of mica and they have a different surface texture. Although no remains of kilns have yet been discovered at Aphrodisias, the discovery of waster fragments indicates that

---

man villa at Jekmejeh village during the 1939 field season at Antioch. Height = 17.7 cm, D = 14.4 cm, thickness = 9 cm and D of the rim = 3.9 cm. Reg. No. C626-P2653. Excavation photographs of the Princeton Art Museum'. Although it has a different rim and slightly higher spout, its characteristic features are the same as far as one could judge from an old black and white photograph.

168 Corresponds to Bloch 2006, type 1; Osband and Eisenberg 2018, 210–275, esp. Plate 9, no. 32—mid seventh to eighth century AD.
169 SAg.17.1.4442.1. To restore the complete vessels a few fragments are missing, but the form can easily be reconstructed—an almost unique exception regarding the pottery material from the excavations of the Place of Palms in general.
170 Byzantine ceramics were noted in contexts 4408, 4416, 4419, and 4426, which all equate to 4089, and 4281 (Beylik, *Phases 6–7*), 4233, 4266 and 4271, which equate to 4255 (Ottoman, *Phase 8*), and 4076 (= 4012) (Ottoman, *Phase 9*).
171 Cormack 1990a, 36; Jeffery 2022.

172 Hayes 1992, 29–30.
173 Doğer 2000; Waksman and von Wartburg 2006; François 2018.

some workshops were close to the city or even within it. The local Sgrafitto with Relief Ware has an interesting decorative technique: the stamps showing small animal figures, such as griffins or the struggle between an eagle and a gazelle, are directly applied to the inner surface after forming on the wheel. On some of the fragments further details are completed with sgrafitto lines. A wide iconographic repertoire can be observed among the examples found in Aphrodisias.

Very few fragments of ceramics of Seljuk date were found during the excavations, which again demonstrates that the area of the former Place of Palms was only settled intensively from the Beylik period (*Phases 6–7*) onwards. One fragment of a glazed bowl, belonging to the Seljuk period, however, is of special interest (Colour Pl. 4, 9): its inner surface has a light green glaze layer and decoration in the sgrafitto technique. The thick slip decoration on the outer surface comprises a geometric pattern with waves. It was found in a context, 4095, dated to the Ottoman period, which again contains material redeposited from the Theatre Hill and finds ranging in date from the twelfth to the fifteenth or sixteenth centuries. There is no indication of an established permanent Seljuk settlement in the area. According to detailed studies the range of data of Byzantine seals is interrupted well before the raid of 1188, perhaps as much as a century earlier,[174] while the Seljuks took control of the north-east part of Karia and took the population of Aphrodisias captive in 1197.[175]

Beylik period

Domination by the Seljuks and local Byzantine rulers continued until the site came under the administration of the Menteshe beylik in the second half of the thirteenth century, as noted above. At the beginning of the fourteenth century, the beylik of the Aydinids expanded into this territory, taking control of Karia/Stavropolis.[176] By this date, equivalent to *Phase 6* in the stratigraphic discussion above, the area of the former Place of Palms appears to have begun to dry out and to have become habitable again, as discussed above. This is further indicated by the large amount of Beylik pottery recovered during the excavations: glazed table wares, storage wares, kitchen wares, and imported glazed table wares.

The influence of Byzantine coloured sgrafitto styles can be clearly identified in the early glazed productions of Beylik period. The earliest glazed table wares, belonging to the end of the thirteenth century and the beginning of the fourteenth, are mostly deep bowl forms, decorated with concentric geometric bands in sgrafitto technique on the inner surfaces. In the fourteenth century, the most common forms among the glazed vessels are large plates and bowls with floral and geometric patterns arranged radially from the centre. These wares were produced and designed under the influence of the Islamic pottery repertoire. However, as the diversity in numismatic data shows, close commercial relations between beyliks make it difficult to distinguish between the products of different workshops or territories. Fragments of tripods and unglazed waster fragments (Colour Pl. 5, 7–8), suggest that at least some of these glazed wares were produced in Aphrodisias. The local glazed table wares can be classified as Green Flecked Sgrafitto Ware (Colour Pl. 5, 1–4), Green and Brown Flecked Sgrafitto Ware (Colour Pl. 5, 5–6) and Plain Glazed Sgrafitto Ware (Colour Pl. 6, 1–3). The glaze is transparent and usually contains coloured flecks. The clay is of red or reddish brown colour—typical of and particular to the post-antique products of Aphrodisias. The clay is not well-processed; mica and lime can be recognized in large particles. The slip is white and cream. Along with bowls a piece of a mould belonging to Relief Decorated Ware was found during the excavation (Colour Pl. 6, 4). These ornamented mould-made jugs were used as table ware. Relief-decorated and green glazed body sherds were also found in very small quantities but the find of another mould fragment further suggests that these two were locally made. Similar vessels of the same period were produced also in Ephesos and Miletos.[177]

Popular serving vessels of the period were also imported to Aphrodisias. Among these a small number of fragments in the underglaze painting technique, of the so-called Miletos Ware, produced by using blue, dark blue, and purple painting under transparent glaze were found (Colour Pl. 6, 5–6). The clay is densely micaceous and contains small lime inclusions. The exterior is glazed in green to halfway down the vessel. These characteristics indicate that it was imported from a workshop in coastal western Anatolia.[178] Import of this ware started at the end of the fourteenth century and continued until the middle of sixteenth century; it was very popular in the Ottoman period.

During the Beylik period more generally, there is an important emphasis on production of both local glazed and unglazed pottery, especially in the fourteenth and first half of the fifteenth centuries. In this period unglazed vessels were manufactured on a large, almost industrial, scale in various shapes. Prominent among these are two-handled storage vessels and *pithoi* used for storing large quantities of foodstuffs, and finally thin-walled cooking pots and their associated lids.

A distinctive feature of all the large two-handled storage vessels (Colour Pl. 7.A, 1–5), is their bright red clay and the high density of mica and lime particles of considerable coarseness in it. These vessels are marked by colour changes during firing: in profile, the fabric of these vessels is grey, due to inadequate oxygenation in the kiln. As their globular body fragments are very thin and fragile it is not possible to reconstruct a complete shape. The base fragments are flat and the body ends with a long neck; the handles are wide and thick for carrying. Lid fragments are not common among the pottery finds but, when they are found, usually have a concave body with a handle (Colour Pl. 7.A, 1). Contemporary parallels for this type of storage vessels have been discovered during the excavations in Manisa at the Gülgün Hatun Hamamı.[179]

Two types of local *pithoi* are very common: Type 1 has a wide rim and a short globular body (Colour Pl. 7.A, 6–7), Type 2 a narrow and thick rim which rises from a long neck and oval-shaped body (Colour Pl. 7.A, 8–11). Both are durable storage vessels with thick walls and could well have been in use for a long

---

174 Nesbitt 1983, 160.
175 Vryonis 1971, 184.
176 Akın 1968, 29.

177 Burlot *et al.* 2018, 427–428.
178 Burlot *et al.* 2018, 429.
179 Gök Gürhan 2011, 196–197, cat. no. 131–134.

time. Their bases are usually flat, though some of them are also carinated (Colour Pl. 7.A, 12, Colour Pl. 7.B). Most of the fragments have handmade relief decoration with vertical ridges, finger-pressed circles or incised decoration in the form of wavy lines. Similar contemporary examples have been also discovered during the Gülgün Hatun Hamamı excavations and in the Crimea.[180]

The thin-walled cooking pots are commonly found in contexts together with storage vessels (Colour Pl. 7.A, 13). Most of the fragments, particularly the bases, have a slag-like surface due to their use directly on or in an open fire. The spherical body narrows slightly towards the rim and the flattened handle joins at the middle of the body. One of the heavy and flat lid fragments has several holes pierced through it to allow steam to escape during cooking (Colour Pl. 7.A, 14).

Ottoman period

In the course of the first quarter of the fifteenth century the Ottoman empire absorbed all of the Beyliks in western Anatolia and this period can be regarded as the beginning of the Ottoman domination of Aphrodisias. Coinciding with this political change, a sudden increase in local pottery production can be noted, especially from the first quarter of the fifteenth century to the middle of the sixteenth century. The largest quantity of pottery finds from the post-antique period from the area of the Place of Palms, in fact, derive from Ottoman layers. The local wares are of a micaceous red, reddish brown, or light brown fabric with small lime inclusions similar to local productions of earlier periods. The white slip is applied on the interior surface and on the rim down to the halfway point of the vessel's body on the exterior surface. The glazes used comprise various shades, from light green to dark green and orange-brown. The classical Ottoman glazed table ware is mainly represented by two forms: bowls with a globular, carinated body and plates with a conical body and thick ribbed rim. This type of serving dish is the most popular in the Ottoman period and the size of the vessels is quite large compared to examples from earlier periods.

Ottoman Plain Glazed Ware is the largest group found during the excavations (Colour Pl. 8.A, 1–2). The green and orange-brown coloured transparent glaze usually has an inhomogeneous texture. Very close parallels are known from Miletos, Ephesos, Pergamon, and Saraçhane.[181] Ottoman Slip-Painted Ware is less common among the glazed table ware. Examples with patchy yellow, yellowish-brown, or green glaze covering the interior are found and were serially produced (Colour Pl. 8.A, 3). The majority of sgrafitto decorated pottery consists of Aphrodisias Spotted Ware (Colour Pl. 8.A, 4–5). The whole interior surface of this locally produced ware is covered with green and brown dots and lines following the geometrical sgrafitto lines on a light green surface. A large amount of green glazed spouted pitcher fragments found together with serving dishes suggest their use together at the same time (Colour Pl. 8.A, 6–7); these were used for serving liquids as well as for washing hands after the meal. The style of these forms imitates the metal ware of the same period and similar vessels are known from Pergamon and Saraçhane.[182]

At the end of the fifteenth century a decrease in imported pottery with underglaze technique can be noted at Aphrodisias. Under the influence of Chinese imports, the Ottoman vessels from the site change in style through to the sixteenth century. The cobalt blue painted decoration comprises flower and leaf motifs on both sides. A large bowl fragment (Colour Pl. 8.A, 9) is an excellent example of this development in style and decoration. Belonging to the same period are a small number of fragments of Celadon Ware (Colour Pl. 8.A, 8) with the typical fabric of greyish-white colour with thick transparent light green glaze.

For the material of the fifteenth to sixteenth centuries, several observations can be made. First, most of the local glazed vessels were used as cooking and storage wares and it seems to have been typical practice to cover the whole interior surface and the exterior of the rim with green glaze (Colour Pl. 8.A, 10–13), while the white slip with the green glaze is mostly applied only around the rim. The most common of these forms is a cooking pot with broad rim and globular body (Colour Pl. 8.A, 10). Storage vessels with small capacity have exactly the same form (Colour Pl. 8.A, 11). The cooking pots can be distinguished only by the brittle texture of their fabric and burn marks on the exterior surface because of their use over an open fire. The two-handled storage vessels with narrow rim and long body are made of a similar fabric to the local kitchen wares. Large amounts of these storage vessels have been found, for example during excavations in Saraçhane.[183]

When it comes to seventeenth-century material, the ceramic finds from the area are mostly water containers, which were used for agricultural production or animal husbandry. These vessels have a simple rim, one handle, and a spherical body. The final group of ceramic objects to come from the most recent layers in the area of the Place of Palms is a small but very distinctive set of wheel-made glazed tobacco pipes (Colour Pl. 8.B, 1–2), which are nineteenth-century in date. The clay of these type of sieved tobacco pipes with bases is micaceous, contains small lime particles, and is of reddish-brown colour. The exterior surface is covered with white slip and green glaze. Similar tobacco pipes have been found in Tel Aphek and Horvat Zikhrin,[184] as well as many Ottoman sites all over Anatolia.[185] An even smaller quantity of fragments belongs to a group of mould-made pipes with red slip, the globular bowls of which are generally decorated with stamped floral elements (Colour Pl. 8.B, 3).

E. POST-ANTIQUE SMALL FINDS AND GLASS
(TP & HJ)

The middle Byzantine period

Contexts dated to the middle Byzantine period yielded relatively few small finds, but a number of artefacts that may be dated to this period were residual finds in later contexts, and are

---

180 Gök Gürhan 2011, 215, cat. no. 166; on the Crimea, Teslenko 2016.
181 Böhlendorf-Arslan 2008, fig. 10, 12; Vroom and Fındık 2015, 223–224; Mania 2006, fig. 28; Hayes 1992, fig. 113.
182 Mania 2006, fig. 30/53, 55; Hayes 1992, fig. 127.
183 Hayes 1992, fig. 126.
184 Taxel 2008, fig. 1–2.
185 Ayhan 2015, fig. 2–10.

discussed here as they significantly enhance our understanding of the middle Byzantine settlement. As in the chapter on late antique small finds, only a selection of the most informative finds is presented here.

A spearhead was recovered in the thick sediment layer, **4442**, immediately overlying the *Phase 4* clearance deposits which probably date to the tenth or eleventh centuries. This spearhead takes the form of a conical iron head with a circular socket (Pl. 91.A).[186] This object appears to be broken part way down the socket and may have originally been substantially longer. This spearhead is broadly similar to some conical spearheads from Avar contexts (*c.* AD 650–700), although it is about half the size of its Avar cousins, even accounting for its partial survival; it could therefore be a residual find from one of the seventh-century destructions.[187] A high-quality glass bottle of particular note was found in a classical Ottoman context belonging to *Phase 8*.[188] This flared bottle in a deep olive-green fabric has a flaring neck which bulges towards the bottom before giving way to a piriform body (see above, Fig. 65, Inv. 15-077/SAg.15.1.4076.F335). Its small, almost square, base may indicate that it was not intended to stand independently and was perhaps supported by a stand or suspended from above. This item was probably imported: vessels of this broad shape, sometimes referred to as 'spearlike flasks', were produced during the eleventh and twelfth centuries, especially in Egypt, and are traditionally considered to be containers for kohl.[189] The quality of this vessel indicates the probable import of small quantities of luxury goods—both the vessel itself as well as its former contents, that is kohl. François has published two examples of ceramic bowls from the Bishop's Palace at Aphrodisias likewise imported from Fatimid Egypt, testifying to ongoing contact with the wider Eastern Mediterranean.[190]

Two interesting copper alloy finger rings from a Late Ottoman (*Phase 10*) context probably date to the tenth through twelfth centuries, since they conform to Corinth type Q (Pl. 91.B–C).[191] Flat bezels, in one case square and the other circular, are soldered onto a simple hoop.[192] The bezels are decorated with incuse circular motifs. A very similar example from Sardis is assigned a 'Turkish' date. However, this seems to be on the basis of depositional context, which may well be significantly more recent than their date of manufacture.[193] The prominence of the bezel may indicate that these are sealing rings with a practical function, in addition to personal adornment.

An early discovery, made while removing modern topsoil, was a copper-alloy book ring (Fig. 85, Inv. 14-046).[194] The small piece would have been used to fasten the leather straps of a book cover.[195] Christopher Lightfoot has assembled well-dated examples from Corinth, Constantinople, and Amorium, all from tenth- to twelfth-century contexts.[196] Several more are known from the collection of the Afyon Museum.[197] A small silver cross pendant was also found in topsoil (Fig. 85, Inv. 14-039).[198] Four narrow cylindrical arms protrude from a square at centre. The arms terminate in round knobs. The central square is inlaid with a niello design, comprising four tiny squares arranged to form a square cruciform motif. The upper left and lower right squares are once again subdivided into four squares, multiplying and integrating cruciform elements. Several parallels in copper alloy have been found in burials in the middle Byzantine cemeteries of Aphrodisias.[199]

Further middle Byzantine artefacts were discovered within collapse deposits over the southern portion of the urban park. The deposits were mostly composed of rubble from *petit appareil* masonry that had fallen from the Theatre Hill to the south, and contained ceramics of the Beylik period (equivalent to **4420** and **4089**). It is likely that the small finds recovered in the collapse layers derive from settlement on the hilltop. A large bronze cross once formed one half of a pectoral reliquary dating to the tenth or eleventh century (Fig. 85, Inv. 17-034).[200] The slightly flared arms show no signs of engraved decoration. A small perforation at the end of one of the longer vertical arms attests to a secondary use as a pendant or wall fixture. Two ceramic stamps are both cut with crude Greek crosses with a pellet in each angle. One has a large oval face and a round handle (Fig. 85, Inv. 16-056).[201] Its form and engraved motif conform to a common type of bread stamp attested at middle Byzantine sites across Asia Minor, Constantinople, and mainland Greece.[202] The fabric and firing technique suggest a date in the tenth to twelfth centuries.[203] Similar stamps are often found in ecclesiastical contexts and associated with the preparation of Eucharistic bread, though the practice of stamping food using Christian signs probably extended to food preparation in domestic contexts too.[204] The second stamp has a much smaller face, a cylindrical form, and a fabric that resembles that of ancient brick or tile (Fig. 85, Inv. 15-037).[205]

Some finds from the middle Byzantine period onwards, especially those of an everyday nature, are difficult to date with a high degree of certainty, and the nature of the stratigraphy may mean that they are either of Byzantine or Turkish date.

---

186 SAg.17.1.4442.F757 (Inv. 17-86): L: 12.0 cm, W: 2.4 cm, D: 0.4 cm. An outside possibility remains that rather than a spearhead, this item was in fact a spear butt; even if this option is entertained, the fact remains that the item is of a military nature.
187 Csiky 2015, 106, fig 33, no. 3.
188 SAg.15.1.4076.F335 (Inv. 15-077): H: 14.0 cm, ⌀ (rim): 1.5 cm, ⌀ (base): *c.* 1.0 cm.
189 Carboni and Whitehouse 2001, 139, cat. 55 with further references.
190 François 2001, 152.
191 Davidson 1952, 231.
192 SAg.15.1.4075.F133 (Inv. 15-18): ⌀ (ring): 2.2 cm, W (bezel): 1.4 cm; SAg.15.1.4075.F149 (Inv. 15-36): ⌀ (ring): 1.5–2.1 cm, ⌀ (bezel): 1.5 cm.
193 Waldbaum 1983, 130, cat. 840 with pl. 48.
194 SAg.14.1.4000.F19 (Inv. 14-046): H: 2.1 cm, W: 1.5cm, D: 0.25 cm.
195 Lightfoot 2014.
196 Lightfoot 2014, 383 no. 7; Davidson 1952, 272, nos. 2197–2200; Gill 1986, 266, no. 579.
197 Lightfoot 2003, 100, nos. 21–23.
198 SAg.14.1.4000.F29 (Inv. 14-039): H: 2.9 cm, W: 2.8 cm, D: 0.4 cm.
199 For example, Inv. 65–183; Inv. 83–045.
200 SAg.17.1.4416.F649 (Inv. 17-034). Pitarakis 2006, 30–31.
201 SAg.16.1.4293.F560 (Inv. 16-056): H: 3.3 cm, ⌀ (handle): 3.0 cm, ⌀ (base): 6.8 cm.
202 Ricci 2012, 159 fig. 13; Kontogiannis and Arvaniti 2012, 251 fig. 3; Mercangöz 2007, 73; Köroğlu 2007.
203 We thank Muradiye Bursalı for this observation.
204 Galavaris 1970; Caseau 2014.
205 SAg.15.1.4092.F251 (Inv. 15-037): H: 4.7 cm, ⌀: 2.1 cm.

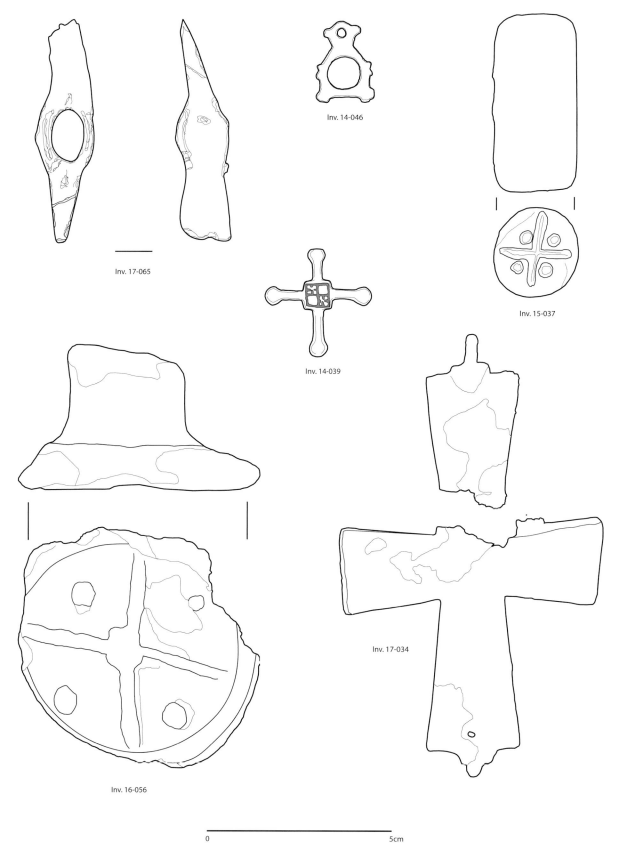

Fig. 85. Selected middle Byzantine-period finds.

The same collapse layer deposit of Beylik date discussed above (**4420** and **4089**) contained several further items of probable middle Byzantine manufacture and use. These included a small iron pickaxe, with a flat pick, slightly curved head, and an oval-shaped eye (Fig. 85, Inv. 17-065).[206] We cannot be sure about the precise use to which this object was put but it is clearly for relatively fine work; we might hypothesise it served for the roughing-out of larger rock crystal fragments or the recutting of bricks into loomweights, as described elsewhere in this section, though neither possibility can be confirmed at present. The relative instability of this period is perhaps illustrated by a small iron spearhead, with a leaf-shaped blade, subtriangular section and round, tapering socket (**4420**).[207] This weapon may hint at the militarised nature of Aphrodisias at this time.

Rock crystal, either colourless or with a slight pinkish tinge, was consistently found in modest quantities throughout all phases of the excavation from the earliest fill of the pool onwards.[208] The fragmentary nature of the crystals recovered may indicate that these minerals were being worked, possibly for the production of jewellery. The earliest finds of rock crystal fragments are from the bottom fills of the pool created by the seventh-century clean-up.[209] It is likely that rock crystal was employed in jewellery production in antiquity, and that some fragments from medieval contexts are residual. However, several fragments of rock crystal vessels (unpublished) were excavated in Byzantine and later contexts in the neighbouring Agora.[210] There is also evidence for rock crystal being utilised in middle Byzantine jewellery at Aphrodisias. A silver button or pendant with a rock crystal setting was discovered in 1962 in a tomb placed within the ruins of the Triconch Church.[211] The burial was made in the thirteenth century, though the pendant may be slightly earlier. Rock crystal was probably employed in craft production from antiquity throughout the middle ages.

The Seljuk, Beylik, and Ottoman periods

Finds of the Seljuk and later periods inform us about life in Aphrodisias after it fell out of Byzantine control. However, the number of objects whose date of manufacture can be securely attributed to the Seljuk or Beylik periods is limited. This reflects a basic continuity in the material practices of everyday life in a rural settlement regardless of the dominant culture of the political elite. It is easier to distinguish objects of the Ottoman period; as a result, finds of this later period predominate in the discussion below.

Tools and implements. A range of metal finds hints at agricultural and production activities, as well as personal grooming and food preparation in Aphrodisias/Geyre throughout the Turkish period. These objects provide insights into day-to-day activities, particularly of non-elite groups, in domestic and productive/agricultural contexts, though it is worth noting that there these two spheres overlap, with production probably taking place in or around domestic space. More work remains to be done on metal finds of late date, and the following summarises some of the best-preserved and most informative identifiable artefacts.

Small-scale artisanal activity, particularly the working of leather and perhaps metal, is suggested by a modest group of tools. The most easily identifiable of these items is an iron leather-cutting knife with a curved blade projecting from a long, narrow stem terminating in a long thin tang (Pl. 97.D), found in an alluvial build-up layer probably dating to the eighteenth century (equal to **4006**).[212] Broadly comparable items have been identified at Pergamon.[213] A substantial copper alloy needle with rounded head, oval-shaped eye and tapering body, which may have been suitable for working leather or heavy textiles (Pl. 91.E), was recovered from a classical Ottoman context (equal to **4012**).[214] A more unusual iron tool, now in a very poor state of preservation, comprises a fluted rotary blade set into a square-sectioned, gently tapering handle, and was found in the same context (Pl. 91.F).[215] The function of this item is not immediately obvious, but it could have been used in leatherworking, though alternative applications, such as food preparation or pottery decoration (for example on sgraffito wares) cannot be excluded.

These metal finds are complemented by a fragment of a leather knife or dagger sheath from another Ottoman layer (Pl. 91.G).[216] The sheath terminates in a small sub-spherical leather pommel, presumably intended to prevent the knife from cutting through the main body of the sheath. Metalworking might be implied by a single metal tong found in a late Ottoman context (equal to **4048**) belonging to *Phase 9*, probably originally part of pair, with a flattened profile and circular perforation; at the other end a pointed tip projects perpendicular from the shaft (Pl. 91.H).[217] Certainly, the presence of several horse shoes (discussed below) would imply the presence of a smith or farrier able to work and fit shoes in Aphrodisias at some point during the Turkish period. Several iron finds may also be linked to agricultural work. An iron billhook with a conical iron socket, both heavily corroded, was recovered in a layer dated to the Beylik period, and may have been used for pruning or felling vegetation (Pl. 91.I).[218]

A few other Turkish-period finds hint at the broader aspects of village life, including hygiene maintenance and food preparation. A close attention to personal hygiene is suggested by a copper alloy ear spoon with straight handle terminating in a folded loop found in a late Ottoman context (**4048**) (Pl.

---

206 SAg.17.1.4420.F675 (Inv. 17-065): H: 1.5 cm, W: 5.85 cm, D: 1.4 cm, H (eye): 0.95 cm, W (eye): 1.4 cm.
207 SAg.17.1.4420.F665 (Inv. 17-025): H: 10.2 cm, W: 1.9 cm, D: 0.4 cm.
208 Contexts including rock crystal: **4048**, **4052**, **4064**, **4065**, **4075**, **4091**, **4095**, **4203**, **4253**, **4255**, **4260**, **4271**, **4317**, **4342**, **4328**, **4403**, **4415**, **4420**, **4442** and **4466**.
209 For example, SAg.17.1.4328.F980.
210 Katherine Larson, personal communication (November 2018).
211 Caruso 2016, 358, fig. 25.15.

212 SAg.15.1.4064.F59 (Inv. 15-40): H: 10.5 cm, W: 4.0 cm, D: 1.0 cm.
213 For example, Gaitzsch 2005, 183, LE 3, LE 5.
214 SAg.15.1.4076.F316 (Inv. 15-48): H: 8.8 cm, W (at eye): 0.4 cm, D: 0.2 cm.
215 SAg.13.2.4016.F021 (Inv. 13-140): L: 7.0 cm, W: 1.6 cm, D: 1.9 cm.
216 SAg.15.1.4064.F61 (Inv. 15-20): L: 4.5 cm, W: 1.5 cm, D: 0.8 cm.
217 SAg.15.1.4085.F247 (Inv. 15-38): H: 14.4 cm, W: 1.4 cm, D: 1.5 cm.
218 SAg.16.1.4339.F550 (Inv. 16-55): H: 23.9 cm, W: 3.0–6.2 cm, D (blade): 0.3 cm, D (socket): 2.6 cm.

91.J).[219] Food preparation, presumably in a domestic setting, is evidenced by an iron pan scraper featuring a long, round handle culminating at one end in a flat oval-shaped projection and at the other in a flattened, roughly triangular head which served as an implement for cleaning cooking vessels (Pl. 92.A).[220] Similar items are found in middle and late Byzantine layers at Pergamon and Djadovo, a Byzantine village in the Balkans,[221] and thereby reflect some broad continuities in material cultural between the Byzantine and Turkish periods. A fragment of copper alloy S-shaped handle, terminating in a flattened-kite-shaped projection, which appears to be decorated with an incised vine leaf, came from context **4048** (Pl. 92.B).[222] Perhaps originally belonging to a spoon, this item may be related to either the preparation and administering of cosmetics or medicines, or have been a relatively luxurious item of cutlery.

Concerns for the security of personal possessions is suggested by a probable decorative tee hinge recovered from another Late Ottoman context.[223] This takes the form of a thin, flat iron object, starting with a teardrop-shaped finial perforated by a small circular hole, probably for the insertion of a thin nail (Pl. 92.C). Probably part of a strong box or door, this item is again a relatively simple but aesthetically pleasing embellishment of an otherwise functional object.

Quernstone. Food production is evidenced by the recovery of a fragmentary schist rotary quern in a context of Late Ottoman date (Pl. 92.D)[224] Approximately half of this millstone survives; it was originally approximately circular, with gently curved top and a flattened bottom, indicating that it was originally an upper quernstone. The millstone has a funnel-shaped eye, joining with a rynd slot at the bottom, and a circular handle socket. As the millstone fractured across the eye, this probably reflects failure during use.

Textile production. Common finds, appearing from the early sedimentation of the pool through to the Turkish period, are loomweights made from recut ancient bricks. These take two basic forms, the first roughly square and the second approximately wedge-shaped, both with central perforations for the attachment of threads (Pl. 92.E). The objects vary considerably in size and weight, with a sample of items from two contexts ranging between 86 g and 350 g.[225] Several unfinished examples were identified, where the central perforation was apparently cut too close to the edge of the reused brick to be viable.[226] This suggests that these devices were being made out of reused material in the Place of Palms or its immediate vicinity, though it is not clear whether they were also being used or sold in the same area.

A similar approach to reuse of obsolete ceramic materials for textile manufacturing can be seen in the case of a recut glazed ceramic vessel base with sgraffito decoration (Pl. 92.F).[227] This was found in the rubble of a wall, which accumulated in the Beylik period and probably through to the early Ottoman. The interior of the footed base still features the remains of green glaze over a white slip layer and circular incisions filled with line of black glaze, now punctured by a hole. The decoration suggests an early Ottoman date. Such an item arguably provided a more aesthetically pleasing alternative to brick loomweights (at least to modern eyes), though it may also reflect the relative ease with which broken bases were converted into loomweights, as the foot of the base provided guidelines which prevented a perforation from being created too close to the edge and thereby breaking the object.

Further evidence for textile production is provided by two spindle-whorls found in a late Beylik or early Ottoman context belonging to *Phase 7*. The first, biconical, example in a reddish grey ceramic fabric is decorated with four pairs of incised lines radiating out from the central perforation on the obverse; the reverse appears to be undecorated with apparent lines only reflecting post-depositional damage (Pl. 92.G).[228] The second is made from a highly polished dark brownish-red soapstone with whitish inclusions (Pl. 92.H).[229] This spindle-whorl is discoid in form, with one rounded side and one flattened side.

Two fine worked bone objects, both probably lathe-turned, may also be related to textile working, perhaps serving as thread spools, bobbins, or needle cases, though the relative merits of these possible identifications deserve further consideration in future. It is worth noting, additionally, that due to the dearth of publications concerning late antique and medieval worked bone objects in the Eastern Mediterranean, the date of manufacture of these items cannot be neatly circumscribed.[230] The first of these, recovered in a fifteenth- or sixteenth-century context (**4233**), is a cylindrical object with outward tapering ends, featuring a group of four bands of incised decoration running around the object close to each extremity (Pl. 92.I).[231] The ends are each perforated with a small hole. The second, recovered in the collapse of an Ottoman wall, dating to the sixteenth century (**4013**), is slightly larger at the extremity (Pl. 92.J).[232] This item is probably functionally similar to the first, as it has a similarly tapering form and a group of two bands of incised decoration near both of the flaring ends and in the centre of the object. In contrast to the first example, this item also features further inserts in the space of a cylindrical drum which terminates in a protruding semi-spherical knob.

---

219 SAg.15.1.4048.F210 (Inv. 15-42): H: 9.0 cm, W: 0.5 cm, D: 0.5 cm. It is possible that this item is residual from the Roman or late antique phases of activity in the Place of Palms.
220 SAg.15.1.4065.F92 (Inv. 15-22): H: 16.0 cm, W: 4.5 cm, D: 0.8 cm.
221 For Pergamon, see Gaitzsch 2005, 180–1, KÜ 1–2, KÜ 5. For Djadovo see Pitarakis 2005, 252, fig. 8.
222 SAg.15.1.4048.F178 (Inv. 15-45): H: 4.5 cm, W: 1.4 cm, D: 1.5 cm.
223 SAg.15.1.4043.F66 (Inv. 15-21): H: 6.5 cm, W: 3.4 cm, D: 0.3 cm.
224 SAg.15.1.4075.M737. Overall dimensions ø: 34.5 cm H: 8 cm, weight: 9.93 kg. Eye ø: top: 6.5 cm, waist: 4.1 cm, bottom: 8.1 cm. Rynd slot: W: 5.1 cm D: 3 cm H: 2 cm. Handle: W: 5.1 cm, D: 3.0 cm, H: 2.0 cm, handle socket: ø: 3.4 cm h4 cm, H: 3.5cm 5 cm. We thank Andrew Wilson for his advice on this object.
225 For example, SAg.17.1.4416.F638–642; SAg.17.1.4416.F644; SAg.17.1.4416.F646–648; SAg.17.1.4416.F650; SAg.17.1.4420.F669–671; SAg.17.1.4420.F673; SAg.17.1.4420.F674.
226 For example, SAg.17.1.4420.F674; SAg.17.1.4420.F671.
227 SAg.17.2.5013.F73 (Inv. 17-18): weight: 200.2 g.
228 SAg.17.1.4404.F600/SAg.17.1.4404.F605 (Inv. 17-10): H: 2.5 cm, ø: 4.5 cm.
229 SAg.17.1.4405.F616 (Inv. 17-16): H: 1.5 cm, ø: 3.3 cm.
230 Stephen Greep, personal communication (January 2019).
231 SAg.16.1.4233.F383 (Inv. 16-5): L: 5.8 cm, ø: 1.1 cm.
232 SAg.16.1.4013.F381 (Inv. 16-6): L: 5.4 cm, ø: 0.8 cm.

Horseshoes. Sporadic finds of horseshoes reflect the ongoing role of horses in the life of the Turkish town. At least two complete horseshoes were recovered in Beylik-period contexts (equal to **4089**, **4438**), though one of these examples may have been residual from a middle Byzantine context as it was found in a collapse layer containing abundant earlier material; several further fragmentary examples are known from another late Beylik or early Ottoman context (equal to **4281**) (for an example, Pl. 93.A).[233] These horseshoes were probably made for light riding horses as they correspond in size with modern horseshoes most commonly used for pleasure-riding breeds including Arabians, Quarter Horses, and Thoroughbreds. The lack of clear evidence for external traction devices (for example caulkins or toe grabs) implies that these horses were travelling over gentle terrain, such as the plain around Aphrodisias. These shoes were therefore for riding animals, perhaps belonging to pastoral farmers, rather than for draught animals used in agricultural or load transportation.

Dress accessories. Dress accessories included a rectangular copper alloy belt buckle, with scalloping along one of the long ends, recovered in a late Ottoman, probably eighteenth-century, context (**4006**) (Pl. 93.B).[234] The design of the obverse is dominated by six rosettes in low relief, possibly repoussé, disposed in two uneven but approximately horizontal rows. The rosettes of the upper row are connected by stems or branches, above which appears a design in very shallow chasing, featuring groups of circles disposed in areas defined by curved lines. On the reverse of the buckle is an applied horizontal slide or pin for attachment purposes. Buckles with comparable shapes have been reported at Amorium[235] and Corinth,[236] though it has not yet been possible to find specimens with similar decorative motifs. Lightfoot dates the Amorium examples to the seventeenth or eighteenth centuries, and a similar date may be appropriate for the Aphrodisian buckle.[237] A strap fitting, which is probably made of silver, and was recovered in topsoil, is executed in a similar style (Pl. 93.C).[238] It takes the form of a hollow prism, rectangular in section and hourglass in plan. A rosette at the centre is flanked by vegetal motifs consisting of three adjacent leaves. The similarity between buckle and strap fitting is so marked that they may even belong to the same set. The presence of these items indicates that at least some members of the community inhabiting Aphrodisias during the Early Modern period were sufficiently wealthy to be able to afford relatively showy elements of dress.

Glass bangles. Vessel glass of a securely Turkish manufacture date has been challenging to identify. This is due, in part, to the highly fragmentary nature of these finds and the typological similarities between the bases from Turkish layers, which survive best, and bases of probable late antique date (see the section on late antique glass, above). None of the characteristic Ottoman-period mould-blown styles identified at Constantinople was observed in the Place of Palms, but it is hoped that in the future, chemical analyses will allow easier differentiation of late antique and medieval glass on the basis of their relative chemical compositions.[239]

Glass bangles, however, are an easily identifiable class of Ottoman find and are common throughout the Beylik period and later with over 200 fragments attested in the Place of Palms (selected examples are illustrated in Fig. 86).[240] A substantial proportion of these items was concentrated in a single Late Ottoman context comprising colluvial deposits washed down from the Theatre Hill, and other debris (**4048**).[241] While further analysis is necessary to provide clarity, it may be that this glass-rich context reflects the gathering of earlier glass destined for recycling. It is only possible to publish a selection of the bangles discovered here, though the assemblage merits a systematic typological study in future. As such, we have not attempted exhaustive presentation of comparable pieces. The bangles attested here fall into at least six principal groupings, differentiated by their decorative techniques. These included undecorated bangles, either with a circular section, such as an example in a black or very dark green fabric (Fig. 86, 4409 (bulk find)),[242] or a sub-rectangular section, as seen in an example now weathered to a metallic grey, and of uncertain original colour (Fig. 86, SAg.15.1.4048.F228).[243]

Twisted bangles appear in a variety of styles, utilising both monochrome and polychrome tones. Examples of the former include a thickly twisted bangle with a subcircular section in a pale blueish-green glass (Fig. 86, SAg.15.1.4048.F77),[244] and a finer example with a circular section in a very pale blueish-green fabric (Fig. 86, SAg.15.1.4048.F98).[245] The latter category features a thin twisted bangle with a circular section comprising a pale blue core wound with occasional very fine opaque mid-red threads (Fig. 86, SAg.15.1.4048.F221),[246] and a twisted bangle, again with a circular section, which was probably originally made of two different colours of glass, as indicated by differential weathering, though the exact colours are unclear (Fig. 86, SAg.15.1.4048.F199).[247]

Tooled bangles appear in a variety of forms, with varying degrees of complexity. Among the simpler specimens are a grooved bangle in a mid-yellowish-green glass, with a semi-circular section whose inner face is concave (Fig. 86, SAg.15.1.4048.F234),[248] or an object with a similar section but in a dark brownish-red fabric, which appears black (Fig. 86, SAg.15.1.4075.F171).[249] More intricate examples include an example with four grooves and a sub-rectangular section in light yellowish-green

---

233 Complete examples: SAg.17.1.4438.F683: H: 11.7 cm, W: 11.7 cm; SAg.17.1.4419.F654: H: 11.0 cm, W: 10.6 cm. Fragmentary examples include SAg.17.1.4404.F603 (Inv. 17-012); SAg.17.1.3311.F627 (n.b. measurements are not provided as these items are heavily damaged).
234 SAg.14.1.4006.F47 (Inv. 15-44): H: 4.0 cm, W: 3.5 cm, D: 0.5 cm.
235 Lightfoot 2003, 92, Appendix 1, cat. 1/SF2578.
236 Davidson 1952, 275, cat. 2252, pl. 116.
237 Lightfoot 2003, 92.
238 SAg.14.1.4000.F30 (Inv. 14-42): H: 2.8 cm, W (maximum): 2.5 cm, D: 0.35–4 cm, plate thickness: 0.1 cm.
239 For Ottoman mould-blown glass from Constantinople, see Özgümüş 2010, 126–129.
240 Dimensions are not supplied for these items as they are, without exception, highly fragmentary.
241 86 of these glass bangle fragments were recorded in **4048**.
242 SAg.17.1.4409 (bulk find).
243 SAg.15.1.4048.F228.
244 SAg.15.1.4048.F77.
245 SAg.15.1.4048.F98.
246 SAg.15.1.4048.F221.
247 SAg.15.1.4048.F199.
248 SAg.15.1.4048.F234.
249 SAg.15.1.4075.F171.

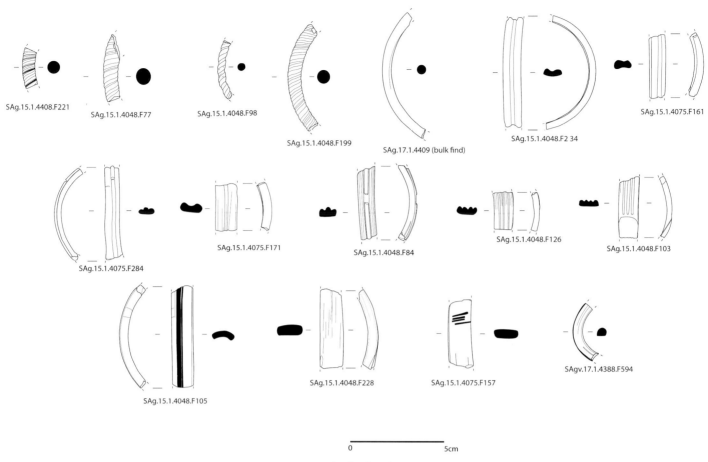

Fig. 86. Glass bangles.

glass (Fig. 86, SAg.15.1.4048.F126),[250] and with three grooves and a rounded rectangular section in a reddish-brown translucent fabric (Fig. 86, SAg.15.1.4048.F103),[251] the latter preserving a seam join.

Bangles with applied decoration, typically in the form of threads which protrude from the core, appear in monochrome and polychrome varieties. One monochrome bangle features two grooves and an applied rod, all in a colourless fabric (Fig. 86, SAg.15.1.4075.F284).[252] A polychrome example with two grooves comprises a dark brownish-red core, which appears black, and a raised band of mid-red opaque glass running around the exterior (Fig. 86, SAg.15.1.4048.F84).[253]

In other cases, applied decoration which comprises a series of differently coloured fused rods is flush with the core rod. This is the case with a bangle with a slightly sub-rectangular section, concave on the inside, and very thin red and silver threads running down the centre of a mid to dark-bluish green core, which appears black (Fig. 86, SAg.15.1.4048.F105).[254] Another example features a single groove and a semi-circular section which is concave on the interior (Fig. 86, SAg.15.1.4075.F161).[255] This item is decorated with applied canes in mid-red and cream running around the exterior of a black core. A similar technique may also have been used for the manufacture of rings, as is attested by a poorly preserved example, which may originally have been sub-circular, and which is made up of a thin red cane flush with a black core; this item came from a cleaning layer, so its exact date is uncertain (Fig. 86, 4388.F594).[256]

Evidence for silver stain decoration of bangles is limited to one highly weathered example with a flattened sub-rectangular section (Fig. 86, SAg.15.1.4075.F157).[257] The opaque black glass preserves very slight remnants of painted decoration visible in the form of four slightly diagonal lines running across the surface of the object. Although further details of this item's decoration cannot be discerned, silver staining can generally be dated to the tenth to twelfth centuries; bangles decorated using this technique have been identified in the Metropolitan Museum of Art in New York.[258] In archaeological contexts, examples of silver stain bangles as well as similarly decorated items using other painting techniques and colours are attested at Amorium,[259] Corinth,[260] and many other sites.[261]

250 SAg.15.1.4048.F126.
251 SAg.15.1.4048.F103.
252 SAg.15.1.4075.F284.
253 SAg.15.1.4048.F84.
254 SAg.15.1.4048.F105.
255 SAg.15.1.4075.F161.
256 SAg.17.1.4388.F594.
257 SAg.15.1.4075.F157.
258 Whitehouse, Pilosi, and Wypyski 2000, 93–95, especially 93, figs. 4–5.
259 Gill 2002, 92–98, cat. 489–556, with 109–111, figs. 1/24–1/29; 207–219, cat. 649–768, with 231–233, figs. 2/33–2/37.
260 Davidson 1952, particularly 264–265, cat. 2148–2159.
261 Zanon 2013, 188–189, fig. 5, no. 20 with further references.

Pictorial evidence of the eleventh and twelfth centuries demonstrates that such bangles were worn by women, predominantly individuals of lower social status, either around the wrist or the upper arm.[262] This view is sometimes corroborated by archaeological evidence, particularly from graves, where glass bangles appear in both poorer female burials and the burials of children. Parani hypothesises that the growing popularity of these items in the tenth to twelfth or thirteenth centuries may have partly arisen from a type of female dress with wide 'trumpet-shaped' sleeves, which could be tied back between the shoulders, exposing the arms and granting increased opportunities for display.[263]

Individuals in eight medieval inhumation burials at Aphrodisias were interred wearing glass bangles.[264] On the basis of the available archival data, none of these skeletons can definitely be said to be adults, and five are definitely non-adults.[265] They are generally examples of child graves with substantial quantities of dress accessories. Parani's thesis that glass bangles were worn on upper and lower arms simultaneously is confirmed by the find positions in the tombs. Sometimes they are in combination with iron or copper alloy bangles, and where this is the case the metal tends to be worn at the wrist beneath the glass.

It is worth noting that as glass bangles do not disappear in Turkish-period sites this probably reflects a strong element of cultural continuity in dress amongst the communities of Byzantine- and Turkish-controlled western Anatolia. Indeed, in all probability, some of these bangles were produced while Aphrodisias was still under Byzantine control, and others may have been made in the Turkish period. As a result, the current state of our knowledge does not allow us to pin down the exact date of manufacture in the majority of cases—with the exception, perhaps, of the possible silver stain example, due to the short lifespan of this technique in the tenth to twelfth centuries. At present, the precise place of production of these items is unclear, and it is hoped that future chemical analyses may help to clarify this. However, we may propose that the concentration of many of these bangles in a single Ottoman context (**4048** and its equivalents), as mentioned above, could reflect stockpiling, perhaps as cullet for recycling. Such a hypothesis may be supported by the highly fragmentary state of preservation of almost all of the bangles, which suggests that they were probably not being stored for sale or distribution.

Charms. Two phalli were recovered in late layers. The first was an alabaster phallus, found directly under a wall of *Phase 10*, datable to the classical or late Ottoman period (Pl. 93.D).[266] This apparently circumcised male member, sculpted in the round, is completely straight and appears to be erect. There are no clear signs of breakage on the base. The item appears to have been left deliberately unfinished, which creates a highly veined effect uncharacteristic of classical depictions of phalluses. The function of this item remains obscure. One possibility, based on its shape alone, is that it was a pestle, though it shows no evidence of wear. Alternatively, this may be a highly residual element created in antiquity, perhaps as a visual joke by a junior sculptor. Alabaster is not commonly used in ancient sculpture; this would therefore be perhaps an improbable use of such a material. However, the recovery of this object directly below a subsequent wall may indicate that it formed part of some kind of foundation deposit. Depictions of phalluses are rare though not unknown in Ottoman art, especially manuscript painting of the erotic *bâhnâme* genre.[267] As a result, we cannot exclude that this item is of Turkish date.

A second phallic object is known in the form of a ceramic pendant shaped in the round, with two suspension holes: one in the glans and one at the base, which was made in a red micaceous fabric that could be either of late Roman or medieval manufacture (Pl. 93.E).[268] This object was recovered in a layer dating to *Phase 10* (equal to **4007**). The item is difficult to identify securely in the absence of immediately obvious close parallels from other sites. It can perhaps be connected to an apotropaic function—almost certainly so if it is in fact a residual Roman piece.

Another curious object was a small bird-shaped ceramic whistle in an orangey-red fabric, recovered in a context dating to the early classical Ottoman period (**4255**). The whistle has an aperture in the neck and an air hole near the top of the belly, and still functions effectively, emitting a sharp, shrill sound when blown (Pl. 93.F).[269] While zoomorphic whistles of this period have not been studied in great detail, several whistles in the shape of rams, now held in the Sadberk collection, have been attributed to the fifteenth century and a further example is known from medieval layers (probably eleventh- to thirteen-century) in the old town of Baku.[270] Ceramic whistles in the shape of birds are still produced and sold in the nearby market town of Karacasu; this may therefore represent an ancestor of these modern whistles. Its original use is unclear. It may have been a child's toy, a shepherd's instrument, or some variety of good-luck charm.

Weaponry. A small assemblage of projectile weapons appear throughout the Turkish period; these items may reflect either the insecure and occasionally violent nature of life in medieval and early modern Geyre or hunting as a subsistence activity.[271] These include an iron lozenge-bladed arrowhead with a flaring shoulder and circular tang (Pl. 93.G) which was recovered in a sixteenth-century Ottoman wall collapse; broadly comparable arrows are found in association with Islamic-period coins at

---

262 Parani 2005, 152–153.
263 *Ibid.*, see also Parani 2003, 73–74.
264 Cath.61.01 (Inv.61–92/93), Cath.61.03 (Inv.61–98/99/100/101), Cath.64.29 (not catalogued), Cat.64.41 (Inv.64–397/99), Cath.65.61 (Inv.65–082a-d), Cath.66.86 (Inv.66–356–58), Tet.84.45 (Inv.84–114), Tet.85.71 (Inv.85–026).
265 Tetrapylon: Nbk 246: *Tetrapylon: S I, II* (G. Paul, 1984), 23; Nbk 267: *S Tetrapylon I, II* (G. Paul, 1985), 47. Cathedral: Nbk 4: *Temple of Aphrodite* (E. Ochsenschlager, 1961), 55–56 (Grave A), 60–61 (Grave C); Nbk 31: *Temple of Aphrodite*, 1 (P.W. Pick, 1964), 67 (Tomb B); Nbk 36: *Temple of Aphrodite; N Odeion (Bouleuterion) I*, 1 (A. Özet), 13 (Tomb D); Nbk 44: *Temple of Aphrodite: N Temenos* (A. Kennedy-Cooke et al., 1966), 113 (Tomb D).
266 SAg.15.1.4121.M869 (Inv. 15-72): H: 9.4 cm, ⌀ (base): 3.0 cm.
267 For discussion see Schick 2004, 83–86.
268 SAg.15.1.4077.F320 (Inv. 15-55): H: 6.5 cm, W: 2.8 cm, D: 2.7 cm.
269 SAg.16.1.4255.F424 (Inv. 16-11): H: 2.9 cm, W: 1.85 cm, D: 3.65 cm.
270 Sadberk 1995, 109–9, cat. 1–2; İbrahimov and Farhadoglu 2002, 21, 59.
271 The fact that hunting was practised is demonstrated by the presence of game animal bones, as discussed in Ch. 10 §C.

Sardis,[272] and in a late medieval context on Andros.[273] An iron arrowhead with a leaf-shaped blade, flat section, and circular socket was found in an early Ottoman context (Pl. 93.H).[274] A further arrowhead, this one with a sub-elliptical blade which tapers to a point, a flat section, and a circular tang, was recovered in a late Ottoman alluvial layer (Pl. 93.I).[275] Finally, a single lead musket ball (not illustrated) with a cast-seam was also found in a late Beylik or early Ottoman context.[276] The latest coins in this deposit date to 1429. Since the earliest use of arquebuses by Ottoman armies dates from the first half of the fifteenth century, this is an early example of firearms technology.[277] The musket ball indicates a degree of economic clout in Ottoman Geyre, since it is associated with costly weaponry.

Residual finds. Some items with ritual connotations and probably of Roman imperial date, but found in highly residual contexts also merit mention. A fragment of a miniature terracotta mask or figure was found in a layer dating to the early Beylik period (Pl. 93.J).[278] The face has a round, cherubic profile with puffy cheeks, full, parted lips, and a double chin, which in conjunction with the carefully delineated eyelashes indicates femininity. The mask's concave profile suggest it was mould-pressed. This mask may be of late hellenistic or early Roman date, in line with similar mould-made masks known from Amorium, Tarsus, and elsewhere.[279] Although the purpose of this item is difficult to discern while it is in such a fragmentary state and because it was found in a highly residual context, we might hypothesize a votive function.

A fragment of a miniature Ionic column in a buff ceramic fabric, with a bulging capital and slightly tapering drum, was found in a modern topsoil context (Pl. 93.K)[280] The details of the column and drum are picked out with incised decoration on the obverse, while the reverse is flattened and undecorated. The fabric of this object may indicate an imperial date and suggests the item is of a votive nature.[281] Ionic was the preferred order in Asia Minor for religious settings and for temple constructions, with the exception of the Imperial cult.[282]

Also worthy of mention is a fragment of a mortarium in white Aphrodisian marble, recovered in topsoil (Pl. 93.L).[283] The preserved piece comprises a semi-circular handle with incised geometric decoration in the form of squares bisected by lines running at a 45-degree angle away from the vessel rim. Numerous fragments of similar design, albeit in blue marble, were found in a large rectangular structure of medieval date in the theatre cavea.[284] Pottery associated with this structure may imply a date either in the final centuries of Byzantine rule at Aphrodisias or during the Seljuk period. But the durable nature of these mortaria means they would be suitable for long-term use and an origin as early as late antiquity cannot be excluded.

One other evocative find from a late context, **4281**, is a square ceramic floor tile, broken on one corner. It is incised with three concentric squares bisected at the middle of each side with perpendicular line (Pl. 93.M).[285] The incisions were made before firing. This motif is traditionally associated with the game known as merels or Nine Men's Morris.[286] However, more recent scholarship has underlined that a range of other meanings and uses, including devotional and apotropaic ones, can be linked to this design.[287] It is possible though not proven that this object is highly residual—the tile could be as early as late antique in origin, though it could also be later as this game has a long lifespan—and its presence reflects the use of portable yet durable gaming boards at Aphrodisias, alongside the fixed ones discussed elsewhere in this book (see Ch. 5 §F).

F. CONCLUSIONS (AK & BR)

There is no reason to think that the picture of post-antique settlement uncovered during the excavations in the Place of Palms is exceptional for Aphrodisias, or indeed wider Asia Minor. Where efforts have been taken to systematically record medieval and later field walls and structures at Aphrodisias—as along the line of the Tetrapylon Street in recent excavations—a similar pattern of lively, often intense, post-antique occupation has been identified. Data from Hierapolis, as noted above, show that comparable medieval occupation layers have been identified in areas of that city. One might expect to find similar evidence for medieval settlement at most other large classical cities in Asia Minor, but traditionally the remains of this period, which are often more ephemeral than those of the Roman period, have been poorly recorded, ignored, or removed. The result of this myopic focus on the 'classical' is that our understanding of the transition from the Byzantine to early Turkish period in the old cities of western Asia Minor remains poor.

The Place of Palms never regained its monumental character after the destruction of the seventh century. In the Byzantine period it remained a jumble of ruins surrounding an increasingly stagnant and overgrown pool—it largely returned, in other words, to the marsh it had been prior to the Tiberian period. The key nodal points of Byzantine activity in the city were located elsewhere, including on the summit of the Theatre Hill. The activities that did take place in the former Place of Palms in this period were temporary and utilitarian. Only with the complete

---

272 SAg.15.1.4017.F273 (Inv. 15-47): H: 6.0 cm, W: 1.8 cm, D: 0.5 cm. For Sardis, see Waldbaum 198, 37, cat. 56, with pl. 4.
273 Kontogiannis and Arvaniti 2012, 252, fig. 5.
274 SAg.17.1.4404.F619 (Inv. 17-19): H: 8.2 cm, W: 2.5 cm, D: not available.
275 SAg.15.1.4064.F60 (Inv. 15-17): H: 4.5 cm, W: 1.0 cm, D: 0.4 cm.
276 SAg.17.1.4403.F602 (Inv. 17-11): ø: 1.9 cm.
277 On early arquebuses, see Ágoston 2014, 88–92. They were introduced probably under Mehmed II, whose armies used them at the Battle of Varna in 1444 and in the Battle of Kosovo in 1448.
278 SAg.15.1.4075.F262 (Inv. 15-16): H: 4.5 cm, W: 5.5 cm, D: 3.0 cm.
279 Lightfoot 2012, 234, cat. 3–4 with further references.
280 SAg.17.1.4405.F622 (Inv. 17-17): H: 6.7 cm, W: 1.5 cm, D: 1.0 cm.
281 Elcin Dogan Gürbüzer, personal communication (August 2018).
282 Whereas most of the major cult buildings in Asia Minor had been built prior to Roman rule, and thus relied on the Ionic order, most religious architecture in Asia Minor remained resistant to change through to late antiquity: Yegül and Favro 2019, 630 ff.
283 SAg.16.1.4200.M1247 (Inv. 16-53).

284 Nbk 116: *Theatre: Surface Area VI* (J. Conger, 1971), 26–33.
285 SAg.16.1.4281.F492, h: 21.4 cm w: 20.3 cm d: 5.6 cm.
286 Parlett 1999, 116–119; for a recent synthesis focussing on these boards in Asia Minor see Crist 2020, 344–346.
287 Berger 2004.

silting up of the pool could the space be put to other uses, and this only seems to have occurred in the thirteenth to fourteenth centuries, when the city oscillated between Byzantine, Seljuk, and more local Beylik control. By this date, this was one of the few open areas in the centre of the city, along with the Agora to the north, which was free from substantial ruins; farmers could lay out fields here without having to remove huge quantities of Roman masonry. The sediments that filled the basin of the pool, and the presence of a high water table, would have make the ground suitable for various crops. It is no surprise, therefore, to see a range of plots develop in the area in the later Beylik and early Ottoman periods, each with their own associated dwellings. By the sixteenth century the village that these plots belonged to—'Gerye', later Geyre—seems to have been quite substantial, extending from here, along the Tetrapylon Street to the north, and east across 'Pekmez Hill'. As the fortunes of this settlement declined, after the late sixteenth or early seventeenth century, so the area of the former Place of Palms reverted to more open land-holdings, free of domestic structures. Little changed in this area between the seventeenth and twentieth centuries, with many field walls standing in place throughout this period and up to the start of the recent excavations.

CHAPTER 10

Faunal Remains from the Late Antique to Ottoman Periods

Angela Trentacoste

Faunal remains document over 1500 years of human–animal relationships in the Place of Palms. Zooarchaeological analysis of this material has been able to reveal changing patterns in animal use, from food consumption to tool production, which in turn reflects the changing landscape and nature of the Place of Palms itself. As the first systemic analysis of faunal material from Aphrodisias for the late antique and later periods, this chapter focuses on broad, general patterns of animal exploitation over the long chronological frame represented by the material. This study offers a 'first look' at these topics, since logistical constraints precluded full and detailed analysis of the entirety of the excavated assemblage (see below). The main aims of this initial analysis were better to understand human diet, animal husbandry strategies, and patterns of processing and discard, and to examine how these practices varied through time and between Aphrodisias and other relevant sites. The results of this zooarchaeological analysis are presented in this chapter alongside discussion and suggestion of further directions for future work. Further zooarchaeological research into the assemblage would certainly be fruitful: in particular, the abundant and well-preserved Ottoman materials offer a rare opportunity to investigate a period and region under-represented in the wider literature.

Animal remains were recovered from throughout the fill of the pool, from the earliest deposits of the seventh century AD through to its complete infilling by the thirteenth or fourteenth century, as well as from the levels of the Ottoman village which came to occupy the site. These faunal materials were grouped into seven analysis groups to facilitate diachronic and spatial comparisons (Table 14). Materials from within and outside the pool were considered separately on account of the different taphonomic histories represented by these contexts: remains from within the pool typically represented dumping events, while those from other contexts derived from various fills and occupation-related accumulations. Most of the remains in the assemblage derived from the late antique, classical Ottoman, and late Ottoman periods; consequently these phases are discussed in the most detail. After introducing the materials and methods, this chapter presents the results of the quantitative zooarchaeological analysis, followed by interpretations and a discussion with broader contextualisation of the assemblage.

A. MATERIALS AND METHODS

Faunal remains from the Place of Palms were hand-collected during excavation between 2012 and 2017, and then recorded over a two-week period on site during the 2018 post-excavation season. Bulk samples taken for flotation[1] also yielded tiny faunal remains. Heavy fractions from these samples were washed over a 2 mm mesh and scanned for the presence/absence of mammals, birds, fish, reptiles/amphibians, and eggshell.

Considering the quantity of hand-collected animal remains and the limited time and availability of osteological reference material in the field, a targeted, diagnostic-zone recording protocol was employed.[2] This protocol was designed to sub-sample the assemblage vertically, recording a limited, pre-selected suite of elements from as many contexts as possible, in order to provide a first look at the faunal material and general spatial and diachronic patterns within the assemblage. Materials were recorded as encountered: logistical constraints precluded laying out all materials from contemporaneous contexts. Consequently, bone groups and articulating remains distributed across several crates or contexts may not have been identified as such. It was decided to approach the assemblage from bottom to top, beginning with the earlier, late antique contexts from the bottom of the pool and progressing to Ottoman levels. As a result, not all classical Ottoman and late Ottoman materials were examined. It should also be noted that this study also does not include faunal material from excavations prior to 2012 in the area of the Place of Palms, even though these produced faunal material. Cursory examination of remains from earlier excavations yielded animals not identified in this analysis, for example several well-preserved *Camelus* bones from the fill of the pool excavated in 1990.[3]

Details on the recording methodology and recorded data are given in online Supplement 1.[4] In brief, all specimens were examined, but only a subset was recorded: (1) those containing one or more of the predefined diagnostic zones, and (2) individual specimens of special interest.[5] Diagnostic zones included upper and lower canines, premolars, and molars; proximal and distal articulations of the long bones; ischium (Z1) and ilium (Z2) of the pelvis; articulations of the ulna, calcaneum, and

---

1 See Ch. 4 §J.
2 Quantification methods based on diagnostic zones or distinct skeletal elements aim to record and count a pre-determined list of skeletal parts. Such approaches can better control for specimen interdependence and aggregation, improve the comparability of recorded material, and simplify calculation of element distribution. See Watson 1979.
3 A complete metacarpal and fragments of a proximal ulna and distal tibia from the 1990 excavations, PTE 1–90.
4 Supplemental files are available via the Oxford University Research Archive: https://doi.org/10.5287/bodleian:ORJB5yRq0
5 For example rare taxa, pathological specimens, worked bone, etc.

Table 14. Analysis groups used in the study of faunal remains.

Period	Analysis Group	Description	Excavation Phases	Context types represented in the zooarchaeological analysis
Imperial to late antique	A	First- to fifth-century AD levels from outside the pool	Phase 1	Planting trenches
Late antique	B1	Late fifth- to early sixth-century AD levels from outside the pool	Phase 2	Ring drain deposits, construction and level fills, planting trenches
	B2	Seventh-century AD pool deposits	Phase 3	First and second pool clearance deposits, first phase of sedimentation
Byzantine	C	Eighth- to twelfth-century AD pool deposits	Phase 4	Pool deposits, siltation layers
Seljuk–Beylik	D	Thirteenth- to late fourteenth-century AD pool and drain deposits	Phases 5–6	Pool and ring drain deposits
Classical Ottoman	E	Village deposits from the fifteenth- to seventeenth-century period	Phases 8–9	Accumulation
Late Ottoman	F	Village deposits from the first phase in the seventeenth- to twentieth-century period	Phases 10	Accumulation

phalanges; articulation (Z1) and neck (Z2) of the scapula; astragalus; horncores/antlers; and cranial zygomaticus. In order to be counted, more than 50% of the specific zone needed to be present, or a complete transverse section of horn cores/antlers. Pigs were recorded without distinction between wild and domestic types, with a note added if they appeared large enough to represent wild boar. Sheep and goat were distinguished following the criteria in Zeder and Lapham 2010 and Zeder and Pilaar 2010, and equids were identified on the basis of enamel folds.[6] The presence of ribs and vertebrae was noted by context according to size classes (large, medium, small mammal). Shells were counted based on presence of an umbo (bivalves) or apex (gastropods). Measurements were taken following von den Driesch 1976 and Payne and Bull 1988. Tooth-wear stages followed Grant for cattle and pigs and Payne for sheep/goat,[7] with mandibles assigned to age groups based on Payne 1973 and O'Connor 2003. Bone fusion was investigated through early, middle, and late fusion groups following Silver 1969 for cattle and equids, Zeder 2006 for sheep/goats, and Zeder, Lemoine, and Payne 2015 for pigs.[8] Skeletal element abundance was quantified using the minimum number of elements (MNE) to calculate the minimum animal units (MAU) represented by different body parts.[9]

Only specimens with diagnostic zones were included in quantitative analyses; material of interest without zones was considered qualitatively. Relative proportions were only routinely calculated for samples with more than 50 specimens; consequently, most analyses consider abundance counts rather than percentages. Specimens recorded as fusing or fused/fusing were grouped with fused during analysis. Figures and summary tables for body part distribution only depict fourth deciduous premolars (dP4) and molars (M); full results are available in the online supplements (see below). Animal size and shape was evaluated using scatterplots of different measurements. For pigs, Log Standard Index (LSI) values[10] were calculated in order to compare *Sus* biometric data from Aphrodisias with those of Ottoman pigs from Kaman-Kalehöyük in central Anatolia.[11] LSI values were calculated following the standards in Hongo 1997. Equid measurements were compared to those from the area of the Harbour of Theodosius in Istanbul[12] and Johnstone's analysis of equids throughout the Roman world.[13] Equid withers heights were estimated using the multiplication factors from May (1985).[14]

B. RESULTS

Original data and large metadata/summary tables are presented in the online supplements.[15] Supplement 2 contains the complete faunal assemblage in tabular format, including measurements. Body part distribution for the main taxa with MNE and MAU counts is presented in Supplements 3–5. Bone fusion is quantified in Supplements 6–9. Figures and selected tables are presented in this volume. Table 15 lists the analysis groups used, and presents the number of specimens with diagnostic zones for each.

---

6 Davis 1980.
7 Grant 1982; Payne 1973.
8 To produce the early, middle, and late fusion groups corresponding to the following ages: Cattle = <18 months, 24–42 months, 42–48 months. Equids = <20 months (early), 36+ months (late). Sheep/goats (based on the fusion sequence for goats) = <12 months, 12–30 months, 30–48+ months. Pigs = <18 months, 18–48 months, 48–60 months.
9 Following Binford 1984.
10 See Meadow 1999.
11 Hongo 1997. LSI values for measurements from pigs were calculated using the same standard as at Kaman-Kalehöyük (published in Hongo 1997).
12 Onar *et al.* 2015.
13 Johnstone 2004.
14 Cited in Johnstone 2004, 156—with the following factors: metacarpal, 6.102; metatarsal, 5.239; radius, 4.111.
15 https://doi.org/10.5287/bodleian:ORJB5yRq0

Table 15. Hand-collected faunal remains: number of quantified specimens by period.

Contribution of antlers to taxon total in parentheses. See text for additional taxa recovered from flotation samples.

	Imperial to late antique	Late antique		Byzantine	Seljuk–Beylik	Classical Ottoman	Late Ottoman
	A	B1	B2	C	D	E	F
	Outside the pool	Outside the pool	Pool deposits	Pool deposits	Pool and ring drain	Village deposits	Village deposits
Cattle (*Bos taurus*)	11	64	178	36	39	116	199
Sheep/goat	5	45	42	21	13	342	231
Sheep (*Ovis aries*)		3	6	2	3	33	23
Goat (*Capra hircus*)	2	23	26	12	6	92	92
Pig (*Sus* sp.)		1	32	16	14	39	110
Pig – large-sized			1		3	10	35
Horse (*Equus caballus*)		1	18	4		9	13
Donkey (*Equus asinus*)		8				9	16
Equid (*Equus* sp.)		7	20	5	1	6	10
Equid – donkey-sized		2	32	8	6	21	40
Equid – horse-sized	1	2	32	12		16	9
Dog (*Canis familiaris*)		4	11	2		20	21
Dog/fox			1	1			
Fox (*Vulpes vulpes*)					1		
Canid							1
Chicken (*Gallus gallus*)		2	4	2			
Red deer (*Cervus eleaphus*)				1 (1)	1	2 (1)	3
Red deer/Fallow deer			1 (1)			2	2 (1)
Fallow deer (*Dama dama*)		2 (1)	5 (2)	2 (1)	3 (1)	10 (1)	14 (1)
Roe deer (*Capreolus capreolus*)			1				
Hare (*Lepus* sp.)		1	1				
Mole rat (*Nannospalax* sp.)							1
Large rodent (Rodentia)							1
Pond turtle (*Mauremys* sp.)			6	4	2	2	
Tortoise/turtle (Testudinidae)		2	16	25	2	1	7
Cattle/deer						1	1
Large mammal			1			1	1
Total	19	167	433	152	94	732	830

Preservation and modifications

Hand collection can lead to the under-representation of small taxa and parts of the skeleton, which may be missed during excavation.[16] Comparison of adjacent small and large bones (for example distal radius, third carpal, proximal metacarpal) demonstrated an under-representation of some small elements (for example loose teeth), with the effect more pronounced in sheep/goat and pigs than in cattle. The presence of bones of microfauna and small livestock (pisiforms, phalanges, unfused metapodial condyles) recovered in flotation samples demonstrated these small and delicate elements did indeed survive in at least some levels, but were not routinely recovered. Small livestock (that is sheep/goat and pigs, especially immature ani-

16 Payne 1972; 1975.

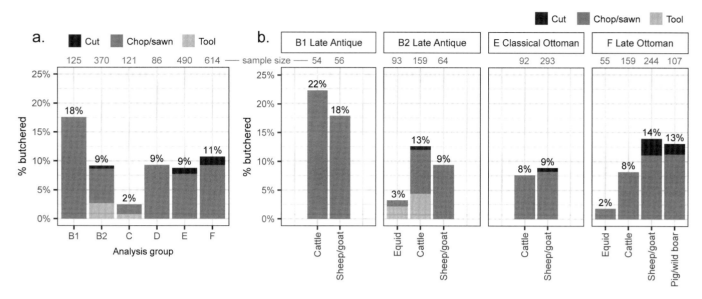

Fig. 87. Proportion of butchered post-cranial bones: (a) by analysis group and (b) for the main taxa (excluding taxa with a zone count less than 50).

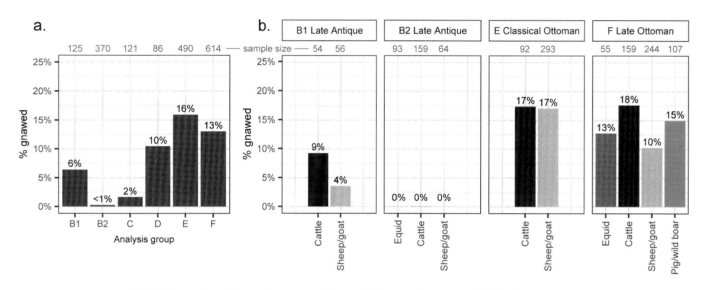

Fig. 88. Proportion of gnawed post-cranial bones: (a) by analysis group and (b) for the main taxa (excluding taxa with a zone count less than 50).

mals) and microfauna should therefore be considered somewhat under-represented compared to cattle and equids in this study.

Natural and anthropogenic modifications to post-cranial bones varied across analysis groups. Surface preservation was generally good, without significant degradation from weathering or root etching (Pl. 94.A).[17] Late antique and Byzantine pool deposits (groups B2 and C) contained the lowest proportions of butchered remains, while late antique contexts from outside the pool (B1) produced the highest percentage of butchered bones (excluding tools, Fig. 87, a). Chop marks were the most common type of butchery modification in all periods. Cut marks were generally rare, albeit more common in later periods. The distribution of cut marks also changed through time (Fig. 87, b). Most bones with cut marks from Ottoman and Late Ottoman phases were from sheep/goat, while no cut marks were identified on sheep/goat bones from earlier periods. Evidence of sawing was recorded on a few late antique goat horn cores and a fallow deer antler from the Seljuk–Beylik period. Seventeen large mammal bones from late antique and Byzantine pool deposits (including six without quantified zones) had wear or modifications suggesting their use as tools (see below).

All periods produced quantified post-cranial specimens with evidence of carnivore gnawing, most likely the result of action by dogs or other canids. Gnawed material was rare in late antique and Byzantine pool deposits (Fig. 88, a). Ottoman and Seljuk–Beylik contexts produced a higher proportion of gnawed bones than earlier periods. This higher prevalence of gnawing was noted across all taxa represented by >50 quantified specimens (Fig. 88, b). When concentrated on the epiphyses of

17 >98% of counted bones in each analysis group had their surface preservation recorded as 'good'.

a. Relative proportions of main taxa

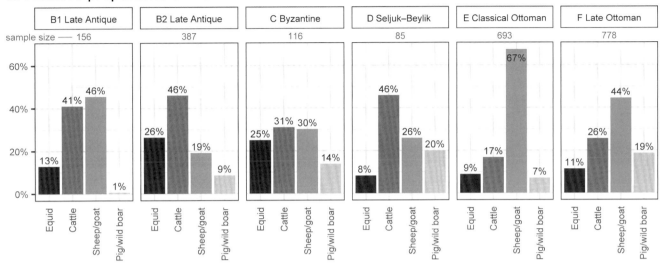

b. Maximum MAU

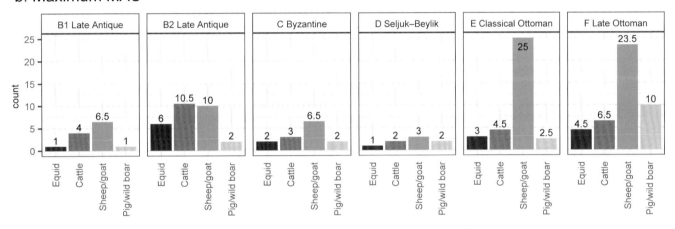

Fig. 89. (a) Relative proportions of main taxa (as a percentage of zone counts) and (b) maximum MAU counts.

long bones, carnivore gnawing can selectively destroy the diagnostic zone registered by the recording protocol, leading to an under-representation of such specimens in the recorded assemblage.[18] This phenomenon was observed in classical Ottoman and late Ottoman contexts,[19] which contained numerous sheep/goat limb bone shaft fragments whose epiphyses (and counted diagnostic zones) had been gnawed away. No instances of burning were recorded.

Counted specimens and taxonomic abundance

Classical Ottoman (E) and late Ottoman (F) features contained the majority of quantified remains, representing 30% and 34% of the counted assemblage, followed by late antique deposits (B1 and B2, 25%). Fewer specimens were associated with other analysis groups, which together represented 11% of the quanti-

---

18 Particularly in the case of less dense parts of the skeleton. See Lyman 1994.
19 Contexts 4015, 4075, 4095, 4808.

fied assemblage. Imperial to late antique contexts from outside the pool (A) produced only a few remains, all from common domestic livestock; these are not discussed in further detail because of the small sample size (n=19).

Domestic taxa comprised the majority of remains in all periods. Goat remains were more abundant than those of sheep in all analysis groups, including when horn cores were excluded. The relative abundance of remains from large pigs increased through time, representing around a fifth of *Sus* bones in the classical Ottoman period (E) and rising to a quarter in late Ottoman times (F). The large size of many pig remains indicates that a significant portion of the pigs in these later periods were wild boar rather than domestic pigs. This distinction is investigated in the sub-section on pigs below.

The relationship between the remains of the main taxa varied through time and between analysis groups (Fig. 89, a). Cattle, sheep/goat and equids comprised the majority of the late antique samples (B1 and B2), with bones from large livestock, especially equids, more abundant within the pool (B2). Byzantine pool deposits (C) produced a different profile, with similar percentages of equids and pigs, but fewer cattle and more sheep/

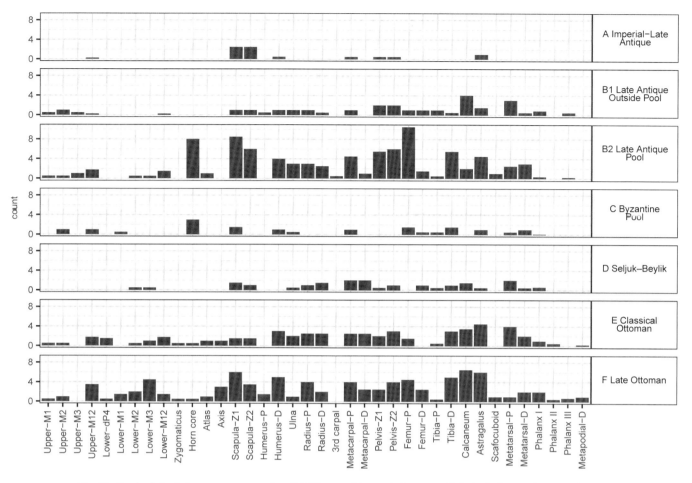

Fig. 90. Cattle skeletal element representation (MAU counts) by analysis group. Only includes specimens with zones. Excludes unfused epiphyses. P: proximal. D: distal. See online Supplement 3 for counts.

goat remains. Sheep/goat remains predominated in classical Ottoman (E) and late Ottoman (F) groups, followed by modest proportions of cattle. Excluding pig bones, which may derive from wild or domestic animals, wild mammals accounted for 5% or fewer of counted specimens in all analysis groups. Turtles were especially abundant in pool deposits, especially in Byzantine levels (C).

Consideration of maximum MAU values for the main taxa (Fig. 89, b), which mitigate specimen interdependence better than NISP, produced taxonomic profiles in which small livestock were better represented. In MAU profiles, sheep/goat was the predominant taxon for all analysis groups except the late antique pool group (B2), and a greater proportion of pigs was documented in the late Ottoman group F. This increase in the relative abundance of small livestock in MAU profiles compared to those from specimen counts is a common occurrence in hand-collected assemblages, where the bones of large animals are more easily identified during excavation, thus recovering a greater proportion of the large mammal skeleton. It suggests that sheep/goat may have been more abundant than suggested by NISP values, which probably under-represent smaller taxa.

Cattle

Body parts and butchery. Cattle element representation varied across the analysis groups, partially as a function of sample size (Fig. 90). Late antique deposits from outside the pool (B1) produced elements from across the skeleton, but with a slight predominance of bones from the hind limb. Within late antique pool deposits (B2), the proximal femur, scapula, and horn cores were the most abundant elements; the proximal parts of the humerus and tibia, as well as the distal femur, were notably under-represented compared to adjacent elements. Their under-representation may reflect differential transport of a portion of the upper limb; however the low density of these elements will also have influenced their survival and chance of being registered by the recording protocol. Cranial elements with the exception of horn cores were also under-represented in late antique pool deposits (B2), as were phalanges. Element distribution was more even across Ottoman analysis groups (E and F), which also contained a greater abundance of teeth.

Butchery marks, predominantly from cleavers, were distributed across the cattle skeleton. Sample sizes were too small to confidently identify more detailed patterns. Longitudinally-split metapodials were recorded in late Ottoman (F) and late antique contexts, with a small concentration in late antique pool depos-

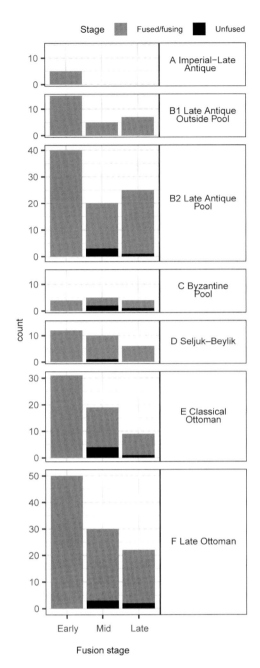

Fig. 91. Counts of fused and unfused cattle bones by analysis group. Only includes specimens with zones. Excludes unfused epiphyses. See online Supplement 6 for counts.

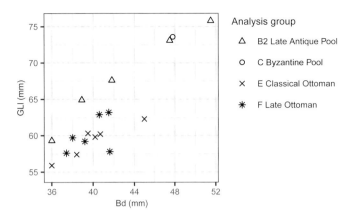

Fig. 92. Cattle astragalus distal breadth (Bd) versus greatest lateral length (GLl).

its (B2, n=8). Articulating elements were noted in groups B2 (horn cores, pelvis and femur, radius and ulna), C (mandible), D (metacarpal and first phalanges), and F (second and third phalanges).[20] A partial cranium was recovered from Byzantine pool deposits (C).[21]

Age and sex. Cattle mandibles provided little information on diachronic trends in cattle age (Table 16), although they demonstrated a predominance of adult and elderly animals in Late

20 From contexts B2: **1016**, **4448**, **4466**. C: **4329**. D: **4419**. F: **4048**.
21 Context **4329**: 17.1.4329.F706.

Ottoman times (F). Bone fusion indicated that the majority of cattle in all periods were slaughtered in adulthood after 48 months (Fig. 91). Unfused bones in the middle fusion group demonstrated that a small but significant proportion of cattle was slaughtered between 24 and 48 months in groups B2–E, suggesting a proportion of cattle culled for meat. Unfused bones under *c.* 18 months of age were absent from all periods. No neonatal cattle bones were recorded. No bones were attributed as male or female based on morphology.

Pathologies. All groups except C produced cattle bones with pathological conditions. The most common conditions encountered were articular exostosis and ossification of muscle attachments on metapodials, tarsals, and phalanges. Metapodials with splayed condyles were noted in groups D–F. These phenomena are associated with stress and old age, and suggest that these individuals were working cattle.[22]

Size. Measurements from cattle astragali illustrated diachronic variation in cattle size (Fig. 92). The late antique and Byzantine periods produced some very large astragali measurements, which were absent from Ottoman levels. Late antique measurements also follow a different regression line from the Ottoman knucklebones, implying a change in animal shape through time. Late antique cattle astragali have a greater lateral length (GLl), and are thus taller and more gracile than Ottoman astragali of a similar width. If the largest late antique individuals are interpreted as males (bulls or oxen), the three smaller late antique astragali could be suggestive of female cattle. As the Ottoman cattle are comparable to these smaller individuals, it may suggest Ottoman assemblages were composed primarily of female individuals.

Sheep and goats

Goats were more common than sheep across all periods. The ratio of goats to sheep in late antiquity (B1 and B2) was approximately 5:1 (n=58); for the classical Ottoman period the ratio

22 De Cupere *et al.* 2000.

Table 16. Mandible wear stages for cattle following O'Connor (1988).

		Wear stage					
Analysis group		Neonatal	Juvenile	Immature	Sub-adult	Adult	Elderly
C	Byzantine – pool deposits		1				
D	Seljuk–Beylik – pool and ring drain deposits					1	
E	Classical Ottoman – village layers				1		
F	Late Ottoman – village layers					3	2

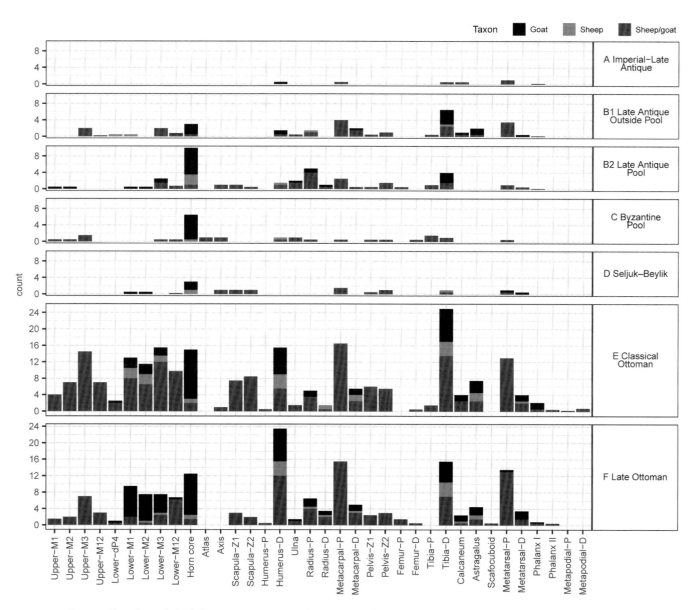

Fig. 93. Sheep/goat skeletal element representation (MAU counts) by analysis group. Only includes specimens with zones. Excludes unfused epiphyses. P: proximal. D: distal. See online Supplement 3 for counts.

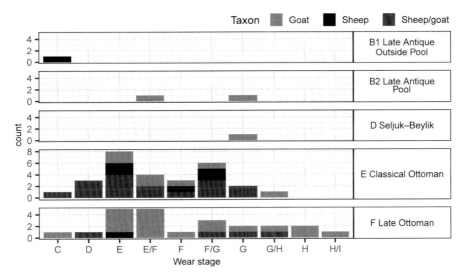

Fig. 94. Counts of mandible wear stages for sheep/goat by analysis group. Wear stages follow Payne 1973.

was 3:1 (n=125), and in late Ottoman times the ratio was 4:1 (n=115).

Body parts and butchery. The distribution of different skeletal parts (Fig. 93) did not demonstrate significant differences in the treatment of the sheep versus goat carcass. The distribution of sheep, goat, and sheep/goat bones was comparable in the classical and late Ottoman analysis groups (E and F). The most abundant elements in these groups were the distal parts of the tibia and humerus, proximal metapodials, and horn cores. Teeth were also well represented, especially in classical Ottoman levels (E). As stated above, Ottoman groups E and F were significantly affected by carnivore gnawing. As anticipated, the densest parts of the post-cranial skeleton, which better survive ravaging by carnivores, were amongst the best represented elements. Within the Ottoman periods, butchery marks clustered on horn cores, humeri, tibiae, and metapodials. Humerus fragments were chopped across the mid-shaft and on the medial side of the distal epiphyses. Metapodials (Pl. 94.B) and tibiae were chopped across their shaft. The position of these modifications demonstrates segmentation of the limbs and removal of the foot at the mid-metapodial. Considering the under-representation of distal metapodials and phalanges, elements robust enough to survive some gnawing, these elements appear to have been disposed of elsewhere.

Distal tibiae and horn cores were also relatively abundant in late antique, Byzantine, and Seljuk–Beylik layers (B1, B2, C, and D). Although the sample was small, materials from within the late antique pool (B2) differed somewhat from other analysis groups, due to a relatively greater abundance of sheep/goat radii and the predominance of horn core fragments. Butchery marks in groups A–B2 clustered on goat horn cores. Marks were predominantly chop marks from heavy tools, but four goat horn core fragments from B1 had saw marks. A set of joining goat horn cores was noted in Byzantine pool deposits (C).

Age and sex. Mandible wear stages for sheep/goat teeth provided little information on culling patterns in between late antique and Seljuk–Beylik periods (Fig. 94, Table 17). More data were available for the classical Ottoman and late Ottoman periods, which demonstrated peaks at wear stages E and F (2–4 years) and F/G (3–5 years), with approximately half of the attributed mandibles documented at wear stages E–F. Compared to the classical Ottoman period, the late Ottoman group contained more mandibles at wear stage E/F (2–4 years) as well as in the advanced wear stags of H and H/I (6+ years). No clear trends were identifiable in sheep versus goat mandible wear stages. This age distribution indicates a management strategy focused on secondary products (milk, fleece, hair) alongside mutton and goat, rather than kid or lamb, meat.

Fig. 95 presents counts of fused and unfused sheep/goat post-cranial bones. Classical Ottoman and late Ottoman analysis groups produced enough material (n>50) to merit consideration of relative proportions of unfused bones at different fusion stages. In classical Ottoman deposits, 0% of early-fusing bones (<12 months) and 11% of middle-fusing bones (12–30 months) were unfused; the late-fusing group (30–48+ months) did not contain enough bones to consider percentages, but unfused bones made up a significant part of the sample. Late Ottoman levels produced similar results: 2% of early-fusing bones and 14% of the middle group were unfused; again, the late group did not have enough material to calculate percentages, but unfused bones constituted about half of the elements in the group. One perinatal sheep/goat bone was recovered from Byzantine pool deposits (C), suggesting lambing in the vicinity during this period.

Compared to mortality profiles based on tooth wear, results from bone fusion under-represented immature individuals in classical Ottoman and late Ottoman samples. Mandible wear stages suggested approximately a third or more of the population was culled before three years: a proportion significantly higher than the 11–14% registered by bones in the middle-fusing group. Young individuals also appeared to be under-represented amongst early-fusing and late-fusing bones, although in these categories the discrepancy was less pronounced. Considering the evidence for gnawing in classical Ottoman and late

Table 17. Mandible wear stages for sheep/goat following Payne (1973).

	Analysis group	Taxon	C	D	E	E/F	F	F/G	G	G/H	H/I	Total
B1	Late antique – ring drain and outside pool	Sheep	1									1
B2	Late antique – pool deposits	Goat				1			1			2
D	Seljuk–Beylik – pool and ring drain deposits	Goat							1			1
E	Classical Ottoman – village layers	Goat			2	2	1	1		1		7
		Sheep			2		1	2				5
		Sheep/goat	1	3	4	?	1	3	?			16
F	Late Ottoman – village layers	Goat	1		4	5	1	2		1	1	18
		Sheep			1							1
		Sheep/goat		1				1	1	1		4

Ottoman contexts, the under-representation of unfused bones in the middle fusing group may result from selective destruction of unfused bones by carnivore-mediated attrition. Alternatively, it may suggest individuals assigned to mandible wear stages E and E/F were slaughtered in the later part of the middle-fusing period, that is late in their third year, when more bones from the middle-fusing group would be in the process of fusing or fully fused.

Pathologies. The most common pathology noted for sheep/goats was the occurrence of coral-roots: abnormal growth of the tooth root thought to result from low-grade infection or inflammation, possibly related to penetration of the alveolus by foreign material.[23] This condition was noted on sheep/goat and goat, but not sheep, teeth in groups B1 (n=2), C (n=1), E (n=13, 7% of counted teeth/jaws), F (n=5, 5% of counted teeth/jaws). Ante-mortem loss of the first molar, probably resulting from an infection of the alveolous was recorded for a classical Ottoman (E) sheep/goat mandible. No post-cranial pathologies were recorded.

Size. Measurements from post-cranial bones demonstrated an increase in the size of sheep and goats between late antique and Ottoman times. Amongst post-cranial bones, the distal tibia produced the most measurements (Fig. 96), which illustrated the presence of few large individuals in late antique contexts, with a general size increase in the later periods. Based on these data, both sheep and goat appear to have experienced this size increase. Other analysis groups produced too few measurements to consider in detail; these fell within the range of late antique and Ottoman values.

Wild and domestic pigs

Body parts and butchery. Fig. 97 presents MAU counts of *Sus* skeletal elements by analysis group. Sample sizes were low in all periods. As in other taxa, the low presence of less-dense and late-fusing bones, like the proximal humerus and femur, probably results from carnivore attrition. Large *Sus* specimens had a similar distribution to other pig bones. Butchery marks encountered on *Sus* bones were predominantly chop marks. In late antique and Byzantine deposits (B1, B2, and C) butchery modifications were noted on the pelvis, ulna, and atlas; in classical Ottoman and late Ottoman levels (E and F) chop marks were especially common on the humerus. Their location on the midshaft suggests the chopping action was used to split the bone transversally. A similar pattern was noted on two tibiae, and two fourth metacarpals were chopped at their distal end. As was observed for sheep/goat butchery within the Ottoman analysis groups, removal of the foot at the lower part of the metapodial may account for the low representation of distal metapodials and phalanges. Articulating fragments of a maxilla and mandible were recorded amongst materials from the late antique pool deposits (B2), and sets of joining third and fourth metacarpals were noted in both Ottoman and Late Ottoman analysis groups (E and F).[24]

Age and sex. Mandible wear stages for pigs were only available for a few individuals (Table 18), which indicated that pigs were culled across a range of ages. Local breeding is indicated by two perinatal pig bones recovered from the late antique pool deposits (B2). Two bones from an infant individual were also found. Analysis of bone fusion (Fig. 98) suggested that pigs under 48 months of age were relatively more abundant in late antique compared to Ottoman levels. In the latter of these periods, bone fusion suggests that most pigs were killed after the early fusing stage but before the end of the late stage. In wild boar this

---

23 Baker and Brothwell 1980, 151; Chilardi and Viglio 2010.

24 B2: **1016**. E: **4076**. F: **4048**.

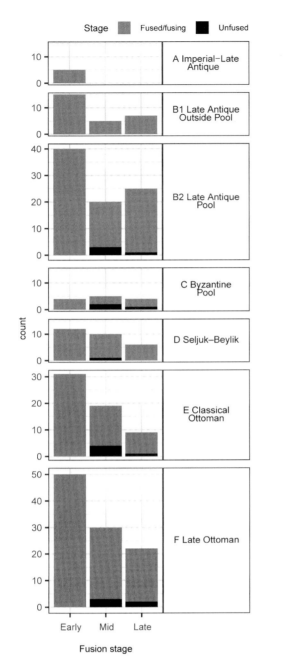

Fig. 95. Counts of fused and unfused sheep/goat bones by analysis group. Only includes specimens with zones. Excludes unfused epiphyses. See online Supplement 7 for counts.

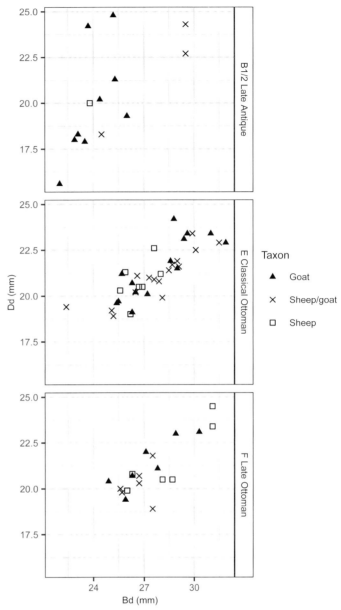

Fig. 96. Sheep/goat tibia distal breadth (Bd) versus distal depth (Dd).

period would represent about 18–60 months of age, while in modern pigs it would align with 12–42 months.[25]

Male pig canines were more abundant than those of females in all periods (Table 19). However, female alveoli without teeth were as abundant as those of males or more so. Preferential recovery of the large male canine would contribute to this phenomenon, privileging the collection of larger male teeth.

Pathologies. Exostosis was recorded on two tibiae and an ulna from the classical Ottoman period (E). On one of the tibiae this extra bone growth occurred at mid-shaft and was suggestive

25 Zeder, Lemoine, and Payne 2015.

of an infection, possibly after a break. On the ulna, exostosis covered the surface. Evidence of an abscess was recorded on a mandible from the late Ottoman analysis group (F).

Size. Few measurements were recorded on pig bones other than in Ottoman analysis groups E and F. Comparison of measurements from the distal humerus and mandibular third molar (Fig. 99) documented the presence of very large *Sus* in classical Ottoman and late Ottoman times, potentially from wild boar. LSI length and width values from late Ottoman pigs (F) produced a bi-modal distribution with two groups (Figs 100 and 101): a group of large-bodied pigs with LSI values >0.06 and a

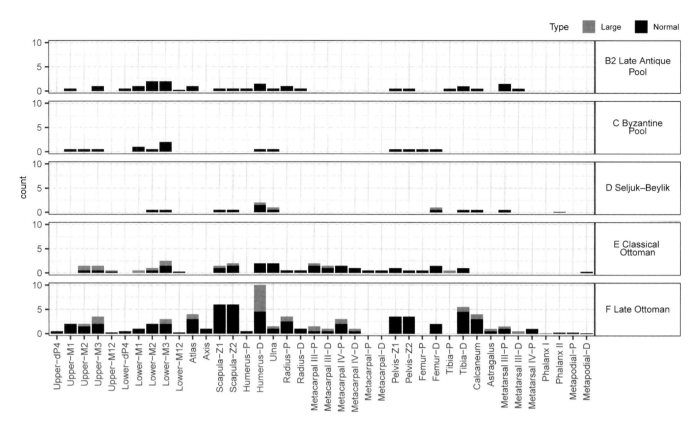

Fig. 97. Pig skeletal element representation (MAU counts) by analysis group. Pig 'types' indicate those specimens perceived as especially large. Only includes specimens with zones. Excludes unfused epiphyses. P: proximal. D: distal. See online Supplement 4 for counts.

Table 18. Mandible wear stages for pigs following O'Connor (1988).

	Analysis group	Mandible wear stage			
		Immature	Sub-adult	Adult I (M3 at wear stage a)	Adult II (M3 at wear stages b–g)
B2	Late antique pool deposits	1		1	2
C	Byzantine – pool deposits			2	1
D	Seljuk–Beylik – pool and ring drain deposits				1
E	Classical Ottoman – village layers			1	
F	Late Ottoman – village layers		2	1	

group of smaller pigs with LSI values <0.04. The classical Ottoman period (E) yielded fewer LSI values, but their distribution also suggested the presence of two pig populations, with greater separation between the groups. In contrast, length and breadth LSI values from Kaman-Kalehöyük had a normal distribution, comprising a main group alongside a few outliers. Mean LSI values were also lower at Kaman-Kalehöyük for both lengths (–0.11) and widths (–0.09), compared to classical Ottoman (E) (lengths: 0.001, widths: –0.021) and late Ottoman (F) (lengths: 0.054, widths: 0.022) values.

The classical Ottoman group (E) included large LSI values (>0.06) comparable with large outliers from Kaman-Kalehöyük, suggesting that these values represent wild boar. The smaller classical Ottoman LSI values (<–0.02) overlapped with the main population from Kaman-Kalehöyük, indicating that these lower values represent domestic pigs. These results broadly concur with the visual impression that large, wild-size remains accounted for about a fifth of pig bones from group E (see Table 15).

LSI values from the late Ottoman period (F), were larger than those from group E, both in terms of means and minimum values. As in the classical Ottoman period (E), LSI values greater than 0.06 may represent wild boar; if so, wild boar would account for a larger proportion of pig remains in the late Ottoman (F) compared to the classical Ottoman (E) times. Late Ottoman LSI values less than 0.06 are difficult to interpret. Length values

Table 19. Distribution of male and female pig canines and alveoli by analysis group.

	Analysis group	Element	Teeth Female	Teeth Male	Alveoli without teeth Female	Alveoli without teeth Male	Total Female	Total Male
B1	Late antique – ring drain and outside pool	Lower	1				1	
B2	Late antique – pool deposits	Lower		1	1	1	1	2
B2		Upper		2				2
C	Byzantine – pool deposits	Lower		3				3
C		Upper		1				1
D	Seljuk–Beylik – pool and ring drain deposits	Lower		1	1		1	1
E	Classical Ottoman – village layers	Lower		1				1
F	Late Ottoman – village layers	Lower	4	4	1		5	4
F		Upper	1	4			1	4

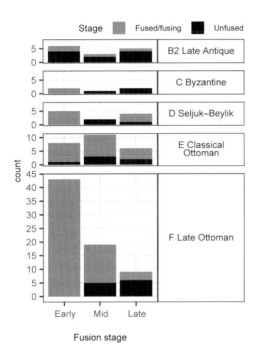

Fig. 98. Counts of fused and unfused pig bones by analysis group. Only includes specimens with zones. Excludes unfused epiphyses. See online Supplement 8 for counts.

from late Ottoman times exceeded all comparative values from Kaman-Kalehöyük, while width values overlapped with the upper range of domestic pigs from Kaman-Kalehöyük. In this context, late Ottoman (F) LSI values less than 0.06 may represent large domestic pigs, for example a modern large-bodied type of the nineteenth or twentieth century, greater in size than earlier Ottoman pigs from the fifteenth to seventeenth centuries. Alternatively, LSI values may reflect a mix of large domestic pigs and small wild boar (for example, males and females).

Equids

Equid remains were recorded in all analysis groups. Equid specimens included horse, donkey, and large and small equids not attributed to either species (which may include mules and hinnies). Based on tooth enamel patterns, donkeys were identified in groups B1, E, and F, and horses were noted in groups B2, C, E, and F. Counted specimens demonstrated that donkeys and small equids were more abundant than horses and large equids in groups B1, D, E and F; large equids predominated in Late Antique and Byzantine pool deposits (B2 and C).

Body parts and butchery. Small equid and donkey remains were more abundant than large equids in the classical and late Ottoman analysis groups (Fig. 102). All parts of the skeleton were represented, with a preponderance of lower third molars in Late Ottoman levels (F). A large metapodial from this period was split longitudinally at its distal end. Late Ottoman deposits also produced two bone groups probably from a single small equid,[26] and classical Ottoman levels (E) yielded an articulating metapodial and first phalanx.[27] In contrast, large equids were relatively more abundant in the late antique pool deposits (B2), with the radius and tibia particularly well represented and mandibular teeth rare (save two loose undetermined premolars/molars). Five sets of articulating remains, predominantly metapodials and phalanges, but also an elbow joint, were found in late antique contexts within the pool (B2).[28] A partial horse cranium and a chopped equid bone were also found in group B2.[29] Additional joins may be present in the assemblage, but logistical constraints precluded further reconstruction of bone groups.

Compared to the other taxa in the late antique pool deposits (B2), equids produced the greatest quantity of joining bones and the fewest butchery modifications. These characteristics, as well as the general impression of the material, suggested a high-

26 Context **4048**.
27 Context **4076**.
28 Contexts **4448**, **4466**, **4482**. Also a joining right and left maxilla from **4328** (17.1.4328.F968; LAB 2017.455).
29 17.1.4328.F968; LAB 2017.455.

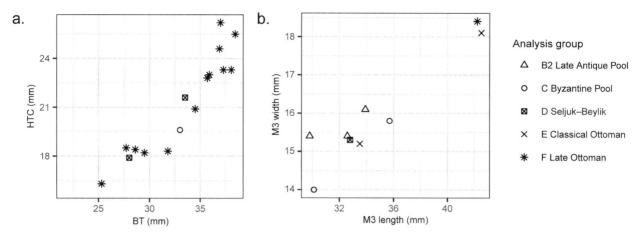

Fig. 99. Pig (a) humerus HTC (diameter of the trochlea at the central constriction) versus BT (breadth of the trochlea) and (b) mandibular third molar width (M3W) versus length (M3L).

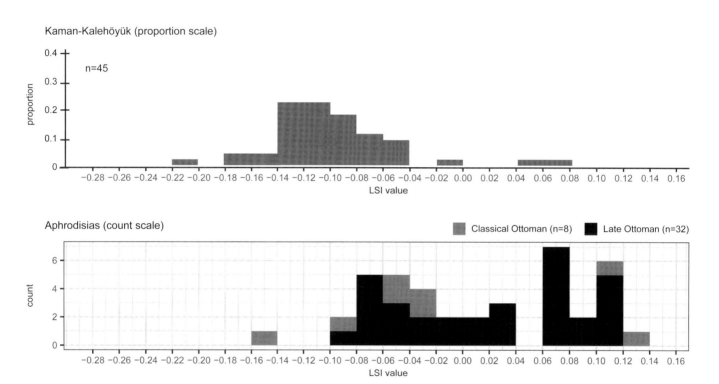

Fig. 100. Pig LSI breadth values from Ottoman Kaman-Kalehöyük and Aphrodisias.

er degree of interdependence between equid remains than for other livestock. Measurements from equid bones demonstrated right/left pairs of very similar size (see below). Consideration of right- and left-sided bones indicated a minimum of seven equids in these late antique pool deposits (quantified using the right proximal radius). These individuals included two horses, three large equids (horses or hybrids), and two small equids (probably donkeys). Considering the under-representation of cranial—especially mandibular—fragments compared to other elements, and presence of a chop mark, it appears that the equid carcasses were processed to some degree before deposition in the pool as bone groups or loose elements, rather than complete skeletons in articulation.

Age and sex. The recovery of deciduous equid teeth from Late Ottoman deposits (F) demonstrated the presence of juvenile equids. Bone fusion (Fig. 103) also demonstrated the presence of equids that died before 3.5 years of age. Unfused equid bones were also recorded in groups B2 and D. Within the late antique pool contexts (B2), unfused bones accounted for 2% of quantified remains from the early-fusing group; unfused bones from

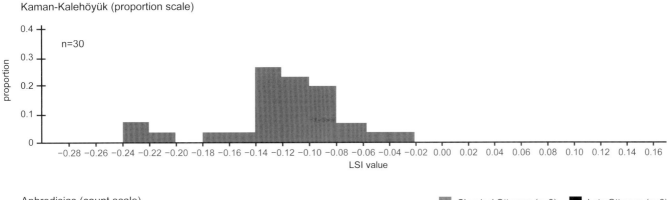

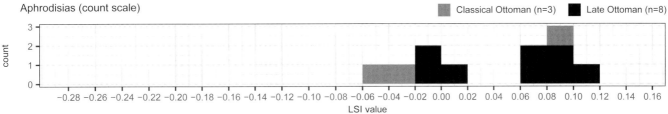

FIg. 101. Pig LSI length values from Ottoman Kaman-Kalehöyük and Aphrodisias.

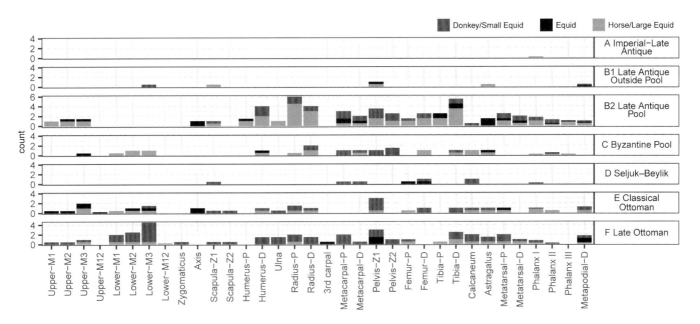

Fig. 102. Equid skeletal element representation (MAU counts) by analysis group. Only includes specimens with zones. Excludes unfused epiphyses. P: proximal. D: distal. See online Supplement 5 for counts.

the late fusing group were also identified. No equid remains were attributed as male or female based on morphology.

Pathologies. Exostosis was recorded on an articulating first and second phalanx from a large equid in B2 and on a pelvis from B1. Late Ottoman levels (F) produced a partial equid cranium with exostosis along the crista temporalis and frontal linea temporalis, as well as a pelvis with pathological bony growth along the ridge.

Size. Consideration of biometry revealed small equids consistent with measurements from modern donkeys (B2 and D) as well as larger individuals comparable to horses and mules (A, B2, C, and E) (Fig. 104).[30] Measurements did not suggest significant diachronic changes in equid size; the sample, however, was small.

Withers heights were calculated from long bones where the greatest length could be measured (Table 20). All heights were below the 14 hands 2 inches height used to distinguish ponies

30 Compared to data from Johnstone 2004. Roman horse withers max 154.3 cm.

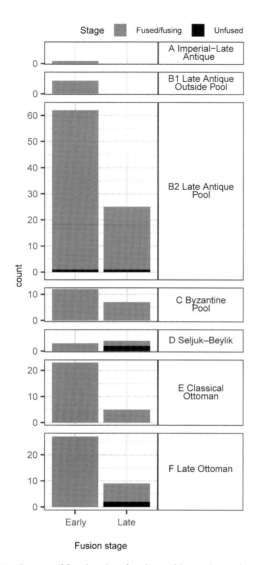

Fig. 103. Counts of fused and unfused equid bones by analysis group. Only includes specimens with zones. Excludes unfused epiphyses. See online Supplement 9 for counts.

from modern standard horses. Late antique measurements all fall within the range of withers heights documented in Johnston's study of Roman equids.[31] The tallest individual from Aphrodisias (146.7 cm) lies at the upper end of the spectrum of Roman horse withers heights, and well above the regional averages for Britain, Egypt, Gaul, the Danube/Balkans, the Rhineland, and Italy (131.2–138.5 cm), though still within the upper size range of large donkeys. Mules were generally taller, with average withers heights between 136.2–144.4 cm, and they could reach withers heights over 160 cm. Excluding the smallest equids—which are probably donkeys judging by their slenderness and size (for examples, see Table 20)—the majority of withers height reconstructions demonstrate animals of medium size, comparable in stature and slenderness with the horses recovered from the Harbour of Theodosius in Istanbul. There, 20 horses from the Byzantine period (fourth to fifteenth centuries AD) produced withers height calculations between 140 cm and 152 cm.[32]

Other mammals

Canids. Canid remains were identified as dogs, foxes, and intermediate canids. Counted specimens from canids represented a low but constant presence across analysis groups, without major inter-period differences. All canid post-cranial bones were fused; and a deciduous premolar from late antique pool deposits (B2) was the only evidence for a juvenile animal. The presence of these animals is further attested by abundant evidence for gnawing, particularly in later periods. A dog humerus from group E was chopped on its distal end.

The only pathology noted was the antemortem loss of a fourth premolar from a dog mandible with crowded teeth (group B1). Measurements from dog bones represented individuals of different sizes, although the sample was too small to identify diachronic trends.

Cervids. Deer remains were present in low proportions in all analysis groups. Fallow deer were the most common species; remains of red deer (groups C–F) and roe deer (group B2) were also present. Antler fragments accounted for a significant proportion of cervid remains (see Table 15). Fallow or red deer antlers from groups B1, C, D, and F contained chop and saw marks, modifications indicative of antler working. Butchered post-cranial bones from fallow deer were recorded in groups D–F. Some of the antlers were shed, including an especially large red deer specimen from the Byzantine analysis group (C).[33] Antlers were thus collected as well as acquired from hunted animals. Joining bones from a fallow deer ankle were recovered from the late antique pool deposits (B2).[34]

Small mammals. Individual hare bones were identified in groups B2 and C. The late Ottoman group (F) produced the cranium and an incisor from a mole rat, most likely the intrusive remains of this tunnelling rodent.

Birds

Chicken bones were recorded in groups B1, B2, and C. Leg bones were more common than wing bones. A tibiotarsus from group B2 contained medullary bone, evidence of an egg-laying hen. A tarsometarus from group C had a spur scar. No modifications were noted on the remains of domestic fowl. Like other taxa, measurements are reported in Supplement 2.

---

31 Johnstone 2004.
32 Onar *et al.* 2015.
33 Find: 17.1.4442.F760; LAB 2017.251. Approximate breadth and depth of shed articular surface: 61 × 70+ mm.
34 Context 4466; 17.1.4442.F760; LAB 2017.251.

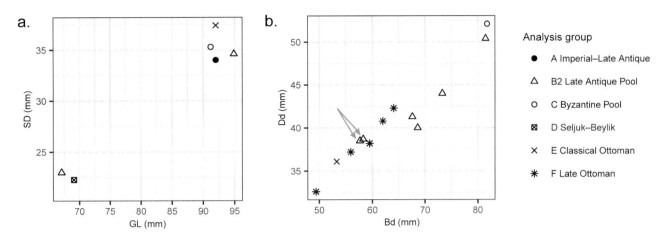

Fig. 104. Equid (a) first phalanx greatest length (GL) versus smallest breadth of the diaphysis (SD), and (b) tibia distal breadth (Bd) versus distal depth (Dd). Grey arrows identify bones potentially from the same individual.

Table 20. Equid withers height estimations and metapodial slenderness indices based on greatest length (GL), proximal breadth (Bp), smallest breadth of the diaphysis (SD), and distal breath (Bd).

	Recorded Taxon	Element	GL	Withers height		Size class	Bp	SD	Bd	Metapodial slenderness indices			Probable id
										Bp/GL *100	SD/GL *100	Bd/GL *100	
			mm	mm	hands		mm	mm	mm				
	Small Equid	Metacarpal	202	1232.6	12	small	41.2	26.1	37.5	20.4	12.9	18.6	Donkey?
	Large Equid	Metacarpal	231	1409.6	14	average	47.9	33.2	46.3	20.7	14.4	20.0	
	Small Equid	Metatarsal	230	1205.0	12	very small/small	38.6		35.2	16.8		15.3	Donkey?
	Small Equid	Metatarsal	254	1330.7	13	smaller than average	35.3	33.2			13.1		Horse?
B	Equid	Metatarsal	270	1414.5	14	average		30.4	44.1		11.3	16.3	
	Large Equid	Metatarsal	280	1466.9	14 2in	larger than average			51.2			18.3	
	Equus caballus	Radius	337	1385.4	13 2in	average		35.9					
	Large Equid	Radius	338.5	1393.6	13 3in	average		39.4	79.8				
	Large Equid	Radius	343	1410.1	14	average			73.8				
D	Small Equid	Metacarpal	180	1098.4	10 3in	very small		23.8	33.8		13.2	18.8	Donkey?
F	Small Equid	Metatarsal	216	1131.6	11 1in	very small	34.3	21.6	30.1	15.9	10.0	13.9	Donkey?

Reptiles

Turtle/tortoise remains were recorded in all analysis groups, although they were most abundant in the Byzantine pool deposits (C). Both pond turtles and tortoises are common on the site today. All remains identified to genus-level were attributed to *Mauremys* sp., Balkan or Caspian pond turtle. With the exception of a humerus from group C, all specimens were carapace or plastron fragments. Curved breaks around the plastron bridge, demonstrating breakage of fresh bone, were recorded on 6 fragments from group B2 and 1 from group C. In prehistoric contexts similar fractures have been interpreted as anthropogenic breakage, produced by laying the turtle on its side and striking the opposite side at the bridge.[35] This action would split the ventral and dorsal shells. However, storks (*Ciconia* sp.), eagle

35 Biton *et al.* 2017.

Table 21. Marine shells by analysis group.

Diagnostic zones only.

	Imperial to late antique	Late antique		Byzantine	Late Ottoman
	A	B1	B2	C	F
Oyster (*Ostrea edulis*)	1	1			
Banded dye murex (*Hexaplex trunculus*)			2	1	
European thorny oyster (*Spondylus gaederopus*)			2	1	1
Atlantic triton (*Charonia variegata*)			1	1	

owl (*Bubo bubo*), and other large birds will also eat *Mauremys* turtles,[36] and if the turtles were dropped or cracked against hard surfaces by birds, similar breakage patterns may, in theory, be produced. Tortoises may also be present in the assemblages, especially in later periods; the lack of reference material on site did not allow finer taxonomic identification.

Marine shells

Four species of marine mollusc were documented in the assemblage (Table 21). Shells were more common in earlier periods compared to Ottoman times. Oyster, thorny oyster, and banded murex are edible species, while the Atlantic triton is not. The remains of edible taxa may have been imported foods. Oysters were widely transported in antiquity, and could survive for days or longer out of water if properly maintained.[37] Shells could also represent decorative or even souvenir items. The Atlantic triton in particular is a large and attractive shell, which can be modified to produce a trumpet noise (giving the 'triton's trumpet' shell its common name). One *Charonia* sp. fragment was recovered from the late fifth-century layer dumped to raise the ground level around the pool (see Ch. 4 §K), and another from the first clearance deposit in the pool.

Bone tools

Seventeen large mammal bones were modified and worn in a manner suggestive of their use as tools (Pl. 94.B). These were recovered from late antique and Byzantine pool deposits (B2 and C),[38] which included 9 cattle metacarpals and 3 metatarsals, 2 unidentified limb shaft fragments and a scapula from indeterminate large mammals, as well as an equid metacarpal and distal radius. These bones had been shaped into rough points or spat-

36 Bertolero and Busack 2017.
37 Marzano 2013, 191–192.
38 Late antique pool deposits (B2): 12 from the first phase of deposits within the pool (**4328**, **4466**, **4482**); 4 from the second phase of deposits within the pool (**4448**, **5028**). Byzantine pool deposits (C): 1 from Byzantine occupation levels (**4442**).

ula-like forms, and they had wear across the cortical surface of the bone. In some specimens this wear was particularly focused on the area of the epiphysis, causing erosion of the entire section (for example, Pl. 94.B, b). While the all-over wear resembles sea-worn material tumbled in the waves, no other elements demonstrated this type of wear or lesser degrees of it, and most examples had been shaped prior to wear. Such modifications therefore appear to result from anthropogenic rather than natural factors. No exact parallels from other sites were identified, but the wear pattern would be consistent with a burnishing or polishing function, perhaps associated with leather or perhaps even stone working (if used with an abrasive).[39]

Animal remains from bulk flotation samples

Table 22 reports the presence of different fauna from flotation samples from 29 floated contexts by analysis group. Bulk samples recovered taxa and elements absent from the hand-collected assemblage, most notably the remains of fish (mostly spines, some small vertebrae), small birds, eggshell, and small rodents. Frog/toad bones were particularly abundant. Rodents included small Murinae (rats/mice) and Arvicolinae (vole). Small elements like loose teeth, unfused epiphyses, phalanges, and pisiforms from medium domestic mammals (sheep/goat, pigs, and dogs) were registered in approximately a third of scanned contexts, demonstrating the survival of many small elements missed during hand collection.

Samples from the ring drain were particularly rich in faunal remains, especially contexts **8007** and **1043**. Of the 28 contexts considered, 10 contexts from phases A–B2 contained the remains of small fish, including a small cyprinid pharyngeal (**4448**). Such bones indicate that small fish lived in the pool during antiquity. It is easy to see how small freshwater fish could have entered the pool or its drains through the aqueduct and pipeline system that fed it, especially if the second-century aqueduct that drew water from the Timeles river was connected to the pool at some point—a situation which was almost certain in the case of the late antique renovations of the water supply of the pool. Compared to the quantity of amphibian remains fish

39 For similar examples see Semeyov 1964; Struckmeyer 2011.

Table 22. Presence of faunal material in flotation heavy fractions by analysis group.

	Analysis group	Total number of contexts scanned	Number of scanned contexts with material type					
			Med/large mammal	Micro-mammal	Amphibian/reptile	Bird	Fish	Eggshell	Snails
A	Imperial – late antique – outside the pool	5	5	5	5	5	5	1	
B1	Late antique – ring drain and outside pool	12	12	5	6	6	4	4	
B2	Late antique – pool deposits	6	4	3	6		2		
C	Byzantine – pool deposits	1						1	1
D	Seljuk–Beylik – pool and ring drain deposits	1	1						
E	Classical Ottoman – village layers	3	3	1	2			3	
F	Late Ottoman – village layers	1	1		1			1	

were much rarer, possibly as a function of a lower population density, or because frogs/toads were more likely to live and die within the protected environment of the ring drain, rather than the open area of the pool itself. It is also possible that some fish remains represent food debris that washed into the pool/drain, similar to some of the botanical material found in the same contexts.[40] However the very small size of the fish remains points to a natural rather than culinary origin.

C. DISCUSSION

Imperial to late antique levels outside the pool (A)

This period encompassed the construction and life of the pool in the Place of Palms. Few remains dating to the imperial to late antique period deposits outside the pool (A) were recovered, all of which represented common domestic livestock. These remains represent loose rubbish incorporated into the planting trenches around the pool. Nothing unusual was noted in the sample, and little else can be said about this collection of material.

Late antique levels outside (B1) and within (B2) the pool

With the decline of the late antique city, the pool was no longer maintained, and, from the seventh century AD, it became pro-

gressively filled by dumped materials and sedimentation. Environmental analysis[41] has suggested that until this point, the pool was fed by clean slow-moving water, and it was vegetated although not necessarily overgrown. Dumps of rubble and burnt timber found on the floor of the pool dated to the seventh century signal a change in the nature of the space. The assemblage from within the pool (B2) included a mix of non-food and food debris representing bone groups/parts of carcasses, consumption refuse, bone tools, raw materials, and local fauna. Articulating remains from cattle and equids were particularly abundant in late antique pool deposits (B2). These carcass segments were not wholly processed and probably still held together by soft tissue when they came to rest in the basin. Considering the lack of gnawed bones, much of this material was probably deposited directly into the pool as part of the seventh-century AD clearance deposits in the lowest levels. The materials in these deposits attest to the destruction of parts of the Place of Palms, and finds of weapons suggest that this end resulted from a violent raid.[42] To what extent the animal remains in these deposits were linked with this particular destruction event is unclear, but the recovery of a stirrup from the same layers suggests that animals may have participated in these events directly as military mounts.[43]

Large livestock, especially equids (which were not typically consumed as food), presented challenges in terms of disposal and may have been dumped into the pool out of convenience. Urban re-organisation in other Roman and late antique cities in Asia Minor offered similar opportunities to dispose of such material. Partial or complete cattle, equid, and camel carcasses have

40 Ch. 4 §J.
41 Robinson 2016.
42 See Ch. 8 §F.
43 Penn, Russell, and Wilson 2021.

been identified at Sagalassos, Pessinus, and Amorium, dumped in abandoned buildings and incorporated into the construction fills of structures.[44] Similarly at Ephesos, a deposit rich in equid remains (though not complete carcasses), interpreted as the debris from a slaughterhouse, was used as a fill in Hanghaus 1 following a fourth-century AD earthquake.[45]

Cattle body part distribution in B2 demonstrated an abundance of horn cores, alongside some emphasis on meaty body parts: the femur and scapula were especially abundant, while low-utility parts like teeth and phalanges were less common. The remains of meaty bones may represent consumption debris, or skeletal parts discarded at early stage of butchery, for example if the carcass was portioned into smaller, more manageable cuts of beef that were transported elsewhere.[46] An interesting point of comparison is offered by a dump of dining debris from the eastern suburb of Sagalassos, interpreted as the remains of meals held in a communal dining space.[47] The heavily butchered/processed bones were predominantly from cattle, resembling 'soup kitchen' deposits found in the western Empire.[48] Several body parts were conspicuously rare, leading to the conclusion that butchery took place elsewhere and certain portions of beef were brought to the dining building. The head of the femur—the most abundant cattle element in late antique pool deposits (B2) in the Place of Palms—was one of the under-represented body parts. Meaty cattle bones from B2 may represent off-cuts removed as an early part of the butchery process. The similar abundance of meaty equid parts, a butchery mark on an equid bone, and similar use of equid bones as tools demonstrates that equids were treated similar to cattle, suggesting that butchers also processed non-food animals. The under-representation of cattle and equid foot bones and teeth suggests that the head (save for the horn cores) and feet, probably with hides attached, were sent elsewhere.

Horn cores, especially those from goats, were abundant in group B2. The predominance of horn cores amongst sheep/goat bones, including several with chop marks, suggests horn removal for craft purposes. As at Sagalassos, this activity was focused on goat horns, although other horn types were also used.[49] Deer antlers from late antique pool deposits presented similar modifications and cattle horn cores were also abundant. Considering the modifications to turtle plastrons, turtle shell or leather may also have been exploited, although their use as an opportunistic food source cannot be excluded.[50] While bone wasters and off-cuts from bone working are richly documented at Pergamon[51] and Sagalassos,[52] there is no evidence for bone object production in the Place of Palms. Rather, the materials point from the late antique pool point to a cache or dump of material resulting from carcass, hide, and horn processing. The rough bone tools from B2 also suggest some type of industrial activity, even if its nature remains unclear. Intriguingly, the closest parallels for their shape and wear are prehistoric lissoirs used in hide working.[53] This activity may have been pursued by a slaughterhouse, butcher, and/or craftsperson involved in transforming carcasses—especially of cattle and equids, but also of other domestic and possibly wild animals—into meat, hide, horn, and possibly other products. Blades recovered from the lowest layers of the pool may also relate to this type of activity, and finds from these levels include small quantities of industrial waste.[54] The location of this activity cannot be deduced from the material, but the pool would have provided a useful water source for various stages in this process.

Late antique animal remains from outside the pool (B1)—that is those recovered from the ring drain, construction/level fills, and planting trenches—had different taphonomic histories from those within the pool (B2), with greater exposure to carnivores and more evidence of butchery. Alongside horn cores, dense post-cranial elements from cattle and sheep/goat, like phalanges and metapodials, were slightly better represented, probably due the better survival of robust remains in deposits subject to re-working and exposure to carnivores.

Overall, the faunal remains from these late antique contexts provide evidence for a diet in which beef was the most important meat source, and butchery was conducted primarily with large cleavers. Goats constituted the majority of sheep/goat herds, suggesting management in rough environments, like the elevated slopes around the valley, while lower fertile areas were reserved for arable agriculture and cattle pasture.[55] Cattle, sheep, goat, and chickens were slaughtered for meat as well as being kept for secondary products. Cattle provided traction power, their role as draught animals evidenced by the presence of large individuals and lower-limb pathologies. Large equids were more common than small equids/donkeys, and their carcasses were exploited for tools and probably hide as well. Red deer, fallow deer, hare, and wild boar were hunted or trapped, for instance in the mixed pine-oak forests of the surrounding upland regions[56] or more locally to protect crops. Such upland environments may also have provided pannage for swine herding.[57] The pool itself was home to pond turtles, numerous frogs/toads, and small fish. Dogs and probably foxes scavenged in the city's streets and alleys. Marine shells, and probably other marine foods, were imported, if rarely. Oysters, a popular food throughout the Roman world,[58] and triton trumpet shell were also identified at Sagalassos.[59] Excavations at Sagalassos also produced fish imported from as far away as Egypt,[60] and fish consumption is also well documented at Ephesos.[61] The rarity of

44 De Cupere 1994; De Cupere *et al.* 2003; Ioannidou 2012.
45 Forstenpointner 1996.
46 Similarly, the under-representation of heads and feet at Ephesos was interpreted as the result of slaughter and butchery happening elsewhere: Forstenpointner, Galik, and Weissengruber 2008.
47 De Cupere *et al.* 2015.
48 van Mensch 1974; Johnstone and Albarella 2002, 228; Maltby 2007. Although similar materials may result from marrow processing and glue production: Groot 2016, 184–185.
49 De Cupere 2001, 156–7.
50 As documented in Roman Portugal: Nabais, Boneta, and Soares 2019.
51 Von den Driesch and Boessneck 1982.
52 De Cupere, Van Neer, and Lentacker 1993; De Cupere 2001.

53 See note 44.
54 See Ch. 8 §D.
55 As suggested by landscape survey: Adkins 2012, 102–106.
56 See Kaniewski *et al.* 2007; Adkins 2012.
57 For example as at Sagalassos: Vanhaverbeke *et al.* 2011; Frémondeau *et al.* 2017.
58 Marzano 2013.
59 De Cupere 2001.
60 Arndt *et al.* 2003.
61 Forstenpointner, Galik, and Weissengruber 2008.

fish remains at Aphrodisias certainly relates to the limited use of sieving and flotation,[62] precluding assessment of fish consumption practices.

Together, animal remains from the two late antique assemblages from the Place of Palms provide an indication of animal exploitation and the kinds of local fauna present at Aphrodisias. Considering the central, monumental context of the excavations and the nature of the assemblage, the extent to which these reflect wider, domestic patterns of urban consumption practices has yet to be determined. Activities associated with the monumental centre of Aphrodisias and particular discard strategies related to the changing nature of this space could reflect very different patterns from those practiced in domestic areas of the same city. At Sagalassos, different areas produced distinct taxon frequencies, with a higher proportion of sheep/goat remains associated with houses compared to communal dining activities.[63] Assemblages with large proportions of cattle bones (>40% of counted specimens) are relatively rare in Anatolian contexts of Roman to Byzantine date outside Sagalassos and Aphrodisias (Table 23): the former records high percentages of cattle in the fourth and fifth centuries AD, but sheep/goat clearly predominate during the sixth to seventh centuries AD. In contrast, animal remains from houses at Ephesos (fifth–seventh centuries AD) demonstrate high levels of pork consumption. If faunal remains from the Place of Palms do provide an indication of wider dietary patterns, the focus on cattle would suggest that relatively large-scale and centralised animal processing and good pasture availability continued after the fourth century AD.[64]

Byzantine pool deposits (C)

Similarities between materials from late antique and Byzantine pool deposits suggested a degree of mixing across these levels. Body part distribution was comparable in analysis groups B2 and C, and a rough bone tool from Byzantine levels was probably recontextualized from the larger group of bone implements found in lower levels of B2. The ramp added at the north-eastern curve of the pool (see Ch. 8 §A) is interpreted as a means of allowing livestock to drink in the pool, and animals, especially large animals like cattle, wading through the shallow water of the pool could have contributed to the mixing of materials from earlier levels.

Turtles were particularly abundant in these deposits. This collection of chelonian carapace and plastron fragments represents individuals that lived in the fresh-water habitat furnished by the overgrown pool.[65] A break on one fragment suggests that turtles may have continued to be exploited as in the previous period, either for food (for humans or birds) or turtle shell. *Mauremys* turtles have also been documented at late antique and early medieval Tarsus, although an explanation for their presence in the assemblage (for example, for food, craft material, natural fauna) was not offered.[66]

Byzantine levels contained relatively more sheep/goat remains than the late antique pool deposits (B2); maximum MAU counts were similar to late antique levels outside the pool (B1), albeit with more pig remains. The extent to which this reflects real changes in meat diet at Aphrodisias in the Byzantine period is difficult to determine on account of the relatively modest size of the assemblage, potential for mixing within the pool, and particular character of deposits in B2, which reflect a mix of food and non-food debris. Sheep/goat remains typically dominate Byzantine assemblages from Anatolia, for example at Amorium, Tarsus, and Beşik Tepe,[67] although cattle continued to make an important contribution to central inland sites like Pessinus and Çadır Höyük (Table 23).

Seljuk and early Beylik use of the space (D)

Seljuk and Beylik levels produced relatively few remains. The frequency of gnawed bones was considerably higher than earlier deposits, indicating a change in disposal practices with greater exposure of rubbish to scavengers. Gnawing probably contributes to the high proportion of cattle in the assemblage, with greater destruction of the remains of smaller taxa, especially juveniles. Compared to earlier periods, pig bones were more abundant and equid remains relatively rare. However, very large pigs accounted for a higher proportion of *Sus* bones than in previous periods, potentially signalling an increased emphasis on wild boar, rather than domestic pigs, as a food source. Other wild taxa, including turtles, were present in similar proportions to earlier periods. Marine shells, which were found in all previous periods, were absent from group D, indicating a deterioration of coastal links that does not appear to recover: after the Seljuk and early Beylik period marine fauna are represented by a single shell from analysis group F.

Classical (E) and late Ottoman (F) village layers

By the fifteenth century AD the basin of the pool was completely covered by siltation and sediment run-off, and an Ottoman village came to occupy the site. The area remained inhabited, first as a village and then as gardens, until the 1960s, at which point the village of 'Old Geyre' was removed from the archaeological site. Animal remains from analysis groups E and F reflected the different economic, cultural, and environmental situation at Aphrodisias in Ottoman times compared to late antiquity. Gnawed bones were more common than earlier periods, demonstrating the repeated exposure of waste material to scavengers. Sheep/goat were the most abundant domestic taxon by a clear margin, with a notable focus on goats, which are better suited to marginal and degraded landscapes.[68]

---

62   Hand collection at Sagalassos also produced few fish bones; see Van Neer, De Cupere, and Waelkens 1997.
63   De Cupere 2001: 139–140; De Cupere *et al.* 2015.
64   At which point it begins to decline at Sagalassos; see De Cupere 2001.
65   See Robinson 2016.
66   Omar 2017.
67   Pişkin 2016.
68   Lebbie 2004; Rosa García *et al.* 2012.

Table 23. Comparative assemblages: number of identified specimens (NISP) of the main livestock.

Site	Type/area	Period	n	Sheep:goat	Cattle%	Sheep/goat%	Pig%	Reference
Gordion	Rural military settlement	Roman	1069	3.1	12%	62%	26%	Çakırlar and Marston 2017
Sagalassos		Roman	12,058		31%	46%	23%	De Cupere 2001
Ephesos	City – Hanghaus 2: Living Unit 7	Roman	265	0.7	6%	28%	66%	Galik, Forstenpointner, and Weissengruber 2016
Ephesos	City – Hanghaus 2: Living Unit 6	Roman	704	1.4	9%	24%	67%	Galik, Forstenpointner, and Weissengruber 2014
Ephesos	City – Hanghaus 2: Living Unit 1 (samples A and B)	Roman	1345	1.4	13%	25%	61%	Forstenpointner, Weissengruber, and Galik 2002
Sagalassos	City – eastern suburbium	Roman	1800	0.8	59%	14%	27%	De Cupere et al. 2015
Pessinus	City – houses (Trench K)	Roman	3053		28%	64%	8%	De Cupere 1995; de Cupere 1994
Limyra	City – southern city – domestic	Roman	125	0.2	14%	54%	33%	Galik, Forstenpointner, and Weissengruber 2012
Sagalassos		Roman	18,267		52%	25%	23%	De Cupere 2001
Tarsus - Gözlüküle Mound	Town	Byzantine	182	1	5%	80%	15%	Omar 2017
Aphrodisias	Place of Palms – B1	Late antique	136	0.1	47%	52%	1%	
Aphrodisias	Place of Palms – B2	Late antique	285	0.2	62%	26%	12%	
Ephesos	City – Vedius Gymnasium: canal fill (sample C)	Late antique	1519	1.2	15%	42%	43%	Forstenpointner, Galik, and Weissengruber 2008
Sagalassos		Late antique	15,673		25%	48%	26%	De Cupere 2001
Ephesos	City – Hanghaus 2: Living Unit 6	Late antique	557	1.8	5%	46%	49%	Galik, Forstenpointner, and Weissengruber 2014
Limyra	City – domestic	Late antique	286	0.2	21%	52%	27%	Galik, Forstenpointner, and Weissengruber 2012
Amorium	City – lower city enclosure area	Late antique	266	1.9	8%	89%	3%	Ioannidou 2012
Aphrodisias	Place of Palms – C	Byzantine	86	0.2	42%	40%	19%	
Amorium	City – lower city enclosure area	Byzantine	317	1.4	5%	74%	21%	Ioannidou 2012
Çadır Höyük	Village	Byzantine	343	1.6	68%	14%	18%	Arbuckle 2009
Beşik-Tepe	Occupation/settlement	Byzantine	79	4	25%	46%	29%	Von den Driesch and Boessneck 1982
Pessinus	City – 'acropolis'	Byzantine	500		62%	20%	18%	Ervynck, Van Neer, and de Cupere 2003; Ervynck, De Cupere, and Van Neer 1993
Amorium	City – lower city enclosure area	Byzantine	153	2	7%	85%	8%	Silibolatlaz-Baykara 2012
Amorium	City – lower city enclosure area	Byzantine	468	2.1	15%	73%	12%	Ioannidou 2012
Tarsus – Gözlüküle Mound	Town	Medieval	2219	2.6	11%	86%	4%	Omar 2017
Gritille	Rural settlement	Medieval	7832	0.5	21%	32%	48%	Stein 1998
Horum Höyük	Village	Medieval	135	1.6	20%	67%	13%	Bartosiewicz 2005

Site	Type/area	Period	n	Sheep:goat	Cattle%	Sheep/goat%	Pig%	Reference
Tilbeşar	Fortified town	Medieval	736	1.4	17%	73%	10%	Mashkour and Berthon 2008
Korucutepe	Selçuk settlement	Medieval	998	0.6	53%	46%	1%	Boessneck and von den Driesch 1975
Aphrodisias	Place of Palms – D	Medieval	87	0.2	41%	40%	18%	
Kaman-Kalehöyük	Settlement	Ottoman	502	2.2	40%	51%	9%	Hongo 1997
Aphrodisias	Place of Palms – E	Classical Ottoman	632	0.4	18%	74%	8%	
Aphrodisias	Place of Palms – F	Late Ottoman	690	0.3	29%	50%	21%	

Over-exploitation of the landscape after AD 650 has been documented elsewhere in Anatolia, leading to the spread of forest steppe environments as a result of human impact on the landscape.[69] The reduction in numbers of cattle and large equids—livestock requiring significant amounts of drinking water and fodder—may also reflect adaptations to a less forested environment. Pig remains were rare in group E but increased in abundance in group F. Wild boar, identified based on size comparisons and impressions during recording, accounted for a quarter or more of pig bones/teeth. LSI analysis suggested that in the late Ottoman times (F) wild pigs may account for an even higher proportion of the assemblage, closer to half the pig bones. This would put the relative importance of domestic pigs at approximately 6% of the classical Ottoman and c. 8–17% of the late Ottoman assemblage. This adjustment brings the percentages more into line with pig frequencies from Ottoman Hungary, where percentages up to c. 12% of NISP are not uncommon.[70] Slightly higher percentages of pigs are found on urban sites in this area, suggesting a more mixed population from a culinary point of view.

Ottoman sheep/goats and pigs were larger than late antique livestock, while cattle were relatively shorter and more robust. Knives became more important as butchery tools, especially on sheep/goat bones: a reflection of differences in processing style between the centralised operations the late antique city, and the smaller-scale practices of the Ottoman periods. Distinct butchery styles are visible in the removal of the foot at the mid-metapodial. These lower limb sections may have travelled connected to the hide or may simply have been discarded.[71]

Juvenile cattle were consumed for meat. Biometry suggests a change in sex ratios to a population of mostly female animals: cattle of a similar size at Ottoman Kaman-Kalehöyük were also interpreted as cows.[72] Lower limb pathologies continue to suggest use of some cattle for traction. Cows may have been used for agricultural labour, and locally oriented stock economies would promote keeping multi-purpose animals. Goats made up the majority of small livestock herds. Sheep/goats were predominantly killed as adults, suggesting a herding strategy aimed at meat, milk, and hair. The peak at mandible wear stage E/F demonstrates a culling strategy focused on adult animals, around 2–4 years of age, after which milk production decreases.[73] Further thinning of the herd continued after this point, as the hair quality or health of older animals decreased. Low juvenile mortality demonstrates that lambs/kids would be kept alive beyond the first year. This management strategy is similar to that employed for modern hair goats near Sagalassos.[74] There, herders kept herds of about 120 female and 5 male animals, raised for meat, milk, and hair used for rough textiles like tent cloth, sacks and kilim.

The only comparative data for the Ottoman period from Anatolia were furnished by Kaman-Kalehöyük, a sixteenth- to seventeenth-century settlement about 100 km southeast of Ankara (see Fig. 105). As at Aphrodisias, sheep/goat remains were the most abundant, but sheep bones were over twice as common as those from goats. Cattle were relatively more abundant, and while pig remains were present in similar proportions, these derived from domestic animals; wild boar made little contribution to the Kaman-Kalehöyük Ottoman assemblage. Mortality patterns demonstrate greater exploitation of young cattle for meat and as well as lambs/kids. Differences in animal usage between Ottoman Kaman-Kalehöyük and Aphrodisias would be expected to reflect differences in local landscape as well as culinary traditions: traditions influenced by ethnic, religious, and cultural diversity.[75] Dietary practices of non-Muslim inhabitants might explain the continued consumption of pigs in Ottoman periods;[76] however even within Islamic communities, dietary rules may have been treated with flexibility at certain periods and by particular groups of people[77] and wild boar meat may also

69 Kaniewski et al. 2007.
70 Bartosiewicz and Gál 2018.
71 As is the practice of some Islamic butchers in Syria (Loyet 2000). Phalanges were also rare at Caesarea in Palestine, again due to differential transport or discard of ungulate feet (Cope 2002).
72 Hongo 1997.
73 Helmer, Gourichon, and Vila 2007.
74 Beuls et al. 2000.
75 Hongo 1997.
76 As has been argued for Ottoman Hungary: Bartosiewicz and Gál 2003. Pigs also make up a significant portion of the assemblage from seventh- to tenth-century Zeugma: Rousseau, Guintard, and Abadie-Reynal 2008.
77 MacLean and Insoll 2003.

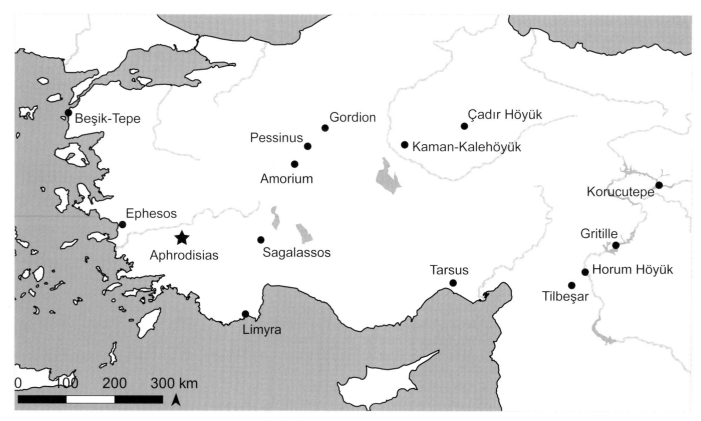

Fig. 105. Location of Aphrodisias and sites with comparative faunal assemblages.

have been treated differently from that of domestic pigs.[78] Such a case is documented in the Rif mountains of Morocco, where some Muslim communities do consume wild boar meat, which is not viewed as falling under the same prohibitions as pork.[79] In certain circumstances, domestic pigs have been similarly treated due to necessity or local tradition.[80] Of course consumption by Christians or other individuals/groups following different dietary guidelines could also contribute—situations probably reflected in the low, but nonetheless persistent, percentages of pig bones found at sites throughout medieval and later Islamic periods.[81]

D. CONCLUSION

Faunal remains from the Place of Palms offer an important perspective on changing patterns of animal usage and discard between late antiquity and the modern period. In all periods animal exploitation was focused on domestic livestock, which were raised for meat and secondary products. Goat-herding had a long history in the area, exploiting rough environments offered by the surrounding landscape. This activity offered material for craft production in the form of horn and hair, as well as a dietary contribution from meat and milk. The monumental pool in the Place of Palms provided a habitat for frogs, turtles, and small fish. Changes in the abundance of livestock bones and their treatment allude to environmental and economic changes over the millennia. If the faunal assemblage is taken to reflect general consumption patterns in the late antique city, beef was primary source of meat consumed, processed by specialized establishments which dealt with large animal carcasses and worked across the horn and hide trade. Cattle remained important into the sixth and seventh centuries AD, after even their use began to decline at Sagalassos, possibly suggesting different land-use situations in these areas. The landscape around Aphrodisias also offered opportunities for hunting wild animals that prefer forested habitats, which may have occupied the rugged foothills a few kilometres to the northeast.[82] In Ottoman times, small livestock were more abundant: animals better adapted to the smaller-scale village economies in terms of their management and processing. Consumption of pork and wild boar may suggest religious diversity amongst the village's inhabitants, or local interpretation of dietary restrictions.

Although the overall samples were modest, this analysis provides the first systematic evidence of animal usage in the late antique city and later periods. It demonstrates the value of these faunal materials and significant future potential should more intensive recovery strategies like flotation and sieving be employed. There is ample scope to expand and deepen the zooarchaeological research. First, further work on the abundant Ot-

78 For example, Taxel, Glick, and Pines 2017.
79 Moreno-García 2004.
80 Simoons 1994, 35–36.
81 For example, Price 2021, 178; Grau-Sologestoa 2017; Bartosiewicz and Gál 2018.

82 Adkins 2012.

toman samples, which were only partly studied for this analysis, is warranted, and it is hoped that this will be possible in future seasons. Secondly, additional attention to the equid remains would doubtless reveal more about their individual life histories as well as more robust identification of donkeys versus horses and hybrids. Lastly, the limited recording protocol employed leaves ample room for more targeted analysis of biometry and butchery patterns. Nonetheless, the results presented here provide a thought-provoking first look at changing human–animal relationships across the millennia in the Place of Palms.

Conclusions

Ben Russell and Andrew Wilson

The major public piazza to the south of the Agora, with its colossal pool, flanking stoas and propylon, is one of the most striking and enigmatic monuments of central Aphrodisias. First referred to in scholarship in the 1740s, this space has been known since the 1930s as the 'South Agora' and identified variously as a second agora, a gymnasium, and an urban park. Although its origins can be dated back to the Tiberian period, the complex was progressively monumentalized, maintained, and reconfigured over at least six centuries.

Between 2012 and 2017 a major campaign of excavation, architectural survey, and analysis was instigated to better understand the 'South Agora' and its role at Aphrodisias. The results generated show that, rather than an agora or gymnasium, this was indeed an elaborate urban park, analogous in form, function, and appearance to the late republican and early imperial *porticus*-monuments of Rome. By late antiquity this garden *porticus* was known poetically as the 'Place of Palms'; it may always have had this name, or something similar, like 'the palm grove'. New data provide insights into the conception and evolution of this complex in the first two centuries AD, its restoration and re-modelling in the fifth and early sixth centuries, and its final destruction in the seventh. So long-lived was the space and its associated structures that the wider fortunes of the city of Aphrodisias over this timeframe can be charted through the evolution of this space. And the occupation of this area of the city did not end in the seventh century: the excavations have shown that the former area of the Place of Palms was re-occupied and intensively settled in the Beylik and Ottoman periods, revealing the medieval landscape of central Aphrodisias on a scale never before uncovered.

Construction and inspiration: a first-century garden *porticus*

The earliest components of this grand new civic space were planned and built at some point between AD 14 and 29 (Ch. 2 §A). This date is provided by the dedicatory inscription on the complex's North Stoa, which was offered by Diogenes son of Menandros to Aphrodite, the deified Augustus, the current emperor Tiberius, Livia, and the People (Pl. 10.B; Appendix 1, In1). The decision to build a public space of this scale, in this area and at this date, was presumably motivated by a desire to connect the already monumentalized zone of the Agora and Temple of Aphrodite with the Theatre to the south. Large-scale construction in this part of the city centre, however, necessitated the drainage of what was seemingly a marshy area and the cutting back of the northward projection of the Theatre Hill itself, which then had to be consolidated with a substantial masonry retaining wall.

The most significant building belonging to this first phase of the complex was the already-mentioned North Stoa, which divided it from the existing Agora (Pl. 10.A; Fig. 5). Despite several adjustments to its ends, this first-century stoa remained in place and functioning until the seventh century, and only collapsed fully in the tenth or eleventh century. Facing the North Stoa was probably also a first-phase South Stoa of indeterminate length, the existence of which can be deduced from cuttings in the Theatre Hill's retaining wall (Fig. 9).

The North and South Stoas framed a substantial open area, down the centre of which ran the new complex's most defining architectural feature, its pool (Pl. 1.A) (Ch. 2 §B). This structure, nearly 174 m long and 25 m wide, has a surface area of just over 3,000 m^2, making it one of the largest known ornamental pools in the empire outside Rome (Fig. 14) (Ch. 2 §D). Although later dates for this pool have been proposed, four factors suggest it belongs to the first phase: its positioning indicates that it was laid out prior to the Hadrianic Baths and centred with respect to the North Stoa; aquatic themes in the decoration of the Propylon, which is Flavian, suggest that the pool already existed by this date (Ch. 7 §C); ceramics from the bedding layer for the marble paving of the path around the pool provide a first-century date (Ch. 2 §C); and most significantly, though decorative in design, the pool played a vital water management role that was a necessary prerequisite to the construction of the entire complex (Ch. 2 §C). The pool walls enclosed a ring drain designed to collect ground water and channel it away from the city centre (Pl. 15.B); and without this drain, the newly opened up construction site would not have been dry enough to be useable (Ch. 2 §B). Above the ring drain, supported on schist slabs, ran a series of pipes that fed fountains around the pool. These two layers of hydraulic infrastructure were hidden from view by marble cover slabs that connected the inner and outer pool walls. These walls were themselves designed as seats, facing both inwards and outwards. Corresponding seats ran along the line of the North Stoa, beneath the level of the stylobate. That a range of sculpture was set up around the pool over time is demonstrated by the discovery of forty-two recessed settings for statue bases on the pool walls (Ch. 7 §B) and finds of sculpture within the pool (Ch. 7 §E). Sculptural displays were also set up elsewhere in the complex, including a group of statues of Hermes, Aphrodite, and three Erotes, attested epigraphically, and perhaps also the Achilles and Troilos group later redisplayed in the Civil Basilica and a statue group representing Polyphemos (Ch. 7 §A).

What the name of this monumental new complex was in the Julio-Claudian period, when it was planned and laid out, is unknown. The fact that it was adjacent to the Agora proper and that much of its open area was taken up by a substantial pool make it unlikely that this space was designed simply as a second agora (though it may have acquired a role as a commercial and gathering space over time). The pool is too shallow to have been a swimming pool of the sort suitable for a gymnasium, and since the complex was directly accessible from the Agora, Theatre, and (later) the Civil Basilica, the suggestion that this could have been a space for exercise and sport is improbable. The excavation in 2012–2014, in the open area between the pool and the North Stoa, of parallel rows of planting trenches provided final proof that this was neither an agora nor a gymnasium (Ch. 2 §C). Like the contemporary *porticus* of Rome, this space contained gardens.

What was planted in this *porticus* could not be confirmed during excavation; hollows left by roots are not preserved at Aphrodisias in the same way that they are at the Vesuvian sites, where Roman horticultural practices have been well studied. The best evidence for what was planted in these planting trenches is provided by archaeobotanical analysis of waterlogged remains from the bottom of the pool, which identified a fragment of Cretan date palm. This came from a seventh-century context but is suggestive evidence of how the complex was planted in this period at least.

Further evidence for the character of these gardens comes from the epigraphy. The key source here is the northernmost of the three inscriptions carved into the façade of the Propylon in the late fifth/early sixth century (Ch. 2 §D, Ch. 4 §A). These texts honour the two individuals, Doulkitios and Ampelios, credited with the restoration of the complex at this date (Appendix 1, In10–12). In the text honouring Ampelios, he is thanked on behalf of the nymphs 'because he gave wonder and splendid beauty to the place of palms (χῶρος φυνικόεις), so that anyone who, among our waters, turns his glance around, may always sing the praise both of him, and of the place, and of the Nymphs as well.' By this date, then, the complex was known as the Place of Palms. This is not the only text to mention a palm grove in the city: an earlier inscription, of the first or second century AD, found re-used in the city wall, refers to a φοινεικοῦς, a palm grove (Ch. 2 §D). Assuming that Aphrodisias did not have two palm groves, we argue that this complex, which was known as the Place of Palms by at least the late fifth century, had always been designed as a garden and was probably always planted with palm trees. In the absence of indigenous species of palms, these trees would have to have been imported to Aphrodisias, and south-western coastal Asia Minor, where the Cretan date palm is a native species, would have been the closest source of palms. The discovery of a fragment Cretan date palm at the bottom of the pool, therefore, is significant (Ch. 2 §C). The *porticus*-monuments of Rome similarly contained a wealth of imported species and the builders of the later palm grove at Smyrna, known to us epigraphically, must also have imported their trees. From its inception, therefore, the complex that we refer to as the Place of Palms was an Aphrodisian response to metropolitan models, which brought together monumental architecture, sculpture, water displays, and greenery, providing a lavish new public piazza in the heart of the city.

The Place of Palms in the first four centuries AD

The complex laid out in the early Julio-Claudian period began to attract new construction almost as soon as its first-phase components were completed. The first major addition to the space was probably the Propylon at its eastern end (Fig. 15; Pl. 22.A) (Ch. 3 §A). Although conventionally dated in previous scholarship to the Antonine period, a re-reading of the dedicatory inscription on this two-storey monument suggests it must have been complete before the reign of Nerva (Appendix 1, In2). This indicates that the monument is Flavian and so is contemporary with or earlier than many of the famous columnar screen monuments known from other cities in Asia Minor, such as Miletos and Ephesos. A full architectural study of this monument was beyond the scope of this study but a new assessment of the sculpture that adorned it shows that it quickly developed into a vital display location for portrait statuary of emperors (Nerva, Hadrian, and Antoninus Pius) and members of the Aphrodisias elite (Ch. 7 §C). Many of these statues were still in place in late antiquity, when a range of other works, including a statue of a river god, was added to the ensemble following Doulkitios' restoration work.

Soon after construction of the Propylon had begun, and still in the Flavian period, work started on the Civil Basilica, which opened on to the south-west corner of the Place of Palms. In practice much of the southern side of the complex was probably a building site in this period (Ch. 3 §B). An extension of the auditorium of the Theatre in the third or fourth quarter of the first century necessitated the extension and partial rebuilding of the Theatre Hill retaining wall and the construction of a series of barrel-vaulted chambers along the north side of this hill. The first-phase South Stoa was probably dismantled in this period and then rebuilt along the full length of this newly remodelled Theatre Hill. Evidence for this second-phase stoa is again provided by the cuttings in the retaining wall. It was probably completed at the same time as the Propylon at its eastern end, to which it was connected.

By the second century AD, with its northern, eastern, and southern sides bristling with new monuments, attention shifted to the western end of the Place of Palms. The construction of the Hadrianic Baths and its East Court demanded that the western end of the North Stoa be truncated and a new West Stoa built to provide a connection between the new structures and the Place of Palms (Ch. 3 §C). This West Stoa largely followed the morphology of the North Stoa, except that its twenty columns were raised on pedestals and the central four formed a propylon supporting a pediment with Syrian gable (Fig. 17). This propylon allowed access to a three-aisled gateway connecting to the East Court beyond. The rear wall of this West Stoa was adorned with polychrome marble revetment, which was also then carried down the length of the North Stoa, providing a decorative link between the two, now interconnected, structures (Ch. 3 §D).

In the three centuries following the construction of the Hadrianic Baths, no new structures were added to the Place of Palms. Periodic earthquake damage, however, led to repairs to the North and the West Stoas (Ch. 3 §C–D). These structures continued to function in their first- and second-century forms, as open-fronted colonnades providing respite from the sun, until the fourth century. At this date, perhaps in response to further earthquake damage, the intercolumniations of the West Stoa were filled with doorways, its interior paved in mosaic, and the whole structure turned into an enclosed hall. Various statues were set up in this space, including a series honouring the Theodosian emperors (Ch. 7 §D). Similar but less wholesale changes were made to the parts of the North Stoa and *topos* inscriptions on the columns of this structure suggest it became a more commercial space in this period (Ch. 3 §D, Ch. 5 §D).

While the shifting architectural landscape of the Place of Palms between the first and fourth centuries can be carefully mapped, our best evidence for the intense use of this space by the Aphrodisian public is provided by the coin finds (Ch. 3 §E) and especially the rich epigraphy from the complex. Aside from the monumental texts that are often our best evidence for the chronology of the complex's buildings, hundreds of more informal texts are revealing of their everyday use. These include a range of textual graffiti, comprising acclamations, prayers, labels, names, abbreviations, and obscene texts (Ch. 5 §B). *Topos* inscriptions are especially useful for unravelling the later use of the complex by various professionals (a sophist, teacher of rhetoric or lawyer, a retailer or tavern keeper, a chairman of a guild, and a possible food-seller) (Ch. 5 §D), but pictorial graffiti (Ch. 5 §C) also show this was a leisure space, where the ordinary citizens of Aphrodisias spent considerable time. This is most clearly demonstrated by 532 gameboards documented in the complex, which represent the highest concentration of gameboards recorded anywhere in the Roman world (Ch. 5 §F). There is good evidence to indicate that many of these belong to the fourth and perhaps fifth centuries, though gaming certainly also continued after the next major phase of building activity in the Place of Palms, in the late fifth and early sixth centuries.

Late antique renewal

The bulk of the structures comprising the Place of Palms were first erected in the first and second centuries AD, but perhaps the most striking result of the new excavations is the revelation that the complex reached its most monumental, architecturally-unified state only in the late fifth or early sixth century AD. At this date, following a major earthquake in the late fifth century from which some areas of the city never recovered (Ch. 4 §M), a vast campaign of restoration was carried out, and in relatively short order. This included repairs to the pool walls and floor (possibly even its total re-surfacing) (Ch. 4 §B); the laying of new pipelines (Ch. 4 §C); the raising of the ground level between the pool walls and the surrounding stoas (Ch. 4 §C); the restoration of the Propylon (Ch. 4 §A); the construction of a new and enlarged South Stoa, probably divided into two stretches, which was, in part at least, two-storeyed (Ch. 4 §F); refurbishment of the interior of the North Stoa (Ch. 4 §E); and the rebuilding and repaving of the West Stoa (Ch. 4 §D). Masons' marks provide some insight into the logistics that this renovation work involved (Ch. 5 §E).

That the Aphrodisians could carry out a building campaign of this scale, and that they committed to new construction alongside restoration work, is testimony both to the vibrancy of the city in this period, in its role as provincial capital, and to the importance of the Place of Palms. Such was the status of the project that it attracted attention from a range of authorities. Instrumental in this process were the provincial governor Doulkitios and the 'father of the city' Ampelios, who are honoured in the three epigrams on the façade of the Propylon (Ch. 4 §A; Appendix 1, In10–12). The acclamations on the columns of the West Stoa show that Albinos was also a crucial player in this process (Ch. 4 §D), while a Philippos is mentioned on an inscription from the South Stoa (Ch. 4 §F; Appendix 1, In9). The monograms of the emperor Anastasius and possibly the *praefectus praetorio per Orientem* on the columns of the new South Stoa reveal an even higher level of patronage (Ch. 4 §A; §F).

The thick deposits of rubble laid over the open area of the complex during this restoration work and the occupation layers on top of them produced numerous coin finds that have added considerably to our numismatic picture of late antique Aphrodisias (Ch. 4 §G). The ceramics from these same layers show the importance of local pottery production, which was only occasionally supplemented by imports (of ARS, LRC, and Cypriot Sigillata) (Ch. 4 §H). Although few small finds came from these deposits (Ch. 4 §I), the fills of the ring drain around the pool provide a valuable dataset for reconstructing diet and food production practices in the city at this date (Ch. 4 §J). Some of the burnt remains from the ring drain may even attest to gardening activities in the Place of Palms, while others probably relate to ritual activity in this area of the city or nearby. Animal bones from the late antique layers around the pool also provide key insights into diet at Aphrodisias in this period (Ch. 10 §C).

Quite why the Place of Palms received so much attention in the late fifth century, when much of the city would also have experienced earthquake damage, is hinted at by the epigraphy from the complex. The fact that Doulkitios is specifically described as Maioumarch in the second epigram relating to him on the Propylon is suggestive (Ch. 4 §M). The Maiouma festival, which so incensed Christian writers of the late Roman period, was enormously popular in Asia Minor and the Levant and often involved aquatic ceremonies. It is plausible that the pool in the Place of Palms became a venue for the festival in this period. This does not mean that the Place of Palms was a pagan cult complex in this period, however: while evidence of religious tension is apparent in the epigraphy (Ch. 5 §G), Ampelios and Albinos were both Christian and keen to invest in the complex's reconstruction; and the numbers of Christian crosses and Jewish symbols inscribed on the pool walls and steps of the North Stoa indicate that the space was used by a cross-section of society. The goal of this investment is clear: this was not about repurposing the Place of Palms or changing its use but reviving and updating a much-loved public space. The key features of the complex, its pool and gardens, despite the effort involved, were renewed; indeed much of what remains of the pool's structure dates from this period. Finds of late antique sculpture in the pool, including the striking portrait head of an early sixth-century notable, show that the area continued to attract high-end statuary displays in this period (Ch. 7 §E).

The Place of Palms was not substantially altered again after the renovations of Doulkitios and his colleagues. The only addition to the complex was a basin, probably a large reservoir, which was built in front of the Propylon in or after the mid sixth century (Ch. 4 §N, Ch. 6 §A). This seems to have been constructed to ensure sufficient water was available for the continued functioning of the pool and its foundation following the earlier reforms. The basin's walls were faced with a range of spoliated reliefs and statue bases, most notably a grand series of mythological reliefs (Ch. 6 §B–C). At the centre of this decorative scheme was a base for a statue of a seated statue, perhaps of Ampelios or another sixth-century Aphrodisian grandee (Ch. 6 §E). There is even evidence for later repairs to the pool and modifications to its supply and drainage arrangements, which attests continued efforts to maintain this urban feature even after an earthquake of *c.* AD 620 (Ch. 4 §O).

Destruction of the Place of Palms

Fine-grained evidence for the violent end of the Place of Palms was discovered in the stratigraphy revealed at the bottom of its pool. Here multiple phases of deposits relating to the clearance of the areas north and south of the pool were uncovered. These constitute a rich material record containing large quantities of architectural remains, sculpture, ceramics, and small finds; they also produced significant quantities of animal bones and carbonized plant remains. The first of these clearance deposits comprises a scatter of material across the full extent of the pool floor as well as a more substantial accumulation of debris adjacent to the northern pool wall (Ch. 8 §A). Archaeobotanical analysis shows that the pool contained clean water at this date; there is no evidence for siltation or the growth of water plants (Ch. 8 §E). Very large quantities of roof tiles and broken marble architecture were recovered from this deposit, as well as burnt timbers (Ch. 8 §A).

After the accumulation of the first clearance deposit, the pool was neglected. Silt began to accumulate (Ch. 8 §A) and reeds and other water plants took hold (Ch. 8 §E). A second clearance deposit, this time along the pool's southern wall, indicates that further efforts were made to tidy up here. The bulk finds were comparable to those found in the similar deposit on the northern side of the pool, and again include burnt timbers and substantial quantities of roof tiles (Ch. 8 §A). Various animal bones, including articulated remains from cattle and equids, were also dumped into the pool at this date (Ch. 10 §C). A considerable range of ceramics and small finds was recovered from these deposits, including stamped unguentaria (Ch. 8 §C), glass, metal elements from the stoas, marketplace and religious items (Ch. 8 §D). Among the most arresting finds were a number of weapons, including arrowheads and javelin- or spearheads; a stirrup, which was probably a piece of military equipment, was also recovered from the pool floor during excavations in 1990 (Ch. 8 §D).

The finds from the first and second clearance deposits in the pool suggest that substantial damage to the structures of the Places of Palms occurred prior to their accumulation. The North and South Stoas were burned and probably lost their roofs; some of their architecture also seems to have come down. When considered alongside the weaponry from the pool floor, these observations suggest the Place of Palms was destroyed by enemy action. When did this occur? The finds from the first clearance deposit mostly date to the sixth and first half of the seventh century (Ch. 8 §B–D). The latest coin dates to AD 643/644, providing a *terminus post quem* for the deposit (Ch. 8 §B). The second clearance deposit in the pool, on the other hand, contains a coin of Heraclius, itself datable to 632–635, which has an Umayyad countermark on it that probably dates to between the 660s and *c.* 685 (Ch. 8 §B). Elsewhere at Aphrodisias there is substantial evidence for fire destruction that can be dated to between 614 and 620, and probably specifically to 617, during a Persian invasion of southern Asia Minor. This fire damage appears to have been followed only a few years later by an earthquake, in *c.* 620 (Ch. 8 §F).

The fire damage in the Place of Palms has also previously been connected to Persian incursions into this territory in the first half of the seventh century. It is perhaps possible that the first clearance deposit in the pool relates to these events and reveals an attempt to make the Place of Palms useable again. If this was the case, however, then it took the Aphrodisians twenty years or more to get around to the task, after the Persian sack of 617 and the earthquake *c.* 620, and this is not supported by the archaeobotanical evidence, which indicates that the pool was functioning up until the point the first clearance deposit was dumped into it. A more plausible reconstruction is that the evidence for fire damage from the Place of Palms, and the weapons from the pool floor, relate to a separate destructive episode that occurred after AD 643/644, in which the North Stoa was burned. The layer of silt between the two clean-up deposits suggests that they were separated by a period of time, and here the Arab-countermarked coin from the second clearance deposit (which relates to the clearing up of damage from the South Stoa), dated to the 660s or later, is the key dating evidence. Such a coin would not have been legal tender in Byzantine Asia Minor. We thus postulate two separate Arab raids, one in the late 640s/early 650s, or in the 660s, and another later in the seventh century. Read in this light, the deposits from the bottom of the pool of the Place of Palms may represent the most convincing evidence recovered to date for the destructive impact of Arab raids in this part of Asia Minor in the second half of the seventh century.

Whatever the exact cause and date of the destruction of the Place of Palms, the complex never recovered its monumental character. The pool began to silt up and soon turned into a marsh. The stoas stayed standing, but without their roofs. Postholes cut into the northern pool walls and the ground to the north of them indicate that temporary structures, perhaps market stalls, were erected here (Ch. 8 §A). A small basin was inserted along the southern side of the pool, while a ramp was added in its north-eastern corner, probably to allow cattle to access what was left of its water. Bone finds from the debris at the base of the pool might point to butchery activities and perhaps the working of hides nearby (Ch. 10 §C). The Place of Palms started the seventh century as a recently renovated and remodelled public space, with a functioning and still impressive central pool; by the end of the same century, it had become an overgrown, part-ruined space, centred on a silted-up bog, now used for temporary markets and watering and processing animals.

Medieval and later occupation

Prior to the commencement of excavations in the Place of Palms in 2012, our knowledge of urban development at Aphrodisias after the seventh century was limited to evidence of Byzantine activity on the Theatre Hill, and in the areas of the Triconch Church, Bishop's Palace, and Cathedral.[1] About occupation in the Seljuk, Beylik, and Ottoman periods we were relatively ignorant. Occasional medieval-period walls constructed out of spoliated architectural elements had been noted in different areas of the city centre, and are sometimes planned in excavation notebooks, but they were rarely afforded much attention; when the trenches in which such structures were uncovered were small, excavators often struggled to clarify whether these were field boundaries or the walls of buildings. For the first time, therefore, the excavations in the Place of Palms offered an opportunity to explore the Turkish settlement at Aphrodisias over a large open area. While it had been assumed that this area was probably farmed in the post-Byzantine period, and divided into small plots of land as it still was in the 1960s, the excavations revealed a much more complicated picture of occupation, which can be traced from the eighth century through to the twentieth. The new excavations provide remarkable insight into the development of this space and the emergence of a new post-antique settlement at Stavropolis, as the city was renamed from around 629.

Between the eighth and twelfth centuries (our *Phase 4*), the area of the former pool developed into a kind of localised swampy marshland around which the middle Byzantine settlement developed (Ch. 9 §A–B). Zooarchaeological analysis indicates that turtles took up residence in the abandoned pool and were perhaps even consumed (Ch. 10 §C). Limited Byzantine finds were recovered during the excavations, with the exception of several eighth-century finds and middle Byzantine material that seems to have slipped down the northern side of the Theatre Hill from the important Byzantine fortifications there (Ch. 9 §C); Byzantine small finds were similarly concentrated along the southern edge of the space (Ch. 9 §E). In the tenth or eleventh century the structures surrounding the former Place of Palms, which had been standing as ruins since the seventh century, were brought down by a major earthquake. Some efforts were made to keep the areas around the pool clear of debris even after this date but overall activity in this area was limited in the middle Byzantine period.

By the Seljuk and early Beylik period (*Phase 5–6*), in the thirteenth to fourteenth centuries, the siltation of the former pool had advanced to such a stage that the pool walls were no longer visible and the basin had filled in; the resulting vacant space was developed for the first time as agricultural land (Ch. 9 §B). Initial trackways across the area of the former pool connected areas of more intensive Seljuk or Beylik occupation, including along the line of the former Tetrapylon Street. These trackways were followed by early field walls, which divided the open land into plots. The beginnings of a settlement proper, defined by a more complex series of boundary walls delimiting narrow streets or lanes, gradually appeared over the course of the Beylik period and into the early Ottoman era (*Phase 7*, fourteenth to fifteenth centuries) (Ch. 9 §B). The first significant quantities of medieval ceramics from the area correspondingly date to the Beylik period (Ch. 9 §D). These provide a crucial dataset for understanding the influence of Byzantine sgraffito styles on Beylik glazed pottery, the commercial connections between the site and other areas of western Anatolia, and continued local production.

The settlement that first appeared in the fourteenth century gradually developed into a village comprising multiple parcels of land, or enclosures, with houses within them, divided from each other by narrow walled lanes (*Phases 8–9*, fifteenth to seventeenth centuries) (Ch. 9 §B). The houses of this date had walls constructed, at least in their lower courses, out of re-purposed Roman architectural elements; their superstructures were probably of timber and earth. These buildings were mostly located in the area between the former pool and the collapsed North Stoa, where the land was presumably drier and firmer than further south. The structures of this period provide the clearest evidence exposed to date for the character of the Ottoman settlement at the site, which is recorded in Ottoman cadastral records as 'Gerye', a name seemingly derived from 'Karia'.

Ottoman deposits associated with this settlement provided the largest quantity of ceramics documented in any of occupation phases of the Place of Palms (Ch. 9 §D). These again demonstrated the continuing vitality of local ceramic production in the territory of the site, as well as a range of imports. That the settlement was primarily an agricultural centre is demonstrated by the range of metal tools and implements related to farming and small-scale artisanal work (Ch. 9 §E). Only the substantial number of glass bangles from both Beylik and Ottoman periods paints a different picture, and it is possible these were made by recycling ancient glass. The animal bones from this period indicate a reduction in the number of cattle and equids compared to the late antique period and an increase in sheep and goats, especially the latter; pigs continued to feature (as did wild boar), which may indicate religious diversity at the site or particular interpretations of dietary restrictions (Ch. 10 §C).

While these Ottoman village houses, on the western outskirts of the settlement proper, were occupied for two centuries, they were mostly abandoned following another major earthquake, in either the late sixteenth or early seventeenth century. The ceramic record trails off substantially in this period (Ch. 9 §B). After this date the area was turned over almost exclusively to horticulture or arboriculture, being transformed into a series

---

[1] For a thorough analysis of all Byzantine evidence from the site, see Jeffery 2022.

of orchards or market gardens for the residents of the village that at some point in this period became known as 'Geyre'. The centre of the village at this date seems to have been located further to the east; indeed the houses of Geyre that were closest to the area of the former Place of Palms were built on top of the base of the former Propylon (*Phases 10–11*, seventeenth to twentieth centuries) (Ch. 9 §B). This was the state in which antiquarians visiting Aphrodisias in the nineteenth century described the area north of the Theatre Hill, and it was this landscape—of fields in the area of the former Place of Palms and houses further east—that Jacopi and other excavators encountered in the early twentieth century (Ch. 9 §B).

From Roman urban park to Ottoman village

In its monumentalisation as an urban park in the Julio-Claudian to Flavian periods, the Place of Palms displays a concentration of evidence for surprisingly precocious urban and architectural development at Aphrodisias, sometimes following fashions directly borrowed from Rome, and sometimes appearing at the forefront of the dissemination of new architectural trends. The overall design of a portico with large central ornamental pool, the space around which was planted to shady trees, all ornamented with sculpture, is clearly inspired by the *porticus*-monuments of Augustan Rome (but the pool is without parallel for its size); and the palm grove thus created long predates the Hadrianic urban palm grove at Smyrna. Likewise the columnar monument of the Place of Palms' Propylon (and indeed the even earlier mid-first-century Sebasteion Propylon) is contemporary with or pre-dates better-known models of such marble 'façade' architecture elsewhere.

The excavations of the pool and its surroundings allow us to chart the evolution of this urban space over some six centuries until the end of antiquity. We can detect earthquake damage and subsequent repairs in the second or third centuries, modifications to the surrounding porticoes, and their development into commercial space with *topos* inscriptions for stallholders. A striking and particularly significant finding of the excavation project was the recognition of evidence for widespread destruction by an earthquake—and, as importantly, the evidence for a large-scale programme of repair and reconstruction within a decade or so either side of AD 500. The urban vitality of Aphrodisias at the start of the sixth century is now not in question. A large corpus of masons' marks belongs to this period, as does a wealth of other graffiti and also gameboards that allow us to populate the urban park in our imagination with citizens playing games on the gameboards around the pool and ordering drinks from sellers of refreshments in the surrounding porticoes, all the while surrounded by an increasing array of honorific and mythical statuary, some of it curated or repurposed from an earlier period of the high empire, and some of it new in the sixth century. The pool appears to have been the setting for celebrations of the Maiouma as late as the sixth century. Further works in the course of the sixth century or possibly the early seventh seem aimed at the maintenance of the water supply to the pool and confirm the importance of this public space to the city's sense of identity.

The relative prosperity of the city at the start of the sixth century makes the end of urban monumentality in the early seventh century all the more in demand of explanation. Newly recognised evidence from the city centre of Aphrodisias, but mostly outside the Place of Palms, suggests a sack by the Persians in 617 swiftly followed by an earthquake *c.* 620, which brought down the Propylon. The city never recovered from this sequence of destructive events, and the probable depopulation as a result of slaughter or deportation that went with them. But clearance deposits of architectural debris thrown into the pool indicate more than one further destructive event, towards the middle of the seventh century, and apparently again in the later seventh century, probably to be interpreted as Arab raids. The teasing apart of the various strands of evidence for seventh-century destruction at Aphrodisias illuminates the complexity of the processes that led to the end of the classical city here, and may help our understanding of similar processes at other cities in Asia Minor in the seventh century.

After the middle of the seventh century, the pool began to silt up, and was apparently used as a pond for watering cattle, with temporary structures, perhaps market stalls, erected around it. Over the course of the following centuries it filled in completely, until by the thirteenth or fourteenth centuries it could be divided into field plots, and then in the fourteenth century a settlement developed over the area of the former pool. This formed part of the Beylik and Ottoman village of Gerye/Geyre, a collection of dwellings largely in timber, traceable through the chocks for their post supports, with some of the larger or more robust buildings having stone footings. Streets or lanes were defined by drystone walls. The abandonment of these buildings following an earthquake in the sixteenth or seventeenth century completed the cycle of transformation of the Roman urban park into abandoned space in the early middle ages, and then into settlement, reverting to orchards and fields on the outskirts of the modern village of Geyre again, as it remained until the twentieth century.

The excavation of the Place of Palms and the overall story that emerges thus shed light on a wide range of aspects of Roman and early Byzantine urban form, architectural development, and the use of civic space between the first and seventh centuries AD. The excavations contribute to histories of leisure, as well as to histories of architecture and sculpture; to stories of urban renewal, and, in the seventh century, to the wider debate on the reasons for the end of classical urbanism in Asia Minor. Most unexpectedly, they have provided perhaps the largest area of fourteenth- to sixteenth- or seventeenth-century village settlement yet excavated in Asia Minor.

Özet

Agora'nın güneyinde bulunan büyük meydan, merkezindeki devasa havuzu, stoaları ve propylonu ile Aphrodisias'ın en dikkat çekici ve karmaşık anıtsal yapı komplekslerinden biridir. Literatürde ilk olarak 1740'larda sözü geçen alan, 1930'larda "Güney Agora" olarak isimlendirilmiş ve o zamandan bu yana agora, gymnasion ve kent parkı olarak tanımlanmıştır. İlk kuruluşu Tiberius dönemine tarihlense de kompleks en az altı yüzyıl boyunca farklı aşamalarla anıtsal hale getirilmiş, sürekli bakım görmüş ve zaman zaman yeniden düzenlenmiştir.

2012 ve 2017 yılları arasında, "Güney Agora"yı ve bu alanın Aphrodisias'taki rolünü daha iyi anlamak için kapsamlı bir kazı, mimari araştırma ve analiz çalışması gerçekleştirilmiştir. Elde edilen sonuçlar burasının biçim, işlev ve görünüm bakımından bir agora veya gymnasiondan ziyade Roma'nın geç Cumhuriyet dönemi ve erken İmparatorluk dönemi *porticus* anıtlarına benzeyen gösterişli bir kent parkı olduğunu ortaya koymuştur. Bu bahçe *porticus*u Geç Antik Çağda "Palmiye Parkı" olarak biliniyordu. Fakat daha önceki dönemlerde de bu isme veya "palmiye korusu" gibi bir isme sahip olmuş olabilir. Yeni veriler bu kompleksin MS 1. ve 2. yüzyıllardaki tasarımı ve evrimi, 5. ve erken 6. yüzyıldaki restorasyonu ve yeniden modellenmesi ile 7. yüzyıldaki son yıkımı hakkındaki bilgilerimize katkı sağlamıştır. Alanın kendisi ve dahilindeki yapılar çok uzun süre kullanıldığından Aphrodisias'ın bu zaman diliminde yaşadığı olayların izleri burada gerçekleşen değişimler üzerinden açıkça okunabilmektedir. Bu alanın kullanımı ve şehirdeki yaşam 7. yüzyılda sona ermemiştir. Kazılarda elde edilen veriler Palmiye Parkı'nın olduğu alanda Beylikler ve Osmanlı dönemlerinde yeniden yoğun bir yerleşim olduğunu göstermiş, Aphrodisias'ın Orta Çağdaki görünümü hakkında hiç olmadığı kadar detaylı bir resim sunmuştur.

MS 1. yüzyıla ait bir bahçe *porticus*u: ilham kaynakları ve yapımı

Bu yeni ve büyük kentsel alanın ilk unsurları MS 14 ve 29 yılları arasında planlanmış ve inşa edilmiştir (Bölüm 2 §A). Bu tarih kompleksin Kuzey Stoasındaki adak yazıtı sayesinde elde edilmiştir. Bu yazıta göre Menandros oğlu Diogenes, Kuzey Stoa'yı Aphrodite'ye, tanrısal Augustus'a, dönemin imparatoru Tiberius'a, Livia'ya ve halka adamıştır. (Pl. 10.B; Appendix 1, In1). Bu tarihte ve bu alanda böylesi ölçekte bir kamusal alan inşa etme kararının arkasında olasılıkla halihazırda anıtsal görünüme sahip Agora'yı ve Aphrodite Tapınağı'nı güneydeki Tiyatro ile birleştirme isteği yatmaktadır. Fakat şehir merkezinin bu kısmında büyük ölçekli bir inşaat projesi, bataklık olduğu anlaşılan bu alanın kurtulmasını, Tiyatro Tepesi'nin kuzeye doğru uzayan kısmının tıraşlanmasını ve daha sonra yamacın sağlamlaştırılması için güçlü bir istinat duvarı yapılmasını gerektirmiştir.

Kompleksin bu ilk evresine ait en önemli yapı, Agora ile arasında bir ayrım sağlayan, yukarıda bahsi geçen Kuzey Stoa idi (Pl. 10.A; Fig. 5). MS 1. yüzyıla ait bu stoa, uçlarına sonradan yapılan çeşitli düzenlemelerle 7. yüzyıla kadar ayakta ve faal durumda kalmış ve ancak 10. veya 11. yüzyılda tamamen yıkılmıştır. Kuzey Stoa'nın karşısında uzunluğu tam anlaşılamayan Güney Stoa'nın ilk evresi yer alıyor olmalıydı. Bu durum Tiyatro Tepesi'nin istinat duvarındaki deliklerden anlaşılmaktadır (Fig. 9).

Kuzey ve Güney Stoalar oldukça büyük bir açık alanı sınırlıyordu. Bu alanın ortasında ise yeni kompleksin en belirgin mimari unsuru olan havuz bulunmaktaydı (Pl. 1.A) (Bölüm 2 §B). Yaklaşık 174 m uzunluğunda ve 25 m genişliğinde olan bu yapı, 3.000 m²'nin biraz üzerinde bir yüz ölçümüyle imparatorlukta Roma dışında bilinen en büyük süs havuzlarından biridir (Fig. 14) (Bölüm 2 §D). Bu havuz için daha geç tarihler önerilmiş olsa da, dört farklı faktör havuzun birinci evreye ait olduğunu düşündürmektedir. 1) Konumu, Hadrianus Hamamı'ndan önce yapıldığını ve Kuzey Stoa'ya göre ortalandığını göstermektedir. 2) Propylon'un süslemelerinde görülen Flaviuslar dönemine ait su temaları, havuzun bu tarihte halihazırda var olduğuna işaret etmektedir (Bölüm 7 §C). 3) Havuzun etrafındaki yürüme yolundaki mermer kaldırım taşlarının altındaki döşeme tabakasında bulunan seramikler MS 1. yüzyıla tarihlendirilmektedir (Bölüm 2 §C). 4) Dördüncü ve en önemli faktör ise, tüm kompleksin inşası için su yönetiminin şart olması ve tasarımı dekoratif olsa da havuzun elzem olan bu su yönetiminde büyük rol oynamış olmasıdır (Bölüm 2 §C). Havuz duvarlarının içerisinde, yeraltı suyunu toplamak ve şehir merkezinden uzaklaştırmak için tasarlanmış bir halka kanal bulunuyordu (Pl. 15.B). Böylesi bir drenaj sistemi olmadan buradaki şantiye sahasının inşaata el verecek kadar kurutulması mümkün olamazdı (Bölüm 2 §B). Halka kanalın üstünde, şist levhalar üzerinde havuzun etrafındaki fıskiyeleri besleyen borular uzanmaktaydı. Bu iki hidrolik altyapı katmanı, havuzun iç ve dış duvarlarını birbirine bağlayan mermer kaplama plakaları ile gizlenmiştir. Duvarlar ise hem içe hem de dışa bakan oturaklar şeklinde tasarlanmıştır. Bunun karşısında, Kuzey Stoa hattı boyunca da stylobat seviyesinin altında oturma yerleri uzanmaktaydı. Havuz duvarları boyunca heykel kaideleri için hazırlanmış 42 adet girintinin varlığı (Bölüm 7 §B) ve havuzdan ele geçen buluntular (Bölüm 7 §E) sayesinde havuzun etrafına zaman içerisinde heykellerin yerleştirildiği kanıtlanmıştır. Kompleksin başka noktalarında da heykellerin sergilendiği anlaşılmaktadır. Bunların arasında

301

varlığı şimdilik yalnızca yazıtlardan bilinen Hermes, Aphrodite ve üç Eros heykelinden oluşan bir grup ile Polyphemos'un betimlendiği bir heykel grubu ve olasılıkla daha sonra Bazilika'ya yerleştirilen Akhilleus ve Troilos grubu sayılabilir (Bölüm 7 §A).

Julius-Claudiuslar döneminde bu yeni anıtsal kompleksin adının ne olduğu ve ne zaman planlanıp inşa edildiği hakkında bilgimiz yoktur. Agoraya bitişik olması ve sahip olduğu açık alanının büyük kısmının büyük bir havuza tahsis edilmiş olması, bu alanın ikinci bir agora olarak tasarlanmış olduğu fikrini zayıflatmaktadır (ama elbette burası zaman içinde insanların ticaret yaptığı ve toplandığı bir alana dönüşmüş olabilir). Havuzun gymnasionlarda yapılan spor faaliyetlerine uygun olamayacak kadar sığ olduğu ve Agora, Tiyatro ve (daha sonra) Bazilika'dan komplekse doğrudan erişim olduğu dikkate alındığında, buranın antrenman ve spor faaliyetleri için kullanıldığı önerisi olasılık dışıdır. Havuz ile Kuzey Stoa arasındaki açık alanda 2012–2014 yıllarında yapılan kazılarda ortaya çıkarılan birbirine paralel sıralanmış ağaç dikim çukurları sayesinde kompleksin agora veya gymnasion olmadığını kesin bir şekilde kanıtlanmıştır. (Bölüm 2 §C). Roma'da aynı döneme ait *porticus*larda olduğu gibi bu alanın da bahçesi vardı.

Bu *porticus*'ta ne tür bitkilerin yetiştirildiği kazılar sırasında belirlenememiştir. Ne yazık ki Aphrodisias'taki kök kalıntıları Romalıların bahçecilik uygulamalarının iyi izlenebildiği Vezüv Yanardağı eteklerindeki yerleşimlerde olduğu kadar iyi korunmamıştır. Ancak buradaki bitki yataklarında nelerin yetiştirildiğini anlamak amacıyla havuz tabanından alınan suya doymuş kalıntılar üzerinde yapılan arkeobotanik analizlerde Girit hurması kalıntısına rastlanmıştır. 7. yüzyıl kontekstinden elde edilen bu veri komplekste en azından bu dönemde yetiştirilen bitkiler hakkında oldukça net bilgiler vermektedir.

Buradaki bahçelerin özelliklerine dair ilave bilgiler epigrafik kanıtlardan gelmektedir. Bu konudaki en önemli kaynak Propylonun ön cephesindeki MS 5. yüzyıl sonu / 6. yüzyıl başına tarihlenen üç yazıttan en kuzeyde olanıdır (Bölüm 2 §D, Bölüm 4 §A). Bu metinler, sözü geçen dönemde kompleksin restorasyonu ile anılan iki isim olan Doulkitios ve Ampelios'u onurlandırmaktadır (Appendix 1, In10–12). Ampelios'u onurlandıran metinde su perileri adına kendisine teşekkür edilir, "çünkü o, sularımızda durup gözünü etrafta gezdiren herkes kendisinden ve buradan ve de Nymphelerden daima övgü ile söz etsin diye palmiye parkına (χῶρος φυνικόεις) harikalar ve muhteşem güzellikler bahşetmiştir." Bu yazıttan anlaşıldığı kadarıyla bu tarihte kompleks artık Palmiye Parkı olarak biliniyordu. Ancak kentte bir hurma korusundan söz eden tek metin bu değildir. Kent surlarında devşirme malzeme olarak bulunan, MS 1. veya 2. yüzyıla ait bir yazıtta da bir hurma korusundan (φοινεικοῦς) söz edilmektedir (Bölüm 2 §D). Aphrodisias'ta iki farklı hurma korusu olmadığını varsayarsak, en azından MS 5. yüzyılın sonlarından beri Palmiye Parkı olarak bilinen bu kompleksin en başından beri bir bahçe olarak tasarlandığını ve burada muhtemelen her zaman hurma ağaçlarının yetiştiğini düşünmekteyiz. Bölgede yerli palmiye türleri olmadığına göre, bu ağaçlar Aphrodisias'a güneybatı Anadolu'nun kıyı bölgelerinden getirilmiş olmalıdır, çünkü o bölge Girit hurmasının Aphrodisias'a en yakın doğal yayılım alanıdır. Nitekim, havuz tabanında Girit hurmasına ait bir parçanın bulunması önemlidir (Bölüm 2 §C). Roma'daki *porticus*-anıtları da ithal bitki türleri bakımından çok zengindi ve Smyrna'da varlığını yazıtlardan bildiğimiz daha geç döneme ait palmiye korusundaki ağaçlar da aynı şekilde ithal edilmiş olmalıydı. Bu bilgilerden anlaşıldığı kadarıyla, Palmiye Parkı olarak isimlendirdiğimiz bu kompleks, anıtsal mimariyi, heykel sanatını, su unsurlarını ve yeşil alanları bir araya getiren metropolis örneklerinin Aphrodisias uyarlamasıdır ve kentin tam kalbinde yepyeni ve şaşaalı bir kamusal meydan olarak işlev görmüştür.

Palmiye Parkı'nda milattan sonra ilk dört yüzyıl

Julius-Claudius döneminin başlarında tasarlanıp inşa edilen kompleks birinci evre unsurlarının tamamlanmasından hemen sonra yeni inşaatlara sahne olmuştur. Alana eklenen ilk büyük yapı muhtemelen doğu ucundaki Propylon'dur (Fig. 15; Pl. 22.A) (Bölüm 3 §A). Geçmiş araştırmalarda Antoninus dönemine tarihlenen bu iki katlı anıtın üzerindeki ithaf yazıtı son dönem araştırmalarında yeniden incelenmiştir. Yazıt, yapının Nerva'nın tahta çıkışından önce tamamlanmış olması gerektiğine işaret etmektedir (Appendix 1, In2). Bu durum, anıtın Flaviuslar döneminde yapıldığını, dolayısıyla Miletos ve Ephesos gibi Anadolu kentlerinden bilinen ünlü sütunlu cephe anıtlarının birçoğu ile çağdaş veya onlardan daha önce inşa edildiğini göstermektedir. Anıtın detaylı mimari incelemesi bu çalışmanın kapsamı dışında olsa da onu süsleyen heykeltıraşlık eserleri üzerinde yapılan güncel değerlendirmeler bu alanın kısa sürede imparatorların (Nerva, Hadrianus ve Antoninus Pius) ve Aphrodisiaslı seçkinlerin portre heykellerinin sergilendiği önemli bir yer haline geldiğine işaret etmektedir (Bölüm 7 §C). Geç Antik Çağda Doulkitios'un restorasyon çalışmalarının ardından bu yapı, aralarında bir nehir tanrısı heykelinin de bulunduğu yeni heykellerle donatılmıştı ve bu dönemde dahi ilk evreye ait heykellerin çoğu hala yerinde durmaktaydı.

Propylon'un inşasından kısa süre sonra, yine Flaviuslar döneminde cephesi Palmiye Parkı'nın güneybatı köşesine bakan Bazilika'nın inşasına başlanmıştır. Parkın güney tarafı bu dönemde olasılıkla hala büyük ölçüde inşaat halindeydi (Bölüm 3 §B). MS 1. yüzyılın üçüncü veya dördüncü çeyreğinde Tiyatro auditoriumuna ek yapmak için Tiyatro Tepesi istinat duvarının uzatılması ve kısmen yeniden yapılması, ayrıca da bu tepenin kuzey yamacına boylu boyunca uzanan bir dizi beşik tonozlu odanın eklenmesi icap etmiştir. Parkın birinci evresinde inşa edilen ilk Güney Stoa muhtemelen bu dönemde sökülmüş ve yenilenen Tiyatro Tepesi'nin kuzey yamacı boyunca yeniden inşa edilmiştir. İkinci evrede de burada bir stoanın var olduğu yine istinat duvarındaki deliklerle kanıtlanmaktadır. Güney Stoa, doğu ucunda bulunan ve bağlantılı olduğu Propylon ile aynı zamanda tamamlanmış olmalıdır.

MS 2. yüzyıla gelindiğinde alanın kuzey, doğu ve güney kenarlarının yeni anıtlarla dolmasıyla odak noktası Palmiye Parkı'nın batı tarafına kaymıştır. Hadrianus Hamamı ve doğusundaki avlunun inşası, Kuzey Stoa'nın batı ucunun kısaltılmasını ve bu yeni yapılar ile Palmiye Parkı arasında bağlantı sağlamak için batı kenarda yeni bir stoanın yapımını gerektirmiştir (Bölüm 3 §C). Söz konusu Batı Stoa büyük ölçüde Kuzey Stoa'nın morfolojisini takip etmiştir ancak farklı olarak Batı

302

Stoa'da yirmi adet sütun kaideler üzerinde yükseltilmiş ve ortadaki dört sütun Syria stilinde beşik çatılı bir alınlığı destekleyen bir propylon oluşturmuştur (Fig. 17). Bu propylon, hemen ardındaki hamamın doğu avlusuna bağlanan üç nefli bir geçide erişim sağlıyordu. Batı Stoa'nın arka duvarı daha sonra Kuzey Stoa'ya da uygulanan ve artık birbiriyle bağlantılı bu iki yapı arasında dekoratif bir bağ oluşturan renkli mermer kaplamalar ile süslenmişti (Bölüm 3 §D).

Hadrianus Hamamı'nın tamamlanmasını takip eden üç yüzyıl boyunca Palmiye Parkı'na herhangi bir yeni yapı eklenmemiştir. Bununla birlikte, depremlerin neden olduğu hasarlar nedeniyle Kuzey ve Batı Stoalar'da onarımlar yapılmıştır (Bölüm 3 §C, §D). Güneşten koruma sağlayan önü açık kolonadlardan oluşan bu yapılar, 1. ve 2. yüzyıldaki formlarını 4. yüzyıla kadar değişmeden korumuşlardır. Olasılıkla yeni depremlerin neden olduğu hasar nedeniyle bu tarihte Batı Stoa'nın sütun aralarına kapılar eklenmiş, iç mekânı mozaikle kaplanmış ve yapı bütünüyle kapalı bir salon haline getirilmiştir. Buraya Theodosiuslar dönemi imparatorlarını onurlandıran heykelleri de içeren yeni heykeller dikilmiştir (Bölüm 7 §D). Kuzey Stoa'nın da bazı kısımlarında benzer değişiklikler yapılmıştır. Buranın sütunlarında görülen *topos* yazıtları, 4. yüzyılda mekânın daha çok ticari amaçlarla kullanıldığını düşündürmektedir (Bölüm 3 §D, Bölüm 5 §D).

Palmiye Parkı'nın MS 1. ve 4. yüzyıllar arasında değişen mimari görünümü hakkında oldukça detaylı bilgiye sahibiz, ancak bu alanın Aphrodisias halkı tarafından yoğun bir şekilde kullanıldığına dair en sağlam kanıtlar sikkeler ve özellikle kompleksin zengin epigrafik bulgularıdır (Bölüm 3 §E). Anıtsal yazıtlar, kompleksteki binaların kronolojisini belirlemek için en iyi kanıtlar olsa da yüzlerce sıradan yazıt binaların günlük kullanımları hakkında önemli bilgiler içermektedir. Bunlar arasında övgüler, dualar, unvanlar, isimler, kısaltmalar ve müstehcen metinler içeren grafiti vardır (Bölüm 5 §B). *Topos* yazıtları, kompleksin daha sonraki dönemlerde çeşitli meslek erbapları (sofist, retorik hocası veya avukat, tüccar veya meyhaneci, lonca başkanı ve olasılıkla bir yiyecek satıcısı) tarafından kullanıldığını göstermesi nedeniyle önemlidir (Bölüm 5 § D), ancak resimli graffitolar (Bölüm 5 §C) bu mekânın sıradan Aphrodisias halkının bolca zaman geçirdiği bir eğlence yeri olduğunu da göstermektedir. Komplekste belgelenen 532 oyun tablası bunun en belirgin kanıtıdır. Burası, Roma sınırları içinde en fazla oyun tablasının bir arada bulunduğu yer olma özelliğine sahiptir (Bölüm 5 §F). Tabaların birçoğu, MS 4. ve belki de 5. yüzyıllara oldukça kesin bir şekilde tarihlenebilmektedir ancak oyun oynama alışkanlığının Palmiye Parkı'ndaki bir sonraki büyük inşaat safhası olan 5. yüzyılın sonları ve 6. yüzyıl başlarından sonra da devam ettiği kesindir.

Geç Antik Çağ yenileme faaliyetleri

Palmiye Parkı'ndaki yapıların büyük bir kısmı ilk olarak MS 1. ve 2. yüzyıllarda inşa edilmiş olsa da yakın zamanda yapılan kazılar buranın anıtsallık ve mimari bütünlük anlamında zirve yaptığı dönemin MS 5. yüzyıl sonları veya 6. yüzyıl başları olduğunu ortaya koymuştur. 5. yüzyılın sonlarında meydana gelen ve kentin bazı yerlerinde tamir edilemeyecek kadar yıkıcı tahribatlar yaratan büyük bir depremin ardından (Bölüm 4 §M) nispeten kısa sürede kapsamlı bir restorasyon projesi hayata geçirilmiştir. Yapılan işler arasında havuz duvarları ve zemininde onarımlar (belki de bütünüyle yeniden kaplanması) (Bölüm 4 §B), yeni boru hatlarının döşenmesi (Bölüm 4 §C), havuz duvarları ile havuzu çevreleyen stoalar arasındaki zemin kotunun yükseltilmesi (Bölüm 4 §C), Propylon'un restorasyonu (Bölüm 4 §A), olasılıkla uzunlamasına ikiye bölünmüş ve en azından kısmen iki katlı, yeni ve genişletilmiş bir Güney Stoa'nın inşası (Bölüm 4 §F), Kuzey Stoa'nın içinin yenilenmesi (Bölüm 4 §E) ile Batı Stoa'nın yeniden inşası ve yeniden döşenmesi (Bölüm 4 §D) sayılabilir. Taş ustalarının bıraktığı işaretler bu yenileme çalışmasının lojistik arka planı hakkında bazı bilgiler vermektedir (Bölüm 5 §E).

Aphrodisias halkının bu ölçekte bir inşa seferberliğine girişmesi ve restorasyon çalışmalarının yanında yeni binalar yapabilmesi kentin bu dönemdeki canlılığına olduğu kadar eyalet başkenti olma rolüne ve de alanın önemine işaret etmektedir. Proje birçok yetkilinin de dikkatini çekmeyi başarmıştır. Propylonun ön cephesindeki üç yazıtta onurlandırılan eyalet valisi Doulkitios ile "şehrin babası" Ampelios bu süreçte önemli rol oynamıştır (Bölüm 4 §A; Ek 1, In10–12). Batı Stoa sütunları üzerindeki övgü yazıtları Albinos'un bu süreçte önemli görevler üstlendiğini gösterirken (Bölüm 4 §D), Güney Stoa'daki bir yazıtta Philippos adlı birinden söz edilmektedir (Bölüm 4 §F; Ek 1, In9). Yeni Güney Stoa'nın sütunları üzerindeki imparator Anastasius ve olasılıkla *praefectus praetorio per Orientem*'e ait monogramlar, hamilikte daha da yüksek bir hiyerarşik seviyeyi ortaya koymaktadır (Bölüm 4 §A; §F).

Bu restorasyon çalışması sırasında kompleksin açık alanında kalın moloz depozitleri oluşmuştur. Bu depozitlerde ve üzerlerindeki yerleşim katmanları içerisinde bulunan çok sayıdaki sikke Aphrodisias'ın Geç Antik Çağda nümizmatiği hakkında önemli bilgiler sağlamıştır (Bölüm 4 §G). Aynı katmanlardan ele geçen seramiklerin arasında ithal mal azdır (ARS, LRC, Kıbrıs Sigillatası) ve buluntular yerel üretiminin önemini kanıtlar niteliktedir (Bölüm 4 §H). Havuzu çevreleyen halka kanalın içindeki dolguda küçük buluntu sayısı az olsa da (Bölüm 4 §I), buradaki bulgular kentin bu dönemdeki beslenme alışkanlıkları ve gıda üretim faaliyetleri hakkında önemli veriler sunmaktadır (Bölüm 4 §J). Halka kanaldan elde edilen yanmış kalıntıların bir kısmı Palmiye Parkı'nda bahçecilik yapıldığını düşündürürken diğer kısmı olasılıkla kentin bu bölgesindeki veya yakınlardaki ritüel faaliyetlerle ilgilidir. Havuzun etrafındaki Geç Antik Çağ tabakalarına ait hayvan kemikleri de Aphrodisias'ın bu dönemdeki beslenme alışkanlıklarına dair önemli bilgiler sağlamaktadır (Bölüm 10 §C).

Palmiye Parkı'ndaki epigrafik bulgular kompleksin MS 5. yüzyılın sonlarında, üstelik kentte depremler nedeniyle önemli hasarların oluştuğu bir dönemde neden bu kadar ilgi gördüğünü daha iyi açıklamaktadır. Propylon'da Doulkitios'un adının geçtiği ikinci yazıtta onun özellikle Maioumarkhes olarak tanımlanması dikkat çekicidir (Bölüm 4 §M). Geç Roma döneminin Hıristiyan yazarlarını çok kızdıran Maiouma Festivali, Anadolu'da ve doğu Akdeniz'de son derece popülerdi ve genellikle su temalı törenler içeriyordu. Palmiye Parkı'ndaki havuzun bu dönemde Maiouma Festival alanı olarak kullanılmış olması olasıdır. Ancak bu durum, Palmiye Parkı'nın bu dönemde bir pagan kült merkezi olduğu anlamına gelmez. İnanca dayalı gerilimler yazıtlardan anlaşılmaktadır (Bölüm 5 §G). Bununla birlikte, Hristiyan oldukları anlaşılan Ampelios ve Albinos, kompleksin yeniden inşasına yatırım yapmaya istekli görünmektedirler. Ayrıca, Kuzey Stoa'nın havuz duvarlarına ve basamaklarına kazınmış Hıristiyan haçları ve Yahudi sembolleri çok yoğundur. Tüm bunlar mekânın toplumun her kesiminden insanlar tarafından kullanıldığını göstermektedir. Muhtemelen bu yatırımın amacı Palmiye Parkı'nı yeniden tasarlamak veya kullanım amacını değiştirmekten ziyade, çok sevilen bir kamusal alanı canlandırmak ve günün koşullarına uygun hale getirmekti. Bu dönemde kompleksin ana unsurları olan havuz ve bahçeler tüm zorluklara rağmen yenilenmiştir. Havuzun günümüze ulaşan kısımlarının çoğu bu döneme aittir. MS 6. yüzyılın başlarına tarihlenen önde gelen bir kişinin portre heykel başı da dahil olmak üzere havuzda bulunan Geç Antik Çağ heykel buluntuları alanın bu dönemde üst düzey heykel sergilerine ev sahipliği yapmaya devam ettiğini göstermektedir (Bölüm 7 §E).

Doulkitios ve meslektaşlarının yenileme çalışmalarından sonra Palmiye Parkı'nda bir daha büyük ölçekli değişiklik yapılmamıştır. Komplekse yapılan tek ekleme, MS 6. yüzyılın ortalarında veya hemen sonrasında Propylon'un önüne inşa edilmiş ve olasılıkla bir rezervuar olarak kullanılan su haznesidir (Bölüm 4 §N, Bölüm 6 §A). Bu hazne, daha önce yapılan yenilemelerin ardından havuzun ve temelinin sağlıklı işleyişi için yeterli suyu yedekte tutmak için inşa edilmiş gibi görünmektedir. Haznenin duvarları, gösterişli bir mitolojik kabartma serisi başta olmak üzere devşirme kullanılmış kabartmalar ve heykel kaideleriyle kaplıydı (Bölüm 6 §B, §C). Bu dekoratif uygulamanın merkezinde, olasılıkla Ampelios ya da başka bir 6. yüzyıl Aphrodisias soylusuna ait oturur pozisyonda bir heykelin kaidesi bulunmaktadır (Bölüm 6 §E). Havuzda daha sonra yapılan onarımlar ile tedarik ve drenaj sistemlerinde yapılan değişikliklere dair kanıtlar bu önemli kompleksin MS 620 yılı civarında meydana gelen depremden sonra bile faal tutulmaya çalışıldığını göstermektedir (Bölüm 4 §O).

Palmiye Parkı'nın yıkılışı

Palmiye Parkı'nın feci sonuyla ilgili somut kanıtlar havuz dibinde ortaya çıkan stratigrafide tespit edilmiştir. Burada, havuzun kuzey ve güneyindeki alanların temizlenmesiyle bağlantılı çok evreli depozitler ortaya çıkarılmıştır. İçlerinde çok sayıda mimari kalıntı, heykel, seramik ve küçük buluntunun yanı sıra, önemli miktarda hayvan kemiği ve karbonlaşmış birki kalıntısı da tespit edilmiştir. Temizlik çalışmaları sonucu oluşan bu depozitlerin ilki havuzun tüm zemini boyunca yayılmış karışık malzemeden ve havuzun kuzey duvarına dayanmış daha yoğun bir moloz yığınından oluşmaktadır (Bölüm 8 §A). Arkeobotanik analizler havuzun bu tarihte temiz su içerdiğini göstermektedir zira siltlenmeye veya havuz içinde su bitkisi yetiştiğine dair bir iz yoktur (Bölüm 8 §E). Bu tabakadan çok miktarda çatı kiremidi, kırık mermer mimari unsurlar ile yanmış ahşap ele geçmiştir (Bölüm 8 §A).

Temizlik çalışmaları sırasında havuz içine moloz atılmaya başlandıktan sonra havuz bakımsız kalmıştır. Alüvyon birikmeye başlamış (Bölüm 8 §A), sazlar ve diğer su bitkileri kök salmıştır (Bölüm 8 §E). Yeni bir moloz tabakası bu sefer havuzun güney duvarı boyunca oluşmuştur. Bu durum güney kısmın temizliği için de büyük emek harcandığını göstermektedir. Buluntuların çoğunluğu havuzun kuzey ucundaki dolguya benzer özellikler göstermektedir ve yine yanmış ahşap parçaları ile çok miktarda çatı kiremidi içermektedir (Bölüm 8 §A). Sığır ve atgillere ait kemikler de dahil olmak üzere çeşitli hayvan kemiklerinin de bu tarihte havuza atıldığı anlaşılmıştır (Bölüm 10 §C). Bu dolgu tabakalarında çok çeşitli seramik ve küçük buluntu tespit edilmiştir. Buluntular arasında damgalı unguentaria (Bölüm 8 §C), cam, stoalara ait metal parçalar, ticari ve dini objeler sayılabilir (Bölüm 8 §D). Dikkat çekici buluntu gruplarından biri de aralarında ok uçları ve cirit veya mızrak uçları da bulunan silahlardır. 1990 yılındaki kazılarda havuz tabanında olasılıkla askeri teçhizat parçası olan bir üzengi de ele geçmiştir (Bölüm 8 §D).

Havuzdaki birinci ve ikinci moloz depozitlerinden elde edilen buluntular Palmiye Parkı'ndaki yapıların bu moloz dolgusunu oluşturan temizlik çalışmalarından önce ciddi oranda hasar gördüğünü düşündürmektedir. Kuzey ve Güney Stoaların yanmış olduğu ve olasılıkla çatılarının çöktüğü, mimari unsurların bir kısmının da yıkıldığı anlaşılmaktadır. Bu durum havuz tabanındaki silah kalıntılarıyla birlikte ele alındığında, Palmiye Parkı'nın bir düşman saldırısı sırasında tahrip olduğuna işaret etmektedir. Bu olay ne zaman olmuştur? İlk moloz depozitinde elde edilen buluntular çoğunlukla MS 6. yüzyıla ve 7. yüzyılın ilk yarısına aittir (Bölüm 8 §B–D). En geç sikkelerin tarihi MS 643/644'tür ve depozit için bir *terminus post quem* sağlar (Bölüm 8 §B). Havuzdaki ikinci moloz depozitinde ise MS 632–635 tarihli bir Herakliusz sikkesi bulunmuştur ancak üzerinde olasılıkla MS 660–685 arası bir döneme ait Emevi kontrmarkı vardır (Bölüm 8 §B). Aphrodisias'ın başka alanlarında MS 614 ile 620 arasında, olasılıkla da MS 617 yılında güney Anadolu'nun Pers istilası esnasında yangın tahribatı yaşandığına dair önemli kanıtlar vardır. Bunun hemen ardından da MS 620 dolaylarında bir deprem meydana gelmiştir (Bölüm 8 §F).

Önceki araştırmalarda Palmiye Parkı'nda görülen yangın tahribatı da MS 7. yüzyılın ilk yarısında Perslerin bölgede gerçekleştirdiği akınlarla ilişkilendirilmişti. Havuzdaki ilk moloz depozitinin Perslerle bağlantılı olması mümkündür ve Palmiye Parkı'nı akınların ardından yeniden kullanılabilir kılma girişimine işaret ediyor olabilir. Ancak bu varsayım doğru ise, 617'deki Pers istilası ve 620'deki depremin ardından Aphrodisias halkı bu temizlik işine kalkışmak için 20 yıl beklemiş olmalıdır. Ama arkeobotanik kanıtlar bu düşünceyi desteklememektedir. Bu kalıntılara göre havuz, içerisine ilk moloz atılana kadar faal kalmıştır. Palmiye Parkı'ndaki yangın izleri ve havuz tabanındaki silah kalıntılarıyla ilgili daha olası bir öneri bunların Kuzey Stoa'nın da yanmasına neden olan, MS 643/644'ten sonra meydana gelen başka bir yıkıcı bir olayla bağlantılı olduğudur. İki moloz depoziti arasındaki alüvyon tabakası iki temizlik işlemi arasında zaman geçtiğini düşündürmektedir. Güney Stoa'daki tahribatın temizlenmesi sonucu oluşan ikinci moloz depozitinde bulunan ve MS 660'lar veya sonrasına tarihlenen Arap kontrmarklı sikke kesin tarihleme konusunda en önemli buluntudur. Böyle bir sikke Bizans döneminde Anadolu'da geçerli bir para birimi değildi. Bu nedenle, biri MS 640'lar sonu / 650'ler başı veya 660'larda ve diğeri 7. yüzyılın sonlarında olmak üzere iki ayrı Arap akını olduğunu düşünmekteyiz. Buna göre, Palmiye Parkı havuz tabanındaki depozitler, MS 7. yüzyılın ikinci yarısında Batı Anadolu'daki Arap akınlarının neden olduğu yıkıma dair bugüne kadar elde edilen en kesin kanıtları barındırıyor olabilir.

Palmiye Parkı'nın yıkımının kesin nedeni ve tarihi netlik kazanmasa da kompleksin bu tarihten sonra anıtsal karakterini asla geri kazanamadığı kesindir. Havuz içerisinde alüvyon birikmeye başlamış ve kısa sürede bataklığa dönüşmüştür. Stoalar ise çatısız olarak ayakta kalmıştır. Havuzun kuzey duvarlarına ve bunların kuzeyindeki zemine açılan direk delikleri, burada geçici yapıların, belki de pazar tezgahlarının kurulduğunu düşündürmektedir (Bölüm 8 §A). Havuzun güney tarafına küçük bir hazne açılmış, kuzeydoğu köşesine ise olasılıkla sığırların havuz içinde kalan sudan içmesi için bir rampa eklenmiştir. Havuz tabanındaki molozlardan elde edilen kemik buluntuları kasaplık faaliyetleri ve belki de derilerin işlenmesiyle ilgili olabilir (Bölüm 10 §C). Palmiye Parkı yedinci yüzyıla, baştan tasarlanmış, yenilenmiş, merkezinde faal durumda ve etkileyici bir havuza sahip kamusal bir alan olarak girmiştir. Fakat aynı yüzyılın sonuna gelindiğinde, ot ve bitkilerin bürüdüğü, kısmen harabe olan bu alan artık geçici bir pazaryeri olmanın yanında hayvanların su içmeye getirildiği ve hayvansal ürünlerin işlendiği, alüvyonla dolmuş bir bataklığa dönüşmüştür.

Alanın Orta Çağ ve sonrasındaki kullanımı

2012 yılında Palmiye Parkı'ndaki kazı çalışmaları başlayana kadar Aphrodisias'ın 7. yüzyıldan sonraki kentsel gelişimi hakkındaki bilgilerimiz Tiyatro Tepesi'ndeki Bizans dönemine ait izler ile Triconch Kilisesi, Piskopos Sarayı ve Katedral çevresinden gelen verilerden ibaretti.[1] Selçuklu, Beylikler ve Osmanlı dönemlerine ait veriler ise çok sınırlıydı. Kent merkezinin farklı yerlerinde zaman zaman devşirme mimari elemanlardan inşa edilen Orta Çağ duvarları kayıt altına alınmış, bazılarının plan çizimleri kazı defterlerine işlenmiştir ancak detaylı olarak incelenmemişlerdir. Bu tür yapıların küçük boyutlu açmalarda ortaya çıkarıldığı durumlarda arkeologlar çoğu zaman bunların tarla sınırı mı bina duvarı mı olduğunu anlamakta zorlanmıştır. Bu nedenle Palmiye Parkı'nda yapılan kazılar Aphrodisias'taki Türk yerleşiminin katmanlarını ilk defa geniş bir açık alan üzerinde araştırma fırsatı sunması açısından önemlidir. Yaygın düşünce, bu alanın Bizans dönemi sonrasında tarım amaçlı kullanıldığını ve 1960'larda olduğu gibi küçük parsellere bölündüğü yönündeydi, fakat yapılan kazılar ortaya MS 8. yüzyıldan 20. yüzyıla kadar takip edilebilen, çok daha karmaşık bir yerleşim süreci olduğunu göstermektedir. Yeni kazılar bu alandaki gelişmeleri ve adı MS 629 yılı civarında Stavropolis olarak değiştirilen kentte antik çağ sonrası yerleşimin başlangıcı hakkında önemli bilgiler sunmaktadır.

Havuzun olduğu alan, MS 8. ve 12. yüzyıllar arasında (bu yayında *4. Evre*), etrafında Orta Bizans Dönemi yerleşiminin geliştiği bir tür küçük bataklığa dönüşmüştür (Bölüm 9 §B).

1 Kentte bulunan Bizans dönemine ait verilerinin detaylı analizi için bkz. Jeffery 2022.

Zooarkeolojik analizlere göre su kaplumbağaları terk edilmiş havuzu mesken tutmuş, hatta muhtemelen kent halkı tarafından yiyecek olarak tüketilmiştir (Bölüm 10 §C). Kazılar sırasında bulunan birkaç 8. yüzyıl buluntusu ve Tiyatro Tepesi'nin kuzey yamacındaki Bizans surlarından aşağı kaymış gibi görünen Orta Bizans dönemi malzemesi dışında Bizans eseri sayısı sınırlıdır (Bölüm 9 §C). Bizans dönemi küçük buluntularının da benzer şekilde alanın güney kenarı boyunca yoğunlaştığı görülmüştür (Bölüm 9 §E). Palmiye Parkı çevresinde MS 7. yüzyıldan beri harabe halde duran eski yapılar 10. veya 11. yüzyılda büyük bir depremle yıkılmıştır. Sonraki dönemde havuz çevresinin molozdan arındırılması için yapılan sınırlı sayıdaki çalışmanın çoğunun Orta Bizans döneminde yapıldığı anlaşılmaktadır.

Selçuklu ve erken Beylikler döneminde (13. ve 14. yy. / *5.–6. Evreler*) siltasyon eski havuzu doldurup duvarlarını kaplayacak seviyeye gelmişti. Geride kalan açık alan ilk defa bu tarihte tarım amacıyla kullanılmaya başlandı (Bölüm 9 §B). Eski havuz alanı boyunca uzanan ilk yollar başta eski Tetrapylon Caddesi hattı boyunca olmak üzere Selçuklu veya Beylikler dönemi yerleşimin yoğun olduğu alanları birbirine bağlamaktaydı. Bu yolları daha sonra, açık araziyi parsellere bölen erken dönem tarla sınır duvarları takip etmiştir. Dar sokakları ve ara yolları çevreleyen daha gelişmiş sınır duvarlarına sahip gerçek bir yerleşim Beylikler dönemi boyunca ve erken Osmanlı döneminde (*7. Evre*, 14.–15. yy.) yavaş yavaş ortaya çıkmıştır (Bölüm 9 §B). Alanda yoğun olarak ele geçen Orta Çağ seramiklerinin en erkenleri Beylikler dönemine aittir (Bölüm 9 §D). Bu keşifler, Bizans sgraffito stillerinin Beylikler dönemi sırlı seramikleri üzerindeki etkisini, bölge ile Batı Anadolu'nun diğer yöreleri arasındaki ticaret ilişkilerini ve devam eden yerel üretimi anlamak açısından çok değerlidir.

İlk olarak 14. yüzyılda ortaya çıkan yerleşim zaman içerisinde bir köye dönüşmüştür. Genel görünümü itibariyle bu köy, içlerinde evler olan çok sayıda parsel veya sınırlandırılmış alan ve bunları birbirinden ayıran, iki yanında duvarlar olan dar yollardan oluşmaktadır (*8.–9. Evreler*, 15.–17. yy.) (Bölüm 9 §B). Bu tarihte evlerin duvarlarında, en azından alt sıralarda, devşirme Roma dönemi mimari parçalar, üst kısımlarda ise muhtemelen ahşap ve toprak kullanılmıştır. Arazi yapısının olasılıkla güneydekinden daha kuru ve sağlam olması nedeniyle bu binaların çoğu eski havuz ile çökmüş Kuzey Stoa arasındaki bölgede yoğunlaşmıştır. Bu yerleşim Osmanlı kadastro kayıtlarında Karia'dan türemiş bir isim olan "Gerye" olarak anılmaktadır. Buradaki yapılar ören yerinde Osmanlı yerleşiminin özellikleri hakkında bugüne kadar ortaya çıkan en net verileri sunmaktadır.

Bu yerleşimle ilişkilendirilen Osmanlı depozitlerindeki seramik malzeme miktarı Palmiye Parkı'nın hiçbir yerleşim evresinde görülmediği kadar çoktur (Bölüm 9 §D). Bu bulgular bazı ithal ürünlerin yanında yerleşimde yerel seramik üretiminin canlı bir şekilde devam ettiğini göstermektedir. Yerleşimde temel uğraşının tarım olduğu çiftçilik ve küçük ölçekli zanaatkarlık faaliyetlerine özgü çeşitli metal alet edevat ile kanıtlanmaktadır (Bölüm 9 §E). Bu duruma tek istisna Beylikler ve Osmanlı dönemlerine tarihlenen çok sayıdaki cam bileziktir. Bunların eski cam malzemelerin geri dönüştürülmesiyle yapılmış olması olasıdır. Bu döneme ait hayvan kemikleri Geç Antik Çağa kıyasla sığır ve atgillerin sayısında azalmaya, koyun ve özellikle de keçi sayısında da artışa işaret etmektedir. Buluntular arasında domuz ve yaban domuzu kalıntılarının da olması bölgedeki dini çeşitliliğe işaret ediyor olabilir veya beslenme alışkanlıklarındaki kısıtlamalarla ilgili olarak farklı yorumlara olanak sağlayabilir (Bölüm 10 §C).

Yerleşimin batı eteklerinde yer alan Osmanlı köy evlerinde yaşam 200 yıl kadar devam etmiş, 16. yüzyılın sonlarında veya 17. yüzyılın başlarında meydana gelen bir başka büyük depremin ardından terk edilmiştir. Seramik malzemede de bu dönemde ciddi bir azalma gözlemlenmektedir (Bölüm 9 §D). Bu tarihten sonra alan, tarihin bir noktasında "Geyre" olarak anılmaya başlanan köyün sakinleri tarafından işlenen bostan ve meyve bahçelerine dönüştürülmüştür. Bu tarihte köy merkezinin daha doğuda olduğu anlaşılmaktadır; zira eski Palmiye Parkı alanına en yakın Geyre evleri Propylon temelinin üzerine inşa edilmiştir (*10.–11. Evreler*, 17.–20. yy.) (Bölüm 9 §B). 19. yüzyılda Aphrodisias'ı ziyaret eden Antik Çağ uzmanları Tiyatro Tepesi'nin kuzeyindeki bölgeyi böyle tarif etmişti. 20. yüzyılın başlarında Palmiye Parkı'nın olduğu alana bakan Jacopi ve diğer kazıcılar da Palmiye Parkı'nın olduğu yerde tarlalar ve doğusundaki evlerden oluşan bu manzarayı görmüşlerdi (Bölüm 9 §B).

Roma dönemi kent parkından Osmanlı köyüne dönüşüm

Palmiye Parkı'nın Julius-Claudiuslar ile Flaviuslar arasındaki dönemde anıtsal bir nitelik kazanması süreci Aphrodisias'ta zamanının ötesinde kentsel ve mimari bir gelişim örneğidir. Kente kimi zaman Roma'daki mimari moda birebir taklit edilirken, kent kimi zaman da yeni mimari akımların yayılmasında öncü bir görev üstlenmiş gibi görünmektedir. Ortasında büyük bir süs havuzu ve bunun çevresindeki açık alanda gölge sağlayan ağaçlar tüm alanı süsleyen heykellerin olduğu bu portikonun tasarımının Augustus dönemi Roma'sının *porticus* anıtlarından esinlendiği aşikâr olsa da büyüklük açısından Aphrodisias'taki havuzun benzeri yoktur. Burada kurulan kentsel hurma bahçesi ise Smyrna'daki Hadrianus dönemi hurma bahçesinden daha erkendir. Benzer şekilde, cephe sütunlu bir yapı olan Palmiye Parkı Propylonu ve hatta MS 1. yy. ortasına tarihlenen Sebasteion Propylonu bile başka yerlerdeki benzer ve iyi bilinen mermer "cephe" mimarisi örneklerinin öncesine tarihlendirilmektedir.

Havuz ve çevresinde gerçekleştirilen kazılar bu kentsel mekânın yaklaşık altı yüzyıl boyunca, Antik Çağın sonuna kadar geçirdiği değişimleri okumamıza olanak sağlamaktadır. MS 2. ve 3. yüzyıllarda meydana gelen depremlerin neden olduğu hasar ve yapılan onarımlar, çevredeki portikolarda yapılan değişiklikler ve pazar esnafı için kullanılan *topos* yazıtları ile alanın ticari bir alana dönüşmesi tespit edilebilmektedir. Kazılar sırasında elde edilen önemli bulgular arasında bu dönemde meydana gelen büyük bir depremin izleri ve MS 495–505 yılları civarında bir süreçte hayata geçirilen büyük ölçekli onarım ve yenileme çalışmalarına dair izlerdir. MS 6. yüzyılın başında Aphrodisias'ın canlı bir kent olduğu artık kanıtlanmıştır. Dönemin taş ustalarının bıraktığı işaretler, diğer graffitolar ve oyun tablaları açısından bu alan çok zengindir. Onurlandırma amaçlı ve mitolojik konuların betimlendiği hem devşirme hem yeni heykellerin oluşturduğu giderek büyüyen bir heykel koleksiyonu ile çevrelenmiş bu kent parkında insanların havuz etrafında oyunlar oynadığı, portikolar altındaki seyyar satıcılardan içecek ısmarladığı anlar artık gözümüzde canlanabiliyor. Elde edilen bulgular havuzun MS 6. yüzyılın sonlarına kadar Maiouma şenliklerine ev sahipliği yapmış olduğunu göstermektedir. MS 6. yüzyıl boyunca veya olasılıkla 7. yüzyılın başında yapılan diğer çalışmalar havuzu besleyen su kaynağının devamlılığını amaçlıyor gibi görünmekte olup bu kamusal alanın kentsel kimlik için süregelen önemini de teyit etmektedir.

MS 6. yüzyılın başında kentin elde ettiği refah seviyesine karşılık 7. yüzyılın başlarında kentsel anıtsallığın aniden sona ermesi açıklık getirilmesi gereken bir durumdur. Aphrodisias'ın merkezinden, ama çoğunlukla da Palmiye Parkı'nın dışından elde edilen yeni bulgular kentin 617'de Persler tarafından yağmalandığını ve hemen ardından MS 620 dolaylarında Propylon'un yıkılmasına neden olan bir depremin meydana geldiğini göstermektedir. Kent bu yıkıcı olaylardan ve neden oldukları yaşam kaybı veya göçlerden sonra bir daha toparlanmamıştır. Ancak havuza atılmış mimari molozların oluşturduğu dolgular bu dönemden sonra da biri MS 7. yüzyılın ortasında, diğeri de olasılıkla aynı yüzyılın sonlarında olmak üzere birden fazla yıkıcı olayın yaşandığını göstermektedir. Bunlar iki farklı Arap akını olarak yorumlanabilir. Aphrodisias'ta MS 7. yüzyılda meydana gelen yıkımla ilgili kanıtları sınıflandırmak, kentteki klasik dönemin sona ermesine neden olan olayların ne kadar karmaşık olduğunu ortaya koymanın yanında, diğer Anadolu kentlerinde 7. yüzyılda yaşanan benzer süreçlerin anlaşılmasına yardımcı olabilir.

MS 7. yüzyılın ortalarından sonra havuz alüvyonla dolmaya başlamıştır ve görünüşe göre büyükbaş hayvanların su içmeye getirildiği bu yerin etrafına barakalar, belki de pazar tezgâhları kurulmuştur. Havuz, sonraki yüzyıllar boyunca dolmaya devam etmiş, 13. veya 14. yüzyıllara gelindiğinde tarım amaçlı parsellere bölünebilecek hale gelmiştir. 14. yüzyılda ise eskiden havuzun olduğu alan üzerinde bir yerleşim yeri gelişmiştir. Burası, Beylikler ve Osmanlı dönemi köyü Gerye/Geyre'nin bir bölümünü oluşturuyordu. Köydeki evlerin çoğu destek direkleri için kullanılan takozlardan da anlaşılacağı üzere ahşaptı fakat bazı büyük binalar taş temeller üzerine yükseliyordu. Sokak ve patikalar kuru taş duvarlarla belirlenmişti. 16. veya 17. yüzyıldaki depremin ardından evlerin boşalmasıyla Roma dönemi kent parkının Orta Çağın başlarında terk edilmesi, sonrasında bir yerleşime dönüşmesi ve ardından 20. yüzyıla kadar aralıksız şekilde tarım arazisi olarak kullanılmasını kapsayan döngü tamamlanmıştır.

Palmiye Parkı'nda gerçekleştirilen kazılarda elde edilen veriler, Roma ve erken Bizans dönemindeki kentsel gelişime, mimari ilerlemelere ve MS 1. ve 7. yüzyıllar arasında kamusal alan kullanımına ilişkin bilgimize katkı sağlamıştır. Kazılar, mimarlık ve heykel sanatının gelişimine olduğu kadar dönemin eğlence anlayışına, kentsel dönüşüm süreçlerine ve Anadolu'da klasik anlamdaki kent yapısının 7. yüzyılda neden sona erdiğine dair daha kapsamlı tartışmalara da açıklık getirmektedir. En büyük sürpriz ise kazıların Anadolu'da belki de bugüne kadar bilinen en büyük 14.–16./17. yüzyıl köy yerleşimini ortaya çıkarmış olmasıdır.

APPENDIX 1

Inscriptions from the Place of Palms

Angelos Chaniotis

This appendix contains a selection of inscriptions found in the area of the Place of Palms that have either not been studied in detail or about which new things can be said. Not included are certain inscriptions discussed elsewhere in this volume in sufficient detail (in Ch. 7, for example) or texts that are better examined in separate studies.[1] In many cases these inscriptions were not originally set up in the Place of Palms. Of course, the building inscriptions and the commemorative epigrams that concern the construction and reconstruction of the stoas and of the Propylon (In1–In2, In4, In9–In12) were originally displayed in this area, and the same applies to inscriptions commemorating the erection or restoration of decorative statues and reliefs (In3, In6–In8). Also at least some honorific statues (In13–In30) must have originally stood in this area, and certainly the three honorific statues of Antonine emperors (In13–In15). The numerous dedications from the Place of Palms (In31–In35) were not found *in situ*. We may assume that the sanctuaries and shrines where they originally stood were in the unexcavated area of the Agora. We know that a small sanctuary of Hephaistos existed in that area, since an inscribed architrave block recording the dedication of a building to Hephaistos was found in the northwest corner of the Agora.[2] There are strong indications that sanctuaries of Zeus Nineudios and Asklepios existed in this area (see In1 and In33). We can be certain that the epitaphs found in the Place of Palms (In36–In48) were moved to this area in secondary use.

The texts are presented according to the subject matter, not according to the place of their discovery, and within each category according to date: inscriptions concerning the construction and restoration of buildings and their sculptural decoration (In1–In12); honorific inscriptions for emperors and imperial officers (In13–In18); honorific decrees and honorific inscriptions for citizens (In19–In28); sculptors' signatures on honorific statues (In29–In30); dedicatory inscriptions (In31–In35); epitaphs (In36–In48); and a fragment (In49).

A. INSCRIPTIONS CONCERNING THE CONSTRUCTION AND RESTORATION OF BUILDINGS AND THEIR DECORATION

In1. Building inscription of the North Stoa (so-called 'Portico of Tiberius') (Pl. 10.B)

Thirteen white marble architrave blocks with cornice and three fasciae; inscribed in the uppermost fascia; on one block, on the top, a gameboard ('Nine Men's Morris') was cut. H 29 cm, W 2.84 m, D 1.04 m each, Lt. 9.5 cm.

Found in 1937 at the west end of the North Stoa; further fragments found in 1986–1988.

Date: *c.* AD 14–29.

Bibliography: Jacopi 1939, 86–96 no. 1 [*BE* 1948, no. 211]; Reynolds 1980, 77–78 no. 6 [*SEG* XXX 1244; *An.Ép* 1980, no. 870]; *IAph2007* 4.4 (photo). Autopsy (only fr. i).

i *vacat* Ἀφροδίτηι καὶ | Αὐτοκράτορι Καίσαρι Θεῶι | [Σεβαστῶι Δι]ὶ Πατρώωι καὶ | Αὐτοκράτορι Τιβερίωι Καίσα[ρι] | [Θεο]ῦ Σεβαστοῦ υἱῶι Σε|βαστῶι *stop* καὶ *stop* Ἰουλίαι Σεβασ|τῆι *stop* καὶ τῶι Δήμωι τὴν στοὰ[ν] | vv Διογένης Μενάνδρου τοῦ | [Δ]ιογένους τοῦ Ἀρτεμιδώρ|[ου καὶ ·· *c.* 13 ·· ἱέρ]|ηα Ἀφροδίτης *stop* καὶ *stop* Μένανδ|[ρος ·· ? ··]

ii [- - -]ΑΙΙΑΛ[- - -]
iii [- - -]ΤΑ[- - -]
iv [- - -]ΤΙ[- - -]

ii. Perhaps to be read as Ἀτταλ[ο- -].

'To Aphrodite and Imperator Caesar Divus Augustus Zeus Patroios and to Imperator Tiberius Caesar Augustus, son of Divus Augustus and to Iulia Augusta and to the People Diogenes, son of Menandros, grandson of Diogenes, great-grandson of Artemidoros, and [- - -], priestess of Aphrodite, and Menandros [- - -] (dedicated) the stoa.'

The inscription commemorates the construction of the North Stoa of the Place of Palms at the expense of Diogenes, son of Menandros. As we may infer from a still unpublished honorific decree (found in 1994), this Diogenes belongs to the family that provided the funds for the construction of the South Building of the Sebasteion and the Sebasteion Temple (see Ch. 2 §A). This new inscription makes a revision of the

---

1 The catalogue, therefore, does not include several fragments of Diocletian's Edict of Maximum Prices, originally inscribed on the west façade of the Civic Basilica and found in the Place of Palms (Inv. nos. 2017-32, 2017-40, 2018-19, 2018-68, I16.01) and a fragment of Diocletian's currency regulation (Chaniotis and Fujii 2015). Also excluded from this catalogue is a fragment of the base of a statue of the *ethnos* of the Maezei found on 25 July 2016 in the South Agora, trench 16.1 (M013), but originally from the Sebasteion. I have also not included a small fragment, probably from the Hadrianic Baths (*IAph2007* 4.102), two caryatid dedications (*IAph2007* 4.108 and the unpublished inscription 'Portico of Tiberius 4'), and two small inscribed panels from *opus sectile* paving (*IAph2007* 4.106–106). Three statue bases from the Propylon (Ch. 7 §C, **4, 5, 7**) and three from the West Stoa (Ch. 7 §D, **41–43**) are examined earlier in this volume.
2 Chaniotis 2004, 395–396 no. 15; *SEG* LIV 1041.

prosopography of the Sebasteion sponsors necessary. The text honours a man whose name is not preserved. Among other benefactions, he funded the construction of the Sebasteion temple (τὸ γεινόμενον ὑπ' αὐτοῦ Σεβαστεῖον Ἡρακλεῖον ἐντεμενιζόμενον λευκολίθῳ ναῷ καὶ περιστύλῳ ποικίλῳ; 'the Sebasteion Herakleion [or: a Herculean work], which was being constructed by him, by being elevated as a sanctuary through the construction of a marble temple and a richly decorated peristyle'); the same man had also completed the construction of a stoa that had shamed the city by remaining unfinished: τὴν πρὸ τοῦ Διὸς στοὰν ἀτελῆ τυγχάνουσαν καὶ τὸ σῶμα τῆς πόλεως ὑβρίζουσαν ἐκ τῶν ἰδίων μετὰ πολλῶν ἀναλωμάτων κατασκευάσας ('the stoa in front of (the temple/sanctuary/statue of) Zeus, which happened to be incomplete and was an insult to the body of the city, he constructed using his own fortune with many expenses').

The unfinished stoa, a very significant building in the heart of the city, must be the building consisting of the South Stoa of the Agora and the North Stoa (or 'Portico of Tiberius') of the Place of Palms. The cult place of Zeus, probably the sanctuary of Zeus Nineudios, must have been in the unexcavated area of the Agora.[3] The identity of this anonymous honorand is revealed by the building inscription of the North Stoa of the Place of Palms: Diogenes, son of Menandros, grandson of Diogenes, great grandson of Artemidoros. His name can also be restored in an inscribed architrave block from the South Stoa of the Agora, found in 2002:[4] [- - Διογένης Μενάνδρου τοῦ Δ]ιογένους τ[οῦ Ἀρτεμιδώρου - -]). At least two other individuals contributed to the construction of the stoa: a woman, priestess of Aphrodite, probably Diogenes' wife, and a certain Menandros, possibly an otherwise unattested son; it is less likely that this Menandros was Diogenes' father, because in that case he would have been mentioned earlier. Further contributors may have been mentioned in the lost part of the architrave, possibly an Attalos, Diogenes' brother (see the critical apparatus and below).

Diogenes' involvement in the construction of the Sebasteion may be inferred from the relevant building inscriptions of the Sebasteion. The inscription referring to the restoration of the South Building mentions two sponsors (in the reign of Claudius or early reign of Nero): Tiberius Claudius Diogenes, who fulfilled the promises made by his homonymous father and his uncle Attalos, and an Attalis (Τιβέριος Κλαύδιος Διογένης φιλοπολίτης, ἃ ἐπηγγείλατο Διογένης, ὁ πατὴ[ρ α]ὐτοῦ, καὶ Ἀτταλὶς καὶ ὑπὲρ Ἀττάλου τοῦ θείου).[5] Diogenes was, therefore, the brother of Attalos and the father of a homonymous son, who acquired Roman citizenship. Both Attalos and Attalis are mentioned in the original building inscription of the South Building (reign of Tiberius): [Ἄτταλος Μενάνδρου τ]οῦ [- - - καὶ Ἀτταλὶς Μενεκράτους τ]οῦ Ἄνδρω[νος Ἀ]πφιον).[6] The full name of Attalos' wife is given as Attalis Apphion, daughter of Menekrates. The names of Attalos' (and Diogenes') father and grandfather are not preserved. J. Reynolds suggested restoring

them as [Μενάνδρου τ]οῦ [Ἀττάλου]. She identifed Attalos' father with a certain Menandros, son of Attalos, known to have dedicated an epistyle.[7] Now that the honorific decree establishes the identity of the sponsor of the Portico of Tiberius with one of the sponsors of the Sebasteion, we know that the grandfather of Attalos and Diogenes was a Diogenes and we must, therefore, restore [Διογένους]. This restoration is two letters longer, but this is outbalanced by the fact that Ἀττάλου has two wide *taus* and Διογένους a narrow *iota*.

This identification also permits a better understanding of the fragmentary building inscription of the Sebasteion temple (reign of Tiberius). The sponsors were, again, Attalis Apphion on behalf of her deceased husband ([ὑπὲ]ρ Ἀττάλου τοῦ Μ[ενάνδρ]ου τοῦ ἀν[δρός]) and another individual on behalf of a relative (ὑπὲρ τοῦ [. . [5]. . .]οῦ).[8] This individual must be [Διογένης Μενάνδρου], who contributed money ὑπὲρ τοῦ [ἀδελφ]οῦ.

The building activities of the brothers Diogenes and Attalos and their families can be reconstructed as follows:[9] early in the reign of Tiberius, Diogenes, joined by other family members, contributed to the completion of the stoas in the area between the Agora and the Place of Palms. His brother Attalos and his wife provided funds for the South Building of the Sebasteion and promised funds for the Sebasteion temple. When Attalos died, still during Tiberius' reign, his widow and his brother Diogenes completed the construction of the temple. After the South Building had been damaged during an earthquake, Diogenes also promised to contribute to the restoration. However, he died, and his promise was fulfilled by his son Tiberius Claudius Diogenes, who provided the necessary funds on behalf of his deceased father and uncle, as well as by Attalos' widow, Attalis.

In2. Building inscription of the Propylon of the Place of Palms, the towers, and its decoration

Fifteen partly joining fragments of 7 architrave blocks; an inscription on the upper fascia. W (standard) *c.* 2.50 m, H 49 cm, D *c.* 76 cm, Lt. 9–10 cm.

Found during the excavation of the Propylon from 1975 to 1984.

Date: First century AD (before AD 96).

Unpublished. The text was transcribed by Joyce Reynolds (Unpublished inscriptions 77.47 + 77.48, 80.15, 27, 30, 31, 32, 83.?; 84.?) and Brian Rose (Notebook 253, p. 13). Andrew Wilson and Ben Russell added fr. 77.134 (the first block) and restored the text. Autopsy.

Τῇ προμήτορι Ἀφροδίτῃ καὶ Θεοῖς Σεβασ[τοῖς] καὶ τῷ δήμῳ Διογένης Μενάνδρ[ου] τοῦ Διογένους νεώτερος ἀνέθηκεν καὶ ἔκτισε[ν ἐκ τῶν] ἰδίων τὸ πρόπυλον ἐκ θεμε[λίων] σὺν τοῖς πύργοις καὶ ταῖς τειμαῖς τῶν Σεβαστῶν καὶ τῷ λοιπῷ κόσμῳ παντ[ὶ . . .]

'To the ancestral mother Aphrodite and the Divi Augusti and to the People, Diogenes 'the Younger', son of Menan-

---

3   Smith 2013, 22–23.
4   Fragment of an architrave block, broken on the right side (H 38 cm, W at least 2.16 m, D 60 cm, Lt. 14 cm); found in the centre of the South Stoa of the Agora (trench NAG 02.3). Mentioned by Ratté and Smith 2008, 720.
5   Smith 2013.
6   *SEG* LXIII 848.

7   Smith 2013.
8   *SEG* LXIII 849.
9   The reconstruction of the prosopography in Smith 2013, 22–23, should be modified accordingly.

dros son of Diogenes, dedicated and constructed from his own finances the propylon from its foundations with the towers and the honorific statues of the Augusti and all the rest of the decoration [- - -]'.

This inscription commemorates the construction of the Propylon, the towers, and statues of emperors (see Ch. 3 §A). The sponsor, Diogenes the Younger, cannot be identified with certainty, because both his name and the name of his father are very common in Aphrodisias.[10] The names Diogenes and Menandros were often used by members of a prominent family engaged in the building of the Sebasteion and the North Stoa of the Place of Palms (In1)[11] and honoured for service in public offices and benefactions.[12] Given the fact that Aphrodisian elite families were often engaged in building projects in the same area over more than one generation,[13] it is probable that this Diogenes is a relative of the homonymous benefactor who sponsored the construction of the earlier North Stoa. The following considerations suggest that he was his grandson.

1. The sponsor of the North Stoa (and the Temple of the Sebasteion) was Diogenes, son of Menandros, son of Diogenes, son of Artemidoros (see In1). His son, who participated in the restoration of the South Building of the Sebasteion, acquired Roman citizenship under Claudius. His name is Tiberius Claudius Diogenes, son of Diogenes (*IAph2007* 9.25; cf. 8.23). Diogenes the Younger can be identified neither as him nor as one of his descendants, since he lacked Roman citizenship. He must belong to a different line of this family (see below).
2. The sponsor of the Propylon is called νεώτερος. The word νεώτερος is often used to distinguish between homonymous fathers and sons.[14] This is not the case here since Diogenes' father was not homonymous. The word νεώτερος is, therefore, used to distinguish Diogenes (II), son of Menandros, from another Diogenes (I), son of Menandros, either a homonymous older brother[15] or, more likely, another older relative. Diogenes I must have been a well-known personality, possibly the sponsor of the North Stoa. The proximity of the building inscription of the North Stoa may have necessitated this clarification.
3. The North Stoa was funded by Diogenes, son of Menandros, together with another Menandros (In1). According to a well-attested pattern in Aphrodisian building projects, this Menandros must have been a relative, a younger brother or a son. This Menandros could have been the father of Diogenes the Younger.
4. One of the statues that decorated the Propylon was a statue of Emperor Nerva, erected still in his lifetime (In13). It was dedicated by the *demos* from the bequest of Diogenes the Younger, who must have been dead by that time. His lifespan can easily be reconciled with the hypothesis that he was a grandson or grandnephew of the sponsor of the North Stoa. A grandson or grandnephew of Diogenes I, who was active in *c.* AD 20–30, would have been active in public life under Nero and a senior public figure under the Flavians.

Even if an identification cannot be determined with certitude, it is certain that his building inscription, set up during Diogenes' lifetime, antedates the reign of Nerva (AD 96).

In3. Label of an image of Victoria Augustorum (Pl. 95.A–B)

Complete section of entablature conisting of an architrave-frieze-cornice. H 39 cm, W 2.61 m, D 54 cm. Architrave with three fasciae. Plain frieze. Cornice consisting of a projecting corona with poorly preserved top moulding. In a shallow recess of the entablature, 67 cm in width, there is an inscription on the corona of the cornice. This recess and the inscription indicate that there might have been an aedicula below the entablature. A statue either stood in this hypothetical aedicula, or possibly above on top of the entablature at this location. Future study of the top of the block could reveal more information.[16]

Found in 1971 (PT 71.85c) a little north of the basilica façade and recorded by J. Reynolds as 'Portico of Tiberius 8'. Found again a little west of the Basilica façade by Allison Kidd on Aug. 18, 2018 (Field Reports I 18.30).

Date: late first /early second century AD.

Unpublished. Transcribed by J. Reynolds. Autopsy.

    Ν̣ε̣ίκη Σεβαστῶν

ν[ί]κη Σεβαστῶν, Reynolds.

    'The Victory of the Augusti.'

The text probably is the label of an image (probably a statue) of Victoria Augustorum, either standing on the cornice or in an aedicula below. The letterforms suggest a date in the late first or early second century AD. The setting up of this statue might, therefore, belong to the period of the construction of the Civil Basilica, or restorations after an earthquake under Trajan (see below).

We should consider the possibility that the statue of Victoria Augustorum mentioned here is identical with a statue of Nike mentioned in another text. An inscription on a statue base records the dedication of a statue of Nike in the late first century BC and its restoration and dedication to the Emperors and the People in the first century AD.[17] In both texts we find the association of Nike with the Sebastoi:

    Νίκη πάρειμ[ι] θεογενε[ῖ]
    Καίσαρι ἀεὶ *vacat*

    θεοῖς Σεβαστοῖς καὶ τῶ[ι]
4   Δήμωι τὴν Νίκην καὶ τὸν
    [λ]έοντα vac. Καλ.[λ]ικράτης
    Μολοσσοῦ ἱερ[εὺς] Μηνὸς
    [Ἀσ]καινοῦ καὶ Ἑ[ρμοῦ Ἀ]γοραίου [τὰ]

---

10 Bourtzinakou 2012, lists 63 men with the name Diogenes (nos. 736–798) and 62 men with the name Menandros (nos. 1599–1660); some of her entries may refer to one and the same man. Cf. *LGPN* V.A, s.vv.
11 *IAph2007* 4.4 (here In1) and 9.25.
12 *IAph2007* 8.23 and 15.261.
13 Smith 2013, 22–23; Chaniotis 2018b.
14 Boyaval 2002, 147–8; for example *SEG* LVIII 1613 L. 6; LX 1261.
15 Νεώτερος can also be used to distinguish between two homonymous brothers: Koerner 1961, 73–74.

16 Description and information provided by Philip Stinson.
17 *IAph2007* 13.116.

8   [προ]γονικὰ ἀν[αθή]ματα αὐτὸ[ς]
    [ἐπ]ισκευάσα[ς ἀπο]καθέστησε[ν]

'I am Victory, always at the side of Caesar, the descendant of a god.
Kallikrates, son of Molossos, priest of Men Askainos and of Hermes of the Agora, himself restored and re-erected the dedications of his ancestors, the (statue of) Victory and the lion, for the divine Augusti and the People'.

The original location of the statues of Nike and the lion is not known. Six small fragments of the base were found as stray finds in the northeast necropolis, northeast of the stadium, and in other locations. The base's width (50 cm) is smaller than that of the inscribed recess of the cornice (67 cm), so that it is conceivable that this base and the statue of Nike stood in an aedicula under the cornice—and the statue of the lion in an adjacent aedicula. Of course, this is just a speculation. But the possibility that the cornice may be associated with the statues of the Nike and the lion, which would have stood in the southwest side of the Place of Palms, invites us to consider the history of these dedications in some detail.

The statues of Nike and a lion were originally dedicated by an ancestor (cf. L. 8: [προ]γονικὰ ἀν[αθή]ματα) of Kallikrates, son of Molossos. This original dedicant was a contemporary of Octavian (LL. 1–2: θεογενε[ῖ] Καίσαρι). The dedication of a statue of Victory suggests a military background; Kallikrates' ancestor must have been involved in the civil wars of the Late Republic. For this reason, he may be identified as Kallikrates, son of Pythodoros, known to have dedicated another statue of Victory, 'which accompanied him in all the wars and dangers in which he strove on his country's behalf'.[18] Not only does he share the same name with Kallikrates, son of Molossos, but he also dedicated the same object: a statue of Nike. The similarity of expression further supports this identification: the expression [Ν]ίκην ... συνπ[αραγεγ]ενημένην α[ὐτῶι] in the dedication of Kallikrates, son of Pythodoros, is exactly paralleled by the expression Νίκη πάρειμ[ι] in the dedication of the ancestor of Kallikrates, son of Molossos.

Kallikrates, son of Molossos, is known to have restored not only the statues of Nike and the lion, but also honorific statues of his ancestors (τὰς τῶν προπατόρων τιμὰς ἐπισκευάσας ἀποκαθέστησεν).[19] One of these ancestors was precisely a war hero, a magistrate, and a benefactor, who had been granted the exceptional honour of burial in the gymnasion. It is reasonable to assume that the ancestor of Kallikrates, son of Molossos, was none other than Kallikrates, son of Pythodoros.[20]

18 IAph2007 11.301 (found in the area of the theatre): [Καλ]λικράτης | [Πυ]θοδώρου τὴν | [Ν]ίκην ἐν π[ᾶσι τοῖς] | πολέμο[ις καὶ κιν]|δύνοις ἀγων[ισά]|μεν[ο]ς ὑπὲρ τῆς |[πατρίδ]ος συνπ[αραγεγ]ενημένην α[ὐ|τῶι] ἀνέθηκεν τῶι | Δή[μ]ωι ('Kallikrates, son of Pythodoros, dedicated to the People the Victory which accompanied him in all the wars and dangers in which he strove on his country's behalf').
19 IAph2007 12.402 lines 14–17.
20 The honorific decree survives in two copies: Reynolds 1982, 150–151 no. 28 and 151–154 nos. 29 and 30; Reynolds (following Robert 1937, 312–313) recognized that these texts refer to Kallikrates, son of Pythodoros (1982, 152, 154–155), whom she tentatively identified with the ancestor of Kallikrates, son of Molossos (1982, 156). These

At some point, the dedications and honorific statues of Kallikrates' ancestors were destroyed, and the younger Kallikrates restored them. Reynolds plausibly attributed the destructions to an earthquake, which she dated to the reign of Trajan.[21] This would place the restoration by the younger Kallikrates in the same period as the restoration of the statues of the Cyclops in the Place of Palms (see below In4). The original location of the statue of Nike is not known; it may have been the Place of Palms, but the block may have been brought from another location in the city, because of its length, to be reused for the entablature of the western South Stoa in the late sixth century AD.

In4. Restoration of a building and a statue group.

White marble statue base shaft inscribed on two adjoining faces (a: narrow side; b: long side, to the left of side a); the surface under the inscription on side b has been scraped off, indicating an erasure. H 69 cm, W 62 cm, D 2.21 m, Lt. 2 cm.

Found in 1977 built in secondary use into the western corner of the exterior wall of the late antique collecting basin west of the Propylon (Agora Gate: Trench 5; Inv. 77.134).

Date: AD 102–116.

Bibliography: Reynolds 1980, 73–74, no. 3a [SEG XXX 1254; BE 1982, 355; An.Ép. 1980, 868]; Reynolds 1982, 183–184 no. 55 (only a) [SEG XXXII 1097; BE 1983, 391]; IAph2007 4.308 (photo); Thomas 2018; Wilson 2018a, 473–474. Autopsy.

a   τῇ προμήτορι Ἀφροδε[ίτῃ]
    vac. καὶ τῷ δήμῳ vac.
    Αὐτοκράτωρ Καῖσαρ Νέρου-
4   ας Τραϊανὸς Σεβαστὸς
    Γερμανικὸς Δακικὸς ἐκ τῆς
    Ἀδράστου τοῦ Περείτου Γρύ-
    που διαθήκης ἀποκαθέστη-
8   σεν διὰ Καλλικράτους τοῦ
    Περείτου Γρύπου ἱερέως
    vac. ἐργεπιστάτου vac.

b   ὁ δῆμος τοὺς ἀνδριάντας τοῦ
    «Κύκλωπος» κατενεχθέντας ὑπὸ
    σεισμοῦ καὶ συντριβέντας καὶ ἀ-
4   χρειωθέντας ἐκ τῶν ἰδίων ἐπισ-
    κευάσας ἀποκαθέστησεν –
    erasure?

a: 'To the first mother Aphrodite and the People, Imperator Caesar Nerva Trajan Augustus Germanicus Dacicus restored (this) from the will of Adrastos Grypos, son of Pereitas, through Kallikrates Grypos, son of Pereitas, priest, supervisor of the work.'

texts are published in IAph2007 11.301, 12.103, 12.402, 12.701, but without reference to these connections.
21 Reynolds 1982, 153 and 156. On this earthquake, see Wilson 2018a, 473–474.

b: 'The People repaired and restored the statues of "the Cyclops", thrown down, shattered and made useless by an earthquake, at their own expense' (transl. J. Reynolds, modified).

The similarity of the lettering suggests that both texts refer to construction work carried out at roughly the same time, but not necessarily both of them under Trajan.[22] Both texts refer to repairs (a LL. 7–8: ἀποκαθέστησεν; b LL. 4–5: ἰδίων ἐπισκευάσας ἀποκαθέστησεν), that were funded by two different sources. The repairs of an unidentified object (apparent to the viewer) under Trajan were funded by the bequest of Adrastos Grypos to the emperor (a),[23] whereas the repairs of a statue group were covered by public funds of the city (b). The fact that the two texts are written on the same base suggests that they refer to repairs of the same statue group on two different occasions;[24] this is plausible but not certain. The identity of the first object is not given.

The object of the repairs is only identified by the second inscription: statues destroyed during an earthquake. It has been suggested that these statues were a composition showing the construction of Aeneas' weapons by Vulcan, assisted by the Cyclops, at the request of Venus.[25] However, Joshua Thomas has convincingly identified fragments of a statue group showing Polyphemos eviscerating a companion of Odysseus as part of this composition;[26] the fact that only the Cyclops is mentioned makes clear that he, not Odysseus, was the main subject of the statue group.[27] The plural form (τοὺς ἀνδριάντας τοῦ Κύκλωπος) requires an explanation. Either the Cyclops here is to be understood as the name of a composition ('the statues belonging to the myth/the episode of Cyclops') or various episodes concerning the Cyclops were represented—for example, the Cyclops' love for Galateia that inspired Theocritus' homonymous idyll and is represented in a relief in the Sebasteion.[28] The dimensions of the base rule out the second hypothesis. The phrase τοὺς ἀνδριάντας τοῦ Κύκλωπος should therefore be understood as referring to the name of the composition: 'the statues of (the composition called) "The Cyclops"'.[29] The original location of the monument in which the statue group stood is not known. It may have been the Place of Palms, where the base was found; representations of Polyphemos are often found in association with aquatic display.[30]

What was repaired by the emperor (using a bequest made on his behalf) is not mentioned in the inscription on the narrow side of the base, but it must have been apparent to the reader. The reference to different funds must mean either repairs of the statue group on two different occasions or repairs of two different objects.[31] A significant difference between the two texts is the fact that the restoration of the object to which the first text refers required the service of an ἐργεπιστάτης (a supervisor of the construction). It is true that ἐργεπιστάται could supervise the erection of honorific statues (IAph2007 8.39 and 12.308), but they are more often mentioned in connection with the construction of buildings: the Hadrianic Baths (IAph2007 5.6) and the Theatre (IAph2007 8.108, 8.112, and 8.113). A clue as to what was restored with Adrastos' bequest is provided by the dedicatory formula (A LL. 1–2): τῇ προμήτορι Ἀφροδε[ίτῃ] καὶ τῷ Δήμῳ. It is exactly the same formula as the one used for the original construction of the Propylon a few years earlier (In2): Τῇ προμήτορι Ἀφροδίτῃ καὶ Θεοῖς Σεβασ[τοῖς] καὶ τῷ δήμῳ; the North Stoa was also dedicated to Aphrodite, the Augusti, and the Demos (In1). Only the reference to the Emperors is missing, but this can be easily explained: the reigning emperor could not use funds bequeathed to him to make a dedication to the deified emperors. It is, therefore, possible that Trajan did not restore statues. If we assume that both texts were visible, the base must have originally been placed at a corner, with its long side (a) facing the readers and informing them about the statue, and the narrow side (b) commemorating the restoration of a building or part of a building, possibly in the Place of Palms. We do not know why an imperial text was inscribed on the narrow side, while the broad side was used for the inscription that mentions the *demos*. Presumably, the narrow side was more suitable for the work that Trajan had funded.

Adrastos and his brother Kallikrates belonged to a prominent family whose members used the name Grypos ('hook-nosed') as their second name.[32] Other relatives include Titus Antonius Lysimachos Grypos, son of Adrastos, in the mid-first century AD (IAph2007 12.207) and Pereitas Grypos, son of Adrastos, in the second century AD (IAph2007 12.528), whose son Molossos served as a priest of Hermes Agoraios while still a child. Kallikrates, son of Molossos (In4) may be a member of the same family.

In5. Building inscription

White marble architrave block, slightly chipped on the upper edge and at both sides; an inscription on two fasciae, continuing on an adjacent block to the right. H 40 cm, W 2.05 m, D 64 cm, Lt. 6 cm.[33]

Found in 1969 fallen in the south west corner of the Place of Palms, in front of the Civil Basilica.

Date: early second century AD.

Bibliography: Reynolds 1980, 78 no. 7 [SEG XXX 1255; An.Ép. 1980, no. 871]; IAph2007 4.3 (photo).

    v Αὐτοκράτορι Καίσαρι Θεῷ Σεβαστῷ Π | [- - -]
    vv Ἀντίπατρος πριμοπειλάριος σὺ|[v - - -]

1. π[ατρὶ πατρίδος?], Reynolds.

'To Imperator Caesar Divus Augustus [father of the fatherland? - - -] Antipatros, a *primipilarius*, [together with - - -]'.

---

22 Cf. Reynolds 1982, 183; cf. Reynolds 1986, 111–112.
23 For bequests to the emperor see Rogers 1947; Millar 1977, 153–158.
24 This is assumed by Wilson 2018a, 473.
25 Reynolds 1980, 75.
26 Thomas 2018.
27 Thomas 2018, 156–157.
28 The Sebasteion relief: Smith 2013, 237–239.
29 For a similar reference to the title of a composition cf. for instance F.Delphes III.3.128: ἐπιδοῦναι τῶι θεῶι καὶ τοῖς Ἕλλησι μετὰ τὸν γυμνικὸν τῆι θυσίαι ἐν τῶι σταδίωι τῶι Πυθικῶι ᾆσμα μετὰ χοροῦ «Διόνυσον».
30 Thomas 2018, 161.
31 Cf. Thomas 2018, 148: 'the individuals named on Side A orchestrated repairs of a different kind, perhaps focusing on an accompanying architectural installation.'
32 On second names in Aphrodisias see Chaniotis 2013b. In IAph2007 4.308 the second name is tentatively attributed to Pereitas.
33 The dimensions given by Reynolds 1980 (H 14 cm, D 11 cm), are not correct.

The inscription records the dedication of a building to an emperor. Reynolds noted that the letter-forms, noticeably later than those of the inscriptions concerning Zoilos, exclude an identification of the emperor with Augustus. She suggested identifying Antipatros with the *primipilarius* Marcus Cocceius Antipatros Ulpianus, the father of Cocceia Maxima, who dedicated one of the caryatids in the East Court of the Olympian (Hadrianic) Baths.[34] This identification is nearly certain, since Antipatros Ulpianus is the only *primipilarius* attested in Aphrodisias. The lettering of this inscription and the form of the architrave are very similar to those of an inscribed architrave block found in the arena of the stadium which names a certain [- -] Μᾶρκος Κοκκήιος Οὐλπιαν[ό]ς as sponsor of another building.[35] He must be the same man. He served in the Roman army and, to judge from his *praenomen* and *nomen gentile*, he must have received Roman citizenship under Nerva (M. Cocceius Nerva). Considering the fact that his daughter dedicated a caryatid during the reign of Hadrian at the earliest, his building activities in Aphrodisias can be dated to the early second century AD. It is striking that the full name of the emperor is not given. His identity must somehow have been apparent to the reader. He must have been an emperor with close relations to the dedicant (Nerva, Trajan, or Hadrian) and/or to Aphrodisias. This, and the fact that the construction to which this architrave belongs is to be located in the area of the Hadrianic Baths (see Ch. 3 §C), make an identification with Hadrian very probable. In Hadrian's inscriptions, the title *pater patriae* is usually mentioned after his full name (Αὐτοκράτωρ Καῖσαρ Τραϊανὸς Ἁδριανὸς Σεβαστός),[36] often after references to the number of years he had held the *tribunicia potestas* and the number of his imperatorial acclamations.[37] However, there is an exception, an inscription from Herakleia, in which we find an abbreviated version of his name (Imperator Caesar Augustus), followed by the honorific title *pater patriae*: [Αὐτοκρά]τορι [Σεβαστ?]ῷ Καί[σαρι] π(ατρὶ) π(ατρίδος).[38] Antipatros sponsored the building together with another individual (L. 2: σὺ|[ν - - -]), possibly his daughter.

In6. Dedication by Kapitoleinos of a relief panel re-used in the late antique basin in front of the Propylon

White marble relief panel showing Pan and a seated female figure; inscribed on upper moulding, which is broken away. Lt. 3 cm.

Found in 1978 near the Propylon (Agora Gate 1, previously Nymphaeum 1).

Date: late second century AD.

Bibliography: *IAph2007* 4.306 (text; Reynolds); Linant de Bellefonds 1996, 184; 2009 (relief).

[- - - Καπιτω]λεῖνος υἱὸς Καπιτωλ[είνου - - -]

The text probably mentions the sponsor or one of the sponsors of the decoration of an unidentified building with mythological reliefs with a pastoral scene, Greeks fighting against Amazons, Greeks fighting against Centaurs, and gods fighting against the Giants. The decoration was reused in the late antique basin in front of the Propylon, and in Gaudin's Fountain (see Ch. 6). Capitolinus, son of Capitolinus, cannot be identical with Τιβέριος Κλαύδιος Καπιτωλεῖνος, son of Tib. Claudius Smaragdos, who supervised a dedication to Claudia Antonia Tatiane, but he may well have been a member of the same family. It is not possible to say with certainty whether the Capitolinus who supervised repairs in the North Stoa (see Ch. 3 §D) is the son of Smaragdos or the son of Capitolinus.

In7. Assembly mark on relief panel re-used in the late antique basin in front of the Propylon

White marble relief sculpture panel, showing an Amazonomachy; an inscription on the upper moulding. Lt. 3 cm.

Found in 1978 in the area of the Propylon (Agora Gate 2, previously Nymphaeum 2)

Date: late second century AD.

Bibliography: *IAph2007* 4.307 (text; Reynolds; photo). Linant de Bellefonds 1996, 175–177; 2009 (relief).

vac. Θ *vac.* [- - -]

The original location of this relief panel is not known; it was reused in the late antique basin in front of the Propylon. J. Reynolds observed that the letter *theta* could be an assembly mark, indicating the position of the panel (ninth panel),[39] but in view of the its size, visibility, and clear cutting she also entertained the thought that it may be an abbreviated label for the young hero depicted below, label, for example Θ(ησεύς). An assembly mark is the more probable interpretation.

In8. Dedication of a statue (?) by Helladios

White marble block with projecting moulding; possibly the upper part of a statue base; inscribed on the upper fascia. H 39, W 76, D 65, Lt. 3 cm.[40]

Found during Mendel's excavations of the Hadrianic Baths in 1905; copied by Boulanger (notebook A, 65 no. 29; 'Galerie de l'E(st), N(ord)' = our West Stoa). Recorded by the NYU expedition in 1975, lying against the wall between the East Court of the Baths and West Stoa (Inv. 75.278), then brought to the excavation house. Found again in August 2019 by Ahmet Tolga Tek among the blocks in the field outside the excavation house.

Date: *c.* AD 325–350.

Bibliography: Robert 1948, 14 note 3 (from Boulanger's notes); [cf. Robert and Robert 1960, 25; 1965, 157]; Roueché 1989, 32 no. 17; *ala2004* 17; *IAph2007* 4.120 (photo). Autopsy.

---

34 The inscription is mentioned by Smith 2007, B21 and Wilson 2016a, 187 no. 14.
35 Chaniotis 2004, 397 no. 19; *SEG* LIV 1027.
36 For example, *TAM* II 1191–1193; III.1.10.
37 For example, *IGBulg* IV 2057; *TAM* II 1187.
38 *I.Heraclea Pontica* 57.

39 On such assembly marks see Ch. 5 and Weber 2015.
40 The dimensions given in Roueché 1989, *ala2004* and *IAph2007* are not correct. The stone was studied and measured by Özge Acar in August 2019.

θῆκε κἀμὲ ἐνθάδε Ἑλλάδιος ὁ
ἀνανεωτὴς τῆς λαμπρᾶς μητροπόλεως.

'Helladios, the renovator of the splendid metropolis, set me up, too, here'.

The object of Helladios' dedication is not named, since it was obvious from the inscription. Although the use of the verb τίθημι in connection with the erection of a building would not be unparalleled in a late antique context,[41] the dimensions of the block suggest that the 'speaking object' was a statue.[42]

The expression 'me, too' and similar expressions (for example καὶ τοῦτο τὸ ἔργον) are very common in late antique epigraphy in connection with the contributions of governors and benefactors to the adornment of a city with new or restored buildings and statuary.[43] Helladios' dedication was, therefore, part of a more extensive programme. Indeed, a second dedication by Helladios, also using the expression κἀμέ was found in the Hadrianic 'Olympian' Baths;[44] in this dedication he is designated as ἁγνός (pure), a common attribute of high officials and governors. This makes the identification with Helladios, a governor (μέγαν ἡγεμονῆα), honoured by the province of Karia ([Κ]ᾶρες στῆ[σα]ν), certain.[45]

Rouché observed that the lettering of the two Helladios dedications is very similar to a dedication made by Flavius Zenon, a high priest, who can be dated to *c.* AD 325–350 (*IAph2007* 5.302). This provides an approximate date for Helladios' governorship and activities in the area of the Baths and the west part of the Place of the Palms.

In9. Building inscription concerning the roofing of part of the South Stoa.

White marble architrave block with simple moulding above two stepped fasciae; an inscription on the upper fascia. H 42 cm, W 2.71 m, D 64.5 cm, Lt. 5–7 cm.

Found in 1971 towards the west end of the South Stoa.

Date: Late fifth century AD.

Bibliography: Rouché 1989, no. 66; *ala2004* 66; *IAph2007* 4.19 (photo).

† Φίλιππος Ἡροδιαν(οῦ) ὁ θαυμ(ασιώτατος) εὐχαριστῶν τῇ οἰκίᾳ πατρίδι τὰ β΄ διάχωρα ἐσκέπασεν †

'Philippos, son of Herodianos, *admirandissimus*, expressing his gratitude to his own fatherland, roofed the two sections.'

---

41 For a bath: *IGUR* 69 (Rome, early fifth century AD): με ... ξεινοδόκον θῆκ[ε λοετρόν]. For a spring: *I.Didyma* 159 II (Didyma, late third century AD): θῆκεν ἄγαλμα πόλει, πηγὴν κοσμήσας.
42 Cf. *IG* II² 3553, 3998; *IG* V.2.312; *IG* IX.4.1163; *IG* X.2.2.261; *IG* XII.1.806 II; *SEG* XIX 538; XXVI 1835; XXVIII 21; LV 617; *I.Beroia* 37; *IGUR* III 1365; *I.Cilicie* 100 bis. Pont 2010, 450, also takes the block to be a statue base, but assumed that Helladios restored the Hadrianic Baths (Pont 2010, 140 and 155).
43 Examples from Aphrodisias: *ala2004* 42, 43 83 xv. For statues, see *SEG* LXVI 1722–1723 (καὶ τοῦτο τὸ ἄγαλμα).
44 Rouché 1989, 32 no. 18; *ala2004* 18; *IAph2007* 5.118.
45 Robert 1965, 157; Rouché 1989, 31–32 no. 16; *ala2004* §6; *IAph2007* 1.131 ii. Rouché 1989, 32, suggested that the three inscriptions refer to the same individual (cf. *ala2004* ii.35).

The dedicant is not otherwise attested.[46] The superlative θαυμασιώτατος is attested already in the imperial period as a praise for members of the civic and provincial elites.[47] Its use was formalized in the fourth century AD as the translation of the Latin *admirandissimus*.[48] Used in the fourth and fifth centuries for members of the higher imperial administration,[49] later it is mostly attested for minor imperial officers and prominent citizens, especially ἔκδικοι/*defensores civitatis*.[50] The fact that Philippos does not mention an office suggests that he only held a civic or minor imperial office.[51]

To judge from the findspot, the two διάχωρα roofed by Philippos, were probably the two sections of the South Stoa, eastern and western (see Ch. 4 §F).[52] The word διάχωρον is attested in inscriptions to indicate the section of a building that was covered with a mosaic or with revetment plaques.[53] It is not clear whether the text refers to repairs of the roof of part of the Stoa or the construction of the late antique South Stoa.

In10. Commemorative epigram for the reconstruction of the Place of Palms honouring Ampelios (Pl. 28.A)

Inscribed on the second bastion of the Propylon (counting from the north), on the highest remaining course of blocks. Lt. 4 cm.

Date: Late fifth century AD.

Bibliography: Rouché 1989, 68 no. 38 [*An.Ép.* 1990, 961]; Merkelbach and Stauber 1998, 232 no. 02/09/03; Puech 2002, 433–434 no. 233; *ala2004* 38; *IAph2007* 4.202 i (Rouché; photo).

†
ἴδμονι θεσμοσύνης γλυκερῷ γενετῆρι τιθήνης
Ἀμπελίῳ Νύμφαι χάριν ἴσχομεν οὕνεκα θάμβος
χώρῳ φυνικόεντι καὶ ἀγλαὸν ὤπασε κάλλος

---

46 The name Philippos is rare in Aphrodisias (Bourtzinakou 2012, nos. 2286–2289; *LGPN* V.A, s.v.), but attested several times in late antique contexts (Rouché 1989, 122, 129 iii, 134 v, 198, 211; cf. *ala2004* V.42); Herodianos is unattested, but cf. Herodes (Bourtzinakou 2012, nos. 1279–1281; *LGPN* V.A, s.v.).
47 Three attestations in the second century AD: Oliver 1970, 113–114 no. 28; Lewartowski 2003, 218 (an archon of the Panhellenion); *TAM* V.3.1472 (an Asiarches and orator); Ferrary 2014, 568–569 no. 289 L. 19 (local magistrate and benefactor of Laodikeia).
48 Koch 1902 Koch 1903, 74 (with references to literary sources); Hornickel 1930, 15–16 (with references to papyri); cf. Rouché 1989, 108. The epigraphic attestations have increased since the last studies. See the following notes.
49 *Praefectus praetorio*: *SEG* LXI 1155 (*c.* AD 354–358), 1156 (AD 350–352). Ἀνθύπατος Ἀσίας: *I.Ephesos* 44+add. L. 8 (*c.* AD 439–442). Ἡγεμών: *TAM* II 553 (fifth century AD). Δοὺξ Ἰσαυρίας: *MAMA* III 73 (*c.* AD 395–408).
50 *Defensores civitatis* (ἔκδικοι): *Sardis* VII.1.18 = *SEG* LII 1177 (AD 459); *SEG* XXXVII 500 (sixth century AD). Ἐπαρχικός: *IG* X.2.1804. Πρωτεύων: *IGLS* VI 2831 (AD 430/431). A priest (πρεσβύτερος): *SEG* LIII 1800 (seventh century AD).
51 Rouché 1989, 108; *ala2004* V.42; cf. Trombley 2001, II 64: *defensor civitatis*.
52 For a different interpretation (intercolumniations) see Rouché 1989, 109; *ala2004* V.42.
53 Mosaic: Orlandos 1929, 39–41 nos. 2, 3, 6, 7 (Eresos, fifth century AD); *SEG* LI 1647 (Sardis, early third century AD; διαχώρημα). Revetment: *SEG* XLV 1647 = LI 1641 bis; LI 1642, 1646 (Sardis, fourth century AD).

313

4 ὄφρα καὶ ἡμετέροις τις ἐν ὕδασιν ὄμμα τιταίνων
   αὐτὸν ἀεὶ καὶ χῶρον ὁμοῦ Νύμφας τε λιγαίνοι.
   Τραλλιανὸς ῥητὴρ τάδ᾽ ἐγράψατο Πυθιόδωρος

'To Ampelios, learned in law, sweet father of his nurse, we Nymphs are grateful; for he gave wonder and splendid beauty to (this) place of palms, so that anyone who, standing among our waters, turns his glance around, may always sing the praise of him and of the place and of the Nymphs as well. Pythiodoros, the orator from Tralles, wrote this.' (transl. Roueché, slightly modified)

The orator and poet Pythiodoros of Tralles is known only from this source.[54] Unlike the epigrams for Doulkitios (In11–In12), presumably written by local poets who remain anonymous, this epigram was commissioned (by Ampelios himself?) from a scholar from a neighboring city. The literary qualities of this epigram, with the use of the rare words ἴδμων (L. 1) and ῥητήρ (L. 6), and the oxymoron 'father of his nurse' (L. 1)—a witty variation on the old honorific title πατὴρ πατρίδος and Ampelios' function as πατὴρ τῆς πόλεως (cf. IAph2007 12.19; ala2004 43)—are higher than than those of the other two epigrams.[55]

Ampelios is known as a lawyer (IAph2007 12.19; ala2004 43: ἐλλογιμότατος σχολαστικός), and served as πατὴρ τῆς πόλεως (pater civitatis), that is he supervised the civic finances and construction works.[56] He is mentioned in connection with various building activities and repairs of buildings in the late fifth/early sixth century AD: the 'palaestra' in the Bouleuterion (IAph2007 2.19; ala2004 43), the Theatre Baths (IAph2007 8.609; ala2004 44), the city walls (IAph2007 12.101 ii; ala2004 22), and probably has some connection to the Sebasteion Temple (see Ch. 5 §E). None of the relevant inscriptions states that Ampelios provided the funds for these building works. The 'palaestra' was constructed and the city walls were repaired 'under' Ampelios (ἐπί Φλαβίου Ἀμπελίου), and this formulation, which is used in connection with several other σχολαστικοὶ καὶ πατέρες in late antiquity,[57] suggests supervision not funding. As was the general practice in the fifth century,[58] Ampelios must have been the governor's agent.

In the Place of Palms, to which the epigram refers with the words χῶρος φοινικόεις (L. 3; cf. L. 5: χῶρον), the object of his repairs and reconstruction was probably the main pool (L. 4: ἐν ὕδασιν)[59] and the palm grove. Other parts of the construction work in this area are attributed to the governor Doulkitios (see In11 and In12). For the date, see In11. See also the discussion in Ch. 4 §A.

In11. Commemorative epigram for the precinct of the Place of Palms honoring the governor Doulkitios (Pl. 28.B)

Three partly joining fragments of a block of the third bastion of the Propylon (counting from north); traces of red paint in the letters. Lt. 5.5–6 cm.

Found in 1980 by the NYU excavation (Inv. 80.28, 80.29 and 80.53).

Date: Late fifth century AD.

Bibliography: Roueché 1993, 68 no. 39; Merkelbach and Stauber 1998, 236–237 no. 02/09/07; ala2004 39; IAph2007 4.202 ii (Roueché; photo).

   καὶ τόδε [Νυμφάων τ]έμενος Κ[. . .^{c. 5–6}. .]. ἔγειρε |
   Δουλκί[τιος κτίστη?]ς τῆς ⟨Ἀ⟩φ[ρ]οδισιάδος |
   οὐδὲν [φεισάμενος] πλούτου δόξης χάριν ἐσθλῆς· |
4 ἥδε γὰρ [ἀίδ]ιον μ[ν]ῆμα βροτοῖσιν πέλει.

1. [Νυμφάων τ]έμενος, D. Feissel (apud Roueché); in fine, Roueché reads Λ, but only the right bottom apex of a letter is preserved and other restorations are possible (including Ν); in the lacuna we expect an attribute of the Nymphs or the temenos; but for example κ[αλλικόμω]ν, κ[αλλίδενρο]ν, and κ[αλλίκρηνο]ν are too long. Gianfranco Agosti suggested κ[αθαρῶν ἀ]νέγειρε, which would make good sense in the case of a fountain (cf. Greek Anthology 9.257 and 9.327), less so in the case of the pool. The poet may have mentioned the recipent of Doulkitios' generosity, that is the Karians. Κ[άρεσσι]ν ἔγειρε is a possibility; the form Κάρεσσι appears for example in an epigram of Gregory of Nazianzos (Greek Anthology 8.184: Μαυσώλου τάφος ἐστὶ πελώριος, ἀλλὰ Κάρεσσι | τίμιος; I owe this reference to Gianfranco Agosti (Rome), with whom I have discussed possible restorations) and in the manuscripts of Theokritos' praise of Ptolemy (Id. 17.89); Agosti suggests instead Κ[αρῶν ἀ]νέγειρε; but in that case we would have two genitives referring to the τέμενος (Νυμφάων and Καρῶν). || The initial Α in Ἀφροδισίαδος is written Λ, and the remaining traces of the first Ο look more like an Α. || 3. [φεισάμενος], Merkelbach. || 4. [ἀίδ]ιον, Merkelbach.

'Doulkitios, [builder] of Aphrodisias, raised up also this precinct [of the Nymphs for the Karians?], not at all sparing with wealth for the sake of noble fame; for fame is what remains an eternal memorial for the mortals.'

This epigram commemorates the construction of the 'precinct of the Nymphs'. If we take the word τέμενος literally, it is a reference to the entire area of the Place of Palms, not only the pool (see also Ch. 4 §A). The fact that a statue of Doulkitios was erected as 'a witness of his labours' (μάρτυς σῶν καμάτων) in front of the Baths, at the other end of the Place of Palms, supports this assumption.[60] On this interpretation, the epigram that commemorates the reshaping of the entire area is flanked

---

54 Puech 2002, 434, tentatively suggests a relation between Pythiodoros of Tralles and the grammarian Flavius Pythiodoros attested in Hermoupolis in the late fifth century AD.
55 Puech 2002, 434.
56 On this office see Jones 1964, I, 726–731, 736, 758–759, who equates the pater civitatis with the curator (λογιστής); cf. Martindale 1980, 74. This view has been challenged by Roueché 1979, 176–185. For σχολαστικοὶ καὶ πατέρες as curators of building works see the next note. For πατέρες πόλεως in late antique Aphrodisias see Roueché 1979, 176–177.
57 For example, Aphrodisias: IAph2007 5.10 ii and 5.14: ἐπὶ Φλ. Φωτίου σχο(λαστικοῦ) κ(αὶ) πατρός); Ephesos: SEG XXXIII 961; Mopsuestia: SEG XXVIII 1287 iii; Tarsus: SEG XXIX 1530; XXXVII 1348; CIG 4438; Side: I.Side 164a; Attaleia: Petersen 1890, 163 no. 68. Further examples in Roueché 1979, 177–179.
58 See Jones 1964, I, 726–758.
59 Construction and restoration of fountains in late antiquity: Pont 2010, 172–174; Puech 2002, 434 note 4, stresses the need to collect late antique epigrams that celebrate baths, fountains, and aqueducts.
60 Roueché 1989, 73–75 no. 41; ala2004 41; IAph2007 8.608.

by epigrams that refer to the construction of parts of it: the pool and the palm grove (left) and the Propylon (right). It seems that the governor Doulkitios (see In12) used private funds for this building program.

In12. Commemorative epigram for the Propylon honoring the governor Doulkitios (Pl. 28.C)

Inscribed on the fifth bastion of the Propylon (counting from the north), on the highest remaining course of blocks; remains of red paint in the letters. Lt. 4–5 cm (*phi*: 9 cm).

Date: Late fifth century AD.

Bibliography: Roueché 1989, 69 no. 40; Roueché 1993, 188–189 no. 65; Mentzu-Meimare *BZ* 89 (1996), 58–73; [*SEG* XLVI 1395]; Merkelbach and Stauber 1998, 02/09/07; *ala2004* no. 40; *IAph2007* 4.202 iii (Roueché; photo).

> τὸν καὶ ἀγωνοθέτην καὶ κτίστην καὶ φιλότιμον καὶ
>   Μαιουμάρχην |
> Δουλκίτιον, ξεῖνε, μέλπε τὸν ἡγεμόνα |
> ὅστις κἀμὲ καμοῦσαν ἀμετρήτοις ἐνιαυτοῖς |
> 4   ἤγειρεν κρατερὴν χεῖρ᾽ ἐπορεξάμενος.

'Stranger, sing the praise of Doulkitios, governor, also, president of contests, builder, lover of honour, and Maioumarch. Stretching out his mighty hand, he raised me too, who had suffered for innumerable years.'

While the other two epigrams from this wall (In10 and In11) identify the object of the construction, this epigram has the form of a 'speaking object' (L. 3: κἀμέ). This makes clear that the epigram is inscribed on the object of the construction, which must be the Propylon.[61] Since the construction is feminine (L. 3: καμοῦσαν), the Greek word implied must be πύλη (Gate).

This epigram provides more information on Doulkitios.[62] He was governor of the province of Karia (ἡγεμών), who had organized contests (ἀγωνοθέτης) and the festival of *maioumas* (Μαϊουμάρχης), a nocturnal celebration during which the celebrants immersed themselves in water, certainly in the pool of the Place of Palms (see Ch. 4 §M). The epigrams in his honour praise him for his generosity (In11), ambition to leave a good reputation (In11, In12), building works (In11, In12), and justice (*ala2004* 41; *IAph2007* 8.608: εὐνομίη).

The three epigrams do not provide absolutely secure dating criteria. Doulkitios' title is given as ἡγεμών (*praeses*). As Roueché pointed out, the title and rank of the governors of Karia was raised to that of an ὑπατικός (*consularis*) some time during the reign of Anastasius I (491–518). But there is a *caveat*: the term ἡγεμών is used here in a poetic text that must respect the metre and may still use a familiar term some time after the governor's title changed. For evidence supporting a date in the late fifth century AD (under Anastasius I) see the discussion in Ch. 4 §A.

---

61 Cf. Roueché 1989, 69, without further discussion.
62 See the detailed discussion by Roueché 1989, 71–72 and *ala2004* iv.19.

B. HONORIFIC INSCRIPTIONS FOR EMPERORS AND IMPERIAL OFFICERS

In13. Honorific inscription for Emperor Nerva (Pl. 95.C)

Marble base with moulding above. The lines are not centred. H 1.30 m (1 m without the moulding), W 86 cm (60 cm without the moulding), D 77 cm. Lt. 5.5–6 cm. See also Ch. 7 §C – **1**.

Found in 1977 in rubble southeast of the Propylon (Inv. 77.34). Autopsy.

Date: AD 96–98.

Unpublished. Transcribed by J. Reynolds.

> Αὐτοκράτορα
> Νέρβαν ❦ Καίσα-
> ρα ~ Σεβαστὸν
> 4   ὁ δῆμος ἐκ τῶν
> Διογένους · τοῦ
> Μενάνδρου *vac.*
> τοῦ Διογένους
> 8   νεωτέρου *vac.*
> *vacat*

2. Ligature of NE.

'The People (set up the statue of) Imperator Nerva Caesar Augustus from the bequest of Diogenes the Younger, son of Menandros, son of Diogenes.'

The funds for the statue of the reigning emperor were provided by the bequest of Diogenes the Younger, whose identity is discussed above (see In2).

In14. Honorific inscription for Emperor Hadrian (Pl. 95.D)

Marble statue base with a large moulded capital; the capital has been damaged. H 1.02 m, W 61 cm, D 66 cm, Lt. 5.5–6 cm. See also Ch. 7 §C – **2**.

Found in 1983 at the Propylon (Inv. 83.75).

Date: *c.* AD 117–123.

Unpublished. Transcribed by J. Reynolds. Autopsy.

> Αὐτοκράτο-
> ρα Καίσαρα
> θεοῦ Τραϊα-
> 4   νοῦ Παρθι-
> κοῦ υἱὸν θεοῦ
> Νέρουα υἱω-
> νὸν Τραϊα-
> 8   νὸν Ἁδρια-
> νὸν Σεβασ-
> τὸν ὁ δῆμος

'The People (set up the statue of) Imperator Caesar Hadrianus Augustus, son of Divus Traianus Parthicus, grandson of Divus Nerva.'

The fact that no praising epithet is attributed to Hadrian (Σωτήρ, Ὀλύμπιος, Πανελλήνιος)[63] suggests that the statue was probably dedicated early in his reign, before his first journey to Asia Minor in AD 123.

In15. Honours for Emperor Antoninus Pius.

Four joining fragments of a white marble statue base shaft; on the top holes for the attachment of a crowning element; the two bottom corners are broken. H 1.15 m, W 75.5 cm, D 52 cm. Lt. 5.5–6 cm (LL. 1–6), 4.5–5 cm (LL. 7–13). The statue has survived. See also Ch. 7 §C – **3**, **10**.

Found in 1980 together with the accompanying statue of Antoninus Pius, at the Propylon, its original location (inv. no. 80.24; SBI 32).

Date: AD 138–161.

Bibliography: *IAph2007* 4.201 (Reynolds; text; photo); Smith *et al.* 2006, no. 17 (statue). Autopsy.

  Αὐτοκράτορα
  Καίσαρα Τίτον
  Αἴλιον Ἁδρια-
4 νὸν Ἀντωνεῖ-
  νον Σεβασ-
  τὸν Εὐσεβῆ
  ὁ δῆμ[ο]ς
8 ἐξ ὧν ὑπ[έ]σχε-
  το Ἄδραστος
  Ἀδράστου τοῦ
  [Ἀ]πολλωνίου
12 [τ]οῦ Ἄνδρωνος
  [Ἀ]ττάλου

'The people (set up the statue of) Imperator Caesar Titus Aelius Hadrianus Antoninus Augustus Pius from the (funds) which Adrastos, son of Adrastos Attalos, son of Apollonios, son of Andron, promised.'

The statue of the emperor was funded from a gift promised and made by a certain Adrastos. Promises of gifts (ὑπόσχεσις, ἐπαγγελία) are attested in Aphrodisias.[64] It is conceivable that some of these statue dedications had been promised by candidates for public office, as a sort of *summa honoraria*, that is, as a part of the contributions expected from an office-holder.[65] We know that the donor served as a *stephanephoros* and endowed funds for a 'perpetual *stephanephoria*'; an early third-century epitaph mentions, his second, posthumous, *stephanephoria*—the cost for the office in that year was covered through his endowment.[66]

Adrastos' homonymous father had the second name Attalos.[67] Since three of the names used in this family (Attalos, Adrastos, and Apollonios) are among the most common names in Aphrodisias—although Andron is less common—[68] it is not possible to establish a relationship between this family and other Aphrodisian families in which these names occur.

In16. Honorific inscription for T. Oppius Aelianus Asklepiodotos

White marble statue base with capital with moulding on three sides and shaft with raised double frame; an inscription on the moulding of the capital (LL. 1–2) and within the panel of the shaft (LL. 3–12). H 84 cm, H 1.10, W 84 cm, D 84, Lt. 2 cm. See also Ch. 6 §B – **B 2**.

Found in 1977 re-used in the late antique basin in front of the Propylon (inv. no. 77.135).

Date: *c.* AD 250–280.

Bibliography: Roueché 1981, 108–113 no. 6 [*SEG* XXXI 910; *BE* 1982, 357; *An.Ép.* 1981, 770; *An.Ép.* 1982, 893]; Roueché 1989, 16–19 no. 7 [Christol 1986, 219 no. 47]; *ala2004* 7; *IAph2007* 4.309 (Roueché; photo). Autopsy.

  ἡ πατρὶς
  Ἀγαθῇ Τύχῃ
  Τ(ίτον) Ὄππ(ιον) Αἰλιανὸν
4 Ἀσκληπιόδοτον
  τὸν λαμπρότατον
  ὑπατικὸν ἡγεμόνα
  Καρίας καὶ Φρυγίας
8 ἀνθύπατον καὶ ἐπα-
  νορθωτὴν Ἀσίας, κτί-
  στην καὶ σωτῆρα καὶ
  τῆς ἑαυτοῦ πατρίδος
12 Τιβ(έριος) Κλ(αύδιος) Μαρκιανὸς ὁ
  πρῶτος ἄρχων

Ligatures of NH (L. 6), NK (L. 8), THN (L. 9), HN (L. 10).

'The fatherland, with good fortune, (set up the statue of) T(itus) Opp(ius) Aelianus Asklepiodotos, the most splendid consular, governor of Karia and Phrygia, proconsul and *cor-*

---

63 Σωτὴρ Ζεὺς Ὀλύμπιος: 8.708; 9.119; Σωτήρ: unpublished inscription (I 18.12); Ὀλύμπιος Πανελλήνιος: 5.5.
64 For example, *IAph2007* 1.109; 8.52; 11.104; 11.401; 12.204. For funds provided by individuals for the erection of statues see Chaniotis 2020, 112.
65 For example, *IAph2007* 4.308 mentions the promise made by the strategos Artemidoros Pedisas during his term in office to dedicate statues: καθὼς ὑπέσχετο καὶ αὐτὸς κατασκευαζομένου τοῦ φοινεικοῦντος ἐν τῷ τῆς στρατηγίας αὐτοῦ χρόν[ῳ] ('as also he himself promised while the palm grove was being constructed during his service as a strategos').

66 *IAph2007* 11.31: ἐπὶ στεφανηφόρου Ἀδράστου τοῦ Ἀδράστου τοῦ Ἀπολλωνίου τὸ β΄ ἥρωος. The identity of the stephanephoros and the donor can be regarded as certain, in view of the names of the father and the grandfather; the identity was suggested by Bourtzinakou 2012, nos. 62 and 72, whereas *LGPN* V.B, s.v. Ἄδραστος nos. 47, 48, and 54, regards them as two different individuals.
67 *IAph2007 ad loc.*, does not exclude the possibility that 'it was the benefactor's grandfather who was called Apollonios Attalos'. This can be ruled out. The second name of an individual is given at the end of filiations that are introduced with the article τοῦ. See Chaniotis 2013b.
68 Adrastos: Bourtzinakou 2012, nos. 31–99; *LGPN* V.B, s.v. nos. 4–66; Apollonios: Bourtzinakou 2012, nos. 287–399; *LGPN* V.B, s.v. nos. 50–148; Attalos: Bourtzinakou 2012, nos. 574–624; *LGPN* V.B, s.v. nos. 3–58; cf. Attalis: Bourtzinakou 2012, nos. 566–573; *LGPN* V.B, s.v. nos. 1–9. Andron: Bourtzinakou 2012, 223–229; *LGPN* V.B, s.v. nos. 2–8.

rector of Asia, builder and saviour also of his own fatherland; Tib(erius) Cl(audius) Markianos, the first archon (was in charge)' (transl. C. Roueché, slightly modified).

T. Oppius Aelianus Asklepiodotos was a citizen of Aphrodisias with a distinguished career in the imperial administration.[69] After serving as a governor of the joint province of Karia and Phrygia, he served as proconsul and *corrector* of Asia—the formulation of the text does not prove that he served as governor and *corrector* at the same time. C. Roueché and M. Christol have proposed two different chronologies, depending on whether he can be identified with a governor of Karia and Phrygia, the *vir perfectissimus* Asklepiodotos mentioned in a milestone from the area of Apamea erected under Carus, Carinus, and Numerianus (AD 282/283).[70] According to Roueché, who accepts the identification, Asklepiodotos was appointed governor under these emperors with the equestrian rank of a *perfectissimus* (διασημότατος ἡγεμών); during his governorship, possibly under Diocletian, he was promoted to the rank of a *clarissimus* and admitted into the senate; this explains why the honorific inscription mentions his title as λαμπρότατος ὑπατικὸς ἡγεμών. As a governor of Asia, he also served as *corrector* to oversee the further subdivision of the province of Asia under Diocletian, perhaps in AD 293.[71] M. Christol favoured, instead, the hypothesis that the equestrian Asklepiodotos of the milestone and the senator Asklepiodotos are two different individuals.[72]

The senator's governorship should be dated in the period c. AD 250–283, in which the province of Karia and Phrygia was ruled by a *consularis*. This date is more plausible and can be supported by the fact that there is no evidence for *curatores* under Diocletian. On the contrary, there is evidence for the assignment of *consulares* as curators of whole provinces (Achaia and Asia) from the late second century AD to the mid-third century AD.[73] As Roueché noted, this is the last appearance of the office of first archon and Markianos, whose family had acquired Roman citizenship in the early Imperial period, and is the latest identifiable member of the traditional civic elite; in later inscriptions, citizens only have the *nomina* Aurelius and Flavius.[74] This too favours an earlier date (in the 250s) rather than a later date (under Diocletian). Markianos may be identical with the Tiberius Claudius Markianos mentioned in *IAph2007* 11.60 (c. AD 240–260).[75] Finally, the fact that Asklepiodotos is praised as a rescuer of the city makes more sense in the period in which Aphrodisias was facing the challenges posed by the creation of the province of Karia and Phrygia and struggling for a privileged position.

69 See the detailed commentary of C. Roueché in *ala2004* II.4–II.11. Cf. Pont 2020, 232, 313, 331–332, who follows Roueché's date.
70 *SEG* XXXI 1101 iii: διασ(ημοτάτου) Ἀσκληπιοδότου (sic).
71 *ala2004* II.4, II.7, and II.10.
72 Christol 1986, 219–221.
73 Achaia: *IG* IV².1.694 (c. AD 200); *F.Delphes* III.4.269 (late second/early third century AD); *IG* VII 2510; *SEG* XLI 456 (early third century AD). Asia: *I.Didyma* 156 (c. AD 250); *I.Milet* I.7.266 (restored; third century AD).
74 *ala2004* II.5.
75 Roueché 1981, 108, considered but rejected this identification, because in *IAph2007* 11.60 she restored the name of Markianos as Tiberius Claudius Apollonios Markianos. However, Apollonios may be the name of his father ([ἀγω]νοθετοῦ[ντος Τιβερί]ου] Κλαυδίου [·· ? ·· υἱοῦ | Ἀπολ]λωνίου Μα[ρκιανοῦ ·· ? ··]).

In17. Honorific inscription for an emperor (Julian or Justinian?) (Pl. 68.B)

Eight joining fragments of the upper part of a white marble revetment plaque of a statue base, broken at the corners. H 76 cm, W 74 cm, D 2.5 cm, Lt. 9.5 cm.[76] See also Ch. 7 §C – **8**.

Found in 1983 at the Propylon (Agora Gate: II.83. IV.C at c. 3.00) during the dismantling of the wall (83.127).

Date: AD 361–363 or AD 527–565.

Bibliography: Roueché 1989, 125 no. 81; *ala2004* 81; *IAph2007* 4.311 (Roueché; photo).

    τὸν εὐσεβέστ[α]-
    τον καὶ καλλί -
    νικον ἡμῶν
4   [δεσπό]την Φλ(άουιον)
    [c. 5–6 -ια]νόν
    [- - - - - - -]

4. Abbreviation sign ϛ || 5. [Ἰουστινια]νόν?, Roueché; [Κλ.ς Ἰουλια]νόν?, Chaniotis.

'[The city?] (set up the statue of) our most pious lord and winner of fair victories Flavius [- -ia]nus.'

The number of letters per line varies (9–12). C. Roueché estimated 12 letters for line 5, ruling out the restorations [Κωνσταντῖ]νον (12 letters) and [Οὐαλεντια]νόν (12 letters) as too long, and [Μαρκια]νόν (9 letters) and [Ἰουστῖ]νον (9 letters) as too short. She also ruled out [Κλ. Ἰουλια]νόν (11 letters) because Julian's name was erased in other inscriptions in Aphrodisias.[77] She tentatively suggested restoring [Ἰουστινια]νόν, which also has 12 letters, exactly as [Κωνσταντῖ]νον and [Οὐαλεντια]νόν, but three of them are narrow iotas. She admitted, however, that 'the elegant appearance of the text might suggest an earlier rather than a later date, and there is certainly a great contrast between this text and some others which we have dated to the later fifth or early sixth century'.[78]

Roueché's argument for ruling out Julian can be discarded. The two inscriptions in which Julian's name was erased are written on the lintel block of the West Gate and on the shaft of a large statue base (H 1.16 m). After Julian's *damnatio memoriae*, the erasure of his name, not the destruction of the entire monuments, was the only option the authorities had. By contrast, in this case the name of the emperor appears on the thin revetment plaque of a statue base; to remove the revetment plaque and replace it was not a difficult task. Since it is unlikely that the line containing the emperor's name was very crowded, Julian's name (11 letters, including two iotas) better fits the limited space of the lacuna. The praising epithets, quite common for emperors since the third century AD, do not permit a decision. Julian is called εὐσεβέστατος in Magnesia and καλλίνικος in Samos,[79] and

76 The measurements given in *ala2004* and *IAph2007* (0.16 × 0.74 × 0.025) are not correct. To judge from the photograph, the height is slightly larger than the width; since the letters are 9.5 cm high, the height must be 76 cm.
77 *ala2004* 19 = *IAph2007* 12.1001; *ala2004* 20 = *IAph2007* 8.405.
78 *ala2004* VI.5.
79 Magnesia: *I.Magnesia* 201. Samos: *IG* XII.6.427.

these attributes are also epigraphically attested for Justinian.[80] As Roueché observed, the elegant appearance of the text would rather support a date in the fourth century AD,[81] and moreover the individual letter-forms find parallels in public inscriptions securely dated to the fourth century AD.[82] The letter beta has two separate bowls, as in inscriptions of the late fifth century AD,[83] but this form also appears in the honorific epigram for Ioannes, chairman of the council, dated by Roueché to the sixth century AD on very shaky grounds;[84] on the contrary, the lettering favours a much earlier date. For these reasons (length of lacuna, lettering), I am more inclined to restore Julian's name rather than that of Justinian (see also Ch. 7 §C).

In18. Honorific epigram for the *praefectus praetorio* Anthemios (i) and Christian acclamations (ii) (Pl. 60.C)

Two joining fragments of a rectangular statue base without moulding; an inscription on the front (i), possibly engraved after an earlier inscription had been erased; a second inscription and a cross on the right side (ii), after an earlier inscription had been erased. H 1.05 m, W 61 cm, D 57.5 cm, Lt. 3.5 cm (i), 3.5–6.5 cm (ii), 17 cm (cross). See also Ch. 6 §B – **B 3**.

Found in 1977 near the Propylon, during the excavation of the collecting basin (Inv. 77.76, SBI 47).

Date: *c.* AD 405–414 (i); *c.* fifth/sixth century AD (ii).

Bibliography: Roueché 1989, 61–63 no. 36 (i) and 188–189 no. 144 (ii); Merkelbach and Stauber 1998, 233 no. 02/09/04 (i); Feissel 1991, 372 (i); *ala2004* 36 (i) and 144 (ii); *IAph2007* 4.310 i/ii (Roueché; photo).

    i   ΘΕΜ[·]ΙΙΙ[·]ΚΑΙΙΙΙΝ σε φάλαγξ ἔστησεν, ὕπαρχε, |
        ἀντ᾽ εὐεργεσιῶν μικρὰ δίδουσα γέρα, |
        Ἀνθέμιε, [σ]ῴζων γὰρ ὁμοῦ δήμους τε πόλεις τε |
        ῥύσαο καὶ Καρῶν τάξιν ἀπολλυμένην, |
        ἣν Βερονικιανὸς διέπων θρόνον | ν ἡγεμονῆος ν |
        ἤνωγεν τεύχειν εἰκόνα μαρμαρέη[ν]

    ii Φῶς † ΧΜΓ
        Ζωή

80 *IGLS* IV 1809: ὁ εὐσεβέστατος καὶ καλλίνικος ἡμῶν βασιλεύς. Anderson, Cumont, and Grégoire 1910, III, no. 255.
81 Cf. the honorific inscription for Helladios: *ala2004* 16. Cf. also *ala2004* 21, 22, 116, and 235.
82 Cursive epsilon and sigma: *ala2004* 13, 14, 16, 17, 31, 153. The square omega is used in two inscriptions that mention the governor Constantius (mid-fourth century AD): *ala2004* 140 (acclamation) and 235 (mosaic inscription); cf. *ala2004* 154.
83 Palmatus: *ala2004* 62; Albinos: *ala2004* 82–83. The beta has a continuous curved line in inscriptions of the third and fourth century AD: *ala2004* 7, 14, 15, 19, 24, 152, 154.
84 *ala2004* 73 with commentary in VI.51: 'Texts 73 and 74 both honour local citizens, John and Hermias; their lettering and layout resemble one another. Neither text includes any clear indication of date, but both are written in hexameters which conform to Nonnan metrical practice. The structure of 73, v.1 is not dissimilar to that of a line of Nonnus' *Paraphrase*: γερόντων εἰς ἓν ἀγειρομένων πρωτόθρονος ἕζετο βουλή (*Par. Jo.* 30. 189–90). … Nonnus' influence on other writers can probably first be observed in the last decades of the fifth century. In short verses such resemblances cannot be considered conclusive, but I would favour a sixth-century date for both these texts.'

i. L. 1, initio, θεμ[ί]στῳ[ρ] (with square sigma and omega) would fit the lacuna and make sense, but causes a metrical problem (as any word starting with θεμ- and a short syllable does), Chaniotis; perhaps Καρῶν σε φάλαγξ, although this seems clumsily repetitious, Roueché. || ii. There are traces around the cross which might be decoration or a monogram, Roueché || ii. L. 1, perhaps Χ(ριστὸν) Μ(αρία) γ(εννᾷ), Roueché.

Translation:

i. 'The array of the Karians, knowledgeable in law (?), set up your statue, prefect, giving a small reward for your benefactions; for, Anthemios, saving peoples and cities, you also rescued the order of the Karians, which was being destroyed; this (the order of the Karians) Veronicianus, occupying the seat of governor, urged to make a marble statue' (transl. C. Roueché, modified).

ii. 'Light! Life! Mary gives birth to Christ (?).

Anthemios served as *prefectus praetorio* in AD 405–414.[85] Here, he is honoured as a protector of δῆμοι, probably provinces, and cities[86] and as rescuer of the τάξις Καρῶν. The identity of those who set up his statue—the provincial council of Karia or the governor's *officium*—is disputed. Pointing to the fact that a governor could not order the provincial council to set up a statue, D. Feissel suggested that the statue was erected by the *officium* (L. 1: φάλαγξ); he adduced as a parallel another honorific inscription from Aphrodisias set up for the governor by his *officium* (στρατεία).[87] Although C. Roueché recognized that 'the governor should not have been in a position to give orders to the provincial council', she preferred to identify the φάλαγξ (L.1) and the τάξις Καρῶν (L. 4) with the provincial assembly of Karia, consisting of the members of the local *ordines* (τάξεις) *decurionum*. Her arguments carry weight: 'firstly, it is hard to see the circumstances in which the *officium* might be being destroyed; while such language might well be used by the upper class of Karia, feeling under pressure from taxation, it seems unlikely that government servants would use it of themselves. Secondly, the *officium* was normally perceived as being the *officium* of the governor—rather than of the province. If a governor ordered his *officium* to erect a statue, therefore, this would presumably be equivalent to erecting it himself.'[88] Since there were restraints on the erection of honorific statues in that period, she argued that the erection of Anthemios' statue required the governor's authorization (ἤνωγεν). As a parallel, she adduced a roughly contemporary inscription from Athens that commemorates the dedication of a statue of the governor by a certain Themistokles: 'The dedicator honoured Theodore (proconsul of Achaea …) εἰκόνι λαϊνέῃ, τὼς γὰρ ἄνωγε πόλις—with a marble statue, for thus the city instructed. The same idea is paraphrased as νεύματι Κεκροπίης and balanced with the obtaining of imperial permission for a bronze statue, νεύματι Θευδοσίου. ἤνωγε in our inscription may well have the same sense as ἄνωγε in the text from Athens, where it appears to mean authorise. As the legislation on the erection of statues became more restrictive, the Carians

85 Roueché in *ala2004* IV.4; *PLRE* II, Anthemius 1.
86 Cf. Roueché in *ala2004* IV.4, who adduces as a parallels *ala2004* 37 (πτολίεθρα σαώσας) and 14 (σωτῆρα τῶν ἐθνῶν). Merkelbach and Stauber 1998, 233, translate δῆμοι as 'Dörfer' (villages).
87 Feissel 1991, 372, with reference to *ala2004* 41.
88 Roueché in *ala2004* IV.5–6.

may have needed the governor's authority to put up a marble statue of Anthemius.'[89]

The difficulty discussed by Feissel and Rouché disappears if one does not translate ἤνωγεν as 'commanded, instructed', but as 'urged'.[90] This is the meaning that the verb has in one of the responses recorded in a dice oracle of the third century AD, preserved in many copies: οὐκ ἔστιν σπεύδοντα τυχεῖν ὅσα καιρὸς ἀνώγει.[91] A somewhat free translation would be: 'even if you exert yourself, it is not possible for you to achieve what the opportunity/circumstances urge you to strive for'; the καιρός does not command, it prompts. Similarly, in the Athenian inscription there is a difference between νεύματι (vote, approval) and ἄνωγε: the statue was erected by Themistokles upon a vote in the Athenian council (στῆσε Θεμιστοκλέης νεύματι Κεκροπίης), responding to a request (not a command) by the city (Θεμιστοκλέης ἀνέθηκε εἰκόνι λαινέη· τὼς γὰρ ἄνωγε πόλις) and promising to set up also a bronze statue with the emperor's approval (εὐχόμενος μετέπιτα θεῷ γεννήτορι πάντων καὶ χαλκοῦ<ν> στήσ<ε>ιν νεύματι Θευδοσίου). In Aphrodisias, the governor did not give an order, he made a recommendation. If we accept that the statue was erected by the provincial council, it is quite possible that the fragmentary word at the beginning of the epigram is an attribute of φάλαγξ, clarifying what this 'array' was. A possible, although metrically incorrect, restoration would be θεμίστωρ ('experienced in law'), an adjective that might describe the legal competence of the provincial assembly.

The governor Veronicianus is otherwise unattested. Also, the dangers from which Anthemios saved the cities cannot be determined with certainty, possibly the Isaurian raids of AD 404–407 or the burden of taxation.[92]

The Christian acclamations inscribed later on the right side of the base are quite common. The acclamations 'light' and 'life', deriving from the Gospel of John,[93] are found in numerous Christian inscriptions, in Aphrodisias and elsewhere, both separately and combined.[94] The Christian acronym ΧΜΓ is very common throughout the Roman East, and in Aphrodisias it appears both in public places and incised on the heads of statues.[95] It is usually interpreted as standing for the phrase Χριστὸν Μαρία γεννᾷ ('Maria gives birth to Christ') or a similar phrase (Χριστὸς Μαρίας γέννα γέννημα, Χριστοῦ Μαρία γεννήτρια γενέτειρα), but other interpretations have been proposed, ranging from the implausible Χριστός, Μιχαήλ, Γαβριήλ, and Χριστὸς μάρτυς γένοιτο to the isopsephism χμγ' = 643 (Θεὸς βοηθός).[96]

---

89 Rouché in *ala2004* IV.6 with reference to *IG* II² 4223 (AD 379–395).
90 See *LSJ*, s.v.; cf. Montanari 2015, 215, s.v. ἀνώγω: 'to command, order, invite, exhort'.
91 For example, *TAM* III.1.34 L. 58.
92 Rouché in *ala2004* IV.7.
93 John 1.4: ἐν αὐτῷ ζωὴ ἦν καὶ ἡ ζωὴ ἦν τὸ φῶς τῶν ἀνθρώπων; cf. John 8.12.
94 Φῶς, ζωή: for example *SEG* XLVI 1973; XLVII 263, 1172; L 658; LIII 1787, 2040(5); LIV 1652; LV 1950; LVI 1851(2); LIX 826; LX 1427; LXI 1575(5). In Aphrodisias: *IAph2007* 4.310 and 12.401; see also Rouché in *ala2004* VIII.16. For ζωή alone see for example *SEG* XLVI 1985(1).
95 *IAph2007* 3.8.ii; 15.102. For the heads of statues, see Smith 2002 (more cases have been identified since that publication).
96 For recent overviews see Derda 1992, 21–27; Llewelyn 1997, 156–168; see also Robert and Robert 1960, 300–311; Rouché in *ala2004* VIII.20.

C. HONORIFIC DECREES AND HONORIFIC INSCRIPTIONS FOR CITIZENS

In19. Honorific decree?

Small marble fragment broken on all sides. H 15.5 cm, W 24 cm, D 3 cm, Lt. 1.8 cm.

Found in 1980 near the Propylon (1 IIIA; Inv. 80.11).

Date: first century BC/AD.

Bibliography: *IAph2007* 4.301 (Reynolds; photo).

```
[- - - - - - - - - - - - - - -]
[- - - π]ολέμωι Υ[- - - - -]
[- - - εἰκόν]ι χαλκῆ[ι- - - -]
[- - - - - - - - - - - - - - -]
```

1. Read by Reynolds; *in fine*, the last letter may be Χ. ‖ 2. A form of χαλκή, Reynolds; [- - - εἰκόν]ι χαλκῆ[ι- - - -], Chaniotis.

'- - - in the war - - - (honour him) with a bronze [statue - - -].'

Reynolds plausibly recognized this fragment as part of a text honouring a man for his services during a war; she commented: 'although the lettering suggests the first century AD, references to war are more common in texts of the first century BC'. In fact, there are no references to wars in the Imperial period, and the singular πολέμωι in L. 1 (instead of, for example, ἐν τοῖς πολέμοις) refers to services in one particular war, certainly a war in the late first century BC (possibly Labienus' attack). The man was honoured for his services with a bronze statue.

In20. Honorific decree for a benefactor.

White marble block, chipped along all edges and on the surface; on top, dowel-holes for an attachment. Dimensions unrecorded. Lt. 0.5 cm.

Found in 1978 'near the east entrance to the Place of Palms, in an area containing re-used material' (Inv. 78.2).

Date: first century BC/AD.

Bibliography: Reynolds 1982, no. 41 [*SEG* XXXII 1097; *BE* 1983 no. 390]; *IAph2007* 4.101 (photo).

```
      vacat
      [γ]ενόμενος δὲ καὶ ἀστυνόμος καὶ νεωπο[ιὸ]ς καὶ
          στρατηγὸ[ς]
      ἐπὶ χώρας, ν στρατηγήσας δὲ πλεονάκις τῆς πόλεως,
          πρεσβεύ-
      [σ]ας δὲ πλείστας καὶ μεγίστας πρεσβήας ἐπιτυχῶς ὑπὲρ
          τῆς πατ-
 4    [ρί]δος ν ἀγωνισάμενος δὲ καὶ περὶ τῆς ἐλευθερίας καὶ
          τῶν
      [ἰδίων?] νόμων καὶ τῆς ἀσυλίας ν καὶ τῶν δεδομένων
          [ἡμῖν?]
      [φι]λανθρώπων ν καὶ ἐπὶ πᾶσιν τούτοις τοῖς γενομένοις
      ὑπ' αὐτοῦ καὶ τ[αῖς ἀρχ]αῖς καὶ λιτουργίαις τιμηθείς
      [vacat]
```

5. *Initio*, [*vacat*?]; *in fine*, *vacat*, Reynolds; [ἰδίων] and [ἡμῖν], Chaniotis. ‖ 6. ἐνὶ πᾶσιν, Reynolds; ἐπὶ πᾶσιν, Chaniotis (read on the photograph).

'[- - -] having also served as *astynomos* and *neopoios* and *strategos* in charge of the territory, and many times *strategos* in charge of the city, and having successfully carried out numerous and very important embassies on behalf of his fatherland; and having toiled for the freedom and our own laws and the inviolability and the privileges granted to us; and been honoured for all his achievements and in the magistracies and the liturgies [- - -]'.

This block contains part of a text that certainly started on another block to the left and probably continued on a third block.[97] Since the text summarizes the career and services of a prominent citizen and magistrate using participles in the nominative, it most probably is a posthumous honorific decree, comparable for example with the honorific decree for Hermogenes.[98] The text must be the *narratio* of the decree.

From the letter-forms, comparable to those of inscriptions honouring Zoilos, Reynolds suggested that the anonymous man was involved in the embassies during of the last years of the Republic, when the privileges of Plarasa/Aphrodisias were granted by the senate. She tentatively identified the honorand as Solon, son of Demetrios, known to have been involved in the first grant of privileges to Aphrodisias in 39 BC and who was the leading statesman in other embassies.[99] Although the identification cannot be proven, there is a detail that may confirm the historical context: the reference to laws (L. 5) is paralleled by a reference in the *senatus consultum* concerning Plarasa/Aphrodisias: <ἀ>λλὰ ἐλεύθεροι καὶ ἀτελεῖς ὦσιν νόμοις | τε ἰδίοις π[ατρί]|οις καὶ οὓς ἂν μετὰ ταῦτα ἐν ἑαυτοῖς κυρ<ώ>σ<ω>ινν χρῶν[ται].[100] At the beginning and the end of L. 5, Reynolds assumed that a longer space of 4–5 letters remained uninscribed. There are vacats in this inscription, but only of one letter; and the end of line 5 is not uninscribed but damaged. At the beginning of L. 5 one cannot restore [πατρίων] because it is too long, but one may restore [ἰδίων] as in the *senatus consultum*.

In21. Posthumous honorific inscription for Timokles
(Pl. 96.A–B)

Three non-joining fragments of two adjoining marble blocks, with the upper edge surviving. H 29.5 cm; fr. a: W 19 cm, D 25 cm; fr. b: W 67 cm, D 67 cm; fr. c: W 18 cm, D 24 cm; Lt. 2 cm. See also Ch. 7 §C – 6.

Fr. a: stray find in 1964 (Inv. 64.117); fr. b: found in 1975 during the excavation of the west facade of the Propylon (Inv. 75.198); fr. c: stray find in 1982.

Date: first century AD?

Unpublished: Transcribed and restored by J. Reynolds.

[? *vac.*] ἡ γε[ρου]σί[α καὶ ἡ βουλὴ καὶ ὁ δῆ]μ[ος ἐτ]είμ[η]-
σ[αν] ταῖς κα[λλίσ]-
[ταις κ]αὶ μεγίσταις τ[ειμαῖς *star* Τειμοκ]λέα Ἀπολλωνίου τοῦ Ὑψικλ[έους]

[? *vac.*] ἄνδρα σοφόν, καλ[ὸν καὶ ἀγαθόν, γ]ένους πρώτου καὶ ἐνδοξοτ[άτου],
4 [γυμνα]σιαρχήσαντα κα[ὶ στεφανηφορήσ]αντα μεγαλοψύχως καὶ φιλο[δόξως]
[καὶ] ἀρχιερατεύσαντ[α τοῦ αὐτοκρά]τορος καὶ ἀγωνοθετήσαντα κα[ὶ δὶς]
[ἑστι]άσαντα τὸν δῆμ[ον καὶ πάντα] ποιήσαντα μεγαλομερῶς λαμ[πρ]-
[ότα]τα καὶ πολυτελέ[στατα ἐκ τῶ]ν ἰδίων ἀξίως καὶ ἀναλογούντω[ς τῇ]
8 *vacat* πα[τρίδι καὶ τῷ γ]ένει *leaf*

8. πα[τρίδι καὶ γ]ένει, Reynolds; πα[τρίδι καὶ τῷ γ]ένει, Chaniotis.

'The gerousia and the council and the people honoured with the fairest and greatest honours Timokles, son of Apollonios, grandson of Hypsikles, a prudent, good, and virtuous man, belonging to one of the foremost and most distinguished families, who served as *gymnasiarchos* and *stephanephoros* with magnanimity and generosity, who served as high priest of the emperor and as *agonothetes*, who offered a banquet to the people twice and who did everything in a generous, most brilliant, and most sumptuous man, spending his own funds, in a manner worthy and fitting to his fatherland and his kin.'

This honorific inscription, apparently written on blocks of a funerary monument, can be safely restored because a second copy was inscribed on a statue base. The statue base was seen and transcribed by Antonio Picenini in 1705 and Robert Wood in 1750; it is now lost. Of course, the division of lines is different, since the statue base was narrower than the block. Moreover, the text on the statue base does not mention the gerousia.[101] It seems that one copy of the honorific inscription was inscribed on the base of Timokles' statue, and the other on his funerary monument. Timokles had a career typical of members of the Aphrodisian elite. He occupied the offices of the *stephanephoros* and the supervisor of the gymnasion,[102] he offered banquets—a common benefaction—,[103] and served as high priest of the imperial cult and chairman of contests. The contests are not identified; since the *agonothesia* is mentioned immediately after the high priesthood, it is possible that the contests in question were in honour of the emperor.[104]

Usually, the high priests and high priestesses of the civic imperial cult are simply designated as ἀρχιερεύς and ἀρχιέρεια, without any reference to the emperor(s).[105] In a few cases, the title is given as ἀρχιερεὺς τῶν Σεβαστῶν,[106] in one case as ἀρχιερεὺς τοῦ κυρίου Σεβαστοῦ (late second century AD).[107] The identity

---

97 Reynolds 1982, 166, thought that this is the conclusion of the text.
98 *SEG* LIV 1020.
99 Reynolds 1982, 166–167, with reference to *IAph2007* 8.25, 8.27, and 8.31.
100 *IAph2007* 8.27 LL. 61–62.
101 *IAph2007* 12.512 with further bibliography.
102 On the gymnasion and the gymnasiarchoi in Aphrodisias see Chaniotis 2015b.
103 For the evidence see Chaniotis 2020, 115–116.
104 Cf. *IAph2007* 12.2 LL. 5–8: ἀρχ[ιερατεύσαντα] τῶν Σεβ[αστῶν ·· c. ·· καὶ ἀ]γωνοθε[τήσαντα τοὺς τῶ]ν Σεβα[στῶν ἀγῶνας?].
105 *IAph2007* 1.158; 1.159; 1.187; 1.189; 4.104; 5.7; 5.10 i; 5.301; 5.302; 8.83; 8.84; 8.85 i; 11.50; 11.58; 11.51; 11.308; 11.414; 11.507; 11.513; 12.35; 12.322; 12.325; 12.417; 12.513; 12.518; 12.520; 12.531; 12.532; 12.533; 12.634; 12.638; 12.644; 12.712; 12.909; 12.1011; 12.1020; 12.1111; 13.205; 13.604; 13.616; 14.18; 15.260; 15.332.
106 *IAph2007* 12.2; 12.206; 12.308; 12.609; 12.1006.
107 *IAph2007* 12.29 iii.

of the emperor is revealed only in inscriptions of the first century AD;[108] This is the only attestation of the expression ἀρχιερεὺς τοῦ Αὐτοκράτορος. Since αὐτοκράτωρ was used to refer to the ruling emperor or past emperors from the early first century AD on,[109] this cannot be used as a dating criterion. The lettering, according to Reynolds, suggests a date in the first century AD.

In22. Honorific inscription (?).

White marble fragment, broken on all sides, probably from the upper part of a statue base with moulding; inscribed under the moulding. H 19 cm, W. 19 cm. D 25 cm, Lt. 1.9 cm.

Found in the Place of Palms in 1971 (South Agora: PT 71.4; Inv. 71.100).

Date: *c.* first/second century AD.

Bibliography: *IAph2007* 4.105 (Reynolds; photo).

> [- - - τ]οῦ Κρατέ[ρου - -]
> [- - -]ΛΗΚΑΙΙ[- - - -]

1. No restoration, Reynolds; restored by Chaniotis. ‖ 2. perhaps [ἡ βουλὴ καὶ ἡ [γερουσία], Chaniotis.

The form of the fragment (statue base) and the remains of the name Krateros, well represented among members of the Aphrodisian elite,[110] suggest that this is the beginning of an honorific inscription.

In23. Honorific inscription for Julia Faustina

White marble statue base with damaged moulding above, broken below and chipped to the right. H 45 cm, W 55 cm, D 26 cm, Lt. 5.5–7 cm. See also Ch. 7 §E – **69**.

Found in 1970 in the south part of the Place of Palms.

Date: *c.* second century AD.

Publication: *IAph2007* 4.118 (Reynolds; photo).

> [- - - - - -]
> Ἰουλίαν Φαυ-
> στεῖναν τὴ[ν]
> γυναῖκα
> αὐτοῦ
> [- - - - - -]

'[NN] (set up the statue of) Julia Faustina, his wife'.

There are another two attestations of the name Faustina in Aphrodisias: a Faustina mentioned in a fragmentary epitaph together with a Papias and a Menandros,[111] and Aurelia Faustina, the wife of Flavius Papias (early third century AD).[112]

In24. Honorific inscription.

Lower left corner of the moulding and the shaft of a white marble statue base. H 25 cm, W 31 cm, D 31 cm, Lt. 2 cm.

Found in 1969 in the southwest corner of the Place of Palms (Inv. 69.485).

Date: second/third century AD.

Bibliography: *IAph2007* 4.119 (Reynolds; photo).

> [- - - - - for example Ἀττά]-
> λου το[ῦ - -]
> Τατιọ[- - -]
> [- - - -]

1–2. λουτο[⋯]|τατιΟ[⋯], Reynolds; restored by Chaniotis. ‖ 2. Τάτιọ[ν] or Τατίọ[υ].

The text must have started on the damaged surface of the moulding. What survives is the ending of a name in the genitive (for example [Ἀττά]λου, [Ζωί]λου, [Ζή]λου, [Παπύ]λου, [Θεοφί]λου, [Τερτύλ]λου, [Παμφί]λου, just to mention the most common names ending in -λος in Aphrodisias). The female name Τάτιον can be recognized in L. 2. A Tation was daughter of Menippos, wife of Papias, and mother of Pyrrhos (*IAph2007* 13.6); she erected the statue of her son. A second Tation, wife of Artemidoros, is known through an epitaph (*IAph2007* 13.120). The woman mentioned in this text cannot be identified with either of them.

In25. Honorific inscription.

Fragment of the right side of a marble statue base. H 38 cm, W 7 cm, D 9 cm, Lt. 2.8 cm.

Found in 1988 in the west section of the North Stoa (NCE 88-1; Inv. 88.14).

Date: second/third century AD.

Bibliography: *IAph2007* 4.110 (Reynolds; photo)

> [- - - - - -]
> [- - - -]ΙΝ
> [- - - -]ΤΑ
> [- - - -]ΑΤ
> 4 [- - - -]ΑΞ
> [- - - -]ΤΡ
> [- - - -]ΣΑ̣
> [- - - - - -]

No restoration is possible.

---

108 ἀρχιερεὺς Θεοῦ Σεβαστοῦ Καίσαρος (Augustus): *IAph2007* 9.19; ἀρχιερεὺς αὐτοῦ (Τιβερίου Κλαυδίου Καίσαρος Σεβαστοῦ Γερμανικοῦ, that is Claudius): *IAph2007* 12.514; ἀρχιερεὺς Οὐεσπασιανοῦ Καίσαρος Σεβαστοῦ (Vespasian): *IAph2007* 12.314.

109 *IAph2007* 12.305 (early first century AD); 8.34 L. 7; 11.412 L. 18 (AD 119); 12.920 LL. 28–29 (mid-second century AD); 12.1111 L. 4 (second century AD); 12.105 L. 10 (second century AD?); 12.921 (late second century AD); 8.37 (AD 198); 8.100 L. 6 (*c.* AD 238–244); 8.114 L. 4 (AD 250); 12.108 (*c.* AD 300); 1.182; 11.31; 12.508; 12.911; 12.1105; 12.1108; 13.11; 15.281 (third century AD).

110 Bourtzinakou 2012, nos. 1486–1495; *LGPN* V.B., s.v. 1–10.

111 Unpublished sarcophagus fragments (69.28 + 71.445); Bourtzinakou 2012, no. 2266.

112 *SEG* LIV 1061; Bourtzinakou 2012, no. 2268.

In26. Honorific inscription

The upper right corner of a white marble statue base with elaborate moulding; an inscription on the upper (LL. 1–2) and lower (L. 3) fasciae. No measurements recorded.

Found in 1989 in the southwest corner of the Place of Palms (PT SW 89 Find 35).

Date: second/third century AD.

Publication: *IAph2007* 4.111 (Reynolds, no restorations; photo).

```
[- - - - - -]ΣΑΝ v. ~
[- - - - - -]ΙΙΙΙΗΤ[..]ΔΟ
[- - - - - -]ΥΤΗ
```

This fragment certainly belongs to an honorific inscription. The verb [ἐτείμη]σαν, rather than [ἀνέστη]σαν, can be recognized in L. 1, probably preceded by for example [ἡ βουλὴ καὶ ὁ δῆμος]. The remains of letters on L. 2 could be reconciled by the reading [το]ῦ Μητ[ρο]δώ[ρου], but this restoration is not certain. The name Metrodoros is common in Aphrodisias. In L. 3 one may think of the praenomen [α]ὑτῇ or [ἐα]υτῇ, but there are other possibilities, for example [ἐπὶ ἤθους πρα]ὐτη|[τι] (as in *IAph2007* 12.22 LL. 22–23) or [τελε]υτή|[σαντα].

In27. Honorific inscription for an anonymous honorand

Rectangular base with panels enclosed in raised frames on three sides; broken at the upper right corner; a clamp hole on top; an inscription on the moulding (L. 1) and the front panel (LL. 2–28); LL. 8, 10, 15 and 26 run onto the right moulding. H 1.07 m, W 48 cm, D 41.5 cm, Lt. 2.2–2.8 cm.

Found in 1977 at the Propylon (Agora Gate, Trench 5, Inv. 77.124).

Date: *c.* AD 250.

Unpublished. Transcribed by J. Reynolds.

```
        ]ΙΟΣΕ[- - - - - -]
        προνοησα[μένου]
        τῆς ἀναστά[σεως]
4       Οὐλ(πίου) Ζήνωνος [τοῦ?]
        καὶ Ζηνᾶ ἀντιπρ[ω]-
        τονεοποιοῦ τῆς
        τρίτης νεοποιίας
8       τοῦ Ποσειδωνίου
        κατὰ τὴν Κλ(αυδίου) Ἀπολ-
        λωνίου Μαρκιανοῦ
        καὶ Κλ(αυδίας) Σελευκεί-
12      ας Τιβερείνης,
        Ἀσίας καὶ τῆς πα-
        τρίδος ἀρχιερεί-
        ας, τῶν ἱερέων
16      τῆς θεοῦ, βούλησιν
        καθὰ καὶ ἡ βουλὴ
        καὶ ὁ δῆμος ἐπε-
        κύρωσαν καὶ νε-
20      οποιῶν Μ. Αὐρ(ηλίου)
        Ζηνοβίου ε΄ Ἐπα-
        φροδείτου καὶ
        Μ. Αὐρ(ηλίου) Κρατέρου ε΄
24      Ἀθηναγόρου καὶ Μ.
        Αὐρ(ηλίου) Ἀν(τωνίου) Μενεσθέως
        τοῦ Μενάνδρου καὶ
        Μ. Αὐρ(ηλίου) Ἐπιγόνου β΄
        τοῦ Ζήνωνος
```

Ligatures: L.3: TH; L. 4: HN; L. 5: HN, NT; L. 6: NE, TH; L. 7: TH, NE; L. 9: THN; L. 15: NTH; L. 21: HN; L. 25: ME; L. 26: ME. ‖ 24. abbreviation sign (a horizontal line) over M.

' - - The erection (of the statue/statues?) was taken care of by Ulpius Zenon, also called Zenas, the deputy chief *neopoios* of the third *neopoiia* of Poseidonios, in accordance with the wish of Claudius Apollonios Markianos and Claudia Seleukeia Tibereine, high priestess of Asia and of the fatherland, the priests of the goddess, and in accordance with what also the council and the people approved, as well as by the *neopoioi* Marcus Aurelius Zenobios V Epaphrodeitos, Marcus Aurelius Krateros V Athenagoras, Marcus Aurelius Antonius Menestheus, son of Menandros, and Marcus Aurelius Epigonos, son of Epigonos, grandson of Zenon.'

The base preserves only the final part of an honorary inscription; since the other sides of the base seem to be uninscribed (according to Reynolds' description), the beginning of the text may have stood on another base. The preserved part preserves the names of the donors who had provided the funds for the statue (or statues) and the men who took care of its erection. We have no clues with regard to the identity of the honorand. Usually, the erection of honorific statues of citizens was taken care of (προνοέω, ἐπιμελέομαι) by friends or family members.[113] When this service was provided by civic magistrates, the honorand could be a member of the imperial family, an imperial official, another city, a member of the local elite, or a victorious athlete.[114] Similarly, funds for the erection of statues were endowed, promised, and donated (ἐπαγγελία, ὑπόσχεσις, διαθήκη, ἀπόλειψις) for a variety of reasons: for the dedication of statues of personifications and gods, for decorative statues, statues of victors in contests, and for statues of emperors.[115] The fact that the donors served as high priests of the provincial imperial cult (see below) is a very uncertain indication that the statue was an imperial one. The donors were also priests of Aphrodite; therefore, the statues may well have been dedications to the goddess. The endowment of the donors had been approved by the council and the assembly (καθὰ καὶ ἡ βουλὴ καὶ ὁ δῆμος ἐπεκύρωσαν), which is a standard procedure in the case of endowments.[116]

---

113 *IAph2007* 1.157; 2.17; 8.709; 11.5; 11.58; 11.223; 12.21; 12.22?; 12.35; 12.104; 12.215; 12.323?; 12.413; 12.513; 12.521; 12.531; 12.623; 12.639; 12.1018; 15.321; 15.329; unclear: 12.317.

114 Member of the imperial family: *IAph2007* 1.189. Imperial official: *IAph2007* 11.414; 12.644; 12.645; 12.931; 12.932. City: *IAph2007* 12.924–929. Citizen: *IAph2007* 5.204; 12.416. Victorious athlete: *IAph2007* 15.364. Undetermined: *IAph2007* 1.118; 12.626.

115 Dedicatory statues: *IAph2007* 1.109; 8.52; 12.204; cf. 12.1002. Emperors: *IAph2007* 4.201; 11.104; 12.641; 12.642. Decorative statues: 4.308; 11.401. Victors in contests: *IAph2007* 11.223; 13.152; 13.616. Unclear: *IAph2007* 3.4; 11.105; 12.712,

116 *IAph2007* 11.105 also mentions the approval of the use of funds for the erection of a statue (κατακεκυρωμένον ὑπό [- -]), but in a fragmentary context.

The board of the χρυσοφόροι νεοποιοὶ τῆς ἁγιωτάτης θεοῦ Ἀφροδείτης was one of the most important civic institutions of Aphrodisias, designated in an inscription as the σεμνότατον καὶ ἀρχαιότατον συνέδριον τῶν χρυσοφόρων νεοποιῶν ('the most solemn and ancient board of the *neopoioi*, who wear gold').[117] Presumably established in order to supervise the funds for the construction of the temple of Aphrodite in the late first century BC,[118] it continued to exist until the third century AD with various competences. The board consisted of five members and was chaired by an ἀρχινεοποιός.[119] From the reference to a *neopoios* who served in this office twice,[120] we may infer that the office was annual. At least two wealthy Aphrodisians endowed funds to be used by the chief *neopoios*: Poseidonios, who is mentioned in this text, and Tiberius Claudius Apollonius Beronikianos Akasson. An honorific inscription reports that a statue was erected by 'Tiberius Claudius Aurelius Mucianus Apollonios Beronikianos, the most distinguished deputy (chief) *neopoios* (ἀντινεοποιός) of Tiberius Claudius Apollonios Beronikianos Akasson, the high priest, his own grandfather, in the first cycle of the chief *neopoiia* that had been funded through the endowment of Apollonios.'[121] If the term ἀντιπρωτονεοποιός (deputy chief *neopoios*) is a synonym of ἀντινεοποιός, this official chaired the board in place of the man who had endowed the funds.[122] The term περίοδος suggests that the endowment was used at regular intervals to cover the expenses of the chairman of the board.[123] In the case of this inscription, Poseidonios' endowment was used for the third time.

The board's main function was to administer the funds (πρόσοδοι) of the sanctuary of Aphrodite,[124] and in this capacity it received fines for the violation of graves.[125] The adverbs used to praise individual *neopoioi*—μεγαλοπρεπῶς (lavishly), κοσμίως (disciplined, decent), ἐπιφανῶς (conspicuously, in a visible manner), εὐσεβῶς (piously), and φιλοτίμως (ambitiously, generously)—[126] suggest that the public activities of the *neopoioi* implied good management of funds for public events, but also personal expenditure. Indeed, the board collectively served as ἀγωνοθέτης (chairman of the contest) of the Aphrodiseia Philemoneia,[127] took care of the erection of statues,[128] and honoured its members.[129] Also individual *neopoioi* dedicated statues.[130] The board received endowments for the distribution of money among its members.[131]

In this inscription, the acting chief *neopoios* Ulpius Zenon, also called Zenas, may be identical with a man honoured with a statue. His name is not preserved, but his second name was Zenas ([- -] τοῦ Ἀπολλωνίου Ζηνᾶν) and he served twice as *neopoios*;[132] additionally, he served as πρῶτος ἄρχων and εἰρηνάρχης. Poseidonios, the sponsor of the perpetual ἀρχινεοποιία, is otherwise unattested.

The individuals who made the bequest for the erection of the statue or statues are well known members of the Aphrodisian elite. Claudius Apollonios Markianos served as Asiarches and high priest of the civic imperial cult in *c.* AD 240,[133] and according to this inscription he also served as priest of Aphrodite together with Claudia Seleukeia Tibereine. Seleukeia must be a close female relative, since the high priesthoods were usually occupied by a husband and a wife or a father and his daughter.[134] She probably is his daughter, since she shares the same gentilicium. A Κλαυδία Σελεύκεια, Ἀπολλωνίου θυγάτηρ appears as a dedicant of a Caryatid in the Hadrianic Baths.[135] Archaeological evidence suggest that the Caryatid series was part of the original construction of the Hadrianic baths in *c.* AD 128–138.[136] One is, therefore, tempted to recognize in Seleukeia Tibereine a third-century member of the dedicant's family. However, the rarity of the name Seleukeia and the relationship of Claudia Seleukeia Tibereine to a Claudius Apollonios invites us to consider another possibility. It is striking that the formulations of the dedicatory inscriptions of the Caryatids are not uniform, as we would expect in inscriptions that were part of a single project. Additionally, in some cases, the carving of the letters is below the usual high standards, creating the impression that it was not done in a workshop, while the bases were being prepared and were lying on their back, but after the bases had been placed in a building. In this interpretation, the bases and statues were part of one (or two) series that date to the time of the Hadrianic construction, but the texts were inscribed over a long period of time, while women made donations of money (not actual dedications of statues);[137] these donations

---

117 *IAph2007* 5.204 and 1.161 (early third century AD).
118 Earliest attestation: *IAph2007* 4.101 (late first century BC).
119 Number of members: *IAph2007* 12.914 and here In25. Chairman: *IAph2007* 11.60; 13.616; 15.364. Deputy: *IAph2007* 13.616.
120 *IAph2007* 12.521.
121 *IAph2007* 13.616: Τιβέριος Κλαύδιος Αὐρήλιος Μουκιανὸς Ἀπολλώνιος Βερονεικιανός, ὁ κράτιστος ἀντινεοποιὸς Τιβερίου Κλαυδίου Ἀπολλωνίου Βερονεικιανοῦ Ἀκάσσωνος, ἀρχιερέως, πάππου ἰδίου, ἐν τῇ πρώτῃ περιόδῳ τῆς ἐπὶ τῇ ἀπολείψει τοῦ Ἀπολλωνίου ἀρχινεοποιίας. Discussed by Roueché 1993, 210.
122 A different interpretation is favoured by Roueché 1993, 200 (without reference to this text): the ἀντινεοποιός 'administered the spending of the money'.
123 Roueché 1993, 200.
124 *IAph2007* 12.914.
125 *IAph2007* 15.245 and 15.247; cf. 11.37; 12.526; 12.1003; 13.154.
126 *IAph2007* 13.105 i and iii.
127 *IAph2007* 11.58; 11.224; 12.35; 13.152; 15.364.
128 *IAph2007* 1.118; 11.60.
129 *IAph2007* 5.204.
130 *IAph2007* 5.108–109.
131 *IAph2007* 1.161; 11.23; 11.403. For such distributions of money in Aphrodisias see Chaniotis 2020, 113–115.
132 *IAph2007* 12.521.
133 *IAph2007* 11.60 and 8.83. Discussion and date in Roueché 1993, 220, who also proposed this identification; cf. Bourtzinakou 2012, no. 389. He may be the father of the πρῶτος ἄρχων Tib. Claudius Markianos in the text In16.
134 See Campanile 1994, 22–25. For fathers and daughters serving as priests see for example *SEG* LIX 1334, 1339, 1342 (cult of Ares in Metropolis).
135 *IAph2007* 5.209, dated by Roueché to the mid-second century. She may also be the woman for whom a seat was reserved in the stadium: Roueché 1993, 88–89; *IAph2007* 10.9.
136 Wilson 2016a, 186–192.
137 A possible parallel is provided by inscriptions on columns of Aphrodite's temple that commemorate the dedication of columns (*IAph2007* 1.4–1.8). The inscriptions, engraved within *tabulae ansatae*, name the donors and mention the dedication of a column; for example *IAph2007* 1.4: Εὔμαχος Ἀθηναγόρου τοῦ Εὐμάχου Διογένης Φιλόκαισαρ καὶ Ἀμιὰς Διονυσίου φύσει δὲ Ἀδρά<σ>του τοῦ Μόλωνος Ὀλυνπιὰς τὸν κίονα θεᾷ Ἀφροδίτῃ καὶ τῷ Δήμῳ. These inscriptions do not mean that the donors donated a particular column, but rather that they donated money for the construction of the tem-

were commemorated on already existing statue bases. A systematic study of this material, that cannot be undertaken here, may shed more light on this problem.

The *neopoios* Marcus Aurelius Zenobios V Epaphrodeitos is the son of Marcus Aurelius Zenobios IV Epaphrodeitos, priest of the Erotes for life, who took care of the dedication of a statue of Ulpia Carminia Claudiana, daughter of Marcus Ulpius Carminius Claudianus (*c*. AD 230–240).[138] The other three *neopoioi*, Marcus Aurelius Krateros V Athenagoras, Marcus Aurelius Antonius Menestheus, son of Menandros, and Marcus Aurelius Epigonos, son of Epigonos, grandson of Zenon, are not known from other sources. The prosopography suggests a date of *c*. AD 240–250.

In28. Honorific epigram for Albinos

Upper part of a columnar statue base shaft of bluish marble, chipped above. H *c*. 40 cm, diam. 50 cm, Lt. 4–4.5 cm. See also Ch. 7 §D – 44.

Found at the southern end of the West Stoa.

Date: Late fifth century

Bibliography: *ALA* 82l; Merkelbach and Stauber 1998, 230 no. 02/09/01; *IAph2007* 4.20 (photo).

Ἀγαθῇ Τύχῃ·
Ἀλβῖνον φι|λόπατριν ἀμει|βομένη πόλις ‖ ἔργοις
αἰνυμένη σ|τῆσε χρυσὸν ἀπει|ρέσιον,
ΟΡΕ[- - - -] | ΑΟΙΣΤ[- - - - - -]

'To Good Fortune. The city set up (the statue of) Albinos, lover of his fatherland, repaying his works, having enjoyed/received immense gold [- - -].'

Albinos, a citizen of Aphrodisias, is honoured with this epigram, written on the base of his statue, and with the acclamations inscribed on the columns of the West Stoa, for his benefactions that included the restoration of the West Stoa (see Appendix 2, W9: αὔξι ὁ κτίστης τῆς στοᾶς), the construction of or rather repairs to other buildings (cf. W20: ὁ κτίστης καὶ τούτου τοῦ ἔργου), and probably donations in cash (cf. LL. 6–7: χρυσὸν ἀπει|ρέσιον) (see Ch. 4 §D). The epigram and the acclamations have been discussed in detail by C. Rouché,[139] and little can be added to her conclusions: Albinos, who is not known from other sources, was a descendant of local benefactors; he was not yet a senator, but bore the honorific title λαμπρότατος/*clarissimus*, which was possible for members of the civic elite (*curiales*) after around the mid-fifth century AD.[140] References to envy and enemies (W16, W17, W25) show that he was involved in some sort of a conflict in Aphrodisias.

Two probable references to the Christian god[141] suggest that he was a Christian. The historical context may well be that of the religious conflicts alluded to in an inscription that refers to a 'civil strife' (*IAph2007* 8.407) and possibly connected with Zenon's *Henotikon* (AD 482) and the conversion of the temple of Aphrodite into a church in the late fifth century AD see Ch. 5 §E).[142] Eight plaques of the pavement of the West Stoa with the abbreviations Ἀλβ(ίνος) and Ἀλβῖν(ος) surely refer to the sponsor of the West Stoa. These plaques were destined 'for (the project) of Albinos' or were 'acquired by (or, on behalf of) Albinos' (see Ch. 5 §E).

Rouché suggested a date in the early sixth century AD, but a date in the late fifth century AD, as part of the reconstruction programme following the late fifth-century earthquake is more likely (see Ch. 4). In this context, the epigram might be seen as a parallel to, or even a response to, those at the other end of the Place of Palms, on the Propylon, commemorating the works of Ampelios (In10) and Doulkitios (In11 and In12). While Ampelios is honoured by the Nymphs, speaking through the verses of the Trallian orator Pythiodoros, and Doulkitios' epigrams are self-praising (In11) and an invitation to the stranger to admire his work (In12), the honorific epigram for Albinos mentions his grateful fatherland as the agent of the honour. This striking emphasis on Albinos' love for his fatherland, also explicitly mentioned in the acclamations in his honour (see Ch. 4 §D) may reflect contemporary discussion in Aphrodisias about the contributions of these three men.

D. SCULPTORS' SIGNATURES ON HONORIFIC STATUES

In29. Signature of the sculptor Apellas Koblanos

Two joining fragments of a white marble statue plinth, carrying two sandalled feet; inscribed on the front face. H 12.5 cm, W 57 cm.

Found in 1987 near the Propylon (Agora BS 87-1; Inv. 87.445).

Date: late first/early second century AD.

Bibliography: Erim, *AS* 39 (1989), 176; Erim and Reynolds 1989, 522–523 no. 4 (*SEG* XL 927); Smith *et al*. 2006, 182–183 no. 54; *IAph2007* 4.303 (Reynolds; photo); Kansteiner *et al*. 2014, 522–523 no. 4133 (K. Hallof and S. Kansteiner)

Ἀπελλᾶς *v* [Κ]ωβλανος ❦
ἐποίει

---

ple, and their donation entitled them to have their names commemorated.

138 *IAph2007* 12.1020: ἐπιμεληθέντος Μ(άρκου) Αὐρ(ηλίου) Ζηνοβίου τετράκις τοῦ Ζηνοβίου τοῦ Ἀρτεμιδώρου Ἐπαφροδείτου, ἱερέως διὰ βίου Θεῶν Ἐρώτων. Bourtzinakou 2012, no. 1100, took the expression Ζηνοβίου τετράκις τοῦ Ζηνοβίου to mean Zenobios V; cf. Reynolds' translation in *IAph2007*: 'fourth of the name from Zenobios son of Artemidoros son of Epaphrodeitos'; τετράκις τοῦ Ζηνοβίου is the equivalent of Ζηνοβίου δ'. On the date of Marcus Ulpius Carminius Claudianus see Pont 2008.
139 Rouché 1989, 125–136.
140 Jones 1964, 529–530.
141 WS16: ὅλη ἡ πόλις τοῦτο λέγι· τοὺς ἐχθρούς σου τῷ ποταμῷ· ὁ μέγας θεὸς τοῦτο παράσχῃ; 'The entire city says this: "Your enemies to the river!" May the great god grant us this!'; and WS25: ἡ πόλις ὅλ]η ὁμοφώνως εὐφη[μ]ή{σα}σα λέγι· ὁ σοῦ ληθαργῶν, Ἀλβῖνε λανπρ(ότατε) θεὸν οὐκ οἶδεν; 'The entire city, having praised you in acclamations in one voice, says: "He who forgets you, Albinos, *clarissimus*, does not know God"'.
142 For discussion of the literary and epigraphic sources: Chaniotis 2002b; Chaniotis 2008a.

'Apellas Koblanos made (this).'

This sculptor is also known from a statue of a victorious athlete found in Sorrento, copy of a fifth-century BC original; this statue may have represented an orator or poet.[143]

In30. Signature of the sculptor Menodotos.

White marble statue of a draped woman (H 1.94 m), on an oval plinth; inscribed on the front face of the plinth. Lt. 1.5 cm.

Date: early second century AD.

Found in 1983 south-east of the Propylon (Inv. 83.122).

Bibliography: Erim and Reynolds 1989, no. 7 (*SEG* XL 930); Smith *et al.* 2006, 204–205 no. 85; *IAph2007* 4.302 (Reynolds; photo); Kansteiner *et al.* 2014, 610 no. 4213 (K. Hallof and S. Kansteiner).

> Μηνόδοτος [Νικο]μάχου τοῦ Μηνοδότ[ου]
> ἐποίει

'Menodotos, son of [Niko]machos, grandson of Menodotos, made (this).'

The sculptor is known from another inscription that reports that he dedicated a statue of Demos, together with his brother Nikomachos.[144] Copying a late hellenistic model, Menodotos made the honorific statue of a woman, certainly a member of the local elite. The original location of the statue's display is not known. It may have been brought to the Propylon in late antiquity.[145]

E. DEDICATORY INSCRIPTIONS

In31. Dedication to an unknown deity (Pl. 30.A, 96.C)

Marble plaque re-cut for reuse as building material in the interior of the pool. H 73 cm, W 72 cm, Lt. 2.7–4 cm.

Found reused in the late fifth-/early sixth-century repairs to the wall of the south side pool, somewhat west of the centre (I 14.04); still *in situ*.

Date: first century AD.

Unpublished. Cf. Wilson 2019, 475 fig. 364 (photo). Autopsy.

> [ ]θέου τοῦ θρέψαντος
> [ ] ἀνέ θη κε ν ❦

Short uninscribed spaces between ΕΘ, ΕΚ, and ΕΝ.

The beginning of the text was written on a block to the left of the preserved block. It contained the name of the dedicant and possibly the name of a deity and/or possibly a designation of the votive. The dedication was made by an alumnus or an alumna for the well-being of the man who raised him/her (ὑπὲρ + name or ὑπὲρ σωτηρίας + name).[146] A restoration is not possible. If the missing block had similar dimensions, *c.* 14 letters are missing in L. 1 and *c.* 8 letters in L. 2 (the text is centered). The remains of a name (L. 1: [- -]θέου) belong either to the name of the man on behalf of whom the dedication was made (without father's name) or to the name of his father. Possible restorations are [Πεισι]θέου, [Τιμο]θέου, and [Φιλο]θέου.[147] Tentative restorations, *exempli gratia*, are

> [... c. 6... ὑπὲρ Τιμο]θέου τοῦ θρέψαντος
> [εὐ χὴ ν] ἀνέ θη κε ν ❦

or

> [... c. 6... ὑπὲρ Τιμο]θέου τοῦ θρέψαντος
> [Ἀσκληπιῷ] ἀνέ θη κε ν ❦

Dedications for the well-being of relatives were made to Asklepios (see below In33) and Zeus Nineudios.[148]

In32. Dedication

Small white marble stele consisting of a square base, and a relief panel; a nude male figure in frontal position is represented in relief from the knees up; the base is broken on left and right; the relief panel is damaged on top; the arms are broken below the elbows; the penis is also broken off; on top, a disproportionally long neck is preserved; it is not certain that a head was represented, and not just a torso.[149] H 21 cm, W 13 cm, D 9.5,[150] Lt. 08.–1.2 cm.

Found in 1986 during excavation in the Place of Palms (P. of T. SE 86-1; Inv. 86.28).

Date: first/second century AD.

Bibliography: *IAph2007* 4.109 (Reynolds; photo).

> [. .]φροδ[.. c. 4..]
> [. .]ΧΗΑΙ[.. c. 4..]

Reynolds's transcription (*stop* Ἀφροδ[ίτη ··] | *vac.* ΧΗΑΝ[·· c. 4 ··]) is not confirmed by the photo; the left side is broken and there is neither a 'stop' in L. 1 nor a vacat in L. 2.

Based on the assumption that the left side of the inscribed base is complete, Reynolds assumed that this is a dedication to Aphrodite. She further speculated that 'Aphrodite's name may have been followed by a cult title, or by the name of a female dedicator, with ἀνέθηκε in full or incomplete'. To judge from the photo, the left part of the inscribed base is not preserved. Additionally, in Reynolds' reading there would be no space for the name of the dedicant. Apart from the fact that private

---

143 Smith *et al.* 2006, 182–183.
144 *IAph2007* 8.52.
145 Smith *et al.* 2006, 204–205; K. Hallof and S. Kansteiner in Kansteiner *et al.* 2014, 610.
146 For such dedications in Aphrodisias see Chaniotis 2011a.
147 Bourtzinakou 2012, nos. 1991, 2187, 2292.
148 Chaniotis 2011a.
149 Reynolds' description is misleading: 'Small white marble stele (W. 0.13 × H. 0.21 × D. 0.95), damaged above and at the bottom right corner, consisting of an inscribed base with oblique left side (right side lost) carrying a nude male three-quarter figure with head surviving as far as the chin only, arms as far as the elbows and legs as far as the knees'. The left side of the base is not oblique but broken; the male figure is in frontal position.
150 The dimensions given in *IAph2007* 4.109 (W. 0.13 × H. 0.21 × D. 0.95) cannot be correct. Unfortunately, I could not study this find in the Museum. The dimensions are estimated on the basis of the photo and the letter-size.

dedications to Aphrodite are extremely rare in Aphrodisias, the representation of a naked male torso would be an unusual dedication to the goddess. The relief resembles an anatomical votive. Anatomical votives showing only part of a naked body, either male or female, usually including the upper legs and the torso but without the head, are not uncommon.[151] The text cannot be restored with certainty. L. 1 probably contains the name of the dedicant, probably [Ἐπ]αφρόδ[ιτος], and L. 2 a dedicatory formula. One would be tempted to restore [εὐ]χή at the beginning, instead of the more common εὐχήν.[152] However, when εὐχή is used, it is usually the last word of the dedication.[153] At the end, there is no space for Reynold's restoration ἀν[έθηκε], and the formula would have been εὐχήν ἀνέθηκε. The restoration [τύ]χῃ ἀγ[αθῇ] can be better reconciled with the remains of letters and the available space.[154] So, a very tentative restoration would be:

[Ἐπ]αφρόδ[ιτος]
[τύ]χῃ ἀγ[αθῇ]

If this object is an anatomical votive, it comes from the (unlocated) sanctuary of Asklepios, just like further finds from the Place of Palms and the Hadrianic Baths (see below no. In33).

In33. Dedication to Asklepios

Small white marble moulded base, oval with flattened back; an inscription on the moulding. H 35 cm, W 65 cm (base)–85 cm (top), Lt. 5–8 cm.

Found in 1990 the southwest section of the pool (Portico of Tiberius WII-90; Inv. 90.26).

Date: *c.* second century AD.

Bibliography: *IAph2007* 4.113 (Reynolds; photo).

θεῷ
Ἀσκληπ[ίῳ]
[ε]ὐχή[ν]

'To the god Asklepios in fulfillment of a vow.'

The cult of Asklepios, jointly with Hygieia and Hypnos, is securely attested through the following inscriptions:
1) an inscription recording the dedication of a statue of Hygieia to Augustus and the Demos by Molossos, the priest of Hygieia (late first century BC/early first century AD; *IAph2007* 8.211);
2) an anatomical votive with the representation of a pair of eyes dedicated to Asklepios by Eleuther[- -] (first century AD; *IAph2007* 15.240);
3) an inscription recording the dedication of statues of Asklepios and Hygieia and of two altars by the doctor T. Flavius Staberianos in accordance with a promise made by his homonymous father, the city's chief doctor (first/second century AD; *IAph2007* 11.401);
4) an anatomical votive with the representation of breasts, dedicated to Asklepios by Amias (second century AD; *IAph2007* 5.111);
5) a dedication to Hypnos by the priest of Asklepios Septimius Aurelius Flavius Venidius Hypsikles (second/third century AD; *IAph2007* 12.638);
6) an anatomical votive with the representation of breasts dedicated to Asklepios Euepekoos by Eugenia (third century AD; *IAph2007* 11.117).

Except for the statue base of Hygieia, which was found in the theatre, none of these inscriptions was found *in situ*. Two were found in the Hadrianic Baths, one in the Place of Palms (this text), three in the southern part of the city, and one is a stray find.[155] Although the exact location of the sanctuary of Asklepios is not known, the discovery of two votives in the Hadrianic Baths and another one in the Place of Palms suggest that it was located near the Baths, either in the area of the Agora or to the south of the Baths. The existence of a sanctuary of a healing god in the vicinity of the baths would not be surprising. The dedication to Hypnos is a strong indication that incubation was practised in this sanctuary.[156]

In34. Dedication?

Fragment of a white marble moulding, probably of a base, broken on right and left, damaged on top. H 16 cm, W 16 cm, D 19cm, Lt. 2.5 cm.

Found in 1969 near the Place of Palms (Inv. 69.487). Recorded by the NYU expedition in 1969 (69.487).

Date: first/second century AD.

Bibliography: *IAph2007* 4.103 (Reynolds; photo).

[- - - - - - - - - - - - -]
[- - - ἀνέ]θηκεν[- - -]
[- - - - -] *vac.* [- - - -]

Neither the recipient of the dedication nor the original location of the base, which probably supported a votive, can be determined.[157]

In35. Dedication of a sundial

Lower part of a white marble spherical sundial supported by a marble base with moulding; broken across the dial; the lower right corner of the base is damaged; an inscription under

---

151 For example Forsén 1996, figs. 20, 21, 26.
152 Examples of εὐχή in the nominative: *SEG* XXIII 515a; *EAM* 20; *IG-Bulg* II 759 and 847; V 5313; *IAph2007* 2.516.
153 Christian dedications consisting of εὐχή + a name in the genitive are a different matter; in Christian dedications εὐχή means 'prayer', not 'vow'.
154 Dedications sometimes end with τύχηι ἀγαθῆι: for example *IG* II² 4761; *I.Stratonikeia* 442; *TAM* III.1.915.
155 Hadrianic Baths: *IAph2007* 5.111 and 117 (southwest sector). Walls: *IAph2007* 12.638 (southeast section). Stray finds: *IAph2007* 11.401 (southwest part of the city); 15.240.
156 On incubation rituals see Ehrenheim 2015; Renberg 2017. Renberg 2017, 677–688, is sceptical about whether a dedication to Hypnos and Oneiros can be taken as evidence for incubation. But in this case, I do not see how else one can interpret a dedication to Hypnos by a priest of Asklepios.
157 Reynolds (*IAph2007*) suspected that this fragment may be from the French excavations of the Hadrianic Baths in the early twentieth century.

the fascia of the moulding. H 35 cm, W 32 cm, D 21 cm, Lt. 1.5–2 cm. See also Ch. 7 §B – **107**.

Found in 1992 in a spoil heap to the east of the Propylon (Inv. 92.53).

Date: *c.* third century AD.

Bibliography: Mentioned by Gates 1994, 267 and fig. 11 [*BE* 1995, 136]; *IAph2007* 4.114 (Reynolds; photo).

Κλ(αύδιος) Δ[..^{c. 3-5}..]

'Cl(audius) D[…]'

Abbreviation sign ς.

Sundials of this type are widely known and have been found in Aphrodisias as well.[158] The letterforms and the use of an abbreviation sign suggest a date in the third century AD at the earliest. The dedicant cannot be identified. There are numerous men in Aphrodisias with the gentilicium Claudius and a name starting with delta (Διαδούμενος, Διογᾶς, and Διογένης).[159] Since the dedicant had a short name, the restoration Δ[ιογᾶς] is possible but far from certain. A certain Claudius Diogas was the father of Marcus Aurelius Claudius Ktesias, a prominent citizen in the early third century AD. The dedicant may have been member of this family.

F. EPITAPHS

In36. Epitaph of a Roman soldier

Body of a marble ossuary without lid; most of the front is lost; decorated with reliefs of rams' heads joined by a swag on the front face (the ram on the right is not preserved); leaves and fruit under the ram's head; inscribed above and below the swag on the front face (possibly also within it). H 33 cm, W 56.5 cm, D 34 cm, Lt. 1.5–2 cm.

Recorded by the *MAMA* expedition in a house yard; found in 1983 near the Propylon, during the demolition of a village house, where it had been re-used in the wall (Inv. 83.66).

Date: first century AD?

Bibliography: *MAMA* VIII 558 (J.M.R. Cormack); *IAph2007* 4.304 (Reynolds; photo).

L[- - - - - - - - - - - - - - - - - - -]
speculator legion(is) III Gallicae

L. 1. Read by Cormack; this reading was rejected by Reynolds: '*MAMA* printed an initial *L* above the opening letter. This is presumably an interpretation of a mark just above the surviving ram's head, on the left'; but in fact, it is not a mark but a letter, probably L(ucius), Chaniotis.

L[(ucius?) - - -], scout of the Gallic Third legion.'

The epitaph is dated by J. Reynolds to the first to second century AD on the basis of the lettering.[160] Because of the lack of comparanda from Aphrodisias (Latin inscriptions, ossuaria), one must look for a plausible historical context for the presence of a soldier of the legio III Gallica in Aphrodisias. This legion participated in the Parthian campaigns of Mark Antony (36 BC), Cn. Domitius Corbulo (*c.* AD 58–63), Lucius Verus (AD 161–165), and Septimius Severus (AD 197–198); it was mainly stationed in Syria, except for a short period during Nero's reign, when it was transferred to Moesia.[161] Other evidence for Roman soldiers in Aphrodisias is rather limited; only the *primus pilus* Antipatros (see In5), the *primus pilus* and *praefectus castrorum* Ulpius Apollonios (*SEG* LVIII 1152, second century AD), and a veteran of *Legio Prima Parthica Severiana Antoniniana*, who served at Singara on the Tigris probably in connection with the defence of the eastern front against the Parthians.[162] We also know of *centuriones frumentarii* stationed in the city in the early third century AD.[163] Of course, a Roman soldier could have died anytime on his way to or from his legion, but it is more likely that this happened during one of the Parthian campaigns. The inscription was carved by a local mason who cannot have been familiar with Latin inscriptions; he must have copied a text written on perishable material. The absence of cursive letters and the use of broad letters make a date in the second century AD or later unlikely.

In37. Gladiatorial memorial for the *familia* of Tiberius Claudius Pauleinos

Fragment of a white marble stele broken on top and bottom; on bottom, an inscription within a framed tabula (H 21 cm, W 33 cm); on top, the lower part of the panel that carried a relief (not preserved). H 30 cm, W 41 cm, D 18 cm, Lt. 2 cm.

Found in 1974 in the West Stoa (Inv. 74.292).

Date: early second century AD.

Bibliography: Roueché 1993, 62–63 no. 13; *IAph2007* 4.104 (photo); Hrychuk Kontokosta 2008, 205–206 no. 3. Autopsy.

  Φαμιλίας · μονομά-
  χων · καὶ καταδίκ-
  ων · Τιβερίου · Κλαυ-
4 δίου · Παυλείνου,
  ἀρχιερέως, · υἱοῦ · Τι-
  [β]ερίου · Κλαυδίου
  [- - - - - - - - - -]

There is a stop, in the form of a small circle, after every word, except for καί (L. 2).

'(Memorial of) the *familia* of gladiators and convicts belonging to Tiberius Claudius Pauleinos, high-priest, son of Tiberius Claudius [- - -].'

---

158 For a list of sundials from Aphrodisias see Chaniotis 2004, 414. For spherical sundials see Gibbs 1976, 12–30.
159 For references see Bourtzinakou 2012, nos. 727, 730, 745, 753, 755, 767–769, 783, 789.
160 Comment in *IAph2007*: 'the rather naive style of the relief suggests the same time-period as the lettering (so Nathalie de Chaisemartin).'
161 Kubitschek and Ritterling 1924, 1518–1531.
162 *IAph2007* 11.30.
163 Chaniotis 2013a.

This stele belongs to a group of gladiatorial reliefs recently studied by A. Hrychuk Kontokosta, who has plausibly suggested that they were erected near the tombs of the high priests, who had organized a *munus*. The *munus* organized by Tiberius Claudius Pauleinos included gladiatorial combats and the execution of convicts.[164] C. Roueché identified Tiberius Claudius Pauleinos with the husband of a certain Claudia Pauleina, known from a posthumous honorific inscription; she dated both inscriptions to the first century AD.[165] Later, J. Reynolds dated the honorific inscription to the late second/early third century AD and did not propose an identification of Claudia Pauleina and Tib. Claudius Pauleinos with any other individuals by these names.[166] Since this gladiatorial monument is regarded as the earliest testimony for gladiatorial combats in Aphrodisias in connection with the imperial cult,[167] its date deserves a detailed discussion.

Claudia Pauleina (*IAph2007* 11.50) must have played a significant role in the public life of Aphrodisias, since she had been honored with the title 'daughter of the city' (θυγάτηρ πόλεως). This is a strong argument in favor of her identification with the Claudia Pauleina who served as *stephanephoros* in AD 119; she probably endowed an αἰώνιος στεφηνφορία (funds to be used in the future for this office), since her fifth, posthumous, *stephanephoria* is mentioned in an epitaph of the early third century AD. She may also be the dedicant of a caryatid in the Hadrianic Baths.[168] In her honorific inscription, Pauleina's husband is referred to as Τιβέριος Κλαύδιος Παυλεῖνος, ἀρχιερεύς, exactly as in the gladiatorial monument—with none of the Latin names abbreviated and with reference to his office. Therefore, the identity of Pauleina's husband with the owner of the *familia* is very probable; in that case, he served as high priest during the reign of Hadrian. The letter-forms on the gladiatorial memorial—especially the square sigma—can be better reconciled with a second-century date than a date in the first century AD.

No matter whether or not Tib. Claudius Pauleinos is the husband of the *stephanephoros* Claudia Pauleina, there is no argument in favour of dating this text to the first century AD. If he is the husband of the *stephanephoros*, the text should be dated to the reign of Hadrian. Since there is no secure evidence for

munera in the first century AD,[169] it is possible that when Hadrian allowed the city to receive money instead of gladiatorial shows from the high priests (AD 125), gladiatorial events were a relatively recent development, of the late first century AD.[170]

In38. Epitaph (?) of Titus Flavius and his family (Pl. 96.D)

Fragment of a marble block stele (?) with a frame; broken on left and top right; the upper and bottom surface are partly preserved (roughly carved); the back is preserved. H 24 cm, W 27 cm, D 20 cm, Lt. 2.4–3.2 cm.

Found in Trench 15.2, re-used in a post-antique structure (6 August 2015; SAg 15.2.M112, Inv. 15-027; I 15.05).

Date: *c.* AD 150–200.

Unpublished. Autopsy.

    [- - -]ΤΙΝΔ.[- - -]
    [- - Τ]ίτου Φλ^αβί-
    [- - -] γυναικὸς
4 [- - -].ΩΝ αὐτοῦ

The letters of LL. 1–2 are more deeply cut than those of LL. 3–4. The last two lines are not straight but slightly drop to the right. ‖ 1. *Initio* a Γ or Τ; *in fine*, the bottom serif of a letter, probably part of a vertical line. ‖ 2. Remains of a small alpha written between the lines. ‖ 4. *Initio*, remains of the lower right part of an oblique line (Α, Λ, Κ, Μ); a small Ο is inserted between Τ und Υ. Line 4 is possibly the last line, since the preserved space below line 4 is wider than the spaces between the other lines.

This fragment seems to be part of an epitaph. Because of the depth of the fragment (20 cm), we may rule out the possibility of a sarcophagus. The first line probably described the type of monument, while the last three lines mentioned the individuals allowed to be buried in the grave: Titus Flavius [- - -] and his wife, possibly also his children and his slaves ([δού]λων rather than [φί]λων).[171] The following resoration is presented only *exempli gratia*:

    [- ἐσ]τὶν Δ.[. .]
    [- Τ]ίτου Φλ^αβί-
    [ου - - - - - - - - καὶ - - - - - - - τῆς] γυναικὸς
4 [αὐτοῦ καὶ τῶν τέκνων καὶ τῶν δού]λων αὐτοῦ

---

164 On the gladiatorial reliefs from Aphrodisias: Hrychuk Kontokosta 2008. On the epigraphic evidence see Roueché 1993, 61–80; Reynolds 2000; Coleman 2008; Chaniotis 2004, 398–399 nos. 21–22. On pictorial graffiti see Chaniotis and De Staebler 2018.
165 Roueché 1993, 62. The honorific inscription (Inv. 63.434) was later published by J. Reynolds (*IAph2007* 11.50). The first-century date for the gladiatorial memorial is still found in Hrychuk Kontokosta 2008, 205–206.
166 *IAph2007* 11.50.
167 Roueché 1993, 62; Welch 1998, 558–561; Hrychuk Kontokosta 2008, 192. For another text from the late first or early second century AD, see Roueché 1993, 63 no. 14; *IAph2007* 11.507; Hrychuk Kontokosta 2008, 205 no. 2.
168 *Stephanephoria* of AD 119: *IAph2007* 11.412. Posthumous *stephanephoria*: *IAph2007* 13.618. Dedication in the Baths: Baths 12 (found by Boulanger in 1904); see Smith 2017, B.16; Wilson 2016a, 187, 9.7. That the three attestations of a Claudia Pauleina may refer to the same woman is tentatively suggested by Bourtzinakou 2012, nos. 1980, 1981, 1982.

169 Gladiatorial events took place in the stadium. For its date, see Welch 1998, 554–556. There is no conclusive epigraphic evidence for a date in the early Imperial period. Comparisons with other stadia only permit the conclusion that the construction of the stadium should be dated 'to sometime in the first century AD'.
170 Hadrian's letter: *IAph2007* 11.412 LL. 27–41. Discussions: Reynolds 2000; Chaniotis 2005, 58–59; Coleman 2008.
171 Owners of graves often allowed the burial of freedmen (*IAph2007* 11.34; 13.150; 15.246) and alumni (*IAph2007* 8.504; 11.59; 12.507; 13.150; 13.702). The burial of slaves in the grave is not explicitly attested, but they may be included in the formulation οἱ ἴδιοι: *IAph2007* 11.103. The burial of friends is attested in one text: *IAph2007* 12.1017: ἐξέσται δὲ ἑκάστῳ φίλους θῖναι δύο.

In39. Epitaph (Pl. 96.E)

Fragment of the body of a marble sarcophagus with moulding on top; broken on all sides except for the back; inscribed on the moulding (L. 1) and the panel (LL. 2–3); signs of later reuse and carving.

Found in 2014 the northeast quadrant of Trench 14.1 (removal of topsoil). M5588. I 14.12. H 15, W 35, D 9.5 cm, LH 2 cm.

Date: *c.* second century AD.

Unpublished. Autopsy.

[- - -]ΕΙΣΤΗ[- - - - - - - - προ]-
δηλουμ[- - - - - -]
[-]ΙΔ[.].[- - - - - -]

1. for example [- -] εἰς τὴ[ν σορὸν ταύτην] ‖ 3. or Λ.

This small fragment belongs to the section of an epitaph that states who is allowed to be buried in the sarcophagus (L. 1: [ἐνταφ- -] εἰς τὴ[ν σορὸν ταύτην]). The participle προδηλούμενος ('aforementioned') refers to the owner of the sarcophagus and either to his right of burial or his exclusive right to determine who can be buried in the sarcophagus.[172] But it may also refer to the sarcophagus.[173]

In40. Epitaph of Polykrates

Upper part of a marble stele; with a pediment in relief; within the pediment a phiale or a crown in relief; an inscription in a framed panel. H. 38 cm, W 41 cm, D 18 cm, Lt. 2.6–3.5 cm.

Found built into a house wall in 1983 southeast of the Propylon (Inv. 83.70).

Date: late second century AD.

Bibliography: *IAph2007* 4.305 (Reynolds; photo).

    ὁ πλάτας ἐσ-
    τιν Πολυκρά-
    τους ο δ' ο τοῦ Ἀ-
4 [πολ]λωνίου
     vacat
    [- - - - - - -]Ο
    [- - - - - - - -]

5. The circular element, *in fine*, may be a decorative element.

'The platform belongs to Polykrates, son of Polykrates, grandson of Polykrates, great grandson of Polykrates the son of Apollonios [- - -].'

Neither Polykrates nor any of his ancestors is otherwise known. A Polykrates, son of Pythion, is known from a first-century AD coin.[174] Apollonios is one of the most common names in Aphrodisias.

In41. Epitaph

Upper edge of the front of a white marble sarcophagus, broken on left, right, and bottom; remains of a sculpted area; inscribed on the upper lip above a sculpted area. H 12.5 cm, W 12 cm, D 7–11.5 cm, Lt. 2 cm.

Found in 1990 in the pool (PT.SW III.90, F.44; Inv. 90.k.).

Date: *c.* second century AD.

Bibliography: *IAph2007* 4.112 (Reynolds; photo).

[- - - ἀσε]βὴς καὶ [ἐπάρατος?- - -]

Restorations suggested by Reynolds, who also considers [Εὐσέ]βης καὶ [- -] or [Εὐσέ]βης Κἀν[διδος].

If the names of the owner of the sarcophagus and those who were allowed to be buried in it were written on the lid, as often is the case, this fragment contains the standard formula that those who violated the burial would be impious and accursed.

In42. Epitaph

Fragment of a sarcophagus lid inscribed on the rim; H 13 cm, W 56 cm, D 29 cm, Lt. 2 cm.

Found in the Place of Palms.

Date: second/third century AD.

Bibliography: *IAph2007* 4.115 (Reynolds; photo).

[- - - ἐν ᾗ σο]ρῷ κηδευθήσεται αὐτό[ς - - -]
[- - - - - - - -]ΚΟΥ καὶ ΦΛΙΔΙΟΣΕΔ[- - -]

1. [π]ροκηδευθήσεται, Reynolds, who also considers [ἐν τῇ σο]ρῷ κηδευθήσεται. But in an epitaph, προκηδεύομαι ('be buried before') always refers to a burial that has already taken place in the past (for example *CIG* 313; *SEG* II 603), never to a future burial; hence, [ἐν ᾗ σο]ρῷ κηδευθήσεται, Chaniotis. ‖ 2. Φλ(άβιος)?, Reynolds.

This small fragment belongs to the section of an epitaph that gives the name of the owner of the sarcophagus, who is to be buried there, and the names of relatives for whom burial was permitted.

In43. Epitaph

Fragment from the top of a marble sarcophagus front with inscribed upper rim and part of a head in relief. H 13 cm, W 14 cm, D 12 cm, Lt. 2.2 cm.

Found in 1986 in the Place of Palms (SE 86-I; Inv. 86.62).

Date: second/third century AD.

Unpublished. Transcribed by J. Reynolds.

[- - -]ΣΟΜΕΝ[- - -]

---

172 Cf. *CIG* 2835a LL. 4–7: [οὐδὲ ἐξουσίαν οὗτοι ἕξουσιν ἐνθάψαι | εἰς] τὴν σορὸν ἄλλο σωμάτειον οὔτε αὐτοὶ ταφῆναι [ἐν τῇ σορῷ μετὰ τοὺς προδη|λο]υμένους, οὐδὲ συνχωρῆσίν τινι ποιήσασθαι οὔτε με[τὰ τὸ τεθῆναι τοὺς] προδηλουμένους ἀνοῖξαι] ἢ κεινῆσαι τὴν σορόν. Cf. for example *CIG* 2830; *MAMA* VIII 541, 548, 559, 570.

173 Cf. *MAMA* VIII 577 LL. 16–17: ἐνταφήσεται δὲ μόνη εἰς τὴν προ|δηλουμένην.

174 Bourtzinakou 2012, no. 2035.

In44. Epitaph (grave epigram?) (Pl. 96.F)

Fragment of a marble panel with broad moulding above, and a right-facing male figure with a spear or staff in his right hand (left hand and lower part lost) in relief below; broken on all sides; (0.23 × 0.23 × 0.14) inscribed on the upper moulding (LL. 1–3) and on either side of the figure. H 23 cm, W 23 cm, D 14 cm, Lt. 0.6–1.2 cm.

Found in 1977 during the 'Agora Gate' excavations (Tr. 5, topsoil; Inv. 77.110).

Date: second/third century AD.

Unpublished. Transcribed by J. Reynolds.

```
       [- - - - - - - - - - - - - - - - - - - -]
       [- - - -] vac. ῥέξας ΜΗΝ[- - -]
       [- - - -] vac. ~ σεισμοῦ [- - -]
       [- - - -]ΩΤΙΚΟΤ[- - - - - - -]
  4    [- - - -]ΕΙ head ΤΙΣΑΦ[- - - -]
       [- - - -]ΛΗ head ΛΛΗΝ[- - -]
       [- - τέ]κν head ου ΜΗ[- - -]
       [- - - -] vac. head ΒΙ[- - - - -]
       [- - - - - - - - - - - - - - - - - - -]
```

Readings by Reynolds. ‖ 1. Ligature of ΜΗΝ. ‖ 3. If the last letter is not a tau but an upsilon, probably a personal name in the genitive (for example [Ζ]ωτικοῦ) rather than a word (for example [ἐ]ξωτικοῦ, [ἰ]διωτικοῦ etc.), Chaniotis. ‖ 4. Perhaps εἴ τις ἀφ[- -], with a form of ἀφαιρέω, referring to the violation of the grave, Chaniotis. ‖ 6. Ligature of ΜΗ; [τέ]κνου, Reynolds

To judge from the rare verb ῥέζω (L. 1), exclusively used in metrical texts,[175] the first lines are part of an epigram, probably a grave epigram. An earthquake is mentioned in an unclear context (L. 2).

In45. Epitaph of Aurelius Oreinos and his family

Left end of a sarcophagus lid with a sleeping Eros at the corner, inscribed on the rim and in a prepared area below. H 17 cm, W 62 cm, Lt. 2 cm.

Found in the southwest corner of the Place of Palms.

Date: early third century AD (after AD 212).

Unpublished. Transcribed by J. Reynolds (Portico of Tiberius 7).

```
ἡ σορὸς καὶ τὸ περιοικοδορ[μημένον - - - - - - - - - - - εἰσιν]
Αὐ[ρ]ηλίου Ὀρεινο boss [ῦ - - - ἐν ᾗ σορῷ ἐνταφήσεται ὁ]
π[ρογ]εγραμμέ boss [νος - - - - - - - - - - - - - - - - - -]
```

1. τὸ περιοικοδορ[μημένον - - - εἰσιν], Reynolds. ‖ 2–3. Restored by Chaniotis.

The epitaph describes the funerary complex and names its owner. Usually the verb περιοικοδομημέω ('built around') refers to τόπος, which is masculine.[176] Here it refers to a neuter noun, possibly ἡρῷον or μνημεῖον.[177] Both words can be used as general descriptions of burial complexes.[178] Either word can be be restored in another fragmentary epitaph from Aphrodisias: ἡ σορὸς καὶ τὸ περὶ αὐτ[ὴν ἡρῷον/μνημεῖον].[179] The name of the owner is Ὄρεινος.[180] The gentilicium Aurelius is not abbreviated, and this suggests a date shortly after the Constitutio Antoniniana.

In46. Epitaph of a family

White marble fragment with moulding; inscribed on the upper moulding (L. 1) and on the fascia below. H 18 cm, W 38 cm, D 45 cm, Lt. 2.8 cm.

Excavated by Mendel; copied by Boulanger (notebook A.61, no. 21, whence B, 15, no. 21); recorded by the NYU expedition near the West Stoa (Baths 6).

Date: early third century AD (after AD 212).

Bibliography: IAph2007 4.116 (Reynolds; photo).

```
[- - μ]νῆμα ΠΑΝΙΔ[- - - - - -]
[- - - τ]οῦ Διοδώρου ΕΙ[- - - -]
[- - -]ται Αὐρηλία Ε[- - - - - -]
[- - - - - - - - - - - - - - - - - - -]
```

l. 1. [μ]νῆμα?, Reynolds; [μ]νῆμα with ligature of ΝΗ; then perhaps παντα[- -] or πᾶν κα[ὶ], Chaniotis. ‖ 3. καί, Reynolds; the first letter must be a tau, since a horizontal line survives on top; probably [κεκήδευ]ται rather than [κηδευθήσε]ται, Chaniotis.

The grave monument belonged to a son or descendant of a Diodoros—not a very common name in Aphrodisias—[181] and members of his family, including an Aurelia, who seems to have already been buried in the grave (see app. cr.: [κεκήδευ]ται). The gentilicium Aurelius is not abbreviated, and this suggests a date shortly after the Constitutio Antoniniana.

In47. Epitaph of a family (Pl. 96.G)

Marble fragment with frame; broken on left, bottom, and right; inscribed on the frame (L. 1) and within the recessed panel (LL. 2–5); signs of later reuse and carving. H 56 cm, W 36 cm, D 15.5 cm, Lt. 2.7–4 cm.

Found in 2014 in the southeast quadrant of Trench 14.1 (removal of topsoil; I 14.11).

Date: late third/early fourth century AD.

---

175 For example MAMA I 100l; I.Anazarbos 26; I.Ephesos 1625 A.
176 AvHierapolis 58; I.Laodikeia am Lykos 95.
177 Cf. I.Iznik 1231: τὸ μνημεῖον κατεσκεύασεν καθὼς περιοικοδόμηται.
178 In IAph2007 12.524 the burial complex, designated as μνημεῖον (L. 12) and ἡρῷον (L. 17), consists of a σορός, a βωμός, and εἰσῶσται. Cf. IAph2007 2.309: [ἡ]ρῷον ἢ μέρος τι ἀπ' αὐτοῦ; for ἡρῷον see for example IAph2007 11.16 L. 14; 12.322 L. 17; 13.612. Μνημεῖον often designates the structure on which a sarcophagus is placed, but it also means, generally, grave; cf. IAph2007 15.245: εἰς ὃν πλάταν κατεσκεύασεν μνημεῖον τὸ ἐπικείμενον τῷ πλάτᾳ, σορόν τε καὶ ἰσώστας τὰς ἐν αὐτῷ; 15.249: [ὁ β]ωμὸς καὶ ἡ ἐπικειμένη αὐτῷ σορὸς [καὶ] αἱ ἐν τῷ μνημείῳ εἰσῶσται; 15.345: ἡ σορὸς καὶ ὁ περικίμενος τόπος τούτῳ μνημείῳ.
179 IAph2007 15.248 (no restoration); Waddington (LW 1640) restored [περίβολον], but περίβολος is masculine.
180 Bourtzinakou 2012, no. 1909; LGPN V.B., s.v.
181 Bourtzinakou 2012, nos. 799–804; LGPN V.B., s.v. 1–7.

Unpublished. Autopsy.

```
       [- -]ẸΟΥΟΠ.[- - -]
       θυγατρὸ[ς - - - Πολυχρο]-
       νίου δ[ὲ? - - - - - - - Πολυ]-
4      χρόνιο.[- - - - - - - - - - - - -]
       ΣΙΜ.[- - - - - - - - - - - - -]
```

1. *In fine*, an oblique line (alpha or lambda). ‖ 2. The mason omitted the omikron; a small (0.8 cm high) omikron was added later, attached to the rho (0.8 cm) ‖ 3–4. probably Πολυ]χρόνιος.

This fragment of an epitaph lists the family members—probably of a certain Polychronios—allowed to be buried in a funerary monument. The names Πολυχρόνιος/Πολυχρονία are very common in Aphrodisias. Most attestations are from the third and fourth century AD.[182]

In48. Epitaph of Nikolaos

White marble plaque broken on right and left. H 90 cm, W 1.10 m, D 16 cm, Lt. 3–7 cm.

Seen and copied by W. Kubitschek 'w(estlich) von der Säulenruine' (Notebook III, p. 22, Abklatsch viii); recorded in 1980 near the Propylon.

Date: tenth century or later.

Bibliography: Cormack 1964, 11 (from Kubitschek's transcription); Robert 1966, 381 note 3; Rouché 1989, no. 173; *ala2004* 173; *IAph2007* 4.312 (Rouché; photo). Autopsy.

[ἐν]ταῦθ(α) κεῖτ(αι) τὸ λείμψανον *stop* Νικολά(ου)

Apostrophe for abbreviations; the last letter of abbreviated words is inscribed above the line and is smaller (Θ, Τ, Α); the last letter was read by Kubitschek, but the stone has suffered further damage since 1893 and the letter is no longer visible; Νικόλα, Cormack; Νικολᾱ̓(ου), Rouché.

'Here lie the remains of Nikolaos.'

The date is suggested by Rouché on the basis of the letter-forms. One notes an interesting linguistic feature: λείμψανον, instead of λείψανον,[183] with a parasitic mu before the labial. From the Imperial period on, a nasal before a labial is often either omitted or assimilated: for example σύβιος for σύμβιος,[184] συφορά for συμφορά,[185] πέππτη for πέμπτη,[186] etc. Here, the opposite phenomenon occurs: a nasal is inserted. This is a common occurence in the case of the future of λαμβάνω: λήμψομαι for λήψομαι;[187] this may have influenced the form *λείμψανον*, although it derives from a different verb (λείπω).

G. FRAGMENTS

In49. Fragment (honorific inscription or public document).

Upper part of a white marble block, broken on right, left, and bottom; possible moulding on top. H. 27 cm, W 10 cm, D 32 cm, Lt. 1.5 cm.

Found in 1983 during the excavation of the Propylon (Inv. 83.177).

Date: first/second century AD.

Bibliography: *IAph2007* 4.117 (Reynolds; photo).

```
       [- - - - - - - - - - -]
       [- - -]παντ[- - - -]
       [- - -]ṆΤΑΤỊ[- - -]
       [- - -].ις νο[μ- - -]
4      [- - -]ων ΚΛ[- - -]
       [- - -]ΚΑΣ[- - - - -]
       [- - -]. .[- - - - - -]
       [- - - - - - - - - - -]
```

Text in majuscules, no restorations, Reynolds. ‖ 1. [ἄ]παντ[- -] or πάντ[- -]. ‖ 2. Perhaps the end of a participle: [- -]ντα Τ̣Ι or [τὴ]ν Τατί[αν], . ‖ 3. probably a form or a composite of νόμος, Chaniotis.

The nature of the text cannot be determined, probably an honorific inscription or a decree, without excluding the possibility of a letter of a Roman magistrate or emperor.

---

[182] Chaniotis 2002a, 235; Bourtzinakou 2012, nos. 2044–2056.
[183] Cf. λίμψανον: *SEG* XXX 507 (Delphi, fifth century AD); *SEG* XXXI 1419 (fourth century AD).
[184] *SEG* LVI 793 L. 2; 806 (third century AD).
[185] *SEG* LIV A 3 (fourth century AD).
[186] *SEG* LV 1304 LL. 2–3 (first century AD).
[187] For example *TAM* II 83, 123, 215, 322, 437, 957; *SEG* XXXVIII 1000 L. 13; *I.Perge* 430. Cf. *TAM* V.3.1421 L. 13: παράλημψιν.

APPENDIX 2

Catalogue of Informal Writing, Graffiti, Masons' Marks, and Gameboards from the Place of Palms

Angelos Chaniotis

This catalogue contains the graffiti, gameboards, and masons' marks registered by Joyce Reynolds and Charlotte Roueché (1970–1994), Angelos Chaniotis (1996–2018), with the assistance of Takashi Fujii (2014–2015), Benjamin Wieland (2015), Masataka Masunaga (2015), Giorgos Tsolakis (2018), Andrew Wilson, Ben Russell, and Allison Kidd (2014–2018), and Özge Acar (2019). If not otherwise stated, the texts and graffiti are unpublished and belong to late antiquity. The catalogue number indicates their location, as follows: P (Pool), NS (North Stoa), WS (West Stoa), SS (South Stoa), TW (Theatre Hill retaining wall), and Pr (Propylon). Loose fragments are listed separately (L).

A. POOL

If not otherwise stated, the graffiti, gameboards, and masons' marks are on the horizontal surface of seats and blocks of the pool.

P1. Cross. H 7.5 cm.
P2. Cross. H 15.5 cm.
P3 (Pl. 53.K). Mason's mark. Lt. 13–16.5 cm: EY
P4. Mason's mark, very faint, facing P3. Lt. 6: E or Ω
 Either cursive E or *omega*; possibly a second letter.
P5. Gameboard, cross-in-square.
P6. Gameboard, cross-in-circle, very faint.
P7. Gameboard, cross-in-square, faint.
P8. Gameboard, cross-in-circle, very faint.
P9 (Pl. 53.J). Mason's mark. Lt. 7.5–12: EPΩ
 The second letter is written upside-down in relation to the other two letters.
P10. Gameboard, eight-spoke wheel (or cross-in-circle), partly preserved.
P11. Gameboard, mancala, partly preserved.
P12. Gameboard, mancala.
 Possibly remains of a superimposed mancala gameboard.
P13. Gameboard, cross-in-circle, faint.
P14 (Pl. 55.H). Gameboard, mancala; in the middle, an additional hole, between the third hole of the two rows.
P15. Graffito of the letter Y. Lt. 8.5.
P16 (Pl. 48.B). Graffito, monogram consisting of ΚΥ (an abbrebiation of Κυ(ριακός)?). Lt. 10 cm.
P17. Cross, possibly with monogram. H 18.5 cm.
P18. Mason's mark. Lt. 7 cm: EY
P19. Mason's mark. Lt. 5 cm: EY
P20. Mason's mark. Lt. 6 cm: EY
P21. Gameboard, cross-in-square.
P22. Graffito of three unclear letters. Lt. 7 cm.
P23. Cross, very faint. H 14.5
P24. Gameboard, cross-in-circle.
P25. Mason's mark. Lt. 6.5 cm: EY
P26. Gameboard, mancala, partly preserved.
P27. Gameboard, eight-spoke wheel or cross-in-circle; only a circle is partly preserved.
P28. Mason's mark. Lt. 3 cm: M
P29 (Pl. 49.H). Pictorial graffito, probably the representation of a bird; seen from the west, it looks like an ostrich, with long legs, long neck, head, and tail; to its left, an unclear image, possibly a very crude human figure. H 23.5 cm (right), 40 cm (left).
P30. Mason's mark. Lt. 5.5 cm: EY
P31. Mason's mark. Lt. 6 cm: EY
P32 (Pl. 46.A). Mason's mark. Lt. 6.5 cm: EY
P33 (Pl. 46.A). Graffito. Christian prayer of the chief goldsmith Kolotron and drawing of two male busts. The man on the left is bearded; the eyes are attached to the nose; the short lines radiating from his head represent a wreath placed on his bold head or an elaborate hairstyle; his muscular body is indicated through raised shoulders. The man on the right has shaved face and head, with just one strain of hair extending from his head; the eyes are attached to the nose; mouth and ears are indicated. Left bust: H 18.5 cm; right bust: H. 39 cm. Lt. 1.7–5 cm.
 † Κολοτρων προταυράριος | οὗ ὁ Θεὸς μνήσετε
 'Kolotron, the chief goldsmith, whom God shall remember'.
P34. Mason's mark. Lt. 3 cm: M
P35. Gameboard, cross-in-circle.
P36. Gameboard, cross-in-circle.
P37. Cross, faint. H 10.5 cm.
P38. Mason's mark, faint. Lt. 5–5.5 cm: EPΩ
 The second letter is written upside-down in relation to the other two letters.
P39. Mason's mark. Lt. 4 cm: M
P40. Gameboard, cross-in-square, very faint.
P41. Mason's mark. Lt. 4.5 cm.: M
P42. Mason's mark. Lt. 4.5 cm.: M
P43. Mason's mark. Lt. 4.5 cm.: ΑΔ
P44. Gameboard, mancala, faint.
P45 (Pl. 46.E). Graffito consisting of two concentric circles crossed in the middle by a horizontal line; letters at the two ends of the line (Θ on left, C or cursive E on right);

possibly to be read as one word. L 28.5 cm: Θεέ? (or Θεός?)

P46 (Pl. 54.M).   Mason's mark. Lt. 4 cm: M

P47.   Unclear pictorial graffito, possibly the unfinished drawing of an animal or a human figure. L 62 cm.

P48.   Small cross. H 8 cm.

P49.   Pictorial graffito; a roughly circular shape. W 31 cm.

P50.   Mason's mark. Lt. 4.5 cm: M

P51 (Pl. 48.D). Textual graffito; letters arranged vertically in two rows; since the letters of the two rows are not exactly aligned (the letters of the right row are lower than those of the left row), it is not certain that they all belong to the same text. Lt. 4.5–10 cm.

    A   Ι
    Λ   K
  —Ο
    Σ   E

L. 1. the second letter is *iota* or *tau*. L. 3. *omikron* or *theta*. Possibly more letters after L. 4.

P52.   Mason's mark. Lt. 4.5 cm.: M

P53.   Mason's mark, faint. Lt. 9 cm: ΕΡΩ

P54.   Gameboard, cross-in-circle, faint.

P55.   Gameboard, mancala.

P56.   Gameboard, cross-in-circle, faint.

P57.   Gameboard, cross-in-circle.

P58.   Gameboard, cross-in-circle, elaborate, with semicircles at the points where the four spokes touch the periphery.

P59.   Mason's mark. Lt. 5.5 cm: M

P60.   Mason's mark. Lt. 7.5 cm: M

P61.   Mason's mark. Lt. 10 cm: M

P62.   Gameboard, cross-in-circle, very faint.

P63 (Pl. 53.Q). Mason's mark. Lt. 7.5–8.5 cm: ΘΕ

P64 (Pl. 48.C). Monogram: a cursive Ε (or Ω) and a T. H 15.5 cm, L 29.5 cm.

Since part of the periphery of the cursive *epsilon* is missing, this graffito was probably made before the block was cut to be re-used in the pool.

P65.   Graffito of two unclear letters. Lt. 6.5 cm.

P66.   Graffito consisting of a circle and two letters (mason's mark?). Lt. 3.5–5 cm: ΟΠ

P67 (Pl. 47.G). Graffito consisting of a circle and two letters (mason's mark?). Lt. 4.5–6 cm: ΟΠ

P68.   Gameboard, cross-in-square.

P69.   Gameboard, cross-in-circle.

P70.   Mason's mark. Lt. 9 cm: M

P71.   Gameboard, cross-in-circle?, very faint.

P72.   Gameboard, cross-in-circle.

P73.   Unclear graffito, consisting of a semicircle with a horizontal line (the letter Ε?); above the horizontal line two erased letters. Lt. 34.5 cm: ⟦ΑΩ⟧

If the erased letters are ΑΩ, they are a Christian religious symbol.

P74.   Graffito of two unclear letters (if read horizontally) followed by a wavy line. L 36 cm, Lt. 8.5–13.5 cm: ΙΘ?

If read vertically, a line and a Φ (11 cm); but it may be a crude or unfinished pictorial graffito.

P75.   Gameboard, *duodecim scripta*.

P76.   Mason's mark. Lt. 6.5 cm: A

P77.   Mason's mark. Lt. 10 cm: ΕΥ

The Y is written higher than the E.

P78.   Graffito of one letter. Lt. 9 cm: E

P79 (Pl. 43.B). Graffito of three lines of text. Lt. 2.5–5.5 cm: ΠΕ|ΛΑ|ΡΓΟΣ

Probably the word πελαργός ('stork'), since the text is written near drawings of birds.

P80.   Gameboard, cross-in-square.

P81 (Pl. 43.C). Pictorial graffito representing a bird (seen from south); the bird has a long neck and a long beak, possibly a stork (cf. P79) or a heron; the eye is indicated with a dot. H 37 cm.

P82.   Gameboard, eight-spoke wheel.

P83.   Mason's mark. Lt. 10 cm: ΕΥ

P84.   Mason's mark. Lt. 9.5 cm: ΕΥ

P85.   Mason's mark. Lt. 5.5 cm: M

P86.   Mason's mark. Lt. 7 cm: M

P87.   Undetermined pictorial graffito or gameboard. An oblong oval shape divided into four unequal sections through a cross; additional lines outside the periphery; possibly a cross-in-circle gameboard with lines added later. H 42 cm.

P88.   Gameboard, cross-in-square, next to and parallel to P89.

P89.   Gameboard, mancala, next to and parallel to P88.

P90 (Pl. 43.D). Pictorial graffito representing a bird. H. 36 cm. The bird faces left and is represented in outline within a diamond-shaped frame. The head, on top of a long neck, is not preserved. Short, curved lines on the body indicate feathers. The two legs are represented as diagonal lines ending in claws; the long beak suggests a stork or heron. A line to the left possibly represents a branch.

P91 (Pl. 43.E). Pictorial graffito, representing a bird in outline. The bird faces to the right; neck, head (with eye), two short legs, and wings are indicated. H 40 cm.

P92.   Gameboard, eight-spoke wheel.

P93.   Mason's mark. Lt. 5.5 cm: ΘΕ

P94 (Pl. 43.F). Pictorial graffito representing a bird facing right. The bird has a small body, a long neck, small head (the eye is indicated but not the beak), and two long legs. H 40 cm.

P95 (Pl. 43.F). Graffito of two lines of text (read from south). Lt. 5–15 cm.

  ΚΟ K...
  ΚΟΥ K

1. The fourth letter is either a square *sigma* or an *epsilon* without the middle horizontal line or a square *omikron*, not completely closed; possibly remains of one or two further letter (a lunate *sigma* or *epsilon* and a vertical line); possibly remains of a third line. One possible reading is

Κό- κος

κου

That is Κόκος Κόκου. The personal name Κῶκος is mostly attested in Asia Minor, but never in the form Κόκος. However, given the proximity of this graffito to the representations of birds it is possible that the graffito represents the voices of birds κο κο κου (see Ch. 5 §A).

P96 (Pl. 48.E). Cross (H 7 cm) and a graffito of two lines of text, hardly legible. Lt. 7–7.5 cm.

† Ṭ remains of 4–5 letters Η ΙΙ
Ν Ν Ω Ι Ο Α̣ Μ̣ Ν̣ Α̣ Ξ

It is not certain that all the letters belong to the same text; they do not follow the same allignment. ‖ 2. *Initio*, possibly a cross and not a *tau*. ‖ 3. The last letter may be a *sigma*.

P97 (Pl. 56.N). Gameboard, cross-in-circle; a small circle on one of the spokes (perhaps the letter Θ?).

P98. Mason's mark. Lt. 7 cm: Μ

P99. Mason's mark. Lt. 5 cm: ΘΕ

P100 (Pl. 56.E). Gameboard, cross-in-square with added letters and drawings in its four sections; one of the sections has two round letters (Θ?, Ο?), the other additional elements are unclear (drawings?, monograms?). H 14 cm, W 11 cm, Lt. 2.5 cm.

P101 (Pl. 47.E). Graffito of four letters. Lt. 4–5 cm: ΛΑΓΑ

P102. Gameboard, cross-in-square.

P103. Two unclear graffiti (letters or unfinished pictorial graffiti).

P104. Cross. H 12 cm.

P105 (Pl. 57.E). Wavy line, perhaps unfinished calligraphical letter (cf. P396, N235).

P106 (Pl. 45.F). Graffito. Acclamation for the association of litter-bearers. Lt. 9 cm. Date: late fifth or sixth century. Publication: *IAph2007* 4.12: νικᾷ | ἡ τύ|χη | τῶν | σελ|λοφό|ρων

P107 (Pl. 49.E). Pictorial graffito. A bust. The outline of a face on a strong neck. H 23 cm.

P108. Circle (or unfinished gameboard B?). Diam. 11 cm.

P109. Gameboard, cross-in-circle.

P110 (Pl. 43.G–H). Gameboard and obscene graffito. The text is written inside an eight-spoke wheel gameboard, with the text distributed between two segments of the circle. Date: late fifth or early sixth century AD. Publications: *IAph2007* 4.26 iii a/b; Chaniotis 2018a, 87–89. Lt. 2–5 cm.

a [- -]ΥΓΙ b Δουλ-
   [- -]Ο Εὐ-   κίτιν
   [σέ]βις

IAph2007 provides slightly different readings:

a ΥΓΙ b Δουλ-
   ΟΕΥ   κιτιαν-
   ΟΙΣ   οῦ

The text probably reads: [π]υγί|[ζει] or [ἐπ]ύγι[σεν] ὁ Εὐ|[σέ]βις | Δουλ|κίτιν ('Eusebi(o)s buggers/buggered Doulkiti(o)s)').

P111 (Pl. 43.I). Gameboard, *duodecim scripta* (elaborate) and graffiti. The four corners of the gameboard are decorated with diagonal lines ('stars'); the two lateral rows of holes have a semicircle in the middle, the central row has a circle divided by spokes into six segments. There are graffiti along all four sides: north (a), west (b), south (c), and east (d). The graffiti are engraved by three, possibly four, different hands and are very worn. Lt. 3.5–6 cm. Publication: *IAph2007* 4.6 ii.

a Νικᾷ ἡ Τύχη το[ῦ?]
b Νικᾷ [- - ?]
c Εὐσεβίου
d [- -]ΟΑ. Ἀλυπιο[- -]

a + c may belong to one text: 'The Fortune of Eusebios prevails'.

IAph2007 gives slightly different readings: a: Νικᾷ ἡ τύχη Π[.. ? ..]; b: [.. ? .. Νικᾷ ἡ τ]ύ[χη .. ? ..]; c: Εὐσέβιος; d: [..?..] ΟΥΜΟ̣[..?..] Λ̣ΑΥΠΕΩΣ.

P112 (Pl. 45.G). Graffito, acclamation. Lt. 5–6.5 cm: Αὔξι | ἡ τύχη | τῶν | ΔC

4. Written in smaller letters; possibly ligature of delta and another letter.

P113. Gameboard, mancala.

P114. Graffito of one letter (possibly more). Lt. 10 cm. Η or Ν

P115. Unclear graffito (two letters or two lines?). Lt. 8.5 cm.

P116. Gameboard, *duodecim scripta*. A horizontal line divides the three vertical rows of holes into two parts.

P117. Gameboard, cross-in-square, very small.

P118. Gameboard, mancala, partly preserved (only one row of five holes).

P119. Cross. H 11 cm.

P120. Unclear pictorial graffito, perhaps unfinished, on the same plaque as P117 and P118.

P121 (Pl. 54.I). Two mason's marks on adjacent plaques. Lt. 7 and 4.5 cm: Α

P122. Mason's mark. Lt. 7 cm: Μ

P123. Mason's mark. Lt. 18.5 cm: Ε

P124. Gameboard, *duodecim scripta*.

P125. Mason's mark. Lt. 6.5: Α

P126. Cross. H 11.5 cm.

P127. Unclear graffito (letters?), and possibly part of a mancala gameboard. Length of the entire graffito 12.5 cm, Lt. 8 cm.

P128. Mason's mark. Lt. 9 cm: ΕΥ

P129. Mason's mark. Lt. 9 cm: ΕΥ

P130. Gameboard, cross-in-square, next to P131.

P131. Gameboard, cross-in-square, next to P130.

P132 (Pl. 52.B). *Topos* inscription. Lt. 5–8.5 cm: Παύλου τόπος

A vertical line between Λ and Ο may be a small cross: Παύλ†ου.

P133. Pictorial graffito, unclear; a circle encloses two unclear drawings. Diam. 37 cm.

P134. Cross. H 22 cm.

P135. Letter?; perhaps a second faint letter. Lt. 7 cm: Θ?

P136. Mason's mark. Lt. 6.5 cm: Μ

P137. Gameboard, cross-in-square.

P138. Mason's mark. Lt. 5 cm: ΕΥ

P139 (Pl. 49.C). Pictorial graffito representing a human figure; one recognizes two legs, a torso, a strong neck, a head with mouth, nose, eyes, and big right ear; the man holds an object with his right hand; a long line on top of his head may be a strand of hair; probably an athlete holding a branch or a wreath. H 24 (18 cm, without the line on top of the head).

P140 (Pl. 57.A). Gameboard, eight-spoke wheel, elaborate; the centre of the circle is a hole; the circle is divided into five segments; within each segment, two concentric half-circles touch the periphery of the circle.

P141 (Pl. 57.A). Gameboard, eight-spoke wheel; a spoke divides one of the segments into two, resulting in a total of nine (not eight) segments.

P142. Cross and possibly remains of a gameboard D. H 13 cm.

P143. Pictorial graffito, unfinished or unclear. H 12, W 13 cm.

P144. Gameboard, eight-spoke wheel.

P145 (Pl. 56.C). Gameboard, cross-in-square with holes within each square.

P146. Gameboard, cross-in-square.

P147. Graffito of one letter. Lt. 10 cm: Θ
Or Φ?

P148. Graffito of one letter. Lt. 21 cm: N
Or H?

P149. Graffito, semicircle or a lunate sigma. H 18 cm.

P150. Gameboard, cross-in-square.

P151. Gameboard, cross-in-circle.

P152. Gameboard, cross-in-square?, faint (only a square is visible).

P153. Gameboard, mancala, possibly remains of another one.

P154. Cross, on the underside of an inner seat slab. H 8 cm.

P155. Gameboard, cross-in-square.

P156. Mason's mark. Lt. 8 cm: EY

P157 (Pl. 53.I). Mason's mark. Lt. 4–4.5 cm: ΘE

P158 (Pl. 53.I). Mason's mark. Lt. 8 cm: EY

P159 (Pl. 51.A). Pictorial graffito, a phallus; possibly another drawing to the right. H 15.5 (12.5 cm, testicles 5.5–6.5 cm).

P160. Cross, very faint. H 7.5.

P161 (Pl. 51.A). Gameboard, eight-spoke wheel, elaborate; an octagon inside the circle.

P162. Mason's mark. Lt. 7 cm: M

P163. Gameboard, eight-spoke wheel.

P164. Gameboard, cross-in-circle.

P165. Mason's mark. Lt. 7 cm: M

P166. Gameboard, mancala.

P167 (Pl. 47.A). Graffito. Lt. 6.5–8 cm: ἀφετηρία

'Starting point'. The letter forms suggest a date in the second or third century AD; the mason's mark (P168) on the same plaque suggests that the inscription originates in the first use of the stone in a place of athletic or equestrian contests.

P168 (Pl. 47.A). Mason's mark. Lt. 4.5 cm: ΘE

P169. Graffito, two lines of text. Lt. 3.5–5.5 cm.

Φ . . E
ΦΡΕΑ

1. The latters are very faint; the second letter may be an *alpha*. || 2. The beginning of φρέαρ or φρεάτιον?

P170. Graffito, a letter. Lt 9 cm: E or Θ

P171 (Pl. 56.K). Gameboard, cross-in-circle, elaborate; there are semicircles at the point where the four spokes touch the periphery.

P172. Part of a gameboard, cross-in-circle, covered by P171, very faint.

P173. Mason's mark, on the rim of a seat. Lt. 5.5: E

P174. Mason's mark. Lt. 5.5 cm: M

P175. Gameboard, cross-in-square.

P176. Gameboard, eight-spoke wheel.

P177. Pictorial graffito, unclear.

P178. Gameboard, cross-in-circle, faint.

P179. Mason's mark. Lt. 9 cm: M

P180. Cross, on the rim of a seat. H 24 cm

P181. Gameboard, cross-in-square with slightly curved sides.

P182. Graffito of one letter. Lt. 31 cm: A?

P183. Gameboard, eight-spoke wheel, faint.

P184. Pictorial graffito, unclear. It consists of two squares of unequal size; the smaller square has a small line in it.

P185. Gameboard, cross-in-circle?; a circle with irregular lines inside it, instead of a cross.

P186. Gameboard, eight-spoke wheel, elaborate; semicircles are attached to the periphery of the circle.

P187. Gameboard, eight-spoke wheel.

P188. Pictorial graffito; a square.

P189 (Pl. 48.H). Graffito, a menorah. H 22 cm.

P190. Gameboard, cross-in-square.

P191. Mason's mark. Lt. 8 cm: M

P192. Unclear pictorial graffito; an irregular circle with a line attached to the periphery.

P193. Cross. H 13.5 cm.

P194 (Pl. 47.H). Graffito of two letters. Lt. 3.5 cm: κ̄ε̄

The lines above the letters indicate an abbreviation, probably Κ(ύρι)ε, the invocation of Jesus, since it is on the same plaque as the cross P193, rather than Κ(ωνσταντῖν)ε or Κ(υριακ)έ.

P195. Gameboard, cross-in-circle.

P196. Pictorial graffito, a circle (wreath?) and a semicircle?. Diam. of circle 11 cm, H of semicircle 21 cm.

P197. Gameboard, mancala placed in a circle, probably superimposed on a cross-in-circle gameboard.

P198. Gameboard, cross-in-square.

P199. A semicircle, probably part of a gameboard, eight-spoke wheel.

P200. Gameboard, eight-spoke wheel, adjacent to P198 and partly covering P201.

P201. Gameboard, cross-in-circle, partly preserved and partly covered by P200. An irregular shape within a segment (pictorial graffito?, letters?).

P202 (Pl. 56.F). Gameboard, cross-in-square; a small cross (?) in one of the squares.

P203. Mason's mark on loose fragment. Lt. 6.5 cm: M

P204. Gameboard, cross-in-square, very faint; it seems to consist of six sections, instead of four (or a separate gameboard is attached to it).

P205 (Pl. 56.J). Gameboard, cross-in-circle; in two of the segments, two small gameboards, cross-in-circle.

P206. Gameboard, cross-in-circle, very faint.

P207. Gameboard, cross-in-circle.

P208 (Pl. 48.I). Graffito, a menorah with base, shofar, and ethrog. H 28.5 cm.

P209. Gameboard, cross-in-circle, probably superimposed on older one.

P210. Graffito of a letter? Lt. 17 cm: C?

P211. Drawing of two parallel lines. L 19 and 20 cm.

P212. Cross, directly under the menorah P213. H 5–6 cm.

P213 (Pl. 48.J). Graffito, a menorah with 10 branches. H 28 cm.

P214. Gameboard, mancala, partly preserved.

P215. Gameboard, cross-in-circle, small.

P216. Graffito of a letter. Lt. 5 cm: A?

P217. Gameboard, cross-in-square.

P218 (Pl. 55.I). Gameboard, mancala, consisting of two rows of four holes each, surrounded by a circle, probably made separately; on the periphery of the circle an unclear shape (pictorial graffito?); an additional hole at the end and offset to one side of the board probably served as a players' store.

P219. Gameboard, mancala.

P220. Mason's mark. Lt. 8 cm: M

P221. Gameboard, cross-in-square, very faint.

P222. Gameboard, cross-in-circle, very faint.

P223. Unclear pictorial graffito in the shape of a semicircle (resembling the letter D) or unfinished cross-in-circle gameboard.

P224. Gameboard, mancala.

P225. Gameboard, cross-in-circle.

P226. Gameboard, cross-in-square.

P227 (Pl. 43.J). Gameboard, cross-in-square. A graffito inside the gameboard and under it. Lt. 2–3.5 cm.: Νικᾷ ἡ | τύχη τ|οῦ Ἀγ|αθοκλῆ

    Ἀγαθοκλῆς was hitherto unattested in Aphrodisias. The influence of the first and second declension on nouns of the third declension (Ἀγαθοκλῆ instead of Ἀγαθοκλέους) is common in the late Imperial period and in late antiquity; see for example *MAMA* III 302: Διοκλῆ (genitive); *SEG* XXVIII 935: Ἀρτέμωναν; *SEG* LVI 793 L. 5: Σωκράτου μηδέναν (instead of Σωκράτους μηδένα); *SEG* LXI 499 L. 2: Νεικόπολις instead of Νεικοπόλεως.

P228. Mason's mark. Lt. 6.5 cm: M

P229. Mason's mark. Lt. 9 cm: EY

P230 (Pl. 52.A). Graffito, drawing of a *tabula ansata*. L 30 cm, H 12 cm.

P231. Pictorial graffito? A simple square, possibly an unfinished *tabula ansata* (next to P230) rather than an unfinished gameboard; a letter (Γ, Π, or square Σ) is inscribed in it.

P232. Mason's mark. Lt.11 cm: EY

P233. Mason's mark. Lt. 5 cm: M

P234. Gameboard, mancala; two rows of five holes each, enclosed in a rectangle.

P235. Gameboard, mancala; two holes, one at each end and offset to the board, probably served as the players' stores.

P236. Gameboard, cross-in-circle.

P237. Mason's mark. Lt. 9.5 cm: EY

P238. Cross. H 13 cm.

P239. Graffito of one letter. Lt. 8.5 cm: Ω or E

P240. Gameboard, cross-in-circle.

P241. Gameboard, eight-spoke wheel, faint.

P242. Mason's mark. Lt. 7 cm: M

P243. Mason's mark. Lt. 5 cm: EY

P244. Cross? H 5.5 cm.

P245 (Pl. 49.B). Pictorial graffito. A standing male figure, his right arm is raised and extended, the left arm is slightly raised near the body; probably an athlete holding a palm branch or a statue. H 36 cm.

P246. Gameboard, cross-in-square, faint.

P247. Pictorial graffito. A standing male figure, very faint. H cm.

P248. Mason's mark. Lt. 6 cm: M

P249 (Pl. 56.B). Two adjacent cross-in-square gameboards that share one of their sides.

P250. Gameboard, mancala, unfinished? Only two holes are preserved.

P251. Cross?, very faint. H 22 cm.

P252. Mason's mark. Lt. 7.5 cm: M

P253. Cross. H 9 cm.

P254. Cross, very faint. H 11 cm.

P255. Gameboard, cross-in-circle, very faint.

P256 (Pl. 56.G). Cross within a circle (or gameboard?). H 30 cm.

P257 (Pl. 56.D). Gameboard, cross-in-square (variant): two squares with crosses share one of their sides, thus creating a rectangle with eight segments (cf. P249); at least four of the segments have small holes inside them.

P258. Gameboard, cross-in-circle, elaborate, with semicircles at the point where the four spokes touch the periphery.

P259. Gameboard, cross-in-circle or pictorial graffito (circle)?

P260 (Pl. 56.H). Gameboard, cross-in-circle enclosed in a large circle.

P261. Pictorial graffito? An irregular round shape. H 45 cm.

P262. Gameboard, mancala.

P263. Gameboard, mancala.

P264 (Pl. 48.K). Menorah. H 34 cm.

P265. Gameboard, mancala.

P266 (Pl. 48.L). Menorah. H 37 cm.

P267. Cross. H 14 cm.

P268. Cross. H 17 cm.

P269. Gameboard, eight-spoke wheel, partly preserved.

P270. Pictorial graffito, outline of a human figure, consisting of head, body, and legs. H 50 cm.

P271. Mason's mark. Lt. 6 cm: M

P272. Mason's mark. Lt. 10 cm: EY

P273. Mason's mark. Lt. 6.5 cm: M

P274. Mason's mark. Lt. 6 cm: EY

P275. Cross. H 16.5 cm.

P276. Gameboard, cross-in-square.

P277. Cross?, very small. H 4 cm.

P278. Cross. H 8 cm.

P279. Gameboard, cross-in-circle, faint.

P280. Gameboard, mancala, only three holes are well preserved.

P281. Gameboard, mancala.

P282. Gameboard, cross-in-circle?

P283. Gameboard, cross-in-square?

P284. Graffito of three lines of text, very faint and unclear. Lt. 6.5–8 cm.

    . . Ω .
    ṆẸICC
    - - - -

    2. The second letter is a cursive *epsilon*; the last cursive letters may be E, O, or Σ.

P285. Gameboard, cross-in-square.

P286. Mason's mark on loose fragment. Lt 6 cm: M

P287. Mason's mark. Lt. 4 cm: M

P288. Gameboard, eight-spoke wheel.
P289. Mason's mark. Lt. 6 cm: M
P290. Mason's mark. Lt. 6.5 cm: M
P291. Gameboard, mancala.
P292. Mason's mark. Lt. 6 cm: M
P293. Mason's mark. Lt. 6 cm: EY
P294. Mason's mark. Lt. 5 cm: EY
P295. Gameboard, mancala.
P296. Gameboard, mancala.
P297. Gameboard, cross-in-circle.
P298. Gameboard, mancala; the rows of holes are placed within a rectangle that resembles a grid.
P299. Gameboard, mancala.
P300 (Pl. 51.D). Pictorial graffito consisting of two concentric elliptical lines, ending in a curve at one end and a straight line at the other. Drawing of the pool? L 57 cm, W 34 cm.
P301. Gameboard, cross-in-circle.
P302. Graffito of two letters, inscribed on the side of a seat block. Lt. 10–11 cm: AN
P303. Pictorial graffito consisting of a square (unfinished?).
P304. Gameboard, *duodecim scripta*, partly preserved.
P305. Gameboard, cross-in-circle, partly preserved, or a cursive E. H 30 cm.
P306. Gameboard, cross-in-circle?, very faint.
P307. Graffito of one letter. Lt. 4 cm: A
P308. Gameboard, cross-in-circle, elaborate: a small circle, with semicircles at the point where the four spokes touch the periphery, is enclosed within another circle.
P309 (Pl. 47.L). Cross monogram? Small circles (letters?) are attached at the ends of the bars. H 21, Lt. 5 cm.
P310. Unclear pictorial graffito in the shape of a heart or a leaf (unfinished?).
P311. Gameboard, eight-spoke wheel unfinished; elaborate, with a circle in the centre and semicircles at the points where the spokes (not engraved) would have touched the periphery.
P312. Gameboard, mancala.
P313 (Pl. 51.E). Pictorial graffito. Outline of a structure (building?). H 37 cm.
P314. Gameboard, mancala.
P315. Gameboard, mancala.
P316. Gameboard, cross-in-square.
P317. Gameboard, mancala within a square.
P318. Gameboard, cross-in-square.
P319 (Pl. 51.J). Large pictorial graffito. Drawing of an oblong object, possibly a boat. L 1.28 cm.
P320. Gameboard, mancala; two rows of five holes each within a rectangular frame, divided into two by a line parallel to its long sides.
P321. Pictorial graffito, unclear; possibly a bust (left) and the crude outline of a human figure (right). H 34, W 47.
P322. Gameboard, cross-in-square.
P323. Gameboard, cross-in-circle.
P324. Monogram; instead of a cross with letters attached to the ends of the bars, it consists of a vertical line resembling a Ψ, with the letters A (bottom), Ω (right), and an unclear letter (left). H 24 cm.

P325. Gameboard, cross-in-circle, elaborate; semicircles at the points where the four spokes touch the periphery of the circle.
P326. Gameboard, mancala; two rows of holes within a grid.
P327. Gameboard, eight-spoke wheel.
P328. Gameboard, cross-in-circle.
P329. Gameboard, mancala.
P330. Gameboard, mancala; a line divides a rectangle into two parts, each of which is subdivided into five sections; holes are visible only in two of these sections.
P331 (Pl. 51.F). Pictorial graffito, possibly originally a cross-in-circle gameboard to which an arch was added; a small irregular circle to the left may be part of this graffito. H of arch 16 cm, diam. 31 cm.
P332. Gameboard, mancala?, partly preserved.
P333 (Pl. 57.B). Gameboard, eight-spoke wheel, elaborate; a wavy line along the periphery of the circle.
P334. Gameboard, cross-in-circle.
P335. Gameboard, cross-in-circle.
P336. Gameboard, mancala.
P337. Gameboard, cross-in-circle, elaborate; a circle in the center; semicircles at the points where the four spokes touch the periphery of the circle.
P338 (Pl. 53.I). Mason's mark or abbreviated word or name. Lt. 4.5–7 cm: ENI
P339. Gameboard, cross-in-circle; an additional line (parallel to one of the arms of the central cross) separates a small segment.
P340. Gameboard, cross-in-square, very faint.
P341. Gameboard, cross-in-circle, very faint.
P342. Gameboard, cross-in-circle.
P343. Pictorial graffito, unclear; possibly the outline of two busts. H 55, W 31 cm.
P344. Gameboard, cross-in-circle.
P345. Gameboard, cross-in-circle.
P346. Gameboard, cross-in-square.
P347. Gameboard, cross-in-circle.
P348. Gameboard, mancala.
P349. Gameboard, mancala.
P350. Gameboard, cross-in-circle.
P351. Gameboard, cross-in-circle.
P352. Gameboard, cross-in-circle.
P353. Gameboard, mancala; one hole at the end and offset to the side of the board, probably served as a players' store.
P354. Circle. Diam. 16.5 cm.
P355. Gameboard, cross-in-square.
P356. Gameboard, cross-in-circle.
P357. Gameboard, cross-in-circle.
P358. Gameboard, cross-in-square.
P359. Gameboard, cross-in-square.
P360. Mason's mark or abbreviated word or name, on loose fragment. Lt. 6.5–7 cm: ENI
P361. Gameboard, cross-in-square.
P362. Gameboard, cross-in-square.
P363. Gameboard, cross-in-square.
P364 (Pl. 55.J). Gameboard in the shape of a grid, consisting of four rows of 5 sections each (variant of mancala?).

P365. Gameboard or unclear pictorial graffito? Only a rectangle is clear.
P366. Graffito of two letters. Lt. 6.5–8.5: EI?
P367. Gameboard, cross-in-circle.
P368. Gameboard, cross-in-square.
P369. Gameboard, cross-in-circle with a circle attached.
P370. Gameboard, cross-in-square.
P371. Gameboard, cross-in-circle.
P372. Gameboard, cross-in-circle.
P373. Gameboard, mancala within a rectangle divided by a line into two rows.
P374. Gameboard, cross-in-square.
P375. Gameboard, cross-in-circle.
P376. Square. H 9 cm.
P377 (Pl. 45.B). Graffito, acclamation for the circus faction of the Reds. Inscription: H 78 cm, W 34 cm. Lt. 8–10 cm.

N[ι]κ[ᾷ]
ἡ Τύ-
χη
τῶν
Ῥου-
σέων
___
___
_

'The fortune of the Reds prevails'.

P378. Gameboard, cross-in-square?
P379. Gameboard, cross-in-circle.
P380. Gameboard, mancala.
P381. Gameboard, cross-in-circle.
P382. Gameboard, mancala.
P383. Gameboard, cross-in-circle.
P384 (Pl. 45.I). Graffito of five letters; a name? Lt. 3.5–6.5: ΑΧΗΛΙ
P385. Gameboard, cross-in-square, faint.
P386. Pictorial graffito (semicircle) or gameboard?
P387. Gameboard, cross-in-square, faint.
P388. Gameboard, cross-in-square, faint.
P389. Unclear pictorial graffito.
P390. Gameboard, cross-in-circle, small.
P391. A circle, gameboard, cross-in-circle, unfinished? (the cross is missing).
P392. Graffito of one letter. Lt. 11 cm: E
P393. Gameboard, cross-in-square.
P394. Gameboard, cross-in-circle.
P395 (Pl. 44.F). Gameboard, mancala; one row of five holes.
P396 (Pl. 44.F). Graffito. Under a pediment, two calligraphic letters, an alpha, with wavy lines rising from the top, and a lambda. The style resembles that of N235. Possibly an abbreviated name. H 21 Lt. 13 cm.
P397. Gameboard, eight-spoke wheel.
P398 (Pl. 44.B). Gameboard, mancala; two apses with small crosses were added to either end of the two rows of holes, transforming the gameboard into the outline of a church, with the rows of holes resembling columns.
P399. Gameboard, cross-in-circle.
P400. Gameboard, mancala.
P401. Gameboard, cross-in-square.
P402. Graffito, two parallel lines.
P403. Gameboard, cross-in-circle.
P404. Gameboard, cross-in-circle, faint.
P405 (Pl. 44.A). Gameboard, cross-in-square.
P406 (Pl. 44.A). Gameboard, cross-in-square.
P407 (Pl. 44.A). Menorah.
P408 (Pl. 44.A). Gameboard, cross-in-square (the base of the menorah turned into gameboard).
P409 (Pl. 44.A). Drawing of an erect phallus.
P410. Pictorial graffito (or monogram?), consisting of two long parallel lines (on two different plaques); circles at the ends on the second line (from west to east), resembling the letter Φ or Θ (top) and the Ω (bottom); a circle may also have existed at the top end of the first line. H 61 cm.
P411. Gameboard, cross-in-circle.
P412. Unclear pictorial graffito consisting of two adjacent irregular circles.
P413. Gameboard, cross-in-circle.
P414. Gameboard, cross-in-square.
P415. Gameboard, *duodecim scripta*.
P416. Gameboard, eight-spoke wheel.
P417. Gameboard, *duodecim scripta*; three rows of small circles (instead of holes) within a frame.
P418. Gameboard, cross-in-circle, elaborate; with large semicircles at the point where the four spokes touch the periphery.
P419 (Pl. 55.E). Gameboard, mancala; holes within a grid; one hole offset to the side of the grid, probably served as a players' store.
P420 (Pl. 55.E). Gameboard, mancala; holes within in a grid; partly preserved.
P421 (Pl. 55.E). Gameboard, mancala.
P422. Pictorial graffito; it resembles a cross with a large triangular base, but it may be the rough drawing of a bird, with the triangle representing the tail and the arms of the cross representing the open wings. H 27 cm.
P423. Graffito of a letter. Lt. 9 cm: Θ
P424. Gameboard, mancala.
P425. Graffito, one letter? (a lunate sigma?). Lt. 14 cm: C
P426. Gameboard, mancala.
P427. Graffito of a letter. Lt. 3 cm: Θ
P428. Gameboard, cross-in-circle.
P429. Gameboard, cross-in-circle?; one vertical and two horizontal lines divide a circle into six sections.
P430. Gameboard, mancala.
P431. Gameboard, cross-in-circle.
P432. Gameboard, cross-in-circle, elaborate but unfinished; the cross has not been engraved, but there are semicircles at the places where the spokes would have ended.
P433. Gameboard, cross-in-circle, superimposed on P434.
P434. Gameboard, mancala.
P435. Gameboard, cross-in-circle, faint.
P436. Gameboard, mancala.
P437. Cross, next to P436. H 10 cm.
P438. Cross. H 4.5 cm.
P439. Letter M or Σ, next to the cross P438. Lt. 7.5 (M) 4.5.

P440. Gameboard, cross-in-circle.
P441. Three masons' marks on adjacent blocks: i) on the rim of a seat (Π); ii) on the plaque in front of the seat (Π); iii) and on the rim of the seat block to the right (Κ). H 2.5 cm (Κ)–3.5 cm (Π).
P442. Gameboard, mancala.
P443. Gameboard, cross-in-square? faint; the lines are slightly curved.
P444. Gameboard, mancala?, only three holes clearly preserved.
P445. Gameboard, mancala?, only one row of four holes is preserved.
P446 (Pl. 48.M). Pictorial graffito, probably unfinished; it consists of a semicircular base that supports an oblong stem; perhaps an unfinished menorah. H 30.5 cm.
P447. Gameboard, mancala.
P448. Graffito. Lt. 7 cm: Κύριε ΑΠΟΛΙΩ?
P449 (Pl. 50.H). Pictorial graffito. Drawing of a large fish facing right; it has a large trapezoidal tail, oblong body, and a large head with oval eye and open mouth; the pelvic and anal fins are clearly represented; two lines separate the head from the body; three small cavities above the mouth might indicate bubbles. L 40 cm.
P450. Textual graffito. Lt. 5.5–12 cm: ΥΘΟΟΙΒΙ
The first letter may be an Y or a N. The last three letters, which are smaller, may belong to a different graffito. The last, very small, letter may be an I, a K, or a C.
P451. Gameboard, cross-in-circle, faint; the cross is missing.
P452 (Pl. 46.C). Graffito, Christian prayer. Lt. 3.7–7 cm: Κύριε βοήθι Πρίμω?
P453. Gameboard, cross-in-circle?; a semicircle and one arm of the cross (unfinished?).
P454. Graffito or gameboard, cross-in-circle?; a circle with a double cross, which divides the circle into six segments. Diam. 15.5 cm.
P455 (Pl. 55.E). Gameboard, *duodecim scripta* or *tabula*? (see Ch. 5 §F); it has two (not three) rows of 12 holes each; a semicircle in the middle of each row.
P456. Gameboard, *duodecim scripta*?, unfinished; three rows of holes, with three holes each.
P457. Gameboard, cross-in-circle.
P458. Mason's mark, on the rim of a seat, H 3 cm: Κ
P459. Gameboard, cross-in-circle, faint.
P460. Gameboard, mancala.
P461 (Pl. 55.G). Gameboard consisting of two rows of four holes each, placed within a grid, which is open on its long sides.
P462 (Pl. 55.G). Gameboard, eight-spoke wheel, elaborate; a hexagon enclosed within the circle.
P463. Unfinished pictorial graffito (irregular semicircle) or gameboard.
P464. Gameboard, cross-in-circle turned into eight-spoke-wheel with the addition of irregular spokes.
P465 (Pl. 48.M). Cross monogram; the letter N at the left end of the horizontal arm. H 37 cm, Lt. 6 cm.
P466. Gameboard, cross-in-circle, faint.
P467. Gameboard, mancala. two holes at the end and offset to the side of the board probably served as the players' store.
P468 (Pl. 56.M). Gameboard, cross-in-circle, heart-shaped.
P469. Pictorial graffito: circle (?).
P470 (Pl. 50.G). Unclear pictorial graffito; possibly the outline of an animal (with tail, back legs, body, and head). H 23.5, L 47.5 cm.
P471. Gameboard, mancala?; only four holes.
P472. Gameboard, mancala.
P473. Small circle or the letter omikron. Diam. 7.5 cm.
P474. Gameboard, mancala.
P475. Gameboard, eight-spoke wheel.
P476. Gameboard, cross-in-circle, unfinished; only one line, instead of a cross.
P477. Gameboard, cross-in-circle.
P478. Gameboard, cross-in-square.
P479 (Pl. 48.F). Cross, next to P480. H 7 cm.
P480 (Pl. 48.F). Cross, next to P479. H 5.5 cm.
P481. Gameboard, cross-in-circle.
P482. Gameboard, cross-in-circle; the cross is very faint.
P483. Mason's mark, on the rim of a seat, Lt. 3.5 cm: Π
P484. Gameboard, cross-in-circle, very faint.
P485. Gameboard, cross-in-circle.
P486. Mason's mark, on the rim of a seat, Lt. 3.5 cm: Π
P487. Gameboard, cross-in-circle.
P488. Mason's mark or abbreviated word or name. Lt. 5.5 cm: ΕΝΙ
P489. Gameboard, mancala?
P490. Gameboard, cross-in-circle.
P491. Mason's mark, on the rim of a seat, Lt. 2.5 cm: Π
P492. Gameboard, cross-in-square.
P493. Gameboard, cross-in-circle.
P494. Gameboard, cross-in-circle; the periphery has the shape of a fruit.
P495. Gameboard, cross-in-circle; a small 'tail' is attached to the periphery.
P496. Gameboard, cross-in-circle.
P497. Gameboard, cross-in-circle.
P498. Gameboard, cross-in-circle.
P499. Gameboard, cross-in-circle.
P500. Gameboard, cross-in-circle.
P501. Gameboard, cross-in-square.
P502. Gameboard, cross-in-circle.
P503. Gameboard, cross-in-square.
P504. Gameboard, cross-in-circle.
P505. Gameboard, cross-in-circle.
P506. Gameboard, cross-in-circle?, unfinished.
P507. Cross? H 13.5 cm.
P508. Gameboard, cross-in-circle.
P509. Pictorial graffito consisting of two small circles.
P510. Gameboard, cross-in-circle.
P511. Gameboard, cross-in-circle.
P512. Gameboard, mancala.
P513. Gameboard, mancala.

B. NORTH STOA

The graffiti, gameboards, and masons' marks recorded in the North Stoa are located on columns, stylobate blocks, and the top of the seat blocks in front of the stylobate. The NS numbers refer to the location of each item on the plan of the North Stoa. The columns are numbered from the east end of the North Stoa to the west end, from N1 to N71, and the graffiti etc. are likewise presented from east to west. The location of each item on a column is indicated with reference to the side of the column and its distance from the stylobate.

NS1 (Pl. 48.G). N1, southwest, 1.12 m above the stylobate. Christogram consisting of a cross and the letters Α (end of left bar), Ω (end of right bar), and Ρ (top). H 18.5 cm, W 15 cm.

NS2. N2, south, 1.58 m above the stylobate. Graffito of one letter. Lt. 3.5 cm: Τ

NS3. N3, southeast, 1.01 m above the stylobate. Mason's mark (assembly mark) or graffito of one letter; the letter is not written on a straight line; it seems to have been engraved before the column was set up. Lt. 3 cm: Δ

NS4. N5, north, 0.74 m above the stylobate. Pictorial graffito, representing a (female?) head and bust.[1]

NS5. Between N5–N6, on the top of the seat block. Gameboard, mancala.

NS6. N6, on the stylobate. *Topos* inscription. Lt. 2–3 cm: τόπος Παπ[ία?]

NS7 (Pl. 53.D). N7, on lower drum, south, 1.88 m above the stylobate. Christian commemoration. Lt. 3 cm: + Εὐτυχία

NS8. N7, under NS7, 1.06 m above the stylobate. Cross or Christogram, very faint (not seen in 2018). H 14 cm, W 10 cm.

NS9. N7, to the right of NS8, 1.11 m above the stylobate. Graffito of two letters. Lt. 4 cm: ΝΙ

NS10 (Pl. 52.F). N7, northwest, 1.64 m above the stylobate. Lt. 2.0–2.5 cm. *Topos* inscription: Ἀντιόχου

NS11. N7, northwest, under NS10, 0.73 m above the stylobate. Lt. 2.5–3 cm. Difficult to read: Τόπ[ος …]|ΤΩΝ

NS12. N8, north, 1.14 m from the stylobate. Graffito of two letters, roughly pecked. Lt. 5 cm: ΠΕ

NS13. N8, south, at 1.31 m above the stylobate. Siglum like an extended cursive Ν. W 5 cm.

NS14. N8, on the stylobate, southeast corner. Assembly mark or graffito of one letter. Lt. 4 cm: Γ

NS15 (Pl. 52.G). N9, south side (originally northwest?), 1.77 m above the stylobate. *Topos* inscription, engraved with neat, deep letters. Date: c. third century AD. Lt. 4.1–5.3 cm: Διονυσί|ου καὶ Πα|πίου.

NS16. N9, south, 0.50 m above the stylobate. Cross. H 10 m, W 3.5 cm.

NS17. N9, 7 cm southeast of N16. Vertical line. L 56 cm.

NS18 (Pl. 53.E). N9, east (originally south?), 1.77 m above the stylobate. Commemoration. Lt. 2.7–3 cm: + Εὐδοξία.

NS19 (Pl. 53.C). N9, west (originally north?), 1.61 m above the stylobate. *Topos* inscription. Lt. 2–3.3 cm: σοφιστοῦ

NS20 (Pl. 45.H). N9, west (originally north?), 0.90 m above the stylobate. Acclamation. Lt. 1–1.7 cm: Νίκη | Τύχῃ ΤΟ

    Possibly unfinished (νίκη το[ῖς - -].

NS21. N9, on the stylobate, northeast corner. Graffito of one letter. Lt. 4 cm: Γ

NS22. N10, southwest (originally north-northeast?), 1.20 m from the stylobate. Cross, rough-pecked. H 9 cm, W 5 cm.

NS23 (Pl. 51.H). N10, north (originally west?), 0.76 m above the stylobate. Pictorial graffito resembling a ladder. H 34 cm, W 4–5 cm.

NS24. N10, on the stylobate, west of the column. Gameboard, mancala.

NS25. N11, in front of the column. Gameboard, cross-in-circle, partly preserved.

NS26. N11, in front of the column. Graffito of one letter. Lt. 12 cm: Κ

NS27. N12, on the top of the seat block in front of the stylobate. Gameboard, eight-spoke wheel, elaborate, with semicircles attached to the periphery.

NS28. N12, on the top of the seat block, west of the column. Gameboard, mancala.

NS29. N12, on the stylobate, east of the base. Gameboard, cross-in-square.

NS30. N13, on the stylobate, east of the base. Gameboard, cross-in-square.

NS31. N13, on the stylobate, east of the base. Gameboard, mancala, faint, immediately to the east of NS30.

NS32. Between N12–N13, on the top of the seat block. Elaborate cross with small circles at the end of the arms. H 41 cm.

NS33. N13, on the top of the seat block, in front of the column. Gameboard, *duodecim scripta*.

NS34. N13, on the top of the seat block, in front of the column. Gameboard, cross-in-square.

NS35. Between N13–N14, on the foundation below the robbed stylobate. Mason's mark. H 9 cm: Δ

NS36. N14, on the stylobate to east of the base. Abbreviation or Christian invocation. Lt. 4.5 cm: ΘΕ

    Θε(έ), or Θε(ός), or a name beginning with Θεο-.

NS37. Immediately north of NS36, *duodecim scripta* gameboard, partly preserved.

NS38. N14, on the stylobate, east of NS36. *Topos* inscription?, engraved inside a rectangle. Lt. 2 cm: [...] | ΙΟΙΙΟ[...]

    2. Τόπο[ς?].

NS39. N14, on the stylobate, south of NS36. Graffito of one letter. H 3 cm: Ε or Ω

NS40. N14, on the stylobate, south of NS36. Pictorial graffito? An irregular shape. H 5 cm.

NS41. N14, on the top of the seat block in front of the column. Gameboard, cross-in-square.

NS42. N14, on the top of the seat block next to NS41. Gameboard, mancala.

---

[1] Chaniotis, Field reports 2005, fig. 35. Not seen in 2018 and 2019.

NS43 (Pl. 54.A). N15, on the south face of the stylobate, faintly visible in early morning light. Name. Lt. 4.5–5 cm: Ἀν[τω]νίας | ⟦- - - -⟧

> The erasure chiselling starts at 1.01 m from the east end of the stylobate and extends for 0.78 m, and is 10 cm up from the bottom, for a height of 13 cm.

NS44. Between N15–N16, on the top of the seat block. Gameboard, mancala.

NS45. N16, on the stylobate, east of the column. Cross, perhaps with monogram or with crescent decoration at the end of the arms. H 25 cm.

NS46. N16, on the stylobate. Graffito of one letter. Lt. 6.5 cm: Τ

NS47. N16, on the stylobate, south face. Name. Lt. 6–8 cm: Κλαυδίου

NS48. N17, on the stylobate, south face. Abbreviation. The inscription is carved over a chiselled panel, hardly visible. Lt. l10 cm: A N

> Possibly Ἀν[τωνίας]; cf. N43.

NS49. N17, on the top of the seat block, in front of the column. Gameboard, cross-in-circle (superimposed on N50).

NS50. N17, on the top of the seat block, in front of the column. Gameboard, mancala.

NS51. N18, northwest. Name of sponsor, written with deeply engraved letters. Lt. 5–7.5 cm. Date: late second century AD. Publication: *IAph*2007 4.1: Κλ(αυδία) | Ἀντω|νία.

NS52 (Pl. 52.P). N18, south, above a circular hole, 1.66 m above the stylobate. *Topos* inscription. Date: *c.* fifth/sixth century AD. Publication: *ALA* 205; *IAph*2007 4.18. Lt. 2.5–3 cm: Ἰωάνν(ου) | ἐλλ(ογιμωτάτου)

NS53 (Pl. 47.C). N18, east, 0.95 m above the stylobate. Obscene graffito. Lt. 1–1.6 cm: πυγιζ

> The unfinished verb πυγίζω ('to bugger').

NS54 (Pl. 46.D). N18, on base, south. Christian invocation, engraved in square rough-pecked letters. Lt. 6–10 cm: ΜΗ † Θ.[ ]

> Probably Μή(τηρ) † Θε(οῦ).

NS55 (Pl. 26.A–B and 46.D). Between N18–N19, on the stylobate, south side, in spindly large letters. The text begins on the stylobate of N19 (a), carved on a slightly projecting, more roughly tooled panel, and continues on the stylobate of N18 (b). The text was engraved after the robbing of the stylobate blocks between the column bases. Name of sponsor? Lt. 7–8 c, (a) and 8–10 cm (b): Μύ[ω]|νος

NS56. N18, on stylobate east of the column. Gameboard, cross-in-square.

NS57. N18, on the top of the seat block in front of the column. Gameboard, cross-in-circle.

NS58 (Pl. 52.H). N19, south, 1.74 m above the stylobate, above two holes. *Topos* inscription; cf. N67. Lt. 2.0–4.3: † Θεοκτίστου

NS59. N19, northwest, 1.69 m above the stylobate. Name of sponsor. Date: late second century AD. Publication: *IAph*2007 4.1. Lt. 7.5–8.5 cm: Κλ. | Ἀντω|νία

NS60. Near N20, stored against the back of the North Portico. Fragment of lower column drum, part-fluted. It cannot be assigned to a particular column. Name of sponsor. Date: late second century AD. Publication: *IAph*2007 4.1. Lt. 6–8 cm: Κλ. | Ἀντω|νία

NS61. Between N20–N21, on the stylobate. Gameboard, mancala, partly preserved.

NS62. N24, east of the column. Gameboard, cross-in-square.

NS63 (Pl. 52.K). N25, south, 1.74 m above the stylobate, above a circular hole. Abbreviated name. Publication: *ALA* 203; *IAph*2007 4.8. Lt. 3–3.7 cm: ΚΗϹ[s]

> The abbreviation sign [s] marks the end of the abbreviated name, which cannot be determined with certainty. If the *eta* is not the result of a spelling mistake (for -ι, -ει etc.),[2] there are several names starting with Κησ-, all of them very rare.[3] We are probably dealing with the Hellenized form of a Latin name starting with *Ces*-; these names are often rendered in Greek as Κησ-.[4] The most likely candidate is Κησώνιος.[5]

NS64. N25, on the top of the seat block, in front of the column. Two parallel lines. H 25 cm.

NS65. N25, on the top of the seat block, west of the column, mancala gameboard, partly preserved.

NS66 (Pl. 56.I). N26, on the top of the seat block. Gameboard, cross-in-circle, consisting of two concentric circles and a cross.

NS67 (Pl. 52.J). N26, south, 1.66 m above the stylobate, above a circular hole. *Topos* inscription. Publication: *ALA* 204; *IAph*2007 4.17. Lt. 2.4–6 cm: ΘΕΟΚ[s]

> Probably Θεοκ(τίστου); cf. N58.

NS68. N26, on the top of the seat block. Gameboard, eight-spoke wheel, elaborate. There is a small circle in the centre. Instead of the four crossing lines that divide the circle into eight segments, the segments are marked by semicircles attached to the periphery of the circle.

NS69. Between N26–N27, on the top of the seat block. Gameboard, cross-in-square.

NS70. Between N26–N27, on the top of the seat block. Gameboard, cross-in-square.

NS71. Between N26–N27, on the top of the seat block. Gameboard, cross-in-square.

NS72 (Pl. 44.C). N27, on the stylobate, west of the column. Gameboard, cross-in-square; there are small semicircles at the four corners and at the ends of the arms of the cross; possibly a Christian cross turned into a gameboard (or vice versa).

NS73 (Pl. 44.C). N27, on the stylobate, west of the column. Gameboard, mancala; probably an additional hole at one end of the two rows, between the two rows.

NS74. Between N27–N28, on the top of the seat block. Gameboard, cross-in-circle, faint.

NS75. Between N27–N28, on the top of the seat block. Gameboard, mancala, partly preserved.

---

[2] Names deriving from κισσός are quite common (Κίσσος, Κίσσων, Κισσεύς, etc.).

[3] For references see *LGPN* I–Vc: Κησάριος, Κησέρνιος, Κήσης, Κῆσος, Κησσις, Κηστος, Κησώ.

[4] For example Cessorinus/Κησωρεῖνος: *IG* II² 4113; Cessius/Κήσιος: *An.Ép.* (1975) no. 808; Cesernius/Κησέρνιος: *SEG* XXIV 1118.

[5] *IG* XII.4.1660; *SEG* XXXVI 1399 B.

NS76. Between N27–N28, on the top of the seat block. Gameboard, mancala.

NS77. N28, on the top of the seat block in front of the column. Gameboard, mancala.

NS78 (Pl. 43.A). N29, on the top of the seat block, in front of the column, on the same plaque as NS79–NS83. Pictorial graffito and text. The drawing of a structure consisting of an oblong band supported by two poles; it may be the representation of the lintel of a building or, perhaps more likely a table (a merchant's stall). Under the band a text of six letters; the last letter is written outside the structure, after the second pole. Probably a *topos* inscription. H 17.5, W 67 cm. Lt. 4.5–7 cm (Pl. 43.A): ΑΝΑ̣†?ΤΟΛ

The third letter could also be a delta or a lambda, probably followed by a rather crude cross, with an askew horizontal bar. Probably Ἀνα†τόλ(ιος) or Ἀνα†τολ(ίου). The name Ἀνατόλιος (Ἀνατόλις) is attested in late antique Aphrodisias (*IAph2007* 1.18).

NS79. N29, on the top of the seat block, in front of the column. Gameboard, cross-in-square, immediately west of NS78.

NS80. N29, on the top of the seat block, in front of the column. Gameboard, cross-in-square.

NS81. N29, on the top of the seat block, in front of the column. Gameboard, cross-in-square.

NS82. N29, on the top of the seat block, in front of the column. Gameboard, cross-in-square.

NS83. N29, on the top of the seat block, in front of the column. Gameboard, *duodecim scripta*?, partly preserved; only one row of six holes is preserved.

NS84. Between N29–N30, on the top of the seat block. Gameboard, eight-spoke wheel.

NS85. N30, on the top of the seat block. Gameboard, cross-in-square.

NS86. N30, south, 0.83 m above the stylobate. Cross. H 5.5 cm.

NS87. Between N30–N31, on the top of the seat block. Gameboard, cross-in-circle, with irregular periphery.

NS88 (Pl. 57.F). Between N30–N31, on the top of the seat block. Gameboard, cross-in-circle.

NS89 (Pl. 57.F). Between N30–N31, on the top of the seat block. Cross, touching the gameboard NS88. H 23 cm.

NS90 (Pl. 55.A). Between N30–N31, on the top of the seat block. Gameboard, *duodecim scripta*, elaborate. The central row of dots has a circle in the middle; the two lateral rows have a semicircle in the middle.

NS91–NS94. N31, on the stylobate, east of the column. A cluster of parallel rows of holes that probably belong to four mancala gameboards.

NS95. N31. Gameboard, cross-in-square, superimposed on NS91–NS94.

NS96. N31, on the top of the seat block, in front of the column. Gameboard, mancala; two holes, one at each end and offset to different sides of the board, probably served as the players' store.

NS97. N31, on the top of the seat block, in front of the column. Cross, almost touching gameboard NS98. H 22.5 cm.

NS98. N31, on the top of the seat block, in front of the column. Gameboard, cross-in-circle.

NS99. N31, on the top of the seat block, west of the column. Gameboard, cross-in-circle.

NS100. Between N31–N32, on the top of the seat block. Two partly superimposed circles, perhaps unfinished gameboards.

NS101. N32, on the top of the seat block, east of the column. Gameboard, cross-in-square, faint.

NS102. N32, on the top of the seat block. Circle (unfinished cross-in-circle or eight-spoke wheel gameboard?).

NS103. N32, on the top of the seat block, in front of the column. Gameboard, cross-in-square; a variant with a cross with two horizontal arms, that divide the square into six sections.

NS104. Between N32–N33, on the top of the seat block. Gameboard, cross-in-square.

NS105. Between N32–N33, on the top of the seat block. Gameboard, mancala.

NS106. Between N32–N33, on the top of the seat block. Gameboard, mancala.

NS107. Between N32–N33, on the top of the seat block. Probably mancala gameboard, faint holes placed within a rectangle that resembles a grid.

NS108. N33, on the stylobate, east of the column. Gameboard, cross-in-square.

NS109. N33, on the stylobate, east of the column. Gameboard, cross-in-square.

NS110. N33, on the top of the seat block, in front of the column. Gameboard, cross-in-circle.

NS111. N33, on the stylobate, west of the column. Gameboard, mancala.

NS112. N33, on the stylobate, west of the column. Gameboard, mancala.

NS113. N33, on the stylobate, west of the column. Gameboard, mancala enclosed in a rectangle.

NS114. Between N33–N34, on the top of the seat block. Gameboard, cross-in-circle, partly superimposed on NS115.

NS115. Between N33–N34, on the top of the seat block. Pictorial graffito (?); an oval shape and a circle, partly overlapping with NS114.

NS116. N34, south, 90 cm above the stylobate. Graffito of one letter (or circle). Lt. 8.5: O

NS117. N34, on the stylobate, west of the column. Gameboard, cross-in-square.

NS118. N34, on the stylobate, west of the column. Gameboard, mancala.

NS119. N34, on the top of the seat block, west of the column. Gameboard, mancala, partly preserved.

NS120. N34, on the top of the seat block, west of the column. Gameboard, cross-in-square.

NS121. Between N34–N35, on the top of the seat block. Gameboard, cross-in-square.

NS122. Between N34–N35, on the top of the seat block. Pictorial graffito, unclear.

NS123. Between N34–N35, on the top of the seat block. Gameboard, cross-in-square, small.

NS124. N35, on the top of the seat block, in front of the column. Gameboard, mancala.

NS125. N35, on the top of the seat block, in front of the column. Gameboard, mancala.

NS126. N35, on the top of the seat block, west of the column. Cross with circles at the end of the arms. H 27 cm.

NS127. N35, on the top of the seat block, west of the column. Cross (or the cross of a cross-in-square or cross-in-circle gameboard?). H 27 cm.

NS128. N35, on the stylobate, west of the column. Gameboard, mancala, attached to NS129.

NS129. N35, on the stylobate, west of the column. Gameboard, mancala, attached to NS128.

NS130. Between N35–N36, on the top of the seat block. Gameboard, eight-spoke wheel.

NS131. Between N35–N36, on the top of the seat block. Gameboard, mancala.

NS132. Between N35–N36, on the top of the seat block. Gameboard, cross-in-square, faint.

NS133. N36, on the top of the seat block, in front of the column. Gameboard, cross-in-square, joining NS134.

NS134. N36, on the top of the seat block, in front of the column. Gameboard, cross-in-square, joining NS133 and NS135.

NS135. N36, on the top of the seat block, in front of the column. Gameboard, cross-in-square, joining N134.

NS136. Between N36 and N37, on the top of the seat block. Gameboard, eight-spoke wheel, but an additional line divides two of the segments into two resulting in a board with ten instead of eight segments.

NS137 (Pl. 48.N). N37, on the top of the seat block, west of the column. Menorah, flanked by two gameboards (NS138 and NS139). H 21 cm.

NS138. N37, on the top of the seat block, adjacent to NS137. Gameboard, eight-spoke wheel.

NS139. N36, on the top of the seat block, adjacent to NS137. Gameboard, mancala, partly preserved.

NS140. N37, on the top of the seat block. Gameboard, cross-in-square, faint.

NS141 (Pl. 47.K). N37, south, 57 cm above the stylobate. Square with crossing lines (a vertical line crossed by an X); similar to squares with monograms of circus factions (NS243) and acclamations (*ALA* 186) but without any recognizable letters. H 11.5 cm.

NS142 (Pl. 49.I). N37, east side, 0.60 m from the stylobate. Pictorial graffito of a bird; the tail suggests a peacock. Publication: Chaniotis and De Staebler 2018, 40 no. 11, fig. 18a. W 14 cm, H 4 cm.

NS143. N37, east side, 0.63 m from the stylobate, above and to the right of NS142. Cross with small triangles at the end of the arms. H 4 cm.

NS144. N37, on the top of the seat block, next to NS132. Gameboard, mancala.

NS145. N37, on the top of the seat block. Gameboard, cross-in-circle, small.

NS146. N37, on the stylobate, west of the column. Gameboard, mancala; possibly with two holes, one at each end of the board, that served as the players' store.

NS147 (Pl. 55.B). Between N37–N38, on the top of the seat block. Gameboard, *duodecim scripta*, elaborate. Three parallel rows of 12 small circles each; in the middle of the lateral rows a bigger circle, in the middle of the central row a rhombus.

NS148. Between N37–N38, on the stylobate. Gameboard, mancala; two holes, one at each end of the board, probably served as the players' store.

NS149. Between N37–N38, on the stylobate. Gameboard, *duodecim scripta*; in the middle of the rows a bigger circle.

NS150. Between N37–N38, on the stylobate. Gameboard, mancala; probably with additional holes at each end and offset to different sides of the board that served as the players' store.

NS151. Between N37–N38, on the stylobate. Gameboard, cross-in-square.

NS152 (Pl. 51.G). Between N37–N38, on the stylobate. Gameboard, cross-in-square. It is turned into a pictorial graffito through the addition on its top of a rectangle with a line in the middle; this rectangle is connected with an irregular round shape. Possibly representation of a structure?

NS153. Between N37–N38, on the stylobate. Gameboard, cross-in-circle.

NS154. Between N37–N38, on the stylobate. Gameboard, cross-in-square superimposed on N153.

NS155. Between N37–N38, on the stylobate. Gameboard, mancala.

NS156. Between N37–N38, on the stylobate. Gameboard, mancala, partly preserved, next to N155.

NS157. N38, on the top of the seat block. Gameboard, mancala.

NS158. N38, on the top of the seat block. Gameboard, mancala.

NS159. N38, on the top of the seat block. Gameboard, cross-in-square.

NS160. N38, on the top of the seat block. Gameboard, cross-in-circle.

NS161. N38, on the top of the seat block. Gameboard, mancala.

NS162. N38, on the top of the seat block. Gameboard, mancala.

NS163 (Pl. 44.D). N38, on the top of the seat block. Pictorial graffito. Caricature of a male bust; the upper part of the body is dressed; the head is bald; mouth, nose and eyes are indicated; the head is flanked by a circle and a triangle (left) and a semicircle and an oblong strip (right), perhaps indications of big ears and clothing items? On top of the bald head an oval object. It is possible that the graffito originally was a calligraphic alpha (as in P396 and NS235) turned into a caricature with additional lines.[6] H 29 cm.

NS164. N38, on the stylobate, west of the column. Gameboard, mancala (possibly two superimposed mancala gameboards).

---

6 For the use of letters as parts of images in graffiti in Pompeii see Lohmann 2018, 260–271.

NS165 (Pl. 52.I). N39, east, 94 cm above the stylobate. Name (*topos* inscription?). Lt. 4.5 cm: Πισιθέ(ου)?
NS166 (Pl. 56.I). N39, on the top of the seat block. Gameboard, cross-in-circle, joined with the smaller gameboard NS167.
NS167 (Pl. 56.I). N39, on the top of the seat block. Small cross-in-circle gameboard, joined with NS166.
NS168. N39, on the top of the seat block. Pictorial graffito? An irregular square, with slightly curved sides.
NS169. N39, on the top of the seat block. Gameboard, cross-in-circle.
NS170. N39, on the top of the seat block. Gameboard, cross-in-circle.
NS171. N39, on the top of the seat block. Large cross-in-circle gameboard, with NS172 and NS173 superimposed.
NS172. N39, on the top of the seat block. Gameboard, cross-in-square, superimposed on NS171.
NS173. N39, on the top of the seat block. Gameboard, cross-in-square, superimposed on NS171.
NS174. N39, on the top of the seat block. Gameboard, cross-in-square.
NS175. N39, on the top of the seat block. Gameboard, cross-in-square.
NS176. N39, on the top of the seat block. Gameboard, cross-in-square, unfinished; a square without cross and with one side of the square open.
NS177. N40, on the top of the seat block. Gameboard, mancala; two holes, one at each end and offset to different sides of the board, probably served as the players' stores.
NS178. N40, on the top of the seat block. Gameboard, eight-spoke wheel.
NS179. N40, on the top of the seat block. Gameboard, cross-in-circle.
NS180. N40, on the top of the seat block. Pictorial graffito? An irregular square.
NS181. N40, on the top of the seat block. Gameboard, cross-in-circle.
NS182. N40, on the top of the seat block. Gameboard, mancala, very faint.
NS183. Between N40–N41, on the top of the seat block. Gameboard, mancala.
NS184. N41, on the top of the seat block, east of the column. Gameboard, cross-in-square.
NS185. N41, on the top of the seat block, east of the column. Gameboard, cross-in-square.
NS186. N41, on the top of the seat block. Gameboard, mancala.
NS187. N41, on the top of the seat block. Gameboard, mancala.
NS188. N41, on the top of the seat block. Gameboard, mancala, very faint.
NS189. N41, on the top of the seat block. Gameboard, mancala, very faint.
NS190 (Pl. 52.M). N41, east, 94 cm from stylobte. Abbreviated name (*topos* inscription?). Lt. 5 cm: ΕΚ^s
 An abbreviated name, for example Ἑκ(άτωνος) or Ἑκ(αταίου). Cf. NS344.

NS191. N41, west, 84 cm and 65 cm from the stylobate. Two graffiti of isolated letters. Lt. 4 cm: ΠΕ (top) and M or H (bottom)
NS192. Between N41–N42, on the top of the seat block. Gameboard, cross-in-circle.
NS193. Between N41–N42, on the top of the seat block, next to the previous one. Gameboard, cross-in-square.
NS194. N42, on the stylobate, east of the column. Gameboard, mancala, partly covered by NS195.
NS195. N42, on the stylobate, east of the column. Gameboard, cross-in-square (?); the horizontal arm of the cross is curved; the gameboards was turned into a pictorial graffito through the addition of a square which is divided into two sections by a wavy line.
NS196. N42, on the stylobate, east of the column. Gameboard, mancala.
NS197. N43, on the top of the seat block, in front of the column. Gameboard, mancala.
NS198. N43, on the top of the seat block, in front of the column. Gameboard, mancala.
NS199. N43, on the top of the seat block, in front of the column. Gameboard, cross-in-circle, with two concentric circles, instead of one.
NS200. N43, on the top of the seat block, in front of the column. Gameboard, mancala.
NS201. Between N43–N44, on the top of the seat block, in front of the column. Gameboard, cross-in-square, faint.
NS202. Between N43–N44, on the top of the seat block, in front of the column. Gameboard, cross-in-square.
NS203. Between N43–N44, on the top of the seat block. Textual graffito within a rectangle. Lt. 7–10 cm (omikron: 2 cm): ϹΥΤΟΙϹ
NS204 (Pl. 49.F). Between N43–N44, on the top of the seat block, immediately next to N203. Pictorial graffito, outline of a bust; mouth, nose, eyes, and long hair are indicated.
NS205. Between N43–N44, on the top of the seat block. Unclear pictorial graffito consisting of a circle, a square, and an irregular shape.
NS206. N44, on the top of the seat block. Gameboard, cross-in-square.
NS207. N44, on the top of the seat block. Gameboard, cross-in-circle, with a superimposed drawing that resembles a large B (Lt. 39.5 cm).
NS208. N44, on the top of the seat block, in front of the column. Gameboard, mancala, partly preserved, perhaps remains of more.
NS209. N44, on the stylobate, west of the column. Gameboard, cross-in-square.
NS210. N44, on the stylobate, west of the column. Circle (unfinished cross-in-circle gameboard?).
NS211. N45, on the top of the seat block, in front of the column. Graffito of 9 letters. Lt. 7.5–11.5 cm: ΝΡ Ι ΤΟΙΚΡΟ
NS212. N45, on the top of the seat block, in front of the column. Gameboard, cross-in-square.

NS213. N46, on the stylobate, east of the column. Gameboard, cross-in-square.

NS214. N46, on the stylobate. Gameboard, *duodecim scripta*.

NS215. N46, on the top of the seat block, east of the column. Gameboard, mancala; two holes, one at each end and offset to different sides of the board, probably served as the players' stores.

NS216. N46, on the stylobate, west of the column. Gameboard, *duodecim scripta*.

NS217. N46, on the top of the seat block. Gameboard, mancala; a variant with an additional hole between the two rows.

NS218. N46, on the top of the seat block. Gameboard, cross-in-square, faint, next to NS217.

NS219. N46, on the top of the seat block. Gameboard, mancala.

NS220. N46, on the top of the seat block. Small cross-in-circle gameboard (?), possibly next to it a pictorial graffito consisting of circular lines.

NS221. Between N46–N47, on the top of the seat block. Gameboard, mancala.

NS222. N47, on the top of the seat block, east of the column. Gameboard, mancala.

NS223. N47, on the top of the seat block. Pictorial graffito (?); two circles. Diam. 10.5 and 13.5 cm.

NS224. N49, on the stylobate, west of the column. Gameboard, mancala.

NS225. N49, on the stylobate, west of the column. Gameboard, cross-in-square.

NS226. Between N49–N50, on the top of the seat block. Gameboard, cross-in-circle; the circle seems to have been made with the use of a compass.

NS227 (Pl. 47.J). N50, on south face of the base. Acclamation for the circus faction of the Blues. Publication: *ALA* 186 iii. Lt. 13 cm: Νικᾷ ἡ τύχη τῶν | (Βενέτων)
Βενέτων written as a monogram.

NS228. N50, on the top of the seat block, in front of the column. Gameboard, mancala.

NS229. N50, on the top of the seat block, in front of the column. Gameboard, mancala, partly preserved.

NS230 (Pl. 47.I). N50, on the south face of the seat block, in front of the column. Graffito of two lines. L 70 cm, Lt. 3–5.5 cm.

ΑΗ
ΑΝ ΠΗ ΚΕ ΒΟ Β

Possibly a sequence of abbreviated names or words (each abbreviation consisting of two letters).

NS231 (Pl. 44.G). N51, on the top of the seat block, east of the base. Abecedary in the shape of a cross, with the letters Α, Β, Γ, Δ, Ε, Θ arranged horizontally to form the long bar of the cross and the letters Ζ and Η placed on either side of a cursive Β to form the cross-bar. These three letters can be read as the Christian acclamation Ζωή. Lt. 5.5–10.5 cm.

Η
Α Β Γ Δ Ε Θ
Ζ

NS232. N50, to the left of N230. Graffito of one letter. Lt. 12 cm: Ν

NS233. N51, on south face of stylobate. Acclamation. Publication: *ALA* 186.ii. Lt. 12.5 cm: Αὔξι ἡ τύχη τῆς πό(λεως)
Ligature of ΠΟ.

NS234. N51, on the top of the seat block, in front of the column. Gameboard, mancala; two holes, one at each end and offset to different sides of the board, probably served as the players' stores.

NS235 (Pl. 44.E). N51, on the top of the seat block, in front of the column. Acclamation, incomplete, engraved with calligraphic letters: ΑΥΞ

NS236. N51, on the stylobate, west of the column. Gameboard, mancala.

NS237. N51, on the stylobate, west of the column. Gameboard, mancala.

NS238. N51, on the stylobate, west of the column. Pictorial graffito? Two circles of different sizes joined with a line.

NS239. Between N51–N52, on the top of the seat block. Gameboard, cross-in-circle.

NS240. Between N51–N52, on the euthynteria. Mason's mark. Lt. 10 cm: Α

NS241. Between N51–N52, on the top of the seat block. Gameboard, eight-spoke wheel.

NS242. Between N51–N52, on the top of the seat block. Gameboard, cross-in-square, partly engraved on top of NS241.

NS243. N52, south, 0.72 m above the stylobate. *Topos* inscription. Lt. 1–1.5 cm: τόπος

NS244. N52, south face of stylobate. Acclamation for the circus faction of the Greens. Publication: *ALA* 186.i. Lt. 12 cm: Νικᾷ ἡ τύχη τῶν | (Πρασίνων)
1. The middle line of the omega is shaped as a cross. 2. The word Πρασίνων is written as a monogram.

NS245. N52, on the top of the seat block. Pictorial graffito; a small circle.

NS246. N52, on the top of the seat block. Graffito; the letter Β? or a magical symbol ('Brillenbuchstabe'); cf. NS207. Lt. 25.5 cm.

NS247. N52, on the top of the seat block. Graffito; the letter Γ?

NS248. N52, on the top of the seat block. Pictorial graffito? An oval shape.

NS249 (Pl. 56.A). N52, on the top of the seat block, in front of the column. Gameboard, cross-in-square.

NS250 (Pl. 56.A). N52, on the top of the seat block, in front of the column. Gameboard, cross-in-square.

NS251. N52, on the top of the seat block, in front of the column. Gameboard, mancala.

NS252. N52, on the top of the seat block, in front of the column. Gameboard, mancala.

NS253. N52, on the top of the seat block, in front of the column. Cross. H 9.5 cm.

NS254. N52, on the top of the seat block, west of the column. Wavy line resembling a large cursive Ε (perhaps to be associated with NS246 and NS247, forming a partial abecedary). Lt. 26 cm.

NS255. N52, on the top of the seat block, west of the column. Gameboard, cross-in-square (unfinished).

NS256. Between N52–N53, on the top of the seat block. Gameboard, cross-in-square.

NS257. Between N52–N53, on the top of the seat block. Gameboard, cross-in-square.

NS258. Between N52–N53, on the top of the seat block. Gameboard, mancala.

NS259. Between N52–N53, on the top of the seat block. Gameboard, eight-spoke wheel (with a circle in the centre).

NS260 (Pl. 45.D). N53, south face of stylobate. Acclamation for a circus faction? Lt. 13 cm: Νικᾷ ἡ τύ[χη] monogram.

NS261. N53, northwest, 1.41 m above the stylobate. Graffito (label?). Lt. 4–5 cm: λακος

Perhaps (τὸ) λάκος (garment) or (ὁ) λάκος for λάκκος (a pit for the storage of wine).[7] In either case, the text would designate the place where either clothes or wine were stored.

NS262. N53, west, 0.65 m above the stylobate. Graffito of one letter. Lt. 4 cm: M

NS263. N53, on the top of the seat block, in front of the column. Gameboard, eight-spoke wheel.

NS264 (Pl. 46.F). N53, on the top of the seat block. Textual graffito of two letters. Lt. 7–8 cm: ΑΩ

Probably a Christian graffito, a reference to Jesus.

NS265 (Pl. 46.F). Between N53–N54, on the top of the seat block. Cross turned into cross-in-circle gameboard. The arms of the cross do not reach the periphery, which is elliptical, and not a circle. Given the proximity to the Christian graffito NS264, it is possible that a periphery was drawn around a Christian cross creating a gameboard.

NS266. Between N53–N54, on the top of the seat block. Gameboard, mancala.

NS267. Between N53–N54, on the top of the seat block. Gameboard, mancala, superimposed on N268.

NS268. Between N53–N54, on the top of the seat block. Unclear textual graffito: six letters superimposed by N267. Lt. 7.5–11: ΗϘΙΟΙΛ

The first letter may not be an eta, but two crosses.

NS269. N54, southeast, 1.10 m above the stylobate. Graffito of one letter. Lt. 2.8 cm: Δ

NS270. N54, south, 0.69 m above the stylobate. Graffito of two letters. Lt. 2.5–3.5 cm: ΠΟ

An abbreviation (the beginning of a name) rather than the remains of the word [τό]πο[ς].

NS271. N54, south, 1.22 m above the stylobate. Cross. H 15 cm, W 8.5 cm.

NS272 (Pl. 49.J). N54, south, 1.10 m above the stylobate. Pictorial graffito. A bird, facing right; the tail suggests a peacock; the cross N271 is above it, to right. Publication: Chaniotis and De Staebler 2018, 40 no. 11. L 18 cm, H 14 cm.

NS273 (Pl. 50.D). N54, north, 0.70 m above the stylobate. Pictorial graffito. Perhaps a bird (left) and a figure with two long legs and a big head on the right. Publication: Chaniotis and De Staebler 2018, 40 no. 12. H 21 cm. Perhaps representation of a *venatio*.

NS274. N54, on the top of the seat block, in front of the column. Gameboard, eight-spoke wheel superimposed on NS275.

NS275. N54, on the top of the seat block, in front of the column. Gameboard, mancala covered by eight-spoke wheel gameboard NS274.

NS276. N54, on the top of the seat block, in front of the column. Gameboard, cross-in-square.

NS277 (Pl. 48.A). N54, on the top of the seat block, in front of the column. Symbol (monogram?). It consists of superimposed cross and X. At one end the vertical bar of the cross a crescent shape; at the lower ends of the diagonal bars small circles (letters?); perhaps letters attached at the end of the other bars. H *c.* 27 cm.

NS278. N54, on the top of the seat block, west of the column. Gameboard, mancala.

NS279 (Pl. 55.C). N54, on the top of the seat block, west of the column. A variant of a *duodecim scripta* gameboard E. A square (or cross-in-square gameboard) is divided with a cross into four segments. There are three rows, of six 'holes' each; the holes of the two rows along the sides of the square are represented by small circles. The middle row, which is identical with the arm of the cross, has six pairs of small circles, arranged on either side of the arm of the cross.

NS280. N55, north, 1.15 m above the stylobate. Abbreviation. Lt. 5 cm: ΙΝ

NS281. N55, north, 87.5 cm above the stylobate, under NS280. Cross. H 13.8 cm, W 4.1 cm.

NS282. N55, north, 71 cm, above the stylobate. Cross. H 5 cm, W 4 cm.

NS283 (Pl. 47.D). N55, west, 1.45 m above the stylobate. Commemorative graffito. Lt. 3–4 cm: φιλῶ

Mentioned in Chaniotis 2011b, 205.

NS284. N55, on the top of the seat block, west of the column. Gameboard, cross-in-circle, faint.

NS285 (Pl. 55.D). Between N55–N56, on the top of the seat block. Gameboard, *duodecim scripta*, elaborate; a cross divides the rectangle into four sections (cf. NS279); there are three rows of small circles, with 12 circles in each. The middle of the row is highlighted: in the middle row, there is a larger circle at the point where the arms of the cross intersect; in the lateral rows, there are large semicircles at the points where the arm of the cross reaches the sides of the rectangle.

NS286. Between N55–N56, on the top of the seat block. Gameboard, mancala.

NS287. Between N55–N56, on the top of the seat block. Gameboard, mancala.

NS288 (Pl. 49.G). N56, northwest, 0.97 m above the stylobate. Pictorial graffito. A male head in profile. H 8 cm high.

NS289 (Pl. 49.K). N56, north, 0.66–0.69 m above the stylobate. Pictorial graffiti. Crude pecked designs, of three animals, possibly birds; the highlighted tail of one of them suggests a peacock. Publication: Chaniotis and De Staebler 2018, 40 nos. 8–10. L left 27 cm, middle 27 cm, right 22 cm.

---

[7] For τὸ λᾶκος see Lhôte 2006, 248 and *Periplus Maris Erythraei* 6. For ὁ λάκκος see *LSJ*.

NS290 (Pl. 53.F). N56, south, 2.60 m above the stylobate, within flute of the column. Mason's mark. Lt. 8: Π

NS291. N56, on the top of the seat block. Gameboard, *duodecim scripta*, elaborate, similar to NS285; it has semicircles on all four points where the arms of the cross reach the sides of the rectangle.

NS292. N56, on the top of the seat block. Gameboard, mancala.

NS293. N56, on the top of the seat block. Gameboard, cross-in-square.

NS294. Between N56–N57, on the stylobate, east of the column. Gameboard, mancala.

NS295 (Pl. 50.E). N57, east, 0.84 m above the stylobate. Pictorial graffito. Two running animals, a dog or horse (above; L 12 cm, H 10 cm) and an animal with long horns (below), an antelope, a gazelle, or a wild goat (L 10 cm, H 14 cm). A similar animal is represented in a graffito in the stadium. Possibly the representation of a *venatio*. Publication: Chaniotis and De Staebler 2018, 40, no. 7

NS296 (Pl. 54.J). N57, southwest, 2.53 m above the stylobate, within flute of the column. Mason's mark; three letters inscribed within a frame. H of frame 12.5 cm, Lt. 3 cm: XXX

NS297. N57, northwest, 2.70 m above the stylobate, within flute of the column. Mason's mark. Lt. 8.5. cm: Θ

NS298. N57, on the top of the seat block, in front of the column. Gameboard, mancala.

NS299. Between N57–N63, on the top of the seat block. Gameboard, eight-spoke wheel.

NS300. Between N57–N63, on the top of the seat block. Gameboard, cross-in-square.

NS301. Between N57–N63, on the top of the seat block. Gameboard, eight-spoke wheel (partially covered by the gameboards NS302 and NS303).

NS302. Between N57–N63, on the top of the seat block. Gameboard, cross-in-square.

NS303. Between N57–N63, on the top of the seat block. Gameboard, cross-in-square.

NS304. Between N58–N63, on the top of the seat block. Gameboard, cross-in-square.

NS305. Between N57–N63, on the top of the seat block. Gameboard, cross-in-circle.

NS306. Between N57–N63, on the top of the seat block. Gameboard, mancala next to NS305.

NS307. Between N57–N63, on the top of the seat block. Gameboard, cross-in-circle, faint.

NS308. Between N57–N63, on the top of the seat block. Gameboard, cross-in-circle; because of lack of space, near the end of the plaque, one semicircle is compressed.

NS309. Between N57–N63, on the top of the seat block. Gameboard, mancala.

NS310. Between N57–N63, on the top of the seat block. Gameboard, eight-spoke wheel, faint; one of the spokes is curved.

NS311. Between N57–N63, on the top of the seat block. Gameboard, *duodecim scripta*, partly preserved or unfinished; two rows of 12 holes each are preserved. It is also possible that two mancala gameboards are placed one next to another.

NS312. Between N57–N63, on the top of the seat block. Gameboard, cross-in-circle; a line is attached to its periphery.

NS313. Between N57–N63, on the top of the seat block. Gameboard, cross-in-circle; a small circle is attached to the periphery.

NS314. Between N57–N63, on the top of the seat block. One segment of a circle; unfinished gameboard or pictorial graffito.

NS315. Between N57–N63, on the top of the seat block. Gameboard, cross-in-circle.

NS316. Between N57–N63, on the top of the seat block. Gameboard, mancala; two rows of five holes each, connected with lines.

NS317 (Pl. 57.C). Between N57–N63, on the top of the seat block. Gameboard, eight-spoke wheel, very elaborate. It consists of four concentric circles, the smallest one representing the center of the outer periphery. Four crossing lines divide the periphery into eight segments. At the point where the radii touch the outer periphery there is a semicircle; crosses decorate the spaces between these semicircles.

NS318. Between N57–N63, on the top of the seat block. Gameboard, cross-in-square.

NS319. Between N57–N63, on the top of the seat block. Gameboard, cross-in-square.

NS320. Between N57–N63, on the top of the seat block. Gameboard, cross-in-circle, faint, superimposed on NS319.

NS321. Between N57–N63, on the top of the seat block. Gameboard, cross-in-square.

NS322. Between N57–N63, on the top of the seat block. Gameboard, cross-in-circle (superimposed on N323).

NS323. Between N58–N63, on the top of the seat block. Gameboard, *duodecim scripta* (NS322 is superimposed on it).

NS324. N64, on the top of the seat block, east of the column. A circle enclosing a small cross-in-circle gameboard.

NS325. N64, on the top of the seat block, east of the column. Gameboard, mancala, partly preserved.

NS326. N65, on the top of the seat block, in front of the column. Gameboard, cross-in-circle.

NS327. N65, on the top of the seat block, in front of the column. Gameboard, cross-in-circle.

NS328. N65, on the top of the seat block, west of the column. Gameboard, unfinished (only a circle is visible).

NS329. N66, on the top of the seat block, east of the column. Gameboard, cross-in-circle.

NS330 (Pl. 52.N). N67, south, 48 cm above the stylobate. Abbreviated name (*topos* inscription?). Lt. 3–4 cm: ΕΠΙ Ε̣ A short lacuna between the third and the fourth letter; the fourth letter is a cursive Ε, a Θ, O, or a cursive C. Probably an abbreviated name, for example Ἐπιθ(υμήτου) or Ἐπιθ(υμίας), if the four letters belong together. Epithymia is attested in Aphrodisias (*IAph2007* 13.101).

NS331 (Pl. 50.A). N67, south and west, 0.70–1.20 m above the stylobate. Pictorial graffito. Three running lions, from top to bottom: a) *c.* 1.20 cm above the stylobate, L 28 cm, H 22 cm; b) *c.* 1 m above the stylobate, L 35 cm, H 28 cm; c) *c.* 70 cm above the stylobate, L 32 cm, H 27 cm. Mentions: Roueché 2002, 60 fig. 20; Chaniotis 2009a, 208 fig. 9. Publication: Chaniotis and De Staebler 2018, 40 nos. 2–4.

NS332 (Pl. 50.B–C). N67, south, ca. 60 cm above the stylobate, under NS331. Cluster of pictorial graffiti. It is not easy to distinguish between lines drawn intentionally and cracks in the stone. The cluster possibly consists of two or more superimposed representations, made successively (total H 22 cm). A figure on the right consists of two long legs, that recall the legs of an ostrich, a round body, and a small round object to the right. To the far left, one sees an oblong object with parallel vertical lines; it resembles the body of a bird, perhaps an ostrich (H 8 cm, L 10 cm). Above this object, one recognizes a torso covered by horizontal lines and a head. Possibly a representation of a man engaged in battle with an ostrich (represented from the back) or, less likely, a pair of gladiators engaged in close combat. Publication: Chaniotis and De Staebler 2018, 40 no. 1

NS333 (Pl. 49.L). N67, south, 55 cm above the stylobate, under NS299. Pictorial graffito: a peacock. Publication: Chaniotis and De Staebler 2018, 40 no. 5. H 10 cm, L 16 cm.

NS334. N67, on the stylobate, east of the column. Gameboard, mancala.

NS335. N67, on the stylobate, east of the column. Gameboard, mancala.

NS336. N67, on the stylobate, west of the column. Gameboard, mancala.

NS337. N68, on the top of the seat block, east of the column. Gameboard, cross-in-circle.

NS338. N68, on the top of the seat block, in front of the column. Gameboard, cross-in-circle.

NS339. N68, north, 2.12 m above base of the column, within flute. Mason's mark. Lt. 7 cm: Π

NS340. N68, west (originally east), 1.29 m above the stylobate. Graffiti: the letter A written four times, in two groups of two. Lt. 1.5 cm: A A   A A

NS341 (Pl. 52.C). N69, south, 1.59 m above the stylobate. *Topos* inscription. Publication: *ALA* 201 a; *ala2004* 201b; *IAph2007* 4.7 i Lt. 3.8–6.9 cm: [τό]πος | Εὐγρα|φίου | φυλάρ|χου

NS342 (Pl. 52.D). N69, south, ca. 1.10 m above the stylobate. *Topos* inscription. Publication: *ALA* 201 b; *ala2004* 201 b; *IAph2007* 4.7 ii. Cf. NS349. Lt. 2.2–3.9 cm: τόπος | Ζωτικοῦ | ⟦...⟧ | ⟦ ... ⟧

NS343. N69, south, under NS342. Graffiti, individual letters. Lt. 1–2 cm.

To the left of L. 2 of NS342   B
Under NS342
9 cm lower than NS342   Γ /   Υ
4.5 cm lower   Γ [reversed] T
Under NS344
9 cm lower   O
2.5 cm lower   Γ   O
                        T

NS344 (Pl. 52.I). N69, south, 1.32 m from the stylobate. *Topos* inscription. Lt. 1.5: Ἑκαταίου

Due to cracks on the stone and the use of cursive letters, joining each other, the text seems to read EKATMIN. The name Hekataios is attested in Aphrodisias (*IAph2007* 13.109; cf. N190).

NS345. N69, north. Christogram.

Recorded in 1997 but not found in 2018.

NS346. N70, north, 1.46 above the stylobate. Graffito of one letter. Lt.4 cm: A

NS347 (Pl. 57.G). Between N70–N71, on the top of the seat block. Circle, probably unfinished gameboard; the circle seems to have been made with the use of a compass.

NS348. Between N70–N71, on the top of the seat block. Gameboard, mancala.

NS349 (Pl. 52.E). N71, north, 1.47 m above the stylobate. *Topos* inscription, crude engraving. Lt. 2–3.5 cm: Ζωτικοῦ τόπος

After the last letter a small circle. On Zotikos, cf. N342.

For the graffiti on N71, see the catalogue of graffiti of the West Stoa, where N71 = W1.

Architrave blocks from the North Stoa, now stored behind the stoa, at its west end, bear masons' marks, probably from the period of its restoration. They are probably assembly marks/numerals indicating the order in the which the architrave blocks should be put back up (see Ch. 5 §E). The marks were recorded (Lt. 2–3 cm), from east to west (NS350–NS360). Another architrave block from the North Stoa, now stored behind the stoa, around the middle of the stoa, bears masons' marks (N360).

NS350. Mason's mark. Lt. 3 cm: A
NS351. Mason's mark. Lt. 3 cm: B
NS352. Mason's mark. Lt. 1 cm (only the top is preserved): Γ
NS353. Mason's mark. Lt. 2.5 cm: Δ
NS354. Mason's mark. Lt. 3 cm: E
NS355. Mason's mark. Lt. 2.5 cm: C

The number *stigma (6)*, in the form of an angular C).

NS356. Mason's mark. Lt. 2.5 cm: Z
NS357. Mason's mark. Lt. 3 cm: H
NS358. Mason's mark. Lt. 3 cm: I

I and Θ are in the wrong sequence (reversed).

NS359. Mason's mark. Lt. 3 cm: Θ
NS360. Mason's mark at both ends of the block. Lt. 3.5–4 cm.: A   B

B is inscribed upside-down.

C. WEST STOA

The graffiti, gameboards, and mason's marks recorded in the West Stoa are located on the columns and the pavement. The WS Numbers refer to the location of each item on columns of the stoa and the pavement west of the colonnade. The columns are numbered from the north to the south, from 1 to 20 (W1 is the 71st column of the North Stoa, with the columns counted from east to west). The location of each item on a column is indicated with reference to the side of the column and its distance from the stylobate. There are two main groups of texts: acclamations on the columns of the West Stoa and masons' marks on the pavement. The main features of these two groups are summarized here.

The acclamations on the columns of the West Stoa were recorded in 1905, when this building was excavated by Mendel (WS1, WS4–WS6, WS8–WS10, WS13–WS18, WS20–WS25). C. Roueché has offered the most recent publication with detailed commentary and summary of previous research (1989 and 2004). There is an inscription on each column, on the west side (interior of the stoa), engraved below the fluting, at a distance varying from 5 to 30 cm. As Roueché observed, the lettering is at its most formal at the northern end of the portico, and becomes more cursive towards the south. The letter size varies between 3 and 9 cm (mostly 4–7 cm). The inscriptions were sheltered by the roof of the portico, and were originally highlighted with red paint, traces of which was preserved when the columns were excavated.[8] The texts are to be read from north to south or from left to right within the stoa. In addition to these more or less official texts, there are also graffiti on the columns (WS2, WS3, WS7, WS11, WS19, WS26–WS29) and a graffito on the pavement (WS12). Some of them were already noticed by Roueché, but there are a few additions (WS2, WS3, WS11, WS29).

The second group of texts consists of masons' marks on the pavement west of the colonnade. These masons' marks were recorded in 2015 with the assistance of Takashi Fujii, Benjamin Wieland, and Masataka Masunaga. They are on marble plaques placed along the stylobate of the stoa (east) and the wall (west). No masons' marks are visible on the plaques in the middle section of the pavement. The marks were recorded from north to south. WS31–WS58 are in the north section of the hall—WS31–WS54 along the west wall, W55S–WS59 close to the colonnade. WS59–WS115 are in the south section of the hall—WS59–WS87 close to the colonnade, WS88–WS115 close to the wall. In the catalogue, the approximate position of a mason's mark is determined through two coordinates: its position in relation to columns of the colonnade (for example W1 = opposite column W1) and its distance from the wall or the colonnade respectively.

WS1. W1, west. Christian acclamation. Publication: *ALA* 83 i; *ala2004* 83 i; *IAph2007* 4.21 i: εἰς τὸν † κόσμον | ὅλον εἷς ὁ θεός
'In the entire world, there is one God!'

WS2. W1, south, lower end of first drum, 1.32 m above the stylobate. Christogram. H 10.5 cm.

WS3. W1, south, 1.39 m above the stylobate. Two crosses. H 4 cm.

WS4. W2, west. Acclamation for the emperors. Publication: *ALA* 83 ii; *ala2004* 83 ii; *IAph2007* 4.21 ii.: πολλὰ τὰ | ἔτη τῶν | βασιλέων
'Many years for the emperors!'

WS5. W3, west. Acclamation for the prefects. Publication: *ALA* 83 iii; *ala2004* 83 iii; *IAph2007* 4.21 iii.: πολλὰ τὰ | ἔτη τῶν | ἐπάρχων
'Many years for the prefects!'

WS6. W4, west. Acclamation for the senate. Publication: *ALA* 83 iv; *ala2004* 83 iv; *IAph2007* 4.21 iv.: πολλὰ τὰ | ἔτη τῆς | συνκλήτου
'Many years for the senate!'

WS7. W4, south, c. 1.90 m above the stylobate, to the right of WS6. Graffito of three letters, Lt. 3.5–4.5: HNK
Possibly HNIC.

WS8. W5, west. Acclamation for the city. Publication: *ALA* 83 v; *ala2004* 83 v; *IAph2007* 4.21 v.: πολλὰ τὰ | ἔτη τῆς | μητροπό(λεως)
'Many years for the metropolis!'

WS9. W6, west. Acclamation for Albinos. Publication: *ALA* 83 vi; *ala2004* 83 vi; *IAph2007* 4.21 vi.: Πέρδε, | Ἀλβῖνε· | αὔξι ὁ κτίστης | ν τῆς στοᾶς
'Look around, Albinos! May the builder of the stoa prosper!'
Πέρδε for περ(ι)ιδέ; αὔξι for αὔξει. For this meaning of περιοράω see Theophrastos, *Charakters* 25.3.

WS10. W7, west. Acclamation for Albinos. Publication: *ALA* 83 vii; *ala2004* 83 vii; *IAph2007* 4.21 vii.: φιλόπατρει | κύρι, ν διαμίνης | ν ἡμῖν
'Lord, lover of the fatherland, may you remain for us!'
Φιλόπατρει κύρι, διαμίνης for φιλόπατρι κύριε, διαμείνης.

WS11. W7, west. Under WS10, 1.50 m above the stylobate. Drawing of a menorah. H 17 cm.
Mention: Chaniotis 2002, 236 no. 2 (where East Portico should be corrected to West Stoa).

WS12 (Pl. 45.C). Between W7–W8, on a plaque of the pavement west of the columns. Acclamation for the circus faction of the Reds. Publication: Chaniotis and De Staebler 2018, 41 no. 16; cf. Chaniotis 2009, 207 fig. 8. Lt. 2.5–5 cm, L 28 cm: νικ[ᾷ ἡ τύχη] | τῶ Ῥουσέων
'The fortune of the Reds prevails.'
On line 2, τῶ Ῥουσέων for τῶν Ῥουσέων.

WS13. W8, west. Acclamation for Albinos. Publication: *ALA* 83 viii; *ala2004* 83 viii; *IAph2007* 4.21 viii: τὰ σὰ [κτ-]ίσματα | αἰωνία ν ὑπόμνη|νσις, | Ἀλβῖνε, φιλοκτίστα
'Your buildings, Albinos, lover of building works, are an eternal reminder'.

WS14. W9, west. Acclamation for Albinos. Publication: *ALA* 83 ix; *ala2004* 83 ix; *IAph2007* 4.21 ix: [··]ΙΤΙΖΑΣ | [··]Σ | [··]ΗΜΟ | ΓΟ[··]ΟΝ, | Ἀλβῖνε λαμπρ(ότατε)
'Albinos, *clarissimus* (most renowned)!
The first lines were erased when a large cavity was made, probably for a light fitting.

---

[8] Roueché 1989, 126; 2007a, 183–184.

WS15. W10, west. Acclamation for Albinos. Publication: *ALA* 83 x; *ala2004* 83 x; *IAph2007* 4.21 x: Πέρδε,| Ἀλβῖνε, ἠδὲ | τί ἐχαρίσω

   'Look around, Albinos, see what you have donated'.

   To be understood as περιδέ, Ἀλβῖνε, ἰδὲ τί ἐχαρίσω; cf. W9.

WS16. W12, west. Acclamation for Albinos. Publication: *ALA* 83 xi; *ala2004* 83 xi; *IAph2007* 4.21 xi: ὅλη ἡ πόλις τοῦ|το λέγι· τοὺς ἐχθρούς | σου τῷ ποταμῷ· | ὁ μέγας θεὸς τοῦτο | ν παράσχη

   'The entire city says this: "Your enemies to the river!" May the great god grant us this!'

WS17. W13, west. Acclamation for Albinos. Publication: *ALA* 83 xiii ('Up with Albinos *clarissimus*, to the Senate!'); *ala2004* 83 xiii; *IAph2007* 4.21 xiii: αὔξι Ἀλβῖνος· | ὁ λανπρ(ότατος) τῇ συν|νκλήτῳ

   'May Albinos prosper! The *clarissimus* to the senate!'

   I have added the interpunct after Ἀλβῖνος.

WS18. W14, west. Acclamation. Publication: *ALA* 83 xiv; *ala2004* 83 xiv; *IAph2007* 4.21 xiv: [- - -]· | ὁ φθόνος τύχην | ν οὐ νικᾷ

   'Envy shall not prevail over fortune!'

WS19 (Pl. 51.B). W14, west, under WS18. Pictorial graffito. A naked female figure with crossed legs, bringing her arms to her head; carved in low relief. Interpreted as the representation of Tyche[9] or a statue of Aphrodite Anadyomene.[10]

WS20. W15, west. Acclamation for Albinos. Publication: *ALA* 83 xv; *ala2004* 83 xv; *IAph2007* 4.21 xv.: αὔξι Ἀλβῖνος | ὁ κτίστης καὶ τούτου | τοῦ ἔργου

   'May Albinos prosper, the builder also of this work!'

WS21. W16, west. Acclamation for Albinos. Publication: *ALA* 83 xvi; *ala2004* 83 xvi; *IAph2007* 4.21 xvi: χρήματα παρίδες | καὶ δόξαν ἐκτήσω, | [Ἀλβῖ]νε λανπρ(ότατε)

   'You disregarded (your) property and obtained glory, Albinos, *clarissimus*!'

WS22. W17, west. Acclamation for Albinos. Publication: *ALA* 83 xvii; *ala2004* 83 xvii; *IAph2007* 4.21 xvii: ἐκ προγόνων | φιλόπατρι, Ἀλβῖνε | λανπρ(ότατε), ἄφθονά σοι | ν γένοιτο

   'Lover of the fatherland, following your ancestors, Albinos, *clarissimus*, may you receive plenty!'

WS23. W18, west. Acclamation for Albinos. Publication: *ALA* 83 xviii; *ala2004* 83 xviii; *IAph2007* 4.21 xviii: [- - -] πόλι παρέχων | [- - ἐν? τ]ούτῳ εὐφημῖτε

   '[- -] providing to the city, he is being praised in acclamations [in this]'.

   Roueché restores: [?κτίσμα] πόλι παρέχων | [?καὶ ἐν τ]ούτῳ εὐφημῖτε (εὐφημῖτε for εὐφημεῖται). Εὐφημεῖτε (imperative, 2nd person plural) is also possible.

WS24. W19, west. Acclamation for Albinos. Publication: *ALA* 83 xix; *ala2004* 83 xix; *IAph2007* 4.21 xix: τοῖς κτίσμασίν σου | τὴν πόλιν ἐφέδρυνας, | Ἀλβῖνε φιλόπατρι

   'With your buildings you have brightened the city, Albinos, lover of the fatherland!'

WS25. W20, west. Acclamation for Albinos, Publication: *ALA* 83 xx; *ala2004* 83 xx; *IAph2007* 4.21 xx: ἡ πό[λις ὅλ] η ὁμοφώνως | εὐφη[μ]ή{σα}σα λέγι· ὁ σοῦ | ληθαργῶν, Ἀλβῖνε λανπρ(ότατε) | ν θεὸν οὐκ οἶδεν

   'The entire city, having praised you in acclamations in one voice, says: "He who forgets you, Albinos, *clarissimus*, does not know God".'

WS26 (Pl. 51.C). W20, west, under WS25. Pictorial graffito, deeply engraved on the columns. A male seated figure with outstretched legs and a disproportionally large, monstrous head, with large eyes and two projecting ears. The figure holds something in each hand; possibly the representation of a statue of a seated satyr. Publication: *ALA* 83 xx; *ala2004* 83 xx; *IAph2007* 4.21 xx; Chaniotis 2018a, 86. H 11 cm.

WS27 (Pl. 51.C). W20, west, to the left and above WS26, 1.56 m from base of the column. Graffito of two lines. Publication: *ALA* 83 xxi; *ala2004* 83 xxi; *IAph2007* 4.21 xxi; Chaniotis 2018a, 86. Lt. 1.7–3 cm: ΠΑΠΑ | ΑΙ

   Possibly a personal name in the genitive: Πάπα or Παπᾶ.

WS28. W20, west, lower than WS26. Acclamation for the city. Publication: *ALA* 83 xxii; *ala2004* 83 xxii; *IAph2007* 4.21 xxii. Lt. 3.5–5 cm: νικᾷ ἡ | τύχη | τῆς πό|λεως

WS29 (Pl. 49.A). W20, west, under WS28, 1.80 m above the stylobate. Drawing of a menorah and to the left of the menorah the letter Φ. H 20 cm.

   Visible in Roueché 1989, pl. xxii, but not explicitly mentioned. Mentioned by Chaniotis 2002a, 236 no. 2, where East Portico should be corrected to West Stoa.

WS30 (Pl. 47.B). In the staircase that leads from the North Stoa to the Hadrianic Baths, opposite W11, on the north side, under the moulding of the base of a pillar, crudely incised on the stone. Label (?) possibly indicating the place where tablets with edicts were displayed. Lt. 1–2 cm: ἐδίκτου

WS31 (Pl. 53.M). W1, 94 cm from wall. Lt. 5.5–7.5 cm: Εὐσ.
WS32. W1, 60 cm from wall. Lt. 405 cm: Εὐτ.
WS33. W1, south corner, 24 cm from wall. Lt. 5 cm: Ἀλβ.
WS34. W1, south corner, 54 cm from wall. Lt. 4.5 cm: Εὐτ.
WS35. W1, south corner, 93 cm from wall. Lt. 3.5–4 cm: Εὐτ.
WS36. Between W1–W2, 49 cm from wall. Lt. 3 cm: Νον.
WS37. Between W1–W2, 22 cm from wall. Lt. 3–6 cm: Ἀλβ.
WS38. Between W1–W2, 85 cm from wall. Lt. 4–5 cm: Εὐτ.
WS39 (Pl. 53.G). Between W1–W2, 16 cm from wall. Lt. 3–11 cm: Ἀλβιν.
WS40. W2, north corner, 94 cm from wall. Lt. 3 cm: Εὐτ.
WS41. W2, 21 cm from wall. Lt. 4–7 cm: Ἀλβ.
WS42. W2, 95 cm from wall. Lt. 4.5 cm: Θε.
WS43. W2, 58 cm from wall. Lt. 3–5 cm: Εὐτ.
WS44. Between W2–W3, 24 cm from wall. Lt. 2–5 cm: Ἀλβ.
WS45. Between W2–W3, 53 cm from wall. Lt. 5–6 cm: Εὐτ.
WS46. Between W2–W3, 91 cm from wall. Lt. 4 cm: Εὐτ.
WS47. Between W2–W3, 22 cm from wall. Lt. 2–3.5 cm: Ἀλβ.
WS48. Between W2–W3, 50 cm from wall. Lt. 5.5–6.5 cm: Εὐτ.
WS49. W3, 15 cm from wall. Lt. 2–5.5 cm: Ἀλβ.
WS50. W3, 49 cm from wall. Lt. 5–6 cm: Εὐτ.
WS51. W3, 85 cm from wall. Lt. 4.5 cm: Εὐτ.
WS52. W4, north corner, 40 cm from wall. Lt. 4 cm: Γ
WS53. W4, 30 cm from wall. Lt. 4.8 cm: Β

---

9 Roueché 1989, 128.
10 Chaniotis 2018a, 89.

WS54. Between W4–W5, 32 cm from wall. Lt. 3.5–7 cm: Ἀλβ.
WS55. Between W6–W7, 84 cm from the stylobate. Lt. 3.5 cm: Π
WS56. W7, 16 cm from the stylobate. Lt. 3 cm: Α
WS57. W7, 49 cm from the stylobate. Lt. 6.2 cm: Θ
WS58. Between W8–W9, 1.20 m from wall. Lt. 6 cm: ΛΕ
WS59 (Pl. 54.Κ). W11, south corner, 20 cm from the stylobate. Lt. 4.8 cm: S
WS60. Between W11–W12, 18 cm from the stylobate. Lt. 2 cm: Δ
WS61. Between W11–W12, 64 cm from wall. Lt. 6 cm: Β
WS62 (Pl. 53.S). Between W12–W13, 22 cm from the stylobate. Lt. 4–8 cm: Μαρ.
WS63. Between W12–W13, 5 cm from the stylobate. Lt. 5.5 cm: ΥΤ
WS64. Between W12–W13, 19 cm from wall. Lt. 2.5–4 cm: ΚΟΙ
WS65. Between W12–W13, 51 cm from wall. Lt. 6 cm: ΗΛΙ
WS66. Between W12–W13, 89 cm from wall. Lt. 5–7 cm: Εὐτ.
WS67. Between W12–W13, 1.44 m from wall. Lt. 3.5–5 cm: Η̣ΛΙ
WS68. Between W12–W13, 22 cm from wall. Lt. 3–4.5 cm and 2.5–5 cm: ΗΛΙ | ΚΟΙ
WS69. Between W12–W13, 92 cm from wall. Lt. 6–7 cm: Εὐτ.
WS70. W13, north corner, 24 cm from the stylobate. Lt. 2–3.5 cm: ΗΛΙ
WS71. W13, north corner, 1.42 m from wall. Lt. 5–6 cm: Εὐσ.
WS72. W13, 18 cm from the stylobate. Lt. 8 cm: Φ
WS73. W13, 13 cm from the stylobate. Lt. 10 cm: Φ
WS74. W13, 95 cm from wall. Lt. 3–5 cm: Εὐτ.
WS75. W13, 1.31 m from wall. Lt. 3–5 cm: ΗΛΙ
WS76. W13, south corner, 65 cm from the stylobate. Lt. 5–6 cm: Θε.
WS77. W13, south corner, 1.49 m from the stylobate. Lt. 4–5 cm: Νον.
WS78. Between W13–W14, 32 cm from the stylobate. Lt. 8 cm: Φ
WS79 (Pl. 53.P). Between W13–W14, 12 cm from the stylobate. Lt. 4 cm: ΙΛΗ
    ΗΛΙ sinistrorsum.
WS80. Between W13–W14, 51 cm from wall. Lt. 4–5 cm: ΗΛΙ
WS81. Between W13–W14, 21 cm from wall. Lt. 4–5 cm: ΗΛΙ
WS82. Between W13–W14, 48 cm from wall. Lt. 7 cm: Φ
WS83. Between W13–W14, 97 cm from wall. Lt. 2–5 cm: Εὐτ.
WS84. Between W13–W14, 97cm from wall. Lt. 6–7 cm: Σε.
WS85 (Pl. 54.T). W14, north corner, 76 cm from the stylobate. Lt. 3.5 cm: Νον.
WS86. W14, north corner, 51 cm from wall. Lt. 3–8 cm: ΙΛ̣Η̣
WS87. W14, north corner, 1.44 m from wall. Lt. 3–4 cm: Ι̣ΙΛΙ
    ΗΛΙ sinistrorsum.
WS88. W14, 22 cm from the stylobate. Lt. 9 cm: Φ
WS89. W14, 49 cm from wall. Lt. 9 cm: Φ
WS90. W14, 1.37 m from wall. Lt. 4–6 cm: ΗΛΙ
WS91. W14, 1.78 m from wall. Lt. 6.5–7.5 cm: ΓΕ
WS92. W14, south corner, 60 cm from wall. Lt. 4 and 7.5 cm: Π | ΚΦ
WS93. W14, south corner, 1.44 m from wall. Lt. 5.5–7 cm: Εὐτ.
WS94. Between W14–W15, 68 cm from the stylobate. Lt. 3–5 cm: Εὐτ.
WS95. Between W14–W15, 69 cm from the stylobate. Lt. 4.5–6 cm: Εὐτ.
WS96. Between W14–W15, 2.01 m from wall. Lt. 5–10 cm: ΦΙ?
WS97. Between W14–W15, 17.5 cm from the stylobate. Lt. 4–6 cm: Μαρ.
WS98. W15, north corner, 1.40 m from wall. Lt. 3–7 cm: Εὐτ. ΚΦ
WS99 (Pl. 53.R). W15, 15 cm from the stylobate. Lt. 2.5–6.5 cm: Π | ΚΟΥ
WS100. W15, 1.76 m from wall. Lt. 6–10 cm: ΦΙ
WS101 (Pl. 53.N). W15, south corner, 15 cm from the stylobate. Lt. 4.5–5 cm: Εὐτ.
WS102. Between W15–W16, 78.5 cm from the stylobate. Lt. 5–6 cm: Εὐτ.
WS103 (Pl. 53.H). Between W15–W16, 26.5 cm and 28 cm from the stylobate. Lt. 2–5.5 cm and 3–3.5 cm: Εἰω. Κοι.
WS104. W16, 88 cm from the stylobate. Lt. 7 cm: Γε.
WS105. W16, south corner, 43 cm from the stylobate. Lt. 5.5 cm: Εὐτ.
WS106. Between W16–W17, 6 cm from the stylobate. Lt. 6–8 cm: Μαρ.
WS107 (Pl. 53.O). Between W16–W17, 11 cm from the stylobate. Lt. 4–7 cm: Εὐτ. ΚΦ
WS108. Between W16–W17, 34.5 cm from the stylobate. Lt. 2.5–3 cm: Εἰω. Κοι.
WS109. Between W16–W17, 38–54 cm from the stylobate. Lt. 3–4 cm and 2.5–3.5 cm: Εἰω. Κοι.
WS110. Between W16–W17, 16 cm from wall. Lt. 8 cm: Φ
WS111. Between W16–W17, 1.21 m from wall. Lt. 4–6 cm: Εὐτ. ΚΦ
WS112. W17, 43 cm from the stylobate. Lt. 4–4.5 cm: ΚΑ
WS113. W17, south corner, 16 cm from the stylobate. Lt. 8 cm: Φ
WS114. Between W17–W18, 42–59 cm from the stylobate. Lt. 3 cm and 2–4 cm: Εἰω. Κοι.
WS115. W18, south corner, 1 cm from the stylobate. Lt. 5–8 cm: ΚΦ

D. SOUTH STOA

The South Stoa has not been completely excavated. The masons' marks and graffiti were collected by Allison Kidd (2017 and 2018) and Angelos Chaniotis with the assistance of Takashi Fujii (2015 and 2016) and Georgios Tsolakis (2018). A continuous numbering of the columns from west to east is not possible; many masons' marks are on loose column drums, and only an approximate position at the time of their registration can be given. For masons' marks and graffiti recorded by Allison Kidd, a cross-reference to her online catalogue (Kidd 2019) is also given (for example SWPb6). Some column drums carry marks on the top and bottom surface, indicated as 'a' and 'b' respectively.

SS1. Loose column drum, in rubble at the southwest corner of the Place of the Palms. Text of two lines, apparently to be read from different sides. Mason's marks, or names of sponsors or contractors (if inscribed before the column was set up) rather than graffiti (if inscribed after the column had fallen). Lt. 5 cm:

HANHM
ΚΙΛΟΚΥΙΨC or ΚΙΛΟΚΥΡΥC

1. Ligature of NHM.

SS2. Loose column drum, at the westernmost part of the South Stoa (SWP8b). Mason's mark: Θ

SS3. Loose column drum, at the westernmost part of the South Stoa (SWP6b). Mason's mark on bottom: Γ E

Cursive epsilon rather than cursive omega; in that case, '3rd drum out of 5' (see Ch. 5 §E).

SS4 (Pl. 52.O). Column 2 from west end (SWPb5). Christian *topos* inscription and cross. H 26 cm: † M(- -)|ου

OY in ligature written between the cross and mu; cf. SS9.

SS5. Loose column drum, at the westernmost part of the South Stoa (SWP2b). Mason's mark on bottom: Δ E

Cursive epsilon rather than cursive omega; in that case, '4th drum out of 5'; cf. S3.

SS6. Loose column drum, at the westernmost part of the South Stoa (SWP1b). Mason's mark in the flute (Δ) and on bottom: B O?

SS7. Southwest, Column 13, on southwest corner of the upper surface of the base (SW13a). Christian *topos* inscription. Publication: *ALA* 200; *ala2004* 200; *IAph2007* 4.15. Lt. 15–25 cm. Καλλινίκου †

SS8. Southwest, Column 16, on the smooth surface of the lower drum of a shaft (SW16b). Remnants of inscription.

SS9. Southwest, Column SW2, 50 cm below fluting, southeast side (SW2b). Christian *topos* inscription and cross. Publication: *ALA* 199; *ala2004* 199; *IAph2007* 4.14. H 26 cm:

† M(- -)|ου

OY in ligature written between the cross and mu; cf. S4.

SS10. Southwest, Column 25 from west end (or SW1) (SW1b). Mason's mark on top: Δ

SS11. West of the Theatre Hill, in Ottoman building, loose column drum (SCW3b). Mason's marks: Ω Δ Z

The first letter can also be read as an epsilon. In that case, three numerals (5, 4, 6).

SS12. West of the Theatre Hill, loose column drum (SCWTh23b). Mason's mark on top: Δ

SS13. West of the Theatre Hill, loose column drum. Two mason's marks (SCWTh21b). Lt. 9 and 9.5 cm. a: B. b: B

SS14. West of the Theatre Hill, loose column drum. Mason's mark (SCWTh20b): B

SS15 (Pl. 54.D). West of the Theatre Hill, loose column drum. Monogram, possibly the name of a sponsor or contractor (SCWTh18b). Lt. 12.5 cm: ὑπάρχου?

The monogram consists of a large Π with an inscribed X under its horizontal bar and the letters P and K attached on top of the horizontal bar. This constellation creates lines that can be read as the letters A, Γ, I, K, Λ, M, N, O, Π, P, Σ, T, Y, and X. The monogram is similar to monograms of the 6th century that have been interpreted as ὑπάρχου.[11] A *praefectus praetorio per Orientem* (Anthemios) is known to have been active in Aphrodisias in the early fifth century; honoured as a benefactor.[12]

SS16. West of the Theatre Hill, loose column drum. Mason's mark. Lt. 10.5 cm: B

SS17 (Pl. 54.E). West of the Theatre Hill, loose column drum. Monogram, possibly the name of a sponsor or contractor (SCWTh17b); see SS15. Lt. 11 cm: ὑπάρχου?

SS18. West of the Theatre Hill, loose column drum. Mason's mark (SCWTh16b). Lt. 6 cm: X

SS19. West of the Theatre Hill, loose column drum. Two mason's marks (SCWThb15). Lt. 5 and 5.5 cm. a: Γ. b: Γ

SS20. West of the Theatre Hill, loose column drum. Monogram, possibly the name of a sponsor or contractor (SCWTh14b); see SS15. Lt. 13 cm: ὑπάρχου?

SS21 (Pl. 54.L). West of the Theatre Hill, loose column drum. Mason's mark (SCWTh10b). Lt. 7.5 and 8.5 cm. a: B. b: B

SS22. South central area, 8th column from west or Column SC10, on the base (SC10a). Monogram, possibly the name of a sponsor or contractor; see SS15. Lt. 11.5 cm: ὑπάρχου ?

SS23. South central area, 9th column (from west) after the unexcavated area, on the upper surface of the base. Mason's mark (numeral). Lt. 8.5 cm: Γ

SS24 (Pl. 54.C). South central area, in front of 11th column base (from west) after the unexcavated area, loose column drum, close to the pool. Monogram on top surface consisting of the letters A, N, T, O, Y, recognized by Allison Kidd as the monogram of Emperor Anastasius used on his coins (SCWTh21b). Lt. 9 cm: (Ἀναστασίου)

Although there is a long tradition of emperors assisting cities after earthquakes,[13] a significant financial involvement of the emperor is unlikely, since none of the relevant building inscriptions mentions Anastasius. But after an earthquake in the late fifth century (see Ch. 4), Anastasius may have authorized the reuse of the columns from a destroyed building. Anastasius is known to have provided subsidies to regions suffering from earthquakes, for example Rhodes;[14] he may also have assisted Aphrodisias in other ways (for instance with a tax relief). The presence of two acclamations of the faction of the Reds in the Place of Palms (P377, W12), the faction that was supported by Anastasius,[15] is striking, since it was one of the small factions, hardly ever mentioned in inscriptions.[16]

SS25. South central area, loose column drum, in front of 11th column base (from west) after the unexcavated area. Mason's mark (numeral). Lt. 3 cm: O

---

11 Zacos and Veglery 1972, 371 no. 293 (ca. 550–650), 442 no. 473 (6th cent.), 482 no. 577 (6th cent.), pl. 242 nos. 461–463 (Pl. 54.F).
12 *IAph2007* 4.310.
13 Jones 2014.
14 Malalas 406: ἐπὶ δὲ τῆς αὐτοῦ βασιλείας ἔπαθεν ὑπὸ θεομηνίας ἡ Ῥόδος νῆσος τὸ τρίτον αὐτῆς πάθος νυκτός· καὶ πολλὰ αὐτοῖς τοῖς περιλειφθεῖσιν ἐχαρίσατο καὶ τῇ πόλει λόγῳ κτισμάτων; see Nicks 1998, 206, 257–258.
15 Malalas 393. See Cameron 1973, 241; Greatrex 1997, 66.
16 I know of only two other epigraphic attestations: Audollent 1904, no. 242: ρουσσέου; *SEG* LII 998 ll. 25f.: φακτ⟨ί⟩ωνα ρουσί⟨α⟩ν.

SS26. South central area, *in situ*, on the path. Mason's mark (SCWTh4b): Δ
SS27. South central area. Mason's mark (SCWTh1b): B
SS28. South central area, re-erected column SC15. Mason's mark (SC15b): B
SS29. South central area, re-erected column SC14. Acclamation (SC14b): Νίκα
SS30 (Pl. 45.E). South central area, re-erected column SC5, on west side, 1.02 m above the base (II.Aph.2.SC5b). Acclamation for the city. Lt. 4.5–5 cm: Νικ[ᾷ ἡ Τύ]χ[η τῆς] | πόλ[εως]
SS31. Loose column drum, in field near the Propylon (EG1b). Mason's mark: E
   Cursive epsilon or omega?
SS32. Loose column drum, from South Stoa but now stored in the North Stoa (NS2b). Mason's mark: P

E. THEATRE WALL

The Theatre Hill retaining wall closes the southeast section of the Place of the Palms. Graffiti and painted inscriptions are visible on the limestone blocks, listed here from east to west. The position of the texts is indicated through reference to the course of blocks (counted from the ground up), their relation to the columns of the South Stoa (counted from east to west; for example S6 = 6th column from east), and their distance from the east wall of the stoa. These inscriptions are usually badly preserved due to the material (limestone).

TW1. Fourth course, 2.06 m from the east wall, 2.01 m above ground. Large cross painted with red colour. H 59 cm, W c. 63 cm.
TW2 (Pl. 53.A). Third course, opposite S1. *Topos* inscription of Zotikos, a retail-trader or tavern keeper. Publication: *ALA* 206; *ala2004* 206; *IAph2007* 4.9. Lt. 1–4 cm: τόπος | ν Ζοτικοῦ | ν καπήλου *cross* | ν εὐτυχῶς †
TW3. Fourth course, 6.7 m from east wall, 2.30 m above ground. Abbreviation or *topos* inscription. Lt. H 8 cm: ΠΟ
   Either the beginning of a name or part of the erased/damaged word τόπος.
TW4. Third course, 7.20 m. from east wall, 1.68 m above ground. Fragmentary graffito. Lt. 6–7 cm: [- -]ΠΑ[- -?]
   Recorded by Reynolds and Roueché in 1986. They read [...]ΠΑΥ[.], without excluding a second line. Possibly a name (Παύ[λ(ου)?).
TW5. Third course, opposite the intercolumniation of S6 and S7, 1.61 m above ground. Cross. H 6.5 cm.
TW6. Fourth course, opposite S9, 2.30 m above ground. Cross. H 24.5 cm.
TW7 (Pl. 53.B). Second course, opposite the intercolumniation between S9 and S10. *Topos* inscription of Artemon, the retail seller or tavern keeper. Lt. 2.5–4.5 cm. Date: *c*. fourth–fifth century AD: [T]όπος Ἀρτέ[μω]νο[ς κα]|πήλου

TW8. Third course, opposite S13, on upper edge of block. Acclamation for the city. Lt. 2.5–3 cm: Νικᾷ ἡ τύχη τῆς πόλε[ω]ς
   Recorded by Reynolds and Roueché in 1988.
TW9 (Pl. 51.I). Third course, opposite S13, under TW8. Two drawings of measures. L 30.5 cm (1 foot) and 62.5 cm (2 feet).
   Recorded by Reynolds and Roueché in 1988.
TW10. Second course, opposite S13, under TW9. Prayer. Publication: Chaniotis 2002, 236 no. 3. Lt. 2.5–3.5 cm: Εὐχὴ …νηλίου
   Some space between the first word and the name, probably because of ancient damage of the block. The text is very worn. The first letter of the name may be a Δ or Κ. In 2002 I suggested Δανηλίου but it may be Κορνηλίου or Καρμινίου.

F. PROPYLON

The gameboards on the steps of the staircase of the Propylon (Pr) were recorded from top to bottom (that is from east to west) and, on each step, from north to west. Irregular or unclear shapes on the steps are not included in the following list. There are no textual or pictorial graffiti.

Pr1: Step 1, north, a circle and a small square attached to it.
Pr2: Step 1, south, gameboard, cross-in-circle.
Pr3: Step 1, south, gameboard, cross-in-square, with an irregular circle attached to one of its corners.
Pr4: Step 2, an irregular square.
Pr5: Step 4, north, gameboard, mancala, with a circle attached to one of its corners.
Pr6: Step 4, south, gameboard, cross-in-square.
Pr7: Step 5, north, circle, open in small section of the periphery.
Pr8: Step 5, south, gameboard, cross-in-circle.
Pr9: Step 5, south, semicircle.
Pr10: Step 5, south, gameboard, cross-in-circle.
Pr11: Step 6, north, gameboard, cross-in-circle.
Pr12: Step 6, north, small circle.
Pr13: Step 7, north, irregular lines (a letter?).
Pr14: Step 7, centre, circle.
Pr15: Step 7, south, gameboard, cross-in-circle.
Pr16: Step 10, south, gameboard, cross-in-square.
Pr17: Step 11, centre, gameboard, cross-in-circle.
Pr18: Step 12, centre, gameboard, cross-in-square.
Pr19: Step 12, south, gameboard, variant of mancala; the basic form, that is two parallel rows of five squares each, is expanded to include an additional third row, consisting of four squares and an irregular circle at the end.
Pr20: Step 13, north, gameboard, cross-in-circle.
Pr21: Step 13, gameboard, mancala, with a circle attached to one of the narrow sides.
Pr22: Step 14, north, gameboard, cross-in-square with small circle attached to one of its corners.
Pr23: Step 14, north, two joined squares.

G. LOOSE FRAGMENTS

The following loose fragments found in the Place of Palms certainly (L1, L2, L4) or very likely (L3, L5) belong to blocks, columns, and other items originally in display in this area. L1 comes from the pool; L2 can certainly be attributed to the North Stoa. The original position of the small fragment L3 cannot be determined, but its content (acclamation apparently for a sponsor of buldings) suggests that it was the Place of Palms.

L1 (Pl. 47.E). Found on August 8, 2018, in a field immediately to the north of the North Stoa. Seat block from the pool; broken on right and left; a hole on the upper surface (front); H 34 cm, W 89 cm, D 53 cm. Commemorative graffito. Lt 3.5–6.5 cm. Date: *c.* third/fourth century AD: Εὐτύχης

L2. SAg 15.1.4076.M724, August 6, 2015, Trench 15.1. Inv. no. 15–024. Fragment of a marble column drum from the North Stoa. H 25 cm, L 41 cm, D 17 cm. Name of sponsor. Lt. 5.8–6.4 cm. Date: late second century: [Καπε]|τωλ[ῖ]|νος [vac.]

L3 (Pl. 45.A). Trench 14.1 ('collapse starting unit **4053**'). Inv. no. M653. Small marble fragment broken on top, bottom, and left. H 12, W 16.5, D 5 cm. Acclamation for a benefactor? Lt. 2.4–2.8 cm. Date: fourth/fifth century:

[- - -]Ι..Ο[- - - - - -]
[- - -]ΣΤΗΣ τῶν vacat
[- - -]ΟΠΟΛΙΤΑΚΥ

1. A vertical line, two short vertical lines and the lower part of a round letter. ‖ 2. for example [αὔξι ὁ κτί]στης τῶν ‖ 3. possibly [φιλ]οπολῖτα κύ[ρι].

L4 (Pl. 54.G). Trench 15.1, **4005**, August 23, 2015. Fragment of a marble vessel, with a crude inscription on the exterior. H 18 cm, W 28 cm, D 11 cm. Owner's inscription (name of a contractor?). Lt. 2–4 cm: Κρισπίνου

L5. Southeast area of the Place of Palms. Column drum (originally from the South Stoa?). D 58 cm. Mason's mark on a surface (name of sponsor or contractor). Lt. 4.5–6.5 cm: Ξάν(θος) or Ξάν(θου)?

Or a name composed with ξανθός, for example Ξάνθιππος.

L6. Northwest foot of the Theatre Hill. Marble plaque, originally from the pool. H 34 cm, W 41 cm. Pictorial graffito; face of a man. H 13.

APPENDIX 3

Catalogue of Greek, Roman, and Byzantine Coin Finds from the Place of Palms

Ahmet Tolga Tek and Hüseyin Köker

A. A GENERAL CONSPECTUS OF COIN FINDS FROM THE PLACE OF PALMS

During the seasons of 2012–2017, 349 coins were found during the excavation of the Place of Palms trenches. We tried to add to the catalogue all the coins we could identify in the Aphrodisias Museum among those excavated in the 1988–1990 seasons and added 58 further coins to the sum. Although these coins were described in field notebooks as best as the excavators could in those years, the coins were not cleaned at the time and most of these descriptions were inadequate. Therefore we added to the catalogue only coins we could identify with envelopes and find numbers that correspond correctly to field note descriptions. Unfortunately some envelopes were lost in the subsequent years at the museum or the coins were not described with enough details to identify them, and for that reason, only a few coins could be added from those seasons. In total, 407 coins have been recorded from Place of Palms.

In the catalogue, the late hellenistic period is represented by 10 coins. Thirty-two Roman provincial coins represent the period from the first to third centuries AD. Nine Roman imperial and contemporary copies also date from these centuries. One hundred and eighty-three coins are from the late Roman period, from tetrarchic issues to the early fifth century AD. Ninety-four of these can only be attributed only to the late Roman period by their formats (thin and small flans, diameter and weight). Some are corroded beyond recognition by the waterlogged conditions in and around the pool, but many were worn, clipped, badly struck, or unstruck flans. These are followed by 74 Byzantine coins and one late medieval coin of Wallachia. Ninety-eight Islamic and modern coins are represented in this sector, and are catalogued in Appendix 4. Fourteen items listed as coins in the

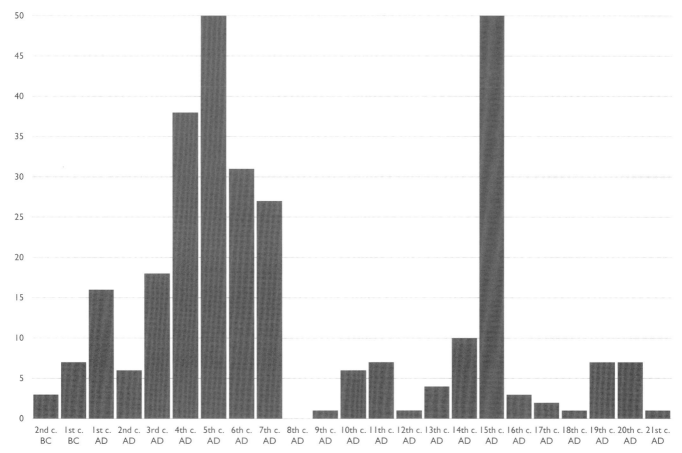

Fig. 106. Dated coin finds from Place of Palms, by century (n = 297).

357

field notes turned out to be other items like nail heads etc., and are not included here.

The chart in Fig. 106 is prepared using 297 exactly dated coins out of 407 in total. Among those that could not be used in the graph are the 95 unidentified late Roman and 12 undated Islamic coins. So there should have been a better representation of the late Roman (especially the fifth century AD) and Islamic periods in the Place of Palms than is shown in the graph.

The graph corresponds to what we know of the Place of Palms perfectly. The construction and early usage phase of the complex is represented by a number of late hellenistic and first-century AD coins seen as a sharp rise in the graph.[1] The first peak in the graph is in the fifth century AD, which corresponds to massive restoration work held around the pool and but is also probably a result of usage of small format and easily losable coins at that time. There is a very sharp break in the finds sequence in the seventh century, corresponding to a city-wide destruction event or various events happening in a short span of time, followed by a gap of no coin finds until the end of the eighth century. A peak corresponding to the fifteenth century shows activity in the late Beylik and early Ottoman periods. The modern finds from the late nineteenth century onwards may be connected to archaeological excavations in the area.

B. GREEK COINS

Mysia
Pergamon
c. 80–10 BC
Obv. Helmeted head of Athena right.
Rev. [AΘH-NAΣ] / [NI]KHΦ[OPOY]; Owl facing, winged open; on palm branch; below wings in left, K and in right, Σ.
Ref. *BMC Mysia*, 197–199; *SNG Cop. Mysia*, 386; *SNG France* 5, 1920–1922; *SNG Ashmolean* IX, 821; Voegtli 1993, 28, 181; Chameroy 2012, 108–112: tab. 1, type 37; Chameroy 2016, 170–173: tab. 1, type 37.
1. AE. 17 mm, 2.00 g, 12h.
Inv. C2015.032; SAg.15.1.4075.C044.

Karia
Alabanda
2nd cent. BC (after 168 BC)
Obv. Head of Apollo, laureate, right.
Rev. [AΛABAN/ΔEΩN]; kithara.
Ref. *BMC Caria*, 15; *SNG Cop. Caria*, 4.
2. AE. 18/19 mm, 6.50 g, 12h.
Inv. C2015.120; SAg.15.4177.C094.

Plarasa and Aphrodisias
1st cent. BC
Obv. Head of Aphrodite wearing *stephane* right.
Rev. ΠΛAPA – AΦPOΔI, eagle on thunderbolt right.
Ref. MacDonald 1992, Type 28, O29/R66.
3. AE. 18/19 mm, 4.04 g, 12h.
Inv. PT.E.90.II, S.8 (Pl. 97).

1 But these were not found in their original contexts, but from later contexts possibly connected with massive earth removal and filling in late antiquity.

1st cent. BC; magistrate(s) M A L
Obv. ΠΛA/P–A / AΦ-PO; double axe.
Rev. M/A-Λ; cuirass in square incuse.
Ref. MacDonald 1992, Type 30.

4. AE. 11 mm, 1.30 g, 12h.
Inv. PT.E.90; [ΠΛA/P]–A / [AΦ-P]O; O-(new variation[2])/R86.
5. AE. 11 mm, 1.31 g, 12h
Inv. PT.E.90; ΠΛA/P–A / AΦ-PO; O50/R89.

1st cent. BC
Obv. [Π]ΛA[PA] / [AΦ-PO]; double axe; two round countermarks; on right field: bunch of grapes, on left field: head right.[3]
Rev. Cuirass (without incuse square).
Ref. MacDonald 1992, Type 31.
6. AE. 11/12 mm, 1.98 g, 12h.
Inv. C2012.196, SAg.12.2.2013.C080.

1st cent. BC
Obv. Draped bust of Aphrodite right.
Rev. [Π]-Λ / A-Φ; thunderbolt in square incuse.
Ref. MacDonald 1992, type 34, R107.
7. AE. 9/10 mm, 0.41 g, 12h.
Inv. C2012.195; SAg.12.2.2015.C079.

1st cent. BC
Obv. Bust of winged Eros right.
Rev. [ΠΛA-AΦPO]; rose.
Ref. MacDonald 1992, Type 36, O68/R112.
8. AE. 10 mm, 0.93 g, 12h.
Inv. C2016.114; SAg.16.2.5002.C005.

Tabai
2nd cent. BC or later
Obv. Veiled female head right.
Rev. TA; forepart of bull right.
Ref. *BMC Caria*, 15–16; *SNG Cop. Caria*, 517–518; Robert and Robert 1954, 127, type T; *SNG Tübingen* 5, 3493; *SNG München* 23, 438; *SNG Ashmolean* XI, 275–276.
9. AE. 12/14 mm, 1.20 g, 12h.
Inv. C2013.104; SAg.13.2.4015.C023.

Lydia
Magnesia ad Sipylum
2nd cent. BC or later
Obv. Turreted head of Kybele right.
Rev. [MAΓNETΩN / ΣIΠY]; Zeus Lydios, wearing chiton and himation, standing left, holding on extended right hand eagle, and in left transverse sceptre; faintly visible monogram in left field. Round countermark on right field, inside scorpion?
Ref. *BMC Lydia*, 4–5; *SNG München* 23, 219.
10. AE. 14/16 mm, 3.59 g, 12h broken.
Inv. C2015.046; SAg.15.1.4048.C054.

2 The same new obverse variation was also observed on another coin: Nümizmatik Lanz München, Auction 131, lot 86 (27 Nov 2006), which should be correctly read as ΠΛA/P-[A].
3 Both countermarks noted as frequent on this type, MacDonald 1992, 70.

C. ROMAN PROVINCIAL COINS

Ionia
Ephesos
Hadrian (AD 117–135)
Obv. [AY KAI TP – AΔPIANOC C]; laureate head right.
Rev. [E]Φ[E]-CIΩN; tetrastyle temple within which cult statue of Artemis Ephesia.
Ref. *BMC Ionia* 229; *RPC* III, 2061; Karwiese 2012, 160–170.
11. AE. 24 mm; 9.23 g, 12h.
Inv. C2016.026; SAg.16.1.4255.C122.

Karia
Antioch ad Maeandrum
Trajan (AD 98–117)
Obv. [AVT NEP TPAIA-NOC KAI CEΓEP ΔAKIK]; laureate head right.
Rev. [MAIANΔPOC AN-TIOXEΩN; river god Maeander reclining left, wearing himation over lower limbs, holding reed each hand, left arm resting on urn.
Ref. Lindgren I, 608; *RPC* III, 2241.
12. AE. 30 mm, 17.17 g, 6h.
Inv. C2012.097; SAg.12.2.2010.C038.

Gordian III (AD 238–244)
Obv. AYT K [M ANT ΓOPΔIANOC]; laureate, draped and cuirassed bust right.
Rev. ANT[IO-X-EΩN]; Tyche standing facing, head left, holding cornucopia and rudder.
Ref. *RPC* VII.1, 612.
13. AE. 22/23 mm, 3.50 g, 6h (holed).
Inv. C2016.005; SAg.16.1.4203.C101.

Philip I (AD 244–249)
Obv. [AYT K M IOY ΦI]ΛIΠΠO[C]; laureate, draped and cuirassed bust right.
Rev. ANTIO-[XE-ΩN]; Tyche standing facing, head left, holding cornucopia and rudder.
Ref. *SNG Cop. Caria*, 59; *RPC* VIII online, unassigned; ID 20562.
14. AE. 20/21 mm, 3.95 g, 7h.
Inv. PT.E.90.III

Aphrodisias
Augustus (27 BC – AD 14)
c. 27 BC?
Obv. Head of Zeus right, laureate.
Rev. A-ΦPOΔI/ΣEIΩN; Cult statue of Aphrodite of Aphrodisias right.
Ref. MacDonald 1992, Type 35, O67/R111; *RPC* I, -.
15. AE. 16/18 mm, 2.82 g, 12h.
Inv. C2016.068; SAg.16.1.4278.C159. A-[ΦPOΔI/ΣIE[ΩN]
16. AE. 16 mm, 2.92 g, h?
Inv. C2013.028, SAg.12.1.1013.C011. A-[ΦPOΔI/ΣIEΩN]
17. AE. 16/19, 3.66 g. h?
Inv. C2016.104; SAg.16.14281.C186. A-ΦPO[ΔI/ΣIEΩN]

c. 2 BC – AD 14; magistrate: Sozon
Obv. [CEBA]-CTOC; head right, laureate.
Rev. [AΦPOΔIC]-I-E-[ΩN CΩZΩN]; double axe bound with fillets.
Ref. MacDonald 1992, Type 45, O94(?)/R156; *RPC* I, 2838.
18. AE. 14 mm, 2.22 g, 6h.
Inv. C2012.088; SAg.12.2.2010.C029.

Mid/Late Augustus – Early Tiberian period (countermark)
Obv. Bust right, worn. (Aphrodite as MacDonald Type 28).
Rev. Obscure (eagle right on thunderbolt as MacDonald 1992, Type 28). Countermark: cult statue of Aphrodite right.
Ref. Howgego 2005, cmk. 227; MacDonald 1992, pl. XXXII, cmk. 13.
19. AE. 18 mm, 3.12 g, 6h.
Inv. C2013.054, SAg.13.1.3022.C010.
20. AE. 17/18 mm; 3.63 g, h?
Inv. C2013.073, SAg.13.1.3020.C014.

Caligula (AD 37–41)
Obv. ΘEOΣ – ΣEBAΣTOΣ; head of Augustus right, laureate.
Rev. AΦPOΔI-ΣIEΩN; cult statue of Aphrodite facing.
Ref. MacDonald, 1992, Type 46. O97/R167; *RPC* I, 2844.
21. AE. 19/20 mm, 4.41 g, 12h.
Inv. C2013.058; SAg.13.2.4006.C008. [ΘEOΣ ΣE]BAΣT[OΣ] / [A]ΦPOΔI[Σ]IEΩ[N]
22. AE. 18/21 mm, 4.65 g, 12h.
Inv. PT.W.88.I; ΘEOΣ – [Σ]EBAΣT[OΣ] / A[ΦPO]ΔI-ΣIE[ΩN]

Uncertain emperor (Nero?)
Late 1st cent. AD
Obv. Humped bull (Zebu / bos indicus / brahman) right.
Rev. AΦPOΔEIΣIEѠN; double axe bound with fillets.
Ref. MacDonald 1992, Type 48; *RPC* II, 1221.
23. AE. 17/19 mm, 3.50 g, 6h.
Inv. C2017.015; SAg.17.1.4404.C214. [AΦPOΔEIΣIEѠN]; O107 /R179
24. AE. 15/16 mm, 2.65 g, ?h.
Inv. PT.E.90, S.5; [AΦ]PO[ΔEIΣIEѠN]; O?/R?

Septimius Severus (AD 193–211)
c. AD 209; magistrate: Tiberius Claudius Zenon
Obv. [ΔHMOC], bust of Demos right, laureate.
Rev. [AΦPOΔI]CIEΩN; in field, [TI K ZH]NΩN]; in ex., [TIMEΛHC]; river god Timeles recumbent left, holding reed and cornucopiae; to right, overturned urn from which water flows.
Ref. MacDonald 1992, Type 107, O153/R275; Johnston 1995, 91, appendix 1.
25. AE. 23/24 mm, 4.39 g, 12h.
Inv. C2015.114; SAg.15.1.4095.C093.

Macrinus (AD 217–218)
Obv. AY K MOC – MAKPE[INOC]; bust right, laureate, wearing cuirass and paludamentum.
Rev. AΦPOΔEI-[CIEΩ]N; cult statue of Aphrodite right; in left, priestess seated right, and upper field, star; in right, sacred well and upper field, crescent.
Ref. MacDonald 1992, Type 160, O214/R398–99; Tek 2016, 177, fig. 16 (this coin).
26. AE. 33/35 mm, 16.15 g, 6h.
Inv. C2016.093; SAg.16.1.4281.C181 (Pl. 97).

Gordian III (AD 238–244)
Obv. [IEPA] – CYNK[ΛHTOC]; head of Synkletos right, draped and diademed.
Rev. AΦPOΔ-[E-I-CIE]ΩN; Three leafless tree trunks inside a lattice enclosure.
Ref. MacDonald 1992, Type 131, O185/ R344; Johnston 1995, 90, appendix 1; *RPC* VII.1, 630.12–15.
27. AE. 23/25 mm, 5.21 g, 12h.
Inv. C2012.146; SAg.12.2.2010.C069.

Salonina (AD 253–268)
Obv. IOY [KO.] – CAΛΩNINA; bust of Salonina right, draped, on crescent.

Rev. ΑΦΡΟ-Δ-Ι-ϹΙΕΩΝ; cult statue of Aphrodite right; to left, priestess seated right, and upper field, star; in right, sacred well, and in upper field, crescent.
Ref. MacDonald 1992, Type 232, O283/R562.
28. AE. 21/22 mm, 4.41 g, 6h.
Inv. C2015.021; SAg.15.1.4075.C035 (Pl. 97).

Obv. [ΙΟΥ] ΚΟΡΝ – [ϹΑΛΩΝΙΝΑ]; bust right draped, on crescent.
Rev. ΑΦΡΟ[Δ-ΙϹΙ]/ΕΩΝ; Hermes advances right; nude but for *petasos*, chlamys and winged *pedilia*; holding caduceus; looking back at ram, which he drags by horn.
Ref. MacDonald 1992, Type 235, O?/R585.
29. AE. 17/22 (broken), 5.17 g, 6h.
Inv. C2016.119; SAg.16.1.4323.C194.

Apollonia Salbake (?)
Antoninus Pius (AD 138–161)
Obv. [.] – ΑΝ[.]; Laureate bust right.
Rev. [Α]ΠΟΛΛΩ-ΝΙΑΤΩ[Ν]; Apollo, nude and Artemis draped, both holding bow and arrow; standing facing each other.
Ref. Robert and Robert 1954, -; *RPC* IV, -.
30. AE. 14/15 mm, 2.19 g, 6h.
Inv. C2013.064; SAg.13.1.3020.C012 (Pl. 97).

Tabai
Domitian AD 81–96
Obv. [ΔΟΜΙ]ΤΙΑ – ϹΕΒ[ΑϹΤΗ]; bust right, draped.
Rev. [ΔΙΑ ΟΡΘΡΙΟΥ] ΙΕΡΩΝ[ΟϹ] / [ΤΑΒΗ]ΝΩΝ; Nike advancing right, holding palm branch and wreath.
Ref. *BMC Caria*, 71; *SNG Cop. Caria*, 557; Robert and Robert 1954, 119, type b; *SNG Aul. Karien*, 2716; *SNG München* 22, 451; *RPC* II, 1255.
31. AE. 19/20 mm, 5.08 g, 12h.
Inv. C2015.005; SAg.15.1.4064.C022.

Lydia
Hypaepa
Septimius Severus (AD 193–211); magistrate: Glykonos, Asiarch
Obv. [Α]ΥΤ Κ[ΑΙ ϹΕΠ] – [ϹΕ]ΟΥ[ΗΡΟϹ]; laureate head right; oval countermark inside which cult figure of Artemis Anaitis facing.
Rev. [ΕΠΙ ΓΛΥΚΩΝΟϹ Α-ϹΙΑ ΥΠΑΙΠΗΝ]/Ω-Ν; Cult statue of Artemis Anaitis standing facing.
Ref. Altınoluk 2013, type 75a; *GRPC Lydia* II, 171; Howgego 2005, cmk. 233.
32. AE. 22 mm, 4.72 g, 5h.
Inv. C2013.136; SAg.13.2.4006.C037.

Sardis
Vespasian (AD 69–79); magistrate: T. Fl. Eisigonos, strategos
Obv. ΑΥΤ[ΟΚ ΚΑΙϹ ΟΥΕϹΠΑϹΙΑΝ]Ω; laureate head right.
Rev. [ΕΠΙ Τ ΦΛ ΕΙϹΙΓΟΝΟΥ ϹΑΡΔΙΑΝΩΝ]; Men standing, left, holding sceptre, and pine cone over altar and staff.
Ref. *RPC* II, 1312.
33. AE. 18/19 mm, 4.76 g, 6h. (holed).
Inv. C2016.109; SAg.16.1.4200.C191.

Tripolis
Marcus Aurelius (AD 161–180)
Obv. Bust of Athena right, with crested helmet, aegis and spear.
Rev. ΤΡΙ-ΠΟ-ΛΕΙΤΩΝ; Hermes standing facing, head turned right, wearing chlamys, holding purse in right hand, caduceus in left.
Ref. *BMC Lydia*, 22; *SNG Cop. Lydia*, 723; *SNG München* 23, 794; *RPC* III, 2559A[4].
34. AE. 21 mm, 4.62 g, 6h.
Inv. C2017.019; SAg.17.1.4393.C221.

Phrygia
Hydrela
Hadrian (AD 117–135); magistrate: Apellas Athenagorou
Obv. ΥΔ[ΡΛΕΙ]ΤΩ-Ν; bust of Athena right, with crested helmet.
Rev. ΑΠΕΛ[ΛΑϹ ΑΝΕ-ΘΗΚΕ]; Hermes standing facing, head turned right, holding purse in right hand, caduceus in left.
Ref. *Von Aulock Phrygiens* I, 312; *RPC* III, 2364.
35. AE. 14/16 mm, 1.95 g, 12h.
Inv. C2015.008; SAg.15.2.3000.C018.

D. UNIDENTIFIED ROMAN PROVINCIAL COINS

Augustus
Obv. Laureate head of Augustus right, countermark? (damaged during holing).
Rev. Worn.
36. AE. 25/26 mm, 7.11 g, 6h. (holed).
Inv. C2015.047; SAg.15.2.3000.C022.

Septimius Severus ?
Obv. Bust, laureate and draped right.
Rev. Worn.
37. AE. 28/31 mm, 14.30 g, h?
Inv. PT.W.88.I, F.44.

1st to 3rd cent. AD
Obv. Worn.
Rev. Worn.
38. AE. 28/30 mm, 11.67 g, 12?h holed Inv. PT.W. 90-III, S.13; Rev. River god reclining left.
39. AE. 29/30 mm, 6.75 g, h?
Inv. C2016.097; SAg.16.1.4281.C185.
40. AE. 18/19 mm, 2.66 g, h?
Inv. C2014.168; SAg.14.2.3045.C016.
41. AE. 28 mm, 3.98 g, h?
Inv. C2012.193; SAg.12.2.2013.C077.
42. AE. 24/25 mm, 5.53 g, h?
Inv. C2013.065; SAg.13.1.3013.C013.

E. ROMAN IMPERIAL COINS

Tiberius (AD 14–37)
Lugdunum
Undated
Obv. TI CAESAR DIVI – AVG F AVGVSTVS; head of Tiberius, laureate, right.
Rev. PONTIF – MAXIM; female figure, draped, seated right on chair with plain legs, holding branch and long sceptre; below chair, double line.
Ref. *BMC* I, 34; *RIC* I, 26.
43. AR denarius, 18 mm, 3.46 g, 12h.
Inv. Ag.BS.88.1.F.5. (Mus. Inv. 3373) (Pl. 97).

---

4   Added coin type after the publication of *RPC* III dated on the website to the period of Trajan or Hadrian.

Unidentified empress (early 3rd cent. AD?)
Obv. Female bust right (Julia Domna?).
Rev. Figure standing.
44. AR Denarius, 16/17 mm, 2.17 g, 12h broken.
Inv. C1995.041, ring drain of the pool.

Claudius II (AD 268–270)
Cyzicus
AD 269
Obv. [IMP C M] AVR CLAVDI[VS AVG]; radiate head right; below head, three dots.
Rev. PAX – [A-E]TERNA; Pax stg, left, holding olive branch and sceptre; in ex., SPQR.
Ref. *RIC* V.1, 237; Gysen 1999 (2nd emission, 1st series).
45. AR Antoninianus, 19/21 mm, 2.84 g, 6h.
Inv. PT.1990, Sondage 1. C001.

Rome
AD 270
Obv. [IMP CLAVDI]VS AVG; radiate, bare bust right.
Rev. ANN[ONA AVG]; Annona standing left, holding corn-ears in right hand and cornucopiae in left hand; at feet to left, prow of ship.
Ref. *RIC* V.1,18.
46. AR Antoninianus, 18 mm, 1.22 g. 2h broken.
Inv. PT.SW.90.III, S.27.

Aurelian (AD 270–275)
Antioch
AD 270–272
Obv. IMP C AVRELIANVS AVG; radiate and cuirassed bust right; below, S.
Rev. VABALATHVS V C R IM D R; laureate, draped and cuirassed bust of Vabalathus right.
Ref. *RIC* V.1, 381; Göbl 1993, 353a (1. Emission).
47. AR Antoninianus 20/22 mm, 3.48 g, 6h.
Inv. C2013.120; SAg.13.2.4006.C033.

Barbarous Radiates
c. AD 270s–*c.* 280s
Prototype Divo Claudio / Funeral pyre, RIC V, 261 (AD 270/1)
Obv. DIVO CLAVDIO; Claudius II, radiate, right.
Rev. CONSECRATIO; Funeral pyre.
Ref. MacDonald 1976, 603–619.
48. AE. 16 mm, 1.22 g, 12h.
Inv. C2015.013; SAg.15.1.4064.C027.
DIVO CLAV[DIO] Rev. [C]ONSECRATI-O (Pl. 97).
49. AE. 11/12 mm, 0.41 g, 6h.
Inv. C2015.104; SAg 15.1, 4076, C085. Obv. CLAVD[IO]

Prototype Divo Claudio / eagle, RIC V, 266 (AD 270/1)
Obv. [DIVO CLAVDIO]; Claudius II, radiate, right.
Rev. [CONSECRATIO]; eagle facing, head turned right.
Ref. MacDonald 1976, 620–640.
50. AE. 12/13 mm, 0.61 g, h?
Inv. C2012.199; SAg.12.2.2028.C083.

Prototype Tetricus II / Spes, RIC V, 272 (AD 273/4)
Obv. C PIV ESV TETRICVS CAES; radiate, draped, bust right.
Rev. [SPES PVBLICA]; Spes, draped, walking left, holding flower in right hand and raising robe with left hand.
Ref. MacDonald 1976, 654; Chameroy 2009, Abb. 25, no 24.
51. AE. 16 mm, 1.50 g, 9h.
Inv. C2012.103; SAg.12.2.2005.C044.
Obv. [C PIV] ESV T[ETRICVS CAES], Rev. [SPES PVBLICA]

Diocletian
Cyzicus
c. AD 295–99
Obv. IMP C C VAL DIOCLETIANVS P F AVG; radiate and cuirassed bust right.
Rev. CONCORDIA MI-LITVM; emperor standing right in military dress receiving small Victory on globe from Jupiter standing left leaning on sceptre; in between, KA.
Ref. *RIC* VI, 15a.
52. AE. 19 mm, 2.48 g, 6h.
Inv. C2016.058; SAg.16.1.4200.C154.

Maximian
Cyzicus
AD 293
Obv. IMP C M AV MAXIMIANVS P F AVG; Bust of Maximian right, radiate and draped; below bust, dot.
Rev. CONCORDIA MILI-TVM; Emperor standing right, holding *parazonium*, receiving Victory on globe from Jupiter standing left, holding sceptre; in left field, H; in ex., XXI.
Ref. *RIC* V.2, 607.
53. AE. 19/20 mm, 2.15g, 2h.
Inv. PT.90, Sondage 1. F.2.

Constantine I (AD 307–337)
Nicomedia, Cyzicus or Antioch
AD 321–324
Obv. [IMP C V]AL CO[NSTANTINVS P] F AVG; bust, radiate, draped, cuirassed right.
Rev. IOVI CON[SERVATORI]; Jupiter standing left, chlamys across left shoulder, holding sceptre with eagle on top, Victory on globe in right hand; eagle with wreath to left; captive to right on ground; in field left [X / IIГ]; in ex. SM[.
Ref. *RIC* VII, Nicomedia 43, Cyzicus 16 or Antioch 34.
54. AE. 16/18 mm, 1.87 g, 12h, broken and holed twice.
Inv. C2013.059; SAg.13.2.4006.C009.

Londinium
AD 323–324
Obv. CONSTAN-TINVS AVG; head right, laureate.
Rev. [SAR]MATIA – DEVICTA; Victory advancing right, holding trophy on right arm, branch in left hand, trampling captive on right on ground; in ex. [PL]ON☽.
Ref. *RIC* VII, 289.
55. AE. 18/19 mm, 2.45 g, 12h.
Inv. C2015.020; SAg.15.1.4075.C033 (Pl. 97).

Constantine I deified
Constantinople
AD 337–340
Obv. DV CONSTAN[TI-NVS PT AVG]; bust right, veiled.
Rev. No legend; emperor in quadriga right, veiled; hand of god reaches down to him; in ex., CONS.
Ref. *RIC* VIII, 37; *LRBC* I, 1041.
56. AE. 14 mm, 1.45 g, 12h.
Inv. C2014.122; SAg.14.3.5001.C001.

Cyzicus
AD 347–348
Obv. DV CONSTANTI-NVS PT AVG; Bust right, veiled.
Rev. VN – MR; emperor standing right, veiled; in ex. SMKA.
Ref. *RIC* VIII, 46; *LRBC* I, 1304.
57. AE. 15 mm, 1.72 g, 12h.
Inv. C2015.014; SAg.15.1.4048.C028.

Constantius II (AD 337–361)
Constantinople
AD 355–361
Obv. D N CONSTAN-TIVS P F AVG; Bust right, pearl diademed, draped and cuirassed.
Rev. FEL TEMP RE-PARATIO; helmeted soldier to left, shield on left arm, spearing falling horseman; shield on ground at right; horseman is bearded and diademed; he turns to face soldier and extends left arm; in ex., CONSB•.
Ref. *RIC* VIII, 135; *LRBC* II, 2041 (FH3).
58. AE. 17 mm, 1.86 g, 12h.
Inv. C2012.143; SAg.12.2.2010.C066.

Nicomedia
AD 336–337
Obv. FL IVL CONSTANTIVS NOB C; bust right, laureate, draped and cuirassed.
Rev. GLOR-IA EXERC-ITVS; two soldiers stg, each holding spear and leaning on shield; between them one standard. in ex., SMNA.
Ref. *RIC* VII, 201; *LRBC* I, 1127.
59. AE. 15 mm, 1.33 g, 6h.
Inv. PT.W.89.I, F.10.

AD 347–348
Obv. DN CONSTAN-TIVS PF AVG; bust right, pearl diademed and draped.
Rev. VOT / XX / MVLT / XXX; all in wreath; in ex., SMNA.
Ref. *RIC* VIII, 49; *LRBC* I, 1149.
60. AE. 15/16 mm, 1.47 g, 6h.
Inv. C2015.011; SAg.15.1.4064.C026.

Cyzicus
AD 355–361
Obv. D N CONSTAN-TIVS P F AVG; bust right, pearl diademed and draped.
Rev. SPES REI – PVBLICE; emperor helmeted in military dress standing left, holding globe and spear; on left field Γ; in ex., SMKA.
Ref. *RIC* VIII, 117; *LRBC* II, 2506 (corr.).
61. AE. 15/16 mm, 1.80 g, 12h.
Inv. C2013.019; SAg.13.1.3012.C004.

Antioch
AD 355–361
Obv. [D N C]ONSTAN-TIVS [P F AVG]; bust pearl-diademed, draped, cuirassed, right.
Rev. [FEL TEMP – RE]PARATIO; helmeted soldier to left, shield on left arm, spearing falling horseman; shield on ground at right; horseman is bearded and bare-headed; he turns to face soldier and extends left arm; in ex., ANH.
Ref. *RIC* VIII, 187A, FH3.
62. AE. 14 mm, 2.07 g,10h.
Inv. PT.1991 (Pl. 97).

Uncertain Mint
AD 355–361
Obv. D N CONSTAN-TIVS P F AVG; bust pearl-diademed, draped, cuirassed, right.
Rev. FEL TEMP RE-PARATIO; helmeted soldier to left, shield on left arm, spearing falling horseman; shield on ground at right; horseman is bearded and bare-headed; he turns to face soldier and extends left arm. (FH 3).
63. AE. 15 mm, 3.04 g, 12h.
Inv. C2015.004; SAg.15.1.4067.C021.
64. AE. 16/18 mm, 1.90 g, 12h.
Inv. C2015.029; SAg.15.1.8006.C001.

65. AE. 16 mm, 1.77 g, 12h.
Inv. C2015.038; SAg.15.1.4064.C047.
66. AE. 14 mm, 1.53 g, 6h.
Inv. C2016.107; SAg 16.1, 4200, C189. Rev. In left field, •M•

Constans (AD 337–350)
Nicomedia
AD 337–340
Obv. CONSTA-NS P F AVG; pearl diademed and draped head right.
Rev. GLOR-IA EXERC-ITVS; two soldiers stg, each holding spear and leaning on shield; between them one standard; in ex., [SM]NA.
Ref. *RIC* VIII, 24; *LRBC* I, 1138.
67. AE. 16/17 mm, 1.38g, 12h.
Inv. C2015.084; SAg.15.1.4076.C008.

Antioch
AD 337–340
Obv. CONST-ANS P F AVG; pearl diademed and draped bust right.
Rev. GLOR-IA EXERC-ITVS; two soldiers stg, each holding spear and leaning on shield; between them one standard; in ex., SMANI.
Ref. *RIC* VIII, 50; *LRBC* I, 1384.
68. AE. 13/15 mm, 0.95 g, 6h.
Inv. PT.SW.89.I, F.41.

Family of Constantine
Uncertain Mint
AD 330–335
Obv. CON[…]; bust right, pearl diademed.
Rev. [GLOR-IA EXERC-ITVS]; two soldiers stg, each holding spear and leaning on shield; between them two standards.
69. AE. 16/18 mm, 1.47 g, 12h.
Inv. C2017.026; SAg.17.1.4420.C226.

Valentinian I (AD 364–375)
Constantinople
AD 364–365
Obv. D N VALENTINI-[ANVS P F AVG]; bust right, pearl diademed, draped and cuirassed.
Rev. GLORIA RO-[MANORVM]; emperor advancing right, with right hand dragging captive and holding *labarum* in left; in left field, wreath and in right field, branch; in ex., CONSA.
Ref. *RIC* IX, 49a; *LRBC* II, 2098.
70. AE. 16 mm, 1.18 g, 6h.
Inv. C2013.017; SAg.13.2.4000.C001.

Valens (AD 364–378)
Nicomedia
AD 367–375
Obv. D N VALEN-S P F AVG; Bust right, pearl diademed and draped.
Rev. SECVRIT[AS – REIPVBLICAE]; Victory left, holding wreath and palm.; in field left, wreath, in field right ₽; in ex. SMNA.
Ref. *LRBC* II, 2341.
71. AE. 16/17 mm, 1.99 g, 12h.
Inv. C2015.006; SAg.15.1.4064.C024 (Pl. 97).

Valentinian I, Valens or Gratian
Uncertain Mint
AD 367–375
Obv. illegible.
Rev. [SECVRITAS – REIPVBLICAE], Victory to left, holding wreath and palm.
72. AE. 15/16 mm, 1.14 g, 6h clipped.
Inv. C1996.220; stray, pool, under drain on west end.

Gratian, Valentinian II or Theodosius I
Uncertain Mint
378–383
AD Obv. Bust right.
Rev. [CONCOR-DIA AVGGG]?, Constantinople or Rome seated facing.
73. AE. 15/16 mm, 0.94 g, h?
Inv. C2012.192; SAg.12.2.2013.C076.

Theodosius I (AD 379–395)
Uncertain Mint
AD 383
Obv. [D N THE]ODO-[SIVS P F AVG]; bust right, pearl diademed and draped.
Rev. VOT / X / MVLT / XX; all in wreath.
74. AE. 13/14 mm, 0.87 g, 12h.
Inv. PT.SW.89.I, F.42.

Uncertain Mint
AD 383–395
Obv. D N THEODO-SIVS P F AVG; bust right, pearl diademed and draped.
Rev. SALVS REI – PVBLICAE; Victory left, trophy on shoulder and dragging captive.
75. AE. 12/13 mm, 0.73 g, 12h.
Inv. C2015.018; SAg.15.1.4065.C034.
76. AE. 14 mm, 0.68 g, 12h.
Inv. C2015.065; SAg.15.1.4065.C060.
77. AE. 11/12 mm, 1.15 g, 12h.
Inv. C2015.068; SAg.15.2.3042.C023.
78. AE. 11/12 mm, 0.49 g, 6h.
Inv. C2015.082; SAg.15.1.4016.C064.

Arcadius (AD 383–408)
Cyzicus
AD 383
Obv. [DN] ARCADI[VS] P F AVG; bust right, pearl diademed and draped.
Rev. VOT / X / MVLT / XX; all in wreath; in ex., SMKΓ.
Ref. *RIC* IX, 21d; *LRBC* II, 2558.
79. AE. 15 mm, 1.04 g, h?
Inv. C2012.024; SAg.12.1.1004.C001.

Uncertain Mint
AD 393–395
Obv. [D N ARCA]DI-VS [P F AVG]; bust right.
Rev. [SALVS REI]-PVBL[ICAE]; Victory left, trophy on shoulder and dragging captive.
80. AE. 11/12 mm; 0.71g, 12h.
Inv. C2015.035; SAg.15.2.3060.C020.

Uncertain Mint:
AD 395–401
Obv. D N ARCADI-[VS P F AVG]; bust right, pearl diademed and draped.
Rev. [VIRT]VS – [EXERCITVS]; emperor stg left, head right, holding spear and resting left hand on shield. Victory, holding palm branch in left hand, crowns him.
Ref. *RIC* X, 56–76 (Virtus Exercitus Type 2).
81. AE. 17/18 mm, 2.20 g, 6h.
Inv. C2013.070; SAg.13.2.4006.C011.
82. AE. 15/16 mm, 1.91 g, 12h. clipped.
Inv. C2014.153; SAg.14.1.4048.C016.

Gratian, Valentinian II, Theodosius I or Arcadius
Cyzicus
AD 383
Obv. Legend illegible. Bust right.
Rev. VOT / X / MVLT / XX; all within wreath; in ex., SMKA.
Ref. *RIC* IX, 21; *LRBC* II, 2555–2558.
83. AE. 12 mm, 1.57 g, 6h.
Inv. C2016.123; SAg.16.1.4376.C201.

Uncertain Mint
AD 383
Obv. Legend illegible. Bust right.
Rev. VOT / X / MVLT / XX; all within wreath.
84. AE. 14 mm, 1.15 g, 12h.
Inv. C2012.048; SAg.12.1.1007.C005.
85. AE. 13 mm, 1.17 g, 6h.
Inv. C2016.089; SAg.16.1.4005.C179.

AD 383
Obv. Legend illegible. Bust right.
Rev. VOT / XX / MVLT / XXX all within wreath.
86. AE. 15 mm, 1.37 g, 6h.
Inv. C2016.124; SAg.16.1.4351.C202.

Valentinian II, Theodosius I, Arcadius
Thessalonica
AD 383–392
Obv. […]VS P F AVG; bust right, pearl diademed and draped.
Rev. [SALVS REI – PVB]LICAE; Victory left, trophy on shoulder, dragging captive; in field left, ⳨; in ex., TES.
Ref. *RIC* IX, 65; *LRBC* II, 1873–1875.
87. AE. 12/13 mm, 1.18 g, 6h.
Inv. C2015.123; SAg.15.1.4076.C097.

Uncertain mint
Obv. Legend illegible. Bust right.
Rev. [SALVS REI – PVBLICAE]; Victory left, trophy on shoulder, dragging captive; in field left, ⳨.
88. AE. 13 mm, 0.71 g, 12h.
Inv. C2012.111; SAg.12.2.2005.C047.

Thessalonica
AD 383–392
Obv. Worn.
Rev. Legend illegible. Two Victories facing one another, each holding wreath.
Ref. as *RIC* IX, 63; as *LRBC* II, 1867–1872 (Victoria Avg type 4).
89. AE. 12 mm, 0.37 g, 6h.
Inv. C2015.007; SAg.15.2.3000.C017.

Uncertain Mint
AD 383–392
Obv. Legend illegible; bust right.
Rev. [VIR]TVS E-[XERCITI]; emperor to right, holding standard and globe and spurning captive with left foot.
Ref. as *LRBC* II, Virtus Exercitus, type 1.
90. AE. 23 mm, 4.69 g, 6h.
Inv. C2012.134; SAg.12.2.2000.C065.

Uncertain Mint
AD 383–392
Obv. Bust right.
Rev. Legend illegible. Victory to left, trophy on shoulder, dragging captive.
Ref. as *LRBC* II, Salus Rei Publicae, type 1.

91. AE. 12/14 mm, 1.55 g, h?
    Inv. C2015.003; SAg.15.1.4064.C020.

Arcadius, Honorius or Theodosius II
Uncertain Mint
AD 406–408
Obv. Legend illegible. Bust right, pearl diademed and draped; star in left, field.
Rev. [GLORI-A ROMA-NORVM]; Legend illegible. Three emperors standing facing; the two outermost are taller, hold spear, rest hand on shield and turn towards each other; the innermost figure is smaller, holds spear and sometimes a globe; his head is turned right.
Ref. *RIC* X, 141a-159; Gloria Romanorum *LRBC* II, Type 21.
92. AE. 15/16 mm, 1.03 g, 6h.
    Inv. C2015.023; SAg.15.1.4065.C031.

Honorius or Theodosius II
Uncertain Mint
AD 408–423
Obv. Legend illegible. Bust right, pearl diademed and draped.
Rev. [GLORI-A ROMA-NORVM]; Legend illegible. Two emperors standing facing, heads turned to one another, each holding spear and resting hand on shield. In ex., SM[..].
Ref. *RIC* X, 395–406; Gloria Romanorum *LRBC* II, Type 22.
93. AE. 11/12 mm, 1.15g, 6h. clipped.
    Inv. C1995.013; PT stray, cleaning at northeast
94. AE. 14 mm, 0.96 g, 12h.
    Inv. C2012.131; SAg.12.2.2005.C064.
95. AE. 14 mm, 0.70 g, ?h. broken.
    Inv. C2012.121; SAg.12.2.2010.C057.

Obv. Legend illegible. Pearl diademed and draped bust right.
Rev. [GLORI-A ROMA-NORVM]; Two emperors facing, heads turned right and left; each hold spear and support globe between.
Ref. *LRBC* II, Gloria Romanorum, Type 23.
96. AE, 15 mm, 1.09g, 12h.
    Inv. PT.W.90, S.21

Theodosius II (AD 402–450)
Nicomedia
AD 402–403
Obv. [D N TH]EODOSI[VS P F AVG]; bust right, facing, helmeted, cuirassed; holding spear in right hand and shield in left.
Rev. CONCOR[DI-A AV]GG; Constantinople enthroned facing, head left, holding long sceptre and Victory on globe; beneath right foot, a prow. in ex., SMNΓ.
Ref. *RIC* X, 93.
97. AE. 15/17 mm, 2.26 g, 6h.
    Inv. PT.W.89.I, F.132.

Cyzicus
AD 402–403
Obv. [DN] THEOD[OSIVS P F AVG]; bust right, facing, helmeted, cuirassed; holding spear in right hand and shield in left.
Rev.[CONCORDI-A AVGG]; Constantinople enthroned facing, head left, holding long sceptre and Victory on globe; beneath right foot, a prow. in ex., SMKA.
Ref. *RIC* X, 96.
98. AE. 16/18 mm, 1.78 g, 6h.
    Inv. C2014.166; SAg.14.2.3045.C014.

Uncertain Mint
AD 425–435
Obv. Legend illegible. Draped and cuirassed bust right.
Rev. Cross within wreath.
Ref. *RIC* X, 440–455.
99. AE. 12 mm, 1.31 g, h?
    Inv. PT.SW.89.I, F.89.
100. AE. 12/13 mm, 1.31g, 12h.
    Inv. PT.W.90.I, S.11 (Pl. 97).
101. AE. 10 mm, 0.72 g, h?
    Inv. C2012.053; SAg.12.2.2005.C008.
102. AE. 11 mm, 0.72 g, 6h.
    Inv. C2012.120; SAg.12.2.2010.C056.

Marcian (AD 450–457)
Nicomedia
Obv. [D N MARCIANVS P F AVG]; draped and cuirassed bust right.
Rev. B, monogram within complete wreath; in ex. [N]ICA.
Ref. *RIC* X, 547 (monogram 5).
103. AE. 8 mm, 0.40 g, h?.
    Inv. C2012.144; SAg.12.2.2011.C067.

Cyzicus
Obv. [D N MARCIANVS P F AVG]; draped and cuirassed bust right.
Rev. D, monogram within broken wreath; in ex. SMKA.
Ref. *RIC* X, 560 (monogram 7).
104. AE. 9/10 mm, 0.96 g, 6h.
    Inv. C2015.034; SAg.15.2.2015.C019.

Leo I (AD 457–474)
Heraclea, Constantinople or Nicomedia?
Obv. Legend illegible; draped and cuirassed bust right.
Rev. Lion standing left; above, star; all within wreath.
Ref. *RIC* X, 666–669.
105. AE. 9 mm, 0.49 g, 12h.
    Inv. PT.90, Sondage 4. S. 1. Obv.]LEO[
106. AE. 8 mm, 0.52 g, 6h.
    Inv. C2016.106; SAg.16.1.4281.C188.

Alexandria?[5]
Obv. Legend illegible; draped and cuirassed bust right.
Rev. Lion standing left; above, cross; all within wreath.
Ref. *RIC* X, 670.
107. AE. 8 mm, 0.40 g, 6h.
    Inv. C2013.053; SAg.13.1.3022.C009.
108. AE. 9 mm, 0.89 g, 12h.
    Inv. C2012.087; SAg.12.2.2011.C028.

Uncertain Mint
Obv. Bust right, worn.
Rev. Leo's Latin monogram (type 1) within wreath.
Ref. Cf. *RIC* X, 681–693.
109. AE. 8 mm, 0.35 g, 12h.
    Inv. C2014.163; SAg.14.2.3045.C011.

Constantinople
Obv. D N – LEO; draped and cuirassed bust right.
Rev. Emperor left, dragging captive; in left field, cross; in ex., [C]ON.
Ref. *RIC* X, 701.

---

5 Although mint marks are not visible, a cross over the lion seems to be used only by Alexandria according to *RIC* X. This should be questioned with the new Aphrodisias evidence, as Alexandria is not represented among its late Roman coins. We have kept the catalogue as it is in order to keep *RIC* X reference numbers.

110. AE. 8 mm, 0.83 g, 12h.
   Inv. C2017.024; SAg.17.1.4419.C223.

Obv. [D N L]EO […]; draped and cuirassed bust right.
Rev. Emperor left, dragging captive; in left field, cross; in ex., CON.
Ref. *RIC* X, 700–702.
111. AE. 8 mm, 0.79 g, h?
   Inv. C2014.156; SAg.14.2.3045.C004.

Obv. D N L-[EO]; draped and cuirassed bust right.
Rev. Emperor left, dragging captive; in left field, star; in ex., CN.
Ref. *RIC* X, 703.
112. AE. 9 mm, 0.19 g, h?
   Inv. C2012.049; SAg.12.2.2005.C007.

Uncertain mint
Obv. Legend illegible; draped and cuirassed bust right.
Rev. Emperor left, dragging captive.
Ref. *RIC* X, 698–712.
113. AE. 9 mm, 0.39 g, 6h.
   Inv. C2016.024; SAg.16.1.4260.C120. *Rev.* in left field, star.
114. AE. 12 mm, 0.95 g, h?
   Inv. C2012.046; SAg.12.2.2007.C005. *Rev.* in left field, star.
115. AE. 9/11 mm, 0.66 g, 12h.
   Inv. C2015.076; SAg.15.2.3042.C031. *Rev.* in left field, cross.
116. AE. 8/9 mm, 0.30 g, h?
   Inv. C2017.052; SAg.17.1.4485.C250. *Rev.* in left field, cross.
117. AE. 9/10 mm, 0.99 g, 12h.
   Inv. C2016.079; SAg.16.1.4255.C170.
118. AE. 9 mm, 0.52 g, 6h.
   Inv. C2015.078; SAg.15.2.3042.C033. *Rev.* in left field, cross.

Uncertain mint
Obv. D N LEO PERPET [AVG]; draped and cuirassed bust right.
Rev. b – E; Empress stg facing, holding cross on globe and transverse sceptre.
Ref. *RIC* X, 718.
119. AE. 10 mm, 0.84 g, 12h.
   Inv. C2015.072; SAg.15.2.3042.C024.

Uncertain mint
Obv. Legend illegible; draped and cuirassed bust right.
Rev. b – E; Empress stg facing, holding cross on globe and transverse sceptre.
Ref. *RIC* X, 713–718.
120. AE. 11 mm, 0.40 g, 12h.
   Inv. C2012.130; SAg.12.2.2005.C063.
121. AE. 9 mm, 0.30 g, 12h.
   Inv. C2015.057; SAg.15.2.3042.C025.

Constantinople
AD 473/4
Obv. Worn.
Rev. No legend. Two emperors or an emperor and an empress, nimbate, enthroned, facing; above, cross.
Ref. *LRBC* II, 2276; *RIC* X, 724.
122. AE. 7/9 mm, 0.54 g, 6h.
   Inv. C2015.070; SAg.15.2.3042.C027.

Zeno (AD 476–491)
Uncertain mint
Obv. Diademed, draped and cuirassed helmeted bust right.
Rev. Victory advancing left head left, holding wreath and dragging captive with left hand cross in left field.
Ref. *RIC* X, 947.
123. AE. 11 mm, 0.43g, 12h.
   Inv. C2012.163; SAg.12.2.2012.C071.

Obv. Legend illegible; draped, cuirassed and helmeted bust right; cross on helmet.
Rev. ZE-NO (various letter arrangements); emperor standing facing, holding standard and cross on globe.
Ref. *RIC* X, 953?
124. AE. 8 mm, 0.47 g, 12h broken.
   Inv. C1995.042; PT, stray, west channel near west exit; rev. [Z/E]-N/[O].
125. AE. 9 mm, 0.85 g, 6h.
   Inv. C2012.082; SAg.12.2.2011.C026; rev. [Z-E]/N-O.
126. AE. 10 mm, 0.75 g, 12h.
   Inv. C2012.129; SAg.12.2.2010.C062.
127. AE. 9/10 mm, 0.84 g 6?
   Inv. C2012.209; SAg.12.1.1015.C013; rev. [Z-E]/N-O.
128. AE. 9 mm, 0.50 g, h?
   Inv. C2014.157; SAg.14.2.3045.C005; rev. [Z]-E/[N]-O.
129. AE. 8 mm, 0.76 g, 6h.
   Inv. C2014.161; SAg.14.2.3045.C009.
130. AE. 8 mm, 0.30 g, 6h, broken.
   Inv. C2014.162; SAg.14.2.3045.C010; rev. Z-E/N-O.
131. AE. 9 mm, 0.25 g, 12h.
   Inv. C2015.077; SAg.15.2.3042.C032; rev. [Z]-E/[N]-O.
132. AE. 9 mm, 0.46 g, h?
   Inv. C2016.073; SAg.16.1.4278.C164. Rev. Z-[E]/N-[O].

Monograms of uncertain emperors
Uncertain mint
AD 450–498
Obv. Bust right.
Rev. Monogram.
133. AE. 7 mm, 0.44 g, h? (holed).
   Inv. C2015.071; SAg.15.2.3042.C026.
134. AE. 9/10 mm, 0.68 g, h?
   Inv. C2014.165; SAg.14.2.3045.C013.
135. AE. 10 mm, 1.00 g, h?
   Inv. C2014.099; SAg.14.2.3002.C002.
136. AE. 9/10 mm, 0.50 g, h?
   Inv. C2014.158; SAg.14.2.3045.C006.
137. AE. 7/8 mm, 0.46 g, h?
   Inv. C2014.160; SAg.14.2.3045.C008.

Kingdom of Italy
Odovacar (AD 476–493)
Ravenna?
AD 477
Obv. [ODO-VAC]; bust draped and cuirassed right.
Rev. Monogram of Odovacar within wreath.
Ref. *BMC Vandals*, 10; as *RIC* X, 3502 (unlisted monogram variation).
138. AE. 9/10 mm, 0.87 g, 6h.
   Inv. C2014.155; SAg.14.2.3045.C003.

Lead Tessera
Fifth cent. AD?
Obv. and rev. unstruck.
139. AE. 10/12 mm, 0.94 g, h?
   Inv. C2015.088; SAg.15.1.4091.C070.

F. UNIDENTIFIED LATE ROMAN COINS

Table 24 contains coins too corroded or worn to be identified but quite possibly belonging to the late Roman period because of their sizes and formats. All coins are AE.

Table 24. Unidentified late Roman coins.

Nr.	Trench	Context	6–10 mm	11–15 mm	16–20 mm	21–25 mm	Total
140–142	PT.SW.89.I			1	2		3
143	PT.W.89.I			1			1
144–155	PT.W.90.I		3	8	1		12
156 157	PT.SW.90.I		1	1			2
158	SAg 12.1	1030		1			1
159	SAg 12.1	1041		1			1
160	SAg 12.1	1043		1			1
161–162	SAg 12.1	1061		2			2
163–173	SAg 12.2	2005	6	5			11
174–190	SAg 12.2	2010	3	10	3	1	17
191–193	SAg 12.2	2012	3				3
194–195	SAg 12.2	2015	1	1			2
196	SAg 12.2	2016		1			1
197	SAg 12.2	2028	1				1
198–199	SAg 13.2	4018		2			2
200	SAg 14.3	5019		1			1
201	SAg 14.2	3002		1			1
202	SAg 14.2	3045	1				1
203	SAg 15.1	8006		1			1
204	SAg 15.1	4048		1			1
205	SAg 15.2	3060		1			1
206–208	SAg 15.2	3042	3				3
209–221	SAg 16.1	4278	10	3			13
222	SAg 16.1	4293			1		1
223	SAg 16.1	4355		1			1
224	SAg 14.3	5000	1				1
225–227	SAg 14.3	5001		2	1		3
228	SAg 17.1	4402		1			1
229	SAg 17.1	4409		1			1
230	SAg 17.1	4419		1			1
231	SAg 17.1	4420			1		1
232	SAg 17.1	4438		1			1
233	SAg 17.1	4482		1			1
234	SAg 17.2	5032		1			1
Total			33	52	9	1	95

G. BYZANTINE COINS

Justin I (AD 518–527)
Constantinople
AD 518–527
Obv. D N IVSTI-NVS P P AVG; bust right, with diadem, cuirass and paludamentum.
Rev. M; above, cross; to left, and right, stars; beneath, Γ; in ex., CON.
Ref. *DOC* I, 8c; *MIBE* I, 11; *Paris* I, 2/8.
235. AE. 31/33 mm, 19.00 g, 6h.
Inv. PT.W.89.I (Pl. 97).

Obv. [D N IVS]TI-[NVS P P AVC]; bust right, wearing diadem with cross, cuirass and paludamentum.
Rev. M; above cross; to left, star and right, cross; beneath, A; in ex., CON.
Ref. *DOC* I, 9a; *MIBE* I, 12; *Paris* I, 2/11–12.
236. AE. 29/33 mm, 13.89 g, 6h.
Inv. C2017.050; SAg.17.1.4485.C249.

Obv. D N IVSTI-[NVS P P AVC]; bust right, with diadem, cuirass and paludamentum.
Rev. ⚹; to left, Γ; to right, Є.
Ref. *DOC* I, 21c, *MIBE* I, 32; *Paris* I, 2/Cp/31–33.
237. AE. 13/15 mm, 1.73 g, 6h.
Inv. C2016.077; SAg.16.1.4278.C168.

Justinian I (AD 527–565)
Constantinople
AD 539/40
Obv. D N IVSTINI-ANVS P P AVC; bust facing, in helmet with plume, diadem and cuirass; in right hand, *globus cruciger*; on left shoulder, shield with horseman device; in right field, cross.
Rev. M; above, cross; to left, A/N/N/O; to right, X/III; beneath, Γ; in ex., CON.
Ref. *DOC* I, 38c; *MIBE* I, 95a¹; *Paris* I, 4/Cp/41–43.
238. AE. 35 mm, 17.03 g, 6h.
Inv. C2012.059; SAg.12.2.2005.C001.
239. AE. 39/41 mm, 20.98 g, 6h.
Inv. C2017.048; SAg.17.1.4402.C247.

AD 541/2
Obv. D N IVSTINI-ANVS P P AVC; bust facing, in helmet with plume, diadem and cuirass; in right hand, *globus cruciger*; on left shoulder, shield with horseman device; in right field, cross.
Rev. M; above, cross; to left, A/N/N/O; to right, X/Ч; beneath, Є; in ex., CON.
Ref. *DOC* I, 40e; *MIBE* I, 95a¹; *Paris* I, 4/Cp/65.
240. AE. 39/40 mm, 22.11 g, 6h.
Inv. C2017.055; SAg.17.1.4482.C237.

AD 547/8
Obv. D N IVSTINI-ANVS P P AVC; bust facing, in helmet with plume, diadem and cuirass; in right hand, *globus cruciger*; on left shoulder, shield with horseman device; in right field, cross.
Rev. K; above, cross; to left, A/N/N/O; to right X/X/I; beneath, Δ.
Ref. as *DOC* I, 70; *MIBE* I, 96.
241. AE. 24/25 mm, 8.42 g, 6h.
Inv. C2015.083; SAg.15.1.4000.C065.

Nicomedia
AD 545/6
Obv. D N IVSTINI-ANVS P P AVC; bust facing, in helmet with plume, diadem and cuirass; in right hand, *globus cruciger*; on left shoulder, shield with horseman device; in right field, cross.
Rev. M; above, ₽; to left, A/N/N/O; to right, X/Ч/II/II; beneath, B; in ex., NIKO.
Ref. *DOC* I, 125b; *MIBE* I, 113b; *Paris* I, 4/Ni/24.
242. AE. 34/35 mm, 18.99 g, 6h.
Inv. C2015.026; SAg.15.1.4000.C038 (Pl. 97).

Antioch
AD 539/40
Obv. D N [IVSTINI-ANVS P P] AVC; bust facing, in helmet with plume, diadem and cuirass; in right hand, *globus cruciger*; on left shoulder, shield with horseman device; in right field, cross.
Rev. K; above cross, A/N/N/O left and year XIII right; below, ΘY.
Ref. *MIBE* I, 152.
243. AE. 29/31 mm, 9.13 g, 12h.
Inv. C1995.012; PT, cleaning, channel west of basin.

AD 542/3
Obv. [D N IVSTINI-ANVS P P AVC]; bust facing, in helmet with plume, diadem and cuirass; in right hand, *globus cruciger*; on left shoulder, shield with horseman device; in right field, cross.
Rev. M; above, cross; to left, [A/N]/N/O; to right, XU/⚹; beneath, Γ; in ex., C̄HЄЧPo.
Ref. As *DOC* I, 216b; *MIBE* I, 144b.
244. AE. 30/33 mm, 5, 15.58 g.
Inv. C2017.023; SAg.17.1.4402.C220.

Carthage
AD 534–537
Obv. Illegible.
Rev. A.
Ref. *MIBE* I, 192–193.
245. AE. 8 mm.; 0.14g.
Inv. C2016.125; SAg.16.1.4319.C200.

AD 539/40
Obv. D N [IVSTINI-A]NV[S P P A]VC; bust facing, in helmet with plume, diadem and cuirass; in right hand, *globus cruciger*; on left shoulder, shield with horseman device; in right field, cross.
Rev. K; above, cross; left, A/N/N/O; beneath S; to right, X/III; in ex., CAR.
Ref. As *DOC* I, 295; *MIBE* I, 197; *Paris* I, 4/Ct/22–24.
246. AE. 31/32 mm, 13.40 g, 2h.
Inv. C2017.054; SAg.17.1.4448.C236.

Vandals of North Africa
Carthage
6th cent. AD (Gelimer? AD 530–533)[6]
Obv. Worn.
Rev. Palm tree, on right inverted G.
Ref. As *BMC Vandals*, 68–72; Morrisson 1990, 243, table 1, 13; Asolati 1995; *MIBEC* II, 134a-b.[7]
247. AE. 10/11 mm, 0.31 g, h?
Inv. PT.W.89.I, F.39.

Justin II (AD 565–578)
Constantinople
AD 567/8
Obv. [D N IVSTI-NVS P P AVC]; Justin, on left and Sophia, on right, seated, nimbate, on double lyre-backed throne; he holds in right hand, *globus cruciger*, she holds cruciform sceptre.

---

6 See Bijovsky 2011: 166–167 for arguments favouring a later dating (Justinianic, after AD 534) for these coins.

7 *MIBEC* II treats these types as even later, contemporary with Maurice Tiberius.

Rev. M; above, cross; to left, A/N/N/O; to right, III; beneath, Γ; in ex., CON.
Ref. *DOC* I, 24c; *MIBE*C II, 43a.
248. AE. 30 mm, 13.79 g, 6h.
Inv. C2012.070; SAg.12.2.2005.C019.

AD 568/9
Obv. [D N IVSTI-NVS P P AVC]; Justin, on left and Sophia, on right, seated, nimbate, on double lyre-backed throne; he holds in right hand, *globus cruciger*, she holds cruciform sceptre.
Rev. M; above, cross; to left, A/N/N/O; to right, II/II; beneath, Γ; in ex., CON.
Ref. *DOC* I, 25c; *MIBE*C II, 43a.
249. AE. 28 mm, 12.23 g, 6h.
Inv. PT.W.88.I.

AD 570/71
Obv. [D N IVSTI-NVS P P AVC]; Justin, on left and Sophia, on right, seated, nimbate, on double lyre-backed throne; he holds in right hand, *globus cruciger*, she holds cruciform sceptre.
Rev. K; above, ✱; to left, A/N/N/O; to right, Ⲩ; in ex., Δ.
Ref. *DOC* I, 49c; *MIBE*C II, 44d.
250. AE. 22/23 mm, 6.13 g, 6h.
Inv. C2017.049; SAg.17.1.4485.C248.

AD 576/7
Obv. D N IVST[I-NVS P P AVC]; Justin, on left and Sophia, on right, seated, nimbate, on double lyre-backed throne; he holds in right hand, *globus cruciger*, she holds cruciform sceptre.
Rev. M; above, cross; to right, A/N/N/O; to right, X/II; beneath, B; in ex., CON.
Ref. *DOC* I, 42b; *MIBE*C II, 43a.
251. AE. 29/31 mm, 12.27 g, 6h.
Inv. C2014.043; SAg.14.1.4000.C010.

Thessalonica
AD 568/9
Obv. [D N I]VSTI-NVS P P A[VI]; Justin, on left and Sophia, on right, seated, nimbate, on double lyre-backed throne; he holds in right hand, *globus cruciger*, she holds cruciform sceptre.
Rev. K; above, cross; to left, A/N/N/O; to right, Δ; in ex., TЄS
Ref. *DOC* I, 65, *MIBE*C II, 70a; *Paris* I, 5/Th/6.
252. AE. 21/22 mm, 4.60 g, 6h.
Inv. C2015.010; SAg.15.1.4064.C025 (Pl. 97).

Nicomedia
AD 565–578
Obv. Monogram.
Rev. Є; to right, N.
Ref. *DOC* I, 116; *MIBE*C II, 49; *Paris* I, 5/Ni/41–44.
253. AE. 15/16 mm, 1.72 g, 6h.
Inv. PT.W.89.I, F.146.

Antioch
AD 565–578
Obv. Monogram.
Rev. Є; to right, ✝.
Ref. *DOC* I, 185 or 186; *MIBE*C II, 65a or 65b; *Paris* I, 5/An/47–50.
254. AE. 11/12 mm, 0, 83 g; h?
Inv. C2016.087; SAg.16.1.4278.C177.

Tiberius II (AD 578–582)
Constantinople
AD 578/9
Obv. [Ỏ] M TIb CONS-TANT P P A[VI]; bust facing, wearing consular robes and crown with cross and *pendilia*; in right hand, *mappa*; in left, sceptre with eagle surmounted by a cross.
Rev. m; above, cross; to left, A/N/N/O; to right, II/II; in ex., CON.
Ref. *MIBE*C II, 24.
255. AE. 34/38 mm, 16.15 g, 6h.
Inv. PT.W.88.I, F. 49 (Pl. 97).

AD 580/1
Obv. [Ỏ] M TI[b CON]- STANT P [P AVI]; bust facing, wearing consular robes and crown with cross and *pendilia*; in right hand, *mappa*; in left, sceptre with eagle surmounted by a cross.
Rev. m; above, cross; to left, A/N/N/O; to right, Ⲩ I; in ex., CONЄ.
Ref. *DOC* I, 13e; *MIBE*C II, 25; *Paris* I, 6/Cp/12–13.
256. AE. 32mm, 11.81 g, 6h.
Inv. PT.W.89.I, F.65.

Nicomedia
AD 580/1
Obv. [Ỏ] M TI[b CONS-TANT P P AVI]; bust facing, wearing consular robes and crown with cross and *pendilia*; in right hand, *mappa*; in left, sceptre with eagle surmounted by a cross.
Rev. m; above, cross; to left, A/N/N/O; to right, Ⲩ I; in ex., NIKOB.
Ref. *DOC* I, 30b; *MIBE*C II, 35; *Paris* I, 6/Ni/2.
257. AE. 27/28 mm, 10.36 g, 6h.
Inv. PT.W.88.I, F. 45.

Maurice (AD 582–602)
Constantinople
AD 582/3
Obv. O N MAV-RIC P P AVC; Bust facing, in cuirass and crown with cross, holding *globus cruciger*
Rev. K; above, cross; to left, A/N/N/O; to right, I; beneath, Δ.
Ref. *DOC* I, 46b, *MIBE*C II, 69B.
258. AE. 20 mm, 4.76 g, 6h.
Inv. C2016.128; SAg.16.1.4320.C201.

AD 587/8
Obv. O N [MAVRC] – TIbЄR P P AV; Bust facing in cuirass and helmet with plume and *pendilia*; in right hand, holds *globus cruciger*; on left shoulder, shield.
Rev. M; above, cross; to left, A/N/N/O; to left, Ⲩ; beneath, A; in ex., CON.
Ref. As *DOC* I, 29a; *MIBE*C II, 67D; *Paris* I, 7/Cp/39.
259. AE. 26/27 mm, 10.34 g, 6h.
Inv. PT.W.88.I, F.43.

AD 589/90
Obv. [O N MAVRC] – TIbЄR P P AV; Bust facing in cuirass and helmet with plume and *pendilia*. In right hand holds *globus cruciger*. On left shoulder shield.
Rev. M; above, cross; to left, A/N/N/O; to right, Ⲩ/II (?); beneath, B; in ex., [C]ON.
Ref. *DOC* I, 31b; *MIB* II, 67D.
260. AE. 28/30 mm, 9.42 g, 6h.
Inv. PT.W.88.I, F.3.

AD 590/91
Obv. D N MAVRIC – TIbЄR P P AVG; Bust facing in cuirass and helmet with plume and *pendilia*. In right hand holds *globus cruciger*. On left shoulder shield. Overstruck.

Rev. M; above, cross; to left, A/N/N/O; to right, Ʉ/II; beneath, Γ; in ex., CON.
Ref. *DOC* I, 32c; *MIBEC* II, 67D.
261. AE. 28/33 mm, 11.66 g, 8h.
                                                    Inv. PT.SE.90.III.

Nicomedia
AD 587/8
Obv. Legend illegible. Bust facing, wearing cuirass and crown. In right hand holds *globus cruciger*. On left shoulder, shield.
Rev. M; to left, A/N/N/O; to right, Ʉ; beneath, B; in ex., NIKO.
Ref. *DOC* I, 96b; *MIBEC* II, 75D; *Paris* I, 7/Ni/4.
262. AE. 29 mm, 8.13 g, 6h.
                     Inv. C2012.052; SAg.12.2.2005.C006.

Cyzicus
AD 585/6
Obv. Legend illegible. Bust facing in cuirass and helmet with plume and *pendilia*. In right hand holds *globus cruciger*. On left shoulder shield with horseman device.
Rev. M; above, cross; to left, A/N/N/O; to right, II/II; beneath, B; in ex., KYZ.
Ref. *DOC* I, 121b; *MIBEC* II, 84D; *Paris* I, 7/Cy/4.
263. AE. 29 mm, 10.17 g, 6h.
                     Inv. C2012.065; SAg.12.2.2005.C015.

Antioch
AD 594/5
Obv. Legend illegible. Bust facing in consular robes and crown with trefoil ornament. In right hand *mappa*, in left, eagle-topped sceptre.
Rev. K; above, cross; to left, A/N/[N/O]; to right, XIII; beneath, Ꝓ; in ex., CON.
Ref. *MIBEC* II, 99C.
264. AE. 21/23 mm, 3.79 g, 12h.
                     Inv. C2013.021; SAg.13.1.3004.C005.

Uncertain Mint
AD 582–602
Obv. [.]TIbЄ[.]; Bust facing.
Rev. M; worn.
265. AE. 30/31 mm, 8.08 g, 12h.
                                      Inv. PT.SW.89.I, F.65.

Phocas (AD 602–610)
Constantinople
AD 603/4
Obv. Worn. To left Phocas stg, wearing chlamys and crown with pendilia; in right hand, *globus cruciger*; to right, Leontia stg, crowned and nimbate, holding cruciform sceptre transversely in right hand; between heads, cross. M overstruck on M.
Rev. m; above, cross; to left, A/N/N/O; to right, II; in ex., CONA; Overstruck on bust right (slightly seen, but pre-Justinian I's coin reform types).
Ref. *DOC* II.I, 25a; *MIBEC* II, 60a.
266. AE. 28/31 mm, 11.18 g, h?
                                     Inv. PT.W.89.I, F.66.

AD 602/3
Obv. [ẟ M FOCA – P P AVC]; To left Phocas stg, crowned, holding *globus cruciger*; to right, Leontia stg, crowned and nimbate holding cruciform sceptre transversely in right hand; between heads, cross.
Rev. XX; above, cross; in ex., CO[N.].
Ref. *DOC* II.I, 35; *MIBEC* II, 64a; *Paris* I, 8/Cp/2 (Off. B).
267. 23 mm, 5.18 g, 6h?
                     Inv. C2016.085; SAg.16.1.4278.C175.

AD 603–610
Obv. ẟ N FOC[AS – PERP AVC]; bust facing, wearing consular robes and crown with cross; in right hand, *mappa*; in left, cross.
Rev. X.X; above, star; in ex., CONA.
Ref. *DOC* II.I, 37a; *MIBEC* II, 65b.
268. AE. 22 mm, 4.13 g, 2h.
                     Inv. C2015.113; SAg.15.1.4177.C092.
269. AE. 23/25 mm, 5.70g, 6h.
                     Inv. C2012.069, SAg.12.2.2005.C018.

Nicomedia
AD 605/6
Obv. [ẟ M FOCA – PER AVϨ]; bust facing, wearing consular robes and crown with *pendilia*; in right hand, *mappa*; in left, cross.
Rev. XXXX; above, ANNO; to right, II/II; in ex. NIKO[.].
Ref. As *DOC* II.I, 57; *MIBEC* II, 69b; *Paris* I, 8/Ni/1–2.
270. AE. 20/32 mm, 11.18 g, 6h.
                     Inv. C2017.002; SAg.17.1.4482.C238.

Obv. [ẟ M FOCA] – PER A[VϨ]; bust facing, wearing consular robes and crown with cross on circlet; in right hand, *mappa*; in left, cross.
Rev. XX; above, cross; to right, II/II; in ex., NIKO[.].
Ref. *DOC* II-1, 65; *MIBEC* II, 73a.
271. AE. 24 mm, 5.12 g, 12h.
                     Inv. C2012.071; SAg.12.2.2005.C020.

Cyzicus
AD 607/8
Obv. [ẟ N] FOCAS – PERP AVC; bust facing, wearing consular robes and crown with cross on circlet; in right hand, *mappa*; in left, cross; in field left, cross.
Rev. XXXX; above, ANNO; to right, Ʉ; in ex., KYZB.
Ref. *DOC* II.I, 73b; *MIBEC* II, 76; *Paris* I, 8/Cy/7–8.
272. AE. 31 mm, 11.01 g, 6h.
                     Inv. C2016.122; SAg.16.1.4318.C193.

Heraclius (AD 610–641)
Constantinople
AD 613
Obv. [dd NN hERACLI]-ɄS ET hER[A CONST P AV]; to left, Heraclius, and to right, Heraclius Constantine, both stg; each wear chlamys and crown with cross and holds *globus cruciger*. In right hand; between heads, cross. Overstruck on M. Tiberius?
Rev. M; above, ✠; to left, A/N/N/O; to right, II/I; beneath, Γ; in ex., CON.
Ref. *DOC* II.I, 76c, Class 2; *MIB* III, 160b[1]; *Paris* I, 10/Cp/17.
273. AE. 29/32 mm, 9.61 g, 7h.
                   Inv. C2015.015; SAg.15.1.4048.C029.

Obv. [dd NN hERACLI-ɄS ET hERA CONST P AV]; to left, Heraclius, and to right, Heraclius Constantine, both stg each wear chlamys and crown with cross and holds *globus cruciger*. In right hand; between heads, cross.
Rev. M; above, ✠; to left, A/N/N/O; to right, II/I; beneath, Δ; in ex., CON.
Ref. *DOC* II.I, 76d, Class 2; *MIB* III, 160b[2].
274. AE. 29/32 mm, 9.59 g, 12h.
                     Inv. C2017.007; SAg.17.1.4482.C239.

AD 613 or 613/4
Obv. [dd NN hERACLI-ɄS ET hERA CONST P AV]; to left, Heraclius, and to right, Heraclius Constantine, both stg; each wear chlamys and crown with cross and holds *globus cruciger*. In right hand; between heads, cross. Overstruck on Phocas XXXX nummi.
Rev. M; above, ✠; to left, A/N/N/O; to right, II/I?; beneath, ?; in ex., [C]ON.

275. AE. 30/31 mm, 10.49 g, 6h.
Inv. C2017.035; SAg.17.1.4482.C231.

AD 613–616
Obv. [dd NN hERACLI-YS ET hERA CONST P AV]; to left, Heraclius, and to right, Heraclius Constantine, both stg; each wears chlamys and crown with cross and holds *globus cruciger*. In right hand; between heads, cross.
Rev. M; above, ⚹; to left, [A/N/N/O]; to right, year ?; beneath, ?; in ex., [CO]N; overstruck on Phocas XXXX nummi.
276. AE. 32/33 mm, 14.02 g, 12h.
Inv. PT.E.90.I, S.4.

AD 624/5
Obv. No inscription. Three figures stg, facing; Heraclius, centre; Heraclius Constantine, to right; Martina, to left; each wear chlamys and crown with cross (Martina's also with loops and pendilia), and holds *globus cruciger*. No crosses in field.
Rev. M; above, cross and [ANN]O; to left ℞; to right, X/Ч; beneath, Γ; in ex., CON.
Ref. *DOC* II.I, 99a, Class 4; *MIB* III, 162a; *Paris* I, 10/Cp/51.
277. AE. 21/24 mm, 5.92 g, 12h.
Inv. C2017.038; SAg.17.1.4402.C230.

AD 631/2
Obv. To left, Heraclius stg, with moustache and long beard, wearing military dress and crown with cross; he holds in right hand long cross, left hand on hip; to right, Heraclius Constantine stg with short beard, wearing chlamys and crown with cross; in right hand, *globus cruciger*; between heads, cross; to left, ℞; to right, K.
Rev. M; above, cross and C; to right, A/N/N/O; to right, [X]/X/II; beneath, Δ; in ex., CON.
Ref. *DOC* II.I, 107b, Class 5; *MIB* III, 164b; *Paris* I, 10/Cp/74.
278. AE. 21/23 mm, 5.31g, 6h.
Inv. C2017.047; SAg.17.1.4466.C244.

AD 632/3
Obv. To left, Heraclius stg, with moustache and long beard, wearing military dress and crown with cross; he holds in right hand long cross, left hand on hip; to right, Heraclius Constantine stg with short beard, wearing chlamys and crown with cross; in right hand, *globus cruciger*; between heads, cross; to left, ℞; to right, K.
Rev. M; above, ⚹; to right, A/N/N/O; to left, [X]/X/II[I]; beneath A; in ex., CON.
Ref. *DOC* II.I, 109a, Class 5, small format; *MIB* III, 164c.
279. AE. 24/26 mm, 4.94 g, 7h.
Inv. C2017.040; SAg.17.1.4482.C233.

AD 634/5
Obv. To left, Heraclius stg, with moustache and long beard, wearing military dress and crown with cross; he holds in right hand long cross, left hand on hip; to right, Heraclius Constantine stg with short beard, wearing chlamys and crown with cross; in right hand, *globus cruciger*; between heads, cross; but no monograms.
Rev. M; above, ℞; to left, [A/N/N/O]; to right, [X]/X/Ч; beneath Є; in ex., CON.
Ref. *DOC* II.I, 112c, Class 5, small format; *MIB* III, 164d.
280. AE. 20/25 mm, 5.80 g, 6h.
Inv. C2017.046; SAg.17.1.4466.C243 (Pl. 97).

AD 632/3 to 634/5 (countermarked in Levant area between *c*. AD 660s to 685)
Obv. To left, Heraclius stg, with moustache and long beard, wearing military dress and crown with cross; he holds in right hand long cross, left hand on hip; to right, Heraclius Constantine (only partly visible) stg with short beard, wearing chlamys and crown with cross; in right hand, *globus cruciger*; between heads, cross. Overstruck.[8]
Rev. M; above, ⚹; to right, [A]/N/N/O; to right, [X/X/III, II/II or Ч]; beneath, Γ; in ex., CON; overstruck; to left elliptic countermark in Arabic *"lillah"* ("for God").
Ref. as *DOC* II.I, Class 5, small format, 109 or 111; *MIB* III, 164c; countermark: Schulze and Goodwin 2005, 42, fig. 1, B2, 44, 47.
281. AE. 22/24 mm, 5.37 g, 6h.
Inv. C2017.053; SAg.17.1.4471.C234 (Pl. 97).

Cyzicus
AD 610/11
Obv. ∂ N hRAC[LI – PERP AVC]; Bust facing, bearded, wearing cuirass and helmet with plume and pendilia; in right hand, *globus cruciger*; on left shoulder, shield with horseman device. Overstruck on M nummi of Maurice Tiberius]IbER[.
Rev. M; above, cross; to left, A/N/[N/O]; to right, I; in ex., KY[Z].
Ref. *DOC* II.I, 167, Class 1; *MIB* III, 184.
282. AE. 27/29 mm, 5.92 g, 6h.
Inv. C2017.014; SAg.17.1.4405.C213.

Anastasius I to Heraclius
Nicomedia
AD 498–641
Obv. Illegible.
Rev. M; in ex., NIKO.
283. AE. 30/33 mm, 7.17 g.
Inv. PT.SW.89.I, F.43.

Unknown Mint
Obv. Illegible.
Rev. M
284. AE. 32 mm, 11.45 g.
Inv. C2012.040; SAg.12.2.2003.C003.
285. AE. 26/29 mm, 10.09 g.
Inv. C2015.101; SAg.15.1.4076.C078.

Obv. Illegible.
Rev. K
286. AE. 18/21 mm, 5.51 g.
Inv. C2012.072; SAg.12.2.2005.C021.

Obv. Illegible.
Rev. I
287. AE. 13/15 mm, 0.82 g.
Inv. C2016.050; SAg.16.1.4268.C146.

Constans II (AD 641–668)
Constantinople
AD 642/3
Obv. [EN TȣTO – NIKA]; Constans standing facing, beardless, wearing chlamys and crown with cross; in right hand, long cross; in left *globus cruciger*.
Rev. m; to left, [O]/Ф/A; above, ANA; to right, N/Є/O/ς; in ex. to left A; to right, II.
Ref. *DOC* II.2, 61a, Class 2; *MIB* III, 163a; *Paris* I, 13/Cp/9 (off. Λ).

---

[8] The obverse of the coin is very worn and very difficult to understand. The size and flan shape of the coin means that it might also belong to Heraclius, Class VI, issued in AD 639/40 to 640/1, with three figures, including Heraclonas, with a similar reverse (*DOC* II.I, 125–127; *MIB* III, 166–167). The third figure on these coins is sometimes not visible because of poor minting. On the other hand, the monogram on top of the M on reverse only appears on Class V coins.

288. AE. 22 mm, 3.94 g, 12h.
Inv. C2012.171; SAg.12.1.1015.C012.

AD 643/44
Obv. [ЄN TȢT]-O NIKA; Constans standing facing, beardless, wearing chlamys and crown with cross; in right hand, stuff surmounted by ⚒; in left *globus cruciger*. Overstruck on Heraclius Class 6, 3 figures.⁹
Rev. ɯ; to left, +/I[II]/+; above, ANA; to right, N/Є/O/ς; in ex., Δ. Overstruck on M nummi; year X/X/[X].
Ref. *DOC* II.2, 62a, Class 3; *MIB* III, 164; *Paris* I, 13/Cp/14 (Off. illegible).
289. AE. 23/26 mm, 4.93 g, 6h.
Inv. C2017.039; SAg.17.1.4482.C232.

AD 645/6
Obv. ЄN T[ȢT-O NIKA]; Constans standing facing, beardless, wearing chlamys and crown with cross; in right hand, long cross; in left *globus cruciger*.
Rev. ɯ; above, cross; to left, [AN]A; to right, [N/Є/O/ς]; in ex. to right, A.
Ref. *DOC* II.2, 64a, Class 4; *MIB* III, 167b.
290. AE. 17/18 mm, 2.29 g, 12h.
Inv. C2013.042; SAg.13.2.4000.C007.

Syracuse
AD 650/1
Obv. Constans facing, with long beard, wearing chlamys and crown with cross on circlet. In right hand globe with cross. Clipped and worn.
Rev. M; above ☓, beneath S[CL].
Ref. *DOC* II.2, 178; *MIB* III, 207.
291. AE. 13/16 mm, 1.89 g, 6h.
Inv. C2017.030; SAg.17.1.4442.C228.

Constans II to Leo III
Uncertain Mint
AD 641–720
Obv. Illegible.
Rev. Small M (unrecognizable type due to corrosion).
292. AE. 17/20 mm, 1.81 g.
Inv. C2017.037; SAg.17.1.4442.C229.

Leo VI (AD 886–912)
Constantinople
Obv. +LЄON BAS-ILЄVS ROM'; Bust of Leo VI with short beard, facing, wearing chlamys and crown with cross; on right shoulder, roundel with central pellet; in left hand, akakia.
Rev. +LЄON / ЄN ΘЄO bA/SILЄVS R/OMЄON.
Ref. *DOC* III.2, 8, Class 3; *Paris* II, 35/Cp/14–55.
293. AE. 23/24 mm, 3.33 g, 6h.
Inv. C2015.045; SAg.15.1.4048.C053 (Pl. 97).
294. AE. 24/26 mm, 7.85 g, 6h.
Inv. C2016.125; SAg 16.1, 4339, C197.

Romanus I (AD 931–944)
Constantinople
AD 931–944
Obv. +RWM[AN · BAS-I]LЄVS [RWM'; Bust of Romanus I facing, bearded, wearing chlamys with tablion and heavy crown with cross; in right hand labarum sceptre topped by trefoil ornament; in left, globe with cross.

---
9 The undertype is a class 6, M nummi of Heraclius from year X/X/[X] (639/40), no mintmark visible; as *DOC* II.I, no 125; as *MIB* III, 166.

Rev. +RWMA/N' ЄN ΘЄW bA/SILЄVS RW/MAIWN
Ref. *DOC* III.2, 25b.
295. AE. 26/27 mm, 6.29 g, 5h.
Inv. C2016.035; SAg.16.1.4251.C131.

Nicephorus II (AD 963–969)
Obv. +NICIF b-ASILЄV RW; bust facing, wearing robe with V-shaped opening and crown with cross and pendilia. In right hand, cross sceptre; in left, globe surmounted by cross. Overstruck on Constantine VII's class V rev. some letters partly visible.
Rev. [+NICHF] / ЄN ΘЄW bA/SILЄVS RW/MAIWN; overstruck on Constantine VII's class V obv. +[CONST' bA]SIL' R[WM']; facing bust with crown partly visible.
Ref. *DOC* III.2, 7 (Class 1).
296. AE. 24/25 mm, 3.50 g, 5h.
Inv. PT.E.90.I, S.3.

Anonymous Follis, Class A2
Constantinople:
AD 976–1030/45
Obv. +ЄMMA-NOVHΛ; Bust of Christ facing, bearded, with nimbus cross having two pellets in each arm, wearing tunic and himation; right hand raised in blessing in sling of cloak, left holds books with ornate cover (central pellets in border of dots) from beneath; in field, IC̅-X̅C̅.
Rev. +IhSꞶS / XRISTꞶS / bASILЄꞶ / bASILЄ'.
297. AE. 29/32 mm, 10.44 g, 10h.
Inv. C2015.105; SAg.15.1.4076.C084.
Ref. *DOC* III.2, A2 var. 20.
298. AE. 23/26 mm, 7.75 g, 6h.
Inv. PT.E.90.II, S.7. Ref. *DOC* III.2, A2 var.24
299. AE. 31/32 mm, 14.27 g, 6h.
Inv. C2014.022; SAg.14.1.4000.C008.
Ref. *DOC* III.2, A2 var. 24b.
300. AE. 26/30 mm, 9.81 g, 6h.
Inv. C2014.004; SAg.14.1.1000.C004.
Ref. *DOC* III.2, A2 var. 32; *Paris* II, 41/Cp/15.
301. AE. 19/29 mm (k), 4.70 g, 11h.
Inv. C2016.014; SAg.16.1.4247.C110.
Ref. *DOC* III.2, A2 var. 42a.
302. AE. 32/34 mm, 14.74 g, h?
Inv. PT.W.88.I, F.4; A2 Var.?
303. AE. 26/30 mm, 7.55 g, 6h.
Inv. PT.SW.89.I, F.38. A2 Var.?
304. AE. 25/31 mm (cut), 8.43 g, 2h. (holed)
Inv. C2016.105; SAg.16.1.4200.C187. A2 Var.?

Anonymous Follis, Class C
Constantinople
AD 1042?–c. 1050
Obv. +ЄMMA-NOVHΛ; Three-quarter-length figure of Christ Antiphonetes facing, bearded, with cross nimbus having pellet in each arm, wearing tunic and himation; right hand raised in blessing in front of body; left holds book with ornate on cover; in field, IC̅-X̅C̅.
Rev. IC̅-X̅C̅ / NI-KA; in angles of jewelled cross with pellet at end of each arm.
Ref. *DOC* III.2, C2.48; *Paris* II, 41/Cp/86–106.
305. AE. 27/29 mm, 8.10 g, 6h.
Inv. C2013.113; SAg.13.2.4042.C032.

Anonymous Follis, Class D
Constantinople
AD *c.* 1050–*c.* 1060

Obv. No inscription. Christ seated on square-backed throne facing, bearded, with cross nimbus having pellet in each arm, wearing tunic and himation; right hand raised in blessing in sling of cloak, left holds books with ∴ on cover, by spine on knee; in field, IC-XC.
Rev. -+- / ISXS / bASILE / bASIL / -ᴗ-.
Ref. *DOC* III.2, D; *Paris* II, 41/Cp/107–119.
306. AE. 31 mm, 7.60 g, 6h.
Inv. C2012.051; SAg.12.1.1007.C006.
307. AE. 29/32 mm, 7.56 g, 6h. (holed).
Inv. C2015.044; SAg.15.1.4048.C052.

Manuel I (AD 1143–1180)
AD 1167–1183
Obv. IC – XC in field; Christ, nimbate, wearing tunic and kolobion, seated upon throne without back; holds Bible in left hand. Pellet in each limb of nimbus cross.
Rev. MANȢH[Λ] – ΔECΠOT; [MP ΘV] in upper right field. Emperor standing facing on left is being crowned by Virgin Mary standing on right.
Ref. *DOC* IV.1, 13a.1–2; *Paris* II, 61/Cp/3.
308. Bill., 28/29 mm, 4.43 g, 6h. (holed).
Inv. C2013.022; SAg.13.2.4000.C002 (Pl. 97).

H. MEDIEVAL EUROPEAN COINS

Wallachia
Mircea I Batran (AD 1386–1418)
AD 1386–1405
Obv. +IѠMY[...а]ΘЕО; coat of arms of Wallachia with sigil X inside the shield right.
Rev. [+]IѠMY[...аΘЕО]; eagle standing left on helmet; head turned right; sigil M on left field.
Ref. MBR, 184; Oberläder-Târnoveanu 2012, VIII.30.
309. AR, ducat, 12/13 mm, 0.32 g, 10h?
Inv. C2016.094; SAg.16.1.4281.C182 (Pl. 97).

APPENDIX 4

Catalogue of Islamic Coin Finds

Betül Teoman and Gültekin Teoman

During our brief visit to Aphrodisias in 2018 we could only study 98 coins excavated from the Place of Palms that belong to the Turkish period. We hope that the following commentary and catalogue is representative of the total finds. These coins cover the period between the Sultanate of Rûm, with the earliest belonging to Sultan Gıyaseddin Keyhüsrev I, dated to 1266–1284, various Anatolian Beyliks, to the Ottoman Empire and the modern Turkish Republic. Eight of the coins could not be identified further, but can be defined as belonging to these periods.

Three fals belong to the Sultanate of Rûm, and were issued under Gıyaseddin Keyhüsrev I, Alaeddin Keykubad I and Gıyaseddin Keyhüsrev III; these are the earliest Turkish coins found in the Place of Palms. Three Beyliks—the Germiyanids, Menteshe and Saruhanids—are each represented by single coins, but the most numerous find groups belong to the Aydinids and the Ottoman Empire. The Aydinids, in whose territory Aphrodisias was situated, are represented by 11 examples. Among these is a rare mangir of Umur II. Two other mangirs belong to Cüneyd Gazi and eight are anonymous examples with no ruler's name on them. Most of the anonymous examples have six-armed star designs, the 'Mühr-i Süleyman'. The motif was even used by pre-Islamic Turkish states and is a common design on western Anatolian Beylik coins, apart from the Saruhanids. It is used as either a central design or a border around the inscription.

A total of 49 Ottoman coins have been recorded in the Place of Palms, belonging to Sultans Bayezid I, Murad II, Mehmed II, Bayezid II, Selim I, Suleyman I, Mehmed III, Ahmed III, Mahmud I, Mahmud II, Abdülmecid, Abdülaziz, and Mehmed V Resad. These coins were minted at various mints including Ayasuluk, Bursa, Enguriye, Halep, Ladik, Tire, Edirne, Serez, Sidrekapsi, Kostantiniyye and Misr (Egypt). On six coins the mints could not be determined. The early anonymous manghirs of the Ottoman Empire, which do not have the names of sultans on them, can be roughly dated by various forms of prayers inscribed on them: for example the 'Hullide Mülkuhu' prayer ('may his reign/governance last long') is commonly used on coins minted between the reigns of Orhan Gazi and Mehmed II. During the last years of Mehmed II's reign, in addition to the 'Hullide Mülkuhu' prayer, with the Mamluk influence, the 'Azze nasruhu' ('May Allah help him to be victorious') prayer also starts to be added to coinage. By this time of Bayezid II only this second prayer remains on the coinage. Therefore, in the catalogue below, we have dated the anonymous mangirs using these criteria.

A. SULTANATE OF RÛM

Keyhüsrev I (1204–1211)
No Mint
(1204–1211)
Obv. Horseman with sword over the right shoulder, galloping to right, two stars either side of rider.
Rev. *Es-sultanu'l muazzam Keyhusrev bin Kilic Arslan.*
Ref. Broome and Novák 2011, 97 Type B; Izmirlier 2009, 152, Hennequin 1985, 1647; Mitchiner 1998, 957.
310. AE. 22 mm, 3.25 g.
Inv. C2014.131; SAg.14.1.4000.C014 (Pl. 98).

Keykubad I (1220–1237)
No Mint
(1220–1237)
Obv. *El-imam el-nasir lidinallah emiru'l muminin.*
Rev. *Es-sultanu'l muazzam Keykubad bin Keyhusrev.*
Ref. Broome and Novák 2011, 231 Type A; Izmirlier 2009, 365.
311. AE. 20 mm, 2.14 g.
Inv. 3572, 85/54; Portico of Tiberius, NCE 85-1 surface (Pl. 98).

Keyhüsrev III (1266–1284)
No Mint
(1266–1284)
Obv. *[El-mulku] lillah.*
Rev. … *gıya[suddunyaveddin]* … .
Ref. Broome and Novák 2011, 802 Type A; Izmirlier 2009, 1162.
312. AE. 15 mm, 1.48 g.
Inv. C2015.042; SAg.15.1.4075.C050 (Pl. 98).

B. AYDINIDS

Umur II (1403–1405)
No Mint
(1403–1405)
Obv. *[U]mur [i]bn Mehmed.*
Rev. *[Hulli]de Mülkuhu.*
Ref. Artuk and Artuk 1971, 1322; Ender 2000, 04-AYD-201; Sağıt and Teoman 2013, HB-238.
313. AE. 18 mm, 1.34 g.
Inv. C2015.091; SAg.15.1.4015.C071 (Pl. 98).

Cüneyd Bey (1405–1425) (Amir of İzmir)
No Mint
(1421–1422)
Obv. Lion walking to the right, head turned left.

Rev. *Aki[bet-i] hayr*.
Ref. Sağıt and Teoman 2013, KE-494.
314. AE. 13 mm, 1.26 g.
                Inv. C2015.066; SAg.15.1.4075.C061 (Pl. 98).

(1421–1422)
Obv. Lion walking to the right, head turned left.
Rev. *Aki[bet-i] hay[r]*.
Ref. Sağıt and Teoman 2013, KE-494.
315. AE. 14 mm, 0.94 g.
                Inv. C2015.067; SAg.15.1.4075.C062 (Pl. 98).

Anonymous (1307–1426)
No Mint
(1307–1426)
Obv. Muhr-i Suleyman motif.
Rev. Worn.
316. AE. 16 mm, 0.61 g.
                Inv. C2017.001; SAg.17.1.4404.C209.

(1307–1426)
Obv. Muhr-i Suleyman motif.
Rev. Worn.
317. AE. 15 mm, 0.50 g.
                Inv. C2017.004; SAg.17.1.4335.C208.

(1307–1426)
Obv. Muhr-i Suleyman motif with star in the centre and single pellets in the border fields.
Rev. Muhr-i Suleyman motif with star in the centre and single pellets in the border fields.
318. AE. 18 mm, 1.33 g.
                Inv. C2016.110; SAg.16.1.4323.C192 (Pl. 98).

(1307–1426)
Obv. Muhr-i Suleyman motif, with single pellets in the centre and in the border fields.
Rev. 7-armed rayed motif with single pellets in field.
319. AE. 18 mm, 0.88 g.
                Inv. C2015.037; SAg.15.1.4075.C046 (Pl. 98).

(1307–1426)
Obv. Star with 8 arms.
Rev. Star with 8 arms.
320. AE. 15 mm, 1.19 g.
                Inv. C2015.027; SAg.15.1.4075.C040.

(1307–1426)
Obv. Floral motif.
Rev. Pinwheel (wheel of fortune) motif.
321. AE. 16 mm, 1.90 g.
                Inv. C2015.060; SAg.15.1.4092.C057 (Pl. 98).

(1307–1426)
Obv. *[Halle]dallahü mülkehu*.
Rev. *Shahada*.
Ref. Sağıt and Teoman 2013, HB-239; Ender 2000, ANM-AYD-1403.
322. AE. 18 mm, 2.83 g.
                Inv. C2016.007; SAg.16.1.4222.C103.

(1307–1426)
Obv. *Es-sultan*.
Rev. … .
323. AE. 21 mm, 1.24 g.
                Inv. C2014.223; SAg.14.1.4006.C018.

C. GERMIYANIDS

Anonymous (1300–1429)
No Mint
(1300–1429)
Obv. *Muhr-i Suleyman*.
Rev. *[Duribe Germiyan]*.
Ref. Teoman and Teoman 2017, 43.
324. AE. 14 mm, 0.75 g.
                Inv. C2017.017; SAg.14.1.4411.C218 (Pl. 98).

D. KARAMANIDS

Anonymous (1300–1466)
Konya
(1421–1471)
Obv. *A[kibet-iHayr]*.
Rev. *[Duribe Konya]*.
Ref. Kürkman 1988, 8.
325. AE. 24 mm, 1.72 g.
                Inv. C2017.022; SAg.17.1.4399.C217 (Pl. 98).

(1350–1351)
Obv. Double-headed eagle (very worn).
Rev. *[Duri]be Konya*.
Ref. Ethem 1918, 60; Ölçer 1975, 249; Perk and Öztürk 2008, 144.
326. AE. 20 mm, 1.27 g.
                Inv. C2017.010; SAg.17.1.4396.C206 (Pl. 98).

E. MENTESHE

Anonymous (1421–1424)
No Mint
(1421–1424)
Obv. Bundle of three laurel branches.
Rev. Worn.
Ref. Teoman and Teoman 2016, 43.
327. AE. 11 mm, 0.60 g.
                Inv. C2016.016; SAg.16.1.4255.C112 (Pl. 98).

F. SARUHANIDS

İshak Bey (1358–1390)
No Mint
(1358–1390)
Obv. *Hullide İsha[k]*.
Rev. *Ha[lledallahü mülkehu]*.
Ref. Hennequin 1985, 1973; Mitchiner 1998, 1202, Ender 2000, 03-SAR-301.
328. AE. 19 mm, 2.53 g.
                Inv. C2015.111; SAg SAg.15.1.4095.C090 (Pl. 98).

G. OTTOMAN EMPIRE

Bayezid I (1389–1402)
No Mint
(1389–1390)
Obv. *[Bayezid] bin Murad.*
Rev. *Hullide mülkuhu 792.*
Ref. Ehlert 2013, 04-000-30-01aa; Pere, 13; Damalı 2010, 4-G1a-792; Artuk and Artuk 1974, 1385.
329. AR. 12 mm, 0.93 g.
Inv. C2015.043; SAg.15.1.4048.C051 (Pl. 98).

(1389–1402)
Obv. *[Bayezid bin Murad].*
Rev. *Hulli[de mülkuhu].*
Ref. Ehlert 2013, 04-000-10-01aa; Kabaklarli 1998, 04-X-01.
330. AE. 13 mm, 0.77 g.
Inv. C2017.003; SAg.17.1.4388.C207.

(1389–1402)
Obv. *[Bayezid] bin Mura[d].*
Rev. *Hullide [mülkuhu].*
Ref. Ehlert 2013, 04-000-10-01aa; Kabaklarli 1998, 04-X-01.
331. AE. 18 mm, 1.45 g.
Inv. C2013.018; SAg.13.1.3008C003.

(1389–1402)
Obv. *Bayezid [bin Murad].*
Rev. *[Hullide mülkuhu].*
Ref. Ehlert 2013, 04-000-10-01aa; Kabaklarli 1998, 04-X-01.
332. AE. 15–17 mm, 2.28 g.
Inv. C2012.038; SAg.12.1.1004.

Murad II (1421–1444) (1446–1451)
Ayasuluk
(1441–1442)
Obv. *Murad bin Mehmed Han 8[45].*
Rev. *[Hullide mülkuhu] duribe Ayasuluk.*
Ref. Ehlert 2013, 06-Aya-10-12a; Kabaklarli 1998, 06-Ay-09.
333. AE. 14 mm, 0.72 g.
Inv. C2013.037; SAg.13.1.3005.C007 (Pl. 98).

Bursa
(1432–1433)
Obv. *[Murad bin Mehmed] Han.*
Rev. *[Hullide mülkuhu] 836 duribe Bursa.*
Ref. Ehlert 2013, 06-Bur-10-11a; Kabaklarli 1998, 06-Br-11; Artuk and Artuk 1974, 1410.
334. AE. 16 mm, 2.12 g.
Inv. C2017.018; SAg.17.1.4411.C219.

(1432–1433)
Obv. *[Murad bin] Mehmed Han.*
Rev. *[Hullide mülkuhu] 83[6 duribe] Bursa.*
Ref. Ehlert 2013, 06-Bur-10-11a; Kabaklarli 1998, 06-Br-11; Artuk and Artuk 1974, 1410.
335. AE. 17 mm, 2.57 g.
Inv. C2016.006; SAg.16.1.4227.C102.

(1432–1433)
Obv. *Mura[d bin] Mehmed Han.*
Rev. *Hullide mülkuhu 83[6] duribe Bursa.*
Ref. Ehlert 2013, 06-Bur-10-11a; Kabaklarli 1998, 06-Br-11; Artuk and Artuk 1974, 1410.
336. AE. 21 mm, 2.60 g.
Inv. C2015.055; SAg.15.1.4000.C056 (Pl. 98).

Ladik
(1434–1435)
Obv. *Murad [bin] Meh[med Han]* in Tugra form.
Rev. *Hullide [mü]lkuhu [38]*, margin *[duribe Ladik].*
Ref. Ehlert 2013, 06-Ladd10-11a; Kabaklarli 1998, 06-Lad-03; Damalı 2010, 6-LD-M1.
337. AE. 18 mm, 1.52 g.
Inv. C2013.096; SAg.13.2.4012.C018 (Pl. 98).

Tire
(1444–1445)
Obv. *Murad [bin Mehmed Han 848].*
Rev. *[Hullide] mülkuhu duribe [Tire].*
Ref. Ehlert 2013, 06-Tir-10-10a; Kabaklarli 1998, 06-Tra-01.
338. AE. 12 mm, 0.60 g.
Inv. C2013.066; SAg.13.2.4008.C010 (Pl. 98).

(1449–1450)
Obv. *Murad bin [Mehmed azze nasruhu].*
Rev. *[Hullide] mülkuhu [853 duribe Tire].*
Ref. Ehlert 2013, 06-Tir-10-102a; Kabaklarli 1998, 06-Tra-07; Damalı 2010, 6-TI-M1-853.
339. AE. 12 mm, 1.29 g.
Inv. C2015.079; SAg.15.1.4076.C077.

(1449–1450)
Obv. *[Mu]rad bin Mehmed [azze nasruhu].*
Rev. *[Hul]lide mülkuhu [853 duribe Tire].*
Ref. Ehlert 2013, 06-Tir-10-102a; Kabaklarli 1998, 06-Tra-07; Damalı 2010, 6-TI-M1-853.
340. AE. 12 mm, 1.27 g.
Inv. C2014.044; SAg.14.1.4000.C009 (Pl. 98).

Unidentified Mints
(1423–1424)
Obv. *[Sultan Murad bin Mehmed Han hullide mülkuhu].*
Rev. *[Duribe "mint name"] hamala usr'[el bab 827].*
Ref. Pere 1968, 65.
341. AE. 17 mm, 1.52 g.
Inv. C2015.033; SAg.15.1.4075.C045.

(1423–1424)
Obv. *[Sultan] Mura[d bin] Mehmed [Han hullide mülkuhu].*
Rev. *[Duribe "mint name" hamala usr'el bab 827].*
Ref. Pere 1968, 65.
342. AE. 18 mm, 2.27 g.
Inv. C2016.023; SAg.16.1.4255.C119 (Pl. 98).

Mehmed II (1444–1446) (1451–1481)
Ayasuluk
(1448–1449)
Obv. [Dragon to r.] margin *[Duribe Ayasuluk 8]52.*
Rev. *[Hullide mülkuhu Mehmed ibn Murad Han].*
Ref. Ehlert 2013, 07-Aya-10-100a; Kabaklarli 1998, 07-Ay-01; Artuk and Artuk 1974, 1440.
343. AE. 13 mm, 0.83 g.
Inv. C2015.099; SAg.15.1.4015.C077.

(1460–1461)
Obv. *[Mehmed bin Murad Han azze nasruhu 865].*
Rev. *[Duribe] Ayasuluk Hullide [mülkuhu].*
Ref. Ehlert 2013, 07-Aya-10-200a; Kabaklarli 1998, 07-Ay-13; Artuk and Artuk 1974, 1442.
344. AE. 15 mm, 2.51 g.
Inv. C2017.016; SAg.17.1.4405.C216.

Bursa
(1456–1457)
Obv. *[Mehmed bin] Murad [Han].*
Rev. *[Hullide] mülkuhu 86[1 duribe Bursa].*
Ref. Ehlert 2013, 07-Bur-10-200a; Kabaklarli 1998, 07-Br-12.
345. AE. 14 mm, 0.95 g.
Inv. C2017.005; SAg.17.1.4405.C210 (Pl. 99).

Edirne
(1460–1461)
Obv. *[Mehmed bin] Murad Han azze [nasruhu 865].*
Rev. *Duribe Edirne Hul[lide mülkuhu].*
Ref. Ehlert 2013, 07-Adr-10-203a.
346. AE. 14 mm, 2.88 g.
Inv. C2013.029; SAg.13.1.3005.C006 (Pl. 99).

Enguriye
(1451–1481)
Obv. *[Mehmed bin] Murad [Han].*
Rev. *Hullide mülkuhu Duribe [En]g[uriye].*
Ref. Kabaklarli, 07-Ang-06; Ehlert 2013, 07-Ank-10-201a.
347. AE. 17 mm, 1.10 g.
Inv. 3585, 85/94; Portico of Tiberius, NC 85-2 (Pl. 99).

Tire
(1451–1481)
Obv. *Mehmed bin [Murad Han].*
Rev. *Hullide mülkuhu [duribe Tire].*
Ref. Ehlert 2013, 07-Tir-10-209c.
348. AE. 13 mm, 0.79 g.
Inv. 3573, 85/57; Portico of Tiberius, NCE 85-1 (Pl. 99).

Unidentified Mints
(1460–1461)
Obv. *Mehmed bin Murad Han [azze] nasruhu [86]5.*
Rev. *[Duribe "mint name"] Hullide mülkuhu.*
Ref. Pere 1968, 86.
349. AR. 11 mm, 0.62 g.
Inv. C2016.053; SAg.16.1.4255.C149 (Pl. 99).

Bayezid II (1481–1512)
Edirne
(1481–1512)
Obv. *Sultan Bayezid bin Mehmed Han.*
Rev. *Azze nasruhu duribe Edirne sene 886.*
Ref. Pere 1968, 105.
350. AR. 11 mm, 0.50 g.
Inv. C2019.125, SAg.19.1.4000.C064 (Pl. 99).

Novar
(1481–1512)
Obv. *Sultan Bayezid bin Mehmed Han.*
Rev. *Azze nasruhu duribe Novar [sen]e 886.*
Ref. Pere 1968, 105.
351. AR. 10 mm, 0.75 g.
Inv. 3574, 85/69; Portico of Tiberius, NCE 85-1, Ext.III (Pl. 99).

Serez
(1481–1512)
Obv. *Sultan Bayezid bin Mehmed Han.*
Rev. *[Azze nasruhu duri]be Serez sene 886.*
Ref. Pere 1968, 105.
352. AR. 10 mm, 0.75 g.
Inv. 3575, 85/70; Portico of Tiberius, NCE 85-1, Ext.III (Pl. 99).

Selim I (1512–1520)
Kostantiniyye
(1516–1517)
Obv. *Fi sene 922.*
Rev. *Fulus duribe Kostantiniyye.*
Ref. Kabaklarli 1998, 09-Qos-17; Ehlert 2013, 09-Kon-10-03a.
353. AE. 15 mm, 2.88 g.
Inv. 3584, 85/93; Portico of Tiberius, NC 85-2 (Pl. 99).

Suleyman I (1520–1566)
Halep
(1531–1532)
Obv. *[Sul]tan Adluhu [ve Tul-u omruhu].*
Rev. *Duribe Ful[us sene 938] Halep.*
Ref. Kabaklarli 1998, 10-Hlb-51.
354. AE. 16 mm, 3.60 g.
Inv. 3583, 85/92; Portico of Tiberius, NC 85-2 (Pl. 99).

H. ORNAMENTAL MANGIRS

Tire
(1444–1512)
Obv. 6 petal floral pattern.
Rev. *[Az]ze nasruhu [duribe Tire].*
Ref. Ölçer 1975, 356.
355. AE. 12 mm, 0.80 g.
Inv. C2015.089; SAg.15.1.4070.C069, C069.

(1444–1512)
Obv. Muhr-i Suleyman motif with 6-armed star in the centre.
Rev. *[Hull]ide mülkuhu [duri]be Tire.*
Ref. Ölçer 1975, 358.
356. AE. 13 mm, 0.86 g.
Inv. C2015.039; SAg.15.1.4075.C048 (Pl. 99).

(1444–1512)
Obv. Entrelac motif, with single pellets in the field.
Rev. *[Hullide mülkuhu] duribe Tir[e].*
Ref. Ölçer 1975, 376.
357. AE. 12 mm, 0.87 g.
Inv. C2015.040; SAg.15.1.4075.C049 (Pl. 99).

(1444–1512)
Obv. Knot of bliss motif.
Rev. *[Azze] nas[ruhu duribe Tire].*
Ref. Ölçer 1975, 360.
358. AE. 15 mm, 1.41 g.
Inv. C2015.080; SAg.15.1.4076.C066 (Pl. 99).

(1444–1512)
Obv. 6 petal floral pattern with 6 palmet motifs.
Rev. *Hulli[de] mulkuhu duribe Tire.*
Ref. Ölçer 1975, 361.
359. AE. 18 mm, 2.77 g.
Inv. 3586, 85/95; Portico of Tiberius, NC 85-2 (Pl. 99).

(1444–1512)
Obv. *Hullide [mülkuhu].*
Rev. *Duri[be] Tir[e].*
Ref. Ölçer 1975, 388.
360. AE. 12 mm, 0.97 g.
Inv. C2015.100; SAg.15.1.4076.C081 (Pl. 99).

(1444–1512)
Obv. *[Hulli]de mülkuhu.*
Rev. *Duribe Tire.*
Ref. Ölçer 1975, 388.
361. AE. 13 mm, 1.04 g.
Inv. C2016.002; SAg.16.1.4200.C098 (Pl. 99).

(1444–1512)
Obv. Lion walking right.
Rev. *[Hullide]mülkuhu duribe Tire.*
Ref. Ölçer 1975, 404.
362. AE. 14 mm, 1.28 g.
Inv. C2015.103; SAg.15.1.4070.C082 (Pl. 99).

(1444–1512)
Obv. Floral pattern.
Rev. *Hullide mülkuhu [duribe Tire].*
Ref. Ölçer 1975, 383.
363. AE. 17 mm, 3.01 g.
Inv. C2013.024; SAg.13.2.4000.C004 (Pl. 99).

Mehmed III (1594–1604)
Sidrekapsi
(1594–1595)
Obv. *[Sultan] Mehmed [bin Mura]d Han.*
Rev. *Azze na[sruhu] duribe Sid[re]kap[si sene 1003].*
Ref. Pere 1968, 340.
364. AR. 13 mm, 0.41 g.
Inv. C2015.030; SAg.15.1.4075.C042 (Pl. 99).

Suleyman II (1687–1691)
Kostantiniyye
(1687–1688)
Obv. Tugra *(Suleyman bin Ibrahim el-muzaffer-ü dâima).*
Rev. *Duribe fi Kostantiniyye [1099].*
Ref. Pere 1968, 471.
365. AE. 20 mm, 1.75 g.
Inv. C2012.026; SAg.12.1.1007 (Pl. 99).

Ahmed III (1703–1730)
Kostantiniyye
(1703–1704)
Obv. Tugra *(Ahmed bin Mehmed Han el-muzaffer-ü dâima).*
Rev. *Duribe fi Kostantiniyye 1115.*
Ref. Pere 1968, 523.
366. AR. 16 mm, 0.43 g.
Inv. C2014.217; SAg.14.1.4006.C017 (Pl. 99).

Mahmud I (1730–1754)
Kostantiniyye
(1730–1731)
Obv. Tugra *(Han-ı Mahmud bin Mustafa el-muzaffer-ü dâima).*
Rev. *Duribe fi Kostantiniyye [1143].*
Ref. Pere 1968, 578.
367. AR. 17 mm, 0.48 g.
Inv. C2013.025; SAg.13.2.4000.C005 (Pl. 99).

Mahmud II (1808–1839)
Kostantiniyye
(1819–1820)
Obv. Tugra *(Han-ı Mahmud bin Abdülhamid el-muzaffer-ü dâima).*
Rev. *Duribe 12 fi Kostantiniyye 1223.*
Ref. Pere 1968, 832.
368. AR. 15 mm, 0.22 g.
Inv. PTSW 89, 03.08.89, F.13 (Pl. 99).

Abdülmecid (1839–1861)
Kostantiniyye
(1839–1861)
Obv. *[Tugra] (Han-ı Abdülmecid bin Mahmud el-muzaffer-ü dâima).*
Rev. [large 5 in centre], surrounded by *azze nasruhu duribe fi Kostantiniyye 1255.*
Ref. Pere 1968, 906.
369. AE. 22 mm, 2.20 g.
Inv. C2013.026; SAg.13.2.4000.C006.

(1839–1861)
Obv. *[Tugra] (Han-ı Abdülmecid bin Mahmud el-muzaffer-ü dâima).*
Rev. [large 5 in centre], surrounded by *azze nasruhu duribe fi Kostantiniyye 1255.*
Ref. Pere 1968, 906.
370. AE. 21 mm, 1.83 g.
Inv. C2013.075; SAg.13.2.4007.C012.

(1857–1858)
Obv. Tugra *(Han-ı Abdülmecid bin Mahmud el-muzaffer-ü dâima)*, year 19.
Rev. Large 5 in centre, surrounded by *azze nasruhu duribe fi Kostantiniyye sene 1255.*
Ref. Pere 1968, 906.
371. AE. 22 mm, 1.97 g.
Inv. C2013.006; SAg.13.1.3000 (Pl. 99).

(1850–1851)
Obv. Tugra *(Han-ı Abdülmecid bin Mahmud el-muzaffer-ü dâima)*, year 12.
Rev. Large 5 in centre, surrounded by *azze nasruhu duribe fi Kostantiniyye sene 1255.*
Ref. Pere 1968, 906.
372. AE. 22 mm, 4.79 g.
Inv. PTSW 89, 03.08.89, F.12 (Pl. 100).

Abdülaziz (1860–1876)
Kostantiniyye
(1863–1864)
Obv. Tugra *(Han-ı Abdülaziz bin Mahmud el-muzaffer-ü dâima)*, year 4.
Rev. Large 5 in centre, surrounded by *azze nasruhu duribe fi Kostantiniyye sene 1277.*
Ref. Pere 1968, 952.
373. AE. 23 mm, 2.27 g.
Inv. C2014.016; SAg.14.1.4000.C007 (Pl. 100).

Mısır
(1863–1864)
Obv. Tugra *(Han-ı Abdülaziz bin Mahmud el-muzaffer-ü dâima)*, 4 P.
Rev. *Duribe 4 fi Mısır 1277.*
Ref. Ölçer 1978, 32 675.
374. AE. 22 mm, 2.23 g.
Inv. C2014.110; SAg.14.1.4000.C012 (Pl. 106).

Mehmed V (1909–1918)
Kostantiniyye
(1911)
Obv. Tugra, Reşad *(Han-ı Mehmed bin Abdülmecid el-muzaffer-ü dâima)*, year 2, surrounded by *Hürriyet, Müsavat, Adalet.*
Rev. Large 10 in centre, surrounded by *duribe fi devlet-i Osmaniye Kostantiniyye 1327.*

Ref. Pere 1968, 1062.
375. Nl. 19 mm, 2.62 g.
Inv. No. PTW-II 89, 13.08.89, F.2 (Pl. 100).

Kostantiniyye
(1913–1914)
Obv. Tugra, Reşad *(Han-ı Mehmed bin Abdülmecid el-muzaffer-ü dâima)*, year 5, surrounded by *Hürriyet, Müsavat, Adalet.*
Rev. Large 5 in centre, surrounded by *duribe fi devlet-i Osmaniye Kostantiniyye 1327.*
Ref. Pere 1968, 1063.
376. Nl. 11 mm, 1.72 g.
Inv. C2012.001; SAg.12.2.2000.

Kostantiniyye
(1913–1914)
Obv. Tugra, Reşad *(Han-ı Mehmed bin Abdülmecid el-muzaffer-ü dâima)*, year 5, surrounded by *Hürriyet, Müsavat, Adalet.*
Rev. Large 5 in centre, surrounded by *duribe fi devlet-i Osmaniye Kostantiniyye 1327.*
Ref. Pere 1968, 1063.
377. Nl. 16 mm, 1.70 g.
Inv. C2018.022; SAg.18.1.4000.C001 (Pl. 100).

I. UNIDENTIFIED ISLAMIC COINS

Table 25 contains coins too corroded or worn to be identified but quite possibly belonging to the Islamic period because of their sizes and formats.

Table 25. Unidentified Islamic coins.

	Inv.	Find No.	Metal	Diameter	Weight	Notes
378	88.320	PTW-I 88	AE	28	1.06	Corroded, Ottoman, 18th–19th century
379	88.321	PTW-I 88	AE	19	1.69	Corroded, Ottoman, Suleyman II ?
380	22.08.89	PTW 89, F.39	AE	10	0.28	Corroded
381	19.08.89	PTW-89, F.12	AE	16/19	0.75	Corroded
382	C2012.025	SAg.12.1.1004	AE	20	5.58	Corroded
383	C2012.050	SAg.12.1.1007	AE	17/19	2.25	Corroded, Ottoman, Bayezid I ?
384	C2012.168	SAg.12.1.1013	AE	13	0.88	Corroded, Ottoman, Ornamental
385	C2012.200	SAg.12.1.2028	AE	13	0.61	Corroded, Ottoman ?
386	C2013.085	SAg.13.2.4012.C013	AE	11	0.99	Corroded
387	C2013.087	SAg.13.2.4012.C014	AE	16	2.79	Corroded, Ottoman
388	C2013.089	SAg.13.2.4015.C015	AE	22	1.97	Corroded, Seljuk of Rûm
389	C2013.093	SAg.13.2.4012.C017	AE	11	0.65	Corroded, Ottoman ?
390	C2013.105	SAg.13.2.4015.C024	AE	13	0.87	Corroded, Ottoman ?
391	C2013.108	SAg.13.2.4015.C027	AE	15	1.85	Corroded, Ottoman, Murad I
392	C2013.110	SAg.13.2.4009.C029	AE	18	1.53	Corroded, Ottoman ?
393	C2016.059	SAg.16.1.4272.C155	AE	15	0.82	Corroded
394	C2017.006	SAg.17.1.4403.C211	AE	13	0.30	Worn, fragment
395	C2017.008	SAg.17.1.4396.C205	AE	13	0.38	Corroded
396	C2017.022	SAg.17.1.4399.C217	AE	24	1.72	Worn
397	C2018.047	SAg.18.1.4000.C011	AE	17	1.69	Worn
398	C2018.074	SAg.18.1.4000.C035	AE	7	0.19	Worn
399	C2019.007	SAg.19.1.4000.C048	AE	15	0.74	Corroded, Ottoman ?
400	C2019.048	SAg.19.1.4000.C066	AE	12	1.17	Worn
401	C2019.062	SAg.19.1.4000.C068	AE	14	1.24	Worn
402	C2019.081	SAg.19.1.4000.C065	AE	13	0.60	Worn

J. MODERN COINS

Table 26. Modern coins.

	Inv.	Find spot	Metal	Diameter	Weight	Notes
403	C2012.213	SAg 12.1, surface find	AE	16	2.13	5 Kurus 1950; Türkiye
404	C2013.023	SAg.13.2.4000.C003	AE	18	2.51	1 Kurus 1943; Türkiye
405	C2014.007	SAg.14.1.1000.C005	AE	18	2.40	1 Kurus 1939; Türkiye
406	C2014.015	SAg.14.1.1000.C006	AE	19	2.00	100 Para 1926; Türkiye
407	C2017.042	SAg.17.1.4402.C246	AE	24	6.91	50 Kurus 2005; Türkiye

APPENDIX 5
Late Roman and Early Byzantine Ceramics – Tables

Ulrike Outschar

Table 27. Late Roman Ceramics (see Ch. 4 §H).

Feature	Context	Overview of ceramics	Catalogued ceramics[1]	
Planting trenches	2015	LRC Form 3, a few diagnostic and a small number of body fragments of plain kitchen and table ware of local/regional production (late 5th–7th century AD). Intrusive: three body fragments of glazed ware (Beylik and classical Ottoman).	12.2.2015.1	basin, rim fragment, D 36 cm, coarse TMC (Fig. 39)
			12.2.2015.2	amphora/storage vessel, rim fragment, D 20 cm, TMW (Fig. 36)
			12.2.2015.4	small basin, rim fragment, D 20 cm, TMW (Fig. 39)
			12.2.2015.6	bowl, imitation of Cypriot Sigillata (?), rim fragment, D 25 cm, TMW (Fig. 37)
			12.2.2015.8	bowl/dish, LRC Form 3, rim fragment, D 26 cm (Fig. 34)
	2017	Small number of body fragments of plain kitchen/table ware of local/regional production (late 5th–7th century AD)		
	3079	Small number of body fragments of plain kitchen/table ware of local/regional production; one very small body fragment of ARS (late 5th–7th century AD).		
Rubble fill to raise ground level	4280 (= 2005 / 2010 / 3027 / 3042 / 3047 / 3048 / 3060 / 3072 / 3073)	LRU, including stamped fragments (late 5th–7th century AD), one fragment of 'simple rim bowl', one small rim fragment ARS/C Form 74(?), one very small rim fragment ARS/D Form 99, 1 (6th century AD), two rim fragments LRC Form 3, and local imitations of LRC; large number of storage vessels, kitchen and plain table ware of local/regional production (late 5th–7th century AD); small number of body fragments of fine ware (late hellenistic/early Roman); two small rim fragments of ESB2 (end of 1st or first half of 2nd century AD); four body fragments of prehistoric date. Intrusive: ten body fragments of Beylik and classical Ottoman glazed wares.	12.2.2005.1	bowl, rim fragment, D 22 cm, TMW (Fig. 38)
			12.2.2005.2	bowl, rim fragment, D 24 cm, TMW (Fig. 38)
			12.2.2005.3	bowl, rim fragment, D 22 cm, TMW (Fig. 38)
			12.2.2005.4	bowl, rim fragment, D 20 cm, TMW (Fig. 38)
			12.2.2005.7	bowl, rim fragment, D 21 cm, TMW (Fig. 38)
			12.2.2005.8	dish/bowl, LRC Form 3, rim fragment, D 26 cm (Fig. 34)
			12.2.2005.9	bowl, rim fragment, D 19 cm, TMW (Fig. 38)
			12.2.2005.11	bowl, rim fragment, D 24 cm, TMW (Fig. 38)
			12.2.2005.14	storage vessel/cooking pot, rim fragment, D 24 cm, TMW (Fig. 41)
			12.2.2005.15	storage vessel/cooking pot, rim fragment, D 25 cm, TMW (Fig. 41)
			12.2.2005.17	bowl, rim fragment, D 16 cm, TMW (Fig. 38)
			12.2.2005.19	simple rim bowl, rim fragment, D 14 cm, hard and dense TMW (Fig. 37)
			12.2.2005.20	storage vessel/cooking pot, rim fragment, D 20 cm, TMW (Fig. 41)
			12.2.2005.21	storage vessel/cooking pot, rim fragment, D 24 cm, TMW (Fig. 41)
			12.2.2005.22	storage vessel/cooking pot, rim fragment, D 24 cm, TMW (Fig. 41)

---

1 Catalogued ceramics are numbered by trench number (for example 12.2), context number (for example 2015), and then a unique identifying number; the last of these numbers is not associated with a letter (unlike small finds (F) or coins (C)).

Feature	Context	Overview of ceramics	Catalogued ceramics	
			12.2.2005.24	storage vessel/cooking pot, rim-handle fragment, D 26 cm, TMW (Fig. 41)
			12.2.2005.27	amphora, rim fragment, D 11 cm, TMW (Fig. 36)
			12.2.2005.29	amphora, rim fragment, D 12 cm, TMW (Fig. 36)
			12.2.2005.32	bowl, imitation of LRC, rim fragment, D 26 cm, TMW (Fig. 37)
			12.2.2005.33	cooking pot, rim fragment, D 10 cm, TMW (Fig. 40)
			12.2.2005.35	bowl, imitation of LRC, rim fragment, D 30 cm, slipped TMW (Fig. 37)
			12.2.2005.36	bowl, imitation of LRC, rim fragment, D 26 cm, slipped TMW (Fig. 37)
			12.2.2005.37	bowl, imitation of LRC, rim fragment, D 22 cm, slipped TMW (Fig. 37)
			12.2.2005.38	bowl, imitation of LRC, rim fragment, D 28 cm, slipped TMW (Fig. 37)
			12.2.2005.40	bowl, imitation Cypriot Sigillata (?), rim fargment with wave pattern on vertical rim outside, D 14 cm, slipped TMW (Fig. 37)
			12.2.2005.41	bowl, imitation of LRC, rim fragment, D 18 cm, slipped TMW (Fig. 37)
			12.2.2005.42	dish, local imitation Cypriot Sigillata (?), rim fragment with wave pattern on horizontal lip, D 32 cm, slipped TMW (Fig. 37)
			12.2.2005.43	bowl, local imitation Cypriot Sigillata, rim fragment, D 28 cm, slipped TMW (Fig. 37)
			12.2.2005.45	small basin, rim fragment, D 24 cm, TMW (Fig. 39)
			12.2.2005.51	cooking pot, rim fragment, D 12 cm, TMW (Fig. 40)
			12.2.2005.53	cooking pot, rim fragment, D 18 cm, TMW (Fig. 40)
			12.2.2005.55	cooking pot, rim fragment, D 18 cm, TMW (Fig. 40)
			12.2.2005.59	amphora, rim fragment, D 12 cm, TMW (Fig. 36)
			12.2.2005.60	bowl/lid (?), imitation of Late Roman Sigillata, rim fragment, D 15 cm, slipped TMW (Fig. 37)
			12.2.2005.63	amphora, rim-handle fragment, D 8.6 cm, TMW (Fig. 36)
			12.2.2005.64	amphora, rim fragment, D 9 cm, TMW (Fig. 36)
			12.2.2005.65	amphora, rim fragment, D 8 cm, TMW (Fig. 36)
			12.2.2005.67	amphora, rim fragment, D 8 cm, TMW (Fig. 36)
			12.2.2005.68	amphora, rim fragment, D 7.6 cm, TMW (Fig. 36)
			12.2.2005.70	amphora, rim fragment, D 13 cm, TMW (Fig. 36)
			12.2.2005.72	amphora, rim frgament, D 10 cm, TMW (Fig. 36)
			12.2.2005.75	amphora, rim-handle fragment, D 12 cm, TMW (Fig. 36)
			12.2.2005.84	basin, rim fragment, D 30 cm, TMW (Fig. 39)
			12.2.2005.86	basin, rim fragment, D 38 cm, coarse TMW (Fig. 39)
			12.2.2005.87	basin, rim fragment, D 33 cm, TMW (Fig. 39)

Feature	Context	Overview of ceramics	Catalogued ceramics	
			12.2.2005.88	basin, rim fragment, D 32 cm, TMW (Fig. 39)
			12.2.2005.90	basin, rim fragment, D 28 cm, TMW (Fig. 39)
			12.2.2055.92	basin, rim fragment, D 36 cm, TMW (Fig. 39)
			12.2.2005.93	basin, rim fragment, D 36 cm, coarse TMW (Fig. 39)
			12.2.2005.94	basin, rim fragment, D 28 cm, TMW (Fig. 39)
			12.2.2005.97	cooking pot, rim fragment, D 14 cm, GCW (Fig. 40)
			12.2.2005.98	cooking pot, rim fragment, D 15 cm, GCW (Fig. 40)
			12.2.2005.99	cooking pot, rim fragment, D 18 cm, GCW (Fig. 40)
			12.2.2005.101	cooking pot, rim fragment, D 13 cm, GCW (Fig. 40)
			12.2.2005.103	cooking pot, rim fragment, D 20 cm, coarse TMW/GCW (Fig. 40)
			12.2.2005.104	cooking pot, rim-handle fragment, D 16 cm, GCW (Fig. 40)
			12.2.2005.105	cooking pot, rim fragment, D 16 cm, coarse TMW (Fig. 40)
			12.2.2005.108	cooking pot, rim fragment, D 19 cm, coarse TMW/GCW (Fig. 40)
			12.2.2005.112	pithos, rim fragment, D 28 cm, coarse TMW (Fig. 41)
			12.2.2005.113	pithos, rim fragment, D 30 cm, coarse TMW (Fig. 41)
			12.2.2005.114	small bowl or lid (?), ARS/C variation to Hayes Form 74 (?) or lid (Fig. 34)
			12.2.2005.115	dish, ARS/D Form 99, rim fragment, D 28 cm (Fig. 34)
			12.2.2005.116	pithos, rim fragment, D 36 cm, coarse TMW (Fig. 41)
			12.2.2005.117	bowl/dish, similar to LRC 3, rim fragment, D 28 cm (Fig. 34)
			12.2.2005.119	dish/bowl, LRC Form 3, D 16 cm (Fig. 34)
			12.2.2005.120	amphora, LRA1, rim-handle fragment, D 9.2 cm (Fig. 36)
			12.2.2005.121	amphora, LRA1, rim-handle fragment, D 9.6 cm (Fig. 36)
			12.2.2005.124	lid, small fragment of upper part, D 2.2 cm, TMW (Fig. 40)
			12.2.2005.128	amphora, base fragment, D 7.4 cm, TMW (Fig. 36)
			12.2.2005.129	amphora, base fragment, D 7 cm, TMW (Fig. 36)
			12.2.2005.130	jug/jar, base fragment, D 4 cm, TMW (Fig. 36)
			12.2.2005.135	amphora, base fragment, D 14 cm, TMW (Fig. 36)
			12.2.2006.136	amphora, base fragment, D 12 cm, TMW (Fig. 36)
			12.2.2005.138	LRU with flat base, lower third of body, H 6 cm (Fig. 35)
			12.2.2005.139	LRU with flat base, lower third of body, H 5.5 cm (Fig. 35)
			15.2.3042.1	amphora, rim-handle fragment, D 11 cm, TMW (Fig. 36)
			15.2.3042.7	basin, rim fragment, D 36 cm, coarse TMW (Fig. 39)
			15.2.3042.8	storage vessel/cooking pot, rim fragment, D 16 cm, coarse TMW (Fig. 41)

Feature	Context	Overview of ceramics	Catalogued ceramics	
			15.2.3047.1	storage vessel/cooking pot, rim fragment, D 20 cm, TMW (Fig. 41)
			15.2.3047.2	lid, rim fragment with burned edges, D 20 cm, TMW (Fig. 40)
			15.2.3060.1	storage vessel/cooking pot, rim fragment, D 18 cm, coarse TMW (Fig. 40)
			15.2.3060.2	storage vessel/cooking pot, rim fragment, D 16 cm, coarse TMW (Fig. 40)
			15.2.3060.3	cooking pot, rim-handle fragment, D 12 cm, GCW (Fig. 40)
			15.2.3060.4	jug/jar, base fragment, D 5 cm, TMW (Fig. 36)
			15.2.3060.5	jug/jar, base fragment, D 5 cm, TMW (Fig. 36)
			15.2.3060.7	amphora, base fragment, D 9 cm, TMW (Fig. 36)
			15.2.3060.11	amphora, rim fragment, D 11 cm, TMW (Fig. 36)
			15.2.3073.1	bowl, rim fragment, D 20 cm, TMW (Fig. 38)
			15.2.3073.3	cooking pot, rim fragment, D 22 cm, coarse TMW (Fig. 40)
			15.2.3073.5	amphora, base fragment, D 8 cm, TMW (Fig. 36)
Planting pits	3062	Small number of body fragments of plain ware of local/regional production (late 5th–7th century AD)		
	3067	Small number of body fragments of plain kitchen and table ware of local/regional production (late 5th–7th century AD)		
	3076	Body fragments of plain kitchen and table ware of local/regional production (late 5th–7th century AD)		
	3078	Body fragments of plain kitchen and table ware of local/regional production (late 5th–7th century AD)		
	3081	Small number of body fragments of plain kitchen and table ware of local/regional production (late 5th–7th century AD)		
Layer of alluvial on top of late antique ground level	4278 (= 4279)	Two fragments LRC Form 3, small number of diagnostic fragments and larger number of body fragments of amphorae, plain kitchen- and table ware of local/regional production (late 5th–7th century AD); two body fragments (prehistoric). Intrusive: two body fragments of Beylik glazed ware.	16.1.4278.1	storage vessel/cooking pot, rim fragment, D 20 cm, TMW (Fig. 41)
			16.1.4278.3	storage vessel/cooking pot, rim fragment, D 24 cm, TMW (Fig. 41)
			16.1.4278.18	dish/bowl, Cypriot Sigillata (?), rim fragment, D 24 cm (Fig. 34)
			16.1.4278.19	dish/bowl, Cypriot Sigillata (?), rim fragment, D 26 cm (Fig. 34)
			16.1.4278.20	cooking pot, rim fragment, D 20 cm, GCW (Fig. 40)

Feature	Context	Overview of ceramics	Catalogued ceramics
Ring drain fills	8009	One small fragment of LRA1 (late 5th–6th century AD) and a small number of body fragments of plain kitchen and table ware of local/regional production (late 5th–7th century AD). Intrusive: five fragments of Beylik and Ottoman glazed wares.	
	8010	Small number of body fragments of plain kitchen and table ware of local/regional production (late 5th–7th century AD). Intrusive: one fragment of Beylik glazed ware.	
	8011	Small number of body fragments of plain kitchen and table ware of local/regional production (late 5th–7th century AD). Intrusive: three fragments of Beylik glazed ware and fifteen fragments of Byzantine/Beylik storage and kitchen vessels.	

Table 28. Ceramics from the Clearance Deposits within the Pool (see Ch. 8 §C).

Feature	Context	Overview of ceramics	Catalogued ceramics	
Deposit on pool floor	4482 (= 4484 / 5029 / 5031)	Large number of LRU (total 32 fragments, four stamped bases, 6th – early 7th century AD), one fragment LRA1 (late 5th – early 7th century AD), one rim fragment LRC Form 3 (6th century AD), one lamp (Miltner Typus IV, middle 6th – middle 7th century AD); large number of mainly body fragments of amphorae, storage vessels, kitchen and plain table ware of local/regional production (late 5th – first half of 7th century AD); six fragments of late hellenistic/early Roman kitchen wares; eight body fragments of prehistoric wares. Intrusive: two body fragments of Beylik glazed ware.	17.1.4482.1	LRU, lower half of body, H 9 cm (Fig. 63)
			17.1.4482.2	LRU, lower half of body, H 9 cm (Fig. 63)
			17.1.4482.3	LRU, lower half of body, H 8.6 cm (Fig. 63)
			17.1.4482.4	LRU, lower half of body, H 7 cm (Fig. 63)
			17.1.4482.5	LRU, lower half of body, H 7.6 cm (Fig. 63)
			17.1.4482.6	LRU, lower third of body, H 5.7 cm (Fig. 63)
			17.1.4482.7	LRU, lower third of body, H 6 cm (Fig. 63)
			17.1.4482.8	dish, LRC Form 3F/17, rim fragment, D 18 cm (Fig. 61)
			17.1.4482.9	amphora, rim fragment, D 9 cm, TMW (Fig. 61)
First clearance deposit	4328 (= 1032 / 4466 / 5027 / 5030 / 5033)	One body and handle fragment of LRA1 (early 6th–7th century AD) and LRU (6th – early 7th century AD); large number of storage vessels, amphorae, cook and plain table ware (mainly body fragments) of local/regional production (late 5th–7th century AD); three fragments of late hellenistic/early Roman kitchen wares; two body fragments of prehistoric wares, including a pithos. Intrusive: two fragments of plain Byzantine table ware.	17.1.4328.3	cooking pot, almost complete form (bottom missing), D 14 cm, H 15.5 cm (reconstructed), GCW (Fig. 61)
			12.2.1032.1	LRU, lower third of body, H 5.6 cm (Fig. 63)
			17.1.4466.1	cooking pot, rim fragment, D 14 cm, GCW (Fig. 61)
			17.1.4466.2	basin, rim fragment, D 28 cm, TMW (Fig. 61)
			17.1.4466.3	basin, rim with simple wave pattern, D 34 cm, TMW (Fig. 61)
			17.1.4466.4	basin, rim with two grooves, D 36 cm, TMW (Fig. 61)

Feature	Context	Overview of ceramics	Catalogued ceramics	
Layer of silt over first clearance deposit	4448 (= 1016 / 5028)	LRU (6th – early 7th century AD), one body fragment LRA4/Agora M373 (late 6th/7th century AD), small number of amphorae/jars and kitchen ware of local/regional production (late 5th–7th century AD); two storage vessel fragments (prehistoric). Intrusive: three fragments of plain Byzantine kitchen ware.	17.1.4448.1	pitcher, rim-neck-handle fragment, H 6.9 cm, TMW (Fig. 61)
			17.1.4448.2	amphora, rim-neck-handle fragment, D 16 cm, TMW (Fig. 61)
			17.1.4448.3	amphora, neck fragment, D 18 cm, TMW (Fig. 61)
			17.1.4448.4	pitcher, spout-neck-handle fragment, H 9.2 cm, TMW (Fig. 61)
			17.1.4448.5	amphora, LRA4 (=Peacock 45, Agora M373), bottom fragment, H 4.5 cm, TMW (Fig. 61)
			17.1.4448.6	LRU, lower half of body, stamped (?), H 10 cm (Fig. 63)
			17.1.4448.7	LRU, complete body, spout missing, H 12.8 cm (Fig. 63)
			17.1.4448.8	LRU, lower half of body, H 7.5 cm (Fig. 63)

Table 29. Late Roman Ceramics from Deposits belonging to *Phases 4–6* (see Ch. 8 §C and Ch. 9 §C).

Feature	Context	Overview of ceramics	Catalogued ceramics	
Thick layer of silt across pool interior	4480 (= 1015 / 4470 / 4479 / 17.2.5024)	LRU (6th – 7th century AD), small number (mainly body fragments) of amphorae, storage vessels, kitchen- and plain table ware of local/regional production (late 5th–7th century AD); three body and one handle fragment of prehistoric wares. Intrusive: one fragment of Beylik storage vessel.	17.1.4480.1	jug/jar or storage pot, base fragment and lower part of body, D 7 cm, H 5 cm (Fig. 62)
Clearance deposit along south side of pool	4461 (= 4467 / 4469)	LRU (6th–7th century AD), small amount of locally/regionally produced storage, cooking- and plain table ware (late 5th–7th century AD).	17.1.4461.1	cooking pot, rim-body fragment, D 18 cm, GCW (Fig. 84)
			17.1.4461.2	jug/jar/amphora, base fragment, D 6.6 cm, TMW (Fig. 62)
			17.1.4461.3	jug/jar, base fragment, D 4.4 cm, TMW (Fig. 62)
Clearance deposit along north side of pool	4329 (= 1019 / 17.2.5023)	Small number of amphorae/jars, storage and kitchen ware of local/regional production (late 5th–7th century AD); one large fragment cooking pot (late 6th–7th century AD). Intrusive: six body fragments of glazed ware (Beylik to classical Ottoman).	12.1.1019.1	cooking pot, almost complete form, lowest part and bottom missing, D 18 cm, H 11.5 cm, GCW

Feature	Context	Overview of ceramics	Catalogued ceramics	
Thick layer of silt across pool interior, above southern clearance deposit	4442	One pilgrim flask (almost complete form; Umayyad period, 8th century AD), several LRU, one body fragment LRA1 (late 5th–early 7th century AD), one base fragment of an amphora Yassi Ada 159 C19 (first half of 7th century AD), storage vessels, amphorae, cook and plain kitchen and table ware of local/regional production (late 5th–7th century AD); one base of late hellenistic/early Roman fine ware; two body fragments (prehistoric).	17.1.4442.1	cooking pot, almost complete, D 12 cm, H 14 cm, GCW (Fig. 84)
			17.1.4442.2	pilgrim flask, almost complete, H 25.4 cm, D (body) 23 cm, D (spout) 4 cm (Fig. 84)
			17.1.4442.3	LRU, spout and upper body, D 2.8 cm, H 5.3 cm (Fig. 62)
			17.1.4442.6	bowl, rim fragment, D 24 cm, TMW (Fig. 62)
			17.1.4442.7	storage pot, rim fragment, D 17 cm, TMW (Fig. 62)
			17.1.4442.9	cooking pot, rim and handle fragment, D 16 cm, GCW (Fig. 84)
			17.1.4442.10	small basin/dish, rim fragment, D 24 cm, TMW (Fig. 62)
			17.1.4442.11	bowl, rim fragment, D 20 cm, poorly slipped TMW (Fig. 62)
			17.1.4442.F790	amphora, base, D 8.6 cm, coarse TMW (Fig. 62)

APPENDIX 6
Context Descriptions

Allison Kidd and Ben Russell

Table 30. Phases.

Phase	Key features	Period	Date Range	Ch. ref.
1	Construction and use of Place of Palms	Roman imperial	1st to 5th/6th cent. AD	2, 3
2	Restoration and continued use	Late antique	5th/6th to 7th cent. AD	4
3	Destruction, clearance, and change of use of area around pool	Late antique – early Byzantine	7th to 9th cent. AD	8
4	Pool as a swamp, limited occupation around it; collapse of stoas	Middle Byzantine	9th cent. to 1197	9
5	Drying out of pool, paths laid across it	Seljuk	Late 12th to late 13th cent.	9
6	Division of area into agricultural plots for the first time	Beylik	Late 13th to late 14th cent.	9
7	Further development of land units and trackways across area	Late Beylik – early Ottoman	Late 14th to early 15th cent.	9
8	First phase of village	Early – classical Ottoman	Early 15th to mid 16th cent.	9
9	Later phase of village	Classical to late Ottoman	Mid 16th to 17th cent.	9
10	Limited occupation of village area	Late Ottoman	17th to 18th cent.	9
11	Field walls	Late Ottoman	19th to early 20th cent.	9
12	Field walls and modern excavation	Turkish Republic	1922 to present	1, 9

Table 31. Principal Stratigraphic Units.

Phase	Context	Equal to	Location	Description and interpretation	Dating elements
1	1034		Pool	Layer of flat stones laid in earth to form substrate for pool floor.	
1	1035		Pool	Layer of small stones and tile fragments, originally set in pinkish mortar, overlying **1034**.	
1	1036		Pool	*Cocciopesto* mortar forming upper level of original pool floor.	
1	1040	1033	North ring drain	Sandy layer within the north ring drain; fourth level of fill within the ring drain.	
1	1041	1033	North ring drain	Silty, wet, dark brown layer of varying thickness rich in charcoal; third level of fill within the north ring drain.	Unidentified late Roman coin (cat. 159).

Phase	Context	Equal to	Location	Description and interpretation	Dating elements
1	1042	1033	North ring drain	Yellowish brown sandy layer, 5–10 cm thick; second level of fill within the north ring drain.	
1	1043	1033	North ring drain	Thin, dark silty layer situated just above the schist paving stones of ring drain floor; first layer of fill within the north ring drain.	Ceramics of first and second centuries AD; unidentified late Roman coin (cat. 160).
1	2011		North of pool	Mortar skim on top of **2013**; mortar on top of which paving of paved path was set.	
1	2013		North of pool	Preparation layer of large rubble stones set in loose to firm mid greyish brown silty clay, 26–30 cm thick and extending for a width of 2.80 m north of the pool wall; preparation for paved path.	
1	2014		North of pool	Firm redeposited light greyish brown clay, 14–27 cm thick, with inclusions of brick, tile, and pottery; interpreted as the original ground surface of the Place of Palms.	
1	2016	16.2.5002	North of pool	Compacted pale stone and lime layer, c. 0.36 cm thick, between **2024** and **2017**; possible path running between planting trenches.	
1	2017		North of pool	Mounded east–west feature, up to 1.65 m wide and 4.5 m north of **2024**, comprising pinkish earth with brick dust; interpreted as upper fill of northern planting trench in area north of pool.	
1	2019		North of pool	Light greyish brown clay layer, overlying **2025**, in area between northern planting trench (**2017**) and North Stoa; possible original ground surface.	
1	2024		North of pool	East–west trench, 1.10–1.30 m wide and 0.45 m deep, cut into **2025** and **2014**; interpreted as southern planting trench in area north of pool.	
1	2025	16.2.5007	North of pool	Mid yellowish brown clay found north of pool, probably natural.	
1	2028		North of pool	Dark greyish brown clay containing large stones and fragments of tile set in base of **2024**; lower fill of southern planting trench.	
1	14.3.5003	14.3.5006, 14.3.5010	North Stoa	Grey silty fill packed behind seat blocks of the North Stoa; original fill beneath floor of North Stoa.	
2	1029, 1022	3022, 4487	North ring drain	Thin layers of grey clay fill in the northern ring drain; fills space of the original pipe duct.	
2	1030	1031	North ring drain	Compact, artificial deposit of clay in northern ring drain, 60 cm thick, with stones and brick tile fragments, and occasional pottery.	Ceramics, last quarter of the fifth or the first quarter of the sixth cent.

Phase	Context	Equal to	Location	Description and interpretation	Dating elements
2	2015		North of pool	Dark reddish brown silt mixed with pink sandy soil and crushed brick dust, overlying **2028**; upper fill of southern planting trench, which was re-cut in the Late Roman period. This deposit is probably the same as **16.2.5001**, which filled **16.2.5010**, but a cut for it could not be identified when it was excavated in 2012.	Ceramics, fifth cent.; coin of Marcian (cat. 104, AD 450–457).
2	3061		North of pool	Large circular pit, overlapping in plan the line of the southernmost planting trench; cut into upper surface of **4280**.	
2	3062		North of pool	Fill of pit **3061**, containing ceramics of the same range as **4280**.	
2	3063, 3065, 3069, 3071, 3075, 3077		North of pool	Line of small holes running on an east-west line equidistant between two larger pits, **3061** and **16.2.5003**; cut into upper surface of **4280**.	
2	3064, 3066, 3068, 3070, 3072, 3076, 3078		North of pool	Fills of pits **3063, 3065, 3069, 3071, 3075, 3077**, containing ceramics of the same range as **4280**.	Ceramics, late fifth- or early sixth cent.
2	4278	**4279**, as well as the lower levels of **2003, 2007, 3013**	North of pool	Alluvial deposit, *c.* 25 cm thick, built up on top of late antique ground surface. Lower levels contain sixth- and seventh-cent. materials, but this deposit clearly continued to build up through the Byzantine period and after the collapse of the North Stoa. Owing to the highly disturbed nature of the stratigraphy in this area this deposit could not be subdivided and so material from this unit could belong to Phases 2–6.	Sixth- and seventh-cent. ceramics with some later Beylik period material in upper portions (fourteenth cent.).
2	4280	2005, 2010, 2012, 3027, 3042, 3047, 3048, 3060, 3072, 3073	North of pool	Artificial deposit of brick and tile fragments, stones, chunks of mortar, and relatively limited amounts of pottery and bone, *c.* 30–40 cm thick outside of the pool, across the whole of the Place of Palms; constitutes the raising of the area's ground level.	Ceramics, late fifth- or early sixth cent.; 64 coins, 57 dating before the end of the fifth cent., the latest being two datable to the reign of Phocas (cat. 169 and 171)
2	14.3.5001		North Stoa	Thin grey silt layer, 2–3 cm thick, over **14.3.5002**.	Ceramics, fifth and sixth cent.; coin (cat. 56), dated to AD 337–340.
2	14.3.5002		North Stoa	Friable pinkish mortar surface with inclusions of small brick/tile fragments and pieces of wall plaster and revetment, 2–3 cm thick, to which **5012** was concreted.	Ceramics, fifth and sixth cent.
2	14.3.5004		North Stoa	Dark brown silt layer, up to 25 cm thick, including stones and large fragments of an earlier ceramic pipeline filling **14.3.5011**.	
2	14.3.5005		North Stoa	Compact grey silty layer, 3–8 cm thick, over **14.3.5004** containing abundant fragments of tile and filling **14.3.5011**.	

Phase	Context	Equal to	Location	Description and interpretation	Dating elements
2	14.3.5011, 14.3.5016	14.3.5017	North Stoa	East-west trenches cut into 14.3.5003, located inside the North Stoa, into which two pipes (14.3.5022 and 14.3.5008) were laid.	
2	14.3.5012		North Stoa	Thin grey mortar construction dump, 1 cm thick, over 14.3.5013.	Ceramics, fifth and sixth cent.
2	14.3.5013		North Stoa	Compact grey silty construction dump, up to 7 cm thick, over 14.3.5018.	Ceramics, fifth and sixth cent.
2	14.3.5014		North Stoa	Sharply sloping cut, 60 by 40 cm, running along the south side of the rear wall of the North Stoa.	
2	14.3.5015, 14.3.5007		North Stoa	The two fills of cut 14.3.5014, running under the threshold of the central door through the North Stoa's back wall.	Fifth-cent. large closed vessel.
2	14.3.5018		North Stoa	Light grey mortar layer, generally 3–4 cm thick, containing numerous pieces of rubble and sealing 14.3.5019.	
2	14.3.5019		North Stoa	Compact orange-brown fill within 14.3.5016, up to 13 cm thick, full of bricks and roof tile fragments	Unidentified late Roman coin (cat. 200).
2	14.3.5020	6004	North Stoa	Dark greyish brown layer of clay with inclusions of charcoal, mortar and tile at the bottom of 14.3.5014; unexcavated.	
2	16.2.5001	3079, 16.2.5012	North of pool	Deposit of dark greyish brown sandy silt containing large quantities of mortar, brick and tile; fills 16.2.5010, the late antique re-cutting of 2024. Probably the same as 2015, the fill of 2024 identified in 2012.	Three unidentified late Roman coins (cat. 225–227).
2	16.2.5003		North of pool	Planting pit to the north-west of 3061, 1.04 m in diameter and 28.5 cm deep; cut into upper surface of 4280.	
2	16.2.5010		North of pool	Linear re-cutting of 2024, the southern planting trench, made in the first phase of the renovations to the planting scheme.	
2	6001		North Stoa	Highly disturbed deposit of greyish-yellow clay covering 6003.	
2	6002		North Stoa	Compact, medium greyish-brown clay deposit with inclusions of brick, mortar, and charcoal filling the bottom of cut 14.3.5014.	Late Roman cooking wares.
2	6003		North Stoa	Spills of hard, medium brownish-grey mortar trampled into the upper surface of 6002.	
2	8001		South ring drain	Layer of rubble and refuse fill in southern ring drain; fills most of the original pipe duct.	
2	8002	4485	South ring drain	Layer of loose, light grey silty fill in southern ring drain.	Ceramics, fifth cent.
2	8005		South ring drain	Layer rubble and refuse mixed with blackish grey soil; fifth layer of deliberate fill in southern ring drain.	Late Roman A1 amphora, end of the fourth cent.; relative stratigraphy, fifth cent.

Phase	Context	Equal to	Location	Description and interpretation	Dating elements
2	8006		South ring drain	Layer of rubble and refuse, 10 cm thick, containing a rich layer of organic material; fourth layer of deliberate fill in southern ring drain.	Ceramics, fifth cent.
2	8007		South ring drain	Sandy accumulation of sediment; formed when drain was left open between episodes of filling.	
2	8008		South ring drain	Layer of rubble and refuse mixed with silt; third and final layer of deliberate fill in southern ring drain.	Ceramics, fifth cent.
2	8009		South ring drain	Layer of rubble and refuse mixed with light grey silt and clay, 32 cm thick; second layer of deliberate fill in the southern ring drain.	
2	8010		South ring drain	Layer of rubble and thick, light grey silt, 7 cm thick; lowest layer of deliberate fill in southern ring drain.	Ceramics, fifth cent.
2	8011		South ring drain	Dense, natural deposit of light grey silt, 14.5 cm thick, with few finds; first phase of siltation in the southern ring drain.	
3	4328	1032, 4466, 17.2.5027, 17.2.5030, 17.2.5033	Pool	Refuse deposit along the interior north side of the pool, 49 cm thick at its deepest point and 7.39 m at its widest, comprising debris gathered from the northern area of the Place of Palms, mainly roof tiles, marble and stone architectural elements, and a substantial number of metal artefacts; first deposition layer in the pool.	Two coins of Heraclius, the latest of which dates to AD 634/5 (cat. 280); ceramics, LRU (1 stamped base fragment; early 6th – early 7th cent. AD).
3	4448	1016, 17.2.5028	Pool	Layer of viscous, dark grey silt and yellowish-tan clay, 10–15 cm thick, found across interior of pool; first phase of major siltation as pool turned into a swamp.	Ceramics, LRU and LRA4/Agora M373 (late 6th/7th cent. AD); coin of Justinian, AD 539/540 (cat. 246).
3	4471	4474	Pool	Refuse deposit along the interior south side of the pool, 50 cm thick at its deepest point and 1.66 m at its widest, comprising debris gathered from the southern area of the Place of Palms, mainly ceramic building material, burnt timber, and marble sculptural fragments; second deposition layer in the pool.	Coin of Heraclius countermarked with Arabic legend (cat. 281), datable to between the AD 660s and c. AD 685.
3	4482	4484, 5029, 5031, 5032	Pool	Refuse deposit lying directly on the pool floor across its central and southern sectors, comprising mainly marble and metal architectural elements, wooden planks and rafters, and small artefacts relating to commerce; first deposition layer in the pool.	Seven coins, the latest of which dates to AD 643/4 (cat. 289); ceramics, LRU (6th – early 7th cent. AD).
4	3001		North of pool	Collapse of North Stoa on to **2005** in area north of pool.	
4	4329	1019, 17.2.5023	Pool	Rubble deposit, up to 42 cm thick, comprising mostly architectural fragments along north side of pool on top of **4480**; clearance deposit.	Ceramics and coins, which are late Roman residual finds.
4	4461	4467, 4469	Pool	Rubble deposit, 20 cm thick, along south side of pool on top of **4480**; clearance deposit.	

Phase	Context	Equal to	Location	Description and interpretation	Dating elements
4	4442	1005, 1028, 3035, 4446, 4450, 4457, 4465, 4468, 4475, 17.2.5020, 17.2.5021	Pool	Layer of sticky grey silt, 20–25 cm thick, found across interior of pool; third phase of major siltation within the pool.	Ceramics generally dated to the late Roman period; coins of the seventh to early eighth cent. (for example cat. 292); pilgrim flask, broadly eighth cent.
4	4480	1015, 4470, 4479, 17.2.5024	Pool	Compact layer of fine-grained, greyish brown silt, 15–20 cm thick, found across interior of pool; second phase of major siltation as pool turned into a swamp.	Coin of Constans II (cat. 288), AD 642/643.
5	4341	3024, 4342, 4366, 4371, 4441, 4463	South of pool/ Pool	Partial clearance deposit of collapse debris 4358, up to 43 cm thick, comprising mostly rubble, river stones, and ceramic building material dumped over the southern pool walls.	
5	4358		South of pool	Collapse of the Theatre Hill, and defensive structures built on it, to the south of the pool; the interface of the collapse unit was cleaned but the unit itself remains unexcavated.	
5	4420	1003, 1024, 3033, 4345, 4421, 4422, 4423, 4445, 4460, 4462, 17.2.5015	Pool	Layer of silt, 30 cm thick containing few small finds, found across interior of pool; fourth phase of major siltation of pool area.	Glazed table ware, Seljuk and early Beylik periods (mid to late thirteenth century).
6	4089	4293, 4309, 4317, 4385, 4393, 4408, 4416, 4417, 4418, 4419, 4424, 4426	Pool	Collapse debris sloping down toward the north along the south side of the pool, 35 cm thick at its thickest point, comprising massive quantities of smooth river stones, worked *petit appareil* blocks, architectural fragments, and ceramic building material; partly cleared after its formation during phase 7 activity.	Pectoral reliquary cross and a bread stamp, middle Byzantine period; relative stratigraphy and glazed table ware, Beylik period (fourteenth century).
6	4316	4339, 4365, 4409, 4010, 17.2.5011, 17.2.5012, 17.2.5014, and the lower levels of 1007/1023	Pool	Layer of silt, 15 cm thick, containing numerous architectural and sculptural fragments found across interior of pool; fifth phase of major siltation of pool area.	Ceramics, Beylik period (fourteenth century).
6	4438	4319, 4320, 4370, 4455, 4458	South of pool/ Pool	Mixed deposit of colluvial material, a loose brownish-grey silt up to 53 cm thick, formed by erosion from the Theatre Hill and the clearance of debris formed over the south pool walls.	Ceramics, Beylik period (fourteenth century).
7	4281	4403, 4404, 4405, 4411, 4415, 17.2.5001, 17.2.5002 as well as the lower levels of 3020 and upper levels of 1007/1023.	Pool	Layer of silt, 15–35 cm thick, found across interior of pool containing numerous small finds and ceramics; sixth phase of major siltation of pool area.	Coins, the two closely datable ones of 1456–1457 (cat. 345) and 1460–1461 (cat. 344); glazed Beylik table ware and early Ottoman ceramics; a seventeenth-century coin must be intrusive (cat. 365).
8	4012	4015, 4016, 4076, 4079, 4091, 4098, 4177, 4203, 4204, 4205, 4206, 4207, 4209, 4211, 4212, 4218, 4220, 4222, 4227, 4240, 4244, 4247, 4248, 4346, 4382, 4351	Open area	A 20 cm thick layer of firm, dark brownish-grey silt found both within and around the Ottoman structures, comprising a substantial quantity and diverse array of small artefacts associated with the Ottoman occupation of the area; seventh phase of major siltation of pool area.	Coins, the latest datable to 1444–1512 (cat. 358); Beylik and classical Ottoman glazed table ware.

Phase	Context	Equal to	Location	Description and interpretation	Dating elements
8	4019	4253	Open area	Accumulated soil within the walls of Building XI.	
8	4095	4369, 4384, 4398	Open area	Loose and sandy colluvial deposit, approx. 15 cm thick, of eroded debris from the Theatre Hill along the southern excavated area.	Ceramics, early Ottoman period; residual coins, including a Saruhanid coin of İshak Bey dating to 1358–1390 (cat. 328).
8	4238	4260/4268	Open area	Accumulated soils within and immediately outside the walls of Building I.	
8	4255	3020, 4026, 4069, 4147, 4210, 4213, 4214, 4215, 4216, 4217, 4223, 4233, 4236, 4245, 4246, 4251, 4265, 4266, 4271, 4327, 4376, 4381, 4387, 4388, 4390, 4392, 4396, as well as 1001, 1004, 2001, 3004, 3005, though these contexts were disturbed by later excavation activity	Open area	Layer of dark greyish-brown silt, c. 10–15 cm thick, found covering the pool walls; this layer was an artificial stratigraphic division of soil due to its exposure during post-season work.	Several coins dating up to 1461 (cat. 349); ceramics, Beylik and early classical Ottoman kitchen ware and glazed table ware.
9	4048	4051, 4052, 4053, 4054, 4107, 4232	Open area	Deposit of refuse and debris in the southeast area of the Ottoman settlement containing a considerable amount of glass, charcoal, mortar, and metal slag refuse; probably an area where the recycling of glass took place.	Beylik ceramics, unglazed storage ware and glazed table ware.
9	4085	4005, 4102, 4285	Open area	Collapse layer comprising a substantial portion of the Theatre Hill retaining wall and *summa cavea*, comprising several large marble architectural elements.	Ceramics, classical Ottoman.
9	4092		Open area	Colluvial deposit in the southeast area of the Ottoman settlement, sloping north over **4048**.	Ceramics, classical Ottoman glazed table ware.
10	4007	1018, 4009, 4060, 4063, 4065, 4075, 4077, 4101, 4202, 4225, 4356	Open area	Layer of silt c. 30–40 cm thick across the whole of the Ottoman settlement area; rich in animal bones and small finds associated with village life, especially in the northeast sector of the area; eighth phase of major siltation of pool area.	Ceramics, classical Ottoman glazed table ware; residual coins, with latest datable to AD 1594–1595 (cat. 364).
11	4006	4027, 4037, 4064, 4066, 4067, 4100, 4201, 4323, 4331	Open area	Layer of silt, 50–70 cm cm thick, across the whole of the Ottoman settlement area; heavily ploughed, with numerous fragmentary residual items and debris; ninth phase of major siltation of pool area.	Copper alloy belt buckle, seventeenth or eighteenth cent. (SAg.14.1.4006. F47 (Inv. 15-044)); latest coin datable to 1703–1704 (cat. 366).
12	4000	1000, 2000, 3000, 3002, 4200, 4318, 4334, 4402, 14.3.5000, 16.2.5000, 17.2.5000	Open area	Topsoil and cleaning layer, c. 30–60 cm thick, of crumbly soil with a high amount of vegetal material and ceramics of mixed date through to the modern era across the whole of the excavated area; tenth and final phase of major siltation of pool area.	Modern objects, such as a screw and metal shoe sole, and a 2005 50 kuruş coin of the Republic of Türkiye (cat. 407).

Bibliography

Abbasoglu 2001 = Abbasoglu, H., 'The founding of Perge and its development in the Hellenistic and Roman periods', in D. Parrish (ed.), *Urbanism in Western Asia Minor, New Studies on Aphrodisias, Ephesos, Hierapolis, Pergamon, Perge and Xanthos* (JRA Supplementary Series 45, Portsmouth 2001), 173–188.

Adam-Veleni 2012 = Adam-Veleni, P., 'Εἰκονογραφημένη πρόσκληση σὲ μονομαχικοὺς ἀγῶνες ἀπὸ τὴν Ἀγορὰ τῆς Θεσσαλονίκης καὶ ρωμαϊκὰ θεάματα στὴ Μακεδονία', in M. Tiverios, P. Nigdelis, and P. Adam-Veleni (eds), Θρεπτήρια. Μελέτες γιὰ τὴν ἀρχαία Μακεδονία (Thessaloniki 2012), 280–315.

Adkins 2012 = Adkins, E., 'The intensive survey', in C. Ratté and P. D. De Staebler (eds), *The Aphrodisias Regional Survey* (Aphrodisias Final Reports, 5. Darmstadt/Mainz 2012), 87–134.

Ágoston 2014 = Ágoston, G., 'Firearms and Military Adaptation: The Ottomans and the European Military Revolution, 1450–1800', *Journal of World History* 25.1 (2014), 85–124.

Akçay-Güven 2018 = Akçay-Güven, B., 'A reworked group of emperor statues from the theatre of Perge', in M. Aurenhammer (ed.), *Sculpture in Roman Asia: Proceedings of the International Conference at Selçuk 2013* (Sonderschriften des Österreichischen Archäologischen Institutes der Österreichischen Akademie der Wissenschaften, 56. Vienna 2018), 365–376.

Akın 1968 = Akın, H., *Aydın Oğulları Tarihi Hakkında Bir Araştırma* [*Results of Studies in the History of the "Aydin Oğulları"*] (Dil ve Tarih-Coğrafya Fakültesi yayınları, 60. Ankara 1968).

Altınoluk 2013 = Altınoluk, S., *Hypaipa. A Lydian City during the Roman Imperial Period* (Istanbul 2013).

Alvino 1996 = Alvino, G., 'Il IX libro dell'Odissea: l'offerta della coppa di vino. Il gruppo fittile di Colle Cesarano e il gruppo scultoreo di Efeso', in B. Andreae and C. Parisi Presicce (eds), *Ulisse: il mito e la memoria. Roma, Palazzo delle Esposizioni, 22 febbraio – 2 settembre 1996* (Rome 1996), 200–209.

Ambraseys 2009 = Ambraseys, N. N., *Earthquakes in the Mediterranean and Middle East: A Multidisciplinary Study of Seismicity up to 1900* (Cambridge 2009).

Ameling 1987 = Ameling, W., 'Maximinus Thrax als Herakles', in *Bonner Historia-Augusta Colloquium 1984/1985*, vol. 5 (1987. Bonn 1987), 1–12.

Anderson 1982 = Anderson, J. C., Jr, 'Domitian, the Argiletum and the Temple of Peace', *AJA* 86 (1982), 101–110.

Anderson, Cumont, and Grégoire 1910 = Anderson, J. G. C., Cumont, F., and Grégoire, H., *Recueil des inscriptions grecques et latines du Pont et de l'Arménie* (Studia Pontica, 3. Brussels 1910).

Andreae 1977 = Andreae, B., 'Vorschlag für eine Rekonstruktion der Polyphemgruppe von Ephesos', in U. Höckmann and A. Krug (eds), *Festschrift für Frank Brommer* (Mainz 1977), 1–11.

Andreae 1982 = Andreae, B., *Odysseus: Archäologie des europäischen Menschenbildes* (Frankfurt 1982).

Andreae 1985 = Andreae, B., 'Die Polyphem-Gruppe von Ephesos', in H. Vetters, M. Kandler, S. Karweise, and R. Pillinger (eds), *Lebendige Altertumswissenschaft: Festgabe zur Vollendung des 70. Lebensjahres von Hermann Vetters* (Vienna 1985), 209–211.

Andreae 1999 = Andreae, B., 'Ist die Hypothese vom Polyphem-Giebel in Ephesos bereits falsifiziert?', in H. Friesinger and F. Frinzinger (eds), *100 Jahre österreichische Forschungen in Ephesos, Akten des Symposiums Wien 1995* (Wien 1999), 531–533.

Antonaras 2010 = Antonaras, A. C., 'Early Christian and Byzantine glass vessels: forms and uses', in F. Daim and J. Drauschke (eds), *Byzanz – das Römerreich im Mittelalter*. Teil 1: *Welt der Ideen, Welt der Dinge* (Mainz 2010), 383–430.

Antonaras 2012 = Antonaras, A. C., 'Gold-glass tile decoration in the St. Demetrios Basilica, Thessaloniki', in D. Ignatiadou and A. C. Antonaras (eds), *Annales du 18e Congrès de l'Association Internationale pour l'Histoire du Verre, Thessaloniki 2009* (Thessaloniki 2012), 301–306.

Arbuckle 2009 = Arbuckle, B., 'Chalcolithic caprines, Dark Age dairy, and Byzantine beef: A first look at animal exploitation at middle and late Holocene Çadır Höyük, north central Turkey.' *Anatolica* 35 (2009), 179–224.

Arndt et al. 2003 = Arndt, A., Van Neer, W., Hellemans, B., Robben, J., Volckaert, F., and Waelkens, M., 'Roman trade relationships at Sagalassos (Turkey) elucidated by ancient DNA of fish remains', *JAS* 30.9 (2003), 1095–1105.

Arslan 1992 = Arslan, M., *Roman Coins, Museum of Anatolian Civilizations* (Ankara 1992).

Arthur 1998 = Arthur, P., 'Eastern Mediterranean amphorae between 500 and 700: A view from Italy', in L. Saguì (ed.), *Ceramica in Italia: VI–VII secolo: atti del convegno in onore di John W. Hayes: Roma, 11–13 maggio 1995*, vol. 1 (Biblioteca di archeologia medievale, Firenze 1998), 157–184.

Arthur 2006 = Arthur, P., *Byzantine and Turkish Hierapolis (Pamukkale): An Archaeological Guide* (Hierapolis archaeological guides, Istanbul 2006).

Arthur 2012 = Arthur, P., 'Hierapolis of Phrygia: the drawn-out demise of an Anatolian city', in N. Christie and A. Augenti (eds), *Vrbes Extinctae: Archaeologies of Abandoned Classical Towns* (Farnham 2012), 275–305.

Arthur *et al.* 2012 = Arthur, P., Bruno, B., Imperiale, M. L., and Tinelli, M., 'Hierapolis bizantina e turca', in F. D'Andria, M. P. Caggia, and T. Ismaelli (eds), *Hierapolis di Frigia V. Le attività delle campagne di scavo e restauro 2004–2006* (Istanbul 2012), 565–583.

Artuk and Artuk 1971 = Artuk, I. and Artuk, C., *İstanbul Arkeoloji Müzeleri Teşhirdeki İslâmî Sikkeler Kataloğu*, vol. 1 (Istanbul 1971).

Artuk and Artuk 1974 = Artuk, I. and Artuk, C., *İstanbul Arkeoloji Müzeleri Teşhirdeki İslâmî Sikkeler Kataloğu*, vol. 2 (Istanbul 1974).

Asolati 1995 = Asolati, M., 'L'emissione vandala con il palmizio: prototipi punici e l'evidenza dei ripostigli', *RIN* 96 (1994/1995) (1995), 187–202.

Asolati and Crisafulli 2015 = Asolati, M. and Crisafulli, C., 'Tyana bizantina: circolazione e tesaurizzazione monetaria,' in D. Beyer, O. Henry, and A. Tibet (eds), *La Cappadoce méridionale de la préhistoire à la période byzantine, 3èmes Rencontres d'Archéologie de l'IFÉA, Istanbul, 8–9 novembre 2012* (Istanbul 2015), 233–249.

Atalay, Efe, and Soykan 2008 = Atalay, I., Efe, R., and Soykan, A., 'Mediterranean ecosystems of Turkey: ecology of the Taurus Mountains', in R. Efe, G. Cravins, M. Ozturk, and I. Atalay (eds), *Natural Environment and Culture in the Mediterranean Region*, vol. 1 (Newcastle-upon-Tyne 2008), 3–37.

Atik, Ortaçeşme, and Erdoğan 2011 = Atik, M. O., V. and R. Erdoğan, 'Landscape diversity in the Mediterranean region of Turkey', in R. Efe, M. Ozturk, and I. Atalay (eds), *Natural Environment and Culture in the Mediterranean Region*, vol. 2 (Newcastle-upon-Tyne 2011), 101–127.

Atik 2012 = Atik, Ş., 'Three Byzantine gold-glass pieces', in D. Ignatiadou and A. Antonaras (eds), *Annales du 18e Congrès de L'association Internationale pour L'histoire du Verre* (Thessaloniki 2012), 309–314.

Atlante 1981 = Atlante, *Atlante delle Forme Ceramiche I, Ceramica Fine Romana nel Bacino Mediterraneo (Medio e Tardo Impero)* (Enciclopedia dell'Arte Antica, Roma 1981).

Attanasio *et al.* 2015 = Attanasio, D., Bruno, M., Prochaska, W., and Yavuz, A., 'Analysis and discrimination of Phrygian and other Pavonazzetto-like marbles', in P. Pensabene and E. Gasparini (eds), *Interdisciplinary Studies on Ancient Stone. ASMOSIA X: Proceedings of the Tenth International Conference of ASMOSIA Association for the Study of Marble & Other Stones in Antiquity, Rome, 21–26 May 2012* (Roma 2015), 753–764.

Audollent 1904 = Audollent, A. M. H., *Defixionum tabellae quotquot innotuerunt: tam in Graecis Orientis quam in totius Occidentis partibus praeter Atticas in Corpore inscriptionum atticarum editas* (Paris 1904).

Aurenhammer 1990 = Aurenhammer, M., *Die Skulpturen von Ephesos: Bildwerke aus Stein. Idealplastik*, vol. 1 (Forschungen in Ephesos, 10/1. Wien 1990).

Austin 1934 = Austin, R. G., 'Zeno's game of τάβλη (A.P. ix. 482)', *The Journal of Hellenic Studies* 54 (1934), 202–205.

Austin 1935a = Austin, R. G., 'Roman board games, I', *Greece & Rome* 4.10 (1935), 24–34.

Austin 1935b = Austin, R. G., 'Roman board games, II', *Greece & Rome* 5.11 (1935), 76–82.

Avşar and Genç 2016 = Avşar, O. B. and Genç, U. D., 'A Multi-Layered Cultural Site in Muğla: Eskihisar Village', in Z. Ahunbay, D. Mazlum, Z. Eres, L. Thys-Şenocak, and E. Yıldırım (eds), *Conservation of Cultural Heritage in Turkey* (Istanbul 2016), 388–400.

Avşar and Genç 2018 = Avşar, O. B. and Genç, U. D., 'Vernacular houses of Stratonikeia: Architectural typology, materials and techniques', in C. Mileto, F. V. López-Manzanares, L. García-Soriano, and V. Cristini (eds), *Vernacular and Earthen Architecture: Conservation and Sustainability: Proceedings of SosTierra 2017 (Valencia, Spain, 14–16 September 2017)* (London 2018), 35–40.

Ayhan 2015 = Ayhan, G., 'Ayasuluk İç Kalesi "Süzgeç Çanaklı" ve "Kaideli Süzgeç Çanaklı" Lüle Buluntular', in C. Şimşek, B. Duman, and E. Konakçı (eds), *Mustafa Büyükkolancı'ya Armağan* (Istanbul 2015), 41–51.

Bachmann and Lorentzen 2017 = Bachmann, M. and Lorentzen, J., 'Steinmetzmarken als Quellen zum Baugeschehen in Pergamon', in D. Kurapkat and U. Wulf-Rheidt (eds), *Werkspuren. Materialverarbeitung und handwerkliches Wissen im antiken Bauwesen* (Diskussionen zur archäologischen Bauforschung, 12. Regensburg 2017), 427–434.

Baeten *et al.* 2012 = Baeten, J., Marinova, E., De Laet, V., Degryse, P., De Vos, D., and Waelkens, M., 'Faecal biomarker and archaeobotanical analyses of sediments from a public latrine shed new light on ruralisation in Sagalassos, Turkey', *JAS* 39.4 (2012), 1143–1159.

Bagnall 2011 = Bagnall, R. S., *Everyday Writing in the Graeco-Roman East* (Berkeley 2011).

Bagnall *et al.* 2016 = Bagnall, R. S., Casagrande-Kim, R., Ersoy, A., and Tanrıver, C., *Graffiti from the Basilica in the Agora of Smyrna* (New York 2016).

Bain 1997 = Bain, D., 'Two submerged items of Greek sexual vocabulary from Aphrodisias', *ZPE* 117 (1997), 81–84.

Baker and Brothwell 1980 = Baker, J. and Brothwell, D. R., *Animal Diseases in Archaeology* (London 1980).

Baldoni and Franco 1995 = Baldoni, D. and Franco, C., 'Unguentaria tardoantichi di Iasos', *Rivista di Archaeologia* 19 (1995), 121–128.

Bartoccini 1929 = Bartoccini, R., *Le terme di Leptis* (L'Africa italiana, Bergamo 1929).

Bartosiewicz 2005 = Bartosiewicz, L., 'Animal remains from the excavations of Horum Höyük, southeast Anatolia, Turkey', in H. Buitenhuis, A. M. Choyke, L. Martin, L. Bartosiewicz and M. Mashkour (eds), *Archaeozoology of the Near East VI: Proceedings of the Sixth International Symposium on the Archaeozoology of Southwestern Asia and Adjacent Areas* (Groningen 2005), 150–162.

Bartosiewicz and Gál 2003 = Bartosiewicz, L. and Gál, E., 'Ottoman Period Animal Exploitation in Hungary', in I. Gerelyes and G. Kovács (eds), *Archeology of the Ottoman Pe-*

riod in Hungary (Opuscula Hungarica 3, Budapest 2003), 365–376.

Bartosiewicz and Gál 2018 = Bartosiewicz, L. and Gál, E., 'Ottoman Turkish influences on animal exploitation in 16th–17th century Hungary', in C. Çakırlar, C. Chahoud, R. Berthon, and S. Pilaar Birch (eds), *Archaeozoology of the Near East XII* (Groningen 2018), 191–206.

Bates 1971 = Bates, G. E., *Byzantine coins* (Archaeological Exploration of Sardis, 1. Cambridge, MA / London 1971).

Bedal 2004 = Bedal, L.-A., *The Petra Pool-complex: A Hellenistic Paradeisos in the Nabataean Capital* (Piscataway, N.J. 2004).

Behling 2014 = Behling, C.-M., 'Der sog. Rundmühle auf der Spur-Zug um Zug zur Neudeutung römischer Radmuster', in E. Trinkl (ed.), *Akten des 14. Österreichischen Archäologentages am Institut für Archäologie der Universität Graz vom 19. bis 21. April 2012* (Vienna 2014), 63–70.

Beihammer 2017 = Beihammer, A. D., *Byzantium and the Emergence of Muslim-Turkish Anatolia, ca. 1040–1130* (Birmingham Byzantine and Ottoman Studies, London and New York 2017).

Belayche 2004a = Belayche, N., 'Pagan festivals in fourth-century Gaza', in B. B. Ashkelony and A. Kofsky (eds), *Christian Gaza In Late Antiquity* (Jerusalem Studies in Religion and Culture, 3. Leiden 2004), 5–22.

Belayche 2004b = Belayche, N., 'Une panégyrie antiochéenne: le *Maïouma*', *Topoi. Orient-Occident* Supplément 5 (2004), 401–415.

Bell and Roueché 2007 = Bell, R. C. and Roueché, C., 'Graeco-Roman pavement signs and game boards: a British Museum working typology', in I. L. Finkel (ed.), *Ancient Board Games in Perspective* (London 2007), 106–109.

Bellinger 1966 = Bellinger, A. R., *Catalogue of the Byzantine coins in the Dumbarton Oaks Collection and in the Whittemore Collection*, vol. 1: *Anastasius to Maurice, 491–602* (Washington, DC 1966).

Bendall 1996 = Bendall, S., *Byzantine Weights: an Introduction* (London 1996).

Berenfeld 2009 = Berenfeld, M. L., 'The Triconch House and the predecessors of the Bishop's Palace at Aphrodisias', *AJA* 113.2 (2009), 203–230.

Berenfeld 2019 = Berenfeld, M. L., *The Triconch House* (Aphrodisias, 11. Wiesbaden 2019).

Berger 2004 = Berger, F., 'From circle and square to the image of the world: a possible interpretation for some petroglyphs of merels boards', *Rock Art Research* 21.1 (2004), 11–25.

Bergmann 1999 = Bergmann, M., *Chiragan, Aphrodisias, Konstantinopel: Zur mythologischen Skulptur der Spätantike*: *Palilia* (Palilia, 7. Wiesbaden 1999).

Bernand 1984 = Bernand, A., *Les portes du désert: recueil des inscriptions grecques d'Antinooupolis, Tentyris, Koptos, Apollonopolis Parva et Apollonopolis Magna* (Paris 1984).

Bertolero and Busack 2017 = Bertolero, A. and Busack, S., '*Mauremys leprosa* (Schoepff in Schweigger 1812) – Mediterranean Pond Turtle, Spanish Terrapin, Mediterranean Stripe-Necked Terrapin', in A. Rhodin, J. Iverson, P. Van Dijk, K. Buhlmann, P. Pritchard, and R. Mittermeier (eds), *Conservation Biology of Freshwater Turtles and Tortoises: A Compilation Project of the IUCN SSC Tortoise and Freshwater Turtle Specialist Group* (2017), 102.1–19.

Beuls *et al.* 2000 = Beuls, I., De Cupere, B., Vermoere, M., Vanhecke, L., Doutrelepont, H., Vrydaghs, L., Librecht, I., and Waelkens, M., 'Modern sheep and goat herding near Sagalassos and its relevance to the reconstruction of pastoral practices in Roman times', in M. Waelkens and L. Loots (eds), *Sagalassos V. Report on the Survey and Excavation Campaigns of 1996 and 1997*, vol. 2 (Leuven 2000), 847–861.

Bezeczky 2013 = Bezeczky, T., *The Amphorae of Roman Ephesus* (Forschungen in Ephesos, 15 part 1 Wien 2013).

Bier 2008 = Bier, L., 'The Bouleuterion', in C. Ratté and R. R. R. Smith (eds), *Aphrodisias Papers 4: New Research on the City and its Monuments* (JRA Supplementary Series, 70. Portsmouth, Rhode Island 2008), 144–168.

Bierbrauer and Bosio 1987 = Bierbrauer, V. and Bosio, L., *Invillino-Ibligo in Friaul: die römische Siedlung und das spätantik-frühmittelalterliche Castrum* (Veröffentlichung der Kommission zur Archäologischen Erforschung des Spätrömischen Raetien der Bayerischen Akademie der Wissenschaften, 33–34. München 1987).

Bijovsky 1998 = Bijovsky, G., 'The Gush Ḥalav Hoard Reconsidered', *'Atiqot* 35 (1998), 77–106.

Bijovsky 2002 = Bijovsky, G., 'The currency of the fifth century CE in Palestine–some reflections in light of the numismatic evidence', *INJ* 14.2000–2002 (2002), 196–210.

Bijovsky 2011 = Bijovsky, G., 'From Carthage to the Holy Land: the 'palm tree' *nummus*', *Israel Numismatic Research* 6 (2011), 163–173.

Bijovsky 2012 = Bijovsky, G., *Gold Coin and Small Change: Monetary Circulation in Fifth–Seventh Century Byzantine Palestine* (Polymnia Numismatica antica e medievale Studi, 2. Trieste 2012).

Binford 1984 = Binford, L., *Faunal Remains from Klasies River Mouth* (Orlando 1984).

Bingöl 1980 = Bingöl, O., *Das ionische Normalkapitell in hellenistischer und römischer Zeit in Kleinasien* (Istanbuler Mitteilungen Beiheft, 20. Tübingen 1980).

Bishop and Coulston 2006 = Bishop, M. C. and Coulston, J. C. N., *Roman Military Equipment from the Punic Wars to the Fall of Rome* (Oxford 2006).

Biton *et al.* 2017 = Biton, R., Sharon, G., Oron, M., Steiner, T., and Rabinovich, R., 'Freshwater turtle or tortoise? The exploitation of testudines at the Mousterian site of Nahal Mahanayeem Outlet, Hula Valley, Israel', *Journal of Archaeological Science: Reports* 14 (2017), 409–419.

Bloch 2006 = Bloch, F., 'Ḫirbat al-Minya. Die unglasierte Keramik', in F. Bloch, V. Daiber, and P. Knötzele (eds), *Studien zur spätantiken und islamischen Keramik. Ḫirbat al-Minya – Baalbek – Resafa* (Orient Archäologie, 18. Rahden 2006), 1–110.

Blümlein 1918 = Blümlein, C., *Bilder aus dem römisch-germanischen Kulturleben (nach Funden und Denkmälern)* (München 1918).

Boessneck and von den Driesch 1975 = Boessneck, J. and von den Driesch, V., 'Tierknochenfunde vom Korucutepe bei Elazig in Ostanatolien', in M. N. Van Loon (ed.), *Korucutepe. Final Report on the Excavations of the Universities of Chi-*

cago, California (Los Angeles) and Amsterdam in the Keban Reservoir, Eastern Anatolia 1968–1970, vol. 1 (Amsterdam and Oxford 1975), 1–220.

Boeswillwald, Cagnat, and Ballu 1905 = Boeswillwald, E., Cagnat, R., and Ballu, A., *Timgad, une cité africaine sous l'empire romain* (Paris 1905).

Böhlendorf-Arslan 2008 = Böhlendorf-Arslan, B., 'Keramikproduktion im byzantinischen und türkischen Milet', *IstMitt* 58 (2008), 371–407.

Bol 2011 = Bol, R., *Funde aus Milet*, vol. 2: *Marmorskulpturen der römischen Kaiserzeit aus Milet* (Milet, 5. Berlin; New York 2011).

Bonner 1950 = Bonner, C., *Studies in Magical Amulets, chiefly Graeco-Egyptian* (Ann Arbor, MI 1950).

Borg 2007 = Borg, B. E., 'Aphrodisians on display: the public image of a local elite', *JRA* 20 (2007), 583–588.

Borg-Cardona, A. 2013 = Borg-Cardona, A., 'The Marine Shell in and around the Maltese Islands', *The Galpin Society Journal* (2013), 185–261.

Boschung 2002 = Boschung, D., *Gens Augusta: Untersuchungen zu Aufstellung, Wirkung und Bedeutung der Statuengruppen des julisch-claudischen Kaiserhauses* (Monumenta artis Romanae, Mainz am Rhein 2002).

Boulanger 1914 = Boulanger, A., 'Note sur les fouilles exécutées à Aphrodisias en 1913', *Comptes rendus de l'Académie des inscriptions et belles-lettres* 58.1 (1914), 46–53.

Bourtzinakou 2012 = Bourtzinakou, I., *Die Prosopographie von Aphrodisias*. Ph.D. thesis, Ruprecht-Karls-Universität, Heidelberg.

Bowie 2012 = Bowie, E. L., 'Hadrien et Smyrne', in A. Hostein and S. Lalanne (eds), *Les voyages des empereurs dans l'orient romain. Époques antonine et sévérienne* (Paris 2012), 247–261.

Boyaval 2002 = Boyaval, B., 'Notes égyptiennes', *Kentron. Revue pluridisciplinaire du monde antique*.18 (2002), 145–174.

Boydak 1985 = Boydak, M., 'The distribution of Phoenix theophrasti in the Datça Peninsula, Turkey', *Biological Conservation* 32 (1985), 129–135.

Boydak 1987 = Boydak, M., 'A new occurrence of Phoenix theophrasti in Kumluca – Karaöz, Turkey', *Principes* 31.2 (1987), 89–95.

Boydak 2000 = Boydak, M., 'Plant Diversity, Phoenix theophrasti and Pinus brutia in Turkey', in A. J. Karamanos and C. A. Thanos (eds), *Biodiversity and Natural Heritage in the Aegean. Proceedings of the Conference "Theophrastus 2000" (July 6–8, 2000, Eressos, Sigri, Lesbos – Greece)* (Athens 2000), 251–259.

Boydak and Barrow 1995 = Boydak, M. and Barrow, S., 'A new locality of Phoenix in Turkey; Gölköy-Bodrum', *Principes* 39.3 (1995), 117–122.

Brandes 1989 = Brandes, W., *Die Städte Kleinasiens im 7. und 8. Jahrhundert* (Berliner byzantinistische Arbeiten, 56. Amsterdam 1989).

Brenk 1987 = Brenk, B., '*Spolia* from Constantine to Charlemagne: aesthetics versus ideology', *DOP* 41 (1987), 103–111.

Brilliant and Kinney 2011 = Brilliant, R. and Kinney, D. (eds), *Reuse Value: Spolia and Appropriation in Art and Architecture from Constantine to Sherrie Levine* (Farnham 2011).

Brody 2007 = Brody, L. R., *The Aphrodite of Aphrodisias* (Aphrodisias, 3. Mainz am Rhein 2007).

Broome and Novák 2011 = Broome, M. and Novák, V., *A Survey of the Coinage of the Seljuqs of Rum* (Royal Numismatic Society special publication, 48. London 2011).

Bruns 1935 = Bruns, G., *Der Obelisk und seine Basis auf dem Hippodrom zu Konstantinopel* (Istanbuler Forschungen, 7. Istanbul 1935).

Burlot *et al.* 2018 = Burlot, J., Waksman, S. Y., Böhlendorf-Arslan, B., Vroom, J., Japp, S., and Teslenko, I., 'The early Turkish pottery productions in western Anatolia: provenances, contextualization and techniques', in F. Yenişehirlioğlu (ed.), *XIth Congress AIECM3 on Medieval and Modern Period Mediterranean Ceramics: Proceedings*, vol. 1 (Antalya 2018), 427–430.

Burrell 2008 = Burrell, B., 'Small bronze hoards at late fifth century CE Sardis', in N. D. Cahill (ed.), *Love for Lydia, A Sardis anniversary volume presented to Crawford H. Greenewalt, Jr* (Archaeological Exploration of Sardis, 4. Cambridge, MA, and London 2008), 159–169.

Buttrey *et al.* 1981 = Buttrey, T. V., Johnston, A., MacKenzie, K. M., and Bates, M. L., *Greek, Roman, and Islamic Coins from Sardis* (Archaeological Exploration of Sardis, Monograph, 7. Cambridge, MA and London 1981).

Cahill 2010 = Cahill, N., *Lidyalılar ve dünyaları = The Lydians and their world* (Yapı Kredi Yayınları, Istanbul 2010).

Cahill 2018 = Cahill, N., 'Sardis, 2016', in *39. Kazı Sonuçları Toplantısı. 22–26 Mayis 2017, Bursa*, vol. 3 (Bursa 2018), 327–344.

Cahill 2019 = Cahill, N., 'Recent fieldwork at Sardis', in S. R. Steadman and G. McMahon (eds), *The Archaeology of Anatolia*, vol. III: *Recent Discoveries (2017–2018)* (Newcastle-upon-Tyne 2019), 122–138.

Çakırlar and Marston 2019 = Çakırlar, C. and Marston, J. M., 'Rural agricultural economies and military provisioning at Roman Gordion (central Turkey)', *Environmental Archaeology* 24.1 (2019), 91–105.

Çakmaklı 2014 = Çakmaklı, O. D., 'Roman and Byzantine glass workshop in Caria. An assessment of new finds and evidence', *Anatolia* 40 (2014), 131–141.

Cameron 1973 = Cameron, A., *Porphyrius the Charioteer* (Oxford 1973).

Campanile 1994 = Campanile, M. D., *I sacerdoti del koinon d'Asia (I sec. a.C.–III sec. d.C.): contributo allo studio della romanizzazione delle élites provinciali nell'Oriente greco* (Studi ellenistici, 7. Pisa 1994).

Canav Özgümüş 2009 = Canav Özgümüş, U., 'Late Roman/Early Byzantine glass from the Marmaray rescue excavations at Sirkeci, Istanbul', in E. Laflı (ed.), *Late Antique/Early Byzantine Glass in the Eastern Mediterranean* (Colloquia Anatolica et Aegaea – Acta Congressus Communis Omnium Gentium Smyrnae, 2. Istanbul 2009), 17–24.

Cappers, Neef, and Bekker 2019 = Cappers, R. T. J., Neef, R., and Bekker, R. M., *Digital Plant Atlas*, (2019), University of Groningen and Deutsches Archäologisches Institut. Accessed 11 November 2021

Carboni and Whitehouse 2001 = Carboni, S. and Whitehouse, D. B., *Glass of the Sultans* (New York 2001).

Carey 2002 = Carey, S., 'A tradition of adventures in the imperial grotto', *Greece & Rome* 49.1 (2002), 44–61.

Carroll 2010 = Carroll, M., 'Exploring the sanctuary of Venus and its sacred grove: politics, cult and identity in Roman Pompeii', *PBSR* 78 (2010), 63–106, 347–351.

Carroll 2018 = Carroll, M., 'Temple gardens and sacred groves', in W. F. Jashemski, K. L. Gleason, K. J. Hartswick, and A. A. Malek (eds), *Gardens of the Roman Empire* (Cambridge 2018), 152–164.

Caruso 2016 = Caruso, S., 'Middle Byzantine jewelry assemblages', in R. R. R. Smith, J. Lenaghan, A. Sokolicek, and E. Welch (eds), *Aphrodisias Papers 5: Excavation and Research at Aphrodisias, 2006–2012* (JRA Supplementary Series, 103. Portsmouth, R.I. 2016), 353–367.

Caseau 2014 = Caseau, B., 'Les marqueurs de pain, objets rituels dans le christianisme antique et byzantin', *Revue de l'histoire des religions* 4 (2014), 599–617.

Casey 2010 = Casey, J., *Sinope – A catalogue of The Greek, Roman and Byzantine Coins in Sinop Museum (Turkey) and Related Historical and Numismatic Studies* (Royal Numismatic Society Special Publication, 44. London 2010).

Cassis et al. 2018 = Cassis, M., Doonan, O., Elton, H., and Newhard, J., 'Evaluating archaeological evidence for demographics, abandonment, and recovery in Late Antique and Byzantine Anatolia', *Human Ecology* 46.3 (2018), 381–398.

Chameroy 2009 = Chameroy, J., 'Von Gallien nach Nordafrika münzen der Gallischen Usurpatoren (260–274 n. Chr.) außerhalb des Gallischen Sonderreichs', *JRGZM* 56 (2009), 321–394.

Chameroy 2012 = Chameroy, J., 'Chronologie und Verbreitung der hellenistischen Bronzeprägungen von Pergamon: der Beitrag der Fundmünzen', *Chiron* 42 (2012), 131–181.

Chameroy 2018 = Chameroy, J., 'The circulation of Gallic Empire coins in western Asia Minor in light of excavated coins', in O. Tekin (ed.), *Second International Congress on the History of Money and Numismatics in the Mediterranean World* (Istanbul 2018), 389–411.

Chaniotis 2002a = Chaniotis, A., 'The Jews of Aphrodisias: new evidence and old problems', *Scripta Classica Israelica* 21 (2002), 209–242.

Chaniotis 2002b = Chaniotis, A., 'Zwischen Konfrontation und Interaktion: Christen, Juden und Heiden im spätantiken Aphrodisias', in A. Ackermann and K. E. Müller (eds), *Patchwork. Dimensionen multikultureller Gesellschaften: Geschichte, Problematik und Chancen* (Bielefeld 2002), 83–128.

Chaniotis 2004 = Chaniotis, A., 'New inscriptions from Aphrodisias (1995–2001)', *AJA* 108.3 (2004), 377–416.

Chaniotis 2005 = Chaniotis, A., 'Macht und Volk in den kaiserzeitlichen Inschriften von Aphrodisias', in G. Urso (ed.), *Popolo e potere nel mondo antico. Atti del convegno internazionale, Cividale del Friuli, 23–25 settembre 2004* (I convegni della Fondazione Niccolò Canussio, 4. Pisa 2005), 47–61.

Chaniotis 2008a = Chaniotis, A., 'The conversion of the temple of Aphrodite at Aphrodisias in context', in J. Hahn, S. Emmel, and U. Gotter (eds), *From Temple to Church: Destruction and Renewal of Local Cultic Topography in Late Antiquity* (Religions in the Graeco-Roman World, 163. Leiden 2008), 243–273.

Chaniotis 2008b = Chaniotis, A., 'Twelve buildings in search of locations: known and unknown buildings in the inscriptions of Aphrodisias', in C. Ratté and R. R. R. Smith (eds), *Aphrodisias Papers 4: New Research on the City and its Monuments* (JRA Supplementary Series, 70. Portsmouth, Rhode Island 2008), 61–78.

Chaniotis 2009a = Chaniotis, A., 'Acclamations as a form of religious communication', in H. Cancik and J. Rüpke (eds), *Die Religion des Imperium Romanum: Koine und Konfrontationen* (Tübingen 2009), 199–218.

Chaniotis 2009b = Chaniotis, A., 'Myths and contexts in Aphrodisias', in U. Dill and C. Walde (eds), *Antike Mythen: Medien, Transformationen und Konstruktionen* (Berlin 2009), 313–338.

Chaniotis 2011a = Chaniotis, A., 'Aphrodite's rivals: devotion to local and other gods at Aphrodisias', *Cahiers du Centre Gustave Glotz* 21 (2010 [2011]), 235–248.

Chaniotis 2011b = Chaniotis, A., 'Graffiti in Aphrodisias: images—texts—contexts', in J. A. Baird and C. Taylor (eds), *Ancient Graffiti in Context* (London 2011), 191–207.

Chaniotis 2013a = Chaniotis, A., 'Roman Army in Aphrodisias', *Revue des Études Militaires Anciennes* 6 (2013), 151–158.

Chaniotis 2013b = Chaniotis, A., 'Second thoughts on second names in Aphrodisias', in R. Parker (ed.), *Personal Names in Ancient Anatolia* (Proceedings of the British Academy, 191. Oxford 2013), 207–229.

Chaniotis 2015a = Chaniotis, A., *Aphrodisias, 2015 Field Report on Inscriptions* (Unpublished project report 2015).

Chaniotis 2015b = Chaniotis, A., 'Das kaiserzeitliche Gymnasion in Aphrodisias', in P. Scholz and D. Wiegandt (eds), *Das kaiserzeitliche Gymnasion* (Wissenskultur und gesellschaftlicher Wandel, 34. Berlin / Boston 2015), 111–131.

Chaniotis 2018a = Chaniotis, A., 'Alltagsskizzen aus Aphrodisias', in P. Lohmann (ed.), *Historische Graffiti als Quellen. Methoden und Perspektiven eines jungen Forschungsgebereiches* (Stuttgart 2018), 77–91.

Chaniotis 2018b = Chaniotis, A., 'Myon, a true *ktistes*: a new inscription from Aphrodisias and its context', in C. M. Draycott, R. Raja, K. Welch, and W. T. Wootton (eds), *Visual Histories of the Classical World: Essays in Honour of R.R.R. Smith* (Studies in Classical Archaeology, 4. Turnhout 2018), 449–458.

Chaniotis 2019 = Chaniotis, A., 'The Epigraphy of the Night', in C. F. Noreña and N. Papazarkadas (eds), *From Document to History: Epigraphic Insights into the Greco-Roman World* (Brill Studies in Greek and Roman Epigraphy, Leiden 2019), 13–36.

Chaniotis 2020 = Chaniotis, A., 'Benefactors in Aphrodisias and the socio-cultural limits of philanthropy', in O. Tekin, C. H. Roosevelt, and A. Engin (eds), *Philanthropy in Anatolia Through the Ages. The First International Suna & İnan Kıraç Symposium on Mediterranean Civilizations, March 26–29, 2019* (Istanbul 2020), 111–120.

Chaniotis 2021 = Chaniotis, A., '"Those who jointly built the city": Epigraphic sources for the urban development of Aphrodisias', in K. Kalogeropoulos, D. Vassilikou, and M. Tiverios (eds), *Sidelights on Greek Antiquity: Archaeological and Epigraphical Essays in Honour of Vasileios Petrakos* (Berlin 2021), 179–193.

Chaniotis and De Staebler 2018 = Chaniotis, A. and De Staebler, P. D., 'Gladiators and animals. New pictorial graffiti from Aphrodisias and their contexts', *PHILIA* 4 (2018), 31–54.

Chaniotis and Fujii 2015 = Chaniotis, A. and Fujii, T., 'A new fragment of Diocletian's currency regulation from Aphrodisias', *JRS* 105 (2015), 227–233.

Chao and Kruger 2007 = Chao, C. T. and Kruger, R. R., 'The date palm (*Phoenix dactylifera* L.): overview of biology, uses and cultivation', *Horticultural Science* 42 (2007), 1077–1082.

Chavane 1975 = Chavane, M.-J., *Salamine de Chypre*, vol. 6: *Les petits objets* (Paris 1975).

Chilardi and Viglio 2010 = Chilardi, S. and Viglio, F., 'Patologie dentarie nei resti animali provenienti dalle UUSS 1–16 del fossato neolitico di Contrada Stretto Partanna (Trapani)', in A. Tagliacozzo, I. Fiore, S. Marconi, and U. Tecchiati (eds), *Atti del 5° Convengo Nazionale di Archeozoologia, Rovereto, 10–12 novembre 2006* (Rovereto 2010), 119–127.

Christol 1986 = Christol, M., *Essai sur l'évolution des carrières sénatoriales dans la seconde moitié du IIIe siècle ap. J.C.* (Études prosopographiques, 6. Paris 1986).

Ciaraldi and Richardson 2000 = Ciaraldi, M. and Richardson, J., 'Food, ritual and rubbish in the making of Pompeii', in G. Fincham, G. Harrison, R. R. Holland, and L. Revel (eds), *TRAC 99. Proceedings of the 9th Annual Theoretical Roman Archaeology Conference, Durham April 1999* (Oxford 2000), 74–82.

Clark 1995 = Clark, J., 'Currycombs', in J. Clark (ed.), *The Medieval Horse and Its Equipment c.1150–c.1450* (Medieval Finds from Excavations in London, 5. London 1995), 157–168.

Cleymans and Talloen 2018 = Cleymans, S. and Talloen, P., 'Protection in life and death: pendant crosses from the cemetery of Apollo Klarios at Sagalassos, Turkey', *EJA* 21.2 (2018), 280–298.

Coarelli 1972 = Coarelli, F., 'Il complesso pompeiano del Campo Marzio e la sua decorazione scultorea', *RendPontAcc* 44 (1971–1972) (1972), 99–122.

Coarelli 1977 = Coarelli, F., 'Il Campo Marzio occidentale. Storia e topografia', *Mélanges de l'école française de Rome* 89.2 (1977), 807–846.

Coarelli 1993 = Coarelli, F., 'I luci di Lazio: la documentazione archeologica', in O. de Cazanove and J. Scheid (eds), *Les bois sacrés: Actes du Colloque international organisé par le Centre Jean Bérard et l'École pratique des Hautes Études (Ve section), Naples, 23–25 Novembre 1989* (Naples 1993), 45–52.

Coarelli 1999 = Coarelli, F., 'Pax, Templum', in E. M. Steinby (ed.), *Lexicon Topographicum Urbis Romae*, vol. 4 (Roma 1999), 67–70.

Coates-Stephens 2003 = Coates-Stephens, R., 'Attitudes to spolia in some late antique texts', in L. Lavan and W. Bowden (eds), *Theory and Practice in Late Antique Archaeology*, vol. 1 (Late Antique Archaeology, 1. Leiden 2003), 341–358.

Coleman 1993 = Coleman, K. M., 'Launching into history: aquatic displays in the early empire', *JRS* 83 (1993), 48–74.

Coleman 2008 = Coleman, K. M., 'Exchanging gladiators for an aqueduct at Aphrodisias (SEG 50.1096)', *Acta Classica* 51 (2008), 31–46.

Collignon 1904 = Collignon, M., 'Note sur les fouilles exécutées à Aphrodisias par M. Paul Gaudin', *Comptes rendus de l'Académie des inscriptions et belles-lettres* 48.6 (1904), 703–711.

Collignon 1906 = Collignon, M., 'Les fouilles d'Aphrodisias', *Revue de l'Art Français Ancien et Moderne* 19 (1906), 33–50.

Commito 2019 = Commito, A. R., 'The cities of southern Asia Minor in the sixth century', in I. Jacobs and H. Elton (eds), *Asia Minor in the Long Sixth Century: Current Research and Future Directions* (Oxford & Philadelphia 2019), 109–142.

Commito and Rojas 2012 = Commito, A. R. and Rojas, F., 'The Aqueducts of Aphrodisias', in C. Ratté and P. D. De Staebler (eds), *Aphrodisias V. The Aphrodisias Regional Survey* (Mainz 2012), 239–307.

Contardi 2009 = Contardi, S., 'Late Antique glass from Iasos (Caria)', in E. Laflı (ed.), *Late Antique/Early Byzantine Glass in the Eastern Mediterranean* (Izmir 2009), 123–132.

Cope 2002 = Cope, C. R., 'Palestinian butchering patterns: Their relation to traditional marketing of meat', in H. Buitenhuis, A. M. Choyke, M. Mashkour, and A. H. Al-Shiyab (eds), *Archaeozoology of the Near East V. Proceedings of the Fifth International Symposium on the Archaeozoology of Southwestern Asia and Adjacent Areas* (Groningen 2002), 316–319.

Cormack 1964 = Cormack, J. M. R., 'Inscriptions from Aphrodisias', *BSA* 59 (1964), 16–29.

Cormack 1990a = Cormack, R., 'Byzantine Aphrodisias: changing the symbolic map of a city', *The Cambridge Classical Journal* 36 (1990), 26–41.

Cormack 1990b = Cormack, R., 'The temple as the cathedral', in C. Roueché and K. T. Erim (eds), *Aphrodisias Papers. Recent Work on Architecture and Sculpture* (JRA Supplementary Series, 1. Ann Arbor, MI 1990), 75–88.

Cormack 1991 = Cormack, R., 'The wall-painting of St. Michael in the theatre', in R. R. R. Smith and K. T. Erim (eds), *Aphrodisias Papers 2: The Theatre, a Sculptor's Workshop, Philosophers, and Coin-types* (JRA Supplementary Series, 2. Ann Arbor, MI 1991), 109–126.

Cottica 1998 = Cottica, D., 'Ceramiche bizantine dipinte ed unguentari tardo antichi dalla "Casa dei capitelli ionici" a Hierapolis', *Rivista di Archeologia* 22 (1998), 81–90.

Coulton 1976 = Coulton, J. J., *The Architectural Development of the Greek Stoa* (Oxford 1976).

Cox 1950 = Cox, D. H., 'The coins', in H. Goldman (ed.), *Excavations at Gözlü Kule, Tarsus*, vol. 1.2: *The Hellenistic and Roman Periods* (Princeton 1950), 38–83.

Crawford 1990 = Crawford, J. S., *The Byzantine Shops at Sardis* (Archaeological Exploration of Sardis, 9. Cambridge, MA, and London 1990).

Crawford 2002 = Crawford, M. H., 'Discovery, autopsy and progress: Diocletian's jigsaw puzzles', in T. P. Wiseman (ed.), *Classics in Progress: Essays on Ancient Greece and Rome* (Oxford 2002).

Crawford and Stinson 2023 = Crawford, M. H. and Stinson, P., *Diocletian's Edict of Maximum Prices at the Civil Basilica in Aphrodisias* (Aphrodisias, 13. Wiesbaden 2023).

Crema 1939 = Crema, L., 'I monumenti architettonici afrodisiensi', *MonAnt* 38 (1939), 233–312.

Crist 2020 = Crist, W., 'Scratching the surface: graffiti games in the Byzantine Empire', in V. Kopp and E. Lapina (eds), *Games and Visual Culture in the Middle Ages and the Renaissance* (Studies in the History of Daily Life (800–1600), 8. Turnhout 2020), 333–353.

Csallány 1954 = Csallány, D., 'Les monuments de l'industrie byzantine des métaux I', *Acta Antiqua Academiae Scientiarum Hungaricae* 2 (1954), 311–340.

Csiky 2015 = Csiky, G., *Avar-Age Polearms and Edged Weapons: Classification, Typology, Chronology and Technology* (East Central and Eastern Europe in the Middle Ages, 450–1450, 32. Leiden / Boston 2015).

Curta 2008 = Curta, F., 'The earliest Avar-age stirrups, or the "stirrup controversy" revisited', in F. Curta (ed.), *The Other Europe in the Middle Ages: Avars, Bulgars, Khazars and Cumans* (East Central and Eastern Europe in the Middle Ages, 450–1450, 2. Leiden / Boston 2008), 297–326.

Curta 2013 = Curta, F., 'Horsemen in forts or peasants in villages? Remarks on the archaeology of warfare in the 6th to 7th c. Balkans', in A. Sarantis and N. Christie (eds), *War and Warfare in Late Antiquity. Current Perspectives*, vol. 2 (Late Antique Archaeology, 8. Leiden 2013), 809–850.

Dalgıç and Sokolicek 2017 = Dalgıç, Ö. and Sokolicek, A., 'Aphrodisias', in P. Niewöhner (ed.), *The Archaeology of Byzantine Anatolia* (Oxford 2017), 269–278.

Damalı 2010 = Damalı, A., *Osmanlı Sikkeleri Tarihi / History of Ottoman Coins*, vol. 1 (Istanbul 2010).

Darwall-Smith 1996 = Darwall-Smith, R. H., *Emperors and Architecture: A Study of Flavian Rome* (Collection Latomus, Brussels 1996).

Davidson 1952 = Davidson, G. R., *Corinth*, vol. 12: *The Minor Objects* (Princeton, N. J. 1952).

Davies 2017 = Davies, P. J. E., *Architecture and Politics in Republican Rome* (Cambridge 2017).

Davis 1980 = Davis, S., 'Late Pleistocene and Holocene equid remains from Israel', *Zoological Journal of the Linnean Society* 70.3 (1980), 289–312.

De Bernardi Ferrero 2002 = De Bernardi Ferrero, D., 'Architettura e decorazione di età flavia a Hierapolis di Frigia', in *Hierapolis IV: Saggi in onore di Paolo Verzone* (Archaeologica, 137. Rome 2002), 1–43.

de Chaisemartin 1987 = de Chaisemartin, N., 'Recherches sur la frise de l'Agora de Tibère', in J. De la Genière and K. T. Erim (eds), *Aphrodisias de Carie, Colloque de l'Université de Lille III, 13 novembre 1985* (Paris 1987), 135–154.

de Chaisemartin 1989a = de Chaisemartin, N., 'Le Portique de Tibère', *DossPar* 139 (1989), 60–73.

de Chaisemartin 1989b = de Chaisemartin, N., 'Le Portique de Tibère à Aphrodisias: problèmes d'identification et de fonction', *RÉA* 91 (1989), 23–45.

de Chaisemartin 1998 = de Chaisemartin, N., 'Mission française d'Aphrodisias: Aperçu sur les recherches en cours', *Anatolia Antiqua* 6 (1998), 203–225.

de Chaisemartin 1999 = de Chaisemartin, N., 'Technical aspects of the sculptural decoration at Aphrodisias in Caria', in M. Schvoerer (ed.), *Archéomatériaux: marbres et autres roches* (ASMOSIA, IV. Bordeaux 1999), 261–267.

de Chaisemartin forthcoming = de Chaisemartin, N., *Les frises à guirlandes d'Aphrodisias de Carie* (Bordeaux forthcoming).

de Chaisemartin and Lemaire 1996 = de Chaisemartin, N. and Lemaire, A., 'Le Portique de Tibère: recherches sur son architecture et sa fonction', in C. Roueché and R. R. R. Smith (eds), *Aphrodisias Papers 3: The Setting and Quarries, Mythological and other Sculptural Decoration, Architectural Development, Portico of Tiberius, and Tetrapylon* (JRA Supplementary Series, Ann Arbor, MI 1996), 149–172.

de Chaisemartin et al. 2017 = de Chaisemartin, N., Theodorescu, D., Goubin, Y., and Lemaire, A., *Le théâtre d'Aphrodisias: les structures scéniques* (Aphrodisias, 8. 2017).

De Cupere 1994 = De Cupere, B., 'Report on the faunal remains from trench K (Roman Pessinus, Central Anatolia)', *Archaeofauna* 3 (1994), 63–75.

De Cupere 2001 = De Cupere, B., *Animals at Ancient Sagalassos: Evidence of the Faunal Remains* (Studies in Eastern Mediterranean Archaeology 4. Turnhout 2001).

De Cupere et al. 2000 = De Cupere, B., Lentacker, A., Van Neer, W., Waelkens, M., and Verslype, L., 'Osteological evidence for the draught exploitation of cattle: first applications of a new methodology', *International Journal of Osteoarchaeology* 10.4 (2000), 254–267.

De Cupere et al. 2003 = De Cupere, B., Fabienne, P., Mircea, U., and Van Neer, W., *Report of the 2003 Archaeozoological team, Sagalassos Archaeological Research Project, Leuven, Belgium* (unpublished report 2003).

De Cupere et al. 2015 = De Cupere, B., Poblome, J., Hamilton-Dyer, S., and Van Haelst, S., 'Communal dining in the eastern suburbium of ancient Sagalassos. The evidence of animal remains and material culture', *HEROM. Journal on Hellenistic and Roman Material Culture* 4.2 (2015), 173–197.

De Cupere et al. 2017 = De Cupere, B., Frémondeau, D., Kaptijn, E., Marinova, E., Poblome, J., Vandam, R., and Van Neer, W., 'Subsistence economy and land use strategies in the Burdur province (SW Anatolia) from prehistory to the Byzantine period', *Quaternary International* 436 (2017), 4–17.

De Cupere, Van Neer, and Lentacker, 1993 = De Cupere, B., Van Neer, W., and Lentacker, A., 'Some aspects of the bone-working industry in Roman Sagalassos (Burdur Province, Turkey)', in M. Waelkens and J. Poblome (eds), *Sagalassos II. Report on the third excavation campaign 1992* (Acta Archaeologica Lovaniensia Monographiae, 6. 1993), 269–278.

De Staebler 2008 = De Staebler, P. D., 'The city wall and the making of a late antique provincial capital', in C. Ratté and R. R. R. Smith (eds), *Aphrodisias Papers 4: New Research on the City and its Monuments* (JRA Supplementary Series, 70. Portsmouth, Rhode Island 2008), 284–318.

De Staebler 2012 = De Staebler, P. D., 'Roman Pottery', in C. Ratté and P. D. De Staebler (eds), *The Aphrodisias Regional Survey* (Aphrodisias, 5. Mainz 2012), 59–86.

de Voogt 2010 = de Voogt, A. J., 'Mancala players at Palmyra', *Antiquity* 84.326 (2010), 1055–1066.

Degeest 2000 = Degeest, R., *The Common Wares of Sagalassos* (Studies in Eastern Mediterranean Archaeology, 3. Turnhout 2000).

Degeest *et al.* 1999 = Degeest, R., Ottenburgs, R., Kucha, H., Viaene, W., Degryse, P., and Waelkens, M., 'The Late Roman unguentaria of Sagalassos', *BABesch* 74 (1999), 247–262.

Degryse *et al.* 2004 = Degryse, P., Muchez, P., de Cupere, B., van Neer, W., and Waelkens, M., 'Statistical treatment of trace element data from modern and ancient animal bone: evaluation of Roman and Byzantine environmental pollution', *Analytical Letters* 37.13 (2004), 2819–2834.

Deiss 1985 = Deiss, J. J., *Herculaneum. Italy's buried treasure* (Malibu 1985).

Dell'Era 2012 = Dell'Era, F., 'Small finds from Zeytinli Bahçe-Birecik (Urfa)', in B. Bohlendorf-Arslan and A. Ricci (eds), *Byzantine Small Finds in Archaeological Contexts* (Byzas, 15. Istanbul 2012), 393–406.

Delrieux 2011 = Delrieux, F., *Les monnaies du Fonds Louis Robert* (Mémoires de l'Académie des inscriptions et belles-lettres, 45. Paris 2011).

Deppmeyer 2008 = Deppmeyer, K., *Kaisergruppen von Vespasian bis Konstantin: eine Untersuchung zu Aufstellungskontexten und Intentionen der statuarischen Präsentation kaiserlicher Familien*, 2 vols. (Schriftenreihe Antiquitates, Hamburg 2008).

Derda 1992 = Derda, T., 'Some remarks on the Christian symbol XMΓ', *The Journal of Juristic Papyrology* 22 (1992), 21–27.

Dey 2015 = Dey, H. W., *The Afterlife of the Roman City: Architecture and Ceremony in Late Antiquity and the Early Middle Ages* (New York 2015).

Dillon 1997 = Dillon, S. A., 'Figured pilaster capitals from Aphrodisias', *AJA* 101.4 (1997), 731–769.

Doğer 2000 = Doğer, L., *İzmir Arkeoloji Müzesi Örnekleriyle Kazıma Dekorlu Ege-Bizans Seramikleri* (Ege Üniversitesi Edebiyat Fakültesi Yayınları, Izmir 2000).

Donners *et al.* 2000 = Donners, K., Waelkens, M., Celis, D., Nackaerts, K., Deckers, J. A., Vermoere, M., and Vanhaverbeke, H., 'Towards a land evaluation of the territory of ancient Sagalassos', in M. Waelkens and L. Loots (eds), *Sagalassos V. Report on the Survey and Excavation Campaigns of 1996 and 1997*, vol. 2 (Acta Archaeologica Lovaniensia Monographiae, 11. Leuven 2000), 723–756.

Dorl-Klingenschmid 2001 = Dorl-Klingenschmid, C., *Prunkbrunnen in kleinasiatischen Städten. Funktion im Kontext* (Studien zur antiken Stadt, 7. Munich 2001).

Dossey 2018 = Dossey, L., 'Shedding light on the Late Antique night', in A. Chaniotis (ed.), *La nuit: imaginaire et réalités nocturnes dans la monde gréco-romaine* (Entretiens sur l'Antiquité classique, 64. Vandoeuvres 2018), 293–322.

Doxa *et al.* 2019 = Doxa, C. K., Sterioti, A., Divanach, P., and Kentouri, M., 'Reproductive behavior of the marine gastropod Charonia seguenzae (Aradas & Benoit, 1870) in captivity', *Mediterranean Marine Science* 20.1 (2019), 49–55.

Duman 2018 = Duman, B., 'Geç antik çağ'da Lydia Tripolis'i (ms 4. Yy'dan Sasani tahribati'na kadar)', in C. Şimşek and T. Kaçar (eds), *Geç antik çağ'da Lykos vadisi ve çevresi / The Lykos Valley and Neighbourhood in Late Antiquity* (Laodikeia Çalışmaları: Ek Yayın Dizisi / Supplementary series, 1. İstanbul 2018), 343–364.

Dunbabin 2017 = Dunbabin, K. M. D., 'Athletes, acclamations, and imagery from the end of antiquity', *JRA* 30 (2017), 151–174.

Duncan-Jones 1982 = Duncan-Jones, R. P., *The Economy of the Roman Empire: Quantitative studies.* 2nd edn. (Cambridge 1982).

Dündar 2007 = Dündar, E., 'Late Roman stamped unguentaria from Kibyra – Kibyra Geç Roma – Erken Doğu Roma Dönemi Mühürlü Unguentariumları', *Olba* 15 (2007), 145–178.

Duthoy 2012 = Duthoy, F., *Sculpteurs et commanditaires au IIe siècle après J.-C: Rome et Tivoli* (Collection de l'École française de Rome, 465. Rome 2012).

Ehlert 2013 = Ehlert, R., *Umlaufgeld im Osmanischen Reich*, vol. 1 (Heidelberg 2013).

Ehrenheim 2015 = Ehrenheim, H. von, *Greek Incubation Rituals in Classical and Hellenistic Times* (Kernos Supplément, 29. Liège 2015).

Eisenmenger and Zäh 1999 = Eisenmenger, U. and Zäh, A., 'Ampullae tardoantiche dell'Asia Minore. Nuovi esempi da Cnido e Limyra', *Quaderni friulani di archeologia* 9 (1999), 113–130.

Ender 2000 = Ender, C., *Karesi, Saruhan, Aydın ve Mentese Beylikleri Paralari* (Ender Nümismatik Yayınları, 2. Istanbul 2000).

Entwistle and Meek 2015 = Entwistle, C. and Meek, A., 'Early Byzantine glass weights: aspects of function, chronology and composition', *British Museum Technical Research Bulletin* 9 (2015), 1–14.

Erdem and Yergün 2016 = Erdem, A. and Yergün, U., 'Some examples of Turkish houses with wooden frame in the seismic zone Anatolia', in H. Cruz, J. Saporiti Machado, A. Campos Costa, P. Xavier Candeias, and N. Ruggieri (eds), *Historical Earthquake-Resistant Timber Framing in the Mediterranean Area. Lecture Notes in Civil Engineering*, vol. 1 (Lecture Notes in Civil Engineering, Springer 2016), 55–73.

Erdim 1985 = Erdim, M., 'Ege Bölgesi Bağ Evleri Mimari Geleneği', in M. Başakman and M. Başakman (eds), *Ege'de Mimarlık, Bildiri Kitabı* (Izmir 1985), 165–178.

Erim 1967 = Erim, K. T., 'De Aphrodisiade', *AJA* 71.3 (1967), 233–243.

Erim 1969 = Erim, K. T., 'Aphrodisias, results of the 1968 campaign', *TürkArkDerg* 17.1 (1969), 43–57.

Erim 1970 = Erim, K. T., 'The ninth campaign of excavations at Aphrodisias in Caria 1969', *TürkArkDerg* 18.2 (1970), 87–110.

Erim 1971 = Erim, K. T., 'Recent archaeological research in Turkey, Aphrodisias, 1970', *Anatolian Studies* 21 (1971), 25–31.

Erim 1972 = Erim, K. T., 'Aphrodisias in Caria. Results of the 1970 campaign', *TürkArkDerg* 19.1 (1972), 55–85.

Erim 1973 = Erim, K. T., '1971 Excavations at Aphrodisias in Caria', *TürkArkDerg* 20.1 (1973), 63–87.

Erim 1974 = Erim, K. T., 'Aphrodisias in Caria. The 1972 campaign of excavations', *TürkArkDerg* 21.1 (1974), 37–57.

Erim 1975 = Erim, K. T., 'Aphrodisias in Caria. The 1973 campaign', *TürkArkDerg* 22.2 (1975), 73–92.

Erim 1976 = Erim, K. T., 'Aphrodisias 1975 (Recent Archaeological Research in Turkey)', *Anatolian Studies* 26 (1976), 24–30.

Erim 1981 = Erim, K. T., 'Aphrodisias 1980 (Recent Archaeological Research in Turkey)', *Anatolian Studies* 31 (1981), 177–181.

Erim 1984 = Erim, K. T., 'Aphrodisias 1983 (Recent Archaeological Research in Turkey)', *Anatolian Studies* 34 (1984), 203–207.

Erim 1985 = Erim, K. T., 'Aphrodisias 1984 (Recent Archaeological Research in Turkey)', *Anatolian Studies* 35 (1985), 176–181.

Erim 1986a = Erim, K. T., 'Aphrodisias 1985 (Recent Archaeological Research in Turkey)', *Anatolian Studies* 36 (1986), 176–181.

Erim 1986b = Erim, K. T., *Aphrodisias: City of Venus Aphrodite* (New York 1986).

Erim 1987 = Erim, K. T., '25 ans de fouilles à Aphrodisias', in J. De la Genière and K. T. Erim (eds), *Aphrodisias de Carie, Colloque de l'Université de Lille III, 13 novembre 1985* (Paris 1987), 7–30.

Erim 1988 = Erim, K. T., 'Recherches récentes et découvertes à Aphrodisias de Carie', *Comptes rendus de l'Académie des inscriptions et belles-lettres* (1988), 734–757.

Erim 1990 = Erim, K. T., 'Recent work at Aphrodisias 1986–1988', in C. Roueché and K. T. Erim (eds), *Aphrodisias Papers. Recent work on architecture and sculpture* (JRA Supplementary Series, 1. Ann Arbor, MI 1990), 9–36.

Erim and Reynolds 1989 = Erim, K. T. and Reynolds, J., 'Sculptors of Aphrodisias in the inscriptions of the city', in N. Başgelen and M. Lugal (eds), *Festschrift für Jale Inan* (Istanbul 1989), 517–538.

Erim and Roueché 1982 = Erim, K. T. and Roueché, C. M., 'Sculptors from Aphrodisias: some new inscriptions', *PBSR* 50 (1982), 102–115.

Erim and Smith 1991 = Erim, K. T. and Smith, R. R. R., 'Sculpture from the theatre: a preliminary report', in R. R. R. Smith and K. T. Erim (eds), *Aphrodisias Papers 2: The Theatre, a Sculptor's Workshop, Philosophers, and Coin-types* (JRA Supplementary Series, 2. Ann Arbor, MI 1991), 67–98.

Ersoy, Önder, and Turan 2014 = Ersoy, A., Önder, M., and Turan, H., *Antik Smyrna Sikkeleri (2008–2012) / Coins from Ancient Smyrna Excavations (2008–2012)* (Izmir 2014).

Ervynck, De Cupere and Van Neer 1993 = Ervynck, A., De Cupere, B. and Van Neer, W., 'Consumption refuse from the Byzantine castle at Pessinus, Central-Anatolia, Turkey', in H. Buitenhuis and A. T. Clason (eds), *Archaeozoology of the Near East. Proceedings of the First International Symposium on the Archaeozoology of Southwestern Asia and Adjacent Areas* (Leiden 1993), 119–127.

Ervynck, Van Neer and de Cupere 2003 = Ervynck, A., Van Neer, W. and de Cupere, B., 'Animal remains from the Byzantine Castle', in J. Devreker, H. Thoen and F. Vermeulen (eds), *Excavations in Pessinus: The So-Called Acropolis. From Hellenistic and Roman Cemetery to Byzantine Castle* (Ghent 2003), 375–382.

Ethem 1918 = Ethem, H., *Müze-i Hümayun Meskukat-ı Kadime-i İslamiye Kataloğu, Kısm-ı Sadis* (Istanbul [Konstantiyye] 1918 [AH 1334]).

Evans 2006 = Evans, J. D., *The Coins and the Hellenistic, Roman, and Byzantine Economy of Palestine* (The Joint Expedition to Caesarea Maritima, Excavation Reports, 6. Boston 2006).

Evans 2013 = Evans, J. D., 'Five Small Bronze Hoards from Sardis and Their Implications for Coin Circulation in the Fifth Century CE', *BASOR* 369.1 (2013), 137–156.

Evans 2018 = Evans, J. D., *Coins from The Excavations at Sardis, Their Archaeological and Economic Contexts: Coins from the 1973 to 2013 Excavations* (Archaeological Exploration of Sardis, Monograph, 13. Cambridge, MA 2018).

Favro 1996 = Favro, D., *The Urban Image of Augustan Rome* (Cambridge 1996).

Fear 1991 = Fear, A. T., 'Religious graffiti in two Spanish amphitheatres', *OJA* 10.1 (1991), 123–125.

Feissel 1991 = Feissel, D., 'Les inscriptions d'Aphrodisias (250–641 ap. J.-C.)', *JRA* 4 (1991), 369–377.

Feldherr 1995 = Feldherr, A., 'Ships of state: Aeneid 5 and Augustan circus spectacle', *ClAnt* 14.2 (1995), 245–265.

Fellows 1852 = Fellows, C., *Travels and Researches in Asia Minor: more particularly in the province of Lycia* (London 1852).

Fentress and Wilson 2021 = Fentress, E. W. B. and Wilson, A. I., '*Terra septem diebus mugitum dedit*: North African earthquakes revisited', in X. Dupuis, V. Fauvinet-Ranson, C. J. Goddard, and H. Inglebert (eds), *L'automne de l'Afrique romaine. Hommages à Claude Lepelley* (Collection Histoire et Archéologie, Paris 2021), 133–153.

Fernández 2014 = Fernández, A., *El comercio tardoantiguo (ss. IV–VII) en el Noroeste peninsular a través del registro cerámico de la ría de Vigo* (Roman and Late Antique Mediterranean Pottery, 5. Oxford 2014).

Ferrary 2014 = Ferrary, J.-L., *Les mémoriaux de délégations du sanctuaire oraculaire de Claros, d'après la documentation conservée dans le Fonds Louis Robert*, 2 vols. (Mémoires de l'Académie des inscriptions et belles-lettres, 49. Paris 2014).

Ferrazzoli 2012 = Ferrazzoli, A. F., 'Byzantine small finds from Elaiussa Sebaste', in B. Bohlendorf-Arslan and A. Ricci (eds), *Byzantine Small Finds in Archaeological Contexts* (Byzas, 15. Istanbul 2012), 289–307.

Ferri 1938 = Ferri, S., 'Il Diogenianon di Afrodisia', *Rivista Filologia* (1938), 59–60.

Feuser 2013 = Feuser, S., *Monopodia–Figürliche Tischfüße aus Kleinasien. Ein Beitrag zum Ausstattungsluxus der römischen Kaiserzeit* (Byzas 17. Istanbul 2013).

Fittschen and Zanker 1985 = Fittschen, K. and Zanker, P., *Katalog der römischen Porträts in den Capitolinischen Museen*, vol. 1: *Kaiser-und Prinzenbildnisse* (Mainz am Rhein 1985).

Fleischer 1971 = Fleischer, R., 'Späthellenistische Gruppe von Pollionymphaeum in Ephesos mit dem Polyphemabenteuer des Odysseus', *Jahresheften des Österreichischen Archäologischen Institutes in Wien* 49. Beiheft 2 (1971), 137–164.

Forsén 1996 = Forsén, B., *Griechische gliederweihungen: eine Untersuchung zu ihrer Typologie und ihrer religions- und sozi-*

algeschichtlichen Bedeutung, vol. 4 (Papers and monographs of the Finnish Institute at Athens, Helsinki 1996).

Forstenpointner 1996 = Forstenpointner, G., 'Die Tierknochenfunde aus dem Sehachtbrunnen im Atrium', in C. Lang-Auinger (ed.), *Hanghaus 1 in Ephesos. Der Baubefund* (Forschungen in Ephesos 8.3, Wien 1996), 209–218.

Forstenpointner, Galik, and Weissengruber 2008 = Forstenpointner, G., Galik, A., and Weissengruber, G., 'Archäozoologie', in M. Steskal and M. La Torre (eds), *Das Vediusgymnasium in Ephesos. Archäologie und Baubefund* (Wien 2008), 211–234.

Foss 1975a = Foss, C., 'The fall of Sardis in 616 and the value of evidence', *Jahrbuch der Österreichischen Byzantinistik* 24 (1975), 11–22.

Foss 1975b = Foss, C., 'The Persians in Asia Minor and the end of Antiquity', *The English Historical Review* 90.357 (1975), 721–747.

Foss 1976 = Foss, C., *Byzantine and Turkish Sardis* (Monograph (Archaeological Exploration of Sardis (Program), 4. Cambridge, Mass. – London 1976).

Fox 2023 = Fox, A., *Trees in Ancient Rome: Growing an Empire in the Late Republic and Early Principate* (London 2023).

François 2001 = François, V., 'Éléments pour l'histoire ottomane d'Aphrodisias: la vaisselle de terre', *Anatolia Antiqua* 9 (2001), 147–190.

François 2018 = François, V., 'Aegean Ware: how a typology became inoperative', in F. Yenişehirlioğlu (ed.), *XIth Congress AIECM3 on Medieval and Modern Period Mediterranean Ceramics: Proceedings*, vol. 1 (Antalya 2018), 197–202.

François and Spieser 2002 = François, V. and Spieser, J.-M., 'Pottery and glass in Byzantium', in A. Laiou (ed.), *The Economic History of Byzantium. From the Seventh through the Fifteenth Century* vol. 1 (Washington D.C. 2002), 593–610.

Frémondeau *et al.* 2017 = Frémondeau, D., De Cupere, B., Evin, A., and Van Neer, W., 'Diversity in pig husbandry from the Classical-Hellenistic to the Byzantine periods: An integrated dental analysis of Düzen Tepe and Sagalassos assemblages (Turkey)', *Journal of Archaeological Science: Reports* 11 (2017), 38–52.

Fuchs 1982 = Fuchs, M., 'Eine Musengruppe aus dem Pompeius-Theater', *RM* 89 (1982), 69–80.

Fuller *et al.* 2012 = Fuller, B. T., De Cupere, B., Marinova, E., Van Neer, W., Waelkens, M., and Richards, M. P., 'Isotopic reconstruction of human diet and animal husbandry practices during the Classical-Hellenistic, imperial, and Byzantine periods at Sagalassos, Turkey', *American Journal of Physical Anthropology* 149.2 (2012), 157–171.

Fünfschilling 2014 = Fünfschilling, S., 'Glass from the Byzantine Palace at Ephesus in Turkey', in D. Keller, J. Price, and C. M. Jackson (eds), *Neighbours and Successors of Rome: Traditions of Glass Production and Use in Europe and the Middle East in the Later 1st millennium AD* (Oxford 2014), 137–146.

Gager 1992 = Gager, J. G. (ed.) *Curse Tablets and Binding Spells from the Ancient World* (Oxford 1992).

Gaitzsch 2005 = Gaitzsch, W., *Eisenfunde aus Pergamon: Geräte, Werkzeuge und Waffen* (Pergamenische Forschungen, 14. Berlin and New York 2005).

Galavaris 1970 = Galavaris, G., *Bread and the Liturgy. The Symbolism of Early Christian and Byzantine Bread Stamps* (Madison 1970).

Galik *et al.* 2020 = Galik, A., González Cesteros, H., Heiss, A. G., Ladstätter, S., and Alice, W., 'Der Rest vom Fest. Die Grubenverfüllung in Raum 12a der Wohneinheit 5 im Hanghaus 2 – Archäologische Evidenz einer Cena Publica in Ephesos?', in S. Ladstätter (ed.), *Eine frühkaiserzeitliche Grubenverfüllung aus dem Hanghaus 2 in Ephesos* (Ergänzungshefte der Jahreshefte des Österreichischen Archäologischen Instituts, 18. Vienna 2020), 257–264.

Galili, Zemer, and Rosen 2013 = Galili, E., Zemer, A., and Rosen, B., 'Ancient fishing gear and associated artifacts from underwater explorations in Israel – a comparative study', *Archaeofauna* 22 (2013), 145–166.

Gândila 2016 = Gândila, A., 'Going East: Western money in the early Byzantine Balkans, Asia Minor and the circumpontic Region (6th–7th c.)', *RIN* 117 (2016), 129–188.

Gärtner 2012 = Gärtner, J., 'Architectural decoration of the Cardo', in O. Gutfeld (ed.), *Jewish Quarter Excavations in the Old City of Jerusalem, conducted by Nahman Avigad, 1969–1982*, vol. 5: *The Cardo (Area X) and the Nea Church (Areas D and T)* (Jerusalem 2012), 101–110.

Gassner 1997 = Gassner, V., *Das Südtor der Tetragonos-Agora: Keramik und Kleinfunde* (Forschungen in Ephesos, 13/1.1. Wien 1997).

Gates 1994 = Gates, M. H., 'Archaeology in Turkey', *AJA* 98.2 (1994), 249–278.

Gelzer 1901 = Gelzer, H., 'Ungedruckte und ungenügend veröffentlichte Texte der Notitiae episcopatuum', *Abhandlungen der philosophisch-historischen Classe der bayerischen Akademie der Wissenschaften* 21.3 (1901), 529–641.

Gençler-Güray 2010 = Gençler-Güray, Ç., 'The glass finds', in E. Equini Schneider (ed.), *Elaiussa Sebaste*, vol. 3: *L'Agora romana* (Istanbul 2010), 234–245.

Gensheimer and Welch 2013 = Gensheimer, M. B. and Welch, K. E., 'The Achilles and Penthesilea statue group from the tetrastyle court of the Hadrianic Baths at Aphrodisias', *IstMitt* 63 (2013), 325–377.

Germer-Durand 1899 = Germer-Durand, J., 'Nouvelle exploration épigraphique de Gérasa', *RBibl* 8.1 (1899), 5–39.

Gibbs 1976 = Gibbs, S. L., *Greek and Roman Sundials* (New Haven 1976).

Gill 1958 = Gill, J., 'A Tractate about the Council of Florence attributed to George Amiroutzes', *The Journal of Ecclesiastical History* 9.1 (1958), 30–37.

Gill 2002 = Gill, M. A. V., *Amorium Reports, Finds I: The Glass (1987–1997)* (BAR International Series, 1070. Oxford 2002).

Gill 1986 = Gill, M. V., 'The small finds', in R. M. Harrison (ed.), *Excavations at Saraçhane in Istanbul*, vol. 1: *The Excavations, Structures, Architectural Decoration, Small Finds, Coins, Bones, and Molluscs* (Princeton, N. J. 1986), 226–277.

Glad 2015 = Glad, D., *L'armement dans la région balkanique à l'époque romaine tardive et protobyzantine (284–641): héritage, adaptation et innovation* (30, Bibliothèque de l'Antiquité Tardive. Turnhout 2015).

Gleason 1993 = Gleason, K. L., 'A garden excavation in the Oasis Palace of Herod the Great at Jericho', *Landscape Journal* 12.2 (1993), 156–167.

Gleason 1994 = Gleason, K. L., '*Porticus Pompeiana*: a new perspective on the first public park of ancient Rome', *Journal of Garden History* 14.1 (1994), 13–27.

Gleason 2010 = Gleason, K. L., 'Constructing nature: The built garden. With notice of a new monumental garden at the Villa Arianna, *Stabiae*', *Bollettino di Archeologia on line* 1. Volume speciale D / D9 / 3 (2010), 8–15.

Gleason 2016 = Gleason, K. L., 'The garden surface', in T. N. Howe, K. L. Gleason, P. Gardelli, L. Toniolo, N. Langobardi, and A. Raimondi (eds), *Excavation and Study of the Garden of the Great Peristyle of the Villa Arianna, Stabiae, 2007–2012* (Quaderni di Studi Pompeiani, 7. Napoli 2016), 67–81.

Gleason and Sutherland 2016 = Gleason, K. L. and Sutherland, I., 'Garden methodology', in T. N. Howe, K. L. Gleason, P. Gardelli, L. Toniolo, N. Langobardi, and A. Raimondi (eds), *Excavation and Study of the Garden of the Great Peristyle of the Villa Arianna, Stabiae, 2007–2012* (Quaderni di Studi Pompeiani, 7. Napoli 2016), 25–36.

Gnoli 1988 = Gnoli, R., *Marmora romana*. 2nd edn. (Rome 1988).

Göbl 1993 = Göbl, R., *Die Münzpragung des Kaisers Aurelianus (270/75)*, 2 vols. (Moneta Imperii Romani 47 / Denkschriften der philosophisch-historischen Klasse, 233. Vienna 1993).

Godefroy 1665 = Godefroy, J., *Codex Theodosianus cum perpetuis commentariis Iacobi Gothofredi viri senatorij & iurisconsulti huius sæculi eximij.: Præmittuntur chronologia accuratior, cum chronico historico, & prolegomena: subijciuntur notitia dignitatum, prosopographia, topographia, index rerum, & glossarium nomicum. Opus posthumum; diu in foro et schola desideratum* (Lyons 1665).

Gogräfe 2016 = Gogräfe, R., 'Isriye-Seriana. Heiligtum, Siedlung und Militärstation in Zentralsyrien von der frühen römischen Kaiserzeit bis in die mamlukische Epoche. Keramik', *Damaszener Forschungen* 17 (2016), 134–159.

Gök Gürhan 2011 = Gök Gürhan, S., *Bir Seramik Definesinin Öyküsü, Saruhanoğlu Beyliği'nin Mirası Manisa Gülgün Hatun Hamamı Seramikleri* (Manisa 2011).

Gökalp 2018 = Gökalp, Z. D., 'Anadolu'nun Ege Kıyılarında Erken Bizans Dönemi Sikke Dolaşımı', in C. Ünal, A. Ersoy, C. Gürbıyık, and B. K. Kasalı (eds), *Ege Dünyası Liman Kentleri: Sikke, Mühür ve Ağırlıkları / Port Cities of the Aegean World: Coins, Seals and Weights* (Manisa Celal Bayar Üniversitesi Yayınlari, 32. Manisa 2018), 83–98.

Goldman 1950 = Goldman, H., *Excavations at Gözlü Kule, Tarsus*, vol. 1: *The Hellenistic and Roman Periods* (Princeton, N. J. 1950).

Gorin-Rosen 2015 = Gorin-Rosen, Y., 'Byzantine gold glass from excavations in the Holy Land', *JGS* 57 (2015), 97–119.

Gorny & Mosch Giessener Münzhandlung 2010 = Gorny & Mosch Giessener Münzhandlung, *Auktion 191. Antike Münzen und Lots, 11/12 Oktober 2010* (Munich 2010).

Graf 2011 = Graf, F., 'Myth in Christian authors', in K. Dowden and N. Livingstone (eds), *A Companion to Greek Mythology* (Blackwell Companions to the Ancient World, Malden 2011), 319–337.

Grant 1982 = Grant, A., 'The use of tooth wear as a guide to the age of domestic ungulates', in R. Wilson, C. Grigson, and S. Payne (eds), *Ageing and Sexing Animal Bones from Archaeological Sites* (Oxford 1982), 91–108.

Grau-Sologestoa 2017 = Grau-Sologestoa, I., 'Socio-economic status and religious identity in medieval Iberia: the zooarchaeological evidence', *Environmental Archaeology* 22.2 (2017), 189–199.

Greatrex 1997 = Greatrex, G., 'The Nika riot: A reappraisal', *The Journal of Hellenic Studies* 117 (1997), 60–86.

Greatrex 2018 = Greatrex, G., 'The impact on Asia Minor of the Persian invasions in the early seventh century', in C. Şimşek and T. Kaçar (eds), *Geç antik çağ'da Lykos vadisi ve çevresi / The Lykos Valley and Neighbourhood in Late Antiquity* (Laodikeia Çalışmaları: Ek Yayın Dizisi / Supplementary series, 1. İstanbul 2018), 13–26.

Greatrex and Watt 1999 = Greatrex, G. and Watt, J. W., 'One, two or three feasts? The Brytae, the Maiuma and the May festival at Edessa', *OC* 83 (1999), 1–21.

Greenewalt 2007 = Greenewalt, C. H., 'Sardis: archaeological research and conservation projects in 2005', in *29. Kazı Sonuçları Toplantısı. 28 Mayis – 1 Haziran 2007, Kocaeli*, vol. 3 (2007), 743–756.

Greenfield 1989 = Greenfield, R. P. H., 'Saint Sisinnios, the Archangel Michael and the Female Demon Gylou: The Typology of the Greek Literary Stories', Βυζαντινά 15 (1989), 83–142.

Grierson 1965 = Grierson, P., 'Two Byzantine coin hoards of the seventh and eighth centuries at Dumbarton Oaks', *DOP* 19 (1965), 207–228.

Groot 2016 = Groot, M., *Livestock for Sale: Animal Husbandry in a Roman Frontier Zone* (Amsterdam 2016).

Gros 1976 = Gros, P., *Aurea templa. Recherches sur l'architecture religieuse de Rome à l'époque d'Auguste* (Rome 1976).

Groupe de Recherches sur l'Afrique antique 1993 = Groupe de Recherches sur l'Afrique antique, *Les Flavii de Cillium. Étude architecturale, épigraphique, historique et littéraire du mausolée de Kasserine (CIL VIII, 211–216)*: Collection de l'École française de Rome (Rome 1993).

Gülmez 2007 = Gülmez, G., 'A case study: the village of Eskihisar/Stratonikeia as an example of urban continuity', in *Proceedings of the 1st Euro-Mediterranean Regional Conference Traditional Mediterranean Architecture: Present and Future. Barcelona, 12–15 July 2007.* (Barcelona 2007), 330–331.

Gysen 1999 = Gysen, P., 'À propos des ateliers de Smyrne et de Cyzique sous Claude II le Gothique', *Cercle d'Études Numismatiques, Bulletin* 36.2 (1999), 29–41.

Haldon 2008 = Haldon, J., 'Military technology and warfare', in E. Jeffreys (ed.), *The Oxford Handbook of Byzantine Studies* (Oxford 2008), 473–481.

Hall et al. 2017 = Hall, M. R., Motti, C., and Kroon, F., *The Potential Role of the Giant Triton Snail,* Charonia tritonis *(Gastropoda: Ranellidae) in Mitigating Populations of the Crown-

of-Thorns Starfish (Tropical Water Quality Hub, Technical Report, Cairns 2017).

Hallett 2005 = Hallett, C. H., *The Roman Nude: Heroic Portrait Statuary, 200 BC–AD 300* (Oxford 2005).

Hallett 2017 = Hallett, C. H., 'The Greek and Roman "statue habit": the last hurrah – R. R. R. SMITH and BRYAN WARD-PERKINS (edd.), THE LAST STATUES OF ANTIQUITY (Oxford University Press 2016). Pp. xxxiii + 410, figs. 209. ISBN 978-0-19-875332-2', *JRA* 30 (2017), 875–890.

Hallett 2021 = Hallett, C. H., 'The wood comes to the city: ancient trees, sacred groves, and the "greening" of early Augustan Rome', *Religion of the Roman Empire* 7.2 (2021), 221–274.

Hallett and Quatember 2018 = Hallett, C. H. and Quatember, U., 'Three bouleuteria from Roman and late antique Aphrodisias', in M. Aurenhammer (ed.), *Sculpture in Roman Asia: Proceedings of the International Conference at Selçuk 2013* (Sonderschriften des Österreichischen Archäologischen Institutes der Österreichischen Akademie der Wissenschaften, 56. Wien 2018), 353–364.

Hallmannsecker 2017 = Hallmannsecker, M., 'Heracles Hoplophylax, Iudaioi, and a palm grove. A fresh look at *I.Smyrna* 697', *Epigraphica Anatolica* 50 (2017), 109–127.

Hannestad 1994 = Hannestad, N., *Tradition in Late Antique Sculpture: Conservation, Modernization, Production* (Acta Jutlandica Humanities series, 69. Aarhus 1994).

Hannestad 2001 = Hannestad, N., 'Sculptural genres in Late Antiquity: continuity or discontinuity?', *Hefte Des Archäologischen Seminars Des Universität Bern* 4 (2001), 137–145.

Hannestad 2012 = Hannestad, N., 'Mythological marble sculpture of late antiquity and the question of workshops', in T. M. Kristensen and B. Poulsen (eds), *Ateliers and Artisans in Roman Art and Archaeology* (JRA Supplementary Series, 45. Portsmouth, R.I. 2012), 77–112.

Hansen 2001 = Hansen, M. F., 'Meanings of style: on the "interiorization" of late antique architecture', in J. Fleischer, N. Hannestad, J. Lund, and M. Nielsen (eds), *Late Antiquity: Art in Context* (Acta Hyperborea, 8. Copenhagen 2001), 71–84.

Harper 2015 = Harper, K., 'Pandemics and passages to late antiquity: rethinking the plague of c.249–270 described by Cyprian', *JRA* 28 (2015), 223–260.

Harrison 1986 = Harrison, R. M., *Excavations at Saraçhane in Istanbul*, vol. 1: *The Excavations, Structures, Architectural Decoration, Small Finds, Coins, Bones, and Molluscs* (Dumbarton Oaks Research Library and Collection, Princeton, NJ 1986).

Harrison *et al.* 1993 = Harrison, R. M., Christie, N. *et al.*, 'Excavations at Amorium: 1992 interim report', *Anatolian Studies* 43 (1993), 147–162.

Harrison and Gill 1986 = Harrison, R. M. and Gill, M. V., 'The inlays and revetment', in R. M. Harrison (ed.), *Excavations at Saraçhane in Istanbul*, vol. 1: *The Excavations, Structures, Architectural Decoration, Small Finds, Coins, Bones, and Molluscs* (Princeton, N. J. 1986), 168–181.

Hayes 1968 = Hayes, J. W., 'A seventh-century pottery group', *DOP* 22 (1968), 203–216.

Hayes 1971 = Hayes, J. W., 'A new type of early Christian ampulla', *BSA* 66 (1971), 243–248.

Hayes 1972 = Hayes, J. W., *Late Roman Pottery* (London 1972).

Hayes 1980 = Hayes, J. W., *A Supplement to Late Roman Pottery* (London 1980).

Hayes 1992 = Hayes, J. W., *Excavations at Saraçhane in Istanbul*, vol. 2: *The Pottery* (Princeton, N.J. 1992).

Hayes 2005 = Hayes, J. W., 'Late Hellenistic and Roman pottery in the eastern Mediterranean: an overview of recent developments', in M. Berg Briese and L. E. Vaag (eds), *Trade Relations in the Eastern Mediterranean from the Late Hellenistic Period to Late Antiquity: the Ceramic Evidence. Acts from a Ph. D. Seminar for Young Scholars (Sandbjerg Manorhouse, 12–15 February 1998)* (Odense 2005), 11–26.

Heberdey 1912 = Heberdey, R., ' IX. Vorläufiger Bericht über die Grabungen in Ephesos 1907–1911', *Jahreshefte des Österreichischen Archäologischen Institutes in Wien* 15. Beiblatt (1912), 157–182.

Hebert 2000 = Hebert, L., *The Temple-Church at Aphrodisias*. Ph.D. dissertation, Institute of Fine Arts, New York University.

Heidemann 2002 = Heidemann, S., 'Die Fundmünzen von Ḥarrān und ihr Verhältnis zur lokalen Geschichte', *Bulletin of the School of Oriental and African Studies, University of London* 65.2 (2002), 267–299.

Heil 1995 = Heil, M., 'Zwei spatantike Statthalter aus Epirus und Achaia', *ZPE* 108 (1995), 159–165.

Heimann and Schädler 2014 = Heimann, F. U. M. and Schädler, U., 'The loop within circular three mens morris', *Board Games Studies Journal online* 8 (2014), 51–61.

Heiss and Thanheiser 2016 = Heiss, A. G. and Thanheiser, U., 'Unters Mosaik geschaut – Hellenistische und Römerzeitliche Pflanzenreste', in E. Rathmayr (ed.), *Hanghaus 2 in Ephesos. Die Wohneinheit 7* (Vienna 2016), 625–641.

Heiss and Thanheiser 2020 = Heiss, A. G. and Thanheiser, U., 'Die Pflanzenreste', in S. Ladstätter (ed.), *Eine frühkaiserzeitliche Grubenverfüllung aus dem Hanghaus 2 in Ephesos* (Ergänzungshefte der Jahreshefte des Österreichischen Archäologischen Instituts, 18. Vienna 2020), 207–238.

Helmer, Gourichon, and Vila 2007 = Helmer, D., Gourichon, L., and Vila, E., 'The development of the exploitation of products from *Capra* and *Ovis* (meat, milk and fleece) from the PPNB to the Early Bronze in the northern Near East (8700 to 2000 BC cal.)', *Anthropozoologica* 42.2 (2007), 41–69.

Hennequin 1985 = Hennequin, G., *Catalogue des monnaies musulmanes de la Bibliothèque Nationale* (Paris 1985).

Herrmann 1992 = Herrmann, J., 'Karasura 1981–1991. Zu den bisherigen Ergebnissen von Ausgrabungen und Forschungsarbeiten in Südthrakien zwischen Stara Zagora und Plovdiv', *ZfA* 26 (1992), 153–180.

Herrmann 1988 = Herrmann, J. J., Jr., *The Ionic Capital in Late Antique Rome* (Archaeologica, 56. Rome 1988).

Homolle 1892 = Homolle, T. (ed.) *Mélanges d'Archéologie et d'Épigraphie par A. Dumont* (Paris 1892).

Hongo 1997 = Hongo, H., 'Patterns of animal husbandry, environment, and ethnicity in central Anatolia in the Ottoman Empire period: faunal remains from Islamic layers at Kaman-Kalehöyük', *Japan Review* 8 (1997), 275–307.

Hoover 2000 = Hoover, O. D., 'Three late Roman 'purse' hoards from Aphrodisias', *The Numismatic Chronicle* 160 (2000), 292–297.

Horbury and Noy 1992 = Horbury, W. and Noy, D., *Jewish Inscriptions of Graeco-Roman Egypt* (Cambridge 1992).

Hornickel 1930 = Hornickel, O., *Ehren- und Rangprädikate in den Papyrusurkunden: ein Beitrag zum römischen und byzantinischen Titelwesen* (Borna, Leipzig, 1930).

Howard-Johnston 2021 = Howard-Johnston, J., *The Last Great War of Antiquity* (Oxford 2021).

Howard 2017 = Howard, D. A., *A History of the Ottoman Empire* (Cambridge 2017).

Howgego 1985 = Howgego, C. J., *Greek Imperial Countermarks: Studies in the Provincial Coinage of the Roman Empire* (Royal Numismatic Society, special publication, 17. London 1985).

Hrychuk Kontokosta 2008 = Hrychuk Kontokosta, A., 'Gladiatorial reliefs and élite funerary monuments', in C. Ratté and R. R. R. Smith (eds), *Aphrodisias Papers 4: New Research on the City and its Monuments*, vol. 4 (JRA Supplementary Series, 70. Portsmouth, Rhode Island 2008), 190–229.

Hudson 2008 = Hudson, N., 'Three centuries of Late Roman pottery', in C. Ratté and R. R. R. Smith (eds), *Aphrodisias Papers 4: New Research on the City and its Monuments*, vol. 4 (JRA Supplementary Series, 70. Portsmouth, Rhode Island 2008), 319–345.

Huttner 2019 = Huttner, U., 'Griechische Graffiti-Cluster', in U. Ehming (ed.), *Vergesellschaftete Schriften. Beiträge zum internationalen Workshop der Arbeitsgruppe 11 am SFB 933* (Philippika, 128. Wiesbaden 2019), 63–84.

Ibrahim, Scranton, and Brill 1976 = Ibrahim, L., Scranton, R., and Brill, R., *Kenchreai: Eastern Port of Corinth. Results of Investigations by The University of Chicago and Indiana University for the American School of Classical Studies at Athens*, vol. 2: *The Panels of Opus Sectile Glass* (Leiden 1976).

İbrahimov and Farhadoglu 2002 = İbrahimov, F. A. and Farhadoglu, K., *Bakı İçərişəhər (Baku`s Old City) Archaeological Album* (Baku 2002).

Ihm 1890 = Ihm, M., 'Römische Spieltafeln', in *Bonner Studien: Aufsatze aus der Altertumswissenschaft, Reinhard Kekule gewidmet* (Berlin 1890), 223–239.

Ihm 1891 = Ihm, M., 'Delle tavole lusorie romane', *Mitteilungen des Deutschen Archäologischen Instituts (Römische Abteilung)* 6 (1891), 208–220.

Imbert 2013 = Imbert, F., 'Graffiti arabes de Cnide et de Kos: Premières traces épigraphiques de la conquête musulmane en mer Égée', in C. Zuckerman (ed.), *Constructing the Seventh Century* (Travaux et Mémoires, 17. Paris 2013), 731–758.

Imhoof-Blumer 1923 = Imhoof-Blumer, F., 'Fluss-und Meergötter auf griechischen und römischen Münzen (Personifikationen der Gewässer)', *Revue suisse de numismatique* 23 (1923), 173–421.

İnan and Alföldi-Rosenbaum 1966 = İnan, J. and Alföldi-Rosenbaum, E., *Roman and Early Byzantine Portrait Sculpture in Asia Minor* (London 1966).

İnan and Alföldi-Rosenbaum 1979 = İnan, J. and Alföldi-Rosenbaum, E., *Römische und frühbyzantinische Porträtplastik aus der Türkei: neue Funde* (Mainz am Rhein 1979).

Ioannidou 2012 = Ioannidou, E., 'Animal husbandry', in C. S. Lightfoot and E. A. Ivison (eds), *Amorium Reports 3, The Lower City Enclosure, Finds and Technical Studies* (Istanbul 2012), 419–442.

Isings 1957 = Isings, C., *Roman Glass from Dated Finds* (Archaeologica Traiectina, 2. Groningen 1957).

Ismaelli 2011 = Ismaelli, T., 'Una nuova proposta di interpretazione per il *Sebasteion* di Aphrodisias: attività commerciali e bancarie nel santuario del culto imperiale', *Mediterraneo Antico: Economie, Società, Culture* 14.1–2 (2011), 149–201.

Ivanišević and Bugarski 2012 = Ivanišević, V. and Bugarski, I., 'Les étriers byzantins: la documentation du Balkan central', in S. Lazaris (ed.), *Le cheval, animal de guerre et de loisir dans l'Antiquité et au Moyen Âge: Actes des Journées d'étude internationales organisées par l'UMR 7044 (Étude des civilisations de l'Antiquité), Strasbourg, 6–7 novembre 2009* (Bibliothèque de l'antiquité tardive, 22. Turnhout 2012), 135–142.

Izmirlier 2009 = Izmirlier, Y., *Anadolu Selçuklu Paraları* [*The coins of Anatolian Seljuqs*] (Istanbul 2009).

Jacobs 2010 = Jacobs, I., 'Production to destruction? Pagan and mythological statuary in Asia Minor', *AJA* 114.2 (2010), 267–304.

Jacobs 2013 = Jacobs, I., *Aesthetic Maintenance of Civic Space: The 'Classical' City from the 4th to the 7th c. AD* (Orientalia Lovaniensia Analecta, 193. Leuven; Paris; Walpole, MA 2013).

Jacobs and Richard 2012 = Jacobs, I. and Richard, J., '"We surpass the beautiful waters of other cities by the abundance of ours": Reconciling function and decoration in late antique fountains', *Journal of Late Antiquity* 5.1 (2012), 3–71.

Jacobs and Waelkens 2013 = Jacobs, I. and Waelkens, M., 'Five centuries of glory. The North-South Colonnaded Street of Sagalassos in the first and the sixth century AD', *IstMitt* 63 (2013), 119–266.

Jacomet 2006 = Jacomet, S., *Identification of Cereal Remains from Archaeological Sites*. 2nd edn. (Basel 2006).

Jacopi 1932 = Jacopi, G., *Esplorazione archeologica di Camiro*, vol. 2: *Necropoli* (ClRh, 6. Bergamo 1932).

Jacopi 1939 = Jacopi, G., 'Gli scavi della Missione Archeologica Italiana ad Afrodisiade nel 1937 (XV–XVI)', *MonAnt* 38 (1939), 73–232.

Jankowiak 2013 = Jankowiak, M., 'Notitia 1 and the impact of the Arab invasions on Asia Minor', *Millennium* 10.1 (2013), 435–462.

Jantzen 2004 = Jantzen, U., *Die Wasserleitung des Eupalinos: die Funde* (Samos, 20. Bonn 2004).

Japp 2007 = Japp, S., 'Late Roman, Byzantine and Ottoman Pottery from Alexandreia Troas', in B. Böhlendorf-Aslan, A. O. Uysal, and J. Witte-Ott (eds), *Çanak. Late Antique and Medieval Pottery and Tiles in Mediterranean Archaeological Contexts: Proceedings of the First International Symposium on Late Antique, Byzantine, Seljuk, and Ottoman Pottery and Tiles in Archaeological Context (Çanakkale, 1–3 June 2005)* (Byzas, 7. 2007), 55–71.

Jarry 1967 = Jarry, J., 'Inscriptions arabes, syriaques et grecques du Massif du Bélus en Syrie du nord', *Annales Islamologiques* 7 (1967), 139–220.

Jashemski 1979 = Jashemski, W. F., *The Gardens of Pompeii, Herculaneum and the Villas Destroyed by Vesuvius* (New Rochelle, N.Y. 1979).

Jashemski and Salza Prina Ricotti 1992 = Jashemski, W. F. and Salza Prina Ricotti, E., 'Preliminary excavations in the gardens of Hadrian's Villa: the Canopus area and the Piazza d'Oro', *AJA* 96.4 (1992), 579–597.

Jeffery 2019 = Jeffery, H. G., *The Archaeology of Middle Byzantine Aphrodisias*. D.Phil. thesis, University of Oxford.

Jeffery 2020 = Jeffery, H. G., 'New lead seals from Aphrodisias', *DOP* 73 (2020), 127–140.

Jeffery 2022 = Jeffery, H. G., *Middle Byzantine Aphrodisias: The Episcopal Village, AD 700–1250* (Aphrodisias, 12. Wiesbaden 2022).

Johnston 1995 = Johnston, A., 'Aphrodisias reconsidered', *The Numismatic Chronicle* 155 (1995), 43–100.

Johnston 2007 = Johnston, A., *Greek Imperial Denominations, ca 200–275: A Study of the Roman Provincial Bronze Coinages of Asia Minor* (Royal Numismatic Society Special Publication, 43. London 2007).

Johnstone and Albarella 2002 = Johnstone, C. and Albarella, U., *The Late Iron Age and Romano-British Mammal and Bird Bone Assemblage from Elms Farm, Heybridge, Essex (Site code: Hyef93-95)* (Centre for Archaeology Report, 45. Portsmouth 2002).

Johnstone 2004 = Johnstone, C. J., *A Biometric Study of Equids in the Roman World*. University of York, PhD thesis: https://etheses.whiterose.ac.uk/14188/.

Jones 1964 = Jones, A. H. M., *The Later Roman Empire, 284–602: A Social, Economic and Administrative Survey*, 3 vols. (Oxford 1964).

Jones 2014 = Jones, C. P., 'Earthquakes and emperors', in A. Kolb (ed.), *Infrastruktur und Herrschaftsorganisation im Imperium Romanum. Herrschaftsstrukturen und Herrschaftspraxis III. Akten der Tagung in Zürich 19.–20.10.2012* (Berlin ; Boston (Mass.) 2014), 52–65.

Kabaklarli 1998 = Kabaklarli, N., *Mangir, Osmanli Imparatorlugu Bakir Paralari 1299–1808* [*Mangir, Copper Coins of Ottoman Empire 1299–1808*], vol. 1 (Uşaklılar Eğitim ve Kültür Vakfı yayınları, Istanbul 1998).

Kaegi 2006 = Kaegi, W. E., 'The early Muslim raids into Anatolia and Byzantine reactions under Emperor Constans II', in E. Grypeou, M. N. Swanson, and D. Thomas (eds), *The Encounter of Eastern Christianity with Early Islam* (The History of Christian-Muslim Relations, 5. Leiden 2006), 73–94.

Kanavou 2013 = Kanavou, N., '"Negative" emotions and Greek names', in A. Chaniotis and P. Ducrey (eds), *Unveiling Emotions*, vol. 2: *Emotions in Greece and Rome: Texts, Images, Material Culture* (HABES, 55. Stuttgart 2013), 167–189.

Kaniewski *et al.* 2007 = Kaniewski, D., De Laet, V., Paulissen, E., and Waelkens, M., 'Long-term effects of human impact on mountainous ecosystems, western Taurus Mountains, Turkey', *Journal of Biogeography* 34.11 (2007), 1975–1997.

Kansteiner *et al.* 2014 = Kansteiner, S., Hallof, K., Lehmann, L., Seidensticker, B., Stemmer, K., and Overbeck, J. A., *Der neue Overbeck (DNO): die antiken Schriftquellen zu den bildenden Künsten der Griechen*, vol. 5: *Späthellenismus, Kaiserzeit. Bildhauer und Maler vom 2. Jh. v. Chr. bis zum 5 Jh. n.Chr.* (Berlin 2014).

Kappel and Loeben 2011 = Kappel, S. and Loeben, C. E., *Gärten im alten Ägypten und in Nubien 2000 v. Chr. – 250 n. Chr* (Archäologie, Inschriften und Denkmäler Altägyptens, 1. Rahden 2011).

Karaman and Zeren 2015 = Karaman, Ö. Y. and Zeren, M. T., 'Case study: Examples of wooden vernacular architecture – Turkish houses in Western Anatolia', *Journal of Built Environment* 3.1–2 (2015), 77–87.

Karwiese 2012 = Karwiese, S., *Die Münzprägung von Ephesos. Katalog und Aufbau der römerzeitlichen Stadtprägung mit allen erfassbaren Stempelnachweisen*, vol. 5.1: *Katalog und Aufbau der römerzeitlichen Stadtprägung mit allen erfassbaren Stempelnachweisen* (Veröffentlichungen des Instituts für Numismatik und Geldgeschichte der Universität Wien Vienna 2012).

Kazanski and Blanc 2003 = Kazanski, M. and Blanc, P. M., *Qal'at Sem'an* (Beyrouth 2003).

Keegan 2014 = Keegan, P., *Graffiti in Antiquity* (London/New York 2014).

Keleş and Oyarçin 2019 = Keleş, V. and Oyarçin, K., 'Parion Odeion'undan Bir Geç Roma Definesi', *TÜBA-AR* 24 (2019), 189–208.

Kenkel 2007 = Kenkel, F., 'The Cypriot Red Slip Ware and its derivatives from Pednelissos in Pisidia', in B. Böhlendorf-Aslan, A. O. Uysal, and J. Witte-Ott (eds), *Çanak. Late Antique and Medieval Pottery and Tiles in Mediterranean Archaeological Contexts: Proceedings of the First International Symposium on Late Antique, Byzantine, Seljuk, and Ottoman Pottery and Tiles in Archaeological Context (Çanakkale, 1–3 June 2005)* (Byzas, 7. 2007), 131–146.

Khairedinova 2012 = Khairedinova, E., 'Early medieval crosses from the south-western Crimea', in B. Bohlendorf-Arslan and A. Ricci (eds), *Byzantine Small Finds in Archaeological Contexts* (Byzas, 15. Istanbul 2012), 417–440.

Kidd 2018 = Kidd, A., 'The Ionic capitals from the South Stoa of Aphrodisias' urban park: a case study of urban design in Late Antiquity', *IstMitt* 68 (2018), 209–244.

Kidd 2019 = Kidd, A., *Ordering Architecture in Late Antiquity: Photo Archive and Database*, (2019). Accessed 14/08/2020

Kiilerich 1998 = Kiilerich, B., *The Obelisk Base in Constantinople: Court Art and Imperial Ideology* (Rome 1998).

Kinney 2006 = Kinney, D., 'The concept of Spolia', in C. Rudolph (ed.), *A Companion to Medieval Art: Romanesque and Gothic in Northern Europe* (Oxford 2006), 233–252.

Kirmaci, Agcagil, and Aslan, 2013 = Kirmaci, M., Agcagil, E., and Aslan, G., 'The bryophyte flora of ancient cities of Aydın Province (Turkey)', *Botanica Serbica* 37.1 (2013), 31–38.

Klar Phillips 2008 = Klar Phillips, L., 'Figural table supports: the archaeology of dining in the Roman world', in C. Ratté and R. R. R. Smith (eds), *Aphrodisias Papers 4: New Research on the City and its Monuments* (JRA Supplementary Series, 70. Portsmouth, Rhode Island 2008), 253–283.

Klementa 1993 = Klementa, S., *Gelagerte Flussgötter des Späthellenismus und der römischen Kaiserzeit* (Arbeiten zur Archäologie, 11. Köln 1993).

Klimek 2013 = Klimek, A. U., 'A system of stonemason marks applied in columns of the tetrastyle courtyard in the House of Leukatios in Ptolemais, Cyrenaica', *Światowit. Annual of the Institute of Archaeology of the University of Warsaw* 10 (2012) (2013), 11–21.

Knipping, Müllenhoff, and Brückner 2008 = Knipping, M., Müllenhoff, M., and Brückner, H., 'Human induced landscape changes around Bafa Gölü (western Turkey)', *Vegetation History and Archaeobotany* 17.4 (2008), 365–380.

Koch 1903 = Koch, P., *Die byzantinischen Beamtentitel von 400 bis 700* (Jena 1903).

Koder 2012 = Koder, J., 'Regional networks in Asia Minor during the Middle Byzantine period, seventh–eleventh centuries', in C. Morrisson (ed.), *Trade and Markets in Byzantium* (Dumbarton Oaks Byzantine Symposia & Colloquia Washington, DC 2012), 147–175.

Koerner 1961 = Koerner, R., *Die Abkürzung der Homonymität in griechischen Inschriften* (Sitzungsberichte der Deutschen Akademie der Wissenschaften zu Berlin, 2. Berlin 1961).

Kontogiannis and Arvaniti 2012 = Kontogiannis, N. D. and Arvaniti, S. I., 'Placing "contexts" in a context: minor objects from medieval Andros', in B. Bohlendorf-Arslan and A. Ricci (eds), *Byzantine Small Finds in Archaeological Contexts* (Byzas, 15. Istanbul 2012), 249–261.

Korkut 2015 = Korkut, T., 'Arkeolojik kalıntılar', in T. Korkut (ed.), *Arkeoloji, Epigrafi, Jeoloji, Doğal ve Kültürel Peyzaj Yapısıyla Tlos Antik Kenti ve Teritoryumu* (Seydikemer Kaymakamlığı Yayınları, 1. Ankara 2015), 12–64.

Köroğlu 2007 = Köroğlu, G., 'Yumuktepe Höyüğü Kazısından İki Ekmek Mührü', in M. Alparslan, M. Doğan-Alparslan, and H. Peker (eds), *Vita: Belkıs Dinçol ve Ali Dinçol'a Armağan/Festschrift in Honour of Belkıs Dinçol and Ali Dinçol* (Istanbul 2007), 433–443.

Kotansky 1994 = Kotansky, R., *Greek Magical Amulets: The Inscribed Gold, Silver, Copper and Bronze Lamellae*, vol. 1: *Published Texts of Known Provenance* (Abhandlungen der Rheinisch-Westfälischen Akademie der Wissenschaften, Opladen 1994).

Kraeling 1938 = Kraeling, C. H., 'The history of Gerasa', in *Gerasa. City of the Decapolis* (New Haven 1938), 27–69.

Kristensen 2018 = Kristensen, T. M., 'Earthquakes and Late Antique urbanism: some observations on the case of the Lykos Valley', in C. Şimşek and T. Kaçar (eds), *Geç antik çağda Lykos vadisi ve çevresi / The Lykos Valley and Neighbourhood in Late Antiquity* (Laodikeia Çalışmaları: Ek Yayın Dizisi / Supplementary series, 1. İstanbul 2018), 71–78.

Kristensen and Stirling 2016 = Kristensen, T. M. and Stirling, L., *The Afterlife of Greek and Roman Sculpture: Late Antique Responses and Practices* (Ann Arbor, MI 2016).

Kropp 2009 = Kropp, A. J. M., 'Nabataean Petra: the royal palace and the Herod connection', *Boreas* 32 (2009), 43–59.

Kruse 2006 = Kruse, T., 'The magistrate and the ocean: acclamations and ritualised communication in town gatherings in Roman Egypt', in *Ritual and Communication in the Graeco-Roman World* (Kernos Supplement, 16. Liège 2006), 297–315.

Kuban 1965 = Kuban, D., *Anadolu-Türk Mimarisinin Kaynak ve Sorunları* (Istanbul 1965).

Kubitschek and Ritterling 1924 = Kubitschek, W. and Ritterling, E., 'Legio', in A. Pauly, G. Wissowa, and W. Kroll (eds), *Real-Encyclopädie der classischen Altertumswissenschaft*, vol. 12 (Stuttgart 1924), 1330–1838.

Kuhn 2012 = Kuhn, C. T., 'Emotionality in the political culture of the Graeco-Roman East: the role of acclamations', in A. Chaniotis (ed.), *Unveiling Emotions. Sources and Methods for the Study of Emotions in the Greek World* (Stuttgart 2012), 295–316.

Külzer 2010 = Külzer, A., 'Ephesos in byzantinischer Zeit: ein historischer Überblick', in F. Daim and J. Drauschke (eds), *Byzanz–Das Römerreich im Mittelalter: Schauplätze* (Monographien RGZM, 2.2. Mainz 2010), 521–539.

Külzer 2011 = Külzer, A., 'Bizans Dönemi Ephesos'u: Tarihine Bir Genel Bakış', in F. Daim and S. Ladstätter (eds), *Bizans Dönemi Ephesos* (Istanbul 2011), 29–46.

Külzer 2013 = Külzer, A., 'Ephesos im siebten Jahrhundert: Notizen zur Stadtgeschichte', *Porphyra* 20 (2013), 4–16.

Kumsar et al. 2016 = Kumsar, H., Aydan, Ö., Şimşek, C., and D'Andria, F., 'Historical earthquakes that damaged Hierapolis and Laodikeia antique cities and their implications for earthquake potential of Denizli basin in western Turkey', *Bulletin of Engineering Geology and the Environment* 75.2 (2016), 519–536.

Kurke 1999 = Kurke, L., 'Ancient Greek board games and how to play them', *CP* 94.3 (1999), 247–267.

Kürkman 1988 = Kürkman, G., 'Karaman Beyliğinin Bakır Paraları Üzerine Tetkikler', in *Türk Nümismatik Derneğinin 20. Kuruluş Yılında İbrahim Artuk'a Armağan* (Istanbul 1988), 163–173.

Kuttner 1999 = Kuttner, A. L., 'Culture and History at Pompey's Museum', *Transactions and Proceedings of the American Philological Association* 129 (1999), 343–373.

Laborde 1838 = Laborde, L. E. S. J., *Voyage de l'Asie Mineure par Messeurs Alexandre de Laborde, Becker, Hall, et Léon de Laborde* (Paris 1838).

Ladstätter 2008 = Ladstätter, S., 'Funde', in M. Steskal and M. La Torre (eds), *Das Vediusgymnasium in Ephesos. Archäologie und Baubefund* (Forschungen in Ephesos, 14/1. Wien 2008), 97–189.

Ladstätter 2010 = Ladstätter, S., 'Keramik', in A. Pülz (ed.), *Das sogenannte Lukasgrab in Ephesos. Eine Fallstudie zur Adaption antiker Monumente in byzantinischer Zeit* (Forschungen in Ephesos, 4/4. Wien 2010), 250–350.

Ladstätter 2017 = Ladstätter, S., 'Ephesus', in P. Niewöhner (ed.), *The Archaeology of Byzantine Anatolia: From the End of Late Antiquity until the Coming of the Turks* (Oxford 2017), 238–248.

Ladstätter and Sauer 2005a = Ladstätter, S. and Sauer, R., 'Late Roman C-Ware und lokale spätantike Feinware aus Ephesos', in F. Krinzinger (ed.), *Spätantike und Mittelalterliche Keramik aus Ephesos, 125–201* (Archäologische Forschungen, 13. Vienna 2005), 143–201.

Ladstätter and Sauer 2005b = Ladstätter, S. and Sauer, R., 'Mineralogisch-petrographische Analysen von frühbyzantinischen Ampullen und Amphoriskoi aus Ephesos', in F. Krinzinger (ed.), *Spätantike und mittelalterliche Keramik in Ephesos* (Archäologische Forschungen, 13. Vienna 2005), 125–135.

Lamer 1927 = Lamer, H., 'Lusoria tabula', in G. Wissowa and W. Kroll (eds), *Paulys Real-Encyclopädie der classischen Altertumswissenschaft*, vol. 13: *Libanius – Lysimachides* (Stuttgart 1927), 1900–2029.

Langner 2001 = Langner, M., *Antike Graffitizeichnungen. Motive, Gestaltung und Bedeutung* (Palilia, 11. Wiesbaden 2001).

Laurent 1963 = Laurent, V., *Le corpus des sceaux de l'Empire byzantin*, vol. 5: *L'Église. Première partie: L'Église du Constantinople* (Paris 1963).

Lauritsen 1984 = Lauritsen, F. M., 'A late Roman hoard from Aphrodisias, Turkey', in W. Heckel and R. Sullivan (eds), *Ancient Coins of the Graeco-Roman World: The Nickle Numismatic Papers* (Waterloo, Ontario 1984), 295.

Lauritsen 1993 = Lauritsen, F. M., 'A mid-third century hoard of antoniniani from Karacasu, Turkey', in M. Kubelík and M. Schwartz (eds), *Von der Bauforschung zur Denkmalpflege, Festschrift für Alois Machatschek zum 65. Geburtstag* (Vienna 1993), 153–155.

Lavagne 1988 = Lavagne, H., *Operosa antra. Recherches sur la grotte à Rome, de Sylla à Hadrien* (Rome 1988).

Lavan 2012 = Lavan, L. A., 'From polis to emporion? Retail and regulation in the late antique city', in C. Morrison (ed.), *Trade and Markets in Byzantium* (Dumbarton Oaks Byzantine Symposia and Colloquia, Washington DC 2012), 333–377.

Lebbie 2004 = Lebbie, S. H. B., 'Goats under household conditions', *Small Ruminant Research* 51.2 (2004), 131–136.

Lenaghan 2007 = Lenaghan, J., 'On the use of Roman copies: Two new examples of the Doryphoros and Westmacott Ephebe', *Eidola* 4 (2007), 147–172.

Lenaghan 2008 = Lenaghan, J., 'A statue of Julia Hera Sebaste (Livia)', in C. Ratté and R. R. R. Smith (eds), *Aphrodisias Papers 4: New Research on the City and its Monuments* (JRA Supplementary Series, 70. Portsmouth, Rhode Island 2008), 37–50.

Lenaghan 2019 = Lenaghan, J., 'Another statue in context: Rhodopaios of Aphrodisias', in C. M. Draycott, R. Raja, K. Welch, and W. T. Wootton (eds), *Visual Histories of the Classical World: Essays in Honour of R.R.R. Smith* (Studies in Classical Archaeology, 4. Turnhout 2019), 503–518.

Lenaghan forthcoming = Lenaghan, J., 'The Monument for Menandros (*ALA* 24)', in G. Agosti and I. Tantillo (eds), *Iscrizioni metriche nel tardo impero romano: società, politica e cultura fra Oriente e Occidente. Settant'anni dopo Louis Robert, Hellenica IV (1948)* (Rome forthcoming 2024).

Lenz 1998 = Lenz, D., 'Ein Gallier unter den Gefährten des Odysseus. Zur Polyphemgruppe aus dem Pollio-Nymphaeum in Ephesos', *IstMitt* 48 (1998), 237–248.

Leppin 2015 = Leppin, H. (ed.) *Antike Mythologie in christlichen Kontexten der Spätantike*, vol. 54 (Berlin 2015).

Lewartowski 2003 = Lewartowski, É., 'Les membres des Koina sous le Principat (Ier–IIIe siècles): quelques exemples d'intégration dans la vie locale', in M. Cébeillac-Gervasoni and L. Lamoine (eds), *Les élites et leurs facettes: les élites locales dans le monde hellénistique et romain* (Collection de l'École française de Rome, 309. Rome 2003), 207–221.

Lhôte 2006 = Lhôte, É., *Les lamelles oraculaires de Dodone* (Geneva 2006).

Lichtenberger and Raja 2016 = Lichtenberger, A. and Raja, R., 'Living with and on the river-side: the example of Roman Antiochia-on-the-Chrysorrhoas-formerly-called-Gerasa', in J. Kuhlmann Madsen, N. Overgaard Andersen, and I. Thuesen (eds), *Water of Life* (Copenhagen 2016), 98–115.

Lightfoot 2002 = Lightfoot, C. S., 'Byzantine Anatolia: reassessing the numismatic evidence', *RN* 6.158 (2002), 229–239.

Lightfoot 2014 = Lightfoot, C. S., 'Learning and literacy in Byzantine Amorium', in A. Özfırat (ed.), *Scripta: Arkeolojiyle Geçen Bir Yaşam İçin Yazılar Veli Sevin'e Armağan - Essays in Honour of Veli Sevin, A Life Immersed in Archaeology* (Istanbul 2014), 381–387.

Lightfoot 2003 = Lightfoot, M., 'Belt buckles from Amorium and in the Afyon museum', in C. S. Lightfoot (ed.), *Amorium Reports II: Research papers and Technical Reports (BAR International Series 1170)* (Oxford 2003), 81–103.

Lilie 1976 = Lilie, R.-J., *Die byzantinische Reaktion auf die Ausbreitung der Araber: Studien zur Strukturwandlung des byzantinischen Staates im 7. und 8. Jhd* (Miscellenea Byzantina Monacensia, 22. München 1976).

Linant de Bellefonds 1996 = Linant de Bellefonds, P., 'The Mythological Reliefs from the Agora Gate', in C. Roueché and R. R. R. Smith (eds), *Aphrodisias Papers 3: The Setting and Quarries, Mythological and other Sculptural Decoration, Architectural Development, Portico of Tiberius, and Tetrapylon* (JRA Supplementary Series, 20. Ann Arbor, MI 1996), 174–186.

Linant de Bellefonds 2009 = Linant de Bellefonds, P., *The Mythological Reliefs from the Agora Gate* (Aphrodisias, 4. Mainz 2009).

Lindros Wohl 2001 = Lindros Wohl, B., 'Constantine's Use of Spolia', in J. Fleischer, J. Lund, and M. Nielsen (eds), *Late Antiquity: Art in Context* (Acta Hyperborea, 8. Copenhagen 2001), 85–115.

Llewelyn 1997 = Llewelyn, S. R., *New Documents Illustrating Early Christianity* vol. 8: *A review of Greek and other inscriptions and papyri published in 1984–1985* (Grand Rapids, Michigan 1997).

Lochner, Sauer, and Linke 2005 = Lochner, S., Sauer, R., and Linke, R., 'Late Roman "Unguentaria"?: a contribution to Early Byzantine wares from the view of Ephesos', in J. M. Gurt i Esparraguera, J. Buxeda i Garrigos, and M. A. Cau Ontiveros (eds), *LRCW I: Late Roman Coarse Wares, Cooking Wares and Amphorae in the Mediterranean: Archaeology and Archaeometry* (BAR International Series, 1340. Oxford 2005), 647–654.

Lockey 2012 = Lockey, I., 'Olive oil production and rural settlement', in C. Ratté and P. D. De Staebler (eds), *The Aphrodisias Regional Survey* (Aphrodisias, 5. Darmstadt/Mainz 2012), 203–237.

Lodwick 2015 = Lodwick, L., 'Identifying ritual deposition of plant remains: a case study of stone pine cones in Roman

Britain', in T. Brindle, M. Allen, E. Durham, and A. Smith (eds), *TRAC 2014: Proceedings of the Twenty-Fourth Annual Theoretical Roman Archaeology Conference, Reading 2014* (Oxford 2015), 54–69.

Lohmann 2018 = Lohmann, P., *Graffiti als Interaktionsform: Geritzte Inschriften in den Wohnhäusern Pompejis* (Materiale Textkulturen, 16. Berlin 2018).

Long 2012 = Long, L. E., 'Regional marble quarries', in C. Ratté and P. D. De Staebler (eds), *The Aphrodisias Regional Survey* (Aphrodisias, 5. Darmstadt/Mainz 2012), 165–201.

Longfellow 2011 = Longfellow, B., *Roman Imperialism and Civic Patronage: Form, Meaning, and Ideology in Monumental Fountain Complexes* (Cambridge 2011).

Loyet 2000 = Loyet, M. A., 'The potential for within-site variation of faunal remains: a case study from the Islamic period urban center of Tell Tuneinir, Syria', *BASOR* 320 (2000), 23–48.

Lund 1996 = Lund, J., 'From archaeology to history? Reflections on the chronological distribution of ceramic finewares in South Western and Southern Asia Minor from the 1st to the 7th century AD', in M. Herfort-Koch, U. Mandel, and U. Schädler (eds), *Hellenistische und kaiserzeitliche Keramik des östlichen Mittelmeergebietes. Kolloquium, Frankfurt 24.–25. April 1995* (Frankfurt am Main 1996), 105–125.

Lyman 1994 = Lyman, R. L., *Vertebrate Taphonomy* (Cambridge 1994).

Macaulay-Lewis 2006 = Macaulay-Lewis, E., 'The role of *ollae perforatae* in understanding horticulture, planting techniques, garden design, and plant trade in the Roman World', in J.-P. Morel, J. T. Juan, and J. C. Matamala (eds), *The Archaeology of Crop Fields and Gardens. Proceedings from 1st Conference on Crop Fields and Gardens Archaeology, University of Barcelona (Barcelona, Spain, June 1–3rd 2006)* (Bari 2006), 207–219.

Macaulay-Lewis 2017 = Macaulay-Lewis, E., 'The archaeology of gardens in the Roman villa', in A.-A. Malek, K. L. Gleason, K. J. Hartswick, and W. F. Jashemski (eds), *Gardens of the Roman Empire* (Cambridge 2017), 87–120.

MacDonald 1974 = MacDonald, D. J., 'Aphrodisias and Currency in the East, AD 259–305', *AJA* 78.3 (1974), 279–286.

MacDonald 1976 = MacDonald, D. J., *Greek and Roman Coins from Aphrodisias* (BAR Supplementary Series, 9. Oxford 1976).

MacDonald 1992 = MacDonald, D. J., *The Coinage of Aphrodisias* (Royal Numismatic Society: Special publication, 23. London 1992).

MacLean and Insoll 2003 = MacLean, R. and Insoll, T., 'Archaeology, luxury and the exotic: the examples of Islamic Gao (Mali) and Bahrain', *WorldArch* 34.3 (2003), 558–570.

Maderna 1988 = Maderna, C., *Iuppiter Diomedes und Merkur als Vorbilder für römische Bildnisstatuen: Untersuchungen zum römischen statuarischen Idealporträt* (Archäologie und Geschichte, 1. Heidelberg 1988).

Maiuro 2007 = Maiuro, M., 'Oltre il Pasquino. Achille, il culto imperiale e l'istituzione ginnasiale tra oriente e occidente nell'Impero romano', *Archaeologia Classica* 58 (2007), 165–246.

Maltby 2007 = Maltby, M., 'Chop and change: specialist cattle carcass processing in Roman Britain', in B. Croxford, N. Ray, and R. Roth (eds), *TRAC 2006: Proceedings of the 16th Annual Theoretical Roman Archaeology Conference* (Oxford 2007), 59–76.

Mania 2006 = Mania, U., 'Eine neue Werkstatt früher türkischer Keramik – Miletware aus Pergamon', *IstMitt* 56 (2006), 473–499.

Manning 1985 = Manning, W. H., 'The iron objects', in L. F. Pitts and J. K. St Joseph (eds), *Inchtuthil. The Roman Legionary Fortress: Excavations 1952–65* (Britannia Monograph Series, London 1985), 289–299.

Marsili 2019 = Marsili, G., *Archeologia del cantiere protobizantino: cave, maestranze e committenti attraverso i marchi dei marmorari* (Bologna 2019).

Marston 2017 = Marston, J. M., *Agricultural Sustainability and Environmental Change at Ancient Gordion* (Gordion special studies, 8. Philadelphia 2017).

Marston and Miller 2014 = Marston, J. M. and Miller, N. F., 'Intensive agriculture and land use at Roman Gordion, central Turkey', *Vegetation History and Archaeobotany* 23.6 (2014), 761–773.

Martindale 1980 = Martindale, J. R., *The Prosopography of the Later Roman Empire*, vol. 2: *A.D. 395–527* (Cambridge 1980).

Marzano 2013 = Marzano, A., *Harvesting the Sea: The Exploitation of Marine Resources in the Roman Mediterranean* (Oxford Studies on the Roman Economy, Oxford 2013).

Marzano 2022 = Marzano, A., *Plants, Politics and Empire in Ancient Rome* (Cambridge 2022).

Mashkour and Berthon 2008 = Mashkour, M. and Berthon, R., 'Animal remains from Tilbeşar excavations, Southeast Anatolia, Turkey', *Anatolia Antiqua* 16 (2008), 23–51.

Massner 1982 = Massner, A.-K., *Bildnisangleichung: Untersuchungen zur Entstehungs- und Wirkungsgeschichte der Augustusporträts (43 v. Chr.–68 n. Chr.)* (Berlin 1982).

McCown 1938a = McCown, C. C., 'The festival theater at the Birketein', in *Gerasa. City of the Decapolis* (New Haven 1938), 159–170.

McCown 1938b = McCown, C. C., 'The Maiumas inscription, pool and theatre at Jerash', in *Atti del XIX Congresso Internazionale degli Orientalisti: Roma 23–29 settembre 1935* (Rome 1938), 685–689.

McDavid 2016 = McDavid, A., 'Renovation of the Hadrianic Baths in late antiquity', in R. R. R. Smith, J. Lenaghan, A. Sokolicek, and K. Welch (eds), *Aphrodisias Papers 5: Excavation and Research at Aphrodisias, 2006–2012* (JRA Supplementary Series, 103. Portsmouth, Rhode Island 2016), 209–224.

Meadow 1999 = Meadow, R., 'The use of size index scaling techniques for research on archaeozoological collections from the Middle East', in C. Becker, H. Manhart, J. Peters, and J. Schibler (eds), *Historia Animalium ex Ossibus. Festschrift für Angela von den Driesch* (Rahden/Westf. 1999), 285–300.

Mendel 1906 = Mendel, G., 'Seconde note sur les fouilles exécutées à Aphrodisias par M. Paul Gaudin. Campagne de 1905', *Comptes rendus de l'Académie des inscriptions et belles-lettres* 4 (1906), 158–184.

Meneghini and Santangeli Valenzani 1996 = Meneghini, R. and Santangeli Valenzani, R., 'Episodi di trasformazione del paesaggio urbano nella Roma altomedievale attraverso l'analisi di due contesti: un isolato in Piazza dei Cinquecento e l'area dei Fori Imperiali', *Archeologia medievale* 23 (1996), 53–99.

Meneghini and Santangeli Valenzani 2004 = Meneghini, R. and Santangeli Valenzani, R., *Roma nell'Altomedioevo: topografia e urbanistica della città dal V al X secolo* (Archeologia del territorio, Rome 2004).

Meneghini and Santangeli Valenzani 2006 = Meneghini, R. and Santangeli Valenzani, R., *Formae Urbis Romae: nuovi frammenti di piante marmoree dallo scavo dei Fori Imperiali*, vol. 15 (Bulletino della Commissione archeologica comunale di Roma, Supplementi, Roma 2006).

Mentzu-Meimare 1996 = Mentzu-Meimare, K., 'Der 'ΧΑΡΙΕΣΤΑΤΟΣ ΜΑΙΟΥΜΑΣ'', *Byzantinische Zeitschrift* 89 (1996), 58–73.

Mercangöz 2007 = Mercangöz, Z., 'Stamp seal', in A. Ödekan (ed.), *The Remnants: 12th and 13th Centuries Byzantine Objects in Turkey* (Istanbul 2007), 73–74.

Merkelbach and Stauber 1998 = Merkelbach, R. and Stauber, J., *Steinepigramme aus dem griechischen Osten*, vol. 1: *Die Westküste Kleinasiens von Knidos bis Ilion* (Stuttgart–Leipzig 1998).

Metaxas 2005 = Metaxas, S., 'Frühbyzantinische Ampullen und Amphoriskoi aus Ephesos', in F. Krinzinger (ed.), *Spätantike und mittelalterliche Keramik aus Ephesos*, vol. 13 (Denkschriften der phil.-hist. Klasse, 332. Wien 2005), 67–123.

Métivier and Prigent 2010 = Métivier, S. and Prigent, V., 'La circulation monétaire dans la Cappadoce byzantine d'après les collections des musées de Kayseri et de Niğde', in *Mélanges Cécile Morrisson* (Travaux et mémoires du Centre d'histoire et civilisation de Byzance, 16. Paris 2010), 577–618.

Millar 1977 = Millar, F., *The Emperor in the Roman World (31 B.C.–A.D. 337)* (London 1977).

Miller 2011 = Miller, N. F., 'Managing predictable unpredictability: agricultural sustainability at Gordion, Turkey', in N. F. Miller, K. M. Moore, and K. Ryan (eds), *Sustainable Lifeways: Cultural Persistence in an Ever-Changing Environment* (Penn Museum International Research Conferences, 3. Philadelphia, PA 2011), 310–324.

Mitchiner 1998 = Mitchiner, M. B., *The World of Islam* (London 1998).

Möbius 1970 = Möbius, H., 'Vier hellenistische Skulpturen', *AntP* 10 (1970), 39–54.

Moltesen 2000 = Moltesen, M., 'The Esquiline Group: Aphrodisian statues in the Ny Carlsberg Glyptotek', *AntP* 27 (2000), 111–131.

Montanari 2015 = Montanari, F., *The Brill Dictionary of Ancient Greek* (Leiden 2015).

Moreno-García 2004 = Moreno-García, M., 'Hunting practices and consumption patterns in rural communities in the Rif mountains (Morocco) – some ethno-zoological notes', in S. J. O'Day, W. Van Neer, and A. Ervynck (eds), *Behavior Behind Bones. The Zooarchaeology of Ritual, Religion, Status and Identity* (2004), 327–334.

Morrisson 1990 = Morrisson, C., 'Carthage, production et circulation du bronze à l'époque byzantine d'après les trouvailles et les fouilles', *BAntFr* 1988.1 (1990), 239–253.

Morrisson 2012 = Morrisson, C., 'Weighing, measuring, paying: exchanges in the market and the marketplace', in C. Morrisson (ed.), *Trade and Markets in Byzantium* (Dumbarton Oaks Byzantine symposia and colloquia, Washington, D.C. 2012), 379–398.

Morrisson 2017 = Morrisson, C., 'Coins', in P. Niewöhner (ed.), *The Archaeology of Byzantine Anatolia: From the End of Late Antiquity until the Coming of the Turks* (Oxford 2017), 71–81.

Morrisson, Popović, and Ivanišević 2006 = Morrisson, C., Popović, V., and Ivanišević, V., *Les trésors monétaires byzantins des Balkans et d'Asie Mineure (491–713)* (Réalités byzantines, 13. Paris 2006).

Mynott 2018 = Mynott, J., *Birds in the Ancient World: Winged Words* (Oxford 2018).

Nabais, Boneta, and Soares 2019 = Nabais, M., Boneta, I., and Soares, R., 'Chelonian use in Portugal: Evidence from Castelo Velho de Safara', *Journal of Archaeological Science: Reports* 28 (2019), 102054.

Nesbitt 1983 = Nesbitt, J. W., 'Byzantine lead seals from Aphrodisias', *DOP* 37 (1983), 159–164.

Netzer 1975 = Netzer, E., 'The Hasmonean and Herodian winter palaces at Jericho', *IEJ* 25.2–3 (1975), 89–100.

Netzer 1981 = Netzer, E., *Greater Herodium* (Qedem, 13. Jerusalem 1981).

Netzer 1986 = Netzer, E., 'The swimming pools of the Hasmonean period at Jericho', in G. Garbrecht (ed.), *Geschichtliche Wasserbauten in Ägypten: Vorträge der Tagung, Kairo 10. bis 17. Februar 1986* (Leichtweiß-Institut für Wasserbau: Mitteilungen, 89. Braunschweig 1986), 1–12.

Netzer 1996a = Netzer, E., 'The Hasmonean palaces in Palestina', in W. Hoepfner and G. Brands (eds), *Basileia: Die Paläste der hellenistischen Könige: Internationales Symposion in Berlin vom 16.12.1992 bis 20.12.1992* (Mainz 1996), 203–208.

Netzer 1996b = Netzer, E., 'The Promontory Palace', in A. Raban and K. G. Holum (eds), *Caesarea Maritima: A Retrospective after Two Millennia* (Leiden 1996), 193–207.

Netzer 1999 = Netzer, E., *Die Paläste der Hasmonäer und Herodes' des Grossen* (Sonderhefte der antiken Welt/Zaberns Bildbände zur Archäologie, Mainz 1999).

Netzer 2001 = Netzer, E., *The Palaces of the Hasmoneans and Herod the Great*. Translated by R. Amoils (Jerusalem 2001).

Neudecker 2014 = Neudecker, R., 'Collecting culture: statues and fragments in Roman gardens', in M. Wellington Gahtan and D. Pegazzan (eds), *Museum Archetypes and Collecting in the Ancient World* (Monumenta Graeca et Romana, 21. Leiden 2014), 129–136.

Ng and Swetnam-Burland 2018 = Ng, D. Y. and Swetnam-Burland, M., *Reuse and Renovation in Roman Material Culture: Functions, Aesthetics, Interpretations* (Cambridge 2018).

Nicks 1998 = Nicks, F. K., *The Reign of Anastasius I, 491–518*. D.Phil. thesis, University of Oxford.

Niebuhr 1835 = Niebuhr, B. G., *Georgius Pachymeres*, vol. 1 (Corpus scriptorum historiae byzantinae, 36. Bonn 1835).

Nielsen 1990 = Nielsen, I., *Thermae et Balnea. The Architecture and Cultural History of Roman Public Baths*, 2 vols. (Aarhus 1990).

Nielsen 1999 = Nielsen, I., *Hellenistic Palaces: Tradition and Renewal*. 2nd edn. (Studies in Hellenistic Civilization 5. Aarhus 1999).

Nielsen 2001 = Nielsen, I., 'The gardens of the Hellenistic palaces', in I. Nielsen (ed.), *The Royal Palace Institution in the First Millennium BC: Regional Development and Cultural Interchange between East and West* (Aarhus 2001), 165–187.

Niewöhner 2007 = Niewöhner, P., *Aizanoi, Dokimion und Anatolien: Stadt und Land, Siedlungs- und Steinmetzwesen vom späteren 4. bis ins 6. Jahrhundert n. Chr.* (Wiesbaden 2007).

Niewöhner 2016 = Niewöhner, P., 'The Byzantine Settlement History of Miletus and Its Hinterland–Quantitative Aspects. Stratigraphy, Pottery, Anthropology, Coins, and Palynology, with contributions by Arzu Demirel, Adam Izdebski, Hacer Sancaktar, Nico Schwerdt, and Harald Stümpel', *AA* 2016.2 (2016), 225–290.

Niewöhner 2017a = Niewöhner, P., 'Miletus', in P. Niewöhner (ed.), *The Archaeology of Byzantine Anatolia: From the End of Late Antiquity until the Coming of the Turks* (Oxford 2017), 255–263.

Niewöhner 2017b = Niewöhner, P., 'Urbanism', in P. Niewöhner (ed.), *The Archaeology of Byzantine Anatolia: From the End of Late Antiquity until the Coming of the Turks* (Oxford 2017), 39–59.

Nollé 1993 = Nollé, J., *Side im Altertum. Geschichte und Zeugnisse*, vol. 1 (Inschriften griechischer Städte aus Kleinasien, 43. Bonn 1993).

Noy 1993 = Noy, D., *Jewish Inscriptions of Western Europe*, vol. 1: *Italy (excluding the city of Rome), Spain and Gaul* (Cambridge 1993).

O'Connor 2003 = O'Connor, T. P., *The Analysis of Urban Animal Bone Assemblages: A Handbook for Archaeologists* (The Archaeology of York, Principles and Methods, 19/2. York 2003).

Oberläder-Târnoveanu 2012 = Oberläder-Târnoveanu, E., 'Untangling Ariadne's Thread – Contributions to the "Archaeology" of the Romanian Medieval Numismatics, Part I, The Early Stage of Wallachian Coinage – from Vladislav I to Mircea the Elder (c. 1364–1418)', *Cercetări Numismatice* 18 (2012), 27–76.

Oeconomides and Drossoyianni 1989 = Oeconomides, M. and Drossoyianni, P., 'A hoard of gold Byzantine coins from Samos', *RN* 6e série, 31 (1989), 145–182.

Oellacher 1948 = Oellacher, H., 'Cocococo', *Glotta* 31.1–2 (1948), 70–72.

Öğüş 2014 = Öğüş, E., 'The rise and fall of sarcophagus production at Aphrodisias', *Phoenix: Journal of the Classical Association of Canada = Revue de la Société Canadienne des Études Classiques* 68.1–2 (2014), 137–156.

Öğüş 2015 = Öğüş, E., 'A late-antique fountain at Aphrodisias and its implications for spoliation practices', *JRA* 28 (2015), 302–324.

Öğüş 2016 = Öğüş, E., 'Excavations on the Tetrapylon Street, 2010–11', in R. R. R. Smith, J. Lenaghan, A. Sokolicek, and K. Welch (eds), *Aphrodisias Papers 5: Excavation and Research at Aphrodisias, 2006–2012* (JRA Supplementary Series, 103. Portsmouth, Rhode Island 2016), 48–57.

Olcay 2001 = Olcay, B. Y., 'Lighting methods in the Byzantine period and findings of glass lamps in Anatolia', *JGS* 43 (2001), 77–87.

Ölçer 1975 = Ölçer, C., *Nakışlı Osmanlı Mangırları* (Istanbul 1975).

Ölçer 1978 = Ölçer, C., *Sultan Abdülmecid Devri Osmanlı Madeni Paraları* [*Ottoman coinage during the reign of Sultan Abdülmecid Han*] (Istanbul 1978).

Oliver 1970 = Oliver, J. H., *Marcus Aurelius: Aspects of Civic and Cultural Policy in the East* (Hesperia Supplement, 13. Princeton, N.J 1970).

Omar 2017 = Omar, L., 'Approaching Medieval cuisine: Employing zoo-archaeological methods on Anatolian faunal assemblages', in J. Vroom, Y. Waksman, and R. v. Oosten (eds), *Medieval MasterChef: Archaeological and Historical Perspectives on Eastern Cuisine and Western Foodways* (Turnhout 2017), 95–115.

Onar et al. 2015 = Onar, V., Pazvant, G., Pasicka, E., Armutak, A., and Alpak, H., 'Byzantine horse skeletons of Theodosius Harbour: 2. Withers height estimation', *Revue de Medecine Veterinaire* 166.1–2 (2015), 30–42.

Onians 1988 = Onians, J., *Bearers of Meaning. The Classical Orders in Antiquity, the Middle Ages, and the Renaissance* (Cambridge 1988).

Orlandos 1929 = Orlandos, A., 'Αἱ παλαιοχριστιανικαὶ βασιλικαὶ τῆς Λέσβου', *ArchDelt* 12 (1929), 1–72.

Osband and Eisenberg 2018 = Osband, M. and Eisenberg, M., 'Summary of the pottery finds', in M. Eisenberg (ed.), *Hippos-Sussita of the Decapolis: The First Twelve Seasons of Excavations 2000–2011*, vol. 2 (Haifa 2018), 210–275.

Ostroumov 1861 = Ostroumov, I. N., *The History of the Council of Florence*. Translated by B. Popoff (London 1861).

Outschar 1991 = Outschar, U., 'Exportorientierte Keramikproduktion auch noch im spâtantiken Ephesos?', *RCRFActa* 29–30 (1991), 317–327.

Outschar 1993 = Outschar, U., 'Produkte aus Ephesos in alle Welt? Ephesische Amphoren', in D. Beyll, U. Outschar, and F. Soykal (eds), *Terra Sigillata aus der Marienkirche in Ephesos: erste Zwischenbilanz* (Berichte und Materialien des Österreichisches Archäologisches Institut, 5. Wien 1993), 47–52.

Outschar 1996a = Outschar, U., 'Dokumentation exemplarisch ausgewählter keramischer Fundkomplexe', in C. Lang-Auinger (ed.), *Hanghaus 1 in Ephesos. Der Baubefund*, vol. 1 (Forschungen in Ephesos, 8/3. Wien 1996), 27–85.

Outschar 1996b = Outschar, U., 'Zur Baudekoration und typologischen Stellung des Tetrapylons', in C. Roueché and R. R. R. Smith (eds), *Aphrodisias Papers 3: The Setting and Quarries, Mythological and other Sculptural Decoration, Architectural Development, Portico of Tiberius, and Tetrapylon* (JRA Supplementary Series, 20. Ann Arbor, MI 1996), 215–224.

Outschar 2016 = Outschar, U., 'Ceramics', in P. Stinson (ed.), *The Civil Basilica* (Aphrodisias, 7. Wiesbaden 2016), 104–122.

Owens 2002 = Owens, E. J., 'The water supply of Antioch', in T. Drew-Bear, M. Tashalan, and C. M. Thomas (eds), *Actes du Ier Congrès international sur Antioche de Pisidie* (Lyon; Paris 2002), 337–348.

Özgümüş 2008 = Özgümüş, Ü., 'Byzantine Glass Finds in the Roman Theater at İznik (Nicaea)', *ByzZeit* 101.2 (2008), 727–735.

Özgümüş 2010 = Özgümüş, U. C., 'Marmaray Sirkeci kurtarma kazıları cam buluntularının değerlendirilmesi / Evaluation of glass finds from Marmaray Sirkeci salvage excavations', in U. Kocabaş and Z. Kızıltan (eds), *İstanbul Arkeoloji Müzeleri 1. Marmaray-Metro Kurtarma Kazıları Sempozyumu bildiriler kitabı 5–6 Mayıs 2008 = Istanbul Archaeological Museums Proceedings of the 1st Symposium on Marmaray-Metro Salvage Expedition 5th–6th May 2008* (Istanbul 2010), 121–134.

Özgür 2008 = Özgür, M. E., *Sculptures of the Museum in Antalya* (Ankara 2008).

Öztaşkın 2017 = Öztaşkın, M., 'Byzantine and Turkish glazed pottery finds from Aphrodisias', in S. Bocharov, V. François, and A. Sitdikov (eds), *Поливная керамика Средиземноморья и Причерноморья X—XVIII вв. / Glazed Pottery of the Mediterranean and the Black Sea region, 10th–18th centuries*, vol. 2 (Archaeological Records of Eastern Europe, Kazan – Kishinev 2017), 165–188.

Öztürk 2016 = Öztürk, A., 'The architecture of the Hadrianic Baths in their original phase', in R. R. R. Smith, J. Lenaghan, A. Sokolicek, and K. Welch (eds), *Aphrodisias Papers 5: Excavation and Research at Aphrodisias, 2006–2012* (JRA Supplementary Series, 103. Portsmouth, Rhode Island 2016), 195–208.

Panella 1995 = Panella, C., 'Domus Aurea: area dello stagnum', in E. M. Steinby (ed.), *Lexicon topographicum urbis Romae*, vol. 2 (Roma 1995), 51–55.

Parani 2003 = Parani, M. G., *Reconstructing the Reality of Images: Byzantine Material Culture and Religious Iconography (11th–15th Centuries)* (The Medieval Mediterranean, 41. Leiden 2003).

Parani 2005 = Parani, M. G., 'Representations of glass objects as a source on Byzantine glass: how useful are they?', *DOP* 59 (2005), 147–171.

Parenzan, P. 1970 = Parenzan, P., *Carta d'identità della conchiglie del Mediterraneo*, vol. 1: *Gasteropodi* (Taranto 1970).

Parlett 1999 = Parlett, D., *The Oxford History of Board Games* (Oxford 1999).

Paul 1996 = Paul, G., 'Die Anastylose des Tetrapylons', in C. Roueché and R. R. R. Smith (eds), *Aphrodisias Papers 3: The Setting and Quarries, Mythological and other Sculptural Decoration, Architectural Development, Portico of Tiberius, and Tetrapylon* (JRA Supplementary Series, 20. Ann Arbor, MI 1996), 201–214.

Payne 1972 = Payne, S., 'Partial recovery and sample bias: the results of some sieving experiments', in E. Higgs (ed.), *Papers in Economic Prehistory* (Cambridge 1972), 49–64.

Payne 1973 = Payne, S., 'Kill-off patterns in sheep and goats', *Anatolian Studies* 23 (1973), 281–303.

Payne 1975 = Payne, S., 'Partial recovery and sample bias', in A. T. Clason (ed.), *Archaeozoological Studies* (Amsterdam 1975), 7–17.

Payne and Bull 1988 = Payne, S. and Bull, G., 'Components of variation in measurements of pig bones and teeth, and the use of measurements to distinguish wild from domestic pig remains', *Archaeozoologia* 2 (1988), 27–65.

Peacock and Williams 1986 = Peacock, D. P. S. and Williams, D. F., *Amphorae and the Roman Economy. An Introductory Guide* (Longman Archaeology Series. London and New York 1986).

Penn, Russell, and Wilson 2021 = Penn, T., Russell, B., and Wilson, A. I., 'On the Roman-Byzantine adoption of the stirrup once more: a new find from seventh-century Aphrodisias', *Anatolian Studies* 71 (2021), 129–139.

Pensabene, 1973 = Pensabene, P., *Scavi Di Ostia*, vol. 7: *I Capitelli* (Rome 1973).

Pensabene, 2017 = Pensabene, P., 'Architectural Spolia and Urban Transformation in Rome from the Fourth to the Thirteenth Century', in *Perspektiven der Spolienforschung*, vol. 2: *Zentren und Konjunkturen der Spoliierung* (Berlin Studies of the Ancient World, 40. Berlin 2017), 177–233.

Pensabene and Bruno 1998 = Pensabene, P. and Bruno, M. (eds), *Il marmo e il colore. Guida fotografica. I marmi della collezione Podesti* (Roma 1998).

Pere 1968 = Pere, N., *Osmanlilarda madenî paralar: Yapi ve Kredi Bankasinin Osmanli Madenî Paralari Koleksiyonu* (Istanbul 1968).

Perk and Öztürk 2008 = Perk, H. and Öztürk, H., *Eretna Kadı Burhanettin ve Erzincan (Mutahharten) Emirliği Sikkeleri* (Anadolu sikkeleri serisi, Istanbul 2008).

Pesce 1950 = Pesce, G., *Il "Palazzo delle Colonne" in Tolemaide di Cirenaica* (Roma 1950).

Peschlow 1998 = Peschlow, U., 'Tradition und Innovation: Kapitellskulptur in Lykien', in *Spätantike und Byzantinische Bauskulptur. Beiträge eines Symposions in Mainz, Februar 1994* (Stuttgart 1998), 67–76.

Petersen 1890 = Petersen, E. A. H., 'Inschriften', in K. Lanckoroński-Brzezie (ed.), *Städte Pamphyliens und Pisidiens*, vol. 1: *Pamphylien* (Leipzig 1890), 153–186.

Peterson *et al.* 2012 = Peterson, E., Markschies, C., Hildebrandt, H., and Nichtweiß, B., *Heis Theos: Epigraphische, formgeschichtliche und religionsgeschichtliche Untersuchungen zur antiken „Ein-Gott"-Akklamation* (Würzburg 2012).

Petsalis-Diomidis 2010 = Petsalis-Diomidis, A., *Truly Beyond Wonders: Aelius Aristides and the Cult of Asklepios* (Oxford Studies in Ancient Culture & Representation, Oxford 2010).

Petzl 2019 = Petzl, G., *Sardis: Greek and Latin Inscriptions*, vol. 2: *Finds from 1958 to 2017* (Archaeological Exploration of Sardis Monographs 14. Cambridge, MA 2019).

Pişkin 2016 = Pişkin, E., 'Urban patterns of animal husbandry on three sites in medieval Anatolia', in B. Jervis, L. Broderick, and I. Grau Sologestoa (eds), *Objects, Environment, and Everyday Life in Medieval Europe* (Studies in the History of Daily Life (800–1600), 3. Turnhout 2016), 93–110.

Pitarakis 2005 = Pitarakis, B., 'Témoignage des objets métalliques dans le village médiéval (Xe – XIVe siècle)', in J. Lefort, C. Morrisson, and J. P. Sodini (eds), *Les Villages dans l'Empire byzantin, IVe–XVe siècle* (Paris 2005), 247–265.

Pitarakis 2006 = Pitarakis, B., *Les croix-reliquaires pectorales byzantines en bronze* (Bibliothèque des cahiers archéologiques, 16. Paris 2006).

Pococke 1745 = Pococke, R., *A Description of the East, and Some Other Countries*, vol. 2, Part II: *Observations on the Islands of the Archipelago, Asia Minor, Thrace, Greece, and Some Other Parts of Europe* (London 1745).

Pollard 2009 = Pollard, E. A., 'Pliny's *Natural History* and the Flavian *Templum Pacis*: botanical imperialism in first-century CE Rome', *Journal of World History* 20 (2009), 309–338.

Pollitt 1986 = Pollitt, J. J., *Art in the Hellenistic Age* (Cambridge 1986).

Pont 2008 = Pont, A.-V., 'L'inscription en l'honneur de M. Vlpivs Carminivs Clavdianvs à Aphrodisias (*CIG*, 2782)', *Cahiers du Centre Gustave Glotz* 19 (2008), 219–245.

Pont 2010 = Pont, A.-V., *Orner la cité. Enjeux culturels et politiques du paysage urbain dans l'Asie gréco-romaine* (Scripta Antiqua, 24. Bordeaux 2010).

Pont 2020 = Pont, A.-V., *La fin de la cité grecque. Métamorphoses et disparition d'un modelle politique et institutionelle local un Asie Mineure, de Dèce à Constantine* (Geneva 2020).

Pottier, Schulze, and Schulze 2008 = Pottier, H., Schulze, I., and Schulze, W., 'Pseudo-Byzantine coinage in Syria under Arab Rule (638–c. 670): classification and dating', *Revue belge de numismatique* 154 (2008), 87–155.

Poulsen 1951 = Poulsen, F., *Catalogue of Ancient Sculpture in the Ny Carlsberg Glyptothek* (Copenhagen 1951).

Preisendanz and Jacoby 1930 = Preisendanz, K. and Jacoby, F., 'Maïumas', in G. Wissowa and W. Kroll (eds), *Paulys Real-Encyclopädie der classischen Altertumswissenschaft*, vol. 14: *Lysimachos – Mazaion* (Stuttgart 1930), col. 610–613.

Price 2021 = Price, M. D., *Evolution of a Taboo: Pigs and People in the Ancient Near East* (Oxford 2021).

Puech 2002 = Puech, B., *Orateurs et sophistes grecs dans les inscriptions d'époque impériale* (Textes et Traditions, 4. Paris 2002).

Purcell 1995 = Purcell, N., 'Literate games: Roman urban society and the game of *alea*', *P&P* 147 (1995), 3–37.

Putzeys and Lavan 2008 = Putzeys, T. and Lavan, L., 'Commercial Space in Late Antiquity', in L. Lavan, E. Swift, and T. Putzeys (eds), *Objects in Context, Objects in Use* (Late Antique Archaeology, 5. Leiden 2008), 81–109.

Putzeys *et al.* 2004 = Putzeys, T., Van Thuyne, T., Poblome, J., Uytterhoeven, I., Waelkens, M., and Degeest, R., 'Analyzing domestic contexts at Sagalassos: developing a methodology using ceramics and macro-botanical remains', *JMA* 17.1 (2004), 31–57.

Quatember 2011 = Quatember, U., *Das Nymphaeum Traiani in Ephesos* (Forschungen in Ephesos XI/2. Vienna 2011).

Quatember, Scheibelreiter, and Sokolicek 2009 = Quatember, U., Scheibelreiter, V., and Sokolicek, A., 'Die sogenannte Alytarchenstoa an der Kuretenstrasse von Ephesos', in S. Ladstätter (ed.), *Neue Forschungen in der Kuretenstrasse von Ephesos*: *Akten des Symposiums für Hilke Thür vom 13. Dezember 2006 an der Österreichischen Akademie der Wissenschaften* (Archäologische Forschungen, 15. Vienna 2009), 111–154.

Raeder 1983 = Raeder, J., *Die statuarische Ausstattung der Villa Hadriana bei Tivoli* (Europäische Hochschulschriften Reihe XXXVIII, Archäologie, Bd 4. Frankfurt am Main 1983).

Raja 2012 = Raja, R., *Urban Development and Regional Identity in the Eastern Roman Provinces, 50 BC – AD 250: Aphrodisias, Ephesos, Athens, Gerasa* (Copenhagen 2012).

Ratté 2001 = Ratté, C., 'New research on the urban development of Aphrodisias in late antiquity', in D. Parrish (ed.), *Urbanism in Western Asia Minor, New Studies on Aphrodisias, Ephesos, Hierapolis, Pergamon, Perge and Xanthos* (JRA Supplement, Portsmouth 2001), 116–147.

Ratté 2002 = Ratté, C., 'The urban development of Aphrodisias in the late Hellenistic and early Imperial periods', in C. Berns, H. von Hesberg, L. Vandeput, and M. Waelkens (eds), *Patris und Imperium: kulturelle und politische Identität in den Städten der römischen Provinzen Kleinasiens in der frühen Kaiserzeit: Kolloquium Köln, November 1998* (Bulletin antieke beschaving. Supplement, 8. Leuven; Paris; Dudley, MA 2002), 5–32.

Ratté 2008 = Ratté, C., 'The founding of Aphrodisias', in C. Ratté and R. R. R. Smith (eds), *Aphrodisias Papers 4: New Research on the City and its Monuments* (JRA Supplementary Series, 70. Portsmouth, Rhode Island 2008), 7–36.

Ratté and De Staebler 2011 = Ratté, C. and De Staebler, P. D., 'Survey evidence for late antique settlement in the region around Aphrodisias', in O. Dally and C. Ratté (eds), *Archaeology and the Cities of Asia Minor in Late Antiquity* (Kelsey Museum Publication 6, Kelsey Museum, Ann Arbor, MI 2011), 123–136.

Ratté and Smith 2004 = Ratté, C. and Smith, R. R. R., 'Archaeological research at Aphrodisias in Caria, 1999–2001', *AJA* 108.2 (2004), 145–186.

Ratté and Smith 2008 = Ratté, C. and Smith, R. R. R., 'Archaeological Research at Aphrodisias in Caria, 2002–2005', *AJA* 112.4 (2008), 713–751.

Rautman 2017 = Rautman, M. L., 'Sardis', in P. Niewöhner (ed.), *The Archaeology of Byzantine Anatolia: From the End of Late Antiquity until the Coming of the Turks* (Oxford 2017), 231–237.

Reed and Leleković 2019 = Reed, K. and Leleković, T., 'First evidence of rice (*Oryza* cf. *sativa* L.) and black pepper (*Piper nigrum*) in Roman Mursa, Croatia', *Archaeological and Anthropological Sciences* 11.1 (2019), 271–278.

Rehm 1941 = Rehm, A., 'ΜΝΗΣΘΗ', *Philologus* 94 (1941), 1–30.

Renberg 2017 = Renberg, G. H., *Where Dreams May Come: Incubation Sanctuaries in the Greco-Roman World*, 2 vols. (Religions in the Graeco-Roman World, 184. Leiden and Boston 2017).

Reese, D. S. 2002 = Reese, D. S., 'Marine invertebrates, freshwater shells, and land snails. Evidence from specimens, mosaics, wall paintings, sculpture, jewelry, and Roman authors', in W. F. Jashemski and F. G. Meyer (eds), *The Natural History of Pompeii* (Cambridge 2002), 292–314.

Rey-Coquais 1977 = Rey-Coquais, J. P., *Inscriptions grecques et latines découvertes dans les fouilles de Tyr (1963–1974)*, vol. 1: *Inscriptions de la nécropole* (BMusBeyr, 29. Paris 1977).

Reynolds 1980 = Reynolds, J. M., 'The origins and beginning of imperial cult at Aphrodisias', *PCPS* (new series 26), 206 (1980), 70–84.

Reynolds 1982 = Reynolds, J. M., *Aphrodisias and Rome* (Journal of Roman Studies Monographs, 1. London 1982).

Reynolds 1986 = Reynolds, J. M., 'Further information on imperial cult at Aphrodisias', in *Festschrift D. M. Pippidi* (Studii clasice, 24. Bucharest 1986), 109–117.

Reynolds 1987 = Reynolds, J. M., 'New evidence for the social history of Aphrodisias', in E. Frézouls (ed.), *Sociétés urbaines, sociétés rurales dans l'Asie Mineure et la Syrie hellénistiques et romaines* (Contributions et travaux de l'Institut d'Histoire Romaine, 4. Strasbourg 1987), 107–113.

Reynolds 1989 = Reynolds, J. M., 'The regulations of Diocletian', in C. Roueché (ed.), *Aphrodisias in Late Antiquity* (Journal of Roman Studies Monograph, 5. London 1989), 252–318.

Reynolds 1995 = Reynolds, J. M., 'The dedication of a bath building at Carian Aphrodisias', in A. Fol, B. Bogdanov, P. Dimitrov, and D. Bojadžiev (eds), *Studia in honorem Georgii Mihailov* (Sofia 1995), 397–402.

Reynolds 1996 = Reynolds, J. M., 'Ruler-cult at Aphrodisias in the Late Republic and under the Julio-Claudian Emperors', in A. Small (ed.), *Subject and Ruler: The Cult of the Ruling Power in Classical Antiquity: Papers Presented at a Conference Held in the University of Alberta on April 13–15, 1994, to Celebrate the 65th Anniversary of Duncan Fishwick* (JRA Supplementary Series, 17. Ann Arbor, MI 1996), 41–50.

Reynolds 1997 = Reynolds, J. M., 'Sculpture in bronze: an inscription from Aphrodisias', *ArchCl* 49 (1997), 423–428.

Reynolds 2000 = Reynolds, J. M., 'New letters from Hadrian to Aphrodisias: trials, taxes, gladiators and an aqueduct', *JRA* 13 (2000), 5–20.

Reynolds 2002 = Reynolds, J. M., 'A new inscription from Carian Aphrodisias', in P. McKechnie (ed.), *Thinking Like a Lawyer: Essays on Legal History and General History for John Crook on his Eightieth Birthday* (Leiden 2002), 247–251.

Reynolds and Tannenbaum 1987 = Reynolds, J. M. and Tannenbaum, R. F., *Jews and God-Fearers at Aphrodisias: Greek Inscriptions with Commentary: Texts from the Excavations at Aphrodisias Conducted by Kenan T. Erim* (Cambridge Philological Society, Supplementary volume, 12. Cambridge 1987).

Reynolds 2018 = Reynolds, P., 'The supply networks of the Roman East and West: interaction, fragmentation, and the origins of the Byzantine economy', in A. I. Wilson and A. K. Bowman (eds), *Trade, Commerce, and the State in the Roman World* (Oxford Studies on the Roman Economy, Oxford 2018), 353–396.

Rheidt 1995 = Rheidt, K., 'Aizanoi: Bericht über die Ausgrabungen un Untersuchungen 1992 und 1993', *AA* (1995), 693–718.

Ricci 2012 = Ricci, A., 'Left behind: small sized objects from the middle Byzantine monastic complex of Satyros (Küçükyali, Istanbul)', in B. Bohlendorf-Arslan and A. Ricci (eds), *Byzantine Small Finds in Archaeological Contexts* (Byzas, 15. Istanbul 2012), 147–161.

Richardson 1977 = Richardson, L., Jr, 'Hercules Musarum and the Porticus Philippi in Rome', *AJA* 81.3 (1977), 355–361.

Richter 1954 = Richter, G. M. A., *Catalogue of Greek Sculptures, Metropolitan Museum of Art, New York* (Cambridge, MA 1954).

Riffle and Craft 2003 = Riffle, R. L. and Craft, P., *An Encyclopedia of Cultivated Palms* (Portland, OR 2003).

Robert 1936 = Robert, L., 'Epigraphica. Inscription de Nicée', *RÉG* 49 (1936), 9–14.

Robert 1937 = Robert, L., Études anatoliennes: recherches sur les inscriptions grecques de l'Asie mineure (Paris 1937).

Robert 1948 = Robert, L., 'Épigrammes du Bas-Empire', *Hellenica* 4 (1948), 5–151.

Robert 1965 = Robert, J., *Hellenica: Recueil d'épigraphie de numismatique et d'antiquités grecques*, vol. 13 (Paris 1965).

Robert 1966 = Robert, L., 'Inscriptions d'Aphrodisias', *Antiquité Classique* 35.2 (1966), 377–432.

Robert 1971 = Robert, L., 'Les colombes d'Anastase et autres volatiles', *JSav* 2.1 (1971), 81–105.

Robert and Robert 1954 = Robert, L. and Robert, J., *La Carie*, vol. 2: *Le plateau de Tabai et ses environs* (Paris 1954).

Robert and Robert 1960 = Robert, L. and Robert, J., *Hellenica: Recueil d'épigraphie de numismatique et d'antiquités grecques*, vol. 11–12 (1960).

Robert and Robert 1978 = Robert, J. and Robert, L., 'Bulletin épigraphique', *RÉG* 91 (1978), 385–510.

Robinson 2002 = Robinson, M., 'Domestic burnt offerings and sacrifices at Roman and pre-Roman Pompeii, Italy', *Vegetation History and Archaeobotany* 11.1–2 (2002), 93–100.

Robinson 2016 = Robinson, M., 'The environmental archaeology of the pool', in R. R. R. Smith, J. Lenaghan, A. Sokolicck, and K. Welch (eds), *Aphrodisias Papers 5: Excavation and Research at Aphrodisias, 2006–2012* (JRA Supplementary Series, 103. Portsmouth, Rhode Island 2016), 91–99.

Roddaz 1984 = Roddaz, J.-M., *Marcus Agrippa* (BÉFAR, 253. Rome 1984).

Rogers 2018 = Rogers, D. K., *Water Culture in Roman Society*, vol. 1 (Brill Research Perspectives in Ancient History, 1. Leiden 2018).

Rogers 1947 = Rogers, R. S., 'The Roman emperors as heirs and legatees', *Transactions and Proceedings of the American Philological Association* 78 (1947), 140–158.

Rosa García et al. 2012 = Rosa García, R., Celaya, R., García, U., and Osoro, K., 'Goat grazing, its interactions with other herbivores and biodiversity conservation issues', *Small Ruminant Research* 107.2 (2012), 49–64.

Rose 1997 = Rose, C. B., *Dynastic Commemoration and Imperial Portraiture in the Julio-Claudian period* (Cambridge 1997).

Rothaus 1992 = Rothaus, R. M., 'Omne ignotum pro sacro: Quadrisected gameboards and religious graffiti', *OJA* 11.3 (1992), 365–368.

Rottoli and Castiglioni 2011 = Rottoli, M. and Castiglioni, E., 'Plant offerings from Roman cremations in northern Italy: a review', *Vegetation History and Archaeobotany* 20.5 (2011), 495–506.

Roueché 1979 = Roueché, C., 'A new inscription from Aphrodisias and the title πατὴρ τῆς πόλεως', *Greek, Roman, and Byzantine Studies* 20.2 (1979), 173–185.

Roueché 1981 = Roueché, C., 'Rome, Asia and Aphrodisias in the third century', *JRS* 71 (1981), 103–120.

Roueché 1984 = Roueché, C., 'Acclamations in the later Roman Empire – new evidence from Aphrodisias', *JRS* 74 (1984), 181–199.

Roueché 1989 = Roueché, C., *Aphrodisias in Late Antiquity* (Journal of Roman Studies Monograph, 5. London 1989).

Roueché 1993 = Roueché, C., *Performers and Partisans at Aphrodisias in the Roman and Late Roman Periods* (Journal of Roman Studies Monograph, 6. London 1993).

Roueché 2002 = Roueché, C., 'Texts and stones: reading the past at Aphrodisias in Caria', in *Greek Archaeology without Frontiers* (Athens 2002), 47–66.

Roueché 2004 = Roueché, C., *Aphrodisias in Late Antiquity*. Electronic 2nd edn. http://insaph.kcl.ac.uk/ala2004/ (London 2004).

Roueché 2007a = Roueché, C., 'From Aphrodisias to Stauropolis', in J. F. Drinkwater and B. Salway (eds), *Wolf Liebeschuetz Reflected: Essays Presented by Colleagues, Friends, & Pupils* (Bulletin of the Institute of Classical Studies, Supplement, 91. London 2007), 183–192.

Roueché 2007b = Roueché, C., 'Late Roman and Byzantine game boards at Aphrodisias', in I. L. Finkel (ed.), *Ancient Board Games in Perspective* (London 2007), 100–105.

Roueché 2014 = Roueché, C., 'Using civic space: identifying the evidence', in W. Eck and P. Funke (ed.), *Öffentichkeit – Monument – Text* (Berlin 2014), 135–158.

Rousseau, Guintard, and Abadie-Reynal 2008 = Rousseau, G., Guintard, C., and Abadie-Reynal, C., 'La gestion des animaux á Zeugma (Turquie): étude des restes fauniques du chantier 9 (époques hellénistique, romaine, byzantine et islamique)', *Revue de Médecine Vétérinaire* 159.5 (2008), 251–275.

Rovira and Chabal 2008 = Rovira, N. and Chabal, L., 'A foundation offering at the Roman port of Lattara (Lattes, France): the plant remains', *Vegetation History and Archaeobotany* 17.1 (2008), 191–200.

Rowan 2014 = Rowan, E., *Roman Diet and Nutrition in the Vesuvian Region: A Study of the Bioarchaeological Remains from the Cardo V Sewer at Herculaneum*. D.Phil. thesis, University of Oxford.

Rowan 2015 = Rowan, E., 'Olive oil pressing waste as a fuel source in Antiquity', *AJA* 119.4 (2015), 465–482.

Ruggieri 1992 = Ruggieri, V., 'I graffiti umayyadi a Cnidos', *Orientalia christiana periodica* 58.1/2 (1992), 549–551.

Ruggieri 2005 = Ruggieri, V., *La Caria Bizantina: topografia, archeologia ed arte (Mylasa, Stratonikeia, Bargylia, Myndus, Halicarnassus)* (Soveria Mannelli 2005).

Ruggieri 2009 = Ruggieri, V., 'The Carians in the Byzantine period', in F. Rumscheid (ed.), *Die Karer und die Anderen. Internationales Kolloquium an der Freien Universität Berlin 13. bis 15. Oktober 2005* (Bonn 2009).

Russell 1982 = Russell, J., 'Byzantine instrumenta domestica from Anemurium: the significance of context', in R. Hohlfelder (ed.), *City, Town and Countryside in the Early Byzantine Era* (New York 1982), 133–163.

Russell 1995 = Russell, J., 'The archaeological context of magic in the early Byzantine period', in H. Maguire (ed.), *Byzantine Magic* (Washington, D.C. 1995), 35–50.

Russell 2001 = Russell, J., 'The Persian Invasions of Syria/Palestine and Asia Minor in the reign of Heraclius: archaeological, numismatic and epigraphic evidence', in E. Kontoura-Galake (ed.), Οι Σκοτεινοι Αιωνες του Βυζαντιου (7ος–9ος αι.) / The Dark *Centuries of Byzantium (7th–9th c.)* (International Symposium, 9. Athens 2001), 41–71.

Russell 2013 = Russell, B., *The Economics of the Roman Stone Trade* (Oxford Studies on the Roman Economy, Oxford 2013).

Russell, A. 2016 = Russell, A., *The Politics of Public Space in Republican Rome* (Cambridge 2016).

Russell, B. 2016 = Russell, B., 'Mapping the marble quarries', in R. R. R. Smith, J. Lenaghan, A. Sokolicek, and K. Welch (eds), *Aphrodisias Papers 5: Excavation and Research at Aphrodisias, 2006–2012* (JRA Supplementary Series, 103. Portsmouth, Rhode Island 2016), 255–267.

Ryan 2016 = Ryan, P., 'Phytolith report: analyses of the samples from Villa Arianna at Stabiae', in T. N. Howe, K. L. Gleason, P. Gardelli, L. Toniolo, N. Langobardi, and A. Raimondi (eds), *Excavation and Study of the Garden of the Great Peristyle of the Villa Arianna, Stabiae, 2007–2012* (Quaderni di Studi Pompeiani, 7. Napoli 2016), 104–105.

Sağıt and Teoman 2013 = Sağıt, B. and Teoman, G., 'Aydınoğlu Beyliği Sikkeleri ve Beyliğin Tarihine Yeni Bir Bakış', in *Uluslararası Batı Anadolu Beylikleri Tarih Kültür ve Medeniyeti Sempozyumu I, (04–06 Kasım 2010)* (Ankara 2013), 309–339.

Saliou 2017 = Saliou, C., 'Toposinschriften. Écriture et usages de l'espace urbain', *ZPE* 202 (2017), 125–154.

Sams 1982 = Sams, G. K., 'The weighing implements', in G. F. Bass and F. H. Van Doorninck (eds), *Yassi Ada: A Seventh-Century Byzantine Shipwreck*, vol. 1 (Ed Rachal Foundation Nautical Archaeology Series Book 1. College Station, Texas 1982), 202–230.

Sancaktar 2011 = Sancaktar, H., 'Yılı Arykanda Kazısı TK3 Definesi: Bir Ön Değerlendirme', *Mediterranean Journal of Humanities* 2.2 (2011), 219–228.

Saradi-Mendelovici 1990 = Saradi-Mendelovici, H., 'Christian attitudes toward pagan monuments in Late Antiquity and their legacy in later Byzantine centuries', *DOP* 44 (1990), 47–61.

Sauron 1987 = Sauron, G., 'Le complexe pompéien du Champ de Mars: nouveauté urbanistique à finalité idéologique', in *L'Urbs : espace urbain et histoire (Ier siècle av. J.-C. – IIIe siècle ap. J.-C.). Actes du colloque international de Rome (8–12 mai 1985)* (Collection de l'École Française de Rome, 98. Rome 1987), 457–473.

Schachinger 2014 = Schachinger, U., 'The coin finds from the Theatre in Ephesus and some remarks on coin circulation in Ephesus', in K. Dörtlük, O. Tekin, and B. Seyhan (eds), *First International Congress of the Anatolian Monetary History and Numismatics, 25–28 February 2013* (Antalya 2014), 525–540.

Schädler 1998 = Schädler, U., 'Mancala in Roman Asia Minor?', *Board Games Studies* 1 (1998), 10–25.

Schädler 2012 = Schädler, U., 'Games, Greek and Roman', in R. S. Bagnall, K. Brodersen, C. B. Champion, A. Erskine, and S. R. Huebner (eds), *The Encyclopedia of Ancient History* (2012).

Schädler 2018 = Schädler, U., 'Encore sur la «marelle ronde»: cent ans après Carl Blümlein', *Kentron. Revue pluridisciplinaire du monde antique* 34 (2018), 87–98.

Schick 2004 = Schick, İ. C., 'Representation of gender and sexuality in Ottoman and Turkish erotic literature', *The Turkish Studies Association Journal* 28.1/2 (2004), 81–103.

Schindel 2009 = Schindel, N., 'Die Fundmünzen von der Kuretenstraße 2005 und 2006. Numismatische und historische Auswertung', in S. Ladstätter (ed.), *Neue Forschungen in der Kuretenstrasse von Ephesos: Akten des Symposiums für Hilke Thür vom 13. Dezember 2006 an der Österreichischen Akademie der Wissenschaften* (Archäologische Forschungen, 15. Vienna 2009), 171–245.

Schindel and Ladstätter 2016 = Schindel, N. and Ladstätter, S., 'An early Byzantine hoard from Ephesus', *The Numismatic Chronicle* 176 (2016), 390–398.

Schopenus 1828 = Schopenus, L., *Ioannis Cantacuzeni eximperatoris historiarum libri IV: Graece et latine*, vol. 1 (Corpus scriptorum historiae Byzantinae, 20. Bonn 1828).

Schulze-Dörrlamm 2009 = Schulze-Dörrlamm, M., *Byzantinische Gürtelschnallen und Gürtelbeschläge im Römisch-Germanischen Zentralmuseum*, vol. 30 (Kataloge vor- und frühgeschichtlicher Altertümer, Mainz; Bonn 2009).

Schulze and Goodwin 2005 = Schulze, W. and Goodwin, T., 'Countermarking in seventh century Syria', *Oriental Numismatic Society Newsletter*.183 (2005), 23–56 (Supplement).

Segre and Pugliese Carratelli 1952 = Segre, M. and Pugliese Carratelli, G., 'Tituli Camirenscs', *ASAtene* n.s., 27–29 (1949–51) (1952), 141–318.

Seigne 2004 = Seigne, J., 'Remarques préliminaires à une étude sur l'eau dans la Gerasa antique', in H.-D. Bienert and J. Häser (eds), *Men of Dikes and Canals. The Archaeology of Water in the Middle East. International Symposium held at Petra, Wadi Musa (H.K. of Jordan), 15–20 June, 1999* (Orient-Archäologie, 13. Rahden 2004), 173–185.

Semeyov 1964 = Semeyov, S. A., *Prehistoric Technology* (London 1964).

Sheppard 1981 = Sheppard, A. R. R., 'RECAM Notes and Studies No. 8: The River God of Heraclea-on-Salbace', *Anatolian Studies* 31 (1981), 29.

Silibolatlaz-Baykara 2012 = Silibolatlaz-Baykara, D., 'Faunal studies on Byzantine city of the Amorium', *Ankara Üniversitesi Dil ve Tarih-Coğrafya Fakültesi Dergisi* 52.1 (2012), 71–82.

Silver 1969 = Silver, I. A., 'The ageing of domestic animals', in D. Brothwell and E. Higgs (eds), *Science in Archaeology: A Survey of Progress and Research* (London 1969), 283–302.

Simoons 1994 = Simoons, F. J., *Eat Not this Flesh. Food Avoidances from Prehistory to the Present* (Madison 1994).

Şimşek 2008 = Şimşek, C., '2007 yılı Laodikeia antik kenti kazıları', in *30. Kazı Sonuçları Toplantısı*, vol. 2 (Ankara 2008), 409–436.

Şimşek 2009 = Şimşek, C., '2008 yılı Laodikeia antik kenti kazıları', in *31. Kazı Sonuçları Toplantısı*, vol. 4 (Ankara 2009), 101–134.

Şimşek 2013 = Şimşek, C., *Laodikeia (Laodiceia ad Lycum)* (Laodikeia Çalışmaları, 2. Istanbul 2013).

Şimşek 2014 = Şimşek, C., 'Lykos Vadisi içinde yer alan Laodikeia (Laodikeia in the Lycos Valley)', in C. Şimşek (ed.), *10. Yılında Laodikeia (2003–2013 Yılları)* (Laodikeia Çalışmaları, 3. Istanbul 2014), 33–69.

Sisson 1929 = Sisson, M. A., 'The stoa of Hadrian at Athens', *PBSR* 11 (1929), 50–72.

Smith 1991 = Smith, R. R. R., *Hellenistic Sculpture: A Handbook* (London 1991).

Smith 1996 = Smith, R. R. R., 'Archaeological Research at Aphrodisias, 1989–1992', in C. Roueché and R. R. R. Smith (eds), *Aphrodisias Papers 3: The Setting and Quarries, Mythological and other Sculptural Decoration, Architectural Development, Portico of Tiberius, and Tetrapylon* (JRA Supplementary Series, 20. Ann Arbor, MI 1996), 11–72.

Smith 1998 = Smith, R. R. R., 'Hellenistic sculpture under the Roman Empire: fishermen and satyrs at Aphrodisias', in O. Palagia and W. D. E. Coulson (eds), *Regional Schools in Hellenistic Sculpture* (Oxford 1998), 253–260.

Smith 1999a = Smith, R. R. R., 'Late antique portraits in a public context: Honorific statuary at Aphrodisias in Caria, A.D. 300–600', *JRS* 89 (1999), 155–189.

Smith 1999b = Smith, R. R. R., 'A late Roman portrait and a himation statue from Aphrodisias', in H. Friesinger and F. Krinzinger (eds), *100 Jahre österreichische Forschungen in Ephesos. Akten des Symposions Wien 1995* (Denkschriften / Österreichische Akademie der Wissenschaften, Philosophisch-Historische Klasse, Vienna 1999), 713–719.

Smith 2001 = Smith, R. R. R., 'A portrait monument for Julian and Theodosius at Aphrodisias', in C. Reusser (ed.), *Griechenland in der Kaiserzeit: neue Funde und Forschungen zu Skulptur, Architektur und Topographie: Kolloquium zum sechzigsten Geburtstag von Prof. Dietrich Willers, Bern, 12.–13. Juni 1998*, vol. 4 (Hefte des archäologischen Seminars der Universität Bern. Beiheft, Bern 2001), 125–136.

Smith 2002 = Smith, R. R. R., 'The statue monument of Oecumenius: a new portrait of a late antique governor from Aphrodisias', *JRS* 92 (2002), 134–156.

Smith 2007 = Smith, R. R. R., 'Statue life in the Hadrianic Baths at Aphrodisias, AD 100–600: Local context and historical meaning', in F. A. Bauer and C. Witschel (eds), *Statuen in der Spätantike* (Wiesbaden 2007), 203–235.

Smith 2011 = Smith, R. R. R., 'Marble workshops at Aphrodisias', in F. D'Andria and I. Romeo (eds), *Roman sculpture in Asia Minor. Proceedings of the international conference to celebrate the 50th anniversary of the Italian excavations at Hierapolis in Phrygia, held on May 24–26, 2007, in Cavallino (Lecce)* (JRA Supplementary Series, 80. Portsmouth, RI 2011), 62–76.

Smith 2012 = Smith, R. R. R., 'Defacing the gods at Aphrodisias', in B. Dignas and R. R. R. Smith (eds), *Historical and Religious Memory in the Ancient World* (Clarendon Press 2012), 283–326.

Smith 2013 = Smith, R. R. R., *The Marble Reliefs from the Julio-Claudian Sebasteion* (Aphrodisias, VI. Darmstadt/Mainz 2013).

Smith 2016a = Smith, R. R. R., 'Aphrodisias', in R. R. R. Smith and B. Ward-Perkins (eds), *The Last Statues of Antiquity* (Oxford 2016), 145–159.

Smith 2016b = Smith, R. R. R., 'Statue practice in the late Roman empire: numbers, costumes and style', in R. R. R. Smith and B. Ward-Perkins (eds), *The Last Statues of Antiquity* (Oxford 2016), 1–27.

Smith 2016c = Smith, R. R. R., 'Three statues and a portrait head: four new finds of public statuary', in R. R. R. Smith, J. Lenaghan, A. Sokolicek, and K. Welch (eds), *Aphrodisias Papers 5: Excavation and Research at Aphrodisias, 2006–2012* (JRA Supplementary Series, 103. Portsmouth, Rhode Island 2016), 292–302.

Smith 2018a = Smith, R. R. R., 'Aphrodisias 2016', in *39. Kazı Sonuçları Toplantısı. 22–26 Mayis 2017, Bursa*, vol. 2 (Bursa 2018), 263–283.

Smith 2018b = Smith, R. R. R., *Aphrodisias 2018: A report on the archaeological field season* (annual project report, 2018).

Smith 2018c = Smith, R. R. R., 'The long lives of Roman statues: Public monuments in late antique Aphrodisias', in M. Aurenhammer (ed.), *Sculpture in Roman Asia (Proceedings of the Conference in Selcuk 2013)* (Vienna 2018), 331–352.

Smith 2021 = Smith, R. R. R., 'The tail of Troilos' horse from Aphrodisias', in K. Koller, U. Quatember, and E. Trinkl (eds), *Stein auf Stein: Festschrift für Hilke Thür zum 80. Geburtstag* (Keryx, 9. Graz 2021), 225–231.

Smith *et al.* 2006 = Smith, R. R. R., Dillon, S., Hallett, C. H., Lenaghan, J., and Van Voorhis, J., *Roman Portrait Statuary from Aphrodisias* (Aphrodisias, 2. Mainz am Rhein 2006).

Smith *et al.* 2016 = Smith, R. R. R., Lenaghan, J., Sokolicek, A., and Welch, K. (eds), *Aphrodisias Papers 5: Excavation and Research at Aphrodisias, 2006–2012* (JRA Supplementary Series 103. Portsmouth, Rhode Island 2016).

Smith and Hallett 2015 = Smith, R. R. R. and Hallett, C. H., 'Troilos and Achilles: a monumental statue group from Aphrodisias', *JRS* 105 (2015), 124–182.

Smith and Lenaghan 2008 = Smith, R. R. R. and Lenaghan, J. (eds), *Aphrodisias'tan Roma portreleri. Roman portraits from Aphrodisias* (Istanbul 2008).

Smith and Ratté 1995 = Smith, R. R. R. and Ratté, C., 'Archaeological research at Aphrodisias in Caria, 1993', *AJA* 99.1 (1995), 33–58.

Smith and Ratté 1998 = Smith, R. R. R. and Ratté, C., 'Archaeological research at Aphrodisias in Caria, 1996', *AJA* 102.2 (1998), 225–250.

Smith and Ratté 2000 = Smith, R. R. R. and Ratté, C., 'Archaeological research at Aphrodisias in Caria, 1997 and 1998', *AJA* 104.2 (2000), 221–254.

Snijder 1935 = Snijder, G. A. S., 'Ein römisches bronzeportrait aus Aphrodisias', *La critica d'arte* 1.1 (1935), 30–33.

Society of Dilettanti 1840 = Society of Dilettanti, *Antiquities of Ionia*, vol. 3 (London 1840).

Sokolicek 2016 = Sokolicek, A., 'Excavations on the Tetrapylon Street, 2012–14', in R. R. R. Smith, J. Lenaghan, A. Sokolicek, and K. Welch (eds), *Aphrodisias Papers 5: Excavation and Research at Aphrodisias, 2006–2012* (JRA Supplementary Series, 103. Portsmouth, Rhode Island 2016), 58–75.

Spier 1993 = Spier, J., 'Medieval Byzantine magical amulets and their tradition', *JWarb* 56 (1993), 25–62.

Stearns 2012 = Stearns, C., 'Geoarchaeological Investigations', in C. Ratté and P. D. De Staebler (eds), *The Aphrodisias Regional Survey* (Aphrodisias, 5. Darmstadt/Mainz 2012), 135–164.

Stein 1998 = Stein, G., 'Medieval pastoral production systems at Gritille', in S. Redford (ed.), *The Archaeology of the Frontier in the Medieval Near East: Excavations at Gritille, Turkey* (Philadelphia 1998), 181–209.

Stewart 1990 = Stewart, A. F., *Greek Sculpture: An Exploration*, 2 vols. (New Haven 1990).

Stichel 1982 = Stichel, R. H. W., *Die römische Kaiserstatue am Ausgang der Antike: Untersuchungen zum plastischen Kaiserporträt seit Valentinian I. (364–375 v. Chr.)* (Rome 1982).

Stinson 2008 = Stinson, P., 'The Civil Basilica of Aphrodisias: urban context, design, and significance', in C. Ratté and R. R. R. Smith (eds), *Aphrodisias Papers 4: New Research on the City and its Monuments* (JRA Supplementary Series, 70. Portsmouth, Rhode Island 2008), 79–107.

Stinson 2016 = Stinson, P., *The Civil Basilica* (Aphrodisias, 7. Wiesbaden 2016).

Stiros 1995 = Stiros, S. C., 'Archaeological evidence of antiseismic constructions in antiquity', *Annali di Geofisica* 38.5–6 (1995), 725–736.

Stronach 1990 = Stronach, D., 'The garden as a political statement: some case studies from the Near East in the first millennium BC', *Bulletin of the Asia Institute* 4 (1990), 171–180.

Struckmeyer 2011 = Struckmeyer, K., 'The bone tools from the dwelling mound Feddersen Wierde, Germany, and their functions', in J. Baron and B. Kufel-Diakowska (eds), *Written in Bones: Studies on Technological and Social Contexts of Past Faunal Skeletal Remains* (Wrocław 2011), 187–196.

Talloen 2018 = Talloen, P., 'Rolling the dice: public game boards from Sagalassos', *HEROM* 7 (2018), 97–132.

Tamsü Polat 2014 = Tamsü Polat, R., 'Metal Finds', in M. Kadioğlu (ed.), *Das Gerontikon von Nysa am Mäander* (Forschungen in Nysa am Mäander, Band 3. Darmstadt 2014), 147–151.

Taşdöğen 2006 = Taşdöğen, F. S., *Traditional Karacassu (Aydın) Dwellings: an Investigation into their Architectural and Social Characteristics*. MA thesis, Middle East Technical University.

Taxel 2008 = Taxel, I., 'An uncommon type of smoking implement from Ottoman Palestine', *PEQ* 140.1 (2008), 39–53.

Taxel, Glick, and Pines 2017 = Taxel, I., Glick, A., and Pines, M., 'Majdal Yābā: More insights on the site in medieval and late Ottoman to Mandatory times', *Journal of Islamic Archaeology* 4.1 (2017), 49–86.

Taylor 2014 = Taylor, R., 'Movement, vision, and quotation in the gardens of Herod the Great', in K. M. Coleman and P. Derron (eds), *Le jardin dans l'antiquité* (Entretiens sur l'Antiquité Classique 60. Geneva 2014), 145–185.

Taylor, Rinne, and Kostoff 2016 = Taylor, R., Rinne, K. W., and Kostoff, S., *Rome: An Urban History from Antiquity to the Present* (Cambridge 2016).

Tek 2002 = Tek, A. T., *Arykanda Kazılarında Bulunan Antik Sikkeler Üzerinde Yeni İncelemeler: 1971–2000 Sezonları*. Ph.D. dissertation Ankara University

Tek 2015 = Tek, A. T., 'Side Sikke Buluntuları Işığında MS 622/3'de Pamphylia'ya "Olası" Bir Sasani Saldırısı', in *Colloquium Anatolicum 14, 2015* (İstanbul 2015), 123–136.

Tek 2016 = Tek, A. T., 'Coin finds from Side in Pamphylia: a preliminary assessment of finds made between 1947–2015', *Annali dell'Istituto Italiano di Numismatica* 62 (2016), 231–250.

Tek 2019 = Tek, A. T., 'Greek and Roman provincial coins found at Aphrodisias: preliminary results from the 1998–2019 seasons', *Colloquium Anatolicum* 18 (2019), 155–182.

Tek, Köker, and Sariiz 2015 = Tek, A. T., Köker, H., and Sariiz, E., 'Stratonikeia 2008–2014 Sezonları Sikke Buluntuları Hakkında Ön Rappor', in B. Söğüt (ed.), *Stratonikeia Çalışmaları 1, Stratonikeia ve Çevresi Araştırmaları* (Istanbul 2015), 137–142.

Tek, Köker, and Sariiz 2019 = Tek, A. T., Köker, H., and Sariiz, E., 'Stratonikeia 2008–2018 Yılları Kazılarında Bulunan Erken Bizans Sikkeleri / Early Byzantine Coins found at Stratonikeia during the Campaigns of 2008–2018', in B. Söğüt (ed.), *Stratonikeia Çalışmaları 4, Mimari, Heykel ve Küçük Buluntu Araştırmaları* (Istanbul 2019), 175–209.

Teoman and Teoman 2016 = Teoman, B. and Teoman, G., 'Sahillerin Sultanları ve Sikkeleri', in *Uluslararası Batı Anadolu Tarih Kültür ve Medeniyeti Sempozyumu II, (25–27 Nisan 2012)* (Ankara 2016), 469–499.

Teoman and Teoman 2017 = Teoman, B. and Teoman, G., 'Germiyanoğulları Beyliği Sikkeleri', in *Uluslararası Batı Anadolu Tarih Kültür ve Medeniyeti Sempozyumu III, (8–10 Mayıs 2014)* (Ankara 2017), 169–200.

Teslenko 2016 = Teslenko, I., 'Пифосы из археологических комплексов Таврики XIV—XV вв', in H. Amouric, V. François, and L. Vallauri (eds), *Jarres et grands contenants entre Moyen Age et Époque Moderne: Actes du Ier Congrès international thématique de l'AIECM3, Montpellier-Lattes 19–21 novembre 2014 / Jars and Large Containers Between the Middle Ages and the Modern Era: Conference Proceedings of the First International Topical Congress of the AIECM3, Montpellier-Lattes 19–21 November 2014* (Aix-en-Provence 2016), 319–324.

Texier 1849 = Texier, C., *Description de l'Asie Mineure: faite par ordre du gouvernement français, de 1833 à 1837, et publiée par le Ministère de l'instruction publique … Beaux-arts, monuments historiques, plans et topographie des cités antiques*, vol. 3 (Paris 1849).

Thédenat 1923 = Thédenat, H., *Le forum romain et les forums impériaux*. 6th edn. (Paris 1923).

Theotokos 2018 = Theotokos, G., 'Military technology: production and use of weapons', in Y. Stouraitis (ed.), *A Companion to the Byzantine Culture of War, ca. 300–1204* (Brill's Companions to the Byzantine World, 3. Leiden 2018), 440–472.

Thomas 2018 = Thomas, J. J., '"The Statues of the Cyclops": Reconstructing a public monument from Aphrodisias in Caria', *IstMitt* 68 (2018), 143–172.

Thomas 2022 = Thomas, J. J., 'The colossal figured consoles of the Hadrianic Baths at Aphrodisias', *Istanbuler Mitteilungen* 72 (2022), 116–168.

Thompson 1937 = Thompson, D. B., 'The garden of Hephaistos', *Hesperia: The Journal of the American School of Classical Studies at Athens* 6.3 (1937), 396–425.

Thomson, Howard-Johnston, and Greenwood 1999 = Thomson, R. W., Howard-Johnston, J., and Greenwood, T., *The Armenian History Attributed to Sebeos: Part 2. Historical Commentary* (Translated Texts for Historians, 31. Liverpool 1999).

Traversari 1960 = Traversari, G., *Gli spettacoli in acqua nel teatro tardo-antico* (Roma 1960).

Trifilò 2011 = Trifilò, F., 'Movement, gaming, and the use of space in the forum', in R. Laurence and D. J. Newsome (eds), *Rome, Ostia, Pompeii: Movement and Space* (Oxford 2011), 312–331.

Trombley 1985 = Trombley, F., 'The decline of the seventh-century town: the exception of Euchaita', in S. Vryonis (ed.), *Byzantine Studies in Honor of Milton V. Anastos* (Byzantina kai Metabyzantina, 4. Malibu, CA 1985), 65–90.

Trombley 2001 = Trombley, F. R., *Hellenic Religion and Christianization, c. 370–529*, 2 vols. reprint edn. (Religions in the Graeco-Roman world, 115. Leiden 2001).

Tsafrir and Foerster 1997 = Tsafrir, Y. and Foerster, G., 'Urbanism at Scythopolis: Bet Shean in the fourth to seventh centuries', *DOP* 51 (1997).

Tucci 2017 = Tucci, P. L., *The Temple of Peace in Rome* (Cambridge 2017).

Turnovsky 2005a = Turnovsky, P., 'Late Antique and Byzantine pottery of the Church of St. Mary in Ephesos. An introduction', *RCRF Acta* 30 (2005), 217–224.

Turnovsky 2005b = Turnovsky, P., 'The morphological repertory of Late Roman/Early Byzantine Coarse Wares in Ephesos', in J. M. Gurt i Esparraguera, J. Buxeda i Garrigos, and M. A. Cau Ontiveros (eds), *LRCW I: Late Roman Coarse Wares, Cooking Wares and Amphorae in the Mediterranean: Archaeology and Archaeometry* (BAR International Series, 1340. Oxford 2005), 635–645.

Ünal and Bülbül 2005 = Ünal, C. and Bülbül, A., 'Kuşadası, Kadıkalesi / Anaia Kazısı, 2001–2004 Yılları Buluntusu Bizans Sikkelerinin Sayısal ve Grafik Destekli Ön Değerlendirmesi', *Sanat Tarihi Dergisi* 14.1 (2005), 111–123.

Uygur 2017 = Uygur, O., *Bodrum Sualtı Arkeoloji Müzesinde Bulunan Bir Grup Bizans Sikkesi*. unpublished MA Thesis, Muğla Sıtkı Koçman Üniversitesi, Sosyal Bilimler Enstitüsü.

Uytterhoeven 2009 = Uytterhoeven, I., 'Know your classics! Manifestations of 'classical culture' in late antique domestic contexts', in P. van Nuffelen (ed.), *Faces of Hellenism. Studies in the History of the Eastern Mediterranean (4th Century B.C. – 5th Century A.D.)* (Studia Hellenistica, 48. Leuven 2009), 321–342.

Vaag 2003 = Vaag, L. E., 'A closer look at the making of Phocaean Red Slip Ware bowls', in C. Abadie-Reynal (ed.), *Les céramiques en Anatolie aux époques hellénistique et romaine. Actes de la table ronde d'Istanbul, 22–24 mai 1996*, vol. 15 (Varia Anatolica, Istanbul 2003), 203–207.

Vallois 1923 = Vallois, R., *Les portiques au sud du Hiéron*, vol. 1: *Le portique de Philippe* (Exploration Archéologique de Délos, 7.1. Paris 1923).

van Alfen 1996 = van Alfen, P. G., 'New light on the 7th-c. Yassi Ada shipwreck: capacities and standard sizes of LRA1 amphoras', *JRA* 9 (1996), 189–213.

van Dieten 1971 = van Dieten, J.-L. (ed.) *Niketas Choniates* (Supplementa Byzantina 2. Berlin 1971).

van Mensch 1974 = van Mensch, P. J. A., 'A Roman soup-kitchen at Zwammerdam?', *Bericht van de Rijksdienst Oudheidkundig Bodemonderzoek (Amersfoort)* 24 (1974), 159–165.

Van Neer, De Cupere, and Waelkens 1997 = Van Neer, W., De Cupere, B., and Waelkens, M., 'Remains of local and imported fish at the ancient site of Sagalassos (Burdur Prov., Turkey)', in M. Waelkens and J. Poblome (eds), *Sagalassos IV. Report on the Survey and Excavation Campaigns of 1994 and 1995* (Acta Archaeologica Lovaniensia Monographiae 9, Leuven 1997), 571–586.

Van Nijf 1997 = Van Nijf, O. M., *The Civic World of Professional Associations in the Roman East* (Dutch Monographs on Ancient History and Archaeology, 17. Amsterdam 1997).

Van Voorhis 2018 = Van Voorhis, J., *The Sculptor's Workshop* (Aphrodisias, 10. Wiesbaden 2018).

Vanhaverbeke et al. 2009 = Vanhaverbeke, H., Vionis, A. K., Poblome, J., and Waelkens, M., 'What happened after the 7th century AD? A different perspective on post-Roman Anatolia', in T. Vorderstrasse and J. Roodenberg (eds), *Archaeology of the Countryside in Medieval Anatolia* (Leiden 2009), 177–190.

Vanhaverbeke et al. 2011 = Vanhaverbeke, H., Degryse, P., Cupere, B. D., Neer, W. V., Waelkens, M., and Muchez, P., 'Urban-Rural Integration at Ancient Sagalassos (SW Turkey). Archaeological, Archaeozoological and Geochemical Evidence', *Archaeofauna* 20 (2011), 73–83.

Varkıvanç 2017 = Varkıvanç, B., 'The stone architecture of the proskene of the theater in Kaunos', *Adalya*.20 (2017), 267–289.

Vermoere 2004 = Vermoere, M., *Holocene Vegetation History in the Territory of Sagalassos (Southwest Turkey): A Palynological Approach* (Studies in Eastern Mediterranean Archaeology, 6. Turnhout 2004).

Vetters 1977a = Vetters, H., 'Zur Baugeschichte der Hanghäuser', in V. M. Strocka (ed.), *Die Wandmalerei der Hanghäuser in Ephesos* (Forschungen in Ephesos, 8.1. Wien 1977), 12–28.

Vetters 1977b = Vetters, H., 'Zur Baugeschichte der Hanghäuser', in W. Jobst (ed.), *Römische Mosaiken aus Ephesos 1. Die Hanghäuser des Embolos* (Forschungen in Ephesos, 8.2. Wien 1977), 17–28.

Vetters 1981 = Vetters, H., 'Ephesos, Vorläufiger Grabungsbericht 1980', *Anzeiger der Österreichischen Akademie der Wissenschaften, Wien, Philologisch-historische Klasse* 118.4 (1981), 137–168.

Vetters 1982 = Vetters, H., 'Ephesos, Vorläufiger Grabungsbericht 1981', *Anzeiger der Österreichischen Akademie der Wissenschaften, Wien, Philologisch-historische Klasse* 119 (1982), 62–101.

Vikan 1984 = Vikan, G., 'Art, medicine, and magic in early Byzantium', *DOP* 38 (1984), 65–86.

Vikan and Nesbitt 1980 = Vikan, G. and Nesbitt, J., *Security in Byzantium: Locking, Sealing and Weighing* (Dumbarton Oaks Collection Publications, 2. Washington, D.C. 1980).

Viscogliosi 1996 = Viscogliosi, A., 'Antra cyclopis: Osservazioni su una tipologia di coenatio', in B. Andreae and C. Parisi Presicce (eds), *Ulisse, il mito e la memoria. Roma, Palazzo delle Esposizioni, 22 febbraio – 2 settembre 1996* (Rome 1996), 252–269.

Vitto 1980 = Vitto, F., 'Notes and News: Tel Naharon', *IEJ* 30.3–4 (1980), 214.

Voegtli 1993 = Voegtli, H., *Die Fundmünzen aus der Stadtgrabung von Pergamon* (Pergamenische Forschungen, 8. Berlin / New York 1993).

von den Driesch 1976 = von den Driesch, A., *A Guide to the Measurement of Animal Bones from Archaeological Sites* (Harvard 1976).

von den Driesch and Boessneck 1982 = von den Driesch, A. and Boessneck, J., 'Tierknochenabfall einer spätrömischen Werkstatt in Pergamon', *AA* (1982), 563–574.

Von Saldern 1980 = Von Saldern, A., *Ancient and Byzantine Glass from Sardis* (Archaeological Exploration of Sardis Monographs, 6. Cambridge, M.A. 1980).

Vorderstrasse 2006 = Vorderstrasse, T., 'A Countermarked Byzantine coin of Heraclius (610–41) from Tell Kurdu', *The Numismatic Chronicle* 166 (2006), 433–438.

Vroom 2017 = Vroom, J., 'Ceramics', in P. Niewöhner (ed.), *The Archaeology of Byzantine Anatolia: From the end of Late Antiquity until the coming of the Turks* (Oxford 2017), 176–194.

Vroom and Fındık 2015 = Vroom, J. and Fındık, E., 'The pottery finds', in S. Ladstätter (ed.), *Die Türbe im Artemision. Ein frühosmanischer Grabbau in Ayasuluk/Selçuk und sein kulturhistorisches Umfeld* (Österreichisches Archäologisches Institut Sonderschriften, 53. Vienna 2015), 205–292.

Vryonis 1971 = Vryonis, S., *The Decline of Medieval Hellenism in Asia Minor and the Process of Islamization from the Eleventh through the Fifteenth Century* (Publications of the Center for Medieval and Renaissance Studies, 4. Berkeley and Los Angeles 1971).

Waage 1952 = Waage, D. B., *Antioch-on-the-Orontes*, vol. 4.2: *Greek, Roman, Byzantine and Crusaders' coins* (Publications of the Committee for the excavation of Antioch and its vicinity, Princeton, London, The Hague 1952).

Waelkens 1987 = Waelkens, M., 'Notes d'architecture sur l'agora et le portique de Tibère à Aphrodisias de Carie', in J. De la Genière and K. T. Erim (eds), *Aphrodisias de Carie, Colloque de l'Université de Lille III, 13 novembre 1985* (Paris 1987), 123–134.

Waelkens, Donners, and van Thuyne 2003 = Waelkens, M., Donners, K., and van Thuyne, T., 'Farming and land use', in H. Vanhaverbeke and M. Waelkens (eds), *The Chora of Sagalassos: The Evolution of the Settlement Pattern from Prehistoric until Recent Times* (Studies in Eastern Mediterranean Archaeology, 5. Turnhout 2003).

Waelkens and Poblome 1997 = Waelkens, M. and Poblome, J. (eds), *Sagalassos IV: Report on the Survey and Excavation*

Campaigns of 1994 and 1995 (Acta archaeologica Lovaniensia. Monographiae 9. Leuven 1997).

Wahlgren 2006 = Wahlgren, S. (ed.) *Symeonis Magistri et Logothetae Chronicon*, vol. 1 (Corpus Fontium Historiae Byzantinae 44. Berlin and New York 2006).

Waksman and von Wartburg 2006 = Waksman, S. Y. and von Wartburg, M. L., '"Fine-sgrafitto ware", "Aegean ware", and other wares: New evidence for a major production of Byzantine ceramics', *RDAC* (2006), 369–388.

Waldbaum 1983 = Waldbaum, J. C., *Metalwork from Sardis: The Finds through 1974* (Archaeological Exploration of Sardis Monograph, 8. Cambridge, MA 1983).

Waldner 2016 = Waldner, A., 'Keramik', in E. Rathmayr (ed.), *Hanghaus 2 in Ephesos: die Wohneinheit 7: Baubefund, Ausstattung, Funde* (Forschungen in Ephesos, 8/10. Wien 2016), 311–423.

Waldner and Ladstätter 2014 = Waldner, A. and Ladstätter, S., 'Keramik', in H. Thür and E. Rathmayr (eds), *Hanghaus 2 in Ephesos: die Wohneinheit 6: Baubefund, Ausstattung, Funde* (Forschungen in Ephesos, 8/9. Wien 2014), 435–588.

Ward-Perkins 1981 = Ward-Perkins, J. B., *Roman Imperial Architecture*. 2nd edn. (Pelican History of Art, Harmondsworth 1981).

Watson 1979 = Watson, J. P. N., 'The estimation of the relative frequencies of mammalian species: Khirokitia 1972', *JAS* 6 (1979), 127–137.

Weber 2013 = Weber, U., *Versatzmarken im antiken griechischen Bauwesen* (Philippika, 58. Wiesbaden 2013).

Weber 2014 = Weber, U., 'Marques d'assemblage dans les édifices du sanctuaire d'Apollon à Claros', in J.-C. Moretti (ed.), *Le sanctuaire de Claros et son oracle. Actes du colloque international de Lyon, 13–14 janvier 2012* (Travaux de la Maison de l'Orient et de la Méditerranée, 65. Lyon 2014), 75–84.

Weber 2015 = Weber, U., 'Building with assembly marks: prefabrication of architectural blocks on building sites at Delos and Pergamon in the IIIrd c. a.C.', in J. des Courtils (ed.), *L'architecture monumentale grecque au IIIe s. a.C.* (40. Bordeaux 2015), 305–316.

Weiss 2014 = Weiss, Z., *Public spectacles in Roman and late antique Palestine* (Harvard University Press, Cambridge, Mass. 2014).

Welch 1998 = Welch, K., 'The stadium at Aphrodisias', *AJA* 102.3 (1998), 547–569.

Welles 1938 = Welles, C. B., 'The inscriptions', in *Gerasa. City of the Decapolis* (New Haven 1938), 355–494.

Werner 1984 = Werner, J., 'Ein byzantinischer 'Steigbügel' aus Caričin Grad', in N. D. a. V. Popović (ed.), *Caričin Grad I. Les basiliques B et J de Caričin Grad, quatre objets remarquables de Caričin Grad, le trésor de Hajdučka Vodenica* (Collection de l'École Française de Rome 75. Rome 1984), 147–155.

Whitehouse, Pilosi, and Wypyski 2000 = Whitehouse, D., Pilosi, L., and Wypyski, M. T., 'Byzantine silver stain', *JGS* 42 (2000), 85–96.

Whittow 2001 = Whittow, M., 'Recent research on the late-antique city in Asia Minor: the second half of the 6th-c. revisited', in L. Lavan and W. Bowden (eds), *Recent Research in Late-Antique Urbanism* (Journal of Roman Archaeology Supplementary Series, 42. Portsmouth, R.I. 2001), 137–153.

Whittow 2018 = Whittow, M., 'The end of antiquity in the Lykos Valley: setting a new agenda', in C. Şimşek and T. Kaçar (eds), *Geç antik çağda Lykos vadisi ve çevresi / The Lykos Valley and Neighbourhood in Late Antiquity* (Laodikeia Çalışmaları: Ek Yayın Dizisi / Supplementary series, 1. İstanbul 2018), 37–53.

Wiegand 1916 = Wiegand, T., 'Torso eines Fischers aus Aphrodisias', *Jahrbuch der Königlich Preussischen Kunstsammlungen* 37 (1916), 1–13.

Wiemer 2004 = Wiemer, H.-U., 'Akklamationen im spätrömischen Reich', *Archiv für Kulturgeschichte* 86.1 (2004), 27–74.

Wilkinson 1998 = Wilkinson, A., *The Garden in Ancient Egypt* (London 1998).

Williams 2005 = Williams, D., 'Late Roman Amphora 1: A study of diversification', in M. Berg Briese and L. E. Vaag (eds), *Trade Relations in the Eastern Mediterranean from the Late Hellenistic Period to Late Antiquity: the Ceramic Evidence Acts from a Ph. D. seminar for young scholars (Sandbjerg Manorhouse, 12–15 February 1998)* (Odense 2005), 157–168.

Wilson 2016a = Wilson, A. I., 'The Olympian (Hadrianic) Baths: layout, operation, and financing', in R. R. R. Smith, J. Lenaghan, A. Sokolicek, and K. Welch (eds), *Aphrodisias Papers 5: Excavation and Research at Aphrodisias, 2006–2012* (JRA Supplementary Series, 103. Portsmouth, Rhode Island 2016), 168–194.

Wilson 2016b = Wilson, A. I., 'Water, nymphs, and a palm grove: monumental water display at Aphrodisias', in R. R. R. Smith, J. Lenaghan, A. Sokolicek, and K. Welch (eds), *Aphrodisias Papers 5: Excavation and Research at Aphrodisias, 2006–2012* (JRA Supplementary Series, 103. Portsmouth, Rhode Island 2016), 100–135.

Wilson 2018a = Wilson, A. I., 'Earthquakes at Aphrodisias', in C. M. Draycott, R. Raja, K. Welch, and W. T. Wootton (eds), *Visual Histories of the Classical World: Essays in Honour of R.R.R. Smith* (Studies in Classical Archaeology, 4. Turnhout 2018), 469–488.

Wilson 2018b = Wilson, A. I., 'Roman nightlife', in A. Chaniotis (ed.), *La nuit: imaginaire et réalités nocturnes dans la monde gréco-romaine* (Entretiens sur l'Antiquité classique, 64. Vandoeuvres 2018), 59–81.

Wilson 2019 = Wilson, A. I., 'Aphrodisias in the long sixth century', in I. Jacobs and H. Elton (eds), *Asia Minor in the Long Sixth Century: Current Research and Future Directions* (Oxford & Philadelphia 2019), 197–221.

Wilson 2020 = Wilson, A. I., 'Roman water-power: chronological trends and geographical spread', in P. Erdkamp, K. Verboven, and A. Zuiderhoek (eds), *Capital, Investment, and Innovation in the Roman World* (Oxford Studies on the Roman Economy. Oxford 2020), 147–194.

Wilson 2022 = Wilson, A. I., 'A Series of Unfortunate Events: The end of classical urbanism in southwestern Asia Minor in the early seventh century AD', in M. Whitby and P.

Booth (eds), *Mélanges James Howard-Johnston* (Travaux et mémoires, 26. Paris 2022), 565–594.

Wilson, Russell, and Proudfoot in preparation = Wilson, A. I., Russell, B., and Proudfoot, T., 'Water-powered marble sawing at Aphrodisias', (in preparation).

Wilson, Russell, and Ward 2016 = Wilson, A. I., Russell, B., and Ward, A., 'Excavations in an urban park ("South Agora"), 2012', in R. R. R. Smith, J. Lenaghan, A. Sokolicek, and K. Welch (eds), *Aphrodisias Papers 5: Excavation and Research at Aphrodisias, 2006–2012* (JRA Supplementary Series, 103. Portsmouth, Rhode Island 2016), 77–90.

Winter 2006 = Winter, F. E., *Studies in Hellenistic architecture* (Phoenix, Supplementary volume, 42. Toronto 2006).

Witte 2012 = Witte, J., 'Counters and stoppers in terracotta and stone', in C. S. Lightfoot and E. A. Ivison (eds), *Amorium Reports*, vol. 3: *Finds Reports and Technical Studies* (Amorium Monograph Series, Istanbul 2012), 243–262.

Yaltirik and Boydak 1991 = Yaltirik, F. and Boydak, M., 'Distribution and ecology of the palm Phoenix theophrasti (Palmae) in Turkey', *Botanica Chronika* 10 (1991), 869–872.

Yegül 1992 = Yegül, F., *Baths and Bathing in Classical Antiquity* (Cambridge (Mass.) and London 1992).

Yegül and Favro 2019 = Yegül, F. and Favro, D., *Roman Architecture and Urbanism: From the Origins to Late Antiquity* (Cambridge 2019).

Yegül 1974 = Yegül, F. K., 'Early Byzantine capitals from Sardis. a study on the Ionic impost type', *DOP* 28 (1974), 265–274.

Yıldırım 2016 = Yıldırım, B., 'Excavations on the Tetrapylon Street, 2008–9', in R. R. R. Smith, J. Lenaghan, A. Sokolicek, and K. Welch (eds), *Aphrodisias Papers 5: Excavation and Research at Aphrodisias, 2006–2012* (JRA Supplementary Series, 103. Portsmouth, Rhode Island 2016), 36–47.

Yılmaz 2008 = Yılmaz, Z., 'Spätantike Sigillaten aus Priene', in B. Böhlendorf-Arslan (ed.), Çanak: Late Antique and Medieval Pottery and Tiles in Mediterranean Archaeological Contexts. Proceedings of the First International Symposium on Late Antique, Byzantine, Seljuk, and Ottoman Pottery and Tiles in Archaeological Context (Çanakkale, 1–3 June 2005) (Byzas, 7. Istanbul 2008), 123–129.

Zach 2002 = Zach, B., 'Vegetable offerings on the Roman sacrificial site in Mainz, Germany—short report on the first results', *Vegetation History and Archaeobotany* 11.1–2 (2002), 101–106.

Zachos 2003 = Zachos, K. L., 'The tropaeum of the sea battle of Actium at Nikopolis: interim report', *JRA* 16 (2003), 64–92.

Zacos and Veglery 1972 = Zacos, G. and Veglery, A., *Byzantine Lead Seals* (Basel 1972).

Zanker 1995 = Zanker, P., *The Mask of Socrates: The Image of the Intellectual in Antiquity*. Translated by A. Shapiro (Sather Classical Lectures, 59. Berkeley – Los Angeles – Oxford 1995).

Zanon 2013 = Zanon, M., 'Tyana/Kemerhisar (Niğde): glass bracelets of the Byzantine and Islamic period', *Anatolia Antiqua. Eski Anadolu* 21.1 (2013), 181–197.

Zarmakoupi 2014 = Zarmakoupi, M., *Designing for Luxury on the Bay of Naples. Villas and Landscapes (c.100 BCE–79 CE)* (Oxford Studies in Ancient Culture and Representation, Oxford 2014).

Zeder 2006 = Zeder, M., 'Reconciling rates of long bone fusion and tooth eruption and wear in sheep (*Ovis*) and goat (*Capra*)', in D. Ruscillo (ed.), *Recent Advances in Ageing and Sexing Animal Bones. 9th ICAZ Conference, Durham 2002* (Oxford 2006), 87–118.

Zeder and Lapham 2010 = Zeder, M. A. and Lapham, H. A., 'Assessing the reliability of criteria used to identify postcranial bones in sheep, Ovis, and goats, Capra', *JAS* 37.11 (2010), 2887–2905.

Zeder, Lemoine, and Payne 2015 = Zeder, M. A., Lemoine, X., and Payne, S., 'A new system for computing long-bone fusion age profiles in Sus scrofa', *JAS* 55 (2015), 135–150.

Zeder and Pilaar 2010 = Zeder, M. A. and Pilaar, S. E., 'Assessing the reliability of criteria used to identify mandibles and mandibular teeth in sheep, *Ovis*, and goats, *Capra*', *JAS* 37.2 (2010), 225–242.

Zemer 1977 = Zemer, A., *Storage Jars in Ancient Sea Trade* (Publications of the Maritime Museum Foundation, Haifa 1977).

Image Credits

Fig. 1, 2, 4, 5, 8, 12, 17, 23, 46, and 75 were created by B. Russell from original drawings by H. Mark, L. Aguilar, E. Brown, and D. Horwitz; Fig. 3 is from Jacopi 1939; Fig. 6 and 7 were drawn by N. de Chaisemartin; Fig. 9 was drawn by L. Wong and annotated by B. Russell; Fig. 11 and 25–26 are by E. Davidson; Fig. 47 and 51 by H. Mark; Fig. 13–14, 18–20 and 27–28 by B. Russell; Fig. 15 by K. Webb; Fig. 21–22, 31–33, 60 and 106 by A. T. Tek; Fig. 24 and 30 by A. Kidd; Fig. 29 by A. Kidd and D. Horwitz; Fig. 34–42, 48–49, 61–63 and 84 by U. Outschar; Fig. 43 and 69–71 by E. Rowan; Fig. 45 by L. Aguilar; Fig. 52 by P. Linant de Bellefonds; Fig. 53 by A. Leung; Fig. 54 and 56–58 were created by J. Thomas and B. Russell from original drawings by H. Mark; Fig. 55 was drawn by H. Morales; Fig. 59 and 74–83 were created by B. Russell and A. Kidd based on an original drawing by H. Mark; Fig. 64–67 and 85 by T. Penn and H. Jeffery; Fig. 86 by T. Penn; Fig. 68 by E. Rowan and B. Russell; Fig. 44 and 72–73 were created by A. Wilson and B. Russell based on original drawings by H. Mark; Fig. 87–106 by A. Trentacoste; the foldout was created by B. Russell and A. Chaniotis based on the original drawing by H. Mark. Fig. 10 is from Nbk 298: *Agora Gate: Basin Front II* (F. Thode, 1988), 34, fig. 9; Fig. 16 is from Erim 1986b; Fig. 50 is from Nbk 240: *South East Agora Gate (SEAG) I* (B. Rose and G. Paul), 77.

The images in Pl. 1.B, 6.A–B, 9.A–B, 10.A–B, 11.A, 11.D, 12.C, 14.C–D, 15.B–C, 16.A–C, 16.E, 17.A, 17.C–E, 18.A–B, 18.D–F, 19.A–C, 20.A–D, 21.C, 22.A, 23.A, 25.B–C, 26.A–B, 28.A–C, 29.A–E, 30.A–D, 31.A–C, 31.F–G, 32.A–C, 33.A–C, 34.B, 35.A, 40.F, 41.A–C, 42.A–C, 78.A–B, 79.A–B, 80.B, 85.A, 86.A, 86.C, 87.A, 89.A are by A. Wilson; Pl. 10.D, 11.B–C, 11.E–F, 12.A, 13.B, 13.D, 16.D, 21.B, 22.C–G, 23.B–C, 23.E, 24.A–B, 25.A, 26.C–G, 29.A–G, 34.C–E, Pl. 57.H, 87.B by B. Russell; Pl. 15.A, 22.B, 34.A, 35.B–C, 36.A–B, 37.A–B, 37.F–J, 38.A–C, 38.E–F, 38.I, 39.A–B, 80.C, 85.B–D, 86.B, 87.D–E, 88.A–B, 89.C–D, 90.B, 90.D by A. Kidd; Pl. 79.C by B. Russell and A. Kidd; Pl. 25.D, 43.A–J, 44.A–G, 45.A–I, 46.A–F, 47.A–M, 48.A–N, 49.A–L, 50.A–G, 51.A–J, 52.A–P, 53.A–T, 54.A–E, 54.G–M, 55.A–J, 56.A–N, Pl. 57.A–G, Pl. 95.A–D, 96.A–G by A. Chaniotis; Pl. 39.C–F, 81.A–K, 82.A–I, 83.A–J, 84.A, 91.A–J, 92.A–J, 93.A–L by I. Cartwright, T. Penn and H. Jeffery; Pl. 1.A, 2.A, 6.C, 7.A–C, 8, 18.C, 24.C–H, 37.D–E, 38.D, 58.A, 59.A, 66.C–D, 67, 80.A by I. Cartwright; Pl. 60.A–B, 61.B, 62–65, 66.A–B, 68–77 by M. Ali Döğenci, G. Petruccioli and I. Cartwright; Colour Pl. 3–7, 8.A–B by M. Bursalı; Pl. 40.A–C, 84.A–G by E. Rowan; 2.B, 3.A, 3.B, 9.C, 13.A, 80.D by Skypro; Pl. 98–100 by B. and G. Teoman; Pl. 37.C, 38.G–H by N. Gier and A. Kidd; Pl. 13.C, 13.E, 14.B by H. Mark; Pl. 94.A–B by A. Trentacoste; Pl. 59.B–C, 60.A–B, 61.A by R. R. R. Smith; Pl. 40.D–E by M. Robinson; Pl. 89.B by M. Miller; Pl. 90.C by M. Klosowski; Pl. 90.A by J. Thomas; Pl. 99.M by A. Sarıönder; Pl. 97 by A. T. Tek. L. Aguilar produced the render shown on the frontispiece. Pl. 4.A is from Society of Dilettanti 1840, pl. VI; Pl. 21.A is © APAAME, photograph by R. Bewley; Pl. 54.F is from Zacos and Veglery 1972, pl. 242; Pl. 56.O was provided by R. J. A. Wilson. Pl. 4.B–D, 5.A–C, 12.B, 14.A, 58.B, 90.E–F are from the excavation photo archive; Pl. 10.C is from Nbk 323: *Portico of Tiberius Sondages* (D. Theodorescu et al., 1991), p. 58; Pl. 17.B is from Nbk 298: *Agora Gate: Basin Front II* (F. Thode, 1988), 34, fig. 9; Pl. 23.D is from Nbk 76: *NE Nymphaeum / SW Portico of Tiberius* (S. Kulaklı, 1969): p. 36; Pl. 31.D–E are from Nbk 298: *Agora Gate: Basin Front II* (F. Thode, 1988), 34; Pl. 58.C is from Nbk 240: *South East Agora Gate (SEAG) I* (B. Rose and G. Paul, 1983), 74–79; Pl. 84.B is from Nbk 316: *Portico of Tiberius: W Pool, Book I; E Pool* (A.T. Tek, 1990), F24, Photo 22; Pl. 87.C is from Nbk 318: *Portico of Tiberius: E Pool* (A. Önce, 1990), 38.

Index

abacus, 19, 50, 53, 85–6, 88, 91
abecedary, 128, 130, 132, 346
acanthus, 19–20, 50, 172
acclamation, 71, 77, 121, 127–31, 136, 138, 149–50, 297, 318–19, 324, 335, 339, 341, 344, 346–7, 350–1, 353–5
Aceruntia, 169
Achaemenid, 36
Achaia, 139, 317
Achilles, 160, 165, 176, 179, 187, 295
Acholios, 149
acropolis, 6, 58, 290
acroterion, 172
admirandissimus, 89, 313
Adrastos, 41, 52, 171, 310–11, 316
    Adrastos Attalos, 316
    Adrastos Grypos, 310–11
Aegean, 62, 102, 110, 219–20, 226, 256
Aelia Stateilia Stratonike, 178
Aeneas, 311
Aeneid, 130
Africa, *see* North Africa
Afyon Museum, 206, 259
Agathias, 142
Agathicum, 116
agriculture, 218–19, 241, 288
Agrippa, 36
Agrippina, 61
Ahmed III (Sultan), 252, 373, 377
Aizanoi, 88
al-Mara, 226
Alabanda, 55, 358
Alaeddin Keykubad I (Sultan), 373
Albinos, 21, 43, 45, 47–8, 54, 66, 77, 79, 89, 121, 125, 129, 138–40, 149–50, 162, 172, 174–5, 297, 318, 324, 350–1
alea, *see* gameboards
Alexandria, 94–5, 134, 189, 191, 364
Alexandria Troas, 63
Alexandros, 161
algae, 186, 209–10, 215
almond, 107–9, 111–12
alveoli, 279, 281
Amazonomachy, 123, 155, 157–9
Amazons, 157–8, 165, 312
ambulatory, 118
Amias, 326
Ammia, 171, 176, 178
Amorgos, 35

Amorium, 188, 196, 198–9, 207, 226, 259, 263, 266, 288–90, 292
Ampelios (*pater civitatis*), 5, 9, 25, 34, 65–7, 75–7, 79, 91, 114, 116–18, 121, 123–5, 138–9, 149, 151, 153, 161–2, 174, 204, 296–8, 313–14, 324
    Publius Ampelios (proconsul of Achaia), 139
amphibian, 269, 286–7
amphorae, 97–8, 103, 113, 192, 384–7
amulet, 127, 205, 251
Anaia, 63
Anaphe, 35
Anastasius, 66, 90, 92, 94, 116–17, 119–20, 125, 189, 191, 297, 315, 353, 370
anathyrosis, 84, 166
Anatolia, 4, 111–13, 218–19, 229–30, 246, 257–8, 265, 270, 289, 291, 299
ancestors, 41, 77, 104, 265, 310, 329, 351
Anchises, 130, 158
Ancyra, 219
Andron, 41, 171, 316
    Andron Attalos, 41, 171
Andronikos, Fl. Andronikos (scupltor), 166, 178
Andronikos II (Byzantine emperor), 230
Andros, 266
Anemurium, 196, 206
animals, 11, 32, 114, 133–5, 158, 160, 165, 188, 205–6, 215, 218, 230, 234, 246, 251–2, 256–8, 263, 265, 269–70, 274–5, 284, 286–9, 291–3, 297–9, 334, 340, 347–8, 395
Ankara, 63, 169, 249
Annona, 361
antelope, 134, 348
Anthemios, 154, 159, 167, 318–19, 353
Antinoopolis, 172
Antioch, 38, 94–5, 119–21, 131, 189–92, 255–6, 361–2, 367, 369
Antioch ad Maeandrum, 60, 359
Antiochus Chuzon, 121
Antipatros, 45, 311–12, 327
antiquities, 1, 55
antlers, 270–1, 284, 288
Antonine, 41, 296, 307
Antoniniana, 327, 330
antoniniani, 62, 361
Antoninus Pius, 41, 60, 62, 167, 169–71, 296, 316, 360
Antonius Claudius Diogenes Dometeinos, 8
Apamea, 90, 317
Apellas Athenagorou, 360

Apellas Koblanos, 171, 324–5
Aphrodiseia Philemoneia, 323
Aphrodisias, *passim*
    Agora, 1, 4, 6, 8–9, 11, 15–16, 18, 20, 26, 34, 43, 53, 75, 79, 94, 114, 116–17, 125, 147–8, 155, 158, 161 n. 29, 174, 181, 189 n. 73, 196, 199, 218–9 221–2, 225–8, 234, 252, 261, 267, 295–6, 307–8, 310, 326
    'Agora Gate', *see* Propylon (Place of Palms)
    aqueducts, 32, 119, 123, 170, 286
        Işıklar, 32
        Seki, 32
        Tavas, 32, 170
        Timeles, 32, 170, 172, 254, 286, 359
    Basilica, 1, 5, 9, 20, 23, 25, 30, 39, 41–5, 47–8, 51, 63, 67, 72, 80–3, 85–6, 89, 93, 116, 124–6, 145, 148, 160, 165, 169, 176, 179, 187, 201, 205, 218, 223–5, 235, 237, 239, 252, 295–6, 307, 309, 311
    Bishop's Palace, 235, 254, 259, 299
    Bouleuterion, 18, 52, 59, 65–7, 77–9, 114, 116–17, 119, 121, 125, 129, 131–4, 138, 161, 169–70, 219, 221–3, 225, 227, 234, 254, 265, 314
    Cathedral, 89–90, 229, 235, 254, 265, 299
    City Walls, 32, 34, 48, 52, 58, 62, 65–6, 92, 110, 116, 118, 125, 131, 134, 138, 159, 163, 219–21, 228, 296, 314
    council of elders, 169
    Diogenianon, 4
    Eusebian Baths, 32
    Gaudin's Fountain, 159, 312
    Hadrianic 'Olympian' Baths, 1, 4, 8–9, 11, 15, 18, 25, 30, 32, 42, 44–5, 48, 50–1, 63, 71, 77, 84–5, 116, 119, 125–6, 121, 130, 135, 140, 142, 147–8, 160, 165, 167, 170, 172, 174–6, 180, 191, 199, 206, 221, 222, 227, 228, 254, 295–7, 307, 311–13, 323, 326, 328, 351
    House of Kybele, 178, 221–3, 225, 227
    North Agora, *see* Agora
    North Stoa (Place of Palms), 1, 4–6, 8–11, 15–21, 23, 30, 32–4, 41–5, 47–57, 63, 65, 67, 69, 73–9, 82–4, 86, 88–9, 91, 114, 116–17, 125, 127–8, 131, 133–4, 136–7, 139–40, 145–9, 153, 171, 174, 176, 178–81, 183, 185–7, 189, 199, 201, 204, 206, 213, 217–18, 221, 223, 225–7, 231, 233–4, 237, 239, 241, 243, 245–6, 251, 254, 295–9, 307–9, 311–12, 321, 341, 349–51, 354–5, 390–3
    Place of Palms, *passim*; *see also* 'Portico of Tiberius', 'South Agora'
    'Portico of Tiberius' (old name for Place of Palms), 1, 5–6, 13, 15–16, 24, 29, 32, 47, 69–70, 72, 75, 80, 84, 183, 186, 188, 204, 207–8, 219, 225, 231, 235, 237, 245, 249, 307–9, 330, 373, 376
    Propylon (Place of Palms), 1, 5–6, 9–11, 13, 15–16, 21, 23, 26, 32, 34, 36, 39–45, 63, 65–6, 74, 79–80, 91, 114, 116, 118–19, 121–7, 132, 139–40, 147–8, 151, 153–5, 158, 161–3, 165, 167, 169–72, 174, 176, 181, 185, 187, 189, 219, 223–8, 230, 234, 237, 254, 295–8, 300, 307–20, 322, 324–5, 327, 329–31, 333, 354
    Propylon basin, 5–6, 9–10, 13, 26, 36, 71, 74–5, 121, 123–4, 126, 135, 139, 151–62, 165, 167–8, 170–2, 176, 223, 226, 228, 298, 310, 312, 316, 318, 367
    Sculptor's Workshop, 116–17, 125
    Sebasteion, 39, 41–2, 48, 63, 71, 75, 113, 118, 131–3, 138–40, 153–4, 157, 159–60, 163, 167, 169, 176, 199, 219, 221–3, 225, 227, 300, 307–9, 311, 314
    'South Agora' (old name for Place of Palms), 1, 4–6, 8–9, 11, 13, 39, 295, 307, 321; *see* Place of Palms
    South Stoa (Place of Palms), 1, 4–6, 10–11, 15, 21, 23, 32, 39, 41–3, 45, 48, 50, 53, 63, 65–7, 69, 72, 79–91, 114, 116–18, 123, 125–7, 135–40, 147, 167, 174, 178–80, 183, 187–9, 201, 217, 223, 225, 227, 231, 234–5, 249, 254, 295–8, 308, 310, 313, 333, 352–5
    Stadium, 35, 38, 92, 118, 129, 134, 136, 140, 149–50, 310, 312, 323, 328, 348
    Temple of Aphrodite, 6, 58, 90–1, 119, 121, 125, 265, 295, 323
    Tetrapylon, 44, 116, 118, 125, 129, 132–3, 140, 146, 221
    Tetrapylon Street, 9, 39, 70–1, 75, 92, 113, 124–5, 133, 135, 138–40, 146, 148, 167, 169, 192, 219, 221–5, 227–8, 230, 239, 254, 266–7, 299
    Tetrastoon, 5, 67, 89, 132, 136, 138, 147–8, 169, 178, 223
    Theatre, 1, 5–6, 8–11, 15, 18, 20–4, 29, 32, 35, 39, 41–3, 50–1, 63–4, 67, 79, 88–9, 116, 121, 128–34, 136, 139–40, 144, 148–9, 159 n. 20, 161, 167, 169, 176 n. 64, 178, 191, 198, 219, 223–4, 228, 230, 241 n. 68, 249, 266, 295–6, 310 n. 18, 311, 326
    Theatre Baths, 5, 8, 50–1, 63, 65, 116–17, 138, 161, 178, 223, 314
    Theatre Hill, 1, 9–11, 15, 21–3, 29, 32, 39, 41–3, 58, 60, 67, 80, 85–6, 125, 130, 167, 179, 215, 223, 228, 235, 237, 239, 241, 243, 246, 248–9, 252, 254, 256, 259, 263, 266, 295–6, 299–300, 333, 353–5, 394–5
    Theatre Wall, 21, 23, 41–2, 80–1, 127, 136, 189, 231, 354
    town council, 64, 119
    Triconch Church, 25, 261
    Triconch House, 118–19, 125
    West Stoa (Place of Palms), 1, 4–6, 11, 13, 15–16, 18, 21, 30, 32, 34–5, 39, 42–9, 51, 53–5, 63, 65–7, 69, 71–2, 74, 77, 79–80, 83, 89, 91, 114, 116–18, 121, 125, 127, 129–30, 133, 135–8, 140, 147, 149, 163, 165, 172, 174–6, 179, 181, 196, 199, 227, 296–7, 307, 312, 324, 327, 330, 333, 350–1
Aphrodite, 4, 6, 16, 34, 39, 58–9, 90–1, 114, 116, 118–19, 121, 125, 135, 158, 160, 163, 178, 180, 228, 265, 295, 307–8, 310–11, 322–6, 351, 358–60
Apollo, 61, 139, 157–8, 160, 163, 358, 360
Apollonia Salbake, 60–1, 360
Apollonios, 41, 171, 316–17, 320, 322–3, 327, 329
Apollonios Attalos, 316
apses, 128, 135, 339
Aquileia, 94
Arabic, 120, 188, 191–2, 226–8, 370, 393
    countermark, 192 n. 86, 226–8, 298, 393
    graffiti, 226 n. 382
Arabs, 143, 183, 187, 189, 191–2, 219–20, 225–8, 298, 300
Araq el-Emir (Jordan), 36

Arcadius, 92, 94, 118, 172, 174–5, 363–4
archaeobotanical material, 10, 70, 77, 105–6, 110–13, 126, 186, 208–10, 218, 226, 296, 298; *see also* plants
arches, 132, 135, 146
architrave, 4–5, 20–1, 42, 44–5, 50–2, 67, 69, 77, 79–80, 82–3, 85–6, 88–91, 114, 116–18, 137, 139–40, 145, 189, 231, 233, 307–9, 311–13, 349
archon, 313, 317
arena, 92, 117–18, 312
Ares, 165, 323
Aristokles Molossos, 42
Aristophanes, *Birds*, 128
Armenia, 220
Armenian History of Ps.-Sebeos, 220–1
army, 189, 219–20, 226–8, 266, 312
Artemidoros, 33–4, 118, 163, 307–9, 316, 321, 324
    Artemidoros Pedisas, 34, 163, 316
Artemis, 50, 61–2, 155, 157, 160, 219, 360
    Artemis Anaitis, 360
Artemon (*kapelos*), 136
artisans, 90
Arykanda, 58, 62–3, 92, 94
ashlar, 18, 21, 23, 41–2, 48, 80, 123
Asia Minor, 35, 38, 49, 51, 53, 58, 62–3, 78–9, 84, 86, 88, 91, 93–4, 96–7, 105, 118, 125, 140, 142–3, 145, 149, 169–70, 183, 189, 191–2, 195, 207, 219–20, 225–7, 235, 239, 254, 256, 259, 266, 287, 296–8, 300, 334
Asklepiodotos, 153, 155, 316–17
Asklepios, 59, 67, 167, 178, 206, 307, 325–6
    Asklepios Euepekoos, 326
Aspendos, 41
assembly marks, 52, 79, 127, 139, 312, 349
astragalus, 275
Athena, 59, 62, 165, 358, 360
Athens, 6, 36, 165, 195, 318
    Areopagos, 204
    Athenian Agora, 36
    Erechtheion, 165
    Hephasteion, 36
    Library of Hadrian, 6
athletes, 128–30, 133, 149–50
Atlantic triton (*Charonia variegata*), *see* Triton's trumpet
atrium, 119, 135
Attaleia, 314
Attalis, 176, 178, 308, 316
Attalis Apphion, 308
Attalos, 41, 52, 171, 178, 308, 316
Augusta Treverorum, 94; *see also* Trier
Augustus, 4, 16, 36, 45, 59–61, 169, 295, 307, 310–12, 315–16, 321, 326, 359–60
Aurelia Faustina, 321
Aurelian, 60, 62, 93, 361
Aurelius, 52, 60, 62, 129, 317, 322–4, 326–7, 330, 360
Aurelius Achilleus, 129
Aurelius Flavius Venidius Hypsikles, 326
Aurelius Oreinos, 330
Avars, 207–8, 219–20, 259
axe, 132, 358–9

Aydın, 218–19, 230, 251
Aydinids, 230, 257, 373

Bacchus, 1
backgammon, 142
Baiae, 165
Baku, 265
Balkan, 94–5, 207–8, 262, 284–5
balteus, 19, 45, 47, 53–4, 73, 85
bangles, 241, 243, 248–9, 251–2, 263–5, 299
Barberini faun, 135
barley (*Hordeum vulgare*), 106–8, 110–13, 214, 218
    hulled, 106, 111–12, 214
basin, at the Propylon, *see* Aphrodisias, Propylon basin
basin (early medieval, water-drawing) 188, 215, 227, 231, 234–5, 298
basins (marble), *see* louteria 119
basins (pottery vessels), 100–1, 192, 381–3, 385, 387
bath-gymnasium, 4, 85, 91
bathhouse, 4, 8, 169, 239
Bayezid I, 373, 375, 378
Bayezid II, 373, 376
bead-and-reel, 18–19
beads, 239, 243, 248, 251
beak, 334
beakers, 196, 198
bedding, 30, 32, 295
beef, 288, 292
Beirut, 100
Belisarius, 189
Bell, Malcolm, 25, 235
bells, 183, 205
bequest, 41, 167, 309, 311, 315, 323
Beroia, 313
Beronikianos, 323; *see also* Veronicianus (governor)
berries, 112
Beşik Tepe, 289
Beylik period, 13, 50, 60, 74, 219, 229–31, 235, 237, 239, 241, 246, 251–2, 256–7, 259, 261–3, 266–7, 270–2, 276–8, 280–1, 287, 289, 295, 299–300, 358, 373, 381, 384–6, 389, 391, 394–5
beyliks, 229, 230, 257–8, 373
birds, 110, 128, 130, 133–4, 149, 218, 243, 265, 269, 284, 286–7, 289, 333–4, 339, 344, 347, 349
Birketein, 36, 120–1
bishops, 192, 227, 229–30
blockwork, 21, 48
Blue Horse, 48, 176, 179, 187
Blümlein, Carl, 145–6
boats, 130, 135, 150, 338
Bodrum, 35, 189
bolsters, 84–5, 88
bone (objects), 70, 104, 243, 248 nn. 104 and 116, 252 n. 152, 262, 286–9, 299
bones (animal), 32, 69–70, 74, 106, 186, 209, 234 n. 19, 251–2, 265 n, 271, 269–70, 273, 275, 277–92, 297–9, 391, 395
    gnawed, 272–3, 287, 289
bones (fish), 113

431

Bosphorus, 219, 226
bottles, 196, 199, 259
Boulanger, André, 4, 48, 312, 328, 330
Boule (town council), 61
bowls, 97–100, 198, 256–9, 318
bracts (pine), 108–9, 112–13, 212, 214
Brassica (sp.), 108, 110, 211, 216
bread, 108, 110, 113, 239, 259, 394
    Eucharistic, 259
bread stamp, 239, 259, 394
bread wheat, 108
bricks, 10, 32, 70, 74, 78, 80, 86, 90–1, 97, 124, 187, 204, 221, 234, 239, 241, 246, 259, 261–2, 390–2
Brillenbuchstabe, 132, 346
bronze, 26, 34, 58–60, 70, 91–2, 94, 118, 135, 149, 154, 163, 167, 170, 180, 221, 239, 241, 245, 248, 251, 259, 318–19
bronzes, 59, 205
buckles, 206, 263
buds, 76, 106–7, 109–10, 112–13, 214, 216
buggers/buggered, 121, 131, 150, 335
buildings, 1, 4–5, 8–9, 11, 13, 18, 23, 34–5, 39, 42–3, 45, 48, 51–3, 58, 63–7, 72, 75, 77–80, 84–6, 88–91, 114, 116–19, 121, 123, 125–9, 131–2, 134–6, 138–9, 144, 151, 153–4, 159, 161, 165, 167, 169–70, 172, 174, 176, 187, 189, 196, 201, 209, 217–25, 227–8, 230–1, 237, 239, 241, 243, 245–6, 248–9, 251–2, 254, 266, 288, 295–7, 299–300, 307–15, 323–5, 343, 350–1, 353, 394–5
    Building II, 245–6, 248
    Building III, 245, 248
    Building IV, 245, 248, 252
    Building IX, 245, 248, 252
    Building VI, 245
    Building VII, 245
    Building VIII, 245–6
    Building XI, 248, 395
burials, 205, 265
burning, 76, 106, 109–10, 112–13, 126, 185, 187, 189, 217, 219, 226–7
butchery, 204, 272, 274, 277–8, 281, 288, 291, 293, 299
Byzantine empire, Byzantines, 192, 226, 229

caduceus, 360
Caelius Montius, 169
Caesarea in Cappadocia, 220
Caesarea Maritima, 36, 291 n. 71
Calama (Guelma, Algeria), 35
calcaneum, 269
Caligula, 59–60, 359
Calvisius Ruso, 165
camel, *camelus*, 269
Çamova Tepe, 49, 51
canids, 271–2, 284
    canis familiaris, 271
canines, 269, 279, 281
Canopus, 6, 36, 165, 170
Capernaum, 94
capitals, 5, 18–20, 35, 43–5, 47, 49–51, 53–4, 82, 84–6, 88–91, 183, 185, 221, 234–5

Capitolinus, 52, 79, 148, 312
    Tiberius Claudius Capitolinus, 79
Cappadocia, 220
Capra hircus, 271
Capreolus capreolus, 271
Caracalla, 120
carcasses, 277, 282, 287–8, 292
Caria, *see* Karia
Caričin Grad, 208
Carminius, Marcus Ulpius Carminius Claudianus, 8, 64, 324
carnivores, 272–3, 277–8, 288
Çarşamba, 142
Carthage, 189–90, 367
caryatids, 45, 165, 175–6, 178, 180, 307, 312, 323, 328
caryopsis, 107–9, 214
Castelgandolfo (Villa of Domitian), 165
cats, 166–7, 170, 176, 320
cattle, 6, 188, 192, 206, 219, 225–8, 231, 234–5, 270–6, 286–92, 298–9
centauromachy, 155, 157–9
centaurs, 157–8, 160, 312
Cephisus (river), 66
ceramics, 10, 24, 43, 70, 73–5, 78–9, 86, 94–5, 104–6, 116, 118, 146, 186–8, 192–4, 204, 209, 225, 229–30, 234–5, 237, 239, 241, 243, 246, 248–9, 251–2, 254, 256–9, 262, 265–6, 295, 297–9, 381–7, 390–5; *see also* pottery
Cerberus, 157
cereals, 106–8, 110–13, 187, 214–15, 218–19; *see also* barley, wheat, spelt
Ceres, 175
cervids, *see* deer
chains, 105, 243, 248, 251
Chalcedon, 219, 226
Chalkis, 139
Chameroy, Jérémie, 59, 62–3, 93, 358, 361
chariot, 92, 149, 157–8
Charonia sp., 113–14, 286
    Charonia seguenzae, 114; *see* Triton's trumpet
    Charonia variegata, 186, 286, 288
Chersiphron, 35
chest, 159–60, 171, 179, 204
chestnut (*Castanea sativa*), 111, 217–18
chicken (*Gallus gallus*), 271, 284, 288
Chios, 49, 226
chips (marble), 6, 8, 33
chisel, 83, 85, 88, 117, 202
chop marks, 272, 277–8, 288
Christ, 130, 134, 176, 318–19, 371–2
Christian, Christians, 29, 52, 55, 116, 120–1, 128–32, 134–5, 144–6, 149–50, 154, 160, 176, 178, 195, 205, 228, 259, 292, 297, 318–19, 324, 326, 333–4, 340–2, 346–7, 350, 353
Christianity, 149
Christograms, 130, 132–3, 150, 341, 349–50
church, 25, 84–6, 88–91, 116, 118–19, 121, 128, 132, 135, 146, 196, 201, 206, 220, 227, 230, 261, 324, 339
Cilicia, 191
Cilician Gates (Byzantine defeat at), 219, 221

circlet, 369, 371
circus factions, 129, 132–3, 149
    Blues, 129, 132, 346
    Greens, 129, 132, 346
    Reds, 129, 339, 350, 353
citizenship, 176, 308–9, 312
Claudia Antonia Tatiane, 52, 148–9
Claudia Pauleina, 328
Claudia Seleukeia Tibereine, 323
Claudia Tatiana Antonia, 234
Claudius Apollonios Markianos, 317, 322–3
Claudius Aurelius Ktesias, 52
Claudius Diogas, 327
Claudius Diogenes, 8, 52, 234, 308–9
Claudius II, 60, 62, 361
Claudius Pauleinos, 327–8
Claudius Smaragdos, 52
climate, 110–13
Cocceia Maxima, 312
cocciopesto, 25, 69, 389
Codex Justinianus, 120
Codex Theodosianus, 90, 120
coin types, 61
    Fel Temp Reparatio, 92
    Gloria Exercitus, 92
    Gloria Romanorum, 364
    Salus Rei Publicae, 92, 363
    Victoria Augustorum, 92, 309, 363
    Virtus Exercitus, 94, 363
coins, 24, 30, 32, 39, 55, 58–63, 70, 73–5, 78, 90–5, 104, 116–19, 124–6, 135, 145, 170, 183, 185, 187–92, 201–2, 219–21, 223, 226–8, 230–1, 234, 239, 241, 243, 248–9, 251–2, 254, 265–6, 297–8, 329, 353, 357–60, 364, 366–7, 369–70, 372–3, 378–9, 381, 389–95
    Arabic-countermarked, 188, 227–8
    barbarous radiates, 60, 62, 93, 95, 361
    clipped, 91–2, 94, 357, 362–4, 371
    countermarked, 59, 187–8, 190, 192, 227, 298, 358–60, 370
    follis, 223, 371
    Gallic Empire, 62–3, 93
    Lycian Federation, 58–9
    mangirs, 373, 376
    overstruck, 187, 368–71
    Turkish Republic, 231, 373, 389
colonnade, 1, 4–5, 11, 16, 18, 20, 32, 39, 43–8, 51, 53–7, 66, 79–82, 85–6, 88–90, 114, 117–19, 124–5, 133, 138–9, 148, 165, 172, 189, 206, 219, 221, 228, 231, 234, 297, 350
colonnettes, 82, 86, 88
colours, 196, 201, 263–4
columella, 113–14
columns, 1, 4–5, 8, 13, 15–16, 18, 20–1, 23, 32, 35, 39, 43–5, 47–8, 51–5, 63, 66–7, 70, 72–4, 77–84, 86, 88–91, 114, 116–18, 123–5, 127–40, 147–9, 165, 178, 189, 196, 221, 223, 225, 231, 234, 241, 243, 245, 249, 252, 266, 296–7, 323–4, 339, 341–55
Commodus, 119

conflagration, *see* fire
congregation, 119–20
conifer, 109
console, 21, 45, 86, 167, 172, 254
Constans I, 92, 169, 183, 185, 189, 191–2, 220, 226, 231, 362, 370–1, 394
Constans II, 92, 183, 185, 189, 191–2, 220, 226, 231, 370–1, 394
Constantine I, 92–4, 121, 139, 223, 226, 361–2, 369–71
Constantine VI, 226
Constantine Tzouroukkas, 121
Constantinople, 48, 90, 94–5, 119–21, 161, 176, 185, 189, 195–6, 202, 219, 226–7, 256, 259, 263, 361–5, 367–71
    Harbour of Theodosius, 270, 284
    St Polyeuktos, 201
Constantinopolis, 92, 190
Constantinopolitan, 170, 178, 180
Constantius, 42, 47–8, 63, 138–9, 318
Constantius II, 70, 169, 362
Constitutio Antoniniana, 330
consumption (food), 105–6, 109–10, 112–14, 181, 198, 208, 219, 269, 287–9, 291–2
contests, 149, 315, 320, 322, 336
cooking pots/vessels/wares, 70, 78, 97–8, 102–6, 112, 192, 246, 255–8, 262, 381–7, 392
copper, 73, 90, 104–5, 183, 185–6, 191, 199, 201–2, 204–7, 219, 237, 239, 241, 248–9, 252, 259, 261–3, 265, 395
copy, 62, 93, 165, 191, 310, 319–20, 325, 357
Corbulo, Cn. Domitius Corbulo, 327
cores, 270, 272–5, 277, 288
Corinth, 202, 259, 263–4
Corinthian (capitals, order), 20, 39, 45, 50, 90, 167, 185
Cormack, J.M.R., 327
cornice, 20, 44–5, 48, 53, 76, 79, 83, 85, 88, 116–18, 155, 189, 231, 233, 246, 307, 309–10
corrector, 317
corrosion, 202, 208, 371
costs, 35, 90, 96
costume, 161, 167, 169, 171–2, 180, 206
council, 64, 119, 169, 188, 205, 227, 229–30, 318–20, 322
    Council of Florence (AD 1439), 230
    Council of Nicaea (AD 787), 229
    Sixth Ecumenical Council (AD 680), 188, 205, 227
    town council, 64, 119
cows, 291
craftsmen, 20, 80, 88, 90
cranial, 270, 272, 274, 277–8, 282, 284, 288
Crema, Luigi, 4
Crete, 35, 226
Crimea, 205, 258
crops, 106, 110–12, 213, 215, 218, 267, 288
crosses, 26, 55, 65, 86, 91–2, 121–2, 127–8, 130, 132–3, 135, 140, 142–6, 148–50, 153, 183, 185, 195, 205, 228–9, 239, 259, 297, 318, 333–50, 352–4, 364–5, 367–72, 394
crystal, 234–5, 237, 241, 243, 248–9, 251–2, 261
cuirass, 358–9, 367–9
cups, 128, 143, 146
currency, 43, 307

Cyclades, 219, 230
Cyclops, 154, 163, 165, 310–11
Cyperaceae, 109–10, 211–12, 216
cypress, 76, 106–7, 109–10, 112–13, 126, 214, 217–18
    Cupressus sempervirens, 217
Cyprus, 97
Cyrenaica, 44
Cyzicus, 92, 94–5, 189–90, 226, 361–4, 369–70

dado, 50–1
daemon, 205
dagger, 252, 261
Dandalas, 97, 110, 229
Daphne, 120
de Chaisemartin, Nathalie, 4–6, 8–9, 15–16, 18, 20–1, 23, 33–4, 36, 42–3, 45, 74–5, 78, 82, 84, 88, 91, 172, 327
de La Genière, Juliette, 6, 15
deacon, 229
decree, 16, 138, 230, 307–8, 310, 319–20, 331
dedications, dedicatory inscriptions, 15, 16, 20, 34, 39, 41, 43, 45, 52, 67, 89, 117–18, 127, 151, 166, 167, 176, 178, 229, 295–6, 307, 309–13, 316, 318, 322–6, 328
deer, 134, 157, 271–2, 284, 288
    red deer (*Cervus eleaphus*), 271
    roe deer, 271, 284
deified (emperors), 92, 295, 311, 361
deity, 160, 178, 325
Delos, 44, 139
Delphi, 331
demolition, 75, 327
demonetization, 62
demos, 4, 16, 41, 61, 170, 309, 311, 325–6, 359
Demosthenes, 160
denarii, 35, 62, 360–1
depopulation, 225, 227, 300
destruction, 10–11, 13, 16, 49, 62, 65, 69, 80, 88, 117–18, 125, 185, 189, 191, 207, 219–28, 230–1, 235, 259, 266, 278, 287, 289, 295, 298, 300, 310, 317, 358, 389
diadem, 174, 179, 367
dice, 142, 319
Didyma, 143, 145, 226, 313, 317
diet, 105–6, 110–13, 269, 288–9, 297
dining, 98, 288–9
Diocese of Asiana, 94
Diocletian, 5, 43, 234–5, 317, 361
    Currency Edict, 43, 93
    Edict on Maximum Prices, 5, 43, 89, 93, 234–5, 237, 239, 307
Diodoros, 330
Diogenes, 4, 8, 16, 20, 34, 39, 41, 52, 117, 163, 167, 170, 234, 295, 307–9, 315
Diogenes Neoteros, 167, 170
Diogenes son of Menandros, 4, 16, 39, 41
Dionysios, 34, 118, 163
Dionysos, 119, 157, 160
Dioskouroi, 158, 160
dish, 97–8, 113, 210, 256–8, 381–5, 387
dogs, 272, 284, 286, 288

Dometeinos, Lucius Antonius Claudius Diogenes Dometeinos, 8
Domitia, 61
Domitian, 60–1, 165, 360
donkeys, 271, 281–5, 288, 293
doorframes, 21, 45, 47, 54–5, 147, 199, 245
Doulkitios, 5, 65–7, 75–7, 79, 86, 90, 114, 116, 119–21, 123–6, 128, 131, 147, 149–51, 153, 161, 169–70, 174, 204, 296–8, 314–15, 324
dowel holes, 47, 53, 83–4, 88
drain, 11, 15, 24–6, 29–30, 32, 67, 69–76, 95, 103–14, 116, 123–6, 178, 180, 192, 217–18, 237, 239, 270–1, 276, 278, 280–1, 286–8, 295, 297, 361–2, 385, 389–90, 392–3
dung, 110, 112, 215
dung beetle, 215
duribe (mint), 374–8
dust, 32, 390–1
dwellings, 245–6, 252, 267, 300

earthquakes, 5, 11, 39, 42, 48, 63–5, 67, 69, 71–2, 74–5, 77, 79, 85–6, 90, 94, 100, 104–5, 113–19, 124–6, 140, 186, 189, 191, 219–21, 223–9, 231, 234–5, 239, 249, 251–2, 288, 297–300, 308–11, 324, 330, 353
Edessa, 191
egg-and-dart/egg-and-tongue, 20, 44–5, 50, 53, 85–6, 91, 172
eggshell, 106, 269, 286–7
Egypt, 35, 191, 221, 259, 284, 288, 373
Elaiussa Sebaste, 196, 198, 205
elder (*Sambucus* sp.), 213, 216
elegaic couplets, 65–6
elm, 217
embassies, 64, 320
empress, 361, 365
enclosures, 66, 90, 241, 243, 245–6, 248, 252, 290, 299, 359
endocarp, 106–8
endowment, 322–3
entablatures, 4, 16, 20, 44, 51, 80, 84–6, 89, 189, 231, 309–10
entasis, 83–4, 88
entrances, 9, 21, 148
Epaphrodeitos, 322, 324
eparch, 195, 202
Ephesos, 9, 41, 60, 62–3, 84–5, 88–9, 92, 97, 111–13, 142, 145, 161, 165, 167, 169–71, 178, 189, 192, 195, 199, 219–21, 226, 257–8, 288–90, 292, 296, 313–14, 330, 359
    Arkadiane, 220
    Curetes street, 220
    East Baths, 63
    Hanghaus 1, 288
    Hanghaus 2, 290
    Library of Celsus, 41, 63
epigrams, 119, 121, 125, 129, 138, 142, 297, 307, 313–15, 318–19, 324, 330
epiphyses, 272–7, 279–81, 283–4, 286
epitaphs, 127, 130, 307, 321, 327–31
Epithymia, 349
equids, 186, 270–3, 281–9, 291, 293, 298–9
equus, 271, 285
Eresos, 313

Erim, Kenan, 5–6, 8, 10, 13, 74 n. 21, 75, 78, 80, 84, 88 n. 71, 181, 191, 219, 230–1, 249, 254
Eros, 34, 50, 123, 137, 152–5, 158–60, 162–3, 167, 172, 176, 330, 358
Eros pillars, 123, 152, 154–5, 158–60
Erotes, 34, 50, 118, 158, 163, 185, 295, 324
Eskihisar, *see* Stratonikeia
Euboea, 49
euergetism, 64, 125
Eugenia, 326
Eugraphios, 130, 136
Europe, 35
Eusebes, 52, 169
Eusebios, 71, 121, 128, 131, 335
Eutolmius Tatianus, 172, 174
exostosis, 275, 279, 283
exploitation, 269, 289, 291–2

farmsteads, 110, 218, 227
fascias, 50
Fatimid Egypt, 259
Faun, 135
fauna, 133, 286–7, 289
faunal remains, material, 269–71, 286–8, 292
Faustina, 170, 174, 179, 321
feasting, 111–12
Fellows, Charles, 1
festivals, 30, 65, 88, 119–21, 126, 131, 140, 149, 297, 315; *see also* Maiouma
    Brytae festival, 120–1
fig (*ficus carica*), 108, 210, 212, 213, 216, 218
fight, 134, 157–8
fire, conflagration, 102, 104, 112, 124, 189, 217, 219–23, 225–8, 252, 258, 298
fish, 113–14, 134–5, 206, 243, 269, 286–9, 292, 340
Fitna, 226
flasks, 195–6, 199, 234, 254–6, 259, 387, 394
Flavia Attalis Ailiane, 176
Flavian (period), 20, 23, 39, 41–2, 44–5, 51, 53, 59–61, 63, 295–6, 300
Flavians, 309
Flavius Ampelios, 117, 125, 138, 149
Flavius Andronikos, 166
Flavius Constantius, 42, 47–8, 63
Flavius Damocharis, 130
Flavius Eutolmius Tatianus, 172, 174
Flavius Ioannes, 116
Flavius Palmatus, 178
Flavius Papias, 321
Flavius Pelagius Ioannes, 117
Flavius Pythiodoros, 314
flots, 106, 209–10
flowers, 35, 110, 112–13
fodder, 106, 110, 112, 291
food production, 110, 262
fortification, 84, 223, 228, 235, 239, 249, 256, 299
Foss, Clive, 219–21

fountains, 10, 23, 25–9, 36, 67, 71, 113, 118, 123–4, 134–5, 151, 159–60, 162–3, 165–7, 180, 226, 228, 295, 312, 314
fox (*Vulpes vulpes*), 271
friezes, 8, 91
frogs, 29, 135, 167, 180, 286–8, 292
fruits, 106–7, 108, 110–13, 121, 144, 214, 218–19, 327, 340; *see also Prunus avium* (sweet cherry); peaches
fuel, 105, 109–10, 112
funeral, 130, 361

Gabii, 36
gable, 39, 44–5, 296
Gaius Caesar, 59
Gallic Empire, 62–3, 93
Gallienus, 60–2, 93
game counters, 51, 63, 143–7, 204
gameboards, 6, 10, 13, 71, 121, 127–36, 140–9, 297, 300, 307, 333–50, 354
    alea, 140, 142–3
    cross-in-circle, 128, 140, 144–6, 333–40, 342–9, 354
    cross-in-square, 128, 140, 143, 145–6, 333–48, 354
    duodecim scripta, 140, 142–3, 146, 204, 334–5, 338–41, 343–4, 346–8
    eight-spoke wheel, 144–6, 333–41, 343–4, 346–8
    mancala, 128, 132, 135, 140, 143, 146, 333–49, 354
    merels, 140, 143–5, 204, 241, 266
    Nine Men's Morris, 140, 145, 266, 307
    round merels (Radmühle, Rundmühle), 140, 145
games, 18, 51, 66, 127–31, 140, 142–50, 204, 234, 237, 239, 241, 243, 248–9, 252, 254, 265–6, 300, 336, 341, 344–6, 349
    three-in-a-row, 144–6
gaming, 147–8, 195, 204, 241, 266, 297
Ganymede, 163
gardens, 10, 11, 13, 30, 33–6, 38, 70, 75–6, 110, 112–13, 204, 246, 251, 254, 289, 295–7, 300
gates, 219, 221, 327
gateway, 44–5, 120, 296
Gaudin, Paul, 4, 16, 44, 159–60, 312
Gaul, 284
Gelimer, 367
genitals, 157–8, 167
gentilicium, 323, 327, 330
genus, 113–14, 285
geographic, 80
Gerasa, 149
Germiyanids, 373–4
gesture, 160, 162, 205
Geta, 120
Geyre, 55, 230, 251–2, 261, 265–7, 289, 300
    Gerye, 230, 249, 252, 267, 299
giants, 155, 157–8, 160, 312
gift, 316
gigantomachy, 123, 157–9
Gıyaseddin Keyhüsrev I (Sultan), 373
Gıyaseddin Keyhüsrev III (Sultan), 373
gladiator, 129–30, 132–4, 327, 349
gladiatorial, 134, 327–8

glass, 70, 78, 104, 106, 143, 183, 185–6, 195–9, 201–2, 206–7, 209, 231, 234–5, 239, 241, 243, 248–9, 251–2, 258–9, 263–5, 298–9, 395; *see also* bangles
    goblets, 196, 198
glaze, 256–8, 262
globe, 361–5
    globus cruciger, 367–71
goats, 134, 158, 205–6, 270–9, 286, 288–92, 299, 348
goblets, 196, 198
godrons taillés, 85, 91
gods, 160, 170, 312, 322
Gordian III (emperor), 60, 359
Gordion, 110–12, 290, 292
Gorence, Justin, 5, 29, 80, 84, 181, 221, 231, 249
Gospel of John, 319
Gothic raids, attacks, 62, 93
governorship, 116, 313, 317
graffiti, 10, 13, 52, 126–37, 140, 144, 146, 147–50, 226, 297, 300, 328, 333–55
grains, 106
grandfather, 308, 316, 323
grapes (*Vitis vinifera*), 50, 106, 107–13, 126, 143, 186–7, 210, 213, 215, 216, 218, 358
grasses, 106–7, 109–10, 212, 214
Gratian, 362–3
grave, 205, 265, 323, 328, 330
Greece, 36, 59, 142, 259
Gregory of Nazianzos, 314
Gritille, 290, 292
grove, 9, 11, 15, 33–6, 38, 63–6, 73, 110, 163, 295–6, 300, 314–16
Grypos, 310–11
Gylou (demon), 205
gymnasium, 4, 6, 8–9, 11, 33, 36, 85, 91, 127, 150, 219, 295–6

Hades, 157, 160
Hadrian, 5–6, 36, 41, 45, 60, 63, 80, 165, 167, 169–70, 172, 296, 312, 315–16, 328, 359–60
hairstyle, 133, 172, 174–6, 178, 180, 333
    bow-knot, 175–6
    Constantinopolitan, 170, 178, 180
    mop, 176, 178, 180
hare (*Lepus* sp.), 271, 284, 288
harvesting, 50
hazelnut (*Corylus avellana*), 108–9, 111–12
Hekataios, 349
Helias (praetorian prefect), 121
Helios, 178
Helladios, 48, 312–13, 318
helmet, 134, 360, 365, 367–70, 372
helmeted, 358, 362, 364–5
hemispherical, 104, 198
Henotikon of Zeno (AD 482), 324
Hephaistos, 157, 160, 307
Heraclea, 95, 312, 364
Heraclian, 192
Heraclius, 185, 187–8, 190–1, 202, 219–21, 223, 227, 298, 369–71, 393

Heraclonas, 370
Herakleia Salbake, 170
Herakles, 45, 155, 157–8, 160
herbs, 110
Herculaneum, 6, 36, 135, 175
    Villa of the Papyri, 6, 36
herds, 288, 291
Hermas, 42
Hermes, 34, 118, 163, 165, 295, 310–11, 360
    Hermes Agoraios, 311
Herod, 36
Herodeion, 36
Herodes Atticus, 63
Herodian, 36, 89
Herodianos, 313
heroes, 157, 160, 162
herons, 133–4
heterogeneity, 91
hexameters, 66, 318
Hierapolis, 20, 49, 90, 116, 125, 220, 223, 235, 239, 266
Hierokles, 171
himation, 123, 155, 158, 160–2, 169–71, 176, 178, 180, 359, 371–2
hinterland, 110, 112–13
Hippos-Sussita, 256
Ḥirbat al-Minya, 255
hoards, 55, 58–9, 62–3, 91–2, 92, 94, 117–18, 191, 219, 221, 223
Honorius, 120, 172, 364
horn cores, 270, 272–5, 277, 288
horses, 48, 121, 134, 158, 165, 176, 179–80, 186–7, 201, 205, 208, 241, 245, 261, 263, 271, 281–5, 293, 348
    thoroughbreds, 263
horseshoes, 239, 248, 251, 263
Horvat Zikhrin, 258
Howard-Johnston, James, 220
'Hullide Mülkuhu' prayer, 373
Hungary (Ottoman), 291
Hydrela, 60, 360
Hygieia, 326
Hypaepa, 60, 360
hypatikos, 66, 116–17
Hypnos, 326

Iasos, 49, 195–6, 198, 226
Iconium, 229, 235
image, imagery, 1, 121, 127–8, 130–1, 133–5, 148–50, 160, 195, 205, 210, 241, 243, 309, 333, 344
impost, 85, 90–1
incubation, 326
indiction, 116–18
inscriptions, 1, 5–6, 9, 16, 34–5, 45, 48, 51–3, 55, 62–3, 65–7, 77, 85, 89, 114, 116–17, 119, 123, 127–8, 130–2, 136, 139, 148–9, 153, 161–2, 172, 205, 296–7, 300, 307–8, 312–15, 317–21, 323, 325–8, 350, 353–4
invasions, 62, 183, 191, 207, 219–21, 227, 298
invocations, 130, 154, 206, 336, 341–2
Ioannes, 116–17, 136, 149, 318

Ionia, 1, 359
Ionic (capitals, colonnade, columns, frieze, order), 1, 18, 20, 39, 43, 47, 53, 73, 80–1, 83–5, 88–91, 183, 235, 241, 243, 245–6, 266
iron, 24, 47, 54, 79, 104, 110, 117, 183, 185, 199, 201–2, 204–8, 225, 235, 237, 239, 248, 251–2, 259, 261–2, 265–6
Isaias of Stavropolis (bishop), 230
Isaurian raids, 319
Isidore of Seville, 142
Israel, 59, 91, 94, 189
Istanbul, 85, 175, 196, 198, 201–2, 217, 284; see Constantinople
Italy, 163, 207, 284, 365
Izmir, 96
Iznik, 130, 330

Jacopi, Giulio, 4–6, 9, 16, 20, 33, 74–5, 231, 252, 254,
javelin, 183, 207–8, 225, 298
Jerash, 36, 119–21
Jericho, 9, 36
Jerusalem, 36, 91, 228
Jesus (invocations of), 130, 134, 336, 347; see also Christ
Jews, 128, 130, 134, 149–50
Johannes (emperor AD 423–5), 94
John Chrysostom, 120, 205
John Malalas, *Chronographia*, 119–21
John the Lydian, *De Mensibus*, 120
Jordan, 36
jug/jar, 383–4, 386
Julia Domna, 361
Julia Faustina, 174, 179, 321
Julian, 119–20, 169, 171, 317–18
Jupiter, 169, 361
Justin I, 189, 202
Justin II, 191, 367–8
Justinian, 169, 183, 185, 189, 191, 221, 318, 367, 369, 393
Justinianic Plague, 126, 219
juvenile, 276, 282, 284, 289, 291

Kallikrates, 310–11
Kallikrates Grypos, 310
Kaman-Kalehöyük, 270, 280–3, 291–2
Kamiros, 128
Karacasu, 55, 62, 246, 265
Karahisar, 49
Karamanids, 374
Karasura (Bulgaria), 208
Karia, 48, 55, 65–6, 91, 116, 131, 183, 189, 191, 195, 202, 220–1, 226–30, 249, 257, 299, 313, 315–18, 358–60
Karians, 65, 314, 318
Karrhae/Harran, 191–2
Kasserine (Tunisia), 66
Katakekaumene, 135
Kaunos, 139
Kay Khusraw(Sultan), 229, 235
Kaystros (river), 170
Kenchreai, 199
Kermes oak, 76, 106, 109–10, 113, 126, 215

Kestros (river), 170
Keykubad I, 373
Kibyra, 142, 195
Klaros, 52, 139
Klaudia Melitine, 176
Knidos, 195, 226
knives, 204, 225, 237, 252, 261, 291
Kolotron, 130, 133, 333
Konya, 229, 374
Koresia, 128
Korucutepe, 291–2
Kos, 36, 142, 226, 230
Kosovo, battle of, AD 1448, 266 n. 277
Krateros, 321–2, 324
Krispos, 139
Kumluca peninsula, 35
Kybele, 178, 221–3, 225, 227, 358
Kyriakos (trouser-maker), 206

Labienus, 319
Laborde, Alexandre, 1, 254
Ladstätter, Sabine, 92, 96–7, 100, 220
Laikanios, 43
lamps, 47, 78, 83, 127, 134, 183, 186, 196, 198, 201, 231, 385
lanes, 230, 241, 243, 246, 248, 299–300
Laodikeia, 38, 116, 125, 135, 142, 145, 220, 223, 235, 313, 330
lapith, 157
latrine, 111, 218
Lauriacum, 207
law, 65–6, 314, 318–20
lead, 24, 53, 91, 94, 130, 146, 185, 188, 198–9, 204–6, 213, 230, 234, 266, 271, 351, 365
leaf, 11, 76, 85, 91, 109, 186, 201, 207, 209, 212, 215, 234, 258, 261–2, 266, 320, 338
leather-cutting, 104, 252, 261
legio III Gallica, 327
Legio Prima Parthica Severiana Antoniniana, 327
legumes, 106–7, 109, 111–13, 214, 219
Lemaire, Anca, 6
Lenaghan, Julia, 169, 172, 174–5, 178, 180
lentils (*lens culinaris*), 106–8, 111–12, 214, 255
Leo III, 371
Leo VI, 371
Leochares, 165
Leontia (wife of Phocas), 369
Lepcis Magna, 9, 145–6
Lepidus, Marcus Lepidus, 154, 159
Lesbian cyma, 19, 53
Levant, 35–6, 121, 191, 297, 370
lewis holes, 53, 84–5
Libanius, 120
Libius Severus, 92, 94
Lightfoot, Christopher, 206, 227, 259, 263, 266
lime, 33, 97, 255–8, 390
Limyra, 58, 86, 195, 290, 292
Linant de Bellefonds, Pascale, 151, 154–5, 157–60, 170, 312
Lindos, 36

437

lions, 18, 20, 67, 94, 116, 134, 149, 310, 349, 364, 373–4, 377
lions'-claw, 67, 116
Livia, 4, 16, 295
Londinium, 93–4, 361
loom, 234, 237, 239, 262
loomweights, 186, 231, 234–5, 237, 239, 241, 243, 245, 248–9, 251–2, 261–2
louteria, 119
Lucius Antonius Claudius Diogenes Dometeinos, 8
Lucius Verus, 62, 327
Lugdunum, 360
Lycia, Lycian, 58–9, 62, 63, 86, 226
Lydia, Lydian, 61, 63, 120, 358, 360
Lykos, Lykos Valley, 220, 223, 330

M. Cocceius Antipatros Ulpianus, 45
Macrinus, 60, 359
Madauros, 35
Maeander, 60, 62, 96–7, 170, 192, 207, 219, 235, 251, 359
Maezei, 307
magical, 132, 195, 205–6, 346
Magnesia, 317
Magnesia ad Sipylum, 55, 59, 358
Mahmud I, 373, 377
Mahmud II, 373, 377
Maiouma, 30, 65, 88, 119–21, 126, 131, 149, 297, 300, 315
mammals, 269, 274, 284, 286
mandibles, 270, 275–80, 281–2, 284, 291
mangirs, 248, 251, 373, 376
Manisa, 246, 257
Manzikert, battle of, AD 1071, 229
mappa, 201, 368–9
marble, 5–6, 8–10, 18, 21, 23–5, 29–30, 33–5, 38, 42–3, 45, 47–51, 63–4, 67, 69–71, 74, 77–8, 80, 82–6, 88–91, 113–14, 117–19, 123–6, 135, 140, 146–7, 149, 151, 153–4, 157, 161–3, 165–7, 169, 175, 178–81, 183, 185–9, 191, 198–9, 204, 206, 209, 217, 221, 225–6, 228, 234, 237, 239, 241, 243, 245–6, 249, 252, 254, 266, 295–6, 298, 300, 307–8, 310–13, 315–22, 324–31, 350, 355, 393, 395
    africano (*marmor luculleum*), 49, 51
    alabastro fiorito, 49–51
    cipollino (*marmor carystium*), 49
    giallo antico (*marmor numidicum*), 49
    granito bianco e nero, 49
    nero antico, 49
    pavonazzetto (*marmor phrygium*), 49–51
    portasanta, 49–51, 69, 204
    rosso antico, 49
    serpentino (*marmor lacadaemonium*), 49–51, 146
    verde antico (*marmor thessalicum*), 49
Marcellinus Comes, 116
Marcian, 73, 92, 104, 364, 391
Marcus Aurelius Claudius Ktesias, 327
Marcus Aurelius Krateros, 324
Marcus Aurelius Krateros V Athenagoras, 324
Marcus Lepidus, 154
marine food, shellfish, shells, 113, 286, 288–9
Mark Antony, 327

markets, 41, 97, 111, 145, 191, 147, 198, 204, 246, 249, 298–9, 300
    marketplace, 5, 9, 188, 195, 200–1, 203, 227–8, 298
Markianos, 317, 322–3
Maron (satyr), 163
Martial, 35, 146
Martina, 370
masks, 20, 91, 266
masons' marks, 52, 67, 89, 127, 132, 136–40, 297, 300, 333, 340–1, 349–50, 352
Mauremys sp., *see* turtles
Maurice, 191, 367–8, 370
    Strategikon, 208
Maximian, 361
meat, 275, 277, 288–9, 291–2
Mehmed II (Sultan), 241, 266, 373, 375
Mehmed III (Sultan), 251, 373, 377
Mehmed V Resad (Sultan), 373
Melitene, 220
Melpomene, 159
Men Askainos, 310
Menander, 47
Menandros, 4, 16, 39, 41, 174–5, 295, 307–9, 315, 321–2, 324
Mendel, Gustave, 4, 312, 330, 350
Menemen, 246
Menodotos (sculptor), 171, 325
menorah, menoroth, 121, 127–8, 130, 132–4, 146, 150, 336–7, 339–40, 344, 350–1
Menteshe beylik, 229–30, 373–4
mesh, 106, 269
metacarpals, 269, 271, 275, 278, 285–6
metal, 29–30, 47, 53–4, 114, 123, 149, 178, 183, 185–6, 188, 196, 198–201, 203, 206–7, 209, 220, 225, 231, 234, 239, 241, 243, 245, 248–9, 251–2, 254, 258, 261, 298–9, 378–9, 393, 395
metalworking, 261
metapodials, 271, 274–5, 277–8, 281, 285, 288
metatarsal, 270, 285–6
Metrodoros, 322
mice, 286
Milas, 189
Milasa, 229
Miletos, 9, 41, 63, 142, 170, 189, 235, 257–8
milk, 277, 291–2
millet, 111–12, 218
millstones, 248–9, 251, 262
mineralized, 105–6, 111
mints, 55, 58–62, 94–5, 185, 189–91, 362–5, 369–71, 373–6
    Ottoman (*see also duribe*)
        Ayasuluk, 373, 375
        Bursa, 373, 375–6
        Edirne, 373, 376
        Enguriye, 373, 376
        Halep, 373, 376
        Kostantiniyye, 373, 376–8
        Ladik, 373, 375
        Misr (Egypt), 373

Novar, 376
Serez, 373,
Sidrekapsi, 251 n. 140, 373, 377
Tire, 248, 373, 375–7
Roman
Arelate (Arles), 94 n. 113
Mircea I Batran, 372
Moesia, 327
molars, 269–70, 278–9, 281–2
mole rat (*Nannospalax* sp.), 271
moles (*Arvicolinae*), 11, 230, 271, 284, 286
Molossos, 42, 310–11, 326
Mongols, 229
monograms, 66, 89–90, 116, 125, 131–2, 136–8, 188, 192, 195, 205, 297, 318, 333–5, 338–40, 342, 344, 346–7, 353, 358, 364–5, 368, 370
Mopsuestia, 314
Morocco, 292
Morsynos, 110, 112–13, 170, 172, 217–18, 227
mortality, 277, 291
mortar, 6, 24–5, 30, 48, 69–70, 74–5, 78, 113, 124–5, 185, 204, 237, 249, 389–92, 395
mosaic, 1, 11, 43, 45, 47, 63, 79, 114, 128, 134, 145, 172, 297, 313, 318
motifs, 84–5, 88, 90–1, 195, 256, 258–9, 263, 376
mould-made, 251, 257–8, 266
mudbrick, 245–6, 248, 252
mules, 281, 283–4
Murad II (Sultan), 241 n. 60, 373, 375–6, 378
murex, 186, 243, 248, 251, 286
Hexaplex trunculus, 286
Muses, 159, 163
musket ball, 241, 266
Myndos, 220
Myon, 52, 79, 148, 169
Myon Adrastos, 52
Myon Eusebes, 169
Myon Eusebes Philopatris, 52
Myra, 198

Nabataea, 36
narthex, 88, 119
Naxos, 135
needle, 202, 248, 261–2
neopoios, neopoioi, 320, 322–4
Nero, 36, 49, 60–1, 308–9, 327, 359
Nerva, 15, 39, 41, 52, 167, 169–71, 296, 309–10, 312, 315
net, 202, 206
Nerva, 312
Nicaea, 119, 121, 196, 198, 229
Nicephorus II, 371
niche, 42, 169, 243, 245–6
Nicomedia, 92, 94–5, 185, 189–90, 361–2, 364, 367–70
Nike, 309–10, 360
Nikephoros, 59
Niketas Choniates, 229
Nikolaos, 331
Nikomachos, 325

Nikopolis, 36
Nile, 170
nimbus, 371–2
North Africa, 35, 49, 62, 110, 189–90, 367
nuts, 106–13, 214–16, 218–19; *see also* hazelnuts, *Prunus dulcis* (almond), walnuts
nymphaeum, 5, 47, 63, 80, 123, 170, 312
nymphs, 9, 34, 36, 65–6, 90, 121, 296, 314, 324
Nysa, 199

oak (*Quercus* sp.), 76, 106, 109–10, 112–13, 126, 205, 212, 214–16, 225, 288
Quercus coccifera, 106, 109, 212, 216
Quercus ilex, 212, 216
oats (*Avena* sp.), 109–10, 214
Octavian, 9, 310
odeion, 221, 265
Odovacar, 94, 365
Odysseus, 163, 165, 311
offerings, 111–13, 121, 126
oil, 47, 78, 110–13, 126, 199
olives (*Olea europaea*), 106–13, 126, 212, 214, 216, 218, 259, 361
orchestra, 67, 117, 120
orders, 91, 318
orthostats, 21, 48
Ostia, 86, 119, 142, 145
ostrich, 134, 333, 349
Ottoman Empire, 258, 373, 375
Ottomans, 230
Ovid, *Ars Amatoria*, 144–5
oysters (*Ostrea edulis*), 254, 286, 288

Pachymeres, 229
painting, 33, 35, 134, 256–7, 264–5
palaces, 36
Palestina Secunda, 202
Palestine, 226, 255, 291
palms, 11, 33, 35, 76, 109, 148, 296
Cretan date palm (*Phoenix theophrasti*), 10, 33, 35, 109, 209, 296
Date palm (*Phoenix dactylifera*), 109
Palmyra, 143
paludamentum, 359, 367
Pamphylia, 62, 189, 220
Panhellenion, 313
Papias, 321
parameters, 80, 83, 157
parapet, 123, 151, 154–5, 159–60, 162
parcels, 239, 243, 252, 299
Parion, 63, 92
park, 9, 13, 34, 43, 65, 73–4, 84, 86, 88, 104, 133, 137, 148–9, 151, 154, 176, 183, 188, 199, 202, 216, 218, 229, 259, 295, 300
Parthians, 327
Pasargadae, 36
pathological, 269, 275, 283
pathologies, 275, 278–9, 283, 288, 291

abscess, 279
exostosis, 275, 279, 283
patris, 178
patrons, 63, 80, 89–90
Paul, Gerhard, 155
Paulleina, 43
peaches (*Prunus persica*), 108, 111–13, 186, 212, 216–18
peacock, 97, 134, 149, 192, 344, 347, 349, 386
pearl, 234, 362–4
pebbles, 25, 143
pedestals, 43–5, 47, 77, 83, 118, 296
pellets, 371, 374, 376
Peloponnese, 146
pelvis, 269, 275, 278, 283
pendant, 166, 179, 185, 188, 205–7, 241, 251, 259, 261, 265
pendilia, 368–71
Pereitas, 310–11
Pereitas Grypos, 311
performances, 119–20
Pergamon, 59, 104, 138, 178, 189, 199, 226, 235, 251, 258, 261–2, 358
Perge, 38, 41, 63, 142, 169–70, 331
Periplus Maris Erythraei, 347
Persia, 228
Persian invasion, war, 183, 191, 207, 219–21, 226–8, 298
personifications, 163, 169–71, 178–80, 322
Pessinus, 288–90, 292
pestle, 185, 243, 249, 251–2, 265
Petra, 36
phalanges, 270–1, 274–5, 277–8, 281, 283, 285, 286, 288, 291
phallus, 121, 128, 133–4, 150, 248, 265, 336, 339
Phaselis, 63
Phellus, 59
Philadelphia, 246
Philip, 42, 60, 62, 66, 125, 139, 309, 359
Philip I, 60, 62, 359
Philippos, 89, 162, 174, 297, 313
Philomelion, 229
Phocaea, 96
Phocas, 74, 126, 185, 191, 220–1, 223, 228, 369–70, 391
Phrygia, 49, 86, 142, 229, 316–17, 360
physiognomy, 176, 178
Piazza Armerina, 145
Picenini, Antonio, 320
pigs (*sus*), 60, 270–1, 273–4, 278–83, 286, 289–92, 299
pilasters, 49–51, 69, 176, 185, 187, 189, 234
pilgrim flask, 234, 254–6, 387, 394
pillars, 1, 123, 133, 134, 139, 152–5, 157–60, 175, 351
pilum, 207, 225
pine, 33, 76, 106–13, 126, 157–8, 186–7, 212, 214–15, 217–18, 288, 292, 360
Pinus sp., 107–8, 212, 214, 216–18
Pinus brutia, 217–18
Pinus pinea, 108, 212, 214, 216–17
Turkish red pine, 217
pine cones, 76, 112, 186–7, 217–18
pins, 47–8, 54, 183, 199
pips, 107–8, 143, 213

pipeline, 25–6, 32–4, 67, 70–1, 74, 78, 113, 123–4, 286, 297, 391
Pisidia, 38, 62, 220–1
pitcher, 97, 386
pithoi, 103, 257, 383, 385
pivot, 202
plague, 62, 93, 126, 219
Justinianic Plague, 126, 219
Plague of Cyprian, 62
plane, 20, 33, 35
planks, 135, 183, 185, 187, 189, 393
planning, 11, 23
planting beds, 32–4, 96
planting pits, 35–6, 75–6, 95, 148, 384
planting trenches, 10, 31, 33–4, 73, 75–6, 106, 270, 288, 296, 381, 390
plants, 10, 32–3, 75–6, 85, 105–6, 110, 112, 186–7, 208–10, 213, 215–19, 225, 298
agrimony (*Agrimonia* sp.), 211, 216
Apiaceae, 109, 211, 216
blackberry (*Rubus fruticosus*), 186, 210, 213, 215–16, 219
black-bindweed (*Fallopia convulvulus*), 109
black horehound (*Ballota nigra*), 211, 213, 216
borage (Boraginaceae), 211
bulrush (*Schoenoplectus lacustris*), 186, 187, 209–11, 215–16
Chara sp., 186, 209–10
chickweed (*Stellaria* sp.), 213, 216
common reed (*Phragmites australis*), 211
corn salad (*Valerianella* sp.), 213, 216
daisy (*asteraceae*), 209, 211, 216
dock (*Rumex* sp.), 109
duckweed (*Lemna* sp.), 209, 211, 213, 215
fabaceae, 107, 109–10, 214
field madder (*Sherardia arvensis*), 106, 109–10
figworts (*Scrophulariaceae*), 213, 216
fleaworts (*Plantago* sp.), 109
fool's watercress (*Apium nodiflorum*), 215
foxtail millet (*Setaria italica*), 112
fumitory (*Fumaria* sp.), 212, 216
goosefoot (*Chenopodium* sp.), 109–10, 211–213, 216, 218
gromwell (*Lithospermum* sp.), 216
gymnospermae, 216
henbane (*Hyoscyamus* sp.), 212, 216
horehound (*Marrubium* sp.), 216
horned pondweed (*Zannichellia* sp.), 211
juniper (*Juniperus* sp.), 109, 217
knotgrass (*Polygonum cf. aviculare*), 109
knotweed (*Persicaria* sp.), 109, 212, 216
madder (*Rubiaceae* sp.), 109
mallow (*Malva* sp.), 209, 212, 216, 218
marigold (*Calendula* sp.), 211
medick (*Medicago*), 109–10, 210, 212, 214, 216, 218
melilot (*Melilotus* sp.), 109–10
mint (*Lamiaceae*), 212, 216
mullein (*Verbascum* sp.), 213, 216
mustard, 106, 108, 110
nettle (*Urtica* sp.), 213, 216

nightshade (*Solanum* sp.), 213, 216, 218
parsley (*Apiaceae*), 109
Poaceae, 107, 109–10, 212, 214, 216
pondweed (*Potamogeton* sp.), 209–11, 215, 218
poppy (*Papaveraceae*; *Papaver* sp.), 109, 209
purslane (*Portulaca* sp.), 212, 216
radish (*Raphanus raphanistrum*), 109, 212–13, 216, 218
sedges, 109–10, 211–12
sheep's sorrel (*Rumex acetosella*), 109, 213, 215–16, 218
small-flowered buttercup (*Ranunculus parviflorus*), 212, 216, 218
speedwell (*Veronica* sp.), 109
stonewort (*Chara* sp.), 209–10
sun spurge (*Euphorbia helioscopia* sp.), 212–13, 216, 218
thistle (*Cirsium* sp.), 211, 216
vervain (*Verbena officinalis*), 209, 213, 215–16, 218
vetch (*Vicia ervilia*), 106–8, 214
watercress (*Nasturtium* sp.), 211
water horehound (*Lycopus* sp.), 211
weld (*Reseda* sp.), 213, 216
plaques, 136–40, 149, 169, 178, 201, 206, 313, 324, 335, 339, 350
Plarasa, 58–9, 320, 358
plastron, 285, 288–9
Pliny, 35, 111
Pliska, 188
plume, 367–70
plums, 111–12
Plutarch, 131
Pococke, Richard, 1
podia, 151
pollen, 111, 218
Polykrates, 329
Polyphemos, 163, 165, 295, 311
pomegranate (*Punica granatum* sp.), 111–13
Pompeii, 35–6, 112, 114, 344
pond turtle, 271, 285, 288
pool (in Place of Palms), 1, 6, 8–11, 13, 15, 18, 20–1, 23–30, 32–4, 36, 38, 48–51, 58–9, 63–77, 80, 82, 86, 88–9, 104–6, 110, 112–14, 116–21, 123–40, 142–3, 146–51, 161–3, 165–7, 172, 174–6, 178–81, 183–9, 191–6, 198–9, 201–2, 204–10, 213, 215–19, 222–3, 225–31, 234–5, 237, 239, 241, 243, 245–6, 254, 261–2, 266–7, 269–78, 280–2, 284–9, 292, 295–300, 314–15, 325–6, 329, 333–4, 338, 353, 355, 357–8, 361–2, 385–7, 389–95
    cattle ramp, 6, 188, 192, 219, 225–7, 231, 234–5
    overflow, 29–30, 71–2, 124
    ring drain, 15, 24–6, 30, 32, 67, 69–73, 75, 95, 103–6, 110–14, 116, 124–6, 178, 180, 192, 217–18, 237, 239, 270–1, 276, 278, 280–1, 286–8, 295, 297, 361, 385, 389–90, 392–3
    seats, 5–6, 13, 18, 21, 23–6, 29–30, 33–5, 42, 45, 55, 67, 69–72, 74, 77–9, 82, 88–9, 114, 116–17, 123, 127–9, 131–3, 136–7, 139–40, 142–3, 146–8, 153, 166, 187–8, 204, 228, 231, 234, 241, 249, 295, 318, 323, 333, 336, 338, 340–9, 355, 390
    sedimentation, 11, 186, 270, 287

pools (ornamental, outside Aphrodisias), 6, 8, 24, 35–8, 63, 120, 295
pork, 289, 292
porphyry, 50–1, 146, 204
portal, 15, 43–5
portico, 1, 4–6, 8, 13, 15–16, 24, 29, 32–3, 36, 47, 64, 69–70, 72, 75, 80, 84, 120, 136, 139, 163, 175, 181, 183, 186, 188, 199, 204, 207–8, 219, 221, 225, 231, 235, 237, 245, 249, 254, 300, 307–9, 326, 330, 342, 350–1, 373, 376
porticus, 9, 11, 13, 35–6, 163, 295–6, 300
    Porticus Vipsania, 35
portraits, 59, 117, 161, 163, 166–7, 169–72, 174–6, 178–81, 186–7, 243, 296, 298
portraiture, 172, 174
Poseidonios, 322–3
postholes, 11, 230, 246, 298
Postumus, 63
pottery, 11, 32–3, 70–1, 74, 94–7, 104, 116, 126, 146, 186, 188, 204, 209, 221, 246, 254–8, 261, 266, 297, 299, 390–1
    Aegean Ware, 256
    ARS/C, 96, 381, 383
    Biscuit Ware, 255
    Brown Flecked Sgrafitto Ware, 257
    Brown Painted Ware, 256
    Celadon Ware, 258
    Chinese imports, 258
    cooking pots, 102–3, 192, 255, 257–8
    Cypriot Sigillata, 96, 104, 381–2, 384
    Eastern Sigillata B, 32
    glazed, 239, 246, 254, 256–8, 262, 299, 381, 384–6, 394–5
    Green Flecked Sgrafitto Ware, 257
    Gritty Cook Ware, 97
    Late Roman Sigillata, 96, 382
    lids, 102–3, 123, 257
    Local Brittle Ware, 98
    Miletos Ware, 257
    Ottoman Plain Glazed Ware, 258
    Ottoman Slip-Painted Ware, 258
    Painted Fine Sgrafitto Ware, 256
    Phocaean Red Slip, 96, 192
    Slip-Painted Ware, 256, 258
    Spotted Ware, 258
    Stained Sgrafitto Ware, 256
    Tan Micaceous Ware, 97
    unglazed, 254, 256–7
    Zeuxippus Ware, 256
praenomen, 137, 312, 322
Praetorian prefect, 121, 154, 167, 172, 174
prayers, 52, 121, 128, 130, 133, 135, 136, 149–50, 160, 297, 326, 333, 340, 354, 373
presses, 110, 113
prices, *see* Diocletian, Edict on Maximum Prices
Priene, 96
priests, 320, 322–3, 328
Primus, 130, 327
prince, 165, 176, 179
privileges, 320

441

Procopius, 116
Propertius, 35
prow, 25, 361, 364
pruning, 105, 110, 112–13, 202, 261
Prunus avium (sweet cherry), 108
Prunus dulcis (almond), 107–8
Prunus persica, *see* peaches
Pseudo-Sebeos, 220
Ptolemais, 139
    House of Leukatios, 139
pulses, 107–8, 110
pulvinus, 19, 53–4
pyrgos, 171–2
Pyrrhos, 321
Pytheas, 118, 121, 162
Pythiodoros, 65–6, 314, 324
Pythodoros, 310

quarries, 49, 64, 67, 77, 89–90, 130, 138, 172
Quercus, *see* oak
quern, 262

rachis, 108, 214
radiates, 60, 62, 93, 95, 361
rafters, 20–1, 23, 41, 80, 117, 183, 185, 187, 189, 393
raids, 62, 183, 189, 191–2, 207, 219–20, 225–9, 257, 287, 298, 300, 319
rats, 286
Ratté, Christopher, 8, 219
Rautman, Marcus, 220
Ravenna, 94, 365
Red Sea, 114
reeds, 19, 33, 112, 170, 211, 298, 359
reliefs, 10, 18–20, 83, 85, 89, 91, 123, 139, 151–5, 157–60, 162–4, 168, 170, 172–3, 177–9, 205, 223, 256–8, 263, 298, 307, 311–12, 325–7, 327–30, 351, 353
    mythological reliefs, 123, 151, 154–5, 159–60, 162, 223, 298
religious conflict, 121, 129, 150, 324
repairs, 21, 24–5, 34, 39, 41–2, 48, 51–4, 63, 65–9, 71–2, 77, 79, 86, 91, 113–14, 116–18, 121, 124–6, 130, 138–40, 147, 149, 174, 191, 204, 226, 228, 230, 297–8, 300, 311–14, 324–5
reptiles, 269, 285
residues, 106, 209–10
revenues, 139
Reynolds, Joyce, 8, 308, 333
rhetoric, 136, 149
Rhodes, 219, 226, 230, 353
Rhodopaios, 162
rider, 188, 205, 373
rings, 239, 246, 248, 251, 259, 264
rituals, 109, 113, 326
rivers, 15, 66, 77, 110, 112, 129, 170, 172, 217, 227, 237, 239, 286, 296, 324, 351, 359–60, 394
Robert, Louis, 55, 174
rodents, 286
Roman empire, 112, 127, 129–30, 208

Romanus I, 371
Rome, 4, 9, 11, 13, 35, 38, 47, 51, 63–4, 90, 92, 94, 139, 145, 148, 163, 169–70, 295–6, 300, 313–14, 361, 363
    Basilica Julia, 145, 148
    Campus Martius, 36
    Domus Aurea, 36
    Horrea Agrippiana, 145
    Portico of Pompey, 35, 163
    Templum Pacis, 35, 165, 170
root, 32–3, 35, 272, 278
Rose, Brian, 308
Roueché, Charlotte, 333
roundel, 198, 371
rudder, 135, 359
Rupkite/Ripkit, 208

sack, 102, 191, 195, 219–21, 225–8, 291, 298, 300
Sagalassos, 110–12, 125–6, 142–3, 195, 205–6, 218–19, 227, 288–92
Sakarya river, 112
Salamis, 169, 205
Salonina, 60, 62, 359
Samos, 97, 169, 317
Saraçhane, 202, 256, 258
Sardis, 47, 58–60, 63, 85, 91–2, 94, 104–5, 143, 145, 188–9, 192, 196, 198–9, 202, 204, 206–7, 219–21, 259, 266, 313, 360
    Sardis Hoard, 91
Saruhanid, Saruhanids, 243, 373–4
Sasanian, Sasanians, 207, 208, 219–20
satyr, 135, 163, 165, 172, 175, 351
scales, 183, 188, 210
scapula, 270, 274, 286, 288
sceptre, 358, 360–1, 364–5, 367–9, 371
scroll, 50–1, 172, 181, 185, 234
sculptors, 64, 84, 88, 90, 116–17, 125, 149, 165, 171–2, 176, 178, 265, 307, 324–5
sculpture, 25–6, 29, 62, 117, 133–5, 163–8, 172–3, 177–81, 187, 243, 265, 295–6, 298, 300, 312
sculptures, 29, 135, 166–7
sea, 110–11, 113–14, 120, 220, 286
seals, 188, 195, 205, 229, 257
seasonings, 108, 110–11
seed, 76, 106–12, 143, 186, 209–10, 213–15, 218
Selene, 158, 160
Seleukeia, 323
Selim I, 373, 376
Seljuk, 229, 231, 235, 237, 239, 256–7, 261, 266–7, 270–2, 276–8, 280–1, 287, 289, 299, 378, 389, 394
Seljuk Empire, 229
Seljuk-Beylik, 239, 270, 272, 276–8, 280–1, 287
Seljuks, 229, 239, 256–7
Septimius Severus, 60–1, 120, 148, 327, 359–60
Severus Alexander, 62
Severus of Antioch, 120
sewer, 70, 105–6, 113, 126
Shahada, 374
Shahin (Persian general), 220–1, 227

Shahrvaraz (Persian general), 220–1, 227
sheath, 105, 243, 252, 261
sheep, 109, 158, 205–6, 213, 215, 270–9, 286, 288–91, 299
sheep/goats, 270–4, 276–9, 286, 288–9, 291
sheets, 91, 201, 206
shells, 24, 29, 106–9, 113–14, 143, 186, 209, 214, 216, 243, 248, 251, 254, 270, 285–6, 288–9
sherds, 11, 95–7, 106, 257
shield, 134, 206, 208, 362–4, 367–70, 372
shoes, 239, 243, 254, 261, 263, 395
shops, 42, 47, 70, 81, 83, 98, 117, 124–5, 136, 188, 202, 219–21, 223–5, 228
Sicily, 130
Side, 41, 63, 91 n. 107, 94 n. 113, 142, 169, 172 n. 56, 189 n. 74, n. 76, 202, 220, 314 n. 57
Silenoi, 165
silver, 59–60, 62, 188, 205, 259, 261, 264–5, 270
Singara, 327
Sinop, 63
Sisinnios (bishop), 227
skeleton, 234, 265, 271, 273–4, 277, 281–2
Skylla, 165
Skythopolis, 90, 188
Slavs, 219, 220, 225
slaves, 34, 131, 328
slip, 96, 192, 255–8, 262
slope, 15, 18, 21, 23, 82, 217, 288
Smaragdos, 52, 312
Smyrna, 35–6, 62–3, 131, 135, 226, 251, 296, 300
snails, 231, 234, 237, 287
  planorbidae, 234–5
Society of Dilettanti, 1, 15, 254
Solon, son of Demetrios, 320
Sophia, wife of Justin II, 367–8
Sophronius of Jerusalem, 228
Sorrento, 325
Sozon (magistrate), 359
Sperlonga, 165
spindle, 104, 192, 237, 248–9, 251–2, 262
spoon, 249, 261–2
Stabiae (Villa Arianna), 33, 75
stars, 114, 241, 320, 335, 359–60, 364–5, 367, 369, 373–4, 376
statues, statuary, 10, 16, 28–9, 34–5, 39, 41, 43, 45, 47–8, 52, 66, 77, 91, 117–18, 121, 123, 133, 135, 142, 149, 151–5, 157–81, 183, 186, 187, 234, 243, 295–6, 298, 300, 307–26, 337, 351, 359–60
  bare-chested, 151, 160–2
  chlamydatus, 174–5
  Elder Magistrate, 174–5
  himation, 123, 155, 158, 160–2, 169–71, 176, 178, 180, 359, 371–2
  Kore-Persephone, 171
  Large Herculaneum type, 175
  Old Fisherman, 180
  togatus, 169, 172, 174–5, 181
  under-lifesize, 170–2, 175, 178–80
  Younger Magistrate, 174–5
statuette, 29, 135, 163, 165–7, 178, 180, 186
Stavropolis, 132, 183, 188, 192, 205, 227–30, 235, 249, 257, 299
steelyard, 188, 202, 220
stephane, 59, 175, 178, 180, 358
stephanephoria, 316, 328
stephanephoros, 316, 320, 328
stirrups, 183, 208, 225, 287, 298
stoa, 1, 4–6, 8–11, 13, 15–21, 23–4, 30, 32–5, 39, 41–57, 63, 65–7, 69, 71–91, 114, 116–18, 121, 123, 125–40, 145–9, 153, 163, 165, 167, 171–2, 174–6, 178–81, 183, 185–9, 196, 198–9, 201–2, 204, 206, 213, 217–18, 220–1, 223, 225–8, 231, 233–5, 237, 239, 241, 243, 245–6, 249, 251, 254, 295–9, 307–13, 321, 324, 327, 330, 333, 341, 349–55, 389, 390–3; *see also* porticos
stool, 158, 160
storks, 134, 285
Strabo, 36
Strategikon, 208
Stratonikeia (Eskihisar), 63, 145, 220, 246, 326
stream, 15, 26
streets, 21, 25, 35, 38, 90–1, 246, 288, 299–300
  colonnaded streets, 38, 91
stylobate, 5–6, 8, 15–16, 18, 21, 23–4, 34, 42–3, 45, 47, 51–2, 54–5, 63, 67, 71, 75, 77–9, 82–3, 86, 114, 116, 118, 121, 127, 136–40, 147, 153, 175, 221, 295, 341–52
Suleyman, 373–4, 376–8
Suleyman II, 377–8
Sultanate of Rûm, 229, 373
sundials, 327
sword, 175, 219–20, 373
Symeon Logothetes, 136
Synkletos (personification), 61, 359
Syracuse, 189–90, 371
Syria, 97, 119, 191, 291, 327
Syrian gable, 39, 44–5, 296

T. Flavius Staberianos, 326
T. Oppius Aelianus Asklepiodotos, 153, 317
Tabai, 55, 60, 358, 360
tabula ansata, 135, 149, 337
Tantalos, 229
Tarsus, 63, 94, 128, 196, 266, 289–90, 292, 314
Tatianus, 172, 174
Taurus Mountains, 111
Tavas (valley, plain), 32, 170
taxation, 64, 318–19
teeth, 83, 85, 88, 201, 270–1, 274, 277–9, 281–2, 284, 286, 288, 291
Tel Aphek, 258
Tel Naharon, 202
Tell Kurdu, 192
Teos, 49
tesserae, 94, 186, 201, 234, 365
Tetrarchy, Tetrarchic, 60, 91, 92, 93, 357
Tetricus, 62–3, 361
Texier, Charles, 1
textile, 134–5, 149, 204, 206, 221, 261–2, 291

443

Themistokles, 318–19
Theocritus, 311
Theodore, bishop of Stavropolis, 188, 205, 227, 318
Theodorescu, Dinu, 6
Theodoros Mankaphas, 229
Theodosian, 48, 63, 120, 172, 174–5, 180, 186, 297
Theodosioupolis, 220
Theodosius I, 92, 119, 169, 172, 363–4
Theodosius II, 92, 119, 169, 364
Theokritos, 314
Theophrastos, *Characters*, 350
Theophylact (deacon), 229
Theseus, 157
Thessalonica, 92, 189–90, 363, 368
    St Demetrios, 201
Thessaly, 49
Thode, Francis, 6, 13, 24, 26, 69–72, 74, 123, 158, 183, 207, 225
threads, 163, 262–4
Tiberius (emperor), 4, 13, 16, 32, 41, 59–60, 62, 117, 191, 295, 307–8, 360
Tiberius II, 185, Table 7, 191, 368
Tiberius Attalos Agatheinos, 176, 178
Tiberius Capitolinus, 79
Tiberius Claudius Apollonius Beronikianos Akasson, 323
Tiberius Claudius Aurelius Mucianus Apollonius Beronikianos, 323
Tiberius Claudius Markianos, 317, 323, 327
Tiberius Claudius Aurelius, 323
Tiberius Claudius Diogenes, 308
Tiberius Claudius Pauleinos, 327–8
Tiberius Claudius Zenon, 359
Tiberius II, 185, 191, 368
Ticinum, 94
Tigris, 327
tiles, 10, 20, 24–5, 30, 32–3, 49, 69–71, 74–5, 78, 80, 89, 123–4, 140, 183, 185, 187, 189, 196, 221, 234, 246, 252, 259, 266, 298, 389–93
timber, timbers, 20–1, 23, 79, 80, 89, 187, 199, 217, 220–1, 223, 230, 246, 248, 251–2, 287, 299–300, 393
Timeles, 32, 170, 172, 254, 286, 359
Timgad, 148
Timokles, 320
titles, 131, 161–2
Titus (emperor), 43
Titus Antonius Lysimachus Grypos, 311
Titus Flavius, 328
Titus Flavius Athenagoras Agathos, 176
Tivoli, 6, 165, 170
Tlos, 38
tobacco, 258
toga, 161, 169, 171–2, 174
tomb, 261, 265, 328
tong, 205, 249, 261
topos inscription, 9, 47, 52, 55, 63, 127, 131, 136, 140, 149, 297, 300, 335, 341–3, 345–6, 348–9, 353–4
topsoil, 70, 78, 254, 259, 263, 266, 329–30, 395
tortoises, 271, 285–6

torus, 47, 83
tower, 39, 42, 151, 223, 308–9
town, 61, 64, 111, 119, 246, 263, 265, 290–1
Trajan, 43, 52, 60, 62, 145, 167, 309–12, 359–60
Tralles, 59, 65, 219, 230, 314
Trebonianus Gallus, 62
trees, 9, 13, 18, 32–6, 75–7, 109, 111–13, 121, 148, 157–8, 214, 218, 249, 254, 296, 300; *see also* cypress, elm, oaks, pine, palms, willow
Trier, 92, 94
Tripolis, 49, 60–3, 116, 125, 207, 220, 223, 360
Triton, 114
Triton's trumpet (shell), 113–14, 286
Troilos, 160, 165, 176, 179, 187, 295
Trombley, Frank, 219, 313
trophy, 363
True Cross, 228
trumpet, 265, 286, 288; *see also* Triton's trumpet
Tugra, 375, 377–8
tunic, 172, 371–2
Turkomen, 235
Turks, 229
turtles (incl. *Mauremys* sp.), 271, 274, 285–6, 288–9, 292, 299
twigs, 106, 107, 109–10, 112–13, 214
Tyana, 192
Tyche, 135, 359
tympanum, 82–3
Tyre, 119–20

Ulmus, 217
Ulpia Apollonia, 178
Ulpia Carminia Claudiana, 324
Ulpius Apollonios, 327
Ulpius Zenon, 159, 322–3; *see also* Zenas
Umayyad, 188, 190, 255–6, 298, 387
Umur II (Aydinid bey), 373
unguentaria, 96–7, 192, 194–5, 234, 241, 298

Vabalathus, 361
Valens, 362
Valentinian, 94, 172, 174–5, 362–3
Valentinian II, 172, 174–5, 363
Valentinian III, 94
Valerian, 60, 62
Van Voorhis, Julie, 117, 165–6, 174, 180
Vandals, 189–90, 365, 367
Varna, battle of, AD 1444, 266 n. 277
Vegetius, 207
venationes, 134, 149
Venus Genetrix, 180
verandas, 246
Verina, 92
Veronicianus, 318–19
Vespasian, 60, 321, 360
Vesuvian sites, 33, 296
Vesuvius, 75
Vetters, Hermann, 219–20
Victoria, victory, 118, 128, 131, 230, 309–10, 317, 361–5

Vindonissa, 207
vines, 33, 218
Vitis vinifera, see grapes
Vitruvius, 8, 33, 35, 44
votives, 326

Wallachia, 241, 357, 372
walnuts (*Juglans regia*), 107–8, 111–12, 212, 214–16
wars, 220, 228, 310, 319
    civil wars, 310
    Persian wars, 220, 228
waste, 70, 76, 97, 105–6, 109–13, 126, 199, 213, 215, 217–18, 288–9
water, 9, 11, 15, 20, 23–6, 29–30, 32, 35–6, 38, 45, 65, 67, 70–1, 73, 78, 88, 105–6, 113–14, 119–20, 123–6, 130–1, 135, 138, 151, 153, 155, 157, 165–7, 170, 186–8, 192, 208–9, 211, 213, 215–16, 218–19, 221, 226, 228, 234, 254, 258, 267, 286–9, 291, 295–6, 298–300, 314–15, 359
water-powered saw, 67, 77, 118–19
wave, 100, 257, 286, 382, 385
wax, 127, 202
weaponry, 185, 204, 207, 223, 225, 265–6, 298
weeds, 106–7, 109–10, 211, 213–15, 218
Westmacott Ephebe, 171
wheat, 106–8, 110–13, 214, 218, 256
    durum, 107–8
    emmer, 106, 108, 110–12, 214, 218
    free-threshing, 106–8, 110–13, 218
    hulled, 106, 111–12, 214
    spelt, 108
    Triticum, 106–8, 214
    Triticum aestivum, 106–8
Triticum dicoccum, 108
wheel, 131–2, 140, 144–6, 257–8, 333–48, 374
whistles, 243, 265
whorls, 239, 248–9, 251, 262
wick, 112, 198
willow (*Salix* sp.), 213, 216
wine, 110, 112–13, 126, 131, 163, 347
winner, 142–3, 145, 317
withers, 270, 283–5
Wood, Robert, 320

Yassi Ada, 192, 201, 387
Yazid (caliph), 226

Zenas, *see* Zenon, Ulpius Zenon
Zeno (emperor), 94, 116–17, 365; *see also Henotikon*
Zenobios
    Marcus Aurelius Zenobios IV Epaphrodeitos, 324
    Marcus Aurelius Zenobios V Epaphrodeitos, 322, 324
Zenon, 171, 324
    Fl. Zenon, 165–6, 313,
    Tiberius Claudius Zenon, 359
    Ulpius Zenon (also called Zenas), 159, 322–3
Zeugma, 291
Zeus, 16, 132, 167, 307–8, 325, 358–9
    Nineudios, 16, 307–8, 325
    Zeus Lydios, 358
Zeytinlibahçe Höyük, 205
Zoilos, 9, 38, 64, 312, 320
zooarchaeological analysis, 10, 269–70, 299
Zosimus, 62
Zotikos, 136, 349, 354

Pl. 1

A. View down the Place of Palms after excavation in 2017, facing west.

B. View facing east down the Place of Palms, towards the end of excavation in 2017.

PL. 2

A. View down the Place of Palms after excavation in 2017, facing west.

B. View of the western end of the Place of Palms in 2017, facing south.

A. View of city centre in 2017, facing south-west, showing the Place of Palms at upper left.

B. View down Place of Palms and across Theatre in 2017, facing south-west.

Pl. 4

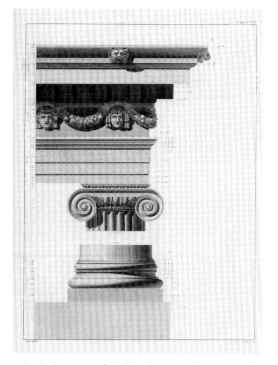

A. Architecture of the North Stoa, as documented by the Society of Dilettanti expedition.

B. View from the Agora south towards the Theatre hill by Alexandre Laborde.

C. Excavations in the west Stoa in 1969, facing north.

D. Excavations along the line of the North Stoa in 1986, facing north-west.

E. Excavations of the fallen colonnade of the North Stoa in 1986, facing north.

Pl. 5

A. Discovery of the late antique inscriptions on the facade of the Propylon in 1980, facing east.

B. Excavation and re-erection of the colonnade of the South Stoa in 1986, facing south-west.

C. Excavation in 1985 of stretch of north side of the pool walls, the function of which at this point was uncertain, facing north-east.

Pl. 6

A. The east end of the Place of Palms in 2011, before the new excavations, looking west.

B. The Place of Palms in 2011, before the new excavations, looking east along the part of the pool excavated in 1988–1990.

C. Zeppelin photograph of the Place of Palms under excavation in 2012, north to top.

PL. 7

A. The centre and western end of the Place of Palms during excavation in 2013, showing trench S.Ag. 13.1 in the foreground with the 2012 trench behind it.

B. The Place of Palms under excavation in 2014, with Ottoman phases being exposed.

C. Excavations of the Phase 9 Ottoman settlement over the pool in the Place of Palms, 2015, facing east.

Pl. 8

Excavation of the Place of Palms in 2016, facing west.

PL. 9

A. Excavation of the rubble deposits at the base of the pool in 2017, facing south-east.

B. The Place of Palms after excavation in 2017, facing west.

C. The Place of Palms during conservation in 2018, facing west.

Pl. 10

A. View down the interior of the North Stoa in 2012, facing east.

B. Part of the dedicatory inscription of the North Stoa, mentioning the emperor Tiberius.

C. Continuation of foundations of North Stoa to the west of the line of the West Stoa, as excavated in 1991, facing north.

D. Steps cut into the stylobate and seat blocks between columns N37 and N38 of the North Stoa, facing north.

A. Bases of columns columns N16 and N17 (in the background) in the North Stoa, facing west.

B. Capital of column N8 of North Stoa, facing north.

C. Variant of standard Ionic capital form from North Stoa.

D. Blocks of the mask and garland frieze of the North Stoa.

E. Cornice block with water spout in the form of a lion's head from the North Stoa.

F. Cornice block with water spout in the form of a lioness's head from the North Stoa.

A. Upper surface of cornice block from North Stoa, showing two phases of cuttings for roof beams.

B. Decorated wooden panel (Inv. 89-1) found in the eastern end of the pool in 1989.

C. Marble doorframe and threshold in North Stoa rear wall, soon after excavation in 1986, facing north-east.

D. View along the interior of the West Stoa, facing north.

PL. 13

A. South end of pool and Theatre Wall in 2017, facing south.

B–E. Cuttings in Theatre Wall: B. Higher row of downward-sloping rafter holes; C. Lower row of downward-sloping rafter holes; D. Slots for struts; E. Later beam holes.

A. Traces of burning visible on surface of highest course of ashlar blocks during excavation in 1984, facing east.

B. Two cuttings showing traces of burning at the far eastern end of the lowest row of beam holes, facing south.

C. Inner face of pool walls, and inner seats, after excavation in 2012, North side of pool, facing north-east.

D. East end of pool showing outer seat blocks, with curvature in their upper surface.

A. Two blocks of the inner lining of the pool, on the north side, towards the east end, clamped together with a lead clamp (2017).

B. The ring drain at the east end of the pool, covered with schist slabs; above these was a duct for terracotta piping, now robbed (2012).

C. Ring drain, showing slabs on floor (2012).

Pl. 16

A.

B.

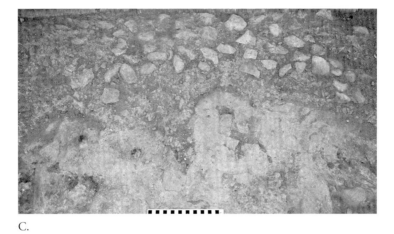

C.

A–C. Pool floor: A) Substrate in large stones with patches of cocciopesto surviving over it; B) Detail of stones laid on edge at sides of pool; C) Cocciopesto skim.

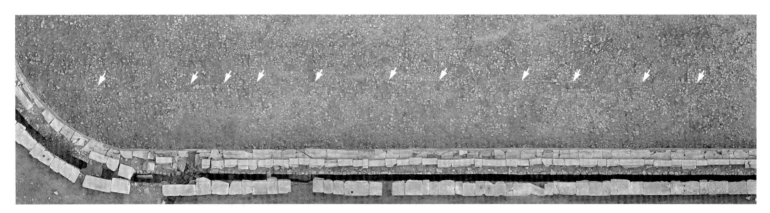

D. Linear traces of setting in pool floor for pipelines.

E. East end of pool, with cutting under seat for inlet (2017).

PL. 17

A. Duct over ring drain at south-east curve of pool, showing connection to fountain.

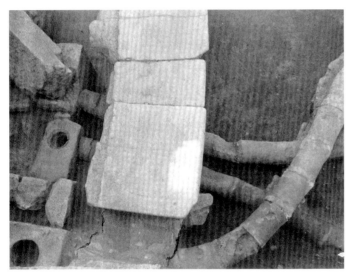

B. Pipelines at east end of pool uncovered during excavations in 1988, north to top of image.

C. Rear side of fountain block (F-1) on south-east curve of pool, facing north-west.

D. Fountain block F-2 on north-east curve of pool, facing west.

E. Fountain block F-3 in centre of north side of pool, facing south.

Pl. 18

A. Fountain block F-4 towards western end of north side of pool, facing south.

B. Possible fountain block (F-5) towards western end of south side of pool, facing west.

C. Marble fountain statue in the form of a frog, found reused in the Theatre.

D. Overlow at western end of pool, facing west.

E. Block with cutting for stopcock or valve at western end of pool, looking west.

F. Outflow drain of pool near west end of pool.

Pl. 19

A. Edging for path around pool at east end.

B. Preparation layer (context **2013**) for paving around pool.

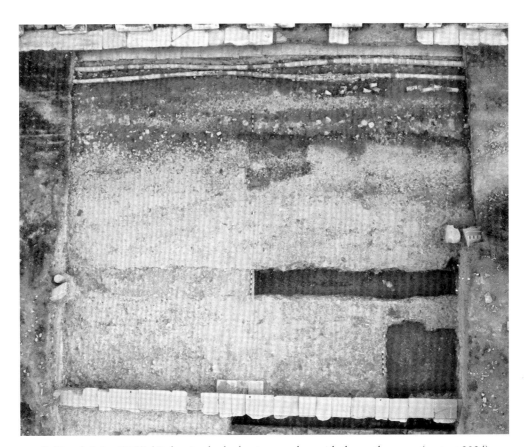

C. Trench S.Ag. 12.2/14.2 showing both planting trenches, with the southern one (context **2024**) excavated for half of its exposed length, north to top.

Pl. 20

A. Trench 12.2/14.2 prior to excavation of southern planting trench, showing path between trenches, north to right.

B. Path between planting trenches, in section, facing west. Scale: 0.5 m in 10 cm units.

C. Cretan date palms (*Phoenix theophrasti*) near Kumluca, Türkiye.

D. Canopus at Hadrian's Villa at Tivoli, Italy.

Pl. 21

A. Aerial view of the pools and theatre at Birketein, Jordan.

B. Stadium pool at Tlos (2022).

C. One of a pair of pools in the North Agora at Laodikeia (2015).

PL. 22

A. View of the Propylon, facing east (2017).

B. Junction between euthynteria of South Stoa and Propylon, looking south-east.

C. Bracket on south tower of Propylon, facing south-west.

D. West Stoa, detail of pedestal.

E. West Stoa, column drum with integrated bracket from West Stoa.

F. Ionic capital on column W15 of West Stoa.

G. Herakles club, on column W13 of West Stoa.

PL. 23

A. Architrave block from the south end of the West Stoa, mentioning Antipater the *primipilarius*.

C. Detail of cuttings, recessed panel, and suspension hole on rear side and South side of column W10, facing north-east.

B. Cuttings for doors and locking mechanism.

D. Mosaic floor inside West Stoa, uncovered in 1969.

E. Rear wall of North Stoa with pin holes for marble revetment, facing north-east.

Pl. 24

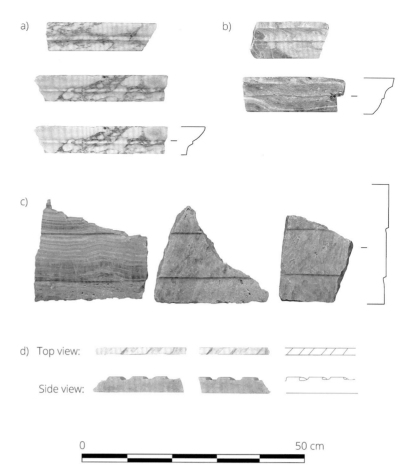

A. Portasanta pilaster shafts found in the lowest pool deposits, from the rear wall of the North Stoa.

B. Marble mouldings found in the lowest pool deposits: a) *Pavonazzetto* crown moulding; b) Alabaster crown moulding; c) Alabaster architrave; d) White fillet with diagonal recesses.

C.

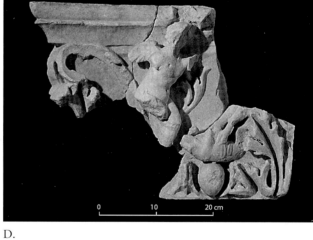

D.

E.

F.

G.

H.

C–H. Figured capitals: C) Inv. 17-29; D) Inv. 17-149/150/152; E) Inv. 12-24; F) Inv. 17-153/155/157; G) Inv. 17-62; H) Inv. 17-54.

PL. 25

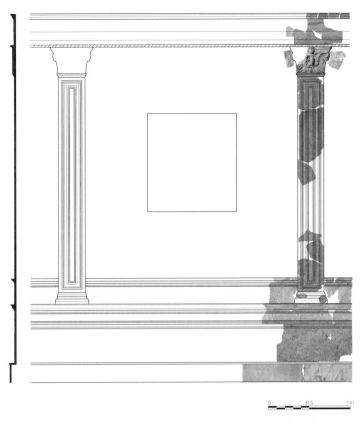

A. Reconstruction of the marble revetment scheme on the rear wall of the North Stoa.

B. Column N19 inscribed with the name of Claudia Antonia in the North Stoa, facing east.

C. Detail of the Claudia Antonia inscription.

D. Detail of the Capitolinus inscription.

PL. 26

A. Stylobate beneath column N19 of the North Stoa inscribed with the first two letters of the name Μύ[ω]|νος, looking north.

B. Stylobate beneath column N18 inscribed with the last three letters of the name Μύ[ω]|νος, looking north.

C. Re-cut pouring channel on upper surface of a column base from the North Stoa.

D. Later variety of capital from the North Stoa.

E. Capital with evidence for a repair to the echinus, from the North Stoa.

F. Capital with evidence for two repairs to the volute, from the North Stoa.

G. Cuttings and recessed strip on column N5 of the North Stoa.

A. Capital with carved-out balteus from North Stoa.

B. Detail of fragmentary capital with carved-out balteus from North Stoa.

C. Cutting through base of column N65 and on stylobate between N65 and N64, facing west

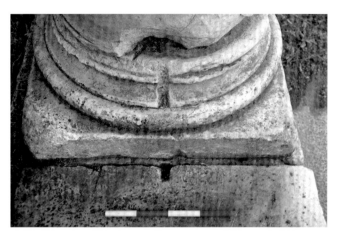

D. Cutting through base of column N70 and on stylobate between N70 and N71, facing east.

E. Groove cut into stylobate between columns N5 and N6, facing east.

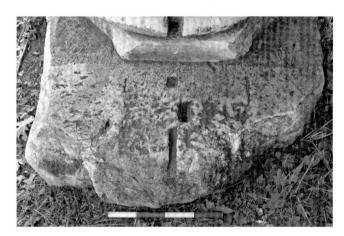

F. Slots for securing thresholds in the intercolumniation between columns N68 and N69.

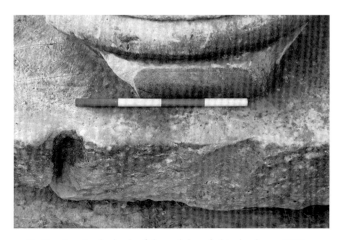

G. Cuttings in the back of the stylobate behind column N52.

Pl. 28

A. Inscription honouring Ampelios on the facade of the second pier of the Propylon of the Place of Palms (In10).

B. Inscription honouring Doulkitios on the facade of the third pier of the Propylon (In11).

C. Inscription honouring Doulkitios on the facade of the fifth pier of the Propylon (In12).

A. Re-used architrave block in the seating on the South side of the pool, facing south.

B. Split column drum re-used over new exit drain of the pool, facing south-west.

C. Stylobate seat benches reused in the south side of the pool, exposed during conservation in 2018, facing north-east.

D. One of the reused stylobate seat blocks temporarily removed during conservation in 2018, for re-setting.

E. Lion's-claw feet block re-used in inner seating on South side of pool, facing north.

PL. 30

A. Inscribed statue base (In31) re-used in the south wall of the pool, facing south-east.

C. Replacement marble slabs on the seats of the south wall of the pool marked with masons' marks, facing east.

B. Detail of sawn blocks re-used in the south wall of the pool.

D. Section of seating raised above ground level along the north wall of the pool, facing south.

A. Detail of late antique pool floor, showing stone fragments.

B. Detail of late antique pool floor, showing alabaster revetment architrave fragment.

C. Detail of late antique pool floor, showing bone.

D. Detail of stone elbow joint pipe block excavated in 1988, north to left.

E. View of stone elbow joint pipe block, facing south.

F. Detail of fountain feature with cutting for pipe, facing south.

G. Late drain approaching East end of pool, facing south.

PL. 32

A. Overflows at west end of pool, facing west.

B. Second-phase overflow drain on north-east curve of pool, facing south-east.

F. Second-phase overflow drain within ring drain, facing west.

PL. 33

A. Second-phase exit drain cut through south-east curve of the pool walls.

B. Trench S.Ag. 13.1/14.2/15.2 showing raised late antique ground level in the area north of the pool, facing east.

C. Late antique pipelines uncovered in trench S.Ag. 12.2, facing west.

PL. 34

A. Late planting pit **3061**, half-sectioned during excavation, facing west.

B. Acclamation (WS9) on column W6 of the West Stoa: 'Look around, Albinos! May the builder of the stoa prosper!'

C. Trench S.Ag. 14.3, facing south.

D. Detail of deposits uncovered beneath door threshold in S.Ag. 14.3, facing north.

E. Marble seats and thrones wedged against foundations of rear wall of North Stoa in trench S.Ag. 14.4, facing west.

Pl. 35

A. Repairs to column N27 in the North Stoa.

B. Late antique eastern South Stoa stylobate and foundation, with preceding stylobate and *euthynteria* blocks below, facing south.

C. Section of the stylobate of the western South Stoa in front of the Basilica, facing north-east.

A. Late antique column base belonging to the late antique eastern South Stoa, facing south-west.

B. Restored late antique column shafts of the eastern South Stoa, facing south-east.

PL. 37

A. Capital from the late antique eastern South Stoa: SE1c.

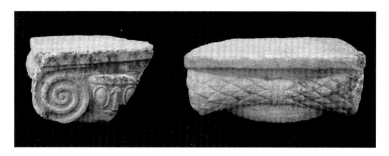

B. SE2c.

C. SE3c.

D. SE4c.

E. SE5c.

F. SE6c.

G. SE7c.

H. SE8c.

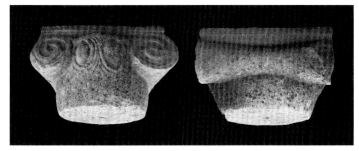

I. SE9c.

J. SE10c.

PL. 38

A. SE11c.

B. SE12c.

C. SE13c.

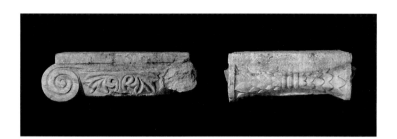

D. SE14c.

E. SE15c.

F. SE16c.

G. SE17c.

H. SE18c.

I. SE19c.

PL. 39

A. Dowel holes on bottom of an Ionic capital from the late antique eastern South Stoa (SE15).

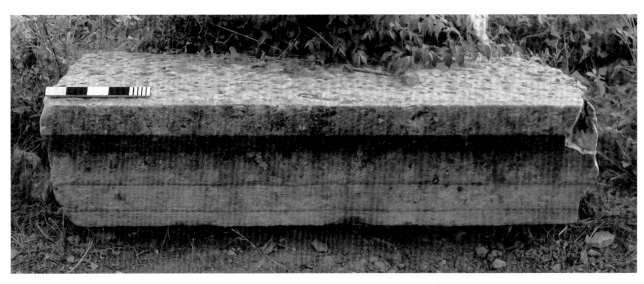

B. Architrave block belonging to the late antique eastern South Stoa.

C.   D.   E.   F.

C–F. Late Roman small finds: C. Iron implement (SAg.12.2.2015.F2017); D. Copper alloy arrowhead (Inv. 16-040);
E. Copper alloy belt buckle (SAg.12.2.2005.F.2014); F. Copper alloy chain (SAg.12.2.1210.F2013).

A. Carbonized date stone fragment (*Phoenix* sp. *theophrasti* or *dactylifera*).

B. Carbonized foodstuffs, from left to right: free-threshing wheat caryopsis (*Triticum aestivum/durum*), olive stone (*Olea europaea*), walnut shell fragment (*Juglans regia*).

C. Carbonized ritual waste, from left to right: Cypress seed (*Cupressus* sp.), fragment of carbonized fig flesh (*Ficus carica*), Kermes oak leaves (*Quercus coccifera*).

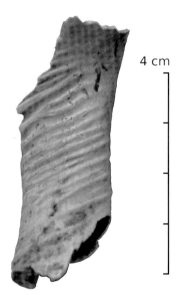

D. Fragment of the columella of a *Charonia* sp. shell from a late antique context.

E. A modern *Charonia lampas* shell sectioned to expose the columella.

F. Octagonal statue base re-used as a junction box.

A. Upper part of the junction box shown in Pl. 40.F.

B. Stone distributor block from the third phase of supply, at the east end of the pool, with the cover tile found in 1988.

C. East end of the pool with stone distributor block of the third phase of supply, with both cover tiles (found in 1988 and 2017).

Pl. 42

A. Late repair in brickwork to the north wall of the pool, post-dating the repairs of Ampelios.

B. Hole for late inlet to pool, in the south-east of the pool.

C. Crudely cut drain at west end of the pool.

Pl. 43

A. North Stoa, place inscription of Anatolios (NS78).

B. Pool, drawing of a bird and graffito 'stork' (P79).

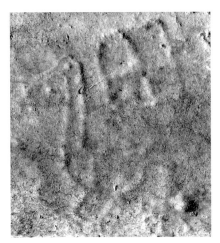
C. Pool, drawing of a bird (P81).

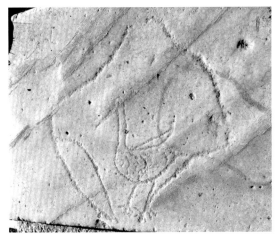
D. Pool, drawing of a bird (P90).

E. Pool, drawing of a bird (P91).

F. Pool, drawing of a bird and graffito (P94–P95).

G–H. Pool, gameboard with graffito naming Doulkitios (P110) and detail.

I. Pool, gameboard with graffiti of the *nika*-type (P111).

J. Pool, gameboard with graffito of the *nika*-type (P227).

PL. 44

A. Cluster of gameboards, a menorah, and a phallus (P405–P409).

B. Pool, mancala gameboard transformed into the outline of a church (P398).

C. North Stoa, Christian cross (?) turned into a gameboard (NS72) and gameboard (NS73).

D. North Stoa, graffito, caricature of a man (NS163).

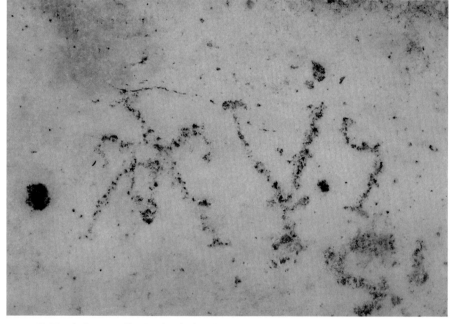

E. North Stoa, graffito (unfinished acclamation) with calligraphic letters (NS235).

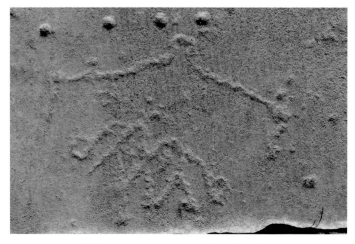

F. Pool, gameboard (mancala) and graffito with calligraphic letters (P395 and P396).

G. North Stoa, abecedary in the shape of a cross; the cross-bar can be read as a Christian acclamation (NS231).

PL. 45

A. Loose fragment with acclamation (L3).

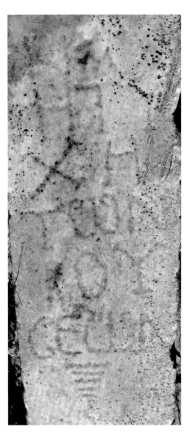

B. Pool, acclamation for the faction of the Reds (P377).

C. West Stoa, acclamation for the faction of the Reds (WS12).

D. North Stoa, acclamation (NS260).

E. South Stoa, acclamation for the city (SS30).

F. Pool, acclamation of the chair-bearers (P106).

G. Pool, acclamation (P112).

H. North Stoa, acclamation (NS20).

I. Pool, personal name (acclamation for Achilleus?) (P384)

Pl. 46

A. Pool, pictorial graffito of two busts and the prayer of a goldsmith (P33), as well as a mason's mark (P32).

B. Theatre, pictorial graffito of a bust and the prayer of a goldsmith (*IAph2007* 8.61.8i.3).

C. Pool, Christian prayer (P452).

D. North Stoa, Christian graffito (top; NS54) and masons' mark (below; NS55).

E. Pool, (Christian?) graffito (P45).

F. North Stoa, Christian graffito (left; NS264) and cross-in-circle gameboard (NS265).

PL. 47

A. Pool, graffito ἀφετηρία and masons' mark (P167, P168).

B. West Stoa, graffito with the word ἐδίκτου (WS30).

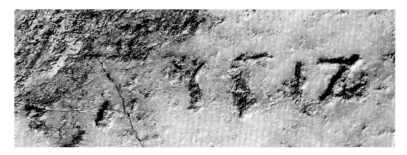
C. North Stoa, obscene graffito (NS53).

D. North Stoa, graffito φιλῶ (NS283).

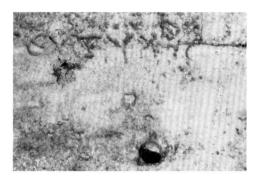
E. Commemorative inscription of Eutyches (L1).

F. Graffito ΛΑΓΑ (P101).

G. Pool, abbreviation, ΟΠ within a circle (P67).

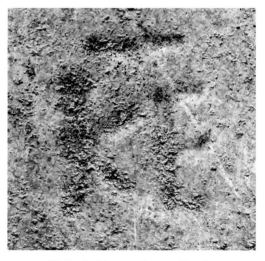
H. Pool, abbreviated name (P194).

I. North Stoa, abbreviations (NS230).

J. Monogram NS227.

K. Monogram NS141.

L. Monogram P309.

M. Monogram P465.

PL. 48

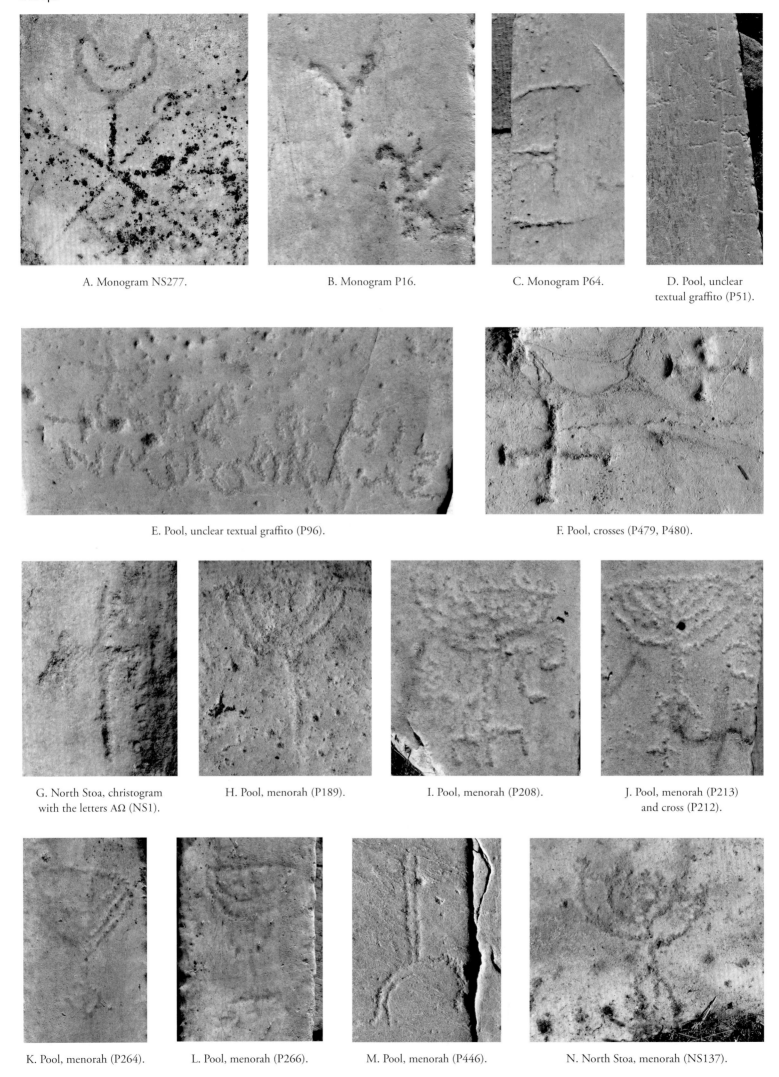

A. Monogram NS277.

B. Monogram P16.

C. Monogram P64.

D. Pool, unclear textual graffito (P51).

E. Pool, unclear textual graffito (P96).

F. Pool, crosses (P479, P480).

G. North Stoa, christogram with the letters AΩ (NS1).

H. Pool, menorah (P189).

I. Pool, menorah (P208).

J. Pool, menorah (P213) and cross (P212).

K. Pool, menorah (P264).

L. Pool, menorah (P266).

M. Pool, menorah (P446).

N. North Stoa, menorah (NS137).

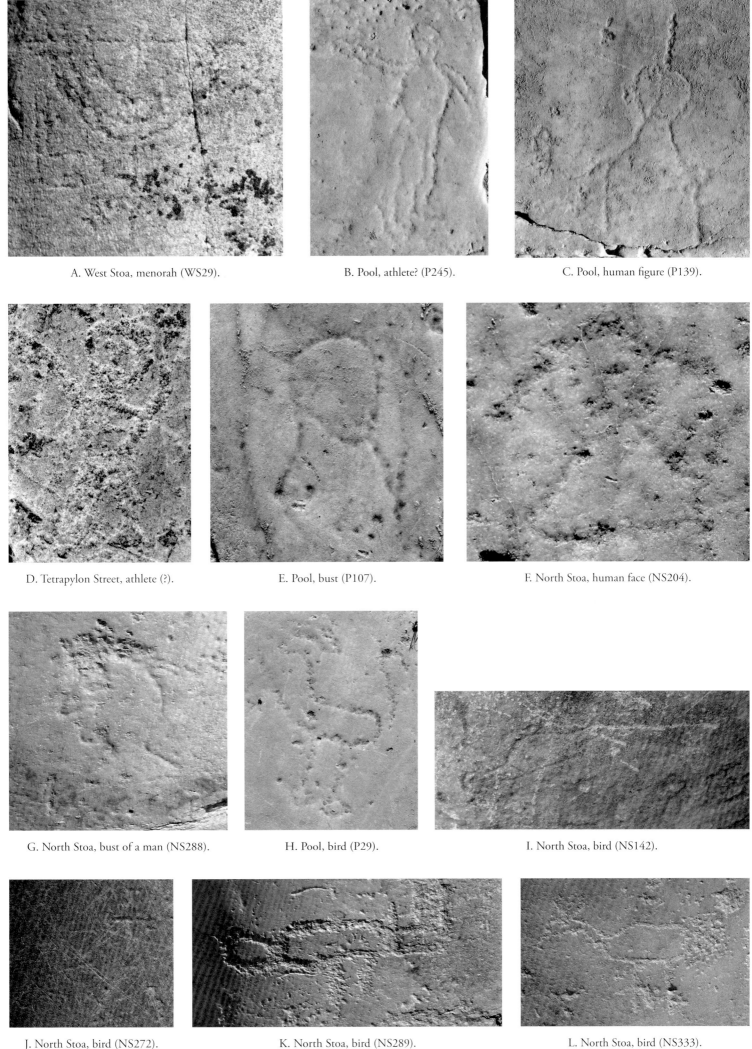

A. West Stoa, menorah (WS29). B. Pool, athlete? (P245). C. Pool, human figure (P139).

D. Tetrapylon Street, athlete (?). E. Pool, bust (P107). F. North Stoa, human face (NS204).

G. North Stoa, bust of a man (NS288). H. Pool, bird (P29). I. North Stoa, bird (NS142).

J. North Stoa, bird (NS272). K. North Stoa, bird (NS289). L. North Stoa, bird (NS333).

A. North Stoa, pictorial graffito of three running lions (NS331).

 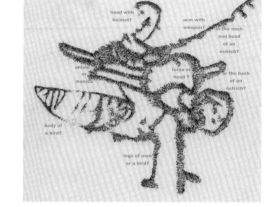

B–C. North Stoa, cluster of pictorial graffiti (*venatio*?) (NS332), with labelled drawing.

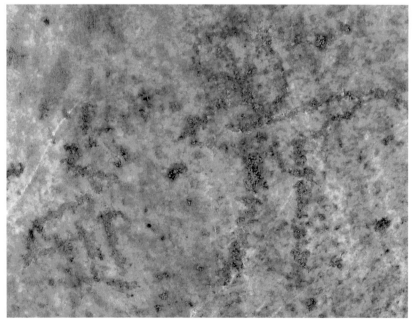

D. North Stoa, pictorial graffito (man and animal) (NS273).

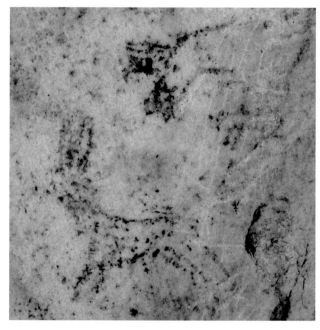

E. North Stoa, pictorial graffito of two running animals (antelope? and dog?) (NS295).

F. Stadium, pictorial graffito of an antelope or wild goat.

G. Pool, animal? (P470).

H. Pool, fish (P449).

Pl. 51

A. Pool, pictorial graffito of a phallus and eight-spoke wheel gameboard (P159, P161).

B. West Stoa, carved figure (Aphrodite Anadyomene?) (WS19).

C. West Stoa, carved figure (satyr) (WS26) and place inscription of Papas (WS27).

D. Pool, graffito, outline of the pool? (P300).

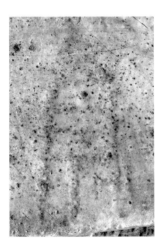

E. Pool, pictorial graffito (building?) (P313).

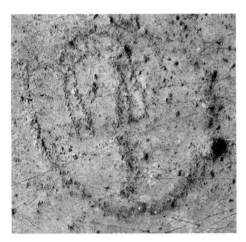

F. Pool, pictorial graffito (arch?) (P331).

G. North Stoa, gameboard (cross-in-square) turned into pictorial graffito (NS152).

H. North Stoa, pictorial graffito (ladder?) (NS23).

I. South Wall, measures (one foot and two feet) (TW9).

J. Pool, pictorial graffito of a boat (P319).

PL. 52

A. Pool, *tabula ansata* (P230).

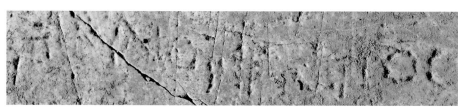

B. Pool, *topos* of Paulos (P132).

C. North Stoa, *topos* of Eugraphios (NS341)

D. North Stoa, *topos* of Zotikos (NS342).

E. North Stoa, *topos* of Zotikos (NS349).

F. North Stoa, *topos* of Antiochos (NS10).

G. North Stoa, place of Dionysios and Papias (NS15).

H. North Stoa, place of Theoktistos (NS58).

I. North Stoa, place of Hekataios (NS344).

J. North Stoa, place of Theok(tistos) (NS67).

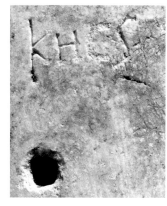

K. North Stoa, place of Kes(onios) (NS63).

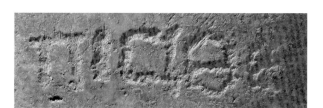

L. North Stoa, place of Pisitheos (NS165).

M. North Stoa, place of Hek. (NS190).

N. North Stoa, place of Epi. (NS330).

O. South Stoa, Place of M. (SS4).

P. Place of Ioann(es) (NS52).

PL. 53

A. Theatre Wall, Place of Zotikos (TW2).(P218).

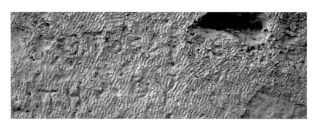

B. Theatre Wall, place of Artemon (TW7).

C. North Stoa, place of the *sophistes* (NS19).

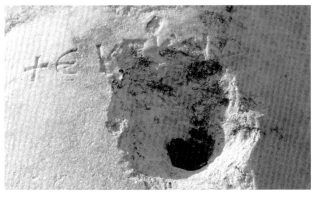

D. North Stoa, place of Eutychia (NS7).

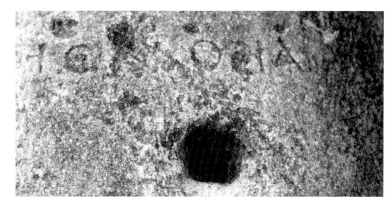

E. North Stoa, place of Eudoxia (NS18).

F. North Stoa, mason's mark (NS290).

G. West Stoa, mason's mark (WS39).

H. West Stoa, mason's mark (WS103).

I. Pool, mason's mark (P338).

J. Pool, mason's mark (P9).

K. Pool, mason's mark (P3).

L. Pool, masons' marks (P157 and P158).

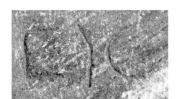

M. West Stoa, mason's mark (WS31).

N. West Stoa, mason's mark (WS101).

O. West Stoa, mason's mark (WS107).

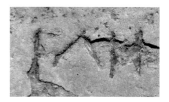

P. West Stoa, mason's mark (WS79).

Q. Pool, mason's mark (P63).

R. West Stoa, mason's mark (WS99).

S. West Stoa, mason's mark (WS62).

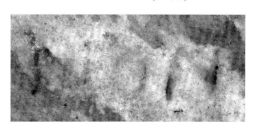

T. West Stoa, mason's mark (WS85).

PL. 54

A. North Stoa, mason's mark (NS43).

B. Sebasteion, column bases allocated for a project of Ampelios.

C. South Stoas, monogram of Anastasius (SS24).

D. South Stoas, monogram (SS15).

E. South Stoas, monogram (SS17).

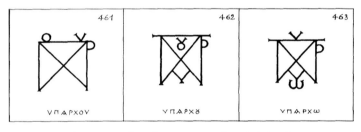

F. Monograms of prefects, ὕπαρχοι, identified elsewhere.

G. Mark of Krispinos (L4).

H. Tetrapylon Street, mark of Krispos.

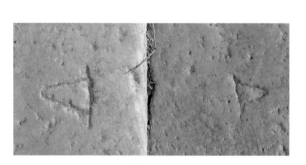

I. Pool, letters (P121).

J. North Stoa, letters (NS296).

K. West Stoa, letter (WS59).

L. South Stoas, letter (SS21).

M. Pool, letter (P46).

A. North Stoa, *duodecim scripta* board (NS90).

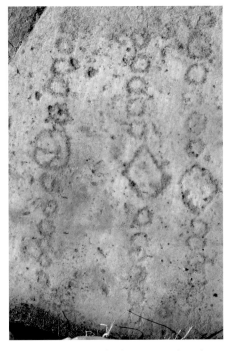

B. North Stoa, *duodecim scripta* board (NS147).

C. North Stoa, *duodecim scripta* board (NS279).

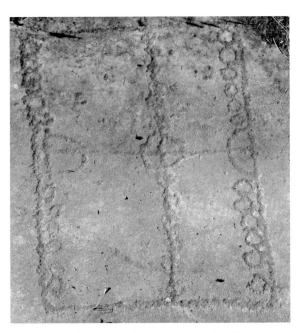

D. North Stoa, *duodecim scripta* board (NS285).

E. Pool, *duodecim scripta* board (P455).

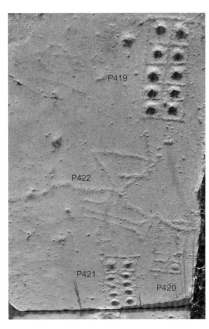

F. Pool, mancala boards and possible cross (P419–422).

G. Pool, mancala and eight-spoke wheel gameboards (P461-462).

H. Pool, mancala board (P14).

I. Pool, mancala board (P218).

J. Pool, variant of mancala board (P364).

PL. 56

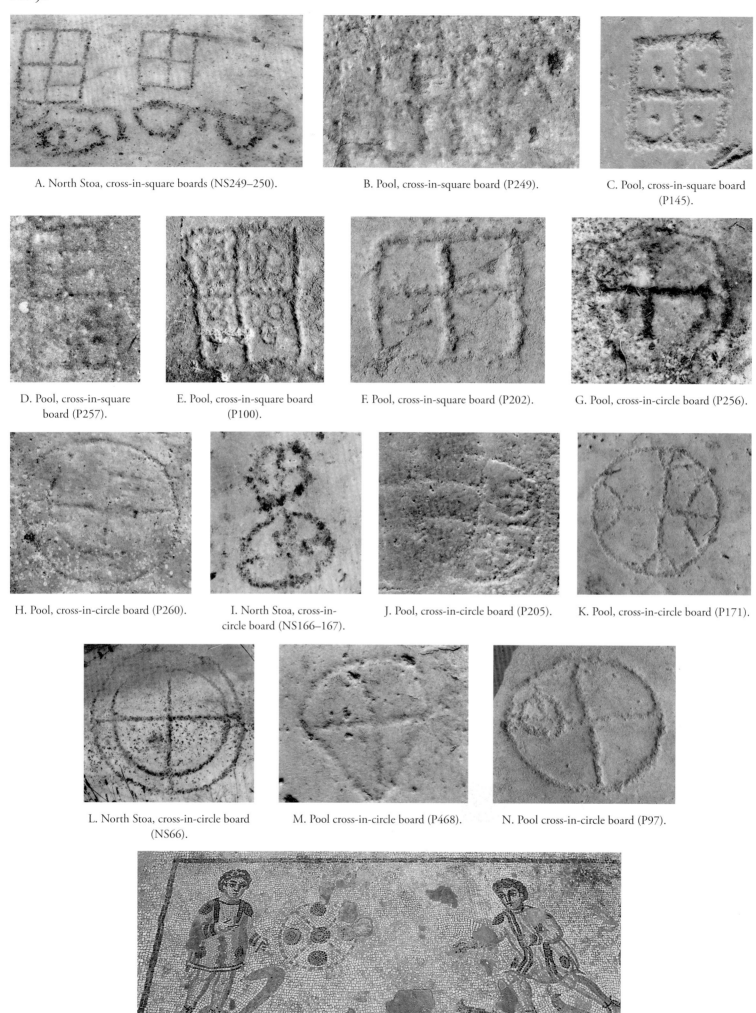

A. North Stoa, cross-in-square boards (NS249–250).

B. Pool, cross-in-square board (P249).

C. Pool, cross-in-square board (P145).

D. Pool, cross-in-square board (P257).

E. Pool, cross-in-square board (P100).

F. Pool, cross-in-square board (P202).

G. Pool, cross-in-circle board (P256).

H. Pool, cross-in-circle board (P260).

I. North Stoa, cross-in-circle board (NS166–167).

J. Pool, cross-in-circle board (P205).

K. Pool, cross-in-circle board (P171).

L. North Stoa, cross-in-circle board (NS66).

M. Pool cross-in-circle board (P468).

N. Pool cross-in-circle board (P97).

O. Mosaic from Piazza Armerina, showing boys apparently playing a game involving throwing counters onto a board consisting of a cross in circle

PL. 57

  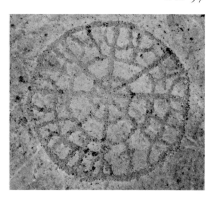

A. Pool, eight-spoke wheel boards (P140–141).   B. Pool, eight-spoke wheel board (P333).   C. North Stoa, eight-spoke wheel board (NS317).

 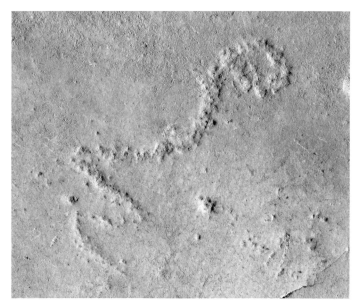

D. Tetrapylon Street, circular gameboard.   E. Pool, graffito (calligraphic letter?) (P105).

 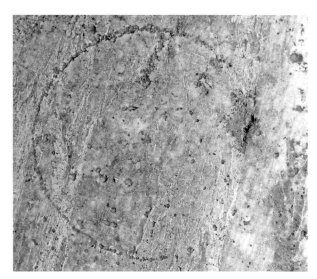

F. North Stoa, cross and cross-in-circle gameboard (NS88 and NS89).   G. North Stoa, circle made with use of a compass (NS347).

Pl. 58

A–B. Propylon of the Place of Palms and basin, facing north.

C. Relief **R 15** and Eros pillar **P 9** *in situ* (excavation photo 1983).

A. Propylon basin, north is to right.

B. Propylon basin, facing south.

C. Short end of basin, lower wall, facing south.

Pl. 60

A. Eros pillar **B 1** in north wall.

B. Base **B 2** in west wall.

C. Anthemios' base **B 3**.

D. Marcus Lepidus' base **B 4**.

A. Base for 'statues of the Cyclops', **B 5**.

B. Ethnos relief **B 6**.

PL. 62

A. **R 2**: Giants vs Hades.

B. **R 3**: Giants vs Hephaistos.

C. **R 4**: Amazons.

D. **R 5**: Centaurs vs Apollo.

E. **R 6**: Centaurs drinking.

F. **R 7**: Centaurs vs Herakles.

A. **R 8**: Amazons vs Dionysos.

B. **R 9**: Pastoral scene.

C. **R 10**: Giants vs Apollo.

D. **R 11**: Giants vs Dioskouroi.

E. **R 12**: Giants vs Selene.

F. **R 13**: Amazons.

G. **R 14**: Amazons.

PL. 64

A. **R 15**: Amazons vs Herakles.

B. **R 16**: Centauromachy.

PL. 65

A. P 1.   B. P 2.   C. P 3.

D. P 4.   E. P 5.   F. P 6.

G. P 7.   H. P 8.   I. P 9.

PL. 66

A–B. Statue **St 1**.

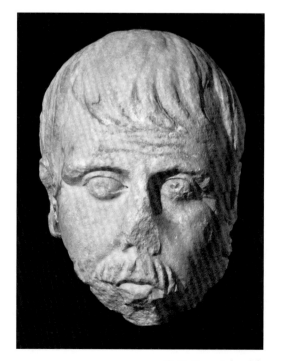 

C–D. Portrait head from pool (Inv. 17-53 and 17-112 [74]).

PL. 67

Reconstructon of statue **St 1** with head Inv. 17-53 and 17-112 (74), carried out in 2018.

Pl. 68

A. Base for Antoninus Pius (**3**).

B. Plaque for Julian (**8**).

C. Young togatus statue (**9**).

D. Colossal statue of Roman emperor (**10**).

PL. 69

A. Lower right torso fragment (**30**).

B. Over-lifesize seated figure (**31**).

C. Head of goddess or personification (**33**).

D. Satyr head (**35**).

E. Reclining river god statue (**34**).

PL. 70

A. Eros-on-dolphin console (**36**).

B–C. Eros heads reattached (**36, 37**).

D. Eros-on-dolphin console (**37**).

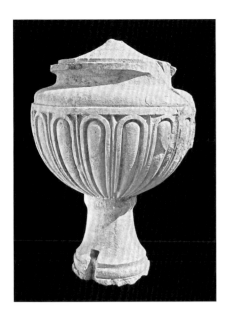

A–C. Krater-like acroteria (**38, 39, 40**).

D. Caryatid from Hadrianic Baths (**50**).

E. Over-lifesize ideal female head (**52**).

F. Under-lifesize ideal female head (**53**).

G. Satyr head (**54**).

PL. 72

A. 'Valentinian II' (57).

B. Fourth-century head (61).

C. Julio-Claudian portrait head (72).

D. Nude torso (79).

E. Cuirass fragment (84).

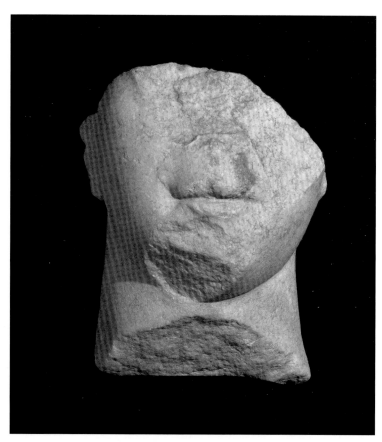

F. Over-lifesize female portrait head (73).

PL. 73

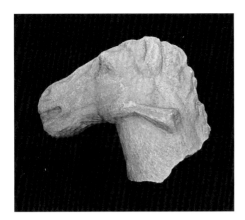

A. Horse's head (**85**).

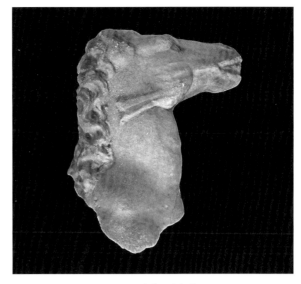

B. Horse's head (**86**).

C. Eagle on plinth (**87**).

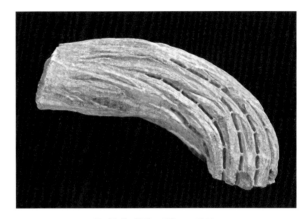

D. Tail of Blue Horse (**88**).

E. Blue Horse with tail reattached (**88**).

PL. 74

A. Under-lifesize ideal female head (**89**).

B. Votive plaque with eyes (**91**).

C. Relief with barbarian (**90**).

D. Classicising caryatid (?) from Hadrianic Baths (**92**).

E. Under-lifesize horse with harness (**96**).

F. Late antique priestess statuette (**97**).

PL. 75

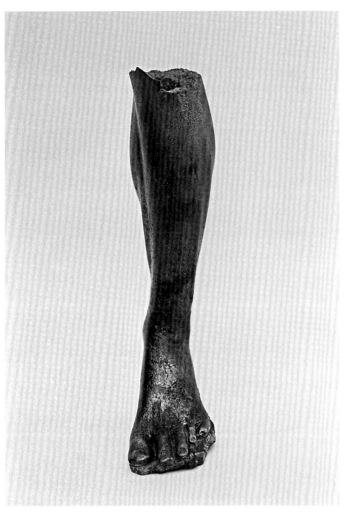

A. Bronze statuette leg (**98**).

B. Ideal female figure with *stephane* (**99**).

C. Battered long-haired youth (**100**).

D. Over-lifesize female head with architectural cuttings at back (**101**).

E. Under-lifesize male head (**102**).

PL. 76

A. Heroic male statuette (**103**).

B. Under-lifesize ideal male head (**104**).

C. Battered double herm (**105**).

D. Frog fountain statuette (**109**).

E. Venus Genetrix statuette (**106**).

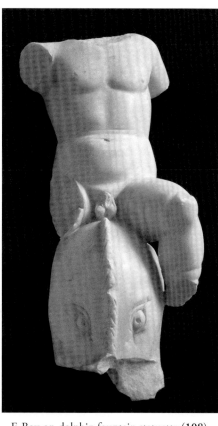
F. Boy-on-dolphin fountain statuette (**108**).

G. Late antique seated statue (**112**).

A. Portrait head with Theodosian hairstyle and beard (**116**).

B. Late antique ankle and scroll support (**118**).

C. Sixth-century portrait head with 'mop' hairstyle (**117**).

PL. 78

A. Deposits directly over the pool floor during excavation: the thick clearance deposit **4328** to the north (left) and the scatter over the pool floor (**4482**) to the south.

B. Drone photo showing extent of first clearance deposit (**4328**), facng West.

Pl. 79

A. The first thick silt layer (**4448**) over the floor of the pool, seen here below **4471**, facing south.

B. Part of the second clearance deposit (**4471**) overlying the silt layer **4448**, facing south-west.

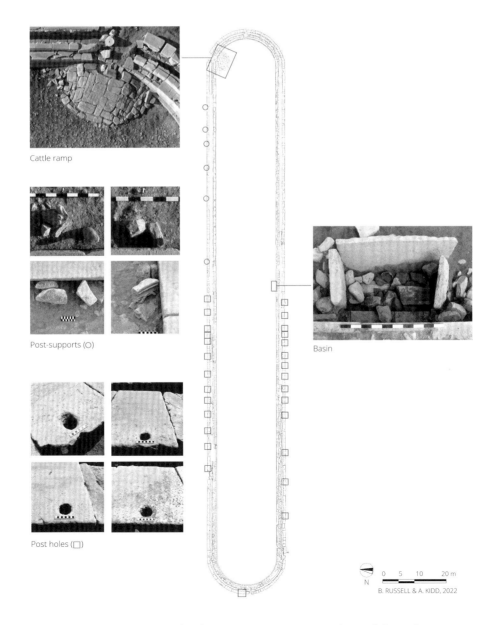

C. Features associated with Byzantine occupation in and around the pool.

PL. 80

A. View along the south side of the pool, facing west, showing holes cut in outer seating.

B. Wooden pole F830 under excavation in context **4448**, facing south-east.

C. Stone basin (**4464**) under excavation, with deposit **4471**, north to top.

D. Late ramp added in north-east arc of pool, probably for watering livestock, north to top.

PL. 81

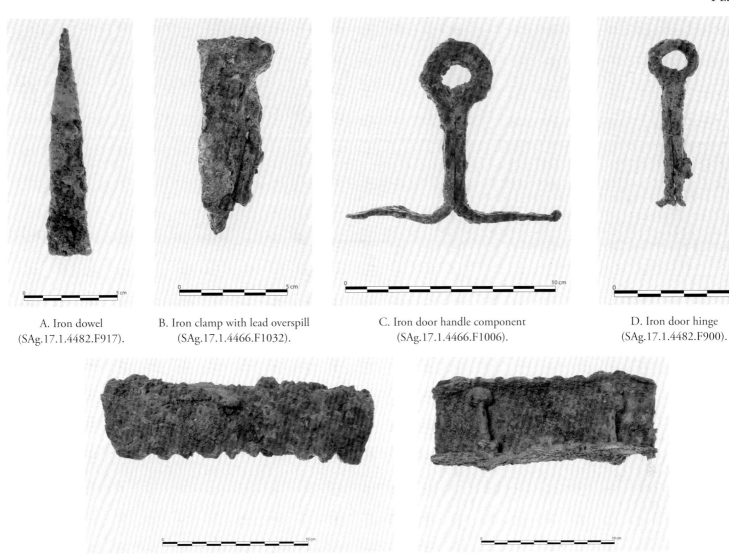

A. Iron dowel (SAg.17.1.4482.F917).

B. Iron clamp with lead overspill (SAg.17.1.4466.F1032).

C. Iron door handle component (SAg.17.1.4466.F1006).

D. Iron door hinge (SAg.17.1.4482.F900).

E–F. Side and underside of iron furniture fitting or utility device (Inv. 17-117).

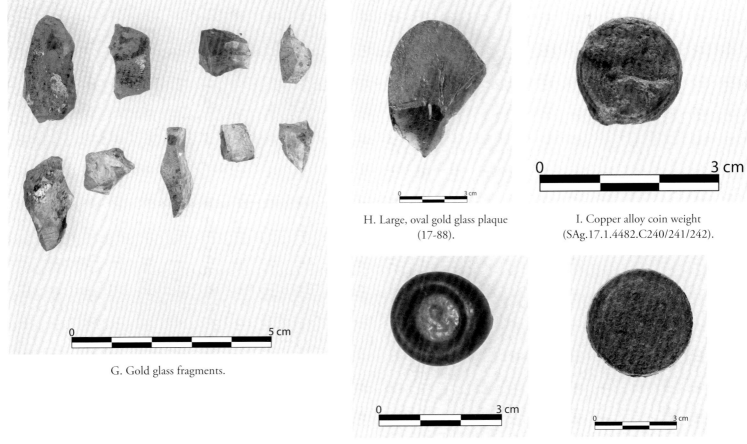

G. Gold glass fragments.

H. Large, oval gold glass plaque (17-88).

I. Copper alloy coin weight (SAg.17.1.4482.C240/241/242).

J. Glass weight (Inv. 18-55).

K. Copper alloy disc-shaped weight (Inv. 17-85).

PL. 82

A. Copper alloy chisel (Inv. 17-170).

B. Iron pruning hook (SAg.17.1.4448.F795).

C. Fragment of iron pan.

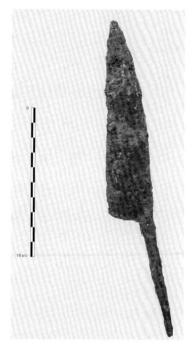

D. Iron knife (SAg.17.1.4328.F985).

E. Iron knife (SAg.17.1.4448.F863).

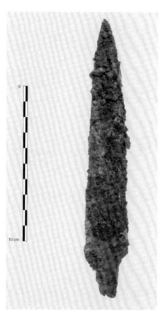

F. Iron knife (SAg.17.1.4448.F850).

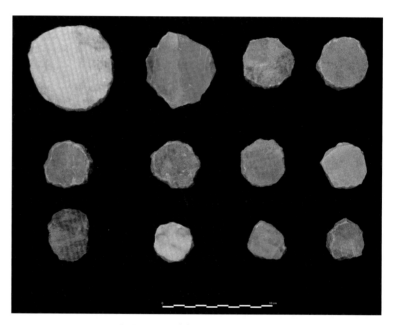

G. Recut marble gaming counters.

H. Monogrammed seal (Inv. 17-94).

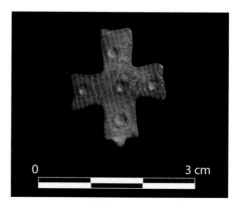

I. Copper alloy cross (Inv. 12-23).

Pl. 83

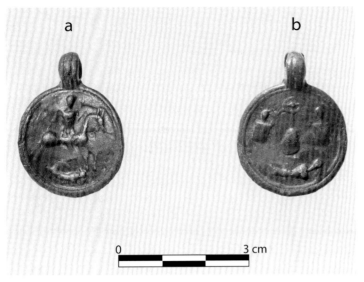

A. Silver pendant (Inv. 17-108).

B. Small copper alloy bell (Inv. 17-176).

C. Small copper alloy bell (Inv. 17-175).

D. Large copper alloy bell (Inv. 17-169).

E. Rolled lead sheets.

F. Iron arrowhead (SAg.17.1.4328.F972).

G. Iron arrowhead (SAg.17.1.4328.F974).

H. Iron arrowhead (SAg 17.1.4466.F1033).

I. Possible iron javelin (PTW.SW.89.1.13.F83).

J. Possible iron spearhead (SAg.17.1.4466.F1031).

Pl. 84

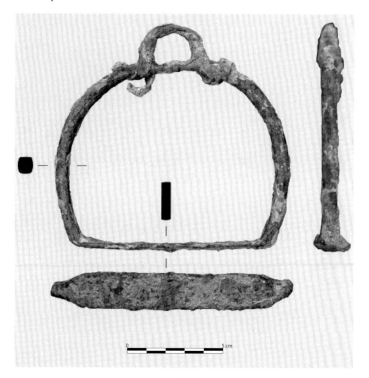

A. Iron stirrup (PTE.1.1990.F24).

B. The stirrup at the moment of its discovery (1990).

C. From left to right: True bulrush seed (*Schoenoplectus lacustris*), pondweed seed (*Potamogeton* sp.), a stonewort algae oospore (*Chara* sp.) and a fool's-water-cress seed (*Apium nodiflorus*).

D. Terrestrial species preserved through waterlogging, from left to right: blackberry endocarp (*Rubus fruticosus* agg.), sun spurge seed (*Euphorbia helioscopia*), and a fragment of peach stone (*Prunus persica*).

E. Waterlogged stone pine pinecone (*Pinus pinea*).

F. Waterlogged peach stones (*Prunus persica*).

A. Clearance deposit (**4329**), facing north-east.

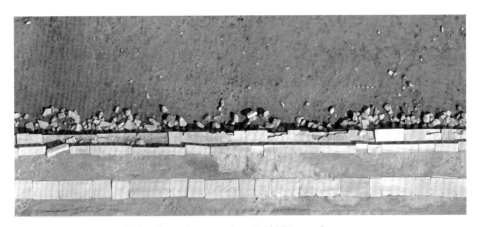

B. Southern clearance deposit (**4461**), north to top.

C. [5.1] facing east.

D. [5.3] facing west.

Pl. 85

PL. 86

A. [5.8] facing west.

B. [6.1] facing north.

C. **4089** facing east.

D. Lanes between [7.7], [8.2], and [8.1] facing north-east.

PL. 87

A. [8.6] with marble torso (79) *in situ*, facing east.

B. Building I, north to top.

C. East wall of Building I, uncovered in 1990.

D. Building I, facing north-east.

E. Buildings II and III, facing north-east.

A. Building IV, north to top.

B. Building IX, north to top.

PL. 89

A. Well, facing south.

B. [8.11], facing south.

C. Phase 9 walls and lanes, facing north-east.

D. Building XI, north to top.

Pl. 90

A. Storage vessel (SAg.15.1.40/6.F137), facing north.

B. Theatre Hill collapse (**4085**) facing north-west.

C. Phase 10 parallel walls, facing north.

D. [10.4]/[10.10] facing south.

E. Balloon photograph of Aphrodisias taken *c.* 1961, showing area of Place of Palms covered in trees (to the east) and small fields (centre and west), north to top.

F. View from the top of the Theatre hill, looking north-west towards the Hadrianic Baths, showing fields in the area of the former Place of Palms (*c.* 1961).

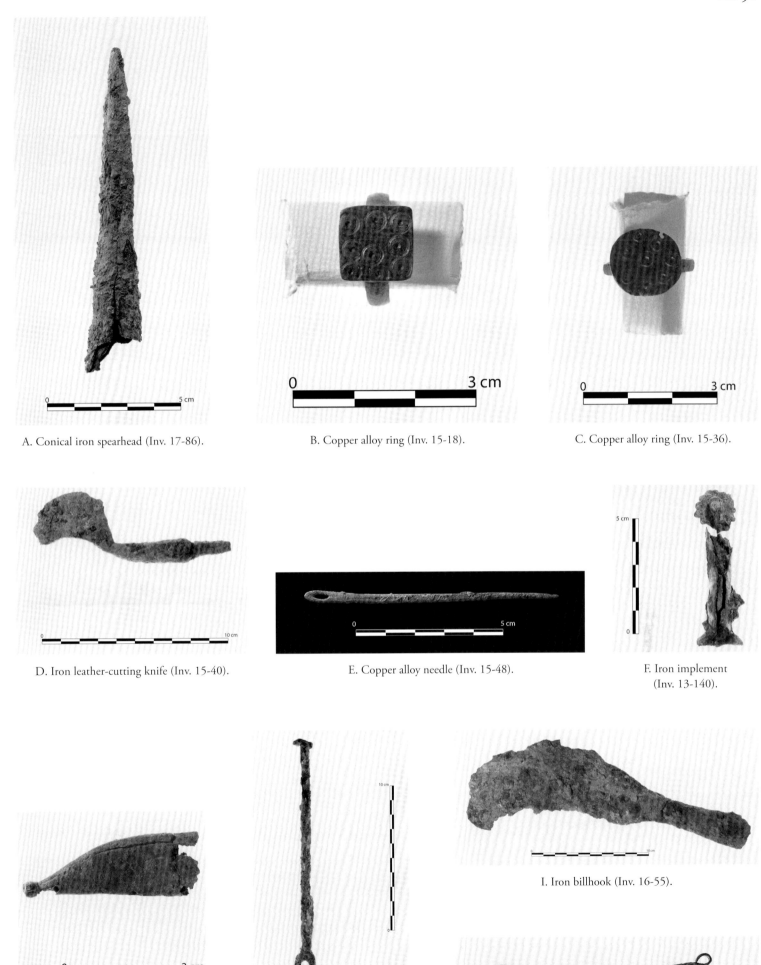

A. Conical iron spearhead (Inv. 17-86).

B. Copper alloy ring (Inv. 15-18).

C. Copper alloy ring (Inv. 15-36).

D. Iron leather-cutting knife (Inv. 15-40).

E. Copper alloy needle (Inv. 15-48).

F. Iron implement (Inv. 13-140).

G. Leather sheath (Inv. 15-20).

H. Iron tong (Inv. 15-38).

I. Iron billhook (Inv. 16-55).

J. Copper alloy earspoon (Inv. 15-42).

PL. 92

 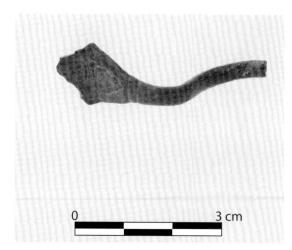 

A. Iron pan scraper (Inv. 15-22).

B. Copper alloy handle fragment (Inv. 15-45).

C. Iron hinge fragment (Inv. 15-21).

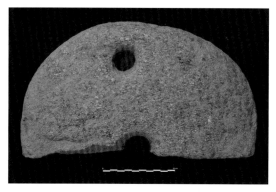 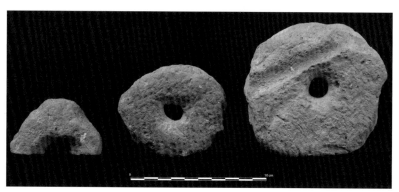

D. Rotary quern fragment (SAg.15.1.4075.M737).

E. Bricks recut as loomweights.

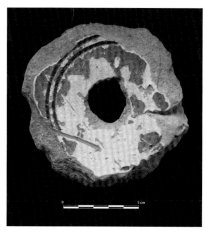 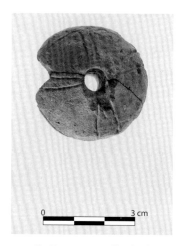 

F. Glazed ceramic vessel base with sgraffito decoration recut as loomweight (Inv. 17-18).

G. Ceramic spindlewhorl (Inv. 17-10).

H. Stone spindlewhorl (Inv. 17-16).

 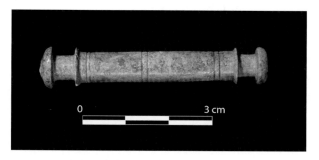

I. Bone lathe-turned object (Inv. 16-5).

J. Bone lathe-turned object (Inv. 16-6).

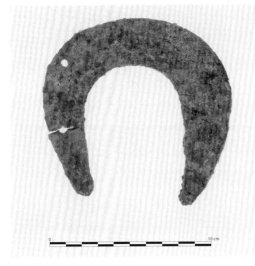
A. Iron horseshoe (SAg.17.1.4438.F683).

B. Copper alloy belt buckle (Inv. 15-44).

C. Silver strap fitting (Inv. 14-42).

D. Alabaster phallus (Inv. 15-72).

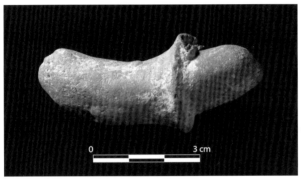
E. Ceramic phallus pendant (Inv. 15-55).

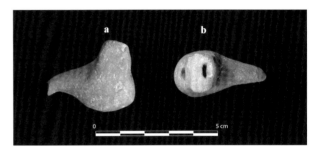
F. Ceramic whistle in the form of a bird (Inv. 16-11).

G. Iron arrowhead (Inv. 15-47).

H. Iron arrowhead (Inv. 17-19).

I. Iron arrowhead (Inv. 15-17).

J. Miniature terracotta mask (Inv. 15-16).

K. Miniature ceramic column (Inv. 17-17).

L. Marble mortarium fragment (Inv. 16-53).

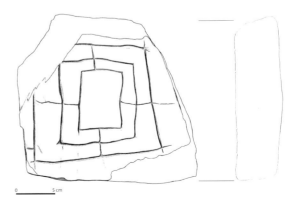
M. Ceramic floor tile inscribed with possible gameboard (SAg.16.1.4281.F492).

PL. 94

A. Typical preservation patterns of sheep/goat metapodials from Ottoman occupation (fifteenth to seventeenth century, context **4091**).
Arrows indicate chop marks. Surface preservation typical of the assemblage.

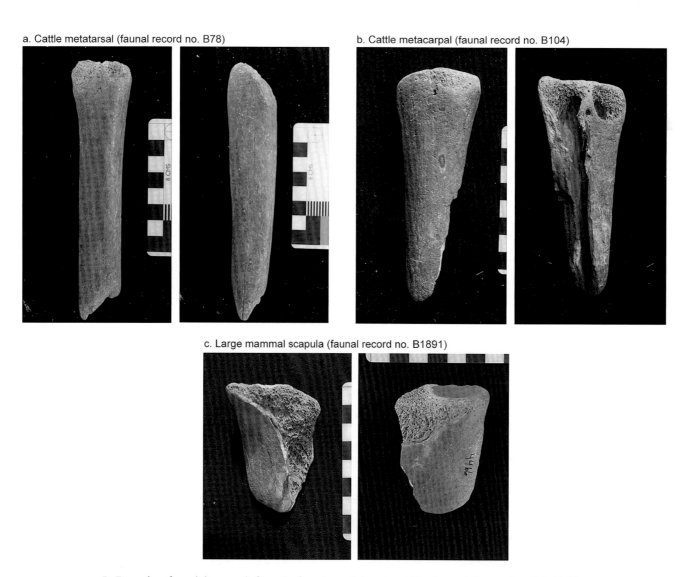

B. Examples of rough bone tools from the first phase of deposits within the pool (late antique B2, **4466**).

Pl. 95

A–B. Label of an image of Victoria Augustorum (In3).

C. Honorific inscription for Emperor Nerva (In13).

D. Honorific inscription for Emperor Hadrian (In14).

PL. 96

A. Posthumous honorific inscription for Timokles (In21) (1).

B. Posthumous honorific inscription for Timokles (In21) (2).

C. Dedication to an unknown deity (In31).

D. Epitaph (?) of Titus Flavius and his family (In38).

E. Epitaph (In39).

F. Epitaph (In44).

G. Epitaph (In47).

PL. 97

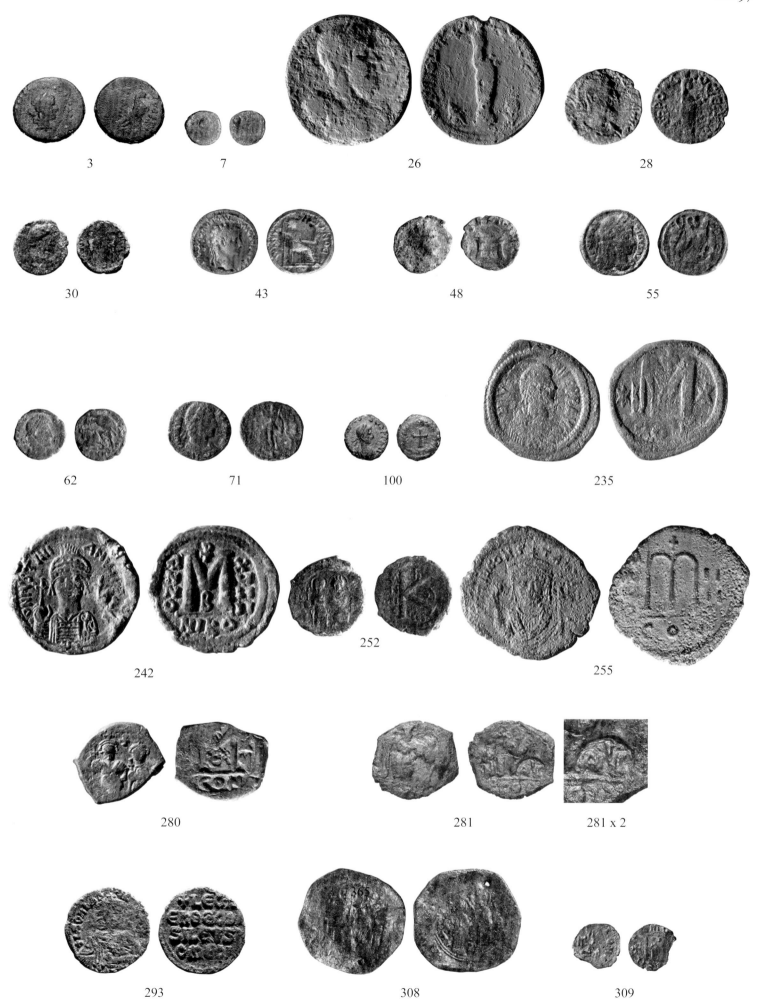

Greek, Roman and Byzantine coins from the Place of Palms (scale 1:1, unless indicated).

PL. 98

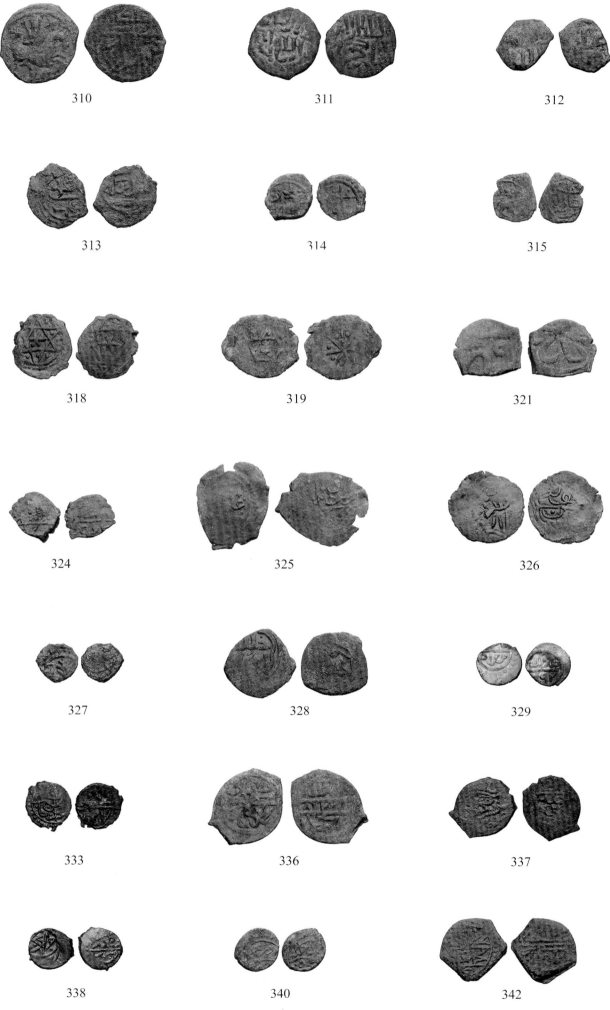

Islamic coins from the Place of Palms (scale 1:1) (1).

PL. 99

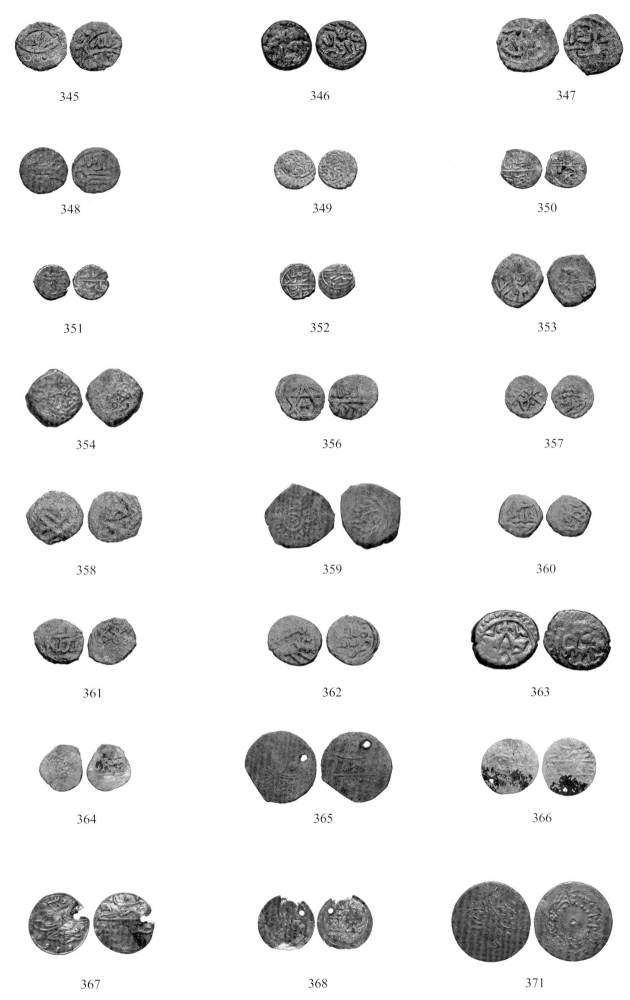

Islamic coins from the Place of Palms (scale 1:1) (2).

Pl. 100

372 373 374

375 377

Islamic coins from the Place of Palms (scale 1:1) (3).

COLOUR PL. 1

A. Portasanta pilaster shafts found in the lowest pool deposits, from the rear wall of the North Stoa.

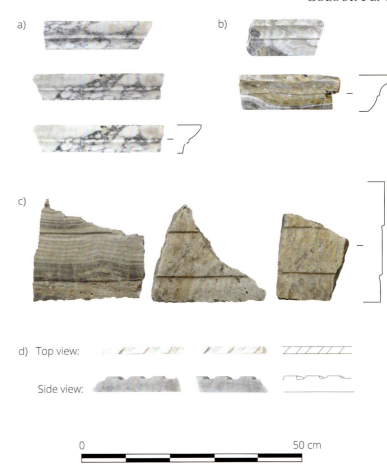

B. Marble mouldings found in the lowest pool deposits: a) *Pavonazzetto* crown moulding; b) Alabaster crown moulding; c) Alabaster architrave; d) White fillet with diagonal recesses.

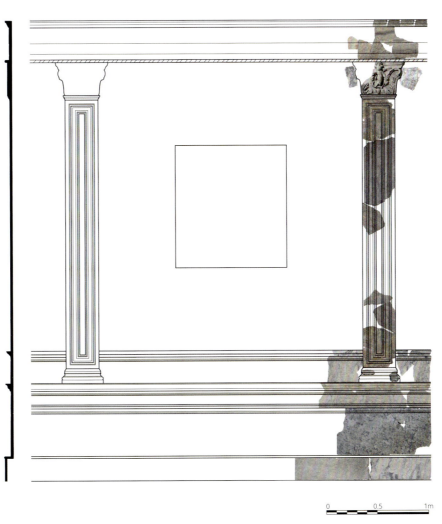

C. Reconstruction of the marble revetment scheme on the rear wall of the North Stoa.

Colour Pl. 2

A. Gold glass fragments.

B. Large, oval gold glass plaque (17-88).

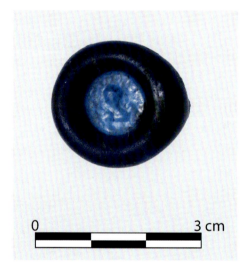

C. Glass weight (Inv. 18-55).

D. Recut marble gaming counters.

COLOUR PL. 3

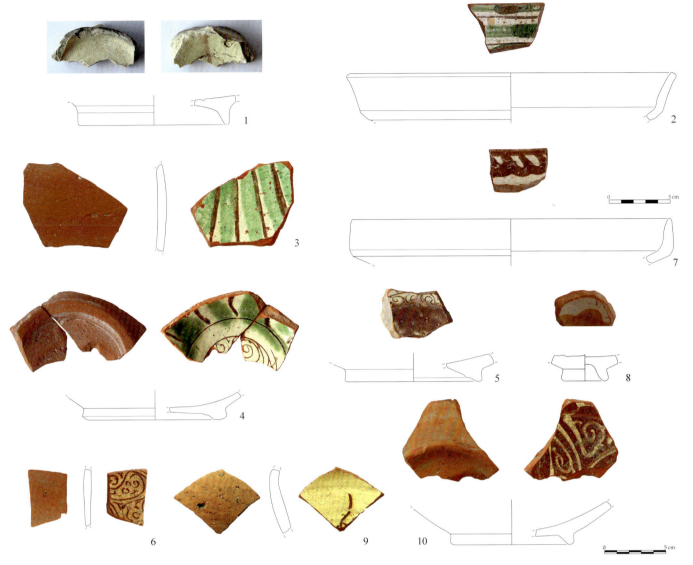

Middle Byzantine ceramics.

COLOUR PL. 4

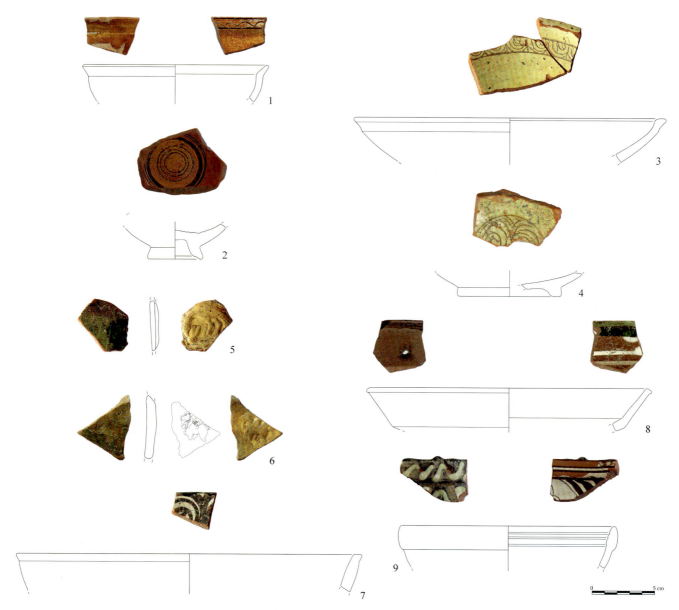

Middle Byzantine and Seljuk ceramics.

COLOUR PL. 5

Beylik ceramics (1).

Colour Pl. 6

Beylik ceramics (2).

COLOUR PL. 7

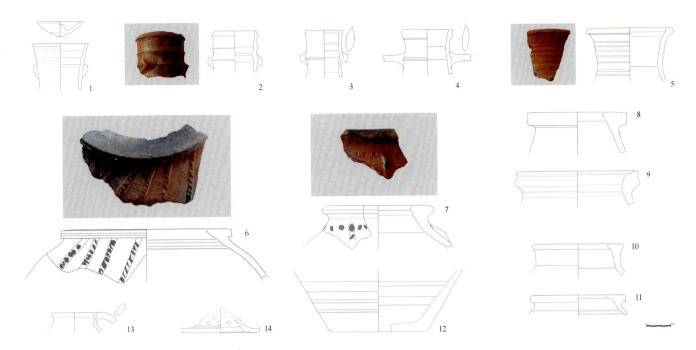

A. Beylik storage and cooking vessels.

B. Base of a Beylik storage vessel (SAg.15.1.4076.F137).

Colour Pl. 8

A. Early and classical Ottoman ceramics.

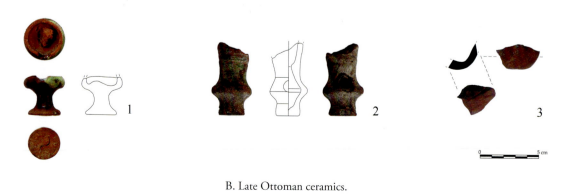

B. Late Ottoman ceramics.